KU-735-702

THE WORLD : Political

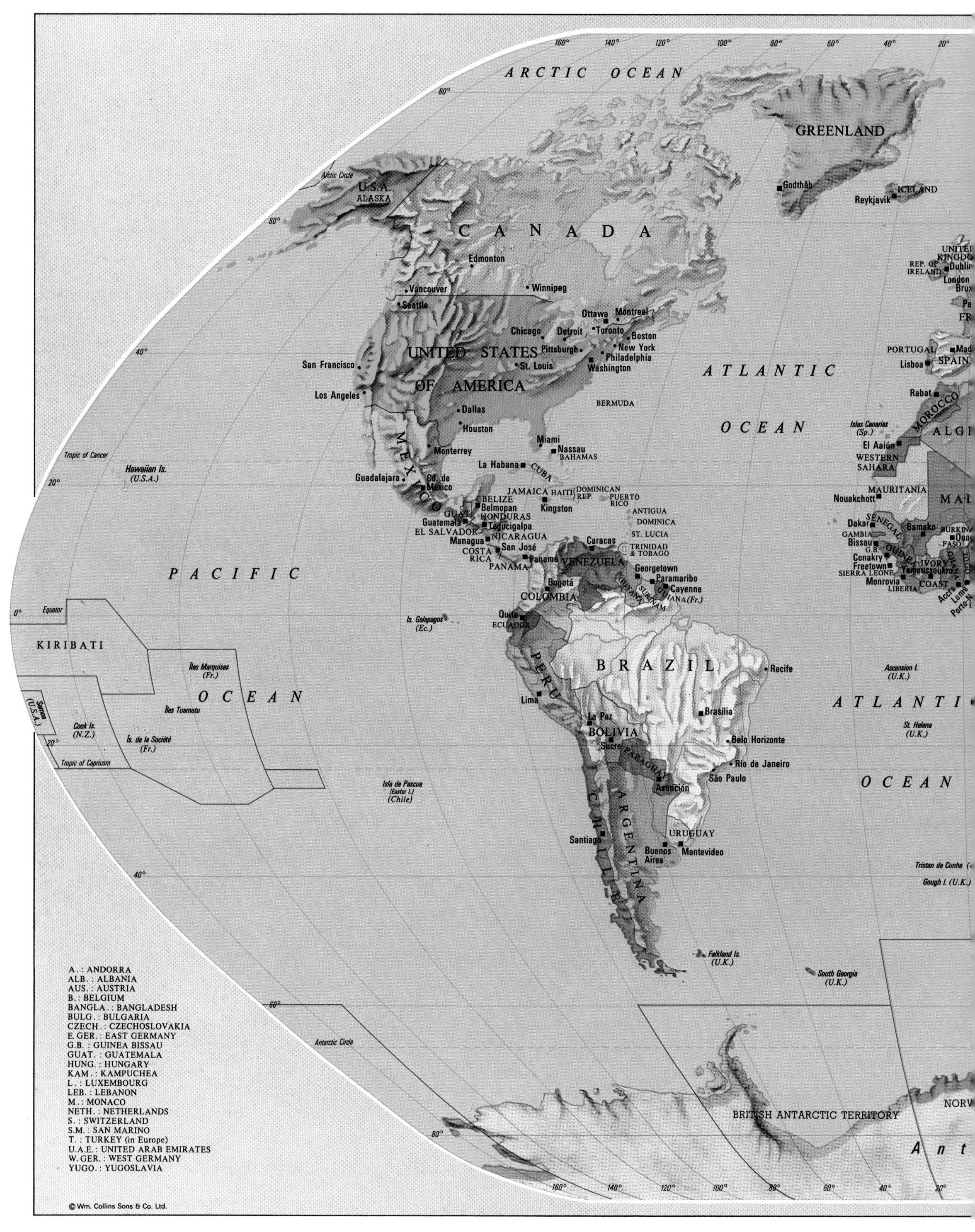

ARCTIC OCEAN
GREENLAND
Godthåb
ICELAND
Reykjavík
U.S.A.
ALASKA
Arctic Circle
CANADA
Edmonton
Vancouver
Winnipeg
Seattle
Ottawa
Montreal
Chicago
Detroit
Toronto
Boston
New York
Philadelphia
Washington
Pittsburgh
UNITED STATES OF AMERICA
St. Louis
San Francisco
Los Angeles
Dallas
Houston
BERMUDA
Miami
Nassau
BAHAMAS
MEXICO
Monterrey
La Habana
CUBA
Guadalajara
Cd. de México
Tropic of Cancer
Hawaiian Is.
(U.S.A.)
JAMAICA
HAITI
DOMINICAN REP.
PUERTO RICO
Kingston
BELIZE
Belmopan
HONDURAS
Tegucigalpa
GUAT.
Guatemala
EL SALVADOR
NICARAGUA
Managua
COSTA RICA
San José
PANAMA
Panamá
ANTIGUA
DOMINICA
ST. LUCIA
TRINIDAD & TOBAGO
Caracas
VENEZUELA
Georgetown
Paramaribo
Cayenne
GUYANA
SURINAM
GUIANA (Fr.)
Bogotá
COLOMBIA
Quito
ECUADOR
Is. Galapagos
(Ec.)
PACIFIC OCEAN
ATLANTIC OCEAN
Equator
KIRIBATI
Îles Marquises
(Fr.)
Îles Tuamotu
Samoa
(U.S.A.)
Cook Is.
(N.Z.)
Îs. de la Société
(Fr.)
Tropic of Capricorn
BRAZIL
Recife
PERU
Lima
Brasilia
La Paz
BOLIVIA
Sucre
Belo Horizonte
Rio de Janeiro
São Paulo
PARAGUAY
Asunción
Isla de Pascua
(Easter I.)
(Chile)
CHILE
ARGENTINA
Santiago
URUGUAY
Buenos Aires
Montevideo
Falkland Is.
(U.K.)
South Georgia
(U.K.)
Ascension I.
(U.K.)
St. Helena
(U.K.)
Tristan da Cunha
Gough I. (U.K.)
REP. OF IRELAND
Dublin
London
PORTUGAL
Lisboa
SPAIN
Rabat
MOROCCO
Islas Canarias
(Sp.)
El Aaiún
WESTERN SAHARA
MAURITANIA
Nouakchott
Dakar
SENEGAL
GAMBIA
Bissau
G.B.
GUINEA
Conakry
Freetown
SIERRA LEONE
Monrovia
LIBERIA
Bamako
IVORY COAST
Yamoussoukro
Antarctic Circle
BRITISH ANTARCTIC TERRITORY
160°
140°
120°
100°
80°
60°
40°
20°
0°
A. : ANDORRA
ALB. : ALBANIA
AUS. : AUSTRIA
B. : BELGIUM
BANGLA. : BANGLADESH
BULG. : BULGARIA
CZECH. : CZECHOSLOVAKIA
E.GER. : EAST GERMANY
G.B. : GUINEA BISSAU
GUAT. : GUATEMALA
HUNG. : HUNGARY
KAM. : KAMPUCHEA
L. : LUXEMBOURG
LEB. : LEBANON
M. : MONACO
NETH. : NETHERLANDS
S. : SWITZERLAND
S.M. : SAN MARINO
T. : TURKEY (in Europe)
U.A.E. : UNITED ARAB EMIRATES
W. GER. : WEST GERMANY
YUGO. : YUGOSLAVIA

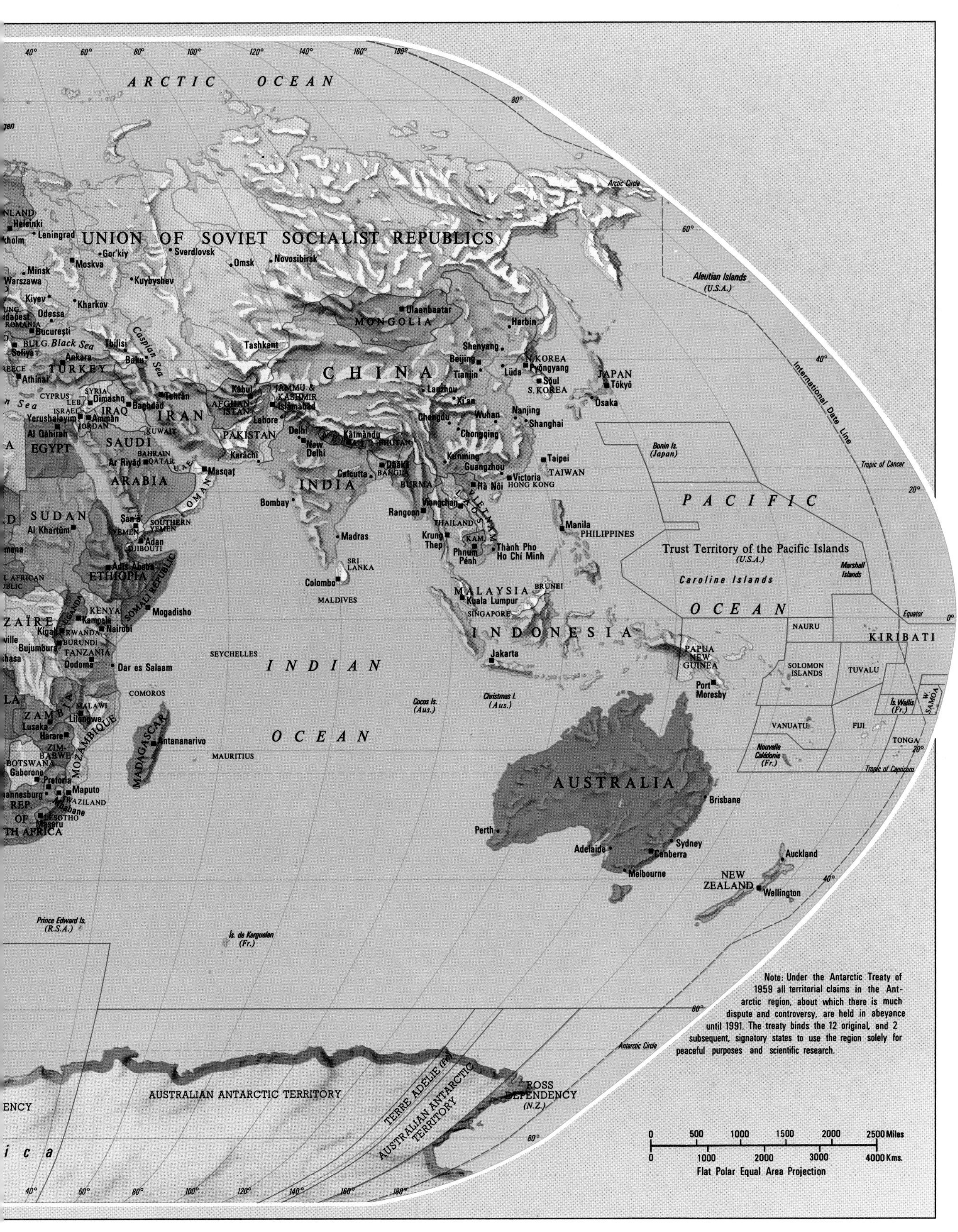
ARCTIC OCEAN
UNION OF SOVIET SOCIALIST REPUBLICS
Leningrad
Helsinki
Moskva
Gor'kiy
Sverdlovsk
Omsk
Novosibirsk
Minsk
Warszawa
Kuybyshev
Kiyev
Kharkov
Odessa
București
ROMANIA
BULG.
Black Sea
Sofiya
Caspian Sea
Tbilisi
Baku
TURKEY
Ankara
Athinai
CYPRUS
SYRIA
LEB.
Dimashq
ISRAEL
Yerushalayim
Ammān
JORDAN
IRAQ
Baghdād
Tehrān
IRAN
KUWAIT
Al Qāhirah
EGYPT
SAUDI
ARABIA
BAHRAIN
QATAR
Ar Riyāḍ
U.A.E.
Masqaț
OMAN
SUDAN
Al Kharțūm
Şan'ā
YEMEN
SOUTHERN YEMEN
Adan
DJIBOUTI
Adis Abeba
ETHIOPIA
SOMALI REPUBLIC
Mogadisho
KENYA
Kampala
Nairobi
UGANDA
ZAÏRE
Kigali
RWANDA
BURUNDI
Bujumbura
TANZANIA
Dodoma
Dar es Salaam
SEYCHELLES
COMOROS
MALAWI
Lilongwe
ZAMBIA
Lusaka
Harare
ZIMBABWE
MOZAMBIQUE
MADAGASCAR
Antananarivo
MAURITIUS
BOTSWANA
Gaborone
Pretoria
Maputo
SWAZILAND
Mbabane
LESOTHO
Maseru
REP. OF SOUTH AFRICA
Tashkent
Kābul
AFGHANISTAN
JAMMU & KASHMIR
Islāmābād
Lahore
PAKISTAN
Karāchi
Delhi
New Delhi
Kātmāndu
BHUTAN
Dhaka
BANGLA.
Calcutta
INDIA
Bombay
Madras
SRI LANKA
Colombo
MALDIVES
MONGOLIA
Ulaanbaatar
CHINA
Harbin
Shenyang
Beijing
Tianjin
Lüda
N. KOREA
Pyŏngyang
Sŏul
S. KOREA
JAPAN
Tōkyō
Ōsaka
Lanzhou
Xi'an
Chengdu
Wuhan
Nanjing
Shanghai
Chongqing
Kunming
Guangzhou
Taipei
TAIWAN
Victoria
HONG KONG
Hà Nôi
BURMA
Rangoon
Viangchan
LAOS
THAILAND
VIETNAM
Krung Thep
KAM.
Phnum Pénh
Thành Pho Ho Chí Minh
Manila
PHILIPPINES
MALAYSIA
BRUNEI
Kuala Lumpur
SINGAPORE
INDONESIA
Jakarta
PAPUA NEW GUINEA
Port Moresby
Bonin Is. (Japan)
Aleutian Islands (U.S.A.)
International Date Line
Arctic Circle
Tropic of Cancer
Equator
Tropic of Capricorn
Antarctic Circle
PACIFIC OCEAN
Trust Territory of the Pacific Islands (U.S.A.)
Caroline Islands
Marshall Islands
NAURU
KIRIBATI
SOLOMON ISLANDS
TUVALU
Is. Wallis (Fr.)
W. SAMOA
VANUATU
FIJI
TONGA
Nouvelle Calédonie (Fr.)
INDIAN OCEAN
Cocos Is. (Aus.)
Christmas I. (Aus.)
AUSTRALIA
Brisbane
Perth
Sydney
Adelaide
Canberra
Melbourne
NEW ZEALAND
Auckland
Wellington
Prince Edward Is. (R.S.A.)
Îs. de Kerguelen (Fr.)
AUSTRALIAN ANTARCTIC TERRITORY
TERRE ADÉLIE (Fr.)
AUSTRALIAN ANTARCTIC TERRITORY
ROSS DEPENDENCY (N.Z.)
Note: Under the Antarctic Treaty of 1959 all territorial claims in the Antarctic region, about which there is much dispute and controversy, are held in abeyance until 1991. The treaty binds the 12 original, and 2 subsequent, signatory states to use the region solely for peaceful purposes and scientific research.
0 500 1000 1500 2000 2500 Miles
0 1000 2000 3000 4000 Kms.
Flat Polar Equal Area Projection

COLLINS

PAPERBACK ATLAS

OF THE WORLD

COLLINS
LONDON · GLASGOW · SYDNEY · AUCKLAND · TORONTO · JOHANNESBURG

CONTENTS

IV-V Guide to the Atlas

OUR PLANET EARTH

VI-VII Introduction
VIII-IX The Solar System
X-XI The Whirling Earth
XII-XIII The Earth's Structure
XIV-XV The Atmosphere and Clouds
XVI-XVII The Water of Life
XVIII-XIX The Population Explosion
XX-XXI Alternative Energy
XXII-XXIII Environment in Danger
XXIV Postscript

WORLD ATLAS

1 Symbols Legend

EUROPE

2 Europe *Political*
3 British Isles
4-5 England and Wales
6 Scotland
7 Ireland
8 The Low Countries
9 Paris Basin and Po Valley
10 Spain and Portugal
11 France
12-13 Italy and the Balkans
14-15 Central Europe
16-17 Scandinavia and Baltic Lands
18-19 U.S.S.R. in Europe
20-21 U.S.S.R.

Collins Paperback Atlas of the World, first published 1988 by William Collins Sons & Co. Ltd., P.O. Box, Glasgow G4 0NB. Reprinted 1989.

Prepared and designed by Collins Cartographic under the direction of Andrew M Currie, M.A., Managing Editor.

Printed and bound in Scotland by William Collins Sons & Co. Ltd.

ISBN 0 00 447742 1

Photograph Credits
Credits read from top to bottom and left to right on each page. VI Space Frontiers. VIII Lockheed Solar Laboratory. XV NASA. XVI Robert Harding; Zefa; Grisewood & Dempsey. XVII Pat Morris; Robert Harding; Zefa. XIX M. Borland. XX National Coal Board; Grisewood & Dempsey (2). XXI Nasou; Atomic Energy Authority. XXII Photo Library International; Zefa; Daily Telegraph Library. XXIII Picturepoint; U.S. Environmental Protection Society. XXIV NASA.

ASIA

22 Asia *Political*
23 Japan
24-25 East Asia
26-27 Southeast Asia
28-29 South Asia
30-31 Southwest Asia
32 The Levant

AFRICA

33 Africa *Political*
34-35 Northern Africa
36 Central and Southern Africa
37 East Africa
38 West Africa - East
39 South Africa

OCEANIA

40 Oceania *Political*
41 Australia
42-43 Western Australia
44-45 Eastern Australia
46-47 Southeast Australia
48 New Zealand

NORTH AMERICA

49 North America *Political*
50-51 Canada and Alaska
52-53 United States
54 Western United States
55 Northeast U.S.A. - South Central Canada
56-57 Central America and the Caribbean

SOUTH AMERICA

58 South America *Political*
59 South America - East
60-61 South America - North
62-63 South America - South
64 Polar Regions

WORLD DATA

WORLD FACTS & FIGURES

66 World Physical Data
67 World Political Data
68-70 Nations of the World

WORLD INDEX

71 Introduction/Abbreviations
72-112 Alphabetical Index

WORLD MAPS (Endpapers)

Front The World: Political
Back The World: Physical

GUIDE TO THE ATLAS

COLLINS PAPERBACK ATLAS OF THE WORLD consists of three self-contained but interrelated sections, as is clearly indicated in the preceding list of contents.

OUR PLANET EARTH

This concise encyclopaedia section, by use of stimulating illustration and informative text, brings together many of the latest scientific discoveries and conclusions about our world; our place in the universe, our neighbours in space, the origin, structure and dynamics of our planet, the distribution of peoples and resources, and the increasingly significant effects of man on his environment. Each double-page opening has been carefully designed to highlight an important facet of our world as we know it today. As a special feature, every subject presentation includes a *Factfinder* panel, to which quick and easy reference can be made in order to find out particularly notable facts. All statistics quoted in this section are presented in metric terms in accordance with the System International d'Unites (S.I. units).

WORLD ATLAS

The main section of 64 pages of maps has been carefully planned and designed to meet the contemporary needs of the atlas user. Full recognition has been given to the many different purposes that currently call for map reference.

Map coverage extends to every part of the world in a balanced scheme that avoids any individual country or regional bias. Map areas are chosen to reflect the social, economic, cultural or historical importance of a particular region. Each double spread or single page map has been planned deliberately to cover an entire physical or political unit. Generous map overlaps are included to maintain continuity. Each of the continents is treated systematically in a subsection of its own. As an aid to the reader in locating the required area, a postage stamp key map is incorporated into the title margin of each map page.

Map projections have been chosen to reflect the different requirements of particular areas. No map can be absolutely true on account of the impossibility of representing a spheroid accurately on a flat surface without some distortion in either area, distance, direction or shape. In a general world atlas it is the equal area property that is most important to retain for comparative map studies and feature size evaluation and this principle has been followed wherever possible in this map section. As a special feature of this atlas, the *Global View* projections used for each continental political map have been specially devised to allow for a realistic area comparison between the land areas of each continent and also between land and sea.

Map scales, as expressions of the relationship which the distance between any two points of the map bears to the corresponding distance on the ground, are in the context of this atlas grouped into three distinct categories.

Large scales, of between 1 : 2 000 000 (1 centimetre to 20 kilometres or 1 inch to 32 miles) and 1 : 3 000 000 (1 centimetre to 30 kilometres or 1 inch to 48 miles), are used to cover particularly dense populated areas of Western Europe and Japan.

Medium scales, of between 1 : 3 000 000 and 1 : 10 000 000 are used for maps of important parts of Europe, North America, Australasia, etc.

Small scales, of less than 1 : 10 000 000 (1 centimetre to 100 kilometres or 1 inch to 160 miles), are selected for maps of the complete world, continents, polar regions and many of the larger countries.

The actual scale at which a particular area is mapped therefore reflects its shape, size and density of detail, and as a basic principle the more detail required to be shown of an area, the greater its scale. However, throughout this atlas, map scales have been limited in number, as far as possible, in order to facilitate comparison between maps.

Map measurements give preference to the metric system which is now used in nearly every country throughout the world. All spot heights and ocean depths are shown in metres and the relief and submarine layer delineation is based on metric contour levels. However, all linear scalebar and height reference column figures are given in metric and Imperial equivalents to facilitate conversion of measurements for the non-metric reader.

Map symbols used are fully explained in the legend to be found on the first page of the World Atlas section. Careful study and frequent reference to this legend will aid in the reader's ability to extract maximum information.

Topography is shown by the combined means of precise spot heights, contouring, layer tinting and three-dimensional hill shading. Similar techniques are also used to depict the sea bed on the World Physical map and those of the polar regions.

Hydrographic features such as coastlines, rivers, lakes, swamps and canals are clearly differentiated.

Communications are particularly well represented with the contemporary importance of airports and road networks duly emphasized.

International boundaries and national capitals are fully documented and internal administrative divisions are shown with the maximum detail that the scale will allow. Boundary delineation reflects the 'de facto' rather than the 'de jure' political interpretation and where relevant an undefined or disputed boundary is distinguished. However there is no intended implication that the publishers necessarily endorse or accept the status of any political entity recorded on the maps.

Settlements are shown by a series of graded town stamps, each representing a population size category, based on the latest census figures.

Other features, such as notable ancient monuments, oases, national parks, oil and gas fields, are selectively included on particular maps that merit their identification.

Lettering styles used in the maps have been chosen with great care to ensure maximum legibility and clear distinction of named feature categories. The size and weight of the various typefaces reflect the relative importance of the features. Town names are graded to correspond with the appropriate town stamp.

Map place names have been selected in accordance with maintaining legibility at a given scale and at the same time striking an appropriate balance between natural and man-made features worthy of note. Name forms have been standardized according to the widely accepted principle, now well established in international reference atlases, of including place names and geographical terms in the local language of the country in question. In the case of non-Roman scripts (e.g. Arabic), transliteration and transcription have either been based on the rules recommended by the Permanent Committee on Geographical Names and the United States Board on Geographic Names, or as in the case of the adopted Pinyin transcription of Chinese names, a system officially proposed by the country concerned. The diacritical signs used in each language or transliteration have been retained on all the maps and throughout the index. However the English language reader's requirements have also been recognised in that the names of all countries, oceans, major seas and land features as well as familiar alternative name versions of important towns are presented in English.

Map sources used in the compilation of this atlas were many and varied, but always of the latest available information. At each stage of their preparation the maps were submitted to a thorough process of research and continual revision to ensure that on publication all data would be as accurate as practicable. A well-documented data bank was created to ensure consistency and validity of all information represented on the maps.

WORLD DATA

This detailed data section forms an appropriate compliment to the preceding maps and illustrated texts. There are three parts, each providing a different type of essential geographical information.

World Facts and Figures Drawn from the latest available official sources, these tables present an easy reference profile of significant world physical, political and demographic as well as national data.

World Index This concluding part of the atlas lists in alphabetical order all individual place names to be found on the maps, which total over 20,000. Each entry in the index is referenced to the appropriate map page number, the country or region in which the name is located and the position of the name on the map, given by its co-ordinates of latitude and longitude. A full explanation of how to use the index is to be found on page 71.

World Maps Finally two summary maps giving separate coverage of the main political and physical features of the world are to be found on the front and back endpapers.

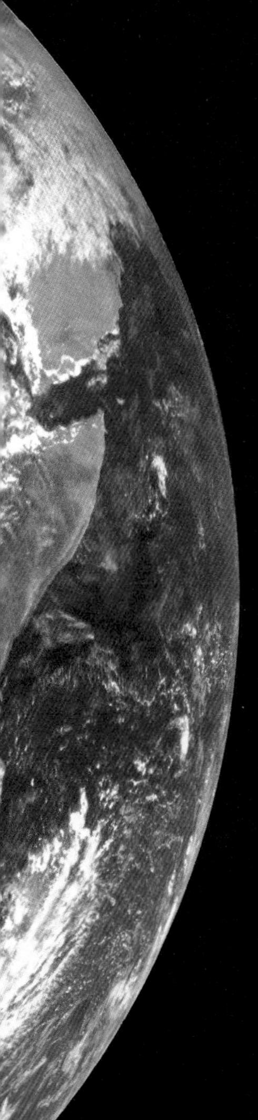

OUR PLANET EARTH

The Space Age, which began in 1957 with the triumphant launch of the Russian satellite Sputnik I, has already greatly enriched our understanding of the Solar System. It has also afforded us a new perspective on our own planet, not least through photographs taken by astronauts that remind us that the Earth is a mere speck in space. These photographs have dispelled the dangerous notion that our world is boundless in extent, with limitless resources. To view our planet from space is to recognize its finite nature and that we misuse it at our peril.

The Earth is a dynamic planet, with an ever-changing face. Movements in the restless atmosphere and hydrosphere are plain to see, while cataclysmic volcanic eruptions and earthquakes testify to the massive forces that operate beneath the Earth's crust. Continental drift is slowly but inexorably changing the world map, creating new ocean basins and lofty mountain ranges. Change ensures that the Earth's resources are constantly renewed. But nature works slowly, while our exploitation of those resources increases year by year – a consequence of a massive population explosion, which is most marked in the poorer nations, where malnutrition and short average life expectancies are features of everyday life. For example, an expanding population must be fed. But in many areas, over-intensive farming and over-grazing can rapidly transform once lush farmland into bleak desert.

Many question marks hang over the future of mankind, divided as it is by race, religion, language and political philosophies. And the plunder of our planet home is threatening many other life forms with extinction. One contribution we can all make to the survival of our world is to study and comprehend the delicate and infinitely varied environments that make Earth such a fascinating planet on which to live. Perhaps then our world can be preserved as, in the words of astronaut Neil Armstrong, a beautiful jewel in space.'

THE SOLAR SYSTEM

The Solar System rotates once around the centre of the Milky Way galaxy every 200 million years. The Solar System consists principally of the Sun and the nine planets that orbit around it, but it also includes moons and much debris, such as the spectacular rings of Saturn, and asteroids, which are called minor planets because they measure up to about 1000 km across. Other rocky matter and frozen gas form comets, which are even more numerous than asteroids. Comets have extremely elongated orbits, the farthest point of which may be in the vicinity of the outer planets. The path of one is shown by the red line in the diagram below. As the comets near the Sun, the frozen matter vaporizes to form a tail that is millions of kilometres long. If the orbit of a comet crosses that of the Earth, loose particles may be ejected into the atmosphere. There, they burn up in meteor showers. Fragments large enough to reach Earth are called meteorites.

Many solar systems probably exist in the Universe. In 1982 Russian astronomers estimated that 130 solar systems similar to our own lie within the observable part of the Milky Way galaxy. But their presence can only be inferred.

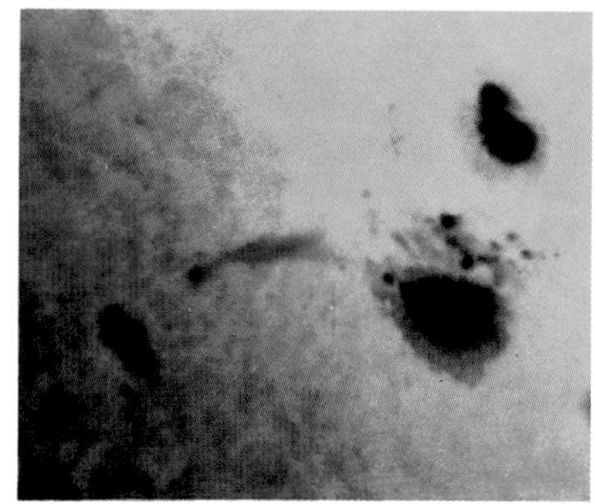

Groups of sunspots are dark areas on the Sun's surface that are around 1000° cooler than surrounding areas. The largest recorded sunspot covered 10,000 million km^2. Sunspots probably result from magnetic fields that cause local cooling. Sunspots may last for months, but small ones vanish after a few days.

Our Sun probably began to form about 4600 million years ago from the solar nebula, a huge cloud of dust and gas. The planets formed somewhat later from the debris that was left over. The Sun consists mainly of hydrogen that is being turned into a central core of helium. The reactions involved in this process generate energy, giving the Sun a surface temperature of 6000°C. Prominences, eruptions of gas from the surface, may reach 50,000°C or more. They are often associated with sunspots, cooler patches possibly caused by strong magnetic fields that block the outward flow of heat. The Sun is surrounded by a thin atmosphere, the corona, which can be seen during a total eclipse. Eventually, the Sun, like all stars, will use up most of its hydrogen and will become a red giant star, engulfing the Solar System. But this will not occur for another 5000 million years.

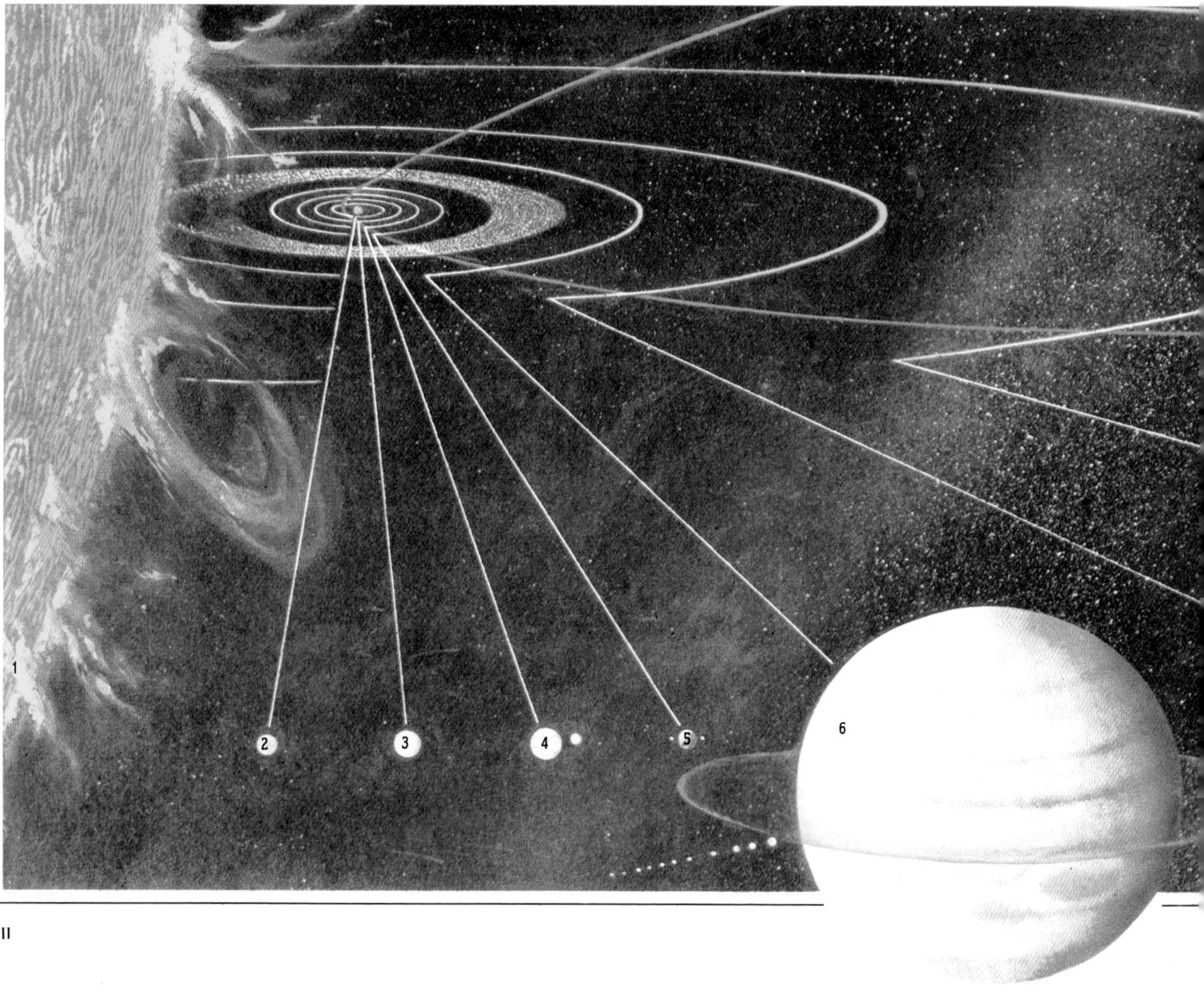

1

2

3

4

5

6

The Inner Planets

The planets differ in many ways in their makeup, appearance, size and temperature. The four inner planets are the cratered Mercury, whose surface resembles that of our Moon; Venus, which is swathed by a cloudy atmosphere containing much carbon dioxide; Earth; and Mars, which also has a cratered surface. These four, comparatively small, rocky bodies are called terrestrial planets.

The Outer Planets

Most of the asteroids in the Solar System lie between Mars, the outermost of the terrestrial planets, and Jupiter, the innermost of the outer planets. The outer planets include three others – the ringed Saturn, Uranus and Neptune – which, like Jupiter, are huge balls of gas, mainly hydrogen and its compounds, with nitrogen (giving ammonia), carbon (giving methane) and helium. Rocky cores may exist beneath the gases. Pluto, which was discovered in 1930, is probably a rocky body with a methane-type atmosphere.

FACTFINDER

		Mean distance from the Sun (millions of km)	Equatorial diameter (km)	Period of rotation on axis	Surface °C temperature	Mass (Earth = 1)	Sidereal Period
1	Sun	—	1,392,000	25d 9h	6000°	333,434.00	—
2	Mercury	58	4,850	58d 14h	350/–170°	0·04	88d
3	Venus	108	12,104	243d	480°	0·83	225d
4	Earth	149·5	12,756	23h56m	22°	1·00	1y
5	Mars	228	6,790	24h 37m	–50°	0·11	1y 322d
6	Jupiter	778·5	142,600	9h 50m	–150°	318.00	11y 315d
7	Saturn	1427	120,000	10h 14m	–180°	95.00	29y 167d
8	Uranus	2870	52,000?	24h(?)	–210°	15.00	84y 6d
9	Neptune	4497	48,000?	22h(?)	–220°	17.00	164y 288d
10	Pluto	5900	3,000?	6d 9h	–230°?	0·06	247y 255d

Number of satellites: Mercury and Venus – 0; Earth – 1; Mars – 2; Jupiter – 14?; Saturn – 17?; Uranus – 5; Neptune – 2; Pluto – 1.

Orbital inclination: Mercury – 7°; Venus – 3°24′; Mars – 1°51′; Jupiter – 1°18′; Saturn – 2°29′; Uranus – 0°46′; Neptune – 1°46′; Pluto – 17°06′.

7
8
9
10

THE WHIRLING EARTH

The Earth moves in three ways: it spins on its axis; it orbits the Sun; and it moves around the Milky Way galaxy with the rest of the Solar System. As it spins on its axis, the Sun appears to move around the sky once every 24 hours. This, the mean solar day, is slightly longer than the sidereal day of 23 hours, 56 minutes and 4 seconds. The difference between the two is explained by the fact that the Earth is orbiting the Sun while it spins on its axis, with the effect that it must rotate 1/365th of a revolution more than a sidereal day in order that the same meridian exactly faces the Sun again.

As the Earth spins on its axis, the time at any point on the surface is calculated from the position of the Sun in the sky. This is called the local or apparent time. Because the Earth rotates 360° in 24 hours, local time changes by one hour for every 15° of longitude or 4 minutes for every 1° of longitude. For practical purposes, however, we use standard or zone time, so that the times are fixed over extensive north-south zones that also take account of national boundaries. By an international agreement in 1884, time zones are measured east and west of the prime meridian (0° longitude) which passes through Greenwich, London. Because clocks are advanced by 12 hours 180° east of Greenwich, but put back by 12 hours 180° west of Greenwich, there is a time difference of 24 hours at the International Date Line. This is approximately 180°W or E, although internationally agreed deviations prevent confusion of dates in island groups and land areas. People crossing the International Date Line from west to east gain a day. Those going from east to west lose a day.

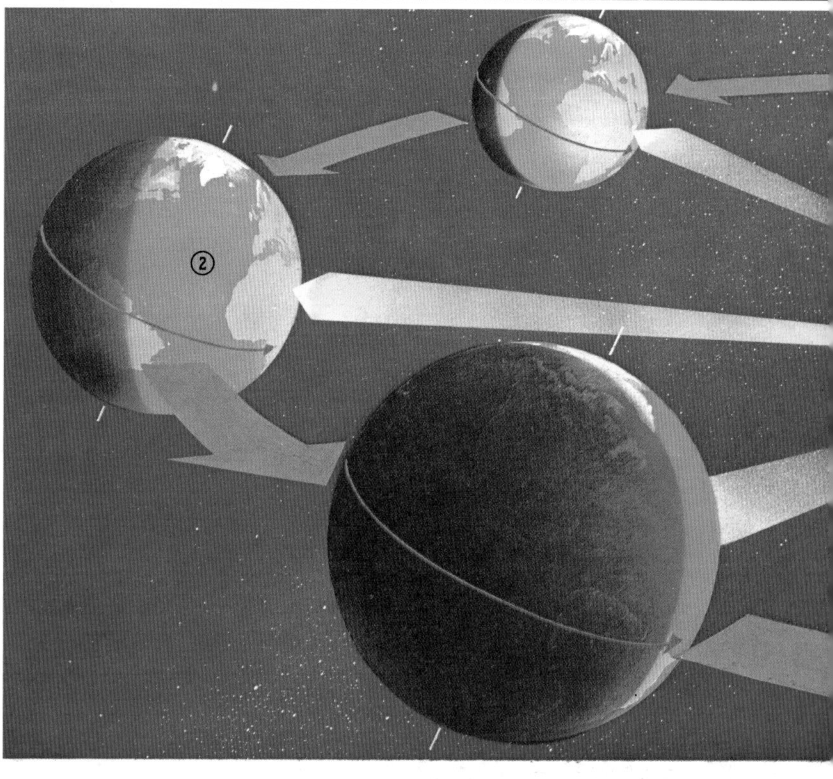
②

The Seasons

Because the Earth's axis is tilted by 23½°, the Sun appears to travel in a higher or lower path across the sky at various times of the year, giving differing lengths of daylight. The diagram at the top of the page shows that, at the spring equinox in the northern hemisphere (March 21), the Sun is overhead at the Equator. After March 21, the overhead Sun moves northwards as the northern hemisphere tilts towards the Sun. On June 21, the summer solstice in the northern hemisphere, the Sun is overhead at the Tropic of Cancer (latitude 23½° North). By September 23, the Sun is again overhead at the Equator. By about December 21, the Sun is overhead at the Tropic of Capricorn (23½° S). This is the winter solstice in the northern hemisphere. The seasons are reversed in the southern hemisphere.

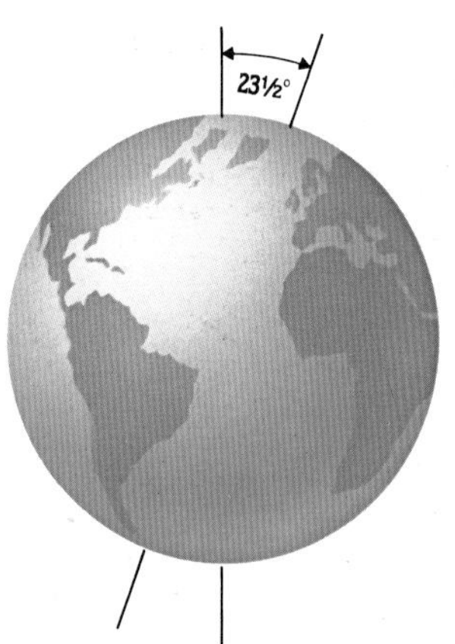
23½°

Above: The Earth's axis (joining the North and South poles via the centre of the Earth) is tilted by 23½°. The Earth rotates on its axis once every 23 hours, 56 minutes and 4 seconds. The tilt of the axis remains constant as the Earth orbits the Sun.

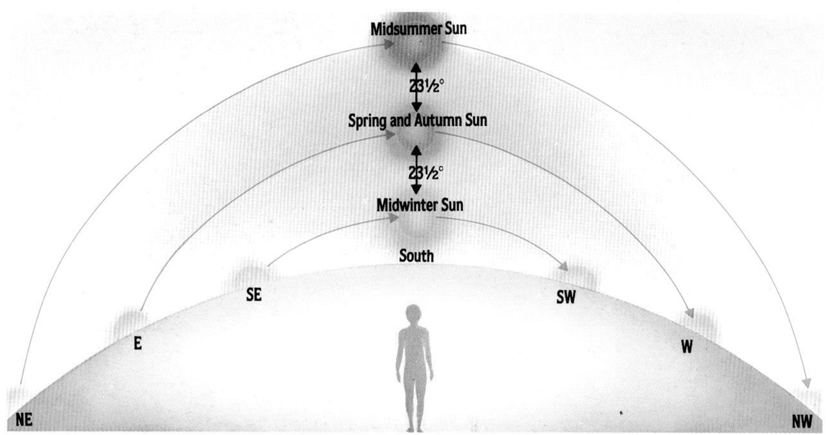
Midsummer Sun
23½°
Spring and Autumn Sun
23½°
Midwinter Sun
South
SE
SW
E
W
NE
NW

Right: The path of the Sun across the sky is highest on Midsummer Day, the longest day, and lowest at midwinter (December 21), the shortest day. The total variation in altitude is 47°, which is twice the angle by which the Earth's axis is tilted.

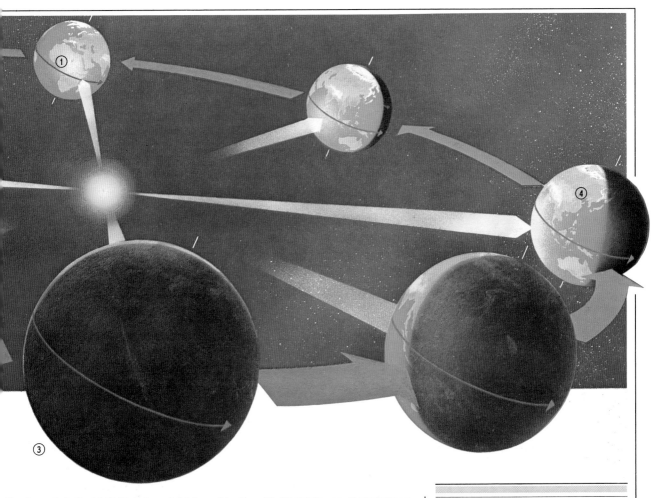

Above: Because the Earth's axis is tilted during its annual orbit of the Sun, there are variations in solar radiation that cause seasons. On March 21, the spring or vernal equinox in the northern hemisphere, the Sun is overhead at the Equator (1). On June 21, it is overhead at the Tropic of Cancer, the summer solstice (2). On September 23, it is overhead at the Equator, the autumn equinox (3). On December 21, it is overhead at the Tropic of Capricorn, the winter solstice (4).

Below: The world is divided into time zones. The standard time at Greenwich (0° longitude) on the map is 12.00 Greenwich Mean Time (not British Summer Time). East of Greenwich, standard times are ahead of GMT, while west of Greenwich, they are behind it. Ideally, time zones should be longitudinal bands of 15° or 7½° (representing time differences of 1 hour or 30 minutes). But time zones are irregular in shape to prevent small countries having two standard times.

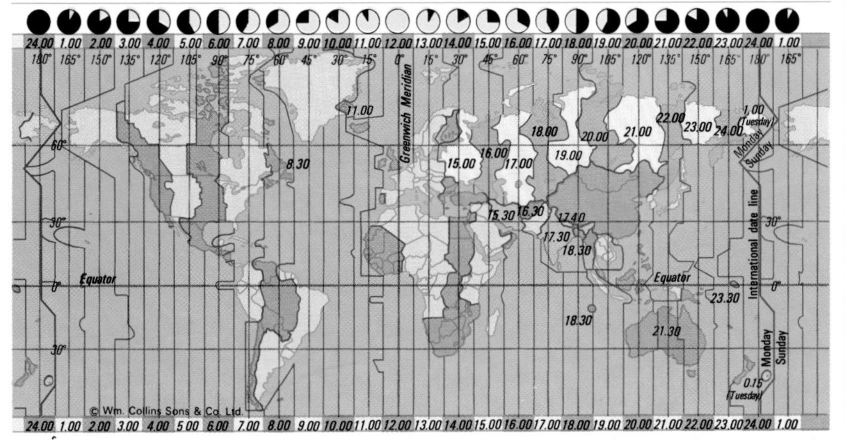
24.00 1.00 2.00 3.00 4.00 5.00 6.00 7.00 8.00 9.00 10.00 11.00 12.00 13.00 14.00 15.00 16.00 17.00 18.00 19.00 20.00 21.00 22.00 23.00 24.00 1.00
180° 165° 150° 135° 120° 105° 90° 75° 60° 45° 30° 15° 0° 15° 30° 45° 60° 75° 90° 105° 120° 135° 150° 165° 180° 165°
Greenwich Meridian
International date line
11.00
8.30
15.00
16.00
17.00
18.00
19.00
20.00
21.00
22.00
23.00
24.00
1.00 (Tuesday)
Monday
Sunday
15.30
16.30
17.40
17.30
18.30
60°
30°
0°
Equator
23.30
18.30
21.30
0.15 (Tuesday)
© Wm. Collins Sons & Co. Ltd.
24.00 1.00 2.00 3.00 4.00 5.00 6.00 7.00 8.00 9.00 10.00 11.00 12.00 13.00 14.00 15.00 16.00 17.00 18.00 19.00 20.00 21.00 22.00 23.00 24.00 1.00

FACTFINDER

Length of day: Mean solar day, 24 hours. Sidereal day (measured against fixed stars) 23·93 hours.

Speed of the Earth's rotation on its axis: At the Equator, it is rotating at 1660 km/h. It is less away from the Equator: at 30°N and S, it is 1438 km/h; at 60° N and S, it is 990 km/h.

Equinoxes: The vernal equinox is on March 21, and the autumn equinox on September 23 in the northern hemisphere. The equinoxes are reversed in the southern hemisphere.

Solstices: In the northern hemisphere, the summer solstice is on June 21 and the winter solstice on December 21. The reverse applies in the southern hemisphere.

THE EARTH'S STRUCTURE

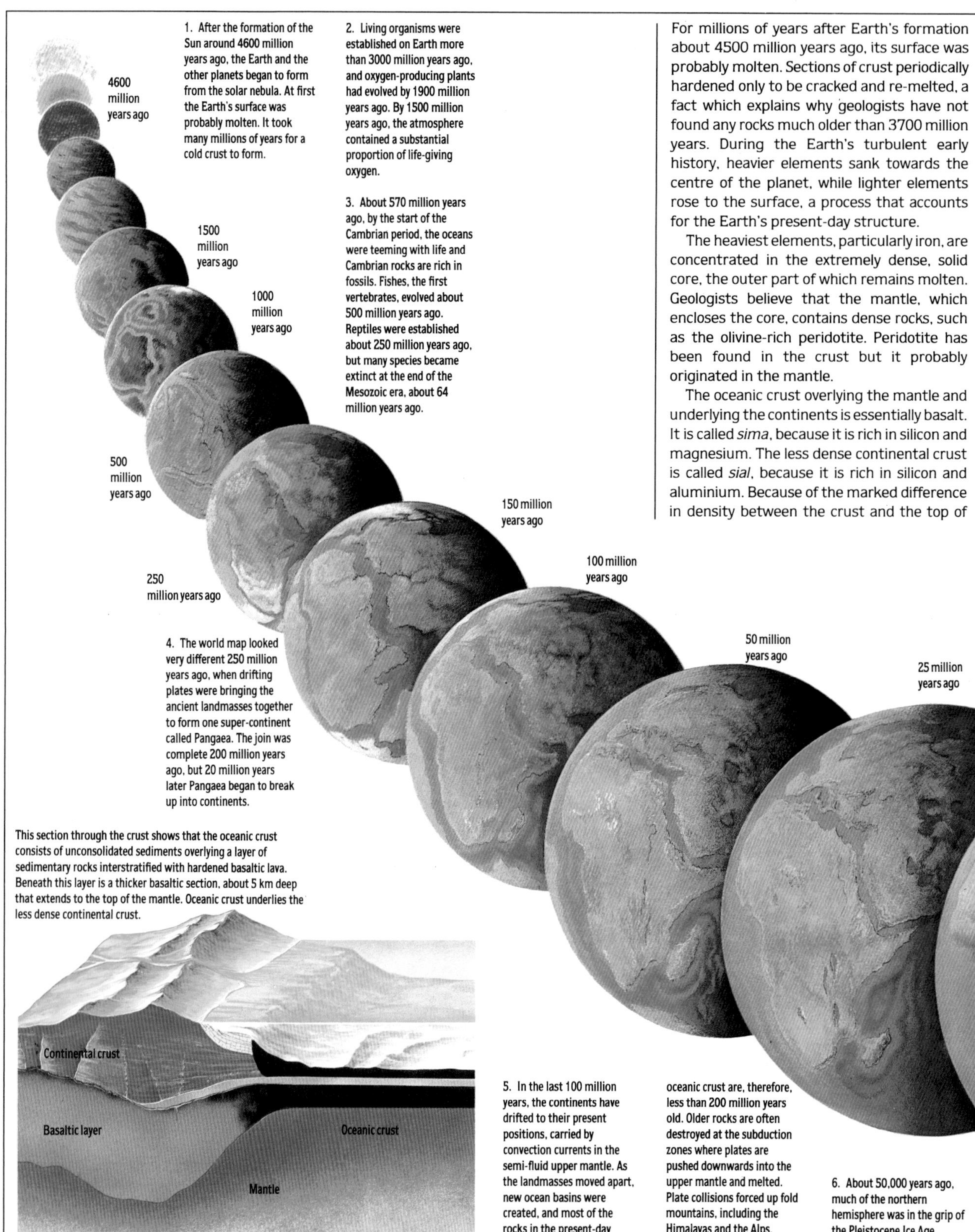
4600 million years ago
1500 million years ago
1000 million years ago
500 million years ago
250 million years ago
150 million years ago
100 million years ago
50 million years ago
25 million years ago
Continental crust
Basaltic layer
Oceanic crust
Mantle

1. After the formation of the Sun around 4600 million years ago, the Earth and the other planets began to form from the solar nebula. At first the Earth's surface was probably molten. It took many millions of years for a cold crust to form.

2. Living organisms were established on Earth more than 3000 million years ago, and oxygen-producing plants had evolved by 1900 million years ago. By 1500 million years ago, the atmosphere contained a substantial proportion of life-giving oxygen.

3. About 570 million years ago, by the start of the Cambrian period, the oceans were teeming with life and Cambrian rocks are rich in fossils. Fishes, the first vertebrates, evolved about 500 million years ago. Reptiles were established about 250 million years ago, but many species became extinct at the end of the Mesozoic era, about 64 million years ago.

4. The world map looked very different 250 million years ago, when drifting plates were bringing the ancient landmasses together to form one super-continent called Pangaea. The join was complete 200 million years ago, but 20 million years later Pangaea began to break up into continents.

5. In the last 100 million years, the continents have drifted to their present positions, carried by convection currents in the semi-fluid upper mantle. As the landmasses moved apart, new ocean basins were created, and most of the rocks in the present-day oceanic crust are, therefore, less than 200 million years old. Older rocks are often destroyed at the subduction zones where plates are pushed downwards into the upper mantle and melted. Plate collisions forced up fold mountains, including the Himalayas and the Alps.

6. About 50,000 years ago, much of the northern hemisphere was in the grip of the Pleistocene Ice Age.

This section through the crust shows that the oceanic crust consists of unconsolidated sediments overlying a layer of sedimentary rocks interstratified with hardened basaltic lava. Beneath this layer is a thicker basaltic section, about 5 km deep that extends to the top of the mantle. Oceanic crust underlies the less dense continental crust.

For millions of years after Earth's formation about 4500 million years ago, its surface was probably molten. Sections of crust periodically hardened only to be cracked and re-melted, a fact which explains why geologists have not found any rocks much older than 3700 million years. During the Earth's turbulent early history, heavier elements sank towards the centre of the planet, while lighter elements rose to the surface, a process that accounts for the Earth's present-day structure.

The heaviest elements, particularly iron, are concentrated in the extremely dense, solid core, the outer part of which remains molten. Geologists believe that the mantle, which encloses the core, contains dense rocks, such as the olivine-rich peridotite. Peridotite has been found in the crust but it probably originated in the mantle.

The oceanic crust overlying the mantle and underlying the continents is essentially basalt. It is called *sima*, because it is rich in silicon and magnesium. The less dense continental crust is called *sial*, because it is rich in silicon and aluminium. Because of the marked difference in density between the crust and the top of

FACTFINDER

The Earth's crust: The oceanic crust averages 6 km thick; density, 3·0 g/cm³. The continental crust averages 35–40 km, reaching 60–70 km under high mountains; density 2·7 g/cm³.

Mantle: About 2900 km thick; density, 3·4–4·5 g/cm³.

Core: Diameter 6740 km. Outer core 2000 km thick, molten iron and nickel. Inner core, a solid metal ball, 1370 km thick. Density of core, 10–13 g/cm³. Temperature at 2700°C, under pressure of 3800 tonnes per sq cm.

Surface area of the Earth: 510,066,000 km². About 148,326,000 km², or just over 29 per cent of the Earth's surface, is land.

Mass: 5976 million million million tonnes.

Shape and size: Oblate spheroid, slightly flattened at the poles and bulging at the Equator. So, at sea level, the diameter of the Earth between the poles is 12,713 km, as compared with a diameter of 12,756 km across the plane of the Equator. Similarly, the equatorial circumference of 40,075 km is greater than the polar circumference of 40,007 km.

the mantle, the crust cannot sink. It is split into large, rigid plates that 'float' on the denser mantle. Plate movements cause earthquakes, mountain building and volcanic activity – occurrences that remind us of the restless nature of our world.

About 85 per cent of the top 16 km of the crust are either igneous rocks (rocks formed from molten magma) or metamorphic rocks (igneous or sedimentary rocks that have been changed by heat, pressure or, sometimes, chemical action). However, sedimentary rocks cover 75 per cent of the surface of landmasses. Many sedimentary rocks are clastic (formed from eroded rock fragments), some, such as coal, are organic, and some are formed by chemical action, such as rock salt precipitated from water.

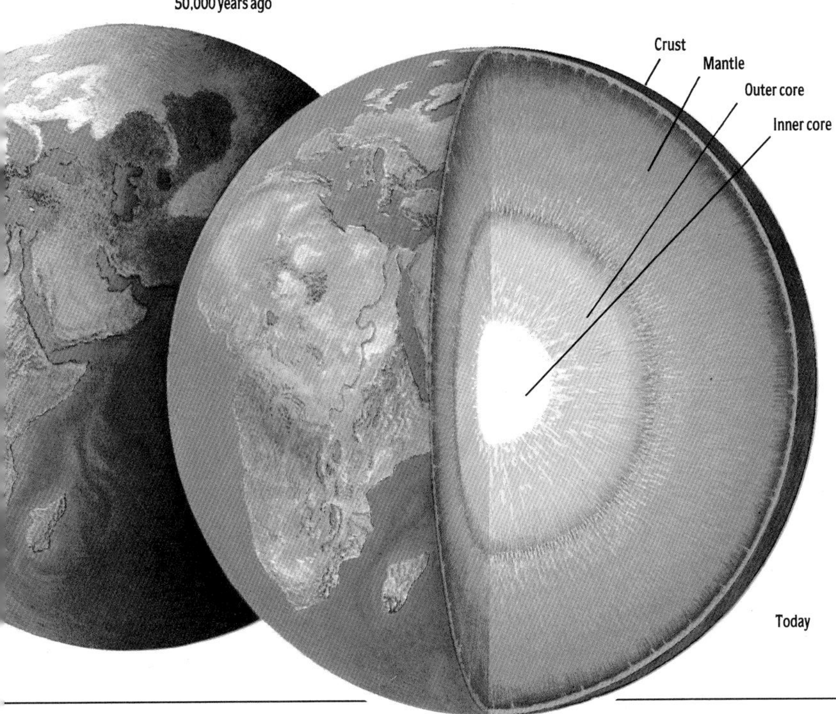
50,000 years ago
Crust
Mantle
Outer core
Inner core
Today

Below are eight rocks found in the Earth's crust. There are three main kinds of rocks: igneous, sedimentary and metamorphic. Igneous rocks, including obsidian and granite, are forms of hardened magma. Many sedimentary rocks, such as sandstone and conglomorate, are composed of worn fragments of other rocks, while coal is compressed plant remains. Metamorphic rocks, such as marble and slate, are formed when great heat and pressure alter igneous or sedimentary rocks.

Obsidian is a glassy, extrusive igneous rock, formed on the surface.

Granite is a coarse-grained, intrusive igneous rock, which forms in huge underground masses.

Marble is formed by the action of great heat and pressure on limestone.

Slate is usually formed by the metamorphism of shale.

Coal is a fossil fuel formed in ancient swamps.

Limestones are sedimentary rocks composed mainly of calcium carbonate.

Sandstone contains grains of quartz and other minerals bound together by tough mineral cements.

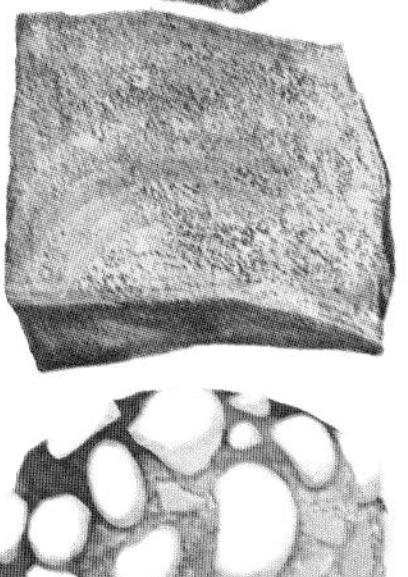

Conglomerates contain pebbles cemented in a fine silt or sand matrix.

THE ATMOSPHERE AND CLOUDS

The atmosphere is a thin skin of gases, chiefly nitrogen and life-giving oxygen, that encircles and protects the Earth. It moderates temperatures, preventing enormous diurnal changes in heating that would destroy life on Earth. And, in the stratosphere, one of the five main layers of the atmosphere, is a belt of ozone that absorbs most of the Sun's dangerous ultraviolet radiation. The depth of the atmosphere cannot be defined precisely, because it becomes increasingly rarefied with height. But more than 99 per cent of its mass is within 40 km of the surface.

Air Pressure

Air has weight and the total weight of the atmosphere is about 5000 million million tonnes. However, we do not feel the constant pressure of about one tonne of air on our shoulders, because there is an equal air pressure inside our bodies. Air pressure varies, a major factor in weather. Generally, pressures are lower in warm, expanding air which tends to rise, as at the doldrums. It is higher in cold, dense air which sinks downwards, as at the high pressure horse latitudes.

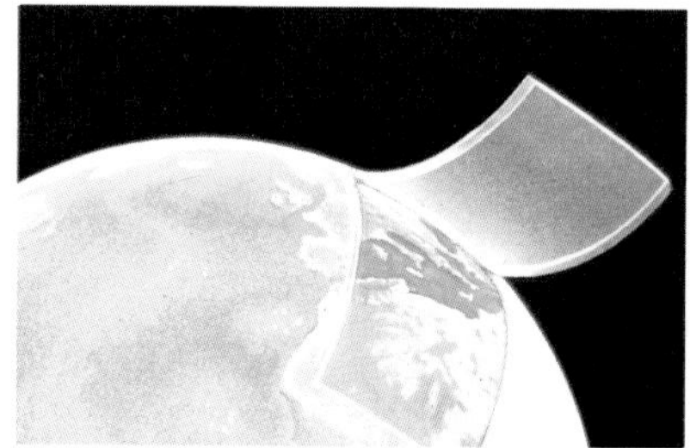

The Earth is surrounded by a thin layer of gases, known as the atmosphere.

This section through the atmosphere shows its five main layers.

EXOSPHERE, which begins at about 500 km above the surface, is extremely rarefied and composed mainly of hydrogen and helium. The exosphere merges into space.

IONOSPHERE, between 80 and 500 km, contains gas molecules that are ionized, or electrically charged, by cosmic or solar rays. Disturbances in the ionosphere cause glowing lights, called aurorae. Temperatures rise steadily with height from about –80°C at 80 km to 2200°C at 400 km.

MESOSPHERE, between 50 and 80 km, is marked by a fall in temperature from 10°C at 50 km to –80°C.

STRATOSPHERE, stretches above the tropopause (the name for the upper boundary of the troposphere) to 50 km height. It has a layer of ozone (oxygen with three rather than two atoms) that filters out most of the Sun's ultraviolet rays. Temperatures rise from –55°C to 10°C at 50 km. The noctilucent clouds are probably composed of meteoric dust.

TROPOSPHERE is the lowest 18km of the atmosphere over the Equator, the lowest 10 to 11 km in the middle latitudes, and the lowest 8 km over the poles. It contains most of the atmosphere's mass. Temperatures fall with height, but stabilize at the tropopause.

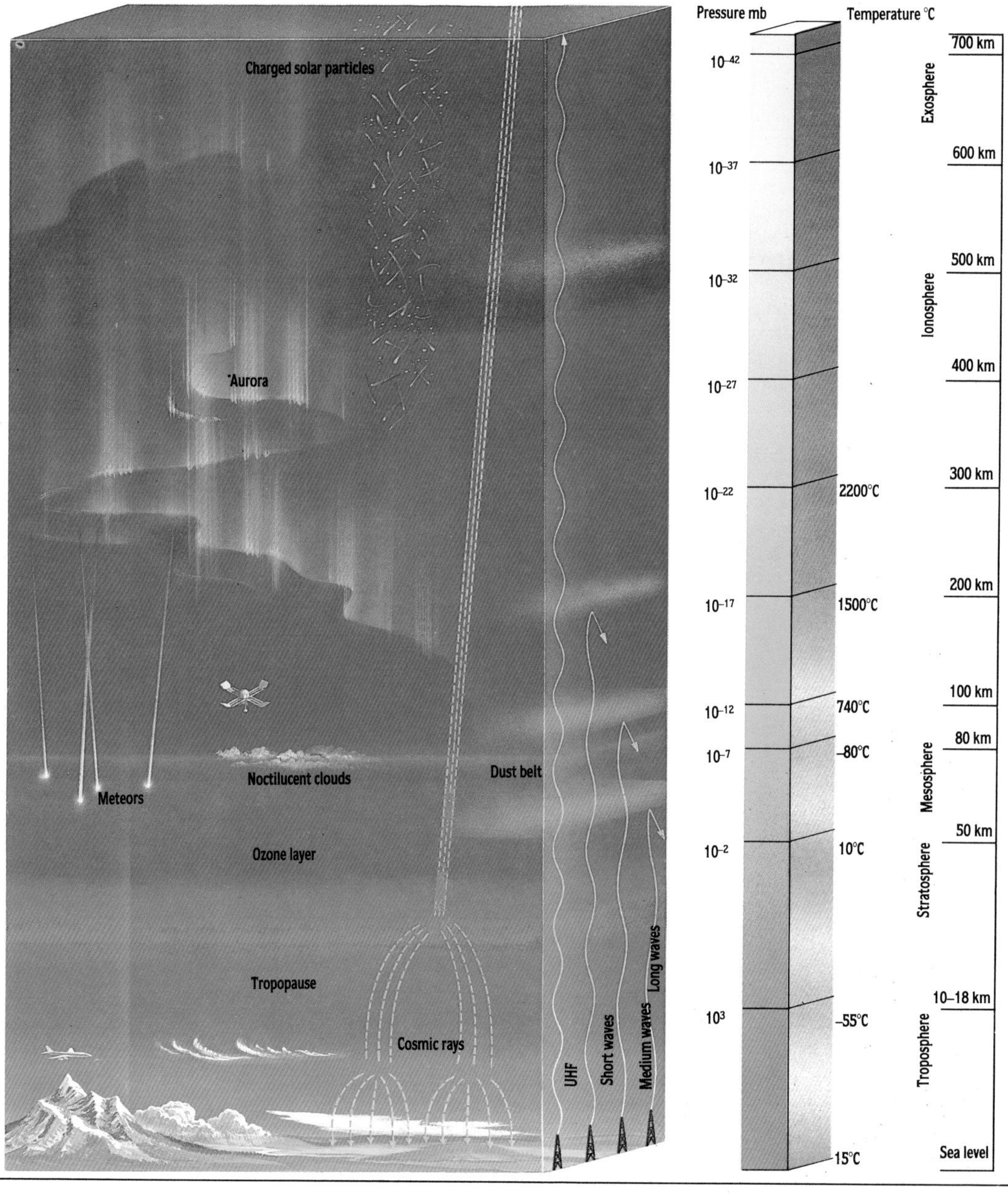

Charged solar particles

Aurora

Noctilucent clouds

Meteors

Dust belt

Ozone layer

Tropopause

Cosmic rays

UHF

Short waves

Medium waves

Long waves

Pressure mb	Temperature °C		
		Exosphere	700 km
10^{-42}			
10^{-37}			600 km
10^{-32}		Ionosphere	500 km
10^{-27}			400 km
10^{-22}	2200°C		300 km
10^{-17}	1500°C		200 km
10^{-12}	740°C		100 km
10^{-7}	–80°C	Mesosphere	80 km
10^{-2}	10°C	Stratosphere	50 km
10^{3}	–55°C	Troposphere	10–18 km
	15°C		Sea level

The clouds on this photograph reveal a hurricane, a rotating low pressure air system.

Cloud Formation

All air contains water vapour, but warm air holds much more than cold air. When air is cooled it can hold less water vapour. At dew point, it is saturated, containing all the water vapour it can at that temperature. Further cooling causes water vapour to condense around specks of dust or salt in the air to form tiny, visible water droplets or ice crystals, masses of which form clouds.

Circulation of Air

Air is invisible but, powered by energy from the Sun, it is always moving. Generally, winds blow from areas of high air pressure, such as the horse latitudes, towards areas of low pressure, such as the doldrums. Winds are deflected by the Coriolis effect, which is caused by the Earth's rotation. Local factors, such as mountains, also affect winds. Monsoons are seasonal reversals of winds. For example, over northern India in winter, cold, dense air masses develop, from which winds blow outwards. But heating in summer creates low air pressure and moist winds are sucked on to the land.

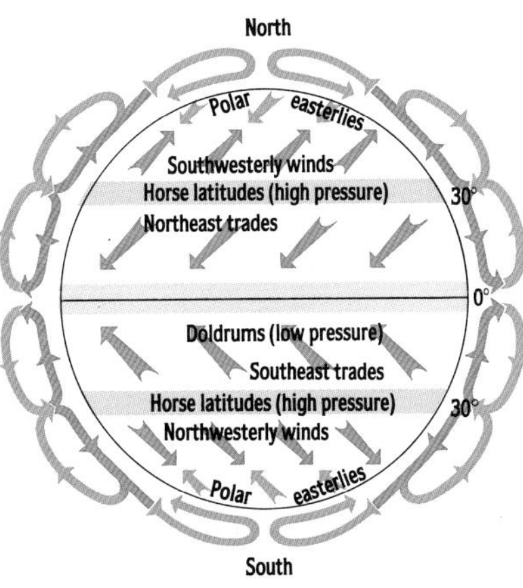
North
Polar easterlies
Southwesterly winds
Horse latitudes (high pressure)
30°
Northeast trades
0°
Doldrums (low pressure)
Southeast trades
Horse latitudes (high pressure)
30°
Northwesterly winds
Polar easterlies
South

Above: The diagram shows the main movements of air in the atmosphere and across the surface in the prevailing wind systems. Winds generally blow towards low pressure regions, such as the doldrums, and outwards from high pressure systems at the horse latitudes and the poles.

FACTFINDER

Composition of the air: Nitrogen (78·09 per cent); oxygen (20·95 per cent); argon (0·93 per cent).
Other gases include carbon dioxide, helium, hydrogen, krypton, methane, neon, ozone, and xenon.

Average surface pressure: 1013 mb.

Atmospheric level reached by radio waves (frequency in kilohertz)

Long waves (below 500 kHz)	: 50 km
Medium waves (500 – 1500 kHz)	: 95 km
Short (1500 – 30,000 kHz by day)	:200 km
waves (1500 – 30,000 kHz by night)	:280 km

Very short wavelengths (UHF) penetrate all layers.

Cloud Types

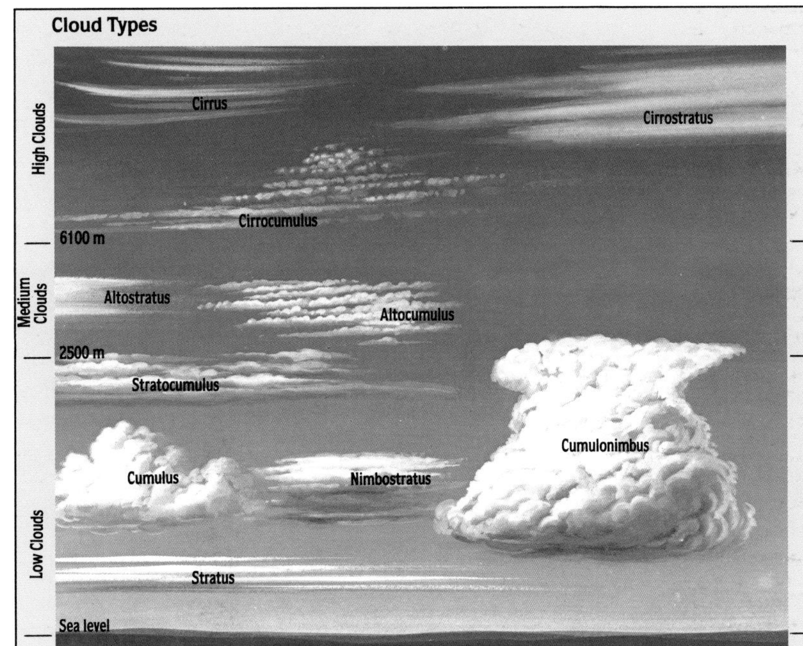
High Clouds
Cirrus
Cirrostratus
Cirrocumulus
6100 m
Medium Clouds
Altostratus
Altocumulus
2500 m
Stratocumulus
Cumulonimbus
Cumulus
Nimbostratus
Low Clouds
Stratus
Sea level

High Clouds

High clouds form above 6100 metres above ground level, as follows:
CIRRUS is a delicate feathery cloud, sometimes called mares' tails or ice banners. It is often the first sign of an approaching depression.
CIRROSTRATUS is a thin layer cloud, with ripples and rounded masses. It veils but does not block out the Sun.
CIRROCUMULUS is a patchy cloud composed of small white balls. Formed from ice crystals, it is often called mackerel sky.

Medium Clouds

Medium clouds occur between about 2500 and 6100 metres, as follows:
ALTOSTRATUS is a greyish or bluish layer cloud that may become so thick that it blocks out the Sun. It is a sign of an advancing depression.
ALTOCUMULUS resembles a mass of tiny clouds. It indicates unsettled weather.

Low Clouds

Low clouds form below 2500 metres above ground level as follows:
STRATOCUMULUS is a greyish-white cloud, consisting of rounded masses.
NIMBOSTRATUS is a dark cloud, associated with rain and snow, which often occurs along the warm fronts of depressions.
CUMULUS is a white, heap cloud, usually with a flat base and a dome-shaped top. In summer, fluffy cumulus is a feature of fine weather. Heavy cumulus can develop into cumulonimbus cloud.
STRATUS is a grey layer cloud that often forms ahead of warm fronts in depressions where warm air is rising fairly slowly over cold air. Such clouds bring drizzle, rain and snow.
CUMULONIMBUS is a dark, heavy cloud. It may rise 4500 metres or more from its ragged base to its often anvil-shaped top. It is associated with thunder, lightning, rain and snow.

Cloud Classification. There are three main types of cloud shapes: feathery cirrus; heap or cumuliform clouds; and layer or stratiform clouds.

THE WATER OF LIFE

In some countries, people take their regular supply of fresh water for granted, while elsewhere, in desert lands, it is a prized commodity. Water reaches us, in one way or another, through the hydrological, or water, cycle, whereby land areas are supplied with precipitation that originates in the saline oceans, where more than 97 per cent of the world's water is found.

Another vital resource, also taken for granted in many places, is the soil, the character of which is largely determined by the climate. The delicate balance between climate, water, and plant life is something that we disturb at our peril.

Soil is the thin layer of loose material derived from and overlying the bedrock. Soils vary in thickness. Mineral grains, the product of weathering, make up more than 90 per cent of most dry soils. Soil also contains humus, including the remains of dead plants and animals. About 40 per cent of moist soils is made up of spaces, occupied by air or water. Soils vary according to the climate, for example, soils in tropical rainy regions are leached by heavy rain. By contrast, some soils in arid regions contain mineral salts deposited by water rising *upwards* towards the surface.

Plant life shows remarkable adaptations to a vast variety of environments. The main vegetation zones are largely determined by climate. But, like climatic regions, vegetation zones have no marked boundaries; they merge imperceptibly with one another.

Vegetation zones usually refer to the original plant cover, or optimum growth, before it was altered by human activity. Human interference with nature can be disastrous. For example, semi-arid grasslands have been ploughed up. Prolonged droughts have reduced the exposed soil to a powdery dust which is removed by the wind, creating dust bowls and encouraging the spread of deserts. The destruction of tropical forests, such as in Brazil, is a matter of concern today. Plants that have never been identified are being destroyed for ever, when they might be sources of new drugs. A massive forest clearance might change world climates.

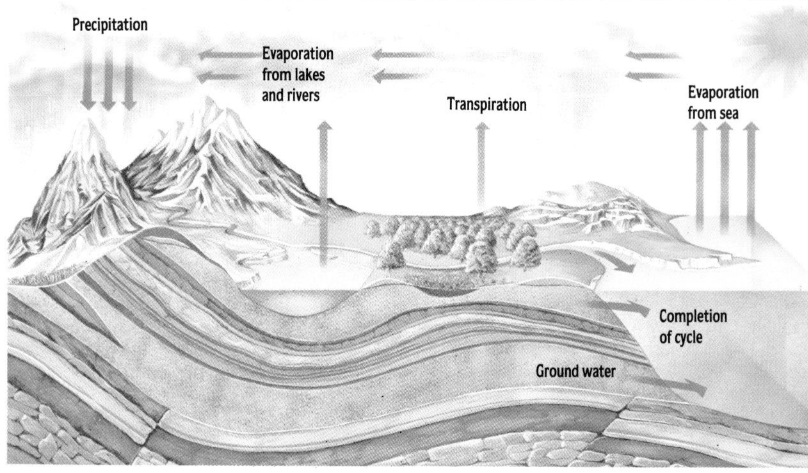
Precipitation
Evaporation from lakes and rivers
Transpiration
Evaporation from sea
Completion of cycle
Ground water

Above: The water cycle provides landmasses with fresh water. The water comes mainly from moisture evaporated from the oceans, to which the water eventually returns.

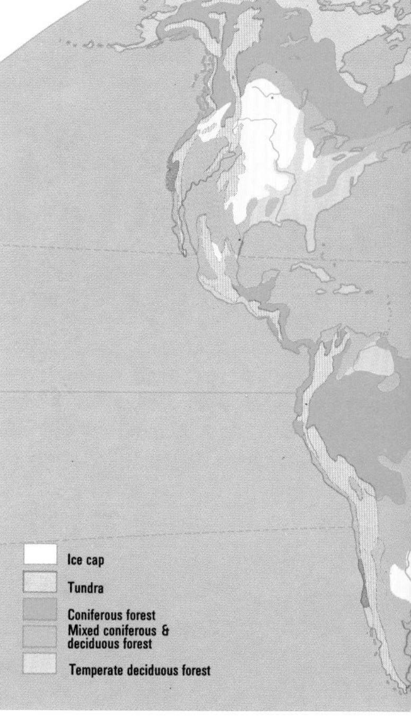
Ice cap
Tundra
Coniferous forest
Mixed coniferous & deciduous forest
Temperate deciduous forest

Right: The map shows the world's chief vegetation zones.

Below: The photographs show major vegetation regions:
1. Tundra is the name for treeless regions near the poles and near the tops of high mountains that are snow-covered for most of the year. But mosses, lichens and some flowering plants flourish in the short summer.
2. Coniferous forests, or taiga, cover a broad belt south of the tundra in the northern hemisphere. The shapes of conifers prevent their being overloaded by snow. The needle-like leaves reduce transpiration, while the thick bark and pitch-like sap reduce evaporation.
3. Broadleaf, or deciduous, forests grow in warm temperate regions. By shedding their leaves, deciduous trees are better able to survive the winter.
4. Scrub and semi-arid grasslands cover large areas of the world. They are highly susceptible to soil erosion if the vegetation cover is removed. Scrub, called maquis, fynbos, chaparral and mallee scrub, are typical of Mediterranean lands where the original forest cover has been destroyed.
5. Tropical grassland includes the llanos of Venezuela. The palm trees in the photograph are growing in a swamp. Tropical grassland is also called campos or savanna.
6. Evergreen tropical rain forest flourishes in regions which are hot and have ample rain throughout the year.

1

2

3

FACTFINDER

Water distribution: 97·2% is in the oceans (about 1360 million km^3); 2·15% is frozen in bodies of ice; 0·625% is ground water; 0·171% is in rivers and lakes; 0·001 is water vapour in the atmosphere.

Average daily water consumption: In the United States: about 200 litres (flushing toilet, washing and bathing, 78%; kitchen use, 6%; drinking, 5%; other, 11%). In many hot countries, the daily per capita water consumption is less than 4 litres.

Common soils: Laterites (leached soils in tropical rainy regions); grey marginal soils (deserts); chestnut-brown soils (arid grasslands); brown forest earths (Mediterranean lands); podsols (cold temperate regions).

Vegetation: Ice covers about 10% of the world's land surfaces and hot deserts 20%. The largest forest is the coniferous forest of the northern USSR, which covers 1100 million hectares – 27% of the world's total forests.

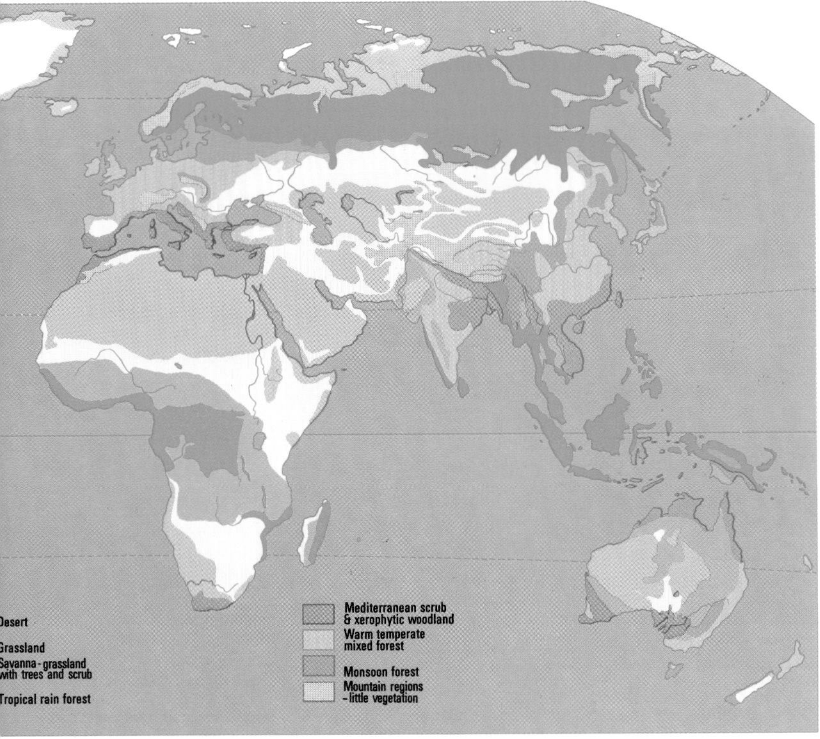
esert
rassland
avanna-grassland with trees and scrub
Tropical rain forest
Mediterranean scrub & xerophytic woodland
Warm temperate mixed forest
Monsoon forest
Mountain regions – little vegetation

Below: Well-developed soils have three layers, called the A, B and C horizons, overlying the parent rock.

Right: Prairie soils occur in regions that are wet enough in places to support woodland. The A horizon contains much humus, but it is also much leached by seeping water.

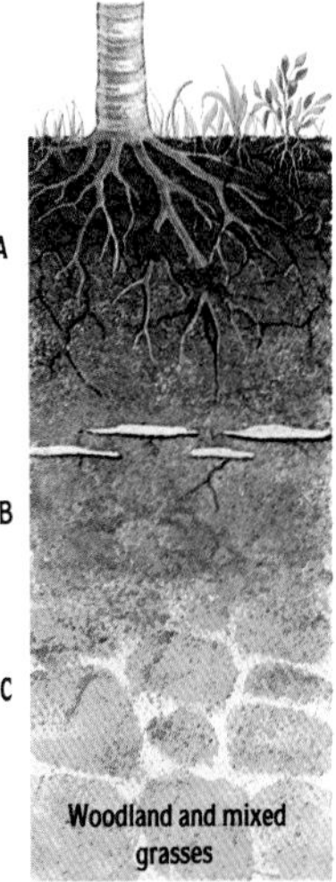
A
B
C
Woodland and mixed grasses

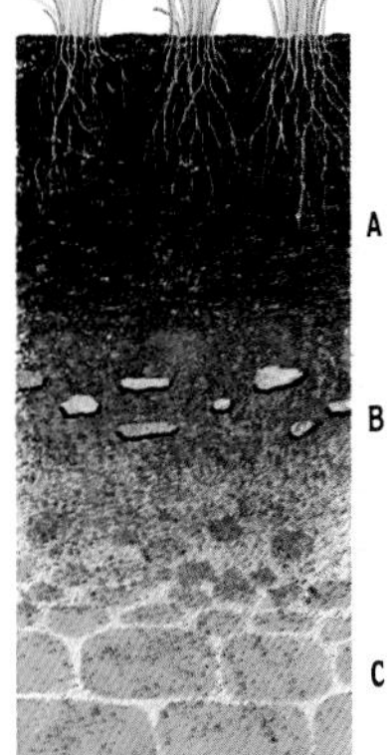
A
B
C
Tall bunch grass

Chernozem soils, sometimes called black earths, contain much humus (mainly decomposed grass). They occur in steppelands which have less rainfall than prairies.

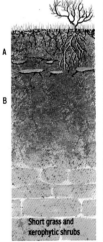

A
B
Short grass and xerophytic shrubs

Chestnut-brown soils are typical of particularly arid grasslands. They occur south of the Russian steppes and in the drier parts of Argentina, South Africa and the United States.

4

5

6

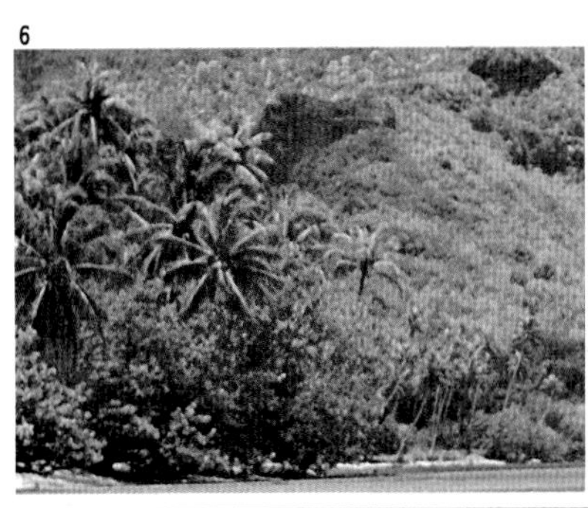

THE POPULATION EXPLOSION

One of the world's most serious problems is the population explosion and the difficulties that can be foreseen in feeding the people of the world in the future. On an average estimated rate of population increase of 1·8 per cent a year between 1970 and 1975, the world's population will double in the next 39 years, although recent data suggests that the rate in the 1970s is less than that in the 1960s. The problems arising from the population explosion are most marked in the developing world and least in the industrial nations where people see advantages in population control.

Population explosions occur when average birth rates far exceed death rates. In recent years, death rates have everywhere declined mainly because of improved medical care. In industrial countries, birth rates have also fallen so that a growing proportion of people is in the senior age groups. But while such countries must finance retirement pensions, developing nations have the highest expenditures on health and other children's services, because 40 per cent or more of their population is under 15. This contrast between developing and developed nations is also illustrated by the average life expectancies of 52 years in India and 74 years in the United States.

The distribution of people throughout the world is uneven, because few people live in the vast hot and cold deserts, mountain regions and rain forests. In the world's most densely populated areas, the proportions of urban dwellers is increasing quickly. Urban growth is also a problem in developing nations where unqualified youngsters flock to the cities only to become unemployed occupants of unhealthy shanty towns.

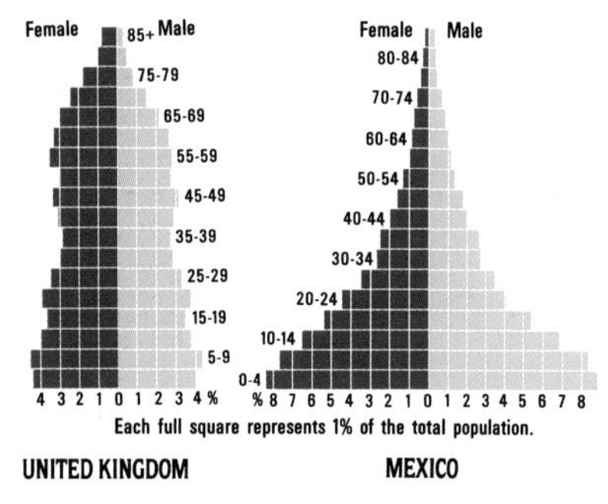
Female
Male
85+
75-79
65-69
55-59
45-49
35-39
25-29
15-19
5-9
4 3 2 1 0 1 2 3 4 %
80-84
70-74
60-64
50-54
40-44
30-34
20-24
10-14
0-4
% 8 7 6 5 4 3 2 1 0 1 2 3 4 5 6 7 8
Each full square represents 1% of the total population.
UNITED KINGDOM
MEXICO

Left: The graphs depict the population structures of two nations according to sex and age. Developed nations, such as the United Kingdom (left), have a high proportion of older people, while developing nations such as Mexico (right) have a young population, with as many as 40 per cent of the people being under 15 years of age.

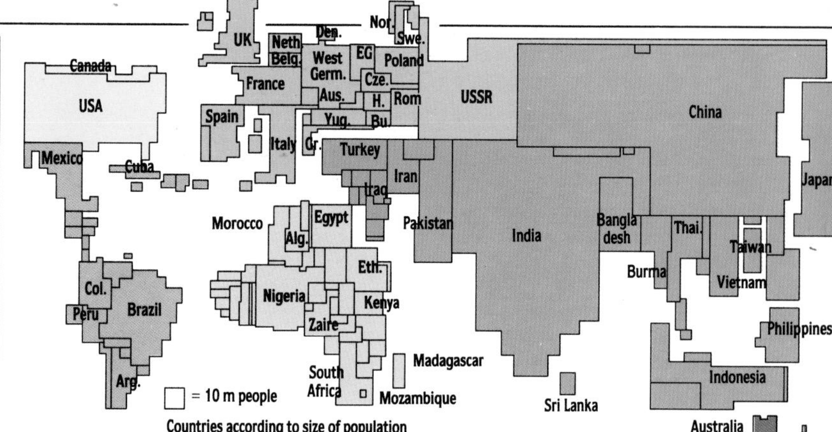
UK
Neth.
Belg.
Den.
Nor.
Swe.
West Germ.
EG
Poland
Canada
France
Cze.
Aus.
H.
Rom
USSR
China
USA
Spain
Italy
Yug.
Bu.
Gr.
Turkey
Mexico
Cuba
Iran
Iraq
Japan
Morocco
Alg.
Egypt
Pakistan
India
Bangla desh
Thai.
Taiwan
Eth.
Burma
Vietnam
Col.
Peru
Brazil
Nigeria
Kenya
Zaire
Philippines
Madagascar
Arg.
South Africa
Mozambique
Sri Lanka
Indonesia
= 10 m people
Countries according to size of population
Australia

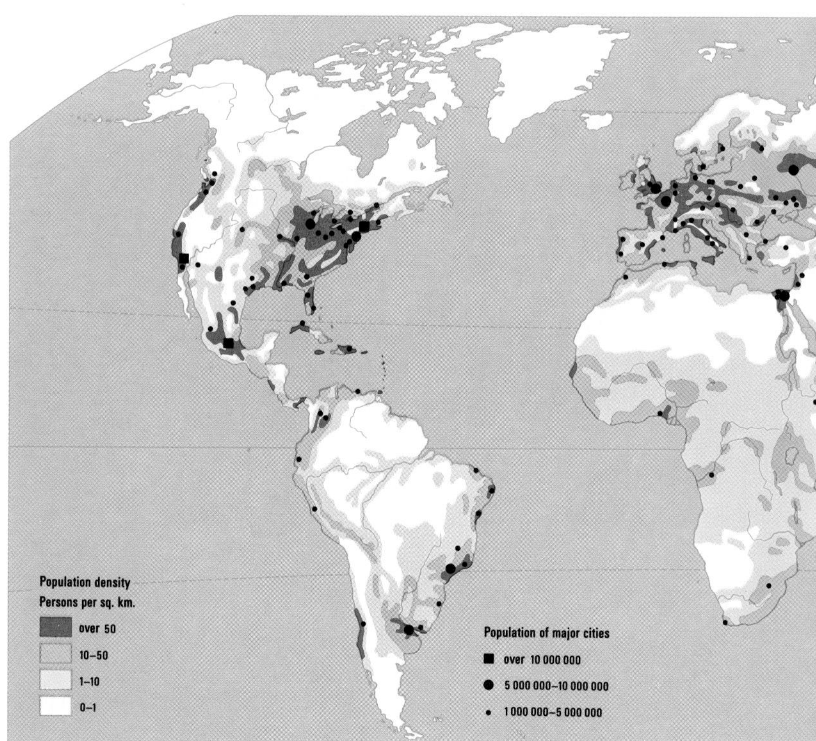
Population density
Persons per sq. km.
over 50
10–50
1–10
0–1
Population of major cities
over 10 000 000
5 000 000–10 000 000
1 000 000–5 000 000

Above: The map shows the uneven distribution of the world's population, a feature that is emphasized by the cartogram, top, which represents the size of nations by their populations rather than by their areas.

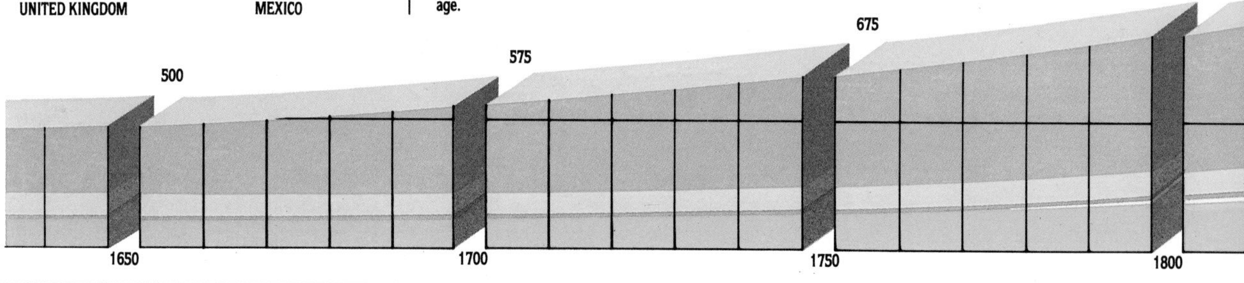
500
575
675
825
1650
1700
1750
1800

FACTFINDER

Population distribution: The mainly developed continents of North America, Europe and Oceania and the USSR contain 23% of the world's people. The rest live in the mainly developing continents of Africa, Latin America and Asia.

Urbanization: Ranges from 2% in Burundi to 90% in the United Kingdom (1980).

Population density: Gibraltar had 5333 people per sq km in 1979, as compared with 2 per sq km in Australia.

Largest country: USSR (by area): China (by population).

Largest metropolitan area: New York 16,479,000.

The world's population was around 300 million in AD 1000. It passed the 1000 million mark around 1850, but the Industrial Revolution led to an acceleration of population growth. The 2000 million mark was passed in the 1920s and the 4000 million mark in the 1970s. By the year 2000, if the present growth rates of 1·8% per year continue, there will be more than 6000 million people on Earth. (for the purposes of this graph, the Americas have been divided into Anglo-Saxon – and Spanish-speaking America).

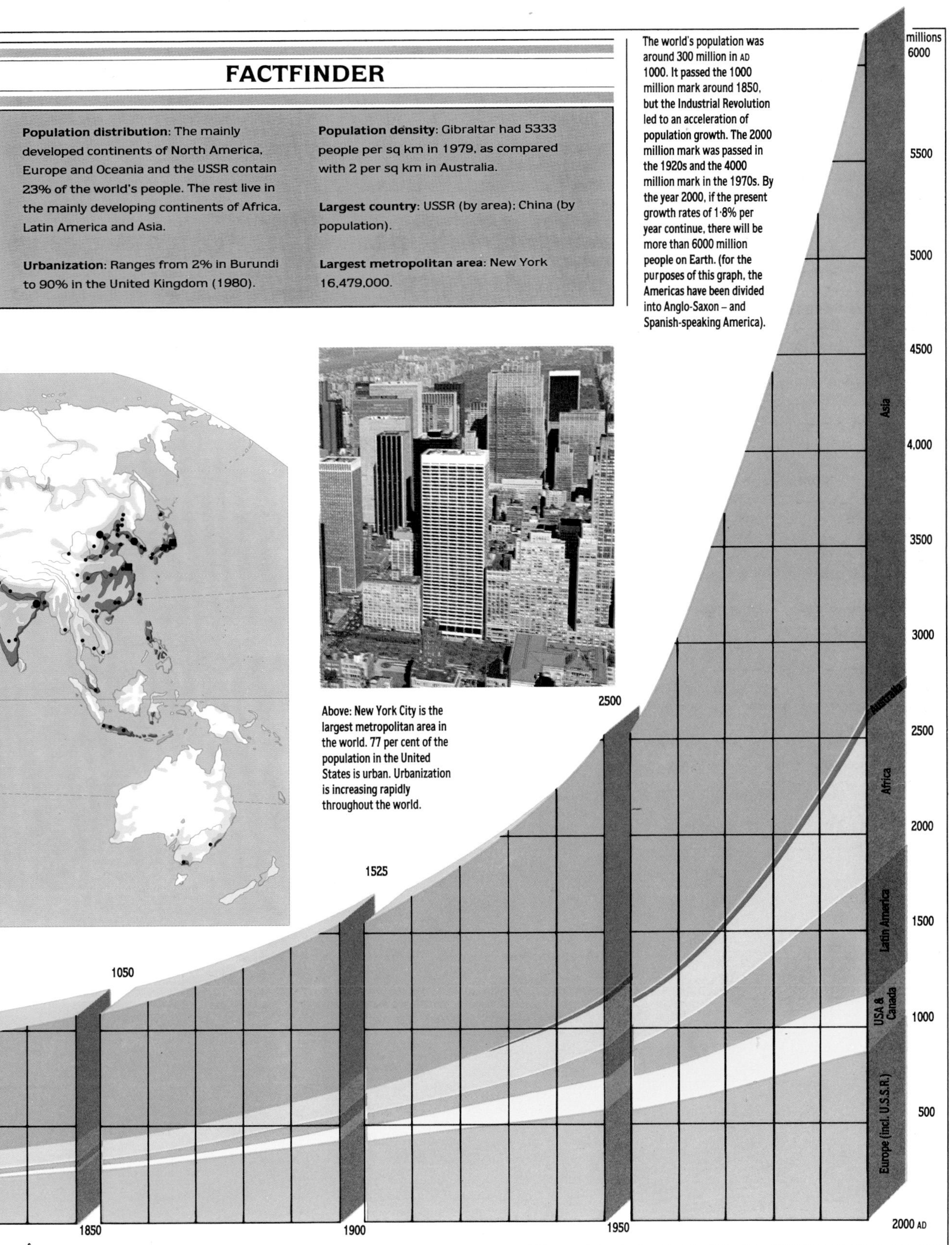

millions
6000
5500
5000
4500
4,000
3500
3000
2500
2000
1500
1000
500
Asia
Australia
Africa
Latin America
USA & Canada
Europe (incl. U.S.S.R.)
1050
1525
2500
1850
1900
1950
2000 AD

Above: New York City is the largest metropolitan area in the world. 77 per cent of the population in the United States is urban. Urbanization is increasing rapidly throughout the world.

ALTERNATIVE ENERGY

All forms of energy come directly or indirectly from the Sun. Prehistoric people had only their own labour, but as life styles changed and technology developed, draught animals, the burning of wood, windmills, waterwheels and sails to propel ships were all employed. With the onset of the Industrial Revolution, another abundant source of energy, the fossil fuel coal, was used to power 'the age of steam'. And recently, oil and natural gas have become the main fossil fuels, chiefly because they are fairly cheap to extract, easy to transport, and weight for weight they are more heat-efficient than coal. In consequence, world coal production has remained roughly stable over the last thirty years, although in some industrial nations, such as France, West Germany and the United Kingdom, it has declined. And yet coal may again become important if the existing reserves of oil start to run out, as predicted on current levels of consumption, in the early 21st century.

Despite the recent pre-eminence of oil and natural gas, alternative forms of energy that could replace fossil fuels have been successfully developed, notably hydro-electricity and, in the last thirty years, nuclear power. Hydro-electricity is now the chief form of electrical energy in such countries as Norway, where it supplies 100 per cent of the nation's electrical supply, Brazil (93 per cent), Switzerland (79 per cent) and Canada (70 per cent). But hydro-electricity is clearly unsuited to flat nations, such as the Netherlands.

Nuclear power, using the heat of nuclear fission, can be generated anywhere and, in several Western nations, including the United States and the United Kingdom, it already supplies more than one tenth of the total electrical supply. Uranium, the raw material used in nuclear fission, is generally abundant, and is produced in the West by the United States, South Africa and Canada.

But nuclear power is surrounded by controversy, particularly concerning the disposal of radioactive nuclear wastes. This factor, together with the finite nature of fossil fuel reserves, have led conservationists to explore many other possible forms of energy, employing the latest modern technology. The diagram, right, summarizes the main possibilities that are currently under investigation, including the harnessing of solar radiation, the power of winds and moving water, and the exploitation of the heat that exists not far beneath the Earth's surface.

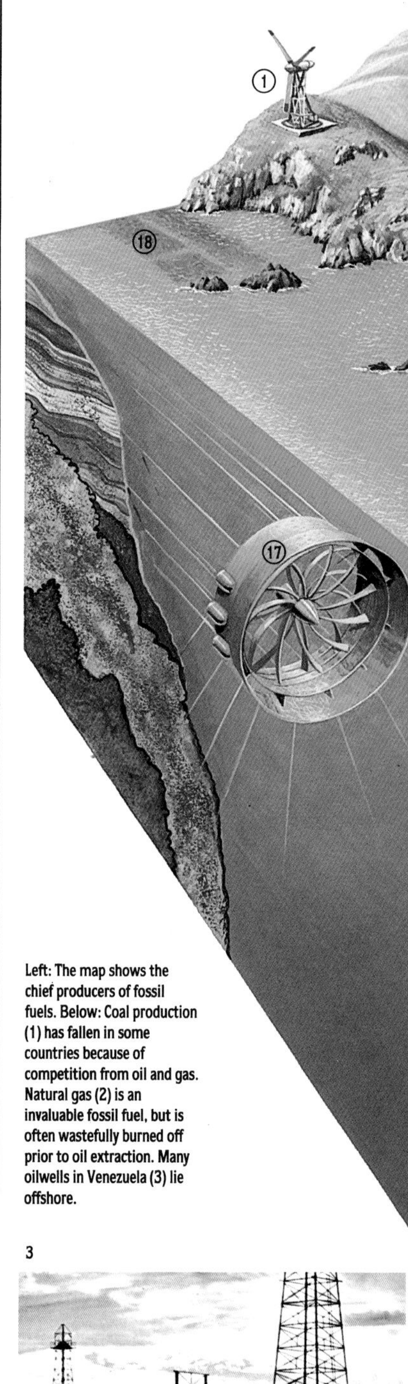
1
18
17

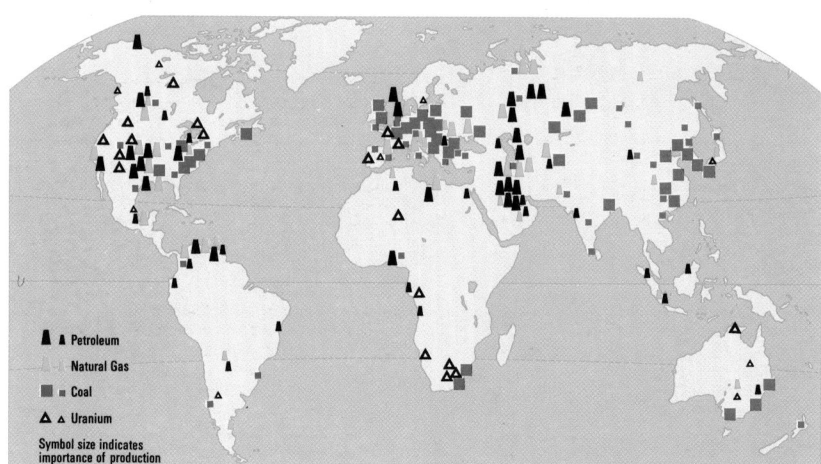
Petroleum
Natural Gas
Coal
Uranium
Symbol size indicates importance of production

Left: The map shows the chief producers of fossil fuels. Below: Coal production (1) has fallen in some countries because of competition from oil and gas. Natural gas (2) is an invaluable fossil fuel, but is often wastefully burned off prior to oil extraction. Many oilwells in Venezuela (3) lie offshore.

1

2

3

FACTFINDER

Energy consumption (per capita, in equivalents of kg of coal, 1980): Africa 370; Far East 544; Middle East 1123; Oceania 3247; Western Europe 4204; North America 10,394.

Largest oil producers (1981): USSR (21 per cent of world production); Saudi Arabia (17 per cent); United States (17 per cent); Rest of Middle East (9 per cent); Mexico (4 per cent); Venezuela (4 per cent); United Kingdom (3 per cent).

Oil reserves (1978): Saudia Arabia (20 per cent); Kuwait (13 per cent); USSR (10 per cent); Iran (8 per cent); Iraq (6 per cent); United Arab Emirates (6 per cent); Mexico, United States and Malaysia (5 per cent each).

Nuclear power: Belgium (25 per cent of its electrical energy production in 1978); Sweden (22 per cent); Bulgaria (20 per cent); Switzerland (17 per cent); United Kingdom (14 per cent).

Left: Alternative energy sources include improved windmills (1) and pump storage reservoirs (2), into which water is pumped when energy is abundant and then used to drive turbine generators. Hydro-electric stations (3) are important in many countries, while solar power stations, powered by concentrated sunlight, could get microwave energy beamed from a satellite (4) or from banks of angled mirrors or heliostats (5). Decaying waste (6) is a source of heat, as are geysers (7) in volcanic areas. Mud (8) can be used to store heat, while greenhouses (9) are familiar ways of utilizing solar energy. Shallow solar ponds (10) produce heated water to drive generators, and solar houses (11) are self-supporting. Geothermal energy (12) comes from heat inside the Earth. Tidal power stations (13) have much potential, and wave power (14) could be harnessed by moving floats ('bobbing ducks'). Ordinary powered ships might use aluminium sails (15) as an extra form of energy. Floating thermal stations (16) could tap heat under the sea, while huge underwater turbines (17) could be driven by ocean currents. Even kelp (18), a seaweed, could be cultivated as a plant fuel. Solar furnaces (19) can produce temperatures of 4000°C by concentrating the Sun's rays with a paraboloid mirror.

Below: Hydro-electricity is a major alternative to fossil fuels in upland areas with abundant rivers that can be dammed (4). Nuclear power stations (5), a recent development, now supply a substantial proportion of the total electrical energy in several developed nations.

4

5

ENVIRONMENT IN DANGER

Because of the population explosion and the industrial and technological developments of the last 200 years, great damage has been done to the environment in many areas by the disruption of the balance of nature.

Pollution has become a major problem particularly in modern industrial societies. For example, air pollution in the form of smog has made cities unpleasant and unhealthy. It causes bronchitis and various other respiratory diseases – the London smog of 1952 killed an estimated 4000 people.

Water pollution by sewage and industrial wastes has fouled rivers, lakes and even seas, notably parts of the almost tideless Mediterranean. The flora and fauna have been destroyed and people's health has been directly affected as at Minamata in Japan in the 1950s. Here perhaps as many as 10,000 people suffered death, deformity or acute illness after eating fish poisoned by acetaldehyde waste pumped into the sea by a chemical company.

The land, too, has been polluted in many ways. For example, the pesticide DDT was once regarded as a means of raising food production. But it has also wiped out large populations of birds and, because of its persistence, it has damaged the fragile ecology of soils by weakening the micro-organisms in it.

Steps have been taken in many places to control the dangers of smog, Minamata disease and DDT. But many other, perhaps even more serious, problems lie ahead if the balance of nature is disturbed. For example, if jet airliners and rocket discharges damage the ozone layer in the stratosphere, it could expose the Earth to the Sun's broiling ultraviolet rays. And no one is sure of the consequences of the rising content in the air of carbon dioxide, which increased by seven per cent between 1958 and 1980. One estimate is that it could double by the year 2030. The atmosphere would then increasingly block long-wave radiation from the Earth, like the glass roof of a greenhouse, and temperatures would rise by an average of 3°C. Climatic zones would change and ice sheets would melt, submerging coastal plains and cities.

1
4
12
19
18
11
23
24
25

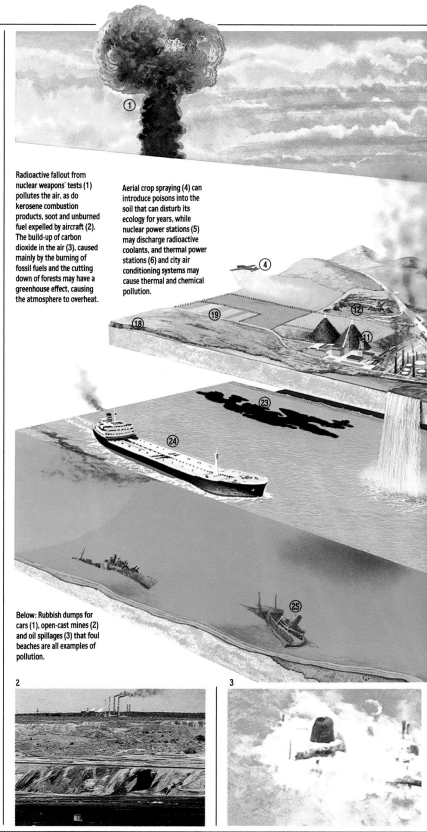

Radioactive fallout from nuclear weapons' tests (1) pollutes the air, as do kerosene combustion products, soot and unburned fuel expelled by aircraft (2). The build-up of carbon dioxide in the air (3), caused mainly by the burning of fossil fuels and the cutting down of forests may have a greenhouse effect, causing the atmosphere to overheat.

Aerial crop spraying (4) can introduce poisons into the soil that can disturb its ecology for years, while nuclear power stations (5) may discharge radioactive coolants, and thermal power stations (6) and city air conditioning systems may cause thermal and chemical pollution.

Below: Rubbish dumps for cars (1), open-cast mines (2) and oil spillages (3) that foul beaches are all examples of pollution.

1

2

3

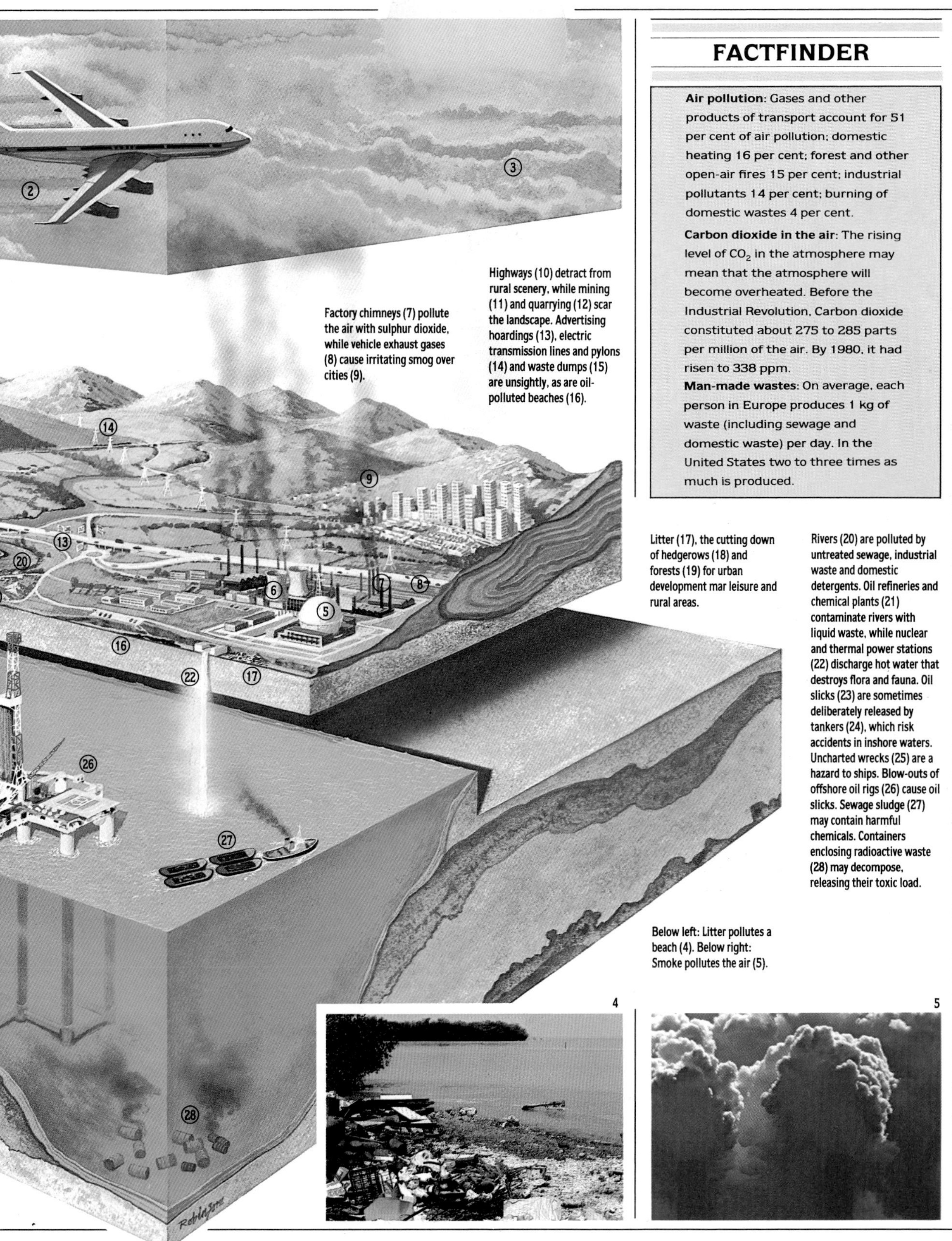

Factory chimneys (7) pollute the air with sulphur dioxide, while vehicle exhaust gases (8) cause irritating smog over cities (9).

Highways (10) detract from rural scenery, while mining (11) and quarrying (12) scar the landscape. Advertising hoardings (13), electric transmission lines and pylons (14) and waste dumps (15) are unsightly, as are oil-polluted beaches (16).

Litter (17), the cutting down of hedgerows (18) and forests (19) for urban development mar leisure and rural areas.

Rivers (20) are polluted by untreated sewage, industrial waste and domestic detergents. Oil refineries and chemical plants (21) contaminate rivers with liquid waste, while nuclear and thermal power stations (22) discharge hot water that destroys flora and fauna. Oil slicks (23) are sometimes deliberately released by tankers (24), which risk accidents in inshore waters. Uncharted wrecks (25) are a hazard to ships. Blow-outs of offshore oil rigs (26) cause oil slicks. Sewage sludge (27) may contain harmful chemicals. Containers enclosing radioactive waste (28) may decompose, releasing their toxic load.

FACTFINDER

Air pollution: Gases and other products of transport account for 51 per cent of air pollution; domestic heating 16 per cent; forest and other open-air fires 15 per cent; industrial pollutants 14 per cent; burning of domestic wastes 4 per cent.

Carbon dioxide in the air: The rising level of CO_2 in the atmosphere may mean that the atmosphere will become overheated. Before the Industrial Revolution, Carbon dioxide constituted about 275 to 285 parts per million of the air. By 1980, it had risen to 338 ppm.

Man-made wastes: On average, each person in Europe produces 1 kg of waste (including sewage and domestic waste) per day. In the United States two to three times as much is produced.

Below left: Litter pollutes a beach (4). Below right: Smoke pollutes the air (5).

4

5

The problems that face mankind are truly monumental. According to the United Nations Environment Programme (UNEP), a recently established agency, soil erosion and soil degradation were still widespread in the early 1980s, and one third of the world's arable land was at risk of becoming desert because of human misuse. Tropical forests were disappearing at an estimated rate of 50 hectares a minute – a rate that, if it continues, will eliminate all tropical forests in forty years. One plant or animal species was also being lost per day – a rate that was accelerating. And in human terms, UNEP estimated that every day some 40,000 infants and young children were dying from hunger or from pollution-related disease.

Disease and malnutrition are features of everyday life in the developing world and, despite all the aid that goes to developing nations, the economic gap between them and the developed world is enormous and increasing. In 1980, the per capita gross national products of the United Kingdom, United States and Switzerland were, respectively, US $7920, $11,360 and $16,440. By contrast, the per capita GNPs of Chad, Burma and India were $120, $170 and $240. A world split into two sectors – one rich and one poor – is a world fraught with danger. And the population explosion, which is most marked in the poorest countries, could cause global chaos.

The world's problems must be tackled with a real understanding of all the factors involved. People once talked of 'taming' Nature, as if Nature were hostile towards and separate from them. However, in recent years, we have begun to realize that the key to our future lies not in 'taming' but in comprehending Nature, particularly the highly complex ecological relationships that exist between us, the Earth and the millions of animals and plant species that the Earth supports. A view from space has made us realize that damage has been and is still being done. But hopefully it is not too late for us to heal the wounds we have inflicted.

WORLD ATLAS

SYMBOLS

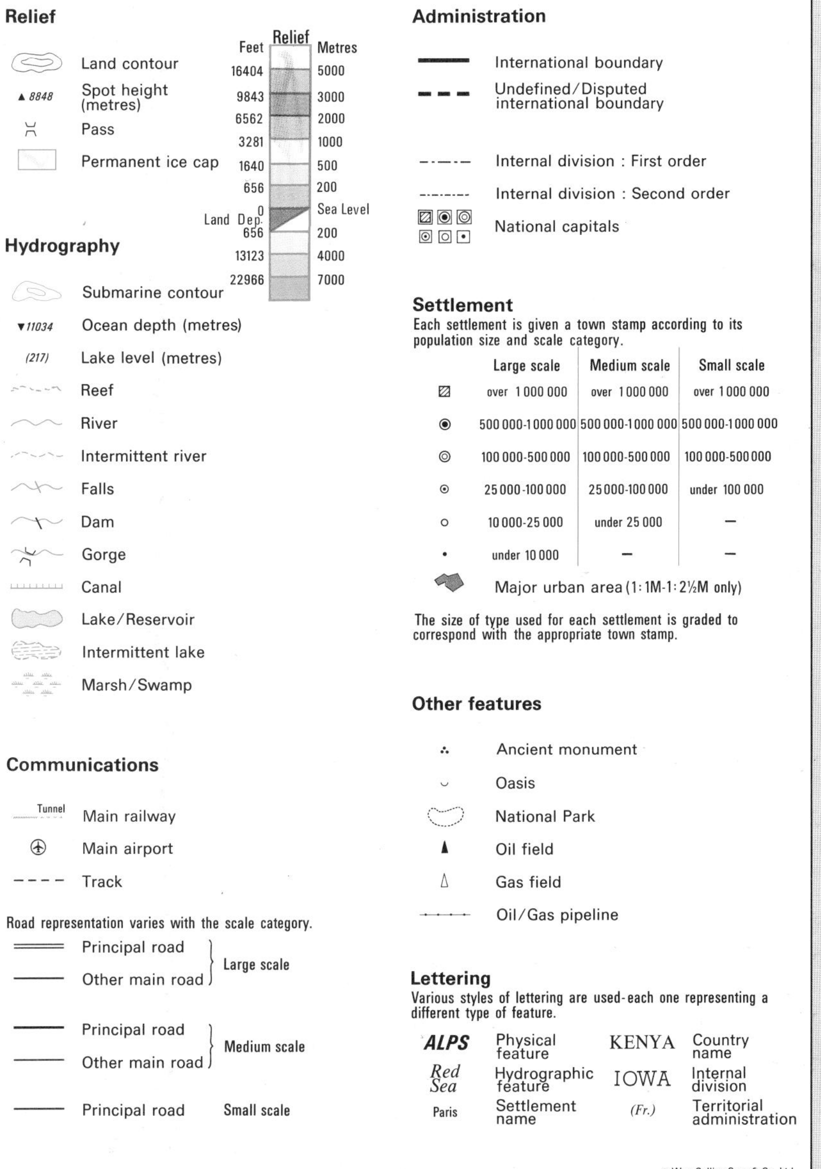

Relief

Land contour

8848 Spot height (metres)

Pass

Permanent ice cap

Feet	Relief	Metres
16404		5000
9843		3000
6562		2000
3281		1000
1640		500
656		200
0		Sea Level
Land Dep. 656		200
13123		4000
22966		7000

Hydrography

Submarine contour

11034 Ocean depth (metres)

(217) Lake level (metres)

Reef

River

Intermittent river

Falls

Dam

Gorge

Canal

Lake/Reservoir

Intermittent lake

Marsh/Swamp

Communications

Tunnel

Main railway

Main airport

Track

Road representation varies with the scale category.

Principal road
Other main road } Large scale

Principal road
Other main road } Medium scale

Principal road Small scale

Administration

International boundary

Undefined/Disputed international boundary

Internal division : First order

Internal division : Second order

National capitals

Settlement

Each settlement is given a town stamp according to its population size and scale category.

	Large scale	Medium scale	Small scale
	over 1 000 000	over 1 000 000	over 1 000 000
	500 000-1 000 000	500 000-1 000 000	500 000-1 000 000
	100 000-500 000	100 000-500 000	100 000-500 000
	25 000-100 000	25 000-100 000	under 100 000
	10 000-25 000	under 25 000	–
	under 10 000	–	–

Major urban area (1: 1M-1: 2½M only)

The size of type used for each settlement is graded to correspond with the appropriate town stamp.

Other features

Ancient monument

Oasis

National Park

Oil field

Gas field

Oil/Gas pipeline

Lettering

Various styles of lettering are used-each one representing a different type of feature.

ALPS	Physical feature	KENYA	Country name
Red Sea	Hydrographic feature	IOWA	Internal division
Paris	Settlement name	*(Fr.)*	Territorial administration

EUROPE

North America
South America
ARCTIC OCEAN
Spitsbergen (Nor.)
Barents Sea
Novaya Zemlya (U.S.S.R.)
Denmark Strait
Arctic Circle
ICELAND
Reykjavik
ATLANTIC OCEAN
NORWAY
SWEDEN
FINLAND
Helsinki
Bergen
Oslo
Stockholm
Leningrad
U. S. S. R.
(in Europe)
Moskva
Gor'kiy
Kuybyshev
North Sea
Göteborg
Århus
DENMARK
København
REP. OF IRE.
Dublin
UNITED KINGDOM
Birmingham
London
Hamburg
Berlin
EAST GERMANY
POLAND
Warszawa
Łódź
Minsk
Kiyev
Khar'kov
NETH.
Amsterdam
B.
LUX.
Bruxelles
Bonn
Leipzig
Praha
Brno
CZECH.
WEST GERMANY
Paris
FRANCE
Lyon
Zürich
Bern
SW.
L.
AUSTRIA
Wien
Budapest
HUNGARY
ROMANIA
București
Odessa
Bay of Biscay
Milano
M.
AN.
Zagreb
Beograd
S.M.
YUGOSLAVIA
ITALY
Oporto
Lisboa
PORTUGAL
Madrid
SPAIN
Barcelona
Corse (Fr.)
Sardegna (It.)
Is. Baleares (Sp.)
Roma
Tiranë
ALB.
Sofiya
BULGARIA
Istanbul
T.
Thessaloníki
GREECE
Athínai
Black Sea
Caspian Sea
Asia
Madeira (Port.)
Islas Canarias (Sp.)
Sicilia
MALTA
Kriti
Mediterranean Sea
Tropic of Cancer
Equator
Tropic of Capricorn
Africa
INDI
OCE

ALB. : ALBANIA
AN. : ANDORRA
B. : BELGIUM
CZECH. : CZECHOSLOVAKIA
L. : LIECHTENSTEIN
LUX. : LUXEMBOURG
M. : MONACO
NETH. : NETHERLANDS
REP. OF IRE. : REPUBLIC OF IRELAND
S.M. : SAN MARINO
SW. : SWITZERLAND
T. : TURKEY *(in Europe)*

BRITISH ISLES

ATLANTIC OCEAN
NORTH SEA
IRISH SEA
English Channel
Celtic Sea
SCOTLAND
UNITED KINGDOM
NORTHERN IRELAND
REPUBLIC OF IRELAND
ENGLAND
WALES
FRANCE
BELGIUM
NETHERLANDS
WEST GERMANY
DENMARK
NORWAY
LUXEMBOURG
London
Dublin
Edinburgh
Glasgow
Belfast
Paris
Amsterdam
Bruxelles
Relief
Feet
Metres
Sea Level
Land Dep.
Conic Projection
© Collins ◇ Longman Atlases Cbii

ENGLAND AND WALES

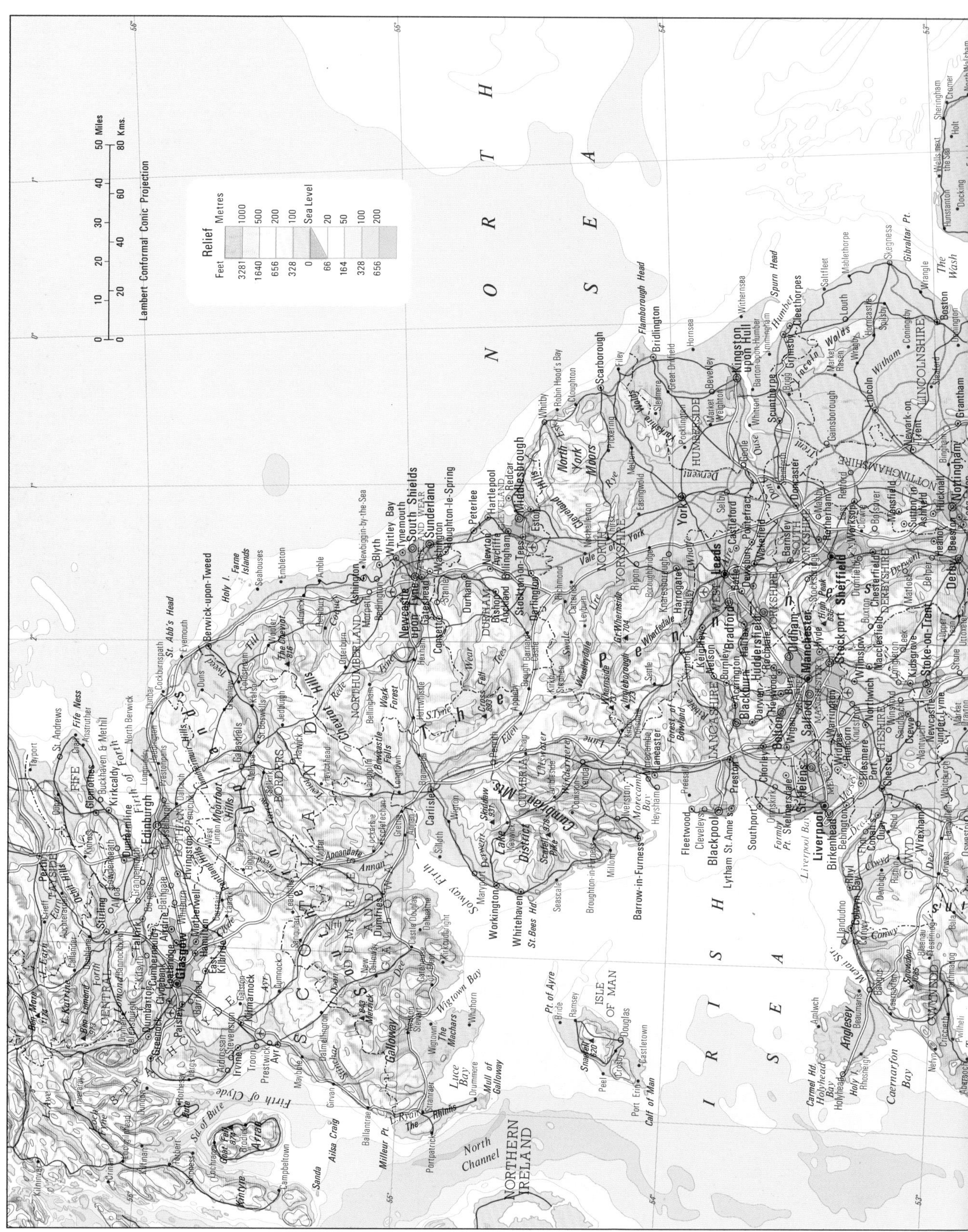

Lambert Conformal Conic Projection
0 10 20 30 40 50 Miles
0 20 40 60 80 Kms.
Relief
Feet Metres
3281 1000
1640 500
656 200
328 100
0 Sea Level 0
66 20
164 50
328 100
656 200
N O R T H S E A
I R I S H S E A

ENGLISH CHANNEL
Bristol Channel
Baie de la Seine
Passage de la Déroute
Strait of Dover
Baie de la Somme
Lyme Bay
Cardigan Bay
Carmarthen Bay
WALES
FRANCE
CHANNEL ISLANDS
Alderney
Guernsey
Jersey
Sark
St. Peter Port
St. Helier
London
Birmingham
Cardiff
Bristol
Swansea
Newport
Plymouth
Exeter
Torbay
Southampton
Portsmouth
Bournemouth
Poole
Brighton
Oxford
Reading
Cambridge
Ipswich
Northampton
Coventry
Gloucester
Cheltenham
Swindon
Salisbury
Weymouth
Taunton
Chelmsford
Southend-on-Sea
Maidstone
Canterbury
Dover
Folkestone
Hastings
Eastbourne
Margate
Ramsgate
Le Havre
Rouen
Caen
Cherbourg
Dieppe
Boulogne
Lisieux
SEINE MARITIME
CALVADOS
MANCHE
EURE
ISLE OF WIGHT
CORNWALL
DEVON
DORSET
SOMERSET
WILTSHIRE
HAMPSHIRE
KENT
ESSEX
SUFFOLK
OXFORDSHIRE
GLOUCESTERSHIRE
WEST SUSSEX
EAST SUSSEX
SURREY
AVON
GWENT
POWYS
DYFED
Dartmoor Forest
Exmoor Forest
Bodmin Moor
Salisbury Plain
Mendip Hills
Cotswold Hills
Chiltern Hills
Lizard Pt.
Land's End
Start Pt.
Dodman Pt.
Hartland Pt.
Lundy
Bill of Portland
Isle of Portland
The Needles
St. Catherine's Pt.
Selsey Bill
Beachy Hd.
Dungeness
North Foreland
C. de la Hague
Pte. de Barfleur
C. d'Antifer
C. Gris-Nez
Isles of Scilly
St. Mary's
St. Martin's
Mount's Bay
Same Scale
© Collins - Longman Atlases

SCOTLAND

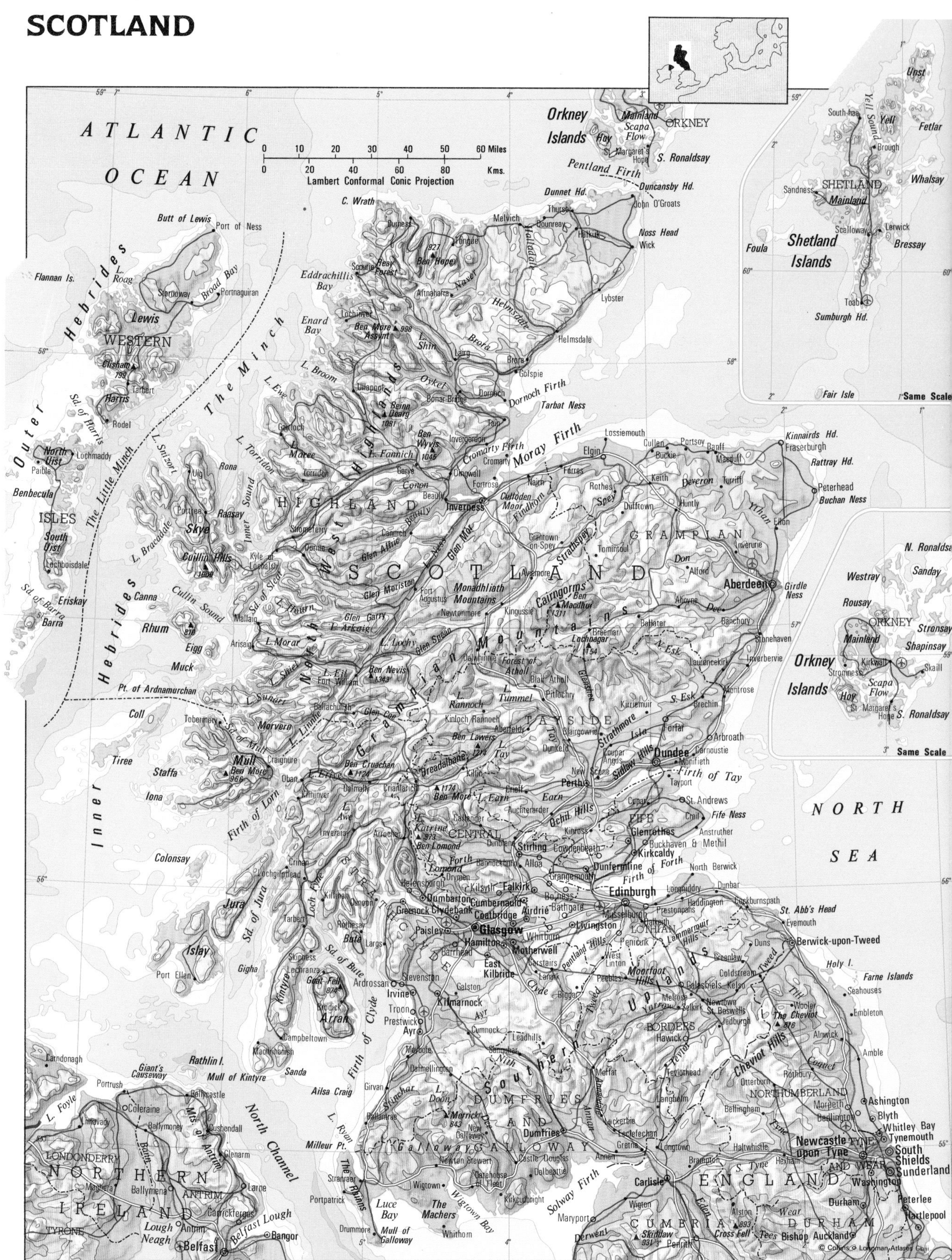

ATLANTIC OCEAN
0 10 20 30 40 50 60 Miles
0 20 40 60 80 Kms.
Lambert Conformal Conic Projection
NORTH SEA
Orkney Islands
Shetland Islands
Same Scale
Pentland Firth
Moray Firth
Firth of Forth
Firth of Tay
Firth of Clyde
Firth of Lorn
Solway Firth
North Channel
The Minch
The Little Minch
Outer Hebrides
Inner Hebrides
WESTERN ISLES
HIGHLAND
SCOTLAND
GRAMPIAN
TAYSIDE
CENTRAL
FIFE
LOTHIAN
STRATHCLYDE
BORDERS
DUMFRIES AND GALLOWAY
NORTHERN IRELAND
ENGLAND
NORTHUMBERLAND
CUMBRIA
DURHAM
TYNE AND WEAR
Grampian Mountains
Cairngorms
Monadhliath Mountains
Southern Uplands
Cheviot Hills
Lammermuir Hills
Pentland Hills
Ochil Hills
Sidlaw Hills
Moorfoot Hills
Cuillin Hills
North West Highlands
Ben Nevis 1343
Ben Macdhui 1311
Ben Hope 927
Ben More Assynt 998
Ben Lawers 1214
Ben Cruachan 1124
Ben More 1174
Ben Lomond 973
Lochnagar 1154
Merrick 843
The Cheviot 816
Goat Fell 874
C. Wrath
Dunnet Hd.
Duncansby Hd.
John O'Groats
Noss Head
Wick
Thurso
Tarbat Ness
Kinnairds Hd.
Fraserburgh
Rattray Hd.
Peterhead
Buchan Ness
Girdle Ness
Fife Ness
St. Abb's Head
Mull of Kintyre
Mull of Galloway
Butt of Lewis
Lewis
Harris
North Uist
Benbecula
South Uist
Barra
Eriskay
Skye
Raasay
Rhum
Eigg
Muck
Canna
Coll
Tiree
Mull
Staffa
Iona
Colonsay
Jura
Islay
Gigha
Arran
Bute
Ailsa Craig
Rathlin I.
Fair Isle
Foula
Unst
Yell
Fetlar
Whalsay
Bressay
Sumburgh Hd.
Westray
Sanday
Stronsay
Shapinsay
Rousay
Hoy
S. Ronaldsay
Scapa Flow
Kirkwall
Lerwick
Stornoway
Inverness
Aberdeen
Dundee
Perth
Stirling
Edinburgh
Glasgow
Paisley
Kilmarnock
Ayr
Dumfries
Falkirk
Kirkcaldy
Dunfermline
Motherwell
Hamilton
Greenock
Oban
Fort William
Elgin
Montrose
Arbroath
St. Andrews
Berwick-upon-Tweed
Newcastle upon Tyne
Carlisle
Sunderland
South Shields
Durham
Belfast
Bangor
Larne
Londonderry
Coleraine
L. Ness
L. Lomond
L. Tay
L. Rannoch
L. Shin
L. Maree
Glen More
Glen Coe
Tay
Tweed
Spey
Dee
Don
Clyde
Forth
Luce Bay
Wigtown Bay
The Machers
The Rhinns
Lough Neagh
Belfast Lough
© Collins-Longman Atlases Gbiii

IRELAND

Relief
Feet
Metres
3281 1000
1640 500
656 200
328 100
0 Sea Level
66 20
164 50
328 100
656 200
ATLANTIC OCEAN
IRISH SEA
North Channel
St. George's Channel
REPUBLIC OF IRELAND
NORTHERN IRELAND
SCOTLAND
WALES
ISLE OF MAN
DONEGAL
LONDONDERRY
ANTRIM
TYRONE
FERMANAGH
ARMAGH
DOWN
MONAGHAN
SLIGO
LEITRIM
MAYO
CAVAN
LOUTH
ROSCOMMON
LONGFORD
MEATH
WEST MEATH
DUBLIN
GALWAY
OFFALY
KILDARE
WICKLOW
LAOIS
CLARE
CARLOW
TIPPERARY
KILKENNY
WEXFORD
LIMERICK
WATERFORD
KERRY
CORK
Dublin
Belfast
Londonderry
Cork
Limerick
Galway
Waterford
Wexford
0 10 20 30 40 Miles
0 20 40 60 Kms.
Lambert Conformal Conic Projection
© Collins ◇ Longman Atlases Cbiii

THE LOW COUNTRIES

0 10 20 30 40 50 60 Miles
0 20 40 60 80 Kms.
Conic Projection
Relief
Feet Metres
16404 5000
9843 3000
6562 2000
3281 1000
1640 500
656 200
0 Sea Level
Land Dep.
656 200
13123 4000
22966 7000
NORTH SEA
NETHERLANDS
BELGIUM
GERMANY
FRANCE
LUXEMBOURG
Waddeneilanden
Waddenzee
IJsselmeer
Ostfriesische Inseln
Ardennes
Eifel
Hunsrück
Westerwald
Ruhr
Amsterdam
Rotterdam
's Gravenhage (The Hague)
Utrecht
Groningen
Antwerpen
Bruxelles
Gent
Brugge
Liège
Lille
Luxembourg
Köln
Düsseldorf
Essen
Dortmund
Münster
Osnabrück
Oldenburg
Wilhelmshaven
Trier
Koblenz
Aachen
Maastricht
Eindhoven
Arnhem
Nijmegen
FRIESLAND
DRENTHE
OVERIJSSEL
GELDERLAND
NOORD HOLLAND
ZUID HOLLAND
ZEELAND
NOORD BRABANT
LIMBURG
NIEDERSACHSEN
NORDRHEIN WESTFALEN
RHEINLAND-PFALZ
SAARLAND
WEST VLAANDEREN
OOST VLAANDEREN
ANTWERPEN
BRABANT
HAINAUT
NAMUR
LIÈGE
LUXEMBOURG
NORD
PICARDIE
CHAMPAGNE ARDENNE
© Collins - Longman Atlases Cbiii

PARIS BASIN AND PO VALLEY

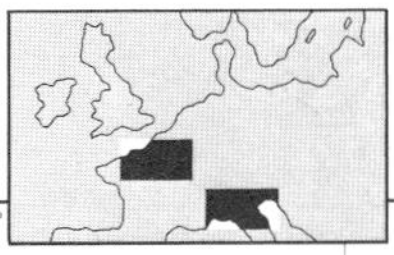

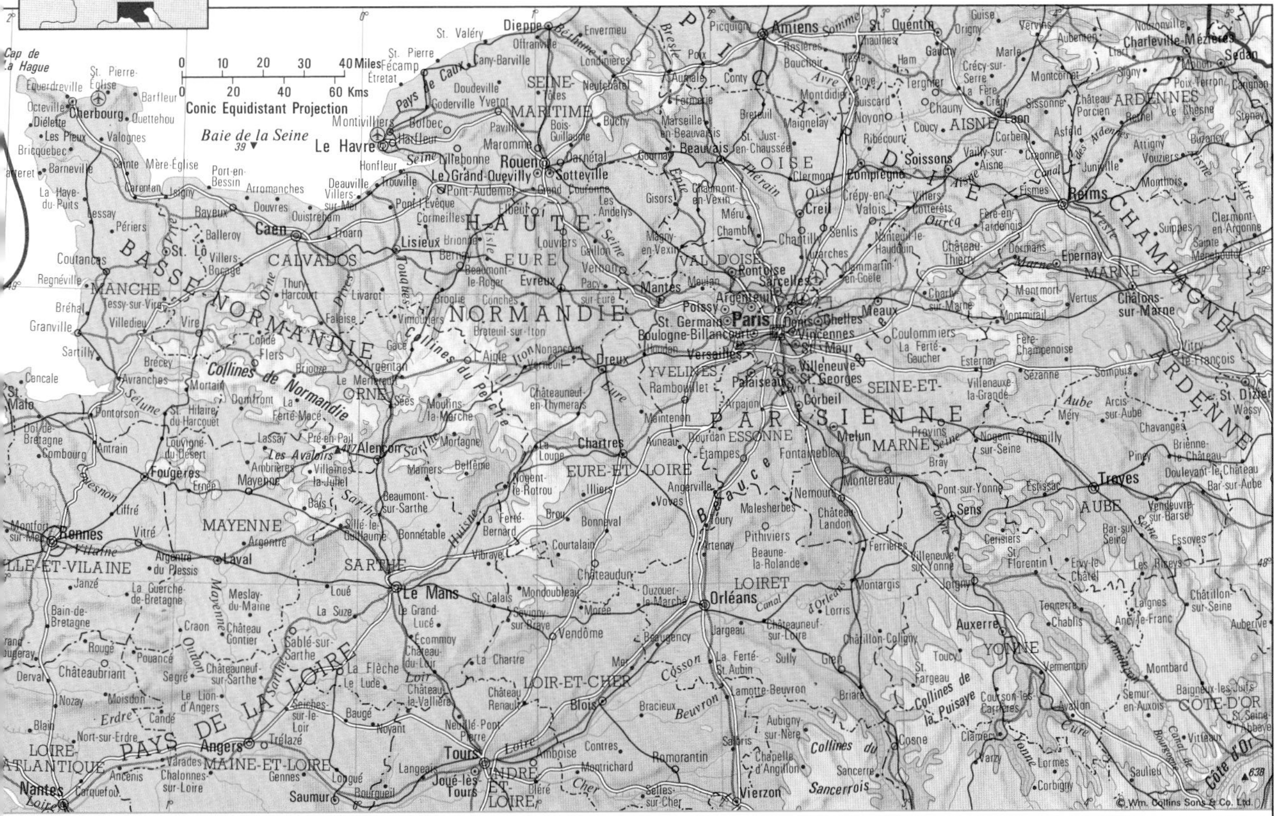

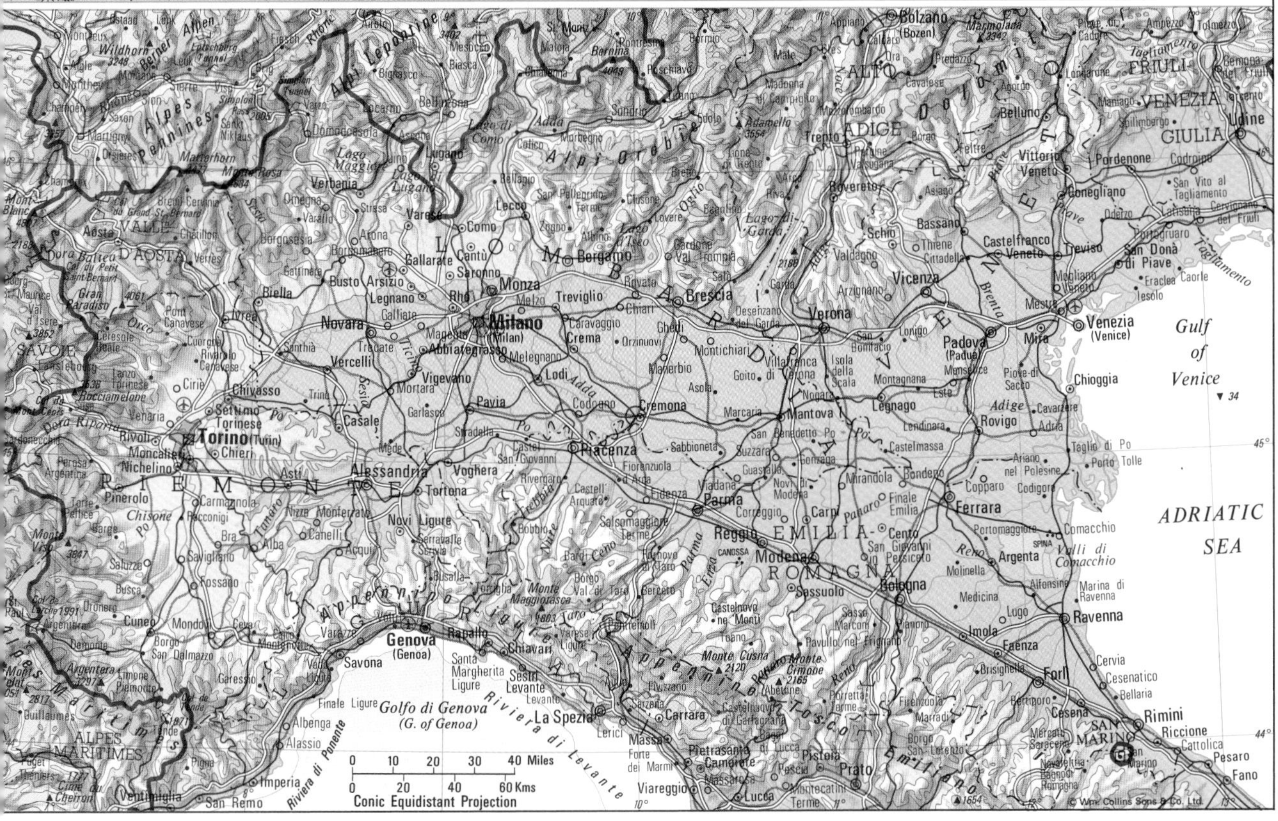

0 10 20 30 40 Miles
0 20 40 60 Kms
Conic Equidistant Projection

0 10 20 30 40 Miles
0 20 40 60 Kms
Conic Equidistant Projection

SPAIN AND PORTUGAL

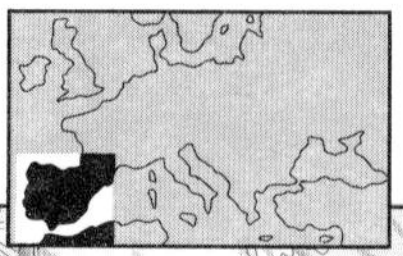

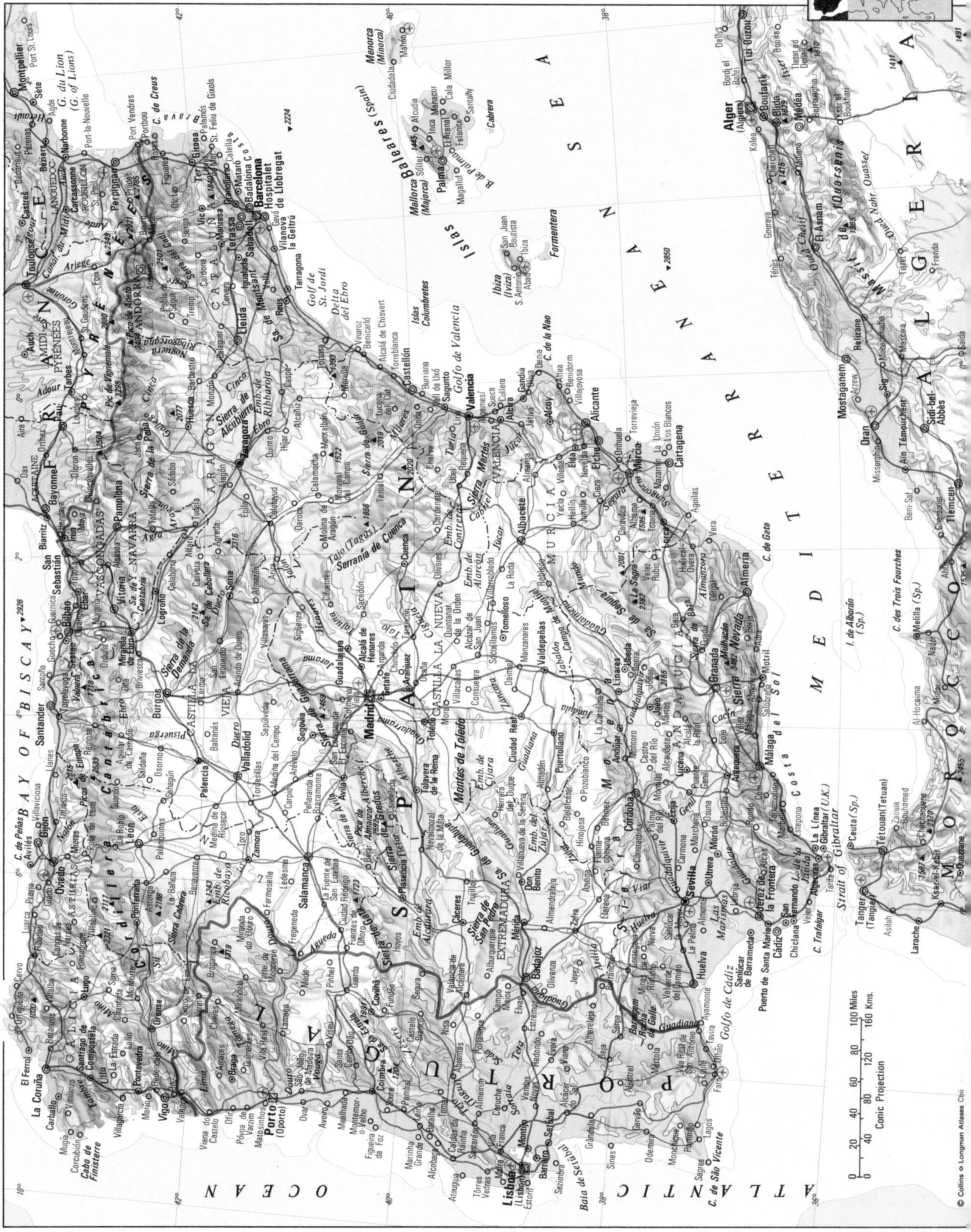

0 20 40 60 80 100 Miles
0 40 80 120 160 Kms.
Conic Projection

FRANCE

FRANCE
BELGIUM
LUXEMBOURG
WEST GERMANY
SWITZERLAND
ITALIA
SPAIN
ANDORRA
MONACO
English Channel
Bay of Biscay
Golfe de Gascogne (G. of Gascony)
Mediterranean Sea
Ligurian Sea
G. du Lion (Gulf of Lions)
G. di Genova (G. of Genoa)
Corse (Corsica) (Fr.)
Channel Islands Jersey (U.K.)
Massif Central
Paris
Lyon
Marseille
Bordeaux
Toulouse
Nantes
0 20 40 60 80 100 Miles
0 40 80 120 160 Kms.
Conic Projection
© Collins • Longman Atlases

ITALY AND THE BALKANS

AUSTRIA
SWITZ.
FRANCE
ALPS
ITALIA
SLOVENIJA
MONACO
SAN MARINO
ALGERIA
TUNISIA
MALTA
LIGURIAN SEA
TYRRHENIAN SEA
MEDITERRANEAN SEA
ADRIATIC
Gulf of Venice
Golfo di Genova (Gulf of Genoa)
G. du Lion (G. of Lions)
Strait of Bonifacio
Malta Channel
Golfe de Hammamet
G. de Tunis
Corse (Corsica) (Fr.)
Sardegna (Sardinia) (Italy)
Sicilia (Sicily)
Menorca
Mahón
Elba
Capraia
Montecristo
Pianosa
Giglio
Isole Ponziane
Ischia
Capri
I. Eolie
Stromboli 926
Ustica (Italy)
Marettimo
Favignana
Pantelleria (Italy)
Linosa
Lampione
Lampedusa (Italy)
Gozo
Malta
La Galite
Iles d'Hyères
Asinara
Maddalena
Caprera
San Pietro
Relief
Feet
Metres
16404
5000
9843
3000
6562
2000
3281
1000
1640
500
656
200
0
Sea Level
Land Dep.
656
200
13123
4000
22966
7000
Lyon
Villeurbanne
St. Etienne
Clermont Ferrand
Grenoble
Valence
Avignon
Nîmes
Arles
Montpellier
Marseille
Toulon
Aix-en-Provence
Nice
Cannes
Antibes
Genève (Geneva)
Mont Blanc 4807
Matterhorn 4477
Torino (Turin)
Milano (Milan)
Bergamo
Brescia
Verona
Vicenza
Padova (Padua)
Venezia (Venice)
Trieste
Udine
Bolzano
Trento
Genova (Genoa)
La Spezia
Parma
Piacenza
Alessandria
Modena
Bologna
Ferrara
Ravenna
Rimini
Pisa
Livorno (Leghorn)
Firenze (Florence)
Siena
Perugia
Ancona
Pescara
Roma (Rome)
Napoli (Naples)
Salerno
Foggia
Ajaccio
Bastia
Sassari
Cagliari
Oristano
Palermo
Messina
Catania
Siracusa
Marsala
Trapani
Agrigento
Tunis
Bizerte
Annaba
Skikda
Constantine
Sétif
Batna
Sousse
Monastir
Kairouan
Valletta
Ljubljana
Rijeka
Klagenfurt
Zadar
Krk
Cres
Lošinj
Istra
Pula
TOSCANA
UMBRIA
LAZIO
ABRUZZI
MOLISE
CAMPANIA
MARCHE
EMILIA-ROMAGNA
LOMBARDIA
PIEMONTE
LIGURIA
VENETO
TRENTINO-ALTO ADIGE
FRIULI-VENEZIA GIULIA
VALLE D'AOSTA
PROVENCE
CÔTE D'AZUR
LANGUEDOC-ROUSSILLON
AUVERGNE
RHÔNE-ALPES
Monts de Constantine
Monts de la Medjerda
Dolomiti
Alpi Carniche
Alpes Maritimes
Cévennes
Mt. Cimone 2165
Mt. Cinto 2710
Monte Vettore 2476
Mt. Corno 2914
Mt. Amaro 2794
Mt. Etna 3340
Monti Nebrodi
Djebel Mrhila 1378
C. Corse
C. Carbonara
C. Spartivento
C. del Falcone
C. Passero
C. Bon
C. de Fer
C. Serrat
Tevere
Arno
Po
Adige
Rhône
Isère
Durance

HUNGARY
ROMANIA
U.S.S.R.
YUGOSLAVIA
BULGARIA
ALBANIA
GREECE
TURKEY
BLACK SEA
AEGEAN SEA
IONIAN SEA
SEA
Nagykanizsa
Kaposvár
Pécs
Mohács
Szekszárd
Baja
Kiskunhalas
Szeged
Hódmezővásárhely
Makó
Arad
Mureş
Timişoara
Lugoj
Hunedoara
Deva
Alba-Iulia
Sebeş
Sibiu
Sighişoara
Mediaş
Făgăraş
Odorhei
Braşov
Sfîntu-Gheorghe
Focşani
Rîmnicu-Sărat
Tecuci
Galaţi
Brăila
Tulcea
Babadag
Izmail
Kilija
Bolgrad
Delta Dunării (Mouths of the Danube)
Gura Portiţei
Subotica
Senta
Sombor
Kikinda
Bečej
Osijek
Vukovar
Vinkovci
Novi Sad
Zrenjanin
Vršac
Petrovaradin
Brod
Bosanska Gradiška
Beograd (Belgrade)
Šabac
Smederevo
Požarevac
Banja Luka
Tuzla
Brčko
Valjevo
SRBIJA (SERBIA)
BOSNA I HERCEGOVINA
Sarajevo
Kragujevac
Čačak
Kraljevo
Titovo Užice
Kruševac
Niš
Pirot
Leskovac
Mostar
Durmitor 2522
Novi Pazar
Kosovska Mitrovica
Priština
Peć
CRNA GORA (MONTENEGRO)
Nikšić
Titograd
Dubrovnik
Herceg-Novi
Mljet
Kotor
Bar
Ulcinj
Prizren
Skopje
Tetovo
Kumanovo
Titov Veles
Štip
Prilep
Bitola
Ohrid
MAKEDONIJA MACEDONIA
Vardar
Shkodër
Tiranë
Durrës
Elbasan
Berat
Korçë
Vlorë
Kep-i-Rodonit
Kep-i-Palit
Lake Ohrid
Lake Prespa
Str. of Otranto
Petroşani
Caransebeş
Reşiţa
Peleaga 2509
Carpaţii Meridionali
Mindra 2518
Negoiu 2548
Alpi Transilvaniei
Cîmpina
Ploieşti
Buzău
Tîrgovişte
Piteşti
Rîmnicu-Vîlcea
Tîrgu-Jiu
Turnu-Severin
Iron Gate
Craiova
Wallachia
Caracal
Roşiori-de-Vede
Bucureşti (Bucharest)
Călăraşi
Slatina
Olteniţa
Giurgiu
Turnu-Măgurele
Ialomiţa
Feteşti
Medgidia
Constanţa
Mangalia
Mamaia
Dobrogea
Dunărea
Silistra
Ruse
Razgrad
Tolbukhin
Balchik
Ludogorie
Vidin
Lom
Pleven
Svishtov
Gorna Oryakhovitsa
Veliko Tŭrnovo
Tŭrgovishte
Shumen
Varna
Nos Kaliakra
Mikhaylovgrad
Vratsa
Lovech
Gabrovo
Stara Planina (Balkan Mts.)
Sofiya (Sofia)
Pernik
Kyustendil
Blagoevgrad
Musala 2925
Vezhen 2198
Botev 2376
Kazanlŭk
Stara Zagora
Sliven
Yambol
Burgas
Michurin
Plovdiv
Pazardzhik
Asenovgrad
Khaskovo
Kŭrdzhali
Dimitrovgrad
Rhodopi Planina
Maritsa
Arda
Smolyan
Igneada Bur.
İstanbul Boğazı (Bosporus)
Edirne
Kırklareli
Lüleburgaz
Çorlu
İstanbul
Üsküdar
Tekirdağ
Marmara Denizi (Sea of Marmara)
Marmara
Bandırma
Bursa
Mustafakemalpaşa
Çanakkale
Çanakkale Boğazı (Dardanelles)
Gelibolu
Saros Körfezi
Gökçeada (Imroz)
Bozca Ada
Kaz Dağı 1767
Balıkesir
Edremit
Simav
Lésvos
Bergama
Manisa
İzmir
Salihli
Ödemiş
Tire
Aydın
Büyük Menderes
Söke
Muğla
Kerme Körfezi
İzmir Körfezi
Komotini
Xánthi
Dráma
Kavála
Sérrai
Néstos
Strimón
Alexandroúpolis
Thásos
Samothráki
Thessaloníki
Kólpos Orfanoú
Ákra Platí
Áthos 2033
Singitikós Kólpos
Toronaíos Kólpos
Thermaïkós Kólpos
Olimbos (Olympus) 2917
Ossa 1978
Smólikas 2633
Pindhos Mts.
Lárisa
Tríkala
Vólos
Kardhítsa
Lamía
Ioánnina
Kérkira (Corfu)
Kérkira
Paxoí
Préveza
Levkás
Ióniοi Nísoi (Ionian Is.)
Kefallinía
Zákinthos
Pátrai
Kórinthos
Kilíni 2376
Trípolis
Kalámai
Spárti
Pílos
Sparta
Náfplion
Kiparissía
Filiatrá
Néapolis
Lakonikós Kólpos
Messiniakós Kólpos
Ákra Maléa
Ákra Taínaron
Kíthira
Andikíthira
Thermopylae
Gióna 2510
Parnassós 2457
Athinai (Athens)
Piraiévs (Piraeus)
Aíyina
Khalkís
Évvoia (Euboea)
Ákra Kafirévs
Skíros
Vóriai Sporádhes (N. Sporades)
Alónnisos
Límnos
Áyios Evstrátios
Psará
Khíos
Ándros
Tínos
Kéa
Síros
Míkonos
Kíthnos
Kikládhes (Cyclades)
Sérifos
Páros
Náxos
Sífnos
Mílos
Síkinos
Íos
Folégandros
Amorgós
Thíra
Anáfi
Ikaría
Sámos
Foúrnoi
Pátmos
Árki
Kálimnos
Kos
Astipálaia
Dhodhekánisos (Dodecanese)
Tílos
Ródhos (Rhodes)
Kárpathos
Kásos
Ólimbos
Kritikón Pélagos (Sea of Crete)
Ákra Spátha
Kríti (Crete)
Kíssamos
Khaniá
Réthimnon
Iráklion
Ídhi Óros 2456
Ídhra
Spétsai
Monopoli
Ostuni
Brindisi
Martina Franca
Mesagne
Francavilla
Taranto
Manduria
Lecce
Nardò
Galatina
Otranto
Gallipoli
Casarano
Tricase
C. Sta Maria di Leuca
Golfo di Taranto
Cirò Marina
Crotone
C. Rizzuto
1224
4791
50 100 150 200 Miles
50 100 150 200 250 300 Kms.
Conic Projection
© Collins ○ Longman Atlases Cbii

CENTRAL EUROPE

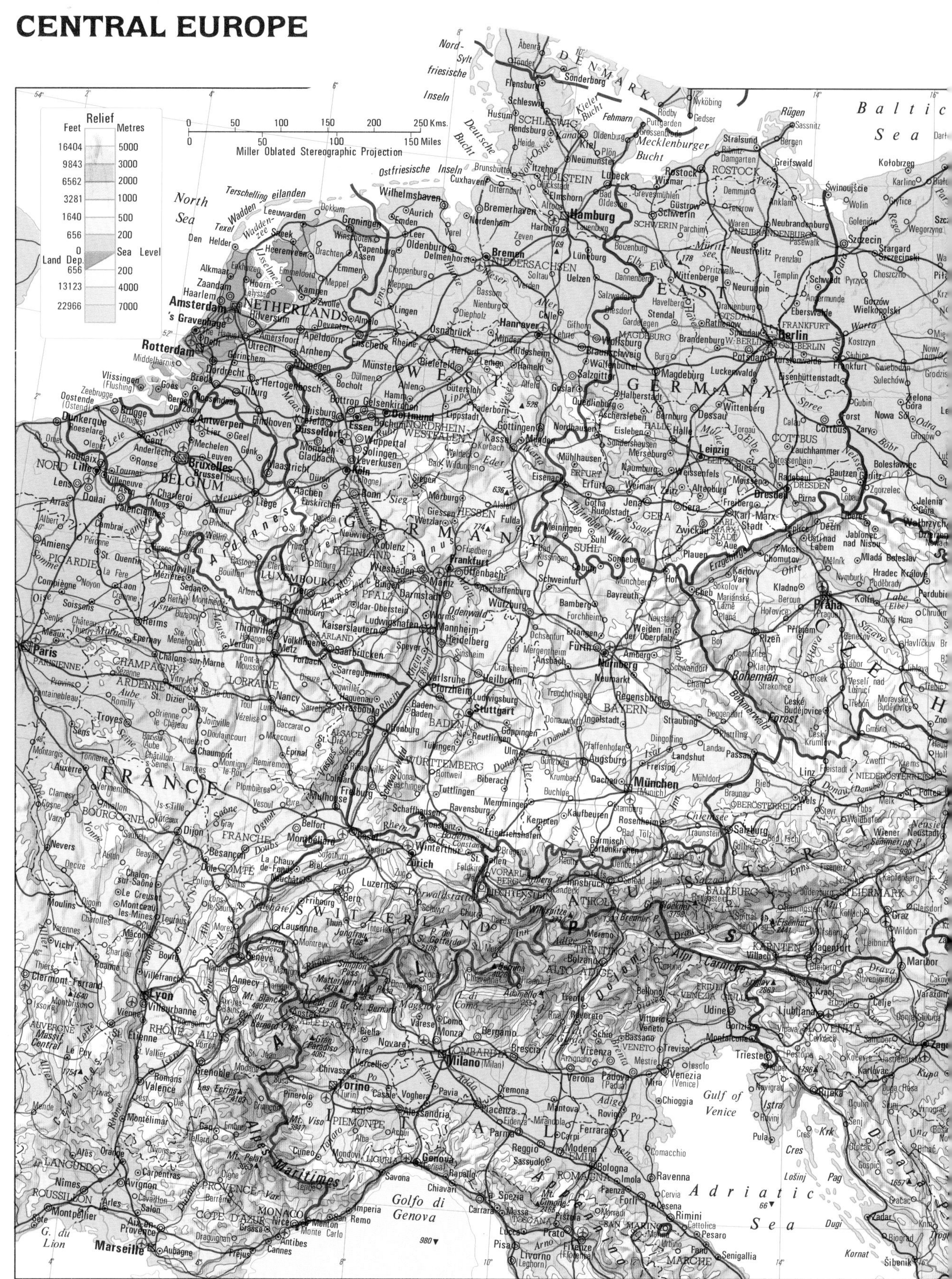
Relief
Feet Metres
16404 5000
9843 3000
6562 2000
3281 1000
1640 500
656 200
0 Sea Level
Land Dep.
656 200
13123 4000
22966 7000
0 50 100 150 200 250 Kms.
0 50 100 150 Miles
Miller Oblated Stereographic Projection
North Sea
Baltic Sea
Deutsche Bucht
Mecklenburger Bucht
Gulf of Venice
Golfo di Genova
Adriatic Sea
G. du Lion
DENMARK
NETHERLANDS
BELGIUM
LUXEMBOURG
WEST GERMANY
EAST GERMANY
FRANCE
SWITZERLAND
AUSTRIA
ITALY
MONACO
SAN MARINO
SLOVENIA
Alpes Maritimes
Ardennes
Erzgebirge
Böhmerwald
Schwarzwald
Vosges
Jura

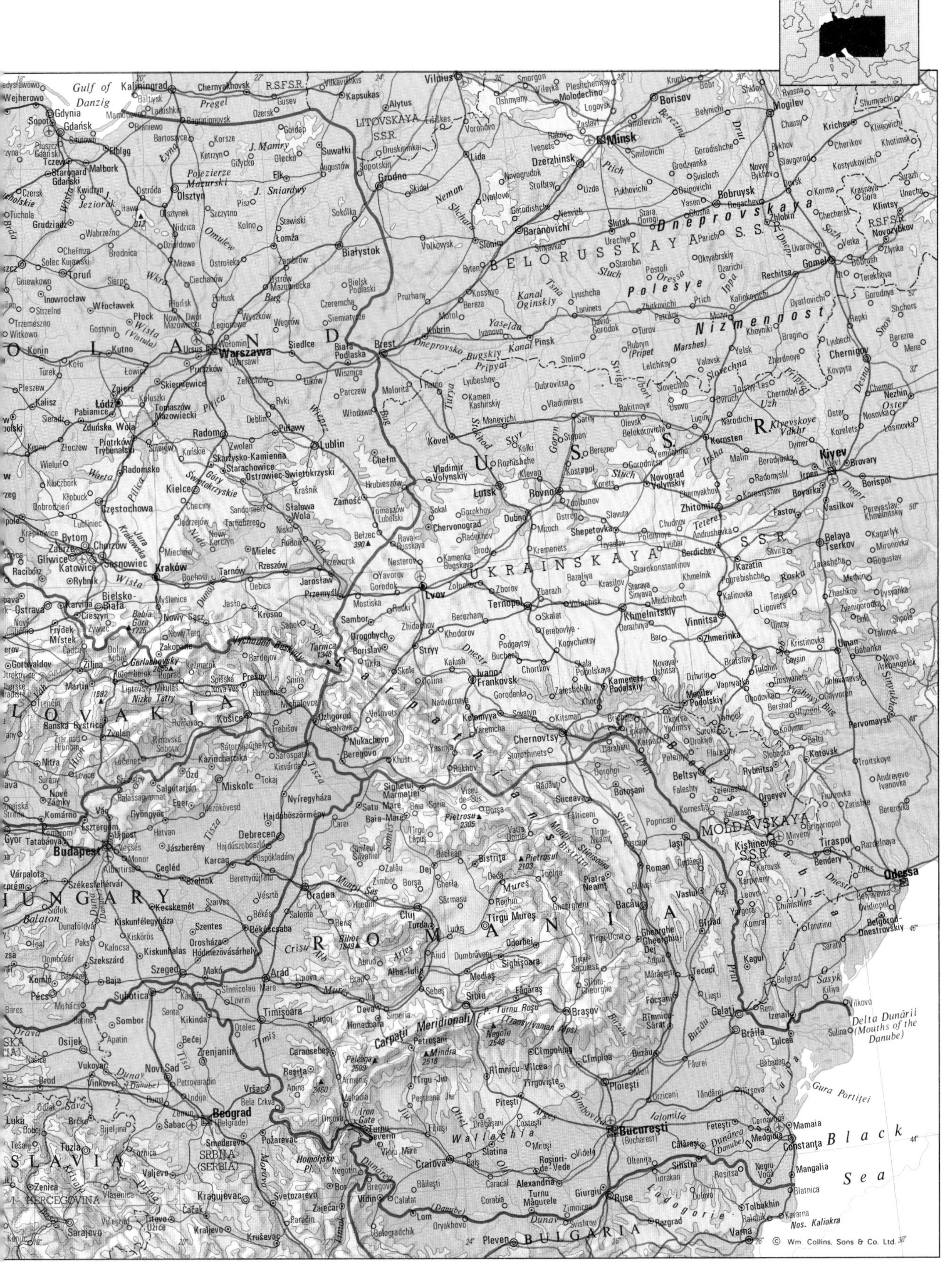
Gulf of Danzig
Kaliningrad
R.S.F.S.R.
Vilnius
LITOVSKAYA S.S.R.
Minsk
Borisov
Mogilev
Gdańsk
Gdynia
Elbląg
Olsztyn
Białystok
Grodno
Baranovichi
Bobruysk
Gomel
BELORUSSKAYA S.S.R.
Dneprovskaya
Polesye
Pripet Marshes
Nizmennost
POLAND
Warszawa (Warsaw)
Łódź
Lublin
Brest
Pinsk
Chernigov
Kiyev (Kiev)
Dnepr
Zhitomir
Rovno
Lutsk
Kraków
Katowice
Częstochowa
Lvov
Ternopol
Vinnitsa
UKRAINSKAYA S.S.R.
Vistula
Ostrava
Karpaty
Carpathians
Košice
SLOVAKIA
Chernovtsy
Uzhgorod
Beltsy
Kishinev
MOLDAVSKAYA S.S.R.
Odessa
Tiraspol
Budapest
HUNGARY
Debrecen
Miskolc
Szeged
Cluj
ROMANIA
Iaşi
Bacău
Braşov
Carpaţii Meridionali
(Transylvanian Alps)
Timişoara
Arad
Oradea
Sibiu
Galaţi
Brăila
Ploieşti
Bucureşti (Bucharest)
Constanţa
Craiova
Wallachia
Delta Dunării (Mouths of the Danube)
Black Sea
Beograd (Belgrade)
SRBIJA (SERBIA)
Novi Sad
Sarajevo
Dunav
Dunărea (Danube)
BULGARIA
Ruse
Varna
Pleven
Vidin
© Wm. Collins, Sons & Co. Ltd.

SCANDINAVIA AND BALTIC LANDS

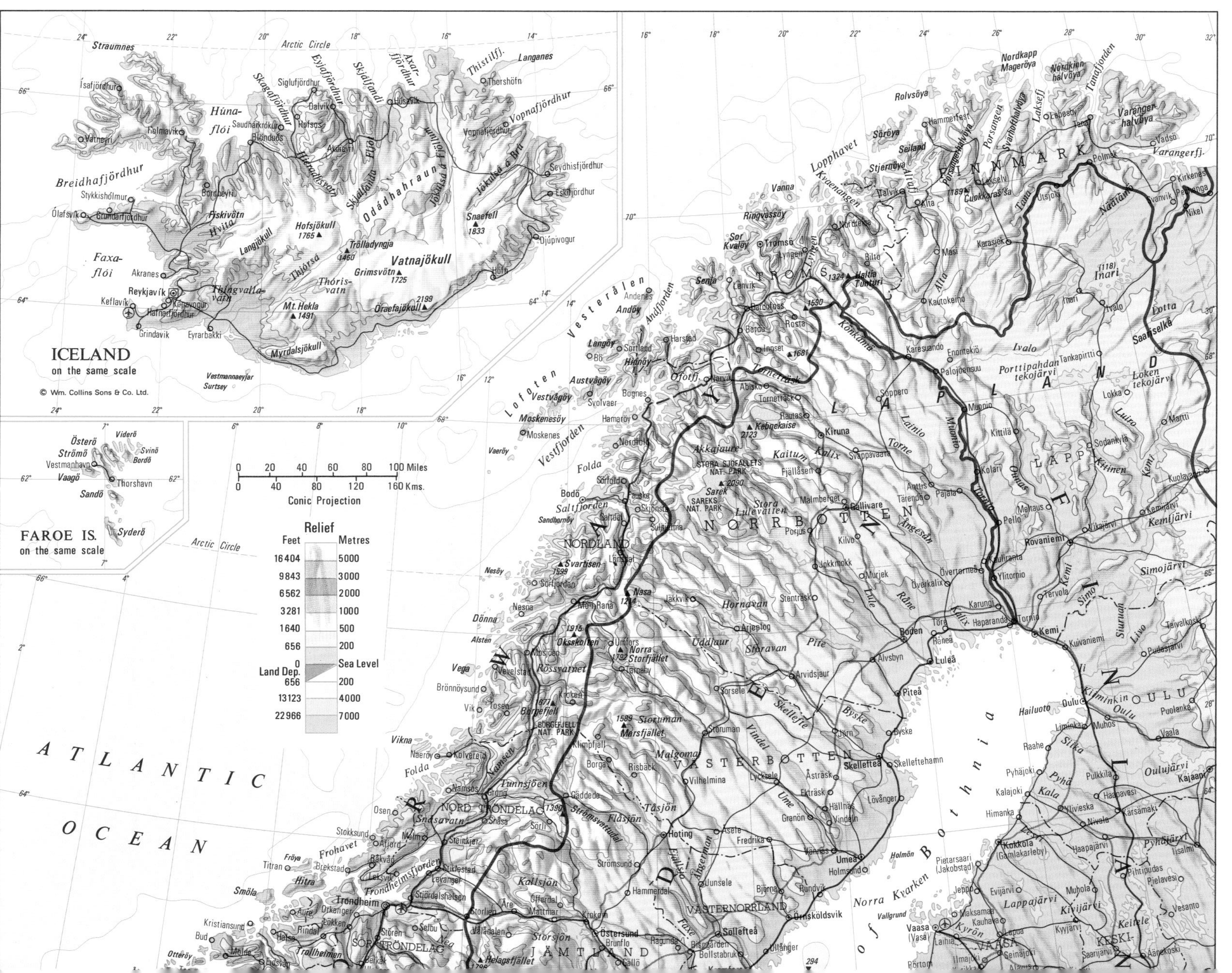
ICELAND
on the same scale
© Wm. Collins Sons & Co. Ltd.
FAROE IS.
on the same scale
0 20 40 60 80 100 Miles
0 40 80 120 160 Kms.
Conic Projection
Relief
Feet
Metres
16404 5000
9843 3000
6562 2000
3281 1000
1640 500
656 200
0 Sea Level
Land Dep. 656 200
13123 4000
22966 7000
ATLANTIC
OCEAN
Gulf of Bothnia
Vatnajökull
Reykjavík
Arctic Circle
FINNMARK
NORRBOTTEN
VÄSTERBOTTEN
NORDLAND
TROMS
LAPP
OULU
NORD TRÖNDELAG
SÖR TRÖNDELAG
JÄMTLAND
VÄSTERNORRLAND
Lofoten
Vesterålen
Trondheim
Luleå
Umeå
Oulu
Kiruna
Tromsö
Bodö

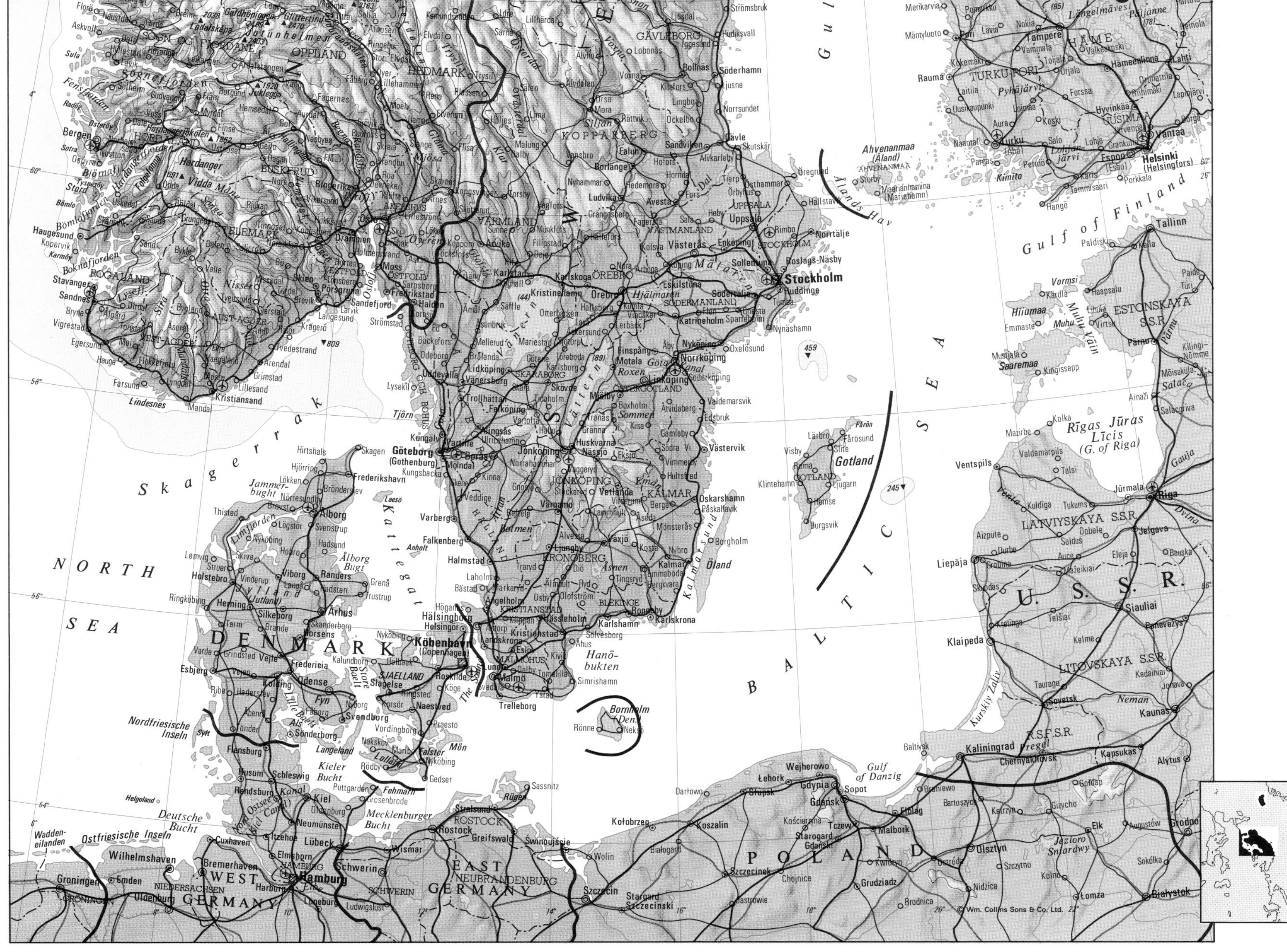

Gulf of Finland
BALTIC SEA
Skagerrak
Kattegat
NORTH SEA
DENMARK
POLAND
U.S.S.R.
EAST GERMANY
WEST GERMANY
Stockholm
Helsinki (Helsingfors)
Tallinn
Riga
Gotland
Öland
Bornholm (Den.)
København (Copenhagen)
Göteborg (Gothenburg)
Gulf of Danzig
Rīgas Jūras Līcis (G. of Riga)
© Wm. Collins Sons & Co. Ltd.

U.S.S.R. IN EUROPE

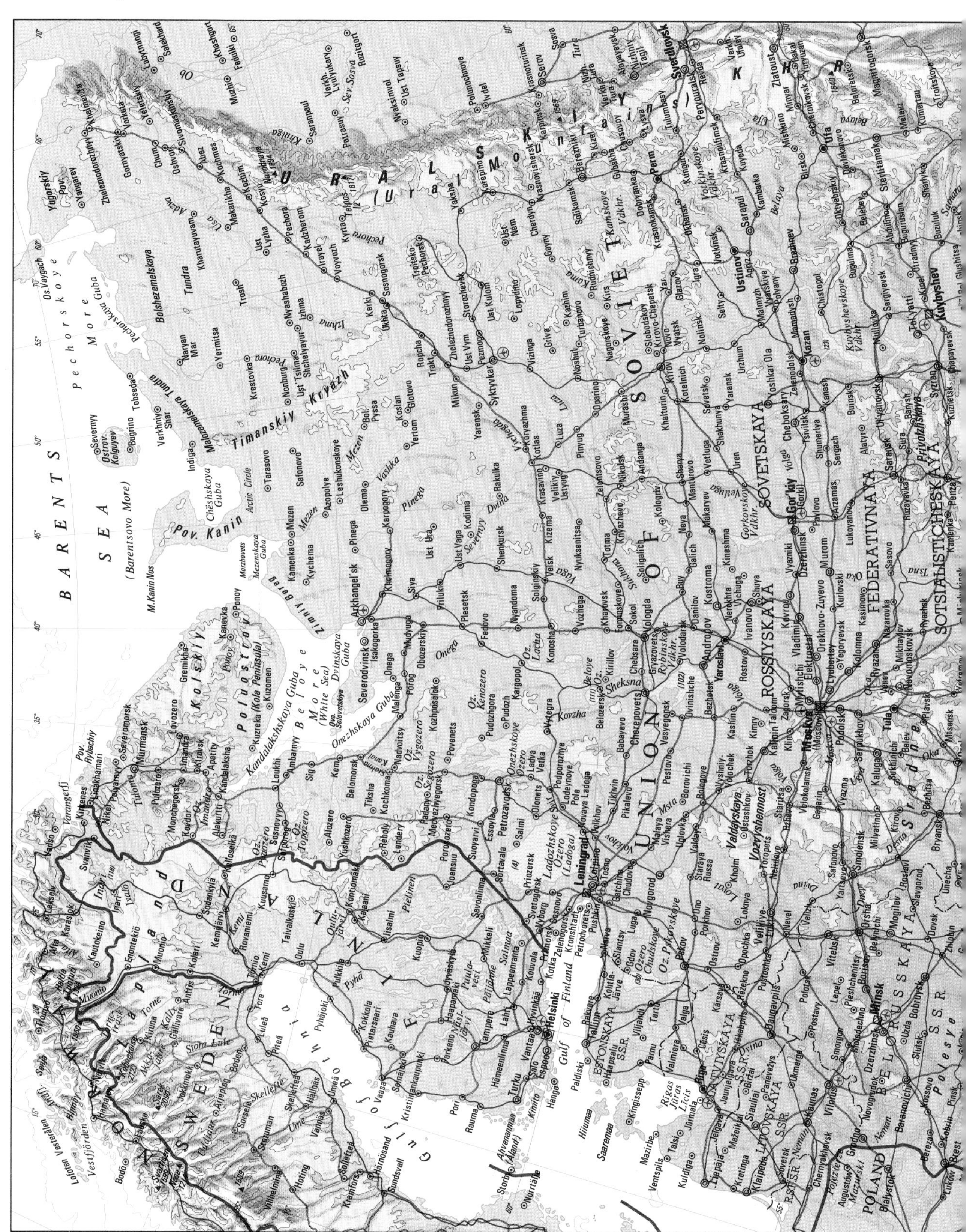
BARENTS SEA
(Barentsovo More)
Pechorskoye More
UNION OF SOVIET
ROSSIYSKAYA
SOVETSKAYA
FEDERATIVNAYA
SOTSIALISTICHESKAYA
Timanskiy Kryazh
Pov. Kanin
Beloye More
(White Sea)
Poluostrov Kol'skiy
(Kola Peninsula)
Ladozhskoye Ozero
(Ladoga)
Onezhskoye Ozero
Gulf of Finland
Gulf of Bothnia
FINLAND
SWEDEN
NORWAY
POLAND
Leningrad
Moskva
Helsinki
Arkhangel'sk
Murmansk
Gor'kiy
Kazan
Perm
Sverdlovsk
Kuybyshev
Ufa
Ustinov
Yaroslavl
Tula
Minsk
Riga
Tallinn
Kaunas
Vilnius
Syktyvkar
Kirov
Vologda
Petrozavodsk
Severodvinsk

SOCIALIST REPUBLICS
UKRAINSKAYA S.S.R.
KAZAKHSKAYA S.S.R.
ROMANIA
BULGARIA
TURKEY
SYRIA
IRAQ
IRAN
LEBANON
CYPRUS
BLACK SEA
CASPIAN SEA
MEDITERRANEAN SEA
Azovskoye More (Sea of Azov)
Prikaspiyskaya Nizmennost (Caspian Depression)
Mesopotamia
Kiyev
Khar'kov
Odessa
Volgograd
Astrakhan'
Rostov
Krasnodar
Tbilisi
Yerevan
Baku
Tehrān
Baghdād
Ankara
İstanbul
İzmir
Bucureşti (Bucharest)
Dimashq (Damascus)
Halab (Aleppo)
Bayrūt (Beirut)
0 100 200 300 Miles
0 100 200 300 400 Kms.
Conic Projection
© Wm. Collins, Sons & Co. Ltd.

U.S.S.R.

BARENTS SEA
BLACK SEA
CASPIAN SEA
Conic Projection
© Collins • Longman Atlases

Relief
Feet
Metres
16404
5000
9843
3000
6562
2000
3281
1000
1640
500
656
200
0
Sea Level
Land Dep.
656
200
13123
4000
22966
7000
Bering Str.
O. Komsomolets
O. Oktyabr'skoy Revolyutsii
O. Bol'shevik
Severnaya Zemlya
Proliv Vil'kitskogo
M. Chelyuskin
Novosibirskiye Ostrova
O. Novaya Sibir
O. Kotel'nyy
O. Bol. Lyakhovskiy
Proliv Dmitriya Lapteva
MORE LAPTEVYKH
VOSTOCHNO SIBIRSKOYE MORE
O. Vrangelya
Proliv Longa
O. Ayon
Chukotskiy Poluostrov
Anadyrskiy Zaliv
Poluostrov Taymyr
Gory Byrranga
Ozero Taymyr
Khatangskiy Zaliv
Nordvik
Oleněkskiy Zaliv
Ust Olenëk
Tiksi
Yanskiy Zaliv
Kazachye
Bulun
Khatanga
Volochanka
Anabar
Kokuora
Kondakovo
Yarcha
Srednekolymsk
Nizhne Kolymsk
Ambarchik
Bilibino
Pevek
Yentubol
Anadyr
Markovo
Omolon
Kolyma
Indigirka
Khonu
G. Pobeda
Khrebet Cherskogo
Verkhoyansk
Verkhoyanskiy Khrebet
Yana
Lena
Dzhelinde
Dzhardzhan
Olenëk
Zhigansk
Kamen
Putorana
Yessey
Sredne Sibirskoye Ploskogor'ye
(Central Siberian Plateau)
SOCIALIST REPUBLICS
RESPUBLIKA
ROSSIYSKAYA SOTSIALISTICHESKAYA
Markha
Nyurba
Vilyuysk
Suntar
Tura
Tunguska
Simenga
Tuoy-Khaya
Atara
Aldan
Yakutsk
Okhotskiy Perevoz
Amga
Ust'Maya
Oymyakon
Ust-Omchug
Magadan
Seymchan
Okhotsk
Khrebet Dzhugdzhur
Ayan
Nelkan
Aim
Chagda
Buyaga
Olekminsk
Baykit
Mutoray
Podkamennaya Tunguska
Nizh. Tunguska
Vitim
Mama
Yenyuka
Olekma
Chulman
Stanovoy Khrebet
Gelets Skalistyy
Kezhma
Angara
Chuna
Kondratyevo
Kirensk
Ust Kut
Nevanka
Kansk
Tayshet
Bratsk
Ust'-Ilga
Nizhneangarsk
Muya
Kalakan
Ust-Tungir
Tynda
Skovorodino
Zeya
Norsk
Ekimchan
Chumikan
Tugur
Nikolayevsk-na-Amure
Okha
Shantarskiy Ostrova
Aleksandrovsk Sakhalinskiy
Sakhalin
Poronaysk
Uglegorsk
Yuzhno Sakhalinsk
Tatarskiy Proliv
La Perouse Str.
Kurilskiye Ostrova
SEA OF OKHOTSK
BERING SEA
Gizhiga
Penzhinskaya Guba
Gizhiginskaya Guba
Kamenskoye
Koryakskiy Khrebet
Kichiga
O. Karaginskiy
Palana
Ust-Kamchatsk
Tigil
Poluostrov Kamchatka
Klyuchevskaya
Petropavlovsk Kamchatskiy
Kirovskiy
Opala
Bratsk Vdkhr.
Bol'shoy Onguren
Barguzin
Bagdarin
Ozero Baykal
Tulun
Nizhneudinsk
Zima
Cheremkhovo
Angarsk
Irkutsk
Ulan-Ude
Chita
Sretensk
Shilka
Yablonovyy Khrebet
Mongolia
Munku Sardyk
Hövsgöl Nuur
Kyakhta
Altanbulag
Petrovsk Zabaykal'skiy
Aginskoye
Olovyannaya
Borzya
Khapcheranga
Erzin
Mörön
Selenge Mörön
Darhan
Bulgan
Ulaanbaatar (Ulan Bator)
Tuul Gol
Kerulen
Tamsagbulag
Uliastay
Altay
MONGOLIA
Mandalgovi
Saynshand
Dalandzadgad
Gobi
Erenhot
Ejin Qi
Hanggin Houqi
Baotou
Hohhot
Guyang
Jining
Huade
Zhangjiakou
Beijing (Peking)
HEBEI
NEI MONGGOL
Qagan Nur
Hexigten Qi
Weichang
LIAONING
Jinzhou
Jinxi
Xingcheng
Liaodong Wan
Lüda
Huang Hai
Shenyang
Fushun
Anshan
Tieling
Siping
Kaiyuan
Shuangliao
Changchun
JILIN
Jilin
Baicheng
Da Hinggan Ling
Manzhouli
Hailar
Hulun Nur
Oroqen Zizhiqi
Gulian
Ushumun
Amur
Aihui
Blagoveshchensk
Svobodnyy
HEILONGJIANG
Bei'an
Nenjiang
Fuyu
Qiqihar
Hailun
Suihua
Harbin
Acheng
Da'an
Mudanjiang
Jixi
Songhua Jiang
Shuangyashan
Fuyuan
Khabarovsk
Birobidzhan
Zavitinsk
Amurzet
Chegdomyn
Komsomol'sk-na-Amure
Sofiysk
Sovetskaya Gavan
Bikin
Lesozavodsk
Ussuriysk
Vladivostok
Nakhodka
Olga
Rudnaya Pristan
Amgu
Sikhote Alin
Kraskino
CHINA
NORTH KOREA
Hŭngnam
Wŏnsan
Pyŏngyang
Dandong
Namp'o
Sŏul (Seoul)
Inch'ŏn
SOUTH KOREA
SEA OF JAPAN
Hokkaidō
Wakkanai
Asahikawa
Sapporo
Otaru
Hakodate
Aomori
Hachinohe
Akita
Morioka
Sendai
Yamagata
Niigata
Honshū
Toyama
Kanazawa
Tōkyō
Yokohama
Fuji san
Nagoya
Kyōto
Kōbe
Ōsaka
JAPAN

ASIA

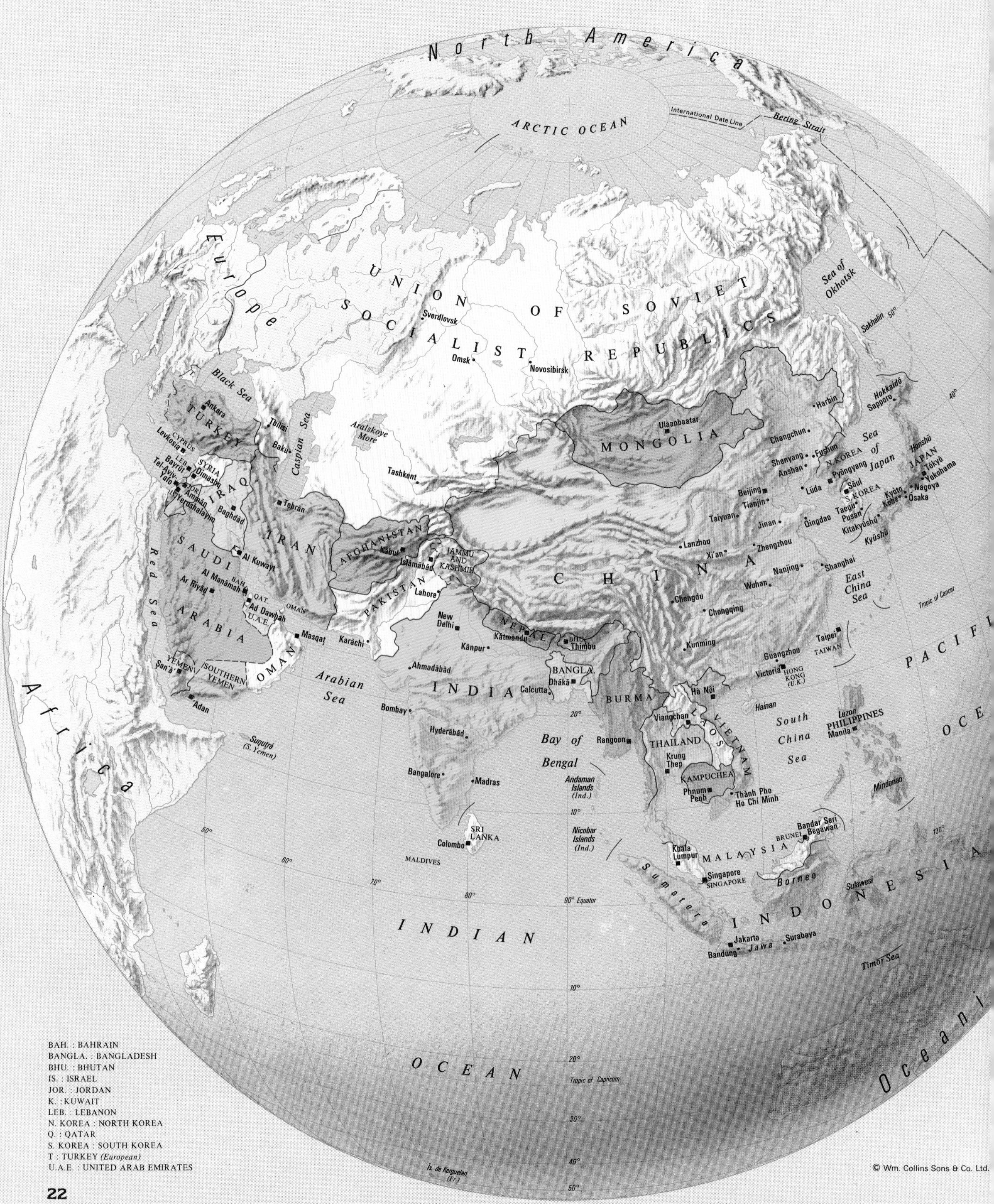
North America
ARCTIC OCEAN
International Date Line
Bering Strait
Europe
UNION OF SOVIET SOCIALIST REPUBLICS
Sverdlovsk
Omsk
Novosibirsk
Sea of Okhotsk
Sakhalin
Black Sea
Caspian Sea
Aralskoye More
Ankara
TURKEY
Tbilisi
Baku
CYPRUS
Levkosia
LEB.
SYRIA
Bayrūt
Dimashq
Tel Aviv-Yafo
IS.
JOR.
'Ammān
Yerushalayim
IRAQ
Baghdād
Tehrān
IRAN
Tashkent
MONGOLIA
Ulaanbaatar
Harbin
Changchun
Shenyang
Fushun
Anshan
Lüda
N.KOREA
Pyŏngyang
Sŏul
S.KOREA
Taegu
Pusan
Sea of Japan
Hokkaidō
Sapporo
Honshū
JAPAN
Tōkyō
Yokohama
Nagoya
Kyōto
Kobe
Ōsaka
Kitakyūshū
Kyūshū
Beijing
Tianjin
Taiyuan
Jinan
Qingdao
Lanzhou
Xi'an
Zhengzhou
Nanjing
Shanghai
Wuhan
Chengdu
Chongqing
Kunming
CHINA
East China Sea
Tropic of Cancer
Taipei
TAIWAN
Guangzhou
Victoria
HONG KONG (U.K.)
AFGHANISTAN
Kābul
Islāmābād
JAMMU AND KASHMIR
PAKISTAN
Lahore
Karāchi
New Delhi
Kānpur
NEPAL
Kātmāndu
BHU.
Thimbu
BANGLA.
Dhākā
Calcutta
INDIA
Ahmadābād
Bombay
Hyderābād
Bangalore
Madras
SRI LANKA
Colombo
MALDIVES
Red Sea
SAUDI ARABIA
K.
Al Kuwayt
BAH.
Al Manāmah
Ar Riyād
QAT.
Ad Dawḥah
U.A.E.
OMAN
Masqaṭ
YEMEN
Ṣan'ā'
SOUTHERN YEMEN
Adan
Suquṭrā (S. Yemen)
Arabian Sea
Africa
BURMA
Rangoon
Bay of Bengal
Andaman Islands (Ind.)
Nicobar Islands (Ind.)
THAILAND
Krung Thep
Viangchan
LAOS
Hà Nôi
VIETNAM
Hainan
KAMPUCHEA
Phnum Penh
Thành Phô Hồ Chí Minh
South China Sea
PHILIPPINES
Luzon
Manila
Mindanao
PACIFIC OCEAN
Kuala Lumpur
MALAYSIA
BRUNEI
Bandar Seri Begawan
Singapore
SINGAPORE
Sumatera
Borneo
Sulawesi
INDONESIA
Jakarta
Bandung
Jawa
Surabaya
Timor Sea
Oceania
INDIAN OCEAN
Equator
Tropic of Capricorn
Is. de Kerguelen (Fr.)
50°
60°
70°
80°
90°
130°
40°
20°
10°

BAH. : BAHRAIN
BANGLA. : BANGLADESH
BHU. : BHUTAN
IS. : ISRAEL
JOR. : JORDAN
K. : KUWAIT
LEB. : LEBANON
N. KOREA : NORTH KOREA
Q. : QATAR
S. KOREA : SOUTH KOREA
T : TURKEY *(European)*
U.A.E. : UNITED ARAB EMIRATES

JAPAN

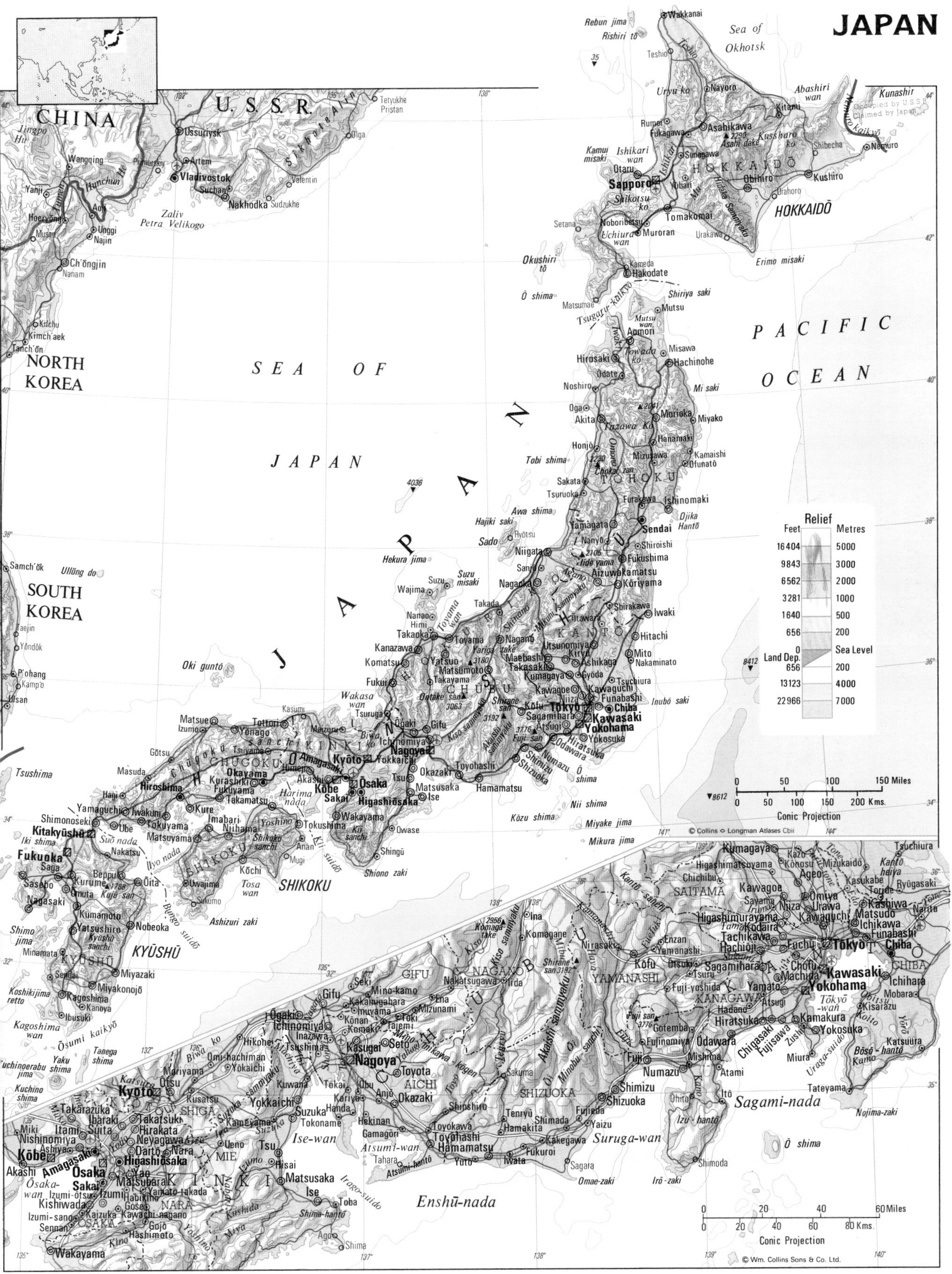

EAST ASIA

KAZAKHSKAYA S.S.R.
U.S.S.R.
UZBEKSKAYA S.S.R.
KIRGIZSKAYA S.S.R.
TADZHIKSKAYA S.S.R.
MONGOLIA
Gobi
XINJIANG UYGUR
Taklimakan Shamo
Tarim He
Junggar Pendi
Tian Shan
Altai
Kunlun Shan
Altun Shan
Qing Zang Gaoyuan (Tibetan Plateau)
XIZANG (TIBET)
QINGHAI
GANSU
NINGXIA
SICHUAN
YUNNAN
GUIZHOU
CHINA
HIMALAYA
NEPAL
BHUTAN
BANGLADESH
BURMA
THAILAND
LAOS
VIETNAM
INDIA
PAKISTAN
JAMMU AND KASHMIR
PUNJAB
HARYANA
RAJASTHAN
UTTAR PRADESH
MADHYA PRADESH
BIHAR
W. BENGAL
ORISSA
MAHARASHTRA
ANDHRA PRADESH
ASSAM
MEGHALAYA
ARUNACHAL PRADESH
BAY OF BENGAL
Ozero Balkhash
Ozero Baykal
Tashkent
Alma Ata
Frunze
Ürümqi
Kashi
Lhasa
Katmandu
Thimbu
Dhākā (Dacca)
Calcutta
Delhi
New Delhi
Lahore
Lucknow
Kānpur
Patna
Mandalay
Kunming
Chengdu
Chongqing
Lanzhou
Xining
Golmud
Hami
Dunhuang
Ulaangom
Irkutsk
Hà Nôi (Hanoi)
Viangchan (Vientiane)
Chiang Mai
Pegu
Akyab
Chittagong
Mt. Everest
K2 8611
Qinghai Hu
Bosten Hu
Lop Nur
Qaidam
Yarkant He
Brahmaputra
Ganga
Yamuna
Chambal
Narmada
Godavari
Irrawaddy
Salween
Mekong
Huang He
Jinsha Jiang
Lancang Jiang
Nu Jiang
Yarlung Zangbo Jiang
Palmyras Pt.
Ramree I.

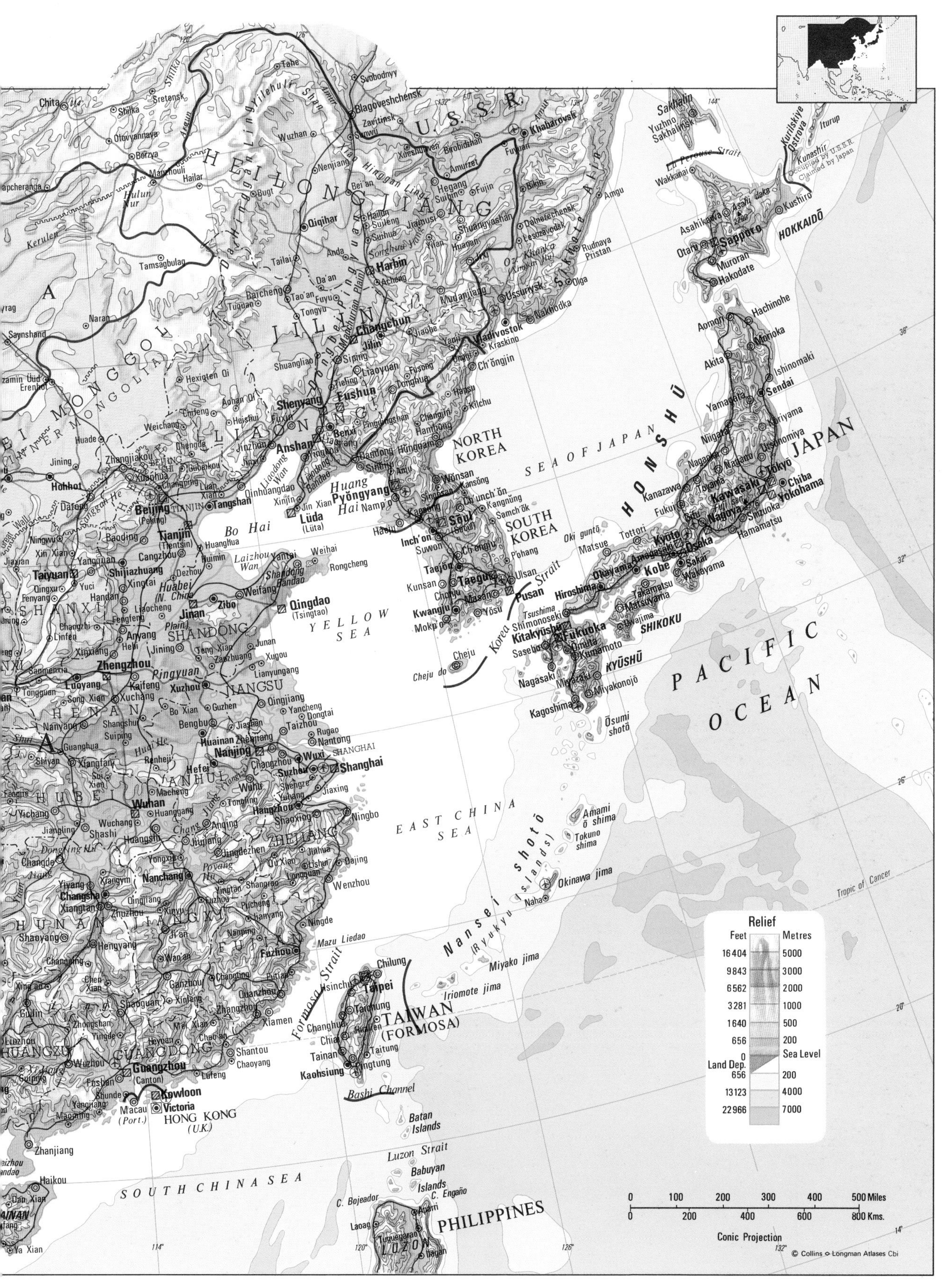
U.S.S.R.
HEILONGJIANG
JILIN
LIAONING
NEI MONGGOL
INNER MONGOLIA
NORTH KOREA
SOUTH KOREA
JAPAN
HONSHŪ
HOKKAIDŌ
SHIKOKU
KYŪSHŪ
SEA OF JAPAN
PACIFIC OCEAN
YELLOW SEA
EAST CHINA SEA
SOUTH CHINA SEA
Bo Hai
Huang Hai
TAIWAN (FORMOSA)
HONG KONG (U.K.)
PHILIPPINES
LUZON
SHANDONG
JIANGSU
HENAN
HUBEI
ANHUI
ZHEJIANG
JIANGXI
FUJIAN
HUNAN
GUANGDONG
GUANGXI
SHANXI
HEBEI
Beijing (Peking)
Tianjin (Tientsin)
Shanghai
Nanjing
Wuhan
Guangzhou (Canton)
Harbin
Changchun
Shenyang
Qingdao (Tsingtao)
Lüda (Lüta)
Fuzhou
Taipei
Kaohsiung
Kowloon
Victoria
Macau (Port.)
P'yŏngyang
Sŏul (Seoul)
Pusan
Tokyo
Yokohama
Kawasaki
Nagoya
Kyoto
Osaka
Kobe
Hiroshima
Fukuoka
Kitakyūshū
Sapporo
Sendai
Vladivostok
Khabarovsk
Blagoveshchensk
Sakhalin
Kuril'skiye Ostrova
Kunashir Occupied by U.S.S.R. Claimed by Japan
La Perouse Strait
Korea Strait
Formosa Strait
Bashi Channel
Luzon Strait
Nansei shotō (Ryukyu Islands)
Okinawa jima
Amami ō shima
Ōsumi shotō
Cheju do
Tropic of Cancer
Relief
Feet
Metres
16404
5000
9843
3000
6562
2000
3281
1000
1640
500
656
200
0
Sea Level
Land Dep.
656
200
13123
4000
22966
7000
0
100
200
300
400
500 Miles
0
200
400
600
800 Kms.
Conic Projection
© Collins · Longman Atlases Cbi

SOUTHEAST ASIA

CHINA
BURMA
THAILAND
LAOS
VIETNAM
KAMPUCHEA
MALAYSIA
BRUNEI
SINGAPORE
HONG KONG
INDIAN OCEAN
SOUTH CHINA SEA
ANDAMAN SEA
Gulf of Thailand
Gulf of Tongking
Gulf of Martaban
LAUT JAWA (JAVA SEA)
HAINAN
BORNEO
SUMATERA
JAWA (JAVA)
Andaman Islands (India)
Nicobar Islands (India)
Rangoon
Krung Thep (Bangkok)
Hà Nôi (Hanoi)
Thành Phô Ho Chí Minh (Ho Chi Minh City)
Phnum Pénh (Phnom Penh)
Viangchan (Vientiane)
Kuala Lumpur
Singapore
Jakarta
Guangzhou (Canton)
Victoria (U.K.)
Macau (Port.)
0 100 200 300 400 500 Miles
0 200 400 600 800 Kms.
Bonne Projection
© Collins-Longman Atlases Cbi

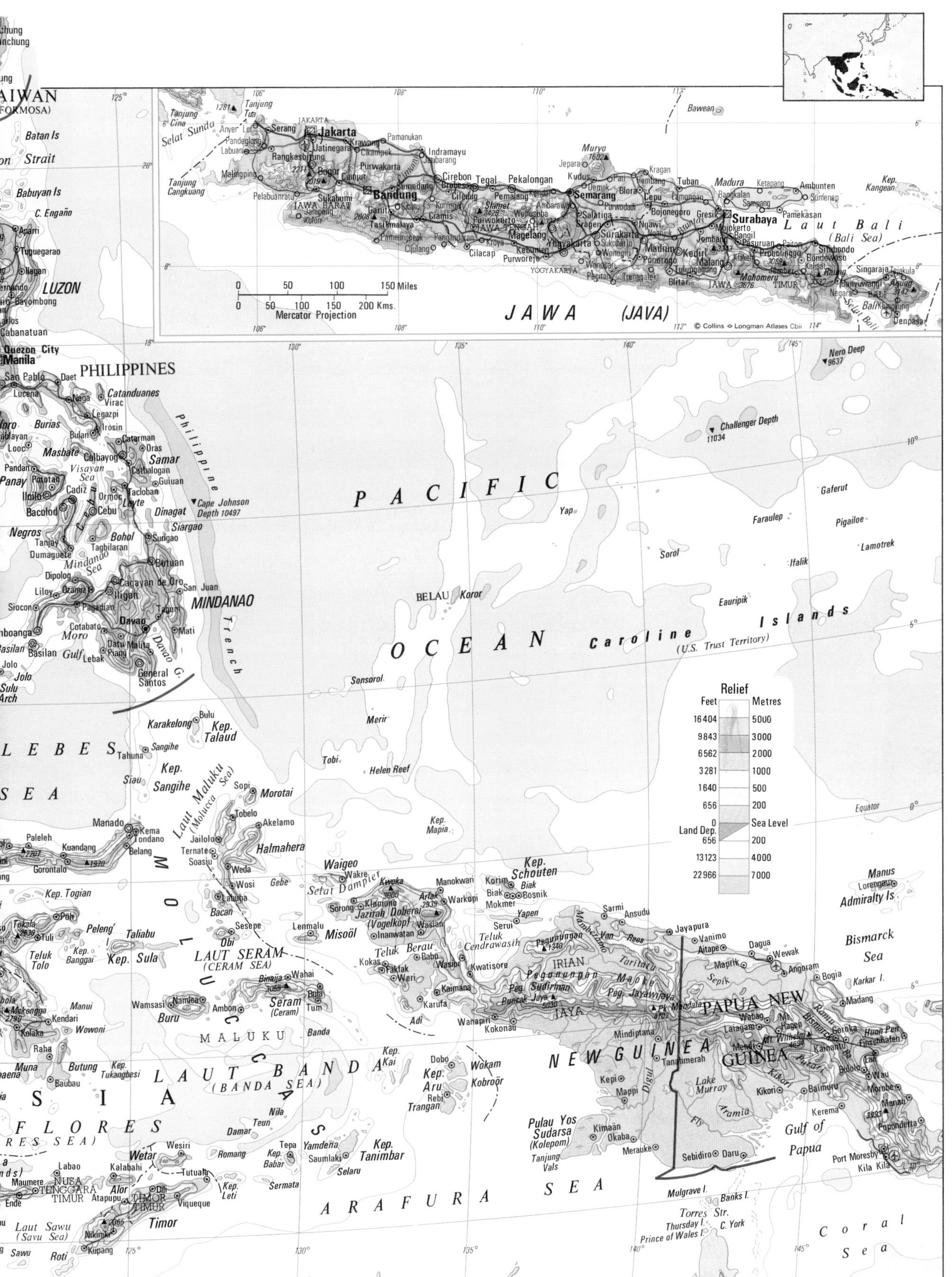
PACIFIC OCEAN
PHILIPPINES
LUZON
MINDANAO
Philippine Trench
Caroline Islands
(U.S. Trust Territory)
JAWA (JAVA)
Laut Bali (Bali Sea)
Mercator Projection
© Collins · Longman Atlases Cbii
Relief
Feet
Metres
16404
5000
9843
3000
6562
2000
3281
1000
1640
500
656
200
0
Sea Level
Land Dep.
656
200
13123
4000
22966
7000
MOLUCCAS
LAUT SERAM (CERAM SEA)
LAUT BANDA (BANDA SEA)
ARAFURA SEA
NEW GUINEA
PAPUA NEW GUINEA
IRIAN JAYA
Bismarck Sea
Coral Sea
Gulf of Papua
Torres Str.
Jakarta
Bandung
Semarang
Surabaya
Yogyakarta
Manila
Quezon City
Davao
Jayapura
Port Moresby
Challenger Depth 11034
Equator

SOUTH ASIA

IRAN
AFGHANISTAN
PAKISTAN
SAUDI ARABIA
OMAN
UNITED ARAB EMIRATES
QATAR
BAHRAIN
SOUTHERN YEMEN
IRAQ
U.S.S.R.
THE GULF
Gulf of Oman
ARABIAN SEA
INDIAN OCEAN
MALDIVES
Lakshadweep Is. (India)
Tropic of Cancer
Karāchi
Bombay
Tehrān
Kābul
Lahore
Quetta
Kermān
Eşfahān
Rann of Kutch
Thar Desert
Rub' al Khālī
Suquţrá (Socotra) (S. Yemen)
© Collins ◇ Longman Atlases Cbi

Kunlun Shan
Qing Zang Gaoyuan
(Tibetan Plateau)
Tanggula Shan
Bayan Har Shan
QINGHAI
XIZANG
(TIBET)
Gangdisê Shan
Nyainqêntanglha Shan
Hengduan Shan
CHINA
SICHUAN
YUNNAN
GUIZHOU
GANSU
SHAANXI
Qinling
HIMALAYA
NEPAL
BHUTAN
INDIA
BANGLADESH
BURMA
LAOS
VIETNAM
THAILAND
KAMPUCHEA
MALAYSIA
INDONESIA
SRI LANKA
BAY OF BENGAL
ANDAMAN SEA
GULF OF THAILAND
Gulf of Martaban
Andaman Islands (India)
Nicobar Islands (India)
Ten Degree Channel
Mergui Archipelago
Isthmus of Kra
Lhasa
Chengdu
Chongqing
Kunming
Guiyang
Katmandu
Lucknow
Kanpur
Allahabad
Varanasi (Benares)
Patna
Calcutta
Howrah
Dhaka (Dacca)
Chittagong
Mandalay
Rangoon
Moulmein
Bassein
Madras
Jaffna
Hà Nôi (Hanoi)
Hai Phong
Vientiane
Krung Thep (Bangkok)
Thonburi
Phnom Penh
Relief
Feet
Metres
16404
5000
9843
3000
6562
2000
3281
1000
1640
500
656
200
0
Sea Level
Land Dep.
656
200
13123
4000
22966
7000
0
100
200
300
400
500 Miles
0
200
400
600
800 Kms.
Conic Projection

SOUTHWEST ASIA

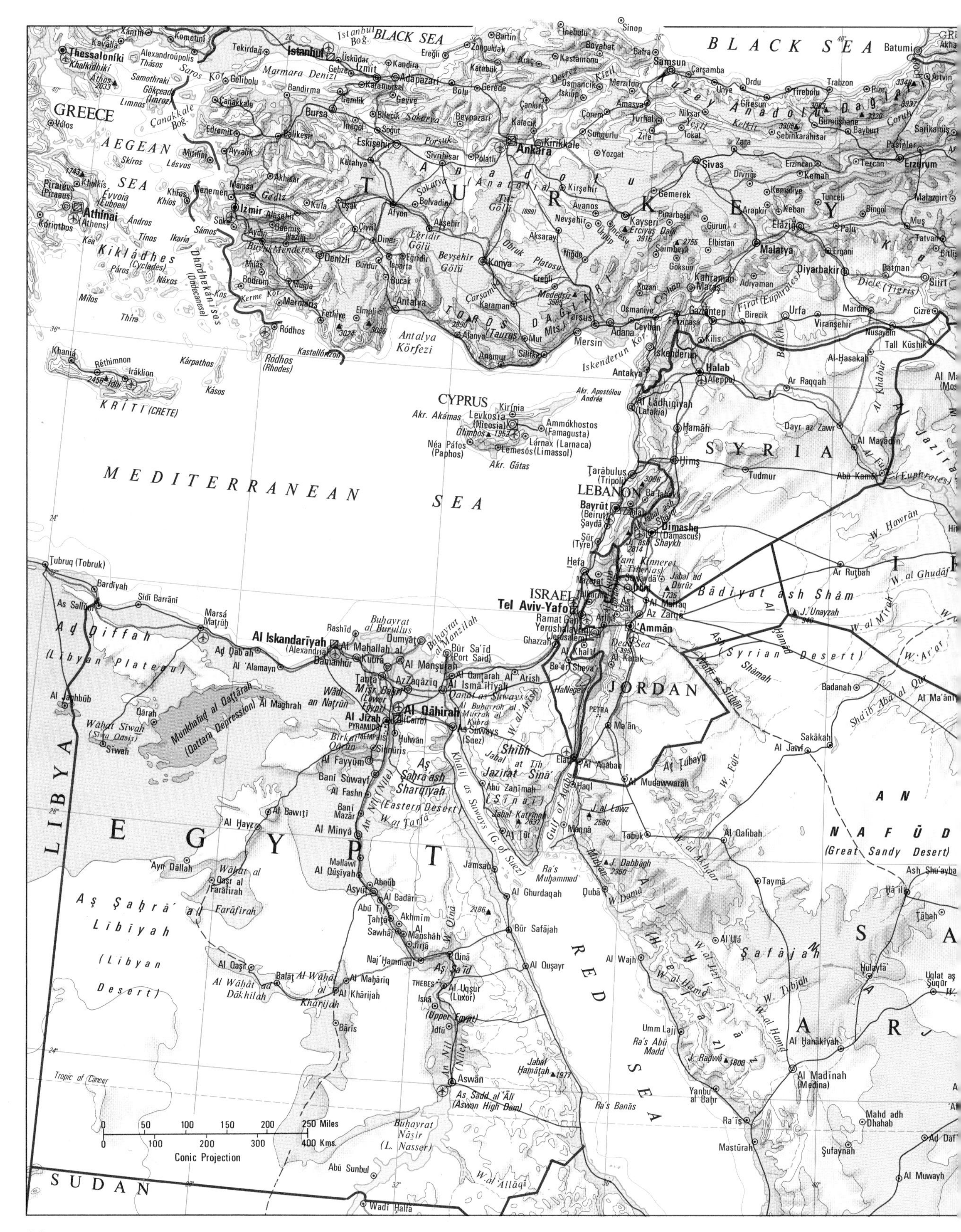

BLACK SEA
Istanbul
Marmara Denizi
GREECE
AEGEAN SEA
Athínai
(Athens)
Thessaloníki
Izmir
Bursa
Ankara
TURKEY
Konya
Antalya
Adana
Kayseri
Sivas
Samsun
Malatya
Diyarbakir
Erzurum
Kríti (CRETE)
Ródhos (Rhodes)
CYPRUS
Levkosia (Nicosia)
MEDITERRANEAN SEA
SYRIA
Halab (Aleppo)
Dimashq (Damascus)
LEBANON
Bayrūt (Beirut)
ISRAEL
Tel Aviv-Yafo
Yerushalayim (Jerusalem)
JORDAN
'Ammān
Dead Sea
Bādiyat ash Shām
Syrian Desert
EGYPT
Al Iskandarīyah (Alexandria)
Al Qāhirah (Cairo)
Būr Sa'īd (Port Said)
As Suways (Suez)
Aswān
Al Uqşur (Luxor)
Buhayrat Nāşir (L. Nasser)
Munkhafad al Qaţţārah (Qattara Depression)
Aş Şaḩrā' al Lībīyah (Libyan Desert)
Aş Şaḩrā' ash Sharqīyah (Eastern Desert)
Jazīrat Sīnā' (Sinai)
Gulf of Aqaba
RED SEA
LIBYA
Ţubruq (Tobruk)
SUDAN
Wadi Ḩalfa
AN NAFŪD (Great Sandy Desert)
Al Madinah (Medina)
Tropic of Cancer
0 50 100 150 200 250 Miles
0 100 200 300 400 Kms.
Conic Projection

CASPIAN
SEA
Zaliv Kara Bogaz Gol
U. S. S. R.
TURKMENSKAYA S. S. R.
PESKI KARAKUMY
(Black Sand Desert)
AZERBAYDZHANSKAYA S.S.R.
Relief
Feet
Metres
16404
5000
9843
3000
6562
2000
3281
1000
1640
500
656
200
0
Sea Level
Land Dep.
656
200
13123
4000
22966
7000
Karakumskiy Kanal
Baku
Sumgait
Apsheronskiy Pov.
Krasnovodsk
Krasnovodskiy Pov.
Krasnovodskiy Zaliv
Cheleken
Nebit-Dag
Kum Dag
Ashkhabad
Khiva
Bukhara
Chardzhou
Yerbent
Tabriz
Ardabīl
Rasht
Bandar-e Anzalī
Qazvīn
Tehrān
Rey
Tajrīsh
Qolleh-ye Damāvand
5601
RESHTEH-YE KŪHHĀ-YE ALBORZ
(Elburz Mts)
Semnān
Dāmghān
Mashhad
Neyshābūr
Sabzevār
Gorgān
Bandar-e Torkeman
DASHT-E KAVĪR
(Salt Desert)
Daryācheh-ye Namak
Qom
Kāshān
Hamadān
Kermānshāh
Esfahān
Yazd
Kermān
Shīrāz
Ahvāz
Ābādān
Khorramshahr
Al Başrah
Baghdād
IRAN
IRAQ
KŪHHĀ-YE ZĀGROS
(ZAGROS MTS)
DASHT-E LŪT
(Barren Desert)
AFGHANISTAN
Herāt
Farāh
PAKISTAN
Zāhedān
Kūh-e Taftān
4042
Daryācheh-ye Reẕā'īyeh
(L. Urmia)
Reẕā'īyeh
Dijlah (Tigris)
Al Kuwayt (Kuwait)
KUWAIT
Būshehr
Bandar-e Rīg
Bandar-e Abbās
Qeshm
Str. of Hormuz
THE GULF
BAHRAIN
Al Manāmah
Ad Dammām
QATAR
Ad Dawḩah (Doha)
Abū Ẓaby (Abu Dhabi)
Dubayy (Dubai)
UNITED ARAB EMIRATES
GULF OF OMAN
Masqaṭ (Muscat)
OMAN
ARABIAN SEA
Tropic of Cancer
Ar Riyāḑ (Riyadh)
SAUDI ARABIA
Al Hufūf
Al Jubayl
Jāsk
Chāh Bahār
Makran
Ra's al Ḩadd
Al Jabal al Akhḑar
3017
Al Jawb
Al Qafā'
© Collins ◇ Longman Atlases

THE LEVANT

Relief
Feet
Metres
16404
5000
9843
3000
6562
2000
3281
1000
1640
500
656
200
0
Sea Level
Land Dep.
656
200
13123
4000
22966
7000
0 20 40 60 80 100 Miles
0 50 100 150 Kms.
Polyconic Projection
M E D I T E R R A N E A N
S E A
C Y P R U S
Kólpos Mórfou
Akr. Akámas
Akr. Apostólou Andréa
Rizokárpason
Leonárison
Kólpos Ammókhostou
Ammókhostos (Famagusta)
Akr. Pidálion
Lefkosía (Nicosia)
Mórfou
Tróodos
Lárnax (Larnaca)
Néa Páfos (Paphos)
Koúklia
Akrotíri
Lemesós (Limassol)
Akr. Gátas
Al Lādhiqīyah (Latakia)
Jablah
Bāniyās
Ḩamāh
Ţarţūs
Al Ḩamīdīyah
Ḩimş
Shinshār
Ţarābulus (Tripoli)
Al Batrūn
LEBANON
Jūnīyah
Bayrūt (Beirut)
Al 'Atīqah
Şaydā (Sidon)
Aş Şarafand
Şūr (Tyre)
Dimashq (Damascus)
Buhayrat al 'Utaybah
Al Kiswah
Al Mismīyah
Nahariyya
Hefa (Haifa)
'Akko
Tirat Karmel
Golan Heights
Yam Kinneret
ISRAEL
Umm el Fahm
Hadera
Netanya
Herzliyya
Bene Beraq
Ramat Gan
Tel Aviv-Yafo
Bat Yam
Holon
Rishon LeZiyyon
Rehovot
Ashdod
Ashqelon
Jabālyah
Gaza Strip
Khān Yūnus
Rafah
Ghazzah (Gaza)
Ofaqim
Be'er Sheva'
Yerushalayim (Jerusalem)
Dead Sea
Al Khalīl (Hebron)
Nazerat
Dar'ā
Irbid
Jarash
Az Zarqā'
'Ammān
Ard al Jabbān
Mādabā
Aţ Ţunayb
JORDAN
Al Qaţrānah
Al Karak
Al Manzil
Aţ Ţafīlah
Ard aş Şawwān
Bā'ir
Ash Shawbak
Petra
Wādī Mūsā
Al Jafr
Ma'ān
Ra's an Naqb
Abū Ţarafah
Al 'Aqabah
Al Mudawwarah
Ḩaql
Al Bi'r
SAUDI ARABIA
J. al Lawz 2580
Ḩismá
Al Bad'
Maqnā
Tabūk
Ash Sharmah
J. Dabbāgh 2350
Ḩarrat ar Raḩā
Jabal aţ Ţubayq
Mizpe Ramon
Ha Negev (Negev)
Dimona
Elat
Al Kuntillah
Ath Thamad
An Nakhl
Shibh Jazīrat Sīnā' (Sinai Peninsula)
Jabal at Tīh
Gulf of Aqaba
Nuwaybi' al Muzayyinah
Dhahab
J. Mūsā 2285
J. Katrīnah 2637
Aţ Ţūr
Sharm ash Shaykh
Ra's Muḩammad
RED SEA
Jazīrat Tīrān
Madyan
Maḑīq Jūbāl (Str. of Jubal)
Khalīj as Suways (Gulf of Suez)
J. Ghārib 1751
Abū Zanīmah
Abū Dharbah
Bi'r Umm 'Umayyid
Al Burj
Buhayrat al Burullus
Baltīm
Rashīd
Dumyāţ
Al Iskandarīyah (Alexandria)
Kafr ash Shaykh
Buhayrat al Manzilah
Būr Sa'īd (Port Said)
Sabkhat al Bardawīl
Al 'Arīsh
Damanhūr
Al Mahallah al Kubrá
Al Manşūrah
Ţanţā
Misr Bahrī
(Lower Egypt)
Az Zaqāzīq
Shibīn al Kawm
Banhā
Al Ismā'īlīyah
Qanāt as Suways (Suez Canal)
Shubrā al Khaymah
Imbābah
Al Jīzah
Al Qāhirah (Cairo)
Ḩulwān
As Suways (Suez)
Al Buhayrah al Murrah al Kubrá (Great Bitter Lake)
Mamarra Mitla (Mitla Pass)
Wadi an Natrūn
E G Y P T
Birkat Qārūn
Al Fayyūm
Banī Suwayf
Nīl (Nile)
Aş Şahrā ash Sharqīyah (Arabian or Eastern Desert)
Jabal al Jalālat al Qiblīyah
Al Minyā
Mallawī
Samālūt
Maghāghah
© Collins-Longman Atlases

AFRICA

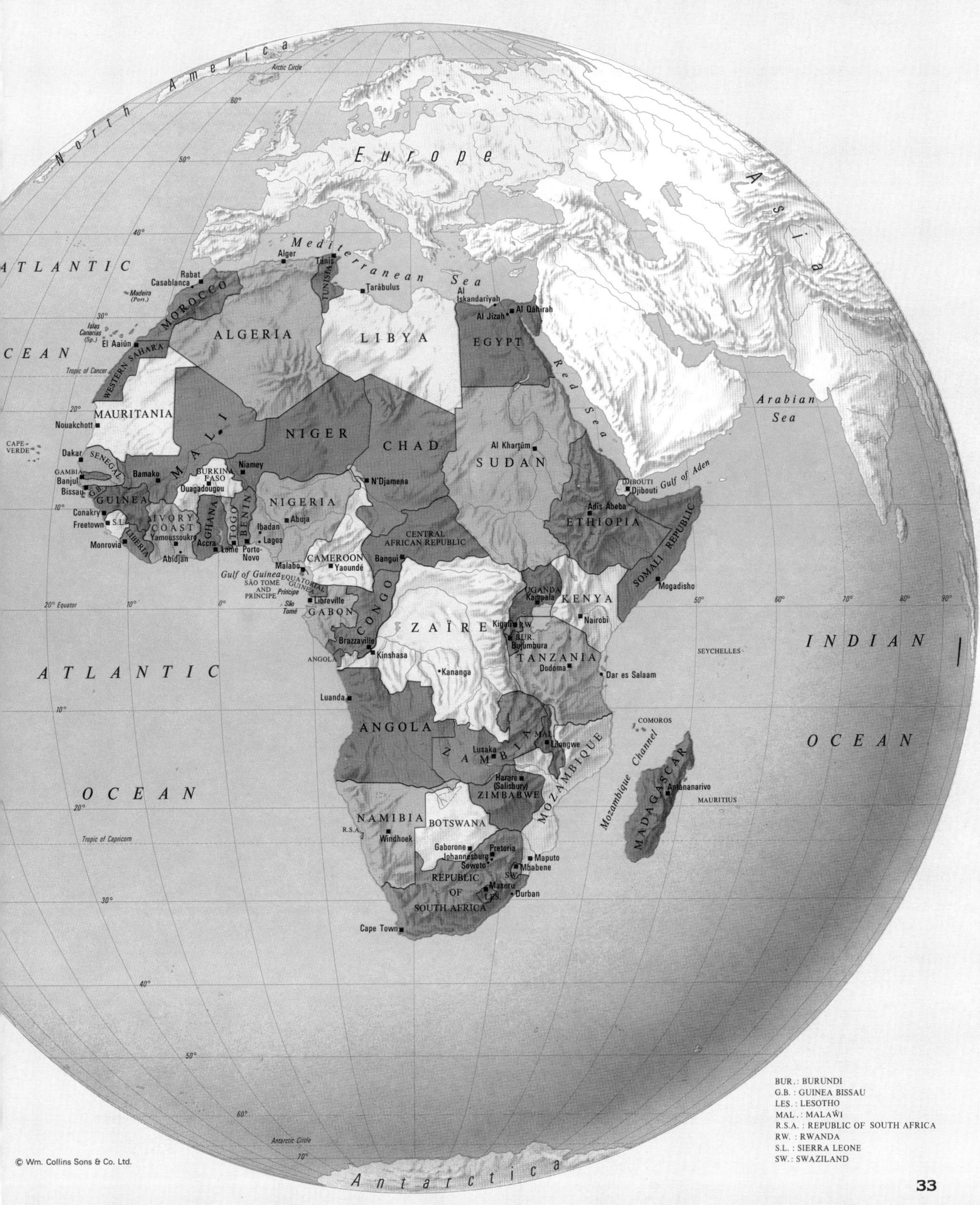

North America
Arctic Circle
Europe
Asia
Mediterranean Sea
ATLANTIC OCEAN
Rabat
Casablanca
Madeira (Port.)
MOROCCO
Alger
Tunis
TUNISIA
Tarābulus
Al Iskandarīyah
Al Qāhirah
Al Jīzah
Islas Canarias (Sp.)
El Aaiún
WESTERN SAHARA
ALGERIA
LIBYA
EGYPT
Tropic of Cancer
Red Sea
Arabian Sea
MAURITANIA
Nouakchott
MALI
NIGER
CHAD
Al Kharṭūm
SUDAN
CAPE VERDE
Dakar
SENEGAL
GAMBIA
Banjul
Bissau
G.B.
GUINEA
Bamako
BURKINA FASO
Ouagadougou
Niamey
N'Djamena
DJIBOUTI
Djibouti
Gulf of Aden
Conakry
S.L.
Freetown
Monrovia
LIBERIA
IVORY COAST
Yamoussoukro
Abidjan
GHANA
Accra
TOGO
Lomé
BENIN
Porto-Novo
NIGERIA
Abuja
Ibadan
Lagos
CENTRAL AFRICAN REPUBLIC
Bangui
Adīs Abeba
ETHIOPIA
SOMALI REPUBLIC
Mogadisho
Malabo
CAMEROON
Yaoundé
Gulf of Guinea
EQUATORIAL GUINEA
SÃO TOMÉ AND PRÍNCIPE
Príncipe
São Tomé
Libreville
GABON
CONGO
UGANDA
Kampala
KENYA
Nairobi
20° Equator
ZAÏRE
Kigali
RW.
BUR.
Bujumbura
Brazzaville
Kinshasa
ANGOLA
TANZANIA
Dodoma
Dar es Salaam
SEYCHELLES
INDIAN OCEAN
Kananga
Luanda
ANGOLA
COMOROS
MAL.
Lilongwe
Lusaka
ZAMBIA
MOZAMBIQUE
Mozambique Channel
Harare (Salisbury)
ZIMBABWE
MADAGASCAR
Antananarivo
MAURITIUS
NAMIBIA
R.S.A.
Windhoek
BOTSWANA
Tropic of Capricorn
Gaborone
Pretoria
Johannesburg
Soweto
Maputo
Mbabane
SW.
REPUBLIC OF SOUTH AFRICA
Maseru
LES.
Durban
Cape Town
Antarctic Circle
Antarctica
BUR.: BURUNDI
G.B.: GUINEA BISSAU
LES.: LESOTHO
MAL.: MALAWI
R.S.A.: REPUBLIC OF SOUTH AFRICA
RW.: RWANDA
S.L.: SIERRA LEONE
SW.: SWAZILAND

NORTHERN AFRICA

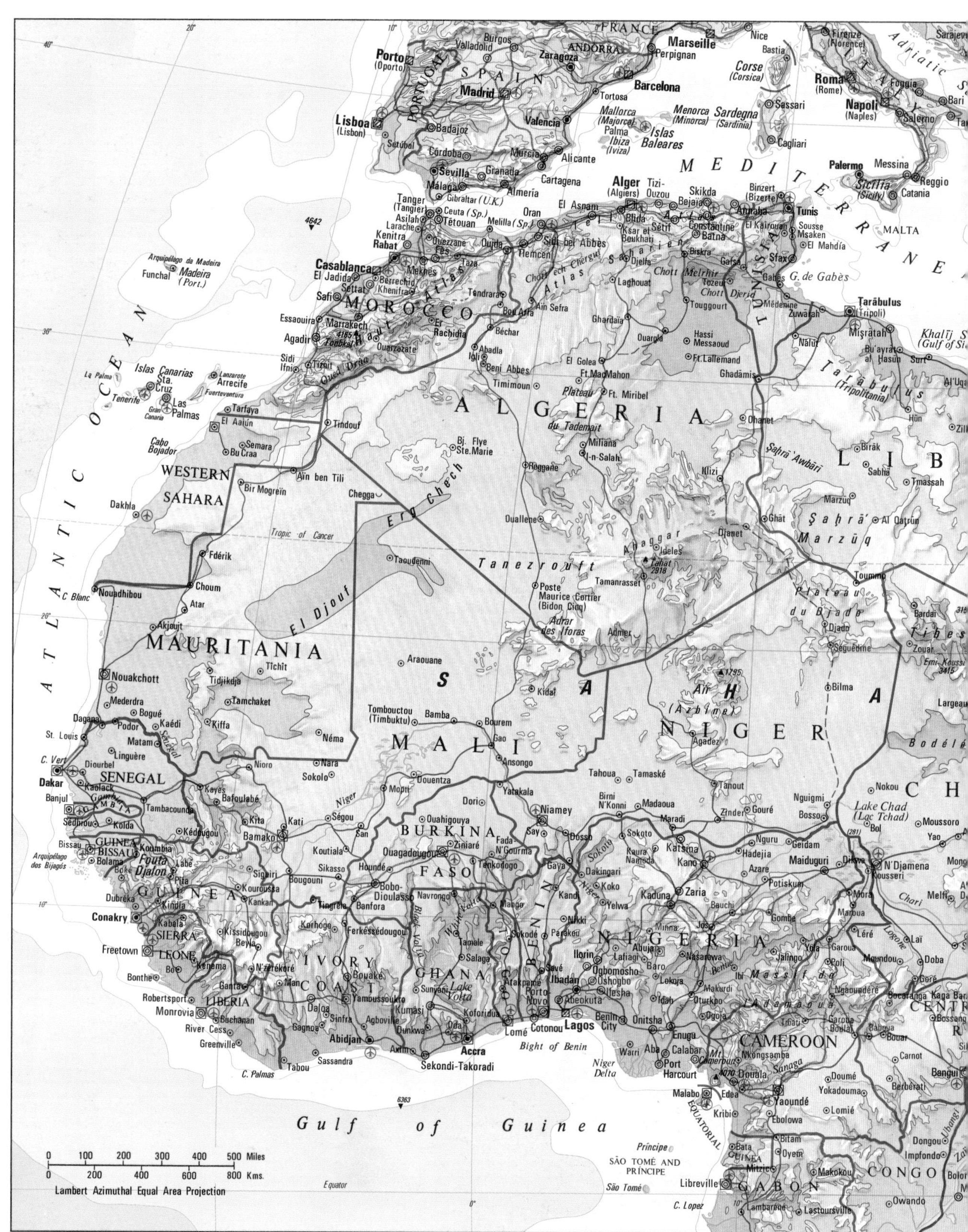
ATLANTIC OCEAN
MEDITERRANEAN
MOROCCO
ALGERIA
WESTERN SAHARA
MAURITANIA
MALI
NIGER
SENEGAL
GAMBIA
GUINEA-BISSAU
GUINEA
SIERRA LEONE
LIBERIA
IVORY COAST
BURKINA FASO
GHANA
TOGO
BENIN
NIGERIA
CAMEROON
EQUATORIAL GUINEA
GABON
CONGO
TUNISIA
SPAIN
PORTUGAL
FRANCE
ANDORRA
ITALY
MALTA
SÃO TOMÉ AND PRÍNCIPE
SAHARA
Gulf of Guinea
Bight of Benin
Tropic of Cancer
Equator
Lisboa (Lisbon)
Madrid
Porto (Oporto)
Barcelona
Marseille
Roma (Rome)
Napoli (Naples)
Alger (Algiers)
Tunis
Tarābulus (Tripoli)
Rabat
Casablanca
Marrakech
Nouakchott
Dakar
Bamako
Niamey
Ouagadougou
Conakry
Freetown
Monrovia
Abidjan
Accra
Lomé
Porto Novo
Lagos
Malabo
Libreville
Yaoundé
N'Djamena
Bangui
0 100 200 300 400 500 Miles
0 200 400 600 800 Kms.
Lambert Azimuthal Equal Area Projection

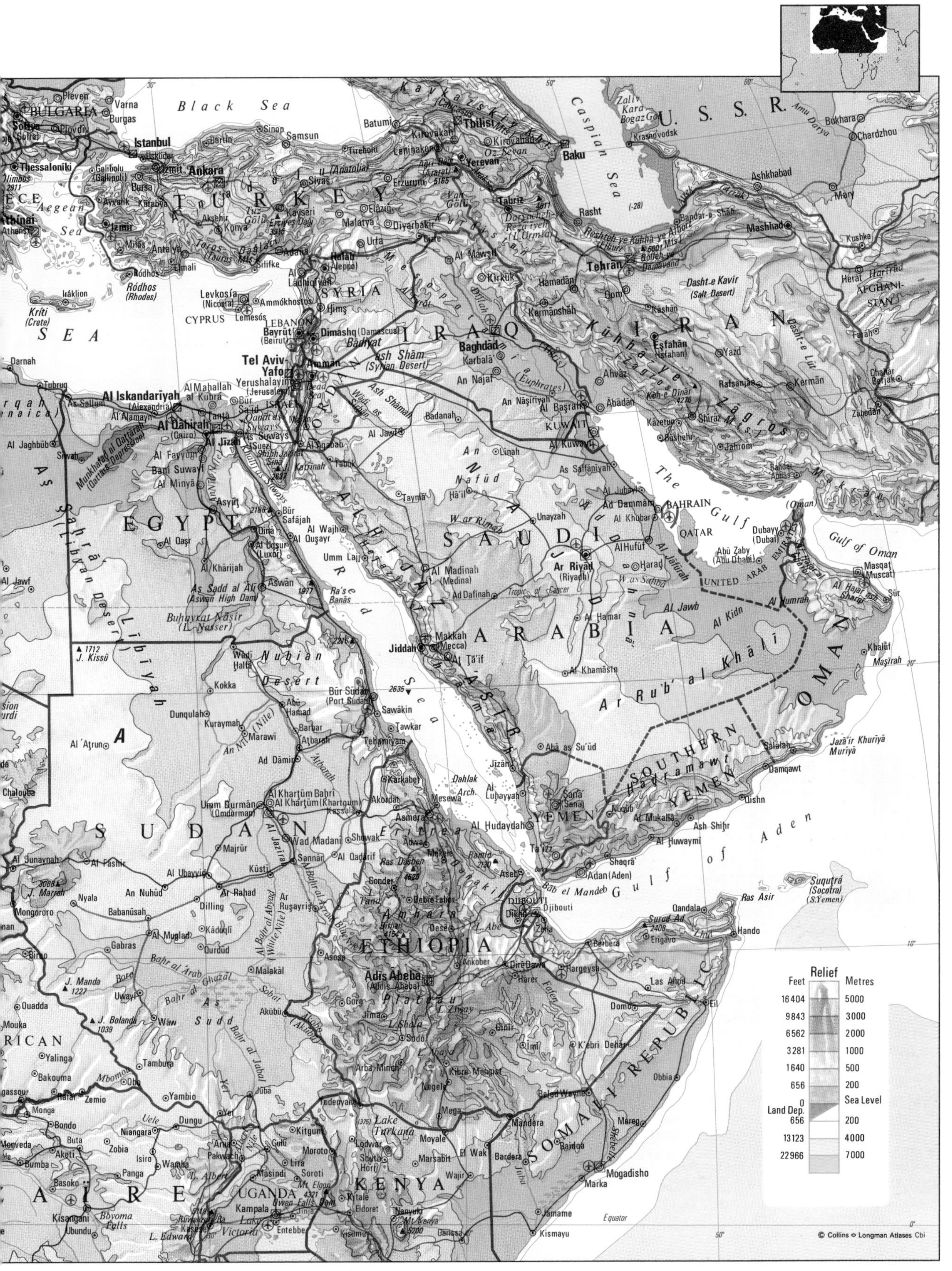

Black Sea
Caspian Sea
U. S. S. R.
BULGARIA
Sofiya (Sofia)
Plovdiv
Varna
Burgas
Istanbul
Thessaloníki
Ankara
İzmir
TURKEY
Anatolia
Samsun
Sinop
Batumi
Tbilisi
Yerevan
Baku
Krasnovodsk
Ashkhabad
Bukhara
Chardzhou
Amu Darya
Mary
Mashhad
Erzurum
Elâzığ
Malatya
Diyarbakir
Kayseri
Konya
Antalya
Adana
Urfa
Halab (Aleppo)
Al Mawşil
Kirkūk
Tabrīz
Rasht
Tehrān
Damavand
Dasht-e Kavir (Salt Desert)
Qom
Hamadān
Kermānshāh
Kāshān
Eşfahān (Isfahan)
Yazd
Kermān
IRAN
Kūhhā-ye Zāgros
Zagros Mts
Shīrāz
Ahvāz
Ābādān
Būshehr
Zāhedān
Herāt
AFGHANISTAN
Farāh
Makran
Ródhos (Rhodes)
Iráklion
Kríti (Crete)
SEA
CYPRUS
Levkosía (Nicosia)
Lemesós
LEBANON
Bayrūt (Beirut)
Dimashq (Damascus)
SYRIA
Ḩimş
IRAQ
Baghdād
Karbalā'
An Najaf
Al Başrah
Euphrates
Badiyat ash Shām (Syrian Desert)
Tel Aviv-Yafo
Yerushalayim (Jerusalem)
ISRAEL
'Ammān
JORDAN
Darnah
Tubruq
Al Iskandarīyah (Alexandria)
Al Qāhirah (Cairo)
Al Jīzah
Bür Sa'īd
Suez
As Suways
Al Fayyūm
Al Minyā
Asyūţ
EGYPT
Munkhafaḑ al Qaţţārah (Qattara Depression)
Aş Şaḩrā' al Lībīyah (Libyan Desert)
Al Jaghbūb
Sīwah
Qinā
Al Uqşur (Luxor)
Al Khārijah
Aswān
As Sadd al 'Ālī (Aswan High Dam)
Buḩayrat Nāşir (L. Nasser)
Sīnā'
KUWAIT
Al Kuwayt
An Nafūd
SAUDI ARABIA
Ḩā'il
Taymā'
Tabūk
Al Wajh
Al Madīnah (Medina)
Makkah (Mecca)
Jiddah
Aţ Ţā'if
Ar Riyāḑ (Riyadh)
Al Hufūf
Ad Dammām
BAHRAIN
QATAR
The Gulf
Dubayy (Dubai)
Abū Zaby (Abu Dhabi)
UNITED ARAB EMIRATES
Gulf of Oman
Masqaţ (Muscat)
OMAN
Ar Rub' al Khālī
Tropic of Cancer
Red Sea
Jīzān
YEMEN
Şan'ā' (Sana)
Al Ḩudaydah
Ta'izz
Adan (Aden)
SOUTHERN YEMEN
Ḩaḑramawt
Al Mukallā
Şalālah
Gulf of Aden
Suquţrā (Socotra) (S.Yemen)
Nubian Desert
Wadi Halfā
Būr Sūdān (Port Sudan)
Sawākin
Al Khartūm (Khartoum)
Umm Durmān (Omdurman)
SUDAN
Wad Madanī
Kassalā
Al Ubayyiḑ
Kūstī
Nyala
Malakāl
As Sudd
Bahr al Jabal
Juba
Eritrea
Asmera
Mits'iwa
Gonder
Ras Dashen
ETHIOPIA
Adis Abeba (Addis Ababa)
Dīre Dawa
Harer
DJIBOUTI
Djibouti
Berbera
Hargeysa
SOMALI REPUBLIC
Mogadisho
Kismayu
Marka
Bardera
KENYA
Mt Kenya
Nairobi
UGANDA
Kampala
L. Victoria
L. Albert
L. Edward
L. Turkana
ZAIRE
Kisangani
CENTRAL AFRICAN
Equator
Relief
Feet
Metres
16404 5000
9843 3000
6562 2000
3281 1000
1640 500
656 200
0 Sea Level
Land Dep.
656 200
13123 4000
22966 7000
© Collins ◇ Longman Atlases Cbi

CENTRAL AND SOUTHERN AFRICA

Relief

Feet	Metres
16404	5000
9843	3000
6562	2000
3281	1000
1640	500
656	200
0	Sea Level
656	200
13123	4000

0 100 200 300 400 500 Miles

0 200 400 600 800 Kms.

Lambert Azimuthal Equal Area Projection

EAST AFRICA

UGANDA
KENYA
TANZANIA
RWANDA
BURUNDI
ZAMBIA
MALAWI
MOZAMBIQUE
ZIMBABWE
SOMALI REP
COMOROS
MADAGASCAR
HAUT-ZAIRE
KIVU
SHABA
INDIAN OCEAN
Mozambique Channel
Lake Victoria
Lake Turkana
Lake Tanganyika
Lake Malawi
Lake Rukwa
Lake Kariba
Nairobi
Kampala
Mogadishu
Dar es Salaam
Mombasa
Dodoma
Harare
Lusaka
Lilongwe
Blantyre
Zanzibar
Moroni
Equator
0 100 200 Miles
0 100 200 300 Kms.
Lambert Azimuthal Equal Area Projection
© Collins ◇ Longman Atlases Cbi

WEST AFRICA – EAST

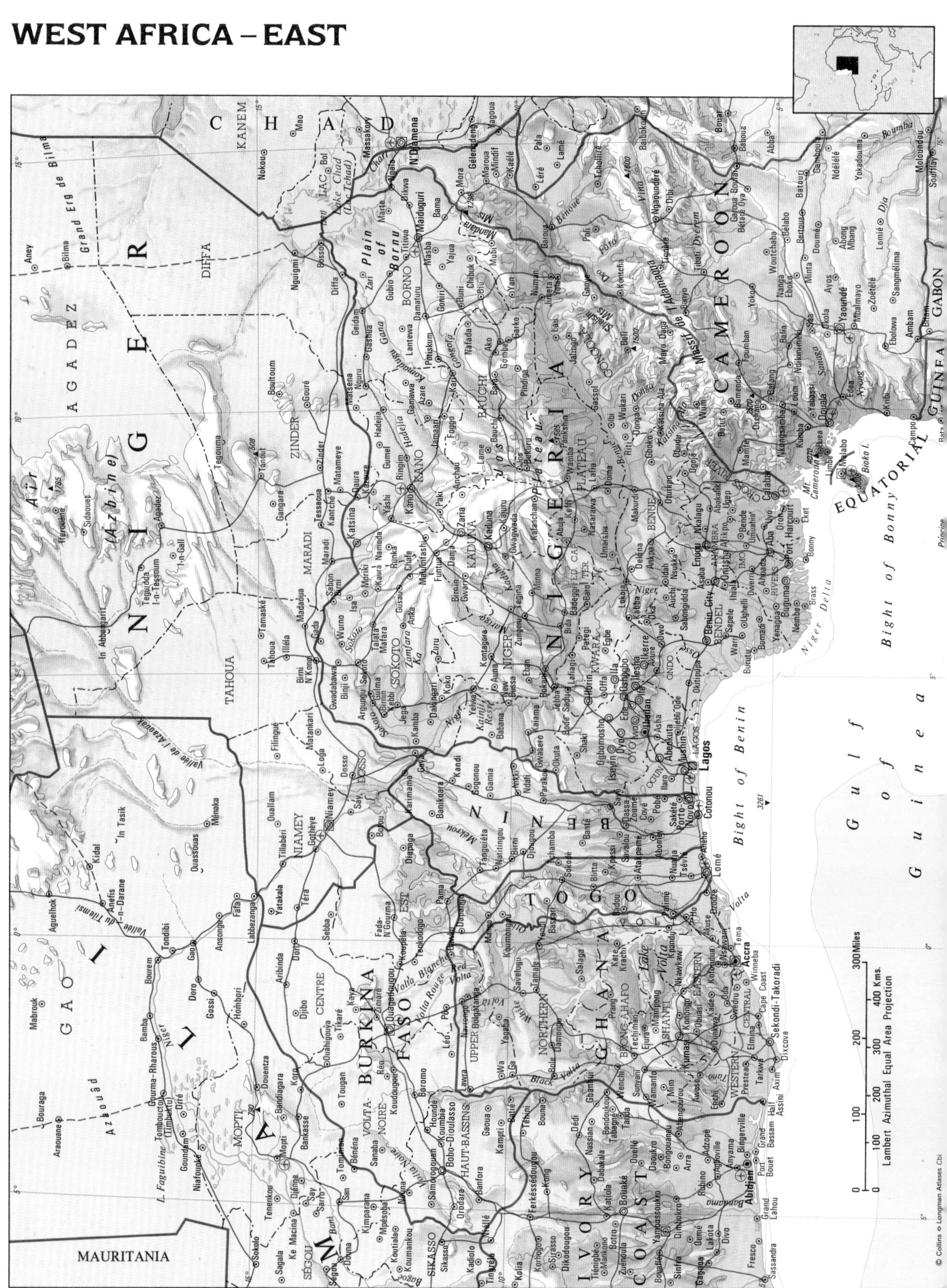

CHAD
NIGER
MALI
BURKINA FASO
NIGERIA
CAMEROON
GHANA
TOGO
BENIN
IVORY COAST
MAURITANIA
EQUATORIAL GUINEA
GABON
Gulf of Guinea
Bight of Benin
Bight of Bonny
Lake Chad
Lagos
Accra
Abidjan
Niamey
N'Djamena
Yaoundé
0 100 200 300 Miles
0 100 200 300 400 Kms.
Lambert Azimuthal Equal Area Projection
© Collins - Longman Atlases Cbi

SOUTH AFRICA

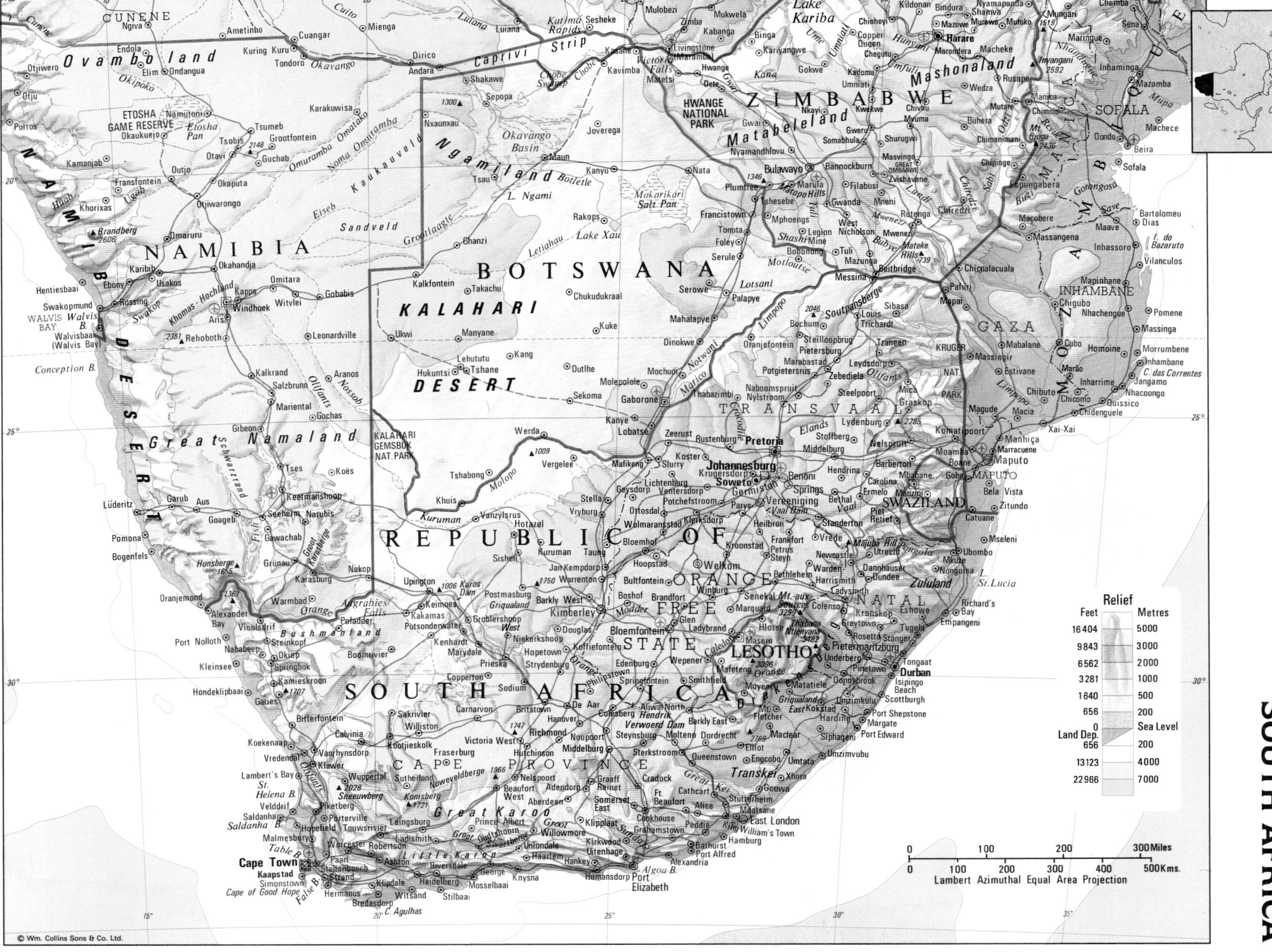

Relief
Feet
Metres
16404
5000
9843
3000
6562
2000
3281
1000
1640
500
656
200
0
Sea Level
Land Dep.
656
200
13123
4000
22966
7000
0
100
200
300Miles
0
100
200
300
400
500Kms.
Lambert Azimuthal Equal Area Projection
NAMIBIA
BOTSWANA
ZIMBABWE
REPUBLIC OF SOUTH AFRICA
ORANGE FREE STATE
TRANSVAAL
NATAL
CAPE PROVINCE
LESOTHO
SWAZILAND
KALAHARI DESERT
NAMIB DESERT
Pretoria
Johannesburg
Soweto
Bloemfontein
Kimberley
Durban
Pietermaritzburg
East London
Port Elizabeth
Cape Town
Kaapstad
Maputo
Windhoek
Gaborone
Bulawayo
Harare
Lüderitz
Walvis Bay
Cape of Good Hope
C. Agulhas
Lake Kariba
© Wm. Collins Sons & Co. Ltd.

OCEANIA

PACIFIC OCEAN
North America
ASIA
(Japan)
Mariana Islands
Guam (U.S.A.)
Philippine Sea
MICRONESIA
Trust Territory of the Pacific Islands (U.S.A.)
Tropic of Cancer
Hawaiian Islands (U.S.A.)
Equator
KIRIBATI
NAURU
Phoenix Island
MELANESIA
New Ireland
New Britain
Bougainville
SOLOMON ISLANDS
Guadalcanal
Santa Cruz Is.
TUVALU
Tokelau Is.
PAPUA NEW GUINEA
Port Moresby
Is. (France) Wallis
WESTERN SAMOA
Apia
(U.S.A.)
Cook (N.Z.) Islands
POLYNESIA
Îles Marquises
Îles Tuamotu
Arafura Sea
Coral Sea
Espiritu Santo
Malekula
VANUATU
Vila
Vanua Levu
FIJI
Suva
TONGA
Alofi
Niue
Nuku'alofa
(France)
Nouvelle Calédonia
Nouméa
Îles Loyauté
Tropic of Capricorn
Avarua
Papeete
Tahiti (France)
Timor Sea
AUSTRALIA
Brisbane
Sydney
Canberra
Adelaide
Melbourne
Perth
Tasmania
Hobart
INDIAN OCEAN
North Island
Auckland
NEW ZEALAND
Wellington
Tasman Sea
South Island
Christchurch
Dunedin
Stewart I.
Chatham Is.
International Date Line
PACIFIC OCEAN
Antarctic Circle
Antarctica

AUSTRALIA

INDONESIA
PAPUA NEW GUINEA
LAUT BANDA
(BANDA SEA)
LAUT FLORES
(FLORES SEA)
ARAFURA SEA
TIMOR SEA
CORAL SEA
Bismarck Sea
Solomon Sea
Gulf of Papua
Torres Strait
Gulf of Carpentaria
Great Barrier Reef
NORTHERN TERRITORY
QUEENSLAND
WESTERN AUSTRALIA
SOUTH AUSTRALIA
NEW SOUTH WALES
VICTORIA
TASMANIA
AUST. CAP. TER.
Great Sandy Desert
Gibson Desert
Great Victoria Desert
Simpson Desert
Nullarbor Plain
Great Artesian Basin
Great Dividing Range
Barkly Tableland
Kimberley Plateau
Macdonnell Ranges
Musgrave Ranges
Hamersley Range
Arnhem Land
Cape York Peninsula
L. Eyre
L. Torrens
L. Gairdner
L. Frome
L. Mackay
L. Amadeus
L. Carnegie
L. Disappointment
Great Australian Bight
Spencer Gulf
Kangaroo I.
Bass Strait
King I.
Flinders I.
INDIAN OCEAN
TASMAN SEA
Darwin
Katherine
Alice Springs
Tennant Creek
Perth
Fremantle
Geraldton
Kalgoorlie
Esperance
Albany
Broome
Port Hedland
Adelaide
Port Augusta
Whyalla
Port Lincoln
Melbourne
Geelong
Ballarat
Sydney
Newcastle
Wollongong
Canberra
Brisbane
Rockhampton
Townsville
Cairns
Mount Isa
Hobart
Launceston
Port Moresby
Lae
Broken Hill
Mt. Kosciusko 2230
Mt. Ossa 1617
Mt. Wilhelm 4694
Puncak Jaya 5030
0 100 200 300 400 500 Miles
0 200 400 600 800 Kms.
Lambert Azimuthal Equal Area Projection
© Collins ◇ Longman Atlases Cbi

WESTERN AUSTRALIA

Relief
Feet
Metres
16404 5000
9843 3000
6562 2000
3281 1000
1640 500
656 200
0 Sea Level
Land Dep. 656 200
13123 4000
22966 7000
TIMOR SEA
OCEAN
NORTHERN TERRITORY
WESTERN AUSTRALIA
Timor
Sumba
Roti
Kupang
Nikiniki
Waingapu
Baing
Darwin
Batchelor
Humpty Doo
Rum Jungle
Pine Creek
Katherine
Mataranka
Larrimah
Birdum
Daly Waters
Oenpelli
Melville I.
Bathurst I.
Cobourg Pen.
Croker I.
Goulburn Is
Van Diemen Gulf
Dundas Str.
Clarence Str.
Arnhem Land
Roper Valley
Newcastle Waters
Powell Creek
Renner Springs
Tennant Creek
Hatches Creek
Barrow Creek
Tea Tree
Mt. Freeling
Alice Springs
Macdonnell Ranges
Hermannsburg
Deep Well
Henbury
Erldunda
Kulgera
Finke
Bloods Creek
Hamilton
Musgrave Ranges
Mt. Woodroffe 1440
L. Amadeus
Palmer
Hugh
Mt. Zeil 1510
Mt. Laughlen
Ewaninga
Lander
The Granites
Tanami
L. Mackay
L. White
L. Macdonald
L. Hopkins
Petermann Ranges
Tomkinson Ranges
Barrow Ra.
Warburton Ra.
Bonython Ra.
Gregory L.
Sturt Plain
L. Woods
Wave Hill
Victoria River Downs
Victoria
Willeroo
Burrundie
Daly
Port Keats
Anson B.
Joseph Bonaparte Gulf
Queens Ch.
Cambridge G.
Wyndham
Kununurra
Ord
Mistake Creek
Inverway
Nicholson
Gordon Downs
Sturt
Turkey Creek
Kimberley Plateau
Halls Creek
Margaret River
C. Londonderry
Drysdale
Kalumburu
Mt. Hann 776
Gibb River
Glenroy
Admiralty G.
King Leopold Ranges
Fitzroy Crossing
Jubilee Downs
Christmas Creek
Noonkanbah
Ellendale
Fitzroy
Bonaparte Archipelago
Brunswick B.
Collier B.
King Sound
Derby
Yeeda River
Dampier Land
C. Lévêque
Beagle Bay Mission
Broome
Roebuck B.
La Grange
Anna Plains
Scott Reef
Rowley Shoals
Eighty Mile Beach
Mandora
Canning Basin
Great Sandy Desert
Southesk Tablelands
Percival Lakes
L. Dora
L. Disappointment
Gibson Desert
Carnegie
L. Carnegie
Granite Peak
Yelma
Wiluna
Mount Goldsworthy
Ningarra
De Grey
Marble Bar
Nullagine
Balfour Downs
Ethel Creek
Mount Nicholas
Opthalmia Range
Mundiwindi
Mount Newman
Wodgina
Wittenoom
Port Hedland
Roebourne
Coolawanyah
Hamersley Range
Mt. Bruce 1227
Tom Price
Ashburton
Mount Vernon
Mt. Egerton 994
Robinson Ranges
Peak Hill
Meekatharra
Mooloogool
Three Rivers
Nannine
Dampier
Fortescue
Deepdale
Boolaloo
Barlee Range
Mt. Augustus 1106
Lyons
Landor
Mooraire
Murchison
Mardie
Onslow
Minderoo
Gascoyne Junction
Barrow I.
Exmouth Gulf
North West C.
Exmouth
Learmonth
Bullara
Cardabia
L. McLeod
Boologooro
Gascoyne
Carnarvon
Wooramel
Meeberrie
Denham
Tamala
Shark B.
Dirk Hartog I.
Geographe Channel
Naturaliste Channel
Tropic of Capricorn
1150
1540

Great Victoria Desert
AUSTRALIA
Nullarbor Plain
Great Australian Bight
INDIAN OCEAN
Perth
Fremantle
Geraldton
Kalgoorlie
Coolgardie
Norseman
Esperance
Albany
Bunbury
Eucla
Port Lincoln
Archipelago of the Recherche
King George Sd.
C. Leeuwin
C. Naturaliste
Lambert Zenithal Equal Area Projection
© Wm. Collins Sons & Co. Ltd.

EASTERN AUSTRALIA

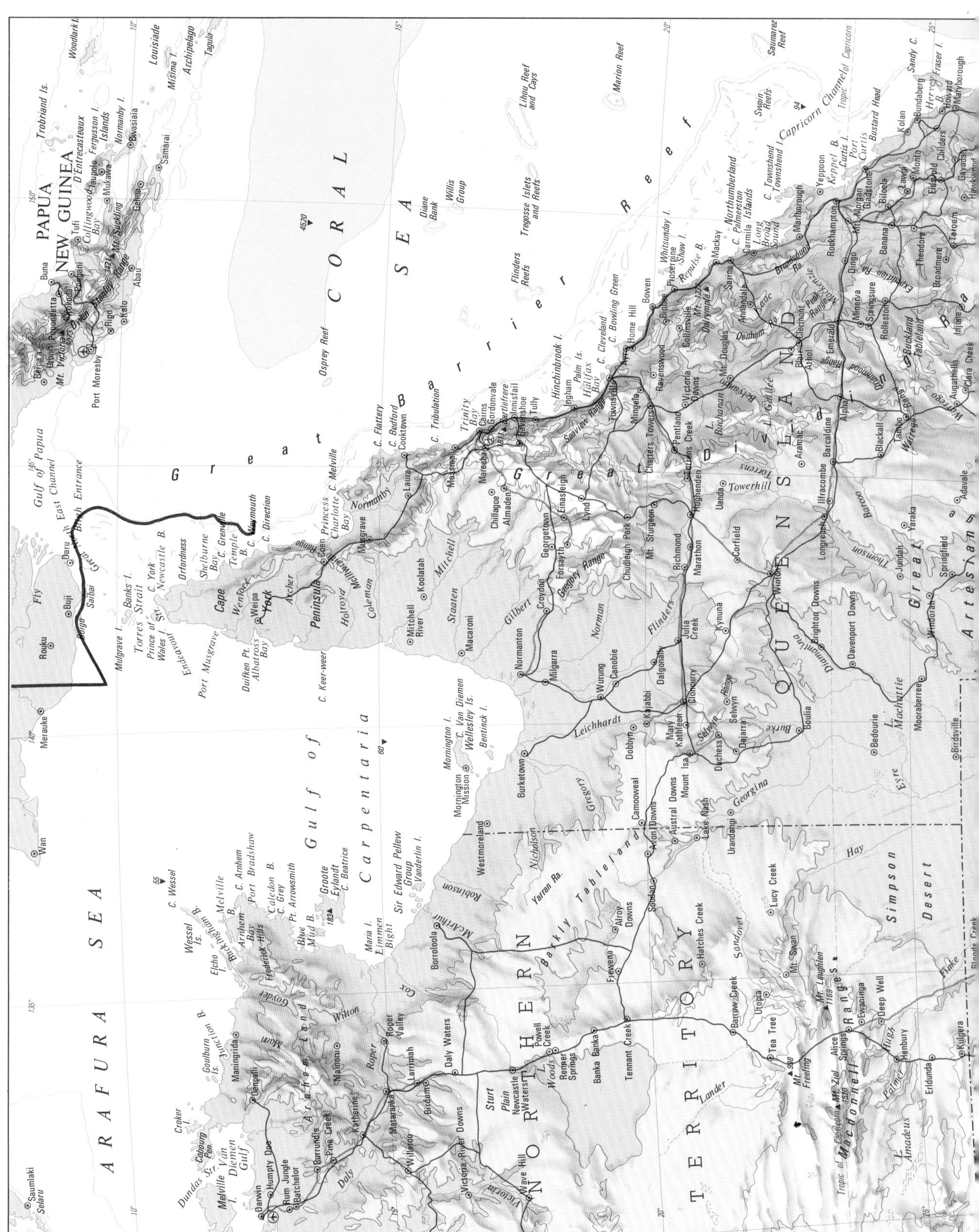

PAPUA NEW GUINEA
Port Moresby
Trobriand Is.
D'Entrecasteaux Islands
Louisiade Archipelago
Gulf of Papua
Torres Strait
Great Barrier Reef
CORAL SEA
ARAFURA SEA
Gulf of Carpentaria
Cape York Peninsula
Groote Eylandt
Arnhem Land
NORTHERN TERRITORY
QUEENSLAND
Barkly Tableland
Great Dividing Range
Great Artesian Basin
Simpson Desert
Macdonnell Ranges
Darwin
Katherine
Daly Waters
Tennant Creek
Alice Springs
Borroloola
Mount Isa
Cloncurry
Normanton
Burketown
Weipa
Cooktown
Cairns
Townsville
Bowen
Mackay
Rockhampton
Gladstone
Bundaberg
Maryborough
Longreach
Winton
Hughenden
Charters Towers
Emerald
Barcaldine
Boulia
Birdsville
Mitchell
Flinders
Leichhardt
Georgina
Diamantina
Thomson
Barcoo
Gilbert
Norman
Roper
Victoria
Tropic of Capricorn

SOUTH AUSTRALIA
NEW SOUTH WALES
VICTORIA
TASMANIA
TASMAN SEA
Great Australian Bight
Bass Strait
Banks Strait
Great Victoria Desert
Sturt Desert
Lake Eyre (North)
L. Eyre (South)
L. Torrens
L. Gairdner
L. Frome
Flinders Ranges
Barrier Range
Spencer Gulf
Gulf St. Vincent
Kangaroo I.
King I.
Flinders I.
Sydney
Melbourne
Adelaide
Brisbane
Canberra
Hobart
Launceston
Newcastle
Wollongong
Geelong
Ballarat
Bendigo
Port Augusta
Whyalla
Broken Hill
Mildura
Wagga Wagga
Albury
Dubbo
Bourke
Toowoomba
Relief
Feet
Metres
16404
9843
6562
3281
1640
656
0
656
13123
22966
5000
3000
2000
1000
500
200
Sea Level
200
4000
7000
Land Dep.
0 50 100 150 200 250 Miles
0 100 200 300 400 Kms.
Lambert Zenithal Equal Area Projection
© Wm. Collins, Sons & Co. Ltd.

SOUTHEAST AUSTRALIA

Lake Eyre (North)
L. Eyre (South)
Madigan Gulf
Sturt Desert
Lake Torrens
Lake Gairdner
Lake Frome
L. Gregory
L. Blanche
Lake Callabonna
Lake Everard
Gawler Ranges
Flinders Ranges
Mt. Lofty Ranges
Grey Range
Main Barrier Range
Eyre Peninsula
Spencer Gulf
Gulf St. Vincent
Investigator Strait
Kangaroo I.
Encounter Bay
Streaky Bay
Anxious Bay
Coffin Bay
Lacepede Bay
Discovery Bay
Murray
Darling
L. Alexandrina
L. Albert
L. Hindmarsh
Adelaide
Port Augusta
Port Pirie
Whyalla
Port Lincoln
Ceduna
Broken Hill
Mildura
Mt. Gambier
Portland
Warrnambool
Coober Pedy
Woomera
Marree
Peterborough
Murray Bridge
Victor Harbour
Kingscote
C. Otway
C. Nelson
C. Bridgewater
C. Northumberland
C. Jaffa
C. Borda
C. du Couëdic
135°
140°
30°
35°

Relief
Feet
Metres
16404
5000
9843
3000
6562
2000
3281
1000
1640
500
656
200
0
Sea Level
Land Dep.
656
200
13123
4000
22966
7000
0
25
50
75
100
125Miles
0
50
100
150
200Kms.
Lambert Zenithal Equal Area Projection
© Wm. Collins, Sons & Co. Ltd.
PACIFIC OCEAN
TASMAN SEA
SOUTH WALES
COMMONWEALTH TERRITORY
AUST. CAPITAL TERRITORY
Brisbane
Sandgate
Ipswich
Beenleigh
Logan
Southport
Surfer's Paradise
Coolangatta
Murwillumbah
Mullumbimby
C. Byron
Byron Bay
Ballina
Lismore
Nimbin
Kyogle
Casino
Broadwater
Evans Hd.
Woodburn
Wooded Bluff
Yamba
Maclean
Grafton
Corindi
Woolgoolga
Green Bluff
Coff's Harbour
Dorrigo
Bellingen
Urunga
Nambucca Heads
Macksville
Smoky Cape
Kempsey
Smithtown
Port Macquarie
Camden Haven
Kendall
Coopernook
Taree
C. Hawke
Sugarloaf Pt.
Port Stephens
Newcastle
Stockton
Maitland
Cessnock
L. Macquarie
Gosford
Broken Bay
Manly
Sydney
Botany Bay
Parramatta
Liverpool
Campbelltown
Wollongong
Shellharbour
Kiama
Gerringong
Nowra
Jervis Bay
St. George Hd.
Ulladulla
Batemans Bay
Burrewarra Pt.
Moruya
Bodalla
Narooma
C. Dromedary
Bermagui
Tathra
Eden
Twofold Bay
Disaster Bay
C. Howe
Mallacoota Inlet
C. Everard
Canberra
Queanbeyan
Goulburn
Yass
L. George
Mt. Bimberi
Mt. Kosciusko
Mt. Townsend
Snowy Mts.
Australian Alps
Eucumbene
Cooma
Albury
Wodonga
Wagga Wagga
Hume Resr.
Murray
Murrumbidgee
Lachlan
Orange
Bathurst
Lithgow
Katoomba
Blue Mts.
Dubbo
Wellington
Mudgee
Tamworth
Armidale
Glen Innes
Inverell
Moree
Narrabri
Gunnedah
Liverpool Plains
Liverpool Ra.
New England Ra.
Nandewar Range
Warrumbungle Range
Darling Downs
Bourke
Brewarrina
Walgett
Cobar
Nyngan
Narromine
Parkes
Forbes
Cowra
Young
Griffith
Leeton
Narrandera
Hay
Deniliquin
Melbourne
Ringwood
Dandenong
Frankston
Mornington
French I.
Wonthaggi
Venus Bay
Waratah Bay
Wilson's Promontory
Corner Inlet
Port Albert
Sale
Traralgon
Morwell
Bairnsdale
Lakes Entrance
Ninety Mile Beach
Orbost
Marlo
Mt. Buller
Mt. Hotham
Mt. Bogong
Mt. Howitt
Eildon Resr.
Shepparton
Wangaratta

NEW ZEALAND

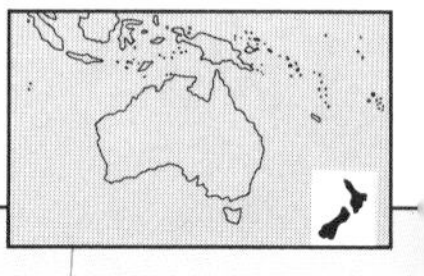

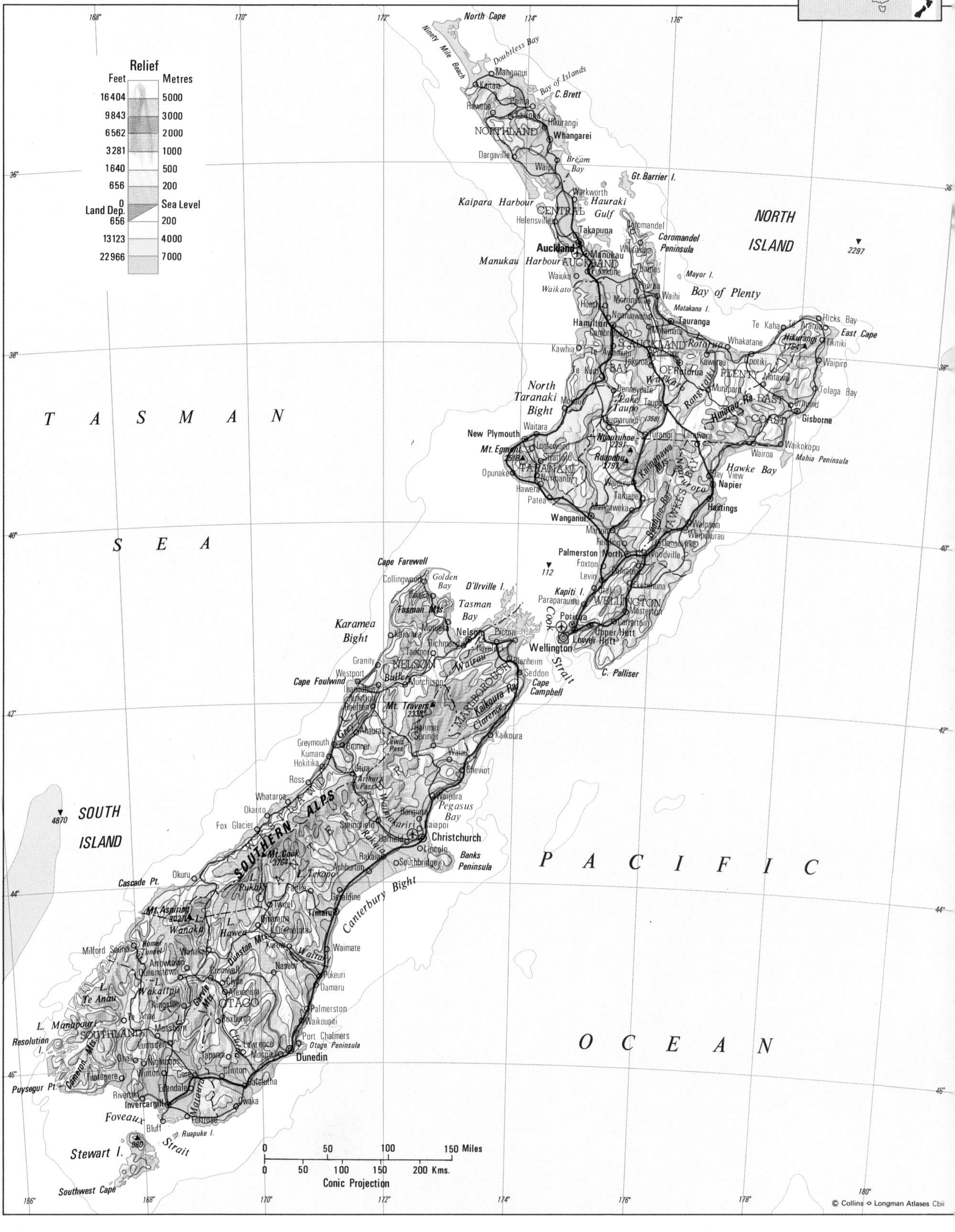

Relief

Feet	Metres
16404	5000
9843	3000
6562	2000
3281	1000
1640	500
656	200
0	Sea Level
Land Dep. 656	200
13123	4000
22966	7000

TASMAN SEA

PACIFIC OCEAN

NORTH ISLAND

SOUTH ISLAND

North Cape
Ninety Mile Beach
Doubtless Bay
Mangonui
Kaitaia
Bay of Islands
C. Brett
Paihia
Rawene
Kaikohe
Hikurangi
NORTHLAND
Whangarei
Dargaville
Bream Bay
Waipu
Gt. Barrier I.
Warkworth
Kaipara Harbour
CENTRAL
Hauraki Gulf
Helensville
Coromandel
Takapuna
Coromandel Peninsula
Auckland
AUCKLAND
Manukau
Manukau Harbour
Whitianga
Waiuku
Pukekohe
Thames
Mayor I.
Waikato
Paeroa
Waihi
Bay of Plenty
Huntly
Morrinsville
Matakana I.
Ngaruawahia
Tauranga
Hamilton
Cambridge
Te Aroha
Te Kaha
Hicks Bay
East Cape
Kawhia
SOUTH AUCKLAND
Rotorua
Whakatane
Hikurangi 1754
Tikitiki
Te Kuiti
BAY OF PLENTY
Opotiki
Waipiro
North Taranaki Bight
Lake Taupo
Taupo
Matawai
Tolaga Bay
Mokau
Taumarunui
(358)
EAST COAST
Gisborne
New Plymouth
Waitara
Ngauruhoe 2291
Tutangi
Mt. Egmont 2518
Inglewood
Stratford
Ruapehu 2797
Kaimanawa Mts.
Waikokopu
Mahia Peninsula
Wairoa
Opunake
TARANAKI
Eltham
Hawke Bay
Bay View
Napier
Hawera
Waiouru
Taihape
Patea
HAWKES BAY
Mangaweka
Hastings
Wanganui
Ruahine Ra.
Marton
Waipawa
Waipukurau
Feilding
Dannevirke
Palmerston North
Woodville
Foxton
Levin
Pahiatua
Eketahuna
Kapiti I.
Paraparaumu
WELLINGTON
Masterton
Carterton
Porirua
Upper Hutt
Lower Hutt
Wellington
Cook Strait
C. Palliser
2297
112
4870
Cape Farewell
Collingwood
Golden Bay
D'Urville I.
Takaka
Tasman Mts.
Tasman Bay
Karamea Bight
Karamea
Motueka
Nelson
Picton
Richmond
Havelock
Tadmor
Granity
Westport
NELSON
Blenheim
Seddon
Cape Foulwind
Buller
Murchison
Cape Campbell
Reefton
Mt. Travers 2338
MARLBOROUGH
Kaikoura Ra.
Clarence
Hanmer Springs
Kaikoura
Greymouth
Kumara
Hokitika
Brunner
Lewis Pass
Waiau
Arthur's Pass
Otira
Cheviot
Ross
Whataroa
Okarito
Waipara
Pegasus Bay
Fox Glacier
SOUTHERN ALPS
Rangiora
Springfield
Kaiapoi
Darfield
Christchurch
Lincoln
Banks Peninsula
Mt. Cook 3764
Rakaia
Southbridge
Ashburton
Okuru
Cascade Pt.
L. Tekapo
L. Pukaki
Fairlie
Geraldine
Twizel
Mt. Aspiring 3027
L. Wanaka
L. Hawea
Omarama
Timaru
Canterbury Bight
Otematata
Milford Sound
Homer Tunnel
Wanaka
Dunstan Mts.
Kurow
Waitaki
Waimate
Arrowtown
Queenstown
Cromwell
Naseby
L. Wakatipu
Clyde
Alexandra
Pukeuri
Oamaru
L. Te Anau
Kingston
Garvie Mts.
OTAGO
Te Anau
Roxburgh
Palmerston
Waikouaiti
L. Manapouri
SOUTHLAND
Mossburn
Resolution I.
Lumsden
Port Chalmers
Otago Peninsula
Lawrence
Mosgiel
Dunedin
Tapanui
Ohai
Nightcaps
Cameron Mts.
Winton
Gore
Clinton
Balclutha
Tuatapere
Puysegur Pt.
Edendale
Riverton
Mataura
Owaka
Invercargill
Fortrose
Foveaux Strait
Bluff
Ruapuke I.
980
Stewart I.
Southwest Cape

166° 168° 170° 172° 174° 176° 178° 180°
36° 38° 40° 42° 44° 46°

0 50 100 150 Miles
0 50 100 150 200 Kms.
Conic Projection

NORTH AMERICA

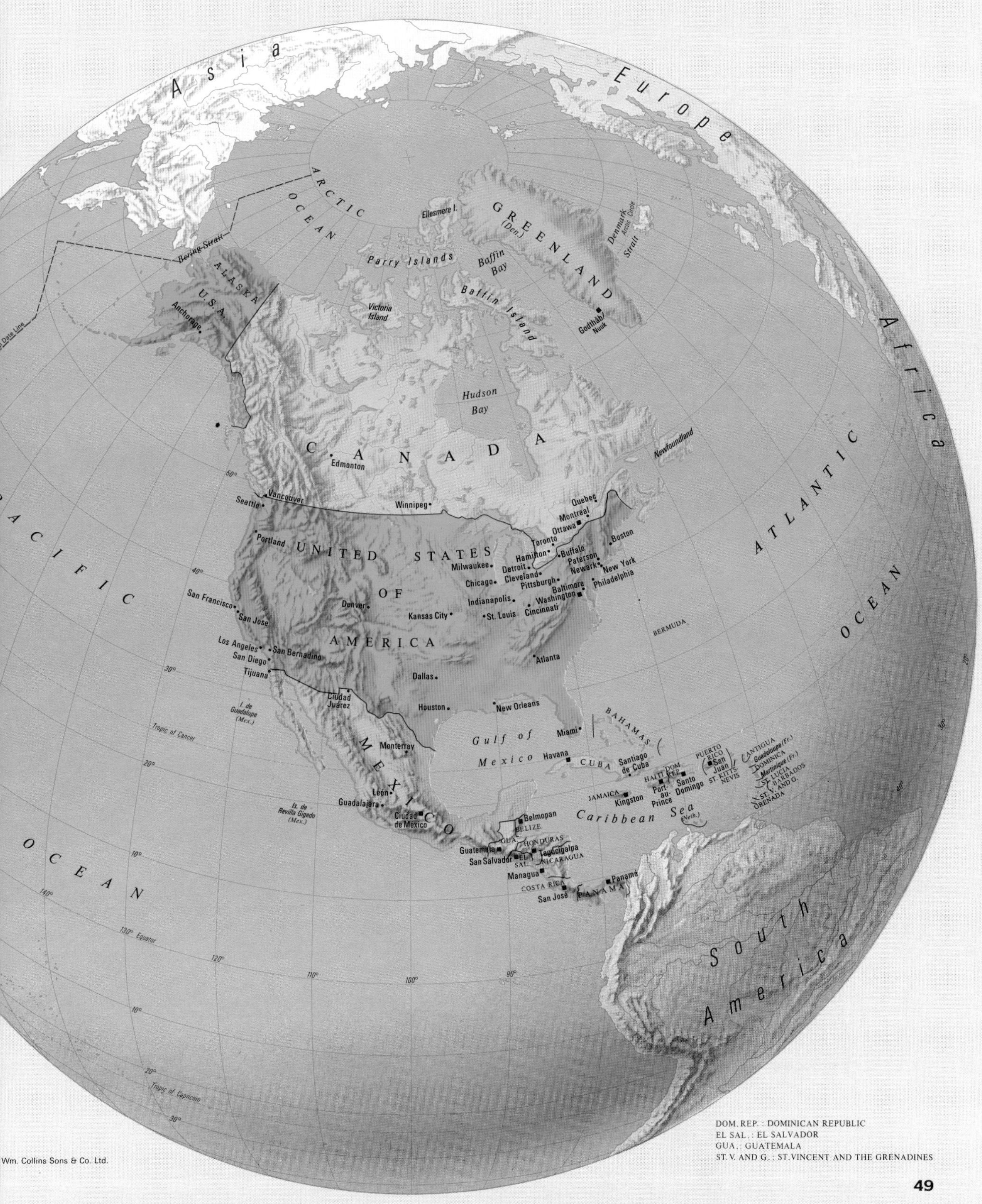

Asia
Europe
Africa
ARCTIC OCEAN
Bering Strait
ALASKA
U.S.A.
Anchorage
Ellesmere I.
GREENLAND (Den.)
Parry Islands
Baffin Bay
Baffin Island
Victoria Island
Godthåb/Nuuk
Denmark Strait
Arctic Circle
Hudson Bay
CANADA
Edmonton
Newfoundland
Vancouver
Seattle
Winnipeg
Quebec
Montreal
Ottawa
Toronto
Boston
Portland
UNITED STATES OF AMERICA
Milwaukee
Detroit
Hamilton
Buffalo
Paterson
Newark
New York
Philadelphia
Chicago
Cleveland
Pittsburgh
Baltimore
Washington
Indianapolis
St. Louis
Cincinnati
Denver
Kansas City
San Francisco
San Jose
Los Angeles
San Bernardino
San Diego
Tijuana
Atlanta
Dallas
Ciudad Juárez
Houston
New Orleans
I. de Guadalupe (Mex.)
Tropic of Cancer
Monterrey
MEXICO
León
Guadalajara
Ciudad de México
Is. de Revilla Gigedo (Mex.)
Miami
BAHAMAS
Gulf of Mexico
Havana
CUBA
Santiago de Cuba
HAITI
DOM. REP.
Port-au-Prince
Santo Domingo
JAMAICA
Kingston
PUERTO RICO
San Juan
ST. KITTS-NEVIS
ANTIGUA
Guadeloupe (Fr.)
DOMINICA
Martinique (Fr.)
ST. LUCIA
BARBADOS
ST. V. AND G.
GRENADA
Caribbean Sea
(Neth.)
Belmopan
BELIZE
GUA.
Guatemala
San Salvador
EL SAL.
HONDURAS
Tegucigalpa
NICARAGUA
Managua
COSTA RICA
San José
PANAMA
Panamá
PACIFIC OCEAN
ATLANTIC OCEAN
BERMUDA
South America
Equator
Tropic of Capricorn
Date Line

DOM. REP. : DOMINICAN REPUBLIC
EL SAL. : EL SALVADOR
GUA. : GUATEMALA
ST. V. AND G. : ST. VINCENT AND THE GRENADINES

CANADA AND ALASKA

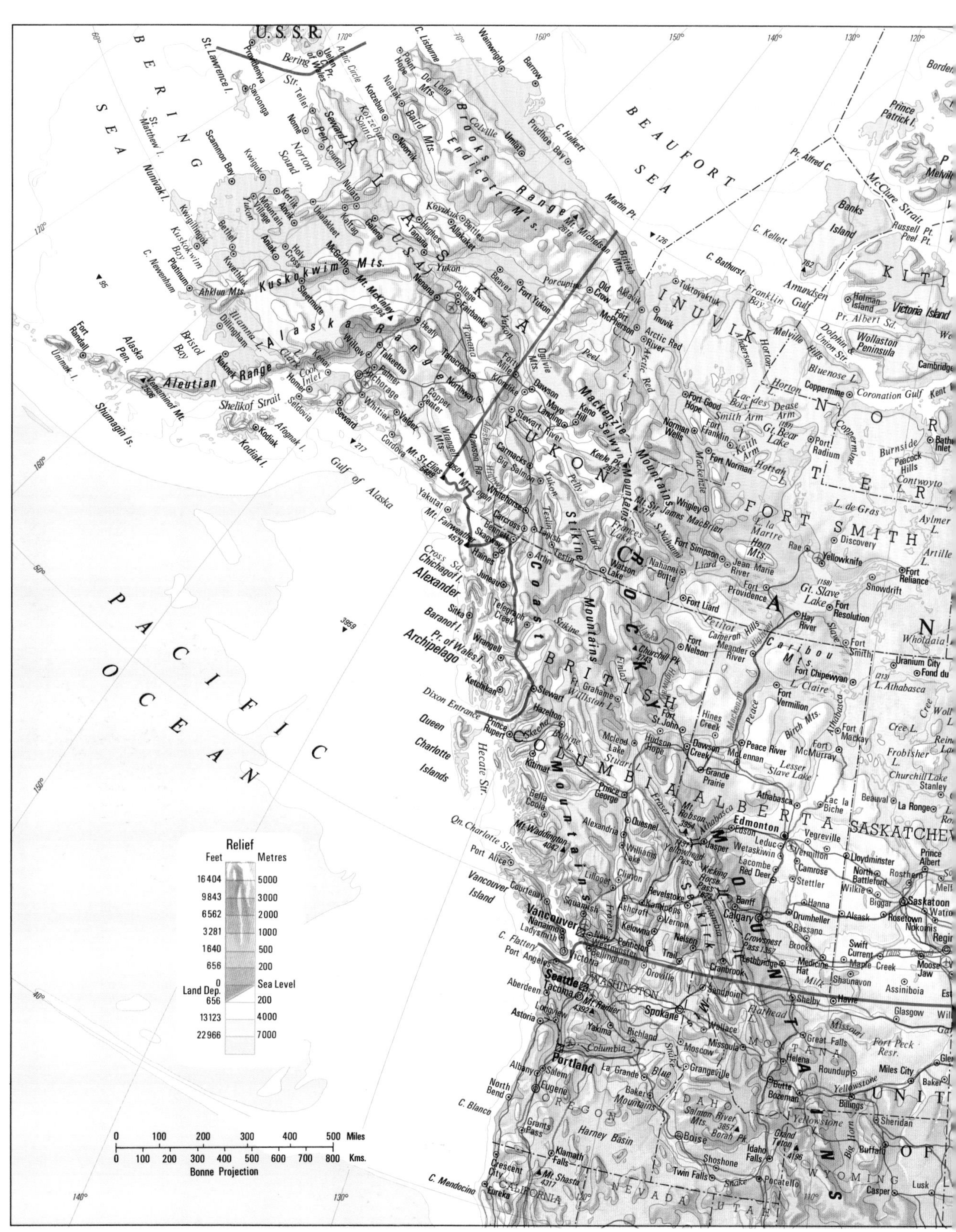
U.S.S.R.
BERING SEA
BEAUFORT SEA
PACIFIC OCEAN
Gulf of Alaska
Bering Str.
Norton Sound
Bristol Bay
Kuskokwim Bay
Shelikof Strait
Cook Inlet
Dixon Entrance
Hecate Str.
Qn. Charlotte Str.
Amundsen Gulf
Franklin Bay
Coronation Gulf
McClure Strait
ALASKA (U.S.A.)
YUKON
BRITISH COLUMBIA
ALBERTA
SASKATCHEWAN
INUVIK
FORT SMITH
WASHINGTON
OREGON
IDAHO
MONTANA
WYOMING
NEVADA
UTAH
CALIFORNIA
Brooks Range
Endicott Mts.
Kuskokwim Mts.
Alaska Range
Aleutian Range
Mackenzie Mountains
Selwyn Mountains
Coast Mountains
ROCKY MOUNTAINS
Cariboo Mts.
Mt. McKinley 6194
Mt. St. Elias 5488
Mt. Logan
Mt. Fairweather 4570
Mt. Robson 3954
Mt. Waddington 4042
Mt. Rainier 4392
Mt. Shasta 4317
Borah Pk. 3857
Grand Teton 4196
Banks Island
Victoria Island
Prince Patrick I.
Melville
Wollaston Peninsula
Alexander Archipelago
Queen Charlotte Islands
Vancouver Island
Kodiak I.
Nunivak I.
St. Lawrence I.
St. Matthew I.
Unimak I.
Shumagin Is.
Barrow
Nome
Fairbanks
Anchorage
Juneau
Sitka
Ketchikan
Whitehorse
Dawson
Inuvik
Tuktoyaktuk
Yellowknife
Fort Simpson
Fort Nelson
Fort St. John
Prince Rupert
Prince George
Edmonton
Calgary
Vancouver
Victoria
Seattle
Tacoma
Spokane
Portland
Boise
Helena
Great Falls
Butte
Billings
Saskatoon
Lloydminster
Medicine Hat
Lethbridge
Eureka
Relief
Feet
Metres
16 404
9843
6562
3281
1640
656
0
Land Dep.
656
13123
22966
5000
3000
2000
1000
500
200
Sea Level
200
4000
7000
0
100
200
300
400
500
Miles
0
100
200
300
400
500
600
700
800
Kms.
Bonne Projection

GREENLAND
Kong Christian den IX Land
Kong Frederik den VI Kyst
Mt. Forel 2850
K. Gustav Holm
Arctic Circle
Ammassalik/ Tasiilaq
Køge Bugt
K. Møsting
Thule/ Qaanaaq
Upernavik
Nunavik
Disko
Godhavn/ Qeqertarsuaq
Christianshåb/ Qasigiannguit
Søndrestrømfjord/ Kangerlussuaq
Holsteinsborg/ Sisimiut
Sukkertoppen/ Maniitsoq
Godthåb/ Nuuk
Fiskenæsset/ Qeqertarsuatsiaat
Frederikshåb/ Paamiut
Ivigtût/ Ivittuut
Julianehåb/ Qaqortoq
Nanortalik
K. Farvel/ Uummannarsuaq (C. Farewell)
Axel Heiberg I.
Ellesmere Island
Nares Strait
K. Parry
Coburg I.
Jones Sd.
C. Parker
Devon Island
Cornwallis I.
Resolute
Lancaster Sound
Somerset Island
Prince Regent Inlet
Brodeur Peninsula
Borden Peninsula
Arctic Bay
Bylot I.
Pond Inlet
C. Liverpool
Baffin Bay
C. Adair
Clyde
C. Hewett
Milne Inlet
Gifford
Davis Strait
Home Bay
Padloping Island
C. Dyer
Cape Dyer
Penny Highland 2591
Cumberland Pen.
Pangnirtung
Hoare Bay
C. Mercy
Cumberland Sound
BAFFIN ISLAND
Gulf of Boothia
Boothia Peninsula
Igloolik Island
Hall Lake
Melville Peninsula
Prince Charles I.
Foxe Basin
Nettilling L.
Amadjuak L.
Frobisher Bay
Hall Pen.
Resolution Island
Lake Harbour
King William I.
Spence Bay
Pelly Bay
Gjoa Haven
Adelaide Pen.
Repulse Bay
Cape Dorchester
Foxe Peninsula
Foxe Channel
Cape Dorset
Amadjuak
Back
Wager Bay
Southampton Island
Coral Harbour
Hudson Strait
Akpatok I.
C. Chidley
Labrador Sea
ATLANTIC OCEAN
Baker Lake
KEEWATIN
Chesterfield Inlet
Rankin Inlet
Whale Cove
Tavani
Fisher Strait
Coats I.
Mansel I.
Ivujivik
Sagfouk
Péninsule D'Ungava
Maricourt
Koartac
Bellin
Ungava Bay
Port-Nouveau Québec
Hebron
Nutak
Nain
Hopedale
C. Harrison
Indian Harbour
Rigolet
Cartwright
Padlei
Eskimo Point
CANADA
Nueltin
Hudson Bay
Ottawa Is.
Inoucdjouac (Port Harrison)
L. Minto
R. aux Feuilles
Fort Chimo
La Baleine
George
L. à l'Eau-Claire
L. Bienville
Schefferville
Michikamau
Labrador
North West River
Battle Harbour
C. Bauld
St. Anthony
Churchill
C. Churchill
Seal
King George Is.
Belcher Is.
C. Tatnam
Port Nelson
York Factory
Fort Severn
Winisk
C. Henrietta Maria
Poste de la Baleine
Fort George
La Grande
Caniapiscau
Petitsikapau L.
Labrador City
Wabush City
Churchill Falls
St. Augustin
Saguenay
Natashquan
Romaine
Str. of Belle Isle
NEWFOUNDLAND
Gander
Bonavista
Carbonear
St. John's
Grand Falls
Buchans
Newfoundland
Corner Brook
Harbour Grace
Placentia
Trepassey
C. Race
Channel-Port aux Basques
St. Pierre and Miquelon (Fr.)
Southern Indian L.
Thompson
Sachigo
Severn
Attawapiskat
James Bay
Akimiski I.
Fort Albany
Moosonee
Eastmain
Nouveau-Comptoir
Fort Rupert
Nottaway
Mistassini
L. Mistassini
Chibougamau
L. Matagami
Gagnon
Mingan
Ile D'Anticosti
P. de l'Est
Sept Iles
Port Cartier
Gaspé
C. de Gaspé
Gulf of St. Lawrence
Cabot Str.
Cape Breton I.
Sydney
Port Hawkesbury
Mulgrave
Sable I.
Iles de la Madeleine
PR. EDWARD I.
Charlottetown
Baie Comeau
Matane
Rimouski
Campbellton
Chatham
Bathurst
Moncton
Truro
Dartmouth
Halifax
Bridgewater
Liverpool
Shelburne
C. Sable
Yarmouth
Bay of Fundy
Saint John
Fredericton
NEW BRUNSWICK
NOVA SCOTIA
MANITOBA
Norway House
Grand Rapids
Island L.
Big Trout L.
Winisk Lake
Sandy L.
L. Winnipeg
Pickle Crow
ONTARIO
Albany
Abitibi
Harricana
QUEBEC
Dolbeau
Chicoutimi-Jonquière
Roberval
Réservoir Gouin
Tadoussac
Québec
Lévis
Edmundston
Thetford Mines
Sherbrooke
Hodgson
Riverton
Victoria Beach
Gimli
Winnipeg
Portage la Prairie
St Boniface
Emerson
Morden
Red Lake
L. St. Joseph
Nakina
Hearst
Cochrane
Amos
Senneterre
Val d'Or
Longlac
Oba
Noranda
Rouyn
Timmins
Kirkland Lake
Cobalt
Sioux Lookout
L. Nipigon
Nipigon
Kenora
L. of the Woods
Dryden
Ignace
Trans Canada Highway
Thunder Bay
Franz
Michipicoten
L. Kipawa
Maniwaki
Réservoir Cabonga
Trois-Rivières
Joliette
Sorel
St. Hyacinthe
Granby
Montreal
Fort Frances
Rainy Lake
Steep Rock Lake
Virginia
L. Superior
Sault Sainte Marie
Copper Cliff
Sudbury
North Bay
Ottawa
Hull
Pembroke
Perth
Brockville
Kingston
Georgian Bay
Huntsville
Red Lake
Bemidji
Hibbing
Duluth
Grand Forks
Grafton
Leech L.
Ironwood
Marquette
Superior
Iron River
Manistique
Fargo
Valley City
MINNESOTA
Rhinelander
Merrill
Green Bay
Cheboygan
Traverse City
Cadillac
Midland
Owen Sound
Barrie
Oshawa
Cobourg
L. Ontario
Toronto
Kitchener
Hamilton
Niagara Falls
St. Catharines
Buffalo
Rochester
Syracuse
Utica
Albany
Burlington
Montpelier
Concord
Manchester
Portland
Bangor
Lawrence
Worcester
Boston
C. Cod
Providence
Hartford
New Haven
Long Island
New York
Newark
Paterson
Scranton
Reading
Philadelphia
Baltimore
Harrisburg
Williamsport
Olean
Erie
L. Erie
Youngstown
Cleveland
Pittsburgh
Toledo
Detroit
Windsor
London
Sarnia
Bay City
Ludington
Grand Rapids
MICHIGAN
L. Michigan
L. Huron
Kalamazoo
Lima
Fort Wayne
INDIANA
OHIO
PENNSYLVANIA
NEW JERSEY
MARYLAND
ILLINOIS
St. Paul
Minneapolis
St. Cloud
Aberdeen
Winona
Mankato
Austin
Worthington
Sioux Falls
Mason City
Waterloo
Cedar Rapids
Sioux City
Mitchell
IOWA
WISCONSIN
Sheboygan
Milwaukee
Madison
Chicago
Gary
Mississippi
UNITED STATES OF AMERICA
NORTH DAKOTA
© Collins ◇ Longman Atlases Cbi

UNITED STATES

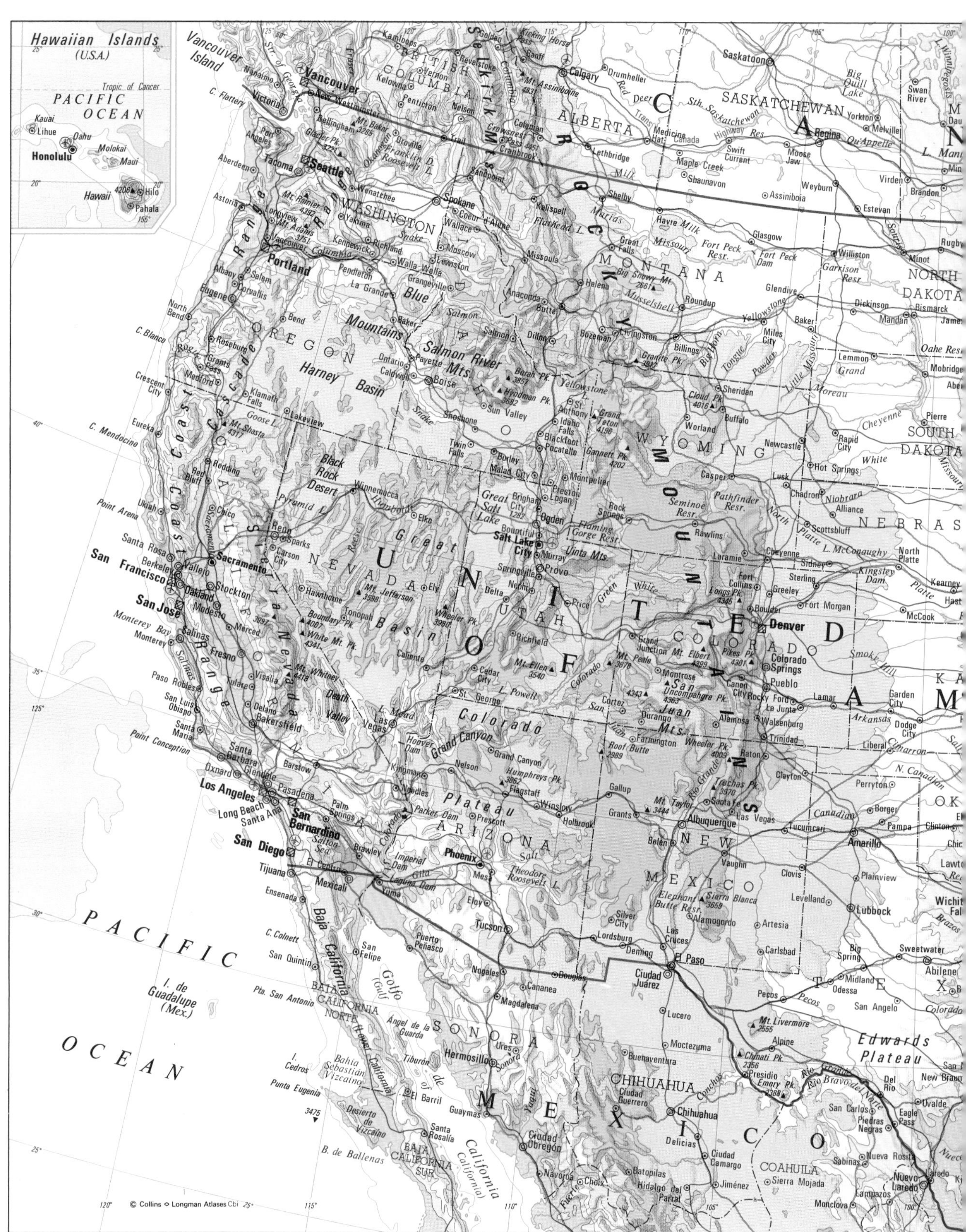

Hawaiian Islands (U.S.A.)

PACIFIC OCEAN

Tropic of Cancer

Kauai
Lihue
Oahu
Honolulu
Molokai
Maui
Hawaii 4206 Hilo
Pahala

Vancouver Island

C. Flattery

PACIFIC OCEAN

I. de Guadalupe (Mex.)

© Collins ◇ Longman Atlases Cbi

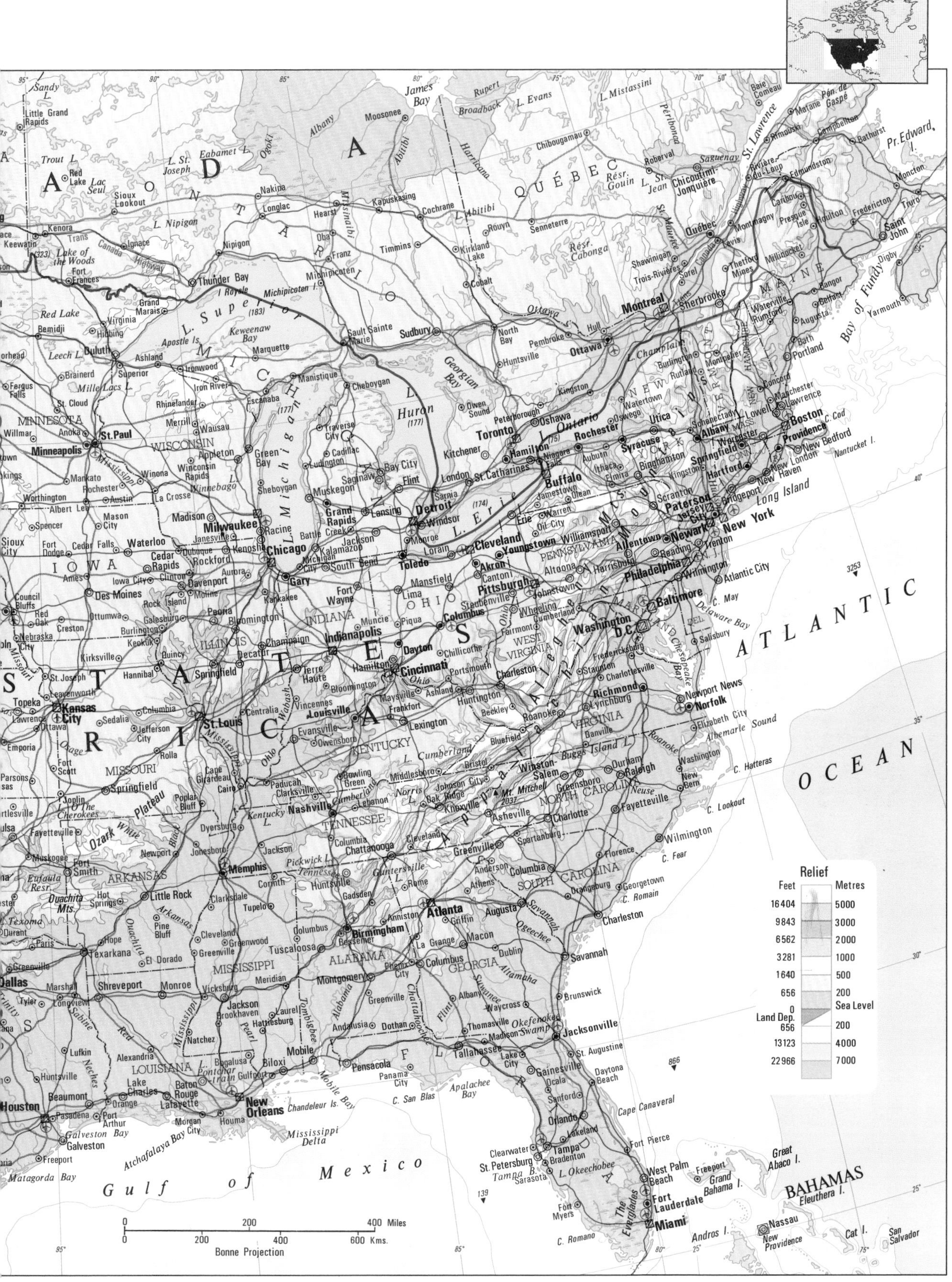
CANADA
UNITED STATES OF AMERICA
ONTARIO
QUÉBEC
James Bay
L. Superior
L. Michigan
L. Huron
L. Erie
L. Ontario
Georgian Bay
Appalachian Mountains
ATLANTIC OCEAN
Gulf of Mexico
BAHAMAS
MINNESOTA
WISCONSIN
MICHIGAN
IOWA
ILLINOIS
INDIANA
OHIO
PENNSYLVANIA
NEW YORK
MAINE
KENTUCKY
WEST VIRGINIA
VIRGINIA
MISSOURI
TENNESSEE
NORTH CAROLINA
SOUTH CAROLINA
ARKANSAS
MISSISSIPPI
ALABAMA
GEORGIA
LOUISIANA
FLORIDA
Thunder Bay
Sault Sainte Marie
Sudbury
Ottawa
Montreal
Québec
Toronto
Hamilton
Kingston
Saint John
Duluth
Minneapolis
St.Paul
Milwaukee
Chicago
Detroit
Toledo
Cleveland
Buffalo
Rochester
Syracuse
Albany
Boston
Providence
Hartford
New York
Newark
Philadelphia
Baltimore
Washington D.C.
Pittsburgh
Columbus
Indianapolis
Cincinnati
Louisville
St.Louis
Kansas City
Memphis
Nashville
Atlanta
Birmingham
Charlotte
Raleigh
Richmond
Norfolk
Charleston
Savannah
Jacksonville
Tampa
Orlando
Miami
Fort Lauderdale
West Palm Beach
New Orleans
Mobile
Houston
Dallas
Shreveport
Little Rock
Jackson
Montgomery
Nassau
Cape Canaveral
C. Hatteras
C. Cod
Long Island
Mississippi Delta
Relief
Feet
Metres
16404
5000
9843
3000
6562
2000
3281
1000
1640
500
656
200
0
Sea Level
Land Dep.
656
200
13123
4000
22966
7000
0
200
400 Miles
0
200
400
600 Kms.
Bonne Projection

WESTERN UNITED STATES

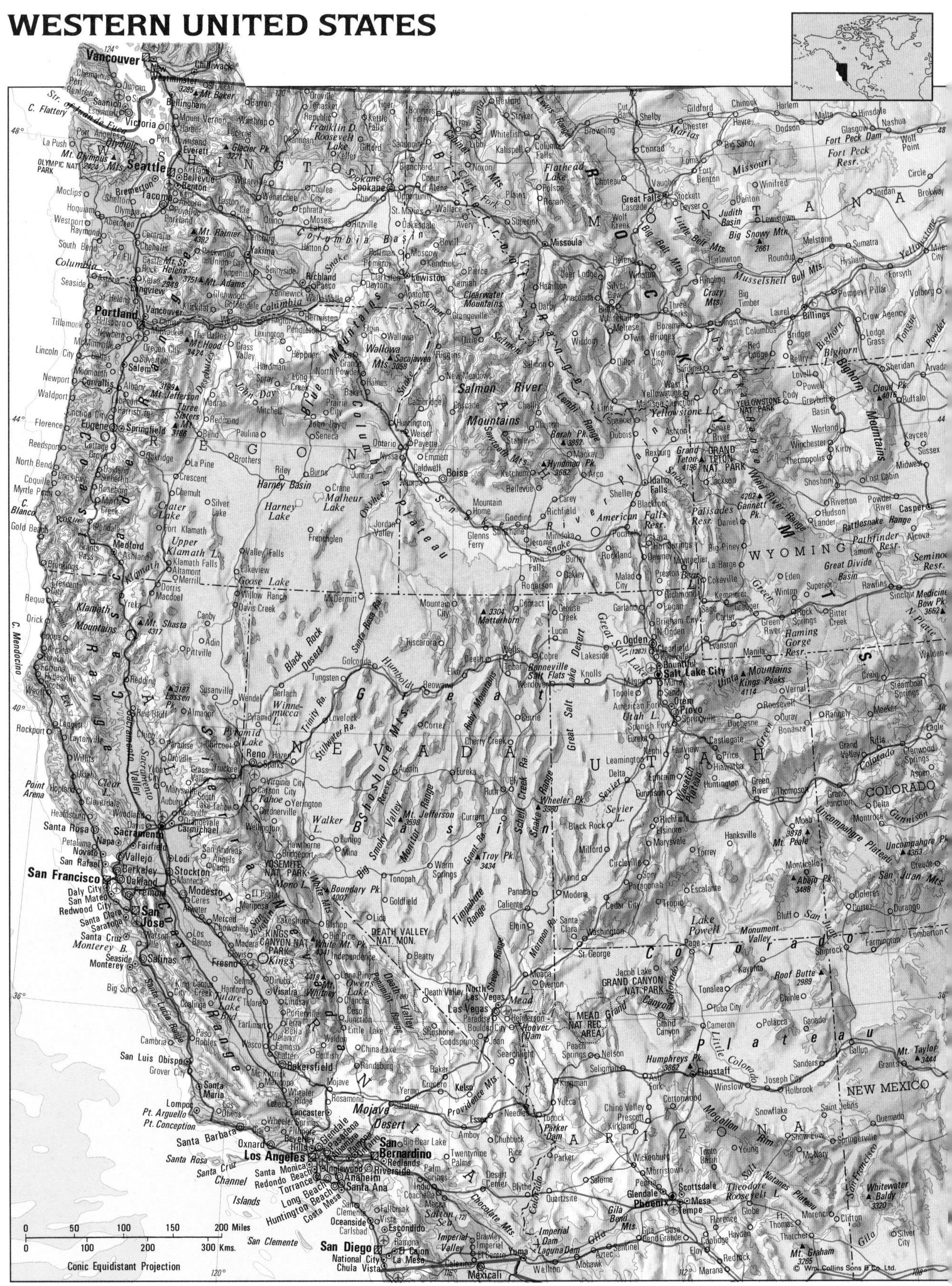

WASHINGTON
OREGON
IDAHO
MONTANA
WYOMING
NEVADA
UTAH
CALIFORNIA
ARIZONA
COLORADO
NEW MEXICO
Vancouver
Victoria
Seattle
Tacoma
Spokane
Portland
Salem
Eugene
Boise
Great Falls
Helena
Missoula
Billings
Salt Lake City
Ogden
Provo
Reno
Sacramento
San Francisco
Oakland
San Jose
Fresno
Bakersfield
Los Angeles
San Bernardino
San Diego
Las Vegas
Phoenix
Flagstaff
Mexicali
ROCKY MOUNTAINS
Cascade Range
Coast Ranges
Sierra Nevada
Great Basin
Columbia Plateau
Snake River Plain
Colorado Plateau
Great Salt Lake
Mojave Desert
Death Valley
Pacific Ocean
0 50 100 150 200 Miles
0 100 200 300 Kms.
Conic Equidistant Projection
© Wm. Collins Sons & Co. Ltd.

NORTHEAST U.S.A. – SOUTH CENTRAL CANADA

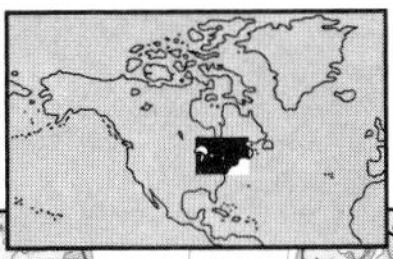

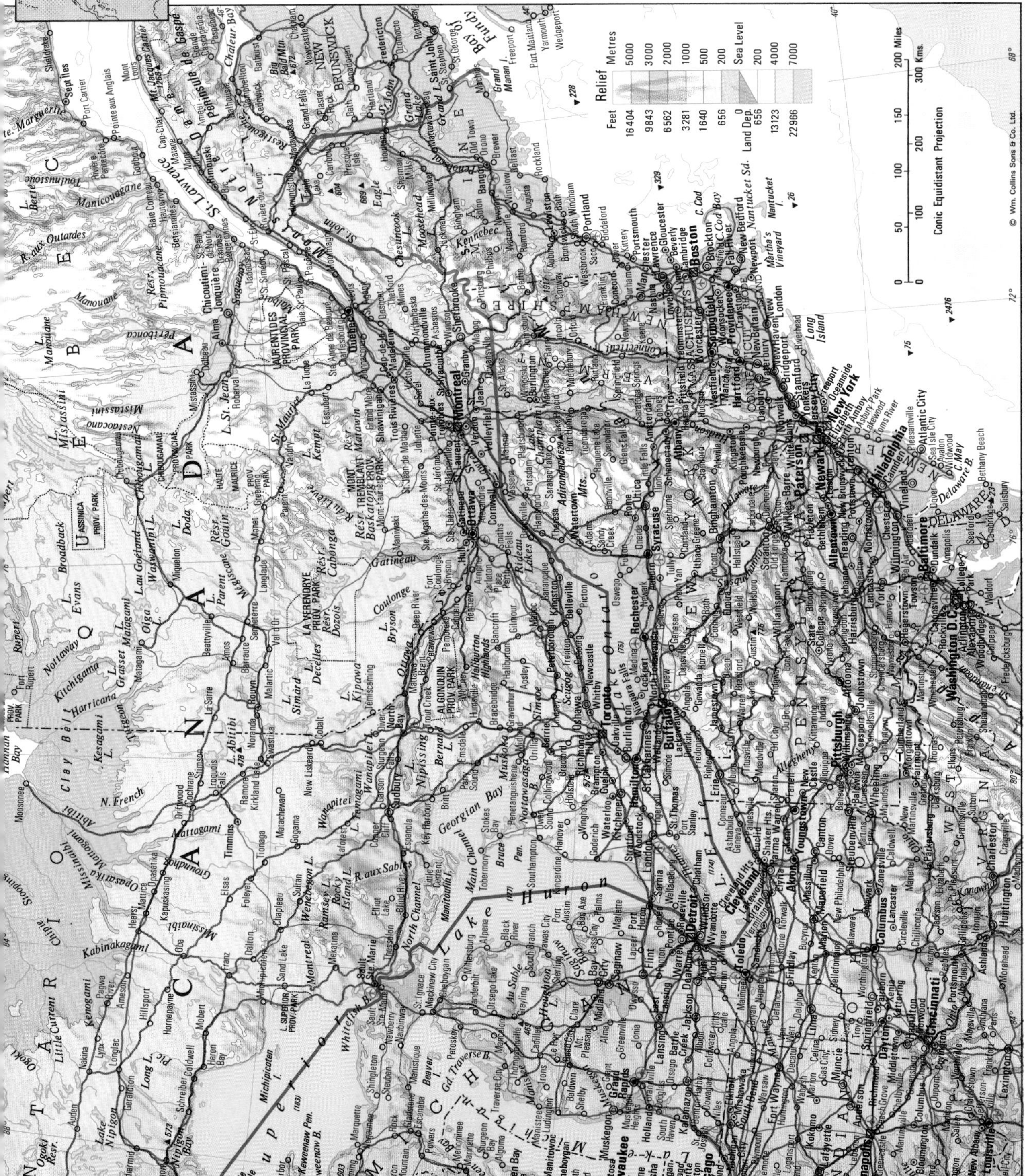

Relief Feet	Metres
16404	5000
9843	3000
6562	2000
3281	1000
1640	500
656	200
0	Sea Level
Land Dep. 656	200
13123	4000
22966	7000

0 50 100 150 200 Miles
0 100 200 300 Kms.
Conic Equidistant Projection

CENTRAL AMERICA AND THE CARIBBEAN

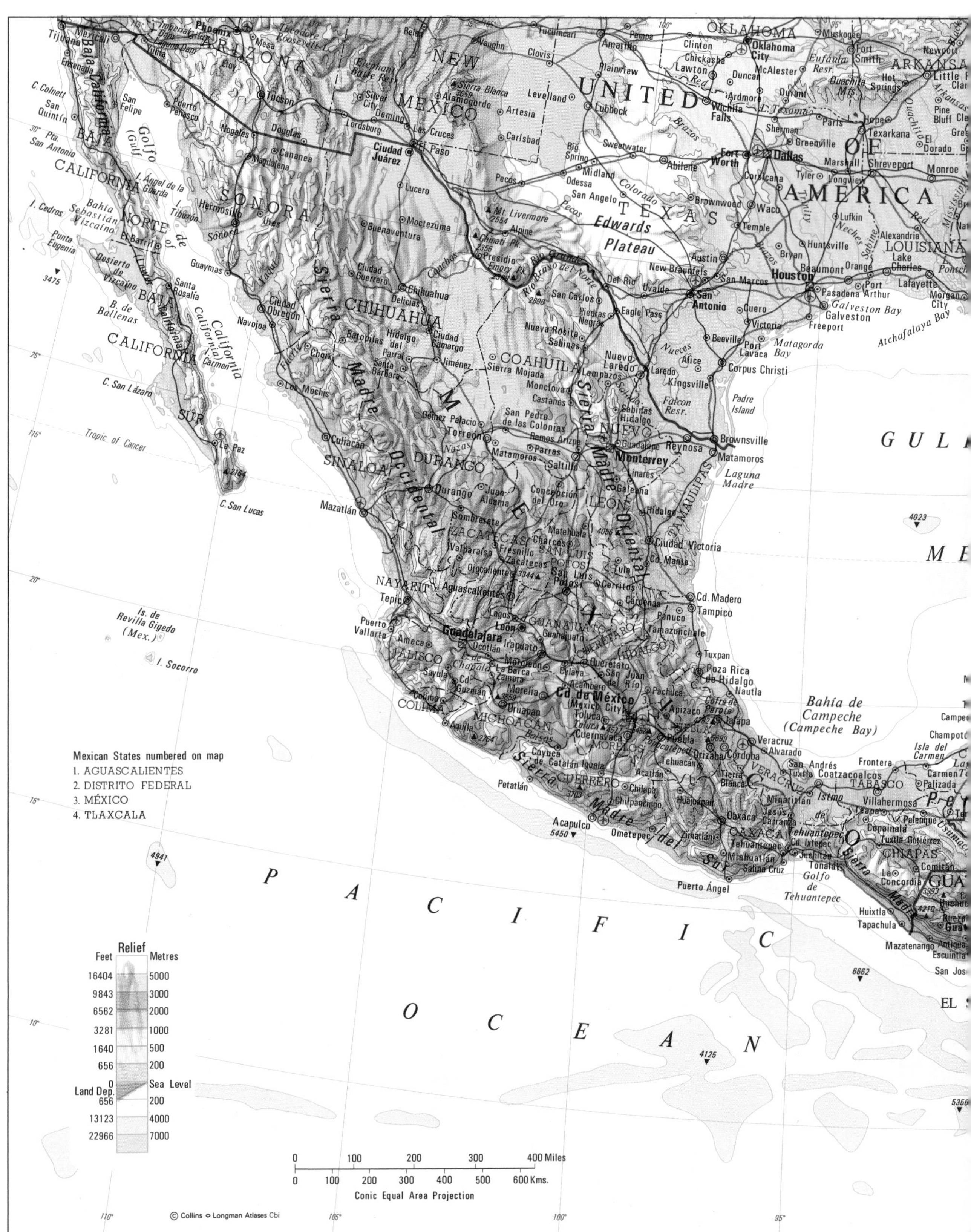

Mexican States numbered on map
1. AGUASCALIENTES
2. DISTRITO FEDERAL
3. MÉXICO
4. TLAXCALA
Relief
Feet
Metres
16404
5000
9843
3000
6562
2000
3281
1000
1640
500
656
200
0
Sea Level
Land Dep.
656
200
13123
4000
22966
7000
0
100
200
300
400 Miles
0
100
200
300
400
500
600 Kms.
Conic Equal Area Projection
© Collins ○ Longman Atlases Cbi
P A C I F I C
O C E A N
UNITED
OF
AMERICA
TEXAS
ARIZONA
NEW MEXICO
OKLAHOMA
ARKANSAS
LOUISIANA
Edwards Plateau
SONORA
CHIHUAHUA
COAHUILA
NUEVO LEÓN
SINALOA
DURANGO
ZACATECAS
SAN LUIS POTOSÍ
NAYARIT
JALISCO
COLIMA
MICHOACÁN
GUANAJUATO
QUERÉTARO
HIDALGO
MORELOS
PUEBLA
GUERRERO
OAXACA
VERACRUZ
TABASCO
CHIAPAS
TAMAULIPAS
BAJA CALIFORNIA NORTE
BAJA CALIFORNIA SUR
Golfo de California
Golfo de Tehuantepec
Bahía de Campeche (Campeche Bay)
Sierra Madre Occidental
Sierra Madre Oriental
Sierra Madre del Sur
Tropic of Cancer
Is. de Revilla Gigedo (Mex.)
I. Socorro
C. San Lucas
C. San Lázaro
Laguna Madre
Galveston Bay
Matagorda Bay
Atchafalaya Bay
Phoenix
Tucson
El Paso
Ciudad Juárez
Chihuahua
Hermosillo
Guaymas
La Paz
Mazatlán
Culiacán
Durango
Torreón
Monterrey
Saltillo
Nuevo Laredo
San Antonio
Houston
Dallas
Fort Worth
Oklahoma City
Austin
Corpus Christi
Brownsville
Matamoros
Reynosa
Ciudad Victoria
Tampico
Cd. Madero
Zacatecas
San Luis Potosí
Aguascalientes
Tepic
Guadalajara
León
Morelia
Querétaro
Pachuca
Cd. de México
Toluca
Cuernavaca
Puebla
Jalapa
Veracruz
Orizaba
Córdoba
Oaxaca
Acapulco
Puerto Ángel
Salina Cruz
Coatzacoalcos
Minatitlán
Villahermosa
Tuxtla Gutiérrez
Tapachula
Lubbock
Amarillo
Abilene
Waco
Shreveport
Lake Charles
Lafayette
Beaumont
Pasadena
Galveston
Freeport
Victoria
Laredo
Del Rio
Eagle Pass
Piedras Negras
Monclova
Tuxpan
Poza Rica de Hidalgo
Puerto Vallarta
Manzanillo
Petatlán
Chilpancingo
Istmo de Tehuantepec
Frontera
Isla del Carmen

SOUTH AMERICA

North America
ATLANTIC OCEAN
Caribbean Sea
Barranquilla
Maracaibo
Caracas
TRINIDAD AND TOBAGO
VENEZUELA
Georgetown
Paramaribo
Cayenne
GUYANA
SURINAM
GUIANA (Fr.)
Medellín
Bogotá
Cali
COLOMBIA
Quito
ECUADOR
Guayaquil
Islas Galapagos (Ec.)
Belém
Fortaleza
Recife
Salvador
BRAZIL
PERU
Lima
La Paz
BOLIVIA
Sucre
Brasília
Belo Horizonte
Rio de Janeiro
São Paulo
Santo André
Curitiba
PARAGUAY
Asunción
PACIFIC OCEAN
San Félix (Chile)
San Ambrosio
CHILE
ARGENTINA
Córdoba
Rosario
Pôrto Alegre
URUGUAY
Valparaíso
Santiago
Islas Juan Fernández (Chile)
Buenos Aires
La Plata
Montevideo
ATLANTIC OCEAN
Falkland Is. (U.K.)
Tierra del Fuego
South Georgia (U.K.)
Tropic of Cancer
Equator
Tropic of Capricorn
Antarctic Circle
International Date Line
Antarctica

SOUTH AMERICA – EAST

Relief
Feet
Metres
16404
5000
9843
3000
6562
2000
3281
1000
1640
500
656
200
0
Sea Level
Land Dep.
656
200
13123
4000
0
100
200
300
400 Miles
0
100
200
300
400
500
600 Kms.
Lambert Azimuthal Equal Area Projection
B R A Z I L
BOLIVIA
PARAGUAY
ARGENTINA
URUGUAY
MATO GROSSO
GOIÁS
MINAS GERAIS
SÃO PAULO
PARANÁ
SANTA CATARINA
RIO GRANDE DO SUL
MATO GROSSO DO SUL
RIO DE JANEIRO
ESPÍRITO SANTO
DISTRITO FEDERAL
BAHIA
SANTA CRUZ
FORMOSA
CHACO
CORRIENTES
MISIONES
ENTRE RÍOS
SANTA FÉ
CÓRDOBA
BUENOS AIRES
LA PAMPA
Planalto do Mato Grosso
Planalto Brasil
(Brazilian Highlands)
Bañados de Izozog
(Izozog Marshes)
Tropic of Capricorn
Brasília
Belo Horizonte
Rio de Janeiro
São Paulo
Sto. André
Curitiba
Pôrto Alegre
Asunción
Buenos Aires
Montevideo
La Plata
Rosario
Goiânia
Cuiabá
Campo Grande
Florianópolis
Vitória
Niterói
Santos
Mar del Plata
Bahía Blanca
Río de la Plata (R. Plate)
Lagoa dos Patos
L. Mirim
L. Mangueira
Salto das Sete Quedas (Guaira Falls)
© Collins ◇ Longman Atlases Cbi
© Wm. Collins Sons & Co. Ltd.
0
40
80 Miles
0
40
80
120 Kms.

COLOMBIA
VENEZUELA
ECUADOR
PERU
BOLIVIA
AMAZONAS
TRINIDAD
TOBAGO
Caracas
Bogotá
Quito
Lima
La Paz
Manaus
© Collins ○ Longman Atlases Cbi

Relief
Feet Metres
16404 5000
9843 3000
6562 2000
3281 1000
1640 500
656 200
0 Sea Level
Land Dep. 656 200
13123 4000
0 100 200 300 400 500 Miles
0 100 200 300 400 500 600 700 800 Kms.
Lambert Azimuthal Equal Area Projection
SURINAM
GUIANA (Fr.)
BRAZIL
PARÁ
AMAPÁ
MARANHÃO
PIAUÍ
CEARÁ
BAHIA
GOIÁS
MINAS GERAIS
PERNAMBUCO
Estuario do Rio Amazonas (Amazon Delta)
Planalto Brasil (Brazilian Highlands)
Belém
Fortaleza
Recife
Salvador
Brasília

SOUTH AMERICA – SOUTH

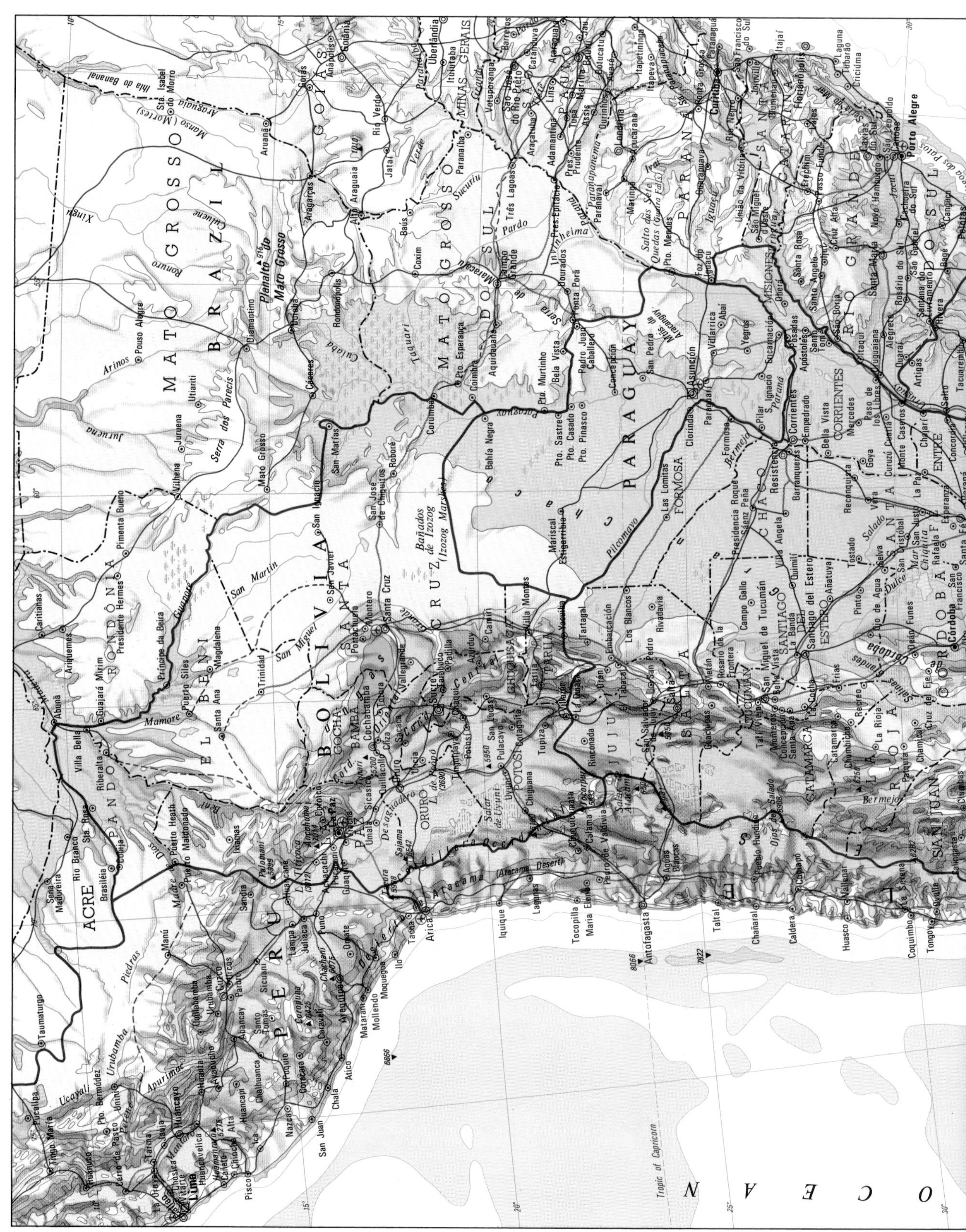
BRAZIL
MATO GROSSO
MATO GROSSO DO SUL
GOIÁS
MINAS GERAIS
SÃO PAULO
PARANÁ
SANTA CATARINA
RIO GRANDE DO SUL
RONDÔNIA
ACRE
BOLIVIA
PARAGUAY
PERU
PANDO
EL BENI
SANTA CRUZ
COCHABAMBA
LA PAZ
ORURO
POTOSÍ
CHUQUISACA
TARIJA
JUJUY
SALTA
FORMOSA
CHACO
CORRIENTES
MISIONES
SANTIAGO DEL ESTERO
TUCUMÁN
CATAMARCA
LA RIOJA
SAN JUAN
CÓRDOBA
SANTA FE
ENTRE RÍOS
OCEAN
Tropic of Capricorn
Lima
Asunción
Curitiba
Porto Alegre
Florianópolis
Cuiabá
Campo Grande
Goiânia
Uberlândia
Corumbá
Santa Cruz
Sucre
Potosí
Cochabamba
Arica
Antofagasta
Iquique
Tocopilla
Taltal
Chañaral
Caldera
Huasco
Coquimbo
Corrientes
Resistencia
Salta
Tucumán
Córdoba
Pisco
Ica
Nazca
Arequipa
Mollendo
Tacna
Cuzco
Huancayo
Ayacucho
Puno
Juliaca
Trinidad
Riberalta
Guajará Mirim
Abunã
Ariquemes
Vilhena
Cáceres
Concepción
Encarnación
Posadas
Formosa
Atacama Desert
Planalto do Mato Grosso
Bañados de Izozog
Serra dos Parecis
Pilcomayo
Paraguay
Paraná
Uruguay
Madre de Dios
Mamoré
Guaporé
Beni
Ucayali
Urubamba
Apurímac
Juruena
Arinos
Xingu
Araguaia
Salado
Bermejo
Titicaca

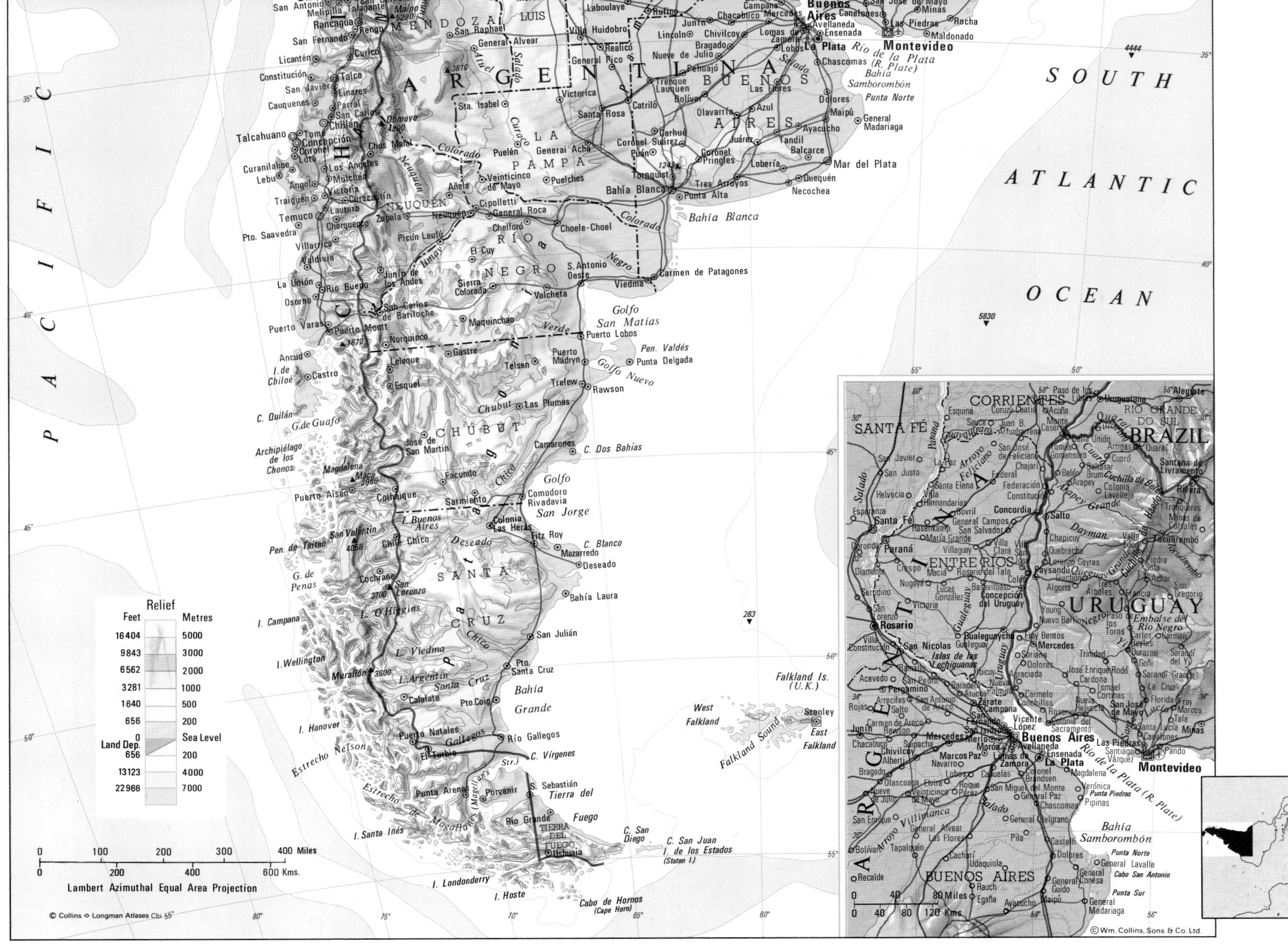
SOUTH ATLANTIC OCEAN
PACIFIC
ARGENTINA
CHILE
URUGUAY
BRAZIL
Falkland Is. (U.K.)
Relief
Feet
Metres
16404 5000
9843 3000
6562 2000
3281 1000
1640 500
656 200
0 Sea Level
Land Dep. 656 200
13123 4000
22966 7000
0 100 200 300 400 Miles
0 200 400 600 Kms.
Lambert Azimuthal Equal Area Projection
© Collins ◇ Longman Atlases Cbi 55°
© Wm. Collins, Sons & Co. Ltd.

POLAR REGIONS

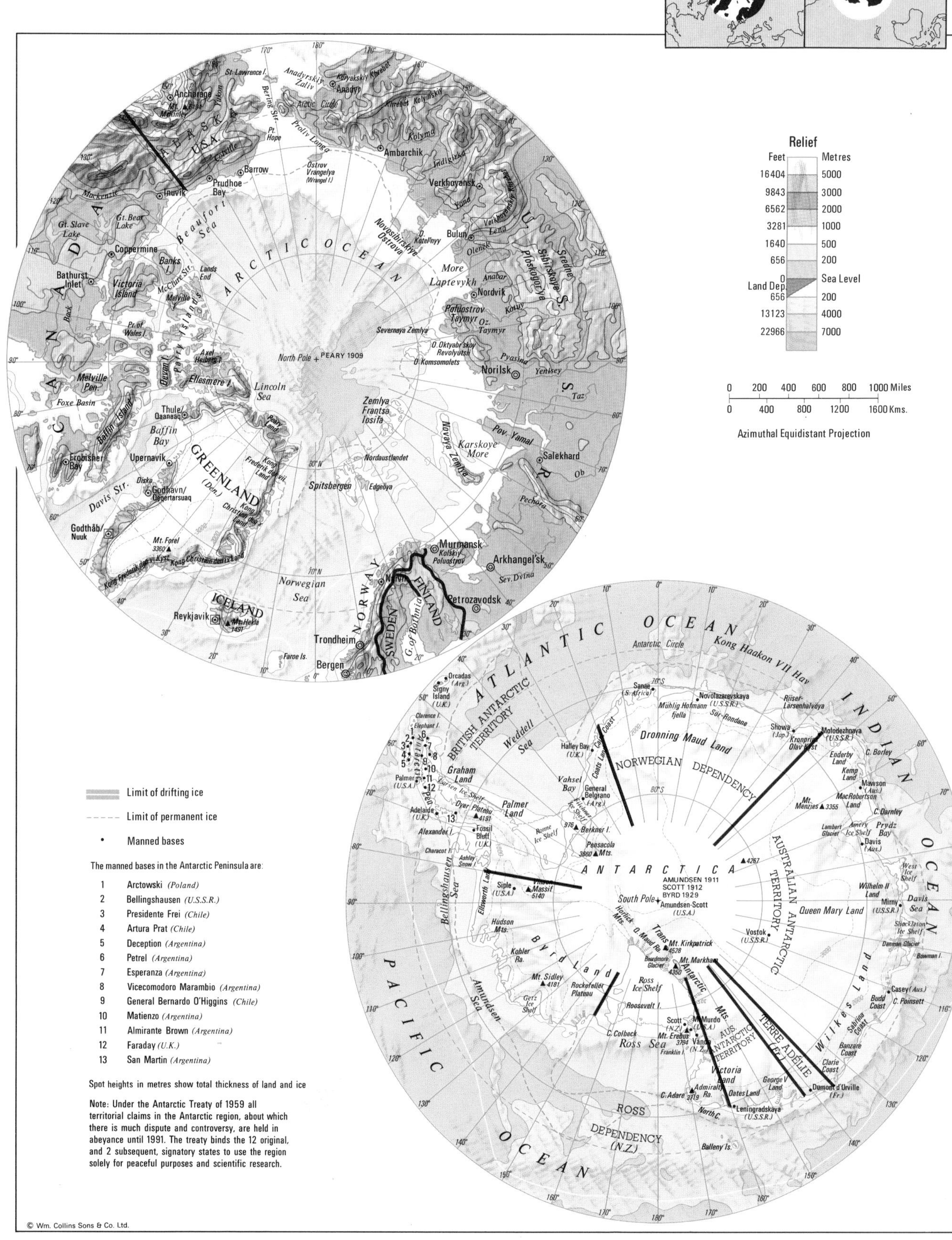
Relief
Feet
Metres
16404
5000
9843
3000
6562
2000
3281
1000
1640
500
656
200
0
Sea Level
Land Dep.
656
200
13123
4000
22966
7000
0 200 400 600 800 1000 Miles
0 400 800 1200 1600 Kms.
Azimuthal Equidistant Projection
ARCTIC OCEAN
North Pole + PEARY 1909
GREENLAND (Den.)
CANADA
ALASKA U.S.A.
ICELAND
NORWAY
SWEDEN
FINLAND
Spitsbergen
Zemlya Frantsa Iosifa
Novaya Zemlya
Severnaya Zemlya
Norwegian Sea
Beaufort Sea
Baffin Bay
Lincoln Sea
Murmansk
Arkhangel'sk
Reykjavik
Anchorage
Barrow
Thule/Qaanaaq
Godthåb/Nuuk
Norilsk
Salekhard
Petrozavodsk
Trondheim
Bergen
ANTARCTICA
AMUNDSEN 1911
SCOTT 1912
BYRD 1929
South Pole
Amundsen-Scott (U.S.A.)
ATLANTIC OCEAN
INDIAN OCEAN
PACIFIC OCEAN
BRITISH ANTARCTIC TERRITORY
NORWEGIAN DEPENDENCY
AUSTRALIAN ANTARCTIC TERRITORY
ROSS DEPENDENCY (N.Z.)
TERRE ADÉLIE (Fr.)
Weddell Sea
Ross Sea
Amundsen Sea
Bellingshausen Sea
Dronning Maud Land
Byrd Land
Wilkes Land
Queen Mary Land
Graham Land
Palmer Land
Ellsworth Land
Victoria Land
Ross Ice Shelf
Ronne Ice Shelf
Vinson Massif 5140
Mt. Kirkpatrick 4528
Mt. Markham
Mt. Erebus 3794
Vostok (U.S.S.R.)
Halley Bay (U.K.)
Mawson (Aus.)
Davis (Aus.)
Casey (Aus.)
Dumont d'Urville (Fr.)
Scott (N.Z.)
McMurdo (U.S.A.)
Limit of drifting ice
Limit of permanent ice
Manned bases
The manned bases in the Antarctic Peninsula are:
1 Arctowski (Poland)
2 Bellingshausen (U.S.S.R.)
3 Presidente Frei (Chile)
4 Artura Prat (Chile)
5 Deception (Argentina)
6 Petrel (Argentina)
7 Esperanza (Argentina)
8 Vicecomodoro Marambio (Argentina)
9 General Bernardo O'Higgins (Chile)
10 Matienzo (Argentina)
11 Almirante Brown (Argentina)
12 Faraday (U.K.)
13 San Martin (Argentina)
Spot heights in metres show total thickness of land and ice
Note: Under the Antarctic Treaty of 1959 all territorial claims in the Antarctic region, about which there is much dispute and controversy, are held in abeyance until 1991. The treaty binds the 12 original, and 2 subsequent, signatory states to use the region solely for peaceful purposes and scientific research.
© Wm. Collins Sons & Co. Ltd.

WORLD DATA

Part 1

WORLD FACTS AND FIGURES 66-70

WORLD PHYSICAL DATA 66

WORLD POLITICAL DATA 67

NATIONS OF THE WORLD 68-70

Part 2

WORLD INDEX 71-112

Part 3

WORLD MAPS–ENDPAPERS

THE WORLD: POLITICAL–FRONT

THE WORLD: PHYSICAL–BACK

WORLD PHYSICAL DATA

Earth's Dimensions

Superficial area	510 066 000 km²
Land surface	148 326 000 km²
Water surface	361 740 000 km²
Equatorial circumference	40 075 km
Meridional circumference	40 007 km
Volume	1 083 230x10⁶ km³
Mass	5.976x10²¹ tonnes

Oceans and Sea Areas

Pacific Ocean	165 384 000 km²
Atlantic Ocean	82 217 000 km²
Indian Ocean	73 481 000 km²
Arctic Ocean	14 056 000 km²
Mediterranean Sea	2 505 000 km²
South China Sea	2 318 000 km²
Bering Sea	2 269 000 km²
Caribbean Sea	1 943 000 km²
Gulf of Mexico	1 544 000 km²
Okhotskoye More (Sea of Okhotsk)	1 528 000 km²
East China Sea	1 248 000 km²
Hudson Bay	1 233 000 km²
Sea of Japan	1 008 000 km²
North Sea	575 000 km²
Black Sea	461 000 km²

River Lengths

An Nīl (Nile); Africa	6695 km
Amazonas (Amazon); South America	6570 km
Mississippi - Missouri; North America	6020 km
Chang Jiang (Yangtze); Asia	5471 km
Ob-Irtysh; Asia	5410 km
Huang He (Hwang Ho); Asia	4840 km
Zaïre; Africa	4630 km
Amur; Asia	4416 km
Lena; Asia	4269 km
Mackenzie; North America	4240 km
Niger; Africa	4183 km
Mekong; Asia	4180 km
Yenisey; Asia	4090 km
Murray - Darling; Oceania	3717 km
Volga; Europe	3688 km

Lake and Inland Sea Areas

Some areas are subject to seasonal variations.

Caspian Sea; U.S.S.R. / Iran	371 795 km²
Lake Superior; U.S.A. / Canada	82 413 km²
Lake Victoria; East Africa	69 485 km²
Aralskoye More (Aral Sea); U.S.S.R.	66 457 km²
Lake Huron; U.S.A. / Canada	59 596 km²
Lake Michigan; U.S.A.	58 016 km²
Lake Tanganyika; East Africa	32 893 km²
Great Bear Lake; Canada	31 792 km²
Ozero Baykal (Lake Baikal); U.S.S.R.	30 510 km²
Great Slave Lake; Canada	28 930 km²
Lake Malaŵi; Malaŵi / Mozambique	28 490 km²
Lake Erie; U.S.A. / Canada	25 667 km²
Lake Winnipeg; Canada	24 514 km²
Lake Ontario; U.S.A. / Canada	19 529 km²
Ladozhskoye Ozero (Lake Ladoga); U.S.S.R.	18 390 km²

The Continents

Asia	44 391 162 km²
Africa	30 244 049 km²
North America	24 247 038 km²
South America	17 821 028 km²
Antarctica	13 338 500 km²
Europe	10 354 636 km²
Oceania	8 547 000 km²

Island Areas

Greenland; Arctic / Atlantic Ocean	2 175 597 km²
New Guinea; Indonesia / Papua New Guinea	828 057 km²
Borneo; Malaysia / Indonesia / Brunei	751 929 km²
Madagascar; Indian Ocean	587 042 km²
Baffin Island; Canada	476 068 km²
Sumatera (Sumatra); Indonesia	422 170 km²
Honshū; Japan	230 455 km²
Great Britain; United Kingdom	229 867 km²
Ellesmere Island; Canada	212 688 km²
Victoria Island; Canada	212 199 km²
Sulawesi (Celebes); Indonesia	179 370 km²
South Island; New Zealand	150 461 km²
Jawa (Java); Indonesia	126 500 km²
North Island; New Zealand	114 688 km²
Cuba; Caribbean Sea	114 525 km²

Mountain Heights (Selected)

Everest; Nepal / China	8848 m
K2; Jammu & Kashmir / China	8611 m
Kānchenjunga; Nepal / India	8586 m
Dhaulāgiri; Nepal	8172 m
Annapurna; Nepal	8078 m
Aconcagua; Argentina	6960 m
Ojos del Salado; Argentina / Chile	6908 m
McKinley; Alaska U.S.A.	6194 m
Logan; Canada	6050 m
Kilimanjaro; Tanzania	5895 m
Elbrus; U.S.S.R.	5633 m
Kenya; Kenya	5200 m
Vinson Massif; Antarctica	5139 m
Puncak Jaya; Indonesia	5030 m
Blanc; France / Italy	4807 m

Volcanoes (Selected)

	Last Eruption	Height
Cameroun; Cameroon	1922	4070 m
Cotopaxi; Ecuador	1975	5897 m
Elbrus; U.S.S.R.	extinct	5633 m
Erebus; Antarctica	1979	3794 m
Etna; Sicilia, Italy	1983	3340 m
Fuji san (Fujiyama); Japan	extinct	3776 m
Hekla; Iceland	1981	1491 m
Kilimanjaro; Tanzania	extinct	5895 m
Mauna Loa; Hawaii	1978	4171 m
Ngauruhoe; New Zealand	1975	2291 m
Popocatépetl; Mexico	1920	5452 m
St. Helens; U.S.A.	1981	2949 m
Stromboli; Italy	1975	926 m
Tristan da Cunha; Atlantic Ocean	1962	2160 m
Vesuvio (Vesuvius); Italy	1944	1277 m

WORLD POLITICAL DATA

National Areas

Union of Soviet Socialist Republics; Asia / Europe	22 402 000 km²
Canada; North America	9 976 000 km²
China; Asia	9 596 961 km²
United States; North America	9 363 123 km²
Brazil; South America	8 511 965 km²
Australia; Oceania	7 686 848 km²
India; Asia	3 287 590 km²
Argentina; South America	2 766 889 km²
Sudan; Africa	2 505 813 km²
Algeria; Africa	2 381 741 km²
Zaïre; Africa	2 345 409 km²
Greenland; North America	2 175 600 km²
Saudi Arabia; Asia	2 149 690 km²
Mexico; North America	1 972 547 km²
Indonesia; Asia	1 904 345 km²
Libya; Africa	1 759 540 km²
Iran; Asia	1 648 000 km²
Mongolia; Asia	1 565 000 km²
Peru; South America	1 285 216 km²
Chad; Africa	1 284 000 km²

National Populations

China; Asia	982 550 000
India; Asia	683 810 000
Union of Soviet Socialist Republics; Asia / Europe	265 542 000
United States; North America	227 640 000
Indonesia; Asia	147 383 000
Brazil; South America	123 032 000
Japan; Asia	117 057 000
Bangladesh; Asia	86 656 000
Pakistan; Asia	82 441 000
Nigeria; Africa	77 082 000
Mexico; North America	71 911 000
West Germany; Europe	61 658 000
Italy; Europe	57 140 000
United Kingdom; Europe	55 945 000
France; Europe	53 788 000
Vietnam; Asia	52 742 000
Philippines; Asia	48 400 000
Thailand; Asia	46 455 000
Turkey; Asia / Europe	45 218 000
Egypt; Africa	41 995 000

World Cities

New York; United States	16 479 000
Ciudad de México (Mexico City); Mexico	13 994 000
Tokyō; Japan	11 695 000
Shanghai; China	10 820 000
Los Angeles; United States	10 607 000
Paris; France	9 863 000
Buenos Aires; Argentina	8 436 000
Moskva (Moscow); U.S.S.R.	8 011 000
Chicago; United States	7 664 000
Beijing (Peking); China	7 570 000
São Paulo; Brazil	7 199 000
Calcutta; India	7 031 000
Sŏul (Seoul); South Korea	6 879 000
London; United Kingdom	6 696 000
Bombay; India	5 971 000

Major International Organisations

United Nations - In December 1984 the United Nations had 159 members. Independent states not represented include Liechtenstein, Monaco, Nauru, North Korea, San Marino, South Korea, Switzerland, Taiwan, Tonga.

Commonwealth

Antigua	Australia	Bahamas	Bangladesh
Barbados	Belize	Botswana	Brunei
Canada	Cyprus	Dominica	Fiji
Gambia	Ghana	Grenada	Guyana
India	Jamaica	Kenya	Kiribati
Lesotho	Malaŵi	Malaysia	Maldives
Malta	Mauritius	Nauru	New Zealand
Nigeria	Papua New Guinea	St. Kitts-Nevis	St. Lucia
St. Vincent	Seychelles	Sierra Leone	Singapore
Solomon Islands	Sri Lanka	Swaziland	Tanzania
Tonga	Trinidad & Tobago	Tuvalu	Uganda
United Kindom	Vanuatu	Western Samoa	Zambia
Zimbabwe			

OAU - Organisation of African Unity

Algeria	Angola	Benin	Botswana
Burkina Faso	Burundi	Cameroon	Cape Verde
Cent. African Rep.	Chad	Comoros	Congo
Djibouti	Egypt	Equatorial Guinea	Ethiopia
Gabon	Gambia	Ghana	Guinea
Guinea Bissau	Ivory Coast	Kenya	Lesotho
Liberia	Libya	Madagascar	Malaŵi
Mali	Mauritania	Mauritius	Morocco
Mozambique	Niger	Nigeria	Rwanda
São Tomé & Príncipe	Senegal	Seychelles	Sierra Leone
Somali Rep.	Sudan	Swaziland	Tanzania
Togo	Tunisia	Uganda	Western Sahara
Zaïre	Zambia	Zimbabwe	

OAS - Organisation of American States

Antigua	Argentina	Bahamas	Barbados
Bolivia	Brazil	Chile	Colombia
Costa Rica	Cuba	Dominica	Dominican Rep.
Ecuador	El Salvador	Grenada	Guatemala
Haiti	Honduras	Jamaica	Mexico
Nicaragua	Panama	Paraguay	Peru
St. Kitts-Nevis	St. Lucia	St. Vincent	Surinam
Trinidad & Tobago	United States	Uruguay	Venezuela

EEC - European Economic Community

Belgium	Denmark	France	Greece
Ireland	Italy	Luxembourg	Netherlands
United Kingdom	West Germany		

EFTA - European Free Trade Association

Austria	Finland (assoc.)	Iceland	Norway
Portugal	Sweden	Switzerland	

COMECON - Council for Mutual Economic Assistance

Bulgaria	Cuba	Czechoslovakia	East Germany
Hungary	Mongolia	Poland	Romania
U.S.S.R.	Vietnam	Yugoslavia (assoc.)	

ASEAN - Association of Southeast Asian Nations

Brunei	Indonesia	Malaysia	Philippines
Singapore	Thailand		

ECOWAS - Economic Community of West African States

Benin	Burkina Faso	Cape Verde	Gambia
Ghana	Guinea	Guinea Bissau	Ivory Coast
Liberia	Mali	Mauritania	Niger
Nigeria	Senegal	Sierra Leone	Togo

CARICOM - Caribbean Community and Common Market

Antigua	Barbados	Belize	Dominica
Grenada	Guyana	Jamaica	Monserrat
St. Kitts - Nevis	St. Lucia	St. Vincent	Trinidad & Tobago

NATIONS OF THE WORLD

COUNTRY	AREA sq. km.	POPULATION total	per sq. km.	FORM OF GOVERNMENT	CAPITAL CITY	MAIN LANGUAGES	CURRENCY
AFGHANISTAN	647 497	15 540 000	24	democratic republic	Kābul	Pushtu, Dari (Persian)	afghani
ALBANIA	28 748	2 734 000	95	socialist people's republic	Tiranë	Albanian	lek
ALGERIA	2 381 741	18 594 000	8	republic	Alger (Algiers)	Arabic	dinar
ANDORRA	453	34 000	75	principality	Andorra	Catalan	French franc, Spanish peseta
ANGOLA	1 246 700	7 078 000	5.6	people's republic	Luanda	Portuguese	kwanza
ANTIGUA AND BARBUDA	442	74 000	167	independent political entity	St John's	English	East Caribbean dollar
ARGENTINA	2 766 889	27 863 000	10	federal republic	Buenos Aires	Spanish	peso
AUSTRALIA	7 686 848	14 727 000	1.9	monarchy (federal)	Canberra	English	dollar
AUSTRIA	83 849	7 507 000	89	federal republic	Wien (Vienna)	German	schilling
BAHAMAS	13 935	223 000	16	constitutional monarchy	Nassau	English	dollar
BAHRAIN	622	364 000	585	emirate	Al Manāmah	Arabic	dinar
BANGLADESH	143 998	86 656 000	601	people's republic	Dhākā	Bengali	taka
BARBADOS	431	250 000	580	independent political entity	Bridgetown	English	dollar
BELGIUM	30 513	9 859 000	323	constitutional monarchy	Bruxelles / Brussel (Brussels)	French, Dutch, German	franc
BELIZE	22 965	145 000	6.3	constitutional monarchy	Belmopan	English	dollar
BENIN	112 622	3 567 000	31	people's republic	Porto-Novo	French	CFA franc
BHUTAN	47 000	1 298 000	27	monarchy (Indian protection)	Thimbu	Dzongkha	Indian rupee, ngultrum
BOLIVIA	1 098 581	5 600 000	5	republic	La Paz / Sucre	Spanish	peso
BOTSWANA	600 372	819 000	1.3	republic	Gaborone	English, Tswana	pula
BRAZIL	8 511 965	123 032 000	14	federal republic	Brasília	Portuguese	cruzeiro
BRUNEI	5 765	213 000	37	sultanate (U.K. protectorate)	Bandar Seri Begawan	Malay	dollar
BULGARIA	110 912	8 862 000	79	people's republic	Sofiya (Sofia)	Bulgarian	lev
BURMA	676 552	35 289 000	52	federal republic	Rangoon	Burmese	kyat
BURUNDI	27 834	4 512 000	162	republic	Bujumbura	French, Kirundi	franc
CAMEROON	475 442	8 503 000	17	republic	Yaoundé	French, English	CFA franc
CANADA	9 976 139	23 941 000	2.4	monarchy (federal)	Ottawa	English, French	dollar
CAPE VERDE	4 033	314 000	78	republic	Praia	Portuguese, Creole	escudo
CENTRAL AFRICAN REPUBLIC	622 984	2 370 000	3.8	republic	Bangui	French, Sango	CFA franc
CHAD	1 284 000	4 524 000	3.5	republic	N'Djamena	French	CFA franc
CHILE	756 945	11 104 000	15	republic	Santiago	Spanish	peso
CHINA	9 596 961	982 550 000	102	people's republic	Beijing (Peking)	Mandarin	yuan
COLOMBIA	1 138 914	27 520 000	24	republic	Bogotá	Spanish	peso
COMOROS	2 171	320 000	147	federal republic	Moroni	Comoran, Arabic, French	CFA Franc
CONGO	342 000	1 537 000	4.4	republic	Brazzaville	French	CFA franc
COSTA RICA	50 700	2 245 000	44	republic	San José	Spanish	colon
CUBA	114 524	9 833 000	86	people's republic	La Habana (Havana)	Spanish	peso
CYPRUS	9 251	629 000	68	republic	Levkosía (Nicosia)	Greek	pound
CZECHOSLOVAKIA	127 869	15 312 000	119	federal socialist republic	Praha (Prague)	Czech, Slovak	koruna
DENMARK	43 069	5 124 000	119	constitutional monarchy	Köbenhavn (Copenhagen)	Danish	krone
DJIBOUTI	22 000	119 000	5.4	republic	Djibouti	French, Somali, Afar	franc
DOMINICA	751	81 000	108	republic	Roseau	English, French	East Caribbean dollar
DOMINICAN REPUBLIC	48 734	5 431 000	111	republic	Santo Domingo	Spanish	peso
EAST GERMANY	108 178	16 737 000	155	people's republic	Berlin	German	mark
ECUADOR	283 561	8 354 000	29	republic	Quito	Spanish	sucre
EGYPT	1 001 449	41 995 000	41	republic	Al Qāhirah (Cairo)	Arabic	pound
EL SALVADOR	21 041	4 813 000	228	republic	San Salvador	Spanish	colón
EQUATORIAL GUINEA	28 051	363 000	13	republic	Malabo	Spanish	ekuele
ETHIOPIA	1 221 900	31 065 000	25	provisional military government	Ādīs Ābeba (Addis Ababa)	Amharic	birr
FIJI	18 272	631 000	34	monarchy (federal)	Suva	English, Fijian, Hindustani	dollar
FINLAND	337 009	4 788 000	14	republic	Helsinki	Finnish, Swedish	mark
FRANCE	547 026	53 788 000	98	republic	Paris	French	franc
GABON	267 667	551 000	2.1	republic	Libreville	French	CFA franc
GAMBIA	11 295	601 000	53	republic	Banjul	English	dalasi
GHANA	238 537	11 450 000	48	republic	Accra	English	cedi
GREECE	131 944	9 599 000	72	republic	Athínai (Athens)	Greek	drachma
GREENLAND	2 175 600	50 000	0.1	overseas territory (Denmark)	Godthåb / Nuuk	Danish, Greenlandic	kroner
GRENADA	344	97 000	281	independent political entity	St George's	English	East Caribbean dollar
GUATEMALA	108 889	7 262 000	66	republic	Guatemala	Spanish	quetzal
GUIANA	91 000	64 000	0.6	overseas department (France)	Cayenne	French	franc

NATIONS OF THE WORLD

COUNTRY	AREA sq. km.	POPULATION total	per sq. km.	FORM OF GOVERNMENT	CAPITAL CITY	MAIN LANGUAGES	CURRENCY
UINEA	245 857	5 014 000	20	republic	Conakry	French	syli
UINEA BISSAU	36 125	777 000	22	republic	Bissau	Portuguese	peso
UYANA	214 969	884 000	4.1	republic	Georgetown	English	dollar
AITI	27 750	5 009 000	180	republic	Port-au-Prince	French, Créole	gourde
ONDURAS	112 088	3 691 000	32	republic	Tegucigalpa	Spanish	lempira
ONG KONG	1 045	5 068 000	4 850	colony (U.K.)		English, Chinese	dollar
UNGARY	93 030	10 711 000	115	republic	Budapest	Magyar	forint
CELAND	103 000	228 000	2.2	republic	Reykjavík	Icelandic	króna
NDIA	3 287 590	683 810 000	208	republic	New Delhi	Hindi	rupee
NDONESIA	1 904 345	147 383 000	77	republic	Jakarta	Bahasa Indonesia	rupiah
RAN	1 648 000	37 447 000	22	islamic republic	Tehrān	Persian	rial
RAQ	434 924	13 084 000	30	republic	Baghdād	Arabic	dinar
RELAND, REPUBLIC OF	70 023	3 365 000	48	republic	Dublin	English, Irish	punt
SRAEL	20 770	3 871 000	186	republic	Yerushalayim (Jerusalem)	Hebrew	shekel
TALY	301 225	57 140 000	189	republic	Roma (Rome)	Italian	lira
VORY COAST	322 462	7 973 000	25	republic	Yamoussoukro	French	CFA franc
AMAICA	10 991	2 192 000	199	constitutional monarchy	Kingston	English	dollar
APAN	372 313	117 057 000	314	monarchy	Tōkyō	Japanese	yen
ORDAN	97 740	2 779 000	28	monarchy	'Ammān	Arabic	dinar
AMPUCHEA	181 035	8 872 000	49	people's republic	Phnum Pénh (Phnom Penh)	Cambodian, Khmer	riel
ENYA	582 646	16 402 000	28	republic	Nairobi	Swahili, English	shilling
IRIBATI	886	63 000	71	republic	Bairiki	English, Gilbertese (I-Kiribati)	Australian dollar
UWAIT	17 818	1 356 000	76	sheikdom	Al Kuwayt (Kuwait)	Arabic	dinar
AOS	236 800	3 721 000	15	people's republic	Viangchan (Vientiane)	Lao	kip
EBANON	10 400	3 161 000	304	republic	Bayrūt (Beirut)	Arabic	pound
ESOTHO	30 355	1 339 000	44	monarchy	Maseru	English, Sesotho	loti
IBERIA	111 369	1 873 000	16	republic	Monrovia	English	dollar
IBYA	1 759 540	2 977 000	1.6	republic	Ṭarābulus (Tripoli)	Arabic	dinar
IECHTENSTEIN	157	26 000	166	constitutional monarchy	Vaduz	German	Swiss franc
UXEMBOURG	2 586	364 000	140	constitutional monarchy	Luxembourg	Letzeburgish, French, German	franc
ADAGASCAR	587 041	8 742 000	14	republic	Antananarivo	Malagasy	Malagasy franc
ALAWI	118 484	5 968 000	50	republic	Lilongwe	English, Chichewa	kwacha
ALAYSIA	329 749	13 436 000	40	constitutional monarchy	Kuala Lumpur	Malay	ringgit
ALDIVES	298	143 046	480	republic	Malé	Divehi	rupee
ALI	1 240 000	6 906 000	5.5	republic	Bamako	French, Bambara	franc
ALTA	316	369 000	1 167	republic	Valletta	Maltese, English	pound
AURITANIA	1 030 700	1 634 000	1.5	republic	Nouakchott	French, Arabic	ouguiya
AURITIUS	2 045	924 000	452	independent political entity	Port Louis	English, Creole	rupee
EXICO	1 972 547	71 911 000	35	federal republic	Ciudad de México (Mexico City)	Spanish	peso
ONACO	1.5	26 000	17 333	constitutional monarchy	Monaco	French	French franc
ONGOLIA	1 565 000	1 595 000	1.1	people's republic	Ulaanbaatar (Ulan Bator)	Mongol	tugrik
OROCCO	446 550	20 242 000	44	monarchy	Rabat	Arabic	dirham
OZAMBIQUE	783 000	12 130 000	13	people's republic	Maputo	Portuguese	escudo
AMIBIA	824 292	852 000	1.1	South African mandate	Windhoek	Afrikaans, English	R.S.A. rand
AURU	21	8 000	381	republic	Nauru	Nauruan, English	Australian dollar
EPAL	140 797	14 010 000	99	monarchy	Kātmāndu	Nepali	rupee
ETHERLANDS	40 844	14 220 000	348	constitutional monarchy	Amsterdam	Dutch	guilder
EW ZEALAND	268 676	3 164 000	12	monarchy	Wellington	English	dollar
ICARAGUA	130 000	2 703 000	20	republic	Managua	Spanish	córdoba
IGER	1 267 000	5 305 000	4.1	republic	Niamey	French	CFA franc
IGERIA	923 768	77 082 000	83	federal republic	Abuja	English	naira
ORTH KOREA	120 538	17 914 000	148	people's republic	Pyŏngyang	Korean	won
ORWAY	324 219	4 092 000	13	constitutional monarchy	Oslo	Norwegian	krone
OMAN	212 457	891 000	4.1	sultanate	Masqaṭ (Muscat)	Arabic	rial
PAKISTAN	803 943	82 441 000	103	federal republic	Islāmābād	Urdu, Punjabi, English	rupee
PANAMA	75 650	1 837 000	24	republic	Panamá	Spanish	balbao
PAPUA NEW GUINEA	461 691	3 082 000	6.7	republic	Port Moresby	English	kina
PARAGUAY	406 752	3 067 000	7.5	republic	Asunción	Spanish, Guaraní	guaraní

NATIONS OF THE WORLD

COUNTRY	AREA sq. km.	POPULATION total	POPULATION per sq. km.	FORM OF GOVERNMENT	CAPITAL CITY	MAIN LANGUAGES	CURRENCY
PERU	1 285 216	17 780 000	14	republic	Lima	Spanish	sol
PHILIPPINES	300 000	48 400 000	161	republic	Manila	Pilipino	peso
POLAND	312 677	35 815 000	115	people's republic	Warszawa (Warsaw)	Polish	zloty
PORTUGAL	92 082	9 933 000	107	republic	Lisboa (Lisbon)	Portuguese	escudo
PUERTO RICO	8 897	3 188 000	358	commonwealth (U.S.A.)	San Juan	Spanish, English	dollar
QATAR	11 000	220 000	20	emirate	Ad Dawḥah (Doha)	Arabic	riyal
ROMANIA	237 500	22 201 000	93	socialist republic	Bucureşti (Bucharest)	Romanian	leu
RWANDA	26 338	5 046 000	191	republic	Kigali	Kinyarwanda, French	franc
ST KITTS - NEVIS	266	62 000	233	independent political entity	Basseterre	English	East Caribbean dollar
ST LUCIA	616	113 000	183	independent political entity	Castries	English, French	East Caribbean dollar
ST VINCENT AND THE GRENADINES	389	96 000	247	independent political entity	Kingstown	English	East Caribbean dollar
SAN MARINO	61	21 000	344	republic	San Marino	Italian	Italian lira
SÃO TOMÉ AND PRÍNCIPE	964	82 750	86	republic	São Tomé	Portuguese, Creole	dobra
SAUDI ARABIA	2 149 690	8 367 000	3.8	monarchy	Ar Riyāḍ (Riyadh)	Arabic	riyal
SENEGAL	196 192	5 661 000	28	republic	Dakar	French	CFA franc
SEYCHELLES	280	61 900	221	republic	Victoria	English, French	rupee
SIERRA LEONE	71 740	3 474 000	48	republic	Freetown	English	leone
SINGAPORE	602	2 391 000	3 972	republic	Singapore	Malay, English, Chinese, Tamil	dollar
SOLOMON ISLANDS	28 446	221 000	7.8	constitutional monarchy	Honiara	English	dollar
SOMALI REPUBLIC	637 657	3 645 000	5.7	republic	Mogadisho	Arabic, Italian, English, Somali	shilling
SOUTH AFRICA, REPUBLIC OF	1 221 037	29 285 000	23	federal republic	Cape Town (Kaapstad) / Pretoria	Afrikaans, English	rand
SOUTH KOREA	98 484	37 605 000	382	republic	Sŏul (Seoul)	Korean	won
SOUTHERN YEMEN	332 968	1 969 000	5.9	people's republic	'Adan (Aden)	Arabic	dinar
SPAIN	504 782	37 430 000	74	constitutional monarchy	Madrid	Spanish	peseta
SRI LANKA	65 610	14 738 000	225	republic	Colombo	Sinhala, Tamil	rupee
SUDAN	2 505 813	18 681 000	7.4	republic	Al Kharṭūm (Khartoum)	Arabic	pound
SURINAM	163 265	352 000	2.1	republic	Paramaribo	Dutch, English	guilder
SWAZILAND	17 363	547 000	31	monarchy	Mbabane	English, Siswati	R.S.A. rand, lilangeni
SWEDEN	449 964	8 320 000	18	constitutional monarchy	Stockholm	Swedish	krona
SWITZERLAND	41 288	6 329 000	153	federal republic	Bern (Berne)	German, French, Italian, Romansh	franc
SYRIA	185 180	8 979 000	48	republic	Dimashq (Damascus)	Arabic	pound
TAIWAN	35 961	17 479 000	486	republic	Taipei	Mandarin	dollar
TANZANIA	945 087	17 982 000	19	republic	Dar es Salaam / Dodoma	Swahili	shilling
THAILAND	514 000	46 455 000	90	monarchy	Krung Thep (Bangkok)	Thai	baht
TOGO	56 000	2 699 000	48	republic	Lomé	French	CFA franc
TONGA	699	97 000	139	monarchy	Nuku'alofa	Tongan, English	dollar
TRINIDAD AND TOBAGO	5 128	1 156 000	225	republic	Port of Spain	English	dollar
TUNISIA	163 610	6 363 000	39	republic	Tunis	Arabic	dinar
TURKEY	780 576	45 218 000	57	republic	Ankara	Turkish	lira
TUVALU	24	7 000	292	constitutional monarchy	Funafuti	Tuvalu, English	dollar
U.S.S.R.	22 402 200	265 542 000	12	federal socialist republic	Moskva (Moscow)	Russian	rouble
UGANDA	236 036	13 225 000	56	republic	Kampala	English	shilling
UNITED ARAB EMIRATES	83 600	1 040 000	12	self-governing union		Arabic	dirham
UNITED KINGDOM	244 046	55 945 000	229	constitutional monarchy	London	English	pound
UNITED STATES OF AMERICA	9 363 123	227 640 000	24	federal republic	Washington	English	dollar
UPPER VOLTA (BURKINA FASO)	274 200	6 908 000	25	republic	Ouagadougou	French	CFA franc
URUGUAY	177 508	2 899 000	16	republic	Montevideo	Spanish	peso
VANUATU	14 763	112 000	7.6	republic	Vila	English, French	vatu
VENEZUELA	912 050	13 913 000	15	federal republic	Caracas	Spanish	bolívar
VIETNAM	333 000	52 742 000	158	people's republic	Hà Nôi (Hanoi)	Vietnamese	dong
WEST GERMANY	248 577	61 658 000	248	federal republic	Bonn	German	mark
WESTERN SAHARA	266 000	135 000	0.5		El Aaiún	Arabic	peseta
WESTERN SAMOA	2 842	156 000	55	constitutional monarchy	Apia	Samoan, English	tala
YEMEN	195 000	5 926 000	30	republic	Şan'ā	Arabic	riyal
YUGOSLAVIA	255 804	22 471 000	87	socialist federal republic	Beograd (Belgrade)	Serbo-Croat, Macedonian, Slovene	dinar
ZAÏRE	2 345 409	28 291 000	12	republic	Kinshasa	French, Lingala	zaïre
ZAMBIA	752 614	5 680 000	7.5	republic	Lusaka	English	kwacha
ZIMBABWE	390 580	7 360 000	18	republic	Harare	English	dollar

WORLD INDEX

Introduction to World Index

The Index includes an alphabetical list of all names appearing on the maps in the World Atlas section. Each entry indicates the country or region of the world in which the name is located. This is followed by a page reference and finally the name's location on the map, given by latitude and longitude co-ordinates. Most features are indexed to the largest scale map on which they appear, however when the name applies to countries or other extensive features it is generally indexed to the map on which it appears in its entirety. Areal features are generally indexed using co-ordinates which indicate the centre of the feature. The latitude and longitude indicated for a point feature gives the location of the point on the map. In the case of rivers the mouth or confluence is always taken as the point of reference.

Names in the Index are generally in the local language and where a conventional English version exists, this is cross referenced to the entry in the local language. Names of features which extend across the boundaries of more than one country are usually named in English if no single official name exists. Names in languages not written in the Roman alphabet have been transliterated using the official system of the country if one exists, e.g. Pinyin system for China, otherwise the systems recognised by the United States Board on Geographical Names have been used.

Names abbreviated on the maps are given in full in the Index. Abbreviations are used for both geographical terms and administrative names in the Index. All abbreviations used in the Index are listed below.

Abbreviations of Geographical Terms

b., **B.**	bay, Bay
c., **C.**	cape, Cape
d.	internal division e.g. county, region, state.
des.	desert
est.	estuary
f.	physical feature e.g. valley, plain, geographic district or region
g., G.	gulf, Gulf
i., I., **is.**, Is.	island, Island, islands, Islands
l., L.	lake, Lake
mtn., Mtn.	mountain, Mountain
mts., Mts.	mountains, Mountains
pen., Pen.	peninsula, Peninsula
Pt.	Point
r.	river
resr., Resr.	reservoir, Reservoir
Sd.	Sound
str., Str.	strait, Strait

Abbreviations of Country / Administrative Names

Afghan.	Afghanistan
Ala.	Alabama
Alas.	Alaska
Alta.	Alberta
Ariz.	Arizona
Ark.	Arkansas
Bangla.	Bangladesh
B.C.	British Columbia
B.S.S.R.	Belorusskaya Sovetskaya Sotsialisticheskaya Respublika
Calif.	California
C.A.R.	Central African Republic
Char. Mar.	Charente Maritime
Colo.	Colorado
Conn.	Connecticut
C.P.	Cape Province
Czech.	Czechoslovakia
D. and G.	Dumfries and Galloway
D.C.	District of Colombia
Del.	Delaware
Derbys.	Derbyshire
Dom. Rep.	Dominican Republic
E. Germany	East Germany
Equat. Guinea	Equatorial Guinea
Fla.	Florida
Ga.	Georgia
Glos.	Gloucestershire
G.M.	Greater Manchester
Guang. Zhuang.	Guangxi Zhuangzu
Himachal P.	Himachal Pradesh
H. Zaïre	Haut Zaïre
Ill.	Illinois
Ind.	Indiana
I.o.M.	Isle of Man
Kans.	Kansas
K. Oriental	Kasai Oriental
Ky.	Kentucky
La.	Lousiana
Liech.	Liechtenstein
Lit. S.S.R.	Litovskaya Sovetskaya Sotsialisticheskaya Respublika
Lux.	Luxembourg
Madhya P.	Madhya Pradesh
Man.	Manitoba
Mass.	Massachusetts
Md.	Maryland
Mich.	Michigan
Minn.	Minnesota
Miss.	Mississippi
Mo.	Missouri
Mont.	Montana
M.S.S.R.	Moldavskaya Sovetskaya Sotsialisticheskaya Respublika
N.B.	New Brunswick
N.C.	North Carolina
N. Dak.	North Dakota
Nebr.	Nebraska
Neth.	Netherlands
Nev.	Nevada
Nfld.	Newfoundland
N.H.	New Hampshire
N.J.	New Jersey
N. Korea	North Korea
N. Mex.	New Mexico
Northum.	Northumberland
N.S.	Nova Scotia
Nschn.	Niedersachen
N.S.W.	New South Wales
N.-Westfalen	Nordrhein-Westfalen
N.W.T.	Northwest Territories
N.Y.	New York State
N. Yorks.	North Yorkshire
O.F.S.	Orange Free State
Okla.	Oklahoma
Ont.	Ontario
Oreg.	Oregon
P.E.I.	Prince Edward Island
Penn.	Pennsylvania
Phil.	Philippines
P.N.G.	Papua New Guinea
Pyr. Or.	Pyrénées Orientales
Qld.	Queensland
Que.	Québec
Raj.	Rājasthān
Rep. of Ire.	Republic of Ireland
Rhein.-Pfalz	Rheinland-Pfalz
R.I.	Rhode Island
R.S.A.	Republic of South Africa
R.S.F.S.R.	Rossiyskaya Sovetskaya Federativnaya Sotsialisticheskaya Respublika
S.A.	South Australia
Sask.	Saskatchewan
S.C.	South Carolina
Sch.-Hol.	Schleswig-Holstein
S. Dak.	South Dakota
Shrops.	Shropshire
S. Korea	South Korea
Sogn og Fj.	Sogn og Fjordane
Somali Rep.	Somali Republic
Strath.	Strathclyde
Switz.	Switzerland
S. Yemen	Southern Yemen
Tas.	Tasmania
Tenn.	Tennessee
Tex.	Texas
Tk. S.S.R.	Turkmenskaya Sovetskaya Sotsialisticheskaya Respublika
Trans.	Transvaal
U.A.E.	United Arab Emirates
U.K.	United Kingdom
Ukr. S.S.R.	Ukrainskaya Sovetskaya Sotsialisticheskaya Respublika
U.S.A.	United States of America
U.S.S.R.	Union of Soviet Socialist Republics
Uttar P.	Uttar Pradesh
Va.	Virginia
Vic.	Victoria
Vt.	Vermont
W.A.	Western Australia
Wash.	Washington
W. Bengal	West Bengal
W. Germany	West Germany
Wisc.	Wisconsin
W. Isles	Western Isles
W. Sahara	Western Sahara
W. Va.	West Virginia
Wyo.	Wyoming
Xin Uygur	Xinjiang Uygur
Yugo.	Yugoslavia

A

Aachen W. Germany 8 50.46N 6.06E
Aalsmeer Neth. 8 52.17N 4.46E
Aalst Belgium 8 50.57N 4.03E
Äänekoski Finland 16 62.36N 25.44E
Aarau Switz. 14 47.24N 8.04E
Aardenburg Neth. 8 51.16N 3.26E
Aare r. Switz. 14 47.37N 8.13E
Aarschot Belgium 8 50.59N 4.50E
Aba China 29 32.55N101.42E
Aba Nigeria 38 5.06N 7.21E
Abā as Su'ūd Saudi Arabia 35 17.28N 44.06E
Ābādān Iran 31 30.21N 48.15E
Abadan, Jazīreh-ye i. Iran 31 30.10N 48.30E
Ābādeh Iran 31 31.10N 52.40E
Abadla Algeria 34 31.01N 2.45W
Abaetetuba Brazil 61 1.45S 48.54W
Abaí Paraguay 62 26.01S 55.57W
Abajo Peak mtn. U.S.A. 54 37.51N109.28W
Abakaliki Nigeria 38 6.17N 8.04E
Abakan U.S.S.R. 21 53.43N 91.25E
Abancay Peru 62 13.35S 72.55W
Abau P.N.G. 44 10.10S148.40E
Abay U.S.S.R. 20 49.40N 72.47E
Abaya, L. Ethiopia 35 6.20N 38.00E
Abayḍ, Al Baḥr al r. Sudan 35 15.45N 32.25E
Abba C.A.R. 38 5.20N 15.11E
Abbeville France 11 50.06N 1.51E
Abbiategrasso Italy 9 45.24N 8.54E
Abbotsbury U.K. 5 50.40N 2.36W
Abdulino U.S.S.R. 18 53.42N 53.40E
Abe, L. Ethiopia 35 11.06N 41.50E
Abéché Chad 35 13.49N 20.49E
Abengourou Ivory Coast 38 6.42N 3.27W
Åbenrå Denmark 17 55.02N 9.26E
Abeokuta Nigeria 38 7.10N 3.26E
Aberayron U.K. 5 52.15N 4.16W
Abercrombie r. Australia 47 33.50S149.10E
Aberdare U.K. 5 51.43N 3.27W
Aberdare Range mts. Kenya 37 0.20S 36.40E
Aberdeen R.S.A. 39 32.28S 24.03E
Aberdeen U.K. 6 57.08N 2.07W
Aberdeen Md. U.S.A. 55 39.30N 76.10W
Aberdeen Ohio U.S.A. 55 38.39N 83.46W
Aberdeen S. Dak. U.S.A. 52 45.28N 98.30W
Aberdeen Wash. U.S.A. 54 46.59N123.50W
Aberdovey U.K. 5 52.33N 4.03W
Aberfeldy U.K. 6 56.37N 3.54W
Abergavenny U.K. 5 51.49N 3.01W
Abersoch U.K. 4 52.50N 4.31W
Aberystwyth U.K. 5 52.25N 4.06W
Abetone Italy 9 44.08N 10.40E
Abez U.S.S.R. 18 66.33N 61.51E
Abhar Iran 31 36.09N 49.13E
Abidjan Ivory Coast 38 5.19N 4.01W
Abilene Tex. U.S.A. 52 32.27N 99.45W
Abingdon U.K. 5 51.40N 1.17W
Abisko Sweden 16 68.20N 18.51E
Abitibi r. Canada 55 51.03N 80.55W
Abitibi, L. Canada 55 48.42N 79.45W
Abnūb Egypt 30 27.16N 31.09E
Åbo see Turku Finland 17
Abomey Benin 38 7.14N 2.00E
Abong Mbang Cameroon 38 3.59N 13.12E
Abou Deïa Chad 34 11.20N 19.20E
Aboyne U.K. 6 57.05N 2.48W
Abrantes Portugal 10 39.28N 8.12W
Abrud Romania 15 46.17N 23.04E
Abruzzi d. Italy 12 42.05N 13.45E
Absaroka Range mts. U.S.A. 54 44.45N109.50W
Abu Dhabi see Abū Ẓaby U.A.E. 31
Abū Dharbah Egypt 32 28.29N 33.20E
Abū Ḥamad Sudan 35 19.32N 33.20E
Abuja Nigeria 38 9.12N 7.11E
Abū Kabīr Egypt 32 30.44N 31.40E
Abū Kamāl Syria 30 34.27N 40.55E
Abū Madd, Ra's c. Saudi Arabia 30 24.50N 37.07E
Abunã Brazil 60 9.41S 65.20W
Abū Qurqāṣ Egypt 32 27.56N 30.50E
Abū Sulṭān Egypt 32 30.25N 32.19E
Abū Sunbul Egypt 30 22.18N 31.40E
Abū Ṭarafah Jordan 32 30.00N 35.56E
Abū Tīj Egypt 30 27.06N 31.17E
Abū Ẓaby U.A.E. 31 24.27N 54.23E
Abū Zanīmah Egypt 32 29.03N 33.06E
Åby Sweden 17 58.40N 16.11E
Acámbaro Mexico 56 20.01N101.42W
Acapulco Mexico 56 16.51N 99.56W
Acará Brazil 61 1.57S 48.11W
Acarigua Venezuela 60 9.35N 69.12W
Acatlán Mexico 56 18.12N 98.02W
Accra Ghana 38 5.33N 0.15W
Accrington U.K. 4 53.46N 2.22W
Aceh d. Indonesia 26 4.00N 97.30E
Acevedo Argentina 63 33.46S 60.27W
Achacachi Bolivia 62 16.03S 68.43W
Achar Uruguay 63 32.25S 56.10W
Acheng China 25 45.32N126.59E
Achill I. Rep. of Ire. 7 53.57N 10.00W
Achinsk U.S.S.R. 20 56.10N 90.10E
Acklin's I. Bahamas 57 22.30N 74.10W
Aconcagua mtn. Argentina 62 32.39S 70.00W
Acqui Italy 9 44.41N 8.28E
Acraman, L. Australia 46 32.02S135.26E
Acre d. Brazil 60 8.50S 71.30W
Açu Brazil 61 5.35S 36.57W
Acuña Argentina 63 29.54S 57.57W
Adair, C. Canada 51 71.24N 71.13W
Adamantina Brazil 59 21.42S 51.04W
Adamaoua, Massif de l' mts. Cameroon / Nigeria 38 7.05N 12.00E
Adamello mtn. Italy 9 46.10N 10.35E
Adaminaby Australia 47 36.04S148.42E
Adamintina Brazil 62 21.42S 51.04W
Adams N.Y. U.S.A. 55 43.49N 76.01W
Adams, Mt. U.S.A. 54 46.12N121.28W
'Adan S. Yemen 35 12.50N 45.00E
Adana Turkey 30 37.00N 35.19E
Adapazari Turkey 30 40.45N 30.23E
Adare, C. Antarctica 64 71.30S171.00E
Adavale Australia 44 25.55S144.36E
Adda r. Italy 9 45.08N 9.55E
Aḍ Ḍab'ah Egypt 30 31.02N 28.26E
Ad Dafīnah Saudi Arabia 30 23.18N 41.58E
Ad Dahnā' des. Saudi Arabia 31 26.00N 47.00E
Ad Dāmir Sudan 35 17.37N 33.59E
Ad Dammām Saudi Arabia 31 26.23N 50.08E
Ad Dawādimī Saudi Arabia 31 24.29N 44.23E
Ad Dawḥah Qatar 31 25.15N 51.34E
Aḍ Ḍiffah f. Africa 30 30.45N 26.00E
Ad Dilam Saudi Arabia 31 23.59N 47.10E
Ad Dimās Syria 32 33.35N 36.05E
Addis Ababa see Ādīs Ābeba Ethiopia 35
Ad Dīwānīyah Iraq 31 31.59N 44.57E
Adelaide Australia 46 34.56S138.36E
Adelaide Pen. Canada 51 68.09N 97.45W
Adelong Australia 47 35.21S148.04E
Aden see 'Adan S. Yemen 35
Aden, G. of Indian Oc. 35 13.00N 50.00E
Adendorp R.S.A. 39 32.18S 24.31E
Adi i. Indonesia 27 4.10S133.10E
Adieu, C. Australia 43 31.59S132.09E
Adige r. Italy 9 45.10N 12.20E
Adilang Uganda 37 2.44N 33.28E
Adin U.S.A. 54 41.12N120.57W
Adirondack Mts. U.S.A. 55 44.00N 74.00W
Ādīs Ābeba Ethiopia 35 9.03N 38.42E
Adiyaman Turkey 30 37.46N 38.15E
Adjud Romania 15 46.04N 27.11E
Admer well Algeria 34 20.23N 5.27E
Admiralty G. Australia 42 14.20S125.50E
Admiralty Is. P.N.G. 27 2.30S147.20E
Admiralty Range mts. Antarctica 64 72.00S164.00E
Adour r. France 11 43.28N 1.35W
Adra Spain 10 36.43N 3.03W
Adrano Italy 12 37.39N 14.49E
Adrar des Iforas mts. Algeria / Mali 34 20.00N 2.30E
Adria Italy 9 45.03N 12.03E
Adrian Mich. U.S.A. 55 41.55N 84.01W
Adriatic Sea Med. Sea 12 42.30N 16.00E
Ādwa Ethiopia 35 14.12N 38.56E
Adzopé Ivory Coast 38 6.07N 3.49W
Adzwa r. U.S.S.R. 18 66.30N 59.30E
Aegean Sea Med. Sea 13 39.00N 25.00E
Afghanistan Asia 28 34.00N 65.30E
'Afif Saudi Arabia 30 23.53N 42.59E
Afikpo Nigeria 38 5.53N 7.55E
Afjord Norway 16 63.57N 10.12E
Afmadu Somali Rep. 37 0.27N 42.05E
Afobaka Surinam 61 5.00N 55.05W
Afognak I. U.S.A. 50 58.15N152.30W
Afonso Cláudio Brazil 59 20.05S 41.06W
Afsluitdijk f. Neth. 8 53.04N 5.11E
'Afula Israel 32 32.36N 35.17E
Afyon Turkey 30 38.46N 30.32E
Agadez Niger 38 17.00N 7.56E
Agadez d. Niger 38 19.25N 11.00E
Agadir Morocco 34 30.26N 9.36W
Agana Guam 27 13.28N144.45E
Agapa U.S.S.R. 21 71.29N 86.16E
Agartala India 29 23.49N 91.15E
Agboville Ivory Coast 38 5.55N 4.15W
Agde France 11 43.19N 3.28E
Agen France 11 44.12N 0.38E
Ageo Japan 23 35.58N139.36E
Agger r. W. Germany 8 50.45N 7.06E
Aghada Rep. of Ire. 7 51.50N 8.13W
Aginskoye U.S.S.R. 21 51.10N114.32E
Agnew Australia 43 28.01S120.30E
Ago Japan 23 34.17N136.48E
Agordo Italy 9 46.17N 12.02E
Āgra India 29 27.09N 78.00E
Agra r. Spain 10 42.12N 1.43W
Agraciada Uruguay 63 33.48S 58.15W
Agreda Spain 10 41.51N 1.55W
Agri r. Italy 13 40.13N 16.45E
Agri Turkey 30 39.44N 43.04E
Agri Daği mtn. Turkey 31 39.45N 44.15E
Agrigento Italy 12 37.19N 13.36E
Agrihan i. Mariana Is. 27 18.44N145.39E
Agropoli Italy 12 40.21N 15.00E
Agryz U.S.S.R. 18 56.30N 53.00E
Aguas Blancas Chile 62 24.13S 69.50W
Aguascalientes Mexico 56 21.51N102.18W
Aguascalientes d. Mexico 56 22.00N102.00W
Agudos Brazil 59 22.27S 49.03W
Agueda r. Spain 10 41.00N 6.56W
Aguelhok Mali 38 19.28N 0.52E
Aguilar de Campóo Spain 10 42.47N 4.15W
Aguilas Spain 10 37.25N 1.35W
Agulhas, C. R.S.A. 39 34.50S 20.00E
Agulhas Negras mtn. Brazil 59 22.20S 44.43W
Ahaggar mts. Algeria 34 24.00N 5.50E
Ahar Iran 31 38.25N 47.07E
Ahaura New Zealand 48 42.21S171.33E
Ahaus W. Germany 8 52.04N 7.01E
Ahklun Mts. U.S.A. 50 59.15N161.00W
Ahlen W. Germany 8 51.47N 7.52E
Ahmadābād India 28 23.03N 72.40E
Ahmadī Iran 31 27.56N 56.42E
Ahmadnagar India 28 19.08N 74.48E
Ahoada Nigeria 38 5.06N 6.39E
Ahr r. W. Germany 8 50.34N 7.16E
Ahram Iran 31 28.52N 51.16E
Aḥsā', Wāḥat al oasis Saudi Arabia 31 25.37N 49.40E
Ähtäri Finland 16 62.34N 24.06E
Åhus Sweden 17 55.55N 14.17E
Ahvāz Iran 31 31.17N 48.44E
Ahvenanmaa d. Finland 17 60.15N 20.00E
Ahvenanmaa is. Finland 17 60.15N 20.00E
Aichi d. Japan 23 35.02N137.15E
Aigle Switz. 9 46.19N 6.58E
Aigues-Mortes France 11 43.34N 4.11E
Ailette r. France 8 49.35N 3.09E
Ailsa Craig i. U.K. 6 55.15N 5.07W
Aim U.S.S.R. 21 58.50N134.15E
Aimorés Brazil 59 19.30S 41.04W
Ain r. France 11 45.47N 5.12E
Ainaži U.S.S.R. 17 57.52N 24.21E
Aïn ben Tili Mauritania 34 26.00N 9.32W
Aïn Sefra Algeria 34 32.45N 0.35W
Aïr mts. Niger 38 18.30N 8.30E
Airdrie U.K. 6 55.52N 3.59W
Aire France 11 43.39N 0.15W
Aire r. France 9 49.19N 4.49E
Aire r. U.K. 4 53.42N 0.54W
Aisne d. France 9 49.30N 3.30E
Aisne r. France 9 49.27N 2.51E
Aitape P.N.G. 27 3.10S142.17E
Aiud Romania 15 46.19N 23.44E
Aix-en-Provence France 11 43.31N 5.27E
Aix-les-Bains France 11 45.42N 5.55E
Aíyina i. Greece 13 37.43N 23.30E
Aíyion Greece 13 38.15N 22.05E
Aizpute U.S.S.R. 17 56.43N 21.38E
Ajaccio France 11 41.55N 8.43E
Ajdābiyā Libya 34 30.48N 20.15E
'Ajlūn Jordan 32 32.20N 35.45E
'Ajmah, Jabal al f. Egypt 32 29.12N 33.58E
'Ajmān U.A.E. 31 25.23N 55.26E
Ajmer India 28 26.29N 74.40E
Akaishi sammyaku mts. Japan 23 35.20N138.10E
Akámas, Akrotírion c. Cyprus 32 35.06N 32.17E
Akashi Japan 23 34.38N134.59E
Akbulak U.S.S.R. 19 51.00N 55.40E
Akelamo Indonesia 27 1.35N129.40E
Akershus d. Norway 17 60.00N 11.10E
Aketi Zaïre 36 2.46N 23.51E
Akhaltsikhe U.S.S.R. 30 41.37N 42.59E
Akhḍar, Al Jabal al mts. Libya 35 32.10N 22.00E
Akhḍar, Al Jabal al mts. Oman 31 23.10N 57.25E
Akhḍar, Wādī r. Egypt 32 28.42N 33.41E
Akhḍar, Wādī al r. Saudi Arabia 32 28.30N 36.48E
Akhelóös Greece 13 38.20N 21.04E
Akhisar Turkey 13 38.54N 27.49E
Akhmīm Egypt 30 26.34N 31.44E
Akhtyrka U.S.S.R. 19 50.19N 34.54E
Akimiski I. Canada 51 53.00N 81.20W
Akita Japan 25 39.44N140.05E
Akjoujt Mauritania 34 19.44N 14.26W
Akkajaure l. Sweden 16 67.40N 17.30E
'Akko Israel 32 32.55N 35.04E
Akkol U.S.S.R. 24 45.04N 75.39E
Aklavik Canada 50 68.12N135.00W
Ako Nigeria 38 10.19N 10.48E
Akobo r. Ethiopia 35 8.30N 33.15E
Akola India 28 20.44N 77.00E
Akordat Ethiopia 35 15.35N 37.55E
Akpatok I. Canada 51 60.30N 68.30W
Akranes Iceland 16 64.19N 22.05W
Akron Ohio U.S.A. 55 41.04N 81.31W
Akrotíri Cyprus 32 34.36N 32.57E
Aksaray Turkey 30 38.22N 34.02E
Aksarka U.S.S.R. 20 66.31N 67.50E
Aksay China 24 39.28N 94.15E
Aksay U.S.S.R. 19 51.24N 52.11E
Akşehir Turkey 30 38.22N 31.24E
Aksu China 24 42.10N 80.00E
Aktag mtn. China 24 36.45N 84.40E
Aktogay U.S.S.R. 24 46.59N 79.42E
Aktyubinsk U.S.S.R. 19 50.16N 57.13E
Akūbū Sudan 36 7.47N 33.01E
Akūbū r. see Akobo r. Sudan 36
Akure Nigeria 38 7.14N 5.08E
Akureyri Iceland 16 65.41N 18.04W
Akuse Ghana 38 6.04N 0.12E
Akxokesay China 24 36.48N 91.06E
Akyab see Sittwe Burma 29
Ål Norway 17 60.38N 8.34E
Alabama d. U.S.A. 53 33.00N 87.00W
Alabama r. U.S.A. 53 31.05N 87.55W
Alādāgh, Kūh-e mts. Iran 31 37.15N 57.30E
Alagoas d. Brazil 61 9.30S 37.00W
Alagoinhas Brazil 61 12.09S 38.21W
Alagón Spain 10 41.46N 1.12W
Alakol, Ozero l. U.S.S.R. 24 46.00N 81.40E
Alakurtti U.S.S.R. 18 67.00N 30.23E
Al 'Alamayn Egypt 30 30.49N 28.57E
Alamagan i. Mariana Is. 27 17.35N145.50E
Al 'Amārah Iraq 31 31.52N 47.50E
Al Āmirīyah Egypt 32 31.01N 29.48E
Alamogordo U.S.A. 52 32.54N105.57W
Alamosa U.S.A. 52 37.28N105.52W
Åland is. see Ahvenanmaa is. Finland 17
Ålands Hav sea Finland 17 60.00N 19.30E
Alanya Turkey 30 36.32N 32.02E
Alapayevsk U.S.S.R. 18 57.55N 61.42E
Al 'Aqabah Jordan 32 29.32N 35.00E
Al 'Aramah f. Saudi Arabia 31 25.30N 46.30E
Alarcón, Embalse de resr. Spain 10 39.36N 2.10W
Al 'Arīsh Egypt 32 31.08N 33.48E
Alaşehir Turkey 13 38.22N 28.29E
Alaska d. U.S.A. 50 65.00N153.00W
Alaska, G. of U.S.A. 50 58.45N145.00W
Alaska Pen. U.S.A. 50 56.00N160.00W
Alaska Range mts. U.S.A. 50 62.10N152.00W
Alassio Italy 9 44.00N 8.10E
Al 'Aṭīqah Lebanon 32 33.42N 35.27E
Al 'Aṭrun Sudan 35 18.11N 26.36E
Alatyr U.S.S.R. 18 54.51N 46.35E
Alausí Ecuador 60 2.00S 78.50W
Alavus Finland 16 62.35N 23.37E
Alawoona Australia 46 34.44S140.33E
Al 'Ayyāṭ Egypt 32 29.37N 31.15E
Alazani r. U.S.S.R. 31 41.06N 46.40E
Alba Italy 9 44.42N 8.02E
Albacete Spain 10 39.00N 1.52W
Al Bad' Saudi Arabia 32 28.29N 35.02E
Al Badārī Egypt 30 26.59N 31.25E
Al Bahnasā Egypt 32 28.32N 30.39E
Alba-lulia Romania 15 46.04N 23.33E
Albania Europe 13 41.00N 20.00E
Albany Australia 43 34.57S117.54E
Albany r. Canada 51 52.10N 82.00W
Albany Ga. U.S.A. 53 31.37N 84.10W
Albany N.Y. U.S.A. 55 42.39N 73.45W
Albany Oreg. U.S.A. 54 44.38N123.06W
Al Baṣrah Iraq 31 30.33N 47.50E
Al Bāṭinah f. Oman 31 24.25N 56.50E
Albatross B. Australia 44 12.45S141.43E
Al Batrūn Lebanon 32 34.16N 35.40E
Al Bawīṭī Egypt 30 28.21N 25.52E
Al Bayḍā' Libya 35 32.50N 21.50E
Albemarle Sd. U.S.A. 53 36.10N 76.00W
Albenga Italy 9 44.03N 8.13E
Alberche r. Spain 10 40.00N 4.45W
Alberga Australia 45 27.12S135.28E
Alberga r. Australia 45 27.12S135.28E
Albert Australia 47 32.21S147.33E
Albert France 8 50.02N 2.38E
Albert, L. Australia 46 35.38S139.17E
Albert, L. Uganda / Zaïre 37 1.45N 31.00E
Alberta d. Canada 50 55.00N115.00W
Alberti Argentina 63 35.01S 60.16W
Albertirsa Hungary 15 47.15N 19.38E
Albert Kanaal canal Belgium 8 51.00N 5.15E
Albert Lea U.S.A. 53 43.38N 93.16W
Albert Nile r. Uganda 37 3.30N 32.00E
Albi France 11 43.56N 2.08E
Albina Surinam 61 5.30N 54.03W
Albino Italy 9 45.46N 9.47E
Albion Mich. U.S.A. 55 42.14N 84.45W
Albion Penn. U.S.A. 55 41.53N 80.22W
Al Bi'r Saudi Arabia 32 28.52N 36.15E
Alborán, Isla de i. Spain 10 35.55N 3.10W
Ålborg Denmark 17 57.03N 9.56E
Ålborg Bugt b. Denmark 17 56.45N 10.30E
Alborz, Reshteh-ye Kūhhā-ye mts. Iran 31 36.00N 52.30E
Albuquerque U.S.A. 52 35.05N106.40W
Al Buraymī U.A.E. 31 24.15N 55.45E
Al Burj Egypt 32 31.35N 30.59E
Alburquerque Spain 10 39.13N 6.59W
Albury Australia 47 36.03S146.53E
Alby Sweden 16 62.30N 15.25E
Alcácer do Sal Portugal 10 38.22N 8.30W
Alcalá de Chisvert Spain 10 40.19N 0.13E
Alcalá de Henares Spain 10 40.28N 3.22W
Alcalá la Real Spain 10 37.28N 3.55W
Alcamo Italy 12 37.59N 12.58E
Alcañiz Spain 10 41.03N 0.09W
Alcántara, Embalse de resr. Spain 10 39.45N 6.25W
Alcaudete Spain 10 37.35N 4.05W
Alcázar de San Juan Spain 10 39.24N 3.12W
Alcira Spain 10 39.10N 0.27W
Alcobaça Portugal 10 39.33N 8.59W
Alcova U.S.A. 54 42.35N106.34W
Alcoy Spain 10 38.42N 0.29W
Alcubierre, Sierra de mts. Spain 10 41.40N 0.20W
Alcudia Spain 10 39.51N 3.09E
Aldan U.S.S.R. 21 58.44N125.22E
Aldan r. U.S.S.R. 21 63.30N130.00E
Aldeburgh U.K. 5 52.09N 1.35E
Alderney i. U.K. 5 49.42N 2.11W
Aldershot U.K. 5 51.15N 0.47W
Aldridge U.K. 5 52.36N 1.55W
Alegre Brazil 59 20.44S 41.30W
Alegrete Brazil 63 29.46S 55.46W
Aleksandrov Gay U.S.S.R. 19 50.08N 48.34E
Aleksandrovsk Sakhalinskiy U.S.S.R. 21 50.55N142.12E
Além Paraíba Brazil 59 21.49S 42.36W
Alençon France 9 48.25N 0.05E
Aleppo see Ḥalab Syria 30
Aléria France 11 42.05N 9.30E
Alès France 11 44.08N 4.05E
Alessandria Italy 9 44.54N 8.37E
Ålesund Norway 16 62.28N 6.11E
Aleutian Range mts. U.S.A. 50 58.00N156.00W
Alexander Archipelago is. U.S.A. 50 56.30N134.30W
Alexander Bay town R.S.A. 39 28.36S 16.26E
Alexander I. Antarctica 64 72.00S 70.00W
Alexandra Australia 47 37.12S145.14E
Alexandra New Zealand 48 45.14S169.26E
Alexandria B.C. Canada 50 52.38N122.27W
Alexandria Ont. Canada 55 45.18N 74.39W
Alexandria see Al Iskandarīyah Egypt 32
Alexandria Romania 15 43.58N 25.20E
Alexandria R.S.A. 39 33.39S 26.24E
Alexandria La. U.S.A. 53 31.19N 92.29W
Alexandria Va. U.S.A. 55 38.48N 77.03W
Alexandrina, L. Australia 46 35.26S139.10E
Alexandroúpolis Greece 13 40.50N 25.53E
Aleysk U.S.S.R. 20 52.32N 82.45E
Al Fant Egypt 32 28.46N 30.53E
Alfaro Spain 10 42.11N 1.45W
Al Fāshir Sudan 35 13.37N 25.22E
Al Fashn Egypt 32 28.49N 30.54E
Al Fāw Iraq 31 29.57N 48.30E
Al Fayyūm Egypt 32 29.19N 30.50E
Alfeld W. Germany 14 51.59N 9.50E
Alfenas Brazil 59 21.28S 45.48W
Alfiós r. Greece 13 37.37N 21.27E
Alfonsine Italy 9 44.30N 12.03E
Alford U.K. 6 57.14N 2.42W
Al Fujayrah U.A.E. 31 25.10N 56.20E
Al Furāt r. Asia 31 31.00N 47.27E
Alga U.S.S.R. 20 49.49N 57.16E
Ålgård Norway 17 58.46N 5.51E
Algeciras Spain 10 36.08N 5.27W
Algemesí Spain 10 39.11N 0.27W
Alger Algeria 34 36.50N 3.00E
Algeria Africa 34 28.00N 2.00E
Al Ghayl Saudi Arabia 31 22.36N 46.19E
Alghero Italy 12 40.33N 8.20E
Al Ghurdaqah Egypt 30 27.14N 33.50E
Algiers see Alger Algeria 34
Algoa B. R.S.A. 39 33.50S 26.00E
Algonquin Prov. Park Canada 55 45.27N 78.26
Algorta Uruguay 63 32.25S 57.23W
Al Ḥajar al Gharbī mts. Oman 31 24.00N 56.30
Al Ḥajar ash Sharqī mts. Oman 31 22.45N 58.45E
Alhama Spain 10 37.51N 1.25W
Al Ḥamād des. Saudi Arabia 30 31.45N 39.00E
Al Ḥamar Saudi Arabia 31 22.26N 46.12E
Alhambra U.S.A. 54 34.06N118.08W
Al Ḥamīdīyah Syria 32 34.43N 35.56E
Al Ḥanākīyah Saudi Arabia 30 24.53N 40.30E
Al Ḥarīq Saudi Arabia 31 23.37N 46.31E
Al Ḥasakah Syria 30 36.29N 40.45E
Al Ḥawāmidīyah Egypt 32 29.54N 31.15E
Al Ḥayz Egypt 30 28.02N 28.39E
Al Ḥijāz f. Saudi Arabia 30 26.00N 37.30E
Al Ḥillah Iraq 31 32.28N 44.29E
Al Ḥillah Saudi Arabia 31 23.30N 46.51E
Al Hirmil Lebanon 32 34.25N 36.23E
Al Ḥudaydah Yemen 35 14.50N 42.58E
Al Hufūf Saudi Arabia 31 25.20N 49.34E
Al Ḥumrah des. U.A.E. 31 22.45N 55.10E
Al Ḥusaynīyah Egypt 32 30.52N 31.55E
Al Ḥuwaymī S. Yemen 35 14.05N 47.44E
Aliābād, Kūh-e mtn. Iran 31 34.09N 50.48E
Aliákmon r. Greece 13 40.30N 22.38E
Alicante Spain 10 38.21N 0.29W
Alice R.S.A. 39 32.47S 26.49E
Alice U.S.A. 52 27.45N 98.06W
Alice Springs town Australia 44 23.42S133.52E
Alīgarh India 29 27.54N 78.04E
Alīgūdarz Iran 31 33.25N 49.38E
'Alījūq, Kūh-e mtn. Iran 31 31.27N 51.43E
Alingsås Sweden 17 57.56N 12.31E
Alīpur Duār India 29 26.29N 89.44E
Aliquippa U.S.A. 55 40.38N 80.16W
Al Iskandarīyah Egypt 32 31.13N 29.55E
Al Ismā'īlīyah Egypt 32 30.36N 32.15E
Aliwal North R.S.A. 39 30.41S 26.41E
Al Jafr Jordan 32 30.16N 36.11E
Al Jāfūrah des. Saudi Arabia 31 24.40N 50.20E
Al Jaghbūb Libya 35 29.42N 24.38E
Al Jahrah Kuwait 31 29.20N 47.41E
Al Jawārah Oman 28 18.55N 57.17E
Al Jawb f. Saudi Arabia 31 23.00N 50.00E
Al Jawf Libya 35 24.09N 23.19E
Al Jawf Saudi Arabia 30 29.49N 39.52E
Al Jazīrah f. Iraq 30 35.00N 41.00E
Al Jazīrah f. Sudan 35 14.30N 33.00E
Al Jifārah Saudi Arabia 31 23.59N 45.11E
Al Jīzah Egypt 32 30.01N 31.12E
Al Jubayl Saudi Arabia 31 27.59N 49.40E
Al Junaynah Sudan 35 13.27N 22.30E
Aljustrel Portugal 10 37.55N 8.10W
Al Karak Jordan 32 31.11N 35.42E
Al Khābūr r. Syria 30 35.07N 40.30E
Al Khābūrah Oman 31 23.58N 57.10E
Al Khalīl Jordan 32 31.32N 35.06E
Al Khamāsīn Saudi Arabia 35 20.29N 44.49E
Al Khānkah Egypt 32 30.12N 31.21E
Al Khārijah Egypt 30 25.26N 30.33E
Al Kharṭūm Sudan 35 15.33N 32.35E
Al Kharṭūm Baḥrī Sudan 35 15.39N 32.34E
Al Khawr Qatar 31 25.39N 51.32E
Al Khirbah as Samrā' Jordan 32 32.11N 36.10
Al Khubar Saudi Arabia 31 26.18N 50.06E
Al Khufayfīyah Saudi Arabia 31 24.55N 44.42E
Al Khunn Saudi Arabia 31 23.18N 49.15E
Al Kidn des. Saudi Arabia 35 22.30N 54.00E
Al Kidn des. Saudi Arabia 31 22.20N 54.20E
Al Kiswah Syria 32 33.21N 36.14E
Alkmaar Neth. 8 52.37N 4.44E
Al Kuntillah Egypt 32 30.00N 34.41E
Al Kūt Iraq 31 32.30N 45.51E
Al Kuwayt Kuwait 31 29.20N 48.00E
Al Labwah Lebanon 32 34.11N 36.21E
Al Lādhiqīyah Syria 32 35.31N 35.47E
Allāhābād India 29 25.57N 81.50E
Allakaket U.S.A. 50 66.30N152.45W
Allanche France 11 45.14N 2.56E
'Allāqī, Wādī al r. Egypt 30 22.55N 33.02E
Allegheny r. U.S.A. 55 40.27N 80.00W
Allegheny Mts. U.S.A. 53 38.30N 80.00W
Allen, Lough Rep. of Ire. 7 54.07N 8.04W
Allentown U.S.A. 55 40.37N 75.30W
Alleppey India 28 9.30N 76.22E
Aller r. W. Germany 14 52.57N 9.11E
Alliance Nebr. U.S.A. 52 42.06N102.52W
Allier r. France 11 46.58N 3.04E
Al Līṭānī r. Lebanon 32 33.22N 35.14E
Alloa U.K. 6 56.07N 3.49W
Allora Australia 45 28.02S151.59E
Allos France 11 44.14N 6.38E
Al Luḥayyah Yemen 35 15.43N 42.42E
Alluitsup-Paa see Sydpröven Greenland 51
Alma Canada 55 48.32N 71.40W
Alma Mich. U.S.A. 55 43.23N 84.40W
Al Ma'ānīyah well Iraq 30 30.44N 43.00E
Alma-Ata U.S.S.R. 24 43.19N 76.55E
Almaden Australia 44 17.20S144.41E
Almadén Spain 10 38.47N 4.50W
Al Madīnah Saudi Arabia 30 24.30N 39.35E
Al Madīnah al Fikrīyah Egypt 32 27.56N 30.49E
Al Mafraq Jordan 32 32.20N 36.12E
Al Maghrah well Egypt 30 30.14N 28.56E
Almagor Israel 32 32.55N 35.36E
Al Maḥallah al Kubrá Egypt 32 30.59N 31.12E
Al Maḥārīq Egypt 30 25.37N 30.39E
Al Maḥmūdīyah Egypt 32 31.10N 30.30E
Al Majma'ah Saudi Arabia 31 25.52N 45.25E
Al Manāmah Bahrain 31 26.12N 50.36E
Almanor U.S.A. 54 40.15N121.08W
Almansa Spain 10 38.52N 1.06W
Al Manshāh Egypt 30 26.28N 31.48E
Al Manṣūrah Egypt 32 31.03N 31.23E

Al Manzil Jordan 32 31.03N 36.01E
Al Manzilah Egypt 32 31.10N 31.56E
Almanzor, Pico de mtn. Spain 10 40.20N 5.22W
Almanzora r. Spain 10 37.16N 1.49W
Al Maţarīyah Egypt 32 31.12N 32.02E
Al Mawşil Iraq 30 36.21N 43.08E
Al Mayādīn Syria 30 35.01N 40.28E
Almazán Spain 10 41.29N 2.31W
Al Mazra'ah Jordan 32 31.16N 35.31E
Almeirim Portugal 10 39.12N 8.37W
Almelo Neth. 8 52.21N 6.40E
Almendralejo Spain 10 38.41N 6.26W
Almería Spain 10 36.50N 2.26W
Älmhult Sweden 17 56.33N 14.08E
Al Midhnab Saudi Arabia 31 25.52N 44.15E
Al Miḩrāḑ des. Saudi Arabia 31 20.00N 52.30E
Al Minyā Egypt 32 28.06N 30.45E
Al Mismīyah Syria 32 33.08N 36.24E
Almonte Spain 10 37.16N 6.31W
Al Mudawwarah Jordan 32 29.20N 36.00E
Al Muglad Sudan 35 11.01N 27.50E
Al Muḩarraq Bahrain 31 26.16N 50.38E
Al Mukallā S. Yemen 35 14.34N 49.09E
Almuñécar Spain 10 36.44N 3.41W
Al Muwayh Saudi Arabia 30 22.41N 41.37E
Alnwick U.K. 4 55.25N 1.41W
Alofi Niue 40 19.03S169.55W
Alónnisos i. Greece 13 39.08N 23.50E
Alor i. Indonesia 27 8.20S124.30E
Alor Setar Malaysia 26 6.06N100.23E
Alozero U.S.S.R. 18 65.02N 31.10E
Alpena U.S.A. 55 45.04N 83.27W
Alpes Maritimes mts. France 11 44.07N 7.08E
Alpha Australia 44 23.39S146.38E
Alphen Neth. 8 52.08N 4.40E
Alpine U.S.A. 52 30.22N103.40W
Alps mts. Europe 11 46.00N 7.30E
Al Qaḑārif Sudan 35 14.02N 35.24E
Al Qafā' des. U.A.E. 28 23.25N 53.50E
Al Qafā' des. U.A.E. 31 23.30N 53.30E
Al Qāhirah Egypt 32 30.03N 31.15E
Al Qā'īyah Saudi Arabia 30 24.18N 43.30E
Al Qā'īyah well Saudi Arabia 31 26.27N 45.35E
Al Qalībah Saudi Arabia 30 28.24N 37.42E
Al Qanāţir al Khayrīyah Egypt 32 30.12N 31.08E
Al Qanţarah Egypt 32 30.52N 32.20E
Al Qaryatayn Syria 32 34.13N 37.13E
Al Qaşr Egypt 30 25.43N 28.54E
Al Qaşşāşīn Egypt 32 30.34N 31.56E
Al Qaţīf Saudi Arabia 31 26.31N 50.00E
Al Qaţrānah Jordan 32 31.15N 36.03E
Al Qaţrūn Libya 34 24.55N 14.38E
Al Qayşūmah Saudi Arabia 31 28.20N 46.07E
Al Qunayţirah Syria 32 33.08N 35.49E
Al Qurnah Iraq 31 31.00N 47.26E
Al Quşaymah Egypt 32 30.40N 34.22E
Al Quşayr Egypt 30 26.06N 34.17E
Al Qūşīyah Egypt 30 27.26N 30.49E
Al Quţayfah Syria 32 33.44N 36.36E
Alroy Downs town Australia 44 19.18S136.04E
Als i. Denmark 17 54.59N 9.55E
Alsace d. France 11 48.25N 7.40E
Alsask Canada 50 51.23N109.59W
Alsasua Spain 10 42.54N 2.10W
Älsborg d. Sweden 17 58.00N 12.20E
Alsfeld W. Germany 14 50.45N 9.16E
Alsten i. Norway 16 65.55N 12.35E
Alston U.K. 6 54.48N 2.26W
Alta Norway 16 70.00N 23.15E
Alta r. Norway 16 69.50N 23.30E
Altafjorden est. Norway 16 70.10N 23.00E
Alta Gracia Argentina 62 31.40S 64.26W
Altagracia de Orituco Venezuela 60 9.54N 66.24W
Altai mts. Mongolia 24 46.30N 93.30E
Altamaha r. U.S.A. 53 31.15N 81.23W
Altamira Brazil 61 3.12S 52.12W
Altamont Oreg. U.S.A. 54 42.12N121.44W
Altamura Italy 13 40.50N 16.32E
Altay China 24 47.48N 88.07E
Altay Mongolia 24 46.20N 97.00E
Altea Spain 10 38.37N 0.03W
Altenburg E. Germany 14 50.59N 12.27E
Altenkirchen W. Germany 8 50.41N 7.40E
Altiboullin, L. Australia 46 29.50S142.50E
Altnaharra U.K. 6 58.16N 4.26W
Alto Araguaia Brazil 61 17.19S 53.10W
Alto Molocue Mozambique 37 15.38S 37.42E
Alton U.K. 5 51.08N 0.59W
Altona Australia 42 27.34S120.00E
Altona W. Germany 14 53.32N 9.56E
Altoona U.S.A. 55 40.30N 78.24W
Altun Shan mts. China 24 38.10N 87.50E
Al Ubayyiḑ Sudan 35 13.11N 30.10E
Al 'Ulá Saudi Arabia 30 26.39N 37.58E
Al' Uqaylah Libya 34 30.15N 19.12E
Al Uqşur Egypt 30 25.41N 32.24E
Al Urduun r. Asia 32 31.47N 35.31E
Al 'Uwaynah well Saudi Arabia 31 26.46N 48.13E
Al 'Uyūn Saudi Arabia 31 26.32N 43.41E
Alva U.S.A. 52 36.48N 98.40W
Alvarado Mexico 56 18.49N 95.46W
Älvdalen Sweden 17 61.14N 14.02E
Alvesta Sweden 17 56.54N 14.33E
Älvho Sweden 17 61.30N 14.46E
Älvkarleby Sweden 17 60.34N 17.27E
Älvsbyn Sweden 16 65.39N 20.59E
Al Wajh Saudi Arabia 30 26.16N 36.28E
Al Wakrah Qatar 31 25.09N 51.36E
Alwar India 28 27.32N 76.35E
Al Yamāmah Saudi Arabia 31 24.11N 47.21E
Alyaty U.S.S.R. 31 39.59N 49.20E
Alytus U.S.S.R. 15 54.24N 24.03E
Alzette r. Lux. 8 49.52N 6.07E
Amadeus, L. Australia 42 24.50S130.45E
Amadjuak Canada 51 64.00N 72.50W
Amadjuak L. Canada 51 65.00N 71.00W
Amagasaki Japan 23 34.43N135.25E
Åmål Sweden 17 59.03N 12.42E
Amaliás Greece 13 37.48N 21.21E
Amami ō shima i. Japan 25 28.20N129.30E
Amamula Zaïre 37 0.17S 27.49E
Amanā, L. Brazil 60 2.35S 64.40W
Amangeldy U.S.S.R. 20 50.12N 65.11E
Amapá Brazil 61 2.00N 50.50W
Amapá d. Brazil 61 2.00N 52.00W
Amarante Brazil 61 6.14S 42.51W
Amareleja Portugal 10 38.12N 7.13W
Amares Portugal 10 41.38N 8.21W
Amarillo U.S.A. 52 35.14N101.50W
Amaro, Monte mtn. Italy 12 42.06N 14.04E
Amasya Turkey 30 40.37N 35.50E
Amazon r. see Amazonas r. Brazil 61
Amazonas d. Brazil 60 4.50S 64.00W
Amazonas r. Brazil 61 2.00S 52.00W
Amazonas, Estuario do Rio f. Brazil 61 0.00 50.30W
Amazon Delta see Amazonas, Estuario do Rio f. Brazil 61
Ambāla India 28 30.19N 76.49E
Ambam Cameroon 38 2.25N 11.16E
Ambarchik U.S.S.R. 21 69.39N162.27E
Ambarnyy U.S.S.R. 18 65.59N 33.53E
Ambato Ecuador 60 1.18S 78.36W
Ambato-Boeni Madagascar 36 16.28S 46.43E
Ambatondrazaka Madagascar 36 17.50S 48.25E
Amberg W. Germany 14 49.27N 11.52E
Ambergris Cay i. Belize 57 18.00N 87.58W
Ambikāpur India 29 23.07N 83.12E
Ambilobe Madagascar 36 13.12S 49.04E
Amble U.K. 4 55.20N 1.34W
Ambleside U.K. 4 54.26N 2.58W
Amboise France 9 47.25N 1.00E
Ambon Indonesia 27 4.50S128.10E
Ambovombe Madagascar 36 25.11S 46.05E
Amboy U.S.A. 54 34.33N115.44W
Ambre, Cap d' c. Madagascar 36 11.57S 49.17E
Ambrières France 9 48.24N 0.38W
Ambriz Angola 36 7.54S 13.12E
Amderma U.S.S.R. 20 69.44N 61.35E
Ameca Mexico 56 20.33N104.02W
Ameland i. Neth. 8 53.28N 5.48E
Americana Brazil 59 22.44S 47.19W
American Falls Resr. U.S.A. 54 43.00N113.00W
American Fork U.S.A. 54 40.23N111.48W
Amersfoort Neth. 8 52.10N 5.23E
Amery Australia 43 31.09S117.05E
Ames U.S.A. 53 42.02N 93.39W
Ameson Canada 55 49.49N 84.34W
Ametinho Angola 39 17.20S 17.20E
Amga U.S.S.R. 21 60.51N131.59E
Amga r. U.S.S.R. 21 62.40N135.20E
Amgu U.S.S.R. 25 45.48N137.36E
Amgun r. U.S.S.R. 21 53.10N139.47E
Amhara Plateau f. Ethiopia 35 10.00N 37.00E
Amiata mtn. Italy 12 42.53N 11.37E
Amiens Australia 47 28.35S151.46E
Amiens France 9 49.54N 2.18E
Åmli Norway 17 58.47N 8.30E
Amlwch U.K. 4 53.24N 4.21W
'Ammān Jordan 32 31.57N 35.56E
Ammanford U.K. 5 51.48N 4.00W
Ammassalik Greenland 51 65.40N 38.00W
Ammókhostos Cyprus 32 35.07N 33.57E
Ammókhostos, Kólpos b. Cyprus 32 35.12N 34.05E
Āmol Iran 31 36.26N 52.24E
Amorgós i. Greece 13 36.50N 25.55E
Amos Canada 55 48.34N 78.07W
Ampala Honduras 57 13.16N 87.39W
Amparo Brazil 59 22.44S 46.44W
Ampezzo Italy 9 46.25N 12.48E
Amphitheatre Australia 46 37.12S143.25E
Ampotaka Madagascar 36 25.03S 44.41E
Amqui Canada 55 48.28N 67.27W
Amrāvati India 28 20.58N 77.50E
Amritsar India 28 31.35N 74.56E
Amstelveen Neth. 8 52.18N 4.51E
Amsterdam Neth. 8 52.22N 4.54E
Amsterdam N.Y. U.S.A. 55 42.57N 74.11W
Am Timan Chad 35 11.02N 20.17E
Amu Darya r. U.S.S.R. 20 43.50N 59.00E
Amundsen G. Canada 50 70.30N122.00W
Amundsen Sea Antarctica 64 72.00S120.00W
Amuntai Indonesia 26 2.24S115.14E
Amur r. U.S.S.R. 21 53.17N140.00E
Amurzet U.S.S.R. 25 47.50N131.05E
Anabar r. U.S.S.R. 21 72.40N113.30E
Ana Branch r. Australia 46 34.08S141.46E
Anaco Venezuela 60 9.27N 64.28W
Anaconda U.S.A. 54 46.08N112.57W
Anadolu f. Turkey 30 38.00N 35.00E
Anadyr U.S.S.R. 21 64.40N177.32E
Anadyr r. U.S.S.R. 21 65.00N176.00E
Anadyrskiy Zaliv g. U.S.S.R. 21 64.30N177.50W
Anáfi i. Greece 13 36.21N 25.50E
Anaheim U.S.A. 54 33.51N117.57W
Analalava Madagascar 36 14.38S 47.45E
Anambas, Kepulauan is. Indonesia 26 3.00N106.10E
Anambra d. Nigeria 38 6.20N 7.25E
Anamur Turkey 30 36.06N 32.49E
Anantapur India 28 14.41N 77.36E
Anápolis Brazil 61 16.19S 48.58W
Anapú r. Brazil 61 1.53S 50.53W
Anār Iran 31 30.54N 55.18E
Anārak Iran 31 33.20N 53.42E
Anatahan i. Mariana Is. 27 16.22N145.38E
Anatolia f. see Anadolu f. Turkey 30
Anatone U.S.A. 54 46.08N117.09W
Añatuya Argentina 62 28.26S 62.48W
Ancenis France 9 47.21N 1.10W
Anchau Nigeria 38 11.00N 8.23E
Anchorage U.S.A. 50 61.10N150.00W
Ancohuma mtn. Bolivia 62 16.05S 68.36W
Ancón Peru 60 11.50S 77.10W
Ancona Italy 12 43.37N 13.33E
Ancuabe Mozambique 37 13.00S 39.50E
Ancud Chile 63 41.05S 73.50W
Ancy-le-Franc France 9 47.46N 4.10E
Anda China 25 46.25N125.20E
Andalsnes Norway 16 62.33N 7.43E
Andalucía d. Spain 10 37.36N 4.30W
Andalusia U.S.A. 53 31.20N 86.30W
Andaman Is. India 29 12.00N 93.00E
Andaman Sea Indian Oc. 29 11.15N 95.30E
Andamooka Australia 46 30.27S137.12E
Andanga U.S.S.R. 18 59.11N 45.44E
Andara Namibia 39 18.04S 21.26E
Andelot France 11 48.15N 5.18E
Andenes Norway 16 69.18N 16.10E
Andenne Belgium 8 50.29N 5.04E
Anderlecht Belgium 8 50.51N 4.18E
Andernach W. Germany 8 50.25N 7.24E
Anderson r. Canada 50 69.45N129.00W
Anderson Ind. U.S.A. 55 40.05N 85.41W
Anderson S.C. U.S.A. 53 34.30N 82.39W
Andes mts. S. America 63 32.40S 70.00W
Andevoranto Madagascar 36 18.57S 49.06E
Andfjorden est. Norway 16 68.55N 16.00E
Andhra Pradesh d. India 29 17.00N 79.00E
Andikíthira i. Greece 13 35.52N 23.18E
Andizhan U.S.S.R. 24 40.48N 72.23E
Andorra town Andorra 11 42.30N 1.31E
Andorra Europe 11 42.30N 1.32E
Andover U.K. 5 51.13N 1.29W
Andöy i. Norway 16 69.05N 15.40E
Andreyevo-Ivanovka U.S.S.R. 15 47.28N 30.29E
Andria Italy 12 41.13N 16.18E
Andropov U.S.S.R. 18 58.01N 38.52E
Ándros Greece 13 37.50N 24.57E
Ándros i. Greece 13 37.50N 24.50E
Andros I. Bahamas 57 24.30N 78.00W
Andros Town Bahamas 57 24.43N 77.47W
Andrushevka U.S.S.R. 15 50.00N 28.59E
Andújar Spain 10 38.02N 4.03W
Anefis I-n-Darane Mali 38 17.57N 0.35E
Anegada i. B.V.Is. 57 18.46N 64.24W
Anécho Togo 38 6.17N 1.40E
Añelo Argentina 63 38.20S 68.45W
Aneto, Pico de mtn. Spain 10 42.40N 0.19E
Aney Niger 38 19.24N 12.56E
Angara r. U.S.S.R. 21 58.00N 93.00E
Angarsk U.S.S.R. 21 52.31N103.55E
Angaston Australia 46 34.30S139.03E
Angatuba Brazil 59 23.27S 48.25W
Ånge Sweden 16 62.31N 15.40E
Ángel de la Guarda, Isla i. Mexico 56 29.20N113.25W
Angel Falls f. Venezuela 60 5.55N 62.30W
Ängelholm Sweden 17 56.15N 12.50E
Angels Camp U.S.A. 54 38.04N120.32W
Ångerman r. Sweden 16 63.00N 17.43E
Angermünde E. Germany 14 53.01N 14.00E
Angers France 9 47.29N 0.32W
Angerville France 9 48.19N 2.00E
Ångesån r. Sweden 16 66.22N 22.58E
Angkor ruins Kampuchea 26 13.26N103.50E
Angledool Australia 47 29.06S147.57E
Anglesey i. U.K. 4 53.16N 4.25W
Angoche Mozambique 37 16.10S 39.57E
Angol Chile 63 37.48S 72.43W
Angola Africa 36 12.00S 18.00E
Angola Ind. U.S.A. 55 41.38N 85.01W
Angola N.Y. U.S.A. 55 42.39N 79.02W
Angoram P.N.G. 27 4.04S144.04E
Angoulême France 11 45.40N 0.10E
Angra dos Reis Brazil 59 22.59S 44.17W
Anguilla i. Leeward Is. 57 18.14N 63.05W
Angumu Zaïre 37 0.10S 27.38E
Anholt i. Denmark 17 56.42N 11.34E
Anholt W. Germany 8 51.51N 6.26E
Anhui d. China 25 31.30N 116.45E
Aniak U.S.A. 50 61.32N159.40W
Anina Romania 15 45.05N 21.51E
Anjō Japan 23 34.57N137.05E
Anjouan i. Comoros 37 12.12S 44.28E
Anju N. Korea 25 39.36N125.42E
Anka Nigeria 38 12.06N 5.56E
Ankara Turkey 30 39.55N 32.50E
Anklam E. Germany 14 53.51N 13.41E
Ānkʼober Ethiopia 35 9.32N 39.43E
Ankpa Nigeria 38 7.26N 7.38E
Annaba Algeria 34 36.55N 7.47E
An Nabk Syria 32 34.02N 36.43E
Anna Creek town Australia 46 28.50S136.07E
An Nafūd des. Saudi Arabia 30 28.40N 41.30E
An Najaf Iraq 31 31.59N 44.19E
An Nakhl Egypt 32 29.55N 33.45E
Annam Highlands see Annamitique, Chaîne mts. Laos / Vietnam 26
Annamitique, Chaîne mts. Laos / Vietnam 26 17.40N105.30E
Annan U.K. 6 54.59N 3.16W
Annan r. U.K. 6 54.58N 3.16W
Annandale Australia 44 21.57S148.18E
Annandale f. U.K. 6 55.12N 3.25W
Anna Plains Australia 42 19.18S121.34E
Annapolis U.S.A. 55 38.59N 76.30W
Annapurna mtn. Nepal 29 28.34N 83.50E
An Naqīrah well Saudi Arabia 31 27.53N 48.15E
Ann Arbor U.S.A. 55 42.18N 83.43W
An Nāşirīyah Iraq 31 31.04N 46.16E
Annecy France 11 45.54N 6.07E
Anniston U.S.A. 53 33.38N 85.50W
Annonay France 11 45.15N 4.40E
Annuello Australia 46 34.52S142.54E
An Nuhūd Sudan 35 12.41N 28.28E
Anoka U.S.A. 53 45.11N 93.20W
Anqing China 25 30.20N116.50E
Ansbach W. Germany 14 49.18N 10.36E
Anshan China 25 41.05N122.58E
Anshun China 29 26.02N105.57E
Anson B. Australia 42 13.10S130.00E
Ansongo Mali 38 15.40N 0.30E
Anstruther U.K. 6 56.14N 2.42W
Ansudu Indonesia 27 2.11S139.22E
Antakya Turkey 30 36.12N 36.10E
Antalya Turkey 30 36.53N 30.42E
Antalya Körfezi g. Turkey 30 36.38N 31.00E
Antananarivo Madagascar 36 18.55S 47.31E
Antarctica 64
Antas Brazil 61 10.20S 38.20W
Antequera Spain 10 37.01N 4.34W
Antibes France 11 43.35N 7.07E
Anticosti, Île d' i. Canada 51 49.20N 63.00W
Antifer, Cap d' c. France 9 49.41N 0.10E
Antigua Guatemala 56 14.33N 90.42W
Antigua i. Leeward Is. 57 17.09N 61.49W
Anti-Lebanon mts. see Sharqī, Al Jabal ash mts. Lebanon 32
Antofagasta Chile 62 23.39S 70.24W
Antônio Bezerra Brazil 61 3.44S 38.35W
Antônio Carlos Brazil 59 21.18S 43.48W
Antrain France 9 48.28N 1.30W
Antrim U.K. 7 54.43N 6.14W
Antrim d. U.K. 7 54.58N 6.20W
Antrim, Mts. of U.K. 7 55.00N 6.10W
Antsiranana Madagascar 36 12.16S 49.17E
Anttis Sweden 16 67.16N 22.52E
Antwerpen Belgium 8 51.13N 4.25E
Antwerpen d. Belgium 8 51.16N 4.45E
Anvik U.S.A. 50 62.38N160.20W
Anxi Gansu China 24 40.32N 95.57E
Anxious B. Australia 46 33.25S134.35E
Anyama Ivory Coast 38 5.30N 4.03W
Anyang China 25 36.04N114.20E
Anzhero-Sudzhensk U.S.S.R. 20 56.10N 86.10E
Anzio Italy 12 41.27N 12.37E
Aohan Qi China 25 42.23N119.59E
Aomori Japan 25 40.50N140.43E
Aosta Italy 9 45.43N 7.19E
Apalachee B. U.S.A. 53 29.30N 84.00W
Apaporis r. Colombia 60 1.40S 69.20W
Aparri Phil. 27 18.22N121.40E
Apatin Yugo. 13 45.40N 18.59E
Apatity U.S.S.R. 18 67.32N 33.21E
Apeldoorn Neth. 8 52.13N 5.57E
Apia W. Samoa 40 13.48S171.45W
Apizaco Mexico 56 19.25N 98.09W
Apollo Bay town Australia 46 38.45S143.40E
Apostle Is. U.S.A. 53 47.00N 90.30W
Apóstoles Argentina 62 27.55S 55.45W
Apostólou Andréa, Akrotírion c. Cyprus 32 35.40N 34.35E
Apoteri Guyana 60 4.02N 58.32W
Appalachian Mts. U.S.A. 53 39.30N 78.00W
Appennino mts. Italy 12 42.00N 13.30E
Appennino Ligure mts. Italy 9 44.30N 9.00E
Appennino Tosco-Emiliano mts. Italy 9 44.05N 11.00E
Appiano Italy 9 46.28N 11.15E
Appingedam Neth. 8 53.18N 6.52E
Appleby U.K. 4 54.35N 2.29W
Appleton U.S.A. 53 44.17N 88.24W
Apsheronsk U.S.S.R. 19 44.26N 39.45E
Apsheronskiy Poluostrov pen. U.S.S.R. 31 40.28N 50.00E
Apsley Australia 46 36.58S141.08E
Apsley Canada 55 44.45N 78.06W
Apucarana Brazil 59 23.34S 51.28W
Apure r. Venezuela 60 7.40N 66.30W
Apurimac r. Peru 60 10.43S 73.55W
Aqaba, G. of Asia 32 28.45N 34.45E
Aqabat al Ḩijāzīyah Jordan 32 29.40N 35.55E
'Aqdā Iran 31 32.25N 33.38E
Aqqikkol Hu l. China 24 35.44N 81.34E
Aquidauana Brazil 62 20.27S 55.45W
Aquila Mexico 56 18.30N103.50W
Aquitaine d. France 11 44.40N 0.00
'Arab, Baḩr al r. Sudan 35 9.02N 29.28E
Arabādād Iran 31 33.02N 57.41E
'Arabah, Wādī r. Egypt 32 29.07N 32.40E
Arabian Sea Asia 28 16.00N 65.00E
Araç Turkey 30 41.14N 33.20E
Aracaju Brazil 61 10.54S 37.07W
Aracanguy, Montañas de mts. Paraguay 62 24.00S 55.50W
Aracati Brazil 61 4.32S 37.45W
Araçatuba Brazil 59 21.12S 50.24W
Arad Romania 15 46.12N 21.19E
Arafura Sea Austa. 44 9.00S133.00E
Aragarças Brazil 61 15.55S 52.12W
Aragats mtn. U.S.S.R. 31 40.32N 44.11E
Aragón d. Spain 10 41.25N 1.00W
Aragón r. Spain 10 42.20N 1.45W
Araguacema Brazil 61 8.50S 49.34W
Araguaia r. Brazil 61 5.20S 48.30W
Araguari Brazil 59 18.38S 48.13W
Araguari r. Brazil 61 1.15N 50.05W
Arāk Iran 31 34.06N 49.44E
Arakan Yoma mts. Burma 29 20.00N 94.00E
Araks r. U.S.S.R. 31 40.00N 48.28E
Aral Sea see Aralskoye More sea U.S.S.R. 20
Aralsk U.S.S.R. 20 46.56N 61.43E
Aralskoye More sea U.S.S.R. 20 45.00N 60.00E
Aralsor, Ozero l. U.S.S.R. 19 49.00N 48.40E
Aramac Australia 44 22.59S145.14E
Aramia r. P.N.G. 27 8.00S143.20E
Aranda de Duero Spain 10 41.40N 3.41W
Aran I. Rep. of Ire. 7 53.07N 9.38W
Aran Is. Rep. of Ire. 7 53.07N 9.38W
Aranjuez Spain 10 40.02N 3.37W
Aranos Namibia 39 24.09S 19.09E
Araouane Mali 38 18.53N 3.31W
Arapey Uruguay 63 30.58S 57.30W
Arapey Grande r. Uruguay 63 30.55S 57.49W
Arapiraca Brazil 61 9.45S 36.40W
Arapkir Turkey 30 39.03N 38.29E
'Ar'ar, Wādī r. Iraq 30 32.00N 42.30E
Araraquara Brazil 59 21.46S 48.08W
Araras Brazil 59 22.20S 47.23W
Ararat Australia 46 37.20S143.00E
Ararat mtn. see Ağri Daği mtn. Turkey 31
Aras r. see Araks r. Turkey 30
Arauca Colombia 60 7.04N 70.41W
Arauca r. Venezuela 60 7.05N 70.45W
Araure Venezuela 60 9.36N 69.15W
Araxá Brazil 59 19.37S 46.50W
Araxes r. Iran see Araks r. Iran 31
Arba Minch Ethiopia 35 6.02N 37.40E
Arbatax Italy 12 39.56N 9.41E
Arboga Sweden 17 59.24N 15.50E
Arbroath U.K. 6 56.34N 2.35W
Arcachon France 11 44.40N 1.11W
Arcata U.S.A. 54 40.52N124.05W
Archer r. Australia 44 13.28S141.41E
Archers Post Kenya 37 0.42N 37.40E
Arcis-sur-Aube France 9 48.32N 4.08E
Arckaringa r. Australia 46 27.56S134.45E
Arco Italy 9 45.55N 10.53E
Arco U.S.A. 54 43.38N113.18W
Arcoona Australia 46 31.06S137.19E
Arcoordaby Australia 46 31.10S135.00E
Arcos Brazil 59 20.12S 45.30W
Arcos Spain 10 36.45N 5.45W
Arcoverde Brazil 61 8.23S 37.00W
Arctic Bay town Canada 51 73.05N 85.20W
Arctic Ocean 64
Arctic Red r. Canada 50 67.26N133.48W
Arctic Red River town Canada 50 67.27N133.46W
Arda r. Greece 13 41.39N 26.30E
Ardabīl Iran 31 38.15N 48.18E
Ardahan Turkey 30 41.08N 42.41E
Årdalstangen Norway 17 61.14N 7.43E
Ardara Rep. of Ire. 7 54.46N 8.25W
Arḑ aş Şawwān f. Jordan 32 30.45N 37.15E
Ardèche r. France 11 44.31N 4.40E
Ardennes mts. Belgium 8 50.10N 5.30E
Ardennes d. France 9 49.40N 4.40E
Ardennes, Canal des France 9 49.26N 4.02E
Ardestān Iran 31 33.22N 52.25E
Ardfert Rep. of Ire. 7 52.20N 9.48W
Ardila r. Portugal 10 38.10N 7.30W
Ardlethan Australia 47 34.20S146.53E
Ardmore Rep. of Ire. 7 51.58N 7.43W
Ardmore Okla. U.S.A. 53 34.11N 97.08W
Ardnamurchan, Pt. of U.K. 6 56.44N 6.14W
Ardrossan Australia 46 34.25S137.55E
Ardrossan U.K. 6 55.38N 4.49W
Ards Pen. U.K. 7 54.30N 5.30W
Åre Sweden 16 63.25N 13.05E
Arecibo Puerto Rico 57 18.29N 66.44W
Areia Branca Brazil 61 4.56S 37.07W
Arena, Pt. U.S.A. 52 38.58N123.44W
Arendal Norway 17 58.27N 8.48E
Arequipa Peru 60 16.25S 71.32W
Arès France 11 44.47N 1.08W
Arévalo Spain 10 41.03N 4.43W
Arezzo Italy 12 43.27N 11.52E
Arfak mtn. Indonesia 27 1.30S133.50E
Arganda Spain 10 40.19N 3.26W
Argelès-sur-Mer France 11 42.33N 3.01E
Argens r. France 11 43.10N 6.45E
Argenta Italy 9 44.37N 11.50E
Argentan France 9 48.45N 0.01W
Argentera Italy 9 44.24N 6.57E
Argentera mtn. Italy 9 44.10N 7.18E
Argenteuil France 9 48.57N 2.15E
Argentina S. America 63 36.00S 63.00W
Argentino, L. Argentina 63 50.15S 72.25W
Argenton France 11 46.36N 1.30E
Argentré France 9 48.05N 0.39W
Argentré du Plessis France 9 48.03N 1.08W
Argeş r. Romania 13 44.13N 26.22E
Árgos Greece 13 37.37N 22.45E
Argostólion Greece 13 38.10N 20.30E
Arguello, Pt. U.S.A. 54 34.35N120.39W
Argun r. U.S.S.R. 25 53.30N121.48E
Argungu Nigeria 38 12.45N 4.35E
Århus Denmark 17 56.09N 10.13E
Ariah Park town Australia 47 34.20S147.10E
Ariano Italy 12 41.04N 15.00E
Ariano nel Polesine Italy 9 44.56N 12.07E
Aribinda Burkina Faso 38 14.17N 0.52W
Arica Chile 62 18.29S 70.20W
Arica Colombia 60 2.07S 71.46W
Arid, C. Australia 43 33.58S123.05E
Arieş r. Romania 15 46.26N 23.59E
Arīḩā Al Quds Jordan 32 31.51N 35.27E
Arima Trinidad 60 10.38N 61.17W
Arinos r. Brazil 61 10.20S 57.35W
Aripuanã Brazil 60 9.10S 60.38W
Aripuanã r. Brazil 60 5.05S 60.30W
Ariquemes Brazil 60 9.56S 63.04W
Aris Namibia 39 22.48S 17.10E
Arisaig U.K. 6 56.55N 5.51W
'Arîsh, Wâdi al r. Egypt 32 31.09N 33.49E
Ariza Spain 10 41.19N 2.03W
Arizona d. U.S.A. 52 34.00N112.00W
Årjäng Sweden 17 59.23N 12.08E
Arjeplog Sweden 16 66.00N 17.58E
Arjona Colombia 60 10.14N 75.22W
Arkaig, Loch U.K. 6 56.58N 5.08W
Arkansas d. U.S.A. 53 35.00N 92.00W
Arkansas r. U.S.A. 53 33.50N 91.00W
Arkansas City U.S.A. 53 37.03N 97.02W
Arkhangel'sk U.S.S.R. 18 64.32N 41.10E
Árki i. Greece 13 37.22N 26.45E
Arklow Rep. of Ire. 7 52.47N 6.10W
Arkville U.S.A. 55 42.09N 74.37W
Arlberg Pass Austria 14 47.00N 10.05E
Arles France 11 43.41N 4.38E
Arlington Oreg. U.S.A. 54 45.16N120.13W
Arlington Va. U.S.A. 55 38.52N 77.05W
Arlon Belgium 8 49.41N 5.49E
Armadale Australia 43 32.10S115.57E
Armagh U.K. 7 54.21N 6.41W
Armagh d. U.K. 7 54.16N 6.35W
Armançon r. France 9 47.57N 3.30E
Armavir U.S.S.R. 19 44.59N 41.10E
Armenia Colombia 60 4.32N 75.40W
Armeniş Romania 15 45.12N 22.19E
Armentières France 8 50.41N 2.53E

Armidale Australia **47** 30.32S151.40E
Armyanskaya S.S.R. *d.* U.S.S.R. **31** 40.00N 45.00E
Arnaud *r.* Canada **51** 60.00N 69.45W
Årnes Norway **17** 60.09N 11.28E
Arnhem Neth. **8** 52.00N 5.55E
Arnhem, C. Australia **44** 12.10S137.00E
Arnhem B. Australia **44** 12.20S136.12E
Arnhem Land *f.* Australia **44** 13.10S134.30E
Arno *r.* Italy **12** 43.43N 10.17E
Arno Bay *town* Australia **46** 33.54S136.34E
Arnprior Canada **55** 45.26N 76.21W
Arnsberg W. Germany **8** 51.24N 8.03E
Arona Italy **9** 45.46N 8.34E
Arpajon France **9** 48.35N 2.15E
Arra Ivory Coast **38** 6.42N 3.57W
Ar Rahad Sudan **35** 12.42N 30.33E
Ar Ramādi Iraq **30** 33.27N 43.19E
Ar Ramthā Jordan **32** 32.34N 36.00E
Arran *i.* U.K. **6** 55.35N 5.14W
Ar Raqqah Syria **30** 35.57N 39.03E
Arras France **8** 50.17N 2.46E
Ar Rass Saudi Arabia **30** 25.54N 43.30E
Ar Rastān Syria **32** 34.55N 36.44E
Arrecife Canary Is. **34** 28.57N 13.32W
Arrecifes Argentina **63** 34.05S 60.05W
Ar Riyāḍ Saudi Arabia **31** 24.39N 46.44E
Arrochar U.K. **6** 56.12N 4.44W
Arromanches France **9** 49.20N 0.38W
Arrow, Lough Rep.of Ire. **7** 54.03N 8.20W
Arrowsmith, Pt. Australia **44** 13.18S136.24E
Arrowtown New Zealand **48** 44.56S168.50E
Arroyo Feliciano *r.* Argentina **63** 31.06S 59.53W
Arroyo Villimanca *r.* Argentina **63** 35.36S 59.05W
Ar Rub' al Khālī *des.* Saudi Arabia **28** 20.20N 52.30E
Ar Rubayqī Egypt **32** 30.10N 31.46E
Ar Rumaythah Iraq **31** 31.32N 45.12E
Ar Ruṣayriṣ Sudan **35** 11.52N 34.23E
Ar Ruṭbah Iraq **30** 33.03N 40.18E
Ar Ruwayḍah Saudi Arabia **31** 23.46N 44.46E
Ársos Cyprus **32** 34.50N 32.46E
Árta Greece **13** 39.10N 20.57E
Artemovsk U.S.S.R. **19** 48.35N 38.00E
Artenay France **9** 48.05N 1.53E
Artesia U.S.A. **52** 32.51N104.24W
Arthabaska Canada **55** 46.03N 71.55W
Arthur's Pass New Zealand **48** 42.50S171.45E
Artigas Uruguay **63** 30.24S 56.28W
Artillery L. Canada **50** 63.09N107.52W
Artois *f.* France **8** 50.16N 2.50E
Artux China **24** 39.40N 75.49E
Artvin Turkey **30** 41.12N 41.48E
Aru, Kepulauan *is.* Indonesia **27** 6.00S134.30E
Arua Uganda **37** 3.02N 30.56E
Aruanã Brazil **61** 14.54S 51.05W
Aruba *i.* Neth. Ant. **57** 12.30N 70.00W
Arunachal Pradesh *d.* India **29** 28.40N 94.60E
Arusha Tanzania **37** 3.21S 36.40E
Arusha *d.* Tanzania **37** 4.00S 37.00E
Arvada Wyo. U.S.A. **54** 44.39N105.05W
Arvagh Rep. of Ire. **7** 53.56N 7.35W
Arvidsjaur Sweden **16** 65.35N 19.07E
Arvika Sweden **17** 59.39N 12.36E
Arzamas U.S.S.R. **18** 55.24N 43.48E
Arzgir U.S.S.R. **19** 45.24N 44.04E
Arzignano Italy **9** 45.31N 11.20E
Asaba Nigeria **38** 6.12N 6.44E
Asahi dake *mtn.* Japan **25** 43.42N142.54E
Asahikawa Japan **25** 43.50N142.20E
Asansol India **29** 23.40N 87.00E
Åsarna Sweden **16** 62.40N 14.20E
Asbestos Canada **55** 45.46N 71.56W
Asbury Park U.S.A. **55** 40.14N 74.00W
Aschaffenburg W. Germany **14** 49.58N 9.10E
Aschendorf W. Germany **8** 53.03N 7.20E
Aschersleben E. Germany **14** 51.46N 11.28E
Ascoli Piceno Italy **12** 42.52N 13.36E
Ascona Switz. **9** 46.09N 8.46E
Aseb Ethiopia **35** 13.01N 42.47E
Åseda Sweden **17** 57.10N 15.20E
Åsele Sweden **16** 64.10N 17.20E
Åsenbruk Sweden **17** 58.54N 12.40E
Asenovgrad Bulgaria **13** 42.00N 24.53E
Åseral Norway **17** 58.37N 7.25E
Asfeld France **9** 49.27N 4.05E
Asha Nigeria **38** 7.07N 3.43E
Ashanti *d.* Ghana **38** 6.30N 1.30W
Ashbourne Rep. of Ire. **7** 53.31N 6.25W
Ashburton *r.* Australia **42** 21.15S115.00E
Ashburton New Zealand **48** 43.54S171.46E
Ashby de la Zouch U.K. **5** 52.45N 1.29W
Ashcroft Canada **50** 50.43N121.17W
Ashdod Israel **32** 31.48N 34.38E
Asheville U.S.A. **53** 35.35N 82.35W
Ashford Kent U.K. **5** 51.08N 0.53E
Ash Fork U.S.A. **54** 35.13N112.29W
Ashington U.K. **4** 55.11N 1.34W
Ashiya Japan **23** 34.43N135.17E
Ashkhabad U.S.S.R. **31** 37.58N 58.24E
Ashland Ky. U.S.A. **55** 38.28N 82.40W
Ashland Oreg. U.S.A. **54** 42.12N122.42W
Ashland Wisc. U.S.A. **53** 46.34N 90.45W
Ashley Australia **47** 29.19S149.52E
Ashley Snow I. Antarctica **64** 72.30S 77.00W
Ashmūn Egypt **32** 30.18N 30.59E
Ashqelon Israel **32** 31.40N 34.35E
Ash Shallūfah Egypt **32** 30.07N 32.34E
Ash Shāmah *des.* Saudi Arabia **30** 31.20N 38.00E
Ash Shāmīyah *des.* Iraq **31** 30.30N 45.30E
Ash Shāriqah U.A.E. **31** 25.20N 55.26E
Ash Sharmah Saudi Arabia **32** 28.01N 35.14E
Ash Shawbak Jordan **32** 30.33N 35.35E
Ash Shaykh Faḍl Egypt **32** 28.29N 30.50E
Ash Shaykh 'Ibādah Egypt **32** 27.48N 30.52E
Ash Shaykh Miskīn Syria **32** 32.49N 36.09E
Ash Shiḥr S. Yemen **35** 14.45N 49.36E
Ash Shu'aybah Iraq **31** 30.30N 47.40E
Ash Shu'aybah Saudi Arabia **30** 27.53N 42.43E
Ash Shumlūl Saudi Arabia **31** 26.29N 47.20E
Ashtabula U.S.A. **55** 41.53N 80.47W
Ashton R.S.A. **39** 33.49S 20.04E
Ashton U.S.A. **54** 44.04N111.27W
'Āṣī *r.* Lebanon **32** 34.37N 36.30E
Asiago Italy **9** 45.52N 11.30E
Asilah Morocco **34** 35.32N 6.00W
Asinara *i.* Italy **12** 41.04N 8.18E
Asinara, Golfo dell' *g.* Italy **12** 41.00N 8.32E
'Asīr *f.* Saudi Arabia **35** 19.00N 42.00E
Asir, Ras *c.* Somali Rep. **35** 12.00N 51.30E
Askeaton Rep. of Ire. **7** 52.36N 9.00W
Askersund Sweden **17** 58.53N 14.54E
Askim Norway **17** 59.35N 11.10E
Askvoll Norway **17** 61.21N 5.04E
Āsmera Ethiopia **35** 15.20N 38.58E
Åsnen *l.* Sweden **17** 56.38N 14.42E
Asola Italy **9** 45.13N 10.24E
Asosa Ethiopia **35** 10.03N 34.32E
Aspen U.S.A. **54** 39.11N106.49W
Aspiring, Mt. New Zealand **48** 44.20S168.45E
As Sadd al 'Ālī *dam* Egypt **30** 23.59N 32.54E
Aş Şaff Egypt **32** 29.34N 31.17E
As Saffānīyah Saudi Arabia **31** 28.00N 48.48E
Aş Şa'īd *f.* Egypt **30** 25.30N 32.00E
Aş Şāliḥīyah Egypt **32** 30.47N 31.59E
As Sallūm Egypt **30** 31.31N 25.09E
As Salṭ Jordan **32** 32.03N 35.44E
As Salwa Saudi Arabia **31** 24.44N 50.50E
Assam *d.* India **29** 26.30N 93.00E
As Samāwah Iraq **31** 31.18N 45.18E
Aş Şarafand Lebanon **32** 33.27N 35.18E
As Sarīrīyah Egypt **32** 28.20N 30.45E
Assebroek Belgium **8** 51.11N 3.16E
Assen Neth. **8** 53.00N 6.34E
As Sinbillāwayn Egypt **32** 30.53N 31.27E
Assiniboia Canada **50** 49.38N105.59W
Assinica Prov. Park Canada **55** 50.24N 75.00W
Assis Brazil **59** 22.37S 50.25W
As Sudd *f.* Sudan **35** 7.50N 30.00E
As Sulaymānīyah Iraq **31** 35.32N 45.27E
As Sulaymānīyah Saudi Arabia **31** 24.10N 47.20E
Aş Şummān *f.* Saudi Arabia **31** 27.00N 47.00E
As Suwaydā' Syria **32** 32.43N 36.33E
As Suways Egypt **32** 29.59N 32.33E
Asti Italy **9** 44.54N 8.13E
Astipálaia *i.* Greece **13** 36.35N 26.25E
Astorga Spain **10** 42.30N 6.02W
Astoria U.S.A. **54** 46.11N123.50W
Åstorp Sweden **17** 56.08N 12.57E
Astrakhan U.S.S.R. **19** 46.22N 48.00E
Åsträsk Sweden **16** 64.38N 20.00E
Asturias *d.* Spain **10** 43.20N 6.00W
Asuncion *i.* Mariana Is. **27** 19.34N145.24E
Asunción Paraguay **59** 25.15S 57.40W
Aswān Egypt **30** 24.05N 32.56E
Aswan High Dam *see* As Sadd al 'Ālī Egypt **30**
Asyūṭ Egypt **30** 27.14N 31.07E
Atacama, Desierto *des.* S. America **62** 20.00S 69.00W
Atacama, Salar de *f.* Chile **62** 23.30S 68.46W
Atacama Desert *see* Atacama, Desierto *des.* S. America **62**
Atakpamé Togo **38** 7.34N 1.14E
Atami Japan **23** 35.05N139.04E
Atapupu Indonesia **27** 9.00S124.51E
Atar Mauritania **34** 20.32N 13.08W
Atara U.S.S.R. **21** 63.10N129.10E
Atasu U.S.S.R. **20** 48.42N 71.38E
'Aṭbarah Sudan **35** 17.42N 34.00E
'Aṭbarah *r.* Sudan **35** 17.47N 34.00E
Atchafalaya B. U.S.A. **53** 29.30N 92.00W
Ath Belgium **8** 50.38N 3.45E
Athabasca Canada **50** 54.44N113.15W
Athabasca *r.* Canada **50** 58.30N111.00W
Athabasca, L. Canada **50** 59.30N109.00W
Athea Rep. of Ire. **7** 52.28N 9.19W
Athenry Rep. of Ire. **7** 53.18N 8.45W
Athens *see* Athinai Greece **13**
Athens Ga. U.S.A. **53** 33.57N 83.24W
Athinai Greece **13** 37.59N 23.42E
Athlone Rep. of Ire. **7** 53.26N 7.57W
Atholl, Forest of U.K. **6** 56.50N 3.55W
Áthos *mtn.* Greece **13** 40.09N 24.19E
Ath Thamad Egypt **32** 29.40N 34.18E
Ati Chad **34** 13.11N 18.20E
Atico Peru **60** 16.12S 73.37W
Atkarsk U.S.S.R. **19** 51.55N 45.00E
Atlanta Ga. U.S.A. **53** 33.45N 84.23W
Atlantic City U.S.A. **55** 39.22N 74.26W
Atlas Saharien *mts.* Algeria **34** 34.20N 2.00E
Atlin Canada **50** 59.35N133.42W
Atnosen Norway **17** 61.44N 10.49E
Atouguia Portugal **10** 39.20N 9.20W
Atrak *r.* Iran *see* Atrek *r.* Asia **31**
Ätran *r.* Sweden **17** 56.53N 12.30E
Atrato *r.* Colombia **60** 8.15N 76.58W
Atrek *r.* Asia **31** 37.23N 54.00E
Atsugi Japan **23** 35.27N139.22E
Atsumi-hantō *pen.* Japan **23** 34.40N137.20E
Atsumi-wan *b.* Japan **23** 34.45N137.10E
Aṭ Ṭafīlah Jordan **32** 30.52N 35.36E
Aṭ Ṭā'if Saudi Arabia **35** 21.15N 40.21E
At Tall Syria **32** 33.36N 36.18E
Attapu Laos **26** 14.51N106.56E
Attawapiskat *r.* Canada **51** 52.57N 82.18W
Aṭ Ṭayrīyah Egypt **32** 30.39N 30.46E
Attendorn W. Germany **8** 51.07N 7.54E
Attigny France **9** 49.29N 4.35E
Attleborough U.K. **5** 52.31N 1.01E
Aṭ Ṭubayq *mts.* Saudi Arabia **30** 29.30N 37.15E
Aṭ Ṭunayb Jordan **32** 31.48N 35.56E
Aṭ Ṭūr Egypt **32** 28.14N 33.36E
Atucha Argentina **63** 33.58S 59.17W
Atuel *r.* Argentina **63** 36.15S 66.55W
Åtvidaberg Sweden **17** 58.12N 16.00E
Atwater U.S.A. **54** 37.21N120.36W
Aubagne France **11** 43.17N 5.35E
Aube *d.* France **9** 48.15N 4.05E
Aube *r.* France **9** 48.30N 3.37E
Aubenton France **9** 49.50N 4.12E
Auberive France **9** 47.47N 5.03E
Aubigny-sur-Nère France **9** 47.29N 2.26E
Aubin France **11** 44.32N 2.14E
Auburn Calif. U.S.A. **54** 38.54N121.04W
Auburn Ind. U.S.A. **55** 41.22N 85.02W
Auburn Maine U.S.A. **55** 44.06N 70.14W
Auburn N.Y. U.S.A. **55** 42.57N 76.34W
Auburn Wash. U.S.A. **54** 47.18N122.13W
Aubusson France **11** 45.57N 2.11E
Auce U.S.S.R. **17** 56.28N 22.53E
Auch France **11** 43.40N 0.36E
Auchi Nigeria **38** 7.05N 6.16E
Auchterarder U.K. **6** 56.18N 3.43W
Auckland New Zealand **48** 36.55S174.45E
Aude *r.* France **11** 43.13N 2.20E
Auden Canada **55** 50.14N 87.50W
Aue E. Germany **14** 50.35N 12.42E
Augathella Australia **44** 25.48S146.35E
Augrabies Falls *f.* R.S.A. **39** 28.33S 20.27E
Augsburg W. Germany **14** 48.21N 10.54E
Augusta Australia **43** 34.19S115.09E
Augusta Italy **12** 37.13N 15.13E
Augusta Ga. U.S.A. **53** 33.29N 82.00W
Augusta Maine U.S.A. **55** 44.19N 69.47W
Augustín Codazzi Colombia **60** 10.01N 73.10W
Augustów Poland **15** 53.51N 22.59E
Augustus, Mt. Australia **42** 24.20S116.49E
Aulla Italy **9** 44.12N 9.58E
Aulnay France **11** 46.02N 0.22W
Aulne *r.* France **11** 48.30N 4.11W
Aulnoye-Aymeries France **8** 50.13N 3.50E
Aumale France **9** 49.46N 1.45E
Aumont-Aubrac France **11** 44.43N 3.17E
Auna Nigeria **38** 10.11N 4.46E
Auneau France **9** 48.27N 1.46E
Aura Finland **17** 60.36N 22.34E
Aurangābād Mahār India **28** 19.52N 75.22E
Aurdal Norway **17** 60.56N 9.24E
Aure Norway **16** 63.16N 8.34E
Aurich W. Germany **8** 53.28N 7.29E
Aurillac France **11** 44.56N 2.26E
Aurora Ill. U.S.A. **53** 41.45N 88.20W
Aursunden *l.* Norway **16** 62.37N 11.40E
Aus Namibia **39** 26.41S 16.14E
Au Sable *r.* U.S.A. **55** 44.27N 83.21W
Aust-Agder *d.* Norway **17** 58.50N 8.20E
Austin Minn. U.S.A. **53** 43.40N 92.58W
Austin Nev. U.S.A. **54** 39.30N117.04W
Austin Penn. U.S.A. **55** 41.38N 78.05W
Austin Tex. U.S.A. **52** 30.18N 97.47W
Austin, L. Australia **42** 27.40S118.00E
Austral Downs *town* Australia **44** 20.28S137.55E
Australia Austa. **41**
Australian Alps *mts.* Australia **47** 36.30S148.30E
Australian Antarctic Territory Antarctica **64** 73.00S 90.00E
Australian Capital Territory *d.* Australia **47** 35.30S149.00E
Austria Europe **14** 47.30N 14.00E
Austvågöy *i.* Norway **16** 68.20N 14.40E
Autun France **11** 46.58N 4.18E
Auvergne *d.* France **11** 45.20N 3.00E
Auxerre France **9** 47.48N 3.35E
Aux Sables *r.* Canada **55** 46.13N 82.04W
Auzances France **11** 46.02N 2.29E
Avallon France **9** 47.30N 3.54E
Avaloirs, Les *hills* France **9** 48.28N 0.07W
Avalon U.S.A. **55** 39.06N 74.43W
Avanos Turkey **30** 38.44N 34.51E
Avaré Brazil **59** 23.06S 48.57W
Avarua Cook Is. **40** 21.12S159.46W
Aveiro Portugal **10** 40.40N 8.35W
Avellaneda Argentina **63** 34.40S 58.20W
Avellino Italy **12** 40.55N 14.46E
Aversa Italy **12** 40.58N 14.12E
Avery U.S.A. **54** 47.15N115.49W
Avesnes France **8** 50.08N 3.57E
Avesta Sweden **17** 60.09N 16.12E
Aveyron *r.* France **11** 44.09N 1.10E
Avezzano Italy **12** 42.03N 13.26E
Aviemore U.K. **6** 57.12N 3.50W
Avignon France **11** 43.56N 4.48E
Ávila Spain **10** 40.39N 4.42W
Ávila, Sierra de *mts.* Spain **10** 40.35N 5.08W
Avilés Spain **10** 43.35N 5.57W
Avoca *r.* Australia **46** 35.56S143.44E
Avon *r.* Australia **43** 31.40S116.07E
Avon *d.* U.K. **5** 51.35N 2.40W
Avon *r.* Dorset U.K. **5** 50.43N 1.45W
Avon *r.* Glos. U.K. **5** 52.00N 2.10W
Avon Downs *town* Australia **44** 20.05S137.30E
Avonmouth U.K. **5** 51.30N 2.42W
Avranches France **9** 48.42N 1.21W
Avre *r.* France **9** 49.53N 2.20E
Awaso Ghana **38** 6.20N 2.22W
Awat China **24** 40.38N 80.22E
Awbārī, Ṣaḥrā' *des.* Libya **34** 27.30N 11.30E
Awdah, Hawr al *l.* Iraq **31** 31.36N 46.53E
Awe, Loch U.K. **6** 56.18N 5.24W
Axarfjördhur *est.* Iceland **16** 66.10N 16.30W
Axat France **11** 42.48N 2.14E
Axel Heiberg I. Canada **51** 79.30N 90.00W
Axim Ghana **38** 4.53N 2.14W
Axiós *r.* Greece **13** 40.31N 22.43E
Axminster U.K. **5** 50.47N 3.01W
Ayabaca Peru **60** 4.40S 79.53W
Ayacucho Argentina **63** 37.10S 58.30W
Ayacucho Peru **60** 13.10S 74.15W
Ayaguz U.S.S.R. **24** 47.59N 80.27E
Ayamonte Spain **10** 37.12N 7.24W
Ayan U.S.S.R. **21** 56.29N138.00E
Aydin Turkey **30** 37.52N 27.50E
Áyios Evstrátios *i.* Greece **13** 39.30N 25.00E
Aylesbury U.K. **5** 51.48N 0.49W
Aylmer L. Canada **50** 64.05N108.30W
Aylsham U.K. **4** 52.48N 1.16E
'Ayn, Wādī al *r.* Oman **31** 22.18N 55.35E
'Ayn Dāllah *well* Egypt **30** 27.19N 27.20E
Ayon, Ostrov *i.* U.S.S.R. **21** 70.00N169.00E
Ayos Cameroon **38** 3.55N 12.30E
Ayr Australia **44** 19.35S147.24E
Ayr U.K. **6** 55.28N 4.37W
Ayr *r.* U.K. **6** 55.28N 4.38W
Ayre, Pt. of U.K. **4** 54.25N 4.22W
Ayutthaya Thailand **29** 14.25N100.30E
Ayvalik Turkey **13** 39.19N 26.42E
Azaouâd *des.* Mali **38** 18.00N 3.00W
Azaouak, Vallée de l' *f.* Mali **38** 16.00N 3.40E
Azare Nigeria **38** 11.40N 10.08E
Azbine *mts. see* Aïr *mts.* Niger **38**
Azerbaydzhanskaya S.S.R. *d.* U.S.S.R. **31** 40.10N 47.50E
Azogues Ecuador **60** 2.35S 78.00W
Azopolye U.S.S.R. **18** 65.15N 45.18E
Azov, Sea of *see* Azovskoye More U.S.S.R. **19**
Azovskoye More *sea* U.S.S.R. **19** 46.00N 36.30E
Azraq, Al Baḥr al *r.* Sudan **35** 15.45N 32.25E
Aztec U.S.A. **54** 32.48N113.26W
Azua Dom. Rep. **57** 18.29N 70.44W
Azuaga Spain **10** 38.16N 5.40W
Azuero, Península de *pen.* Panama **57** 7.30N 80.30W
Azul Argentina **63** 36.46S 59.50W
Azurduy Bolivia **62** 19.59S 64.29W
Az Zāb al Kabīr *r.* Iraq **31** 35.37N 43.20E
Az Zāb aş Şaghīr *r.* Iraq **31** 35.15N 43.27E
Az Zabdānī Syria **32** 33.43N 36.05E
Az Zahrān Saudi Arabia **31** 26.18N 50.08E
Az Zaqāzīq Egypt **32** 30.36N 31.30E
Az Zarqā' Jordan **32** 32.04N 36.05E
Az Zarqā' *r.* Jordan **32** 32.08N 35.32E
Az Zilfī Saudi Arabia **31** 26.15N 44.50E
Az Zrārīyah Lebanon **32** 33.21N 35.20E

B

Baan Baa Australia **47** 30.28S149.58E
Baarle-Hertog Neth. **8** 51.26N 4.56E
Babadag Romania **15** 44.54N 28.43E
Babahoyo Ecuador **60** 1.53S 79.31W
Babakin Australia **43** 32.11S117.58E
Babana Nigeria **38** 10.26N 3.51E
Babanka U.S.S.R. **15** 48.41N 30.30E
Babanūsah Sudan **35** 11.20N 27.48E
Babar, Kepulauan *is.* Indonesia **27** 8.00S129.30E
Babayevo U.S.S.R. **18** 59.24N 35.50E
B'abdā Lebanon **32** 33.50N 35.31E
Bab el Mandeb *str.* Asia **35** 13.00N 43.10E
Babia Gora *mtn.* Czech./Poland **15** 49.38N 19.38E
Babine L. Canada **50** 54.45N126.00W
Babo Indonesia **27** 2.33S133.25E
Bābol Iran **31** 36.32N 52.42E
Baboua C.A.R. **38** 5.49N 14.51E
Babuyan Is. Phil. **27** 19.20N121.30E
Babylon *ruins* Iraq **31** 32.33N 44.25E
Bacabal Maranhão Brazil **61** 4.15S 44.45W
Bacabal Para Brazil **61** 5.20S 56.45W
Bacău Romania **15** 46.32N 26.59E
Baccarat France **11** 48.27N 6.45E
Bacchus Marsh *town* Australia **46** 37.41S144.27E
Bacharach W. Germany **8** 50.03N 7.48E
Bacheli India **29** 18.40N 81.16E
Bachelina U.S.S.R. **20** 57.45N 67.20E
Back *r.* Canada **51** 66.37N 96.00W
Bac Kan Vietnam **26** 22.06N105.57E
Bäckefors Sweden **17** 58.48N 12.10E
Backstairs Passage *str.* Australia **46** 35.42S138.05E
Bac Lieu Vietnam **26** 9.16N105.45E
Bac Ninh Vietnam **26** 21.10N106.04E
Bacolod Phil. **27** 10.38N122.58E
Badagara India **28** 11.36N 75.35E
Badajós, Lago *l.* Brazil **60** 3.15S 62.47W
Badajoz Spain **10** 38.53N 6.58W
Badalona Spain **10** 41.27N 2.15E
Badanah Saudi Arabia **30** 30.59N 41.02E
Bad Axe U.S.A. **55** 43.49N 82.59W
Badeggi Nigeria **38** 9.04N 6.09E
Bad Ems W. Germany **8** 50.21N 7.42E
Baden Austria **14** 48.01N 16.14E
Baden-Baden W. Germany **14** 48.45N 8.15E
Baden-Württemberg *d.* W. Germany **14** 48.30N 9.00E
Badgastein Austria **14** 47.07N 13.09E
Bad Godesberg W. Germany **8** 50.41N 7.09E
Bad Honnef W. Germany **8** 50.39N 7.13E
Bad Ischl Austria **14** 47.43N 13.38E
Bādiyat ash Shām *des.* Asia **30** 32.00N 39.00E
Bad Kissingen W. Germany **14** 50.12N 10.04E
Bad Kreuznach W. Germany **8** 49.51N 7.52E
Bad Mergentheim W. Germany **14** 49.30N 9.46E
Bad Münstereifel W. Germany **8** 50.34N 6.47E
Bad Neuenahr-Ahrweiler W. Germany **8** 50.33N 7.07E
Bad Oldesloe W. Germany **14** 53.48N 10.22E
Badou Togo **38** 7.37N 0.37E
Bad Tölz W. Germany **14** 47.46N 11.34E
Bad Wildungen W. Germany **14** 51.07N 9.07E
Baerami Australia **47** 32.23S150.30E
Baeza Spain **10** 37.57N 3.25W
Bafang Cameroon **38** 5.11N 10.12E
Baffin *d.* Canada **51** 66.00N 72.00W
Baffin B. Canada **51** 74.00N 70.00W
Baffin I. Canada **51** 68.50N 70.00W
Bafia Cameroon **38** 4.39N 11.14E
Bafoulabé Mali **34** 13.49N 10.50W
Bāfq Iran **31** 31.35N 55.21E
Bafra Turkey **30** 41.34N 35.56E
Bafut Cameroon **38** 6.06N 10.02E
Bagamoyo Tanzania **37** 6.26S 38.55E
Bagdarin U.S.S.R. **21** 54.28N113.38E
Bagé Brazil **59** 31.22S 54.06W
Baggy Pt. U.K. **5** 51.08N 4.15W
Baghdād Iraq **31** 33.20N 44.26E
Bagheria Italy **12** 38.05N 13.30E
Baghlān Afghan. **28** 36.11N 68.44E
Bagni di Lucca Italy **9** 44.01N 10.35E
Bagnois-sur-Cèze France **11** 44.10N 4.37E
Bagoé *r.* Mali **38** 12.34N 6.30W
Bagolino Italy **9** 45.49N 10.28E
Bagrationovsk U.S.S.R. **15** 54.26N 20.38E
Baguio Phil. **27** 16.25N120.37E
Bahamas C. America **57** 23.30N 75.00W
Bahāwalpur Pakistan **28** 29.24N 71.47E
Bahi Tanzania **37** 5.59S 35.15E
Bahia *d.* Brazil **61** 12.30S 42.30W
Bahía, Islas de la *is.* Honduras **57** 16.10N 86.30W
Bahía Blanca Argentina **59** 38.45S 62.15W
Bahía de Caráquez Ecuador **60** 0.40S 80.25W
Bahía Laura Argentina **63** 48.18S 66.30W
Bahía Negra Paraguay **59** 20.15S 58.12W
Bahrain Asia **31** 26.00N 50.35E
Bahrāmābād Iran **28** 30.24N 56.00E
Bāhū Kalāt Iran **31** 25.42N 61.28E
Baia-Mare Romania **15** 47.40N 23.35E
Baião Brazil **61** 2.41S 49.41W
Baia Sprie Romania **15** 47.40N 23.42E
Baïbokoum Chad **38** 7.46N 15.43E
Baicheng China **25** 45.40N122.52E
Baidoa Somali Rep. **37** 3.08N 43.34E
Baie Comeau Canada **55** 49.12N 68.10W
Baie St. Paul *town* Canada **55** 47.27N 70.30W
Baigneux-les-Juifs France **9** 47.31N 4.39E
Băileşti Romania **15** 44.02N 23.21E
Bailleul France **8** 50.44N 2.44E
Baimuru P.N.G. **27** 7.30S144.49E
Bain-de-Bretagne France **9** 47.50N 1.41W
Baing Indonesia **42** 10.15S120.34E
Bāir Jordan **32** 30.46N 36.41E
Bā'ir, Wādī *r.* Jordan **32** 31.10N 36.55E
Baird Mts. U.S.A. **50** 67.35N161.30W
Bairnsdale Australia **47** 37.51S147.38E
Bais France **9** 48.15N 0.22W
Baise *r.* France **11** 44.15N 0.20E
Baja Hungary **15** 46.12N 18.58E
Baja California *pen.* Mexico **56** 28.40N114.40W
Baja California Norte *d.* Mexico **56** 29.45N115.30W
Baja California Sur *d.* Mexico **56** 26.00N113.00W
Bakal U.S.S.R. **18** 54.58N 58.45E
Baker Calif. U.S.A. **54** 35.16N116.04W
Baker Mont. U.S.A. **52** 46.22N104.17W
Baker Oreg. U.S.A. **54** 44.47N117.50W
Baker, Mt. U.S.A. **54** 48.47N121.49W
Baker Lake *town* Canada **51** 64.20N 96.10W
Bakersfield U.S.A. **54** 35.23N119.01W
Bakouma C.A.R. **36** 5.42N 22.47E
Baku U.S.S.R. **31** 40.22N 49.53E
Bala U.K. **4** 52.54N 3.36W
Balabac *i.* Phil. **26** 7.57N117.01E
Balabac Str. Malaysia/Phil. **26** 7.30N117.00E
Ba'labakk Lebanon **32** 34.00N 36.12E
Balaclava Australia **46** 32.09S141.25E
Bālāghāt Range *mts.* India **28** 18.45N 76.30E
Balaguer Spain **10** 41.50N 0.50E
Balaka Malaŵi **37** 15.00S 34.56E
Balaklava Australia **46** 34.08S138.24E
Balaklava U.S.S.R. **19** 44.31N 33.35E
Balakovo U.S.S.R. **18** 52.04N 47.46E
Balama Mozambique **37** 13.19S 38.35E
Bālā Morghāb Afghan. **31** 35.34N 63.20E
Balāngīr India **29** 20.41N 83.30E
Balashov U.S.S.R. **19** 51.30N 43.10E
Balasore India **29** 21.31N 86.59E
Balassagyarmat Hungary **15** 48.05N 19.18E
Balāṭ Egypt **30** 25.33N 29.16E
Balaton *l.* Hungary **15** 46.55N 17.50E
Balboa Panama **57** 8.37N 79.33W
Balbriggan Rep. of Ire. **7** 53.36N 6.12W
Balcarce Argentina **63** 37.52S 58.15W
Balchik Bulgaria **15** 43.24N 28.10E
Balclutha New Zealand **48** 46.16S169.46E
Baldwin Mich. U.S.A. **55** 43.54N 85.50W
Baldwin Penn. U.S.A. **55** 40.23N 79.58W
Baleanoona Australia **46** 30.33S139.22E
Baleares, Islas *is.* Spain **10** 39.30N 2.30E
Balfate Honduras **57** 15.48N 86.25W
Balfour Downs *town* Australia **42** 22.57S120.46E
Bali *d.* Indonesia **26** 8.18S115.00E
Bali *i.* Indonesia **26** 8.30S115.05E
Balikesir Turkey **13** 39.38N 27.51E
Balīkh *r.* Syria **30** 35.58N 39.05E
Balikpapan Indonesia **26** 1.15S116.50E
Balkan Mts. *see* Stara Planina *mts.* Bulgaria **13**
Balkhash U.S.S.R. **24** 46.51N 75.00E
Balkhash, Ozero *l.* U.S.S.R. **24** 46.40N 75.00E
Ballachulish U.K. **6** 56.40N 5.08W
Balladonia Australia **43** 32.27S123.51E
Ballandean Australia **47** 28.39S151.50E
Ballantrae U.K. **6** 55.06N 5.01W
Ballarat Australia **46** 37.36S143.58E
Ballard, L. Australia **43** 29.27S120.55E
Ballater U.K. **6** 57.03N 3.03W
Ballenas, Bahía de *b.* Mexico **56** 26.45N113.25W
Balleny Is. Antarctica **64** 66.30S163.00E
Balleroy France **9** 49.11N 0.50W
Ballina Australia **47** 28.50S153.37E
Ballina Rep. of Ire. **7** 54.08N 9.10W
Ballinasloe Rep. of Ire. **7** 53.20N 8.15W
Ballingeary Rep. of Ire. **7** 51.50N 9.15W
Ballybay Rep. of Ire. **7** 54.08N 6.56W
Ballycastle U.K. **7** 55.12N 6.15W
Ballyclare U.K. **7** 54.45N 6.00W
Ballyconnell Rep. of Ire. **7** 54.06N 7.37W
Ballydehob Rep. of Ire. **7** 51.34N 9.28W
Ballydonegan Rep. of Ire. **7** 51.38N 10.04W
Ballygar Rep. of Ire. **7** 53.32N 8.20W
Ballygawley U.K. **7** 54.28N 7.03W

allykelly U.K. 7 55.03N 7.00W
allymena U.K. 7 54.52N 6.17W
allymoney U.K. 7 55.04N 6.31W
allyquintin Pt. U.K. 7 54.40N 5.30W
allyragget Rep. of Ire. 7 52.47N 7.21W
allyshannon Rep. of Ire. 7 54.30N 8.11W
allyvaughan Rep.of Ire. 7 53.06N 9.09W
allyvourney Rep. of Ire. 7 51.57N 9.10W
almoral Australia 46 37.17S141.50E
alonne r. Australia 47 28.30S148.20E
alpunga Australia 46 33.44S141.50E
alrāmpur India 29 27.26N 82.11E
alranald Australia 46 34.37S143.37E
alş Romania 15 44.21N 24.06E
alsas r. Brazil 61 9.00S 48.10W
alsas r. Mexico 56 18.10N102.05W
alta U.S.S.R. 15 47.58N 29.39E
altanás Spain 10 41.56N 4.15W
altasar Brum Uruguay 63 30.44S 57.19W
altic Sea Europe 17 57.00N 20.00E
altîm Egypt 32 31.34N 31.05E
altimore Md. U.S.A. 55 39.17N 76.37W
altiysk U.S.S.R. 17 54.39N 19.55E
aluchistan f. Pakistan 28 28.00N 66.00E
alygychan U.S.S.R. 21 63.55N154.12E
alykshi U.S.S.R. 19 47.04N 51.55E
ām Iran 31 29.07N 58.20E
ama Nigeria 38 11.35N 13.40E
amako Mali 34 12.40N 7.59W
amba Kenya 37 3.33S 39.32E
amba Mali 38 17.05N 1.23W
ambari C.A.R. 36 5.40N 20.37E
amberg W. Germany 14 49.54N 10.53E
ambuí Brazil 59 20.01S 45.59W
am Co l. China 29 31.30N 91.10E
amenda Cameroon 38 5.55N 10.09E
ampton Devon U.K. 5 51.00N 3.29W
ampūr Iran 31 27.13N 60.29E
ampūr r. Iran 31 27.18N 59.02E
āmra Hills India 29 21.30N 84.30E
anagher Rep. of Ire. 7 53.12N 8.00W
anana Australia 44 24.30S150.08E
ananal, Ilha do f. Brazil 61 11.30S 50.15W
anās, Ra's c. Egypt 30 23.54N 35.48E
an Ban Laos 29 19.38N103.34E
anbridge U.K. 7 54.21N 6.17W
Banbury U.K. 5 52.04N 1.21W
Banchory U.K. 6 57.03N 2.30W
Bancroft Canada 55 45.03N 77.51W
Banda Gabon 36 3.47S 11.04E
Banda i. Indonesia 27 4.30S129.55E
Banda, Laut sea Indonesia 27 5.00S128.00E
Banda Aceh Indonesia 26 5.35N 95.20E
Bandama r. Ivory Coast 38 5.10N 4.59W
Bandar 'Abbās Iran 31 27.10N 56.15E
Bandar-e Anzalī Iran 31 37.26N 49.29E
Bandar-e Deylam Iran 31 30.05N 50.11E
Bandar-e Khomeynī Iran 31 30.26N 49.03E
Bandar-e-Lengeh Iran 31 26.34N 54.53E
Bandar-e Rīg Iran 31 29.30N 50.40E
Bandar-e Torkeman Iran 31 36.55N 54.05E
Bandar Seri Begawan Brunei 26 4.56N114.58E
Banda Sea see Banda, Laut sea Indonesia 27
Bandawe Malaŵi 37 11.57S 34.11E
Bandeira mtn. Brazil 59 20.25S 41.45W
Bandiagara Mali 38 14.12N 3.29W
Bandirma Turkey 13 40.22N 28.00E
Bandon Rep. of Ire. 7 51.45N 8.45W
Bandon r. Rep. of Ire. 7 51.43N 8.38W
Bandundu Zaïre 36 3.20S 17.24E
Bandung Indonesia 26 6.57S107.34E
Banes Cuba 57 20.59N 75.24W
Banff Canada 50 51.10N115.34W
Banff U.K. 6 57.40N 2.31W
Banfora Burkina Faso 38 10.36N 4.45W
Bangalore India 28 12.58N 77.35E
Bangassou C.A.R. 35 4.41N 22.48E
Banggai, Kepulauan is. Indonesia 27 1.30S123.10E
Banggi i. Malaysia 26 7.17N117.12E
Banghāzī Libya 34 32.07N 20.05E
Bangka i. Indonesia 26 2.20S106.10E
Bangkok see Krung Thep Thailand 29
Bangladesh Asia 29 24.00N 90.00E
Bangong Co l. China 29 33.45N 79.15E
Bangor Rep. of Ire. 7 54.09N 9.44W
Bangor U.K. 4 53.13N 4.09W
Bangor U.K. 7 54.40N 5.41W
Bangor Maine U.S.A. 55 44.49N 68.47W
Bang Saphan Thailand 29 11.14N 99.31E
Bangui C.A.R. 36 4.23N 18.37E
Bangweulu, L. Zambia 37 11.15S 29.45E
Banhā Egypt 32 30.28N 31.11E
Ban Hat Yai Thailand 26 7.00N100.28E
Ban Houayxay Laos 29 20.21N100.26E
Bani r. Mali 38 14.30N 4.15W
Banikoara Benin 38 11.21N 2.25E
Banī Mazār Egypt 32 28.29N 30.48E
Banī Suwayf Egypt 32 29.05N 31.05E
Bāniyās Syria 32 35.09N 35.58E
Banja Luka Yugo. 13 44.47N 17.10E
Banjarmasin Indonesia 26 3.22S114.36E
Banjul Gambia 34 13.28N 16.39W
Banka Banka Australia 44 18.48S134.01E
Ban Kantang Thailand 29 7.25N 99.30E
Bankasse Mali 38 14.01N 3.29W
Banks Group is. Australia 46 34.35S136.12E
Banks I. Australia 44 10.12S142.16E
Banks I. N.W.T. Canada 50 73.00N122.00W
Banks Pen. New Zealand 48 43.45S173.10E
Banks Str. Australia 45 40.37S148.07E
Ban-m'drack Vietnam 26 12.42N108.47E
Bann r. U.K. 7 55.10N 6.46W
Bannockburn U.K. 6 56.06N 3.55W
Bannockburn Zimbabwe 39 20.16S 29.51E
Banská Bystrica Czech. 15 48.44N 19.07E
Banté Benin 38 8.26N 1.54E
Bantry Rep. of Ire. 7 51.41N 9.27W
Bantry B. Rep. of Ire. 7 51.40N 9.40W
Banyak, Kepulauan is. Indonesia 26 2.15N 97.10E
Banyo Cameroon 38 6.47N 11.50E
Banyuwangi Indonesia 26 8.12S114.22E
Banzare Coast f. Antarctica 64 66.30S125.00E
Baoding China 25 38.54N115.26E
Baoji China 24 34.23N107.16E
Baoshan China 29 25.07N 99.08E
Baotou China 25 40.38N109.59E
Bapaume France 8 50.07N 2.51E
Ba'qūbah Iraq 31 33.45N 44.38E
Bar Albania 13 42.05N 19.06E
Bar U.S.S.R. 15 49.05N 27.40E
Bara Nigeria 38 10.24N 10.43E
Barabinsk U.S.S.R. 20 55.20N 78.18E
Baracoa Cuba 57 20.23N 74.31W
Baradero Argentina 63 33.50S 59.30W
Baradine Australia 47 30.56S149.05E
Baradine r. Australia 47 30.17S148.27E
Barahona Dom. Rep. 57 18.13N 71.07W
Baraka Zaïre 37 4.09S 29.05E
Bāramūla Jammu & Kashmir 28 34.12N 74.21E
Baranoa Colombia 60 10.50N 74.55W
Baranof I. U.S.A. 50 57.05N135.00W
Baranovichi U.S.S.R. 18 53.09N 26.00E
Baratta Australia 46 32.01S139.10E
Barbacena Brazil 59 21.13S 43.47W
Barbados Lesser Antilles 57 13.20N 59.40W
Barbar Sudan 35 18.01N 33.59E
Barbastro Spain 10 42.02N 0.07E
Barberton R.S.A. 39 25.46S 31.02E
Barbezieux France 11 45.28N 0.09W
Barbuda i. Leeward Is. 57 17.41N 61.48W
Barcaldine Australia 44 23.31S145.15E
Barcellona Italy 12 38.10N 15.13E
Barcelona Spain 10 41.25N 2.10E
Barcelona Venezuela 60 10.08N 64.43W
Barcelos Brazil 60 0.59S 62.58W
Barcoo r. Australia 44 25.30S142.50E
Barcs Hungary 15 45.58N 17.28E
Barcs Yugo. 13 45.58N 17.28E
Bardai Chad 34 21.21N 16.56E
Bardejov Czech. 15 49.18N 21.16E
Bardera Somali Rep. 37 2.18N 42.18E
Bardi Italy 9 44.38N 9.44E
Bardnovichi U.S.S.R. 15 53.09N 26.00E
Bardoc Australia 43 30.20S121.17E
Bardsey i. U.K. 4 52.45N 4.48W
Bardu Norway 16 68.54N 18.20E
Bardufoss Norway 16 69.00N 18.30E
Bareilly India 29 28.20N 79.24E
Barellan Australia 47 34.17S146.34E
Barentsovo More see Barents Sea Arctic Oc. 18
Barents Sea Arctic Oc. 18 73.00N 40.00E
Barfleur France 9 49.40N 1.15W
Barge Italy 9 44.43N 7.20E
Barguzin U.S.S.R. 21 53.40N109.35E
Bari Italy 13 41.08N 16.52E
Baricho Kenya 37 3.07S 39.47E
Barim i. S. Yemen 35 12.40N 43.24E
Barinas Venezuela 60 8.36N 70.15W
Bariri Brazil 59 22.04S 48.41W
Bārīs Egypt 30 24.40N 30.36E
Barisāl Bangla. 29 22.41N 90.20E
Barisan, Pegunungan mts. Indonesia 26 3.30S102.30E
Barito r. Indonesia 26 3.35S114.35E
Barker L. Australia 43 31.45S120.05E
Barking U.K. 5 51.32N 0.05E
Barkly East R.S.A. 39 30,58S 27.33E
Barkly Tableland f. Australia 44 19.00S136.40E
Barkly West R.S.A. 39 28.32S 24.29E
Bar-le-Duc France 11 48.46N 5.10E
Barlee, L. Australia 43 29.30S119.30E
Barlee Range mts. Australia 42 23.40S116.00E
Barletta Italy 12 41.20N 16.15E
Barmedman Australia 47 34.08S147.25E
Barmera Australia 46 34.15S140.31E
Barm Fīrūz, Kūh-e mtn. Iran 31 30.21N 52.00E
Barmouth U.K. 4 52.44N 4.03W
Barnard Castle town U.K. 4 54.33N 1.55W
Barnato Australia 47 31.38S144.59E
Barnaul U.S.S.R. 20 53.21N 83.15E
Barnet U.K. 5 51.39N 0.11W
Barneveld Neth. 8 52.10N 5.39E
Barneville France 9 49.23N 1.45W
Barneys L. Australia 46 33.16S144.13E
Barnsley U.K. 4 53.33N 1.29W
Barnstaple U.K. 5 51.05N 4.03W
Baro Nigeria 38 8.37N 6.19E
Barqah f. Libya 35 31.00N 22.10E
Barquisimeto Venezuela 60 10.03N 69.18W
Barra Brazil 61 11.06S 43.15W
Barra i. U.K. 6 56.59N 7.28W
Barra, Sd. of U.K. 6 57.04N 7.20W
Barraba Australia 47 30.24S152.36E
Barra do Corda Brazil 61 5.30S 45.15W
Barra do Piraí Brazil 59 22.28S 43.49W
Barra Mansa Brazil 59 22.35S 44.12W
Barranca Peru 60 4.50S 76.40W
Barrancabermeja Colombia 60 7.06N 73.54W
Barrancas Venezuela 60 8.45N 62.13W
Barrancos Portugal 10 38.10N 7.01W
Barranqueras Argentina 59 27.30S 58.55W
Barranquilla Colombia 60 11.10N 74.50W
Barraute Canada 55 48.26N 77.39W
Barre U.S.A. 55 44.12N 72.30W
Barreiras Brazil 61 12.09S 44.58W
Barreiro Portugal 10 38.40N 9.05W
Barreiros Brazil 61 8.49S 35.12W
Barrême France 14 43.57N 6.22E
Barretos Brazil 59 20.37S 48.38W
Barrhead U.K. 6 55.47N 4.24W
Barrie Canada 55 44.24N 79.40W
Barrington Tops mts. Australia 47 32.30S151.28E
Barringun Australia 47 29.01S145.43E
Barron U.S.A. 54 48.44N120.43W
Barrow r. Rep. of Ire. 7 52.17N 7.00W
Barrow U.S.A. 50 71.16N156.50W
Barrow Creek town Australia 44 21.32S133.53E
Barrow I. Australia 42 21.40S115.27E
Barrow-in-Furness U.K. 4 54.08N 3.15W
Barrow Range mts. Australia 42 26.04S127.28E
Barry U.K. 5 51.23N 3.19W
Barstow U.S.A. 54 34.54N117.01W
Bar-sur-Aube France 9 48.14N 4.43E
Bar-sur-Seine France 9 48.07N 4.22E
Bartica Guyana 60 6.24N 58.38W
Bartin Turkey 30 41.37N 32.20E
Bartlefrere mt. Australia 44 17.23S145.49E
Bartlesville U.S.A. 53 36.44N 95.59W
Bartolomeu Dias Mozambique 39 21.10S 35.09E
Barton-upon-Humber U.K. 4 53.41N 0.27W
Bartoszyce Poland 15 54.16N 20.49E
Barwon r. Australia 47 30.00S148.05E
Barysh U.S.S.R. 18 53.40N 47.09E
Basavilbaso Argentina 63 32.20S 58.52W
Basel Switz. 14 47.33N 7.36E
Bashi Channel Phil./Taiwan 25 21.40N121.20E
Basilan Phil. 27 6.40N121.59E
Basilan i. Phil. 27 6.40N122.10E
Basildon U.K. 5 51.34N 0.25E
Basilicata d. Italy 12 40.30N 16.20E
Basin U.S.A. 54 44.23N108.02W
Basingstoke U.K. 5 51.15N 1.05W
Baskatong, Résr. Canada 55 46.48N 75.50W
Basoko Zaïre 36 1.20N 23.36E
Bassano Canada 50 50.47N112.28W
Bassano Italy 9 45.46N 11.44E
Bassari Togo 38 9.12N 0.18E
Bassein Burma 29 16.45N 94.30E
Basse Normandie d. France 9 49.00N 0.00
Basse-Terre Guadeloupe 57 16.00N 61.43W
Bass Str. Australia 45 39.45S146.00E
Bassum W. Germany 14 52.51N 8.43E
Båstad Sweden 17 56.26N 12.51E
Bastak Iran 31 27.15N 54.26E
Bastelica France 11 42.00N 9.03E
Bastia France 11 42.41N 9.26E
Bastogne Belgium 8 50.00N 5.43E
Basyûn Egypt 32 30.57N 30.49E
Bata Equat. Guinea 38 1.51N 9.49E
Batabanó, Golfo de g. Cuba 57 23.15N 82.30W
Batalha Portugal 10 39.39N 8.50W
Batang China 29 30.02N 99.01E
Batangas Phil. 27 13.46N121.01E
Batan Is. Phil. 27 20.50N121.55E
Bátaszék Hungary 15 46.12N 18.44E
Batatais Brazil 59 20.54S 47.37W
Bataysk U.S.S.R. 19 47.09N 39.46E
Batchelor Australia 44 13.04S131.01E
Bătdâmbâng Kampuchea 26 13.06N103.13E
Bateman's B. Australia 45 35.55S150.09E
Batemans Bay town Australia 47 35.55S150.09E
Bath Canada 55 46.30N 67.36W
Bath U.K. 5 51.22N 2.22W
Bath Maine U.S.A. 55 43.55N 69.49W
Bath N.Y. U.S.A. 55 42.20N 77.19W
Baṭḥā, Wādī al r. Oman 31 20.01N 59.39E
Bathgate U.K. 6 55.44N 3.38W
Bathurst Australia 47 33.27S149.35E
Bathurst Canada 55 47.37N 65.40W
Bathurst R.S.A. 39 33.30S 26.48E
Bathurst, C. Canada 50 70.30N128.00W
Bathurst I. Australia 42 11.45S130.15E
Bathurst I. Canada 51 76.00N100.00W
Bathurst Inlet town Canada 50 66.48N108.00W
Batié Burkina Faso 38 9.42N 2.53W
Batina Yugo. 15 45.51N 18.51E
Batley U.K. 4 53.43N 1.38W
Batlow Australia 47 35.32S148.10E
Batman Turkey 30 37.52N 41.07E
Batna Algeria 34 35.34N 6.11E
Baton Rouge U.S.A. 53 30.30N 91.10W
Batopilas Mexico 56 27.00N107.45W
Batouri Cameroon 38 4.26N 14.27E
Batticaloa Sri Lanka 29 7.43N 81.42E
Battle U.K. 5 50.55N 0.30E
Battle Creek town U.S.A. 55 42.20N 85.11W
Battle Harbour Canada 51 52.16N 55.36W
Batu, Kepulauan is. Indonesia 26 0.30S 98.20E
Batumi U.S.S.R. 30 41.37N 41.36E
Batu Pahat Malaysia 26 1.50N102.48E
Baturaja Indonesia 26 4.10S104.10E
Baturité Brazil 61 4.20S 38.53W
Bat Yam Israel 32 32.01N 34.45E
Baubau Indonesia 27 5.30S122.37E
Bauchi Nigeria 38 10.16N 9.50E
Bauchi d. Nigeria 38 10.40N 10.00E
Baugé France 9 47.33N 0.06W
Bauld, C. Canada 51 51.30N 55.45W
Bauru Brazil 59 22.19S 49.07W
Baús Brazil 59 18.19S 53.10W
Bauska U.S.S.R. 17 56.24N 24.14E
Bautzen E. Germany 14 51.11N 14.29E
Bavay France 8 50.18N 3.48E
Bawean i. Indonesia 26 5.50S112.35E
Bawku Ghana 38 11.05N 0.13W
Bayamo Cuba 57 20.23N 76.39W
Bayamón Puerto Rico 57 18.24N 66.10W
Bayan Har Shan mts. China 24 34.00N 97.20E
Bayburt Turkey 30 40.15N 40.16E
Bay City Mich. U.S.A. 55 43.35N 83.52W
Baydaratskaya Guba b. U.S.S.R. 20 70.00N 66.00E
Bayern d. W. Germany 14 48.30N 11.30E
Bayeux France 9 49.16N 0.42W
Baykal, Ozero l. U.S.S.R. 24 53.30N100.00E
Baykit U.S.S.R. 21 61.45N 96.22E
Bayombong Phil. 27 16.27N121.10E
Bayonne France 11 43.30N 1.28W
Bayovar Peru 60 5.50S 81.03W
Bayreuth W. Germany 14 49.56N 11.35E
Bayrūt Lebanon 32 33.52N 35.30E
Baytik Shan mts. China 24 45.15N 90.50E
Bay View New Zealand 48 39.26S176.52E
Baza Spain 10 37.30N 2.45W
Baza, Sierra de mts. Spain 10 37.15N 2.45W
Bazaliya U.S.S.R. 15 49.42N 26.29E
Bazaruto, Ilha do i. Mozambique 39 21.40S 35.28E
Bazas France 11 44.26N 0.13W
Bazmān Iran 31 27.48N 60.12E
Bazmān, Kūh-e mtn. Iran 31 28.06N 60.00E
Beachport Australia 46 37.29S140.01E
Beachy Head U.K. 5 50.43N 0.15E
Beagle Bay Mission Australia 42 16.58S122.40E
Bear L. U.S.A. 54 42.00N111.20W
Beatrice U.S.A. 53 40.17N 96.45W
Beatrice, C. Australia 44 14.15S136.59E
Beatty U.S.A. 54 36.54N116.46W
Beattyville Canada 55 48.53N 77.10W
Beauce f. France 9 48.22N 1.50E
Beaufort Australia 46 37.28S143.28E
Beaufort Sea N. America 50 72.00N141.00W
Beaufort West R.S.A. 39 32.20S 22.34E
Beaugency France 9 47.47N 1.38E
Beauly U.K. 6 57.29N 4.29W
Beauly r. U.K. 6 57.29N 4.25W
Beaumaris U.K. 4 53.16N 4.07W
Beaumetz-lès-Loges France 8 50.15N 2.36E
Beaumont Belgium 8 50.14N 4.16E
Beaumont Tex. U.S.A. 53 30.04N 94.06W
Beaumont-le-Roger France 9 49.05N 0.47E
Beaumont-sur-Sarthe France 9 48.13N 0.07E
Beaune France 11 47.02N 4.50E
Beaune-la-Rolande France 9 48.04N 2.26E
Beaupréau France 11 47.12N 0.59W
Beauvais France 9 49.26N 2.05E
Beauval Canada 50 55.09N107.35W
Beauvoir France 11 46.55N 2.01W
Beaver Alaska U.S.A. 50 66.22N147.24W
Beaver I. U.S.A. 55 45.42N 85.28W
Beāwar India 28 26.02N 74.20E
Bebedouro Brazil 59 20.54S 48.31W
Bebington U.K. 4 53.23N 3.01W
Beccles U.K. 5 52.27N 1.33E
Bečej Yugo. 15 45.37N 20.03E
Béchar Algeria 34 31.35N 2.17W
Beckley U.S.A. 53 37.46N 81.12W
Beckum W. Germany 8 51.45N 8.02E
Beclean Romania 15 47.11N 24.10E
Bédarieux France 11 43.35N 3.10E
Bedford U.K. 5 52.08N 0.29W
Bedford U.S.A. 55 38.51N 86.30W
Bedford, C. Australia 44 15.14S145.21E
Bedford Levels f. U.K. 5 52.35N 0.08W
Bedfordshire d. U.K. 5 52.04N 0.28W
Bedlington U.K. 4 55.08N 1.34W
Bedourie Australia 44 24.21S139.28E
Beech Grove U.S.A. 55 39.42N 86.06W
Beechworth Australia 47 36.23S146.42E
Beenleigh Australia 47 27.43S153.09E
Be'er Menuha Israel 32 30.19N 35.08E
Be'er Sheva' Israel 32 31.15N 34.47E
Beerta Neth. 8 53.12N 7.07E
Beeston U.K. 4 52.55N 1.11W
Beeville U.S.A. 52 28.25N 97.47W
Beg, Lough U.K. 7 54.47N 6.29W
Bega Australia 47 36.41S149.50E
Bègles France 11 44.48N 0.32W
Begna r. Norway 17 60.32N 10.00E
Behbehān Iran 31 30.35N 50.17E
Bei'an China 25 48.17N126.33E
Beihai China 25 21.29N109.10E
Beijing China 25 39.55N116.25E
Beijing Shi d. China 25 40.15N116.30E
Beilen Neth. 8 52.51N 6.31E
Beinn Dearg mtn. U.K. 6 57.47N 4.55W
Beipa'a P.N.G. 44 8.30S146.35E
Beira Mozambique 39 9.49S 34.52E
Beirut see Bayrūt Lebanon 32
Beitbridge Zimbabwe 39 22.10S 30.01E
Beiuş Romania 15 46.40N 22.21E
Beja Portugal 10 38.01N 7.52W
Bejaïa Algeria 34 36.45N 5.05E
Béjar Spain 10 40.24N 5.45W
Bejestān Iran 31 34.32N 58.08E
Bejoording Australia 43 31.22S116.30E
Békés Hungary 15 46.46N 21.08E
Békéscsaba Hungary 15 46.41N 21.06E
Bela India 29 25.55N 82.00E
Bela Pakistan 28 26.12N 66.20E
Bélabo Cameroon 38 5.00N 13.20E
Bela Crkva Yugo. 15 44.54N 21.26E
Bel Air U.S.A. 55 39.32N 76.21W
Belalcázar Spain 10 38.35N 5.10W
Belang Indonesia 27 0.58N124.56E
Belau Pacific Oc. 27 7.00N134.25E
Bela Vista Brazil 62 22.05S 56.22W
Bela Vista Mozambique 39 26.20S 32.41E
Belaya r. U.S.S.R. 20 55.40N 52.30E
Belaya Glina U.S.S.R. 19 46.04N 40.54E
Belaya Tserkov U.S.S.R. 15 49.49N 30.10E
Belcher Is. Canada 51 56.00N 79.00W
Belcoo U.K. 7 54.18N 7.53W
Belebey U.S.S.R. 18 54.05N 54.07E
Beled Weyne Somali Rep. 35 4.47N 45.12E
Belém Brazil 61 1.27S 48.29W
Belem Mozambique 37 14.11S 35.59E
Belén Uruguay 63 30.47S 57.47W
Belen U.S.A. 52 34.40N106.46W
Belén, Cuchilla de mts. Uruguay 63 30.49S 56.28W
Belev U.S.S.R. 18 53.50N 36.08E
Belfast U.K. 7 54.36N 5.57W
Belfast Maine U.S.A. 55 44.27N 69.01W
Belfast Lough U.K. 7 54.42N 5.45W
Belfort France 11 47.38N 6.52E
Belfry U.S.A. 54 45.09N109.01W
Belgaum India 28 15.54N 74.36E
Belgium Europe 8 51.00N 4.30E
Belgorod U.S.S.R. 19 50.38N 36.36E
Belgorod-Dnestrovskiy U.S.S.R. 15 46.10N 30.19E
Belgrade see Beograd Yugo. 15
Beli Nigeria 38 7.53N 10.59E
Belitung i. Indonesia 26 3.00S108.00E
Belize Belize 57 17.29N 88.20W
Belize C. America 57 17.00N 88.30W
Belka Australia 43 31.45S118.09E
Bellac France 11 46.07N 1.04E
Bella Coola Canada 50 52.22N126.46W
Bellagio Italy 9 45.59N 9.15E
Bellaria Italy 9 44.09N 12.28E
Bellary India 28 15.11N 76.54E
Bellata Australia 47 29.55S149.50E
Bella Unión Uruguay 63 30.15S 57.35W
Bella Vista Corrientes Argentina 62 28.30S 59.00W
Bella Vista Tucuman Argentina 62 27.02S 65.19W
Bellbrook Australia 47 30.48S152.30E
Bellefontaine U.S.A. 55 40.22N 83.45W
Belle Île France 11 47.20N 3.10W
Belle Isle, Str. of Canada 51 51.35N 56.30W
Bellême France 9 48.22N 0.34E
Belleville Canada 55 44.10N 77.23W
Bellevue Idaho U.S.A. 54 43.28N114.16W
Bellevue Penn. U.S.A. 55 40.32N 80.08W
Bellevue Wash. U.S.A. 54 47.37N122.12W
Bellin Canada 51 60.01N 70.01W
Bellingen Australia 47 30.28S152.43E
Bellingham U.K. 4 55.09N 2.15W
Bellingham U.S.A. 54 48.46N122.29W
Bellingshausen Sea Antarctica 64 70.00S 88.00W
Bellinzona Switz. 9 46.11N 9.02E
Bello Colombia 60 6.20N 75.41W
Belluno Italy 9 46.09N 12.13E
Bell Ville Argentina 63 32.35S 62.41W
Bélmez Spain 10 38.17N 5.17W
Belmopan Belize 57 17.25N 88.46W
Belmullet Rep. of Ire. 7 54.14N 10.00W
Belogradchik Bulgaria 15 43.38N 22.41E
Belo Horizonte Brazil 59 19.45S 43.54W
Belo Jardim Brazil 61 8.22S 36.22W
Belokorovichi U.S.S.R. 15 51.04N 28.00E
Belomorsk U.S.S.R. 18 64.34N 34.45E
Beloretsk U.S.S.R. 18 53.59N 58.20E
Belorusskaya S.S.R. d. U.S.S.R. 15 53.30N 28.00E
Beloye More sea U.S.S.R. 18 65.30N 38.00E
Beloye Ozero l. U.S.S.R. 18 60.12N 37.45E
Belozersk U.S.S.R. 18 60.00N 37.49E
Belper U.K. 4 53.02N 1.29W
Beltana Australia 46 30.40S138.27E
Belterra Brazil 61 2.38S 54.57W
Belton Australia 46 32.12S138.45E
Beltsy U.S.S.R. 15 47.45N 27.59E
Belukha, Gora mtn. U.S.S.R. 24 49.48N 86.40E
Belyando r. Australia 44 21.38S146.50E
Belyayevka U.S.S.R. 15 46.30N 30.12E
Belynichi U.S.S.R. 15 54.00N 29.42E
Belyy, Ostrov U.S.S.R. 20 73.10N 70.45E
Belyy Yar U.S.S.R. 20 58.28N 85.03E
Bełżec Poland 15 50.24N 23.26E
Bemidji U.S.A. 53 47.29N 94.52W
Benagerie Australia 46 31.30S140.21E
Benalla Australia 47 36.35S145.58E
Benanee Australia 46 34.32S142.56E
Benares see Vārānasi India 29
Benavente Spain 10 42.00N 5.40W
Benbecula i. U.K. 6 57.26N 7.18W
Ben Cruachan mtn. U.K. 6 56.26N 5.18W
Bencubbin Australia 43 30.48S117.52E
Bend U.S.A. 54 44.03N121.19W
Bende Nigeria 38 5.34N 7.37E
Bendel d. Nigeria 38 6.10N 6.00E
Bendery U.S.S.R. 15 46.50N 29.29E
Bendigo Australia 46 36.48S144.21E
Bendoc Australia 47 37.10S148.55E
Bendorf W. Germany 8 50.26N 7.34E
Bénéna Mali 38 13.09N 4.17W
Benešov Czech. 14 50.45N 14.22E
Benevento Italy 12 41.07N 14.46E
Bengal, B. of Indian Oc. 29 17.00N 89.00E
Bengbu China 25 32.56N117.27E
Benghazi see Banghāzī Libya 34
Bengkulu Indonesia 26 3.46S102.16E
Benguela Angola 36 12.34S 13.24E
Ben Hope mtn. U.K. 6 58.24N 4.36W
Beni r. Bolivia 62 10.23S 65.24W
Beni Zaïre 37 0.29N 29.27E
Beni Abbes Algeria 34 30.08N 2.10W
Benicarló Spain 10 40.25N 0.25E
Benidorm Spain 10 38.33N 0.09W
Benin Africa 38 9.00N 2.30E
Benin, Bight of Africa 38 5.30N 3.00E
Benin City Nigeria 38 6.19N 5.41E
Benjamin Constant Brazil 60 4.22S 70.02W
Ben Lawers mtn. U.K. 6 56.33N 4.14W
Ben Lomond mtn. N.S.W. Australia 47 30.04S151.43E
Ben Lomond mtn. Tas. Australia 45 41.33S147.40E
Ben Lomond mtn. U.K. 6 56.12N 4.38W
Ben Macdhui mtn. U.K. 6 57.04N 3.40W
Ben More mtn. Central U.K. 6 56.23N 4.31W
Ben More mtn. Strath. U.K. 6 56.26N 6.02W
Ben More Assynt mtn. U.K. 6 58.07N 4.52W
Bennett Canada 50 59.49N135.01W
Ben Nevis mtn. U.K. 6 56.48N 5.00W
Benneydale New Zealand 48 38.31S175.21E
Benoni R.S.A. 39 26.12S 28.18E
Bénoué r. Cameroon see Benue r. Nigeria 38
Bentinck I. Australia 44 17.04S139.30E
Benton Harbor U.S.A. 55 42.07N 86.27W
Benue d. Nigeria 38 7.20N 8.00E
Benue r. Nigeria 38 7.52N 6.45E
Ben Wyvis mtn. U.K. 6 57.40N 4.35W
Benxi China 25 41.21N123.45E
Beograd Yugo. 15 44.49N 20.28E
Beowawe U.S.A. 54 40.35N116.29W
Berat Albania 13 42.40N 19.59E

Berau, Teluk *b.* Indonesia **27** 2.20S133.00E
Berbera Somali Rep. **35** 10.28N 45.02E
Berbérati C.A.R. **36** 4.19N 15.51E
Berceto Italy **9** 44.31N 9.59E
Berchem Belgium **8** 50.48N 3.32E
Berck France **11** 50.25N 1.36E
Bercu France **8** 50.32N 3.15E
Berdichev U.S.S.R. **15** 49.54N 28.39E
Berdsk U.S.S.R. **20** 54.51N 82.51E
Berdyansk U.S.S.R. **19** 46.45N 36.47E
Beregovo U.S.S.R. **15** 48.13N 22.39E
Bereko Tanzania **37** 4.27S 35.43E
Beresford Australia **46** 29.14S136.40E
Berettyóújfalu Hungary **15** 47.14N 21.32E
Bereza U.S.S.R. **15** 52.32N 25.00E
Berezhany U.S.S.R. **15** 49.27N 24.56E
Berezina *r.* U.S.S.R. **15** 54.10N 28.10E
Berezna U.S.S.R. **15** 51.34N 31.46E
Berezniki U.S.S.R. **18** 59.26N 56.49E
Berezno U.S.S.R. **15** 51.00N 26.41E
Berezovka U.S.S.R. **15** 47.12N 30.56E
Berezovo U.S.S.R. **20** 63.58N 65.00E
Berga Spain **10** 42.06N 1.48E
Berga Sweden **17** 57.14N 16.03E
Bergama Turkey **13** 39.08N 27.10E
Bergamo Italy **9** 45.42N 9.40E
Bergen E. Germany **14** 54.25N 13.26E
Bergen Neth. **8** 52.40N 4.41E
Bergen Norway **17** 60.23N 5.20E
Bergen op Zoom Neth. **8** 51.30N 4.17E
Bergerac France **11** 44.50N 0.29E
Bergheim W. Germany **8** 50.58N 6.39E
Berghem Neth. **8** 51.46N 5.32E
Bergisch Gladbach W. Germany **8** 50.59N 7.10E
Bergkamen W. Germany **8** 51.35N 7.39E
Bergkvara Sweden **17** 56.23N 16.05E
Bergland U.S.A. **55** 46.36N 89.33W
Bergues France **8** 50.58N 2.21E
Bergum Neth. **8** 53.14N 5.59E
Berhampore India **29** 24.06N 88.18E
Berhampur India **29** 19.21N 84.51E
Bering Sea N. America / Asia **50** 65.00N170.00W
Bering Str. U.S.S.R. / U.S.A. **50** 65.00N170.00W
Berislav U.S.S.R. **19** 46.51N 33.26E
Berja Spain **10** 36.50N 2.56W
Berkåk Norway **16** 62.48N 10.03E
Berkel *r.* Neth. **8** 52.10N 6.12E
Berkeley U.S.A. **54** 37.57N122.18W
Berkner I. Antarctica **64** 79.30S 50.00W
Berkshire *d.* U.K. **5** 51.25N 1.03W
Berkshire Downs *hills* U.K. **5** 51.32N 1.36W
Berlin E. Germany **14** 52.32N 13.25E
Berlin N.H. U.S.A. **55** 44.29N 71.10W
Bermagui Australia **47** 36.28S150.03E
Bermejo *r.* San Juan Argentina **62** 31.40S 67.15W
Bermejo *r.* Tucumán Argentina **62** 26.47S 58.30W
Bern Switz. **14** 46.57N 7.26E
Bernard L. Canada **55** 45.44N 79.24W
Bernay France **9** 48.06N 0.36E
Bernburg E. Germany **14** 51.48N 11.44E
Berne *see* Bern Switz. **11**
Bernina *mtn.* Italy / Switz. **9** 46.22N 9.57E
Bernkastel W. Germany **8** 49.55N 7.05E
Beroun Czech. **14** 49.58N 14.04E
Berrechid Morocco **34** 33.17N 7.35W
Berri Australia **46** 34.17S140.36E
Berrigan Australia **47** 35.41S145.48E
Berry Head U.K. **5** 50.24N 3.28W
Bersenbrück W. Germany **8** 52.36N 7.58E
Bershad U.S.S.R. **15** 48.20N 29.30E
Berté, Lac *l.* Canada **55** 50.47N 68.30W
Bertinoro Italy **9** 44.09N 12.08E
Bertoua Cameroon **38** 4.34N 13.42E
Bertraghboy B. Rep. of Ire. **7** 53.23N 9.52W
Berwick-upon-Tweed U.K. **4** 55.46N 2.00W
Besalampy Madagascar **37** 16.45S 44.30E
Besançon France **11** 47.14N 6.02E
Bessarabia *f.* U.S.S.R. **15** 46.30N 28.40E
Bessemer U.S.A. **53** 33.22N 87.00W
Betanzos Spain **10** 43.17N 8.13W
Bétaré Oya Cameroon **38** 5.34N 14.09E
Bethal R.S.A. **39** 26.26S 29.27E
Bethany Beach *town* U.S.A. **55** 38.31N 75.04W
Bethel Alas. U.S.A. **50** 60.48N161.46W
Bethlehem R.S.A. **39** 28.13S 28.18E
Bethlehem U.S.A. **55** 40.36N 75.22W
Béthune France **8** 50.32N 2.38E
Béthune *r.* France **9** 49.53N 1.09E
Betim Brazil **59** 19.55S 44.07W
Betroka Madagascar **36** 23.16S 46.06E
Bet She'an Israel **32** 32.30N 35.30E
Bet Shemesh Israel **32** 31.45N 35.00E
Betsiamites Canada **55** 48.56N 68.38W
Bettles U.S.A. **50** 66.53N151.51W
Betzdorf W. Germany **8** 50.48N 7.54E
Beulah Australia **46** 35.59S142.26E
Beuvron *r.* France **9** 47.29N 3.31E
Beverley Australia **43** 32.06S116.56E
Beverley U.K. **4** 53.52N 0.26W
Beverley Hills *town* U.S.A. **54** 34.04N118.26W
Beverly Mass. U.S.A. **55** 42.33N 70.53W
Beverwijk Neth. **8** 52.29N 4.40E
Bewcastle Fells *hills* U.K. **4** 55.05N 2.50W
Bexhill U.K. **5** 50.51N 0.29E
Bexley U.K. **5** 51.26N 0.10E
Beyla Guinea **34** 8.42N 8.39W
Beyneu U.S.S.R. **19** 45.16N 55.04E
Beypazari Turkey **30** 40.10N 31.56E
Beyşehir Gölü *l.* Turkey **30** 37.47N 31.30E
Bezhanovo Bulgaria **13** 43.13N 24.26E
Bezhetsk U.S.S.R. **18** 57.49N 36.40E
Bezhitsa U.S.S.R. **18** 53.19N 34.17E
Béziers France **11** 43.21N 3.13E
Bhadrakh India **29** 21.04N 86.30E
Bhāgalpur India **29** 25.14N 86.59E
Bhamo Burma **29** 24.15N 97.15E
Bhatinda India **28** 30.12N 74.57E
Bhatkal India **28** 13.58N 74.34E
Bhātpāra India **29** 22.51N 88.31E
Bhaunagar India **28** 21.46N 72.14E
Bhīlwāra India **28** 25.21N 74.38E
Bhima *r.* India **28** 16.30N 77.10E
Bhopāl India **28** 23.17N 77.28E
Bhor India **28** 18.12N 73.53E
Bhubaneswar India **29** 20.15N 85.50E
Bhuj India **28** 23.12N 69.54E
Bhutan Asia **29** 27.25N 89.50E
Biak Indonesia **27** 1.10S136.05E
Biak *i.* Indonesia **27** 0.55S136.00E
Biała Podlaska Poland **15** 52.02N 23.06E
Białogard Poland **14** 54.00N 16.00E
Białystok Poland **15** 53.09N 23.10E
Biarritz France **11** 43.29N 1.33W
Biasca Switz. **9** 46.22N 8.58E
Bibā Egypt **32** 28.56N 30.59E
Bibbenluke Australia **47** 36.42S149.20E
Biberach W. Germany **14** 48.20N 8.02E
Bic Canada **55** 48.23N 68.43W
Bicas Brazil **59** 21.44S 43.04W
Bicester U.K. **5** 51.53N 1.09W
Bida Nigeria **38** 9.06N 5.59E
Bīdar India **28** 17.54N 77.33E
Biddeford U.S.A. **55** 43.30N 70.26W
Bideford U.K. **5** 51.01N 4.13W
Biel Switz. **11** 47.09N 7.16E
Bielefeld W. Germany **14** 52.02N 8.32E
Biella Italy **9** 45.34N 8.03E
Bielsko-Biała Poland **15** 49.49N 19.02E
Bielsk Podlaski Poland **15** 52.47N 23.12E
Bienville, Lac *l.* Canada **51** 55.05N 72.40W
Bié Plateau *f.* Angola **36** 13.00S 16.00E
Big Bald Mtn. Canada **55** 47.12N 66.25W
Big Bear Lake *town* U.S.A. **54** 34.15N116.53W
Big Belt Mts. U.S.A. **54** 46.40N111.25W
Bigbury B. U.K. **5** 50.15N 3.56W
Biggar Canada **50** 52.04N107.59W
Biggar U.K. **6** 55.38N 3.31W
Bighorn *r.* U.S.A. **54** 46.09N107.28W
Bighorn L. U.S.A. **54** 45.06N108.08W
Bighorn Mts. U.S.A. **54** 44.00N107.30W
Bight, Head of *b.* Australia **45** 31.29S131.16E
Bignasco Switz. **9** 46.20N 8.36E
Big Pine U.S.A. **54** 37.10N118.17W
Big Piney U.S.A. **54** 42.32N110.07W
Big Salmon Canada **50** 61.53N134.55W
Big Sandy U.S.A. **54** 48.11N110.07W
Big Smoky Valley *f.* U.S.A. **54** 38.30N117.15W
Big Snowy Mtn. U.S.A. **54** 46.50N109.30W
Big Spring *town* U.S.A. **52** 32.15N101.30W
Big Sur U.S.A. **54** 36.15N121.48W
Big Timber U.S.A. **54** 45.50N109.57W
Big Trout L. Canada **51** 53.45N 90.00W
Bihać Yugo. **12** 44.49N 15.53E
Bihar India **29** 25.13N 85.31E
Bihar *d.* India **29** 24.15N 86.00E
Biharamulo Tanzania **37** 2.34S 31.20E
Bihor *mtn.* Romania **15** 46.26N 22.43E
Bijagós, Arquipélago dos *is.* Guinea Bissau **34** 11.30N 16.00W
Bijāpur India **28** 16.52N 75.47E
Bijār Iran **31** 35.52N 47.39E
Bijāwar India **29** 24.36N 79.30E
Bijeljina Yugo. **13** 44.45N 19.13E
Bikaner India **28** 28.01N 73.22E
Bikin U.S.S.R. **25** 46.52N134.15E
Bilāspur India **29** 22.03N 82.12E
Bilauktaung Range *mts.* Burma **29** 13.20N 99.30E
Bilbao Spain **10** 43.15N 2.56W
Bilbays Egypt **32** 30.25N 31.34E
Bilecik Turkey **30** 40.10N 29.59E
Bilibino U.S.S.R. **21** 68.02N166.15E
Billabong *r.* Australia **46** 35.04S144.06E
Billeroo Australia **46** 31.13S139.58E
Billingham U.K. **4** 54.36N 1.18W
Billings U.S.A. **54** 45.47N108.27W
Bill of Portland *c.* U.K. **5** 50.32N 2.28W
Bilma Niger **38** 18.46N 12.50E
Biloela Australia **44** 24.24S150.30E
Biloxi U.S.A. **53** 30.30N 88.53W
Bilqās Qism Awwal Egypt **32** 31.14N 31.22E
Bilto Norway **16** 69.26N 21.35E
Bimberi, Mt. Australia **47** 35.40S148.47E
Bina-Etāwa India **29** 24.09N 78.10E
Binaija *mtn.* Indonesia **27** 3.10S129.30E
Bīnālūd, Kūh-e *mts.* Iran **31** 36.15N 59.00E
Binbee Australia **44** 20.20S147.55E
Binche Belgium **8** 50.25N 4.10E
Bindura Zimbabwe **39** 17.18S 31.20E
Binga Zimbabwe **39** 17.38S 27.19E
Binga, Mt. Zimbabwe **39** 19.47S 33.03E
Bingara Australia **47** 29.51S150.38E
Bingen W. Germany **8** 49.58N 7.55E
Bingerville Ivory Coast **38** 5.20N 3.53W
Bingham U.K. **4** 52.57N 0.57W
Bingham U.S.A. **55** 45.03N 69.53W
Binghamton U.S.A. **55** 42.08N 75.54W
Bingkor Malaysia **26** 5.26N116.15E
Bingöl Turkey **19** 38.54N 40.29E
Bingol Dağlari *mtn.* Turkey **30** 39.21N 41.22E
Binh Dinh Vietnam **26** 13.55N109.07E
Binjai Indonesia **26** 3.37N 98.25E
Binji Nigeria **38** 13.12N 4.55E
Binnaway Australia **47** 31.33S148.50E
Bintan *i.* Indonesia **26** 1.10N104.30E
Bintulu Malaysia **26** 3.12N113.01E
Binya Australia **47** 34.14S146.22E
Binzert Tunisia **34** 37.17N 9.51E
Biograd Yugo. **12** 43.56N 15.27E
Bioko *i.* Equat. Guinea **38** 3.25N 8.45E
Bi'r Abū 'Uwayqīlah *well* Egypt **32** 30.50N 34.07E
Bi'r ad Dakhal *well* Egypt **32** 28.40N 32.24E
Birāk Libya **34** 27.32N 14.17E
Bi'r al Jidy *well* Egypt **32** 30.13N 33.03E
Bi'r al Jufayr *well* Egypt **32** 30.49N 32.40E
Bi'r al 'Udayd *well* Egypt **32** 28.59N 34.05E
Birao C.A.R. **35** 10.17N 22.47E
Bi'r aş Şafrā' *well* Egypt **32** 28.46N 34.20E
Bi'r ath Thamadah *well* Egypt **32** 30.10N 33.28E
Bi'r Buerāt *well* Egypt **32** 28.59N 32.10E
Bi'r Bukhayt *well* Egypt **32** 29.13N 32.17E
Birchip Australia **46** 35.59S142.59E
Birch Mts. Canada **50** 57.30N112.30W
Birdsville Australia **44** 25.54S139.22E
Birdum Australia **42** 15.38S133.12E
Birecik Turkey **30** 37.03N 37.59E
Birhan *mtn.* Ethiopia **35** 11.00N 37.50E
Bi'r Ḥasanah *well* Egypt **32** 30.29N 33.47E
Bi'r Hooker *well* Egypt **32** 30.23N 30.20E
Birjand Iran **31** 32.54N 59.10E
Bi'r Jifjafah *well* Egypt **32** 30.28N 33.11E
Birk, Wādī *r.* Saudi Arabia **31** 24.08N 47.35E
Birkenfeld Rhein.-Pfalz W. Germany **8** 49.39N 7.10E
Birkenhead U.K. **4** 53.24N 3.01W
Birksgate Range *mts.* Australia **42** 27.10S129.45E
Bi'r Kusaybah *well* Egypt **32** 22.41N 29.55E
Bîrlad Romania **15** 46.14N 27.40E
Bi'r Lahfān *well* Egypt **32** 31.01N 33.52E
Birmingham U.K. **5** 52.30N 1.55W
Birmingham Ala. U.S.A. **53** 33.30N 86.55W
Bir Mogreïn Mauritania **34** 25.14N 11.35W
Birni Benin **38** 9.59N 1.34E
Birnin Gwari Nigeria **38** 11.02N 6.47E
Birnin Kebbi Nigeria **38** 12.30N 4.11E
Birni N'Konni Niger **38** 13.49N 5.19E
Birobidzhan U.S.S.R. **25** 48.49N132.54E
Birr Rep. of Ire. **7** 53.06N 7.56W
Birrie *r.* Australia **47** 29.43S146.37E
Birsk U.S.S.R. **18** 55.28N 55.31E
Bi'r Tābah *well* Egypt **32** 29.30N 34.53E
Bi'r Umm Sa'īd *well* Egypt **32** 29.40N 33.34E
Bi'r Umm 'Umayyid *well* Egypt **32** 27.53N 32.30E
Biržai U.S.S.R. **18** 56.10N 24.48E
Biscay, B. of France **11** 45.30N 4.00W
Bisceglie Italy **13** 41.14N 16.31E
Bishop Calif. U.S.A. **54** 37.22N118.24W
Bishop Auckland U.K. **4** 54.40N 1.40W
Bishop's Stortford U.K. **5** 51.53N 0.09E
Bisina, L. Uganda **37** 1.35N 34.08E
Biskra Algeria **34** 34.48N 5.40E
Bismarck U.S.A. **52** 46.50N100.48W
Bismarck Range *mts.* P.N.G. **27** 6.00S145.00E
Bismarck Sea Pacific Oc. **27** 4.00S146.30E
Bisotūn Iran **31** 34.22N 47.29E
Bispgården Sweden **16** 63.02N 16.40E
Bissau Guinea Bissau **34** 11.52N 15.39W
Bistrița Romania **15** 47.08N 24.30E
Bistrița *r.* Romania **15** 46.30N 26.54E
Bitam Gabon **36** 2.05N 11.30E
Bitburg W. Germany **8** 49.58N 6.31E
Bitlis Turkey **30** 38.23N 42.04E
Bitola Yugo. **13** 41.02N 21.21E
Bitter Creek *town* U.S.A. **54** 41.31N109.27W
Bitterfontein R.S.A. **39** 31.02S 18.14E
Bitterroot Range *mts.* U.S.A. **54** 47.06N115.10W
Biu Nigeria **38** 10.36N 12.11E
Biumba Rwanda **37** 1.38S 30.02E
Biwa ko *l.* Japan **23** 35.10N136.00E
Biyalā Egypt **32** 31.11N 31.13E
Biysk U.S.S.R. **20** 52.35N 85.16E
Bizerte *see* Binzert Tunisia **34**
Bjelovar Yugo. **13** 45.54N 16.51E
Bjorli Norway **17** 62.16N 8.13E
Björna Sweden **16** 63.32N 18.36E
Björnafjorden *est.* Norway **17** 60.06N 5.22E
Black *r.* Ark. U.S.A. **53** 35.30N 91.20W
Blackall Australia **44** 24.25S145.28E
Blackburn U.K. **4** 53.44N 2.30W
Blackfoot U.S.A. **54** 43.11N112.20W
Black Mtn. U.K. **5** 51.52N 3.50W
Black Mts. U.K. **5** 51.52N 3.09W
Blackpool U.K. **4** 53.48N 3.03W
Black River *town* Jamaica **57** 18.02N 77.52W
Black River *town* Mich. U.S.A. **55** 44.51N 83.21W
Black Rock *town* U.S.A. **54** 38.41N112.59W
Black Rock Desert U.S.A. **54** 41.10N119.00W
Black Sand Desert U.S.S.R. **31** 37.45N 60.00E
Black Sea Europe **15** 44.00N 30.00E
Blacksod B. Rep. of Ire. **7** 54.04N 10.00W
Black Sugarloaf Mt. Australia **47** 31.24S151.34E
Blackville Australia **47** 31.34S150.10E
Black Volta *r.* Ghana **38** 8.14N 2.11W
Blackwater *r.* Waterford Rep. of Ire. **7** 51.58N 7.52W
Blackwood *r.* Australia **43** 34.15S115.10E
Blaenau Ffestiniog U.K. **4** 53.00N 3.57W
Blagoevgrad Bulgaria **13** 42.02N 23.04E
Blagoveshchensk U.S.S.R. **25** 50.19N127.30E
Blain France **9** 47.29N 1.46W
Blair Athol Australia **44** 22.42S147.33E
Blair Atholl U.K. **6** 56.46N 3.51W
Blairgowrie U.K. **6** 56.36N 3.21W
Blanc, Cap *c.* Mauritania **34** 20.44N 17.05W
Blanc, Mont *mtn.* Europe **11** 45.50N 6.52E
Blanca, Bahía *b.* Argentina **63** 39.20S 62.00W
Blanca, Sierra *mtn.* U.S.A. **52** 33.23N105.48W
Blanchard U.S.A. **54** 48.01N116.59W
Blanche, L. Australia **46** 29.15S139.40E
Blanchetown Australia **46** 34.21S139.38E
Blanchewater Australia **46** 29.32S139.28E
Blanco, C. Argentina **63** 47.12S 65.20W
Blanco, C. Costa Rica **57** 9.36N 85.06W
Blanco, C. U.S.A. **54** 42.50N124.34W
Bland *r.* Australia **47** 33.42S147.30E
Blandford Forum U.K. **5** 50.52N 2.10W
Blankenberge Belgium **8** 51.18N 3.08E
Blansko Czech. **14** 49.22N 16.39E
Blantyre Malaŵi **37** 15.46S 35.00E
Blarney Rep. of Ire. **7** 51.56N 8.34W
Blatnica Bulgaria **15** 43.42N 28.31E
Blavet *r.* France **11** 47.43N 3.18W
Blaye France **11** 45.08N 0.40W
Blayney Australia **47** 33.32S149.19E
Blednaya, Gora *mtn.* U.S.S.R. **20** 76.23N 65.08E
Bleiburg Austria **14** 46.35N 14.48E
Blekinge *d.* Sweden **17** 56.20N 15.00E
Blenheim New Zealand **48** 41.32S173.58E
Bléré France **9** 47.20N 0.59E
Blerick Neth. **8** 51.22N 6.08E
Bletchley U.K. **5** 51.59N 0.45W
Blida Algeria **34** 36.30N 2.50E
Bligh Entrance Australia **44** 9.18S144.10E
Blind River *town* Canada **55** 46.16N 82.58W
Blinman Australia **46** 31.05S138.11E
Blitar Indonesia **26** 8.06S112.12E
Blitta Togo **38** 8.23N 1.06E
Bloemfontein R.S.A. **39** 29.07S 26.14E
Bloemhof R.S.A. **39** 27.37S 25.34E
Blois France **9** 47.36N 1.20E
Blönduós Iceland **16** 65.39N 20.18W
Bloods Creek *town* Australia **44** 26.28S135.17E
Bloody Foreland *c.* Rep. of Ire. **7** 55.09N 8.17W
Bloomington Ill. U.S.A. **53** 40.29N 89.00W
Bloomington Ind. U.S.A. **55** 39.10N 86.31W
Bloomsburg U.S.A. **55** 41.00N 76.27W
Bluefield U.S.A. **53** 37.14N 81.17W
Bluefields Nicaragua **57** 12.00N 83.49W
Blue Mts. Australia **47** 33.30S150.15E
Blue Mts. U.S.A. **54** 45.30N118.15W
Blue Mud B. Australia **44** 13.26S135.56E
Blue Nile *r. see* Azraq, Al Baḥr al *r.* Sudan **35**
Bluenose L. Canada **50** 68.30N119.35W
Blue Stack Mts. Rep. of Ire. **7** 54.44N 8.09W
Bluff New Zealand **48** 46.38S168.21E
Bluff U.S.A. **54** 37.17N109.33W
Bluff Knoll *mtn.* Australia **43** 34.25S118.15E
Blumenau Brazil **59** 26.55S 49.07W
Blyth Northum. U.K. **4** 55.07N 1.29W
Blythe U.S.A. **54** 33.37N114.36W
Bö Nordland Norway **16** 68.38N 14.35E
Bö Telemark Norway **17** 59.25N 9.04E
Bo Sierra Leone **34** 7.58N 11.45W
Boa Esperança Brazil **59** 21.03S 45.37W
Boane Mozambique **39** 26.02S 32.19E
Boa Vista Brazil **60** 2.51N 60.43W
Bobadah Australia **47** 32.18S146.42E
Bobadilla Spain **10** 37.02N 4.44W
Bobbili India **29** 18.34N 83.22E
Bobbio Italy **9** 44.46N 9.23E
Bobo-Dioulasso Burkina Faso **38** 11.11N 4.18W
Bobonong Botswana **39** 21.59S 28.29E
Bóbr *r.* Poland **14** 52.04N 15.04E
Bobr U.S.S.R. **15** 54.19N 29.18E
Bobruysk U.S.S.R. **15** 53.08N 29.10E
Bôca do Acre Brazil **60** 8.45S 67.23W
Bocaranga C.A.R. **36** 7.01N 15.35E
Bochnia Poland **15** 49.58N 20.26E
Bocholt W. Germany **8** 51.49N 6.37E
Bochum R.S.A. **39** 23.12S 29.12E
Bochum W. Germany **8** 51.28N 7.11E
Bockum-Hövel W. Germany **8** 51.42N 7.41E
Boconó Venezuela **60** 9.17N 70.17W
Bodalla Australia **47** 36.05S150.03E
Bodallin Australia **43** 31.22S118.52E
Bodélé *f.* Chad **34** 16.50N 17.10E
Boden Sweden **16** 65.50N 21.42E
Bodensee *l.* Europe **14** 47.40N 9.30E
Bode Sadu Nigeria **38** 8.57N 4.49E
Bodfish U.S.A. **54** 35.36N118.30W
Bodmin U.K. **5** 50.28N 4.44W
Bodmin Moor U.K. **5** 50.53N 4.35W
Bodö Norway **16** 67.18N 14.26E
Bodrum Turkey **30** 37.03N 27.28E
Boende Zaïre **36** 0.15S 20.49E
Bogalusa U.S.A. **53** 30.56N 89.53W
Bogan *r.* Australia **47** 30.00S146.20E
Bogan Gate *town* Australia **47** 33.08S147.50E
Bogenfels Namibia **39** 27.26S 15.22E
Boggabilla Australia **47** 28.36S150.21E
Boggabri Australia **47** 30.42S150.02E
Boggeragh Mts. Rep. of Ire. **7** 52.03N 8.53W
Bogia P.N.G. **27** 4.16S145.00E
Bognes Norway **16** 68.15N 16.00E
Bognor Regis U.K. **5** 50.47N 0.40W
Bog of Allen *f.* Rep. of Ire. **7** 53.17N 7.00W
Bogong, Mt. Australia **47** 36.45S147.21E
Bogor Indonesia **26** 6.34S106.45E
Bogotá Colombia **60** 4.38N 74.05W
Bogué Mauritania **34** 16.40N 14.10W
Boguslav U.S.S.R. **15** 49.32N 30.52E
Bo Hai *b.* China **25** 38.30N119.30E
Bohain France **8** 49.59N 3.28E
Bohemian Forest *see* Böhmerwald *mts.* W. Germany / Czech. **14**
Böhmerwald *mts.* W. Germany / Czech. **14** 49.20N 13.10E
Bohol *i.* Phil. **27** 9.45N124.10E
Boiaçu Brazil **60** 0.27S 61.46W
Boigu *i.* Australia **44** 9.16S142.12E
Bois, Lac des *l.* Canada **50** 66.40N125.15W
Boise U.S.A. **54** 43.37N116.13W
Bois-Guillaume France **9** 49.28N 1.08E
Boizenburg E. Germany **14** 53.22N 10.43E
Bojador, Cabo *c.* W. Sahara **34** 26.08N 14.30W
Bojeador, C. Phil. **27** 18.30N120.50E
Bojnūrd Iran **31** 37.28N 57.20E
Bokani Nigeria **38** 9.27N 5.13E
Boké Guinea **34** 10.57N 14.13W
Bokhara *r.* Australia **47** 29.55S146.42E
Boknafjorden *est.* Norway **17** 59.10N 5.35E
Bol Chad **38** 13.27N 14.40E
Bolac, L. Australia **46** 37.45S142.55E
Bolama Guinea Bissau **34** 11.35N 15.30W
Bolanda, Jabal *mtn.* Sudan **35** 7.44N 25.28E
Bolbec France **9** 49.34N 0.28E
Bole Ghana **38** 9.03N 2.23W
Bolesławiec Poland **14** 51.16N 15.34E
Bolgatanga Ghana **38** 10.42N 0.52W
Bolgrad U.S.S.R. **15** 45.42N 28.40E
Bolívar Argentina **63** 36.14S 61.07W
Bolivia S. America **62** 17.00S 65.00W
Bollnäs Sweden **17** 61.21N 16.25E
Bollon Australia **45** 28.02S147.28E
Bollstabruk Sweden **16** 62.59N 17.42E
Bolmen *l.* Sweden **17** 56.55N 13.40E
Bologna Italy **9** 44.30N 11.20E
Bologoye U.S.S.R. **18** 57.58N 34.00E
Bolomba Zaïre **36** 0.30N 19.13E
Bolsena, Lago di *l.* Italy **12** 42.36N 11.55E
Bolshaya Glushitsa U.S.S.R. **18** 52.28N 50.30E
Bolshaya Pyssa U.S.S.R. **18** 64.11N 48.44E
Bolsherechye U.S.S.R. **20** 56.07N 74.40E
Bol'shevik, Ostrov *i.* U.S.S.R. **21** 78.30N102.00E
Bolshezemelskaya Tundra *f.* U.S.S.R. **18** 67.00N 56.10E
Bolshoy Atlym U.S.S.R. **20** 62.17N 66.30E
Bol'shoy Balkhan, Khrebet *mts.* U.S.S.R. **31** 39.38N 54.30E
Bol'shoy Irgiz *r.* U.S.S.R. **18** 52.00N 47.20E
Bol'shoy Lyakhovskiy, Ostrov *i.* U.S.S.R. **21** 73.30N142.00E
Bol'shoy Onguren U.S.S.R. **21** 53.40N107.40E
Bolshoy Uzen *r.* U.S.S.R. **19** 49.00N 49.40E
Bolsover U.K. **4** 53.14N 1.18W
Bolton U.K. **4** 53.35N 2.26W
Bolu Turkey **30** 40.45N 31.38E
Bolus Head Rep. of Ire. **7** 51.47N 10.20W
Bolvadin Turkey **30** 38.43N 31.02E
Bolzano Italy **9** 46.30N 11.20E
Boma Zaïre **36** 5.50S 13.03E
Bomaderry Australia **47** 34.21S150.34E
Bomadi Nigeria **38** 5.13N 6.01E
Bombala Australia **47** 36.55S149.16E
Bombay India **28** 18.56N 72.51E
Bombo Uganda **37** 0.34N 32.32E
Bom Despacho Brazil **59** 19.46S 45.15W
Bomi China **24** 29.50N 95.45E
Bömlafjorden *est.* Norway **17** 59.39N 5.20E
Bömlo *i.* Norway **17** 59.46N 5.13E
Bomokandi *r.* Zaïre **37** 3.37N 26.09E
Bonaire *i.* Neth. Antilles **60** 12.15N 68.27W
Bonanza U.S.A. **54** 40.01N109.11W
Bonaparte Archipelago *is.* Australia **42** 14.17S125.18E
Bonar-Bridge *town* U.K. **6** 57.53N 4.21W
Bonavista Canada **51** 48.38N 53.08W
Bon Bon Australia **46** 30.26S135.28E
Bondeno Italy **9** 44.53N 11.25E
Bondo Zaïre **36** 3.47N 23.45E
Bondoukou Ivory Coast **38** 8.03N 2.15W
Bone, Teluk *b.* Indonesia **27** 4.00S120.50E
Bo'ness U.K. **6** 56.01N 3.36W
Bongouanou Ivory Coast **38** 6.44N 4.10W
Bonifacio, Str. of Med. Sea **12** 41.18N 9.10E
Bonn W. Germany **8** 50.44N 7.06E
Bonners Ferry U.S.A. **54** 48.41N116.18W
Bonnétable France **9** 48.11N 0.26E
Bonneval France **9** 48.11N 1.24E
Bonneville Salt Flats *f.* U.S.A. **54** 40.45N113.52W
Bonney, L. Australia **46** 37.47S140.23E
Bonnie Rock *town* Australia **43** 30.32S118.21E
Bonny Nigeria **38** 4.25N 7.10E
Bonny, Bight of Africa **38** 2.58N 7.00E
Bonshaw Australia **47** 29.08S150.53E
Bontang Indonesia **26** 0.05N117.31E
Bonthain Indonesia **26** 5.32S119.58E
Bonthe Sierra Leone **34** 7.32N 12.30W
Bonython Range *mts.* Australia **42** 23.51S129.00E
Boogah Australia **47** 28.24S147.25E
Bookaloo Australia **46** 31.56S137.21E
Boolabooka, L. Australia **46** 32.40S143.13E
Boolaloo Australia **42** 22.30S115.51E
Booleroo Centre Australia **46** 32.53S138.21E
Booligal Australia **47** 33.54S144.54E
Boologooro Australia **42** 24.21S114.02E
Boom Belgium **8** 51.07N 4.21E
Boomrivier R.S.A. **39** 29.34S 20.26E
Boonah Australia **47** 28.00S152.36E
Boonville N.Y. U.S.A. **55** 43.29N 75.20W
Boorabbin Australia **43** 31.14S120.21E
Boorindal Australia **47** 30.23S146.11E
Booroorban Australia **47** 34.56S144.46E
Boorowa Australia **47** 34.26S148.48E
Boort Australia **46** 36.08S143.46E
Boorthanna Australia **46** 28.32S135.52E
Boothia, G. of Canada **51** 70.00N 90.00W
Boothia Pen. Canada **51** 70.30N 95.00W
Bootra Australia **46** 30.00S143.00E
Bopeechee Australia **46** 29.36S137.23E
Boppard W. Germany **8** 50.13N 7.35E
Bor Czech. **14** 49.43N 12.47E
Bor Yugo. **13** 44.05N 22.07E
Borah Peak *mtn.* U.S.A. **54** 44.08N113.38W
Borås Sweden **17** 57.43N 12.55E
Borāzjān Iran **31** 29.14N 51.12E
Borba Brazil **60** 4.24S 59.35W
Borda, C. Australia **46** 35.45S136.34E
Bordeaux France **11** 44.50N 0.34W
Borden Australia **43** 34.05S118.16E
Borden I. Canada **50** 78.30N111.00W
Borden Pen. Canada **51** 73.00N 83.00W
Borders *d.* U.K. **6** 55.30N 2.53W
Bordertown Australia **46** 36.18S140.49E
Bordheyri Iceland **16** 65.12N 21.06W
Bordighera Italy **9** 43.46N 7.39E
Bordj Flye Sainte Marie Algeria **34** 27.17N 2.59E
Bordö *i.* Faroe Is. **16** 62.10N 7.13W
Borgå Finland **17** 60.24N 25.40E
Borga Sweden **16** 64.49N 15.05E
Börgefjell *mtn.* Norway **16** 65.20N 13.45E
Börgefjell Nat. Park Norway **16** 65.00N 13.58E
Borger Neth. **8** 52.57N 6.46E
Borger U.S.A. **52** 35.39N101.24W
Borgholm Sweden **17** 56.53N 16.39E
Borghorst W. Germany **8** 52.08N 7.27E
Borgo Italy **9** 46.03N 11.27E
Borgomanero Italy **9** 45.42N 8.28E
Borgo San Dalmazzo Italy **9** 44.20N 7.30E
Borgo San Lorenzo Italy **9** 43.57N 11.23E
Borgosesia Italy **9** 45.43N 8.16E

orgo Val di Taro Italy 9 44.29N 9.46E
orgund Norway 17 61.03N 7.49E
orislav U.S.S.R. 15 49.18N 23.28E
orisoglebsk U.S.S.R. 19 51.23N 42.02E
orisov U.S.S.R. 15 54.09N 28.30E
orispol U.S.S.R. 15 50.21N 30.59E
orja Peru 60 4.20S 77.40W
orken W. Germany 8 51.50N 6.52E
orkum W. Germany 8 53.34N 6.41E
orkum i. W. Germany 8 53.35N 6.45E
orlänge Sweden 17 60.29N 15.25E
orley, C. Antarctica 64 66.15S 55.00E
ormio Italy 9 46.28N 10.22E
orndiep g. Neth. 8 53.28N 5.35E
orneo i. Asia 26 1.00N114.00E
ornheim W. Germany 8 50.45N 7.00E
ornholm i. Denmark 17 55.10N 15.00E
orno d. Nigeria 38 12.20N 12.40E
ornu, Plain of f. Nigeria 38 12.30N 13.00E
oro r. Sudan 35 8.50N 28.00E
orodyanka U.S.S.R. 15 50.38N 29.59E
oromo Burkina Faso 38 11.43N 2.53W
oroughbridge U.K. 4 54.06N 1.23W
orovichi U.S.S.R. 18 58.22N 34.00E
orrika Australia 46 35.00S140.05E
orroloola Australia 44 16.04S136.17E
orşa Romania 15 46.56N 23.40E
orşa Romania 15 47.39N 24.40E
orth U.K. 5 52.29N 4.03W
orüjerd Iran 31 33.54N 48.47E
ory Tucholskie f. Poland 15 53.45N 17.30E
orzhomi U.S.S.R. 19 41.49N 43.23E
orzna U.S.S.R. 19 51.15N 32.25E
orzya U.S.S.R. 21 50.24N116.35E
osa Italy 12 40.18N 8.29E
osanska Gradiška Yugo. 13 45.09N 17.15E
osanski Novi Yugo. 14 45.03N 16.23E
oscastle U.K. 5 50.42N 4.42W
oshof R.S.A. 39 28.32S 25.12E
osna r. Yugo. 13 45.04N 18.27E
osna i Hercegovina d. Yugo. 13 44.00N 18.10E
osnik Indonesia 27 1.09S136.14E
ōsō-hantō pen. Japan 23 35.08N140.00E
osporus str. see İstanbul Boğazi str. Turkey 13
ossangoa C.A.R. 36 6.27N 17.21E
osso Niger 38 13.43N 13.19E
osten Hu l. China 24 42.00N 87.00E
oston U.K. 4 52.59N 0.02W
Boston U.S.A. 55 42.21N 71.04W
Boston B. Australia 46 34.35S136.02E
Botany B. Australia 47 34.04S151.08E
Botev mtn. Bulgaria 13 42.43N 24.55E
Botevgrad Bulgaria 13 42.55N 23.57E
Bothnia, G. of Europe 16 63.30N 20.30E
Botletle r. Botswana 39 21.06S 24.47E
Botoşani Romania 15 47.44N 26.41E
Botou Burkina Faso 38 12.47N 2.02E
Botrange mtn. Belgium 8 50.30N 6.04E
Botro Ivory Coast 38 7.51N 5.19W
Botswana Africa 39 22.00S 24.15E
Bottrop W. Germany 8 51.31N 6.55E
Botucatu Brazil 59 22.52S 48.30W
Bouaflé Ivory Coast 38 7.01N 5.47W
Bouaké Ivory Coast 38 7.42N 5.00W
Bouar C.A.R. 38 5.58N 15.35E
Bou Arfa Morocco 34 32.30N 1.59W
Bouchoir France 9 49.45N 2.41E
Bougainville i. Pacific Oc. 40 6.00S155.00E
Bougouni Mali 34 11.25N 7.28W
Bouillon Belgium 8 49.48N 5.03E
Boulder Australia 43 30.55S121.32E
Boulder U.S.A. 52 40.01N105.17W
Boulder City U.S.A. 54 35.59N114.50W
Boulia Australia 44 22.54S139.54E
Boulogne France 11 50.43N 1.37E
Boulogne-Billancourt France 9 48.50N 2.15E
Boultoum Niger 38 14.45N 10.25E
Boumba r. Cameroon 38 2.00N 15.10E
Bouna Ivory Coast 38 9.19N 2.53W
Boundary Peak mtn. U.S.A. 54 37.51N118.21W
Bountiful U.S.A. 54 40.53N111.53W
Bouraga well Mali 38 19.00N 3.36W
Bourem Mali 38 16.59N 0.20W
Bourg France 11 46.12N 5.13E
Bourganeuf France 11 45.57N 1.44E
Bourges France 11 47.05N 2.23E
Bourg Madame France 11 42.26N 1.55E
Bourgogne d. France 11 47.10N 4.20E
Bourgogne, Canal de France 9 47.58N 3.30E
Bourgoin France 11 45.35N 5.17E
Bourgueil France 9 47.17N 0.10E
Bourke Australia 47 30.09S145.59E
Bournemouth U.K. 5 50.43N 1.53W
Boussac France 11 46.22N 2.13E
Bouvard, C. Australia 43 32.40S115.34E
Bovill U.S.A. 54 46.51N116.24W
Bovril Argentina 63 31.22S 59.25W
Bowelling Australia 43 33.25S116.27E
Bowen Australia 44 20.00S148.15E
Bowen, Mt. Australia 47 37.11S148.34E
Bowling Green U.S.A. 53 37.00N 86.29W
Bowling Green, C. Australia 44 19.19S146.25E
Bowman I. Antarctica 64 65.00S104.00E
Bowral Australia 47 34.30S150.24E
Bowser Australia 47 36.19S146.23E
Boxholm Sweden 17 58.12N 15.03E
Bo Xian China 25 33.40N115.50E
Box Tank Australia 46 32.13S142.17E
Boxtel Neth. 8 51.36N 5.20E
Boyabat Turkey 30 41.27N 34.45E
Boyanup Australia 43 33.29S115.40E
Boyarka U.S.S.R. 15 50.20N 30.26E
Boyd r. Australia 47 29.51S152.25E
Boyle Rep. of Ire. 7 53.58N 8.19W
Boyne r. Rep. of Ire. 7 53.43N 6.17W
Boyoma Falls f. Zaïre 36 0.18N 25.30E
Boyup Brook Australia 43 33.50S116.22E
Bozca Ada i. Turkey 13 39.49N 26.03E
Bozeman U.S.A. 54 45.41N111.02W
Bozen see Bolzano Italy 9
Bra Italy 9 44.42N 7.51E
Brabant d. Belgium 8 50.47N 4.30E
Brač i. Yugo. 13 43.20N 16.38E
Bracadale, Loch U.K. 6 57.22N 6.30W
Bracebridge Canada 55 45.02N 79.19W
Bracieux France 9 47.33N 1.33E
Bräcke Sweden 16 62.44N 15.30E
Brad Romania 13 46.06N 22.48E
Bradano r. Italy 13 40.23N 16.52E
Bradenton U.S.A. 53 27.29N 82.33W
Bradford Canada 55 44.07N 79.34W
Bradford U.K. 4 53.47N 1.45W
Bradford Penn. U.S.A. 55 41.58N 78.39W
Bradworthy U.K. 5 50.54N 4.22W
Braemar U.K. 6 57.01N 3.24W
Braga Portugal 10 41.32N 8.26W
Bragado Argentina 63 35.10S 60.30W
Bragança Brazil 61 1.03S 46.46W
Bragança Portugal 10 41.47N 6.46W
Bragança Paulista Brazil 59 22.59S 46.32W
Bragin U.S.S.R. 15 51.49N 30.16E
Brahmaputra r. Asia 29 23.50N 89.45E
Braidwood Australia 47 35.27S149.50E
Brăila Romania 15 45.18N 27.58E
Brainerd U.S.A. 53 46.20N 94.10W
Braintree U.K. 5 51.53N 0.32E
Brålanda Sweden 17 58.34N 12.22E
Brampton Canada 55 43.41N 79.46W
Brampton U.K. 4 54.56N 2.43W
Bramsche W. Germany 8 52.26N 7.59E
Branco r. Brazil 60 1.00S 62.00W
Brandberg mtn. Namibia 39 21.08S 14.35E
Brandbu Norway 17 60.28N 10.30E
Brande Denmark 17 55.57N 9.07E
Brandenburg E. Germany 14 52.25N 12.34E
Brandfort R.S.A. 39 28.41S 26.27E
Brandon Canada 51 49.50N 99.57W
Brandon Mtn. Rep. of Ire. 7 52.14N 10.15W
Brandon Pt. Rep. of Ire. 7 52.17N 10.11W
Braniewo Poland 15 54.24N 19.50E
Bransby Australia 46 28.40S142.00E
Branxholme Australia 46 37.51S141.49E
Brasil, Planalto mts. Brazil 61 17.02S 50.00W
Brasiléia Brazil 60 11.00S 68.44W
Brasília Brazil 61 15.45S 47.57W
Braşov Romania 15 45.40N 25.35E
Brass Nigeria 38 4.20N 6.15E
Brasschaat Belgium 8 51.18N 4.28E
Bratislava Czech. 15 48.10N 17.10E
Bratsk U.S.S.R. 21 56.20N101.15E
Bratsk Vodokhranilishche resr. U.S.S.R. 21 54.40N103.00E
Bratslav U.S.S.R. 15 48.49N 28.51E
Braunau Austria 14 48.15N 13.02E
Braunschweig W. Germany 14 52.15N 10.30E
Braunton U.K. 5 51.06N 4.09W
Brava Somali Rep. 37 1.02N 44.02E
Bravo del Norte, Rio r. Mexico see Rio Grande r. Mexico/U.S.A. 56
Brawley U.S.A. 54 32.59N115.31W
Bray France 9 48.25N 3.14E
Bray Rep. of Ire. 7 53.12N 6.07W
Bray Head Kerry Rep. of Ire. 7 51.53N 10.26W
Brazilian Highlands see Brasil, Planalto mts. Brazil 61
Brazos r. U.S.A. 53 28.55N 95.20W
Brazzaville Congo 36 4.14S 15.14E
Brčko Yugo. 15 44.53N 18.48E
Brda r. Poland 15 53.07N 18.08E
Breadalbane f. U.K. 6 56.30N 4.20W
Bream B. New Zealand 48 36.00S174.30E
Brécey France 9 48.44N 1.10W
Brechin U.K. 6 56.44N 2.40W
Breckland f. U.K. 5 52.28N 0.40E
Břeclav Czech. 14 48.46N 16.53E
Brecon U.K. 5 51.57N 3.23W
Brecon Beacons mts. U.K. 5 51.53N 3.27W
Breda Neth. 8 51.35N 4.46E
Bredasdorp R.S.A. 39 34.31S 20.03E
Bredbo Australia 47 35.57S149.10E
Bregenz Austria 14 47.31N 9.46E
Bregovo Bulgaria 13 44.08N 22.39E
Bréhal France 9 48.53N 1.30W
Breidhafjördhur est. Iceland 16 65.15N 23.00W
Breim Norway 17 61.44N 6.25E
Brekstad Norway 16 63.50N 9.40E
Bremangerland i. Norway 17 61.51N 5.02E
Bremen W. Germany 14 53.05N 8.48E
Bremerhaven W. Germany 14 53.33N 8.35E
Bremer Range mts. Australia 43 32.40S120.55E
Bremerton U.S.A. 54 47.34N122.38W
Brenda Australia 47 29.03S147.12E
Brenner Pass Italy/Austria 14 47.00N 11.30E
Breno Italy 9 45.57N 10.18E
Brent Canada 55 46.02N 78.29W
Brenta r. Italy 9 45.25N 12.15E
Brentwood U.K. 5 51.38N 0.18E
Brescia Italy 9 45.33N 10.12E
Breskens Neth. 8 51.24N 3.34E
Bressay i. U.K. 6 60.08N 1.05W
Bressuire France 11 46.50N 0.28W
Brest France 11 48.23N 4.30W
Brest U.S.S.R. 15 52.08N 23.40E
Bretagne d. France 11 48.15N 2.30W
Breteuil France 9 49.38N 2.18E
Breteuil-sur-Iton France 9 48.50N 0.55E
Brett, C. New Zealand 48 35.15S174.20E
Breuil-Cervinia Italy 9 45.56N 7.38E
Brevik Norway 17 59.04N 9.42E
Brewarrina Australia 47 29.57S147.54E
Brewer U.S.A. 55 44.48N 68.46W
Brezhnev U.S.S.R. 18 55.42N 52.20E
Brezovo Bulgaria 13 42.20N 25.06E
Bria C.A.R. 35 6.32N 21.59E
Briançon France 11 44.53N 6.39E
Briare France 9 47.38N 2.44E
Bribbaree Australia 47 34.07S147.51E
Bribie I. Australia 45 27.00S153.07E
Brichany U.S.S.R. 15 48.20N 27.01E
Bricquebec France 9 49.28N 1.38W
Bride U.K. 4 54.23N 4.24W
Bridgend U.K. 5 51.30N 3.35W
Bridgeport Calif. U.S.A. 54 38.10N119.13W
Bridgeport Conn. U.S.A. 55 41.12N 73.12W
Bridger U.S.A. 54 45.18N108.55W
Bridgetown Australia 43 33.57S116.08E
Bridgetown Barbados 57 13.06N 59.37W
Bridgetown Rep. of Ire. 7 52.14N 6.33W
Bridgewater Canada 51 44.23N 64.31W
Bridgewater, C. Australia 46 38.25S141.28E
Bridgnorth U.K. 5 52.33N 2.25W
Bridgwater U.K. 5 51.08N 3.00W
Bridlington U.K. 4 54.06N 0.11W
Brie f. France 9 48.40N 3.20E
Brienne-le-Château France 9 48.24N 4.32E
Brig Switz. 9 46.19N 8.00E
Brigg U.K. 4 53.33N 0.30W
Brigham City U.S.A. 54 41.31N112.01W
Bright Australia 47 36.42S146.58E
Brighton U.K. 5 50.50N 0.09W
Brighton Downs town Australia 44 23.20S141.34E
Brindisi Italy 13 40.38N 17.57E
Brinkworth Australia 46 33.42S138.24E
Brionne France 9 49.12N 0.43E
Briouze France 9 48.42N 0.22W
Brisbane Australia 47 27.30S153.00E
Brisighella Italy 9 44.13N 11.46E
Bristol U.K. 5 51.26N 2.35W
Bristol Tenn. U.S.A. 53 36.35N 82.12W
Bristol B. U.S.A. 50 58.00N158.50W
Bristol Channel U.K. 5 51.17N 3.20W
British Antarctic Territory Antarctica 64 70.00S 50.00W
British Columbia d. Canada 50 55.00N125.00W
British Mts. Canada 50 69.00N140.20W
British Virgin Is. C. America 57 18.30N 64.30W
Britstown R.S.A. 39 30.34S 23.30E
Britt Canada 55 45.46N 80.35W
Brive France 11 45.09N 1.32E
Briviesca Spain 10 42.33N 3.19W
Brixham U.K. 5 50.24N 3.31W
Brno Czech. 14 49.11N 16.39E
Broach India 28 21.42N 72.58E
Broad Arrow Australia 43 30.32S121.20E
Broad B. U.K. 6 58.15N 6.15W
Broadback r. Canada 55 51.20N 78.50W
Broadford Australia 47 37.16S145.03E
Broadmere Australia 44 25.30S149.30E
Broadsound Range mts. Australia 44 22.30S149.30E
Broadwater Australia 47 28.59S 13.16E
Broadway U.K. 5 52.02N 1.51W
Brochet Canada 51 57.53N101.40W
Brockton U.S.A. 55 42.05N 71.01W
Brockville Canada 55 44.35N 75.41W
Brockway Mont. U.S.A. 54 47.15N105.45W
Brod Hrvatska Yugo. 15 45.09N 18.02E
Brodeur Pen. Canada 51 73.00N 88.00W
Brodick U.K. 6 55.34N 5.09W
Brodnica Poland 15 53.16N 19.23E
Brodribb River town Australia 47 37.42S148.37E
Brody U.S.S.R. 15 50.05N 25.08E
Broglie France 9 49.01N 0.32E
Broken B. Australia 47 33.34S151.18E
Broken Hill town Australia 46 31.57S141.30E
Bromley U.K. 5 51.24N 0.02E
Bromsgrove U.K. 5 52.20N 2.03W
Brønderslev Denmark 17 57.16N 9.58E
Brong-Ahafo d. Ghana 38 7.45N 1.30W
Brönnöysund Norway 16 65.30N 12.10E
Brookes Inlet Australia 43 34.55S116.25E
Brooke's Point town Phil. 26 8.50N117.52E
Brookhaven U.S.A. 53 31.36N 90.28W
Brookings Oreg. U.S.A. 54 42.03N124.17W
Brookings S.Dak. U.S.A. 53 44.19N 96.47W
Brooks Canada 50 50.35N111.53W
Brooks Range mts. U.S.A. 50 68.50N152.00W
Brookton Australia 43 32.22S117.01E
Broom, Loch U.K. 6 57.52N 5.07W
Broome Australia 42 17.58S122.15E
Broome Hill town Australia 43 33.50S117.35E
Brora U.K. 6 58.01N 3.52W
Brora r. U.K. 6 58.00N 3.51W
Brosna r. Rep.of Ire. 7 53.13N 7.58W
Brothers U.S.A. 54 43.49N120.36W
Brou France 9 48.13N 1.11E
Brough England U.K. 4 54.32N 2.19W
Brough Scotland U.K. 6 60.29N 1.12W
Broughton r. Australia 46 33.21S137.46E
Broughton in Furness U.K. 4 54.17N 3.12W
Brouwershaven Neth. 8 51.44N 3.53E
Brovary U.S.S.R. 15 50.30N 30.45E
Brovst Denmark 17 57.06N 9.32E
Brown, Mt. Australia 46 32.33S138.02E
Browning U.S.A. 54 48.34N113.01W
Brownwood U.S.A. 52 31.42N 98.59W
Bruay-en-Artois France 8 50.29N 2.36E
Bruce Pen. Canada 55 44.50N 81.20W
Bruce Rock town Australia 43 31.52S118.09E
Bruges see Brugge Belgium 8
Brugge Belgium 8 51.13N 3.14E
Brühl W. Germany 8 50.50N 6.55E
Brumadinho Brazil 59 20.09S 44.11W
Brumado Brazil 61 14.13S 41.40W
Brunei Asia 26 4.56N114.58E
Brünen W. Germany 8 51.45N 6.41E
Brunflo Sweden 16 63.04N 14.50E
Brunner New Zealand 48 42.28S171.12E
Brunsbüttel W. Germany 14 53.44N 9.05E
Brunssum Neth. 8 50.57N 5.59E
Brunswick Ga. U.S.A. 53 31.09N 81.21W
Brunswick Maine U.S.A. 55 43.55N 69.58W
Brunswick B. Australia 42 15.05S125.00E
Brunswick Junction Australia 43 33.15S115.45E
Bruny I. Australia 45 43.15S147.16E
Brusilovka U.S.S.R. 19 50.39N 54.59E
Brussel see Bruxelles Belgium 8
Brussels see Bruxelles Belgium 8
Bruthen Australia 47 37.44S147.49E
Bruton U.K. 5 51.06N 2.28W
Bruxelles Belgium 8 50.50N 4.23E
Bryan Ohio U.S.A. 55 41.30N 84.34W
Bryan Tex. U.S.A. 53 30.41N 96.24W
Bryan, Mt. Australia 46 33.26S138.27E
Bryansk U.S.S.R. 18 53.15N 34.09E
Bryne Norway 17 58.44N 5.39E
Bryson Canada 55 45.41N 76.37W
Bryson, Lac l. Canada 55 46.19N 77.27W
Brzeg Poland 15 50.52N 17.27E
Bsharrī Lebanon 32 34.15N 36.00E
Bua r. Malaŵi 37 12.42S 34.15E
Bu'ayrāt al Ḥasūn Libya 34 31.24N 15.44E
Būbiyān, Jazīrat i. Kuwait 31 29.45N 48.15E
Bubye r. Zimbabwe 39 22.18S 31.00E
Bucak Turkey 30 37.28N 30.36E
Bucaramanga Colombia 60 7.08N 73.10W
Buchach U.S.S.R. 15 49.09N 25.20E
Buchan Australia 47 37.30S148.09E
Buchanan Liberia 34 5.57N 10.02W
Buchanan, L. Australia 44 21.28S145.52E
Buchan Ness c. U.K. 6 57.28N 1.47W
Buchans Canada 51 48.49N 56.52W
Bucharest see Bucureşti Romania 15
Buchloe W. Germany 14 48.02N 10.44E
Buchy France 9 49.35N 1.22E
Buckambool Mt. Australia 47 31.55S145.40E
Buckhaven and Methil U.K. 4 56.11N 3.03W
Buckie U.K. 6 57.40N 2.58W
Buckingham U.K. 5 52.00N 0.59W
Buckingham B. Australia 44 12.10S135.46E
Buckinghamshire d. U.K. 5 51.50N 0.48W
Buckland Tableland f. Australia 44 25.00S148.00E
Buckleboo Australia 46 32.55S136.12E
Bucquoy France 8 50.09N 2.43E
Bu Craa W. Sahara 34 26.21N 12.57W
Bucureşti Romania 15 44.25N 26.06E
Bucyrus U.S.A. 55 40.47N 82.57W
Bud Norway 16 62.54N 6.56E
Budapest Hungary 15 47.30N 19.03E
Budaun India 29 28.02N 79.07E
Budda Australia 46 31.12S144.16E
Budd Coast f. Antarctica 64 67.00S112.00E
Bude U.K. 5 50.49N 4.33W
Bude B. U.K. 5 50.50N 4.40W
Budennovsk U.S.S.R. 19 44.50N 44.10E
Buea Cameroon 38 4.09N 9.13E
Buenaventura Colombia 60 3.54N 77.02W
Buenaventura Mexico 56 29.51N107.29W
Buenos Aires Argentina 63 34.40S 58.25W
Buenos Aires d. Argentina 63 36.30S 59.00W
Buenos Aires, L. Argentina/Chile 63 46.35S 72.00W
Buffalo N.Y. U.S.A. 55 42.52N 78.55W
Buffalo Wyo. U.S.A. 54 44.21N106.42W
Bug r. Poland 15 52.29N 21.11E
Buga Colombia 60 3.53N 76.17W
Bugaldie Australia 47 31.02S149.08E
Bugembe Uganda 37 0.26N 33.16E
Bugene Tanzania 37 1.34S 31.07E
Buggs Island l. U.S.A. 53 36.35N 78.20W
Bugrino U.S.S.R. 18 68.45N 49.15E
Bugt China 25 48.45N121.58E
Bugulma U.S.S.R. 18 54.32N 52.46E
Buguma Nigeria 38 4.43N 6.53E
Buguruslan U.S.S.R. 18 53.36N 52.30E
Buhera Zimbabwe 39 19.21S 31.25E
Buhuşi Romania 15 46.43N 26.41E
Builth Wells U.K. 5 52.09N 3.24W
Buinsk U.S.S.R. 18 54.58N 48.15E
Buitenpost Neth. 8 53.15N 6.09E
Buji P.N.G. 44 9.07S142.26E
Bujumbura Burundi 37 3.22S 29.21E
Bukavu Zaïre 37 2.30S 28.49E
Bukene Tanzania 37 4.13S 32.52E
Bukhara U.S.S.R. 31 39.47N 64.26E
Buki U.S.S.R. 15 49.02N 30.29E
Bukima Tanzania 37 1.48S 33.25E
Bukittinggi Indonesia 26 0.18S100.20E
Bukoba Tanzania 37 1.20S 31.49E
Bukuru Nigeria 38 9.48N 8.52E
Būl, Kūh-e mtn. Iran 31 30.48N 52.45E
Bula Indonesia 27 3.07S130.27E
Bulan Phil. 27 12.40N123.53E
Bulawayo Zimbabwe 39 20.10S 28.43E
Buldern W. Germany 8 51.52N 7.21E
Bulgan Mongolia 24 48.34N103.12E
Bulgaria Europe 13 42.30N 25.00E
Bullabulling Australia 43 31.05S120.52E
Bullara Australia 42 22.40S114.03E
Buller r. New Zealand 48 41.45S171.35E
Buller, Mt. Australia 47 37.11S146.26E
Bullfinch Australia 43 30.59S119.06E
Bulli Australia 47 34.20S150.55E
Bull Mts. U.S.A. 54 46.05N109.00W
Bulloo r. Australia 46 28.43S142.27E
Bulloo Downs town Australia 46 28.30S142.45E
Bulolo P.N.G. 47 7.13S146.35E
Bulong Australia 43 30.44S121.48E
Bultfontein R.S.A. 39 28.17S 26.09E
Bulu Indonesia 27 4.34N126.45E
Bulu, Gunung mtn. Indonesia 26 3.00N116.00E
Bulun U.S.S.R. 21 70.50N127.20E
Bulunde Tanzania 37 4.19S 32.57E
Bumba Zaïre 35 2.15N 22.32E
Buna Kenya 37 2.49N 39.27E
Buna P.N.G. 44 8.40S148.25E
Bunbury Australia 43 33.20S115.34E
Buncrana Rep. of Ire. 7 55.08N 7.27W
Bundaberg Australia 44 24.50S152.21E
Bundaleer Australia 47 28.39S146.31E
Bundarra Australia 47 30.11S151.04E
Bunde W. Germany 8 53.12N 7.16E
Bundella Australia 47 31.35S149.59E
Bundoran Rep. of Ire. 7 54.28N 8.17W
Bungay U.K. 5 52.27N 1.26E
Bungu Tanzania 37 7.37S 39.07E
Bunguran i. Indonesia 26 4.00N108.20E
Bunguran Selatan i. Indonesia 26 3.00N108.50E
Buni Nigeria 38 11.20N 11.59E
Bunia Zaïre 37 1.30N 30.10E
Buninyong Australia 46 37.41S143.58E
Bunyan Australia 47 36.11S149.09E
Buol Indonesia 27 1.12N121.28E
Buqayq Saudi Arabia 31 25.55N 49.40E
Bura Coast Kenya 37 3.30S 38.19E
Bura Coast Kenya 37 1.09S 39.55E
Burakin Australia 43 30.30S117.08E
Buraydah Saudi Arabia 31 26.18N 43.58E
Burcher Australia 47 33.32S147.18E
Burdur Turkey 19 37.44N 30.17E
Burdwān India 29 23.15N 87.52E
Burg E. Germany 14 52.17N 11.51E
Burgas Bulgaria 13 42.30N 27.29E
Bur Gavo Somali Rep. 37 1.10S 41.50E
Burgenland d. Austria 14 47.30N 16.20E
Burgess Hill U.K. 5 50.57N 0.07W
Burgos Spain 10 42.21N 3.41W
Burgsteinfurt W. Germany 8 52.09N 7.21E
Burgsvik Sweden 17 57.03N 18.16E
Bur Hakkaba Somali Rep. 37 2.43N 44.10E
Burhānpur India 28 21.18N 76.08E
Buri Brazil 59 23.46S 48.39W
Burias i. Phil. 27 12.50N123.10E
Burica, Punta c. Panama 57 8.05N 82.50W
Burke r. Australia 44 23.12S139.33E
Burketown Australia 44 17.44S139.22E
Burkina Faso Africa 38 12.30N 2.00W
Burley U.S.A. 54 42.32N113.48W
Burlington Canada 55 43.19N 79.48W
Burlington Iowa U.S.A. 53 40.50N 91.07W
Burlington Vt. U.S.A. 55 44.29N 73.13W
Burma Asia 29 21.00N 96.30E
Burngup Australia 43 33.00S118.39E
Burnham-on-Crouch U.K. 5 51.37N 0.50E
Burnham-on-Sea U.K. 5 51.15N 3.00W
Burnie Australia 45 41.03S145.55E
Burnley U.K. 4 53.47N 2.15W
Burns Australia 46 32.10S141.03E
Burns Oreg. U.S.A. 54 43.35N119.03W
Burnside r. Canada 50 66.51N108.04W
Burra Australia 46 33.40S138.57E
Burracoppin Australia 43 31.22S118.30E
Burren Junction Australia 47 30.08S148.59E
Burrewarra Pt. Australia 47 35.56S150.12E
Burriana Spain 10 39.54N 0.05W
Burrinjuck Australia 47 35.01S148.33E
Burrinjuck Resr. Australia 47 35.00S148.40E
Burrundie Australia 42 13.32S131.40E
Burry Port U.K. 5 51.41N 4.17W
Bursa Turkey 13 40.11N 29.04E
Būr Safājah Egypt 30 26.44N 33.56E
Būr Sa'īd Egypt 32 31.17N 32.18E
Būr Sūdān Sudan 35 19.39N 37.01E
Burta Australia 46 32.30S141.05E
Būr Tawfīq Egypt 32 29.57N 32.34E
Burton upon Trent U.K. 4 52.58N 1.39W
Burtundy Australia 46 33.45S142.22E
Buru i. Indonesia 27 3.30S126.30E
Burullus, Buḥayrat al l. Egypt 32 31.30N 30.45E
Burundi Africa 37 3.00S 30.00E
Bururi Burundi 37 3.58S 29.35E
Burutu Nigeria 38 5.20N 5.31E
Bury G.M. U.K. 4 53.36N 2.19W
Bury St. Edmunds U.K. 5 52.15N 0.42E
Busalla Italy 9 44.34N 8.57E
Busca Italy 9 44.31N 7.29E
Būsh Egypt 32 29.09N 31.07E
Būshehr Iran 31 28.57N 50.52E
Bushmanland f. R.S.A. 39 29.25S 19.40E
Busigny France 8 50.03N 3.29E
Buskerud Norway 17 60.20N 9.00E
Buşrá ash Shām Syria 32 32.30N 36.29E
Busselton Australia 43 33.43S115.15E
Bussum Neth. 8 52.17N 5.10E
Bustard Head c. Australia 44 24.02S151.48E
Busto Arsizio Italy 9 45.37N 8.51E
Buta Zaïre 35 2.49N 24.50E
Butare Rwanda 37 2.38S 29.43E
Bute Australia 46 33.24S138.01E
Bute i. U.K. 6 55.51N 5.07W
Bute, Sd. of U.K. 6 55.44N 5.10W
Butiaba Uganda 37 1.48N 31.15E
Butte Mont. U.S.A. 54 46.00N112.32W
Butterworth Malaysia 26 5.24N100.22E
Buttevant Rep. of Ire. 7 52.14N 8.41W
Butt of Lewis c. U.K. 6 58.31N 6.15W
Butty Head Australia 43 33.52S121.35E
Butuan Phil. 27 8.56N125.31E
Butung i. Indonesia 27 5.00S122.50E
Buxton U.K. 4 53.16N 1.54W
Buy U.S.S.R. 18 58.23N 41.27E
Buyaga U.S.S.R. 21 59.42N126.59E
Buynaksk U.S.S.R. 19 42.48N 47.07E
Büyük Menderes r. Turkey 13 37.30N 27.05E
Buzachi, Poluostrov pen. U.S.S.R. 19 45.00N 51.55E
Buzancy France 9 49.30N 4.59E
Buzău Romania 15 45.10N 26.49E
Buzău r. Romania 15 45.24N 27.48E
Buzaymah Libya 35 24.55N 22.02E
Buzi r. Mozambique 39 19.52S 34.00E
Buzuluk U.S.S.R. 18 52.49N 52.19E
Bwasiaia P.N.G. 44 10.06S150.48E
Byala Bulgaria 13 42.53N 27.55E
Byam Martin I. Canada 50 75.15N104.00W
Bydgoszcz Poland 15 53.16N 17.33E
Bygland Norway 17 58.48N 7.50E
Bykhov U.S.S.R. 15 53.30N 30.15E
Bykle Norway 17 59.21N 7.20E
Bylot I. Canada 51 73.00N 78.30W
Byrd Land f. Antarctica 64 79.30S125.00W
Byrock Australia 47 30.40S146.25E
Byron, C. Australia 47 28.37S153.40E

Byron Bay *town* Australia **47** 28.43S153.34E
Byrranga, Gory *mts.* U.S.S.R. **21** 74.50N101.00E
Byske Sweden **16** 64.57N 21.12E
Byske *r.* Sweden **16** 64.57N 21.13E
Byten U.S.S.R. **15** 52.50N 25.28E
Bytom Poland **15** 50.22N 18.54E
Bzipi U.S.S.R. **19** 43.15N 40.24E

C

Cabanatuan Phil. **27** 15.30N120.58E
Cabimas Venezuela **60** 10.26N 71.27W
Cabinda Angola **36** 5.34S 12.12E
Cabinet Mts. U.S.A. **54** 48.08N115.46W
Cabo Delgado *d.* Mozambique **37** 12.30S 39.00E
Cabo Frio *town* Brazil **59** 22.51S 42.03W
Cabonga, Résr. Canada **55** 47.35N 76.35W
Caboolture Australia **45** 27.05S152.57E
Cabo Pantoja Peru **60** 1.00S 75.10W
Cabot Str. Canada **51** 47.00N 59.00W
Cabras Italy **12** 39.56N 8.32E
Cabrera *i.* Spain **10** 39.08N 2.56E
Cabrera, Sierra *mts.* Spain **10** 42.10N 6.30W
Cabriel *r.* Spain **10** 39.13N 1.07W
Cabruta Venezuela **60** 7.40N 66.16W
Čačak Yugo. **15** 43.53N 20.21E
Caçapava Brazil **59** 23.05S 45.40W
Cáceres Brazil **61** 16.05S 57.40W
Cáceres Spain **10** 39.29N 6.23W
Cacharí Argentina **63** 36.23S 59.29W
Cachoeira Brazil **61** 12.35S 38.59W
Cachoeira do Sul Brazil **59** 30.03S 52.52W
Cachoeiro de Itapemirim Brazil **59** 20.51S 41.07W
Cacín *r.* Spain **10** 37.10N 4.01W
Caconda Angola **36** 13.46S 15.06E
Čadca Czech. **15** 49.26N 18.48E
Cader Idris *mtn.* U.K. **5** 52.40N 3.55W
Cadí, Serra del *mts.* Spain **10** 42.12N 1.35E
Cadibarrawirracanna, L. Australia **46** 28.52S135.27E
Cadillac U.S.A. **55** 44.15N 85.23W
Cadiz Phil. **27** 10.57N123.18E
Cádiz Spain **10** 36.32N 6.18W
Cádiz, Golfo de *g.* Spain **10** 37.00N 7.10W
Cadoux Australia **43** 30.47S117.05E
Caen France **9** 49.11N 0.22W
Caernarfon U.K. **4** 53.08N 4.17W
Caernarfon B. U.K. **4** 53.05N 4.25W
Caerphilly U.K. **5** 51.34N 3.13W
Caeté Brazil **59** 19.54S 43.37W
Cagayan de Oro Phil. **27** 8.29N124.40E
Cagliari Italy **12** 39.14N 9.07E
Cagliari, Golfo di *g.* Italy **12** 39.07N 9.15E
Cagnes France **9** 43.40N 7.09E
Caguán *r.* Colombia **60** 0.08S 74.18W
Caguas Puerto Rico **57** 18.08N 66.00W
Caha Mts. Rep. of Ire. **7** 51.44N 9.45W
Caherciveen Rep. of Ire. **7** 51.51N 10.14W
Cahir Rep. of Ire. **7** 52.23N 7.56W
Cahora Bassa Dam Mozambique **37** 15.36S 32.41E
Cahore Pt. Rep. of Ire. **7** 52.34N 6.12W
Cahors France **11** 44.28N 0.26E
Cahuapanas Peru **60** 5.15S 77.00W
Caianda Angola **36** 11.02S 23.29E
Caibarién Cuba **57** 22.31N 79.28W
Caicó Brazil **61** 6.25S 37.04W
Caicos Is. Turks & Caicos Is. **57** 21.30N 72.00W
Caird Coast *f.* Antarctica **64** 75.00S 20.00W
Cairngorms *mts.* U.K. **6** 57.04N 3.30W
Cairns Australia **44** 16.51S145.43E
Cairo *see* Al Qāhirah Egypt **32**
Cairo Ill. U.S.A. **53** 37.02N 89.02W
Cairo Montenotte Italy **9** 44.24N 8.16E
Caiwarro Australia **47** 28.38S144.45E
Cajamarca Peru **60** 7.09S 78.32W
Cajàzeiras Brazil **61** 6.52S 38.31W
Cajuru Brazil **59** 21.15S 47.18W
Čakovec Yugo. **14** 46.23N 16.26E
Calabar Nigeria **38** 4.56N 8.22E
Calabozo Venezuela **60** 8.58N 67.28W
Calabria *d.* Italy **13** 39.00N 16.30E
Calafat Romania **15** 43.59N 22.57E
Calafate Argentina **63** 50.20S 72.16W
Calahorra Spain **10** 42.18N 1.58W
Calais France **3** 50.57N 1.52E
Calama Brazil **60** 8.03S 62.53W
Calama Chile **62** 22.30S 68.55W
Calamar Colombia **60** 10.15N 74.55W
Calamian Group *is.* Phil. **27** 12.00N120.05E
Cala Millor Spain **10** 39.35N 3.22E
Calamocha Spain **10** 40.54N 1.18W
Calapan Phil. **27** 13.23N121.10E
Călăraşi Romania **15** 44.11N 27.21E
Calatayud Spain **10** 41.21N 1.39W
Calau E. Germany **14** 51.45N 13.56E
Calbayog Phil. **27** 12.04N124.58E
Calcutta India **29** 22.35N 88.21E
Caldaro Italy **9** 46.25N 11.14E
Caldas Colombia **60** 6.05N 75.36W
Caldas da Rainha Portugal **10** 39.24N 9.08W
Caldera Chile **62** 27.04S 70.50W
Caldwell Idaho U.S.A. **54** 43.40N116.41W
Caldwell Ohio U.S.A. **55** 39.44N 81.32W
Caledon *r.* R.S.A. **39** 30.27S 26.12E
Caledon B. Australia **44** 12.58S136.52E
Calella Spain **10** 41.37N 2.40E
Calexico Mexico **54** 32.40N115.30W
Calf of Man *i.* U.K. **4** 54.03N 4.49W
Calgary Canada **50** 51.05N114.05W
Cali Colombia **60** 3.24N 76.30W
Calicut India **28** 11.15N 75.45E
Caliente U.S.A. **54** 37.37N114.31W
California *d.* U.S.A. **54** 37.29N119.58W
California, G. of *see* California, Golfo de *g.* Mexico **56**
California, Golfo de *g.* Mexico **56** 28.00N112.00W
Calingasta Argentina **62** 31.15S 69.30W
Calingiri Australia **43** 31.07S116.27E
Callabonna *r.* Australia **46** 29.37S140.08E
Callabonna, L. Australia **46** 29.47S140.07E
Callander U.K. **6** 56.15N 4.13W
Callao Peru **62** 12.05S 77.08W
Caloocan Phil. **27** 14.38N120.58E
Caltagirone Italy **12** 37.14N 14.30E
Caltanissetta Italy **12** 37.30N 14.05E
Calulo Angola **36** 10.05S 14.56E
Calvados *d.* France **9** 49.10N 0.30W
Calvi France **11** 42.34N 8.44E
Calvinia R.S.A. **39** 31.29S 19.44E
Cam *r.* U.K. **5** 52.34N 0.21E
Camacupa Angola **36** 12.01S 17.22E
Camagüey Cuba **57** 21.25N 77.55W
Camagüey, Archipiélago de Cuba **57** 22.30N 78.00W
Camaiore Italy **9** 43.56N 10.18E
Camarès France **11** 43.49N 2.53E
Camaret-sur-Mer France **11** 48.16N 4.37W
Camarón, C. Honduras **57** 15.59N 85.00W
Camarones Argentina **63** 44.45S 65.40W
Camas U.S.A. **54** 45.35N122.24W
Cambay India **28** 22.18N 72.37E
Camberley U.K. **5** 51.21N 0.45W
Camborne U.K. **5** 50.12N 5.19W
Cambrai France **11** 50.10N 3.14E
Cambria U.S.A. **54** 35.34N121.05W
Cambrian Mts. U.K. **5** 52.33N 3.33W
Cambridge New Zealand **48** 37.53S175.29E
Cambridge U.K. **5** 52.13N 0.08E
Cambridge Idaho U.S.A. **54** 44.34N116.41W
Cambridge Mass. U.S.A. **55** 42.22N 71.06W
Cambridge Md. U.S.A. **55** 38.34N 76.04W
Cambridge Bay *town* Canada **50** 69.09N105.00W
Cambridge G. Australia **42** 15.00S128.05E
Cambridgeshire *d.* U.K. **5** 52.15N 0.05E
Camden U.K. **5** 51.33N 0.10W
Camden N.J. U.S.A. **55** 39.57N 75.07W
Camden Haven *b.* Australia **47** 31.40S152.49E
Camelford U.K. **5** 50.37N 4.41W
Cameron Ariz. U.S.A. **54** 35.51N111.25W
Cameron Hills Canada **50** 59.48N118.00W
Cameron Mts. New Zealand **48** 45.50S167.00E
Cameroon Africa **34** 6.00N 12.30E
Cameroun, Mont *mtn.* Cameroon **38** 4.20N 9.05E
Cametá Brazil **61** 2.12S 49.30W
Camiri Bolivia **62** 20.03S 63.31W
Camocim Brazil **61** 2.55S 40.50W
Camooweal Australia **44** 19.55S138.07E
Camopi Guiana **61** 3.12N 52.15W
Campana Argentina **63** 34.10S 58.57W
Campana, Isla *i.* Chile **63** 48.25S 75.20W
Campania *d.* Italy **12** 41.00N 14.30E
Campbell, C. New Zealand **48** 41.45S174.15E
Campbellton Canada **55** 48.00N 66.41W
Campbelltown Australia **47** 34.04S150.49E
Campbeltown U.K. **6** 55.25N 5.36W
Campeche Mexico **56** 19.50N 90.30W
Campeche *d.* Mexico **56** 19.00N 90.00W
Campeche, Bahía de *b.* Mexico **56** 19.30N 94.00W
Campeche B. *see* Campeche, Bahía de *b.* Mexico **56**
Camperdown Australia **46** 38.15S143.14E
Campina Grande Brazil **61** 7.15S 35.50W
Campinas Brazil **59** 22.54S 47.06W
Campo Cameroon **38** 2.22N 9.50E
Campobasso Italy **12** 41.34N 14.39E
Campo Belo Brazil **59** 20.52S 45.16W
Campo Gallo Argentina **62** 26.35S 62.50W
Campo Grande Brazil **62** 20.24S 54.35W
Campo Maior Brazil **61** 4.50S 42.12W
Campo Maior Portugal **10** 39.01N 7.04W
Campos Brazil **59** 21.45S 41.18W
Campos Belos Brazil **61** 13.09S 47.03W
Campos do Jordão Brazil **59** 23.28S 46.10W
Cam Ranh Vietnam **26** 11.54N109.14E
Camrose Canada **50** 53.01N112.48W
Canada N. America **50** 60.00N105.00W
Cañada de Gómez Argentina **62** 32.49S 61.25W
Canadian *r.* U.S.A. **53** 35.20N 95.40W
Çanakkale Turkey **13** 40.09N 26.26E
Çanakkale Boğazi *str.* Turkey **13** 40.15N 26.30E
Canal du Midi France **11** 43.18N 2.00E
Cananea Mexico **56** 30.57N110.18W
Canarias, Islas *is.* Atlantic Oc. **34** 29.00N 15.00W
Canastra, Serra da *mts.* Brazil **59** 20.05S 46.30W
Canaveral, C. U.S.A. **53** 28.28N 80.28W
Canavieiras Brazil **61** 15.44S 38.58W
Canbelego Australia **47** 31.33S146.19E
Canberra Australia **47** 35.18S149.08E
Canby Calif. U.S.A. **54** 41.27N120.52W
Cancale France **9** 48.40N 1.50W
Cancon France **11** 44.32N 0.38E
Candé France **9** 47.34N 1.02W
Candeias Brazil **59** 20.44S 45.18W
Candeleda Spain **10** 40.10N 5.14W
Canelli Italy **9** 44.43N 8.17E
Canelones Uruguay **63** 34.32S 56.17W
Cañete Peru **60** 13.00S 76.30W
Cangas de Narcea Spain **10** 43.11N 6.33W
Canguçu Brazil **62** 31.24S 52.41W
Caniapiscau, Lac *l.* Canada **51** 54.10N 69.55W
Çankiri Turkey **30** 40.35N 33.37E
Canna *i.* U.K. **6** 57.03N 6.30W
Cannes France **11** 43.33N 7.00E
Cannich U.K. **6** 57.20N 4.45W
Canning Basin *f.* Australia **42** 19.50S123.35E
Cannock U.K. **5** 52.42N 2.02W
Cann River *town* Australia **47** 37.35S149.06E
Canõas Brazil **59** 29.55S 51.10W
Canobie Australia **44** 19.28S140.38E
Canonba Australia **47** 31.19S147.22E
Canon City U.S.A. **52** 38.27N105.14W
Canopus Australia **46** 33.30S140.57E
Canossa *site* Italy **9** 44.35N 10.27E
Canowindra Australia **47** 33.34S148.30E
Cantabria, Sierra de *mts.* Spain **10** 42.40N 2.30W
Cantábrica, Cordillera *mts.* Spain **10** 42.55N 5.10W
Cantagalo Brazil **59** 21.59S 42.22W
Cantaura Venezuela **60** 9.22N 64.24W
Canterbury *d.* New Zealand **48** 43.30S172.00E
Canterbury U.K. **5** 51.17N 1.05E
Canterbury Bight New Zealand **48** 44.15S172.00E
Can Tho Vietnam **26** 10.03N105.46E
Canton *see* Guangzhou China **25**
Canton Ohio U.S.A. **55** 40.48N 81.23W
Cantù Italy **9** 45.44N 9.08E
Cantua Creek *town* U.S.A. **54** 36.30N120.19W
Cañuelas Argentina **63** 35.03S 58.44W
Canumã *r.* Brazil **60** 3.55S 59.10W
Canutama Brazil **60** 6.32S 64.20W
Cany-Barville France **9** 49.47N 0.38E
Canyon Wyo. U.S.A. **54** 44.43N110.32W
Cao Bang Vietnam **26** 22.40N106.16E
Caorle Italy **9** 45.36N 12.53E
Capanema Brazil **61** 1.08S 47.07W
Cap-Chat Canada **55** 48.56N 66.53W
Cap-de-la-Madeleine *town* Canada **55** 46.22N 72.31W
Cape Barren I. Australia **45** 40.25S148.15E
Cape Breton I. Canada **51** 46.00N 61.00W
Cape Coast *town* Ghana **38** 5.10N 1.13W
Cape Cod B. U.S.A. **55** 41.50N 70.17W
Cape Dyer *town* Canada **51** 66.30N 61.20W
Cape Girardeau *town* U.S.A. **53** 37.19N 89.31W
Cape Johnson Depth Pacific Oc. **27** 10.20N127.20E
Capellen Lux. **8** 49.39N 5.59E
Capelongo Angola **36** 14.28S 16.25E
Cape Province *d.* R.S.A. **39** 31.30S 23.30E
Cape Town R.S.A. **39** 33.55S 18.27E
Cape York Pen. Australia **44** 12.40S142.20E
Cap-Haïtien *town* Haiti **57** 19.47N 72.17W
Capim *r.* Brazil **61** 1.40S 47.47W
Capoompeta, Mt. Australia **47** 29.22S151.59E
Cappoquin Rep. of Ire. **7** 52.09N 7.52W
Capraia *i.* Italy **12** 43.03N 9.50E
Caprera *i.* Italy **12** 41.48N 9.27E
Capri *i.* Italy **12** 40.33N 14.13E
Capricorn Channel Australia **44** 23.00S152.14E
Caprivi Strip *f.* Namibia **39** 17.50S 23.10E
Caqueta *r.* Colombia **60** 1.20S 70.50W
Caracal Romania **15** 44.08N 24.18E
Caracas Venezuela **60** 10.35N 66.56W
Caraghnan Mt. Australia **47** 31.20S149.03E
Caraguatatuba Brazil **59** 23.39S 45.26W
Carandaí Brazil **59** 20.55S 43.46W
Carangola Brazil **59** 20.44S 42.03W
Caransebeş Romania **15** 45.25N 22.13E
Caratasca, Laguna de *b.* Honduras **57** 15.10N 84.00W
Caratinga Brazil **59** 19.50S 42.06W
Caravaca Spain **10** 38.06N 1.51W
Caravaggio Italy **9** 45.30N 9.38E
Caraveli Peru **60** 15.45S 73.25W
Carballo Spain **10** 43.13N 8.41W
Carbonara, Capo *c.* Italy **12** 39.06N 9.32E
Carbondale Penn. U.S.A. **55** 41.35N 75.30W
Carbonear Canada **51** 47.45N 53.13W
Carbonia Italy **12** 39.11N 8.32E
Carcassonne France **11** 43.13N 2.21E
Carcross Canada **50** 60.11N134.41W
Cardabia Australia **42** 23.06S113.48E
Cárdenas Cuba **57** 23.02N 81.12W
Cárdenas Mexico **56** 22.00N 99.40W
Cardenete Spain **10** 39.46N 1.42W
Cardiff U.K. **5** 51.28N 3.11W
Cardigan U.K. **5** 52.06N 4.41W
Cardigan B. U.K. **5** 52.30N 4.30W
Cardona Spain **10** 41.56N 1.40E
Cardona Uruguay **63** 33.53S 57.23W
Carei Romania **15** 47.42N 22.28E
Carentan France **9** 49.18N 1.14W
Carey U.S.A. **54** 43.18N113.56W
Carey, L. Australia **43** 29.05S122.15E
Carhaix France **11** 48.16N 3.35W
Carhué Argentina **63** 37.11S 62.45W
Caribbean Sea C. America **57** 15.00N 75.00W
Caribou U.S.A. **55** 46.52N 68.01W
Caribou Mts. Canada **50** 58.30N115.00W
Carignan France **9** 49.38N 5.10E
Carinda Australia **47** 30.29S147.45E
Carinhanha Brazil **61** 14.18S 43.47W
Carini Italy **12** 38.08N 13.11E
Caritianas Brazil **60** 9.25S 63.06W
Carleton Place Canada **55** 45.08N 76.09W
Carlingford Rep. of Ire. **7** 54.03N 6.12W
Carlingford Lough Rep. of Ire. **7** 54.03N 6.09W
Carlisle U.K. **4** 54.54N 2.55W
Carlos Reyles Uruguay **63** 33.03S 56.29W
Carlow Rep. of Ire. **7** 52.50N 6.46W
Carlow *d.* Rep. of Ire. **7** 52.43N 6.50W
Carlsbad Calif. U.S.A. **54** 33.10N117.21W
Carlsbad N.Mex. U.S.A. **52** 32.25N104.14W
Carmacks Canada **50** 62.04N136.21W
Carmagnola Italy **9** 44.51N 7.43E
Carmarthen U.K. **5** 51.52N 4.20W
Carmarthen B. U.K. **5** 52.30N 4.30W
Carmaux France **11** 44.03N 2.09E
Carmel Head U.K. **4** 53.24N 4.35W
Carmelo Uruguay **63** 34.00S 58.17W
Carmen Colombia **60** 9.46N 75.06W
Carmen Mexico **56** 18.38N 91.50W
Carmen Uruguay **63** 33.15S 56.01W
Carmen, Isla *i.* Mexico **56** 25.55N111.10W
Carmen, Isla del *i.* Mexico **56** 18.35N 91.40W
Carmen de Areco Argentina **63** 34.20S 59.50W
Carmen de Patagones Argentina **63** 40.48S 63.00W
Carmichael U.S.A. **54** 38.38N121.19W
Carmila Australia **44** 21.55S149.25E
Carmo Brazil **59** 21.56S 42.37W
Carmody, L. Australia **43** 32.27S119.20E
Carmona Spain **10** 37.28N 5.38W
Carnac France **11** 47.35N 3.05W
Carnarvon Australia **42** 24.53S113.40E
Carnarvon R.S.A. **39** 30.58S 22.07E
Carndonagh Rep. of Ire. **7** 55.15N 7.15W
Carnegie Australia **42** 25.43S122.59E
Carnegie, L. Australia **42** 26.15S123.00E
Carnew Rep. of Ire. **7** 52.43N 6.31W
Carniche, Alpi *mts.* Austria / Italy **12** 46.40N 12.48E
Car Nicobar *i.* India **29** 9.06N 92.57E
Carnot C.A.R. **36** 4.59N 15.56E
Carnot, C. Australia **46** 34.57S135.38E
Carnoustie U.K. **6** 56.30N 2.44W
Carnsore Pt. Rep. of Ire. **7** 52.10N 6.21W
Carolina Brazil **61** 7.20S 47.25W
Carolina Puerto Rico **57** 18.23N 65.57W
Carolina R.S.A. **39** 26.04S 30.07E
Caroline Is. Pacific Oc. **27** 7.50N145.00E
Caroní *r.* Venezuela **60** 8.20N 62.42W
Carora Venezuela **60** 10.12N 70.07W
Carpathians *mts.* Europe **15** 48.45N 23.45E
Carpaţii Meridionali *mts.* Romania **15** 45.35N 24.40E
Carpentaria, G. of Australia **44** 14.00S139.00E
Carpentras France **11** 44.03N 5.03E
Carpi Italy **9** 44.47N 10.53E
Carpio Spain **10** 41.13N 5.07W
Carpolac Australia **46** 36.45S141.20E
Carquefou France **9** 47.18N 1.30W
Carra, Lough Rep. of Ire. **7** 53.41N 9.15W
Carrara Italy **9** 44.04N 10.06E
Carrathool Australia **47** 34.25S145.24E
Carrauntoohil *mtn.* Rep. of Ire. **7** 52.00N 9.45W
Carrickfergus U.K. **7** 54.43N 5.49W
Carrickmacross Rep. of Ire. **7** 53.58N 6.43W
Carrick-on-Shannon Rep. of Ire. **7** 53.57N 8.06W
Carrick-on-Suir Rep. of Ire. **7** 52.21N 7.26W
Carrieton Australia **46** 32.28S138.34E
Carrowmore Lough Rep. of Ire. **7** 54.11N 9.47W
Çarşamba Turkey **30** 41.13N 36.43E
Çarşamba *r.* Turkey **30** 37.52N 31.48E
Carson City U.S.A. **54** 39.10N119.46W
Carstairs U.K. **6** 55.42N 3.41W
Cartagena Colombia **60** 10.24N 75.33W
Cartagena Spain **10** 37.36N 0.59W
Cartago Colombia **60** 4.45N 75.55W
Cartago Costa Rica **57** 9.50N 83.52W
Carter U.S.A. **54** 41.27N110.25W
Carteret France **9** 49.22N 1.48W
Carterton New Zealand **48** 41.01S175.31E
Cartwright Canada **51** 53.42N 57.01W
Caruarú Brazil **61** 8.15S 35.55W
Carúpano Venezuela **60** 10.39N 63.14W
Carvin France **8** 50.30N 2.58E
Carvoeiro Brazil **60** 1.24S 61.59W
Caryapundy Swamp Australia **46** 29.00S142.36E
Casablanca Morocco **34** 33.39N 7.35W
Casa Branca Brazil **59** 21.45S 47.06W
Casa Grande U.S.A. **54** 32.53N111.45W
Casale Italy **9** 45.08N 8.27E
Casa Nova Brazil **61** 9.25S 41.08W
Casarano Italy **13** 40.00N 18.10E
Cascade Idaho U.S.A. **54** 44.31N116.02W
Cascade Mont. U.S.A. **54** 47.16N111.42W
Cascade Pt. New Zealand **48** 44.01S168.22E
Cascade Range *mts.* U.S.A. **52** 46.15N121.00W
Caserta Italy **12** 41.06N 14.21E
Cashel Tipperary Rep. of Ire. **7** 52.31N 7.54W
Casilda Argentina **63** 33.03S 61.10W
Casimiro de Abreu Brazil **59** 22.28S 42.12W
Casino Australia **47** 28.50S153.02E
Casma Peru **60** 9.30S 78.20W
Caspe Spain **10** 41.14N 0.03W
Casper U.S.A. **54** 42.51N106.19W
Caspian Depression *see* Prikaspiyskaya Nizmennost *ost* U.S.S.R. **19**
Caspian Sea U.S.S.R. **19** 42.00N 51.00E
Cassano allo Ionio Italy **13** 39.47N 16.20E
Cass City U.S.A. **55** 43.37N 83.11W
Cassilis Australia **47** 32.01S149.59E
Castaños Mexico **56** 26.48N101.26W
Castelfranco Veneto Italy **9** 45.40N 11.55E
Casteljaloux France **11** 44.19N 0.06W
Castell' Arquato Italy **9** 44.51N 9.52E
Castelli Argentina **63** 36.07S 57.50W
Castellón Spain **10** 39.59N 0.03W
Castelmassa Italy **9** 45.01N 11.18E
Castelnovo ne'Monti Italy **9** 44.26N 10.24E
Castelnuovo di Garfagnana Italy **9** 44.06N 10.24E
Castelo Brazil **59** 20.33S 41.14W
Castelo Branco Portugal **10** 39.50N 7.30W
Castel San Giovanni Italy **9** 45.04N 9.26E
Castelvetrano Italy **12** 37.41N 12.47E
Casterton Australia **46** 37.35S141.25E
Castets France **11** 43.53N 1.09W
Castilla Peru **60** 5.16S 80.36W
Castilla la Nueva *d.* Spain **10** 40.00N 3.45W
Castilla la Vieja *d.* Spain **10** 41.30N 4.00W
Castilletes Colombia **60** 11.55N 71.20W
Castlebar Rep. of Ire. **7** 53.52N 9.19W
Castleblayney Rep. of Ire. **7** 54.08N 6.46W
Castle Douglas U.K. **6** 54.56N 3.56W
Castleford U.K. **4** 53.43N 1.21W
Castlegate U.S.A. **54** 39.44N110.52W
Castleisland Rep. of Ire. **7** 52.13N 9.28W
Castlemaine Australia **46** 37.05S144.19E
Castlerea Rep. of Ire. **7** 53.45N 8.30W
Castlereagh *r.* Australia **47** 30.12S147.32E
Castle Rock *town* Wash. U.S.A. **54** 46.17N122.54W
Castletown U.K. **4** 54.04N 4.38W
Castletownshend Rep. of Ire. **7** 51.32N 9.12W
Castres France **11** 43.36N 2.14E
Castries St. Lucia **57** 14.01N 60.59W
Castro Chile **63** 42.30S 73.46W
Castro del Río Spain **10** 37.41N 4.29W
Casula Mozambique **37** 15.26S 33.32E
Cataguases Brazil **59** 21.23S 42.39W
Çatalca Turkey **13** 41.09N 28.29E
Cataluña *d.* Spain **10** 42.00N 2.00E
Catamaran Australia **45** 43.33S146.49E
Catamarca Argentina **62** 28.30S 65.45W
Catamarca *d.* Argentina **62** 27.45S 67.00W
Catanduanes *i.* Phil. **27** 13.45N124.20E
Catanduva Brazil **59** 21.03S 49.00W
Catania Italy **12** 37.31N 15.05E
Catanzaro Italy **13** 38.55N 16.35E
Catarman Phil. **27** 12.28N124.50E
Catastrophe, C. Australia **46** 34.59S136.00E
Catbalogan Phil. **27** 11.46N124.55E
Catete Angola **36** 9.09S 13.40E
Cathcart Australia **47** 36.49S149.25E
Cathcart R.S.A. **39** 32.17S 27.08E
Cat I. Bahamas **57** 24.30N 75.30W
Catoche, C. Mexico **57** 21.38N 87.08W
Catonsville U.S.A. **55** 39.16N 76.44W
Catriló Argentina **63** 36.23S 63.24W
Catterick U.K. **4** 54.23N 1.38W
Cattolica Italy **9** 43.58N 12.44E
Catuane Mozambique **39** 26.49S 32.17E
Cauca *r.* Colombia **60** 8.57N 74.30W
Caucasus Mts. *see* Kavkazskiy Khrebet *mts.* U.S.S.R. **19**
Caudry France **11** 50.07N 3.22E
Cauquenes Chile **63** 35.58S 72.21W
Caura *r.* Venezuela **60** 7.38N 64.53W
Cavaillon France **11** 43.50N 5.02E
Cavalese Italy **9** 46.17N 11.26E
Cavan Rep. of Ire. **7** 54.00N 7.22W
Cavan *d.* Rep. of Ire. **7** 53.58N 7.10W
Cavarzere Italy **9** 45.08N 12.05E
Caviana, Ilha *i.* Brazil **61** 0.02N 50.00W
Cavite Phil. **27** 14.30N120.54E
Cawndilla L. Australia **46** 32.30S142.18E
Caxambu Brazil **59** 21.59S 44.54W
Caxias Brazil **61** 4.53S 43.20W
Caxias do Sul Brazil **59** 29.14S 51.10W
Caxito Angola **36** 8.32S 13.38E
Cayambe Ecuador **60** 0.03N 78.08W
Cayenne Guiana **61** 4.55N 52.18W
Cayman Brac *i.* Cayman Is. **57** 19.44N 79.48W
Cayman Is. C. America **57** 19.00N 81.00W
Cazères France **11** 43.13N 1.05E
Ceara *d.* Brazil **61** 4.50S 39.00W
Cebollera, Sierra de *mts.* Spain **10** 41.58N 2.30W
Cebu Phil. **27** 10.17N123.56E
Cebu *i.* Phil. **27** 10.15N123.45E
Cecina Italy **12** 43.18N 10.30E
Cedar City U.S.A. **52** 37.40N113.04W
Cedar City U.S.A. **54** 37.41N113.04W
Cedar Falls *town* U.S.A. **53** 42.34N 92.26W
Cedar Rapids *town* U.S.A. **53** 41.59N 91.31W
Cedros, Isla *i.* Mexico **56** 28.10N115.15W
Ceduna Australia **46** 32.07S133.42E
Cefalù Italy **12** 38.01N 14.03E
Cegléd Hungary **15** 47.10N 19.48E
Celaya Mexico **56** 20.32N100.48W
Celebes *i. see* Sulawesi *i.* Indonesia **27**
Celebes Sea Indonesia **27** 3.00N122.00E
Celina U.S.A. **55** 40.34N 84.35W
Celje Yugo. **12** 46.15N 15.16E
Celle W. Germany **14** 52.37N 10.05E
Celtic Sea Europe **3** 50.00N 8.00W
Cemaes Head U.K. **5** 52.08N 4.42W
Ceno *r.* Italy **9** 44.41N 10.05E
Cento Italy **9** 44.43N 11.17E
Central *d.* Ghana **38** 5.30N 1.10W
Central *d.* Kenya **37** 0.30S 37.00E
Central *d.* U.K. **6** 56.10N 4.20W
Central *d.* Zambia **37** 14.30S 29.30E
Central, Cordillera *mts.* Bolivia **62** 18.30S 65.00W
Central, Cordillera *mts.* Colombia **60** 5.00N 75.20W
Central African Republic Africa **34** 6.30N 20.00E
Central Auckland *d.* New Zealand **48** 36.45S174.45E
Central I. Kenya **37** 3.30N 36.02E
Centralia Ill. U.S.A. **53** 38.32N 89.08W
Centralia Wash. U.S.A. **54** 46.43N122.58W
Central Makrān Range *mts.* Pakistan **28** 26.40N 64.30E
Central Siberian Plateau *see* Sredne Sibirskoyf. *f.* U.S.S.R. **21**
Centre *d.* Burkina Faso **38** 13.30N 1.00W
Centre *d.* France **11** 47.40N 1.45E
Ceram *i. see* Seram *i.* Indonesia **27**
Ceram Sea *see* Seram, Laut *sea* Pacific Oc. **27**
Ceres U.S.A. **54** 37.35N120.57W
Ceresole Reale Italy **9** 45.26N 7.15E
Cereté Colombia **60** 8.54N 75.51W
Cerignola Italy **12** 41.17N 15.53E
Cérilly France **11** 46.37N 2.50E
Cerisiers France **9** 48.08N 3.29E
Cerknica Yugo. **12** 45.48N 14.22E
Cernavodă Romania **15** 44.20N 28.02E
Cerritos Mexico **56** 22.26N100.17W
Cerro de Pasco Peru **60** 10.43S 76.15W
Cervera Lérida Spain **10** 41.40N 1.16E
Cervia Italy **9** 44.15N 12.22E
Cervignano del Friuli Italy **9** 45.49N 13.20E
Cervo Spain **10** 43.40N 7.24W
Cesena Italy **9** 44.08N 12.15E
Cesenatico Italy **9** 44.12N 12.24E
Cēsis U.S.S.R. **18** 57.18N 25.18E
České Budějovice Czech. **14** 49.00N 14.30E
Český Krumlov Czech. **14** 48.49N 14.19E
Cessnock Australia **47** 32.51S151.21E
Cetinje Yugo. **13** 42.24N 18.55E
Ceuta Spain **10** 35.53N 5.19W
Ceva Italy **9** 44.23N 8.01E

evennes *mts.* France 11 44.25N 4.05E
eyhan Turkey 30 37.02N 35.48E
eyhan *r.* Turkey 30 36.54N 34.58E
ablis France 9 47.47N 3.48E
acabuco Argentina 63 34.38S 60.29W
achani *mtn.* Peru 60 16.12S 71.32W
achapoyas Peru 60 6.13S 77.54W
aco *d.* Argentina 62 26.30S 60.00W
ad Africa 34 13.00N 19.00E
ad, L. Africa 38 13.30N 14.00E
adron U.S.A. 52 42.50N103.02W
afe Nigeria 38 11.56N 6.55E
agda U.S.S.R. 21 58.44N130.38E
ahār Borjak Afghan. 28 30.17N 62.03E
āh Bahār Iran 31 25.17N 60.41E
ajarí Argentina 63 30.45S 57.59W
ake Chake Tanzania 37 5.13S 39.46E
akhānsūr Afghan. 31 31.10N 62.02E
ala Peru 60 15.48S 74.20W
aleur B. Canada 55 48.00N 65.45W
alhuanca Peru 60 14.20S 73.10W
allans France 11 46.51N 1.52W
allenger Depth Pacific Oc. 27 11.19N142.15E
allis U.S.A. 54 44.30N114.14W
alonnes-sur-Loire France 9 47.21N 0.46W
âlons-sur-Marne France 9 48.58N 4.22E
alon-sur-Saône France 11 46.47N 4.51E
am W. Germany 14 49.13N 12.41E
ama Zambia 37 11.09S 33.10E
ambal *r.* India 29 26.30N 79.20E
ambersburg U.S.A. 55 39.56N 77.39W
ambéry France 11 45.34N 5.55E
ambeshi Zambia 37 10.57S 31.04E
ambeshi *r.* Zambia 37 11.15S 30.37E
ambly France 9 49.10N 2.15E
amical Argentina 62 30.22S 66.19W
amonix France 11 45.55N 6.52E
ampagne-Ardenne *d.* France 8 49.42N 4.30E
ampaign U.S.A. 53 40.07N 88.14W
ampéry Switz. 9 46.10N 6.52E
amplain, L. U.S.A. 55 44.45N 73.15W
ampotón Mexico 56 19.21N 90.43W
añaral Chile 62 26.21S 70.37W
andeleur Is. U.S.A. 53 29.50N 88.50W
andīgarh India 28 30.44N 76.54E
āndpur Bangla. 29 22.08N 91.55E
andrapur India 29 19.58N 79.21E
ānf Iran 31 26.40N 60.31E
angchun China 25 43.50N125.20E
angde China 25 29.03N111.35E
ang Jiang *r.* China 25 31.40N121.15E
angjin N. Korea 25 40.21N127.20E
angning China 25 26.24N112.24E
angping China 25 40.12N116.12E
angsha China 25 28.10N113.00E
angting China 25 25.47N116.17E
angzhi China 25 36.09N113.12E
angzhou China 25 31.45N119.57E
annel Is. U.K. 5 49.28N 2.13W
annel Is. U.S.A. 54 34.00N120.00W
annel-Port-aux-Basques *town* Canada 51 47.35N 59.10W
anning Mich. U.S.A. 55 46.08N 88.06W
antada Spain 10 42.36N 7.46W
anthaburi Thailand 29 12.38N102.12E
antilly France 9 49.12N 2.28E
ao'an China 25 23.43N116.35E
aonde Mozambique 37 13.43S 40.31E
ao Phraya *r.* Thailand 29 13.30N100.25E
aoyang Guangdong China 25 23.17N116.33E
apada das Mangabeiras *mts.* Brazil 61 10.00S 46.30W
apada Diamantina Brazil 59 13.30S 42.30W
apala, Lago de *l.* Mexico 56 20.00N103.00W
apayevo U.S.S.R 19 50.12N 51.09E
apayevsk U.S.S.R. 18 52.58N 49.44E
apelle-d'Angillon France 9 47.22N 2.26E
apicuy Uruguay 63 31.39S 57.54W
apleau Canada 55 47.50N 83.24W
āpra India 29 25.46N 84.45E
aqui Bolivia 62 19.36S 65.32W
aracot I. Antarctica 64 70.00S 75.00W
arcas Mexico 56 23.08N101.07W
ard U.K. 5 50.52N 2.59W
ardūar India 29 26.52N 92.46E
ardzhou U.S.S.R. 31 39.09N 63.34E
arente *r.* France 11 45.57N 1.00W
ari *r.* Chad 38 13.00N 14.30E
ārīkār Afghan. 28 35.02N 69.13E
aring U.K. 5 51.12N 0.49E
arleroi Belgium 8 50.25N 4.27E
arlesbourg Canada 55 46.53N 71.16W
arleston S.C. U.S.A. 53 32.48N 79.58W
arleston W.Va. U.S.A. 55 38.23N 81.40W
arlestown Rep. of Ire. 7 53.57N 8.48W
arlestown Ind. U.S.A. 55 38.28N 85.40W
arleville Australia 44 26.25S146.13E
arleville-Mézières France 9 49.46N 4.43E
arlieu France 11 46.10N 4.10E
arlotte N.C. U.S.A. 53 35.05N 80.50W
arlottesville U.S.A. 53 38.02N 78.29W
arlottetown Canada 51 46.14N 63.09W
arlton Australia 46 36.18S143.27E
arly-sur-Marne France 9 48.58N 3.17E
arolles France 11 46.26N 4.17E
arters Towers Australia 44 20.05S146.16E
artres France 9 48.27N 1.30E
ascomas Argentina 63 35.35S 58.00W
âteaubriant France 9 47.43N 1.22W
âteau-du-Loir France 9 47.42N 0.25E
âteaudun France 9 48.04N 1.20E
âteau Gontier France 9 47.50N 0.42W
âteau Landon France 9 48.09N 2.42E
âteau-la-Vallière France 9 47.33N 0.19E
âteauneuf-en-Thymerais France 9 48.35N 1.15E
âteauneuf-sur-Loire France 9 47.52N 2.14E
âteauneuf-sur-Sarthe France 9 47.41N 0.30W
âteau-Porcien France 9 49.32N 4.15E
Château Renault France 9 47.35N 0.55E
Châteauroux France 11 46.49N 1.41E
Château-Thierry France 9 49.03N 3.24E
Châtelet Belgium 8 50.24N 4.32E
Châtellerault France 11 46.49N 0.33E
Chatham N.B. Canada 55 47.02N 65.30W
Chatham Ont. Canada 55 42.24N 82.11W
Chatham U.K. 5 51.23N 0.32E
Chatham Is. Pacific Oc. 40 44.00S176.35W
Châtillon Italy 9 45.45N 7.37E
Châtillon-Coligny France 9 47.50N 2.51E
Châtillon-sur-Seine France 9 47.52N 4.35E
Chattahoochee *r.* U.S.A. 53 30.52N 84.57W
Chattanooga U.S.A. 53 35.01N 85.18W
Chatteris U.K. 5 52.27N 0.03E
Chaulnes France 9 49.49N 2.48E
Chaumont France 11 48.07N 5.08E
Chaumont-en-Vexin France 9 49.16N 1.53E
Chauny France 9 49.37N 3.13E
Chausy U.S.S.R. 15 53.49N 30.57E
Chavanges France 9 48.31N 4.34E
Chaves Brazil 61 0.10S 49.55W
Chaves Portugal 10 41.44N 7.28W
Chawang Thailand 29 8.25N 99.32E
Cheb Czech. 14 50.04N 12.20E
Cheboksary U.S.S.R. 18 56.08N 47.12E
Cheboygan U.S.A. 55 45.40N 84.28W
Chebsara U.S.S.R. 18 59.14N 38.59E
Chech, Erg *des.* Africa 34 25.00N 2.15W
Chechersk U.S.S.R. 15 52.54N 30.54E
Checiny Poland 15 50.48N 20.28E
Chegdomyn U.S.S.R. 21 51.09N133.01E
Chegga *well* Mauritania 34 25.30N 5.46W
Chegutu Zimbabwe 39 18.09S 30.07E
Chehalis U.S.A. 54 46.40N122.58W
Cheiron, Cime du *mtn.* France 9 43.49N 6.58E
Cheju S. Korea 25 33.31N126.29E
Cheju do *i.* S. Korea 25 33.20N126.30E
Cheleken U.S.S.R. 31 39.26N 53.11E
Chelforó Argentina 63 39.04S 66.33W
Chelkar U.S.S.R. 20 47.48N 59.39E
Chelles France 9 48.53N 2.36E
Chełm Poland 15 51.10N 23.28E
Chelmsford U.K. 5 51.44N 0.28E
Chełmża Poland 15 53.12N 18.37E
Cheltenham U.K. 5 51.53N 2.07W
Chelva Spain 10 39.45N 1.00W
Chelyabinsk U.S.S.R. 20 55.10N 61.25E
Chelyuskin, Mys *c.* U.S.S.R. 21 77.20N106.00E
Chemainus Canada 54 48.55N123.48W
Chemba Mozambique 37 17.11S 34.53E
Chemult U.S.A. 54 43.13N121.47W
Chën, Gora *mtn.* U.S.S.R. 21 65.30N141.20E
Chenāb *r.* Asia 28 29.26N 71.09E
Cheney U.S.A. 54 47.29N117.34W
Chengde China 25 40.48N118.06E
Chengdu China 29 30.37N104.06E
Chen Xian China 25 25.48N113.02E
Chepen Peru 60 7.15S 79.20W
Chepstow U.K. 5 51.38N 2.40W
Cher *r.* France 9 47.12N 2.04E
Cherbourg France 9 49.38N 1.37W
Cherdyn U.S.S.R. 18 60.25N 55.22E
Cheremkhovo U.S.S.R. 21 53.08N103.01E
Cherepovets U.S.S.R. 18 59.05N 37.55E
Cherikov U.S.S.R. 15 53.35N 31.23E
Cherkassy U.S.S.R. 19 49.27N 32.04E
Cherkessk U.S.S.R. 19 44.14N 42.05E
Cherkovitsa Bulgaria 13 43.41N 24.49E
Cherlak U.S.S.R. 20 54.10N 74.52E
Chernigov U.S.S.R. 15 51.30N 31.18E
Chernikovsk U.S.S.R. 18 54.51N 56.06E
Chernobyl U.S.S.R. 15 51.17N 30.15E
Chernovtsy U.S.S.R. 15 48.19N 25.52E
Chernyakhov U.S.S.R. 15 50.30N 28.38E
Chernyakhovsk U.S.S.R. 17 54.38N 21.49E
Cherquenco Chile 63 38.41S 72.00W
Cherry Creek *town* Nev. U.S.A. 54 39.54N113.53W
Cherskogo, Khrebet *mts.* U.S.S.R. 21 65.50N143.00E
Chertkovo U.S.S.R. 19 49.22N 40.12E
Chertsey U.K. 5 51.23N 0.27W
Chervonograd U.S.S.R. 15 50.25N 24.10E
Cherwell *r.* U.K. 5 51.44N 1.15W
Chesapeake B. U.S.A. 53 38.40N 76.25W
Chesham U.K. 5 51.43N 0.38W
Cheshire *d.* U.K. 4 53.14N 2.30W
Chëshskaya Guba *g.* U.S.S.R. 18 67.20N 46.30E
Chesil Beach *f.* U.K. 5 50.37N 2.33W
Chester U.K. 4 53.12N 2.53W
Chester Mont. U.S.A. 54 48.31N110.58W
Chester Penn. U.S.A. 55 39.51N 75.21W
Chesterfield U.K. 4 53.14N 1.26W
Chesterfield Inlet *town* Canada 51 63.00N 91.00W
Chesuncook L. U.S.A. 55 46.00N 69.20W
Chetumal Mexico 57 18.30N 88.17W
Chetumal B. Mexico 57 18.30N 88.00W
Cheviot New Zealand 48 42.49S173.16E
Cheviot U.S.A. 55 39.10N 84.32W
Cheyenne *r.* U.S.A. 52 44.40N101.15W
Cheyenne Wyo. U.S.A. 52 41.08N104.49W
Cheyne B. Australia 43 34.35S118.50E
Chhindwāra India 29 22.04N 78.58E
Chiang Mai Thailand 29 18.48N 98.59E
Chiapas *d.* Mexico 56 16.30N 93.00W
Chiari Italy 9 45.32N 9.56E
Chiavari Italy 9 44.19N 9.19E
Chiavenna Italy 9 46.19N 9.24E
Chiba Japan 23 35.36N140.07E
Chiba *d.* Japan 23 35.10N140.00E
Chibemba Angola 36 15.43S 14.07E
Chibougamau Canada 55 49.53N 74.24W
Chibougamau Lac *l.* Canada 55 49.50N 74.19W
Chibougamau Prov. Park Canada 55 49.24N 73.48W
Chibuk Nigeria 38 10.52N 12.50E
Chibuto Mozambique 39 24.41S 33.32E
Chicago U.S.A. 53 41.50N 87.45W
Chichagof I. U.S.A. 50 57.55N135.45W
Chichester U.K. 5 50.50N 0.47W
Chichibu Japan 23 35.59N139.05E
Chickasha U.S.A. 52 35.03N 97.57W
Chiclana Spain 10 36.26N 6.09W
Chiclayo Peru 60 6.47S 79.47W
Chico *r.* Chubut Argentina 63 43.45S 66.10W
Chico *r.* Santa Cruz Argentina 63 50.03W 68.35W
Chico U.S.A. 54 39.44N121.50W
Chicomo Mozambique 39 24.33S 34.11E
Chicoutimi-Jonquière Canada 55 48.26N 71.04W
Chicualacuala Mozambique 39 22.06S 31.42E
Chidambarum India 29 11.24N 79.42E
Chidenguele Mozambique 39 24.54S 34.13E
Chidley, C. Canada 51 60.30N 65.00W
Chiemsee *l.* W. Germany 14 47.55N 12.30E
Chiengi Zambia 37 8.42S 29.07E
Chieri Italy 9 45.01N 7.49E
Chieti Italy 12 42.22N 14.12E
Chifeng China 25 41.17N118.56E
Chigasaki Japan 23 35.19N139.24E
Chiguana Bolivia 62 21.05S 67.58W
Chigubo Mozambique 39 22.38S 33.18E
Chihuahua Mexico 56 28.38N106.05W
Chihuahua *d.* Mexico 56 28.40N106.00W
Chiili U.S.S.R. 20 44.10N 66.37E
Chikumbi Zambia 37 15.14S 28.21E
Chikwawa Malaŵi 37 16.00S 34.54E
Chil *r.* Iran 31 25.12N 61.30E
Chilapa Mexico 56 17.38N 99.11W
Chilcoot U.S.A. 54 39.49N120.08W
Childers Australia 44 25.14S152.17E
Chile S. America 62 32.30S 71.00W
Chile Chico Chile 63 46.33S 71.44W
Chilko L. Canada 50 51.20N124.05W
Chillagoe Australia 44 17.09S144.32E
Chillán Chile 63 36.36S 72.07W
Chillicothe Ohio U.S.A. 55 39.20N 82.59W
Chillingollah Australia 46 35.17S143.07E
Chilliwack Canada 54 49.10N122.00W
Chiloé, Isla de *i.* Chile 63 43.00S 73.00W
Chilonga Zambia 37 12.02S 31.17E
Chilpancingo Mexico 56 17.33N 99.30W
Chiltern Australia 47 36.11S146.36E
Chiltern Hills U.K. 5 51.40N 0.53W
Chilumba Malaŵi 37 10.25S 34.18E
Chilwa, L. Malaŵi 37 15.15S 35.45E
Chimanimani Zimbabwe 39 19.48S 32.52E
Chimay Belgium 8 50.03N 4.20E
Chimbas Argentina 62 31.28S 68.30W
Chimborazo *mtn.* Ecuador 60 1.29S 78.52W
Chimbote Peru 60 9.04S 78.34W
Chimishliya U.S.S.R. 15 46.30N 28.50E
Chimkent U.S.S.R. 24 42.16N 69.05E
Chimoio Mozambique 39 19.04S 33.29E
China Asia 24 33.00N103.00E
China Lake *town* U.S.A. 54 35.46N117.39W
Chinandega Nicaragua 57 12.35N 87.10W
Chinati Peak U.S.A. 52 29.57N104.29W
Chincha Alta Peru 60 13.25S 76.07W
Chinchón Spain 10 40.09N 3.26W
Chindio Mozambique 37 17.46S 35.23E
Chindwin *r.* Burma 24 21.30N 95.12E
Chinga Mozambique 37 15.14S 38.40E
Chingleput India 29 12.42N 79.59E
Chingola Zambia 37 12.29S 27.53E
Chingombe Zambia 37 14.25S 29.56E
Chin Hills Burma 29 22.40N 93.30E
Chinhoyi Zimbabwe 39 17.22S 30.10E
Chinle U.S.A. 54 36.09N109.33W
Chinon France 11 47.10N 0.15E
Chinook U.S.A. 54 48.35N109.14W
Chino Valley *town* U.S.A. 54 34.45N112.27W
Chinsali Zambia 37 10.33S 32.05E
Chintheche Malaŵi 37 11.50S 34.13E
Chiny Belgium 8 49.45N 5.20E
Chiôco Mozambique 37 16.27S 32.49E
Chioggia Italy 9 45.13N 12.17E
Chipata Zambia 37 13.37S 32.40E
Chipera Mozambique 37 15.20S 32.35E
Chipie *r.* Canada 55 51.30N 83.16W
Chipinge Zimbabwe 39 20.12S 32.38E
Chippenham U.K. 5 51.27N 2.07W
Chipping Norton U.K. 5 51.56N 1.32W
Chiquian Peru 60 10.10S 77.00W
Chiquinquirá Colombia 60 5.37N 73.50W
Chir *r.* U.S.S.R. 19 48.34N 42.53E
Chirchik U.S.S.R. 24 41.28N 69.31E
Chiredzi Zimbabwe 39 21.03S 31.39E
Chiredzi *r.* Zimbabwe 39 21.10S 31.50E
Chiriquí *mtn.* Panama 57 8.49N 82.38W
Chiriquí, Laguna de *b.* Panama 57 9.00N 82.00W
Chiromo Malaŵi 37 16.28S 35.10E
Chirripó *mtn.* Costa Rica 57 9.31N 83.30W
Chirundu Zimbabwe 37 16.04S 28.51E
Chisamba Zambia 37 14.58S 28.23E
Chisone *r.* Italy 9 44.49N 7.25E
Chistopol U.S.S.R. 18 55.25N 50.38E
Chita U.S.S.R. 25 52.03N113.35E
Chitipa Malaŵi 37 9.41S 33.19E
Chitorgarh India 28 24.53N 74.38E
Chitrāl Pakistan 28 35.52N 71.58E
Chittagong Bangla. 29 22.20N 91.48E
Chittoor India 29 13.13N 79.06E
Chiuta, L. Malaŵi/Mozambique 37 14.45S 35.50E
Chivasso Italy 9 45.11N 7.53E
Chivhu Zimbabwe 39 19.01S 30.53E
Chivilcoy Argentina 63 34.52S 60.02W
Chiwanda Tanzania 37 11.21S 34.55E
Chobe *r.* Namibia/Botswana 39 17.48S 25.12E
Chobe Swamp *f.* Namibia 39 18.20S 23.40E
Chocolate Mts. U.S.A. 54 33.20N115.15W
Chocope Peru 60 7.47S 79.12W
Choele-Choel Argentina 63 39.15S 65.30W
Chōfu Japan 23 35.39N139.33E
Choix Mexico 56 26.43N108.17W
Chojnice Poland 15 53.42N 17.32E
Cholet France 11 47.04N 0.53W
Cholon Vietnam 26 10.45N106.39E
Choluteca Honduras 57 13.16N 87.11W
Choma Zambia 36 16.51S 27.04E
Chomutov Czech. 14 50.28N 13.25E
Chon Buri Thailand 29 13.21N101.01E
Chone Ecuador 60 0.44S 80.04W
Ch'ŏngjin N. Korea 25 41.55N129.50E
Ch'ŏngju S. Korea 25 36.39N127.31E
Chongqing China 29 29.31N106.35E
Chŏnju S. Korea 25 35.50N127.05E
Chonos, Archipelago de los *is.* Chile 63 45.00S 74.00W
Chorley U.K. 4 53.39N 2.39W
Chortkov U.S.S.R. 15 49.01N 25.42E
Chorzów Poland 15 50.19N 18.56E
Chosica Peru 60 11.55S 76.38W
Chos Malal Argentina 63 37.20S 70.15W
Choszczno Poland 14 53.10N 15.26E
Choteau U.S.A. 54 47.49N112.11W
Chott Djerid *f.* Tunisia 34 33.30N 8.30E
Chott ech Chergui *f.* Algeria 34 34.00N 0.30E
Chott Melrhir *f.* Algeria 34 34.15N 7.00E
Choum Mauritania 34 21.10N 13.00W
Chowchilla U.S.A. 54 37.07N120.16W
Christchurch New Zealand 48 43.33S172.40E
Christchurch U.K. 5 50.44N 1.47W
Christianshåb Greenland 51 68.50N 51.00W
Christmas Creek *town* Australia 42 18.55S125.56E
Christmas I. Indian Oc. 26 10.30S105.40E
Chrudim Czech. 14 49.57N 15.48E
Chu *r.* U.S.S.R. 24 42.30N 76.10E
Chubbuck U.S.A. 54 34.22N115.20W
Chūbu *d.* Japan 23 35.25N137.40E
Chubut *d.* Argentina 63 44.00S 68.00W
Chubut *r.* Argentina 63 43.18S 65.06W
Chudleigh U.K. 5 50.35N 3.36W
Chudleigh Park *town* Australia 44 19.41S144.06E
Chudnov U.S.S.R. 15 50.05N 28.01E
Chudovo U.S.S.R. 18 59.10N 31.41E
Chudskoye, Ozero *l.* U.S.S.R. 18 58.30N 27.30E
Chuiquimula Guatemala 57 15.52N 89.50W
Chukai Malaysia 26 4.16N103.24E
Chukotskiy Poluostrov *pen.* U.S.S.R. 21 66.00N174.30W
Chukudukraal Botswana 39 22.30S 23.22E
Chula Vista U.S.A. 54 32.39N117.05W
Chulman U.S.S.R. 21 56.54N124.55E
Chulucanas Peru 60 5.08S 80.00W
Chulym U.S.S.R. 20 55.09N 80.59E
Chum U.S.S.R. 18 67.05N 63.15E
Chumbicha Argentina 62 28.50S 66.18W
Chumikan U.S.S.R. 21 54.40N135.15E
Chumphon Thailand 29 10.35N 99.14E
Chuna *r.* U.S.S.R. 21 58.00N 94.00E
Ch'unch'ŏn S. Korea 25 37.53N127.45E
Chungking *see* Chongqing China 29
Chunya Tanzania 37 8.31S 33.28E
Chuquicamata Chile 62 22.20S 68.56W
Chuquisaca *d.* Bolivia 62 21.00S 64.00W
Chur Switz. 11 46.52N 9.32E
Churchill Canada 51 58.45N 94.00W
Churchill *r.* Man. Canada 51 58.20N 94.15W
Churchill *r.* Nfld. Canada 51 53.20N 60.00W
Churchill, C. Canada 51 58.50N 93.00W
Churchill Falls *f.* Canada 51 53.35N 64.27W
Churchill L. Canada 50 56.00N108.00W
Churchill Peak *mtn.* Canada 50 58.10N125.00W
Church Stretton U.K. 5 52.32N 2.49W
Chusovoy U.S.S.R. 18 58.18N 57.50E
Chuxiong China 29 25.03N101.33E
Ciechanów Poland 15 52.53N 20.38E
Ciego de Avila Cuba 57 21.51N 78.47W
Ciénaga Colombia 60 11.11N 74.15W
Cienfuegos Cuba 57 22.10N 80.27W
Cieszyn Poland 15 49.45N 18.38E
Cieza Spain 10 38.14N 1.25W
Cifuentes Spain 10 40.47N 2.37W
Cigüela *r.* Spain 10 39.47N 3.00W
Cijara, Embalse de *resr.* Spain 10 39.20N 4.50W
Cilacap Indonesia 26 7.44S109.00E
Cimarron *r.* U.S.A. 53 36.15N 96.55W
Cimone, Monte *mtn.* Italy 9 44.12N 10.42E
Cîmpina Romania 13 45.08N 25.44E
Cîmpulung Romania 13 45.16N 25.03E
Cinca *r.* Spain 10 41.22N 0.20E
Cincinnati U.S.A. 55 39.10N 84.30W
Ciney Belgium 8 50.17N 5.06E
Cinto, Monte *mtn.* France 11 42.23N 8.57E
Cipolletti Argentina 63 38.56S 67.59W
Circle U.S.A. 54 47.25N105.35W
Circleville Ohio U.S.A. 55 39.36N 82.57W
Circleville Utah U.S.A. 54 38.10N112.16W
Cirebon Indonesia 26 6.46S108.33E
Cirencester U.K. 5 51.43N 1.59W
Ciriè Italy 9 45.14N 7.36E
Cirò Marina Italy 13 39.22N 17.08E
Cittadella Italy 9 45.39N 11.47E
Cittanova Italy 12 38.21N 16.05E
Ciudad Bolívar Venezuela 60 8.06N 63.36W
Ciudad Camargo Mexico 56 27.40N105.10W
Ciudad de México Mexico 56 19.25N 99.10W
Ciudadela Spain 10 40.00N 3.50E
Ciudad Guayana Venezuela 60 8.22N 62.40W
Ciudad Guerrero Mexico 56 28.33N107.28W
Ciudad Guzmán Mexico 56 19.41N103.29W
Ciudad Ixtepec Mexico 56 16.32N 95.10W
Ciudad Jiménez Mexico 54 27.08N104.55W
Ciudad Juárez Mexico 56 31.44N106.29W
Ciudad Madero Mexico 56 22.19N 97.50W
Ciudad Mante Mexico 56 22.44N 98.57W
Ciudad Obregón Mexico 56 27.29N109.56W
Ciudad Ojeda Venezuela 60 10.05N 71.17W
Ciudad Piar Venezuela 60 7.27N 63.19W
Ciudad Real Spain 10 38.59N 3.55W
Ciudad Rodrigo Spain 10 40.36N 6.33W
Ciudad Victoria Mexico 56 23.43N 99.10W
Civitanova Italy 12 43.19N 13.40E
Civitavecchia Italy 12 42.06N 11.48E
Civray France 11 46.09N 0.18E
Çivril Turkey 30 38.18N 29.43E
Cizre Turkey 30 37.21N 42.11E
Clackline Australia 43 31.43S116.31E
Clacton on Sea U.K. 5 51.47N 1.10E
Claire, L. Canada 50 58.30N112.00W
Clamecy France 9 47.27N 3.31E
Clampton Australia 43 29.56S119.06E
Clara Rep. of Ire. 7 53.21N 7.37W
Clara Creek *town* Australia 44 26.00S146.50E
Clare N.S.W. Australia 46 33.27S143.55E
Clare S.A. Australia 46 33.50S138.38E
Clare *d.* Rep. of Ire. 7 52.52N 8.55W
Clare *r.* Rep. of Ire. 7 53.17N 9.04W
Clare U.S.A. 55 43.49N 84.47W
Clare I. Rep. of Ire. 7 53.48N 10.00W
Claremorris Rep. of Ire. 7 53.44N 9.00W
Clarence *r.* Australia 47 29.25S153.02E
Clarence *r.* New Zealand 48 42.10S173.55E
Clarence I. Antarctica 64 61.30S 53.50W
Clarence Str. Australia 42 12.00S131.00E
Clarie Coast *f.* Antarctica 64 67.00S133.00E
Clark, L. U.S.A. 50 60.15N154.15W
Clarke I. Australia 45 40.30S148.10E
Clark Fork *r.* U.S.A. 54 48.09N116.15W
Clarksburg U.S.A. 55 39.16N 80.22W
Clarksdale U.S.A. 53 34.12N 90.33W
Clarkston U.S.A. 54 46.26N117.02W
Clarksville Tenn. U.S.A. 53 36.31N 87.21W
Clary France 8 50.05N 3.21E
Claverton Australia 45 27.24S145.55E
Clayton *r.* Australia 46 29.06S137.59E
Clayton Idaho U.S.A. 54 44.16N114.25W
Clayton N.Mex. U.S.A. 52 36.27N103.12W
Clear, C. Rep. of Ire. 3 51.25N 9.32W
Clearfield Utah U.S.A. 54 41.07N112.01W
Clear I. Rep. of Ire. 7 51.26N 9.30W
Clear L. U.S.A. 54 39.02N122.50W
Clearwater U.S.A. 53 27.57N 82.48W
Clearwater Mts. U.S.A. 54 46.00N115.30W
Cle Elum U.S.A. 54 47.12N120.56W
Cleethorpes U.K. 4 53.33N 0.02W
Clermont Australia 44 22.49S147.39E
Clermont France 9 49.23N 2.24E
Clermont-en-Argonne France 9 49.05N 5.05E
Clermont-Ferrand France 11 45.47N 3.05E
Clervaux Lux. 8 50.04N 6.01E
Cles Italy 9 46.22N 11.02E
Cleve Australia 46 33.37S136.32E
Clevedon U.K. 5 51.26N 2.52W
Cleveland *d.* U.K. 4 54.37N 1.08W
Cleveland Miss. U.S.A. 53 33.43N 90.46W
Cleveland Ohio U.S.A. 55 41.30N 81.41W
Cleveland Tenn. U.S.A. 53 35.10N 84.51W
Cleveland, C. Australia 44 19.11S147.01E
Cleveland Heights *town* U.S.A. 55 41.30N 81.34W
Cleveland Hills U.K. 4 54.25N 1.10W
Cleveleys U.K. 4 53.52N 3.01W
Clew B. Rep. of Ire. 7 53.50N 9.47W
Clifden Rep. of Ire. 7 53.29N 10.02W
Cliffy Head Australia 43 34.58S116.24E
Clifton Ariz. U.S.A. 54 33.03N109.18W
Clinton B.C. Canada 50 51.05N121.35W
Clinton New Zealand 48 46.13S169.23E
Clinton Iowa U.S.A. 53 41.51N 90.12W
Clinton Okla. U.S.A. 52 35.32N 98.59W
Clisham *mtn.* U.K. 6 57.58N 6.50W
Cliza Bolivia 62 17.36S 65.56W
Cloghan Offaly Rep. of Ire. 7 53.13N 7.54W
Clogher Head Kerry Rep. of Ire. 7 52.09N 10.28W
Clonakilty Rep. of Ire. 7 51.37N 8.54W
Cloncurry Australia 44 20.42S140.30E
Clones Rep. of Ire. 7 54.11N 7.16W
Clonmel Rep. of Ire. 7 52.21N 7.44W
Clonroche Rep. of Ire. 7 52.27N 6.45W
Cloppenburg W. Germany 8 52.52N 8.02E
Clorinda Argentina 62 25.20S 57.40W
Cloud Peak *mtn.* U.S.A. 54 44.25N107.10W
Cloughton U.K. 4 54.20N 0.27W
Cloverdale U.S.A. 54 38.48N123.01W
Clovis Calif. U.S.A. 54 36.49N119.42W
Clovis N.Mex. U.S.A. 52 34.14N103.13W
Clowne U.K. 4 53.18N 1.16W
Cluj Romania 15 46.47N 23.37E
Cluny France 11 46.26N 4.39E
Clusone Italy 9 45.53N 9.57E
Clutha *r.* New Zealand 48 46.18S169.05E
Clwyd *d.* U.K. 4 53.07N 3.20W
Clwyd *r.* U.K. 4 53.19N 3.30W
Clyde Canada 51 70.30N 68.30W
Clyde New Zealand 48 45.11S169.19E
Clyde *r.* U.K. 6 55.58N 4.53W
Clydebank U.K. 6 55.53N 4.23W
Coachella U.S.A. 54 33.41N116.10W
Coahuila *d.* Mexico 56 27.00N103.00W
Coalinga U.S.A. 54 36.09N120.21W
Coalville U.K. 5 52.43N 1.21W
Coast *d.* Kenya 37 3.00S 39.30E
Coast Mts. Canada 50 55.30N128.00W
Coast Range *mts.* U.S.A. 54 42.40N123.30W
Coatbridge U.K. 6 55.52N 4.02W
Coats I. Canada 51 62.30N 83.00W
Coats Land *f.* Antarctica 64 77.00S 25.00W
Coatzacoalcos Mexico 56 18.10N 94.25W
Cobalt Canada 55 47.24N 79.41W
Cobán Guatemala 56 15.28N 90.20W
Cobar Australia 47 31.32S145.51E
Cobargo Australia 47 36.24S149.52E
Cobden Australia 46 38.21S143.07E
Cobden Canada 55 45.38N 76.53W
Cobh Rep. of Ire. 7 51.50N 8.18W
Cobham L. Australia 46 30.09S142.05E
Cobija Bolivia 62 11.02S 68.44W
Cobourg Canada 55 43.58N 78.11W

Cobourg Pen. Australia **44** 11.20S132.15E
Cobram Australia **47** 35.56S145.40E
Cobre U.S.A. **54** 41.07N114.25W
Cobue Mozambique **37** 12.10S 34.50E
Coburg W. Germany **14** 50.15N 10.58E
Coburg I. Canada **51** 76.00N 79.25W
Cochabamba Bolivia **62** 17.24S 66.09W
Cochabamba *d.* Bolivia **62** 17.30S 65.40W
Cochem W. Germany **8** 50.08N 7.10E
Cochin India **28** 9.56N 76.15E
Cochrane Ont. Canada **55** 49.04N 81.02W
Cochrane Chile **63** 47.20S 72.30W
Cockburn Australia **46** 32.05S141.00E
Cockburnspath U.K. **6** 55.56N 2.22W
Coco *r.* Honduras **57** 14.58N 83.15W
Cocoparra Range *mts.* Australia **47** 34.00S146.00E
Cod, C. U.S.A. **55** 41.42N 70.15W
Codăeşti Romania **15** 46.52N 27.46E
Codajás Brazil **60** 3.55S 62.00W
Codigoro Italy **9** 44.49N 12.08E
Codó Brazil **61** 4.28S 43.51W
Codogno Italy **9** 45.09N 9.42E
Codroipo Italy **9** 45.58N 12.59E
Cody U.S.A. **54** 44.32N109.03W
Coen Australia **44** 13.56S143.12E
Coesfeld W. Germany **8** 51.55N 7.13E
Coeur d'Alene U.S.A. **52** 47.40N116.46W
Coevorden Neth. **8** 52.39N 6.45E
Coffin B. Australia **46** 34.27S135.19E
Coff's Harbour Australia **47** 30.19S153.05E
Cofre de Perote *mtn.* Mexico **56** 19.30N 97.10W
Coghinas *r.* Italy **12** 40.57N 8.50E
Cognac France **11** 45.42N 0.19W
Cohoes U.S.A. **55** 42.46N 73.42W
Cohuna Australia **46** 35.47S144.15E
Coiba, Isla de *i.* Panama **57** 7.23N 81.45W
Coihaique Chile **63** 45.35S 72.08W
Coimbatore India **28** 11.00N 76.57E
Coimbra Brazil **59** 19.55S 57.47W
Coimbra Portugal **10** 40.12N 8.25W
Coín Spain **10** 36.40N 4.45W
Cojimies Ecuador **60** 0.20N 80.00W
Cokeville U.S.A. **54** 42.05N110.57W
Coko Range *mts.* Australia **46** 30.35S141.46E
Colac Australia **46** 38.22S143.38E
Colatina Brazil **59** 19.35S 40.37W
Colbeck, C. Antarctica **64** 77.20S159.00W
Colchester U.K. **5** 51.54N 0.55E
Coldstream U.K. **6** 55.39N 2.15W
Coldwater U.S.A. **55** 41.57N 85.01W
Coldwell Canada **55** 48.46N 86.31W
Coleman *r.* Australia **44** 15.06S141.38E
Colenso R.S.A. **39** 28.43S 29.49E
Coleraine Australia **46** 37.36S141.42E
Coleraine U.K. **7** 55.08N 6.40W
Colesberg R.S.A. **39** 30.43S 25.05E
Colico Italy **9** 46.08N 9.22E
Colima Mexico **56** 19.14N103.41W
Colima *d.* Mexico **56** 19.05N104.00W
Colinas Brazil **61** 6.02S 44.14W
Coll *i.* U.K. **6** 56.38N 6.34W
College U.S.A. **50** 64.54N147.55W
College Park *town* Md. U.S.A. **55** 39.00N 76.55W
Collerina Australia **47** 29.22S146.32E
Collie N.S.W. Australia **47** 31.41S148.22E
Collie W.A. Australia **43** 33.21S116.09E
Collie Cardiff Australia **43** 33.27S116.09E
Collier B. Australia **42** 16.10S124.15E
Collingwood Canada **55** 44.29N 80.13W
Collingwood New Zealand **48** 40.41S172.41E
Collingwood B. P.N.G. **44** 9.20S149.30E
Collinsville Australia **44** 20.34S147.51E
Collin Top *mtn.* U.K. **7** 54.58N 6.08W
Collon Rep. of Ire. **7** 53.47N 6.30W
Collooney Rep. of Ire. **7** 54.11N 8.29W
Colmar France **11** 48.05N 7.21E
Colmenar Viejo Spain **10** 40.39N 3.46W
Colne *r.* Essex U.K. **5** 51.50N 0.59E
Colnett, C. Mexico **56** 31.00N116.20W
Colnett, Cabo *c.* Mexico **54** 31.00N116.20W
Colo *r.* Australia **47** 33.26S150.53E
Cologne *see* Köln W. Germany **8**
Colombia S. America **60** 4.00N 72.30W
Colombo Sri Lanka **29** 6.55N 79.52E
Colón Argentina **63** 32.15S 58.10W
Colón Panama **60** 9.21N 79.54W
Colona Australia **45** 31.38S132.05E
Colonia del Sacramento Uruguay **63** 34.28S 57.51W
Colonia Las Heras Argentina **63** 46.33S 68.57W
Colonia Lavelleja Uruguay **63** 31.06S 57.01W
Colonsay *i.* U.K. **6** 56.04N 6.13W
Colorado *r.* Argentina **63** 39.50S 62.02W
Colorado *d.* U.S.A. **52** 39.07N105.27W
Colorado *r.* Ariz. U.S.A. **54** 31.45N114.40W
Colorado *r.* Tex. U.S.A. **53** 28.30N 96.00W
Colorado Plateau *f.* U.S.A. **54** 36.30N108.00W
Colorado Springs *town* U.S.A. **52** 38.50N104.49W
Columbia *r.* U.S.A. **54** 46.15N124.05W
Columbia Mo. U.S.A. **53** 38.58N 92.20W
Columbia S.C. U.S.A. **53** 34.00N 81.00W
Columbia Tenn. U.S.A. **53** 35.37N 87.02W
Columbia Basin *f.* U.S.A. **54** 46.55N117.36W
Columbia Falls *town* U.S.A. **54** 48.23N114.11W
Columbia Plateau *f.* U.S.A. **54** 44.00N117.30W
Columbretes, Islas *is.* Spain **10** 39.50N 0.40E
Columbus Ga. U.S.A. **53** 32.28N 84.59W
Columbus Ind. U.S.A. **55** 39.12N 85.57W
Columbus Miss. U.S.A. **53** 33.30N 88.27W
Columbus Mont. U.S.A. **54** 45.38N109.15W
Columbus Ohio U.S.A. **55** 39.59N 83.03W
Colville *r.* U.S.A. **50** 70.06N151.30W
Colwyn Bay *town* U.K. **4** 53.18N 3.43W
Comacchio Italy **9** 44.42N 12.11E
Comacchio, Valli di *b.* Italy **9** 44.38N 12.06E
Comayagua Honduras **57** 14.30N 87.39W
Comblain-au-Pont Belgium **8** 50.29N 5.32E
Combles France **8** 50.01N 2.52E
Combourg France **9** 48.25N 1.45W
Comboyne Australia **47** 31.35S152.27E
Comeragh Mts. Rep. of Ire. **7** 52.17N 7.34W
Comilla Bangla. **29** 23.28N 91.10E
Comitán Mexico **56** 16.15N 92.08W
Commentry France **11** 46.17N 2.44E
Commonwealth Territory *d.* Australia **47** 35.00S151.00E
Como Italy **9** 45.48N 9.04E
Como, Lago di *l.* Italy **9** 46.05N 9.17E
Comodoro Rivadavia Argentina **63** 45.50S 67.30W
Comorin, C. India **28** 8.04N 77.35E
Comoros Africa **37** 12.15S 44.00E
Compiègne France **9** 49.24N 2.50E
Conakry Guinea **34** 9.30N 13.43W
Concarneau France **11** 47.53N 3.55W
Conceição do Araguaia Brazil **61** 8.15S 49.17W
Concepción Argentina **62** 27.20S 65.36W
Concepción Chile **63** 36.50S 73.03W
Concepción Paraguay **62** 23.22S 57.26W
Concepción del Oro Mexico **56** 24.38N101.25W
Concepción del Uruguay Argentina **63** 32.30S 58.14W
Conception, Pt. U.S.A. **54** 34.27N120.27W
Conception B. Namibia **39** 23.53S 14.28E
Conches France **9** 48.58N 0.58E
Conchillas Uruguay **63** 34.15S 58.04W
Conchos *r.* Mexico **56** 29.32N104.25W
Concord N.H. U.S.A. **55** 43.12N 71.32W
Concordia Argentina **63** 31.24S 58.02W
Concórdia Brazil **60** 4.35S 66.35W
Concordia U.S.A. **52** 39.35N 97.39W
Condé France **9** 48.51N 0.33W
Condé-sur-l'Escaut France **8** 50.28N 3.35E
Condobolin Australia **47** 33.03S147.11E
Condom France **11** 43.58N 0.22E
Conegliano Italy **9** 45.53N 12.18E
Confolens France **11** 46.01N 0.40E
Congleton U.K. **4** 53.10N 2.12W
Congo Africa **36** 1.00S 16.00E
Congonhas Brazil **59** 20.30S 43.53W
Coningsby U.K. **4** 53.07N 0.09W
Coniston U.K. **4** 54.22N 3.06W
Conn, Lough Rep. of Ire. **7** 54.01N 9.15W
Connah's Quay *town* U.K. **4** 53.13N 3.03W
Conneaut U.S.A. **55** 41.58N 80.34W
Connecticut *d.* U.S.A. **55** 41.45N 72.45W
Connecticut *r.* U.S.A. **55** 41.17N 72.21W
Connellsville U.S.A. **55** 40.01N 79.35W
Connemara *f.* Rep. of Ire. **7** 53.32N 9.56W
Conon *r.* U.K. **6** 57.33N 4.33W
Conrad U.S.A. **54** 48.10N111.57W
Conselheiro Lafaiete Brazil **59** 20.40S 43.48W
Consett U.K. **4** 54.52N 1.50W
Con Son *is.* Vietnam **26** 8.30N106.30E
Constance, L. *see* Bodensee Europe **14**
Constanţa Romania **13** 44.10N 28.31E
Constantina Spain **10** 37.54N 5.36W
Constantine Algeria **34** 36.22N 6.38E
Constitución Chile **63** 35.20S 72.25W
Constitución Uruguay **63** 31.05S 57.50W
Consuegra Spain **10** 39.28N 3.43W
Contact U.S.A. **54** 41.48N114.46W
Contamana Peru **60** 7.19S 75.00W
Contas *r.* Brazil **61** 14.15S 39.00W
Contreras, Embalse de *resr.* Spain **10** 39.32N 1.30W
Contres France **9** 47.25N 1.26E
Contwoyto L. Canada **50** 65.42N110.50W
Conty France **9** 49.44N 2.09E
Conway N.H. U.S.A. **55** 43.59N 71.07W
Conway, L. Australia **46** 28.17S135.35E
Coober Pedy Australia **46** 29.01S134.43E
Cook Australia **45** 30.37S130.25E
Cook, C. Canada **50** 50.08N127.55W
Cook, Mt. New Zealand **48** 43.45S170.12E
Cooke, Mt. Australia **43** 32.26S116.18E
Cookhouse R.S.A. **39** 32.44S 25.47E
Cook Inlet U.S.A. **50** 60.30N152.00W
Cook Is. Pacific Oc. **40** 15.00S160.00W
Cookstown U.K. **7** 54.39N 6.46W
Cook Str. New Zealand **48** 41.15S174.30E
Cooktown Australia **44** 15.29S145.15E
Coolabah Australia **47** 31.02S146.45E
Coolah Australia **47** 31.48S149.45E
Coolamara Australia **46** 31.59S143.42E
Coolangatta Australia **47** 28.10S153.26E
Coolawanyah Australia **42** 21.47S117.48E
Coolgardie Australia **43** 31.01S121.12E
Coolidge U.S.A. **54** 32.59N111.31W
Cooma Australia **47** 36.15S149.07E
Coombah Australia **46** 32.58S141.39E
Coomberdale Australia **43** 30.29S116.03E
Coonalpyn Australia **46** 35.41S139.52E
Coonamble Australia **47** 30.55S148.26E
Coonana Australia **43** 31.01S123.05E
Coonawarra Australia **46** 37.16S140.50E
Coondambo Australia **46** 31.07S135.20E
Cooper Creek *r.* Australia **46** 28.33S137.46E
Coopernook Australia **47** 31.49S152.38E
Coorow Australia **43** 29.53S116.01E
Cooroy Australia **44** 26.29S152.50E
Coos Bay *town* U.S.A. **54** 43.22N124.13W
Cootamundra Australia **47** 34.41S148.03E
Cootehill Rep. of Ire. **7** 54.05N 7.05W
Copainalá Mexico **56** 17.05N 93.12W
Copán *ruins* Honduras **57** 14.52N 89.10W
Copenhagen *see* København Denmark **17**
Copiapó Chile **62** 27.22S 70.20W
Copparo Italy **9** 44.54N 11.49E
Copperbelt *d.* Zambia **37** 13.00S 28.00E
Copper Belt *f.* Zambia **37** 12.40S 28.00E
Copper Center U.S.A. **50** 61.58N145.19W
Copper Cliff *town* Canada **55** 46.28N 81.04W
Copper Harbor U.S.A. **55** 47.28N 87.54W
Coppermine *r.* Canada **50** 67.54N115.10W
Coppermine *town* Canada **50** 67.49N115.12W
Copper Queen Zimbabwe **39** 17.31S 29.20E
Copperton R.S.A. **39** 30.00S 22.15E
Coqên China **29** 31.20N 85.25E
Coquet *r.* U.K. **4** 55.21N 1.35W
Coquille U.S.A. **54** 43.11N124.11W
Coquimbo Chile **62** 29.58S 71.21W
Corabia Romania **13** 43.45N 24.29E
Coracora Peru **60** 15.02S 73.48W
Coral Harbour *town* Canada **51** 64.10N 83.15W
Coral Sea Pacific Oc. **44** 14.30S149.30E
Corangamite, L. Australia **46** 38.10S143.25E
Corbeil France **9** 48.37N 2.29E
Corbeny France **9** 49.28N 3.49E
Corbigny France **9** 47.15N 3.40E
Corby U.K. **5** 52.29N 0.41W
Corcubión Spain **10** 42.56N 9.12W
Córdoba Argentina **62** 31.25S 64.10W
Córdoba *d.* Argentina **62** 30.30S 64.30W
Córdoba Mexico **56** 18.55N 96.55W
Córdoba Spain **10** 37.53N 4.46W
Córdoba, Sierras de *mts.* Argentina **62** 30.30S 64.40W
Cordova U.S.A. **50** 60.33N139.44W
Corentyne *r.* Guyana **61** 5.10N 57.20W
Corfield Australia **44** 21.43S143.22E
Corfu *i. see* Kérkira *i.* Greece **13**
Coricudgy, Mt. Australia **47** 32.51S150.25E
Corigliano Italy **13** 39.36N 16.31E
Corindi Australia **47** 30.00S153.21E
Corinth Miss. U.S.A. **53** 34.58N 88.30W
Corinthian Australia **43** 31.05S119.13E
Corinto Nicaragua **57** 12.29N 87.14W
Cork Rep. of Ire. **7** 51.54N 8.28W
Cork *d.* Rep. of Ire. **7** 52.00N 8.40W
Cork Harbour *est.* Rep. of Ire. **7** 51.50N 8.17W
Cormeilles France **9** 49.15N 0.23E
Corner Brook *town* Canada **51** 48.58N 57.58W
Corner Inlet *b.* Australia **47** 38.43S146.20E
Corning N.Y. U.S.A. **55** 42.09N 77.04W
Corno, Monte *mtn.* Italy **12** 42.29N 13.33E
Cornwall Canada **55** 45.02N 74.45W
Cornwall *d.* U.K. **5** 50.26N 4.40W
Cornwallis I. Canada **51** 75.00N 95.00W
Coro Venezuela **60** 11.27N 69.41W
Coroatá Brazil **61** 4.08S 44.08W
Čoroch *r.* U.S.S.R. **19** 41.36N 41.35E
Coroico Bolivia **62** 16.10S 67.44W
Coromandel New Zealand **48** 36.46S175.30E
Coromandel Pen. New Zealand **48** 36.45S175.30E
Coronation G. Canada **50** 68.00N112.00W
Coronda Argentina **63** 31.55S 60.55W
Coronel Chile **63** 37.01S 73.08W
Coronel Brandsen Argentina **63** 35.10S 58.15W
Coronel Pringles Argentina **63** 37.56S 61.25W
Coronel Suárez Argentina **63** 37.30S 61.52W
Coropuna *mtn.* Peru **60** 15.31S 72.45W
Corowa Australia **47** 36.00S146.20E
Corozal Belize **57** 18.23N 88.23W
Corpus Christi U.S.A. **53** 27.47N 97.26W
Correggio Italy **9** 44.46N 10.47E
Correntes, Cabo das *c.* Mozambique **39** 24.11S 35.35E
Corrib, Lough Rep. of Ire. **7** 53.26N 9.14W
Corrientes Argentina **62** 27.30S 58.48W
Corrientes *d.* Argentina **62** 28.00S 57.00W
Corrientes, Cabo *c.* Colombia **60** 5.30N 77.34W
Corrigin Australia **43** 32.21S117.52E
Corrimal Australia **47** 34.21S150.54E
Corry U.S.A. **55** 41.56N 79.39W
Corryong Australia **47** 36.11S147.58E
Corse *d.* France **11** 42.00N 9.10E
Corse *i.* France **11** 42.00N 9.10E
Corse, Cap *c.* France **11** 43.00N 9.21E
Corsham U.K. **5** 51.25N 2.11W
Corsica *i. see* Corse *i.* France **11**
Corsicana U.S.A. **53** 32.05N 96.27W
Corte France **11** 42.18N 9.08E
Cortegana Spain **10** 37.55N 6.49W
Cortez Colo. U.S.A. **54** 37.21N108.35W
Cortez Nev. U.S.A. **54** 40.09N116.38W
Cortina Italy **12** 46.32N 12.08E
Cortland N.Y. U.S.A. **55** 42.36N 76.11W
Cortona Italy **12** 43.16N 11.59E
Coruche Portugal **10** 38.58N 8.31W
Çoruh *r.* Turkey *see* Čoroch *r.* U.S.S.R. **30**
Çorum Turkey **30** 40.31N 34.57E
Corumbá Brazil **62** 19.00S 57.27W
Corumbá *r.* Brazil **59** 18.15S 48.55W
Corunna Australia **46** 32.47S137.08E
Corvallis U.S.A. **54** 44.34N123.16W
Corwen U.K. **4** 52.59N 3.23W
Cosenza Italy **12** 39.17N 16.14E
Cosne France **9** 47.25N 2.55E
Coso Junction U.S.A. **54** 36.03N117.58W
Cosson *r.* France **9** 47.30N 1.15E
Costa Brava *f.* Spain **10** 41.30N 3.00E
Costa del Sol *f.* Spain **10** 36.30N 4.00W
Costa Mesa U.S.A. **54** 33.39N117.55W
Costa Rica C. America **57** 10.00N 84.00W
Costeşti Romania **13** 44.40N 24.53E
Cotabato Phil. **27** 7.14N124.15E
Cotagaita Bolivia **62** 20.50S 65.41W
Côte d'Azur *f.* France **11** 43.20N 6.45E
Côte-d'Or *d.* France **9** 47.30N 4.50E
Côte d'Or *f.* France **9** 47.10N 4.50E
Cotonou Benin **38** 6.24N 2.31E
Cotopaxi *mtn.* Ecuador **60** 0.40S 78.28W
Cotswold Hills U.K. **5** 51.50N 2.00W
Cottage Grove U.S.A. **54** 43.48N123.03W
Cottbus E. Germany **14** 51.43N 14.21E
Cottbus *d.* E. Germany **14** 51.45N 14.00E
Cottonwood U.S.A. **54** 34.45N112.01W
Coucy France **9** 49.31N 3.19E
Couer d'Alene U.S.A. **54** 47.41N117.00W
Couesnon *r.* France **9** 48.37N 1.31W
Coulagh B. Rep. of Ire. **7** 51.42N 10.00W
Coulee City U.S.A. **54** 47.37N119.17W
Coulommiers France **9** 48.49N 3.05E
Coulonge *r.* Canada **55** 45.51N 76.45W
Council U.S.A. **50** 64.55N163.44W
Council Bluffs U.S.A. **53** 41.14N 95.54W
Coupar Angus U.K. **6** 56.33N 3.17W
Courson-les-Carrières France **9** 47.36N 3.30E
Courtalain France **9** 48.05N 1.09E
Courtenay Canada **50** 49.41N125.00W
Coutances France **9** 49.03N 1.29W
Coutras France **11** 45.02N 0.07W
Couvin Belgium **8** 50.03N 4.30E
Covè Benin **38** 7.16N 2.20E
Coventry U.K. **5** 52.25N 1.31W
Covilhã Portugal **10** 40.17N 7.30W
Covington Ky. U.S.A. **55** 39.04N 84.30W
Cowal, L. Australia **47** 33.36S147.22E
Cowan, L. Australia **43** 32.00S122.00E
Cowangie Australia **46** 35.14S141.28E
Cowansville Canada **55** 45.13N 72.44W
Cowcowing, L. Australia **43** 31.01S117.18E
Cowdenbeath U.K. **6** 56.07N 3.21W
Cowell Australia **46** 33.41S136.55E
Cowes U.K. **5** 50.45N 1.18W
Cowra Australia **47** 33.50S148.45E
Cox *r.* Australia **44** 15.19S135.25E
Coxim Brazil **62** 18.28S 54.37W
Cox's Bāzār Bangla. **29** 21.25N 91.59E
Coyuca de Catalán Mexico **56** 18.20N100.39W
Cozes France **11** 45.35N 0.50W
Cozumel, Isla de *i.* Mexico **57** 20.30N 87.00W
Craboon Australia **47** 32.02S149.29E
Cradock R.S.A. **39** 32.10S 25.35E
Craig Colo. U.S.A. **54** 40.31N107.33W
Craigavon U.K. **7** 54.28N 6.25W
Craignure U.K. **6** 56.28N 5.42W
Craigsville U.S.A. **55** 38.04N 79.23W
Crail U.K. **6** 56.16N 2.38W
Crailsheim W. Germany **14** 49.09N 10.06E
Craiova Romania **13** 44.18N 23.46E
Cranbrook Australia **43** 34.15S117.32E
Cranbrook Canada **50** 49.29N115.48W
Crane U.S.A. **54** 43.25N118.34W
Cranston U.S.A. **55** 41.47N 71.26W
Craon France **9** 47.50N 0.58W
Craonne France **9** 49.27N 3.46E
Crater L. U.S.A. **54** 42.56N122.06W
Crateús Brazil **61** 5.10S 40.39W
Crati *r.* Italy **13** 39.43N 16.29E
Crato Amazonas Brazil **60** 7.25S 63.00W
Crato Ceará Brazil **61** 7.10S 39.25W
Craughwell Rep. of Ire. **7** 53.14N 8.44W
Crawfordsville U.S.A. **55** 40.03N 86.54W
Crawley U.K. **5** 51.07N 0.10W
Crazy Mts. U.S.A. **54** 46.08N110.20W
Crécy France **11** 50.15N 1.53E
Crécy-sur-Serre France **9** 49.42N 3.37E
Cree *r.* Canada **50** 59.00N105.47W
Creede U.S.A. **54** 37.51N106.56W
Cree L. Canada **50** 57.20N108.30W
Creil France **9** 49.16N 2.29E
Crema Italy **9** 45.22N 9.41E
Cremona Italy **9** 45.08N 10.03E
Crépy France **9** 49.36N 3.31E
Crépy-en-Valois France **9** 49.14N 2.54E
Cres *i.* Yugo. **12** 44.50N 14.20E
Cres *town* Yugo. **12** 44.58N 14.25E
Crescent U.S.A. **54** 43.29N121.41W
Crescent City U.S.A. **54** 41.45N124.12W
Crespo Argentina **63** 32.02S 60.20W
Cressy Australia **46** 38.02S143.38E
Crest France **11** 44.44N 5.02E
Creston Iowa U.S.A. **53** 41.04N 94.20W
Crete *i. see* Kríti *i.* Greece **13**
Crete, Sea of *see* Kritikón Pélagos *sea* Greece **13**
Creus, Cabo de *c.* Spain **10** 42.20N 3.19E
Creuse *r.* France **11** 47.00N 0.35E
Crewe U.K. **4** 53.06N 2.28W
Crianlarich U.K. **6** 56.23N 4.37W
Criccieth U.K. **4** 52.55N 4.15W
Criciúma Brazil **59** 28.40S 49.23W
Crieff U.K. **6** 56.23N 3.52W
Crimea *pen. see* Krym *pen.* U.S.S.R. **19**
Crinan U.K. **6** 56.06N 5.34W
Cristóbal Colón *mtn.* Colombia **60** 10.53N 73.48W
Crişu Alb *r.* Romania **15** 46.42N 21.17E
Crna *r.* Yugo. **13** 41.33N 21.58E
Crna Gora *d.* Yugo. **13** 43.00N 19.30E
Croaghnameal *mtn.* Rep. of Ire. **7** 54.40N 7.57W
Croatia *d. see* Hrvatska *d.* Yugo. **13**
Crocodile *r.* Trans. R.S.A. **39** 24.11S 26.48E
Croker I. Australia **44** 11.12S132.32E
Cromarty U.K. **6** 57.40N 4.02W
Cromarty Firth *est.* U.K. **6** 57.41N 4.10W
Cromer U.K. **4** 52.56N 1.18E
Cromwell New Zealand **48** 45.03S169.14E
Crooked I. Bahamas **57** 22.45N 74.00W
Crookhaven Rep. of Ire. **7** 51.29N 9.45W
Crookwell Australia **47** 34.27S149.28E
Croom Rep. of Ire. **7** 52.31N 8.43W
Croppa Creek *town* Australia **47** 29.08S150.20E
Crosby U.K. **4** 54.11N 4.34W
Cross Fell *mtn.* U.K. **4** 54.43N 2.28W
Cross River *d.* Nigeria **38** 5.45N 8.25E
Cross Sd. U.S.A. **50** 58.10N136.30W
Crotone Italy **13** 39.05N 17.06E
Crow Agency U.S.A. **54** 45.36N107.27W
Crowes Australia **46** 38.38S143.12E
Crowl *r.* Australia **47** 31.58S144.53E
Crow's Nest Australia **45** 27.16S152.03E
Crowsnest Pass Canada **50** 49.40N114.41W
Croyde U.K. **5** 51.07N 4.13W
Croyden Australia **41** 18.12S142.14E
Croydon Australia **44** 18.12S142.14E
Croydon U.K. **5** 51.23N 0.06W
Crucero U.S.A. **54** 35.03N116.10W
Cruz, Cabo *c.* Cuba **57** 19.52N 77.44W
Cruz Alta Brazil **59** 28.38S 53.38W
Cruz del Eje Argentina **62** 30.44S 64.49W
Cruzeiro Brazil **59** 22.33S 44.59W
Cruzeiro do Sul Brazil **60** 7.40S 72.39W
Crystal Bridge *town* Australia **46** 33.21S138.13E
Csorna Hungary **15** 47.37N 17.16E
Csurgó Hungary **15** 46.16N 17.06E
Cuamba Mozambique **37** 14.48S 36.32E
Cuando *r.* Angola **36** 18.30S 23.32E
Cuangar Angola **39** 17.34S 18.39E
Cuango *r. see* Kwango *r.* Angola **36**
Cuanza *r.* Angola **36** 9.22S 13.09E
Cuaró Uruguay **63** 30.37S 56.54W
Cuaró *r.* Uruguay **63** 30.15S 57.01W
Cuba C. America **57** 22.00N 79.00W
Cuballing Australia **43** 32.50S117.07E
Cubango *r. see* Okavango *r.* Angola **36**
Cubo Mozambique **39** 23.48S 33.55E
Cuckfield U.K. **5** 51.00N 0.08W
Cucuí Brazil **60** 1.12N 66.50W
Cúcuta Colombia **60** 7.55N 72.31W
Cuddalore India **29** 11.43N 79.46E
Cue Australia **42** 27.25S117.54E
Cuenca Ecuador **60** 2.54S 79.00W
Cuenca Spain **10** 40.04N 2.07W
Cuenca, Serranía de *mts.* Spain **10** 40.25N 2.00W
Cuernavaca Mexico **56** 18.57N 99.15W
Cuero U.S.A. **53** 29.06N 97.19W
Cuiabá Brazil **61** 15.32S 56.05W
Cuiabá *r.* Brazil **62** 18.00S 57.25W
Cuillin Hills U.K. **6** 57.12N 6.13W
Cuito *r.* Angola **39** 18.01S 20.50E
Culcairn Australia **47** 35.40S147.03E
Culemborg Neth. **8** 51.57N 5.14E
Culgoa *r.* Australia **47** 29.56S146.20E
Culiacán Mexico **56** 24.48N107.24W
Cullarin Range *mts.* Australia **47** 34.30S149.32E
Cullen U.K. **6** 57.41N 2.50W
Cullera Spain **10** 39.10N 0.15W
Cullin Sd. U.K. **6** 57.03N 6.13W
Culloden Moor U.K. **6** 57.29N 3.55W
Culpeper U.S.A. **55** 38.28N 77.53W
Cultowa Australia **46** 31.24S144.10E
Culuene *r.* Brazil **61** 12.56S 52.51W
Culver, Pt. Australia **43** 32.52S124.41E
Cumaná Venezuela **60** 10.29N 64.12W
Cumberland *r.* U.S.A. **53** 37.16N 88.25W
Cumberland Md. U.S.A. **55** 39.39N 78.46W
Cumberland, L. U.S.A. **53** 37.00N 85.00W
Cumberland Pen. Canada **51** 66.50N 64.00W
Cumberland Sd. Canada **51** 65.00N 65.30W
Cumbernauld U.K. **6** 55.57N 4.00W
Cumbria *d.* U.K. **4** 54.30N 3.00W
Cumbrian Mts. U.K. **4** 54.32N 3.05W
Cuminá *r.* Brazil **61** 1.30S 56.00W
Cummins Australia **46** 34.16S135.44E
Cumnock Australia **47** 32.56S148.46E
Cumnock U.K. **6** 55.27N 4.15W
Cunderdin Australia **43** 31.39S117.15E
Cunene *d.* Angola **39** 16.00S 16.00E
Cunene *r.* Angola **39** 17.15S 11.50E
Cuneo Italy **9** 44.22N 7.32E
Cungena Australia **46** 32.33S134.40E
Cunnamulla Australia **47** 28.04S145.40E
Cuokkaraš'ša *mtn.* Norway **16** 69.57N 24.32E
Cuorgnè Italy **9** 45.23N 7.39E
Cupar U.K. **6** 56.19N 3.01W
Cupica, Golfo de *g.* Colombia **60** 6.35N 77.25W
Curaçao *i.* Neth. Antilles **60** 12.15N 69.00W
Curacautín Chile **63** 38.26S 71.53W
Curaco *r.* Argentina **63** 38.49S 65.01W
Curanilahue Chile **63** 37.28S 73.21W
Curaray *r.* Peru **60** 2.20S 74.05W
Curban Australia **47** 31.33S148.36E
Curdlawidny L. Australia **46** 30.16S136.20E
Cure *r.* France **9** 47.40N 3.41E
Curiapo Venezuela **60** 8.33N 61.05W
Curicó Chile **63** 34.59S 71.14W
Curitiba Brazil **59** 25.24S 49.16W
Curlewis Australia **47** 31.08S150.16E
Curnamona Australia **46** 31.40S139.35E
Currane, Lough Rep. of Ire. **7** 51.50N 10.07W
Currant U.S.A. **54** 38.44N115.30W
Curranyalpa Australia **47** 30.57S144.33E
Currie Australia **45** 39.56S143.52E
Currie U.S.A. **54** 40.17N114.44W
Curtin Australia **43** 30.50S122.05E
Curtis I. Australia **44** 23.38S151.09E
Curuá *r.* Brazil **61** 5.23S 54.22W
Curupu Brazil **61** 1.50S 44.52W
Curuzú Cuatiá Argentina **63** 29.50S 58.05W
Curvelo Brazil **59** 18.45S 44.27W
Cushendall U.K. **7** 55.06N 6.05W
Cusna, Monte *mtn.* Italy **9** 44.17N 10.23E
Cutana Australia **46** 32.14S140.25E
Cut Bank U.S.A. **54** 48.38N112.20W
Cuttaburra *r.* Australia **47** 29.18S145.00E
Cuttack India **29** 20.26N 85.56E
Cuxhaven W. Germany **14** 53.52N 8.42E
Cuyuni *r.* Guyana **60** 6.24N 58.38W
Cuzco Peru **60** 13.32S 71.57W
Cwmbran U.K. **5** 51.39N 3.01W
Cyclades *is. see* Kikládhes *is.* Greece **13**
Cynthiana U.S.A. **55** 38.22N 84.18W
Cyprus Asia **32** 35.00N 33.00E
Cyrenaica *f. see* Barqah *f.* Libya **35**
Czechoslovakia Europe **14** 49.30N 15.00E
Czeremcha Poland **15** 52.32N 23.15E
Czersk Poland **15** 53.48N 18.00E
Częstochowa Poland **15** 50.49N 19.07E

D

Da'an China **25** 45.30N124.18E
Ḑab'ah Jordan **32** 31.36N 36.04E
Dabakala Ivory Coast **38** 8.19N 4.24W
Dabbāgh, Jabal *mtn.* Saudi Arabia **32** 27.51N 35.43E
Dacca *see* Dhākā Bangla. **29**
Dachau W. Germany **14** 48.15N 11.26E
Dadanawa Guyana **60** 2.30N 59.30W

du Pakistan 28 26.44N 67.47E
du He r. China 29 28.47N104.40E
et Phil. 27 14.07N122.58E
gali Norway 17 60.25N 8.27E
gana Senegal 34 16.28N 15.35W
gua P.N.G. 27 3.25S143.20E
guan China 24 27.44N103.53E
gupan Phil. 27 16.02N120.21E
Hinggan Ling mts. China 25 50.00N122.10E
hlak Archipelago is. Ethiopia 35 15.45N).30E
nlem W. Germany 14 50.23N 6.33E
nûk Iraq 30 36.52N 43.00E
miel Spain 10 39.05N 3.35W
tō Japan 23 34.42N135.38E
arra Australia 44 21.42S139.31E
ing China 25 28.24N121.08E
kar Senegal 34 14.38N 17.27W
khal, Wâdi ad r. Egypt 32 28.49N 32.45E
khilah, Al Wāḥāt ad oasis Egypt 30 25.30N 3.10E
khla W. Sahara 34 23.43N 15.57W
kingari Nigeria 38 11.40N 4.06E
kovica Yugo. 13 42.23N 20.25E
kwa Zaïre 36 4.00N 26.26E
r. Sweden 17 60.38N 17.27E
andzadgad Mongolia 24 43.34N104.20E
Lat Vietnam 26 11.56N108.25E
beattie U.K. 6 54.55N 3.49W
by Australia 45 27.11S151.12E
by Sweden 17 55.40N 13.20E
e Hordaland Norway 17 60.35N 5.49E
e Sogn og Fj. Norway 17 61.22N 5.24E
en Norway 17 59.27N 8.00E
gety Australia 47 36.30S148.50E
gonally Australia 44 20.09S141.16E
housie Canada 55 48.03N 66.22W
i China 24 25.42N100.11E
lkeith U.K. 6 55.54N 3.04W
llas Oreg. U.S.A. 54 44.55N123.19W
llas Tex. U.S.A. 53 32.47N 96.48W
lmally U.K. 6 56.25N 4.58W
lmellington U.K. 6 55.19N 4.24W
lnerechensk U.S.S.R. 25 45.55N133.45E
loa Ivory Coast 34 6.56N 6.28W
lou Shan mts. China 24 28.00N106.40E
lrymple, Mt. Australia 44 21.02S148.38E
lton Canada 55 48.10N 84.04W
ltonganj India 29 24.02N 84.07E
lveen Australia 47 28.26S151.55E
lvik Iceland 16 65.58N 18.28W
lwhinnie U.K. 6 56.56N 4.15W
ly r. Australia 42 13.20S130.19E
ly City U.S.A. 54 37.42N122.29W
ly Waters town Australia 44 16.15S133.22E
mā, Wādī r. Saudi Arabia 30 27.04N 35.48E
mān India 28 20.25N 72.58E
manhûr Egypt 32 31.03N 30.28E
mar i. Indonesia 27 7.10S128.30E
mascus see Dimashq Syria 32
maturu Nigeria 38 11.49N 11.50E
māvand, Qolleh-ye mtn. Iran 31 35.47N 2.04E
mba Angola 36 6.44S 15.17E
mghān Iran 31 36.09N 54.22E
mmartin-en-Goële France 9 49.03N 2.41E
mongo Ghana 38 9.06N 1.48W
mpier Australia 42 20.45S116.50E
mpier, Selat str. Pacific Oc. 27 0.30S130.50E
mpier Land Australia 42 17.20S123.00E
mqawt S. Yemen 28 16.34N 52.54E
nakil f. Ethiopia 35 13.00N 41.00E
Nang Vietnam 26 16.04N108.14E
nba China 24 30.57N101.55E
nbury Conn. U.S.A. 55 41.24N 73.26W
ndaragan Australia 43 30.40S115.42E
ndenong Australia 47 37.59S145.14E
ndong China 25 40.06N124.25E
ngriga Belize 57 16.58N 88.13W
niel U.S.A. 54 42.52N110.04W
niell Australia 43 32.37S121.30E
nilov U.S.S.R. 18 58.10N 40.12E
ning China 25 36.32N110.47E
nisa Hills Kenya 37 3.10N 39.37E
nja Nigeria 38 11.29N 7.30E
nlí Honduras 57 14.02N 86.30W
nnenberg W. Germany 14 53.06N 11.05E
nnevirke New Zealand 48 40.12S176.08E
nnhauser R.S.A. 39 28.00S 30.03E
nsville U.S.A. 55 42.34N 77.41W
nube r. Europe 15 45.26N 29.38E
nube, Mouths of the see Dunării, Delta f. Romania 15
nville Va. U.S.A. 53 36.34N 79.25W
n Xian China 25 19.31N109.33E
nzig, G. of Poland 15 54.45N 19.15E
oukro Ivory Coast 38 7.10N 3.58W
pango Togo 38 10.51N 0.15E
Qaidam China 24 37.44N 95.08E
qq-e Patargān f. Iran 31 33.30N 60.40E
r'ā Syria 32 32.37N 36.06E
rāb Iran 31 28.45N 54.34E
rabani Romania 15 48.11N 26.35E
rān Iran 31 33.00N 50.27E
rband, Kūh-e mtn. Iran 31 31.33N 57.08E
rbhanga India 29 26.10N 85.54E
rby Mont. U.S.A. 54 46.01N114.11W
rdanelles see Çanakkale Boğazi str. Turkey 13
reel Australia 47 28.50S148.49E
r es Salaam Tanzania 37 6.51S 39.18E
r es Salaam d. Tanzania 37 6.45S 39.10E
rfield New Zealand 48 43.29S172.07E
rgan Ata U.S.S.R. 20 40.30N 62.10E
rgaville New Zealand 48 35.57S173.53E
rgo Australia 47 37.30S147.16E
rhan Mongolia 24 49.34N106.23E
rién, Golfo del g. Colombia 60 9.20N 77.30W
rjeeling India 29 27.02N 88.20E
rkan Australia 43 33.19S116.42E

Darke Peak *mtn.* Australia 46 33.28S136.12E
Darling *r.* Australia 46 34.05S141.57E
Darling Downs *f.* Australia 45 28.00S149.45E
Darling Range *mts.* Australia 43 32.00S116.30E
Darlington U.K. 4 54.33N 1.33W
Darlington Point *town* Australia 47 34.36S146.01E
Darłowe Poland 14 54.26N 16.23E
Darmstadt W. Germany 14 49.52N 8.30E
Darnah Libya 35 32.45N 22.39E
Darnétal France 9 49.27N 1.09E
Darnick Australia 46 32.55S143.39E
Darnley, C. Antarctica 64 68.00S 69.00E
Daroca Spain 10 41.09N 1.25W
Darreh Gaz Iran 31 37.22N 59.08E
Dartmoor Australia 46 37.58S141.19E
Dartmoor Forest *hills* U.K. 5 50.33N 3.55W
Dartmouth Canada 51 44.40N 63.34W
Dartmouth U.K. 5 50.21N 3.35W
Dartry Mts. Rep. of Ire. 7 54.23N 8.25W
Daru P.N.G. 44 9.04S143.12E
Darvaza U.S.S.R. 20 40.12N 58.24E
Darvel, Teluk *b.* Malaysia 26 4.40N118.30E
Darwen U.K. 4 53.42N 2.29W
Darwin Australia 44 12.23S130.44E
Daryācheh-ye Bakhtegān *l.* Iran 31 29.20N 54.05E
Daryācheh-ye Namak *l.* Iran 31 34.45N 51.36E
Daryācheh-ye Rezā'īyeh *l.* Iran 31 37.40N 45.28E
Daryācheh-ye Sīstān *f.* Iran 31 31.00N 61.15E
Dasht *r.* Pakistan 28 25.07N 61.45E
Dashte-e Mārgow *des.* Afghan. 31 30.45N 63.00E
Dasht-e Kavīr *des.* Iran 31 34.40N 55.00E
Dasht-e Lūt *des.* Iran 31 31.30N 58.00E
Dassa-Zoumé Benin 38 7.50N 2.13E
Dastgardān Iran 31 34.19N 56.51E
Dastjerd Iran 31 34.33N 50.15E
Datong China 25 40.12N113.12E
Datteln W. Germany 8 51.40N 7.20E
Datu, Tanjung *c.* Malaysia 26 2.00N109.30E
Datu Piang Phil. 27 7.02N124.30E
Daugavpils U.S.S.R. 18 55.52N 26.31E
Daun W. Germany 8 50.11N 6.50E
Dauphin Canada 51 51.09N100.05W
Dauphiné, Alpes du *mts.* France 11 44.35N 5.45E
Daura Nigeria 38 13.05N 8.18E
Dāvangere India 28 14.30N 75.52E
Davao Phil. 27 7.05N125.38E
Davao G. Phil. 27 6.30N126.00E
Davenport U.S.A. 53 41.40N 90.36W
Davenport Downs *town* Australia 44 24.09S141.08E
Daventry U.K. 5 52.16N 1.10W
David Panama 57 8.26N 82.26W
David-Gorodok U.S.S.R. 15 52.04N 27.10E
Davis U.S.A. 54 38.33N121.44W
Davis Creek *town* U.S.A. 54 41.44N120.24W
Davis Sea Antarctica 64 66.00S 90.00E
Davis Str. N. America 51 66.00N 58.00W
Davlekanovo U.S.S.R. 18 54.12N 55.00E
Davos Switz. 14 46.47N 9.50E
Dawlish U.K. 5 50.34N 3.28W
Dawna Range *mts.* Burma 29 16.10N 98.30E
Dawson Canada 50 64.04N139.24W
Dawson Creek *town* Canada 50 55.44N120.15W
Dawson Range *f.* Canada 50 62.40N139.00W
Dawu China 24 31.00N101.09E
Dax France 11 43.43N 1.03W
Daxian China 29 31.10N107.28E
Daylesford Australia 46 37.22S144.12E
Dayman *r.* Uruguay 63 31.25S 58.00W
Dayr az Zawr Syria 30 35.20N 40.08E
Dayton Ohio U.S.A. 55 39.45N 84.10W
Dayton Wash. U.S.A. 54 46.19N117.59W
Daytona Beach *town* U.S.A. 53 29.11N 81.01W
De Aar R.S.A. 39 30.39S 24.01E
Dead Sea Jordan 32 31.25N 35.30E
Deakin Australia 43 30.46S128.58E
Deal U.K. 5 51.13N 1.25E
Deán Funes Argentina 62 30.25S 64.20W
Dearborn U.S.A. 55 42.18N 83.14W
Dease Arm *b.* Canada 50 66.52N119.37W
Death Valley *f.* U.S.A. 54 36.30N117.00W
Death Valley *town* U.S.A. 54 36.18N116.25W
Death Valley Nat. Monument U.S.A. 54 36.30N117.00W
Deauville France 9 49.21N 0.04E
Debar Yugo. 13 41.31N 20.31E
Debica Poland 15 50.04N 21.24E
Deblin Poland 15 51.35N 21.50E
Deborah, L. Australia 43 30.45S119.07E
Debrecen Hungary 15 47.30N 21.37E
Debre Tabor Ethiopia 35 11.50N 38.05E
Decatur Ill. U.S.A. 53 39.44N 88.57W
Decatur Ind. U.S.A. 55 40.50N 84.57W
Deccan *f.* India 28 18.30N 77.30E
Decelles, Lac *l.* Canada 55 47.40N 78.08W
Děčín Czech. 14 50.48N 14.15E
Decize France 14 46.50N 3.27E
De Cocksdorp Neth. 8 53.12N 4.52E
Deda Romania 15 46.57N 24.53E
Dédi Ivory Coast 38 8.34N 3.33W
Dedza Malaŵi 37 14.20S 34.24E
Dee *r.* D. and G. U.K. 6 54.50N 4.05W
Dee *r.* Grampian U.K. 6 57.07N 2.04W
Dee *r.* Wales U.K. 4 53.13N 3.05W
Deepdale Australia 42 21.42S116.11E
Deep River *town* Canada 55 46.06N 77.30W
Deep Well Australia 44 24.25S134.05E
Deer Lodge U.S.A. 54 46.24N112.44W
Deesa India 28 24.15N 72.10E
Deeth U.S.A. 54 41.04N115.18W
Defiance U.S.A. 55 41.17N 84.21W
Deggendorf W. Germany 14 48.51N 12.59E
De Grey Aůstralia 42 20.10S119.09E
De Grey *r.* Australia 42 20.12S119.11E

Deh Bīd Iran 31 30.38N 53.12E
Dehra Dūn India 29 30.19N 78.00E
Deinze Belgium 8 50.59N 3.32E
Dej Romania 15 47.08N 23.55E
Deje Sweden 17 59.36N 13.28E
Dekina Nigeria 38 7.43N 7.04E
Delano U.S.A. 54 35.41N119.15W
Delaware *d.* U.S.A. 55 39.10N 75.30W
Delaware *r.* U.S.A. 55 39.20N 75.25W
Delaware *town* U.S.A. 55 40.18N 83.06W
Delaware B. U.S.A. 55 39.05N 75.15W
Delegate Australia 47 37.03S148.58E
Delfinópolis Brazil 59 20.21S 46.51W
Delft Neth. 8 52.01N 4.23E
Delfzijl Neth. 8 53.20N 6.56E
Delgado, C. Mozambique 37 10.45S 40.38E
Delhi India 28 28.40N 77.14E
Delicias Mexico 56 28.13N105.28W
Delingha China 24 37.16N 97.12E
Delmenhorst W. Germany 14 53.03N 8.37E
De Long Mts. U.S.A. 50 68.20N162.00W
Delphos U.S.A. 55 40.50N 84.21W
Del Rio U.S.A. 52 29.23N100.56W
Delta Colo. U.S.A. 54 38.44N108.04W
Delta Utah U.S.A. 54 39.21N112.35W
Delungra Australia 47 29.38S150.50E
Demer *r.* Belgium 8 50.59N 4.42E
Deming U.S.A. 52 32.16N107.45W
Demmin E. Germany 14 53.54N 13.02E
Demonte Italy 9 44.19N 7.17E
Demotte U.S.A. 55 41.07N 87.14W
Denain France 8 50.20N 3.24E
Denbigh U.K. 4 53.11N 3.25W
Den Burg Neth. 8 53.03N 4.47E
Dendermonde Belgium 8 51.01N 4.07E
Dendre *r.* Belgium 8 51.01N 4.07E
Denham Australia 42 25.54S113.35E
Denham Range *mts.* Australia 44 21.55S147.46E
Den Helder Neth. 8 52.58N 4.46E
Denia Spain 10 38.51N 0.07E
Deniliquin Australia 47 35.33S144.58E
Denizli Turkey 30 37.46N 29.05E
Denmark Australia 43 34.54S117.25E
Denmark Europe 17 55.50N 10.00E
Den Oever Neth. 8 52.56N 5.01E
Denpasar Indonesia 26 8.40S115.14E
Denton Mont. U.S.A. 54 47.19N109.57W
D'Entrecasteaux, Pt. Australia 43 34.50S116.00E
D'Entrecasteaux Is. P.N.G. 44 9.30S150.40E
Denver U.S.A. 52 39.43N105.01W
Deo *r.* Cameroon 38 8.33N 12.45E
Deogarh Orissa India 29 21.22N 84.45E
De Peel *f.* Belgium 8 51.30N 5.50E
Depew U.S.A. 55 42.54N 78.41W
Dêqên China 24 28.45N 98.58E
Dera Ghāzi Khān Pakistan 28 30.05N 70.44E
Dera Ismāīl Khān Pakistan 28 31.51N 70.56E
Derazhnya U.S.S.R. 15 49.18N 27.28E
Derbent U.S.S.R. 31 42.03N 48.18E
Derby Tas. Australia 45 41.08S147.47E
Derby W.A. Australia 42 17.19S123.38E
Derby U.K. 4 52.55N 1.28W
Derbyshire *d.* U.K. 4 52.55N 1.28W
Derg, Lough Donegal Rep. of Ire. 7 54.37N 7.55W
Derg, Lough Tipperary Rep. of Ire. 7 52.57N 8.18W
Déroute, Passage de la *str.* France/U.K. 5 49.10N 1.45W
Derrynasaggart Mts. Rep. of Ire. 7 51.58N 9.15W
Derryveagh Mts. Rep. of Ire. 7 55.00N 8.07W
Derval France 9 47.40N 1.40W
Derwent *r.* Cumbria U.K. 4 54.38N 3.34W
Derwent *r.* N. Yorks. U.K. 4 53.44N 0.57W
Desaguadero *r.* Bolivia 62 18.24S 67.05W
Deschutes *r.* U.S.A. 54 45.38N120.54W
Desē Ethiopia 35 11.05N 39.40E
Deseado Argentina 63 47.39S 65.20W
Deseado *r.* Argentina 63 47.45S 65.50W
Desenzano del Garda Italy 9 45.28N 10.32E
Desert Center U.S.A. 54 33.44N115.25W
Des Moines Iowa U.S.A. 53 41.35N 93.35W
Desna *r.* U.S.S.R. 15 50.32N 30.37E
Dessau E. Germany 14 51.51N 12.15E
D'Estrees B. Australia 46 35.50S137.58E
Dete Zimbabwe 39 18.39S 26.49E
Detroit U.S.A. 55 42.23N 83.05W
Deurne Belgium 8 51.13N 4.26E
Deurne Neth. 8 51.29N 5.44E
Deutsche Bucht *b.* W. Germany 14 54.00N 8.15E
Deva Romania 15 45.54N 22.55E
Deventer Neth. 8 52.15N 6.10E
Deveron *r.* U.K. 6 57.40N 2.30W
Devil's Bridge U.K. 5 52.23N 3.50W
Devils Lake *town* U.S.A. 52 48.08N 98.50W
Devin Bulgaria 13 41.44N 24.24E
Devizes U.K. 5 51.21N 2.00W
Devon *d.* U.K. 5 50.50N 3.40W
Devon I. Canada 51 75.00N 86.00W
Devonport Australia 45 41.09S146.16E
Devrez *r.* Turkey 30 41.07N 34.25E
Dewsbury U.K. 4 53.42N 1.38W
Dez *r.* Iran 31 31.38N 48.54E
Dezfūl Iran 31 32.24N 48.27E
Dezhou China 25 37.29N116.11E
Dezh Shāhpūr Iran 31 35.31N 46.10E
Dhahab Egypt 32 28.30N 34.31E
Dhākā Bangla. 29 23.43N 90.25E
Dhānbād India 29 23.47N 86.32E
Dhaulāgiri *mtn.* Nepal 29 28.39N 83.28E
Dhodhekánisos *is.* Greece 13 37.00N 27.00E
Dholpur India 28 26.43N 77.54E
Dhule India 28 20.52N 74.50E
Diamante Argentina 63 32.05S 60.35W
Diamantina *r.* Australia 44 26.45S139.10E
Diamantina Brazil 59 18.17S 43.37W
Diamantina, Chapada *hills* Brazil 61 13.00S 42.30W

Diamantino Brazil 59 14.25S 56.29W
Diane Bank *is.* Australia 44 15.50S149.48E
Diapaga Burkina Faso 38 12.04N 1.48E
Dibi Cameroon 38 7.09N 13.43E
Dibrugarh India 29 27.29N 94.56E
Dickinson U.S.A. 52 46.53N102.47W
Dicle *r.* Turkey *see* Dijlah *r.* Asia 30
Didcot U.K. 5 51.36N 1.14W
Die France 11 44.45N 5.23E
Diekirch Lux. 8 49.52N 6.10E
Diélette France 9 49.33N 1.52W
Diemen Neth. 8 52.22N 4.58E
Diemuchuoke Jammu & Kashmir 29 32.42N 79.29E
Dien Bien Phu Vietnam 26 21.23N103.02E
Diepholz W. Germany 14 52.35N 8.21E
Dieppe France 9 49.55N 1.05E
Dierdorf W. Germany 8 50.33N 7.38E
Dieren Neth. 8 52.03N 6.06E
Diesdorf E. Germany 14 52.45N 10.52E
Diest Belgium 8 50.59N 5.03E
Dieuze France 11 48.49N 6.43E
Dif Kenya 37 1.04N 40.57E
Dif Somali Rep. 37 1.00N 41.00E
Diffa Niger 38 13.19N 12.35E
Diffa *d.* Niger 38 16.00N 13.00E
Digne France 11 44.05N 6.14E
Digoin France 11 46.29N 3.59E
Digul *r.* Indonesia 27 7.10S139.08E
Dijlah *r.* Asia 31 31.00N 47.27E
Dijle *r.* Belgium 8 51.02N 4.25E
Dijon France 11 47.20N 5.02E
Dikhil Djibouti 35 11.06N 42.22E
Dikili Turkey 13 39.05N 26.52E
Dikirnis Egypt 32 31.05N 31.35E
Dikodougou Ivory Coast 38 9.00N 5.45W
Diksmuide Belgium 8 51.01N 2.52E
Dikwa Nigeria 38 12.01N 13.55E
Dili Indonesia 27 8.35S125.35E
Dilling Sudan 35 12.03N 29.39E
Dillingham U.S.A. 50 59.02N158.29W
Dillon U.S.A. 54 45.13N112.38W
Dimashq Syria 32 33.30N 36.19E
Dimbokro Ivory Coast 38 6.43N 4.46W
Dimboola Australia 46 36.27S142.02E
Dîmbovița *r.* Romania 15 44.13N 26.22E
Dimitrovgrad Bulgaria 13 42.01N 25.34E
Dimona Israel 32 31.04N 35.01E
Dinagat *i.* Phil. 27 10.15N125.30E
Dinan France 11 48.27N 2.02W
Dinant Belgium 8 50.16N 4.55E
Dinar Turkey 30 38.05N 30.09E
Dīnār, Kūh-e *mtn.* Iran 31 30.45N 51.39E
Dinara Planina *mts.* Yugo. 14 44.00N 16.30E
Dindigul India 28 10.23N 78.00E
Dingle Rep. of Ire. 7 52.09N 10.17W
Dingle B. Rep. of Ire. 7 52.05N 10.12W
Dingo Australia 44 23.40S149.21E
Dingolfing W. Germany 14 48.38N 12.31E
Dingwall U.K. 6 57.35N 4.26W
Dinokwe Botswana 39 23.24S 26.40E
Dinuba U.S.A. 54 36.32N119.23W
Diö Sweden 17 56.38N 14.13E
Diourbel Senegal 34 14.30N 16.10W
Dipolog Phil. 27 8.34N123.28E
Dirdal Norway 17 58.47N 6.14E
Diré Mali 38 16.16N 3.24W
Direction, C. Australia 44 12.51S143.32E
Dirē Dawa Ethiopia 35 9.35N 41.50E
Dirico Angola 39 17.58S 20.40E
Dirk Hartog I. Australia 42 25.50S113.00E
Dirranbandi Australia 47 28.35S148.10E
Disappointment, L. Australia 42 23.30S122.55E
Disaster B. Australia 47 37.20S149.58E
Discovery Canada 50 63.10N113.58W
Discovery B. Australia 46 38.12S141.07E
Disko *i.* Greenland 51 69.45N 53.00W
Diss U.K. 5 52.23N 1.06E
Distrito Federal *d.* Brazil 61 15.45S 47.50W
Distrito Federal *d.* Mexico 56 19.20N 99.10W
Disūq Egypt 32 31.09N 30.39E
Diu India 28 20.41N 70.59E
Diver Canada 55 46.43N 79.30W
Dives *r.* France 9 49.19N 0.05W
Divinópolis Brazil 59 20.08S 44.55W
Divnoye U.S.S.R. 19 45.55N 43.21E
Divo Ivory Coast 38 5.48N 5.15W
Divriği Turkey 30 39.23N 38.06E
Dixcove Ghana 38 4.49N 1.57W
Dixie U.S.A. 54 45.34N115.28W
Dixon Entrance *str.* Canada/U.S.A. 50 54.10N133.30W
Diyālā *r.* Iraq 31 33.13N 44.33E
Diyarbakir Turkey 30 37.55N 40.14E
Djado Niger 34 21.00N 12.20E
Djado, Plateau du *f.* Niger 34 22.00N 12.30E
Djambala Congo 36 2.33S 14.38E
Djanet Algeria 34 24.34N 9.29E
Djelfa Algeria 34 34.43N 3.14E
Djénne Mali 38 13.55N 4.31W
Djibo Burkina Faso 38 14.09N 1.38W
Djibouti Africa 35 12.00N 42.50E
Djibouti *town* Djibouti 35 11.35N 43.11E
Djougou Benin 38 9.40N 1.47E
Djugu Zaïre 37 1.55N 30.31E
Djúpivogur Iceland 16 64.41N 14.16W
Dmitriya Lapteva, Proliv *str.* U.S.S.R. 21 73.00N142.00E
Dnepr *r.* U.S.S.R. 15 50.00N 31.00E
Dneprodzerzhinsk U.S.S.R. 19 48.30N 34.37E
Dnepropetrovsk U.S.S.R. 19 48.29N 35.00E
Dneprovskaya Nizmennost *f.* U.S.S.R. 15 52.30N 29.45E
Dneprovsko-Bugskiy Kanal U.S.S.R. 15 52.03N 25.35E
Dnestr *r.* U.S.S.R. 15 46.21N 30.20E
Dno U.S.S.R. 18 57.50N 30.00E
Doba Chad 34 8.40N 16.50E
Dobbyn Australia 44 19.48S140.00E

Dobele U.S.S.R. 17 56.37N 23.16E
Dobo Indonesia 27 5.46S134.13E
Doboj Yugo. 15 44.44N 18.02E
Dobrodzień Poland 15 50.44N 18.27E
Dobruja *f.* Romania 15 44.30N 28.15E
Dobrush U.S.S.R. 15 52.24N 31.19E
Dobryanka U.S.S.R. 18 58.30N 56.26E
Doce *r.* Brazil 59 19.32S 39.57W
Docking U.K. 4 52.55N 0.39E
Doda, Lac *l.* Canada 55 49.24N 75.13W
Dodecanese *is. see* Dhodhekánisos *is.* Greece 13
Dodge City U.S.A. 52 37.45N100.02W
Dodman Pt. U.K. 5 50.13N 4.48W
Dodoma Tanzania 37 6.10S 35.40E
Dodoma *d.* Tanzania 37 6.00S 36.00E
Dodson U.S.A. 54 48.24N108.15W
Doetinchem Neth. 8 51.57N 6.17E
Dogai Coring *l.* China 29 34.30N 89.00E
Dogubayazit Turkey 31 39.32N 44.08E
Doha *see* Ad Dawḩah Qatar 31
Dokkum Neth. 8 53.20N 6.00E
Dolbeau Canada 55 48.52N 72.15W
Dol-de-Bretagne France 9 48.33N 1.45W
Dole France 11 47.05N 5.30E
Dolgellau U.K. 5 52.44N 3.53W
Dolina U.S.S.R. 15 49.00N 23.59E
Dolinskaya U.S.S.R. 19 48.06N 32.46E
Dolisie Congo 36 4.09S 12.40E
Dollard *b.* W. Germany 8 53.20N 7.10E
Dolny Kubín Czech. 15 49.12N 19.17E
Dolomiti *mts.* Italy 9 46.25N 11.50E
Dolores Argentina 63 36.19S 57.40W
Dolores Uruguay 63 33.33S 58.13W
Dolores U.S.A. 54 37.28N108.30W
Dolphin and Union Str. Canada 50 69.20N118.00W
Doma Nigeria 38 8.23N 8.21E
Domadare Somali Rep. 37 1.48N 41.13E
Domažlice Czech. 14 49.27N 12.56E
Dombås Norway 17 62.05N 9.08E
Dombey, C. Australia 46 37.12S139.43E
Dombóvár Hungary 15 46.23N 18.08E
Domburg Neth. 8 51.35N 3.31E
Domfront France 9 48.36N 0.39W
Dominica Windward Is. 57 15.30N 61.30W
Dominican Republic C. America 57 18.00N 70.00W
Dommel *r.* Neth. 8 51.44N 5.17E
Domo Ethiopia 35 7.54N 46.52E
Domodossola Italy 9 46.07N 8.17E
Domuyo *mtn.* Argentina 63 36.37S 70.28W
Don *r.* England U.K. 4 53.41N 0.50W
Don *r.* Scotland U.K. 6 57.10N 2.05W
Don *r.* U.S.S.R. 19 47.06N 39.16E
Donaghadee U.K. 7 54.39N 5.33W
Donald Australia 46 36.25S143.04E
Donau *r.* W. Germany *see* Danube *r.* Europe 14
Donaueschingen W. Germany 14 47.57N 8.29E
Donauwörth W. Germany 14 48.44N 10.48E
Don Benito Spain 10 38.57N 5.52W
Doncaster U.K. 4 53.31N 1.09W
Dondo Mozambique 39 19.39S 34.39E
Donegal Rep. of Ire. 7 54.39N 8.06W
Donegal *d.* Rep. of Ire. 7 54.52N 8.00W
Donegal B. Rep. of Ire. 7 54.32N 8.18W
Donegal Pt. Rep. of Ire. 7 52.43N 9.38W
Donetsk U.S.S.R. 19 48.00N 37.50E
Donga Nigeria 38 7.45N 10.05E
Donga *r.* Nigeria 38 8.20N 10.00E
Dongara Australia 43 29.15S114.56E
Dongbei Pingyuan *f.* China 25 42.30N123.00E
Dongchuan China 24 26.10N103.02E
Dongfang China 25 19.04N108.39E
Donggala Indonesia 26 0.48S119.45E
Dong Hoi Vietnam 26 17.32N106.35E
Dongkalang Indonesia 27 0.12N120.07E
Dongou Congo 36 2.05N 18.00E
Dongsheng China 25 39.49N109.59E
Dongtai China 25 32.51N120.18E
Dongting Hu *l.* China 25 29.40N113.00E
Donington U.K. 4 52.55N 0.12W
Donja Stubica Yugo. 14 45.59N 15.58E
Dönna *i.* Norway 16 66.05N 12.30E
Donnacona Canada 55 46.41N 71.45W
Donnybrook Australia 43 33.34S115.47E
Donnybrook R.S.A. 39 29.55S 29.51E
Doodlakine Australia 43 31.41S117.23E
Doon, Loch U.K. 6 55.15N 4.23W
Doondi Australia 47 28.16S148.25E
Dora, L. Australia 42 22.05S122.55E
Dora Baltea *r.* Italy 9 45.11N 8.05E
Dora Riparia *r.* Italy 9 45.05N 7.44E
Dorchester U.K. 5 50.52N 2.28W
Dorchester, C. Canada 51 65.29N 77.30W
Dordogne *r.* France 11 45.03N 0.34W
Dordrecht Neth. 8 51.48N 4.40E
Dordrecht R.S.A. 39 31.22S 27.02E
Dore, Mont *mtn.* France 11 45.32N 2.49E
Dori Burkina Faso 38 14.03N 0.02W
Dorking U.K. 5 51.14N 0.20W
Dormagen W. Germany 8 51.05N 6.50E
Dormans France 9 49.04N 3.38E
Dornie U.K. 6 57.16N 5.31W
Dornoch U.K. 6 57.52N 4.02W
Dornoch Firth *est.* U.K. 6 57.50N 4.04W
Dornum W. Germany 8 53.39N 7.26E
Doro Mali 38 16.09N 0.51W
Dorohoi Romania 15 47.57N 26.24E
Dörpen W. Germany 8 52.58N 7.20E
Dorrigo Australia 47 30.20S152.41E
Dorris U.S.A. 54 41.58N121.55W
Dorset *d.* U.K. 5 50.48N 2.25W
Dorset, C. Canada 51 64.10N 76.40W
Dorsten W. Germany 8 51.38N 6.58E
Dortmund W. Germany 8 51.32N 7.27E
Dortmund-Ems Kanal W. Germany 8 52.20N 7.30E
Dos Bahías, C. Argentina 63 44.55S 65.32W
Dosquet Canada 55 46.28N 71.33W

Dosso Niger 38 13.03N 3.10E
Dosso d. Niger 38 13.00N 3.15E
Dossor U.S.S.R. 19 47.31N 53.01E
Dothan U.S.A. 53 31.12N 85.25W
Douai France 8 50.22N 3.05E
Douala Cameroon 38 4.05N 9.43E
Douarnenez France 11 48.05N 4.20W
Doubs r. France 11 46.57N 5.03E
Doubtful Island B. Australia 43 34.15S119.30E
Doubtless B. New Zealand 48 35.10S173.30E
Doudeville France 9 49.43N 0.48E
Douentza Mali 38 14.58N 2.48W
Douglas r. Australia 46 28.35S136.50E
Douglas R.S.A. 39 29.03S 23.45E
Douglas U.K. 4 54.09N 4.29W
Douglas Ariz. U.S.A. 52 31.21N109.33W
Douglas Mich. U.S.A. 55 42.38N 86.13W
Doulaincourt France 11 48.19N 5.12E
Doulevant-le-Château France 9 48.23N 4.55E
Doumé Cameroon 38 4.13N 13.30E
Douna Mali 38 12.40N 6.00W
Dounreay U.K. 6 58.35N 3.42W
Dourados Brazil 62 22.09S 54.52W
Dourdan France 9 48.32N 2.01E
Douro r. Portugal 10 41.10N 8.40W
Douvres France 9 49.17N 0.23W
Dove r. Derbys. U.K. 4 52.50N 1.35W
Dover U.K. 5 51.07N 1.19E
Dover Del. U.S.A. 55 39.10N 75.32W
Dover N.H. U.S.A. 55 43.12N 70.56W
Dover Ohio U.S.A. 55 40.32N 81.30W
Dover, Pt. Australia 43 32.32S125.30E
Dover, Str. of U.K. 5 51.00N 1.30E
Dovey r. U.K. 5 52.33N 3.56W
Dovrefjell mts. Norway 17 62.06N 9.25E
Dovsk U.S.S.R. 15 53.07N 30.29E
Dowa Malaŵi 37 13.40S 33.55E
Dowagiac U.S.A. 55 41.58N 86.06W
Dowerin Australia 43 31.15S117.00E
Dowlatābād Iran 31 28.19N 56.40E
Down d. U.K. 7 54.20N 6.00W
Downey U.S.A. 54 42.26N112.07W
Downham Market U.K. 5 52.36N 0.22E
Downpatrick U.K. 7 54.21N 5.43W
Downpatrick Head Rep. of Ire. 7 54.20N 9.22W
Dowra Rep. of Ire. 7 54.11N 8.02W
Dozois, Résr. Canada 55 47.30N 77.00W
Drâa, Oued wadi Morocco 34 28.40N 11.06W
Drachten Neth. 8 53.05N 6.06E
Drăgăşani Romania 15 44.40N 24.16E
Dragoman, Pasul pass Bulgaria / Yugo. 13 42.56N 22.52E
Dragon's Mouth str. Trinidad 60 11.00N 61.35W
Dragovishtitsa Bulgaria 13 42.22N 22.39E
Draguignan France 11 43.32N 6.28E
Drake Australia 47 28.55S152.24E
Drakensberg mts. R.S.A. / Lesotho 39 30.00S 29.05E
Dráma Greece 13 41.09N 24.11E
Drammen Norway 17 59.44N 10.15E
Drau r. Austria see Drava r. Yugo. 14
Drava r. Yugo. 15 45.34N 18.56E
Drayton Australia 45 27.40S151.50E
Drenthe d. Neth. 8 52.52N 6.30E
Dresden E. Germany 14 51.03N 13.45E
Dresden d. E. Germany 14 51.10N 14.00E
Dreux France 9 48.44N 1.23E
Driftwood Canada 55 49.08N 81.23W
Drin r. Albania 13 41.45N 19.34E
Drina r. Yugo. 15 44.53N 19.20E
Dröbak Norway 17 59.39N 10.39E
Drogheda Rep. of Ire. 7 53.42N 6.23W
Drogobych U.S.S.R. 15 49.10N 23.30E
Droitwich U.K. 5 52.16N 2.10W
Drokiya U.S.S.R. 15 48.07N 27.49E
Dromedary, C. Australia 47 36.18S150.15E
Dronero Italy 9 44.28N 7.22E
Dronfield U.K. 4 53.18N 1.29W
Dronne r. France 11 45.02N 0.09W
Dronning Maud Land f. Antarctica 64 74.00S 10.00E
Drumheller Canada 50 51.28N112.40W
Drum Hills Rep. of Ire. 7 52.03N 7.42W
Drummond Range mts. Australia 44 23.30S147.15E
Drummondville Canada 55 45.52N 72.30W
Drummore U.K. 6 54.41N 4.54W
Druskininkai U.S.S.R. 15 53.48N 23.58E
Drut r. U.S.S.R. 15 53.03N 30.42E
Drvar Yugo. 14 44.22N 16.24E
Drymen U.K. 6 56.04N 4.27W
Drysdale r. Australia 42 13.59S126.51E
Dschang Cameroon 38 5.28N 10.02E
Ḍubā Saudi Arabia 30 27.21N 35.40E
Dubai see Dubayy U.A.E. 31
Dubawnt r. Canada 51 62.50N102.00W
Dubawnt L. Canada 51 62.50N102.00W
Dubayy U.A.E. 31 25.13N 55.17E
Dubbo Australia 47 32.16S148.41E
Dubica Yugo. 14 45.11N 16.48E
Dublin Rep. of Ire. 7 53.21N 6.18W
Dublin d. Rep. of Ire. 7 53.20N 6.18W
Dublin U.S.A. 53 32.31N 82.54W
Dublin B. Rep. of Ire. 7 53.20N 6.09W
Dubno U.S.S.R. 15 50.28N 25.40E
Dubois Idaho U.S.A. 54 44.10N112.14W
Du Bois Penn. U.S.A. 55 41.07N 78.46W
Dubovka U.S.S.R. 19 49.04N 44.48E
Dubréka Guinea 34 9.50N 13.32W
Dubrovitsa U.S.S.R. 15 51.38N 26.40E
Dubrovnik Yugo. 13 42.40N 18.07E
Dubuque U.S.A. 53 42.31N 90.41W
Duchesne U.S.A. 54 40.10N110.24W
Duchess Australia 41 21.22S139.52E
Duchess Australia 44 21.22S139.52E
Du Couëdic, C. Australia 46 36.00S136.10E
Dudinka U.S.S.R. 21 69.27N 86.13E
Dudley U.K. 5 52.30N 2.05W
Duero r. Spain see Douro r. Portugal 10
Duff Creek town Australia 46 28.28S135.51E
Dufftown U.K. 6 57.27N 3.09W
Duga Resa Yugo. 14 45.27N 15.30E
Dugi i. Yugo. 14 44.04N 15.00E
Duifken Pt. Australia 44 12.33S141.38E
Duisburg W. Germany 8 51.26N 6.45E
Duitama Colombia 60 5.50N 73.01W
Duiveland i. Neth. 8 51.39N 4.00E
Dujuma Somali Rep. 37 1.14N 42.37E
Dukhān Qatar 31 25.24N 50.47E
Dukou China 24 26.33N101.44E
Dulce r. Argentina 62 30.40S 62.00W
Duleek Rep. of Ire. 7 53.39N 6.24W
Dülmen W. Germany 8 51.49N 7.17E
Dulovo Bulgaria 15 43.49N 27.09E
Duluth U.S.A. 53 46.50N 92.10W
Dūmā Syria 32 33.33N 36.24E
Dumaguete Phil. 27 9.20N123.18E
Dumai Indonesia 26 1.41N101.27E
Dumaran i. Phil. 26 10.33N119.50E
Dumaresq r. Australia 47 28.40S150.28E
Dumaring Indonesia 26 1.36N118.12E
Dumbarton U.K. 6 55.57N 4.35W
Dumbleyung Australia 43 33.18S117.42E
Dumbrăveni Romania 15 46.14N 24.35E
Dumfries U.K. 6 55.04N 3.37W
Dumfries and Galloway d. U.K. 6 55.05N 3.40W
Dumyāṭ Egypt 32 31.26N 31.48E
Duna r. Hungary see Danube r. Europe 15
Dunaföldvár Hungary 15 46.48N 18.55E
Dunajec r. Poland 15 50.15N 20.44E
Dunajská Streda Czech. 15 48.01N 17.35E
Dunany Pt. Rep. of Ire. 7 53.51N 6.15W
Dunărea r. Romania see Danube r. Europe 15
Dunării, Delta f. Romania 15 45.05N 29.45E
Dunav r. Bulgaria see Danube r. Europe 15
Dunav r. Yugo. see Danube r. Europe 15
Dunbar U.K. 6 56.00N 2.31W
Dunblane U.K. 6 56.12N 3.59W
Dunboyne Rep. of Ire. 7 53.26N 6.30W
Duncan Canada 54 48.45N123.40W
Duncan U.S.A. 52 34.30N 97.57W
Duncansby Head U.K. 6 58.39N 3.01W
Dundalk Rep. of Ire. 7 54.01N 6.25W
Dundalk U.S.A. 55 39.15N 76.31W
Dundalk B. Rep. of Ire. 7 53.55N 6.17W
Dundas Australia 43 32.20S121.48E
Dundas, L. Australia 43 32.35S121.50E
Dundas Str. Australia 44 11.20S131.35E
Dundee R.S.A. 39 28.09S 30.14E
Dundee U.K. 6 56.28N 3.00W
Dundrum U.K. 7 54.16N 5.51W
Dundrum B. U.K. 7 54.12N 5.46W
Dunedin New Zealand 48 45.52S170.30E
Dunfermline U.K. 6 56.04N 3.29W
Dungannon U.K. 7 54.31N 6.47W
Dungarvan Rep. of Ire. 7 52.06N 7.39W
Dungeness c. U.K. 5 50.55N 0.58E
Dungiven U.K. 7 54.56N 6.56W
Dungog Australia 47 32.24S151.46E
Dungu Zaïre 37 3.40N 28.40E
Dunhuang China 24 40.00N 94.40E
Dunkeld Qld. Australia 45 26.55S148.00E
Dunkeld Vic. Australia 46 37.40S142.23E
Dunkeld U.K. 6 56.34N 3.36W
Dunkerque France 8 51.02N 2.23E
Dunkirk see Dunkerque France 14
Dunkirk U.S.A. 55 42.29N 79.21W
Dunkwa Central Ghana 38 5.59N 1.45W
Dun Laoghaire Rep. of Ire. 7 53.17N 6.09W
Dunleer Rep. of Ire. 7 53.49N 6.24W
Dunmahon Rep. of Ire. 7 52.09N 7.23W
Dunmore U.S.A. 55 41.25N 75.38W
Dunnet Head U.K. 6 58.40N 3.23W
Dunoon U.K. 6 55.57N 4.57W
Dunqulah Sudan 35 19.10N 30.27E
Duns U.K. 6 55.47N 2.20W
Dunsborough Australia 43 33.37S115.06E
Dunshaughlin Rep. of Ire. 7 53.30N 6.34W
Dunstable U.K. 5 51.53N 0.32W
Dunstan Mts. New Zealand 48 44.45S169.45E
Dupont U.S.A. 55 38.53N 85.30W
Duque de Caxias Brazil 59 22.47S 43.18W
Durance r. France 11 43.55N 4.48E
Durango Mexico 56 24.01N104.00W
Durango d. Mexico 56 24.01N104.00W
Durango Spain 10 43.13N 2.40W
Durango U.S.A. 54 37.16N107.53W
Durant U.S.A. 53 33.59N 96.24W
Durazno Uruguay 63 33.22S 56.31W
Durban R.S.A. 39 29.50S 30.59E
Durbe U.S.S.R. 17 56.35N 21.21E
Düren W. Germany 8 50.48N 6.30E
Durg India 29 21.11N 81.17E
Durham U.K. 4 54.47N 1.34W
Durham d. U.K. 4 54.42N 1.45W
Durham N.C. U.S.A. 53 36.00N 78.54W
Durham N.H. U.S.A. 55 43.08N 70.56W
Durlston Head c. U.K. 5 50.35N 1.58W
Durmitor mtn. Yugo. 13 43.08N 19.03E
Durness U.K. 6 58.33N 4.45W
Durrës Albania 13 41.19N 19.27E
Durrow Rep. of Ire. 7 52.51N 7.25W
Dursey Head Rep. of Ire. 7 51.35N 10.15W
Durūz, Jabal ad mtn. Syria 32 32.42N 36.42E
D'Urville I. New Zealand 48 40.45S173.50E
Dushak U.S.S.R. 20 37.13N 60.01E
Dushanbe U.S.S.R. 24 38.38N 68.51E
Dushkotna Bulgaria 13 42.52N 27.10E
Düsseldorf W. Germany 8 51.13N 6.47E
Dutlhe Botswana 39 23.55S 23.47E
Dutton, L. Australia 46 31.49S137.08E
Duvno Yugo. 15 43.43N 17.14E
Duyun China 24 26.16N107.29E
Dvina r. U.S.S.R. 20 57.03N 24.02E
Dvinskaya Guba b. U.S.S.R. 18 64.40N 39.30E
Dwarda Australia 43 32.45S116.23E
Dwārka India 28 22.14N 68.58E
Dwellingup Australia 43 32.42S116.04E
Dyatlovichi U.S.S.R. 15 52.08N 30.49E
Dyatlovo U.S.S.R. 15 53.28N 25.28E
Dyer, C. Canada 51 67.45N 61.45W
Dyérem r. Cameroon 38 6.36N 13.10E
Dyer Plateau Antarctica 64 70.00S 65.00W
Dyersburg U.S.A. 53 36.02N 89.21W
Dyfed d. U.K. 5 52.00N 4.17W
Dykh Tau mtn. U.S.S.R. 19 43.04N 43.10E
Dymer U.S.S.R. 15 50.50N 30.20E
Dyulevo Bulgaria 13 42.22N 27.10E
Dyultydag mtn. U.S.S.R. 31 41.55N 46.52E
Dzamïn Üüd Mongolia 25 43.50N111.53E
Dzerzhinsk B.S.S.R. U.S.S.R. 15 53.40N 27.01E
Dzerzhinsk R.S.F.S.R. U.S.S.R. 18 56.15N 43.30E
Dzhambul U.S.S.R. 24 42.50N 71.25E
Dzhankoy U.S.S.R. 19 45.42N 34.23E
Dzhardzhan U.S.S.R. 21 68.49N124.08E
Dzhelinde U.S.S.R. 21 70.09N114.00E
Dzhetygara U.S.S.R. 20 52.14N 61.10E
Dzhezkazgan U.S.S.R. 20 47.48N 67.24E
Dzhizak U.S.S.R. 20 40.06N 67.45E
Dzhugdzhur, Khrebet mts. U.S.S.R. 21 57.30N138.00E
Dzhurin U.S.S.R. 15 48.40N 28.16E
Działdowo Poland 15 53.15N 20.10E
Dzierżoniów Poland 14 50.44N 16.39E
Dzodze Ghana 38 6.14N 1.00E

E

Eabamet L. Canada 53 51.30N 87.55W
Eagle U.S.A. 54 39.39N106.50W
Eagle L. U.S.A. 55 46.17N 69.20W
Eagle Lake town U.S.A. 55 47.02N 68.36W
Eagle Pass town U.S.A. 52 28.44N100.31W
Ealing U.K. 5 51.31N 0.20W
Earlimart U.S.A. 54 35.53N119.16W
Earn r. U.K. 6 56.21N 3.18W
Earn, Loch U.K. 6 56.23N 4.12W
Easingwold U.K. 4 54.08N 1.11W
Easky Rep. of Ire. 7 54.17N 8.58W
East Anglian Heights hills U.K. 5 52.03N 0.15E
Eastbourne U.K. 5 50.46N 0.18E
East C. New Zealand 48 37.45S178.30E
East China Sea Asia 25 29.00N125.00E
East Coast d. New Zealand 48 38.20S177.45E
Eastern d. Ghana 38 6.20N 0.45W
Eastern d. Kenya 37 0.00 38.00E
Eastern Desert see Sharqīyah, Aş Şaḩrā' ash des. Egypt 32
Eastern Ghāts mts. India 29 16.30N 80.30E
East Falkland i. Falkland Is. 63 51.45W 58.50W
East Germany Europe 14 52.15N 12.30E
East Grinstead U.K. 5 51.08N 0.01W
East Ilsley U.K. 5 51.33N 1.15W
East Kilbride U.K. 6 55.46N 4.09W
East Lansing U.S.A. 55 42.45N 84.30W
Eastleigh U.K. 5 50.58N 1.21W
East London R.S.A. 39 33.00S 27.54E
Eastmain Canada 51 52.15N 78.30W
Eastmain r. Canada 51 52.15N 78.30W
Easton Penn. U.S.A. 55 40.41N 75.13W
Easton Wash. U.S.A. 54 47.14N121.11W
East Retford U.K. 4 53.19N 0.55W
East Sussex d. U.K. 5 50.56N 0.12E
Eau-Claire, Lac à l' l. Canada 51 56.10N 74.30W
Eauripik i. Caroline Is. 27 6.42N143.04E
Eban Nigeria 38 9.41N 4.54E
Ebbw Vale U.K. 5 51.47N 3.12W
Eberswalde E. Germany 14 52.50N 13.50E
Ebinur Hu l. China 24 45.00N 83.00E
Eboli Italy 12 40.37N 15.04E
Ebolowa Cameroon 38 2.56N 11.11E
Ebony Namibia 39 22.05S 15.15E
Ebro r. Spain 10 40.43N 0.54E
Ebro, Delta del f. Spain 10 40.43N 0.54E
Ecclefechan U.K. 4 55.03N 3.18W
Echternach Lux. 8 49.49N 6.25E
Echuca Australia 47 36.10S144.20E
Écija Spain 10 37.33N 5.04W
Écommoy France 9 47.50N 0.16E
Ecuador S. America 60 1.40S 79.00W
Ed Sweden 17 58.55N 11.55E
Edam Neth. 8 52.30N 5.02E
Eddrachillis B. U.K. 6 58.17N 5.15W
Eddystone Pt. Australia 45 40.58S148.12E
Ede Neth. 8 52.03N 5.40E
Ede Nigeria 38 7.45N 4.26E
Edea Cameroon 38 3.47N 10.13E
Eden Australia 47 37.04S149.54E
Eden r. Cumbria U.K. 4 54.57N 3.02W
Eden U.S.A. 54 42.03N109.26W
Edenburg R.S.A. 39 29.44S 25.55E
Edendale New Zealand 48 46.19S168.47E
Edenderry Rep. of Ire. 7 53.21N 7.05W
Edenhope Australia 46 37.04S141.20E
Edeowie Australia 46 31.28S138.29E
Eder r. W. Germany 14 51.13N 9.27E
Ederny U.K. 7 54.32N 7.40W
Edgeöya i. Arctic Oc. 64 77.45N 22.30E
Edgeworthstown Rep. of Ire. 7 53.42N 7.38W
Édhessa Greece 13 40.47N 22.03E
Ediacara Australia 46 30.18S137.50E
Edinburgh U.K. 6 55.57N 3.13W
Edirne Turkey 13 41.40N 26.35E
Edithburgh Australia 46 35.06S137.44E
Edjudina Australia 43 29.48S122.23E
Edmonton Canada 50 53.34N113.25W
Edmundston Canada 55 47.22N 68.20W
Edo r. Japan 23 35.37N139.53E
Edolo Italy 9 46.11N 10.20E
Edremit Turkey 13 39.35N 27.02E
Edsbruk Sweden 17 58.02N 16.28E
Edson Canada 50 53.35N116.26W
Edward, L. Uganda / Zaïre 37 0.30S 29.30E
Edward's Creek town Australia 46 28.15S135.49E
Edwards Plateau f. U.S.A. 52 30.30N100.30W
Eeklo Belgium 8 51.11N 3.34E
Eel r. U.S.A. 54 40.40N124.20W
Egaña Argentina 63 36.57S 59.06W
Egbe Nigeria 38 8.13N 5.31E
Eger Hungary 15 47.54N 20.23E
Egersund Norway 17 58.27N 6.00E
Egerton, Mt. Australia 42 24.44S117.40E
Egmont, Mt. New Zealand 48 39.20S174.05E
Eğridir Turkey 30 37.52N 30.51E
Eğridir Gölü l. Turkey 30 38.04N 30.55E
Egypt Africa 35 26.30N 29.30E
Éibar Spain 10 43.11N 2.28W
Eidsvåg Norway 16 62.47N 8.03E
Eidsvold Australia 44 25.23S151.08E
Eifel f. W. Germany 8 50.10N 6.45E
Eigg i. U.K. 6 56.53N 6.09W
Eighty Mile Beach f. Australia 42 19.00S121.00E
Eil Somali Rep. 35 8.00N 49.51E
Eil, Loch U.K. 6 56.51N 5.12W
Eildon Resr. Australia 47 37.10S146.00E
Einasleigh Australia 44 18.31S144.05E
Eindhoven Neth. 8 51.26N 5.30E
Eirunepé Brazil 60 6.40S 69.52W
Eiseb r. Namibia 39 20.26S 20.05E
Eisenach E. Germany 14 50.59N 10.19E
Eisenerz Austria 14 47.33N 14.53E
Eisenhut mtn. Austria 14 47.00N 13.45E
Eisenhüttenstadt E. Germany 14 52.09N 14.41E
Eišiškes U.S.S.R. 15 54.09N 24.55E
Eisleben E. Germany 14 51.32N 11.33E
Eitorf W. Germany 8 50.46N 7.27E
Ejin Qi China 24 41.50N100.50E
Ejura Ghana 38 7.24N 1.20W
Eket Nigeria 38 4.39N 7.56E
Eketahuna New Zealand 48 40.39S175.44E
Ekibastuz U.S.S.R. 20 51.45N 75.22E
Ekimchan U.S.S.R. 21 53.09N133.00E
Eksjö Sweden 17 57.40N 14.47E
Ekträsk Sweden 16 64.29N 19.50E
El Aaiún W. Sahara 34 27.10N 13.11W
Elands r. Trans. R.S.A. 39 24.52S 29.20E
El Arenal Spain 10 39.30N 2.45E
El Asnam Algeria 34 36.20N 1.30E
Elat Israel 32 29.33N 34.56E
Elâzig Turkey 30 38.41N 39.14E
Elba i. Italy 12 42.47N 10.17E
El Barril Mexico 56 28.22N113.00W
Elbasan Albania 13 41.07N 20.04E
El Baúl Venezuela 60 8.59N 68.16W
Elbe r. W. Germany 14 53.33N 10.00E
El Beni d. Bolivia 62 14.00S 65.30W
Elbert, Mt. U.S.A. 52 39.07N106.27W
Elbeuf France 9 49.17N 1.01E
Elbistan Turkey 30 38.14N 37.11E
Elbląg Poland 15 54.10N 19.25E
Elbrus mtn. U.S.S.R. 19 43.21N 42.29E
Elburg Neth. 8 52.27N 5.50E
Elburz Mts. see Alborz, Reshteh-ye Kūhhā-ye ye Iran 31
El Cajon U.S.A. 54 32.48N116.58W
El Callao Venezuela 60 7.18N 61.48W
El Centro U.S.A. 54 32.48N115.34W
Elche Spain 10 38.16N 0.41W
Elcho I. Australia 44 11.55S135.45E
El Cuy Argentina 63 39.57S 68.20W
Elda Spain 10 38.29N 0.47W
Elde r. E. Germany 14 53.17N 12.40E
Elder, L. Australia 46 30.39S140.13E
El Djouf des. Mauritania 34 20.30N 7.30W
El Dorado Ark. U.S.A. 53 33.12N 92.40W
El Dorado Venezuela 60 6.45N 61.37W
Eldoret Kenya 37 0.31N 35.17E
Eleja U.S.S.R. 17 56.26N 23.42E
Elektrostal U.S.S.R. 18 55.46N 38.30E
Elephant Butte Resr. U.S.A. 52 33.19N107.10W
Elephant I. Antarctica 64 61.00S 55.00W
Eleuthera I. Bahamas 57 25.00N 76.00W
Elevtheroúpolis Greece 13 40.55N 24.16E
El Ferrol Spain 10 43.29N 8.14W
Elgå Norway 17 62.11N 11.07E
Elgin U.K. 6 57.39N 3.20W
Elgin Nev. U.S.A. 54 37.21N114.30W
Elgin Oreg. U.S.A. 54 45.34N117.55W
El Golea Algeria 34 30.35N 2.51E
Elgon, Mt. Kenya / Uganda 37 1.07N 34.35E
Elim Namibia 39 17.47S 15.30E
Elista U.S.S.R. 19 46.18N 44.14E
Elizabeth Australia 46 34.45S138.39E
Elizabeth N.J. U.S.A. 55 40.40N 74.13W
Elizabeth W.Va. U.S.A. 55 39.04N 81.24W
Elizabeth City U.S.A. 53 36.18N 76.18W
El Jadida Morocco 34 33.16N 8.30W
Ełk Poland 15 53.50N 22.22E
El Kairouan Tunisia 34 35.40N 10.04E
Elkhart Ind. U.S.A. 55 41.52N 85.56W
Elkhovo Bulgaria 13 42.10N 26.35E
Elkins W.Va. U.S.A. 55 38.55N 79.51W
Elko U.S.A. 54 40.50N115.46W
Elleker Australia 43 34.55S117.40E
Ellen, Mt. U.S.A. 52 38.06N110.50W
Ellendale Australia 42 17.56S124.48E
Ellensburg U.S.A. 54 47.00N120.32W
Ellesmere I. Canada 51 78.00N 82.00W
Ellesmere Port U.K. 4 53.17N 2.55W
Elliot R.S.A. 39 31.19S 27.49E
Elliot Lake town Canada 55 46.33N 82.39W
Elliston Australia 46 33.39S134.55E
Ellon U.K. 6 57.22N 2.05W
El Mahdia Tunisia 34 35.30N 11.04E
Elmali Turkey 30 36.43N 29.56E
Elmina Ghana 38 5.07N 1.21W
Elmira U.S.A. 55 42.06N 76.49W
Elmore Australia 47 36.30S144.40E
Elmshorn W. Germany 14 53.46N 9.40E
Eloy U.S.A. 54 32.45N111.33W
El Paso U.S.A. 52 31.45N106.29W
El Portal U.S.A. 54 37.41N119.47W
El Real Panama 57 8.06N 77.42W
El Reno U.S.A. 52 35.32N 97.57W
El Roba Kenya 37 3.57N 40.01E
El Salvador C. America 57 13.30N 89.00W
Elsas Canada 55 48.32N 82.55W
Elsdorf W. Germany 8 50.56N 6.35E
Elsinore U.S.A. 54 38.41N112.09W
El Tabacal Argentina 62 23.15S 64.14W
El Tigre Venezuela 60 8.44N 64.18W
Elton, Ozero l. U.S.S.R. 19 49.10N 46.34E
El Turbio Argentina 63 51.41S 72.05W
Elūru India 29 16.45N 81.10E
Elvas Portugal 10 38.53N 7.10W
Elvdal Norway 17 61.38N 11.56E
Elverum Norway 17 60.53N 11.34E
Elvira Argentina 63 35.15S 59.30W
El Wak Kenya 37 2.45N 40.52E
El Wak Somali Rep. 37 2.50N 41.03E
Ely Nev. U.S.A. 54 39.15N114.53W
Elyria U.S.A. 55 41.22N 82.06W
Emån r. Sweden 17 57.08N 16.30E
Emāmshahr Iran 31 36.25N 55.00E
Emba U.S.S.R. 20 48.47N 58.05E
Emba r. U.S.S.R. 19 46.38N 53.00E
Embarcación Argentina 62 23.15S 64.10W
Embleton U.K. 4 55.30N 1.37W
Embrun France 11 44.34N 6.30E
Embu Kenya 37 0.32S 37.28E
Emden W. Germany 8 53.23N 7.13E
Emerald Australia 44 23.32S148.10E
Emerson Canada 51 49.00N 97.12W
Emi Koussi mtn. Chad 34 19.58N 18.30E
Emilia-Romagna d. Italy 9 44.35N 11.00E
Emlichheim W. Germany 8 52.37N 6.50E
Emmaboda Sweden 17 56.38N 15.32E
Emmaste U.S.S.R. 17 58.42N 22.36E
Emmaville Australia 47 29.25S151.39E
Emmeloord Neth. 8 52.43N 5.46E
Emmen Neth. 8 52.48N 6.55E
Emmerich W. Germany 8 51.49N 6.16E
Emmett U.S.A. 54 43.52N116.30W
Emory Peak mtn. U.S.A. 52 29.15N103.19W
Empangeni R.S.A. 39 28.45S 31.54E
Empedrado Argentina 62 27.59S 58.47W
Emporia Kans. U.S.A. 53 38.24N 96.10W
Ems r. W. Germany 8 53.14N 7.25E
Emsdale Canada 55 45.32N 79.19W
Emsdetten W. Germany 8 52.14N 7.32E
Ems-Jade Kanal W. Germany 8 53.28N 7.40E
Emyvale Rep. of Ire. 7 54.20N 6.59W
Enard B. U.K. 6 58.05N 5.20W
Encarnación Paraguay 59 27.20S 55.50W
Enchi Ghana 38 5.53N 2.48W
Encontrados Venezuela 60 9.03N 72.14W
Encounter B. Australia 46 35.35S138.44E
Ende Indonesia 27 8.51S121.40E
Endeavour Str. Australia 44 10.50S142.15E
Enderby Land f. Antarctica 64 67.00S 53.00E
Endicott U.S.A. 55 42.06N 76.03W
Endicott Mts. U.S.A. 50 68.00N152.00W
Endola Namibia 39 17.37S 15.50E
Enfield U.K. 5 51.40N 0.05W
Engaño, C. Phil. 27 18.30N122.20E
Engcobo R.S.A. 39 31.39S 28.01E
'En Gedi Israel 32 31.28N 35.23E
Engels U.S.S.R. 19 51.30N 46.07E
Enggano i. Indonesia 26 5.20S102.15E
Enghien Belgium 8 50.42N 4.02E
England U.K. 4 53.00N 2.00W
English Bāzār India 29 25.00N 88.12E
English Channel U.K. 5 50.15N 1.00W
English River town Canada 55 49.14N 90.58W
Enid U.S.A. 52 36.24N 97.54W
Enkhuizen Neth. 8 52.42N 5.17E
Enköping Sweden 17 59.38N 17.04E
Enna Italy 12 37.34N 14.15E
Ennadai L. Canada 51 60.53N101.15W
Enngonia Australia 47 29.20S145.53E
Ennis Rep. of Ire. 7 52.51N 9.00W
Enniscorthy Rep. of Ire. 7 52.30N 6.35W
Enniskillen U.K. 7 54.21N 7.40W
Ennistymon Rep. of Ire. 7 52.56N 9.18W
Enns r. Austria 14 48.14N 14.22E
Enontekiö Finland 16 68.23N 23.38E
Ensay Australia 47 37.24S147.52E
Enschede Neth. 8 52.13N 6.54E
Ensenada Argentina 63 34.51S 57.55W
Ensenada Baja Calif. Norte Mexico 56 31.52N116.37W
Enshi China 25 30.18N109.29E
Enshū-nada sea Japan 23 34.30N137.30E
Entebbe Uganda 37 0.08N 32.29E
Entre Ríos d. Argentina 63 32.10S 59.00W
Entre Rios de Minas Brazil 59 20.39S 44.06W
Enugu Nigeria 38 6.20N 7.29E
Envermeu France 9 49.53N 1.15E
Envigado Colombia 60 6.09N 75.35W
Enza r. Italy 9 44.54N 10.31E
Enzan Japan 23 35.42N138.44E
Eolie, Isole is. Italy 12 38.35N 14.45E
Epe Neth. 8 52.21N 5.59E
Epernay France 9 49.02N 3.58E
Ephraim U.S.A. 54 39.22N111.35W
Ephrata Wash. U.S.A. 54 47.19N119.33W
Épila Spain 10 41.36N 1.17W
Épinal France 11 48.10N 6.28E
Epping U.K. 5 51.42N 0.07E
Epsom U.K. 5 51.20N 0.16W
Epte r. France 9 49.04N 1.37E
Equatorial Guinea Africa 34 1.30N 10.30E
Equerdreville France 9 49.40N 1.34W
Era, Ozero l. U.S.S.R. 19 47.38N 45.18E
Eraclea Italy 9 45.35N 12.40E
Eradu Australia 43 28.41S115.02E
Erciyaş Daği mtn. Turkey 30 38.33N 35.25E
Erdre r. France 9 47.27N 1.34W
Erebus, Mt. Antarctica 64 77.40S167.20E
Erechim Brazil 59 27.35S 52.15W
Ereğli Konya Turkey 30 37.30N 34.02E
Ereğli Zonguldak Turkey 30 41.17N 31.26E
Erenhot China 25 43.50N112.00E

r. W. Germany 8 51.12N 6.45E
urt E. Germany **14** 50.58N 11.02E
urt *d.* E. Germany **14** 51.10N 10.45E
ani Turkey **30** 38.17N 39.44E
ene *r.* Turkey **13** 41.02N 26.22E
ca Neth. **8** 52.44N 6.56E
e U.S.A. **55** 42.07N 80.05W
e, L. Canada / U.S.A. **55** 42.15N 81.00W
gavo Somali Rep. **35** 10.40N 47.20E
skay *i.* U.K. **6** 57.04N 7.17W
trea *f.* Ethiopia **35** 15.30N 38.00E
kelenz W. Germany **8** 51.05N 6.18E
angen W. Germany **14** 49.36N 11.02E
dunda Australia **44** 25.14S133.12E
nelo Neth. **8** 52.19N 5.38E
nelo R.S.A. **39** 26.30S 29.59E
née France **9** 48.18N 0.56W
ode India **28** 11.21N 77.43E
Rachidia Morocco **34** 31.58N 4.25W
rego Mozambique **37** 16.02S 37.11E
rigal Mtn. Rep. of Ire. **7** 55.02N 8.08W
ris Head Rep. of Ire. **7** 54.19N 10.00W
tix He *r.* U.S.S.R. **24** 48.00N 84.20E
udina Australia **46** 31.30S139.23E
vy-le-Châtel France **9** 48.02N 3.55E
zgebirge *mts.* E. Germany / Czech. **14** 50.30N 2.50E
zin U.S.S.R. **24** 50.16N 95.14E
zincan Turkey **30** 39.44N 39.30E
zurum Turkey **30** 39.57N 41.17E
bjerg Denmark **17** 55.28N 8.27E
bo *see* Espoo Finland **17**
calante U.S.A. **54** 37.47N111.36W
canaba U.S.A. **55** 45.47N 87.04W
ch Lux. **8** 49.31N 5.59E
chweiler W. Germany **8** 50.49N 6.16E
condido *r.* Nicaragua **57** 11.58N 83.45W
condido U.S.A. **54** 33.07N117.05W
cuintla Guatemala **56** 14.18N 90.47W
ens W. Germany **8** 53.40N 7.40E
fahān Iran **31** 32.42N 51.40E
her U.K. **5** 51.23N 0.22W
hkanān Iran **31** 27.10N 53.38E
howe R.S.A. **39** 28.53S 31.29E
k *r.* N. Yorks. U.K. **4** 54.29N 0.37W
kifjördhur *town* Iceland **16** 65.05N 14.00W
kilstuna Sweden **17** 59.22N 16.30E
kimo Point *town* Canada **51** 61.10N 94.15W
kişehir Turkey **30** 39.46N 30.30E
la *r.* Spain **10** 41.29N 6.03W
lāmābād Iran **31** 34.08N 46.35E
löv Sweden **17** 55.50N 13.20E
meraldas Ecuador **60** 0.56N 79.40W
panola Canada **55** 46.15N 81.46W
pe U.S.S.R. **20** 43.50N 74.10E
perance Australia **43** 33.49S121.52E
perance B. Australia **43** 33.51S121.53E
peranza Argentina **63** 31.30S 61.00W
pinal Colombia **60** 4.08N 75.00W
pinhaço, Serra do *mts.* Brazil **59** 17.15S 43.10W
pírito Santo *d.* Brazil **59** 20.00S 40.30W
píritu Santo *i.* Vanuatu **40** 15.50S166.50E
poo Finland **17** 60.13N 24.40E
pungabera Mozambique **39** 20.28S 32.48E
quel Argentina **63** 42.55S 71.20W
quimalt Canada **54** 48.30N123.23W
quina Argentina **63** 30.00S 59.30W
saouira Morocco **34** 31.30N 9.47W
sen W. Germany **8** 51.27N 6.57E
sequibo *r.* Guyana **60** 6.30N 58.40W
ssex *d.* U.K. **5** 51.46N 0.30E
ssex U.S.A. **54** 34.45N115.15W
ssonne *d.* France **9** 48.36N 2.20E
ssoyes France **9** 48.04N 4.32E
ssoyla U.S.S.R. **18** 61.47N 33.11E
st *d.* Burkina Faso **38** 12.45N 0.25E
st, Pointe de l' *c.* Canada **51** 49.08N 61.41W
stados, Isla de los *i.* Argentina **63** 54.45S 64.00W
şţahbānāt Iran **31** 29.05N 54.03E
stância Brazil **61** 11.15S 37.28W
stand, Kūh-e *mtn.* Iran **31** 31.18N 60.03E
ste Italy **9** 45.14N 11.39E
stepona Spain **10** 36.26N 5.09W
sternay France **9** 48.44N 3.34E
stevan Canada **50** 49.09N103.00W
stissac France **9** 48.16N 3.49E
stivane Mozambique **39** 24.07S 32.38E
ston U.K. **4** 54.34N 1.07W
stonskaya S.S.R. *d.* U.S.S.R. **17** 58.35N 24.35E
storil Portugal **10** 38.42N 9.23W
strela, Serra da *mts.* Portugal **10** 40.20N 7.40W
stremoz Portugal **10** 38.50N 7.35W
sztergom Hungary **15** 47.48N 18.45E
tables France **11** 48.37N 2.50W
tadunna Australia **46** 28.43S138.38E
tampes France **9** 48.26N 2.10E
taples France **11** 50.31N 1.39E
thel Creek *town* Australia **42** 23.05S120.14E
thiopia Africa **35** 10.00N 39.00E
tive, Loch U.K. **6** 56.27N 5.15W
tna, Monte *mtn.* Italy **12** 37.43N 14.59E
tosha Game Res. Namibia **39** 18.50S 15.40E
Etosha Pan *f.* Namibia **39** 18.50S 16.20E
Etretat France **9** 49.42N 0.12E
Ettelbrück Lux. **8** 49.51N 6.06E
Euabalong Australia **47** 33.07S146.28E
Euboea *see* Évvoia *i.* Greece **13**
Eucla Australia **43** 31.40S128.51E
Euclid U.S.A. **55** 41.34N 81.33W
Eucumbene, L. Australia **47** 36.05S148.45E
Eudunda Australia **46** 34.09S139.04E
Eufaula Resr. U.S.A. **53** 35.15N 95.35W
Eugene U.S.A. **54** 44.02N123.05W
Eugenia, Punta *c.* Mexico **56** 27.50N115.03W
Eumungerie Australia **47** 31.57S148.39E
Eupen Belgium **8** 50.38N 6.04E
Euphrates *r. see* Al Furāt *r.* Asia **31**
Eure *d.* France **9** 49.10N 1.00E
Eure *r.* France **9** 48.18N 1.12E
Eure et Loire *d.* France **9** 48.30N 1.30E
Eureka Calif. U.S.A. **54** 40.47N124.09W
Eureka Nev. U.S.A. **54** 39.31N115.58W
Eureka Utah U.S.A. **54** 39.57N112.07W
Eurinilla *r.* Australia **46** 30.50S140.01E
Euriowie Australia **46** 31.22S141.42E
Euroa Australia **47** 36.46S145.35E
Europa, Picos de *mts.* Spain **10** 43.10N 4.40W
Euskirchen W. Germany **8** 50.40N 6.47E
Euston Australia **46** 34.34S142.49E
Evans, Lac *l.* Canada **55** 50.50N 77.00W
Evans Head *c.* Australia **47** 29.06S153.25E
Evanston Wyo. U.S.A. **54** 41.16N110.58W
Evansville U.S.A. **55** 38.00N 87.33W
Evelyn Creek *r.* Australia **46** 28.20S134.50E
Everard, C. Australia **47** 37.50S149.16E
Everard, L. Australia **46** 31.25S135.05E
Everard Range *mts.* Australia **45** 27.05S132.28E
Everest, Mt. Asia **29** 27.59N 86.56E
Everett Wash. U.S.A. **54** 47.59N122.13W
Evesham U.K. **5** 52.06N 1.57W
Evijärvi Finland **16** 63.22N 23.29E
Evje Norway **17** 58.36N 7.51E
Évora Portugal **10** 38.34N 7.54W
Évreux France **9** 49.03N 1.11E
Évry France **9** 48.38N 2.27E
Évvoia *i.* Greece **13** 38.30N 23.50E
Ewaninga Australia **44** 23.58S133.58E
Ewe, Loch U.K. **6** 57.48N 5.38W
Exe *r.* U.K. **5** 50.40N 3.28W
Exeter U.K. **5** 50.43N 3.31W
Exmoor Forest *hills* U.K. **5** 51.08N 3.45W
Exmouth Australia **42** 21.54S114.10E
Exmouth U.K. **5** 50.37N 3.24W
Exmouth G. Australia **42** 22.00S114.20E
Expedition Range *mts.* Australia **44** 24.30S149.05E
Extremadura *d.* Spain **10** 39.00N 6.00W
Exuma Is. Bahamas **57** 24.00N 76.00W
Eyasi, L. Tanzania **37** 3.40S 35.00E
Eye U.K. **5** 52.19N 1.09E
Eyemouth U.K. **6** 55.52N 2.05W
Eygurande France **11** 45.40N 2.26E
Eyjafjördhur *est.* Iceland **16** 65.54N 18.15W
Eyrarbakki Iceland **16** 63.52N 21.09W
Eyre Australia **43** 32.15S126.18E
Eyre *r.* Australia **44** 26.40S139.00E
Eyre, L. Australia **46** 28.30S137.25E
Eyre Pen. Australia **46** 34.00S135.45E

F

Fåberg Norway **17** 61.10N 10.22E
Fåborg Denmark **17** 55.06N 10.15E
Fabriano Italy **12** 43.20N 12.54E
Facatativá Colombia **60** 4.48N 74.32W
Facundo Argentina **63** 45.19S 69.59W
Fada Chad **35** 17.13N 21.30E
Fada-N'Gourma Burkina Faso **38** 12.03N 0.22E
Faenza Italy **9** 44.17N 11.52E
Fafa Mali **38** 15.20N 0.43E
Fafen *r.* Ethiopia **35** 6.07N 44.20E
Făgăraş Romania **15** 45.51N 24.58E
Fagernes Norway **17** 60.59N 9.17E
Fagersta Sweden **17** 60.00N 15.47E
Faguibine, Lac *l.* Mali **38** 16.45N 3.54W
Fagus Egypt **32** 30.44N 31.47E
Fā'id Egypt **32** 30.19N 32.19E
Fairbanks U.S.A. **50** 64.50N147.50W
Fairborn U.S.A. **55** 39.48N 84.03W
Fairfield Calif. U.S.A. **54** 38.15N122.03W
Fair Head U.K. **7** 55.13N 6.09W
Fair Isle U.K. **6** 59.32N 1.38W
Fairlie New Zealand **48** 44.06S170.50E
Fairmont W.Va. U.S.A. **55** 39.28N 80.08W
Fairview Utah U.S.A. **54** 39.38N111.26W
Fairweather, Mt. U.S.A. **50** 59.00N137.30W
Faisalābād Pakistan **28** 31.25N 73.09E
Faizābād India **29** 26.46N 82.08E
Fajr, Wādī *r.* Saudi Arabia **30** 30.00N 38.25E
Fakenham U.K. **4** 52.50N 0.51E
Fakfak Indonesia **27** 2.55S132.17E
Falaise France **9** 48.54N 0.11W
Falcarragh Rep. of Ire. **7** 55.08N 8.06W
Falcone, Capo del *c.* Italy **12** 40.57N 8.12E
Faleshty U.S.S.R. **15** 47.30N 27.45E
Falkenberg Sweden **17** 56.54N 12.28E
Falkirk U.K. **6** 56.00N 3.48W
Falkland Is. Atlantic Oc. **63** 51.45W 59.00W
Falkland Sd. *str.* Falkland Is. **63** 51.45W 59.25W
Falköping Sweden **17** 58.10N 13.31E
Fallbrook U.S.A. **54** 33.23N117.15W
Fall River *town* U.S.A. **55** 41.43N 71.08W
Falmouth U.K. **5** 50.09N 5.05W
False B. R.S.A. **39** 34.10S 18.40E
Falster *i.* Denmark **17** 54.48N 11.58E
Fălticeni Romania **15** 47.28N 26.18E
Falun Sweden **17** 60.36N 15.38E
Famagusta *see* Ammókhostos Cyprus **32**
Famoso U.S.A. **54** 35.36N119.14W
Fannich, Loch U.K. **6** 57.38N 5.00W
Fano Italy **9** 43.50N 13.01E
Faradje Zaïre **37** 3.45N 29.43E
Faradofay Madagascar **36** 25.02S 47.00E
Farāfirah, Wāḥāt al *oasis* Egypt **30** 27.15N 28.10E
Farāh Afghan. **31** 32.23N 62.07E
Farāh *r.* Afghan. **31** 31.25N 61.30E
Farallon de Medinilla *i.* Mariana Is. **27** 16.01N146.04E
Farallon de Pajaros *i.* Mariana Is. **27** 20.33N144.59E
Faraulep *is.* Mariana Is. **27** 8.36N144.33E
Fareham U.K. **5** 50.52N 1.11W
Farewell, C. *see* Farvel, Kap *c.* Greenland **51**
Farewell, C. New Zealand **48** 40.30S172.35E
Fargo U.S.A. **53** 46.52N 96.59W
Farina Australia **46** 30.05S138.20E
Farkwa Tanzania **37** 5.26S 35.15E
Farmington N.Mex. U.S.A. **54** 36.44N108.12W
Farnborough U.K. **5** 51.17N 0.46W
Farne Is. U.K. **4** 55.38N 1.36W
Farnham U.K. **5** 51.13N 0.49W
Faro Brazil **61** 2.11S 56.44W
Faro Portugal **10** 37.01N 7.56W
Faroe Is. Europe **16** 62.00N 7.00W
Fårön *i.* Sweden **17** 57.56N 19.08E
Fårösund Sweden **17** 57.52N 19.03E
Farrell U.S.A. **55** 41.13N 80.31W
Farrukhābād India **29** 27.23N 79.35E
Fársala Greece **13** 39.17N 22.22E
Fārsī Afghan. **31** 33.47N 63.12E
Farsund Norway **17** 58.05N 6.48E
Farvel, Kap *c.* Greenland **51** 60.00N 44.20W
Fasā Iran **31** 28.55N 53.38E
Fastov U.S.S.R. **15** 50.08N 29.59E
Făurei Romania **15** 45.04N 27.15E
Fauske Norway **16** 67.17N 15.25E
Favara Italy **12** 37.19N 13.40E
Favignana *i.* Italy **12** 37.57N 12.19E
Faxaflói *b.* Iceland **16** 64.30N 22.50W
Faxe *r.* Sweden **16** 63.15N 17.15E
Fayetteville Ark. U.S.A. **53** 36.03N 94.10W
Fayetteville N.C. U.S.A. **53** 35.03N 78.53W
Fdérik Mauritania **34** 22.35N 12.30W
Feale *r.* Rep. of Ire. **7** 52.28N 9.37W
Fear, C. U.S.A. **53** 33.51N 77.59W
Fécamp France **9** 49.45N 0.23E
Federación Argentina **63** 31.00S 57.55W
Federal Argentina **63** 30.55S 58.45W
Federal Capital Territory *d.* Nigeria **38** 8.50N 7.00E
Fedovo U.S.S.R. **18** 62.22N 39.21E
Fedulki U.S.S.R. **18** 65.00N 66.10E
Feeagh, Lough Rep. of Ire. **7** 53.56N 9.35W
Fehmarn *i.* W. Germany **14** 54.30N 11.05E
Feia, Lagoa *l.* Brazil **59** 22.00S 41.20W
Feijó Brazil **60** 8.09S 70.21W
Feilding New Zealand **48** 40.10S175.25E
Feira Zambia **37** 15.30S 30.27E
Feira de Santana Brazil **61** 12.17S 38.53W
Felanitx Spain **10** 39.27N 3.08E
Feldkirch Austria **14** 47.15N 9.38E
Felixstowe U.K. **5** 51.58N 1.20E
Feltre Italy **9** 46.01N 11.54E
Femunden *l.* Norway **17** 62.12N 11.52E
Femundsenden Norway **17** 61.55N 11.55E
Fengfeng China **25** 36.34N114.19E
Fengjie China **25** 31.00N109.30E
Fensfjorden *est.* Norway **17** 60.51N 4.50E
Fenton U.S.A. **55** 42.48N 83.42W
Fenyang China **25** 37.14N111.43E
Feodosiya U.S.S.R. **19** 45.03N 35.23E
Ferdows Iran **31** 34.00N 58.10E
Fère-Champenoise France **9** 48.45N 3.59E
Fère-en-Tardenois France **9** 48.12N 3.31E
Fergana U.S.S.R. **24** 40.23N 71.19E
Fergus Falls *town* U.S.A. **53** 46.18N 96.00W
Fergusson I. P.N.G. **44** 9.30S150.40E
Ferkéssédougou Ivory Coast **38** 9.30N 5.10W
Fermanagh *d.* U.K. **7** 54.21N 7.40W
Fermo Italy **12** 43.09N 13.43E
Fermoselle Spain **10** 41.19N 6.24W
Fermoy Rep. of Ire. **7** 52.08N 8.17W
Fernlee Australia **47** 28.12S147.05E
Ferrara Italy **9** 44.49N 11.38E
Ferreñafe Peru **60** 6.42S 79.45W
Ferret, Cap *c.* France **11** 44.42N 1.16W
Ferrières France **9** 48.05N 2.48E
Fès Morocco **34** 34.05N 5.00W
Feshi Zaïre **36** 6.08S 18.12E
Festubert Canada **55** 47.12N 72.40W
Feteşti Romania **15** 44.23N 27.50E
Fethiye Turkey **30** 36.37N 29.06E
Fetlar *i.* U.K. **6** 60.37N 0.52W
Feuilles, Rivière aux *r.* Canada **51** 58.47N 70.06W
Fevzipaşa Turkey **30** 37.07N 36.38E
Fianarantsoa Madagascar **36** 21.26S 47.05E
Fidenza Italy **9** 44.52N 10.03E
Fier Albania **13** 40.43N 19.34E
Fife *d.* U.K. **6** 56.10N 3.10W
Fife Ness *c.* U.K. **6** 56.17N 2.36W
Figeac France **11** 44.32N 2.01E
Figueira da Foz Portugal **10** 40.09N 8.51W
Figueres Spain **10** 42.16N 2.57E
Fiji Pacific Oc. **40** 18.00S178.00E
Filabusi Zimbabwe **39** 20.34S 29.20E
Filey U.K. **4** 54.13N 0.18W
Filiaşi Romania **15** 44.33N 23.31E
Filiatrá Greece **13** 37.09N 21.35E
Filingué Niger **38** 14.21N 3.22E
Filipstad Sweden **17** 59.43N 14.10E
Fillmore Calif. U.S.A. **54** 34.24N118.55W
Finale Emilia Italy **9** 44.50N 11.17E
Finale Ligure Italy **9** 44.10N 8.20E
Findhorn *r.* U.K. **6** 57.38N 3.37W
Findlay U.S.A. **55** 41.02N 83.40W
Finisterre, Cabo de *c.* Spain **10** 42.54N 9.16W
Finke *r.* Australia **45** 27.00S136.10E
Finland Europe **16** 64.30N 27.00E
Finland, G. of Finland / U.S.S.R. **17** 59.30N 24.00E
Finlay *r.* Canada **50** 56.30N124.40W
Finley Australia **47** 35.40S145.34E
Finmark Canada **55** 48.36N 89.44W
Finn *r.* Rep. of Ire. **7** 54.50N 7.30W
Finnmark *d.* Norway **16** 70.10N 26.00E
Finschhafen P.N.G. **27** 6.35S147.51E
Finse Norway **17** 60.36N 7.30E
Finspång Sweden **17** 58.43N 15.47E
Fiorenzuola d'Arda Italy **9** 44.56N 9.55E
Firat *r.* Turkey *see* Al Furāt *r.* Asia **30**
Firenze Italy **12** 43.46N 11.15E
Firenzuola Italy **9** 44.07N 11.23E
Firozābād India **29** 27.09N 78.24E
Firozpur India **28** 30.55N 74.38E
Firth of Clyde *est.* U.K. **6** 55.35N 4.53W
Firth of Forth *est.* U.K. **6** 56.05N 3.00W
Firth of Lorn *est.* U.K. **6** 56.20N 5.40W
Firth of Tay *est.* U.K. **6** 56.24N 3.08W
Firūzābād Iran **31** 28.50N 52.35E
Firyuza U.S.S.R. **20** 37.55N 58.03E
Fish *r.* Namibia **39** 28.07S 17.45E
Fisher Str. Canada **51** 63.00N 84.00W
Fishguard U.K. **5** 51.59N 4.59W
Fiskenaesset Greenland **51** 63.05N 50.40W
Fiskivötn *f.* Iceland **16** 64.50N 20.45W
Fismes France **9** 49.18N 3.41E
Fitz Roy Argentina **63** 47.00S 67.15W
Fitzroy *r.* Australia **42** 17.31S123.35E
Fitzroy Crossing Australia **42** 18.13S125.33E
Fivizzano Italy **9** 44.14N 10.08E
Fizi Zaïre **37** 4.18S 28.56E
Fjällåsen Sweden **16** 67.29N 20.10E
Fjällsjo *r.* Sweden **16** 63.27N 17.06E
Flå Norway **17** 60.25N 9.26E
Flagstaff U.S.A. **54** 35.12N111.39W
Flåm Norway **17** 60.50N 7.07E
Flamborough Head U.K. **4** 54.06N 0.05W
Flaming Gorge Resr. U.S.A. **54** 41.15N109.30W
Flandre *f.* Belgium **8** 50.52N 3.00E
Flannan Is. U.K. **6** 58.16N 7.40W
Flåsjön *l.* Sweden **16** 64.06N 15.51E
Flathead L. U.S.A. **54** 47.52N114.08W
Flattery, C. Australia **44** 14.58S145.21E
Flattery, C. U.S.A. **52** 48.23N124.43W
Fleetwood U.K. **4** 53.55N 3.01W
Flekkefjord *town* Norway **17** 58.17N 6.41E
Flen Sweden **17** 59.04N 16.35E
Flensburg W. Germany **14** 54.47N 9.27E
Flers France **9** 48.45N 0.34W
Flinders *r.* Australia **44** 17.30S140.45E
Flinders B. Australia **43** 34.23S115.19E
Flinders I. S.A. Australia **46** 33.44S134.30E
Flinders I. Tas. Australia **45** 40.00S148.00E
Flinders Range *mts.* Australia **46** 31.25S138.45E
Flinders Reefs Australia **44** 17.37S148.31E
Flin Flon Canada **51** 54.47N101.51W
Flint U.K. **4** 53.15N 3.07W
Flint U.S.A. **55** 43.03N 83.40W
Flint *r.* Ga. U.S.A. **53** 30.52N 84.35W
Flinton Australia **45** 27.54S149.34E
Flisa Norway **17** 60.34N 12.06E
Florac France **11** 44.19N 3.36E
Florence *see* Firenze Italy **12**
Florence Ariz. U.S.A. **54** 33.02N111.23W
Florence Oreg. U.S.A. **54** 43.58N124.07W
Florence S.C. U.S.A. **53** 34.12N 79.44W
Florence, L. Australia **46** 28.52S138.08E
Florencia Colombia **60** 1.37N 75.37W
Florennes Belgium **8** 50.14N 4.35E
Florenville Belgium **8** 49.42N 5.19E
Flores *i.* Indonesia **27** 8.40S121.20E
Flores, Laut *sea* Indonesia **27** 7.00S121.00E
Floreshty U.S.S.R. **15** 47.52N 28.12E
Flores Sea *see* Flores, Laut *sea* Indonesia **27**
Floriano Brazil **61** 6.45S 43.00W
Florianópolis Brazil **59** 27.35S 48.34W
Florida Uruguay **63** 34.06S 56.13W
Florida *d.* U.S.A. **53** 29.00N 82.00W
Florina Australia **46** 32.23S139.58E
Flórina Greece **13** 40.48N 21.25E
Florö Norway **17** 61.36N 5.00E
Fluessen *l.* Neth. **8** 52.58N 5.23E
Flushing *see* Vlissingen Neth. **8**
Fly *r.* P.N.G. **44** 8.22S142.23E
Focşani Romania **15** 45.40N 27.12E
Foggia Italy **12** 41.28N 15.33E
Foggo Nigeria **38** 11.21N 9.57E
Foix France **11** 42.57N 1.35E
Folda *est.* Nordland Norway **16** 67.36N 14.50E
Folda *est.* N. Trönd. Norway **16** 64.45N 11.20E
Folégandros *i.* Greece **13** 36.35N 24.55E
Foley Botswana **39** 21.34S 27.21E
Foleyet Canada **55** 48.05N 82.26W
Folgefonna *glacier* Norway **17** 60.00N 6.20E
Foligno Italy **12** 42.56N 12.43E
Folkestone U.K. **5** 51.05N 1.11E
Folsom U.S.A. **54** 38.41N121.15W
Fominskoye U.S.S.R. **18** 59.45N 42.03E
Fond-du Lac Canada **50** 59.20N107.09W
Fonsagrada Spain **10** 43.08N 7.04W
Fonseca, Golfo de *g.* Honduras **57** 13.10N 87.30W
Fontainebleau France **9** 48.24N 2.42E
Fonte Boa Brazil **60** 2.33S 65.59W
Fontenay France **11** 46.28N 0.48W
Forbach France **11** 49.11N 6.54E
Forbes Australia **47** 33.24S148.03E
Forchheim W. Germany **14** 49.43N 11.04E
Förde Norway **17** 61.27N 5.52E
Ford's Bridge Australia **47** 29.46S145.25E
Forel, Mt. Greenland **51** 67.00N 37.00W
Foreland Pt. U.K. **5** 51.15N 3.47W
Forest of Bowland *hills* U.K. **4** 53.57N 2.30W
Forest of Dean *f.* U.K. **5** 51.48N 2.32W
Forfar U.K. **6** 56.38N 2.54W
Forlì Italy **9** 44.13N 12.02E
Formby Pt. U.K. **4** 53.34N 3.07W
Formentera *i.* Spain **10** 38.41N 1.30E
Formerie France **9** 49.39N 1.44E
Formiga Brazil **59** 20.30S 45.27W
Formosa Argentina **62** 26.06S 58.14W
Formosa *d.* Argentina **62** 25.00S 60.00W
Formosa *see* Taiwan Asia **25**
Formosa Brazil **61** 15.30S 47.22W
Formosa, Serra *mts.* Brazil **61** 12.00S 55.20W
Formosa Str. China / Taiwan **25** 25.00N120.00E
Fornovo di Taro Italy **9** 44.42N 10.06E
Forres U.K. **6** 57.37N 3.38W
Forrest Australia **43** 30.49S128.03E
Fors Sweden **17** 60.13N 16.18E
Forsayth Australia **44** 18.35S143.36E
Forssa Finland **17** 60.49N 23.38E
Forst E. Germany **14** 51.46N 14.39E
Forsyth U.S.A. **54** 46.16N106.41W
Fort Albany Canada **51** 52.15N 81.35W
Fortaleza Brazil **61** 3.45S 38.35W
Fort Augustus U.K. **6** 57.09N 4.41W
Fort Beaufort R.S.A. **39** 32.46S 26.36E
Fort Benton U.S.A. **54** 47.49N110.40W
Fort Chimo Canada **51** 58.10N 68.15W
Fort Chipewyan Canada **50** 58.46N111.09W
Fort Collins U.S.A. **52** 40.35N105.05W
Fort Coulonge Canada **55** 45.51N 76.44W
Fort-de-France Martinique **57** 14.36N 61.05W
Fort Dodge U.S.A. **53** 42.31N 94.10W
Forte dei Marmi Italy **9** 43.57N 10.10E
Fortescue *r.* Australia **42** 21.00S116.06E
Fort Frances Canada **51** 48.37N 93.23W
Fort Franklin Canada **50** 65.11N123.45W
Fort George Canada **51** 53.50N 79.01W
Fort Good Hope Canada **50** 66.16N128.37W
Fort Grahame Canada **50** 56.30N124.35W
Fort Grey Australia **46** 29.04S141.13E
Forth *r.* U.K. **6** 56.06N 3.48W
Fort Klamath U.S.A. **54** 42.42N122.00W
Fort Lallemand Algeria **34** 31.13N 6.17E
Fort Lauderdale U.S.A. **53** 26.08N 80.08W
Fort Liard Canada **50** 60.14N123.28W
Fort MacKay Canada **50** 57.12N111.41W
Fort MacMahon Algeria **34** 29.51N 1.45E
Fort Maguire Malaŵi **37** 13.38S 34.59E
Fort McMurray Canada **50** 56.45N111.27W
Fort McPherson Canada **50** 67.29N134.50W
Fort Miribel Algeria **34** 29.31N 2.55E
Fort Morgan U.S.A. **52** 40.15N103.48W
Fort Myers U.S.A. **53** 26.39N 81.51W
Fort Nelson Canada **50** 58.48N122.44W
Fort Norman Canada **50** 64.55N125.29W
Fort Peck Dam U.S.A. **54** 47.52N106.38W
Fort Peck Resr. U.S.A. **54** 47.45N106.50W
Fort Pierce U.S.A. **53** 27.28N 80.20W
Fort Portal Uganda **37** 0.40N 30.17E
Fort Providence Canada **50** 61.21N117.39W
Fort Randall U.S.A. **50** 55.10N162.47W
Fort Reliance Canada **50** 62.45N109.08W
Fort Resolution Canada **50** 61.10N113.39W
Fortrose New Zealand **48** 46.34S168.48E
Fortrose U.K. **6** 57.34N 4.09W
Fort Rousset Congo **36** 0.30S 15.48E
Fort Rupert Que. Canada **55** 51.29N 78.45W
Fort St. John Canada **50** 56.14N120.55W
Fort Scott U.S.A. **53** 37.52N 94.43W
Fort Severn Canada **51** 56.00N 87.40W
Fort Shevchenko U.S.S.R. **19** 44.31N 50.15E
Fort Simpson Canada **50** 61.46N121.15W
Fort Smith Canada **50** 60.00N111.53W
Fort Smith *d.* Canada **50** 63.30N118.00W
Fort Smith U.S.A. **53** 35.22N 94.27W
Fort Thomas U.S.A. **54** 33.02N109.58W
Fortuna Calif. U.S.A. **54** 40.36N124.09W
Fort Vermilion Canada **50** 58.22N115.59W
Fort Wayne U.S.A. **55** 41.05N 85.08W
Fort William U.K. **6** 56.49N 5.07W
Fort Worth U.S.A. **53** 32.45N 97.20W
Forty Mile *town* Canada **50** 64.24N140.31W
Fort Yukon U.S.A. **50** 66.35N145.20W
Foshan China **25** 23.03N113.08E
Fossano Italy **9** 44.33N 7.43E
Foster Australia **47** 38.39S146.12E
Fostoria U.S.A. **55** 41.10N 83.25W
Fougères France **9** 48.21N 1.12W
Foula *i.* U.K. **6** 60.08N 2.05W
Foulness I. U.K. **5** 51.35N 0.55E
Foulwind, C. New Zealand **48** 41.45S171.30E
Foumban Cameroon **38** 5.43N 10.50E
Fourmies France **8** 50.01N 4.02E
Foúrnoi *i.* Greece **13** 37.34N 26.30E
Fouta Djalon *f.* Guinea **34** 11.30N 12.30W
Foveaux Str. New Zealand **48** 46.40S168.00E
Fowey U.K. **5** 50.20N 4.39W
Fowlers B. Australia **45** 31.59S132.27E
Foxe Basin *b.* Canada **51** 67.30N 79.00W
Foxe Channel Canada **51** 65.00N 80.00W
Foxe Pen. Canada **51** 65.00N 76.00W
Fox Glacier *town* New Zealand **48** 43.28S170.01E
Foxton New Zealand **48** 40.27S175.18E
Foyle *r.* U.K. **7** 55.00N 7.20W
Foyle, Lough U.K. **7** 55.05N 7.10W
Foz do Iguaçu Brazil **59** 25.33S 54.31W
Franca Brazil **59** 20.33S 47.27W
Francavilla Fontana Italy **13** 40.31N 17.35E
France Europe **11** 47.00N 2.00E
Frances Australia **46** 36.41S140.59E
Frances L. Canada **50** 61.25N129.30W
Francesville U.S.A. **55** 40.59N 86.54W
Franche-Comté *d.* France **11** 47.10N 6.00E
Francia Uruguay **63** 32.33S 56.37W
Francistown Botswana **39** 21.12S 27.29E
Franeker Neth. **8** 53.13N 5.31E
Frankfort R.S.A. **39** 27.15S 28.30E
Frankfort Ky. U.S.A. **55** 38.11N 84.53W
Frankfurt E. Germany **14** 52.20N 14.32E
Frankfurt *d.* E. Germany **14** 52.30N 14.00E
Frankfurt W. Germany **14** 50.06N 8.41E
Frankland *r.* Australia **43** 34.58S116.49E
Franklin N.H. U.S.A. **55** 43.27N 71.39W
Franklin W.Va. U.S.A. **55** 38.39N 79.20W
Franklin B. Canada **50** 70.00N126.30W
Franklin D. Roosevelt L. U.S.A. **54** 48.20N118.10W
Franklin Harbour Australia **46** 33.42S136.56E
Franklin I. Antarctica **64** 76.10S168.30E
Frankston Australia **47** 38.08S145.07E
Fransfontein Namibia **39** 20.12S 15.01E
Frantsa Iosifa, Zemlya *is.* U.S.S.R. **20** 81.00N 54.00E
Franz Canada **55** 48.28N 84.25W
Franz Josef Land *is. see* Frantsa Iosifa, Zemlya U.S.S.R. **20**
Fraser *r.* B.C. Canada **50** 49.05N123.00W

Fraser, I. Australia **44** 25.15S153.10E
Fraserburg R.S.A. **39** 31.55S 21.29E
Fraserburgh U.K. **6** 57.42N 2.00W
Fray Bentos Uruguay **63** 33.08S 58.18W
Fray Marcos Uruguay **63** 34.11S 55.44W
Fredericia Denmark **17** 55.35N 9.46E
Frederick Hills Australia **44** 12.41S136.00E
Fredericksburg Va. U.S.A. **55** 38.18N 77.30W
Fredericton Canada **55** 45.57N 66.40W
Frederikshåb Greenland **51** 62.05N 49.30W
Frederikshavn Denmark **17** 57.26N 10.32E
Fredonia N.Y. U.S.A. **55** 42.27N 79.22W
Fredrika Sweden **16** 64.05N 18.24E
Fredrikstad Norway **17** 59.13N 10.57E
Freeling, Mt. Australia **44** 22.35S133.06E
Freeling Heights *mts.* Australia **46** 30.10S139.16E
Freeport Bahamas **57** 26.40N 78.30W
Freeport N.S. Canada **55** 44.17N 66.19W
Freeport N.Y. U.S.A. **55** 40.40N 73.35W
Freeport Tex. U.S.A. **53** 28.56N 95.20W
Freetown Sierra Leone **34** 8.30N 13.17W
Freiberg E. Germany **14** 50.54N 13.20E
Freiburg W. Germany **14** 48.00N 7.52E
Freilingen W. Germany **8** 50.33N 7.50E
Freising W. Germany **14** 48.24N 11.45E
Freistadt Austria **14** 48.31N 14.31E
Fréjus France **11** 43.26N 6.44E
Fremantle Australia **43** 32.07S115.44E
Fremont Calif. U.S.A. **54** 37.34N122.01W
Fremont Nebr. U.S.A. **53** 41.26N 96.30W
Fremont Ohio U.S.A. **55** 41.21N 83.08W
Frenchglen U.S.A. **54** 42.48N118.56W
French I. Australia **47** 38.20S145.20E
Freren W. Germany **8** 52.29N 7.32E
Fresco *r.* Brazil **61** 7.10S 52.30W
Fresco Ivory Coast **38** 5.03N 5.31W
Freshford Rep. of Ire. **7** 52.44N 7.23W
Fresnillo Mexico **56** 23.10N102.53W
Fresno U.S.A. **54** 36.45N119.45W
Frewena Australia **44** 19.25S135.25E
Frias Argentina **62** 28.40S 65.10W
Fribourg Switz. **14** 46.50N 7.10E
Friedberg Hessen W. Germany **14** 50.20N 8.45E
Friedrichshafen W. Germany **14** 47.39N 9.29E
Friesland *d.* Neth. **8** 53.05N 5.45E
Friesoythe W. Germany **8** 53.02N 7.52E
Frio, Cabo *c.* Brazil **59** 22.59S 42.00W
Friuli-Venezia Giulia *d.* Italy **9** 46.15N 12.45E
Frobisher B. Canada **51** 63.00N 66.45W
Frobisher Bay *town* Canada **51** 63.45N 68.30W
Frobisher L. Canada **50** 56.25N108.20W
Frohavet *est.* Norway **16** 63.55N 9.05E
Frolovo U.S.S.R. **19** 49.45N 43.40E
Frome *r.* Australia **46** 29.49S138.40E
Frome U.K. **5** 51.16N 2.17W
Frome, L. Australia **46** 30.48S139.48E
Frome Downs *town* Australia **46** 31.13S139.46E
Frontera Mexico **56** 18.32N 92.38W
Frosinone Italy **12** 41.36N 13.21E
Fröya *i.* Norway **16** 63.45N 8.45E
Frunze U.S.S.R. **24** 42.53N 74.46E
Frunzovka U.S.S.R. **15** 47.19N 29.44E
Frýdek-Místek Czech. **15** 49.41N 18.22E
Fuchū Japan **23** 35.40N139.29E
Fuefuki *r.* Japan **23** 35.33N138.28E
Fuente-obejuna Spain **10** 38.15N 5.25W
Fuentes de Oñoro Spain **10** 40.33N 6.52W
Fuerte *r.* Mexico **56** 25.50N109.25W
Fuerteventura *i.* Canary Is. **34** 28.20N 14.10W
Fuji Japan **23** 35.09N138.39E
Fuji *r.* Japan **23** 35.07N138.38E
Fujian *d.* China **25** 26.30N118.00E
Fujieda Japan **23** 34.52N138.16E
Fujin China **25** 47.15N131.59E
Fujinomiya Japan **23** 35.12N138.38E
Fuji san *mtn.* Japan **23** 35.22N138.44E
Fujisawa Japan **23** 35.21N139.29E
Fuji-yoshida Japan **23** 35.38N138.42E
Fukui Japan **25** 36.04N136.12E
Fukuoka Japan **25** 33.39N130.21E
Fukuroi Japan **23** 34.45N137.55E
Fulda W. Germany **14** 50.35N 9.45E
Fulda *r.* W. Germany **14** 50.33N 9.41E
Fuling China **24** 29.43N107.24E
Fulton N.Y. U.S.A. **55** 43.20N 76.26W
Fumay France **8** 49.59N 4.42E
Funabashi Japan **23** 35.42N139.59E
Funchal Madeira Is. **34** 32.38N 16.54W
Fundão Portugal **10** 40.08N 7.30W
Fundy, B. of Canada **55** 45.00N 66.00W
Funing China **24** 23.37N105.36E
Funtua Nigeria **38** 11.34N 7.18E
Furancungo Mozambique **37** 14.51S 33.38E
Fürg Iran **31** 28.19N 55.10E
Furnas, Représa de *resr.* Brazil **59** 20.45S 46.00W
Furneaux Group *is.* Australia **45** 40.15S148.15E
Furqlus Syria **32** 34.38N 37.08E
Fürstenau W. Germany **8** 52.32N 7.41E
Fürstenwalde E. Germany **14** 52.22N 14.04E
Fürth W. Germany **14** 49.28N 11.00E
Furu-tone *r.* Japan **23** 35.58N139.51E
Fusagasugá Colombia **60** 4.22N 74.21W
Fushun China **25** 41.51N123.53E
Fusong China **25** 42.17N127.19E
Fuwah Egypt **32** 31.12N 30.33E
Fuxin China **25** 42.08N121.39E
Fuyu China **25** 45.12N124.49E
Fuyuan Heilongjiang China **25** 48.20N134.18E
Fuyuan Yunnan China **29** 25.40N104.14E
Fuzhou Fujian China **25** 26.01N119.20E
Fuzhou Jiangxi China **25** 28.03N116.15E
Fyn *i.* Denmark **17** 55.20N 10.30E
Fyne, Loch U.K. **6** 55.55N 5.23W

G

Ga Ghana **38** 9.48N 2.28W
Gabès Tunisia **34** 33.52N 10.06E
Gabès, Golfe de *g.* Tunisia **34** 34.00N 10.25E
Gabon Africa **36** 0.00 12.00E
Gaborone Botswana **39** 24.45S 25.55E
Gabras Sudan **35** 10.16N 26.14E
Gabrovo Bulgaria **13** 42.52N 25.19E
Gacé France **9** 48.48N 0.18E
Gach Sārān Iran **31** 30.13N 50.49E
Gada Nigeria **38** 13.50N 5.40E
Gäddede Sweden **16** 64.30N 14.15E
Gadsden U.S.A. **53** 34.00N 86.00W
Gaeta Italy **12** 41.13N 13.35E
Gaeta, Golfo di *g.* Italy **12** 41.05N 13.30E
Gaferut *i.* Caroline Is. **27** 9.14N145.23E
Gafsa Tunisia **34** 34.25N 8.48E
Gagarin U.S.S.R. **18** 55.38N 35.00E
Gagnoa Ivory Coast **38** 6.04N 5.55W
Gagnon Canada **51** 51.55N 68.10W
Gaillac France **11** 43.54N 1.53E
Gaillon France **9** 49.10N 1.20E
Gainesville Fla. U.S.A. **53** 29.37N 82.31W
Gainsborough U.K. **4** 53.23N 0.46W
Gairdner *r.* Australia **43** 34.20S119.30E
Gairdner, L. Australia **46** 31.30S136.00E
Gairloch U.K. **6** 57.43N 5.40W
Galana *r.* Kenya **37** 3.12S 40.09E
Galashiels U.K. **6** 55.37N 2.49W
Galaţi Romania **15** 45.27N 27.59E
Galatina Italy **13** 40.10N 18.10E
Galdhöpiggen *mtn.* Norway **17** 61.37N 8.17E
Galeana Mexico **56** 24.50N100.04W
Galeh Dār Iran **31** 27.36N 52.42E
Galena Australia **43** 27.50S114.41E
Galena Alas. U.S.A. **50** 64.43N157.00W
Galesburg U.S.A. **53** 40.58N 90.22W
Galich U.S.S.R. **18** 58.20N 42.12E
Galicia *d.* Spain **10** 43.00N 8.00W
Galilee, L. Australia **44** 22.21S145.48E
Gallarate Italy **9** 45.40N 8.47E
Galle Sri Lanka **29** 6.01N 80.13E
Gállego *r.* Spain **10** 41.40N 0.55W
Gallegos *r.* Argentina **63** 51.35S 69.00W
Galley Head Rep. of Ire. **7** 51.32N 8.57W
Galliate Italy **9** 45.29N 8.42E
Gallinas, Punta *c.* Colombia **60** 12.20N 71.30W
Gallipoli Italy **13** 40.02N 18.01E
Gallipolis U.S.A. **55** 38.49N 82.14W
Gällivare Sweden **16** 67.07N 20.45E
Gällö Sweden **16** 62.56N 15.15E
Galloway *f.* U.K. **6** 55.00N 4.28W
Gallup U.S.A. **54** 35.32N108.44W
Galong Australia **47** 34.37S148.34E
Galston U.K. **6** 55.36N 4.23W
Galty Mts. Rep. of Ire. **7** 52.20N 8.10W
Galveston U.S.A. **53** 29.17N 94.48W
Galveston B. U.S.A. **53** 29.40N 94.40W
Galvez Argentina **62** 32.03S 61.14W
Galway Rep. of Ire. **7** 53.17N 9.04W
Galway *d.* Rep. of Ire. **7** 53.25N 9.00W
Galway B. Rep. of Ire. **7** 53.12N 9.07W
Gamagōri Japan **23** 34.50N137.14E
Gamawa Nigeria **38** 12.10N 10.31E
Gambia Africa **34** 13.10N 16.00W
Gambia *r.* Gambia **34** 13.28N 15.55W
Gambier I. Australia **46** 35.12S136.32E
Gamboula C.A.R. **38** 4.05N 15.10E
Gamia Benin **38** 10.24N 2.45E
Gamlakarleby *see* Kokkola Finland **16**
Gamleby Sweden **17** 57.54N 16.24E
Ganado U.S.A. **54** 35.43N109.33W
Gananoque Canada **55** 44.20N 76.10W
Ganda Angola **36** 13.02S 14.40E
Gander Canada **51** 48.58N 54.34W
Gandía Spain **10** 38.59N 0.11W
Ganga *r.* India **29** 23.30N 90.25E
Gangara Niger **38** 14.35N 8.40E
Gangdisê Shan *mts.* China **24** 31.00N 82.00E
Ganges *r. see* Ganga *r.* India **29**
Gangtok India **29** 27.20N 88.39E
Ganmain Australia **47** 34.47S147.01E
Gannat France **11** 46.06N 3.11E
Gannett Peak *mtn.* U.S.A. **54** 43.11N109.39W
Gansu *d.* China **24** 36.00N 103.00E
Ganta Liberia **34** 7.15N 8.59W
Gantheaume, C. Australia **46** 36.05S137.27E
Ganye Nigeria **38** 8.24N 12.02E
Ganzhou China **25** 25.52N114.51E
Gao Mali **38** 16.19N 0.09W
Gao *d.* Mali **38** 18.30N 1.15W
Gaotai China **24** 39.20N 99.58E
Gaoua Burkina Faso **38** 10.20N 3.09W
Gaoxiong Taiwan **25** 22.36N120.17E
Gap France **11** 44.33N 6.05E
Gar China **29** 32.10N 79.59E
Gara, Lough Rep. of Ire. **7** 53.57N 8.27W
Garah Australia **47** 29.04S149.38E
Garanhuns Brazil **61** 8.53S 36.28W
Gārbosh, Kūh-e *mtn.* Iran **31** 32.36N 50.02E
Gard *r.* France **11** 43.52N 4.40E
Garda Italy **9** 45.34N 10.42E
Garda, Lago di *l.* Italy **9** 45.40N 10.40E
Gardelegen E. Germany **14** 52.31N 11.23E
Garden City Kans. U.S.A. **52** 37.58N100.53W
Gardiner U.S.A. **54** 45.02N110.42W
Gardnerville U.S.A. **54** 38.56N119.45W
Gardone Val Trompia Italy **9** 45.41N 10.11E
Garessio Italy **9** 44.12N 8.02E
Garies R.S.A. **39** 30.34S 18.00E
Garigliano *r.* Italy **12** 41.13N 13.45E
Garissa Kenya **37** 0.27S 39.49E
Garko Nigeria **38** 11.45N 8.53E
Garland Utah U.S.A. **54** 41.45N112.10W
Garlasco Italy **9** 45.12N 8.55E
Garlin France **11** 43.34N 0.15W
Garmisch Partenkirchen W. Germany **14** 47.30N 11.05E
Garmsār Iran **31** 35.15N 52.21E
Garonne *r.* France **11** 45.00N 0.37W
Garoua Cameroon **38** 9.17N 13.22E
Garoua Boulaï Cameroon **38** 5.54N 14.33E
Garrison Resr. U.S.A. **52** 47.50N102.20W
Garron Pt. U.K. **7** 55.03N 5.57W
Garry L. Canada **51** 66.00N100.00W
Garson Canada **55** 46.34N 80.52W
Garub Namibia **39** 26.33S 16.00E
Garut Indonesia **26** 7.15S107.55E
Garvão Portugal **10** 37.42N 8.21W
Garve U.K. **6** 57.37N 4.41W
Garvie Mts. New Zealand **48** 45.15S169.00E
Gary U.S.A. **55** 41.34N 87.20W
Garyarsa China **24** 31.30N 80.40E
Garzón Colombia **60** 2.14N 75.376
Gas City U.S.A. **55** 40.28N 85.37W
Gascogne, Golfe de *g.* France **11** 44.00N 2.40W
Gascony, G. of *see* Gascogne, Golfe de France **11**
Gascoyne *r.* Australia **42** 25.00S113.40E
Gascoyne Junction Australia **42** 25.02S115.15E
Gashua Nigeria **38** 12.53N 11.02E
Gaspé Canada **51** 48.50N 64.30W
Gaspé, Cap de *c.* Canada **51** 48.45N 64.10W
Gaspé, Péninsule de *pen.* Canada **55** 48.30N 65.00W
Gassol Nigeria **38** 8.34N 10.25E
Gastre Argentina **63** 42.17S 69.15W
Gata, Cabo de *c.* Spain **10** 36.45N 2.11W
Gata, Sierra de *mts.* Spain **10** 40.20N 6.30W
Gátas, Akrotírion *c.* Cyprus **32** 34.33N 33.03E
Gatchina U.S.S.R. **18** 59.32N 30.05E
Gatehouse of Fleet U.K. **6** 54.53N 4.12W
Gateshead U.K. **4** 54.57N 1.35W
Gatineau Canada **55** 45.29N 75.40W
Gatineau *r.* Canada **55** 45.27N 75.40W
Gattinara Italy **9** 45.37N 8.22E
Gatun L. Panama **57** 9.20N 80.00W
Gauchy France **9** 49.49N 3.13E
Gauhāti India **29** 26.05N 91.55E
Gavá Spain **10** 41.18N 2.00E
Gavāter Iran **31** 25.10N 61.31E
Gāv Koshī Iran **31** 28.39N 57.13E
Gävle Sweden **17** 60.40N 17.10E
Gävleborg *d.* Sweden **17** 61.30N 16.15E
Gávrion Greece **13** 37.52N 24.46E
Gawachab Namibia **39** 27.03S 17.50E
Gāwilgarh Hills India **28** 21.20N 77.00E
Gawler Australia **46** 34.38S138.44E
Gawler Ranges *mts.* Australia **46** 32.30S136.00E
Gaya India **29** 24.48N 85.00E
Gaya Niger **38** 11.53N 3.31E
Gayndah Australia **44** 25.37S151.36E
Gayny U.S.S.R. **18** 60.17N 54.15E
Gaysin U.S.S.R. **15** 48.50N 29.29E
Gayvoron U.S.S.R. **15** 48.20N 29.52E
Gaza *see* Ghazzah Egypt **32**
Gaza *d.* Mozambique **39** 23.20S 32.35E
Gaza Strip *f.* Egypt **32** 31.32N 34.23E
Gaziantep Turkey **30** 37.04N 37.21E
Gbanhui Ivory Coast **38** 8.12N 3.02W
Gboko Nigeria **38** 7.22N 8.58E
Gcuwa R.S.A. **39** 32.20S 28.09E
Gdańsk Poland **15** 54.22N 18.38E
Gdov U.S.S.R. **18** 58.48N 27.52E
Gdynia Poland **15** 54.31N 18.30E
Gebe *i.* Indonesia **27** 0.05S129.20E
Gebze Turkey **30** 40.48N 29.26E
Gedera Israel **32** 31.48N 34.46E
Gediz *r.* Turkey **13** 38.37N 26.47E
Gedser Denmark **17** 54.35N 11.57E
Geel Belgium **8** 51.10N 5.00E
Geelong Australia **46** 38.10S144.26E
Gehua P.N.G. **44** 10.20S150.25E
Geidam Nigeria **38** 12.55N 11.55E
Geilenkirchen W. Germany **8** 50.58N 6.08E
Geilo Norway **17** 60.31N 8.12E
Gejiu China **24** 23.25N103.05E
Gela Italy **12** 37.03N 14.15E
Gelai *mtn.* Tanzania **37** 2.37S 36.07E
Gelderland *d.* Neth. **8** 52.05N 6.00E
Geldermalsen Neth. **8** 51.53N 5.17E
Geldern W. Germany **8** 51.31N 6.19E
Geldrop Neth. **8** 51.26N 5.31E
Geleen Neth. **8** 50.58N 5.51E
Gélengdeng Chad **38** 10.56N 15.32E
Gelibolu Turkey **13** 40.25N 26.31E
Gelligaer U.K. **5** 51.40N 3.18W
Gelsenkirchen W. Germany **8** 51.30N 7.05E
Gemas Malaysia **26** 2.35N102.35E
Gembloux Belgium **8** 50.34N 4.42E
Gemerek Turkey **30** 39.13N 36.05E
Gemlik Turkey **30** 40.26N 29.10E
Gemona del Friuli Italy **9** 46.16N 13.09E
Genappe Belgium **8** 50.37N 4.25E
Gendringen Neth. **8** 51.52N 6.26E
General Acha Argentina **63** 37.20S 64.35W
General Alvear Buenos Aires Argentina **63** 36.00S 60.00W
General Alvear Mendoza Argentina **63** 34.59S 67.42W
General Belgrano Argentina **63** 35.45S 58.30W
General Campos Argentina **63** 31.30S 58.25W
General Conesa Argentina **63** 36.30S 57.19W
General Guido Argentina **63** 36.40S 57.45W
General Lavalle Argentina **63** 36.22S 56.55W
General Madariaga Argentina **63** 37.00S 57.05W
General Paz Argentina **63** 35.32S 58.18W
General Pico Argentina **63** 35.38S 63.46W
General Roca Argentina **63** 39.02S 67.33W
General Santos Phil. **27** 6.05N125.15E
Geneseo N.Y. U.S.A. **55** 42.46N 77.49W
Geneva *see* Genève Switz. **14**
Geneva N.Y. U.S.A. **55** 42.53N 76.59W
Geneva Ohio U.S.A. **55** 41.48N 80.57W
Geneva, L. *see* Léman, Lac *l.* Switz. **14**
Genève Switz. **14** 46.13N 6.09E
Genichesk U.S.S.R. **19** 46.10N 34.49E
Genil *r.* Spain **10** 37.42N 5.20W
Genk Belgium **8** 50.58N 5.34E
Gennep Neth. **8** 51.43N 5.58E
Gennes France **9** 47.20N 0.14W
Genoa Australia **47** 37.29S149.35E
Genoa *see* Genova Italy **9**
Genoa, G. of *see* Genova, Golfo di *g.* Italy **9**
Genova Italy **9** 44.24N 8.54E
Genova, Golfo di *g.* Italy **9** 44.12N 8.55E
Gent Belgium **8** 51.02N 3.42E
Geographe B. Australia **43** 33.35S115.15E
Geographe Channel Australia **42** 24.40S113.20E
George *r.* Australia **46** 28.24S136.39E
George *r.* Canada **51** 58.30N 66.00W
George R.S.A. **39** 33.57S 22.27E
George, L. N.S.W. Australia **47** 35.07S149.22E
George, L. S.A. Australia **46** 37.26S140.00E
George, L. Uganda **37** 0.00 30.10E
Georgetown Qld. Australia **44** 18.18S143.33E
George Town Tas. Australia **45** 41.04S146.48E
Georgetown Cayman Is. **57** 19.20N 81.23W
Georgetown Guyana **60** 6.46N 58.10W
George Town Malaysia **26** 5.30N100.16E
Georgetown S.C. U.S.A. **53** 33.23N 79.18W
George V Land *f.* Antarctica **64** 69.00S145.00E
Georgia *d.* U.S.A. **53** 33.00N 83.00W
Georgian B. Canada **55** 45.15N 80.50W
Georgina *r.* Australia **44** 23.12S139.33E
Georgiu-Dezh U.S.S.R. **19** 51.00N 39.30E
Georgiyevsk U.S.S.R. **19** 44.10N 43.30E
Gera E. Germany **14** 50.51N 12.11E
Gera *d.* E. Germany **14** 50.45N 11.45E
Geraardsbergen Belgium **8** 50.47N 3.53E
Geral de Goiás, Serra *mts.* Brazil **61** 13.00S 45.40W
Geraldine New Zealand **48** 44.05S171.15E
Geral do Paraná, Serra *mts.* Brazil **61** 14.40S 47.30W
Geraldton Australia **43** 28.49S114.36E
Geraldton Canada **55** 49.44N 86.59W
Gerede Turkey **30** 40.48N 32.13E
Gereshk Afghan. **28** 31.48N 64.34E
Gérgal Spain **10** 37.07N 2.31W
Gerlach U.S.A. **54** 40.40N119.21W
Gerlachovsky *mtn.* Czech. **15** 49.10N 20.05E
Germiston R.S.A. **39** 26.14S 28.10E
Gerolstein W. Germany **8** 50.14N 6.40E
Gerringong Australia **47** 34.45S150.50E
Gêrzê China **29** 32.16N 84.12E
Gescher W. Germany **8** 51.58N 7.00E
Getafe Spain **10** 40.18N 3.44W
Gete *r.* Belgium **8** 50.58N 5.07E
Gevān Iran **31** 26.03N 57.17E
Gevelsberg W. Germany **8** 51.20N 7.20E
Geysdorp R.S.A. **39** 26.31S 25.17E
Geyser U.S.A. **54** 47.16N110.30W
Geyve Turkey **30** 40.32N 30.18E
Ghadaf, Wādī al *r.* Jordan **32** 31.46N 36.50E
Ghadāmis Libya **34** 30.10N 9.30E
Ghāghra *r.* India **29** 25.45N 84.50E
Ghana Africa **38** 8.00N 1.00W
Ghanzi Botswana **39** 21.42S 21.39E
Ghardaïa Algeria **34** 32.20N 3.40E
Ghārib, Jabal *mtn.* Egypt **32** 28.06N 32.54E
Ghāt Libya **34** 24.59N 10.11E
Ghazāl, Baḩr al *r.* Sudan **35** 9.30N 31.30E
Ghāziābād India **28** 28.37N 77.30E
Ghaznī Afghan. **28** 33.33N 68.28E
Ghazzah Egypt **32** 31.30N 34.28E
Ghedi Italy **9** 45.24N 10.16E
Gheorghe-Gheorghiu-Dej Romania **15** 46.14N 26.44E
Gheorgheni Romania **15** 46.43N 25.36E
Gherla Romania **15** 47.02N 23.55E
Ghudāf, Wādī al *r.* Iraq **30** 32.54N 43.33E
Ghūrīān Afghan. **31** 34.20N 61.25E
Gia Dinh Vietnam **26** 10.48N106.43E
Gibb River *town* Australia **42** 15.39S126.38E
Gibeon Namibia **39** 25.09S 17.44E
Gibraltar Europe **10** 36.07N 5.22W
Gibraltar, Str. of Africa/Europe **10** 36.00N 5.25W
Gibraltar Pt. U.K. **4** 53.05N 0.20E
Gibson Australia **43** 33.39S121.48E
Gibson Desert Australia **42** 24.30S123.00E
Gien France **9** 47.41N 2.37E
Giessen W. Germany **14** 50.35N 8.42E
Gieten Neth. **8** 53.01N 6.45E
Gifford *r.* Canada **51** 70.21N 83.05W
Gifford U.S.A. **54** 48.20N118.08W
Gifhorn W. Germany **14** 52.29N 10.33E
Gifu Japan **23** 35.25N136.45E
Gifu *d.* Japan **23** 35.32N137.15E
Gigha *i.* U.K. **6** 55.41N 5.44W
Giglio *i.* Italy **12** 42.21N 10.53E
Gijón Spain **10** 43.32N 5.40W
Gila *r.* U.S.A. **54** 32.43N114.33W
Gila Bend U.S.A. **54** 32.57N112.43W
Gila Bend Mts. U.S.A. **54** 33.10N113.10W
Gilbert *r.* Australia **44** 16.35S141.15E
Gildford U.S.A. **54** 48.34N110.18W
Gilé Mozambique **37** 16.10S 38.17E
Gilgandra Australia **47** 31.42S148.40E
Gil Gil *r.* Australia **47** 29.10S148.50E
Gilgil Kenya **37** 0.29S 36.19E
Gilgit Jammu & Kashmir **28** 35.54N 74.20E
Gilgunnia Australia **47** 32.25S146.04E
Gill, Lough Rep. of Ire. **7** 54.15N 8.14W
Gilles, L. Australia **46** 32.50S136.45E
Gillingham Kent U.K. **5** 51.24N 0.33E
Gilmour Canada **55** 44.48N 77.37W
Gimli Canada **51** 50.38N 96.59W
Gingin Australia **43** 31.21S115.42E
Ginir Ethiopia **35** 7.07N 40.46E
Ginzo de Limia Spain **10** 42.03N 7.47W
Gióna *mtn.* Greece **13** 38.38N 22.14E
Girardot Colombia **60** 4.19N 74.47W
Girdle Ness U.K. **6** 57.06N 2.02W
Giresun Turkey **30** 40.55N 38.25E
Girilambone Australia **47** 31.14S146.55E
Girona Spain **10** 41.59N 2.49E
Gironde *r.* France **11** 45.35N 1.00W
Girvan U.K. **6** 55.15N 4.51W
Gisborne New Zealand **48** 38.41S178.02E
Gisors France **9** 49.17N 1.47E
Gitega Burundi **37** 3.25S 29.58E
Giulianova Italy **12** 42.45N 13.57E
Giurgiu Romania **15** 43.52N 25.58E
Giv'atayim Israel **32** 32.04N 34.49E
Givet France **11** 50.08N 4.49E
Gizhiga U.S.S.R. **21** 62.00N160.34E
Gizhiginskaya Guba *g.* U.S.S.R. **21** 61.00N158.00E
Giżycko Poland **15** 54.03N 21.47E
Gjerstad Norway **17** 58.54N 9.00E
Gjirokastër Albania **13** 40.05N 20.10E
Gjoa Haven *town* Canada **51** 68.39N 96.08W
Gjövik Norway **17** 60.48N 10.42E
Glacier Peak *mtn.* U.S.A. **54** 48.07N121.06W
Gladstone Qld. Australia **44** 23.52S151.16E
Gladstone S.A. Australia **46** 33.17S138.22E
Gladstone Mich. U.S.A. **55** 45.52N 87.02W
Glafsfjorden *l.* Sweden **17** 59.34N 12.37E
Glåma *r.* Norway **17** 59.15N 10.55E
Glamoč Yugo. **13** 44.03N 16.51E
Glan *r.* W. Germany **8** 49.46N 7.43E
Glanaman U.K. **5** 51.49N 3.54W
Glandorf W. Germany **8** 52.05N 8.00E
Glasgow U.K. **6** 55.52N 4.15W
Glasgow Mont. U.S.A. **54** 48.12N106.38W
Glastonbury U.K. **5** 51.09N 2.42W
Glazov U.S.S.R. **18** 58.09N 52.42E
Gleisdorf Austria **14** 47.06N 15.44E
Glen R.S.A. **39** 28.57S 26.19E
Glen Affric *f.* U.K. **6** 57.15N 5.03W
Glénans, Îles de *is.* France **11** 47.43N 3.57W
Glenarm U.K. **7** 54.57N 5.58W
Glenburnie Australia **46** 37.49S140.56E
Glencoe Australia **46** 37.41S140.05E
Glen Coe *f.* U.K. **6** 56.40N 5.03W
Glendale Ariz. U.S.A. **54** 33.32N112.11W
Glendale Calif. U.S.A. **54** 34.10N118.17W
Glendale Oreg. U.S.A. **54** 42.44N123.26W
Glen Davis Australia **47** 33.07S150.22E
Glendive U.S.A. **52** 47.06N104.43W
Glenelg Australia **46** 34.59S138.31E
Glenelg *r.* Australia **46** 38.03S141.00E
Glengarriff Rep. of Ire. **7** 51.45N 9.33W
Glen Garry *f.* Highland U.K. **6** 57.03N 5.04W
Glen Head Rep. of Ire. **7** 54.44N 8.46W
Glen Ina Australia **46** 31.45S143.33E
Glen Innes Australia **47** 29.42S151.45E
Glen Lyon Australia **46** 31.41S142.06E
Glen Mòr *f.* U.K. **6** 57.15N 4.30W
Glen Moriston U.K. **6** 57.09N 4.50W
Glenns Ferry U.S.A. **54** 42.57N115.18W
Glenrothes U.K. **6** 56.12N 3.10W
Glenroy Australia **42** 17.23S126.01E
Glens Falls *town* U.S.A. **55** 43.19N 73.39W
Glenshee *f.* U.K. **6** 56.45N 3.25W
Glen Spean *f.* U.K. **6** 56.53N 4.40W
Glenwood Oreg. U.S.A. **54** 45.39N123.16W
Glenwood Springs *town* U.S.A. **54** 39.33N107.19W
Glittertind *mtn.* Norway **17** 61.39N 8.33E
Gliwice Poland **15** 50.17N 18.40E
Globe U.S.A. **54** 33.24N110.47W
Głogów Poland **14** 51.40N 16.06E
Glotovo U.S.S.R. **18** 63.25N 49.28E
Gloucester Australia **47** 31.59S151.58E
Gloucester U.K. **5** 51.52N 2.15W
Gloucester U.S.A. **55** 42.41N 70.39W
Gloucestershire *d.* U.K. **5** 51.45N 2.00W
Głubczyce Poland **15** 50.13N 17.49E
Glückstadt W. Germany **14** 53.47N 9.25E
Glusha U.S.S.R. **15** 53.03N 28.55E
Gmünd Austria **14** 48.47N 14.59E
Gnarp Sweden **17** 62.03N 17.16E
Gnesta Sweden **17** 59.03N 17.18E
Gniewkowo Poland **15** 52.24N 18.25E
Gniezno Poland **15** 52.32N 17.32E
Gnjilane Yugo. **13** 42.28N 21.58E
Gnosjö Sweden **17** 57.22N 13.44E
Gnowangerup Australia **43** 33.57S117.58E
Gnuka Australia **43** 31.08S117.24E
Goa *d.* India **28** 15.30N 74.00E
Goageb Namibia **39** 26.45S 17.18E
Goat Fell *mtn.* U.K. **6** 55.37N 5.12W
Goba Mozambique **39** 26.11S 32.08E
Gobabis Namibia **39** 22.28S 18.58E
Gobi *des.* Asia **24** 43.30N103.30E
Goch W. Germany **8** 51.41N 6.09E
Gochas Namibia **39** 24.50S 18.48E
Godalming U.K. **5** 51.11N 0.37W
Godāvari *r.* India **29** 16.40N 82.15E
Godbout Canada **55** 49.20N 67.38W
Goddard Creek *r.* Australia **43** 31.10S124.30E
Goderich Canada **55** 43.45N 81.43W
Goderville France **9** 49.39N 0.22E
Godhavn Greenland **51** 69.20N 53.30W
Godhra India **28** 22.49N 73.40E
Godoy Cruz Argentina **63** 32.55S 68.50W
Gods L. Canada **51** 54.40N 94.20W
Godthåb Greenland **51** 64.10N 51.40W
Goéland, Lac au *l.* Canada **55** 49.47N 76.41W
Goes Neth. **8** 51.30N 3.54E
Gogama Canada **55** 47.35N 81.35W
Gogebic Range *mts.* U.S.A. **55** 46.45N 89.25W
Gogonou Benin **38** 10.50N 2.50E
Gogra *r. see* Ghāghra India **29**
Goiana Brazil **61** 7.30S 35.00W
Goiânia Brazil **61** 16.43S 49.18W
Goiás Brazil **61** 15.57S 50.07W
Goiás *d.* Brazil **61** 12.00S 48.00W
Goito Italy **9** 45.15N 10.40E
Gojō Japan **23** 34.21N135.42E
Gökçeada *i.* Turkey **13** 40.10N 25.51E

ksun Turkey 30 38.03N 36.30E
kteik Burma 29 22.26N 97.00E
kwe Zimbabwe 39 18.14S 28.54E
l Norway 17 60.42N 8.57E
lan Heights mts. Syria 32 32.55N 35.42E
lconda U.S.A. 54 40.57N117.30W
ldap Poland 15 54.19N 22.19E
ld Beach town U.S.A. 54 42.25N124.25W
lden Rep. of Ire. 7 52.30N 7.59W
lden B. New Zealand 48 40.45S172.50E
ldendale U.S.A. 54 45.49N120.50W
lden Ridge town Australia 43 30.51S121.42E
lden Vale f. Rep. of Ire. 7 52.30N 8.07W
ldfield U.S.A. 54 37.42N117.14W
leniów Poland 14 53.36N 14.50E
lets Skalisty mtn. U.S.S.R. 21 56.00N130.40E
lfito Costa Rica 57 8.42N 83.10W
lfo degli Aranci town Italy 12 41.00N 9.38E
l Gol Australia 46 34.10S142.17E
lling Austria 14 47.36N 13.10E
lmud China 24 36.22N 94.55E
lovanevsk U.S.S.R. 15 48.25N 30.30E
lpāyegān Iran 31 33.23N 50.18E
lspie U.K. 6 57.58N 3.58W
ma Zaïre 37 1.37S 29.10E
mbe Nigeria 38 10.17N 11.20E
mbe r. Tanzania 37 4.43S 31.30E
mel U.S.S.R. 15 52.25N 31.00E
mez Palacio Mexico 56 25.39N103.30W
mishān Iran 31 37.04N 54.06E
naïves Haiti 57 19.29N 72.42W
nâve, Golfe de la g. Haiti 57 19.20N 73.00W
nâve, Île de la i. Haiti 57 18.50N 73.00W
nbad-e Kāvūs Iran 31 37.15N 55.11E
nda India 29 27.08N 81.58E
nder Ethiopia 35 12.39N 37.29E
ndia India 29 21.27N 80.12E
ngbo'gyamda China 29 29.56N 93.23E
ngga Shan mtn. China 24 29.30N101.30E
ngola d. Nigeria 38 8.40N 11.30E
ngola r. Nigeria 38 9.30N 12.06E
ngolgon Australia 47 30.22S146.56E
ñi Uruguay 63 33.31S 56.24W
niri Nigeria 38 11.30N 12.15E
nzaga Italy 9 44.57N 10.49E
od Hope, C. of R.S.A. 39 34.21S 18.28E
oding U.S.A. 54 42.56N114.43W
odooga Australia 47 29.08S147.30E
odsprings U.S.A. 54 35.50N115.26W
ole U.K. 4 53.42N 0.52W
olgowi Australia 47 33.59S145.42E
olma Australia 47 32.21S149.20E
oloogong Australia 47 33.37S148.43E
olwa Australia 46 35.31S138.45E
omalling Australia 43 31.19S116.49E
ombalie Australia 47 29.59S145.24E
ondiwindi Australia 47 28.30S150.17E
ongarrie Australia 43 30.03S121.09E
or Neth. 8 52.16N 6.33E
ose L. U.S.A. 54 41.57N120.25W
ppingen W. Germany 14 48.43N 9.39E
rakhpur India 29 26.45N 83.23E
rdon Australia 46 32.05S138.08E
rdon r. Australia 43 34.12S117.00E
rdon Downs town Australia 42 18.43S128.33E
rdonvale Australia 44 17.05S145.47E
ré Chad 34 7.57N 16.31E
re Ethiopia 35 8.08N 35.33E
re New Zealand 48 46.06S168.58E
rgān Iran 31 36.50N 54.29E
rgān r. Iran 31 37.00N 54.00E
ri U.S.S.R. 31 41.59N 44.05E
rinchem Neth. 8 51.50N 4.59E
rizia Italy 12 45.58N 13.37E
rki see Gor'kiy U.S.S.R. 18
r'kiy U.S.S.R. 18 56.20N 44.00E
rkovskoye Vodokhranilishche resr. U.S.S.R.
18 56.49N 43.00E
rlitz E. Germany 14 51.09N 15.00E
rlovka U.S.S.R. 19 48.17N 38.05E
rna Oryakhovitsa Bulgaria 13 43.07N 25.40E
rno Altaysk U.S.S.R. 20 51.59N 85.56E
rno Filinskoye U.S.S.R. 20 60.06N 69.58E
rnyatskiy U.S.S.R. 18 67.30N 64.03E
rodenka U.S.S.R. 15 48.40N 25.30E
rodishche B.S.S.R. U.S.S.R. 15 53.45N
29.45E
rodishche B.S.S.R. U.S.S.R. 15 53.18N
26.00E
rodnitsa U.S.S.R. 15 50.50N 27.19E
rodnya U.S.S.R. 15 51.54N 31.37E
rodok U.S.S.R. 15 49.48N 23.39E
roka P.N.G. 27 6.02S145.22E
roke Australia 46 36.43S141.30E
rokhov U.S.S.R. 15 50.30N 24.46E
rongosa r. Mozambique 39 20.29S 34.36E
rontalo Indonesia 27 0.33N123.05E
rt Rep. of Ire. 7 53.04N 8.49W
ryn r. U.S.S.R. 15 52.08N 27.17E
rzów Wielkopolski Poland 14 52.42N 15.12E
se Japan 23 34.27N135.44E
sford Australia 47 33.25S151.18E
slar W. Germany 14 51.54N 10.25E
spić Yugo. 14 44.34N 15.23E
sport U.K. 5 50.48N 1.08W
ssi Mali 38 15.49N 1.17W
stivar Yugo. 13 41.47N 20.24E
stynin Poland 15 52.26N 19.29E
ta r. Sweden 17 57.42N 11.52E
ta Kanal Sweden 17 58.50N 13.58E
teborg Sweden 17 57.43N 11.58E
teborg och Bohus d. Sweden 17 58.30N
1.30E
temba Japan 23 35.18N138.56E
tene Sweden 17 58.32N 13.29E
tha E. Germany 14 50.57N 10.43E
thenburg see Göteborg Sweden 17
thèye Niger 38 13.51N 1.31E
tland d. Sweden 17 57.30N 18.30E
Gotland i. Sweden 17 57.30N 18.33E
Göttingen W. Germany 14 51.32N 9.57E
Gottwaldov Czech. 15 49.13N 17.41E
Gouda Neth. 8 52.01N 4.43E
Gouin, Résr. Canada 55 48.38N 74.50W
Goulburn Australia 47 34.47S149.43E
Goulburn r. Australia 47 36.08S144.30E
Goulburn Is. Australia 44 11.33S133.26E
Goundam Mali 38 17.27N 3.39W
Gourdon France 11 44.45N 1.22E
Gouré Niger 38 13.59N 10.15E
Gourma-Rharous Mali 38 16.58N 1.50W
Gournay France 9 49.29N 1.44E
Gourock Range mts. Australia 47 35.45S149.25E
Governador Valadares Brazil 59 18.51S 42.00W
Gowanda U.S.A. 55 42.28N 78.57W
Gowd-e Zereh des. Afghan. 31 30.00N 62.00E
Gower pen. U.K. 5 51.37N 4.10W
Goya Argentina 62 29.10S 59.20W
Goyder r. Australia 44 12.38S135.11E
Gozo i. Malta 12 36.03N 14.16E
Graaff Reinet R.S.A. 39 32.15S 24.31E
Gračac Yugo. 14 44.18N 15.51E
Grace, L. Australia 43 33.18S118.15E
Gracias á Dios, Cabo c. Honduras / Nicaragua 57
15.00N 83.10W
Grado Italy 9 45.40N 13.23E
Grado Spain 10 43.23N 6.04W
Grafton Australia 47 29.40S152.56E
Grafton N.Dak. U.S.A. 53 48.28N 97.25W
Grafton W.Va. U.S.A. 55 39.21N 80.03W
Graham, Mt. U.S.A. 54 32.42N109.52W
Graham Land f. Antarctica 64 67.00S 60.00W
Grahamstown R.S.A. 39 33.18S 26.30E
Graiguenamanagh Rep. of Ire. 7 52.33N 6.57W
Grajaú r. Brazil 61 3.41S 44.48W
Grampian d. U.K. 6 57.22N 2.35W
Grampian Mts. U.K. 6 56.55N 4.00W
Grampians mts. Australia 46 37.12S142.34E
Granada Nicaragua 57 11.58N 85.59W
Granada Spain 10 37.10N 3.35W
Granby Canada 55 45.23N 72.44W
Gran Canaria i. Canary Is. 34 28.00N 15.30W
Gran Chaco f. S. America 62 22.00S 60.00W
Grand r. S.Dak. U.S.A. 52 45.40N100.32W
Grand Bahama I. Bahamas 57 26.35N 78.00W
Grand Bassam Ivory Coast 38 5.14N 3.45W
Grand Canyon f. U.S.A. 54 36.10N112.45W
Grand Canyon town U.S.A. 54 36.03N112.09W
Grand Canyon Nat. Park U.S.A. 54
36.15N112.58W
Grand Cayman i. Cayman Is. 57 19.20N 81.30W
Grand Couronne France 9 49.21N 1.00E
Grande r. Bolivia 62 15.10S 64.55W
Grande r. Bahia Brazil 61 11.05S 43.09W
Grande r. Minas Gerais Brazil 62 20.00S 51.00W
Grande, Bahía b. Argentina 63 51.30S 67.30W
Grande, Ilha i. Brazil 59 23.07S 44.16W
Grande Cascapédia Canada 55 48.21N 65.52W
Grande Comore i. Comoros 37 11.35S 43.20E
Grande do Gurupá, Ilha i. Brazil 61 1.00S
51.30W
Grande Prairie town Canada 50 55.10N118.52W
Grand Erg de Bilma des. Niger 38 18.30N
14.00E
Grandes, Salinas f. Argentina 62 29.37S 64.56W
Grandes Bergeronnes Canada 55 48.16N
69.35W
Grand Falls town Nfld. Canada 51 48.57N
55.40W
Grand Falls town N.B. Canada 55 46.55N 67.45W
Grand Forks U.S.A. 53 47.57N 97.05W
Grand Fougeray France 9 47.44N 1.44W
Grand Island town U.S.A. 52 40.56N 98.21W
Grand Junction U.S.A. 54 39.05N108.33W
Grand L. N.B. Canada 55 45.38N 67.38W
Grand L. U.S.A. 55 45.15N 67.50W
Grand Lahou Ivory Coast 38 5.09N 5.01W
Grand Manan I. Canada 55 44.38N 66.50W
Grand Marais U.S.A. 53 47.55N 90.15W
Grand' Mère Canada 55 46.37N 72.41W
Grândola Portugal 10 38.10N 8.34W
Grand Rapids town Canada 51 53.08N 99.20W
Grand Rapids town Mich. U.S.A. 55 42.57N
85.40W
Grand St. Bernard, Col du pass Italy / Switz. 9
45.52N 7.11E
Grand Teton mtn. U.S.A. 54 43.44N110.48W
Grand Teton Nat. Park U.S.A. 54
43.30N110.37W
Grand Traverse B. U.S.A. 55 45.02N 85.30W
Grand Valley town U.S.A. 54 39.27N108.03W
Grandville U.S.A. 55 42.54N 85.48W
Grangemouth U.K. 6 56.01N 3.44W
Granger U.S.A. 54 41.35N109.58W
Grängesberg Sweden 17 60.05N 14.59E
Grangeville U.S.A. 54 45.56N116.07W
Granite Peak town Australia 42 25.38S121.21E
Granite Peak mtn. U.S.A. 52 45.10N109.50W
Granity New Zealand 48 41.38S171.51E
Granja Brazil 61 3.06S 40.50W
Gränna Sweden 17 58.01N 14.28E
Granollers Spain 10 41.37N 2.18E
Granön Sweden 16 64.15N 19.19E
Gran Paradiso mtn. Italy 9 45.31N 7.15E
Grant Mich. U.S.A. 55 43.20N 85.49W
Grantham U.K. 4 52.55N 0.39W
Grantown-on-Spey U.K. 6 57.20N 3.38W
Grant Range mts. U.S.A. 54 38.25N115.30W
Grants U.S.A. 54 35.09N107.52W
Grants Pass town U.S.A. 54 42.26N123.19W
Grantsville U.S.A. 55 38.55N 81.07W
Granville France 9 48.50N 1.35W
Gras, Lac de l. Canada 50 64.30N110.30W
Graskop R.S.A. 39 24.55S 30.50E
Grasse France 11 43.40N 6.56E
Grasset, L. Canada 55 49.53N 78.07W
Grass Patch Australia 43 33.14S121.43E
Grass Valley town Calif. U.S.A. 54
39.13N121.04W
Grass Valley town Oreg. U.S.A. 54
45.22N120.47W
Grave Neth. 8 51.45N 5.45E
Grave, Pointe de c. France 11 45.35N 1.04W
Gravenhurst Canada 55 44.55N 79.22W
Gravesend Australia 47 29.35S150.20E
Gravesend U.K. 5 51.27N 0.24E
Gray France 11 47.27N 5.35E
Grayling U.S.A. 55 44.40N 84.43W
Grays U.K. 5 51.29N 0.20E
Graz Austria 14 47.05N 15.22E
Grdelica Yugo. 13 42.54N 22.04E
Great Abaco I. Bahamas 57 26.30N 77.00W
Great Artesian Basin f. Australia 44
26.30S143.02E
Great Australian Bight Australia 43
33.10S129.30E
Great Barrier I. New Zealand 48 36.15S175.30E
Great Barrier Reef f. Australia 44 16.30S146.30E
Great Basin f. U.S.A. 54 40.35N116.00W
Great Bear L. Canada 50 66.00N120.00W
Great Bend town U.S.A. 52 38.22N 98.47W
Great Bitter L. see Murrah al Kubrá, Al Buḩayrah
al h5ayrah al Egypt 32
Great Blasket I. Rep. of Ire. 7 52.05N 10.32W
Great Coco i. Burma 29 14.10N 93.25E
Great Divide Basin f. U.S.A. 54 42.00N108.10W
Great Dividing Range mts. Australia 47
29.00S152.00E
Great Driffield U.K. 4 54.01N 0.26W
Greater Antilles is. C. America 57 17.00N
70.00W
Greater London d. U.K. 5 51.31N 0.06W
Greater Manchester d. U.K. 4 53.30N 2.18W
Great Exuma i. Bahamas 57 23.00N 76.00W
Great Falls town U.S.A. 54 47.30N111.17W
Great Inagua I. Bahamas 57 21.00N 73.20W
Great Indian Desert see Thar Desert
India / Pakistan 28
Great Karoo f. R.S.A. 39 32.40S 22.20E
Great Kei r. R.S.A. 39 32.39S 28.23E
Great L. Australia 45 41.50S146.43E
Great Malvern U.K. 5 52.07N 2.19W
Great Namaland f. Namibia 39 25.30S 17.20E
Great Nicobar i. India 29 7.00N 93.50E
Great North East Channel P.N.G. / Australia 44
9.00S144.00E
Great Ouse r. U.K. 4 52.47N 0.23E
Great Ruaha r. Tanzania 37 7.55S 37.52E
Great Salt L. U.S.A. 54 41.10N112.30W
Great Salt Lake Desert U.S.A. 54
40.40N113.30W
Great Sandy Desert Australia 42 20.30S123.35E
Great Sandy Desert see An Nafūd des. Saudi
Arabia 30
Great Slave L. Canada 50 61.30N114.20W
Great Victoria Desert Australia 43
29.00S127.30E
Great Whernside mtn. U.K. 4 54.09N 1.59W
Great Yarmouth U.K. 5 52.40N 1.45E
Great Zimbabwe ruins Zimbabwe 39 20.30S
30.30E
Gréboun, Mont mtn. Niger 38 20.01N 8.35E
Gredos, Sierra de mts. Spain 10 40.18N 5.20W
Greece Europe 13 39.00N 22.00E
Greeley U.S.A. 52 40.25N104.42W
Green r. U.S.A. 54 38.11N109.53W
Green Bay town U.S.A. 53 44.32N 88.00W
Green Bluff f. Australia 47 30.10S153.14E
Greenbushes Australia 43 33.50S116.00E
Greencastle Ind. U.S.A. 55 39.39N 86.51W
Greene U.S.A. 55 42.20N 75.46W
Greenhills Australia 43 31.58S117.01E
Greening Canada 55 48.07N 74.55W
Greenland N. America 51 68.00N 45.00W
Greenlaw U.K. 6 55.43N 2.28W
Greenly I. Australia 46 34.39S134.50E
Greenock U.K. 6 55.57N 4.45W
Greenore Pt. Rep. of Ire. 7 52.14N 6.19W
Green River town Utah U.S.A. 54
38.59N110.10W
Green River town Wyo. U.S.A. 54
41.32N109.28W
Greensboro N.C. U.S.A. 53 36.03N 79.50W
Greensburg Ind. U.S.A. 55 39.20N 85.29W
Greenville Liberia 34 5.01N 9.03W
Greenville Ala. U.S.A. 53 31.50N 86.40W
Greenville Mich. U.S.A. 55 43.11N 85.13W
Greenville Miss. U.S.A. 53 33.23N 91.03W
Greenville S.C. U.S.A. 53 34.52N 82.25W
Greenville Tex. U.S.A. 53 33.09N 96.07W
Greenwood Miss. U.S.A. 53 33.31N 90.10W
Gregory r. Australia 44 17.53S139.17E
Gregory, L. S.A. Australia 46 28.55S139.00E
Gregory, L. W.A. Australia 42 20.10S127.20E
Gregory Range mts. Australia 44 19.00S143.05E
Greifswald E. Germany 14 54.06N 13.24E
Gremikha U.S.S.R. 18 68.03N 39.38E
Grenå Denmark 17 56.25N 10.53E
Grenada C. America 60 12.07N 61.40W
Grenada i. Windward Is. 57 12.15N 61.45W
Grenade France 11 43.47N 1.10E
Grenoble France 11 45.11N 5.43E
Grenville, C. Australia 44 12.00S143.13E
Gretna U.K. 6 55.00N 3.04W
Greven W. Germany 8 52.07N 7.38E
Grevenbroich W. Germany 8 51.07N 6.33E
Grevesmühlen E. Germany 14 53.51N 11.10E
Grey r. New Zealand 48 42.28S171.13E
Grey, C. Australia 44 13.00S136.40E
Greybull U.S.A. 54 44.30N108.03W
Greymouth New Zealand 48 42.28S171.12E
Grey Range mts. Australia 45 27.00S143.35E
Greystones Rep. of Ire. 7 53.09N 6.04W
Greytown R.S.A. 39 29.04S 30.36E
Griffin U.S.A. 53 33.15N 84.17W
Griffith Australia 47 34.18S146.04E
Grignan France 11 44.25N 4.54E
Grigoriopol U.S.S.R. 15 47.08N 29.18E
Grim, C. Australia 45 40.45S144.45E
Grimsby U.K. 4 53.35N 0.05W
Grimstad Norway 17 58.20N 8.36E
Grimsvötn mtn. Iceland 16 64.30N 17.10W
Grindavík Iceland 16 63.50N 22.27W
Grindsted Denmark 17 55.45N 8.56E
Griqualand East f. R.S.A. 39 30.40S 29.10E
Griqualand West f. R.S.A. 39 28.50S 23.30E
Griva U.S.S.R. 18 60.35N 50.58E
Grobina U.S.S.R. 17 56.33N 21.10E
Groblershoop R.S.A. 39 28.55S 20.59E
Grodno U.S.S.R. 15 53.40N 23.50E
Grodzisk Poland 14 52.14N 16.22E
Grodzyanka U.S.S.R. 15 53.30N 28.41E
Groenlo Neth. 8 52.02N 6.36E
Groix, Île de i. France 11 47.38N 3.26W
Gronau W. Germany 8 52.14N 7.02E
Grong Norway 16 64.27N 12.19E
Groningen Neth. 8 53.13N 6.35E
Groningen d. Neth. 8 53.15N 6.45E
Groot r. C.P. r. R.S.A. 39 33.58S 25.03E
Groote Eylandt i. Australia 44 14.00S136.40E
Grootfontein Namibia 39 19.32S 18.07E
Groot Karasberge mts. Namibia 39 27.20S
18.50E
Grootlaagte r. Botswana 39 20.58S 21.42E
Groot Swartberge mts. R.S.A. 39 33.20S 22.00E
Grossenbrode W. Germany 14 54.23N 11.07E
Grossenhain E. Germany 14 51.17N 13.31E
Grosseto Italy 12 42.46N 11.08E
Gross Glockner mtn. Austria 14 47.05N 12.50E
Grote Nete r. Belgium 8 51.07N 4.20E
Groundhog r. Canada 55 49.43N 81.58W
Grouse Creek town U.S.A. 54 41.22N113.53W
Grover City U.S.A. 54 35.07N120.37W
Groznyy U.S.S.R. 19 43.21N 45.42E
Grudziądz Poland 15 53.29N 18.45E
Grumeti r. Tanzania 37 2.05S 33.45E
Grünau Namibia 39 27.44S 18.18E
Grundarfjördhur town Iceland 16 64.55N 23.20W
Grungedal Norway 17 59.44N 7.43E
Gruzinskaya S.S.R. d. U.S.S.R. 19 42.00N
43.30E
Gryazovets U.S.S.R. 18 58.52N 40.12E
Gryfice Poland 14 53.56N 15.12E
Guachipas Argentina 62 25.31S 65.31W
Guacuí Brazil 59 20.44S 41.40W
Guadalajara Mexico 56 20.30N103.20W
Guadalajara Spain 10 40.37N 3.10W
Guadalcanal i. Solomon Is. 40 9.32S160.12E
Guadalete r. Spain 10 36.37N 6.15W
Guadalmena r. Spain 10 38.00N 3.50W
Guadalquivir r. Spain 10 36.50N 6.20W
Guadalupe Mexico 56 25.41N100.15W
Guadalupe, Isla de i. Mexico 52 29.00N118.16W
Guadalupe, Sierra de mts. Spain 10 39.30N
5.25W
Guadarrama r. Spain 10 39.55N 4.10W
Guadarrama, Sierra de mts. Spain 10 41.00N
3.50W
Guadeloupe i. Leeward Is. 57 16.20N 61.40W
Guadiana r. Portugal 10 37.10N 7.36W
Guadix Spain 10 37.19N 3.08W
Guafo, Golfo de g. Chile 63 43.35S 74.15W
Guainía r. Colombia 60 2.01N 67.07W
Guaíra Falls see Sete Quedas, Salto das f. Brazil
62
Guajará Mirim Brazil 60 10.48S 65.22W
Guajira, Península de la pen. Colombia 60
12.00N 72.00W
Gualeguay Argentina 63 33.10S 59.20W
Gualeguay r. Argentina 63 33.18S 59.38W
Gualeguaychu Argentina 63 33.00S 58.30W
Guam i. Mariana Is. 40 13.30N144.40E
Guamal Colombia 60 9.10N 74.15W
Guanajuato Mexico 56 21.00N101.16W
Guanajuato d. Mexico 56 21.00N101.00W
Guanare Venezuela 60 9.04N 69.45W
Guanarito Venezuela 60 8.43N 69.12W
Guane Cuba 57 22.13N 84.07W
Guangdong d. China 25 23.00N113.00E
Guanghua China 25 32.30N111.50E
Guangxi Zhuangzu d. China 25 23.50N109.00E
Guangyuan China 29 32.26N105.52E
Guangzhou China 25 23.20N113.30E
Guanling China 29 25.57N105.38E
Guantánamo Cuba 57 20.09N 75.14W
Guan Xian Sichuan China 29 30.59N103.40E
Guaporé r. Bolivia / Brazil 62 12.00S 65.15W
Guaqui Bolivia 62 16.35S 68.51W
Guarabira Brazil 61 6.46S 35.25W
Guarapuava Brazil 59 25.22S 51.28W
Guaratinguetá Brazil 59 22.49S 45.09W
Guarda Portugal 10 40.32N 7.17W
Guardavalle Italy 13 38.30N 16.30E
Guardo Spain 10 42.47N 4.50W
Guareim r. Uruguay see Quarí r. Brazil 63
Guasipati Venezuela 60 7.28N 61.54W
Guastalla Italy 9 44.55N 10.39E
Guatemala C. America 57 15.40N 90.00W
Guatemala town Guatemala 56 14.38N 90.22W
Guatire Venezuela 60 10.28N 66.32W
Guaviare r. Colombia 60 4.00N 67.35W
Guaxupé Brazil 59 21.17S 46.44W
Guayaquil Ecuador 60 2.13S 79.54W
Guayaquil, Golfo de g. Ecuador 60 3.00S
80.35W
Guaymallén Argentina 63 32.54S 68.47W
Guaymas Mexico 56 27.56N110.54W
Guayquiraró r. Argentina 63 30.25S 59.36W
Gubakha U.S.S.R. 18 58.55N 57.30E
Gubeikou China 25 40.41N117.09E
Gubin Poland 14 51.59N 14.42E
Gubio Nigeria 38 12.31N 12.44E
Guchab Namibia 39 19.40S 17.47E
Gúdar, Sierra de mts. Spain 10 40.27N 0.42W
Gudbrandsdalen f. Norway 17 61.30N 10.00E
Gudvangen Norway 17 60.52N 6.50E
Guecho Spain 10 43.21N 3.01W
Guelph Canada 55 43.33N 80.15W
Guémené-sur-Scorff France 11 48.04N 3.13W
Guéret France 11 46.10N 1.52E
Guernica Spain 10 43.19N 2.40W
Guernsey i. U.K. 5 49.27N 2.35W
Guerra Mozambique 37 13.05S 35.12E
Guerrero d. Mexico 56 18.00N100.00W
Guguan i. Mariana Is. 27 17.20N145.51E
Guiana S. America 61 3.40N 53.00W
Guiana Highlands S. America 60 4.00N 59.00W
Guichón Uruguay 63 32.21S 57.12W
Guildford Australia 43 31.55S115.55E
Guildford U.K. 5 51.14N 0.35W
Guilin China 25 25.21N110.11E
Guimarães Brazil 61 2.08S 44.36W
Guimarães Portugal 10 41.27N 8.18W
Guinan China 24 35.20N100.50E
Guinea Africa 34 10.30N 11.30W
Guinea, G. of Africa 38 3.00N 3.00E
Guinea Bissau Africa 34 11.30N 15.00W
Güines Cuba 57 22.50N 82.02W
Guingamp France 11 48.34N 3.09W
Guiping China 25 23.20N110.04E
Güiria Venezuela 60 10.37N 62.21W
Guiscard France 8 49.39N 3.01E
Guiscard France 9 49.39N 3.03E
Guise France 9 49.54N 3.38E
Guiuan Phil. 27 11.02N125.44E
Guiyang China 24 26.35N106.40E
Guizhou d. China 24 27.00N106.30E
Gujarat d. India 28 22.45N 71.30E
Gujrānwāla Pakistan 28 32.06N 74.11E
Gujrāt Pakistan 28 32.35N 74.06E
Gulargambone Australia 47 31.21S148.32E
Gulbarga India 28 17.22N 76.47E
Gulfport U.S.A. 53 30.21N 89.08W
Gulgong Australia 47 32.20S149.49E
Gulma Nigeria 38 12.41N 4.24E
Gulshad U.S.S.R. 24 46.37N 74.22E
Gulu Uganda 37 2.46N 32.21E
Guluguba Australia 44 26.16S150.03E
Gulwe Tanzania 37 6.27S 36.27E
Gumel Nigeria 38 12.39N 9.23E
Gummersbach W. Germany 8 51.03N 7.32E
Gümüşhane Turkey 30 40.26N 39.26E
Guna India 28 24.39N 77.18E
Gunbar Australia 47 34.04S145.25E
Gundagai Australia 47 35.07S148.05E
Gundlupet India 28 11.48N 76.41E
Gungu Zaïre 36 5.43S 19.20E
Gunnedah Australia 47 30.59S150.15E
Gunnison r. U.S.A. 54 39.03N108.35W
Gunnison Utah U.S.A. 54 39.09N111.49W
Guntersville L. U.S.A. 53 34.35N 86.00W
Guntūr India 29 16.20N 80.27E
Gunungsitoli Indonesia 26 1.17N 97.37E
Günzburg W. Germany 14 48.27N 10.16E
Gura Portiţei f. Romania 15 44.40N 29.00E
Gurgueia r. Brazil 61 6.45S 43.35W
Gursköy i. Norway 16 62.16N 5.42E
Gurué Mozambique 37 15.30S 36.58E
Gürün Turkey 30 38.44N 37.15E
Gurupá Brazil 61 1.25S 51.39W
Gurupi r. Brazil 61 1.13S 46.06W
Guruve Zimbabwe 37 16.42S 30.40E
Guryev U.S.S.R. 19 47.08N 51.59E
Gusau Nigeria 38 12.12N 6.40E
Gusev U.S.S.R. 15 54.32N 22.12E
Guspini Italy 12 39.32N 8.38E
Gustav Holm, Kap c. Greenland 51 67.00N
34.00W
Güstrow E. Germany 14 53.48N 12.11E
Gütersloh W. Germany 14 51.54N 8.22E
Guyana S. America 60 4.40N 59.00W
Guyra Australia 47 30.14S151.40E
Guzhen Anhui China 25 33.19N117.19E
Gwa Burma 29 17.36N 94.35E
Gwabegar Australia 47 30.34S149.00E
Gwadabawa Nigeria 38 13.23N 5.15E
Gwādar Pakistan 28 25.09N 62.21E
Gwagwada Nigeria 38 10.15N 7.15E
Gwai Zimbabwe 39 19.15S 27.42E
Gwai r. Zimbabwe 39 17.59S 26.55E
Gwalior India 29 26.12N 78.09E
Gwanda Zimbabwe 39 20.59S 29.00E
Gwasero Nigeria 38 9.30N 8.30E
Gweebarra B. Rep. of Ire. 7 54.52N 8.28W
Gwent d. U.K. 5 51.44N 3.00W
Gweru Zimbabwe 39 19.25S 29.50E
Gwydir r. Australia 47 29.35S148.45E
Gwynedd d. U.K. 4 53.00N 4.00W
Gyangzê China 29 29.00N 89.40E
Gydanskiy Poluostrov pen. U.S.S.R. 20 70.00N
78.30E
Gympie Australia 44 26.11S152.40E
Gyöngyös Hungary 15 47.47N 19.56E
Györ Hungary 15 47.41N 17.40E
Gypsumville Canada 51 51.45N 98.35W

H

Haan W. Germany 8 51.10N 7.02E
Haapajärvi Finland 16 63.45N 25.20E
Haapamäki Finland 16 62.15N 24.28E
Haapavesi Finland 16 64.08N 25.22E
Haapsalu U.S.S.R. 17 58.56N 23.33E
Hā Arava r. Israel / Jordan 32 30.30N 35.10E
Haarlem Neth. 8 52.22N 4.38E
Haarlem R.S.A. 39 33.46S 23.28E
Habahe China 24 47.53N 86.12E
Habarūt S. Yemen 28 17.18N 52.44E
Habaswein Kenya 37 1.06N 39.26E
Habay-la-Neuve Belgium 8 49.45N 5.38E
Habikino Japan 23 34.33N135.37E
Habo Sweden 17 57.55N 14.04E
Hachinohe Japan 25 40.30N141.30E
Hachiōji Japan 23 35.39N139.20E

Hack, Mt. Australia 46 30.44S138.45E
Hadano Japan 23 35.22N139.14E
Ḥadd, Ra's al *c.* Oman 31 22.32N 59.49E
Haddington U.K. 6 55.57N 2.47W
Hadejia Nigeria 38 12.30N 10.03E
Hadejia *r.* Nigeria 38 12.47N 10.44E
Hadera Israel 32 32.26N 34.55E
Haderslev Denmark 17 55.15N 9.30E
Ḥaḍramawt *f.* S. Yemen 35 16.30N 49.30E
Hadsten Denmark 17 56.20N 10.03E
Hadsund Denmark 17 56.43N 10.07E
Haedo, Cuchilla de *mts.* Uruguay 63 31.50S 56.10W
Haegeland Norway 17 58.15N 7.50E
Haeju N. Korea 25 38.04N125.40E
Ḥafar al Bāṭin Saudi Arabia 31 28.28N 46.00E
Hafnarfjördhur *town* Iceland 16 64.04N 21.58W
Haft Gel Iran 31 31.28N 49.35E
Hagen W. Germany 8 51.22N 7.27E
Hagerstown U.S.A. 55 39.39N 77.43W
Hagfors Sweden 17 60.02N 13.42E
Ha Giang Vietnam 26 22.50N105.01E
Hags Head Rep. of Ire. 7 52.56N 9.29W
Hague, Cap de la *c.* France 9 49.44N 1.56W
Haguenau France 11 48.49N 7.47E
Hai Duong Vietnam 26 20.56N106.21E
Haifa *see* Hefa Israel 32
Haikou China 25 20.05N110.25E
Ḥā'il Saudi Arabia 30 27.31N 41.45E
Hailar China 25 49.15N119.41E
Hailsham U.K. 5 50.52N 0.17E
Hailun China 25 47.29N126.58E
Hailuoto *i.* Finland 16 65.02N 24.42E
Hainan *i.* China 25 18.30N109.40E
Hainaut *d.* Belgium 8 50.30N 3.45E
Haines Alas. U.S.A. 50 59.11N135.23W
Haines Oreg. U.S.A. 54 44.55N117.56W
Hai Phòng Vietnam 26 20.48N106.40E
Haiti C. America 57 19.00N 73.00W
Hajdúböszörmény Hungary 15 47.41N 21.30E
Hajdúszoboszló Hungary 15 47.27N 21.24E
Hakkâri Turkey 31 37.36N 43.45E
Hakodate Japan 25 41.46N140.44E
Ḥalab Syria 30 36.14N 37.10E
Ḥalabjah Iraq 31 35.10N 45.59E
Ḥalbā Lebanon 32 34.34N 36.05E
Halberstadt E. Germany 14 51.54N 11.04E
Halden Norway 17 59.09N 11.23E
Half Assini Ghana 38 5.04N 2.53W
Haliburton Canada 55 45.03N 78.03W
Haliburton Highlands Canada 55 45.03N 78.03W
Halifax Canada 51 44.38N 63.35W
Halifax U.K. 4 53.43N 1.51W
Halifax B. Australia 44 18.50S146.30E
Halīl *r.* Iran 28 27.35N 58.44E
Halkett, C. U.S.A. 50 71.00N152.00W
Halkirk U.K. 6 58.30N 3.30W
Halladale *r.* U.K. 6 58.34N 3.54W
Halland *d.* Sweden 17 56.45N 13.00E
Hall B. Australia 46 34.00S135.03E
Halle Belgium 8 50.45N 4.14E
Halle E. Germany 14 51.28N 11.58E
Halle *d.* E. Germany 14 51.30N 11.45E
Hällefors Sweden 17 59.47N 14.30E
Hallingdal *f.* Norway 17 60.30N 9.00E
Hall Lake *town* Canada 51 68.40N 81.30W
Hällnäs Sweden 16 64.19N 19.38E
Hall Pen. Canada 51 63.30N 66.00W
Hallsberg Sweden 17 59.04N 15.07E
Hall's Creek *town* Australia 42 18.17S127.44E
Hallstavik Sweden 17 60.03N 18.36E
Hallstead U.S.A. 55 41.58N 75.45W
Halmahera *i.* Indonesia 27 0.45N128.00E
Halmstad Sweden 17 56.39N 12.50E
Halsa Norway 16 63.03N 8.14E
Hälsingborg Sweden 17 56.03N 12.42E
Haltern W. Germany 8 51.45N 7.10E
Haltia Tunturi *mtn.* Finland 16 69.17N 21.21E
Haltwhistle U.K. 4 54.58N 2.27W
Ham France 9 49.45N 3.04E
Ḥamad, Wādī al *r.* Saudi Arabia 30 25.49N 36.37E
Hamadān Iran 31 34.47N 48.33E
Ḥamāh Syria 32 35.09N 36.44E
Hamakita Japan 23 34.48N137.47E
Hamamatsu Japan 23 34.42N137.44E
Hamar Norway 17 60.48N 11.06E
Hamaröy Norway 16 68.05N 15.40E
Ḥamāṭah, Jabal *mtn.* Egypt 30 24.11N 35.01E
Hamborn W. Germany 8 51.29N 6.46E
Hamburg R.S.A. 39 33.17S 27.27E
Hamburg W. Germany 14 53.33N 10.00E
Häme *d.* Finland 17 61.20N 24.30E
Hämeenlinna Finland 17 61.00N 24.27E
Hamelin B. Australia 43 34.10S115.00E
Hameln W. Germany 14 52.06N 9.21E
Hamersley Range *mts.* Australia 42 22.00S118.00E
Hamhŭng N. Korea 25 39.54N127.35E
Hami China 24 42.40N 93.30E
Hamilton Australia 46 37.45S142.04E
Hamilton *r.* Australia 45 27.12S135.28E
Hamilton Canada 55 43.15N 79.51W
Hamilton New Zealand 48 37.46S175.18E
Hamilton U.K. 6 55.46N 4.10W
Hamilton Mont. U.S.A. 54 46.15N114.09W
Hamilton Ohio U.S.A. 55 39.23N 84.33W
Hamley Bridge *town* Australia 46 34.21S138.41E
Hamm W. Germany 8 51.40N 7.49E
Ḥammār, Hawr al *l.* Iraq 31 30.50N 47.00E
Hammerdal Sweden 16 63.35N 15.20E
Hammerfest Norway 16 70.40N 23.42E
Hammond Australia 46 32.33S138.20E
Hammond N.Y. U.S.A. 55 44.27N 75.42W
Hamoir Belgium 8 50.25N 5.32E
Hampshire *d.* U.K. 5 51.03N 1.20W
Ḥamrīn, Jabal *mts.* Iraq 31 34.40N 44.10E
Hāmūn-e Jaz Mūrīān *l.* Iran 28 27.20N 58.55E
Hanang *mtn.* Tanzania 37 4.30S 35.21E
Hancheng China 25 35.28N110.29E
Hancock Mich. U.S.A. 55 47.08N 88.34W
Handa Japan 23 34.53N136.56E
Handan China 25 36.35N114.29E
Handeni Tanzania 37 5.25S 38.04E
Hando Somali Rep. 35 10.39N 51.08E
HaNegev *des.* Israel 32 30.42N 34.55E
Hanford U.S.A. 54 36.20N119.39W
Hanggin Houqi China 24 40.52N107.04E
Hangö Finland 17 59.50N 22.57E
Hangzhou China 25 30.10N120.07E
Hankey R.S.A. 39 33.50S 24.52E
Hanksville U.S.A. 54 38.21N110.44W
Hānle Jammu & Kashmir 29 32.48N 79.00E
Hanmer Springs *town* New Zealand 48 42.31S172.50E
Hann, Mt. Australia 42 15.55S125.57E
Hanna Canada 50 51.38N111.54W
Hannah B. Canada 55 51.05N 79.45W
Hannibal Mo. U.S.A. 53 39.41N 91.25W
Hannover W. Germany 14 52.23N 9.44E
Hannut Belgium 8 50.40N 5.05E
Hanöbukten *b.* Sweden 17 55.45N 14.30E
Hà Nôi Vietnam 26 21.01N105.53E
Hanoi *see* Hà Nôi Vietnam 26
Hanover Canada 55 44.09N 81.02W
Hanover R.S.A. 39 31.04S 24.25E
Hanover Penn. U.S.A. 55 39.48N 76.59W
Hanover, Isla *i.* Chile 63 50.57S 74.40W
Han Pijesak Yugo. 13 44.04N 18.59E
Han Shui *r.* China 25 30.45N114.24E
Hanson, L. Australia 46 31.02S136.13E
Hantengri Feng *mtn.* China 24 42.09N 80.12E
Hanzhong China 29 33.10N107.02E
Haparanda Sweden 16 65.50N 24.10E
Hapsu N. Korea 25 41.12N128.48E
Ḥaql Saudi Arabia 32 29.14N 34.56E
Ḥaraḍ Saudi Arabia 31 24.12N 49.08E
Harare Zimbabwe 39 17.49S 31.04E
Har-Ayrag Mongolia 25 45.42N109.14E
Harbin China 25 45.45N126.41E
Harbour Grace *town* Canada 51 47.42N 53.13W
Harburg W. Germany 14 53.27N 9.58E
Hardangerfjorden *est.* Norway 17 60.10N 6.00E
Hardangerjökulen *mtn.* Norway 17 60.33N 7.26E
Hardanger Vidda *f.* Norway 17 60.20N 7.30E
Hardenberg Neth. 8 52.36N 6.40E
Harderwijk Neth. 8 52.21N 5.37E
Harding R.S.A. 39 30.34S 29.52E
Hardman U.S.A. 54 45.10N119.40W
Hardwār India 29 29.58N 78.10E
Hardwicke B. Australia 46 34.52S137.10E
Haren W. Germany 8 52.48N 7.15E
Hārer Ethiopia 35 9.20N 42.10E
Harfleur France 9 49.30N 0.12E
Hargeysa Somali Rep. 35 9.31N 44.02E
Har Hu *l.* China 24 38.20N 97.40E
Hari *r.* Indonesia 26 1.00S104.15E
Harīrūd *r.* Afghan. 28 35.42N 61.12E
Harlech U.K. 4 52.52N 4.08W
Harlem U.S.A. 54 48.32N108.47W
Harlingen Neth. 8 53.10N 5.25E
Harlow U.K. 5 51.47N 0.08E
Harlowton U.S.A. 54 46.26N109.50W
Harney Basin *f.* U.S.A. 54 43.15N120.40W
Harney L. U.S.A. 54 43.14N119.07W
Härnösand Sweden 16 62.37N 17.55E
Har Nuur *l.* Mongolia 24 48.00N 93.25E
Harricana *r.* Canada 55 51.10N 79.45W
Harris *i.* U.K. 6 57.50N 6.55W
Harris, L. Australia 45 31.08S135.14E
Harris, Sd. of U.K. 6 57.43N 7.05W
Harrisburg Oreg. U.S.A. 54 44.16N123.10W
Harrisburg Penn. U.S.A. 55 40.16N 76.52W
Harrismith Australia 43 32.55S117.50E
Harrismith R.S.A. 39 28.15S 29.07E
Harrison, C. Canada 51 55.00N 58.00W
Harrogate U.K. 4 53.59N 1.32W
Harrow U.K. 5 51.35N 0.21W
Harstad Norway 16 68.48N 16.30E
Hart, L. Australia 46 31.08S136.24E
Hartford U.S.A. 55 41.45N 72.42W
Hartland Canada 55 46.18N 67.31W
Hartland U.K. 5 50.59N 4.29W
Hartland Pt. U.K. 5 51.01N 4.32W
Hartlepool U.K. 4 54.42N 1.11W
Hartola Finland 17 61.35N 26.01E
Har Us Nuur *l.* Mongolia 24 48.10N 92.10E
Hārūt *r.* Afghan. 31 31.36N 61.12E
Harvey Australia 43 33.06S115.50E
Harwich U.K. 5 51.56N 1.18E
Haryana *d.* India 28 29.15N 76.00E
Ḥasā, Wādī al *r.* Jordan 32 31.01N 35.29E
Hasa Oasis *see* Aḥsā', Wāḥat al *oasis* Saudi Arabia 31
Hase *r.* W. Germany 8 52.42N 7.17E
Haselünne W. Germany 8 52.40N 7.30E
Hasenkamp Argentina 63 31.30S 59.50W
Hashtrūd Iran 31 37.29N 47.05E
Hashimoto Japan 23 34.19N135.37E
Haslemere U.K. 5 51.05N 0.41W
Hasselt Belgium 8 50.56N 5.20E
Hassi Messaoud Algeria 34 31.43N 6.03E
Hässleholm Sweden 17 56.09N 13.46E
Hastings New Zealand 48 39.39S176.52E
Hastings U.K. 5 50.51N 0.36E
Hastings Nebr. U.S.A. 52 40.37N 98.22W
Hastings Range *mts.* Australia 47 31.14S152.00E
Hatches Creek *town* Australia 44 20.56S135.12E
Hatfield Australia 46 33.53S143.47E
Hatfield U.K. 5 51.46N 0.13W
Ha Tinh Vietnam 26 18.21N105.55E
Hattah Australia 46 34.52S142.23E
Hattem Neth. 8 52.29N 6.06E
Hatteras, C. U.S.A. 53 35.14N 75.31W
Hattiesburg U.S.A. 53 31.25N 89.19W
Hattingen W. Germany 8 51.24N 7.09E
Hatton U.S.A. 54 46.46N118.49W
Hatvan Hungary 15 47.40N 19.41E
Hauge Norway 17 58.18N 6.15E
Haugesund Norway 17 59.25N 5.18E
Haugsdorf Austria 14 48.42N 16.05E
Hauraki G. New Zealand 48 36.30S175.00E
Haut Atlas *mts.* Morocco 34 32.00N 5.50W
Haut-Bassins *d.* Burkina Faso 38 10.45N 3.45W
Haute Maurice Prov. Park Canada 55 48.35N 74.21W
Haute-Normandie *d.* France 9 49.30N 1.00E
Hauterive Canada 55 49.11N 68.16W
Hautmont France 8 50.16N 3.52E
Haut Zaïre *d.* Zaïre 37 2.00N 27.00E
Havana *see* La Habana Cuba 57
Havant U.K. 5 50.51N 0.59W
Havel *r.* E. Germany 14 52.51N 11.57E
Havelange Belgium 8 50.23N 5.14E
Havelberg E. Germany 14 52.50N 12.04E
Havelock New Zealand 48 41.17S173.46E
Haverfordwest U.K. 5 51.48N 4.59W
Haverhill U.K. 5 52.06N 0.27E
Havlíčkuv Brod Czech. 14 49.38N 15.35E
Havre U.S.A. 54 48.33N109.41W
Hawaii *d.* U.S.A. 52 21.00N156.00W
Hawaii *i.* Hawaii U.S.A. 52 19.30N155.30W
Hawaiian Is. U.S.A. 52 21.00N157.00W
Hawdon, L. Australia 46 37.09S139.54E
Hawea, L. New Zealand 48 44.30S169.15E
Hawera New Zealand 48 39.35S174.19E
Hawick U.K. 6 55.25N 2.47W
Hawke, C. Australia 47 32.12S152.33E
Hawke B. New Zealand 48 39.18S177.15E
Hawker Australia 46 31.53S138.25E
Hawkers Gate Australia 46 29.46S141.00E
Hawke's Bay *d.* New Zealand 48 39.40S176.35E
Hawkwood Australia 44 25.46S150.48E
Ḥawrān, Wādī *r.* Iraq 30 33.57N 42.35E
Ḥawsh 'Īsá Egypt 32 30.55N 30.17E
Hawthorne U.S.A. 54 38.32N118.38W
Hay Australia 47 34.31S144.31E
Hay *r.* Australia 44 25.00S138.00E
Haya *r.* Japan 23 35.30N138.26E
Hayange France 11 49.20N 6.02E
Hayden U.S.A. 54 33.00N110.47W
Hayes *r.* Canada 51 57.00N 92.30W
Hay-on-Wye U.K. 5 52.04N 3.09W
Hay River *town* Canada 50 60.51N115.42W
Haywards Heath *f.* U.K. 5 51.00N 0.05E
Hazārān, Kūh-e *mtn.* Iran 31 29.30N 57.18E
Hazelton Canada 50 55.15N127.18W
Hazen U.S.A. 54 39.34N119.03W
Hazleton U.S.A. 55 40.58N 75.59W
Healdsburg U.S.A. 54 38.37N122.52W
Healesville Australia 47 37.40S145.31E
Healy U.S.A. 50 63.52N148.58W
Heanor U.K. 4 53.01N 1.20W
Hearst Canada 55 49.42N 83.40W
Heathcote Australia 47 36.54S144.42E
Hebei *d.* China 25 39.20N117.15E
Hebel Australia 47 28.55S147.49E
Hebi China 25 35.57N114.08E
Hebron Canada 51 58.05N 62.30W
Hebron *see* Al Khalīl Jordan 32
Heby Sweden 17 59.56N 16.53E
Hecate Str. Canada 50 53.00N131.00W
Hechtel Belgium 8 51.07N 5.22E
Hechuan China 29 30.00N106.15E
Hede Sweden 17 62.25N 13.30E
Hedemora Sweden 17 60.17N 15.59E
Hedmark *d.* Norway 17 61.20N 11.30E
Heemstede Neth. 8 52.21N 4.38E
Heerde Neth. 8 52.23N 6.02E
Heerenveen Neth. 8 52.57N 5.55E
Heerlen Neth. 8 50.53N 5.59E
Hefa Israel 32 32.49N 34.59E
Hefei China 25 31.55N117.18E
Hegang China 25 47.36N130.30E
Heide W. Germany 14 54.12N 9.06E
Heidelberg C.P. R.S.A. 39 34.05S 20.58E
Heidelberg W. Germany 14 49.25N 8.42E
Heilbron R.S.A. 39 27.16S 27.57E
Heilbronn W. Germany 14 49.08N 9.14E
Heilongjiang *d.* China 25 47.00N126.00E
Heiloo Neth. 8 52.37N 4.43E
Heinola Finland 17 61.13N 26.02E
Heinsberg W. Germany 8 51.04N 6.06E
Heishui China 25 42.06N119.22E
Hejaz *f. see* Al Ḥijāz *f.* Saudi Arabia 30
Hekinan Japan 23 34.51N136.58E
Hekla, Mt. Iceland 16 64.00N 19.45W
Hekou China 29 22.39N103.57E
Helagsfjället *mtn.* Sweden 16 62.58N 12.25E
Helena U.S.A. 54 46.36N112.01W
Helen Reef *i.* Caroline Is. 27 2.43N131.46E
Helensburgh U.K. 6 56.01N 4.44W
Helensville New Zealand 48 36.40S174.27E
Hellendoorn Neth. 8 52.24N 6.29E
Hellenthal W. Germany 8 50.28N 6.25E
Hellesylt Norway 17 62.05N 6.54E
Hellevoetsluis Neth. 8 51.49N 4.08E
Hellín Spain 10 38.31N 1.43W
Helmand *r.* Asia 28 31.10N 61.20E
Helmond Neth. 8 51.28N 5.40E
Helmsdale U.K. 6 58.07N 3.40W
Helmsdale *r.* U.K. 6 58.05N 3.39W
Helsingfors *see* Helsinki Finland 17
Helsingör Denmark 17 56.02N 12.37E
Helsinki Finland 17 60.08N 25.00E
Helston U.K. 5 50.07N 5.17W
Helvecia Argentina 63 31.06S 60.05W
Hemel Hempstead U.K. 5 51.46N 0.28W
Hemse Sweden 17 57.14N 18.22E
Hemsedal Norway 17 60.52N 8.34E
Henan *d.* China 25 33.45N113.00E
Henares *r.* Spain 10 40.26N 3.35W
Henbury Australia 44 24.35S133.15E
Hendaye France 11 43.22N 1.46W
Henderson Ky. U.S.A. 55 37.50N 87.35W
Henderson Nev. U.S.A. 54 36.02N114.59W
Hendrik Verwoerd Dam R.S.A. 39 30.37S 25.29E
Hendrina R.S.A. 39 26.09S 29.42E
Hengelo Neth. 8 52.16N 6.46E
Hengyang China 25 26.58N112.31E
Hénin-Beaumont France 8 50.25N 2.55E
Hennebont France 11 47.48N 3.16W
Henrietta Maria, C. Canada 51 55.00N 82.15W
Hentiesbaai Namibia 39 22.10S 14.19E
Henty Australia 47 35.30S147.03E
Henzada Burma 29 17.38N 95.35E
Heppner U.S.A. 54 45.21N119.33W
Heqing China 29 26.34N100.12E
Herāt Afghan. 31 34.21N 62.10E
Herceg-Novi Yugo. 13 42.27N 18.32E
Hereford U.K. 5 52.04N 2.43W
Hereford and Worcester *d.* U.K. 5 52.08N 2.30W
Herentals Belgium 8 51.12N 4.42E
Herford W. Germany 14 52.07N 8.40E
Hermanus R.S.A. 39 34.24S 19.16E
Hermidale Australia 47 31.33S146.44E
Hermiston U.S.A. 54 45.51N119.17W
Hermosillo Mexico 56 29.04N110.58W
Herne W. Germany 8 51.32N 7.12E
Herne Bay *town* U.K. 5 51.23N 1.10E
Herning Denmark 17 56.08N 8.59E
Heron Bay *town* Canada 55 48.41N 86.28W
Herowābād Iran 31 37.36N 48.36E
Herrera del Duque Spain 10 39.10N 5.03W
Herstal Belgium 8 50.14N 5.38E
Herten W. Germany 8 51.36N 7.08E
Hertford U.K. 5 51.48N 0.05W
Hertfordshire *d.* U.K. 5 51.51N 0.05W
Hervey B. Australia 44 25.00S153.00E
Herzliyya Israel 32 32.10N 34.50E
Hesbaye *f.* Belgium 8 50.32N 5.07E
Hesel W. Germany 8 53.19N 7.35E
Hessen *d.* W. Germany 14 50.30N 9.15E
Hesso Australia 46 32.08S137.58E
Hetzerath W. Germany 8 49.54N 6.50E
Hewett, C. Canada 51 70.20N 68.00W
Hexham U.K. 4 54.58N 2.06W
Hexigten Qi China 25 43.17N117.24E
Heysham U.K. 4 54.03N 2.53W
Heyuan China 25 23.44N114.41E
Heywood Australia 46 38.08S141.38E
Heywood U.K. 4 53.36N 2.13W
Hiawatha Utah U.S.A. 54 39.29N111.01W
Hibbing U.S.A. 53 47.25N 92.55W
Hicks Bay *town* New Zealand 48 37.35S178.18E
Hidalgo *d.* Mexico 56 20.50N 98.30W
Hidalgo Tamaulipas Mexico 56 24.15N 99.26W
Hidalgo del Parral Mexico 56 26.56N105.40W
Hieradhsvotn *r.* Iceland 16 65.45N 18.50W
Higashimatsuyama Japan 23 36.02N139.24E
Higashimurayama Japan 23 35.46N139.29E
Higashiōsaka Japan 23 34.39N135.35E
Higginsville Australia 43 31.46S121.43E
Highland *d.* U.K. 6 57.42N 5.00W
High Peak *mtn.* U.K. 4 53.22N 1.48W
High Willhays *mtn.* U.K. 5 50.41N 4.00W
High Wycombe U.K. 5 51.38N 0.46W
Hiiumaa *i.* U.S.S.R. 17 58.52N 22.40E
Híjar Spain 10 41.10N 0.27W
Hikone Japan 23 35.15N136.15E
Hikurangi New Zealand 48 35.36S174.17E
Hikurangi *mtn.* New Zealand 48 37.50S178.10E
Hilden W. Germany 8 51.10N 6.56E
Hildesheim W. Germany 14 52.09N 9.58E
Hillegom Neth. 8 52.19N 4.35E
Hillsboro Oreg. U.S.A. 54 45.31N122.59W
Hillsdale U.S.A. 55 41.56N 84.37W
Hillsport Canada 55 49.27N 85.34W
Hillston Australia 47 33.30S145.33E
Hilo Hawaii U.S.A. 52 19.42N155.04W
Hiltrup W. Germany 8 51.55N 7.36E
Hilversum Neth. 8 52.14N 5.12E
Himachal Pradesh *d.* India 28 31.45N 77.30E
Himalaya *mts.* Asia 29 29.00N 84.00E
Himanka Finland 16 64.04N 23.39E
Himarë Albania 13 40.07N 19.44E
Ḥimṣ Syria 32 34.44N 36.43E
Hinchinbrook I. Australia 44 18.23S146.17E
Hinckley U.K. 5 52.33N 1.21W
Hindmarsh, L. Australia 46 36.03S141.53E
Hindu Kush *mts.* Asia 28 36.40N 70.00E
Hindupur India 28 13.49N 77.29E
Hines Creek *town* Canada 50 56.15N118.36W
Hingol *r.* Pakistan 28 25.25N 65.32E
Hinnöy *i.* Norway 16 68.35N 15.50E
Hinojosa Spain 10 38.30N 5.17W
Hinsdale Mont. U.S.A. 54 48.24N107.05W
Hippolytushoef Neth. 8 52.57N 4.58E
Hirakata Japan 23 34.48N135.38E
Hirākud *resr.* India 29 21.32N 83.55E
Hiratsuka Japan 23 35.19N139.21E
Hiroshima Japan 25 34.23N132.27E
Hirson France 8 49.56N 4.05E
Hîrşova Romania 15 44.41N 27.57E
Hirtshals Denmark 17 57.35N 9.58E
Hisai Japan 23 34.40N136.28E
Hisār India 28 29.10N 75.43E
Ḥismá *f.* Saudi Arabia 32 28.45N 35.56E
Hispaniola *i.* C. America 57 19.00N 71.00W
Ḥisyah Syria 32 34.24N 36.45E
Hīt Iraq 30 33.38N 42.50E
Hitchin U.K. 5 51.57N 0.16W
Hitra *i.* Norway 16 63.37N 8.46E
Hjälmaren *l.* Sweden 17 59.15N 15.45E
Hjörring Denmark 17 57.28N 9.59E
Hlotse Lesotho 39 28.52S 28.02E
Ho Ghana 38 6.38N 0.38E
Hoare B. Canada 51 65.20N 62.30W
Hobart Australia 45 42.54S147.18E
Hobart Ind. U.S.A. 55 41.32N 87.14W
Hoboken Belgium 8 51.11N 4.21E
Hobro Denmark 17 56.38N 9.48E
Ho Chi Minh City *see* Thành Pho Ho Chí Minh *h* Vietnam 26
Hodgson Canada 51 51.13N 97.34W
Hod HaSharon Israel 32 32.15N 34.55E
Hódmezövásárhely Hungary 13 46.26N 20.21E
Hoek van Holland Neth. 8 51.59N 4.08E
Hof W. Germany 14 50.19N 11.56E
Höfn Iceland 16 64.16N 15.10W
Hofors Sweden 17 60.33N 16.17E
Hofsjökull *mtn.* Iceland 16 64.50N 19.00W
Hofsos Iceland 16 65.53N 19.26W
Höganäs Sweden 17 56.12N 12.33E
Hohhot China 25 40.49N111.37E
Hoi An Vietnam 26 15.54N108.19E
Hoima Uganda 37 1.25N 31.22E
Hokitika New Zealand 48 42.42S170.59E
Hokkaidō *i.* Japan 25 43.30N143.20E
Hokksund Norway 17 59.47N 9.59E
Hola Kenya 37 1.29S 40.02E
Holbaek Denmark 17 55.43N 11.43E
Holbrook Australia 47 35.46S147.20E
Holbrook U.S.A. 54 34.54N110.10W
Holguín Cuba 57 20.54N 76.15W
Höljes Sweden 17 60.54N 12.36E
Hollabrunn Austria 14 48.34N 16.05E
Holland Mich. U.S.A. 55 42.46N 86.06W
Holman Island *town* Canada 50 70.43N117.43W
Holmavik Iceland 16 65.43N 21.39W
Holmestrand Norway 17 59.29N 10.18E
Holmön *i.* Sweden 16 63.47N 20.53E
Holmsund Sweden 16 63.41N 20.20E
Holon Israel 32 32.01N 34.46E
Holroyd *r.* Australia 44 14.10S141.36E
Holstebro Denmark 17 56.21N 8.38E
Holstein Canada 55 44.03N 80.45W
Holsteinsborg Greenland 51 66.55N 53.30W
Holsworthy U.K. 5 50.48N 4.21W
Holt U.K. 4 52.55N 1.04E
Holten Neth. 8 52.18N 6.26E
Holwerd Neth. 8 53.22N 5.54E
Holy Cross U.S.A. 50 62.12N159.47W
Holyhead U.K. 4 53.18N 4.38W
Holyhead B. U.K. 4 53.22N 4.40W
Holy I. England U.K. 4 55.41N 1.47W
Holy I. Wales U.K. 4 53.15N 4.38W
Holywood U.K. 7 54.38N 5.50W
Hombori Mali 38 15.20N 1.38W
Home B. Canada 51 69.00N 66.00W
Home Hill *town* Australia 44 19.40S147.25E
Homer Alas. U.S.A. 50 59.40N151.37W
Homer Tunnel New Zealand 48 44.40S168.15E
Homoine Mozambique 39 23.45S 35.09E
Homoljske Planina *f.* Yugo. 15 44.20N 21.45E
Honda Colombia 60 5.15N 74.50W
Hondeklipbaai R.S.A. 39 30.19S 17.12E
Hondo *r.* Mexico 57 18.33N 88.22W
Honduras C. America 57 14.30N 87.00W
Honduras, G. of Carib. Sea 57 16.20N 87.30W
Honfleur France 9 49.25N 0.14E
Hong Hà *r.* Vietnam 26 20.15N106.36E
Hong Kong Asia 25 22.30N114.10E
Hongshui He *r.* China 25 23.20N110.04E
Honiton U.K. 5 50.48N 3.13W
Honkajoki Finland 17 62.00N 22.15E
Honolulu Hawaii U.S.A. 52 21.19N157.50W
Honshū *i.* Japan 25 36.00N138.00E
Hood Pt. Australia 43 34.23S119.34E
Hood Range *mts.* Australia 47 28.35S144.30E
Hoogeveen Neth. 8 52.44N 6.29E
Hoogezand Neth. 8 53.10N 6.47E
Hoogstade Belgium 8 50.59N 2.42E
Hook Head Rep. of Ire. 7 52.07N 6.55W
Hoopa U.S.A. 54 41.03N123.40W
Hoopstad R.S.A. 39 27.48S 25.52E
Hoorn Neth. 8 52.38N 5.03E
Hoover Dam U.S.A. 54 36.00N114.27W
Hope U.S.A. 53 33.40N 93.36W
Hope, L. Australia 43 32.40S120.10E
Hope, L. Australia 46 28.23S139.19E
Hopedale Canada 51 55.30N 60.10W
Hopefield R.S.A. 39 33.04S 18.19E
Hopetoun Vic. Australia 46 35.43S142.20E
Hopetoun W.A. Australia 43 33.57S120.05E
Hopetown R.S.A. 39 29.37S 24.04E
Hopkins *r.* Australia 46 38.25S142.00E
Hopkins, L. Australia 42 24.15S128.50E
Hopland U.S.A. 54 38.58N123.07W
Hoquiam U.S.A. 54 46.59N123.53W
Hordaland *d.* Norway 17 60.30N 6.30E
Horde W. Germany 8 51.29N 7.30E
Horlick Mts. Antarctica 64 86.00S102.00W
Hormuz, Str. of Asia 31 26.35N 56.20E
Horn Austria 14 48.40N 15.40E
Horn, C. *see* Hornos, Cabo de *c.* S. America 63
Hornavan *l.* Sweden 16 66.10N 17.30E
Horncastle U.K. 4 53.13N 0.08W
Horndal Sweden 17 60.18N 16.25E
Hornell U.S.A. 55 42.19N 77.39W
Hornepayne Canada 55 49.14N 84.48W
Hornindal Norway 17 61.58N 6.31E
Horn Mts. Canada 50 62.15N119.15W
Hornos, Cabo de *c.* S. America 63 55.47S 67.00W
Hornsby Australia 47 33.11S151.06E
Hornsea U.K. 4 53.55N 0.10W
Hořovice Czech. 14 49.50N 13.54E
Horsens Denmark 17 55.52N 9.52E
Horsham Australia 46 36.45S142.15E
Horsham U.K. 5 51.04N 0.20W
Horten Norway 17 59.25N 10.30E
Horton *r.* Canada 50 70.00N127.00W
Horton L. Canada 50 67.30N122.28W
Hose, Pegunungan *mts.* Malaysia 26 1.30N114.10E
Hoshiārpur India 28 31.30N 75.59E
Hôsh 'Isa Egypt 32 30.55N 30.17E
Hoskins P.N.G. 41 5.30S150.27E
Hospitalet de Llobregat Spain 10 41.20N 2.06E
Hoste, Isla *i.* Chile 63 55.10S 69.00W

an China 24 37.07N 79.57E
azel R.S.A. 39 27.16S 22.57E
ham r. Australia 43 32.58S116.22E
ham, Mt. Australia 47 36.58S147.11E
ing Sweden 16 64.07N 16.10E
Springs town Ark. U.S.A. 53 34.30N 93.02W
Springs town S.Dak. U.S.A. 52 .26N103.29W
tah L. Canada 50 65.04N118.29W
dan France 9 48.47N 1.36E
ffalize Belgium 8 50.08N 5.50E
ghton L. U.S.A. 55 44.16N 84.48W
ghton-le-Spring U.K. 4 54.51N 1.28W
ulton U.S.A. 55 46.08N 67.51W
uma U.S.A. 53 29.35N 90.44W
undé Burkina Faso 38 11.34N 3.31W
urn, Loch U.K. 6 57.06N 5.33W
uston Tex. U.S.A. 53 29.45N 95.25W
vd Mongolia 24 46.40N 90.45E
ve U.K. 5 50.50N 0.10W
vlya U.S.S.R. 19 49.19N 44.01E
vsgöl Nuur l. Mongolia 24 51.00N100.30E
ward Australia 44 25.20S152.32E
we, C. Australia 47 37.30S149.59E
well Australia 47 30.00S151.00E
witt, Mt. Australia 47 37.15S146.40E
wrah India 29 22.35N 88.20E
wth Head Rep. of Ire. 7 53.22N 6.03W
y i. U.K. 6 58.51N 3.17W
yanger Norway 17 61.13N 6.05E
yos Spain 10 40.09N 6.45W
dec Králové Czech. 14 50.13N 15.50E
on r. Czech. 15 47.49N 18.45E
ubieszów Poland 15 50.49N 23.55E
vatska d. Yugo. 15 45.10N 15.30E
ab r. Namibia 39 20.55S 13.28E
abei Pingyuan f. China 25 34.30N117.00E
acho Peru 60 11.05S 77.36W
ade China 25 41.57N114.04E
ai He r. China 25 32.58N118.18E
ainan China 25 32.41N117.06E
ajuápan Mexico 56 17.50N 97.48W
alian Taiwan 25 24.00N121.39E
allaga r. Peru 60 5.02S 75.30W
amanrazo mtn. Peru 60 12.54S 75.04W
ambo Angola 36 12.47S 15.44E
anan China 25 46.13N130.31E
ancané Peru 60 15.10S 69.44W
ancapi Peru 60 13.35S 74.05W
ancavelica Peru 60 12.45S 75.03W
ancayo Peru 60 12.05S 75.12W
anggang China 25 30.40N114.50E
ang Hai b. N. Korea 25 39.00N124.00E
ang He r. China 25 37.55N118.46E
anghua China 25 38.22N117.20E
angshi China 25 30.13N115.05E
anta Peru 60 12.54S 74.13W
ánuco Peru 60 9.55S 76.11W
araz Peru 60 9.33S 77.31W
armey Peru 60 10.05S 78.05W
ascaran mtn. Peru 60 9.08S 77.36W
asco Chile 62 28.28S 71.14W
ubei d. China 25 31.15N112.15E
ubli India 28 15.20N 75.14E
ückelhoven W. Germany 8 51.04N 6.10E
ucknall U.K. 4 53.03N 1.12W
uddersfield U.K. 4 53.38N 1.49W
uddinge Sweden 17 59.14N 17.59E
udiksvall Sweden 17 61.44N 17.07E
udson r. U.S.A. 55 40.42N 74.02W
udson N.Y. U.S.A. 55 42.15N 73.47W
udson Wyo. U.S.A. 54 42.54N108.35W
udson B. Canada 51 58.00N 86.00W
udson Hope Canada 50 56.02N121.55W
udson Mts. Antarctica 64 76.00S 99.00W
udson Str. Canada 51 62.00N 70.00W
ue Vietnam 26 16.28N107.35E
uedin Romania 15 46.52N 23.02E
uehuetenango Guatemala 56 15.19N 91.26W
uelva Spain 10 37.15N 6.56W
uelva r. Spain 10 37.25N 6.00W
uércal-Overa Spain 10 37.23N 1.56W
uesca Spain 10 42.02N 0.25W
ugh r. Australia 44 25.01S134.01E
ughenden Australia 44 20.51S144.12E
ugo U.S.A. 50 66.03N154.16W
uiarau Range mts. New Zealand 48 38.20S177.15E
uimin China 25 37.29N117.29E
uisne r. France 9 47.59N 0.11E
uixtla Mexico 56 15.09N 92.30W
uizen Neth. 8 52.18N 5.12E
ukuntsi Botswana 39 24.02S 21.48E
ulayfā' Saudi Arabia 30 26.00N 40.47E
ulín Czech. 15 49.19N 17.28E
ull Canada 55 45.26N 75.45W
üls W. Germany 8 51.23N 6.30E
ulst Neth. 8 51.18N 4.01E
ultsfred Sweden 17 57.29N 15.50E
ulun Nur l. China 25 49.00N117.27E
ulwān Egypt 32 29.51N 31.20E
umaitá Brazil 60 7.31S 63.02W
umansdorp R.S.A. 39 34.02S 24.45E
umber r. U.K. 4 53.40N 0.12W
umberside d. U.K. 4 53.48N 0.35W
umboldt r. U.S.A. 54 40.02N118.31W
umedān Iran 31 25.24N 59.39E
umenné Czech. 15 48.56N 21.55E
ume Resr. Australia 47 36.06S147.05E
umphreys Peak mtn. U.S.A. 54 35.20N111.40W
umpty Doo Australia 42 12.37S131.14E
ūn Libya 34 29.06N 15.57E
únaflói b. Iceland 16 65.45N 20.50W
unan d. China 25 27.30N111.30E
unedoara Romania 15 45.45N 22.54E
ungary Europe 15 47.30N 19.00E
ungerford Australia 46 29.00S144.26E
ungerford U.K. 5 51.25N 1.30W
üngnam N. Korea 25 39.49N127.40E
Hunsberge mts. Namibia 39 27.40S 17.12E
Hunse r. Neth. 8 53.20N 6.18E
Hunsrück mts. W. Germany 8 49.44N 7.05E
Hunstanton U.K. 4 52.57N 0.30E
Hunte r. W. Germany 14 52.30N 8.19E
Hunter r. Australia 47 32.50S151.42E
Hunter I. Australia 45 40.30S144.46E
Hunter Range mts. Australia 47 32.49S150.20E
Huntingdon U.K. 5 52.20N 0.11W
Huntingdon Penn. U.S.A. 55 40.29N 78.01W
Huntington Ind. U.S.A. 55 40.54N 85.30W
Huntington Oreg. U.S.A. 54 44.21N117.16W
Huntington Utah U.S.A. 54 39.20N110.58W
Huntington W.Va. U.S.A. 55 38.24N 82.26W
Huntington Beach town U.S.A. 54 33.39N118.01W
Huntly New Zealand 48 37.35S175.10E
Huntly U.K. 6 57.27N 2.47W
Huntsville Canada 55 45.20N 79.13W
Huntsville Ala. U.S.A. 53 34.44N 86.35W
Huntsville Tex. U.S.A. 53 34.44N 86.35W
Hunyani r. Mozambique 39 15.41S 30.38E
Huon Pen. P.N.G. 27 6.00S147.00E
Huonville Australia 45 43.01S147.01E
Huron S.Dak. U.S.A. 52 44.22N 98.12W
Huron, L. Canada/U.S.A. 55 44.30N 82.15W
Húsavík Iceland 16 66.03N 17.21W
Huşi Romania 15 46.40N 28.04E
Huskvarna Sweden 17 57.48N 14.16E
Husum W. Germany 14 54.29N 9.04E
Hutchinson R.S.A. 39 31.30S 23.10E
Hutchinson U.S.A. 52 38.03N 97.56W
Huy Belgium 8 50.31N 5.14E
Hvar i. Yugo. 13 43.10N 16.45E
Hvita r. Iceland 16 64.33N 21.45W
Hwange Zimbabwe 39 18.20S 26.29E
Hwange Nat. Park Zimbabwe 39 19.00S 26.30E
Hyargas Nuur l. Mongolia 24 49.30N 93.35E
Hyde U.K. 4 53.26N 2.06W
Hyden Australia 43 32.27S118.53E
Hyderābād India 29 17.22N 78.26E
Hyderābād Pakistan 28 25.23N 68.24E
Hydesville U.S.A. 54 40.31N124.00W
Hyères France 11 43.07N 6.08E
Hyères, Îles d' is. France 11 43.01N 6.25E
Hyllestad Norway 17 61.10N 5.18E
Hyndland, Mt. Australia 47 30.09S152.25E
Hyndman Peak U.S.A. 54 43.50N114.10W
Hysham U.S.A. 54 46.18N107.14W
Hythe Kent U.K. 5 51.04N 1.05E
Hyvinkää Finland 17 60.38N 24.52E

I

Ialomiţa r. Romania 15 44.41N 27.52E
Iar Connacht f. Rep. of Ire. 7 53.21N 9.22W
Iaşi Romania 15 47.09N 27.38E
Iauaretê Brazil 60 0.36N 69.12W
Iaupolo P.N.G. 44 9.34S150.30E
Ibadan Nigeria 38 7.23N 3.56E
Ibagué Colombia 60 4.25N 75.20W
Ibar r. Yugo. 13 43.44N 20.44E
Ibaraki Japan 23 34.49N135.34E
Ibarra Ecuador 60 0.23N 78.05W
Ibbenbüren W. Germany 8 52.17N 7.44E
Ibi r. Japan 23 35.03N136.42E
Ibi Nigeria 38 8.11N 9.44E
Ibiapaba, Serra da mts. Brazil 61 5.30S 41.00W
Ibicaraí Brazil 61 14.52S 39.37W
Ibicuy Argentina 63 33.45S 59.13W
Ibina r. Zaïre 37 1.00N 28.40E
Ibitinga Brazil 59 21.43S 48.47W
Ibiza i. Spain 10 39.00N 1.23E
Ibiza town Spain 10 38.55N 1.30E
Ibotirama Brazil 61 12.13S 43.12W
Ibshawāy Egypt 32 29.21N 30.40E
Içá r. Brazil 60 3.07S 67.58W
Ica Peru 60 14.02S 75.48W
Içana Brazil 60 0.21N 67.19W
Içana r. Brazil 60 0.00 67.10W
Iceland Europe 16 64.45N 18.00W
Ichihara Japan 23 35.31N140.05E
Ichikawa Japan 23 35.44N139.55E
Ichinomiya Japan 23 35.18N136.48E
Icoraci Brazil 61 1.16S 48.28W
Idah Nigeria 38 7.05N 6.45E
Idaho d. U.S.A. 54 44.58N115.56W
Idaho Falls town U.S.A. 54 43.30N112.02W
Idar-Oberstein W. Germany 8 49.43N 7.19E
Ideles Algeria 34 23.58N 5.53E
Idfū Egypt 30 24.58N 32.50E
Idhi Oros mtn. Greece 13 35.13N 24.45E
Idhra i. Greece 13 37.20N 23.32E
Idmū Egypt 32 28.09N 30.41E
Idre Sweden 17 61.52N 12.43E
Ieper Belgium 8 50.51N 2.53E
Ierápetra Greece 13 35.00N 25.45E
Iesi Italy 12 43.32N 13.15E
Iesolo Italy 9 45.32N 12.38E
Ifakara Tanzania 37 8.09S 36.41E
Ifalik is. Caroline Is. 27 7.15N144.27E
Ife Oyo Nigeria 38 7.33N 4.34E
Iferouâne Niger 38 19.04N 8.24E
Iga r. Japan 23 34.45N136.01E
Igal Hungary 15 46.31N 17.55E
Iggesund Sweden 17 61.38N 17.04E
Iglesias Italy 12 39.18N 8.32E
Igli Algeria 34 30.25N 2.12W
Igloolik Island town Canada 51 69.05N 81.25W
Ignace Canada 51 49.26N 91.40W
Iğneada Burnu c. Turkey 13 41.50N 28.05E
Igoumenitsa Greece 13 39.32N 20.14E
Igra U.S.S.R. 18 57.31N 53.09E
Iguaçu r. Brazil 59 25.33S 54.35W
Iguala Mexico 56 18.21N 99.31W
Igualada Spain 10 41.35N 1.37E
Iguatu Brazil 61 6.22S 39.20W
Ihiala Nigeria 38 5.51N 6.52E
Ihosy Madagascar 36 22.24S 46.08E
Ii r. Finland 16 65.19N 25.20E
Iida Japan 23 35.31N137.50E
Iisalmi Finland 16 63.34N 27.11E
Ijebu Ode Nigeria 38 6.47N 3.54E
IJmuiden Neth. 8 52.28N 4.37E
IJssel r. Overijssel Neth. 8 52.34N 5.50E
IJssel r. Zuid Holland Neth. 8 51.54N 4.32E
IJsselmeer l. Neth. 8 52.45N 5.20E
Ijuí Brazil 59 28.23S 53.55W
Ijzendijke Neth. 8 51.19N 3.37E
Ijzer r. Belgium 8 51.09N 2.44E
Ikaría i. Greece 13 37.35N 26.10E
Ikdū Egypt 32 31.18N 30.18E
Ikela Zaïre 36 1.06S 23.04E
Ikerre Nigeria 38 7.30N 5.14E
Ila Nigeria 38 8.01N 4.55E
Ilagan Phil. 27 17.07N121.53E
Īlām Iran 31 33.27N 46.27E
Ilangali Tanzania 37 6.50S 35.06E
Ilaro Nigeria 38 6.53N 3.03E
Iława Poland 15 53.37N 19.33E
Ilebo Zaïre 36 4.20S 20.35E
Ilek r. U.S.S.R. 19 51.30N 54.00E
Ileret Kenya 37 4.22N 36.13E
Ilesha Oyo Nigeria 38 7.39N 4.45E
Ilfracombe Australia 44 23.30S144.30E
Ilfracombe U.K. 5 51.13N 4.08W
Ilhabela Brazil 59 23.47S 45.20W
Ilha Grande, Baía da b. Brazil 59 23.09S 44.30W
Ilhéus Brazil 61 14.50S 39.06W
Ili r. U.S.S.R. 24 45.00N 74.20E
Ilia Romania 15 45.56N 22.39E
Iliamna L. U.S.A. 50 59.30N155.00W
Ilich U.S.S.R. 24 40.50N 68.29E
Iligan Phil. 27 8.12N124.13E
Ilintsy U.S.S.R. 15 49.08N 29.11E
Ilion U.S.A. 55 43.01N 75.02W
Ilkley U.K. 4 53.56N 1.49W
Illapel Chile 62 31.38S 71.10W
Ille-et-Vilaine d. France 9 48.10N 1.30W
Illéla Niger 38 14.30N 5.09E
Iller r. W. Germany 14 48.23N 9.58E
Illiers France 9 48.18N 1.15E
Illinois d. U.S.A. 53 40.00N 89.00W
Illizi Algeria 34 26.20N 8.20E
Ilmajoki Finland 16 62.44N 22.34E
Ilminster U.K. 5 50.55N 2.56W
Ilo Peru 62 17.38S 71.20W
Iloilo Phil. 27 10.45N122.33E
Ilorin Nigeria 38 8.32N 4.34E
Imala Mozambique 37 14.39S 39.34E
Imandra U.S.S.R. 18 67.53N 33.30E
Imandra, Ozero l. U.S.S.R. 18 67.30N 32.45E
Imbābah Egypt 32 30.05N 31.12E
Īmī Ethiopia 35 6.28N 42.18E
Immingham U.K. 4 53.37N 0.12W
Imo d. Nigeria 38 5.30N 7.20E
Imola Italy 9 44.21N 11.42E
Imperatriz Brazil 61 5.32S 47.28W
Imperia Italy 9 43.53N 8.01E
Imperial Calif. U.S.A. 54 32.51N115.34W
Imperial Dam U.S.A. 54 32.55N114.30W
Imperial Valley f. U.S.A. 54 32.50N115.30W
Impfondo Congo 36 1.36N 17.58E
Imphāl India 29 24.47N 93.55E
Imroz i. see Gökçeada i. Turkey 13
Ina Japan 23 35.50N137.57E
Ina r. Japan 23 34.43N135.28E
In Abbangarit well Niger 38 17.49N 6.15E
Inangahua Junction New Zealand 48 41.53S171.58E
Inanwatan Indonesia 27 2.08S132.10E
Inari l. Finland 16 69.00N 28.00E
Inari town Finland 16 68.54N 27.01E
Inazawa Japan 23 35.15N136.47E
Inca Spain 10 39.43N 2.54E
Incesu Turkey 30 38.39N 35.12E
Inch'on S. Korea 25 37.30N126.38E
Indals r. Sweden 16 62.30N 17.20E
Indaw Burma 24 24.14N 96.07E
Independence Calif. U.S.A. 54 36.48N118.12W
Inderagiri r. Indonesia 26 0.30S103.08E
Inderborskiy U.S.S.R. 19 48.32N 51.44E
India Asia 29 23.00N 78.30E
Indiana d. U.S.A. 55 40.00N 86.15W
Indiana town U.S.A. 55 40.37N 79.09W
Indianapolis U.S.A. 55 39.45N 86.10W
Indian Harbour Canada 51 54.25N 57.20W
Indiga U.S.S.R. 18 67.40N 49.00E
Indigirka r. U.S.S.R. 21 71.00N148.45E
Indija Yugo. 15 45.03N 20.05E
Indio U.S.A. 54 33.43N116.13W
Indonesia Asia 26 6.00S118.00E
Indore India 28 22.42N 75.54E
Indrāvati r. India 29 18.45N 80.16E
Indre r. France 11 47.16N 0.19W
Indus r. Pakistan 28 24.00N 67.33E
Inebolu Turkey 30 41.57N 33.45E
Inegöl Turkey 30 40.06N 29.31E
Infiesto Spain 10 43.21N 5.21W
I-n-Gall Niger 38 16.47N 6.56E
Ingatestone U.K. 5 51.41N 0.22E
Ingersoll Canada 55 43.02N 80.53W
Ingham Australia 44 18.35S146.12E
Ingleborough mtn. U.K. 4 54.10N 2.23W
Inglewood Australia 47 28.25S151.02E
Inglewood New Zealand 48 39.09S174.12E
Inglewood U.S.A. 54 33.58N118.21W
Ingolstadt W. Germany 14 48.46N 11.27E
Ingomar Australia 46 29.38S134.48E
Ingulets U.S.S.R. 19 47.43N 33.16E
Ingwiller France 11 48.52N 7.29E
Inhambane Mozambique 39 23.51S 35.29E
Inhambane d. Mozambique 39 22.20S 34.00E
Inhaminga Mozambique 39 18.24S 35.00E
Inharrime Mozambique 39 24.29S 35.01E
Inhassoro Mozambique 39 21.32S 35.10E
Inirida r. Colombia 60 3.59N 67.45W
Inishbofin i. Galway Rep. of Ire. 7 53.38N 10.14W
Inisheer i. Rep. of Ire. 7 53.04N 9.32W
Inishmaan i. Rep. of Ire. 7 53.06N 9.36W
Inishmore i. Rep. of Ire. 7 53.08N 9.43W
Inishowen Pen. Rep. of Ire. 7 55.08N 7.20W
Inishturk i. Rep. of Ire. 7 53.43N 10.08W
Injune Australia 44 25.51S148.34E
Inn r. Europe 14 48.33N 13.26E
Inner Hebrides is. U.K. 6 56.50N 6.45W
Inner Mongolia d. see Nei Monggol d. China 25
Inner Sd. U.K. 6 57.30N 5.55W
Innisfail Australia 44 17.32S146.02E
Innsbruck Austria 14 47.17N 11.25E
Innset Norway 16 68.41N 18.50E
Inongo Zaïre 36 1.55S 18.20E
Inoucdjouac Canada 51 58.25N 78.18W
Inowrocław Poland 15 52.49N 18.12E
I-n-Salah Algeria 34 27.12N 2.29E
Insein Burma 26 16.54N 96.08E
In Tasik well Mali 38 18.03N 2.00E
Interlaken Switz. 14 46.42N 7.52E
Intute Mozambique 37 14.08S 39.55E
Inuvik Canada 50 68.16N133.40W
Inuvik d. Canada 50 68.00N130.00W
Inuyama Japan 23 35.23N136.56E
Inveraray U.K. 6 56.24N 5.05W
Inverbervie U.K. 6 56.51N 2.17W
Invercargill New Zealand 48 46.26S168.21E
Inverell Australia 47 29.46S151.10E
Invergordon U.K. 6 57.42N 4.10W
Inverness U.K. 6 57.27N 4.15W
Inverurie U.K. 6 57.17N 2.23W
Inverway Australia 42 17.49S129.40E
Investigator Group is. Australia 46 33.45S134.30E
Investigator Str. Australia 46 35.25S137.10E
Invinheima r. Brazil 62 22.52S 53.20W
Inya U.S.S.R. 20 50.24N 86.47E
Inyangani mtn. Zimbabwe 39 18.18S 32.50E
Inyonga Tanzania 37 6.43S 32.02E
Ioánnina Greece 13 39.39N 20.49E
Iona i. U.K. 6 56.20N 6.25W
Ionia U.S.A. 55 42.58N 85.06W
Ionian Is. see Iónioi Nísoi is. Greece 13
Ionian Sea Med. Sea 13 38.30N 18.45E
Iónioi Nísoi is. Greece 13 38.45N 20.00E
Íos i. Greece 13 36.42N 25.20E
Iowa d. U.S.A. 53 42.00N 93.00W
Iowa City U.S.A. 53 41.39N 91.30W
Ipatovo U.S.S.R. 19 45.44N 42.56E
Ipiales Colombia 60 0.52N 77.38W
Ipiaú Brazil 61 14.07S 39.43W
Ipixuna Brazil 60 7.00S 71.30W
Ipoh Malaysia 26 4.36N101.02E
Ippa r. U.S.S.R. 15 52.13N 29.08E
Ipswich Australia 47 27.38S152.40E
Ipswich U.K. 5 52.04N 1.09E
Ipu Brazil 61 4.23S 40.44W
Ipuh Indonesia 26 2.58S101.28E
Iquique Chile 62 20.13S 70.10W
Iquitos Peru 60 3.51S 73.13W
Irago-suidō str. Japan 23 34.35N137.00E
Iráklion Greece 13 35.20N 25.08E
Iran Asia 31 32.00N 54.30E
Iran, Pegunungan mts. Indonesia/Malaysia 26 3.20N115.00E
Īrānshahr Iran 31 27.14N 60.42E
Irapuato Mexico 56 20.40N101.40W
Iraq Asia 30 33.00N 44.00E
Irayel U.S.S.R. 18 64.23N 55.25E
Irazú mtn. Costa Rica 57 9.59N 83.52W
Irbid Jordan 32 32.33N 35.51E
Irbil Iraq 31 36.12N 44.01E
Irian Jaya d. Indonesia 27 4.00S138.00E
Iringa Tanzania 37 7.49S 35.39E
Iringa d. Tanzania 37 8.30S 35.00E
Iriomote jima i. Japan 25 24.30N124.00E
Iriri r. Brazil 61 3.50S 52.40W
Irish Sea U.K./Rep. of Ire. 7 53.30N 5.40W
Irkutsk U.S.S.R. 24 52.18N104.15E
Iron Baron Australia 46 32.59S137.09E
Iron Gate f. Romania/Yugo. 15 44.40N 22.30E
Iron Knob Australia 46 32.44S137.08E
Iron Mountain town U.S.A. 55 45.51N 88.03W
Iron Mts. Rep. of Ire. 7 54.10N 7.56W
Iron River town U.S.A. 53 46.05N 88.38W
Irons U.S.A. 55 44.08N 85.55W
Ironton U.S.A. 55 38.32N 82.40W
Ironwood U.S.A. 55 46.25N 90.08W
Iroquois Falls town Canada 55 48.47N 80.41W
Irosin Phil. 27 12.45N124.02E
Irō-zaki c. Japan 23 34.36N138.51E
Irpen U.S.S.R. 15 50.31N 30.29E
Irrapatana Australia 46 29.03S136.28E
Irrawaddy r. Burma 29 17.45N 95.25E
Irrawaddy Delta Burma 29 16.30N 95.20E
Irsha r. U.S.S.R. 15 50.45N 29.30E
Irtysh r. U.S.S.R. 20 61.00N 68.40E
Iruma r. Japan 23 35.57N139.30E
Irumu Zaïre 37 1.29N 29.48E
Irún Spain 10 43.20N 1.48W
Irvine U.K. 6 55.37N 4.40W
Irvinestown U.K. 7 54.29N 7.40W
Irwin, Pt. Australia 43 35.03S116.20E
Isa Nigeria 38 13.14N 6.24E
Isaac r. Australia 44 22.52S149.20E
Isabella, Cordillera mts. Nicaragua 57 13.30N 85.00W
Ísafjördhur town Iceland 16 66.05N 23.06W
Isaka Tanzania 37 3.52S 32.54E
Isakogorka U.S.S.R. 18 64.23N 40.31E
Isar r. W. Germany 14 48.48N 12.57E
Isbergues France 8 50.38N 2.24E
Ischia i. Italy 12 40.43N 13.54E
Ise Japan 23 34.29N136.42E
Iseo, Lago d' l. Italy 9 45.43N 10.04E
Isère r. France 11 45.02N 4.54E
Iserlohn W. Germany 8 51.23N 7.42E
Isernia Italy 12 41.36N 14.14E
Ise-wan b. Japan 23 34.45N136.40E
Iseyin Nigeria 38 7.59N 3.36E
Isfahan see Eşfahān Iran 28
Ishim U.S.S.R. 20 56.10N 69.30E
Ishim r. U.S.S.R. 20 57.50N 71.00E
Ishinomaki Japan 25 38.25N141.18E
Ishpeming U.S.A. 55 46.29N 87.40W
Isigny France 9 49.18N 1.06W
Isiolo Kenya 37 0.20N 37.36E
Isipingo Beach town R.S.A. 39 30.00S 30.57E
Isiro Zaïre 37 2.50N 27.40E
Iskenderun Turkey 30 36.37N 36.08E
Iskenderun Körfezi g. Turkey 30 36.40N 35.50E
Iskilip Turkey 30 40.45N 34.28E
Iskūr r. Bulgaria 13 43.42N 24.27E
Isla r. U.K. 6 56.32N 3.22W
Islāmābād Pakistan 28 33.40N 73.08E
Island L. Australia 46 31.30S136.40E
Island L. Canada 51 53.58N 94.47W
Island Magee pen. U.K. 7 54.48N 5.44W
Island Pt. Australia 43 30.21S115.01E
Islands, B. of New Zealand 48 35.15S174.15E
Islay i. U.K. 6 55.45N 6.20W
Isle r. France 11 45.02N 0.08W
Isle of Portland f. U.K. 5 50.32N 2.25W
Isle of Wight d. U.K. 5 50.40N 1.17W
Ismael Cortinas Uruguay 63 33.58S 57.06W
Isnā Egypt 30 25.16N 32.30E
Isoka Zambia 37 10.06S 32.39E
Isola della Scala Italy 9 45.16N 11.00E
Isparta Turkey 30 37.46N 30.32E
Ispica Italy 12 36.46N 14.55E
Israel Asia 32 32.00N 34.50E
Israelite B. Australia 43 33.40S123.55E
Issoire France 11 45.33N 3.15E
Is-sur-Tille France 11 47.30N 5.10E
Issyk Kul l. U.S.S.R. 24 43.30N 77.20E
Istanbul Turkey 13 41.02N 28.58E
Istanbul Boğazi str. Turkey 13 41.07N 29.04E
Isthmus of Kra Thailand 29 10.10N 99.00E
Istiaía Greece 13 38.57N 23.09E
Istok Yugo. 13 42.47N 20.29E
Istra pen. Yugo. 14 45.12N 13.55E
Itabaiana Brazil 61 7.20S 35.20W
Itabira Brazil 59 19.39S 43.14W
Itabirito Brazil 59 20.21S 43.45W
Itabuna Brazil 61 14.48S 39.18W
Itacajuna r. Brazil 61 5.20S 49.08W
Itacoatiara Brazil 60 3.06S 58.22W
Itagüí Colombia 60 6.10N 75.36W
Itaí Brazil 59 23.23S 49.05W
Itaim r. Brazil 61 6.43S 42.48W
Itaituba Brazil 61 4.17S 55.59W
Itajaí Brazil 59 26.50S 48.39W
Itajubá Brazil 59 22.24S 45.25W
Itaka Tanzania 37 8.51S 32.48E
Italy Europe 12 43.00N 12.00E
Itami Japan 23 34.46N135.25E
Itapecerica Brazil 59 20.28S 45.09W
Itapecuru Mirim Brazil 61 3.24S 44.20W
Itaperuna Brazil 59 21.14S 41.51W
Itapetinga Brazil 61 15.17S 40.16W
Itapetininga Brazil 59 23.36S 48.07W
Itapeva Brazil 59 23.59S 48.59W
Itapicuru r. Brazil 61 11.50S 37.30W
Itapira Brazil 59 22.24S 46.56W
Itaqui Brazil 59 29.07S 56.33W
Itatiba Brazil 59 22.59S 46.51W
Itatinga Brazil 59 23.06S 48.36W
Itatuba Brazil 60 5.40S 63.20W
Itaúna Brazil 59 20.04S 44.14W
Ithaca U.S.A. 55 42.26N 76.30W
Itháki Greece 13 38.23N 20.42E
Itmurinkol, Ozero l. U.S.S.R. 19 49.30N 52.17E
Itō Japan 23 34.58N139.05E
Iton r. France 9 49.09N 1.12E
Itsa Egypt 32 29.14N 30.47E
Itu Brazil 59 23.17S 47.18W
Ituí r. Brazil 60 4.38S 70.19W
Ituiutaba Brazil 59 19.00S 49.25W
Ituri r. Zaïre 37 1.45N 27.06E
Iturup i. U.S.S.R. 25 44.00N147.30E
Ituverava Brazil 59 20.22S 47.48W
Ituxi r. Brazil 60 7.20S 64.50W
Ityāy al Bārūd Egypt 32 30.53N 30.40E
Itzehoe W. Germany 14 53.56N 9.32E
Ivaí r. Brazil 59 23.20S 53.23W
Ivalo Finland 16 68.42N 27.30E
Ivalo r. Finland 16 68.43N 27.36E
Ivanhoe Australia 46 32.56S144.22E
Ivano-Frankovsk U.S.S.R. 15 48.55N 24.42E
Ivanovo B.S.S.R. U.S.S.R. 15 52.10N 25.13E
Ivanovo R.S.F.S.R. U.S.S.R. 18 57.00N 41.00E
Ivdel U.S.S.R. 18 60.45N 60.30E
Ivenets U.S.S.R. 15 53.50N 26.40E
Ivigtût Greenland 51 61.10N 48.00W
Ivittuut see Ivigtût Greenland 51
Iviza i. see Ibiza i. Spain 10
Ivory Coast Africa 34 8.00N 5.30W
Ivrea Italy 9 45.28N 7.52E
Ivujivik Canada 51 62.24N 77.55W
Ivybridge U.K. 5 50.24N 3.56W
Iwata Japan 23 34.42N137.48E
Iwo Nigeria 38 7.38N 4.11E
Ixiamas Bolivia 62 13.45S 68.09W
Izabal, Lago de l. Guatemala 57 15.30N 89.00W
Izberbash U.S.S.R. 19 42.31N 47.52E
Izhma U.S.S.R. 18 65.03N 53.48E
Izhma r. U.S.S.R. 18 65.16N 53.18E
Izmail U.S.S.R. 15 45.20N 28.50E
Izmir Turkey 13 38.24N 27.09E
Izmir Körfezi g. Turkey 13 38.30N 26.45E
Izmit Turkey 30 40.48N 29.55E
Izozog, Bañados de f. Bolivia 62 18.30S 62.05W
Izozog Marshes f. see Izozog, Bañados de f. Bolivia 62
Izu-hantō pen. Japan 23 34.53N138.55E
Izumi Japan 23 34.29N135.26E
Izumi-ōtsu Japan 23 34.30N135.24E

Izumi-sano Japan 23 34.25N135.19E
Izumo *r.* Japan 23 34.38N136.33E
Izyaslav U.S.S.R. 15 50.10N 26.46E
Izyum U.S.S.R. 19 49.12N 37.19E

J

Jabal, Baḩr al *r.* Sudan 35 9.30N 30.20E
Jabalón *r.* Spain 10 38.55N 4.07W
Jabalpur India 29 23.10N 79.59E
Jabālyah Egypt 32 31.32N 34.29E
Jabbān, Arḑ al *f.* Jordan 32 32.08N 36.35E
Jablah Syria 32 35.22N 35.56E
Jablonec nad Nisou Czech. 14 50.44N 15.10E
Jaboticabal Brazil 59 21.15S 48.17W
Jaca Spain 10 42.34N 0.33W
Jacareí Brazil 59 23.17S 45.57W
Jackman U.S.A. 55 45.38N 70.16W
Jackson Mich. U.S.A. 55 42.15N 84.24W
Jackson Miss. U.S.A. 53 32.20N 90.11W
Jackson Ohio U.S.A. 55 39.03N 82.40W
Jackson Tenn. U.S.A. 53 35.37N 88.50W
Jackson Wyo. U.S.A. 54 43.29N110.38W
Jacksonville Fla. U.S.A. 53 30.20N 81.40W
Jacobābād Pakistan 28 28.16N 68.30E
Jacobina Brazil 61 11.13S 40.30W
Jacob Lake *town* U.S.A. 54 36.41N112.14W
Jacques Cartier, Mt. Canada 55 49.00N 65.55W
Jacuí *r.* Brazil 59 29.56S 51.13W
Jacundá *r.* Brazil 61 1.57S 50.26W
Jade W. Germany 8 53.21N 8.11E
Jadebusen *b.* W. Germany 8 53.30N 8.12E
Jaén Peru 60 5.21S 78.28W
Jaén Spain 10 37.46N 3.48W
Jaffa, C. Australia 46 36.58S139.39E
Jaffna Sri Lanka 29 9.38N 80.02E
Jagdalpur India 29 19.04N 82.05E
Jaguarão Brazil 59 32.30S 53.25W
Jahrom Iran 31 28.30N 53.30E
Jailolo Indonesia 27 1.05N127.29E
Jaipur India 28 26.53N 75.50E
Jajawijaya Mts. Asia 27 4.20S139.10E
Jājpur India 29 20.50N 86.20E
Jakarta Indonesia 26 6.08S106.45E
Jäkkvik Sweden 16 66.23N 17.00E
Jakobstad *see* Pietarsaari Finland 16
Jalālah al Baḩrīyah, Jabal *mts.* Egypt 32 29.20N 32.12E
Jalālat al Qiblīyah, Jabal al *mts.* Egypt 32 28.42N 32.23E
Jalapa Mexico 56 19.45N 96.48W
Jālgaon India 28 21.01N 75.39E
Jalingo Nigeria 38 8.54N 11.21E
Jalisco *d.* Mexico 56 21.00N103.00W
Jālna India 28 19.50N 75.58E
Jalón *r.* Spain 10 41.47N 1.02W
Jālor India 28 25.21N 72.37E
Jalpaiguri India 29 26.30N 88.50E
Jālū Libya 35 29.00N 21.30E
Jalūlā Iraq 31 34.16N 45.10E
Jamaari Nigeria 38 11.44N 9.53E
Jamaica C. America 57 18.00N 77.00W
Jamālpur Bangla. 29 24.54N 89.57E
Jamame Somali Rep. 37 0.04N 42.46E
Jamanxim *r.* Brazil 61 4.43S 56.18W
Jamberoo Australia 47 34.40S150.44E
Jambes Belgium 8 50.28N 4.52E
Jambi Indonesia 26 1.36S103.39E
Jambi *d.* Indonesia 26 2.00S102.30E
James *r.* S.Dak. U.S.A. 53 42.50N 97.15W
James B. Canada 51 53.00N 80.00W
James Bay Prov. Park Canada 55 51.24N 79.00W
Jamestown Australia 46 33.12S138.38E
Jamestown N.Dak. U.S.A. 52 46.54N 98.42W
Jamestown N.Y. U.S.A. 55 42.06N 79.14W
Jammerbught *b.* Denmark 17 57.20N 9.30E
Jammu Jammu & Kashmir 28 32.44N 74.52E
Jammu & Kashmir Asia 28 33.30N 76.00E
Jāmnagar India 28 22.28N 70.06E
Jamsah Egypt 32 27.39N 33.35E
Jämsänkoski Finland 17 61.55N 25.11E
Jamshedpur India 29 22.47N 86.12E
Jämtland *d.* Sweden 16 63.00N 14.30E
Janda, Laguna de la *l.* Spain 10 36.15N 5.50W
Jándula *r.* Spain 10 38.08N 4.08W
Janesville U.S.A. 53 42.42N 89.02W
Jangamo Mozambique 39 24.06S 35.21E
Janin Jordan 32 32.28N 35.18E
Jan Kempdorp R.S.A. 39 27.55S 24.48E
Januária Brazil 59 15.28S 44.23W
Janzé France 9 47.58N 1.30W
Japan Asia 25 36.00N136.00E
Japan, Sea of Asia 25 40.00N135.00E
Japurá *r.* Brazil 60 3.00S 64.50W
Jarama *r.* Spain 10 40.27N 3.32W
Jarash Jordan 32 32.17N 35.54E
Jardee Australia 43 34.18S116.04E
Jardines de la Reina *is.* Cuba 57 20.30N 79.00W
Jardinópolis Brazil 59 20.59S 47.48W
Jargeau France 9 47.52N 2.07E
Jarocin Poland 15 51.59N 17.31E
Jarosław Poland 15 50.02N 22.42E
Jarrāḩī *r.* Iran 31 30.40N 48.23E
Järvenpää Finland 17 60.28N 25.06E
Jāsk Iran 31 25.40N 57.45E
Jasło Poland 15 49.45N 21.29E
Jasper Canada 50 52.55N118.05W
Jastrebarsko Yugo. 14 45.40N 15.39E
Jastrowie Poland 14 53.26N 16.49E
Jászberény Hungary 15 47.30N 19.55E
Jataí Brazil 59 17.58S 51.45W
Játiva Spain 10 39.00N 0.32W
Jatobá Brazil 61 4.35S 49.33W
Jaú Brazil 59 22.11S 48.35W
Jauja Peru 60 11.50S 75.15W
Jaunjelgava U.S.S.R. 18 56.34N 25.02E
Jaunpur India 29 25.44N 82.41E
Java *i. see* Jawa *i.* Indonesia 26
Javari *r.* Peru 60 4.30S 71.20W
Java Sea *see* Jawa, Laut *sea* Indonesia 26
Java Trench *f.* Indonesia 26 10.00S110.00E
Jawa *i.* Indonesia 26 7.30S110.00E
Jawa, Laut *sea* Indonesia 26 5.00S111.00E
Jawa Barat *d.* Indonesia 26 7.15S107.00E
Jawa Tengah *d.* Indonesia 26 7.40S109.40E
Jawa Timur *d.* Indonesia 26 7.00S112.00E
Jayah, Wādī al *see* Hā 'Arava Jordan/Israel 32
Jayapura Indonesia 27 2.28S140.38E
Jazirah Doberai *f.* Indonesia 27 1.10S132.30E
Jazzīn Lebanon 32 33.32N 35.34E
Jean U.S.A. 54 35.46N115.20W
Jean Marie River *town* Canada 50 61.32N120.40W
Jebāl Bārez, Kūh-e *mts.* Iran 31 28.40N 58.10E
Jebba Nigeria 38 9.11N 4.49E
Jedburgh U.K. 6 55.29N 2.33W
Jędrzejów Poland 15 50.39N 20.18E
Jefferson, Mt. Nev. U.S.A. 54 38.46N116.55W
Jefferson, Mt. Oreg. U.S.A. 54 44.40N121.47W
Jefferson City U.S.A. 53 38.33N 92.10W
Jeffersonville U.S.A. 55 38.16N 85.45W
Jega Nigeria 38 12.12N 4.23E
Jēkabpils U.S.S.R. 18 56.28N 25.58E
Jelenia Góra Poland 14 50.55N 15.45E
Jelgava U.S.S.R. 17 56.39N 23.42E
Jember Indonesia 26 8.07S113.45E
Jena E. Germany 14 50.56N 11.35E
Jenbach Austria 14 47.24N 11.47E
Jenolan Caves *town* Australia 47 33.53S150.03E
Jeparit Australia 46 36.09S141.59E
Jeppo Finland 16 63.24N 22.37E
Jequié Brazil 61 13.52S 40.06W
Jequitinhonha *r.* Brazil 59 16.46S 39.45W
Jerantut Malaysia 26 3.56N102.22E
Jérémie Haiti 57 18.40N 74.09W
Jerez Spain 10 38.20N 6.45W
Jerez de la Frontera Spain 10 36.41N 6.08W
Jericho *see* Arīḩā Jordan 32
Jerilderie Australia 47 35.23S145.41E
Jerome U.S.A. 54 42.43N114.31W
Jersey *i.* U.K. 5 49.13N 2.08W
Jersey City U.S.A. 55 40.44N 74.04W
Jerusalem *see* Yerushalayim Israel/Jordan 32
Jervis B. Australia 47 35.05S150.44E
Jesenice Yugo. 12 46.27N 14.04E
Jessore Bangla. 29 23.10N 89.12E
Jesús Carranza Mexico 56 17.26N 95.02W
Jever W. Germany 8 53.34N 7.54E
Jevnaker Norway 17 60.15N 10.28E
Jeypore India 29 18.51N 82.41E
Jeziorak, Jezioro *l.* Poland 15 53.40N 19.04E
Jhang Sadar Pakistan 28 31.16N 72.19E
Jhānsi India 29 25.27N 78.34E
Jhelum *r.* Pakistan 28 31.04N 72.10E
Jialing Jiang *r.* China 29 29.33N106.30E
Jiamusi China 25 46.50N130.21E
Ji'an China 25 27.08N115.00E
Jiange China 29 32.04N105.26E
Jiangling China 25 30.20N112.20E
Jiangsu *d.* China 25 34.00N119.00E
Jiangxi *d.* China 25 27.25N115.20E
Jianyang Fujian China 25 27.20N117.50E
Jiaohe China 25 43.42N127.19E
Jiashan China 25 32.47N117.59E
Jiaxian China 25 38.02N110.29E
Jiaxing China 25 30.40N120.50E
Jiayi Taiwan 25 23.38N120.27E
Jiddah Saudi Arabia 35 21.30N 39.10E
Jihlava Czech. 14 49.24N 15.35E
Jilib Somali Rep. 37 0.28N 42.50E
Jilin China 25 43.53N126.35E
Jilin *d.* China 25 43.00N127.30E
Jilong Taiwan 25 25.10N121.43E
Jima Ethiopia 35 7.39N 36.47E
Jiménez Mexico 56 27.08N104.55W
Jimeta Nigeria 38 9.19N 12.25E
Jinan China 25 36.50N117.00E
Jingdezhen China 25 29.16N117.11E
Jinggu Yunnan China 29 23.29N100.19E
Jinghong China 24 21.59N100.49E
Jing Xian China 25 26.35N109.41E
Jinhua China 25 29.06N119.40E
Jining Nei Monggol China 25 40.56N113.00E
Jining Shantung China 25 35.25N116.40E
Jinja Uganda 37 0.27N 33.10E
Jinotepe Nicaragua 57 11.50N 86.10W
Jinsha Jiang *r.* China 29 26.30N101.40E
Jinxi Liaoning China 25 40.54N120.36E
Jin Xian Liaoning China 25 39.04N121.45E
Jinzhou China 25 41.07N121.06E
Jipijapa Ecuador 60 1.23S 80.35W
Jirjā Egypt 30 26.20N 31.53E
Jitarning Australia 43 32.48S117.57E
Jiu *r.* Romania 13 43.44N 23.52E
Jiujiang China 25 29.41N116.03E
Jixi China 25 45.17N131.00E
Jīzān Saudi Arabia 35 16.56N 42.33E
Jizl, Wādī al *r.* Saudi Arabia 30 25.37N 38.20E
João Pessoa Brazil 61 7.06S 34.53W
Jódar Spain 10 37.50N 3.21W
Jodhpur India 28 26.18N 73.08E
Jodoigne Belgium 8 50.45N 4.52E
Joensuu Finland 18 62.35N 29.46E
Johannesburg R.S.A. 39 26.11S 28.04E
John Day U.S.A. 54 44.25N118.57W
John Day *r.* U.S.A. 54 45.44N120.39W
John O'Groats U.K. 6 58.39N 3.02W
Johnson City Tenn. U.S.A. 53 36.20N 82.23W
Johnston Lakes, The Australia 43 32.25S120.30E
Johnstown Penn. U.S.A. 55 40.20N 78.55W
Johor Baharu Malaysia 26 1.29N103.40E
Joigny France 9 48.00N 3.20E
Joinville Brazil 59 26.20S 48.49W
Joinville France 11 48.27N 5.08E
Jokkmokk Sweden 16 66.37N 19.50E
Jökulsá á Brú *r.* Iceland 16 65.33N 14.23W
Jökulsá á Fjöllum *r.* Iceland 16 66.05N 16.32W
Jolfa Iran 31 32.40N 51.39E
Joliette Canada 55 46.02N 73.27W
Jolo *i.* Phil. 27 5.55N121.20E
Jolo *town* Phil. 27 6.03N121.00E
Jombang Indonesia 26 7.30S112.21E
Jomda China 29 31.30N 98.16E
Jonava U.S.S.R. 17 55.05N 24.17E
Jonesboro Ark. U.S.A. 53 35.50N 90.41W
Jones Sd. Canada 51 76.00N 85.00W
Jönköping Sweden 17 57.47N 14.11E
Jönköping *d.* Sweden 17 57.30N 14.30E
Joplin U.S.A. 53 37.04N 94.31W
Jordan Asia 30 31.00N 36.00E
Jordan *r. see* Al Urdunn *r.* Asia 32
Jordan Mont. U.S.A. 54 47.19N106.55W
Jordan Valley *town* U.S.A. 54 42.58N117.03W
Jorhāt India 29 26.45N 94.13E
Jörn Sweden 16 65.04N 20.02E
Jos Nigeria 38 9.54N 8.53E
José de San Martín Argentina 63 44.04S 70.26W
José Enrique Rodó Uruguay 63 33.41S 57.34W
Joseph Bonaparte G. Australia 42 14.00S128.30E
Joseph City U.S.A. 54 34.57N110.20W
Jos Plateau *f.* Nigeria 38 10.00N 9.00E
Jotunheimen *mts.* Norway 17 61.38N 8.18E
Joué-lès-Tours France 9 47.21N 0.40E
Joure Neth. 8 52.59N 5.49E
Joverega Botswana 39 19.08S 24.15E
Juan Aldama Mexico 56 24.19N103.21W
Juan B. Arruabarrena Argentina 63 30.25S 58.15W
Juan de Fuca, Str. of Canada/U.S.A. 54 48.15N124.00W
Juan de Nova *i.* Madagascar 37 17.03S 42.45E
Juárez Argentina 63 37.40S 59.48W
Juàzeiro Brazil 61 9.25S 40.30W
Juàzeiro do Norte Brazil 61 7.10S 39.18W
Juba *r.* Somali Rep. 37 0.20S 42.40E
Jūbā Sudan 35 4.50N 31.35E
Jūbāl, Maḑīq *str.* Egypt 32 27.40N 33.55E
Jubal, Str. of *see* Jūbāl, Maḑīq *str.* Egypt 32
Jubilee Downs *town* Australia 42 18.22S125.17E
Júcar *r.* Spain 10 39.10N 0.15W
Juchitán Mexico 56 16.27N 95.05W
Judenburg Austria 14 47.10N 14.40E
Judith Basin *f.* U.S.A. 54 47.10N109.58W
Juist W. Germany 8 53.41N 7.01E
Juist *i.* W. Germany 8 53.43N 7.00E
Juiz de Fora Brazil 59 21.47S 43.23W
Jujuy *d.* Argentina 62 23.00S 66.00W
Juklegga *mtn.* Norway 17 61.03N 8.13E
Juliaca Peru 60 15.29S 70.09W
Julia Creek *town* Australia 44 20.39S141.45E
Juliana Kanaal *canal* Neth. 8 51.00N 5.48E
Julianehåb Greenland 51 60.45N 46.00W
Jülich W. Germany 8 50.55N 6.21E
Jullundur India 28 31.18N 75.40E
Jumbo Somali Rep. 37 0.12S 42.38E
Jumbunna Australia 47 38.30S145.38E
Jumet Belgium 8 50.27N 4.27E
Jumilla Spain 10 38.28N 1.19W
Jumla Nepal 29 29.17N 82.10E
Jumna *r. see* Yamuna India 28
Junāgadh India 28 21.32N 70.32E
Junan China 25 35.11N118.50E
Junction B. Australia 44 11.50S134.15E
Junction City Kans. U.S.A. 53 39.02N 96.51W
Junction City Oreg. U.S.A. 54 44.13N123.12W
Jundah Australia 44 24.50S143.02E
Jundiaí Brazil 59 23.10S 46.54W
Juneau U.S.A. 50 58.20N134.20W
Junee Australia 47 34.51S147.40E
Jungfrau *mtn.* Switz. 11 46.30N 8.00E
Junggar Pendi *f.* Asia 24 44.20N 86.30E
Junglinster Lux. 8 49.41N 6.13E
Junín Argentina 63 34.35S 60.58W
Junín de los Andes Argentina 63 39.57S 71.05W
Juniville France 9 49.24N 4.23E
Jūniyah Lebanon 32 33.59N 35.38E
Junnah, Jabal *mts.* Egypt 32 28.52N 34.15E
Junsele Sweden 16 63.40N 16.55E
Juntura U.S.A. 54 43.46N118.05W
Jura *mts.* Europe 11 46.55N 6.45E
Jura *i.* U.K. 6 55.58N 5.55W
Jura, Sd. of U.K. 6 56.00N 5.45W
Jurado Colombia 60 7.07N 77.46W
Jura Krakowska *mts.* Poland 15 50.30N 19.30E
Jurhen Ul Shan *mts.* China 29 34.00N 91.00E
Jūrmala U.S.S.R. 17 56.58N 23.42E
Juruá *r.* Brazil 60 2.33S 65.50W
Juruena Brazil 62 12.50S 58.58W
Juruena *r.* Brazil 61 7.20S 57.30W
Juruti Brazil 61 2.09S 56.04W
Jussey France 11 47.49N 5.54E
Jutaí *r.* Brazil 60 2.35S 67.00W
Juticalpa Honduras 57 14.45N 86.12W
Jutland *pen. see* Jylland *pen.* Denmark 17
Jūyom Iran 31 28.10N 53.52E
Jwayyā Lebanon 32 33.14N 35.20E
Jylland *pen.* Denmark 17 56.00N 9.15E
Jyväskylä Finland 16 62.14N 25.44E

K

K2 *mtn.* Asia 24 35.53N 76.32E
Ka *r.* Nigeria 38 11.35N 4.10E
Kaabong Uganda 37 3.28N 34.08E
Kaapstad *see* Cape Town R.S.A. 39
Kabaena *i.* Indonesia 27 5.25S122.00E
Kabala Sierra Leone 34 9.40N 11.36W
Kabale Uganda 37 1.13S 30.00E
Kabalega Falls *f.* Uganda 37 2.17N 31.46E
Kabalega Falls Nat. Park Uganda 37 2.15N 31.45E
Kabalo Zaïre 36 6.02S 27.00E
Kabambare Zaïre 37 4.40S 27.41E
Kabanga Zambia 39 17.36S 26.45E
Kabba Nigeria 38 7.50N 6.07E
Kabia *i.* Indonesia 27 6.07S120.28E
Kabinakagami *r.* Canada 55 50.20N 84.20W
Kabīr Kūh *mts.* Iran 31 33.00N 47.00E
Kabongo Zaïre 36 7.22S 25.34E
Kabonzo Zaïre 37 6.41S 27.49E
Kabūd Gonbad Iran 31 37.02N 59.46E
Kābul Afghan. 28 34.30N 69.10E
Kabunda Zaïre 37 12.27S 29.15E
Kabwe Zambia 37 14.27S 28.25E
Kāchā Kūh *mts.* Iran 31 29.30N 61.20E
Kachiry U.S.S.R. 20 53.07N 76.08E
Kade Ghana 38 6.08N 0.51W
Kadina Australia 46 33.58S137.14E
Kadiolí Mali 38 10.38N 5.45W
Kadoma Zimbabwe 39 18.23S 29.52E
Kaduna Nigeria 38 10.28N 7.25E
Kaduna *d.* Nigeria 38 11.00N 7.35E
Kaduna *r.* Nigeria 38 8.45N 5.45E
Kāduqlī Sudan 35 11.01N 29.43E
Kadusam *mtn.* China 29 28.30N 96.45E
Kadzherom U.S.S.R. 18 64.42N 55.59E
Kaédi Mauritania 34 16.12N 13.32W
Kaélé Cameroon 38 10.05N 14.28E
Kaesŏng N. Korea 25 37.59N126.30E
Kafanchan Nigeria 38 9.38N 8.20E
Kafirévs, Ákra *c.* Greece 13 38.11N 24.30E
Kafr ad Dawwār Egypt 32 31.08N 30.08E
Kafr al Baţţīkh Egypt 32 31.24N 31.44E
Kafr ash Shaykh Egypt 32 31.07N 30.56E
Kafr az Zayyāt Egypt 32 30.50N 30.49E
Kafr Salīm Egypt 32 31.09N 30.07E
Kafu *r.* Uganda 37 1.40N 32.07E
Kafue Zambia 37 15.40S 28.13E
Kafue *r.* Zambia 36 15.53S 28.55E
Kafue Dam Zambia 37 15.40S 27.10E
Kafunzo Uganda 37 1.05S 30.26E
Kaga Bandoro C.A.R. 36 7.00N 19.10E
Kagan U.S.S.R. 20 39.45N 64.32E
Kagarlyk U.S.S.R. 15 49.50N 30.50E
Kagera *d.* Tanzania 37 2.00S 31.20E
Kağizman Turkey 30 40.08N 43.07E
Kagoshima Japan 25 31.37N130.32E
Kagul U.S.S.R. 13 45.54N 28.11E
Kahama Tanzania 37 3.48S 32.38E
Kahayan *r.* Indonesia 26 3.20S114.04E
Kahnūj Iran 31 27.55N 57.45E
Kahraman Maraş Turkey 30 37.34N 36.54E
Kai, Kepulauan *is.* Indonesia 27 5.45S132.55E
Kaiama Nigeria 38 9.37N 4.03E
Kaiapoi New Zealand 48 43.23S172.39E
Kaifeng China 25 34.47N114.20E
Kaikohe New Zealand 48 35.25S173.49E
Kaikoura New Zealand 48 42.24S173.41E
Kaikoura Range *mts.* New Zealand 48 42.00S173.40E
Kaimana Indonesia 27 3.39S133.44E
Kaimanawa Mts. New Zealand 48 39.10S176.15E
Kainantu P.N.G. 27 6.16S145.50E
Kainji Resr. Nigeria 38 10.00N 4.35E
Kaipara Harbour New Zealand 48 36.30S174.00E
Kaiserslautern W. Germany 8 49.27N 7.47E
Kaitaia New Zealand 48 35.08S173.18E
Kaitum *r.* Sweden 16 67.30N 21.05E
Kaizuka Japan 23 34.27N135.21E
Kajaani Finland 16 64.14N 27.41E
Kajabbi Australia 44 20.02S140.02E
Kajiado Kenya 37 1.50S 36.48E
Kajuru Nigeria 38 10.19N 7.40E
Kakamas R.S.A. 39 28.44S 20.35E
Kakamega Kenya 37 0.21N 34.47E
Kakamigahara Japan 23 35.28N136.48E
Kakegawa Japan 23 34.46N138.01E
Kakhovskoye Vodokhranilishche *resr.* U.S.S.R. 19 47.33N 34.40E
Kākī Iran 31 28.19N 51.34E
Kākināda India 29 16.59N 82.20E
Kakonko Tanzania 37 3.19S 30.54E
Kakuma Kenya 37 3.38N 34.48E
Kakuto Uganda 37 0.54S 31.26E
Kala *r.* Finland 16 64.17N 23.55E
Kalabahi Indonesia 27 8.13S124.31E
Kalabáka Greece 13 39.42N 21.43E
Kalabity Australia 46 31.53S140.18E
Kalach-na-Donu U.S.S.R. 19 48.43N 43.31E
Kalahari Desert Botswana 39 23.30S 22.00E
Kalahari Gemsbok Nat. Park R.S.A. 39 25.45S 20.25E
Kalajoki Finland 16 64.15N 23.57E
Kalakan U.S.S.R. 21 55.10N116.45E
Kalámai Greece 13 37.02N 22.05E
Kalamazoo U.S.A. 55 42.17N 85.36W
Kalamera Tanzania 37 2.07S 33.43E
Kalamurra, L. Australia 46 28.00S138.00E
Kalannie Australia 43 30.21S117.04E
Kalarash U.S.S.R. 15 47.18N 28.16E
Kalāt Pakistan 28 29.01N 66.38E
Kalecik Turkey 30 40.06N 33.22E
Kalehe Zaïre 37 2.05S 28.53E
Kalemie Zaïre 37 5.57S 29.10E
Kalgan *r.* Australia 43 34.55S117.58E
Kalgoorlie Australia 43 30.49S121.29E
Kaliakra, Nos *c.* Bulgaria 13 43.23N 28.29E
Kalianda Indonesia 26 5.50S105.45E
Kalimantan *d.* Indonesia 26 1.00S113.00E
Kalimantan *f.* Indonesia 26 0.05N112.30E
Kalimantan Barat *d.* Indonesia 26 0.30N110.00E
Kalimantan Selatan *d.* Indonesia 26 2.30S115.30E
Kalimantan Tengah *d.* Indonesia 26 2.00S113.30E
Kalimantan Timur *d.* Indonesia 26 2.20N116.30E
Kálimnos *i.* Greece 13 37.00N 27.00E
Kalinin U.S.S.R. 18 56.47N 35.57E
Kaliningrad U.S.S.R. 17 54.43N 20.30E
Kalinkovichi U.S.S.R. 15 52.10N 29.13E
Kalinovka U.S.S.R. 15 49.29N 28.30E
Kalispell U.S.A. 54 48.12N114.19W
Kalisz Poland 15 51.46N 18.02E
Kaliua Tanzania 37 5.08S 31.50E
Kalix *r.* Sweden 16 65.50N 23.11E
Kalkar W. Germany 8 51.45N 6.17E
Kalkfontein Botswana 39 22.08S 20.54E
Kalkrand Namibia 39 24.05S 17.34E
Kallista Australia 45 42.57S146.10E
Kallsjön *l.* Sweden 16 63.35N 13.00E
Kalmar Sweden 17 56.40N 16.22E
Kalmar *d.* Sweden 17 57.20N 16.00E
Kalmarsund *str.* Sweden 17 56.40N 16.25E
Kalmthout Belgium 8 51.23N 4.28E
Kalmykovo U.S.S.R. 19 49.02N 51.55E
Kalo P.N.G. 44 10.05S147.45E
Kalocsa Hungary 15 46.32N 18.59E
Kalole Zaïre 37 3.40S 27.22E
Kalomo Zambia 36 17.03S 26.29E
Kalonje Zambia 37 12.21S 31.06E
Kaltag U.S.A. 50 64.20N158.44W
Kaluga U.S.S.R. 18 54.31N 36.16E
Kalumburu Australia 42 14.14S126.38E
Kalundborg Denmark 17 55.41N 11.06E
Kalush U.S.S.R. 15 49.02N 24.20E
Kalutara Sri Lanka 29 6.35N 79.58E
Kama *r.* U.S.S.R. 18 55.30N 52.00E
Kamakura Japan 23 35.19N139.33E
Kamanashi *r.* Japan 23 35.33N138.28E
Kamanjab Namibia 39 19.39S 14.50E
Kamba Nigeria 38 11.52N 3.42E
Kambalda Australia 43 31.12S121.40E
Kambarka U.S.S.R. 18 56.18N 54.13E
Kamchatka, Poluostrov *pen.* U.S.S.R. 21 56.00N160.00E
Kamen *mtn.* U.S.S.R. 21 68.40N 94.20E
Kamenets Podolskiy U.S.S.R. 15 48.40N 26.3
Kamenka R.S.F.S.R. U.S.S.R. 18 65.55N 44.02
Kamenka R.S.F.S.R. U.S.S.R. 18 53.10N 44.05
Kamenka Bugskaya U.S.S.R. 15 50.07N 24.30
Kamen Kashirskiy U.S.S.R. 15 51.32N 24.59E
Kamen-na-Obi U.S.S.R. 20 53.46N 81.18E
Kamenskoye U.S.S.R. 21 62.31N165.15E
Kamensk-Shakhtinskiy U.S.S.R. 19 48.20N 40.16E
Kamensk-Ural'skiy U.S.S.R. 20 56.29N 61.49E
Kāmet *mtn.* China 29 31.03N 79.25E
Kameyama Japan 23 34.51N136.27E
Kamiah U.S.A. 54 46.14N116.02W
Kamieskroon R.S.A. 39 30.12S 17.53E
Kamina Zaïre 36 8.46S 25.00E
Kamloops Canada 50 50.39N120.24W
Kamo *r.* Japan 23 35.00N139.52E
Kamp W. Germany 8 50.14N 7.37E
Kampa Indonesia 26 1.46S105.26E
Kampala Uganda 37 0.19N 32.35E
Kampar *r.* Indonesia 26 0.20N102.55E
Kampen Neth. 8 52.33N 5.55E
Kamp-Lintfort W. Germany 8 51.34N 6.38E
Kâmpóng Cham Kampuchea 26 11.59N105.26
Kâmpóng Chhnăng Kampuchea 26 12.16N104.39E
Kâmpóng Saôm Kampuchea 26 10.38N103.30
Kâmpôt Kampuchea 26 10.37N104.11E
Kampti Burkina Faso 38 10.07N 3.22W
Kampuchea Asia 26 12.00N105.00E
Kamsack Canada 51 51.34N101.54W
Kamskoye Vodokhranilishche *resr.* U.S.S.R. 1 58.55N 56.20E
Kamyshin U.S.S.R. 19 50.05N 45.24E
Kana *r.* Zimbabwe 39 18.30S 26.50E
Kanagawa *d.* Japan 23 35.25N139.10E
Kananga Zaïre 36 5.53S 22.26E
Kanash U.S.S.R. 18 55.30N 47.27E
Kanawha *r.* U.S.A. 55 38.50N 82.08W
Kanazawa Japan 25 36.35N136.38E
Kanchanaburi Thailand 29 14.08N 99.31E
Kānchenjunga *mtn.* Asia 29 27.44N 88.11E
Kānchipuram India 29 12.50N 79.44E
Kandalaksha U.S.S.R. 18 67.09N 32.31E
Kandalakshskaya Guba *g.* U.S.S.R. 18 66.30N 34.00E
Kandangan Indonesia 26 2.50S115.15E
Kandi Benin 38 11.05N 2.59E
Kandira Turkey 30 41.05N 30.08E
Kandos Australia 47 32.53S149.59E
Kandrāch Pakistan 28 25.29N 65.29E
Kandreho Madagascar 37 17.29S 46.06E
Kandy Sri Lanka 29 7.18N 80.43E
Kane U.S.A. 55 41.40N 78.49W
Kanem *d.* Chad 38 15.10N 15.30E
Kanevka U.S.S.R. 18 67.08N 39.50E
Kang Botswana 39 23.43S 22.51E
Kangān Iran 31 27.50N 52.07E
Kangar Malaysia 26 6.28N100.10E
Kangaroo I. Australia 46 35.50S137.06E
Kangding China 24 30.05N102.04E
Kangean, Kepulauan *is.* Indonesia 26 7.00S115.45E
Kangerlussuaq *see* Söndreströmfjord Greenland 51
Kanin, Poluostrov *pen.* U.S.S.R. 18 68.00N 45.00E
Kaningo Kenya 37 0.52S 38.31E
Kanin Nos, Mys *c.* U.S.S.R. 18 68.38N 43.20E
Kaniva Australia 46 36.33S141.17E
Kanjiža Yugo. 15 46.04N 20.04E
Kankakee U.S.A. 53 41.08N 87.52W
Kankan Guinea 34 10.22N 9.11W
Kānker India 29 20.17N 81.30E
Kano *r.* Japan 23 35.05N138.52E
Kano Nigeria 38 12.00N 8.31E
Kano *d.* Nigeria 38 12.00N 9.00E
Kanona Zambia 37 13.03S 30.37E
Kanowna Australia 43 30.36S121.36E
Kānpur India 29 26.27N 80.14E
Kansas *d.* U.S.A. 52 38.00N 99.00W
Kansas *r.* U.S.A. 53 39.07N 94.36W
Kansas City Mo. U.S.A. 53 39.02N 94.33W
Kansk U.S.S.R. 21 56.11N 95.20E

Kansŏng S. Korea 25 38.20N128.28E
Kantché Niger 38 13.31N 8.30E
Kantemirovka U.S.S.R. 19 49.40N 39.52E
Kantō d. Japan 23 35.35N139.30E
Kantōheiya f. Japan 23 36.02N140.10E
Kantō-sanchi mts. Japan 23 36.00N138.35E
Kanye Botswana 39 24.58S 25.17E
Kanyu Botswana 39 20.05S 24.39E
Kaolack Senegal 34 14.09N 16.08W
Kapchagay U.S.S.R. 24 43.51N 77.14E
Kapenguria Kenya 37 1.13N 35.07E
Kapfenberg Austria 14 47.27N 15.18E
Kapiri Mposhi Zambia 37 13.59S 28.40E
Kapit Malaysia 26 2.01N112.56E
Kapiti I. New Zealand 48 40.50S174.50E
Kapongolo Zaïre 37 7.51S 28.12E
Kaposvár Hungary 13 46.22N 17.47E
Kapps Namibia 39 22.22S 17.52E
Kapsabet Kenya 37 0.12N 35.05E
Kapsukas U.S.S.R. 17 54.33N 23.21E
Kapuas r. Indonesia 26 0.13S109.12E
Kapunda Australia 46 34.21S138.54E
Kapuskasing Canada 55 49.25N 82.26W
Kaputar, Mt. Australia 47 30.20S150.10E
Kapuvár Hungary 15 47.36N 17.02E
Kara U.S.S.R. 20 69.12N 65.00E
Kara-Bogaz Gol, Zaliv b. U.S.S.R. 31 41.20N 53.40E
Karabük Turkey 30 41.12N 32.36E
Karabutak U.S.S.R. 20 49.55N 60.05E
Karāchi Pakistan 28 24.51N 67.02E
Karād India 28 17.17N 74.12E
Karaganda U.S.S.R. 20 49.53N 73.07E
Karaginskiy, Ostrov i. U.S.S.R. 21 59.00N165.00E
Karakas U.S.S.R. 24 48.20N 83.30E
Karakelong i. Indonesia 27 4.20N126.50E
Karakoram Pass Asia 29 35.53N 77.51E
Karakoram Range mts. Jammu & Kashmir 28 35.30N 76.30E
Karaköse see Ağri Turkey 19
Karakumskiy Kanal canal U.S.S.R. 31 37.30N 65.48E
Karakumy, Peski f. U.S.S.R. 31 37.45N 60.00E
Karakuwisa Namibia 39 18.56S 19.43E
Karaman Turkey 30 37.11N 33.13E
Karamay China 24 45.48N 84.30E
Karamea New Zealand 48 41.15S172.07E
Karamea Bight b. New Zealand 48 41.15S171.30E
Karamürsel Turkey 30 40.42N 29.37E
Karand Iran 31 34.16N 46.15E
Karasburg Namibia 39 28.00S 18.46E
Karasjok Norway 16 69.27N 25.30E
Karasuk U.S.S.R. 20 53.45N 78.01E
Karatau, Khrebet mts. U.S.S.R. 19 44.15N 52.10E
Karatobe U.S.S.R. 19 49.44N 53.30E
Karaton U.S.S.R. 19 46.26N 53.32E
Karazhal U.S.S.R. 20 48.00N 70.55E
Karbalā' Iraq 31 32.37N 44.03E
Karcag Hungary 15 47.19N 20.56E
Kardhítsa Greece 13 39.22N 21.59E
Kärdla U.S.S.R. 17 59.00N 22.42E
Karema Tanzania 37 6.50S 30.25E
Karen India 29 12.50N 92.55E
Karepino U.S.S.R. 18 61.05N 58.02E
Karesuando Finland 16 68.25N 22.30E
Kargasok U.S.S.R. 20 59.07N 80.58E
Kargi Kenya 37 2.31N 37.34E
Kargil Jammu & Kashmir 28 34.32N 76.12E
Kargopol U.S.S.R. 18 61.32N 38.59E
Kari Nigeria 38 11.17N 10.35E
Kariba Zimbabwe 37 16.32S 28.50E
Kariba, L. Zimbabwe/Zambia 37 16.50S 28.00E
Kariba Dam Zimbabwe/Zambia 37 16.15S 28.55E
Karibib Namibia 39 21.56S 15.52E
Kārikāl India 29 10.58N 79.50E
Karimama Benin 38 12.02N 3.15E
Karis Finland 17 60.05N 23.40E
Karisimbi, Mt. Zaïre/Rwanda 37 1.31S 29.25E
Kariya Japan 23 34.59N136.59E
Kariyangwe Zimbabwe 39 17.57S 27.30E
Karkabet Ethiopia 35 16.13N 37.30E
Karkaralinsk U.S.S.R. 20 49.21N 75.27E
Karkar I. P.N.G. 27 4.40S146.00E
Karkas, Kūh-e mtn. Iran 31 33.25N 51.40E
Karkheh r. Iran 31 31.45N 47.52E
Karkinitskiy Zaliv g. U.S.S.R. 19 45.50N 32.45E
Karlino Poland 14 54.03N 15.51E
Karl-Marx-Stadt E. Germany 14 50.50N 12.55E
Karl-Marx-Stadt d. E. Germany 14 50.45N 12.45E
Karlovac Yugo. 12 45.30N 15.34E
Karlovy Vary Czech. 14 50.14N 12.53E
Karlsborg Sweden 17 58.32N 14.31E
Karlshamn Sweden 17 56.10N 14.51E
Karlskoga Sweden 17 59.20N 14.31E
Karlskrona Sweden 17 56.10N 15.35E
Karlsruhe W. Germany 14 49.00N 8.24E
Karlstad Sweden 17 59.22N 13.30E
Karmöy i. Norway 17 59.15N 5.15E
Karnafuli Resr. Bangla. 29 22.40N 92.05E
Karnataka d. India 28 14.45N 76.00E
Karnobat Bulgaria 13 42.40N 27.00E
Kärnten d. Austria 14 46.50N 13.50E
Karonga Malaŵi 37 9.54S 33.55E
Karonie Australia 43 30.58S122.32E
Karoonda Australia 46 35.09S139.54E
Karos Dam R.S.A. 39 28.27S 21.39E
Karpach U.S.S.R. 15 48.00N 27.10E
Kárpathos Greece 13 35.30N 27.14E
Kárpathos i. Greece 13 35.35N 27.08E
Karpineny U.S.S.R. 15 46.46N 28.18E
Karpinsk U.S.S.R. 18 59.48N 59.59E
Karpogory U.S.S.R. 18 64.01N 44.30E
Karragullen Australia 43 32.05S116.03E
Karridale Australia 43 34.12S115.04E
Kars Turkey 30 40.35N 43.05E
Karsakpay U.S.S.R. 20 47.47N 66.43E
Kärsämäki Finland 16 63.58N 25.46E
Kārsava U.S.S.R. 18 56.45N 27.40E
Karskoye More sea U.S.S.R. 20 73.00N 65.00E
Kartaly U.S.S.R. 20 53.06N 60.37E
Karufa Indonesia 27 3.50S133.27E
Kārūn r. Iran 31 30.25N 48.12E
Karungi Sweden 16 66.03N 23.55E
Karungu Kenya 37 0.50S 34.09E
Karviná Czech. 15 49.50N 18.30E
Kasai r. Zaïre 36 3.10S 16.13E
Kasama Zambia 37 10.10S 31.11E
Kasane Botswana 39 17.48S 25.09E
Kasanga Tanzania 37 8.27S 31.10E
Kāsaragod India 28 12.30N 75.00E
Kasba L. Canada 51 60.18N102.07W
Kasese Uganda 37 0.07N 30.06E
Kāshān Iran 31 33.59N 51.31E
Kashi China 24 39.29N 76.02E
Kashin U.S.S.R. 18 57.22N 37.39E
Kashiwa Japan 23 35.52N139.59E
Kāshmar Iran 31 35.12N 58.26E
Kasimov U.S.S.R. 18 54.55N 41.25E
Kaskinen Finland 16 62.23N 21.13E
Kaskö see Kaskinen Finland 16
Kásos i. Greece 13 35.22N 26.56E
Kassalā Sudan 35 15.24N 36.30E
Kassel W. Germany 14 51.18N 9.30E
Kastamonu Turkey 30 41.22N 33.47E
Kastoría Greece 13 40.32N 21.15E
Kasugai Japan 23 35.14N136.58E
Kasukabe Japan 23 35.58N139.45E
Kasulu Tanzania 37 4.34S 30.06E
Kasungu Malaŵi 37 13.04S 33.29E
Kasūr Pakistan 28 31.07N 74.30E
Katanning Australia 43 33.42S117.33E
Katarniān Ghāt India 29 28.20N 81.09E
Katchall i. India 29 7.57N 93.22E
Katete Zambia 37 14.08S 31.50E
Katha Burma 29 24.11N 96.20E
Katherine Australia 44 14.29S132.20E
Kati Mali 34 12.41N 8.04W
Katima Rapids f. Zambia 39 17.27S 24.13E
Katiola Ivory Coast 38 8.10N 5.10W
Kātmāndu Nepal 29 27.42N 85.19E
Katonga r. Uganda 37 0.03N 30.15E
Katoomba Australia 47 33.42S150.23E
Katowice Poland 15 50.15N 18.59E
Katrīnah, Jabal mtn. Egypt 32 28.30N 33.57E
Katrine, Loch U.K. 6 56.15N 4.30W
Katrineholm Sweden 17 59.00N 16.12E
Katsina Nigeria 38 13.00N 7.32E
Katsina Ala Nigeria 38 7.10N 9.30E
Katsina Ala r. Nigeria 38 7.50N 8.58E
Katsura r. Japan 23 34.53N135.42E
Katsuura Japan 23 35.08N140.18E
Kattegat str. Denmark/Sweden 17 57.00N 11.20E
Katwijk aan Zee Neth. 8 52.13N 4.27E
Kauai i. Hawaii U.S.A. 52 22.05N159.30W
Kaub W. Germany 8 50.07N 7.50E
Kaufbeuren W. Germany 14 47.53N 10.37E
Kauhajoki Finland 16 62.26N 22.11E
Kauhava Finland 16 63.06N 23.05E
Kaukauveld mts. Namibia 39 20.00S 20.15E
Kauliranta Finland 16 66.26N 23.40E
Kaunas U.S.S.R. 17 54.54N 23.54E
Kaura Namoda Nigeria 38 12.39N 6.38E
Kautokeino Norway 16 69.00N 23.02E
Kavála Greece 13 40.56N 24.24E
Kāvali India 29 14.55N 80.01E
Kavarna Bulgaria 13 43.26N 28.22E
Kavimba Botswana 39 18.05S 24.34E
Kavkaz U.S.S.R. 19 45.20N 36.39E
Kavkazskiy Khrebet mts. U.S.S.R. 19 43.00N 44.00E
Kaw Guiana 61 4.29N 52.02W
Kawachi-nagano Japan 23 34.25N135.32E
Kawagoe Japan 23 35.55N139.29E
Kawaguchi Japan 23 35.48N139.43E
Kawambwa Zambia 37 9.47S 29.10E
Kawasaki Japan 23 35.32N139.43E
Kawerau New Zealand 48 38.05S176.42E
Kawhia New Zealand 48 38.04S174.49E
Kaya Burkina Faso 38 13.04N 1.04W
Kayambi Zambia 37 9.26S 32.01E
Kayan r. Indonesia 26 2.47N117.46E
Kaycee U.S.A. 54 43.43N106.38W
Kayenta U.S.A. 54 36.44N110.17W
Kayes Mali 34 14.26N 11.28W
Kayseri Turkey 30 38.42N 35.28E
Kaysville U.S.A. 54 41.02N111.56W
Kazachye U.S.S.R. 21 70.46N136.15E
Kazakhskaya S.S.R. d. U.S.S.R. 19 48.00N 52.30E
Kazakhskiy Zaliv b. U.S.S.R. 19 42.43N 52.30E
Kazan U.S.S.R. 18 55.45N 49.10E
Kazanlŭk Bulgaria 13 42.38N 25.26E
Kazatin U.S.S.R. 15 49.41N 28.49E
Kazaure Nigeria 38 12.40N 8.25E
Kazbek mtn. U.S.S.R. 19 42.42N 44.30E
Kāzerūn Iran 31 29.35N 51.39E
Kazhim U.S.S.R. 18 60.18N 51.34E
Kazincbarcika Hungary 15 48.16N 20.37E
Kazo Japan 23 36.07N139.36E
Kéa i. Greece 13 37.36N 24.20E
Kearney U.S.A. 52 40.42N 99.04W
Keban Turkey 30 38.48N 38.45E
Kebnekaise mtn. Sweden 16 67.53N 18.33E
K'ebri Dehar Ethiopia 35 6.47N 44.17E
Kecskemét Hungary 15 46.54N 19.42E
Kedainiai U.S.S.R. 17 55.17N 24.00E
Kedgwick Canada 55 47.38N 67.21W
Kediri Indonesia 26 7.55S112.01E
Kédougou Senegal 34 12.35N 12.09W
Keele Peak mtn. Canada 50 63.15N129.50W
Keene U.S.A. 55 42.56N 72.17W
Keepit Resr. Australia 47 30.52S150.30E
Keer-Weer, C. Australia 44 13.58S141.30E
Keetmanshoop Namibia 39 26.34S 18.07E
Keewatin d. Canada 51 65.00N 90.00W
Kefallinía i. Greece 13 38.15N 20.33E
Kefar Ata Israel 32 32.48N 35.06E
Kefar Sava Israel 32 32.11N 34.54E
Keffi Nigeria 38 8.52N 7.53E
Keflavík Iceland 16 64.01N 22.35W
Keighley U.K. 4 53.52N 1.54W
Keila U.S.S.R. 17 59.18N 24.29E
Keimoes R.S.A. 39 28.41S 20.58E
Keitele l. Finland 16 62.55N 26.00E
Keith Australia 46 36.06S140.22E
Keith U.K. 6 57.32N 2.57W
Keith Arm b. Canada 50 65.20N122.15W
Kelang Malaysia 26 2.57N101.24E
Kelberg W. Germany 8 50.17N 6.56E
Kelkit r. Turkey 30 40.46N 36.32E
Keller U.S.A. 54 48.03N118.40W
Kellerberrin Australia 43 31.38S117.43E
Kellett, C. Canada 50 71.59N125.34W
Kelloselkä Finland 18 66.55N 28.50E
Kells Meath Rep. of Ire. 7 53.44N 6.53W
Kelme U.S.S.R. 17 55.38N 22.56E
Kelowna Canada 50 49.50N119.29W
Kelso U.K. 6 55.36N 2.26W
Kelso Calif. U.S.A. 54 35.01N115.39W
Kelso Wash. U.S.A. 54 46.09N122.54W
Keluang Malaysia 26 2.01N103.18E
Kelvedon U.K. 5 51.50N 0.43E
Kem U.S.S.R. 18 64.58N 34.39E
Kema Indonesia 27 1.22N125.08E
Ke Macina Mali 38 14.05N 5.20W
Kemah Turkey 30 39.35N 39.02E
Kemaliye Turkey 30 39.16N 38.29E
Kemerovo U.S.S.R. 20 55.25N 86.10E
Kemi Finland 16 65.49N 24.32E
Kemi r. Finland 16 65.47N 24.30E
Kemijärvi Finland 16 66.36N 27.24E
Kemmerer U.S.A. 54 41.48N110.32W
Kempen f. Belgium 8 51.05N 5.00E
Kemp Land f. Antarctica 64 69.00S 57.00E
Kempsey Australia 47 31.05S152.50E
Kempt, Lac l. Canada 55 47.26N 74.30W
Kempten W. Germany 14 47.44N 10.19E
Kenai U.S.A. 50 60.33N151.15W
Kendal Australia 47 31.28S152.40E
Kendal U.K. 4 54.19N 2.44W
Kendari Indonesia 27 3.57S122.36E
Kendenup Australia 43 34.28S117.35E
Kendrick U.S.A. 54 46.37N116.39W
Kenebri Australia 47 30.45S149.02E
Kenema Sierra Leone 34 7.57N 11.11W
Kengeja Tanzania 37 5.24S 39.45E
Keng Tung Burma 29 21.16N 99.39E
Kenhardt R.S.A. 39 29.21S 21.08E
Kenilworth U.K. 5 52.22N 1.35W
Kenitra Morocco 34 34.20N 6.34W
Kenmare Rep. of Ire. 7 51.53N 9.36W
Kennebec r. U.S.A. 55 44.00N 69.50W
Kennet r. U.K. 5 51.28N 0.57W
Kennewick U.S.A. 54 46.12N119.07W
Kenogami r. Canada 55 50.24N 84.20W
Keno Hill town Canada 50 63.58N135.22W
Kenora Canada 51 49.47N 94.26W
Kenosha U.S.A. 53 42.34N 87.50W
Kenozero, Ozero l. U.S.S.R. 18 62.20N 37.00E
Kent d. U.K. 5 51.12N 0.40E
Kent Ohio U.S.A. 55 41.10N 81.20W
Kent Wash. U.S.A. 54 47.23N122.14W
Kentau U.S.S.R. 24 43.28N 68.36E
Kentland U.S.A. 55 40.46N 87.23W
Kenton U.S.A. 55 40.38N 83.38W
Kent Pen. Canada 50 68.30N107.00W
Kentucky d. U.S.A. 53 38.00N 85.00W
Kentucky L. U.S.A. 53 36.15N 88.00W
Kenya Africa 37 1.00N 38.00E
Kenya, Mt. Kenya 37 0.10S 37.19E
Keokuk U.S.A. 53 40.23N 91.25W
Kepi Indonesia 27 6.32S139.19E
Kepno Poland 15 51.17N 17.59E
Keppel B. Australia 44 23.21S150.55E
Kerala d. India 28 10.30N 76.30E
Kerang Australia 46 35.42S143.59E
Kerch U.S.S.R. 19 45.22N 36.27E
Kerchenskiy Proliv str. U.S.S.R. 19 45.15N 36.35E
Kerema P.N.G. 27 7.59S145.46E
Kericho Kenya 37 0.22S 35.19E
Kerinci, Gunung mtn. Indonesia 26 1.45S101.20E
Kerio r. Kenya 37 3.00N 36.14E
Kerki R.S.F.S.R. U.S.S.R. 18 63.40N 54.00E
Kerki Tk.S.S.R. U.S.S.R. 20 37.53N 65.10E
Kérkira Greece 13 39.37N 19.50E
Kérkira i. Greece 13 39.35N 19.50E
Kerkrade Neth. 8 50.52N 6.02E
Kermān Iran 31 30.18N 57.05E
Kermānshāh Iran 31 34.19N 47.04E
Kerme Körfezi g. Turkey 13 36.52N 27.53E
Kerpen W. Germany 8 50.52N 6.42E
Kerry d. Rep. of Ire. 7 52.07N 9.35W
Kerry Head Rep. of Ire. 7 52.24N 9.56W
Kerulen r. Mongolia 25 48.45N117.00E
Kesagami L. Canada 55 50.23N 80.15W
Keşan Turkey 13 40.50N 26.39E
Keshod India 28 21.18N 70.15E
Keskal India 29 20.05N 81.35E
Keski-Suomi d. Finland 16 62.30N 25.30E
Keswick U.K. 4 54.35N 3.09W
Keszthely Hungary 15 46.46N 17.15E
Ketapang Kalimantan Indonesia 26 1.50S110.02E
Ketchikan U.S.A. 50 55.25N131.40W
Ketchum U.S.A. 54 43.41N114.22W
Kete Krachi Ghana 38 7.50N 0.03W
Ketrzyn Poland 15 54.06N 21.23E
Kettering U.K. 5 52.24N 0.44W
Kettering U.S.A. 55 39.41N 84.10W
Kettle Falls town U.S.A. 54 48.36N118.03W
Keweenaw B. U.S.A. 55 46.46N 88.26W
Keweenaw Pen. U.S.A. 55 47.10N 88.30W
Key, Lough Rep. of Ire. 7 54.00N 8.15W
Key Harbour Canada 55 45.52N 80.48W
Keynsham U.K. 5 51.25N 2.30W
Kezhma U.S.S.R. 21 58.58N101.08E
Kežmarok Czech. 15 49.08N 20.25E
Khabarovsk U.S.S.R. 25 48.32N135.08E
Khairpur Sind Pakistan 28 27.30N 68.50E
Khalkís Greece 13 38.27N 23.36E
Khalmer Yu U.S.S.R. 18 67.58N 64.48E
Khalturin U.S.S.R. 18 58.38N 48.50E
Khalūf Oman 28 20.31N 58.04E
Khambhāt, G. of India 28 20.30N 72.00E
Khamkeut Laos 29 18.14N104.44E
Khānaqīn Iraq 31 34.22N 45.22E
Khandwa India 28 21.49N 76.23E
Khāneh Khvodī Iran 31 36.05N 56.04E
Khaniá Greece 13 35.30N 24.02E
Khanka, Ozero l. U.S.S.R. 25 45.00N132.30E
Khanty-Mansiysk U.S.S.R. 20 61.00N 69.00E
Khān Yūnus Egypt 32 31.21N 34.18E
Khapcheranga U.S.S.R. 25 49.46N112.20E
Kharagpur India 29 22.23N 87.22E
Khārān r. Iran 31 27.37N 58.48E
Khārijah, Al Wāḥāt al oasis Egypt 30 24.55N 30.35E
Kharkov U.S.S.R. 19 50.00N 36.15E
Khār Kūh mtn. Iran 31 31.37N 53.47E
Kharovsk U.S.S.R. 18 59.67N 40.07E
Khartoum see Al Kharṭūm Sudan 35
Kharutayuvam U.S.S.R. 18 66.51N 59.31E
Khasavyurt U.S.S.R. 19 43.16N 46.36E
Khāsh r. Afghan. 31 31.12N 62.00E
Khāsh Iran 31 28.14N 61.15E
Khashgort U.S.S.R. 18 65.25N 65.40E
Khaskovo Bulgaria 13 41.57N 25.33E
Khatanga U.S.S.R. 21 71.50N102.31E
Khatangskiy Zaliv g. U.S.S.R. 21 75.00N112.10E
Khemmarat Thailand 29 16.04N105.10E
Khenifra Morocco 34 33.00N 5.40W
Khersān r. Iran 31 31.29N 48.53E
Kherson U.S.S.R. 19 46.39N 32.38E
Khíos Greece 13 38.23N 26.07E
Khíos i. Greece 13 38.23N 26.04E
Khiva U.S.S.R. 31 41.25N 60.49E
Khmelnik U.S.S.R. 15 49.36N 27.59E
Khmelnitskiy U.S.S.R. 15 49.25N 26.49E
Khodorov U.S.S.R. 15 49.20N 24.19E
Kholm U.S.S.R. 18 57.10N 31.11E
Kholmogory U.S.S.R. 18 63.51N 41.46E
Khomas-Hochland mts. Namibia 39 22.50S 16.25E
Khonu U.S.S.R. 21 66.29N143.12E
Khoper r. U.S.S.R. 19 49.35N 42.17E
Khorixas Namibia 39 20.24S 14.58E
Khorog U.S.S.R. 24 37.32N 71.32E
Khorramābād Iran 31 33.29N 48.21E
Khorramshahr Iran 31 30.26N 48.09E
Khotimsk U.S.S.R. 15 53.24N 32.36E
Khotin U.S.S.R. 15 48.30N 26.31E
Khowrnag, Kūh-e mtn. Iran 31 32.10N 54.38E
Khoyniki U.S.S.R. 15 51.54N 30.00E
Khuis Botswana 39 26.37S 21.50E
Khulga r. U.S.S.R. 18 63.33N 61.53E
Khulna Bangla. 29 22.49N 89.34E
Khurīyā Murīyā, Jazā'ir is. Oman 28 17.30N 56.00E
Khurra Bārīk r. Iraq 30 32.00N 44.15E
Khust U.S.S.R. 15 48.11N 23.19E
Khvor Iran 31 33.47N 55.06E
Khvormuj Iran 31 28.40N 51.20E
Khvoy Iran 31 38.32N 45.02E
Khyber Pass Asia 28 34.06N 71.05E
Kiama Australia 47 34.41S150.49E
Kibali r. Zaïre 37 3.37N 28.38E
Kibombo Zaïre 36 3.58S 25.57E
Kibondo Tanzania 37 3.35S 30.41E
Kibre Mengist Ethiopia 35 5.52N 39.00E
Kibungu Rwanda 37 2.10S 30.31E
Kibwesa Tanzania 37 6.30S 29.57E
Kibwezi Kenya 37 2.28S 37.57E
Kichiga U.S.S.R. 21 59.50N163.27E
Kicking Horse Pass Canada 50 51.28N116.23W
Kidal Mali 38 18.27N 1.25E
Kidderminster U.K. 5 52.24N 2.13W
Kidete Morogoro Tanzania 37 6.39S 36.42E
Kidsgrove U.K. 4 53.06N 2.15W
Kiel W. Germany 14 54.20N 10.08E
Kielce Poland 15 50.52N 20.37E
Kieler Bucht b. W. Germany 14 54.30N 10.30E
Kiev see Kiyev U.S.S.R. 15
Kiffa Mauritania 34 16.38N 11.28W
Kigali Rwanda 37 1.59S 30.05E
Kigoma Tanzania 37 4.52S 29.36E
Kigoma d. Tanzania 37 4.45S 30.00E
Kigosi r. Tanzania 37 4.37S 31.29E
Kiiminkin r. Finland 16 65.12N 25.18E
Kikinda Yugo. 15 45.51N 20.30E
Kikládhes is. Greece 13 37.00N 25.00E
Kikori P.N.G. 27 7.25S144.13E
Kikori r. P.N.G. 27 7.10S144.05E
Kikwit Zaïre 36 5.02S 18.51E
Kil Sweden 17 59.30N 13.19E
Kilafors Sweden 17 61.14N 16.34E
Kila Kila P.N.G. 27 9.31S147.10E
Kilchu N. Korea 25 40.55N129.21E
Kilcoy Australia 45 26.57S152.33E
Kilcullen Rep. of Ire. 7 53.08N 6.46W
Kildare Rep. of Ire. 7 53.10N 6.55W
Kildare d. Rep. of Ire. 7 53.10N 6.50W
Kildonan Zimbabwe 39 17.22S 30.33E
Kilfinan U.K. 6 55.58N 5.18W
Kilifi Kenya 37 3.30S 39.50E
Kilimanjaro d. Tanzania 37 3.45S 37.40E
Kilimanjaro mtn. Tanzania 37 3.02S 37.20E
Kilindoni Tanzania 37 7.55S 39.39E
Kilingi-Nõmme U.S.S.R. 17 58.09N 24.58E
Kilis Turkey 30 36.43N 37.07E
Kiliya U.S.S.R. 15 45.30N 29.16E
Kilkee Rep. of Ire. 7 52.41N 9.40W
Kilkenny Rep. of Ire. 7 52.39N 7.16W
Kilkenny d. Rep. of Ire. 7 52.35N 7.15W
Kilkieran B. Rep. of Ire. 7 53.20N 9.42W
Kilkís Greece 13 40.59N 22.51E
Killala B. Rep. of Ire. 7 54.15N 9.10W
Killard Pt. U.K. 7 54.19N 5.31W
Killarney Australia 47 28.18S152.15E
Killarney Rep. of Ire. 7 52.04N 9.32W
Killary Harbour est. Rep. of Ire. 7 53.38N 9.56W
Killin U.K. 6 56.29N 4.19W
Killíni mtn. Greece 13 37.56N 22.22E
Killorglin Rep. of Ire. 7 52.07N 9.45W
Killybegs Rep. of Ire. 7 54.38N 8.27W
Killyleagh U.K. 7 54.24N 5.39W
Kilmarnock U.K. 6 55.37N 4.30W
Kilmichael Pt. Rep. of Ire. 7 52.44N 6.09W
Kilmore Australia 47 37.18S144.58E
Kilninver U.K. 6 56.21N 5.30W
Kilombero r. Tanzania 37 8.30S 37.28E
Kilosa Tanzania 37 6.49S 37.00E
Kilronan Rep. of Ire. 7 53.08N 9.41W
Kilrush Rep. of Ire. 7 52.39N 9.30W
Kilsyth U.K. 6 55.59N 4.04W
Kilvo Sweden 16 66.50N 21.04E
Kilwa Kivinje Tanzania 37 8.45S 39.21E
Kilwa Masoko Tanzania 37 8.55S 39.31E
Kimaän Indonesia 27 7.54S138.51E
Kimba Australia 46 33.09S136.25E
Kimberley R.S.A. 39 28.44S 24.44E
Kimberley Plateau Australia 42 17.20S127.20E
Kimito i. Finland 17 60.10N 22.30E
Kimparana Mali 38 12.52N 4.59W
Kimry U.S.S.R. 18 56.51N 37.20E
Kinabalu mtn. Malaysia 26 6.10N116.40E
Kincardine Canada 55 44.11N 81.38W
Kindia Guinea 34 10.03N 12.49W
Kindu Zaïre 36 3.00S 25.56E
Kinel U.S.S.R. 18 53.17N 50.42E
Kineshma U.S.S.R. 18 57.28N 42.08E
Kingaroy Australia 44 26.33S151.50E
King City U.S.A. 54 36.13N121.08W
King George Is. Canada 51 57.20N 78.25W
King George Sd. Australia 43 35.03S117.57E
King I. Australia 45 39.50S144.00E
Kingisepp U.S.S.R. 17 58.12N 22.30E
King Leopold Ranges mts. Australia 42 17.00S125.30E
Kingman Ariz. U.S.A. 54 35.12N114.04W
Kingoonya Australia 46 30.54S135.18E
Kings r. U.S.A. 54 36.03N119.49W
Kingsbridge U.K. 5 50.17N 3.46W
Kings Canyon Nat. Park U.S.A. 54 36.48N118.30W
Kingsclere U.K. 5 51.20N 1.14W
Kingscote Australia 46 35.40S137.38E
King Sd. Australia 42 17.00S123.30E
Kingsdown Kent U.K. 5 51.21N 0.17E
Kingsley Dam U.S.A. 52 41.15N101.30W
King's Lynn U.K. 4 52.45N 0.25E
Kings Peaks mts. U.S.A. 54 40.46N110.23W
Kingston Australia 46 36.50S139.50E
Kingston Canada 55 44.14N 76.30W
Kingston Jamaica 57 17.58N 76.48W
Kingston New Zealand 48 45.20S168.43E
Kingston N.Y. U.S.A. 55 41.55N 74.00W
Kingston upon Hull U.K. 4 53.45N 0.20W
Kingstown St. Vincent 57 13.12N 61.14W
Kingsville U.S.A. 52 27.32N 97.53W
Kingswood Avon U.K. 5 51.27N 2.29W
Kings Worthy U.K. 5 51.06N 1.18W
Kington U.K. 5 52.12N 3.02W
Kingussie U.K. 6 57.05N 4.04W
King William I. Canada 51 69.00N 97.30W
King William's Town R.S.A. 39 32.52S 27.23E
Kinloch Rannoch U.K. 6 56.42N 4.11W
Kinna Sweden 17 57.30N 12.41E
Kinnairds Head U.K. 6 57.42N 2.00W
Kinnegad Rep. of Ire. 7 53.28N 7.08W
Kino r. Japan 23 34.13N135.09E
Kinross U.K. 6 56.13N 3.27W
Kinsale Rep. of Ire. 7 51.42N 8.32W
Kinshasa Zaïre 36 4.18S 15.18E
Kintyre pen. U.K. 6 55.35N 5.35W
Kinvara Rep. of Ire. 7 53.08N 8.56W
Kiparissía Greece 13 37.15N 21.40E
Kipawa, Lac l. Canada 55 46.55N 79.00W
Kipengere Range mts. Tanzania 37 9.15S 34.15E
Kipili Tanzania 37 7.30S 30.39E
Kipini Kenya 37 2.31S 40.32E
Kippure mtn. Rep. of Ire. 7 53.11N 6.20W
Kirby U.S.A. 54 43.49N108.10W
Kircheimbolanden W. Germany 8 49.39N 8.00E
Kirensk U.S.S.R. 21 57.45N108.00E
Kirgiziya Step f. U.S.S.R. 19 50.00N 57.10E
Kirgizskaya S.S.R. d. U.S.S.R. 24 41.30N 75.00E
Kirgiz Steppe see Kirgiziya Step f. U.S.S.R. 19
Kiribati Pacific Oc. 40 2.00S175.00E
Kirikkale Turkey 30 39.51N 33.32E
Kirillov U.S.S.R. 18 59.53N 38.21E
Kirínia Cyprus 32 35.20N 33.20E
Kirkby Lonsdale U.K. 4 54.13N 2.36W
Kirkby Stephen U.K. 4 54.27N 2.23W
Kirkcaldy U.K. 6 56.07N 3.10W
Kirkcudbright U.K. 6 54.50N 4.03W
Kirkenes Norway 16 69.40N 30.03E
Kirkland Ariz. U.S.A. 54 34.26N112.43W
Kirkland Wash. U.S.A. 54 47.41N122.12W
Kirkland Lake town Canada 55 48.10N 80.00W
Kirklareli Turkey 13 41.44N 27.12E
Kirkpatrick, Mt. Antarctica 64 85.00S170.00E
Kirksville U.S.A. 53 40.12N 92.35W
Kirkūk Iraq 31 35.28N 44.26E
Kirkwall U.K. 6 58.59N 2.58W
Kirkwood R.S.A. 39 33.25S 25.24E
Kirn W. Germany 8 49.47N 7.28E
Kirov R.S.F.S.R. U.S.S.R. 18 53.59N 34.20E
Kirov R.S.F.S.R. U.S.S.R. 18 58.38N 49.38E

Kirovabad U.S.S.R. 31 40.39N 46.20E
Kirovakan U.S.S.R. 31 40.49N 44.30E
Kirovo-Chepetsk U.S.S.R. 18 58.40N 50.02E
Kirovograd U.S.S.R. 19 48.31N 32.15E
Kirovsk U.S.S.R. 18 67.37N 33.39E
Kirovskiy U.S.S.R. 21 54.25N155.37E
Kirriemuir U.K. 6 56.41N 3.01W
Kirs U.S.S.R. 18 59.21N 52.10E
Kirsanoy U.S.S.R. 19 51.29N 52.30E
Kırşehir Turkey 30 39.09N 34.08E
Kiruna Sweden 16 67.51N 20.16E
Kisa Sweden 17 57.59N 15.37E
Kisaga Tanzania 37 4.26S 34.26E
Kisangani Zaïre 35 0.33N 25.14E
Kisaran Indonesia 26 2.47N 99.29E
Kisarazu Japan 23 35.23N139.55E
Kiselevsk U.S.S.R. 20 54.01N 86.41E
Kishinev U.S.S.R. 15 47.00N 28.50E
Kishiwada Japan 23 34.28N135.22E
Kishtwār Jammu & Kashmir 28 33.20N 75.48E
Kisii Kenya 37 0.40S 34.44E
Kisiju Tanzania 37 7.23S 39.20E
Kiskörös Hungary 15 46.38N 19.17E
Kiskunfélegyháza Hungary 15 46.43N 19.52E
Kiskunhalas Hungary 15 46.26N 19.30E
Kislovodsk U.S.S.R. 19 43.56N 42.44E
Kismayu Somali Rep. 37 0.25S 42.31E
Kiso Japan 23 35.02N136.45E
Kiso sammyaku *mts.* Japan 23 35.42N137.50E
Kissamos Greece 13 35.30N 23.38E
Kissidougou Guinea 34 9.48N 10.08W
Kissū, Jabal *mtn.* Sudan 35 21.35N 25.09E
Kistna *r. see* Krishna *r.* India 28
Kisumu Kenya 37 0.07S 34.47E
Kisvárda Hungary 15 48.13N 22.05E
Kita Mali 34 13.04N 9.29W
Kitab U.S.S.R. 20 39.08N 66.51E
Kitakyūshū Japan 25 33.52N130.49E
Kitale Kenya 37 1.01N 35.01E
Kitchener Australia 43 31.01S124.20E
Kitchener Canada 55 43.27N 80.29W
Kitchigama *r.* Canada 55 51.12N 78.55W
Kitgum Uganda 37 3.17N 32.54E
Kíthira Greece 13 36.09N 23.00E
Kíthira *i.* Greece 13 36.15N 23.00E
Kíthnos *i.* Greece 13 37.25N 24.25E
Kitikmeot *d.* Canada 50 80.00N105.00W
Kitimat Canada 50 54.05N128.38W
Kitinen *r.* Finland 16 67.20N 27.27E
Kitsman U.S.S.R. 15 48.30N 25.50E
Kittakittaooloo, L. Australia 46 28.09S138.09E
Kittanning U.S.A. 55 40.49N 79.32W
Kittery U.S.A. 55 43.05N 70.45W
Kittilä Finland 16 67.40N 24.54E
Kitui Kenya 37 1.22S 38.01E
Kitunda Tanzania 37 6.48S 33.17E
Kitwe Zambia 37 12.50S 28.04E
Kiunga Kenya 37 1.46S 41.30E
Kivijärvi *l.* Finland 16 63.10N 25.09E
Kivik Sweden 17 55.41N 14.15E
Kivu *d.* Zaïre 37 3.00S 27.00E
Kivu, L. Rwanda/Zaïre 37 2.00S 29.10E
Kiyev U.S.S.R. 15 50.28N 30.29E
Kiyevskoye Vodokhranilishche *resr.* U.S.S.R. 15 51.00N 30.25E
Kizel U.S.S.R. 18 59.01N 57.42E
Kizema U.S.S.R. 18 61.12N 44.52E
Kizil *r.* Turkey 30 41.45N 35.57E
Kizlyar U.S.S.R. 19 43.51N 46.43E
Kizlyarskiy Zaliv *b.* U.S.S.R. 19 44.33N 47.00E
Kizu *r.* Japan 23 34.53N135.42E
Kizyl-Arvat U.S.S.R. 31 39.00N 56.23E
Kizyl Atrek Turkey 31 37.37N 54.49E
Kladno Czech. 14 50.10N 14.05E
Klagenfurt Austria 14 46.38N 14.20E
Klaipeda U.S.S.R. 17 55.43N 21.07E
Klamath *r.* U.S.A. 54 41.33N124.04W
Klamath Falls *town* U.S.A. 54 42.14N121.47W
Klamath Mts. U.S.A. 54 41.40N123.20W
Klamono Indonesia 27 1.08S131.28E
Klar *r.* Sweden 17 59.23N 13.32E
Klatovy Czech. 14 49.24N 13.18E
Klawer R.S.A. 39 31.48S 18.34E
Kleinsee R.S.A. 39 29.41S 17.04E
Klerksdorp R.S.A. 39 26.51S 26.38E
Klevan U.S.S.R. 15 50.44N 25.50E
Kleve W. Germany 8 51.47N 6.11E
Klickitat U.S.A. 54 45.49N121.09W
Klimovichi U.S.S.R. 15 53.36N 31.58E
Klimpfjäll Sweden 16 65.04N 14.52E
Klin U.S.S.R. 18 56.20N 36.45E
Klintehamn Sweden 17 57.24N 18.12E
Klintsy U.S.S.R. 15 52.45N 32.15E
Klipdale R.S.A. 39 34.18S 19.58E
Klippan Sweden 17 56.08N 13.06E
Klipplaat R.S.A. 39 33.01S 24.19E
Kłobuck Poland 15 50.55N 18.57E
Kłodzko Poland 14 50.27N 16.39E
Klöfta Norway 17 60.04N 11.09E
Klondike Canada 50 64.02N139.24W
Kluczbork Poland 15 50.59N 18.13E
Knaresborough U.K. 4 54.01N 1.29W
Knighton U.K. 5 52.21N 3.02W
Knin Yugo. 14 44.02N 16.10E
Knockadoon Head Rep. of Ire. 7 51.52N 7.52W
Knockalongy *mtn.* Rep. of Ire. 7 54.12N 8.45W
Knockmealdown Mts. Rep. of Ire. 7 52.15N 7.55W
Knokke Belgium 8 51.21N 3.17E
Knolls U.S.A. 54 40.44N113.18W
Knossos *site* Greece 13 35.20N 25.10E
Knoxville U.S.A. 53 36.00N 83.57W
Knutsford U.K. 4 53.18N 2.22W
Knyazhevo U.S.S.R. 18 59.40N 43.51E
Knysna R.S.A. 39 34.02S 23.03E
Koartac Canada 51 61.05N 69.36W
Kōbe Japan 23 34.41N135.10E
København Denmark 17 55.43N 12.34E
Koblenz W. Germany 8 50.21N 7.36E
Kobrin U.S.S.R. 15 52.16N 24.22E
Kobroör *i.* Indonesia 27 6.10S134.30E
Kočani Yugo. 13 41.55N 22.24E
Kočevje Yugo. 12 45.38N 14.52E
Kochkoma U.S.S.R. 18 64.03N 34.14E
Kochmes U.S.S.R. 18 66.12N 60.48E
Kodaira Japan 23 35.44N139.29E
Kodiak U.S.A. 50 57.49N152.30W
Kodiak I. U.S.A. 50 57.00N153.50W
Kodima U.S.S.R. 18 62.24N 43.57E
Kodyma U.S.S.R. 15 48.06N 29.04E
Koekelare Belgium 8 51.08N 2.59E
Koekenaap R.S.A. 39 31.30S 18.18E
Koersel Belgium 8 51.04N 5.19E
Koës Namibia 39 25.58S 19.07E
Koffiefontein R.S.A. 39 29.24S 25.00E
Köflach Austria 14 47.04N 15.05E
Koforidua Ghana 38 6.01N 0.12W
Kōfu Japan 23 35.39N138.35E
Koga Tanzania 37 6.10S 32.21E
Køge Denmark 17 55.27N 12.11E
Køge Bugt *b.* Greenland 51 65.00N 40.30W
Kohāt Pakistan 28 33.37N 71.30E
Kohīma India 29 25.40N 94.08E
Kohler Range *mts.* Antarctica 64 77.00S110.00W
Kohtla-Järve U.S.S.R. 18 59.28N 27.20E
Koito *r.* Japan 23 35.21N139.52E
Kojonup Australia 43 33.50S117.05E
Kokand U.S.S.R. 24 40.33N 70.55E
Kokas Indonesia 27 2.45S132.26E
Kokchetav U.S.S.R. 20 53.18N 69.25E
Kokemäki Finland 17 61.15N 22.21E
Kokka Sudan 35 20.00N 30.35E
Kokkola Finland 16 63.50N 23.07E
Koko Sokoto Nigeria 38 11.27N 4.35E
Kokoda P.N.G. 44 8.50S147.45E
Kokomo U.S.A. 55 40.30N 86.09W
Kokonau Indonesia 27 4.42S136.25E
Kokpekty U.S.S.R. 24 48.45N 82.25E
Koksoak *r.* Canada 51 58.30N 68.15W
Kokstad R.S.A. 39 30.32S 29.25E
Kokuora U.S.S.R. 21 71.33N144.50E
Kolaka Indonesia 27 4.04S121.38E
Kolan Australia 44 24.42S152.10E
Kola Pen. *see* Kolskiy Poluostrov *pen.* U.S.S.R. 18
Kolār India 29 13.10N 78.10E
Kolari Finland 16 67.20N 23.48E
Kolāyat India 28 27.50N 72.57E
Kolbio Kenya 37 1.11S 41.10E
Kolda Senegal 34 12.56N 14.55W
Kolding Denmark 17 55.31N 9.29E
Kolepom *i. see* Yos Sudarsa, Pulau *i.* Indonesia 27
Kolguyev, Ostrov *i.* U.S.S.R. 18 69.00N 49.00E
Kolhāpur India 28 16.43N 74.15E
Kolia Ivory Coast 38 9.46N 6.28W
Kolín Czech. 14 50.02N 15.10E
Kolka U.S.S.R. 17 57.45N 22.35E
Kolki U.S.S.R. 15 51.09N 25.40E
Köln W. Germany 8 50.56N 6.57E
Koło Poland 15 53.25N 21.56E
Koło Poland 15 52.12N 18.37E
Kołobrzeg Poland 14 54.10N 15.35E
Kologriv U.S.S.R. 18 58.49N 44.19E
Kolomna U.S.S.R. 18 55.05N 38.45E
Kolomyya U.S.S.R. 15 48.31N 25.00E
Kolpashevo U.S.S.R. 20 58.21N 82.59E
Kolpino U.S.S.R. 18 59.44N 30.39E
Kolskiy Poluostrov *pen.* U.S.S.R. 18 67.00N 38.00E
Kolsva Sweden 17 59.36N 15.50E
Koluszki Poland 15 51.44N 19.49E
Kolvereid Norway 16 64.53N 11.35E
Kolwezi Zaïre 36 10.44S 25.28E
Kolyma *r.* U.S.S.R. 21 68.50N161.00E
Kolymskiy, Khrebet *mts* U.S.S.R. 21 63.00N160.00E
Kom Kenya 37 1.06N 38.00E
Komadugu Gana *r.* Nigeria 38 13.06N 12.23E
Komadugu Yobe *r.* Niger/Nigeria 38 13.43N 13.19E
Komagane Japan 23 35.43N137.55E
Komaga-take *mtn.* Japan 23 35.47N137.48E
Komaki Japan 23 35.17N136.55E
Komárno Czech. 15 47.45N 18.09E
Komarom Hungary 15 47.44N 18.08E
Komatipoort R.S.A. 39 25.25S 31.55E
Komló Hungary 15 46.12N 18.16E
Kommunarsk U.S.S.R. 19 48.30N 38.47E
Kommunizma, Pik *mtn.* U.S.S.R. 24 38.39N 72.01E
Komotiní Greece 13 41.07N 25.26E
Komrat U.S.S.R. 15 46.18N 28.40E
Komsberg *mtn.* R.S.A. 39 32.40S 20.48E
Komsomolets, Ostrov *i.* U.S.S.R. 21 80.20N 96.00E
Komsomolets, Zaliv *g.* U.S.S.R. 19 45.17N 53.30E
Komsomolsk-na-Amure U.S.S.R. 21 50.32N136.59E
Kōnan Japan 23 35.20N136.53E
Kondakovo U.S.S.R. 21 69.38N152.00E
Kondinin Australia 43 32.33S118.13E
Kondoa Tanzania 37 4.54S 35.49E
Kondopoga U.S.S.R. 18 62.12N 34.17E
Kondratyevo U.S.S.R. 21 57.22N 98.15E
Kondut Australia 43 30.44S117.06E
Kong Ivory Coast 38 8.54N 4.36W
Kong Christian den IX Land *f.* Greenland 51 68.20N 37.00W
Kong Frederik den VI Kyst *f.* Greenland 51 63.00N 44.00W
Kong Haakon VII Hav *sea* Antarctica 64 65.00S 25.00E
Kongolo Zaïre 36 5.20S 27.00E
Kongsberg Norway 17 59.39N 9.39E
Kongsvinger Norway 17 60.12N 12.00E
Kongur Shan *mtn.* China 24 38.40N 75.30E
Kongwa Tanzania 37 6.13S 36.28E
Konin Poland 15 52.13N 18.16E
Konjic Yugo. 15 43.39N 17.57E
Könkämä *r.* Sweden/Finland 16 68.29N 22.30E
Konongo Ghana 38 6.38N 1.12W
Konosha U.S.S.R. 18 60.58N 40.08E
Kōnosu Japan 23 36.03N139.31E
Konotop U.S.S.R. 19 51.15N 33.14E
Końskie Poland 15 51.12N 20.26E
Konstanz W. Germany 14 47.40N 9.10E
Kontagora Nigeria 38 10.24N 5.22E
Kontcha Cameroon 38 7.59N 12.15E
Kontiomäki Finland 18 64.21N 28.10E
Kontum Vietnam 26 14.23N108.00E
Konya Turkey 30 37.51N 32.30E
Konz W. Germany 8 49.42N 6.34E
Konza Kenya 37 1.45S 37.07E
Kookynie Australia 43 29.20S121.29E
Koolatah Australia 44 15.53S142.27E
Koolkootinnie L. Australia 46 27.58S137.47E
Koolyanobbing Australia 43 30.48S119.29E
Koondrook Australia 46 35.39S144.11E
Koongawa Australia 46 33.11S135.52E
Koonibba Australia 46 31.58S133.29E
Koorawatha Australia 47 34.02S148.33E
Koorda Australia 43 30.50S117.51E
Kootjieskolk R.S.A. 39 31.14S 20.18E
Kópavogur Iceland 16 64.06N 21.53W
Koper Yugo. 14 45.33N 13.44E
Kopervik Norway 17 59.17N 5.18E
Kopet Dag, Khrebet *mts.* U.S.S.R. 31 38.00N 58.00E
Köping Sweden 17 59.31N 16.00E
Kopparberg *d.* Sweden 17 60.50N 15.00E
Koppom Sweden 17 59.43N 12.09E
Koprivnica Yugo. 14 46.10N 16.50E
Kopychintsy U.S.S.R. 15 49.10N 25.58E
Kor *r.* Iran 31 29.40N 53.17E
Korba India 29 22.21N 82.41E
Korbach W. Germany 14 51.16N 8.53E
Korçë Albania 13 40.37N 20.45E
Korčula *i.* Yugo. 13 42.56N 16.53E
Kord Küy Iran 31 36.48N 54.07E
Korea Str. S. Korea/Japan 25 35.00N129.20E
Korets U.S.S.R. 15 50.39N 27.10E
Korhogo Ivory Coast 38 9.22N 5.31W
Korim Indonesia 27 0.58S136.10E
Korinthiakós Kólpos *g.* Greece 13 38.15N 22.30E
Kórinthos Greece 13 37.56N 22.55E
Kōriyama Japan 25 37.23N140.22E
Korma U.S.S.R. 15 53.08N 30.47E
Körmend Hungary 14 47.01N 16.37E
Kornat *i.* Yugo. 12 43.48N 15.20E
Korneshty U.S.S.R. 15 47.21N 28.00E
Kornsjö Norway 17 58.57N 11.39E
Koro Mali 38 14.01N 2.58W
Korocha U.S.S.R. 19 50.50N 37.13E
Korogwe Tanzania 37 5.10S 38.35E
Koroit Australia 46 38.17S142.26E
Korong Vale *town* Australia 46 36.22S143.45E
Koror *i.* Belau 27 7.30N134.30E
Korosten U.S.S.R. 15 51.00N 28.30E
Korostyshev U.S.S.R. 15 50.19N 29.03E
Korrat *i.* Yugo. 14 43.48N 15.20E
Korsör Denmark 17 55.20N 11.09E
Korsze Poland 15 54.10N 21.09E
Kortrijk Belgium 8 50.49N 3.17E
Koryakskiy Khrebet *mts.* U.S.S.R. 21 62.20N171.00E
Koryazhma U.S.S.R. 18 61.19N 47.12E
Kos *i.* Greece 13 36.48N 27.10E
Kościan Poland 14 52.06N 16.38E
Kościerzyna Poland 15 54.08N 18.00E
Kosciusko, Mt. Australia 47 36.28S148.17E
Koshk-e Kohneh Afghan 31 34.52N 62.29E
Košice Czech. 15 48.44N 21.15E
Koski Finland 17 60.39N 23.09E
Koslan U.S.S.R. 18 63.29N 48.59E
Kosovska-Mitrovica Yugo. 13 42.54N 20.51E
Kossovo U.S.S.R. 15 52.40N 25.18E
Kosta Sweden 17 56.51N 15.23E
Koster R.S.A. 39 25.51S 26.52E
Kostopol U.S.S.R. 15 50.51N 26.22E
Kostroma U.S.S.R. 18 57.46N 40.59E
Kostrzyn Poland 14 52.24N 17.11E
Kostyukovichi U.S.S.R. 15 53.20N 32.01E
Kosyu U.S.S.R. 18 65.36N 59.00E
Koszalin Poland 14 54.12N 16.09E
Kota Rāj. India 28 25.11N 75.58E
Kota Baharu Malaysia 26 6.07N102.15E
Kota Belud Malaysia 26 6.00N116.00E
Kotabumi Indonesia 26 4.52S104.59E
Kota Kinabalu Malaysia 26 5.59N116.04E
Kotelnich U.S.S.R. 18 58.20N 48.10E
Kotelnikovo U.S.S.R. 19 47.39N 43.08E
Kotel'nyy, Ostrov *i.* U.S.S.R. 21 75.30N141.00E
Kotka Finland 18 60.26N 26.55E
Kotlas U.S.S.R. 18 61.15N 46.28E
Kotlik U.S.A. 50 63.02N163.33W
Kotor Yugo. 13 42.28N 18.47E
Kotovsk M.S.S.R. U.S.S.R. 15 46.50N 28.31E
Kotovsk Ukr.S.S.R. U.S.S.R. 15 47.42N 29.30E
Kottagūdem India 29 17.32N 80.39E
Kotuy *r.* U.S.S.R. 21 71.40N103.00E
Kotzebue U.S.A. 50 66.51N162.40W
Kotzebue Sd. U.S.A. 50 66.20N163.00W
Koudougou Burkina Faso 38 12.15N 2.21W
Koúklia Cyprus 32 34.42N 32.34E
Koumankou Mali 38 11.58N 6.06W
Koumbia Burkina Faso 38 11.18N 3.38W
Koumbia Guinea 34 11.54N 13.40W
Koumongou Togo 38 10.10N 0.29E
Koupéla Burkina Faso 38 12.09N 0.22W
Kouroussa Guinea 34 10.40N 9.50W
Kousseri Cameroon 34 12.07N 15.01E
Koutiala Mali 38 12.20N 5.23W
Kouto Ivory Coast 38 9.53N 6.25W
Kouvola Finland 18 60.54N 26.45E
Kovdor U.S.S.R. 18 67.33N 30.30E
Kovel U.S.S.R. 15 51.12N 24.48E
Kovpyta U.S.S.R. 15 51.22N 30.51E
Kovrov U.S.S.R. 18 56.23N 41.21E
Kovzha *r.* U.S.S.R. 18 61.05N 36.27E
Kowloon Hong Kong 25 22.20N114.15E
Koyukuk *r.* U.S.A. 50 64.50N157.30W
Kozan Turkey 30 37.27N 35.47E
Kozáni Greece 13 40.18N 21.48E
Kozelets U.S.S.R. 15 50.54N 31.09E
Kozhim U.S.S.R. 18 65.45N 59.30E
Kozhposelok U.S.S.R. 18 63.10N 38.10E
Kpandu Ghana 38 7.02N 0.17E
Kpessi Togo 38 8.07N 1.17E
Krabi Thailand 26 8.04N 98.52E
Krâchéh Kampuchea 26 12.30N106.03E
Kragerö Norway 17 58.52N 9.25E
Kragujevac Yugo. 13 44.01N 20.55E
Kraków Poland 15 50.03N 19.55E
Kraljevo Yugo. 13 43.44N 20.41E
Kramatorsk U.S.S.R. 19 48.43N 37.33E
Kramfors Sweden 16 62.55N 17.50E
Kranj Yugo. 14 46.15N 14.21E
Kranskop R.S.A. 39 28.58S 30.52E
Krapkowice Poland 15 50.29N 17.56E
Krasavino U.S.S.R. 18 60.58N 46.25E
Krasilov U.S.S.R. 15 49.39N 26.59E
Kraskino U.S.S.R. 25 42.42N130.48E
Krasnaya Gora U.S.S.R. 15 53.00N 31.36E
Kraśnik Poland 15 50.56N 22.13E
Krasnodar U.S.S.R. 19 45.02N 39.00E
Krasnograd U.S.S.R. 19 49.22N 35.28E
Krasnokamsk U.S.S.R. 18 58.05N 55.49E
Krasnoperekopsk U.S.S.R. 19 45.56N 33.47E
Krasnoselkup U.S.S.R. 20 65.45N 82.31E
Krasnoturinsk U.S.S.R. 18 59.46N 60.10E
Krasnoufimsk U.S.S.R. 18 56.40N 57.49E
Krasnouralsk U.S.S.R. 20 58.25N 60.00E
Krasnovishersk U.S.S.R. 18 60.25N 57.02E
Krasnovodsk U.S.S.R. 31 40.01N 53.00E
Krasnovodskiy Poluostrov *pen.* U.S.S.R. 31 40.30N 53.10E
Krasnovodskiy Zaliv *g.* U.S.S.R. 31 39.50N 53.15E
Krasnoyarsk U.S.S.R. 21 56.05N 92.46E
Krasnyy Yar U.S.S.R. 19 46.32N 48.21E
Kratovo Yugo. 13 42.05N 22.11E
Krefeld W. Germany 8 51.20N 6.32E
Kremenchug U.S.S.R. 19 49.03N 33.25E
Kremenchugskoye Vodokhranilishche *resr.* U.S.S.R. 19 49.20N 32.30E
Kremenets U.S.S.R. 15 50.05N 25.48E
Krems Austria 14 48.25N 15.36E
Krestovka U.S.S.R. 18 66.24N 52.31E
Kretinga U.S.S.R. 17 55.53N 21.13E
Kribi Cameroon 38 2.56N 9.56E
Krichev U.S.S.R. 15 53.40N 31.44E
Krishna *r.* India 29 16.00N 81.00E
Kristiansand Norway 17 58.10N 8.00E
Kristianstad Sweden 17 56.02N 14.08E
Kristianstad *d.* Sweden 17 56.15N 13.35E
Kristiansund Norway 16 63.07N 7.45E
Kristiinankaupunki Finland 17 62.17N 21.23E
Kristinehamn Sweden 17 59.20N 14.07E
Kristinestad *see* Kristiinankaupunki Finland 17
Kristinovka U.S.S.R. 15 48.50N 29.58E
Kríti *i.* Greece 13 35.15N 25.00E
Kritikón Pélagos *sea* Greece 13 36.00N 25.00E
Krivaja *r.* Yugo. 15 44.27N 18.09E
Krivoy Rog U.S.S.R. 19 47.55N 33.24E
Krk *i.* Yugo. 14 45.04N 14.36E
Krnov Czech. 15 50.05N 17.41E
Kroken Norway 16 65.23N 14.15E
Krokom Sweden 16 63.20N 14.30E
Kronoberg *d.* Sweden 17 56.45N 14.15E
Kronprins Olav Kyst *f.* Antarctica 64 69.00S 42.00E
Kronshtadt U.S.S.R. 18 60.00N 29.40E
Kroonstad R.S.A. 39 27.38S 27.12E
Kropotkin U.S.S.R. 19 45.25N 40.35E
Krosno Poland 15 49.42N 21.46E
Krotoszyn Poland 15 51.42N 17.26E
Kruger Nat. Park R.S.A. 39 24.10S 31.36E
Krugersdorp R.S.A. 39 26.06S 27.46E
Krujë Albania 13 41.30N 19.48E
Krumbach W. Germany 14 48.14N 10.22E
Krung Thep Thailand 29 13.45N100.35E
Krupki U.S.S.R. 15 54.19N 29.05E
Kruševac Yugo. 15 43.34N 21.20E
Krym *pen.* U.S.S.R. 19 45.30N 34.00E
Krymsk U.S.S.R. 19 44.56N 38.00E
Krzyz Poland 14 52.54N 16.01E
Ksar el Boukhari Algeria 34 35.55N 2.47E
Kuala Dungun Malaysia 26 4.47N103.26E
Kualakapuas Indonesia 26 3.01S114.21E
Kuala Lipis Malaysia 26 4.11N102.00E
Kuala Lumpur Malaysia 26 3.08N101.42E
Kuala Trengganu Malaysia 26 5.10N103.10E
Kuandang Indonesia 27 0.53N122.58E
Kuantan Malaysia 26 3.50N103.19E
Kuba U.S.S.R. 31 41.23N 48.33E
Kuban *r.* U.S.S.R. 19 45.20N 37.17E
Kuching Malaysia 26 1.32N110.20E
Kudat Malaysia 26 6.45N116.47E
Kudus Indonesia 26 6.46S110.48E
Kufstein Austria 14 47.36N 12.11E
Kūhpāyeh Iran 31 32.42N 52.25E
Kūhrān, Kūh-e *mtn.* Iran 31 26.46N 58.15E
Kuivaniemi Finland 16 65.35N 25.11E
Kuke Botswana 39 23.19S 24.29E
Kukerin Australia 43 33.11S118.03E
Kukës Albania 13 42.05N 20.24E
Kūl *r.* Iran 31 28.00N 55.45E
Kula Turkey 30 38.33N 28.38E
Kulakshi U.S.S.R. 19 47.09N 55.22E
Kulal, Mt. Kenya 37 2.44N 36.56E
Kuldiga U.S.S.R. 17 56.58N 21.59E
Kulgera Australia 44 25.50S133.18E
Kulin Australia 43 32.40S118.10E
Kulja Australia 43 30.28S117.17E
Kulkyne *r.* Australia 47 30.16S144.12E
Kulpara Australia 46 34.07S137.59E
Kulsary U.S.S.R. 19 46.59N 54.02E
Kulu Turkey 19 39.06N 33.02E
Kulunda U.S.S.R. 20 52.34N 78.58E
Kulwin Australia 46 35.02S142.40E
Kulyab U.S.S.R. 24 37.55N 69.47E
Kuma *r.* U.S.S.R. 19 44.40N 46.55E
Kumagaya Japan 23 36.08N139.23E
Kumai Indonesia 26 2.45S111.44E
Kumamoto Japan 25 32.50N130.42E
Kumanovo Yugo. 13 42.08N 21.40E
Kumara New Zealand 48 42.38S171.11E
Kumarl Australia 43 32.47S121.33E
Kumasi Ghana 38 6.45N 1.35W
Kumba Cameroon 38 4.39N 9.26E
Kumbakonam India 29 10.59N 79.24E
Kum Dag U.S.S.R. 31 39.14N 54.33E
Kumertau U.S.S.R. 18 52.48N 55.46E
Kumi Uganda 37 1.26N 33.54E
Kumla Sweden 17 59.08N 15.08E
Kunashir *i.* U.S.S.R. 25 44.25N146.00E
Kundelungu Mts. Zaïre 37 9.30S 27.50E
Kundip Australia 43 33.44S120.11E
Kungälv Sweden 17 57.52N 11.58E
Kungsbacka Sweden 17 57.29N 12.04E
Kungur U.S.S.R. 18 57.27N 56.50E
Kunlun Shan *mts.* China 24 36.40N 88.00E
Kunming China 24 25.04N102.41E
Kunsan S. Korea 25 35.57N126.42E
Kununoppin Australia 43 31.09S117.53E
Kununurra Australia 41 15.42S128.50E
Kuolayarvi U.S.S.R. 16 66.58N 29.12E
Kuopio Finland 18 62.51N 27.30E
Kupa *r.* Yugo. 14 45.30N 16.20E
Kupang Indonesia 27 10.13S123.38E
Kupyansk U.S.S.R. 19 49.41N 37.37E
Kuqa China 24 41.43N 82.58E
Kura *r.* U.S.S.R. 31 39.18N 49.22E
Kuraymah Sudan 35 18.32N 31.48E
Kurchum U.S.S.R. 24 48.35N 83.39E
Kurdistan *f.* Asia 31 37.00N 43.30E
Kŭrdzhali Bulgaria 13 41.38N 25.21E
Kurgaldzhino U.S.S.R. 20 50.35N 70.03E
Kurgan U.S.S.R. 20 55.20N 65.20E
Kurikka Finland 16 62.37N 22.25E
Kurilskiye Ostrova *is.* U.S.S.R. 25 46.00N150.30E
Kuring Kuru Namibia 39 17.36S 18.36E
Kurlovski U.S.S.R. 18 55.26N 40.40E
Kurnalpi Australia 43 30.35S121.50E
Kurnool India 29 15.51N 78.01E
Kurow New Zealand 48 44.44S170.28E
Kurri Kurri Australia 47 32.49S151.29E
Kursk U.S.S.R. 19 51.45N 36.14E
Kurškiy Zaliv *b.* U.S.S.R. 17 55.00N 21.00E
Kuršumlija Yugo. 13 43.09N 21.16E
Kuru Finland 17 61.52N 23.44E
Kuruman R.S.A. 39 27.28S 23.25E
Kuruman *r.* R.S.A. 39 26.53S 20.38E
Kusatsu Japan 23 35.02N135.57E
Kusel W. Germany 8 49.32N 7.21E
Kushchevskaya U.S.S.R. 19 46.34N 39.39E
Kushida *r.* Japan 23 34.36N136.34E
Kushiro Japan 25 42.58N144.24E
Kushka U.S.S.R. 31 35.14N 62.15E
Kuskokwim B. U.S.A. 50 59.45N162.25W
Kuskokwim Mts. U.S.A. 50 62.50N156.00W
Kustanay U.S.S.R. 20 53.15N 63.40E
Küstenkanal W. Germany 8 53.05N 7.46E
Kūstī Sudan 35 13.11N 32.38E
Kütahya Turkey 30 39.25N 29.56E
Kutaisi U.S.S.R. 19 42.15N 42.44E
Kutch, G. of India 28 22.30N 69.30E
Kutná Hora Czech. 14 49.57N 15.16E
Kutno Poland 15 52.15N 19.23E
Kutu Zaïre 36 2.42S 18.09E
Kuusamo Finland 18 65.57N 29.15E
Kuwait Asia 31 29.20N 47.40E
Kuwait *town see* Al Kuwayt Kuwait 31
Kuwana Japan 23 35.04N136.42E
Kuybyshev U.S.S.R. 18 53.10N 50.15E
Kuybyshevskoye Vodokhranilishche *resr.* U.S.S.R. 18 55.00N 49.00E
Kuyeda U.S.S.R. 18 56.25N 55.33E
Kuzey Anadolu Dağlari *mts.* Turkey 30 40.32N 38.00E
Kuznetsk U.S.S.R. 18 53.08N 46.36E
Kuzomen U.S.S.R. 18 66.15N 36.51E
Kuzreka U.S.S.R. 18 66.35N 34.48E
Kvaenangen *est.* Norway 16 69.50N 21.30E
Kwale Kenya 37 4.20S 39.25E
Kwangju S. Korea 25 35.07N126.52E
Kwango *r.* Zaïre 36 3.20S 17.23E
Kwara *d.* Nigeria 38 8.20N 5.35E
Kwatisore Indonesia 27 3.18S134.50E
Kwekwe Zimbabwe 39 18.59S 29.46E
Kwethluk U.S.A. 50 60.49N161.27W
Kwidzyn Poland 15 53.45N 18.56E
Kwigillingok U.S.A. 50 59.51N163.08W
Kwiguk U.S.A. 50 62.45N164.28W
Kwinana Australia 43 32.15S115.48E
Kwobrup Australia 43 33.36S117.55E
Kwoka *mtn.* Indonesia 27 1.30S132.30E
Kyabé Chad 34 9.28N 18.54E
Kyaka Tanzania 37 1.16S 31.27E
Kyakhta U.S.S.R. 24 50.22N106.30E
Kyalite Australia 46 34.57S143.31E
Kyancutta Australia 46 33.08S135.34E
Kyaukpyu Burma 29 19.28N 93.30E
Kybybolite Australia 46 36.54S140.58E
Kychema U.S.S.R. 18 65.32N 42.42E
Kyle of Lochalsh *town* U.K. 6 57.17N 5.43W
Kyll *r.* W. Germany 8 49.48N 6.42E
Kyllburg W. Germany 8 50.03N 6.36E
Kyluchevskaya *mtn.* U.S.S.R. 21 56.00N160.30E
Kynuna Australia 44 21.35S141.55E
Kyoga, L. Uganda 37 1.30N 33.00E
Kyogle Australia 47 28.36S152.59E
Kyotera Uganda 37 0.40S 31.31E

Kyōto Japan **23** 35.00N135.45E
Kyōto *d.* Japan **23** 34.55N135.35E
Kyrön *r.* Finland **16** 63.14N 21.45E
Kyrta U.S.S.R. **18** 64.02N 57.40E
Kyūshū *i.* Japan **25** 32.50N130.50E
Kyustendil Bulgaria **13** 42.18N 22.39E
Kywong Australia **47** 35.01S146.45E
Kyyjärvi Finland **16** 63.02N 24.34E
Kyzyl U.S.S.R. **24** 51.42N 94.28E
Kyzyl Kum, Peski *f.* U.S.S.R. **20** 42.00N 64.30E
Kzyl Orda U.S.S.R. **20** 44.52N 65.28E

L

La Asunción Venezuela **60** 11.06N 63.53W
La Baleine *r.* Canada **51** 58.00N 57.50W
La Banda Argentina **62** 27.44S 64.15W
La Bañeza Spain **10** 42.17N 5.55W
Labao Indonesia **27** 8.12S122.49E
La Barca Mexico **56** 20.20N102.33W
La Barge U.S.A. **54** 42.16N110.12W
La Bassée France **8** 50.32N 2.49E
La Baule France **11** 47.18N 2.23W
Labbezanga Mali **38** 14.57N 0.42E
Labé Guinea **34** 11.17N 12.11W
Labe *r.* Czech. *see* Elbe *r.* W. Germany **14**
Labinsk U.S.S.R. **19** 44.39N 40.44E
La Blanquilla *i.* Venezuela **57** 11.53N 64.38W
Labouheyre France **11** 44.13N 0.55W
Laboulaye Argentina **63** 34.05S 63.25W
Labrador *f.* Canada **51** 54.00N 61.30W
Labrador City Canada **51** 52.54N 66.50W
Labrador Sea Canada / Greenland **51** 57.00N 53.00W
Lábrea Brazil **60** 7.16S 64.47W
Labrit France **11** 44.07N 0.33W
Labuan *i.* Malaysia **26** 5.20N115.15E
Labuha Indonesia **27** 0.37S127.29E
Labyrinth, L. Australia **46** 30.43S135.07E
Lac *d.* Chad **38** 13.30N 14.35E
La Calera Chile **63** 32.47S 71.12W
La Capelle France **8** 49.59N 3.57E
La Carlota Argentina **63** 33.25S 63.18W
La Carolina Spain **10** 38.16N 3.36W
Lacaune France **11** 43.42N 2.41E
La Ceiba Honduras **57** 15.45N 86.45W
Lacepede B. Australia **46** 36.47S139.45E
Lac Giao Vietnam **26** 12.41N108.02E
Lacha, Ozero *l.* U.S.S.R. **18** 61.25N 39.00E
La Charité France **11** 47.11N 3.01E
La Chartre France **9** 47.44N 0.35E
La Chaux-de-Fonds Switz. **14** 47.07N 6.51E
Lach Dera *r.* Somali Rep. **37** 0.01S 42.45E
Lachlan *r.* Australia **46** 34.21S143.58E
Lackan Resr. Rep. of Ire. **7** 53.09N 6.31W
Lackawanna U.S.A. **55** 42.49N 78.49W
Lac la Biche *town* Canada **50** 54.46N111.58W
La Cocha Argentina **62** 27.45S 65.35W
Lacombe Canada **50** 52.28N113.44W
La Concepción Venezuela **60** 10.25N 71.41W
La Concordia Mexico **56** 16.05N 92.38W
La Coruña Spain **10** 43.22N 8.24W
La Crosse Wisc. U.S.A. **53** 43.48N 91.15W
La Cruz Uruguay **63** 33.56S 56.15W
La Demanda, Sierra de *mts.* Spain **10** 42.10N 3.20W
Ladismith R.S.A. **39** 33.29S 21.15E
Ladispoli Italy **12** 41.56N 12.05E
Lādīz Iran **31** 28.57N 61.18E
Ladoga *l. see* Ladozhskoye Ozero *l.* U.S.S.R. **18**
La Dorada Colombia **60** 5.27N 74.40W
Ladozhskoye Ozero *l.* U.S.S.R. **18** 61.00N 32.00E
Ladushkin U.S.S.R. **15** 54.30N 20.05E
Ladva Vetka U.S.S.R. **18** 61.16N 34.23E
Ladybrand R.S.A. **39** 29.11S 27.26E
Ladysmith Canada **50** 48.58N123.49W
Ladysmith R.S.A. **39** 28.32S 29.47E
Lae P.N.G. **27** 6.45S146.30E
Laesö *i.* Denmark **17** 57.16N 11.01E
La Estrada Spain **10** 42.40N 8.30W
Lafayette Ind. U.S.A. **55** 40.25N 86.54W
Lafayette La. U.S.A. **53** 30.12N 92.18W
La Fère France **9** 49.40N 3.22E
La Ferté-Bernard France **9** 48.11N 0.40E
La Ferté-Gaucher France **9** 48.47N 3.18E
La Ferté-Macé France **9** 48.36N 0.22W
La Ferté-St. Aubin France **9** 47.43N 1.56E
Lafia Nigeria **38** 8.35N 8.34E
Lafiagi Nigeria **38** 8.50N 5.23E
La Flèche France **9** 47.42N 0.05W
Laforest Canada **55** 47.02N 81.13W
La Fregeneda Spain **10** 40.58N 6.54W
La Fuente de San Esteban Spain **10** 40.48N 6.15W
Lagan *r.* U.K. **7** 54.37N 5.44W
Lågen *r.* Akershus Norway **17** 60.10N 11.28E
Lågen *r.* Vestfold Norway **17** 59.03N 10.05E
Laghouat Algeria **34** 33.50N 2.59E
Lagos Mexico **56** 21.21N101.55W
Lagos Nigeria **38** 6.27N 3.28E
Lagos *d.* Nigeria **38** 6.32N 3.30E
Lagos Portugal **10** 37.05N 8.40W
La Grande *r.* Canada **51** 53.50N 79.00W
La Grande U.S.A. **54** 45.20N118.05W
La Grange Australia **42** 18.46S121.49E
La Grange U.S.A. **53** 33.02N 85.02W
La Guaira Venezuela **60** 10.38N 66.55W
La Guerche-de-Bretagne France **9** 47.56N 1.14W
Laguna Brazil **62** 28.29S 48.47W
Laguna Dam U.S.A. **54** 32.55N114.25W
Lagunas Chile **62** 20.59S 69.37W
Lagunas Peru **60** 5.10S 73.35W
Lagunillas Venezuela **60** 10.07N 71.16W
La Habana Cuba **57** 23.07N 82.25W
Lahad Datu Malaysia **26** 5.05N118.20E
Lahat Indonesia **26** 3.46S103.32E
La Haye-du-Puits France **9** 49.18N 1.33W
Lāhījān Iran **31** 37.12N 50.00E
Lahn *r.* W. Germany **8** 50.18N 7.36E
Lahnstein W. Germany **8** 50.17N 7.38E
Laholm Sweden **17** 56.31N 13.02E
Lahore Pakistan **28** 31.34N 74.22E
Lahti Finland **17** 60.58N 25.40E
Laï Chad **34** 9.22N 16.14E
Laiagam P.N.G. **27** 5.31S143.39E
L'Aigle France **9** 48.45N 0.38E
Laignes France **9** 47.50N 4.22E
Laihia Finland **16** 62.58N 22.01E
Laingsburg R.S.A. **39** 33.11S 20.49E
Lainio *r.* Sweden **16** 67.28N 22.50E
Lairg U.K. **6** 58.01N 4.25W
Laisamis Kenya **37** 1.38N 37.47E
Laissac France **11** 44.23N 2.49E
Laitila Finland **17** 60.53N 21.41E
Laizhou Wan *b.* China **25** 37.30N119.30E
Lajes Brazil **59** 27.48S 50.20W
La Junta U.S.A. **52** 37.59N103.33W
Lak Bor *r.* Somali Rep. **37** 0.32N 42.05E
Lake Biddy *town* Australia **43** 33.01S118.51E
Lake Brown *town* Australia **43** 30.57S118.19E
Lake Cargelligo *town* Australia **47** 33.19S146.23E
Lake Charles *town* U.S.A. **53** 30.13N 93.13W
Lake City U.S.A. **53** 30.05N 82.40W
Lake District *f.* U.K. **4** 54.30N 3.10W
Lake Grace *town* Australia **43** 33.06S118.28E
Lake Harbour *town* Canada **51** 62.50N 69.50W
Lake Hart *town* Australia **46** 31.16S136.21E
Lake King *town* Australia **43** 33.05S119.40E
Lakeland *town* U.S.A. **53** 28.02N 81.59W
Lake Mead Nat. Recreation Area U.S.A. **54** 36.00N114.30W
Lake Nash *town* Australia **44** 21.00S137.55E
Lake Placid *town* U.S.A. **55** 44.17N 73.59W
Lakes Entrance *town* Australia **47** 37.53S147.59E
Lakeshore U.S.A. **54** 37.15N119.12W
Lakeside Utah U.S.A. **54** 41.13N112.54W
Lake Stewart *town* Australia **46** 29.22S140.12E
Lake Superior Prov. Park Canada **55** 47.43N 84.53W
Lake Varley *town* Australia **43** 32.46S119.27E
Lakeview U.S.A. **54** 42.11N120.21W
Lakewood N.J. U.S.A. **55** 40.06N 74.12W
Lakewood Ohio U.S.A. **55** 41.29N 81.50W
Lakhpat India **28** 23.49N 68.47E
Lakonikós Kólpos *g.* Greece **13** 36.35N 22.42E
Lakota Ivory Coast **38** 5.50N 5.30W
Laksefjorden *est.* Norway **16** 70.58N 27.00E
Lakselv Norway **16** 70.03N 24.55E
Lakshadweep Is. Indian Oc. **28** 11.00N 72.00E
Lalaua Mozambique **37** 14.20S 38.30E
Lālehzār, Kūh-e *mtn.* Iran **31** 29.26N 56.48E
La Libertad El Salvador **57** 13.28N 89.20W
Lalín Spain **10** 42.40N 8.05W
La Línea Spain **10** 36.10N 5.21W
Lalitpur India **29** 24.42N 78.24E
La Loupe France **9** 48.28N 1.01E
La Louvière Belgium **8** 50.29N 4.11E
Lamar U.S.A. **52** 38.04N102.37W
Lambaréné Gabon **36** 0.41S 10.13E
Lambayeque Peru **60** 6.36S 79.50W
Lambay I. Rep. of Ire. **7** 53.29N 6.01W
Lambert's Bay *town* R.S.A. **39** 32.06S 18.16E
Lamé Chad **38** 9.14N 14.33E
Lame Nigeria **38** 10.27N 9.12E
Lamego Portugal **10** 41.05N 7.49W
Lameroo Australia **46** 35.20S140.33E
La Mesa Calif. U.S.A. **54** 32.46N117.01W
Lamía Greece **13** 38.53N 22.25E
Lammermuir Hills U.K. **6** 55.51N 2.40W
Lammhult Sweden **17** 57.09N 14.35E
Lamont U.S.A. **54** 42.12N107.28W
Lamotrek *i.* Caroline Is. **27** 7.28N146.23E
Lamotte-Beuvron France **9** 47.37N 2.01E
Lampa Peru **60** 15.10S 70.30W
Lampazos Mexico **56** 27.01N100.31W
Lampedusa *i.* Italy **12** 35.30N 12.35E
Lampeter U.K. **5** 52.06N 4.06W
Lampione *i.* Italy **12** 35.33N 12.18E
Lamu Kenya **37** 2.20S 40.54E
La Mure France **11** 44.54N 5.47E
La Nao, Cabo de Spain **10** 38.42N 0.15E
Lanark U.K. **6** 55.41N 3.47W
Lancang Jiang *r.* China *see* Mekong *r.* Asia **24**
Lancashire *d.* U.K. **4** 53.53N 2.30W
Lancaster U.K. **4** 54.03N 2.48W
Lancaster Calif. U.S.A. **54** 34.42N118.08W
Lancaster Ohio U.S.A. **55** 39.43N 82.37W
Lancaster Penn. U.S.A. **55** 40.02N 76.19W
Lancaster Sd. Canada **51** 74.00N 85.00W
Lancelin Australia **43** 31.01S115.19E
Lanchow *see* Lanzhou China **24**
Landau Bayern W. Germany **14** 48.40N 12.43E
Landeck Austria **14** 47.09N 10.35E
Landen Belgium **8** 50.46N 5.04E
Lander *r.* Australia **44** 20.25S132.00E
Lander U.S.A. **54** 42.50N108.44W
Landerneau France **11** 48.27N 4.16W
Landor Australia **42** 25.06S116.50E
Landrecies France **8** 50.08N 3.40E
Land's End *c.* U.K. **5** 50.03N 5.45W
Landshut W. Germany **14** 48.31N 12.10E
Landskrona Sweden **17** 55.52N 12.50E
Langå Denmark **17** 56.23N 9.55E
Langadhás Greece **13** 40.45N 23.04E
Langanes *c.* Iceland **16** 66.30N 14.30W
Langao China **25** 33.22N109.04E
Langeais France **9** 47.20N 0.24E
Langeland *i.* Denmark **17** 55.00N 10.50E
Längelmävesi *l.* Finland **17** 61.32N 24.22E
Langeoog *i.* W. Germany **8** 53.46N 7.30E
Langesund Norway **17** 59.00N 9.45E
Langholm U.K. **6** 55.09N 3.00W
Langjökull *ice cap* Iceland **16** 63.43N 20.03W
Langkawi *i.* Malaysia **26** 6.20N 99.30E
Langlade Canada **55** 48.14N 75.59W
Langon France **11** 44.33N 0.14W
Langöy *i.* Norway **16** 68.45N 15.00E
Langres France **11** 47.53N 5.20E
Langsa Indonesia **26** 4.28N 97.59E
Lang Son Vietnam **26** 21.50N106.55E
Languedoc-Roussillon *d.* France **11** 43.50N 3.30E
Lannion France **11** 48.44N 3.27W
Lansing U.S.A. **55** 42.44N 84.34W
Lanslebourg France **9** 45.17N 6.52E
Lantewa Nigeria **38** 12.15N 11.45E
Lanzarote *i.* Canary Is. **34** 29.00N 13.55W
Lanzhou China **24** 36.01N103.45E
Lanzo Torinese Italy **9** 45.16N 7.28E
Laoag Phil. **27** 18.14N120.36E
Lào Cai Vietnam **26** 22.30N104.00E
Laois *d.* Rep. of Ire. **7** 53.00N 7.20W
Laon France **9** 49.34N 3.37E
La Oroya Peru **60** 11.36S 75.54W
Laos Asia **26** 19.00N104.00E
Lapage, L. Australia **43** 30.40S121.50E
La Palma *i.* Canary Is. **34** 28.50N 18.00W
La Palma Spain **10** 37.23N 6.33W
La Pampa *d.* Argentina **63** 37.00S 66.00W
La Paragua Venezuela **60** 6.53N 63.22W
La Paz Entre Ríos Argentina **63** 30.45S 59.38W
La Paz Mendoza Argentina **63** 33.28S 67.34W
La Paz Bolivia **62** 16.30S 68.09W
La Paz *d.* Bolivia **62** 16.00S 68.10W
La Paz Mexico **56** 24.10N110.18W
La Pedrera Colombia **60** 1.18S 69.43W
Lapeer U.S.A. **55** 43.03N 83.09W
La Peña, Sierra de *mts.* Spain **10** 42.30N 0.50W
La Perouse Str. U.S.S.R. **21** 45.50N142.30E
La Pine U.S.A. **54** 43.40N121.30W
Lapinjärvi Finland **17** 60.38N 26.13E
Lapland *f.* Sweden / Finland **16** 68.10N 24.10E
La Plata Argentina **63** 34.55S 57.57W
La Plata, Río de *est.* Argentina / Uruguay **63** 35.15S 56.45W
Lappajärvi *l.* Finland **16** 63.08N 23.40E
Lappeenranta Finland **18** 61.04N 28.05E
Lappi *d.* Finland **16** 67.20N 26.00E
Laptevykh, More *sea* U.S.S.R. **21** 74.30N125.00E
Lapua Finland **16** 62.57N 23.00E
La Push U.S.A. **54** 47.55N124.38W
La Quiaca Argentina **62** 22.05S 65.36W
L'Aquila Italy **12** 42.22N 13.25E
Lār Iran **31** 27.37N 54.16E
Larache Morocco **34** 35.12N 6.10W
Laramie U.S.A. **52** 41.19N105.35W
Lärbro Sweden **17** 57.47N 18.47E
Larche, Col de France / Italy **9** 44.25N 6.53E
Laredo U.S.A. **52** 27.32N 99.22W
Largeau Chad **34** 17.55N 19.07E
Largs U.K. **6** 55.48N 4.52W
Lariang Indonesia **26** 1.35S119.25E
La Rioja Argentina **62** 29.25S 66.50W
La Rioja *d.* Argentina **62** 29.00S 66.00W
Lárisa Greece **13** 39.36N 22.24E
Lark *r.* U.K. **5** 52.26N 0.20E
Lārkāna Pakistan **28** 27.32N 68.18E
Larnaca *see* Lárnax Cyprus **32**
Lárnax Cyprus **32** 34.54N 33.39E
Larne U.K. **7** 54.51N 5.49W
La Robla Spain **10** 42.50N 5.41W
La Roche Belgium **8** 50.11N 5.35E
La Rochelle France **11** 46.10N 1.10W
La Roche-sur-Yon France **11** 46.40N 1.25W
La Roda Spain **10** 39.13N 2.10W
La Romana Dom. Rep. **57** 18.27N 68.57W
La Ronge Canada **50** 55.07N105.18W
La Ronge, Lac *l.* Canada **50** 55.07N105.15W
Laroquebrou France **11** 44.58N 2.11E
Larrimah Australia **44** 15.35S133.12E
Larvik Norway **17** 59.04N 10.00E
La Sagra *mtn.* Spain **10** 37.58N 2.35W
Las Anod Somali Rep. **35** 8.26N 47.24E
La Sarre Canada **55** 48.49N 79.12W
Las Cruces U.S.A. **52** 32.23N106.29W
La Seine, Baie de France **11** 49.40N 0.30W
La Serena Chile **62** 29.54S 71.16W
La Seyne France **11** 43.06N 5.53E
Las Flores Argentina **63** 36.02S 59.07W
Lāsh-e Joveyn Afghan. **31** 31.43N 61.39E
Las Heras Argentina **63** 32.50S 68.50W
Lashio Burma **29** 22.58N 97.48E
Las Lomitas Argentina **62** 24.43S 60.35W
Las Marismas *f.* Spain **10** 37.00N 6.15W
Las Palmas Canary Is. **34** 28.08N 15.27W
Las Perlas, Archipelago de Panama **57** 8.45N 79.30W
La Spezia Italy **9** 44.07N 9.49E
Las Piedras Uruguay **63** 34.44S 56.13W
Las Plumas Argentina **63** 43.40S 67.15W
Lassay France **9** 48.26N 0.30W
Lassen Peak *mtn.* U.S.A. **54** 40.29N121.31W
Lastoursville Gabon **36** 0.50S 12.47E
Lastovo *i.* Yugo. **13** 42.45N 16.52E
Lastrup W. Germany **8** 52.48N 7.55E
La Suze France **9** 47.54N 0.02E
Las Vegas Nev. U.S.A. **54** 36.11N115.08W
Las Vegas N.Mex. U.S.A. **52** 35.36N105.13W
Latacunga Ecuador **60** 0.58S 78.36W
La Tagua Colombia **60** 0.03S 74.40W
Latakia *see* Al Lādhiqīyah Syria **32**
La Teste-de-Buch France **11** 44.38N 1.09W
Lathen W. Germany **8** 52.54N 7.20E
Latina Italy **12** 41.28N 12.52E
Latisana Italy **9** 45.47N 13.00E
La Tortuga *i.* Venezuela **60** 11.00N 65.20W
La Tuque Canada **55** 47.26N 72.47W
Latviyskaya S.S.R. *d.* U.S.S.R. **17** 56.45N 23.00E
Lau Nigeria **38** 9.14N 11.15E
Lauchhammer E. Germany **14** 51.30N 13.48E
Lauenburg W. Germany **14** 53.22N 10.33E
Laughlen, Mt. Australia **44** 23.23S134.23E
Launceston Australia **45** 41.25S147.07E
Launceston U.K. **5** 50.38N 4.21W
La Unión Chile **63** 40.15S 73.02W
La Unión Spain **10** 37.38N 0.53W
Laura Australia **46** 33.08S138.19E
La Urbana Venezuela **60** 7.08N 66.56W
Laurel Miss. U.S.A. **53** 31.41N 89.09W
Laurel Mont. U.S.A. **54** 45.40N108.46W
Laurencekirk U.K. **6** 56.50N 2.29W
Laurentides Prov. Park Canada **55** 47.46N 71.40W
Lausanne Switz. **14** 46.32N 6.39E
Laut *i.* Indonesia **26** 3.45S116.20E
Lautaro Chile **63** 38.31S 72.27W
Lauterecken W. Germany **8** 49.39N 7.36E
Lavagh More *mtn.* Rep. of Ire. **7** 54.45N 8.07W
Lava Hot Springs *town* U.S.A. **54** 42.37N112.01W
Laval France **9** 48.04N 0.45W
La Vega Dom. Rep. **57** 19.15N 70.33W
La Vela Venezuela **60** 11.27N 69.34W
La Vérendrye Prov. Park Canada **55** 47.29N 77.06W
Laverton Australia **43** 28.49S122.25E
Lavia Finland **17** 61.36N 22.36E
Lavik Norway **17** 61.06N 5.30E
Lavras Brazil **59** 21.15S 44.59W
Lávrion Greece **13** 37.44N 24.04E
Lawgi Australia **44** 24.34S150.39E
Lawra Ghana **38** 10.40N 2.49W
Lawrence New Zealand **48** 45.55S169.42E
Lawrence Kans. U.S.A. **53** 38.58N 95.15W
Lawrence Mass. U.S.A. **55** 42.42N 71.09W
Lawton Okla. U.S.A. **52** 34.36N 98.25W
Lawz, Jabal al *mtn.* Saudi Arabia **32** 28.40N 35.20E
Laxå Sweden **17** 58.59N 14.37E
Laytonville U.S.A. **54** 39.41N123.29W
Lazio *d.* Italy **12** 42.20N 12.00E
Leadhills U.K. **6** 55.25N 3.46W
Leamington U.S.A. **54** 39.31N112.17W
Learmonth Australia **42** 22.13S114.04E
Leavenworth U.S.A. **53** 39.19N 94.55W
Lebak Phil. **27** 6.32N124.03E
Lebanon Asia **32** 34.00N 36.00E
Lebanon Ind. U.S.A. **55** 40.02N 87.28W
Lebanon Oreg. U.S.A. **54** 44.32N122.54W
Lebanon Penn. U.S.A. **55** 40.20N 76.25W
Lebanon Tenn. U.S.A. **53** 36.11N 86.19W
Lebec U.S.A. **54** 34.50N118.52W
Lebesby Norway **16** 70.34N 27.00E
Le Blanc France **11** 46.37N 1.03E
Łebork Poland **15** 54.33N 17.44E
Lebrija Spain **10** 36.55N 6.10W
Lebu Chile **63** 37.37S 73.39W
Le Bugue France **11** 44.55N 0.56E
Le Cateau France **8** 50.07N 3.33E
Le Catelet France **8** 50.00N 3.12E
Lecce Italy **13** 40.21N 18.11E
Lecco Italy **9** 45.51N 9.23E
Lech *r.* W. Germany **14** 48.45N 10.51E
Le Chesne France **8** 49.31N 4.46E
Lechiguanas, Islas de las *is.* Argentina **63** 33.26S 59.42W
Le Creusot France **11** 46.48N 4.27E
Lectoure France **11** 43.56N 0.38E
Ledbury U.K. **5** 52.03N 2.25W
Ledesma Spain **10** 41.05N 6.00W
Le Dorat France **11** 46.14N 1.05E
Leduc Canada **50** 53.16N113.33W
Lee *r.* Rep. of Ire. **7** 51.53N 8.25W
Leech L. U.S.A. **53** 47.10N 94.30W
Leeds U.K. **4** 53.48N 1.34W
Leek U.K. **4** 53.07N 2.02W
Leer W. Germany **8** 53.14N 7.27E
Leeton Australia **47** 34.33S146.24E
Leeuwarden Neth. **8** 53.12N 5.48E
Leeuwin, C. Australia **43** 34.22S115.08E
Leeward Is. C. America **57** 18.00N 61.00W
Lefroy, L. Australia **43** 31.15S121.40E
Legazpi Phil. **27** 13.10N123.45E
Legget U.S.A. **54** 39.52N123.34W
Leghorn *see* Livorno Italy **12**
Legion Mine Zimbabwe **39** 21.23S 28.33E
Legionowo Poland **15** 52.25N 20.56E
Legnago Italy **9** 45.11N 11.18E
Legnano Italy **9** 45.36N 8.54E
Legnica Poland **14** 51.12N 16.10E
Le Grand-Lucé France **9** 47.52N 0.28E
Le Grand-Quevilly France **9** 49.25N 1.02E
Leh Jammu & Kashmir **28** 34.09N 77.35E
Le Havre France **9** 49.30N 0.06E
Lehrte W. Germany **14** 52.22N 9.59E
Lehututu Botswana **39** 23.54S 21.52E
Leibnitz Austria **14** 46.48N 15.32E
Leicester U.K. **5** 52.39N 1.09W
Leicestershire *d.* U.K. **5** 52.29N 1.10W
Leichardt *r.* Australia **44** 17.35S139.48E
Leiden Neth. **8** 52.10N 4.30E
Leie *r.* Belgium **8** 51.03N 3.44E
Leigh *r.* Australia **46** 29.49S138.10E
Leigh Creek *town* Australia **46** 30.31S138.25E
Leighton Buzzard U.K. **5** 51.55N 0.39W
Leikanger Norway **17** 61.10N 6.52E
Leipzig E. Germany **14** 51.20N 12.20E
Leipzig *d.* E. Germany **14** 51.15N 12.45E
Leiria Portugal **10** 39.45N 8.48W
Leitrim *d.* Rep. of Ire. **7** 54.08N 8.00W
Leizhou Bandao *pen.* China **25** 20.40N109.30E
Lek *r.* Neth. **8** 51.55N 4.29E
Leksvik Norway **16** 63.40N 10.40E
Lelchitsy U.S.S.R. **15** 51.48N 28.20E
Leleque Argentina **63** 42.24S 71.04W
Le Lion-d'Angers France **9** 47.38N 0.43W
Le Lude France **9** 47.39N 0.09E
Lelystad Neth. **8** 52.32N 5.29E
Léman, Lac *l.* Switz. **14** 46.30N 6.30E
Le Mans France **9** 48.01N 0.10E
Leme Brazil **59** 22.10S 47.23W
Le Merlerault France **9** 48.42N 0.18E
Lemesós Cyprus **32** 34.40N 33.03E
Lemgo W. Germany **14** 52.02N 8.54E
Lemhi Range *mts.* U.S.A. **54** 44.30N113.25W
Lemmer Neth. **8** 52.50N 5.43E
Lemmon U.S.A. **52** 45.56N102.10W
Lemvig Denmark **17** 56.32N 8.18E
Lena *r.* U.S.S.R. **21** 72.00N127.10E
Lendery U.S.S.R. **18** 63.24N 31.04E
Lendinara Italy **9** 45.05N 11.36E
Lengerich W. Germany **8** 52.12N 7.52E
Lenina, Kanal *canal* U.S.S.R. **19** 43.46N 45.00E
Lenina, Pik *mtn.* U.S.S.R. **24** 40.14N 69.40E
Leninabad U.S.S.R. **24** 40.14N 69.40E
Leninakan U.S.S.R. **31** 40.47N 43.49E
Leningrad U.S.S.R. **18** 59.55N 30.25E
Leninogorsk U.S.S.R. **20** 50.23N 83.32E
Leninsk U.S.S.R. **19** 48.42N 45.14E
Leninsk Kuznetskiy U.S.S.R. **20** 54.44N 86.13E
Lenkoran U.S.S.R. **31** 38.45N 48.50E
Lenmalu Indonesia **27** 1.58S130.00E
Lenne *r.* W. Germany **8** 51.24N 7.30E
Lennonville Australia **42** 27.58S117.50E
Lens France **8** 50.26N 2.50E
Lentini Italy **12** 37.17N 15.00E
Lenvik Norway **16** 69.22N 18.10E
Léo Burkina Faso **38** 11.05N 2.06W
Leoben Austria **14** 47.23N 15.06E
Leominster U.K. **5** 52.15N 2.43W
Leominster U.S.A. **55** 42.32N 71.45W
León Mexico **56** 21.10N101.42W
León Nicaragua **57** 12.24N 86.52W
León Spain **10** 42.35N 5.34W
León *d.* Spain **10** 41.40N 5.55W
Leonardville Namibia **39** 23.21S 18.47E
Leonárison Cyprus **32** 35.28N 34.08E
Leongatha Australia **47** 38.29S145.57E
Leonora Australia **43** 28.54S121.20E
Leopoldina Brazil **59** 21.30S 42.38W
Leopoldsburg Belgium **8** 51.08N 5.13E
Leovo U.S.S.R. **15** 46.29N 28.12E
Lepel U.S.S.R. **18** 54.48N 28.40E
Le Puy France **11** 45.03N 3.54E
Le Quesnoy France **8** 50.15N 3.39E
Lerbäck Sweden **17** 58.56N 15.02E
Léré Chad **38** 9.41N 14.17E
Lerici Italy **9** 44.04N 9.55E
Lerma Spain **10** 42.02N 3.46W
Le Roy Mich. U.S.A. **55** 44.03N 85.29W
Lerwick U.K. **6** 60.09N 1.09W
Les Andelys France **9** 49.15N 1.25E
Les Cayes Haiti **57** 18.15N 73.46W
Leschenault, C. Australia **43** 31.50S115.23E
Les Ecrins *mtn.* France **11** 44.50N 6.20E
Leshan China **29** 29.34N103.42E
Leshukonskoye U.S.S.R. **18** 64.55N 45.50E
Lesjaskog Norway **17** 62.15N 8.22E
Leskovac Yugo. **13** 43.00N 21.56E
Lesotho Africa **39** 29.00S 28.00E
Lesozavodsk U.S.S.R. **25** 45.30N133.29E
Les Pieux France **9** 49.35N 1.50W
Les Riceys France **9** 47.59N 4.22E
Les Sables d'Olonne France **11** 46.30N 1.47W
Lessay France **9** 49.14N 1.30W
Lesser Antilles *is.* C. America **57** 13.00N 65.00W
Lesser Slave L. Canada **50** 55.30N115.00W
Lesser Sunda Is. *see* Nusa Tenggara *is.* Indonesia **26**
Lessines Belgium **8** 50.43N 3.50E
Lesti *r.* Finland **16** 64.04N 23.38E
Lésvos *i.* Greece **13** 39.10N 26.16E
Leszno Poland **14** 51.51N 16.35E
Letchworth U.K. **5** 51.58N 0.13W
Lethbridge Canada **50** 49.43N112.48W
Lethem Guyana **60** 3.18N 59.46W
Leti, Kepulauan *is.* Indonesia **27** 8.20S128.00E
Letiahau *r.* Botswana **39** 21.16S 24.00E
Leticia Colombia **60** 4.09S 69.57W
Le Tréport France **11** 50.04N 1.22E
Lette Australia **46** 34.22S143.15E
Letterkenny Rep. of Ire. **7** 54.56N 7.45W
Leuk Switz. **9** 46.19N 7.38E
Leuser *mtn.* Indonesia **26** 3.50N 97.10E
Leuven Belgium **8** 50.53N 4.45E
Leuze Hainaut Belgium **8** 50.36N 3.37E
Leuze Namur Belgium **8** 50.34N 4.53E
Levanger Norway **16** 63.45N 11.19E
Levanto Italy **9** 44.10N 9.38E
Levelland U.S.A. **52** 33.35N102.23W
Lévêque, C. Australia **42** 16.25S123.00E
Le Verdon France **11** 45.33N 1.04W
Leverkusen W. Germany **8** 51.02N 6.59E
Levice Czech. **15** 48.13N 18.37E
Levin New Zealand **48** 40.37S175.18E
Lévis Canada **55** 46.49N 71.12W
Lévka Cyprus **32** 35.06N 32.51E
Levkás Greece **13** 38.50N 20.41E
Levkás *i.* Greece **13** 38.44N 20.37E
Levkosía Cyprus **32** 35.11N 33.23E
Lewes U.K. **5** 50.53N 0.02E
Lewis *i.* U.K. **6** 58.10N 6.40W
Lewis Pass *f.* New Zealand **48** 42.30S172.15E
Lewis Range *mts.* U.S.A. **54** 48.30N113.15W
Lewiston Idaho U.S.A. **54** 46.25N117.01W
Lewiston Maine U.S.A. **55** 44.06N 70.13W
Lewistown Mont. U.S.A. **54** 47.04N109.26W
Lewistown Penn. U.S.A. **55** 40.36N 77.31W
Lexington Ky. U.S.A. **55** 38.02N 84.30W
Lexington Oreg. U.S.A. **54** 45.27N119.41W
Leyburn U.K. **4** 54.19N 1.50W
Leydsdorp R.S.A. **39** 23.59S 30.32E
Leyte *i.* Phil. **27** 10.40N124.50E
Lezignan France **11** 43.12N 2.46E
Lhasa China **29** 29.41N 91.10E
Lhazê China **29** 29.10N 87.45E
Lhokseumawe Indonesia **26** 5.09N 97.09E
Lhut *r.* Somali Rep. **35** 10.25N 51.05E
Liangdang China **24** 33.56N106.12E

Lianyungang China 25 34.37N119.10E
Liaocheng China 25 36.29N115.55E
Liaodong Bandao pen. China 25 40.00N122.50E
Liaodong Wan b. China 25 40.20N121.00E
Liaoning d. China 25 41.30N123.00E
Liaoyang China 25 41.16N123.12E
Liaoyuan China 25 42.53N125.10E
Liard r. Canada 50 61.56N120.35W
Liart France 9 49.46N 4.20E
Libby U.S.A. 54 48.23N115.33W
Libenge Zaïre 34 3.39N 18.39E
Liberal U.S.A. 52 37.03N100.56W
Liberdade Brazil 59 22.01S 44.22W
Liberec Czech. 14 50.48N 15.05E
Liberia Africa 34 6.30N 9.30W
Liberia Costa Rica 57 10.39N 85.28W
Lībīyah, Aş Şahrā' al des. Africa 30 24.00N 25.30E
Libourne France 11 44.55N 0.14W
Libramont Belgium 8 49.56N 5.22E
Libreville Gabon 36 0.30N 9.25E
Libya Africa 34 26.30N 17.00E
Libyan Desert see Lībīyah, Aş Şahrā' al a-' al Africa 30
Libyan Plateau see Aḑ Ḑiffah f. Africa 30
Licantén Chile 63 34.59S 72.00W
Licata Italy 12 37.07N 13.58E
Lichfield U.K. 5 52.40N 1.50W
Lichinga Mozambique 37 13.09S 35.17E
Lichtenburg R.S.A. 39 26.08S 26.09E
Lichtenvoorde Neth. 8 51.59N 6.32E
Lida U.S.A. 54 37.29N117.29W
Lida U.S.S.R. 15 53.50N 25.19E
Lidköping Sweden 17 58.30N 13.10E
Liechtenstein Europe 14 47.08N 9.35E
Liège Belgium 8 50.38N 5.35E
Liège d. Belgium 8 50.32N 5.35E
Lienz Austria 14 46.50N 12.47E
Liepāja U.S.S.R. 17 56.31N 21.01E
Lier Belgium 8 51.08N 4.35E
Lierneux Belgium 8 50.18N 5.50E
Lieşti Romania 15 45.38N 27.32E
Liévin France 8 50.27N 2.49E
Lièvre, Rivière du r. Canada 55 45.31N 75.26W
Liffey r. Rep. of Ire. 7 53.21N 6.14W
Liffré France 9 48.13N 1.30W
Liguria d. Italy 9 42.25N 8.40E
Ligurian Sea Med. Sea 12 43.30N 9.00E
Lihou Reef and Cays Australia 44 17.25S151.40E
Lihue Hawaii U.S.A. 52 21.59N159.23W
Lihula U.S.S.R. 17 58.41N 23.50E
Lijiang China 29 26.50N100.15E
Likasi Zaïre 36 10.58S 26.47E
Lille France 8 50.39N 3.05E
Lille Baelt str. Denmark 17 55.20N 9.45E
Lillebonne France 9 49.31N 0.33E
Lillehammer Norway 17 61.08N 10.30E
Lillers France 8 50.34N 2.29E
Lillesand Norway 17 58.15N 8.24E
Lilleström Norway 17 59.57N 11.05E
Lillhärdal Sweden 17 61.51N 14.04E
Lillooet Canada 50 50.42N121.56W
Lilongwe Malaŵi 37 13.58S 33.49E
Liloy Phil. 27 8.08N122.40E
Lilydale Australia 46 32.58S139.59E
Lim r. Yugo. 13 43.45N 19.13E
Lima Peru 60 12.06S 77.03W
Lima r. Portugal 10 41.40N 8.50W
Lima Sweden 17 60.56N 13.26E
Lima Mont. U.S.A. 54 44.38N112.36W
Lima Ohio U.S.A. 55 40.43N 84.06W
Limassol see Lemesós Cyprus 32
Limavady U.K. 7 55.03N 6.57W
Limay r. Argentina 63 39.02S 68.07W
Limbang Malaysia 26 4.50N115.00E
Limbe Cameroon 38 4.01N 9.12E
Limbourg Belgium 8 50.36N 5.57E
Limburg d. Belgium 8 50.36N 5.57E
Limburg d. Neth. 8 51.15N 5.45E
Limeira Brazil 59 22.34S 47.25W
Limerick Rep. of Ire. 7 52.40N 8.37W
Limerick d. Rep. of Ire. 7 52.40N 8.37W
Limfjorden str. Denmark 17 56.55N 9.10E
Liminka Finland 16 64.49N 25.24E
Limmen Bight Australia 44 14.45S135.40E
Límnos i. Greece 13 39.55N 25.14E
Limoges France 11 45.50N 1.15E
Limogne France 11 44.24N 1.46E
Limón Costa Rica 57 10.00N 83.01W
Limone Piemonte Italy 9 44.12N 7.34E
Limousin d. France 11 45.45N 1.30E
Limpopo r. Mozambique 39 25.14S 33.33E
Linah Saudi Arabia 31 28.48N 43.45E
Linakhamari U.S.S.R. 18 69.39N 31.21E
Linares Chile 63 35.51S 71.36W
Linares Mexico 56 24.54N 99.38W
Linares Spain 10 38.05N 3.38W
Lincang China 24 24.00N100.10E
Lincoln Argentina 63 34.55S 61.30W
Lincoln New Zealand 48 43.38S172.29E
Lincoln U.K. 4 53.14N 0.32W
Lincoln Nebr. U.S.A. 53 40.49N 96.41W
Lincoln N.H. U.S.A. 55 44.03N 71.40W
Lincoln City U.S.A. 54 44.59N124.00W
Lincoln Gap town Australia 46 32.45S137.18E
Lincoln Sea Greenland 64 82.00N 55.00W
Lincolnshire d. U.K. 4 53.14N 0.32W
Lincoln Wolds hills U.K. 4 53.22N 0.08W
Lindesnes c. Norway 17 58.00N 7.02E
Lindhos Greece 13 36.05N 28.02E
Lindi Tanzania 37 10.00S 39.41E
Lindsay Canada 55 44.21N 78.44W
Lindsay U.S.A. 54 36.12N119.05W
Linfen China 25 36.05N111.32E
Lingayen Phil. 27 16.02N120.14E
Lingbo Sweden 17 61.03N 16.41E
Lingen W. Germany 8 52.32N 7.19E
Lingga i. Indonesia 26 0.20S104.30E
Linguère Senegal 34 15.22N 15.11W
Linköping Sweden 17 58.25N 15.37E
Linnhe, Loch U.K. 6 56.35N 5.25W
Linosa i. Italy 12 35.52N 12.50E
Lins Brazil 59 21.40S 49.44W
Lintan China 24 34.39N103.40E
Linton Ind. U.S.A. 55 39.01N 87.10W
Lintorf W. Germany 8 51.19N 6.50E
Linxe France 11 43.56N 1.10W
Linxia China 24 35.31N103.08E
Linz Austria 14 48.19N 14.18E
Linz W. Germany 8 50.34N 7.19E
Lion, Golfe du g. France 11 43.12N 4.15E
Lions, G. of see Lion, Golfe du g. France 11
Lipetsk U.S.S.R. 18 52.37N 39.36E
Liphook U.K. 5 51.05N 0.49W
Lipkany U.S.S.R. 15 48.18N 26.48E
Lipova Romania 15 46.05N 21.40E
Lipovets U.S.S.R. 15 49.11N 29.01E
Lippe r. W. Germany 8 51.38N 6.37E
Lippstadt W. Germany 14 51.41N 8.20E
Liptovský Mikuláš Czech. 15 49.06N 19.37E
Lira Uganda 37 2.15N 32.55E
Liri r. Italy 12 41.12N 13.45E
Liria Spain 10 39.37N 0.35W
Lisala Zaïre 35 2.08N 21.37E
Lisboa Portugal 10 38.44N 9.08W
Lisbon see Lisboa Portugal 10
Lisburn U.K. 7 54.30N 6.03W
Lisburne, C. U.S.A. 50 69.00N165.50W
Liscannor B. Rep. of Ire. 7 52.55N 9.24W
Lishui China 25 28.30N119.59E
Lisichansk U.S.S.R. 19 48.53N 38.25E
Lisieux France 9 49.09N 0.14E
Liskeard U.K. 5 50.27N 4.29W
Lismore N.S.W. Australia 47 28.48S153.17E
Lismore Vic. Australia 46 37.58S143.22E
Lismore Rep. of Ire. 7 52.08N 7.57W
Liss U.K. 5 51.03N 0.53W
Lisse Neth. 8 52.18N 4.33E
Listowel Rep. of Ire. 7 52.27N 9.30W
Litang Qu r. China 29 28.09N101.30E
Lithgow Australia 47 33.30S150.09E
Litovskaya S.S.R. d. U.S.S.R. 15 54.30N 24.00E
Little Andaman i. India 29 10.50N 92.38E
Little Belt Mts. U.S.A. 54 46.45N110.35W
Little Cayman i. Cayman Is. 57 19.40N 80.00W
Little Coco i. Burma 26 13.50N 93.10E
Little Colorado r. U.S.A. 54 36.11N111.48W
Little Current r. Canada 55 50.57N 84.36W
Little Current town Canada 55 45.58N 81.56W
Little Falls town N.Y. U.S.A. 55 43.03N 74.52W
Littlehampton U.K. 5 50.48N 0.32W
Little Inagua i. Bahamas 57 21.30N 73.00W
Little Karoo f. R.S.A. 39 33.40S 21.40E
Little Lake town U.S.A. 54 35.58N117.53W
Little Missouri r. U.S.A. 52 47.30N102.25W
Little Nicobar i. India 29 7.20N 93.40E
Little Ouse r. U.K. 5 52.34N 0.20E
Little Rock town U.S.A. 53 34.42N 92.17W
Little Topar Australia 46 31.44S142.14E
Liuli Tanzania 37 11.07S 34.34E
Liuzhou China 25 24.17N109.15E
Livarot France 9 49.01N 0.09E
Livermore, Mt. U.S.A. 52 30.39N104.11W
Liverpool Australia 47 33.57S150.52E
Liverpool Canada 51 44.03N 64.43W
Liverpool U.K. 4 53.25N 3.00W
Liverpool, C. Canada 51 73.38N 78.06W
Liverpool B. U.K. 4 53.30N 3.10W
Liverpool Plains f. Australia 47 31.20S150.00E
Liverpool Range mts. Australia 47 31.45S150.45E
Livingston U.K. 6 55.54N 3.31W
Livingston Mont. U.S.A. 54 45.40N110.34W
Livingstone see Maramba Zambia 39
Livingstonia Malaŵi 37 10.35S 34.10E
Livo r. Finland 16 65.24N 26.48E
Livorno Italy 12 43.33N 10.18E
Liwale Tanzania 37 9.47S 38.00E
Lizard U.K. 5 49.58N 5.12W
Lizard Pt. U.K. 5 49.57N 5.15W
Ljubljana Yugo. 12 46.04N 14.28E
Ljugarn Sweden 17 57.19N 18.42E
Ljungan r. Sweden 17 62.19N 17.23E
Ljungby Sweden 17 56.50N 13.56E
Ljungdalen Sweden 16 62.54N 12.45E
Ljusdal Sweden 17 61.50N 16.05E
Ljusnan r. Sweden 17 61.12N 17.08E
Ljusne Sweden 17 61.13N 17.08E
Llandeilo U.K. 5 51.54N 4.00W
Llandovery U.K. 5 51.59N 3.49W
Llandrindod Wells U.K. 5 52.15N 3.23W
Llandudno U.K. 4 53.19N 3.49W
Llanelli U.K. 5 51.41N 4.11W
Llanes Spain 10 43.25N 4.45W
Llangadfan U.K. 5 52.41N 3.28W
Llangollen U.K. 4 52.58N 3.10W
Llanidloes U.K. 5 52.28N 3.31W
Llanos f. S. America 60 7.30N 70.00W
Llanwrtyd Wells U.K. 5 52.06N 3.39W
Lleida Spain 10 41.37N 0.38E
Llerena Spain 10 38.14N 6.00W
Lloret de Mar Spain 10 41.41N 2.53E
Lloydminster Canada 50 53.18N110.00W
Lobatse Botswana 39 25.12S 25.39E
Löbau E. Germany 14 51.05N 14.40E
Lobería Argentina 63 38.08S 58.48W
Lobito Angola 36 12.20S 13.34E
Lobonäs Sweden 17 61.33N 15.20E
Lobos Argentina 63 35.10S 59.05W
Locarno Switz. 14 46.10N 8.48E
Lochboisdale town U.K. 6 57.09N 7.19W
Lochem Neth. 8 52.10N 6.25E
Loches France 11 47.08N 1.00E
Lochgilphead U.K. 6 56.02N 5.26W
Lochinver U.K. 6 58.09N 5.15W
Lochmaddy town U.K. 6 57.36N 7.10W
Lochnagar mtn. U.K. 6 56.57N 3.15W
Lochranza U.K. 6 55.42N 5.18W
Lochy, Loch U.K. 6 56.58N 4.55W
Lock Australia 46 33.34S135.46E
Lockerbie U.K. 6 55.07N 3.21W
Lockhart Australia 47 35.16S146.42E
Lockhart, L. Australia 43 33.27S119.00E
Lock Haven U.S.A. 55 41.08N 77.27W
Lockport U.S.A. 55 43.11N 78.39W
Loc Ninh Vietnam 26 11.55N106.35E
Lodalskåpa mtn. Norway 17 61.47N 7.13E
Loddon r. Australia 46 35.40S143.59E
Lodeynoye Pole U.S.S.R. 18 60.43N 33.30E
Lodge Grass U.S.A. 54 45.19N107.22W
Lodhrān Pakistan 28 29.32N 71.38E
Lodi Italy 9 45.19N 9.30E
Lodi Calif. U.S.A. 54 38.08N121.16W
Lodja Zaïre 36 3.29S 23.33E
Lodwar Kenya 37 3.06N 35.38E
Łódź Poland 15 51.49N 19.28E
Lofoten Vesterålen is. Norway 16 68.15N 13.50E
Log U.S.S.R. 19 49.28N 43.51E
Loga Niger 38 13.40N 3.15E
Logan Australia 47 27.48S153.04E
Logan Utah U.S.A. 54 41.44N111.50W
Logan, Mt. Canada 50 60.45N140.00W
Logansport U.S.A. 55 40.45N 86.25W
Logone r. Cameroon / Chad 34 12.10N 15.00E
Logoysk U.S.S.R. 15 54.08N 27.42E
Logroño Spain 10 42.28N 2.26W
Lögstör Denmark 17 56.58N 9.15E
Lohja Finland 17 60.15N 24.05E
Lohjanjärvi l. Finland 17 60.15N 23.55E
Loimaa Finland 17 60.51N 23.03E
Loir r. France 9 47.29N 0.32W
Loire r. France 9 47.18N 2.00W
Loiret d. France 9 47.55N 2.20E
Loir-et-Cher d. France 9 47.30N 1.30E
Loja Ecuador 60 3.59S 79.16W
Loja Spain 10 37.10N 4.09W
Löken Norway 17 59.48N 11.29E
Loken tekojärvi resr. Finland 16 67.55N 27.40E
Lokeren Belgium 8 51.06N 3.59E
Lokichar Kenya 37 2.23N 35.39E
Lokitaung Kenya 37 4.15N 35.45E
Lokka Finland 16 67.49N 27.44E
Lökken Denmark 17 57.22N 9.43E
Lökken Norway 16 63.06N 9.43E
Loknya U.S.S.R. 18 56.49N 30.00E
Lokoja Nigeria 38 7.49N 6.44E
Lolland i. Denmark 17 54.46N 11.30E
Lom Bulgaria 15 43.49N 23.13E
Lom Norway 17 61.50N 8.33E
Loma U.S.A. 54 47.57N110.30W
Lomas de Zamora Argentina 63 34.46S 58.24W
Lombardia d. Italy 9 45.25N 10.00E
Lombok i. Indonesia 26 8.30S116.20E
Lomé Togo 38 6.10N 1.21E
Lomela Zaïre 36 2.15S 23.15E
Lomié Cameroon 38 3.09N 13.35E
Lomme France 8 50.38N 2.59E
Lommel Belgium 8 51.15N 5.18E
Lomond, Loch U.K. 6 56.07N 4.36W
Lompoc U.S.A. 54 34.38N120.27W
Łomża Poland 15 53.11N 22.04E
Londinières France 9 49.50N 1.24E
London Canada 55 42.59N 81.14W
London U.K. 5 51.32N 0.06W
Londonderry U.K. 7 55.00N 7.21W
Londonderry d. U.K. 7 55.00N 7.00W
Londonderry, C. Australia 42 13.58S126.55E
Londonderry, Isla i. Chile 63 55.03S 70.40W
Londrina Brazil 62 23.30S 51.13W
Lone Pine U.S.A. 54 36.36N118.04W
Longa, Proliv str. U.S.S.R. 21 70.00N178.00E
Longarone Italy 9 46.16N 12.18E
Long Beach town Calif. U.S.A. 54 33.46N118.11W
Long Broad Sd. Australia 44 22.20S149.50E
Longchamps Belgium 8 50.05N 5.42E
Long Creek town U.S.A. 54 44.43N119.06W
Long Eaton U.K. 4 52.54N 1.16W
Longford Rep. of Ire. 7 53.44N 7.48W
Longford d. Rep. of Ire. 7 53.42N 7.45W
Long I. Bahamas 57 23.00N 75.00W
Long I. U.S.A. 55 40.46N 73.00W
Longido Tanzania 37 2.43S 36.41E
Longiram Indonesia 26 0.05S115.45E
Long L. Canada 55 49.29N 86.44W
Longlac town Canada 55 49.47N 86.24W
Longnawan Indonesia 26 1.54N114.53E
Longniddry U.K. 6 55.58N 2.53W
Longquan China 25 28.05N119.07E
Longreach Australia 44 23.26S144.15E
Longs Peak U.S.A. 52 40.15N105.37W
Longtown U.K. 4 55.01N 2.58W
Longué France 9 47.23N 0.06W
Longuyon France 8 49.27N 5.35E
Longview Tex. U.S.A. 53 32.30N 94.45W
Longview Wash. U.S.A. 54 46.08N122.57W
Longwy France 8 49.32N 5.46E
Longxi China 24 35.00N105.00E
Long Xuyen Vietnam 26 10.23N105.25E
Lonigo Italy 9 45.23N 11.23E
Löningen W. Germany 8 52.44N 7.46E
Lönsdal Norway 16 66.46N 15.26E
Lonsdale, L. Australia 46 37.05S142.15E
Lons-le-Saunier France 11 46.40N 5.33E
Looc Phil. 27 12.20N122.05E
Looe U.K. 5 50.51N 4.26W
Lookout, C. U.S.A. 53 34.34N 76.34W
Loolmalassin mtn. Tanzania 37 3.00S 35.45E
Loongana Australia 43 30.57S127.02E
Loop Head Rep. of Ire. 7 52.33N 9.56W
Lop Buri Thailand 26 14.49N100.37E
Lopez, C. Gabon 36 0.36S 8.45E
Lop Nur l. China 24 40.30N 90.30E
Lopphavet est. Norway 16 70.30N 20.00E
Lopydino U.S.S.R. 18 61.10N 52.02E
Lorain U.S.A. 55 41.28N 82.11W
Loralai Pakistan 28 30.20N 68.41E
Lorca Spain 10 37.40N 1.41W
Lordsburg U.S.A. 52 32.21N108.43W
Lorena Brazil 59 22.44S 45.07W
Lorengau P.N.G. 27 2.01S147.15E
Lorenzo Geyres Uruguay 63 32.05S 57.55W
Loreto Brazil 61 7.05S 45.09W
Loreto Italy 12 43.26N 13.36E
Lorian Swamp Kenya 37 0.35N 39.40E
Lorient France 11 47.45N 3.21W
Lormes France 9 47.17N 3.49E
Lorne Australia 46 38.34S144.01E
Lorraine d. France 11 49.00N 6.20E
Lorris France 9 47.53N 2.31E
Lorup W. Germany 8 52.58N 7.39E
Los Andes Chile 63 32.50S 70.37W
Los Angeles Chile 63 37.28S 72.21W
Los Angeles U.S.A. 52 34.00N118.17W
Los Banos U.S.A. 54 37.04N120.51W
Los Blancos Argentina 62 23.40S 62.35W
Los Blancos Spain 10 37.37N 0.48W
Los Canarreos, Archipiélago de Cuba 57 21.40N 82.30W
Lošinj i. Yugo. 12 44.36N 14.20E
Losinovka U.S.S.R. 15 55.50N 31.57E
Los Mochis Mexico 56 25.45N108.57W
Los Olivos U.S.A. 54 34.40N120.06W
Los Roques is. Venezuela 60 12.00N 67.00W
Lossiemouth U.K. 6 57.43N 3.18W
Lost Cabin U.S.A. 54 43.19N107.36W
Los Teques Venezuela 60 10.25N 67.01W
Los Vilos Chile 62 31.55S 71.31W
Lot r. France 11 44.17N 0.22E
Lota Chile 63 37.05S 73.10W
Lotagipi Swamp Sudan 36 4.36N 34.55E
Lothian d. U.K. 6 55.50N 3.00W
Lotsani r. Botswana 39 22.42S 28.11E
Lötschberg Tunnel Switz. 11 46.25N 7.53E
Louang Namtha Laos 29 20.57N101.25E
Louangphrabang Laos 29 19.53N102.10E
Loudéac France 11 48.11N 2.45W
Loué France 9 48.00N 0.09W
Loughborough U.K. 4 52.47N 1.11W
Loughrea Rep. of Ire. 7 53.12N 8.35W
Loughros More B. Rep. of Ire. 7 54.48N 8.32W
Louisburgh Rep. of Ire. 7 53.46N 9.49W
Louisiade Archipelago is. P.N.G. 44 11.00S153.00E
Louisiana d. U.S.A. 53 31.00N 92.30W
Louis Trichardt R.S.A. 39 23.03S 29.54E
Louisville Ky. U.S.A. 55 38.13N 85.48W
Loukhi U.S.S.R. 18 66.05N 33.04E
Loulé Portugal 10 37.08N 8.02W
Loum Cameroon 38 4.36N 9.45E
Lourches France 8 50.19N 3.20E
Lourdes France 11 43.06N 0.02W
Louth Australia 47 30.34S145.09E
Louth d. Rep. of Ire. 7 53.55N 6.30W
Louth U.K. 4 53.23N 0.00
Louviers France 9 49.13N 1.10E
Louvigné-du-Désert France 9 48.29N 1.08W
Lövånger Sweden 16 64.22N 21.18E
Lovat r. U.S.S.R. 18 58.06N 31.37E
Lovech Bulgaria 13 43.08N 24.44E
Lovell U.S.A. 54 44.50N108.24W
Lovelock U.S.A. 54 40.11N118.28W
Lovere Italy 9 45.49N 10.04E
Lovoi r. Zaïre 37 8.14S 26.40E
Lovozero U.S.S.R. 18 68.01N 35.08E
Lovrin Romania 15 45.58N 20.48E
Lowell U.S.A. 55 42.39N 71.18W
Lower California pen. see Baja California pen. Mexico 56
Lower Egypt see Mişr Baḩrī f. Egypt 32
Lower Hutt New Zealand 48 41.13S174.55E
Lower Lough Erne U.K. 7 54.28N 7.48W
Lowestoft U.K. 5 52.29N 1.44E
Łowicz Poland 15 52.06N 19.55E
Loxton Australia 46 34.38S140.38E
Loyauté, Îles is. N. Cal. 40 21.00S167.00E
Loyoro Uganda 37 3.22N 34.16E
Loznica Yugo. 13 44.32N 19.13E
Luachimo Angola 36 7.25S 20.43E
Lualaba r. Zaïre 36 0.18N 25.30E
Luama r. Zaïre 37 4.45S 26.55E
Luanda Angola 36 8.50S 13.20E
Luangwa r. Central Zambia 37 15.32S 30.28E
Luanshya Zambia 37 13.09S 28.24E
Luan Xian China 25 39.45N118.44E
Luao Angola 36 10.41S 22.09E
Luapula r. Zambia 37 9.25S 28.36E
Luarca Spain 10 43.33N 6.31W
Lubango Angola 36 14.55S 13.30E
Lubbock U.S.A. 52 33.35N101.53W
Lubeck Australia 46 36.47S142.38E
Lübeck W. Germany 14 53.52N 10.40E
Lubenka U.S.S.R. 19 50.22N 54.13E
Lubersac France 11 45.27N 1.24E
Lubika Zaïre 37 7.50S 29.12E
Lubin Poland 14 51.24N 16.13E
Lublin Poland 15 51.18N 22.31E
Lubliniec Poland 15 50.40N 18.41E
Lubny U.S.S.R. 19 50.01N 33.00E
Lubumbashi Zaïre 37 11.44S 27.29E
Lucas González Argentina 63 32.25S 59.33W
Lucca Italy 9 43.50N 10.29E
Luce B. U.K. 6 54.45N 4.47W
Lucena Phil. 27 13.56N121.37E
Lucena Spain 10 37.25N 4.29W
Lucena del Cid Spain 10 40.09N 0.17W
Lučenec Czech. 15 48.20N 19.40E
Lucera Italy 12 41.30N 15.20E
Lucerne U.S.A. 54 48.12N120.36W
Lucero Mexico 56 30.49N106.30W
Lucin U.S.A. 54 41.22N113.55W
Lucindale Australia 46 36.59S140.25E
Luckenwalde E. Germany 14 52.05N 13.11E
Lucknow India 29 26.50N 80.54E
Lucy Creek town Australia 44 22.25S136.20E
Lüda China 25 38.53N121.37E
Lüdenscheid W. Germany 8 51.13N 7.36E
Lüderitz Namibia 39 26.37S 15.09E
Ludhiāna India 28 30.56N 75.52E
Lüdinghausen W. Germany 8 51.46N 7.27E
Ludington U.S.A. 55 43.58N 86.27W
Ludlow U.K. 5 52.23N 2.42W
Ludogorie mts. Bulgaria 15 43.45N 27.00E
Luduş Romania 15 46.29N 24.05E
Ludvika Sweden 17 60.09N 15.11E
Ludwigsburg W. Germany 14 48.53N 9.11E
Ludwigshafen W. Germany 14 49.29N 8.27E
Luena Angola 36 11.46S 19.55E
Luena Zambia 37 10.40S 30.21E
Lufeng China 25 22.57N115.38E
Lufkin U.S.A. 53 31.21N 94.47W
Luga U.S.S.R. 18 58.42N 29.49E
Lugano Switz. 9 46.01N 8.58E
Lugano, Lago di l. Switz. / Italy 9 46.00N 9.00E
Lugela Mozambique 37 16.25S 36.42E
Lugenda r. Mozambique 37 11.23S 38.30E
Lugh Ganane Somali Rep. 37 3.56N 42.32E
Luginy U.S.S.R. 15 51.05N 28.21E
Lugnaquilla Mtn. Rep. of Ire. 7 52.58N 6.28W
Lugo Italy 9 44.25N 11.54E
Lugo Spain 10 43.00N 7.33W
Lugoj Romania 15 45.42N 21.56E
Luiana Angola 39 17.08S 22.59E
Luiana r. Angola 39 17.28S 23.02E
Luino Italy 9 46.00N 8.44E
Luiro r. Finland 16 67.18N 27.28E
Łuków Poland 15 51.56N 22.23E
Lukoyanov U.S.S.R. 18 55.03N 44.29E
Lukuga r. Zaïre 37 5.37S 26.58E
Lukumbule Tanzania 37 11.34S 37.24E
Lule r. Sweden 16 65.35N 22.03E
Luleå Sweden 16 65.34N 22.10E
Lüleburgaz Turkey 13 41.25N 27.23E
Lulua r. Zaïre 36 5.03S 21.07E
Lumberton N.Mex. U.S.A. 54 36.55N106.56W
Lumsden New Zealand 48 45.44S168.26E
Lund Sweden 17 55.42N 13.11E
Lund Nev. U.S.A. 54 38.52N115.00W
Lund Utah U.S.A. 54 38.01N113.28W
Lundazi Zambia 37 12.19S 33.11E
Lundi r. Zimbabwe 39 21.20S 32.23E
Lundy i. U.K. 5 51.10N 4.41W
Lune r. U.K. 4 54.03N 2.49W
Lüneburg W. Germany 14 53.15N 10.24E
Lünen W. Germany 8 51.37N 7.31E
Lunéville France 11 48.36N 6.30E
Luninets U.S.S.R. 15 52.18N 26.50E
Luning U.S.A. 54 38.30N118.10W
Luofo Zaïre 37 0.12S 29.15E
Luogosanto Italy 12 41.02N 9.12E
Luoyang China 25 34.48N112.25E
Lupilichi Mozambique 37 11.45S 35.15E
Luquan China 29 25.35N102.30E
Lure France 11 47.42N 6.30E
Lurgan U.K. 7 54.28N 6.21W
Lurio Mozambique 37 13.30S 40.30E
Lurio r. Mozambique 37 13.32S 40.31E
Lusaka Zambia 37 15.20S 28.14E
Lusambo Zaïre 36 4.59S 23.26E
Lushnje Albania 13 40.56N 19.42E
Lushoto Tanzania 37 4.48S 38.20E
Lusk U.S.A. 52 42.46N104.27W
Lüta see Lüda China 25
Luton U.K. 5 51.53N 0.25W
Lutsk U.S.S.R. 15 50.42N 25.15E
Lutterworth U.K. 5 52.28N 1.12W
Luvua r. Zaïre 37 6.45S 27.00E
Luwegu r. Tanzania 37 8.30S 37.28E
Luwingu Zambia 37 10.13S 30.05E
Luxembourg d. Belgium 8 49.58N 5.30E
Luxembourg Europe 8 49.50N 6.15E
Luxembourg town Lux. 8 49.37N 6.08E
Luxor see Al Uqşur Egypt 30
Luza U.S.S.R. 18 60.41N 47.12E
Luza r. U.S.S.R. 18 60.45N 46.25E
Luzarches France 9 49.07N 2.25E
Luzern Switz. 14 47.03N 8.17E
Luzhou China 29 28.25N105.20E
Luziânia Brazil 61 16.18S 47.57W
Luzon i. Phil. 27 17.50N121.00E
Luzon Str. Pacific Oc. 27 20.20N122.00E
Lvov U.S.S.R. 15 49.50N 24.00E
Lyantonde Uganda 37 0.26S 31.08E
Lybster U.K. 6 58.18N 3.18W
Lycksele Sweden 16 64.36N 18.40E
Lydenburg R.S.A. 39 25.06S 30.27E
Lyme B. U.K. 5 50.40N 2.55W
Lyme Regis U.K. 5 50.44N 2.57W
Lymington U.K. 5 50.46N 1.32W
Łyna r. Poland 15 54.37N 21.14E
Lynchburg U.S.A. 53 37.24N 79.09W
Lynd Australia 44 18.56S144.30E
Lyndhurst Australia 46 30.19S138.24E
Lyngdal Norway 17 58.08N 7.05E
Lyngen Norway 16 69.36N 20.10E
Lyngen est. Norway 16 69.35N 20.20E
Lynn U.S.A. 55 42.28N 70.57W
Lynn Lake town Canada 51 56.51N101.01W
Lynton U.K. 5 51.14N 3.50W
Lynx Canada 55 50.07N 86.00W
Lyon France 11 45.46N 4.50E
Lyons Australia 46 30.34S133.50E
Lyons r. Australia 42 25.02S115.09E
Lysefjorden est. Norway 17 59.00N 6.14E
Lysekil Sweden 17 58.16N 11.26E
Lysva U.S.S.R. 18 58.07N 57.49E
Lysyanka U.S.S.R. 15 49.16N 30.49E
Lysyye Gory U.S.S.R. 19 51.32N 44.48E
Lytham St. Anne's U.K. 4 53.45N 3.01W
Lyubar U.S.S.R. 15 49.58N 27.41E
Lyubech U.S.S.R. 15 51.42N 30.41E
Lyubertsy U.S.S.R. 18 55.38N 37.58E
Lyubeshov U.S.S.R. 15 51.42N 25.32E

ushcha U.S.S.R. 15 52.28N 26.41E

r. Vietnam 26 19.47N105.56E
amakeogh *mtn.* Rep. of Ire. 7 54.17N 9.29W
amturk Mts. Rep. of Ire. 7 53.32N 9.42W
'ân Jordan 32 30.11N 35.43E
arianhamina Finland 17 60.06N 19.57E
as *r.* Neth. 8 51.44N 4.42E
aseik Belgium 8 51.08N 5.48E
assluis Neth. 8 51.58N 4.12E
astricht Neth. 8 50.51N 5.42E
ave Mozambique 39 21.06S 34.48E
aza Plateau Egypt 32 27.39N 31.45E
balane Mozambique 39 23.49S 32.36E
bel Creek *town* Australia 45 29.01S134.17E
blethorpe U.K. 4 53.21N 0.14E
brouk Mali 38 19.29N 1.15W
cá *mtn.* Chile 63 45.06S 73.12W
caé Brazil 59 22.21S 41.48W
calister *r.* Australia 47 37.55S146.50E
capá Brazil 61 0.04N 51.04W
caroni Australia 44 16.36S141.30E
cau Asia 25 22.11N113.33E
cau Brazil 61 5.05S 36.37W
cclesfield U.K. 4 53.16N 2.09W
cdiarmid Canada 55 49.27N 88.08W
cdoel U.S.A. 54 41.50N122.00W
cdonald, L. Australia 42 23.30S129.00E
cdonnell Ranges *mts.* Australia 44 3.45S133.20E
cduff U.K. 6 57.40N 2.29W
cedon *mtn.* Australia 47 37.27S144.34E
cedonia *see* Makedonija *d.* Yugo. 13
ceió Brazil 61 9.40S 35.44W
cerata Italy 12 43.18N 13.30E
cfarlane, L. Australia 46 31.55S136.42E
cgillycuddy's Reeks *mts.* Rep. of Ire. 7 52.00N 9.43W
chado Brazil 59 21.39S 45.33W
chala Ecuador 60 3.20S 79.57W
chattie, L. Australia 44 24.50S139.48E
chece Mozambique 39 19.17S 35.33E
cheke Zimbabwe 39 18.08S 31.49E
cheng China 25 31.11N115.02E
chevna U.S.S.R. 21 60.46N171.40E
chias Maine U.S.A. 55 44.43N 67.28W
chida Japan 23 35.32N139.27E
chilipatnam India 29 16.13N 81.12E
chiques Venezuela 60 10.04N 72.37W
chiya *r.* Japan 23 35.01N136.42E
chrihanish U.K. 6 55.25N 5.44W
chynlleth U.K. 5 52.35N 3.51W
ciá Argentina 63 32.11S 59.25W
cia Mozambique 39 25.03S 33.10E
acintyre *r.* Australia 47 28.50S150.50E
ackay Australia 44 21.09S149.11E
acKay U.S.A. 54 43.55N113.37W
ackay, L. Australia 42 22.30S149.10E
ackenzie *r.* Australia 44 22.48S149.15E
ackenzie *r.* Canada 50 69.20N134.00W
ackenzie King I. Canada 50 77.30N112.00W
ackenzie Mts. Canada 50 64.00N130.00W
ackinaw City U.S.A. 55 45.47N 84.43W
ackinnon Road *town* Kenya 37 3.50S 39.03E
acksville Australia 47 30.43S152.55E
aclean Australia 45 29.27S153.14E
aclear R.S.A. 39 31.04S 28.21E
acleay *r.* Australia 47 30.52S153.01E
açobere Mozambique 39 21.14S 32.50E
acomer Italy 12 40.16N 8.45E
âcon France 11 46.18N 4.50E
acon Ga. U.S.A. 53 32.47N 83.37W
acpherson Range *mts.* Australia 47 28.15S153.00E
acquarie *r.* Australia 47 30.07S147.24E
acquarie, L. Australia 47 33.05S151.35E
acquarie Marshes Australia 47 30.50S147.32E
acRobertson Land *f.* Antarctica 64 69.30S 64.00E
acroom Rep. of Ire. 7 51.54N 8.58W
acumba *r.* Australia 45 27.55S137.15E
a'dabā Jordan 32 31.44N 35.48E
adagascar Africa 36 17.00S 46.00E
adang P.N.G. 27 5.14S145.45E
adaoua Niger 38 14.05N 6.27E
adawaska U.S.A. 55 47.21N 68.20W
adeira *i.* Atlantic Oc. 34 32.45N 17.00W
adeira *r.* Brazil 60 3.20S 59.00W
adeira, Arquipélago da *is.* Atlantic Oc. 34 32.40N 16.45W
adeleine, Îles de la *is.* Canada 51 47.30N 61.45W
adera U.S.A. 54 36.57N120.03W
adgaon India 28 15.26N 73.50E
adhya Pradesh *d.* India 29 23.00N 79.30E
adibira Tanzania 37 8.13S 34.47E
adigan G. Australia 46 28.55S137.48E
adison Fla. U.S.A. 53 30.29N 83.39W
adison Ind. U.S.A. 55 38.46N 85.22W
adison Wisc. U.S.A. 53 43.04N 89.22W
adison W.Va. U.S.A. 55 38.03N 81.50W
adison Junction U.S.A. 54 44.39N110.51W
adiun Indonesia 26 7.37S111.33E
adoc Canada 55 44.30N 77.28W
Mado Gashi Kenya 37 0.40N 39.11E
Madoi China 24 34.28N 98.56E
Madonna di Campiglio Italy 9 46.14N 10.49E
Madrakah, Ra's al *c.* Oman 28 19.00N 57.50E
Madras India 29 13.05N 80.18E
Madras U.S.A. 54 44.38N121.08W
Madre, Laguna *b.* Mexico 56 25.00N 97.30W
Madre, Sierra *mts.* Mexico/Guatemala 56 15.20N 92.20W
Madre de Dios *r.* Bolivia 60 10.24S 65.30W
Madre del Sur, Sierra *mts.* Mexico 56 17.00N100.00W
Madre Occidental, Sierra *mts.* Mexico 56 25.00N105.00W
Madre Oriental, Sierra *mts.* Mexico 56 24.00N 99.00W
Madrid Spain 10 40.25N 3.43W
Madukani Tanzania 37 3.57S 35.49E
Madura *i.* Indonesia 26 7.00S113.30E
Madurai India 29 9.55N 78.07E
Maestra, Sierra *mts.* Cuba 57 20.10N 76.30W
Maevatanana Madagascar 36 16.56S 46.49E
Mafeteng Lesotho 39 29.51S 27.13E
Maffra Australia 47 37.58S146.59E
Mafia I. Tanzania 37 7.50S 39.50E
Mafikeng R.S.A. 39 25.52S 25.36E
Mafra Portugal 10 38.56N 9.20W
Magadan U.S.S.R. 21 59.38N150.50E
Magadi Kenya 37 1.53S 36.18E
Magallanes, Estrecho de *str.* Chile 63 53.00S 71.00W
Magalluf Spain 10 39.30N 2.31E
Magangué Colombia 60 9.14N 74.46W
Magdalena Argentina 63 35.04S 57.32W
Magdalena Bolivia 62 13.50S 64.08W
Magdalena *r.* Colombia 60 10.56N 74.58W
Magdalena Mexico 56 30.38N110.59W
Magdalena, Isla *i.* Chile 63 44.42S 73.10W
Magdalene *mtn.* Malaysia 26 4.25N117.55E
Magdeburg E. Germany 14 52.08N 11.36E
Magdeburg *d.* E. Germany 14 52.15N 11.30E
Magé Brazil 59 22.37S 43.03W
Magelang Indonesia 26 7.28S110.11E
Magellan's Str. *see* Magallanes, Estrecho de *str.* Chile 63
Magenta Italy 9 45.28N 8.53E
Magenta, L. Australia 43 33.26S119.10E
Mageröya *i.* Norway 16 71.03N 25.45E
Maggiorasca, Monte *mtn.* Italy 9 44.33N 9.29E
Maggiore, Lago *l.* Italy 9 46.00N 8.40E
Maghâghah Egypt 32 28.39N 30.50E
Magherafelt U.K. 7 54.45N 6.38W
Magna U.S.A. 54 40.42N112.06W
Magnitogorsk U.S.S.R. 18 53.28N 59.06E
Magny-en-Vexin France 9 49.09N 1.47E
Magog Canada 55 45.16N 72.09W
Magude Mozambique 39 25.01S 32.39E
Magué Mozambique 37 15.46S 31.42E
Magwe Burma 29 20.10N 95.00E
Mahābād Iran 31 36.44N 45.44E
Mahadday Weyne Somali Rep. 37 2.58N 45.32E
Mahagi Zaïre 37 2.16N 30.59E
Mahajanga Madagascar 36 15.43S 46.19E
Mahalapye Botswana 39 23.04S 26.47E
Maḩallāt Iran 31 33.54N 50.28E
Mahānadi *r.* India 29 20.17N 86.43E
Mahārāshtra *d.* India 28 20.00N 77.00E
Mahd adh Dhahab Saudi Arabia 30 23.30N 40.52E
Mahdia Guyana 60 5.10N 59.12W
Mahenge Tanzania 37 8.46S 36.38E
Mahia Pen. New Zealand 48 39.10S177.50E
Maho Sri Lanka 29 7.49N 80.17E
Mahón Spain 10 39.55N 4.18E
Maidenhead U.K. 5 51.32N 0.44W
Maidstone U.K. 5 51.17N 0.32E
Maiduguri Nigeria 38 11.53N 13.16E
Maignelay France 9 49.33N 2.31E
Maihar India 29 24.14N 80.50E
Main *r.* W. Germany 14 50.00N 8.19E
Main Barrier Range *mts.* Australia 46 31.25S141.25E
Main Channel *str.* Canada 55 45.22N 81.50W
Mai Ndombe *l.* Zaïre 36 2.00S 18.20E
Maine *d.* U.S.A. 55 45.15N 69.15W
Mainland *i.* Orkney Is. U.K. 6 59.00N 3.10W
Mainoru Australia 44 14.02S134.05E
Maintenon France 9 48.35N 1.35E
Mainz W. Germany 14 50.00N 8.16E
Maipo *mtn.* Argentina 63 34.10S 69.50W
Maipú Argentina 63 36.52S 57.54W
Maiquetía Venezuela 60 10.03N 66.57W
Maitland N.S.W. Australia 47 32.33S151.33E
Maitland S.A. Australia 46 34.21S137.42E
Majene Indonesia 26 3.33S118.59E
Majorca *i.* *see* Mallorca *i.* Spain 10
Majrūr Sudan 35 15.03N 30.31E
Majuba Hill R.S.A. 39 27.26S 29.48E
Makale Indonesia 26 3.06S119.53E
Makarikari Salt Pan *f.* Botswana 39 20.50S 25.45E
Makarikha U.S.S.R. 18 66.17N 58.28E
Makaryev U.S.S.R. 18 57.52N 43.40E
Makasar, Selat *str.* Indonesia 26 3.00S118.00E
Makassar Str. *see* Makasar, Selat *str.* Indonesia 26
Makat U.S.S.R. 19 47.38N 53.16E
Makedonija *d.* Yugo. 13 41.35N 21.30E
Makere Tanzania 37 4.15S 30.26E
Makeyevka U.S.S.R. 19 48.01N 38.00E
Makhachkala U.S.S.R. 19 42.59N 47.30E
Makhfar al Quwayrah Jordan 32 29.49N 35.18E
Makhrūq, Wādī al *r.* Jordan 32 31.30N 37.10E
Makinsk U.S.S.R. 20 52.40N 70.28E
Makkah Saudi Arabia 35 21.26N 39.49E
Makó Hungary 15 46.13N 20.30E
Makokou Gabon 36 0.38N 12.47E
Makran *f.* Asia 31 26.30N 61.20E
Makrān Coast Range *mts.* Pakistan 28 25.40N 64.00E
Maksamaa Finland 16 63.14N 22.05E
Makuliro Tanzania 37 9.34S 37.26E
Makurdi Nigeria 38 7.44N 8.35E
Malabo Equat. Guinea 38 3.45N 8.48E
Malacca, Str. of Indian Oc. 26 3.00N100.30E
Malad City U.S.A. 54 42.12N112.15W
Málaga Spain 10 36.43N 4.25W
Malakāl Sudan 35 9.31N 31.40E
Malakand Pakistan 28 34.34N 71.57E
Malang Indonesia 26 7.59S112.45E
Malange Angola 36 9.36S 16.21E
Mälaren *l.* Sweden 17 59.30N 17.12E
Malartic Canada 55 48.09N 78.09W
Malatya Turkey 30 38.22N 38.18E
Malaŵi Africa 37 12.00S 34.00E
Malaŵi, L. Africa 37 12.00S 34.30E
Malaya Vishera U.S.S.R. 18 58.53N 32.08E
Malāyer Iran 31 34.19N 48.51E
Malaysia Asia 26 5.00N110.00E
Malazgirt Turkey 30 39.09N 42.31E
Malbaie *r.* Canada 55 47.39N 70.09W
Malbooma Australia 46 30.41S134.11E
Malbork Poland 15 54.02N 19.01E
Malcolm Australia 43 28.56S121.30E
Malcolm, Pt. Australia 43 33.47S123.44E
Maldives Indian Oc. 28 6.20N 73.00E
Maldon U.K. 5 51.43N 0.41E
Maldonado Uruguay 59 34.57S 54.59W
Male Italy 9 46.21N 10.55E
Maléa, Ákra *c.* Greece 13 36.27N 23.11E
Mālegaon India 28 20.32N 74.38E
Malekula *i.* Vanuatu 40 16.15S167.30E
Malema Mozambique 37 14.55S 37.09E
Malenga U.S.S.R. 18 63.50N 36.50E
Malesherbes France 9 48.18N 2.25E
Malgomaj *l.* Sweden 16 64.47N 16.12E
Malheur L. U.S.A. 54 43.20N118.45W
Mali Africa 34 17.30N 2.30E
Malili Indonesia 27 2.38S121.06E
Malin U.S.S.R. 15 50.48N 29.08E
Malinau Indonesia 26 3.35N116.38E
Malindi Kenya 37 3.14S 40.08E
Malin Head Rep. of Ire. 7 55.23N 7.24W
Malin More Rep. of Ire. 7 54.42N 8.48W
Malita Phil. 27 6.19N125.39E
Mallacoota Australia 47 37.34S149.43E
Mallacoota Inlet *b.* Australia 47 37.34S149.43E
Mallaig U.K. 6 57.00N 5.50W
Mallawī Egypt 32 27.44N 30.50E
Mallorca *i.* Spain 10 39.35N 3.00E
Mallow Rep. of Ire. 7 52.08N 8.39W
Malm Norway 16 64.04N 11.12E
Malmberget Sweden 16 67.10N 20.40E
Malmédy Belgium 8 50.25N 6.02E
Malmesbury R.S.A. 39 33.28S 18.43E
Malmö Sweden 17 55.36N 13.00E
Malmöhus *d.* Sweden 17 55.45N 13.30E
Malmyzh U.S.S.R. 18 56.34N 50.41E
Maloja Switz. 9 46.24N 9.41E
Malone U.S.A. 55 44.51N 74.17W
Malonga Zaïre 36 10.26S 23.10E
Malorita U.S.S.R. 15 51.50N 24.08E
Målöy Norway 17 61.56N 5.07E
Malozemelskaya Tundra *f.* U.S.S.R. 18 67.40N 50.10E
Malpas Australia 46 34.44S140.43E
Malta Europe 12 35.55N 14.25E
Malta Mont. U.S.A. 54 48.21N107.52W
Malta Channel Med. Sea 12 36.20N 14.45E
Maltby U.K. 4 53.25N 1.12W
Malton U.K. 4 54.09N 0.48W
Maluku *d.* Indonesia 27 4.00S129.00E
Maluku, Laut *sea* Pacific Oc. 27
Malumfashi Nigeria 38 11.48N 7.36E
Malung Sweden 17 60.40N 13.44E
Malvérnia Mozambique 36 22.06S 31.42E
Mama U.S.S.R. 21 58.20N112.55E
Mamadysh U.S.S.R. 18 55.43N 51.20E
Mamaia Romania 15 44.15N 28.37E
Mambasa Zaïre 37 1.20N 29.05E
Mamberamo *r.* Indonesia 27 1.45S137.25E
Mambilima Falls *town* Zambia 37 10.32S 28.45E
Mamers France 9 48.21N 0.23E
Mamfe Cameroon 38 5.46N 9.18E
Mamonovo U.S.S.R. 15 54.30N 19.59E
Mamore *r.* Bolivia 62 12.00S 65.15W
Mampong Ghana 38 7.06N 1.24W
Mamry, Jezioro *l.* Poland 15 54.08N 21.42E
Mamuju Indonesia 26 2.41S118.55E
Man Ivory Coast 34 7.31N 7.37W
Man, Isle of U.K. 4 54.15N 4.30W
Mana *r.* Guiana 61 5.35N 53.55W
Manacapuru Brazil 60 3.16S 60.37W
Manacor Spain 10 39.32N 3.12E
Manado Indonesia 27 1.30N124.58E
Managua Nicaragua 57 12.06N 86.18W
Managua, Lago de *l.* Nicaragua 57 12.10N 86.30W
Manakara Madagascar 36 22.08S 48.01E
Manapouri, L. New Zealand 48 45.30S167.00E
Manara Australia 46 32.28S143.59E
Manau P.N.G. 27 8.02S148.00E
Manaus Brazil 60 3.06S 60.00W
Mancelona U.S.A. 55 44.54N 85.03W
Manche *d.* France 9 49.00N 1.10W
Manchester U.K. 4 53.30N 2.15W
Manchester Conn. U.S.A. 55 41.47N 72.31W
Manchester N.H. U.S.A. 55 42.59N 71.28W
Manchurian Plain *f.* *see* Dongbei Pingyuan *f.* China 25
Mancia Mozambique 36 19.04S 33.29E
Mand *r.* Iran 31 28.09N 51.16E
Manda Iringa Tanzania 37 10.30S 34.37E
Manda Mbeya Tanzania 37 7.59S 32.27E
Manda, Jabal *mtn.* Sudan 35 8.39N 24.27E
Mandal Norway 17 58.02N 7.27E
Mandala Peak Indonesia 27 4.45S140.15E
Mandalay Burma 29 21.57N 96.04E
Mandalgovi Mongolia 24 45.40N106.10E
Mandals *r.* Norway 17 58.02N 7.28E
Mandan U.S.A. 52 46.50N100.54W
Mandara Mts. Nigeria/Cameroon 38 10.30N 13.30E
Mandera Kenya 37 3.55N 41.50E
Mandora Australia 42 19.45S120.50E
Mandurah Australia 43 32.31S115.41E
Manduria Italy 13 40.24N 17.38E
Mandya India 28 12.33N 76.54E
Måne *r.* Norway 17 59.55N 8.48E
Manerbio Italy 9 45.21N 10.08E
Manevichi U.S.S.R. 15 51.19N 25.35E
Manfred Australia 46 33.21S143.50E
Manfredonia Italy 12 41.38N 15.54E
Manfredonia, Golfo di *g.* Italy 12 41.35N 16.05E
Mangalia Romania 15 43.50N 28.35E
Mangalore Australia 44 26.42S146.08E
Mangalore India 28 12.54N 74.51E
Mangaweka New Zealand 48 38.49S175.48E
Mangnai China 24 37.52N 91.26E
Mango Togo 38 10.23N 0.30E
Mangochi Malaŵi 37 14.29S 35.15E
Mangoky *r.* Madagascar 36 21.29S 43.41E
Mangonui New Zealand 48 35.00S173.34E
Mangueira, L. Brazil 59 33.06S 52.48W
Mangyshlak, Poluostrov *pen.* U.S.S.R. 19 44.00N 52.30E
Manhiça Mozambique 39 25.24S 32.49E
Manhuaçu Brazil 59 20.16S 42.01W
Manhumirim Brazil 59 20.22S 41.57W
Maniago Italy 9 46.10N 12.43E
Maniamba Mozambique 37 12.30S 35.05E
Manica Mozambique 39 19.00S 33.00E
Manica *d.* Mozambique 39 20.00S 34.00E
Manicoré Brazil 60 5.49S 61.17W
Manicouagane *r.* Canada 55 49.15N 68.20W
Maniitsoq *see* Sukkertoppen Greenland 51
Manila Phil. 27 14.36N120.59E
Manila U.S.A. 54 40.59N109.43W
Manildra Australia 47 33.12S148.41E
Manilla Australia 47 30.45S150.45E
Maningrida Australia 44 12.03S134.13E
Manipur *d.* India 29 25.00N 93.40E
Manisa Turkey 13 38.37N 27.28E
Manistee U.S.A. 55 44.14N 86.20W
Manistee *r.* U.S.A. 55 44.14N 86.20W
Manistique U.S.A. 55 45.58N 86.17W
Manitoba *d.* Canada 51 54.00N 96.00W
Manitoba, L. Canada 51 51.35N 99.00W
Manitoulin I. Canada 55 45.45N 82.30W
Maniwaki Canada 55 46.22N 75.58W
Manizales Colombia 60 5.03N 75.32W
Mānjhand Pakistan 28 25.50N 68.10E
Manjil Iran 31 36.44N 49.29E
Manjimup Australia 43 34.14S116.06E
Mankato U.S.A. 53 44.10N 94.00W
Mankono Ivory Coast 38 8.01N 6.09W
Manly Australia 47 33.47S151.17E
Mann *r.* Australia 44 12.20S134.07E
Man Na Burma 29 23.30N 97.13E
Manna Indonesia 26 4.27S102.55E
Mannahill Australia 46 32.26S139.59E
Mannar Sri Lanka 29 8.59N 79.54E
Mannar, G. of India/Sri Lanka 29 8.20N 79.00E
Mannheim W. Germany 14 49.30N 8.28E
Mannin B. Rep. of Ire. 7 53.28N 10.06W
Mannu *r.* Sardegna Italy 12 39.16N 9.00E
Mannum Australia 46 34.50S139.20E
Manokwari Indonesia 27 0.53S134.05E
Manono Zaïre 37 7.18S 27.24E
Manorhamilton Rep. of Ire. 7 54.18N 8.10W
Manosque France 11 43.50N 5.47E
Manouane *r.* Canada 55 49.29N 71.13W
Manouane, Lac *l.* Canada 55 50.40N 70.45W
Mānpur India 29 20.22N 80.44E
Manresa Spain 10 41.43N 1.50E
Mansa Zambia 37 11.10S 28.52E
Mansel I. Canada 51 62.00N 80.00W
Mansfield U.K. 4 53.08N 1.12W
Mansfield Mass. U.S.A. 55 42.02N 71.13W
Mansfield Ohio U.S.A. 55 40.46N 82.31W
Manso *r.* Brazil 62 11.59S 50.25W
Manta Ecuador 60 0.59S 80.44W
Mantaro *r.* Peru 60 12.00S 74.00W
Manteca U.S.A. 54 37.48N121.13W
Mantes France 9 49.00N 1.41E
Mantiqueira, Serra da *mts.* Brazil 59 22.25S 45.00W
Mantova Italy 9 45.09N 10.47E
Mänttä Finland 17 62.02N 24.38E
Manturovo U.S.S.R. 18 58.20N 44.42E
Mäntyluoto Finland 17 61.35N 21.29E
Manú Peru 60 12.14S 70.51W
Manui *i.* Indonesia 27 3.35S123.08E
Manukau Harbour *est.* New Zealand 48 37.10S174.00E
Manunda *r.* Australia 46 32.50S138.58E
Manus *i.* P.N.G. 27 2.00S147.00E
Manuwalkaninna Australia 46 29.00S139.08E
Manyane Botswana 39 23.23S 21.44E
Manyara, L. Tanzania 37 3.40S 35.50E
Manych *r.* U.S.S.R. 19 47.14N 40.20E
Manych Gudilo, Ozero *l.* U.S.S.R. 19 46.20N 42.45E
Manyoni Tanzania 37 5.46S 34.50E
Manzanares Spain 10 39.00N 3.23W
Manzanillo Cuba 57 20.21N 77.21W
Manzhouli China 25 49.36N117.28E
Manzilah, Buḩayrat al *l.* Egypt 32 31.20N 32.00E
Manzini Swaziland 39 26.29S 31.24E
Mao Chad 38 14.06N 15.11E
Maoke, Pegunungan *mts.* Indonesia 27 4.00S137.30E
Maoming China 25 21.50N110.56E
Mapai Mozambique 39 22.51S 32.00E
Mapia, Kepulauan *is.* Indonesia 27 1.00N134.15E
Mapinhane Mozambique 39 22.19S 35.03E
Mapire Venezuela 60 7.46N 64.41W
Maple Creek *town* Canada 50 49.55N109.27W
Mappi Indonesia 27 7.06S139.23E
Maprik P.N.G. 27 3.38S143.02E
Mapuera *r.* Brazil 61 2.00S 55.40W
Maputo Mozambique 39 25.58S 32.35E
Maputo *d.* Mozambique 39 26.00S 32.30E
Maqnā Saudi Arabia 32 28.26N 34.44E
Maqu China 29 34.05N102.15E
Maquela do Zombo Angola 36 6.06S 15.12E
Maquinchao Argentina 63 41.15S 68.44W
Mar, Serra do *mts.* Brazil 59 23.00S 44.40W
Mara Tanzania 37 1.30S 34.31E
Mara *d.* Tanzania 37 1.45S 34.30E
Mara *r.* Tanzania 37 1.30S 33.52E
Maraã Brazil 60 1.50S 65.22W
Marabá Brazil 61 5.23S 49.10W
Marabastad R.S.A. 39 23.58S 29.21E
Maracaibo Venezuela 60 10.44N 71.37W
Maracaibo, Lago de *l.* Venezuela 60 9.50N 71.30W
Maracaju, Serra de *mts.* Brazil 59 21.38S 55.10W
Maracay Venezuela 60 10.20N 67.28W
Maradi Niger 38 13.29N 7.10E
Maradi *d.* Niger 38 14.00N 8.10E
Marāgheh Iran 31 37.25N 46.13E
Maragogipe Brazil 61 12.48S 38.59W
Marahuaca, Cerro *mtn.* Venezuela 60 3.37N 65.25W
Marajó, Ilha de *i.* Brazil 61 1.00S 49.40W
Maralal Kenya 37 1.15N 36.48E
Maralinga Australia 43 30.13S131.32E
Maramba Zambia 39 17.52S 25.52E
Marana U.S.A. 54 32.27N111.13W
Marand Iran 31 38.25N 45.50E
Maranhão *d.* Brazil 61 6.00S 45.30W
Maranoa *r.* Australia 45 27.55S148.30E
Marañón *r.* Peru 60 4.40S 73.20W
Marão Mozambique 39 24.21S 34.07E
Marapi *mtn.* Indonesia 26 0.20S100.45E
Mărăşeşti Romania 15 45.52N 27.14E
Marathon Australia 44 20.49S143.34E
Marathón Greece 13 38.10N 23.59E
Maratua *i.* Indonesia 26 2.10N118.35E
Marāveh Tappeh Iran 31 37.55N 55.57E
Marawī Sudan 35 18.30N 31.49E
Marbella Spain 10 36.31N 4.53W
Marble Bar Australia 42 21.16S119.45E
Marburg W. Germany 14 50.49N 8.36E
Marcaria Italy 9 45.07N 10.32E
March U.K. 5 52.33N 0.05E
Marchant Hill Australia 46 32.16S138.49E
Marche Belgium 8 50.13N 5.21E
Marche *d.* Italy 12 43.35N 13.00E
Marchena Spain 10 37.20N 5.24W
Mar Chiquita *l.* Argentina 62 30.42S 62.36W
Marcos Paz Argentina 63 34.49S 58.51W
Marcq-en-Baroeul France 8 50.40N 3.01E
Mardān Pakistan 28 34.14N 72.05E
Mar del Plata Argentina 63 38.00S 57.32W
Marden U.K. 5 51.11N 0.30E
Mardie Australia 42 21.14S115.57E
Mardin Turkey 30 37.19N 40.43E
Maree, Loch U.K. 6 57.41N 5.28W
Mareeba Australia 44 17.00S145.26E
Mareg Somali Rep. 35 3.47N 47.18E
Marettimo *i.* Italy 12 37.58N 12.05E
Margai Caka *l.* China 29 35.11N 86.57E
Margaret *r.* Australia 46 29.26S137.00E
Margaret River *town* W. Aust. Australia 42 18.38S126.52E
Margaret River *town* W. Aust. Australia 43 33.57S115.04E
Margarita, Isla de *i.* Venezuela 60 11.00N 64.00W
Margate R.S.A. 39 30.51S 30.22E
Margate U.K. 5 51.23N 1.24E
Mārgow, Dasht-e *des.* Afghan. 28 30.45N 63.00E
María Elena Chile 62 22.21S 69.40W
María Grande Argentina 63 31.40S 59.55W
Maria I. Australia 44 14.52S135.40E
Mariana Brazil 59 20.23S 43.23W
Mariana Is. Pacific Oc. 40 15.00N145.00E
Marianao Cuba 57 23.03N 82.29W
Mariánské Lázně Czech. 14 49.59N 12.43E
Marias *r.* U.S.A. 54 47.56N110.30W
Maribo Denmark 17 54.46N 11.31E
Maribor Yugo. 14 46.35N 15.40E
Marico *r.* R.S.A. 39 24.12S 26.57E
Maricopa U.S.A. 54 35.03N119.24W
Maricourt Canada 51 61.30N 72.00W
Marié *r.* Brazil 60 0.27S 66.26W
Marieburg Belgium 8 50.07N 4.30E
Marie-Galante *i.* Guadeloupe 57 15.54N 61.11W
Mariehamn *see* Maarianhamina Finland 17
Mariemberg Neth. 8 52.32N 6.35E
Mariental Namibia 39 24.38S 17.58E
Mariestad Sweden 17 58.43N 13.51E
Marietta Ohio U.S.A. 55 39.26N 81.27W
Mariga *r.* Nigeria 38 9.37N 5.55E
Marília Brazil 59 22.13S 50.20W
Marín Spain 10 42.23N 8.42W
Marina di Ravenna Italy 9 44.29N 12.17E
Maringá Brazil 59 23.36S 52.02W
Maringue Mozambique 39 17.55S 34.24E
Marinha Grande Portugal 10 39.45N 8.55W
Marion Ind. U.S.A. 55 40.33N 85.40W
Marion Ohio U.S.A. 55 40.35N 83.08W
Marion Reef Australia 44 19.10S152.17E
Mariposa U.S.A. 54 37.29N119.58W
Mariscal Estigarribia Paraguay 59 22.03S 60.35W
Maritsa *r.* Turkey 13 41.00N 26.15E
Marka Somali Rep. 37 1.42N 44.47E
Markaryd Sweden 17 56.26N 13.36E
Marken *i.* Neth. 8 52.28N 5.03E
Markerwaard *f.* Neth. 8 52.30N 5.15E
Market Drayton U.K. 4 52.55N 2.30W
Market Harborough U.K. 5 52.29N 0.55W
Market Rasen U.K. 4 53.24N 0.20W
Market Weighton U.K. 4 53.52N 0.04W
Markha *r.* U.S.S.R. 21 63.37N119.00E
Markham, Mt. Antarctica 64 83.00S164.00E
Marks U.S.S.R. 19 51.43N 46.45E
Marl W. Germany 8 51.39N 7.03E
Marlborough Australia 44 22.51S149.50E
Marlborough *d.* New Zealand 48 41.40S173.40E
Marlborough U.K. 5 51.26N 1.44W
Marle France 9 49.44N 3.46E
Marlette U.S.A. 55 43.20N 83.04W
Marlo Australia 47 37.50S148.35E

Marmara i. Turkey **13** 40.38N 27.37E
Marmara, Sea of see Marmara Denizi sea Turkey **13**
Marmara Denizi sea Turkey **13** 40.45N 28.15E
Marmaris Turkey **13** 36.50N 28.17E
Marmolada mtn. Italy **9** 46.26N 11.51E
Marne d. France **9** 48.55N 4.10E
Marne r. France **9** 48.50N 2.25E
Marnoo Australia **46** 36.40S142.55E
Maromme France **9** 49.28N 1.02E
Marondera Zimbabwe **39** 18.11S 31.31E
Maroni r. Guiana **61** 5.30N 54.00W
Maroua Cameroon **38** 10.35N 14.20E
Marquard R.S.A. **39** 28.39S 27.25E
Marquette U.S.A. **55** 46.33N 87.23W
Marra Australia **46** 31.11S144.03E
Marra r. Australia **47** 30.05S147.05E
Marracuene Mozambique **39** 25.44S 32.41E
Marradi Italy **9** 44.04N 11.37E
Marradong Australia **43** 32.49S116.27E
Marrah, Jabal mtn. Sudan **35** 14.04N 24.21E
Marrakech Morocco **34** 31.49N 8.00W
Marree Australia **46** 29.40S138.04E
Marrupa Mozambique **37** 13.10S 37.30E
Marsabit Kenya **37** 2.20N 37.59E
Marsala Italy **12** 37.48N 12.27E
Marsá Maṭrūḥ Egypt **30** 31.21N 27.14E
Marsden Australia **47** 33.46S147.35E
Marseille France **11** 43.18N 5.22E
Marseille-en-Beauvaisis France **9** 49.35N 1.57E
Marsfjället mtn. Sweden **16** 65.05N 15.28E
Marshall Tex. U.S.A. **53** 32.33N 94.22W
Martaban Burma **29** 16.30N 97.35E
Martaban, G. of Burma **29** 15.10N 96.30E
Martapura Indonesia **26** 3.22S114.56E
Marte Nigeria **38** 12.23N 13.46E
Martelange Belgium **8** 49.50N 5.44E
Martés, Sierra mts. Spain **10** 39.10N 1.00W
Marthaguy r. Australia **47** 30.16S147.35E
Martha's Vineyard i. U.S.A. **55** 41.25N 70.40W
Martigny Switz. **14** 46.07N 7.05E
Martin Czech. **15** 49.05N 18.55E
Martina Franca Italy **13** 40.42N 17.21E
Martinique i. Windward Is. **57** 14.40N 61.00W
Martin Pt. U.S.A. **50** 70.10N143.50W
Martinsburg W.Va. U.S.A. **55** 39.27N 77.58W
Martins Ferry town U.S.A. **55** 40.07N 80.45W
Martinsville Ind. U.S.A. **55** 39.25N 86.25W
Marton New Zealand **48** 40.04S175.25E
Martos Spain **10** 37.44N 3.58W
Martre, Lac la l. Canada **50** 63.15N116.55W
Martti Finland **16** 67.28N 28.28E
Marudi Malaysia **26** 4.15N114.19E
Marula Zimbabwe **39** 20.26S 28.06E
Marum Neth. **8** 53.06N 6.16E
Marvejols France **11** 44.33N 3.18E
Marvel Loch town Australia **43** 31.31S119.30E
Mārwār India **28** 25.44N 73.36E
Mary U.S.S.R. **20** 37.42N 61.54E
Maryborough Qld. Australia **44** 25.32S152.36E
Maryborough Vic. Australia **46** 37.05S143.47E
Marydale R.S.A. **39** 29.24S 22.06E
Mary Kathleen Australia **44** 20.49S140.00E
Maryland d. U.S.A. **55** 39.00N 76.45W
Maryport U.K. **4** 54.43N 3.30W
Marysvale U.S.A. **54** 38.27N112.11W
Marysville Calif. U.S.A. **54** 39.09N121.35W
Maryvale Australia **47** 28.04S152.12E
Marzūq Libya **34** 25.56N 13.57E
Marzūq, Ṣaḥrā' des. Libya **34** 24.30N 13.00E
Masāhim, Kūh-e mtn. Iran **31** 30.26N 55.08E
Masai Steppe f. Tanzania **37** 4.30S 37.00E
Masaka Uganda **37** 0.20S 31.46E
Masan S. Korea **25** 35.10N128.35E
Masasi Tanzania **37** 10.43S 38.48E
Masba Nigeria **38** 10.35N 13.01E
Masbate i. Phil. **27** 12.00N123.30E
Maseru Lesotho **39** 29.18S 27.28E
Mashhad Iran **31** 36.16N 59.34E
Mashki Chāh Pakistan **28** 29.01N 62.27E
Mashonaland f. Zimbabwe **39** 18.20S 32.00E
Masi Norway **16** 69.26N 23.40E
Masindi Uganda **37** 1.41N 31.45E
Maṣīrah i. Oman **28** 20.30N 58.50E
Masjed Soleymān Iran **31** 31.59N 49.18E
Mask, Lough Rep. of Ire. **7** 53.38N 9.22W
Mason City U.S.A. **53** 43.10N 93.10W
Masqaṭ Oman **31** 23.36N 58.37E
Massa Italy **9** 44.02N 10.09E
Massachusetts d. U.S.A. **55** 42.15N 71.50W
Massakory Chad **38** 13.02N 15.43E
Massa Marittima Italy **12** 43.03N 10.53E
Massangena Mozambique **39** 21.31S 33.03E
Massangulo Mozambique **37** 13.54S 35.24E
Massarosa Italy **9** 43.52N 10.20E
Massena U.S.A. **55** 44.56N 74.54W
Massif Central mts. France **11** 45.00N 3.30E
Massillon U.S.A. **55** 40.48N 81.32W
Massinga Mozambique **39** 23.20S 35.25E
Massingir Mozambique **39** 23.49S 32.04E
Masterton New Zealand **48** 40.57S175.39E
Mastūrah Saudi Arabia **30** 23.06N 38.50E
Masvingo Zimbabwe **39** 20.10S 30.49E
Maṣyāf Syria **32** 35.03N 36.21E
Matabeleland f. Zimbabwe **39** 19.50S 28.15E
Matachewan Canada **55** 47.56N 80.39W
Matadi Zaïre **36** 5.50S 13.32E
Matagami Canada **55** 49.40N 77.41W
Matagami, L. Canada **55** 49.42N 77.39W
Matagorda B. U.S.A. **53** 28.30N 96.20W
Matakana Australia **47** 32.59S145.53E
Matakana I. New Zealand **48** 37.35S176.15E
Matam Senegal **34** 15.40N 13.18W
Matamata New Zealand **48** 37.49S175.46E
Matameye Niger **38** 13.26N 8.28E
Matamoros Coahuila Mexico **56** 25.33N103.15W
Matamoros Tamaulipas Mexico **56** 25.50N 97.31W
Matandu r. Tanzania **37** 8.44S 39.22E
Matane Canada **55** 48.50N 67.31W
Matankari Niger **38** 13.47N 4.00E
Matanzas Cuba **57** 23.04N 81.35W
Mataram Indonesia **26** 8.36S116.07E
Matarani Peru **62** 16.58S 72.07W
Mataranka Australia **42** 14.56S133.07E
Mataró Spain **10** 41.32N 2.27E
Matatiele R.S.A. **39** 30.19S 28.48E
Mataura r. New Zealand **48** 46.34S168.45E
Matawai New Zealand **48** 38.21S177.32E
Matawin, Résr. Canada **55** 46.43N 73.54W
Maṭāy Egypt **32** 28.25N 30.46E
Matehuala Mexico **56** 23.40N100.40W
Mateke Hills Zimbabwe **39** 21.48S 31.00E
Matera Italy **13** 40.41N 16.36E
Matetsi Zimbabwe **39** 18.17S 25.57E
Matfors Sweden **17** 62.21N 17.02E
Mathews Peak mtn. Kenya **37** 1.18N 37.20E
Mathoura Australia **47** 35.49S144.54E
Mathura India **28** 27.30N 77.42E
Mati Phil. **27** 6.55N126.15E
Matias Barbosa Brazil **59** 21.52S 43.21W
Matipó Brazil **59** 20.16S 42.17W
Matlock U.K. **4** 53.09N 1.32W
Matochkin Shar U.S.S.R. **20** 73.15N 56.35E
Mato Grosso d. Brazil **62** 13.00S 55.00W
Mato Grosso town Brazil **62** 15.05S 59.57W
Mato Grosso, Planalto do f. Brazil **62** 16.00S 54.00W
Mato Grosso do Sul d. Brazil **62** 20.00S 54.30W
Matope Malaŵi **37** 15.20S 34.57E
Matopo Hills Zimbabwe **39** 20.45S 28.30E
Matosinhos Portugal **10** 41.11N 8.42W
Maṭraḥ Oman **31** 23.37N 58.33E
Matsena Nigeria **38** 13.13N 10.04E
Matsubara Japan **23** 34.34N135.33E
Matsudo Japan **23** 35.47N139.54E
Matsue Japan **25** 35.29N133.00E
Matsusaka Japan **23** 34.34N136.32E
Matsuyama Japan **25** 33.50N132.47E
Mattagami r. Canada **55** 50.43N 81.29W
Mattawa Canada **55** 46.19N 78.42W
Mattawamkeag U.S.A. **55** 45.31N 68.21W
Matterhorn mtn. Italy / Switz. **9** 45.58N 7.38E
Matterhorn mtn. U.S.A. **54** 41.49N115.23W
Matthews Ridge town Guyana **60** 7.30N 60.10W
Matthew Town Bahamas **57** 20.57N 73.40W
Mattice Canada **55** 49.36N 83.16W
Mattmar Sweden **16** 63.19N 13.45E
Matua Indonesia **26** 2.58S110.52E
Maturín Venezuela **60** 9.45N 63.10W
Maua Mozambique **37** 13.53S 37.10E
Maubeuge France **8** 50.17N 3.58E
Maude Australia **46** 34.27S144.21E
Maués Brazil **61** 3.24S 57.42W
Maui i. Hawaii U.S.A. **52** 20.45N156.15W
Maumee U.S.A. **55** 41.34N 83.41W
Maumee r. U.S.A. **55** 41.40N 83.35W
Maumere Indonesia **27** 8.35S122.13E
Maun Botswana **39** 19.52S 23.40E
Maurice, L. Australia **45** 29.28S130.58E
Mauritania Africa **34** 20.00N 10.00W
Mawjib, Wādī al r. Jordan **32** 31.28N 35.34E
Mawlaik Burma **29** 23.40N 94.26E
Maxcanú Mexico **56** 20.35N 89.59W
May, C. U.S.A. **55** 38.58N 74.55W
Maya Spain **10** 43.12N 1.29W
Mayaguana I. Bahamas **57** 22.30N 73.00W
Mayagüez Puerto Rico **57** 18.13N 67.09W
Mayāmey Iran **31** 36.27N 55.40E
Maya Mts. Belize **57** 16.30N 89.00W
Maybole U.K. **6** 55.21N 4.41W
Mayen W. Germany **8** 50.19N 7.14E
Mayenne France **9** 48.18N 0.37W
Mayenne d. France **9** 48.05N 0.40W
Mayenne r. France **9** 47.30N 0.37W
Maykop U.S.S.R. **19** 44.37N 40.48E
Maymyo Burma **29** 22.05N 96.33E
Maynooth Rep. of Ire. **7** 53.23N 6.37W
Mayo d. Rep. of Ire. **7** 53.47N 9.07W
Mayo, Plains of f. Rep. of Ire. **7** 53.46N 9.05W
Mayo Daga Nigeria **38** 6.59N 11.25E
Mayo Landing Canada **50** 63.45N135.45W
Mayor I. New Zealand **48** 37.15S176.15E
Mayotte, Île i. Comoros **37** 12.50S 45.10E
May Pen Jamaica **57** 17.58N 77.14W
Maysville U.S.A. **55** 38.38N 83.46W
Mazagão Brazil **61** 0.07S 51.17W
Mazamba Mozambique **39** 18.32S 34.50E
Mazamet France **11** 43.30N 2.24E
Mazán Peru **60** 3.15S 73.00W
Mazarredo Argentina **63** 47.00S 66.45W
Mazarrón Spain **10** 37.38N 1.19W
Mazatenango Guatemala **56** 14.31N 91.30W
Mazatlán Mexico **56** 23.13N106.25W
Mažeikiai U.S.S.R. **17** 56.19N 22.20E
Mazirbe U.S.S.R. **17** 57.41N 22.21E
Mazowe r. Mozambique **37** 16.32S 33.25E
Mazowe Zimbabwe **39** 17.30S 30.58E
Mazu Liedao is. China **25** 26.12N120.00E
Mazunga Zimbabwe **39** 21.45S 29.52E
Mazurski, Pojezierze lakes Poland **15** 53.50N 21.00E
Mbabane Swaziland **39** 26.19S 31.08E
Mbala Zambia **37** 8.50S 31.24E
Mbale Uganda **37** 1.04N 34.12E
Mbalmayo Cameroon **38** 3.35N 11.31E
Mbamba Bay town Tanzania **37** 11.18S 34.50E
Mbandaka Zaïre **34** 0.03N 18.28E
Mbarara Uganda **37** 0.36S 30.40E
Mbeya Tanzania **37** 8.54S 33.29E
Mbeya d. Tanzania **37** 8.30S 32.30E
Mbinda Congo **36** 2.11S 12.55E
Mbogo Tanzania **37** 7.26S 33.26E
Mbomou r. C.A.R. **35** 4.08N 22.25E
Mbuji Mayi Zaïre **36** 6.10S 23.39E
Mbulamuti Uganda **37** 0.50N 33.05E
Mbura Tanzania **37** 11.14S 35.25E
Mbuzi Zambia **37** 12.20S 32.17E
McAlester U.S.A. **53** 34.56N 95.46W
McAlister, Mt. Australia **47** 34.27S149.45E
McArthur r. Australia **44** 15.54S136.40E
McClintock Channel Canada **51** 71.20N102.00W
McClure Str. Canada **50** 74.30N116.00W
McConaughy, L. U.S.A. **52** 41.20N102.00W
McCook U.S.A. **52** 40.15N100.45W
McDermitt U.S.A. **54** 41.59N117.36W
McDouall Peak Australia **46** 29.51S134.55E
McGrath U.S.A. **50** 62.58N155.40W
Mchinja Tanzania **37** 9.44S 39.45E
Mchinji Malaŵi **37** 13.48S 32.55E
McIlwraith Range mts. Australia **44** 14.00S143.10E
McKeesport U.S.A. **55** 40.21N 79.52W
McKinley, Mt. U.S.A. **50** 63.00N151.00W
McKittrick U.S.A. **54** 35.18N119.37W
McLennan Canada **50** 55.42N116.54W
McLeod, L. Australia **42** 24.10S113.35E
McLeod Lake town Canada **50** 54.59N123.02W
McMinnville Oreg. U.S.A. **54** 45.13N123.12W
McNary U.S.A. **54** 34.04N109.51W
Mdatsane R.S.A. **39** 32.54S 27.24E
Mead, L. U.S.A. **54** 36.05N114.25W
Meadville U.S.A. **55** 41.38N 80.09W
Mealhada Portugal **10** 40.22N 8.27W
Meander River town Canada **50** 59.02N117.42W
Mearim r. Brazil **61** 3.20S 44.20W
Meath d. Rep. of Ire. **7** 53.32N 6.40W
Meaux France **9** 48.58N 2.54E
Mecca see Makkah Saudi Arabia **35**
Mecca U.S.A. **54** 33.35N116.03W
Mechelen Belgium **8** 51.01N 4.28E
Mecklenburger Bucht b. E. Germany **14** 54.05N 11.00E
Meconta Mozambique **37** 15.00S 39.50E
Mecufi Mozambique **37** 13.20S 40.32E
Meda Portugal **10** 40.58N 7.16W
Medan Indonesia **26** 3.35N 98.39E
Mede Italy **9** 45.06N 8.44E
Mededsiz mtn. Turkey **30** 37.33N 34.38E
Medellín Colombia **60** 6.15N 75.36W
Medemblik Neth. **8** 52.48N 5.06E
Médenine Tunisia **34** 33.24N 10.25E
Mederdra Mauritania **34** 17.02N 15.41W
Medford Oreg. U.S.A. **54** 42.19N122.52W
Medgidia Romania **15** 44.15N 28.16E
Mediaş Romania **15** 46.10N 24.21E
Medicina Italy **9** 44.28N 11.38E
Medicine Bow Peak mtn. U.S.A. **54** 41.21N106.19W
Medicine Hat Canada **50** 50.03N110.41W
Medina see Al Madīnah Saudi Arabia **30**
Medina N.Y. U.S.A. **55** 43.14N 78.23W
Medina del Campo Spain **10** 41.20N 4.55W
Medina de Rioseco Spain **10** 41.53N 5.03W
Mediterranean Sea **34** 37.00N 15.00E
Mêdog China **24** 29.19N 95.19E
Medveditsa r. U.S.S.R. **19** 49.35N 42.45E
Medvezhyegorsk U.S.S.R. **18** 62.56N 34.28E
Medvin U.S.S.R. **15** 49.25N 30.48E
Medway r. U.K. **5** 51.24N 0.31E
Medzhibozh U.S.S.R. **15** 49.29N 27.28E
Meeberrie Australia **42** 26.58S115.51E
Meekatharra Australia **42** 26.35S118.30E
Meeker U.S.A. **54** 40.02N107.55W
Meer Belgium **8** 51.27N 4.46E
Meerhusener Moor f. W. Germany **8** 53.36N 7.33E
Meerut India **28** 29.00N 77.42E
Mega Ethiopia **35** 4.07N 38.16E
Mégara Greece **13** 38.00N 23.21E
Meghalaya d. India **29** 25.30N 91.00E
Mégiscane r. Canada **55** 48.36N 76.00W
Mehadia Romania **15** 44.55N 22.22E
Meiktila Burma **29** 20.53N 95.54E
Meiningen E. Germany **14** 50.34N 10.25E
Meissen E. Germany **14** 51.10N 13.28E
Mei Xian China **25** 24.19N116.13E
Mekatina Canada **55** 46.58N 84.05W
Mekele Ethiopia **35** 13.33N 39.30E
Meknès Morocco **34** 33.53N 5.37W
Mekong r. Asia **26** 10.00N106.20E
Mekong Delta Vietnam **26** 10.00N106.20E
Mekongga mtn. Indonesia **27** 3.39S121.15E
Mékrou r. Benin **38** 12.20N 2.47E
Melaka Malaysia **26** 2.11N102.16E
Melanesia is. Pacific Oc. **40** 5.00N165.00E
Melbourne Australia **47** 37.45S144.58E
Melegnano Italy **9** 45.21N 9.19E
Meleuz U.S.S.R. **18** 52.58N 55.56E
Mélèzes, Rivière aux r. Canada **51** 57.40N 69.30W
Melfi Chad **34** 11.04N 18.03E
Melfi Italy **12** 40.59N 15.39E
Melfort Canada **50** 52.52N104.36W
Melilla Spain **10** 35.17N 2.57W
Melipilla Chile **63** 33.42S 71.13W
Melitopol U.S.S.R. **19** 46.51N 35.22E
Melk Austria **14** 48.14N 15.20E
Mellerud Sweden **17** 58.42N 12.28E
Melmore Pt. Rep. of Ire. **7** 55.15N 7.49W
Melnik Bulgaria **13** 41.30N 23.22E
Mělník Czech. **14** 50.20N 14.29E
Melo Uruguay **59** 32.22S 54.10W
Melrose U.K. **6** 55.36N 2.43W
Melrose Mont. U.S.A. **54** 45.37N112.41W
Melstone U.S.A. **54** 46.36N107.52W
Meltaus Finland **16** 66.54N 25.22E
Melton Mowbray U.K. **4** 52.46N 0.53W
Melun France **9** 48.32N 2.40E
Melvich U.K. **6** 58.33N 3.55W
Melville, C. Australia **44** 14.11S144.30E
Melville B. Australia **44** 12.10S136.32E
Melville Hills Canada **50** 69.20N122.00W
Melville I. Australia **44** 11.30S131.00E
Melville I. Canada **50** 75.30N110.00W
Melville Pen. Canada **51** 68.00N 84.00W
Melvin, Lough Rep. of Ire. / U.K. **7** 54.26N 8.12W
Melzo Italy **9** 45.30N 9.25E
Memba Mozambique **37** 14.16S 40.30E
Memboro Indonesia **26** 9.22S119.32E
Memmingen W. Germany **14** 47.59N 10.11E
Memphis ruins Egypt **32** 29.52N 31.12E
Memphis Tenn. U.S.A. **53** 35.05N 90.00W
Mena U.S.S.R. **15** 51.30N 32.15E
Menai Str. U.K. **4** 53.17N 4.20W
Ménaka Mali **38** 15.55N 2.24E
Mendawai r. Indonesia **26** 3.17S113.20E
Mende France **11** 44.32N 3.30E
Mendi P.N.G. **27** 6.13S143.39E
Mendip Hills U.K. **5** 51.15N 2.40W
Mendocino, C. U.S.A. **54** 40.25N124.25W
Mendoza Argentina **63** 32.54S 68.50W
Mendoza d. Argentina **63** 34.30S 68.00W
Mendung Indonesia **26** 0.31N103.12E
Mene Grande Venezuela **60** 9.51N 70.57W
Menemen Turkey **30** 38.34N 27.03E
Menen Belgium **8** 50.48N 3.07E
Menfi Italy **12** 37.36N 12.59E
Mengzi China **29** 23.20N103.21E
Menindee Australia **46** 32.23S142.30E
Menindee L. Australia **46** 32.21S142.20E
Menongue Angola **36** 14.36S 17.48E
Menorca i. Spain **10** 40.00N 4.00E
Mentawai, Kepulauan is. Indonesia **26** 2.50S 99.00E
Mentekab Malaysia **26** 3.29N102.21E
Mentok Indonesia **26** 2.04S105.12E
Menton France **11** 43.47N 7.30E
Menyapa, Gunung mtn. Indonesia **26** 1.00N116.20E
Menzies Australia **43** 29.41S121.02E
Menzies, Mt. Antarctica **64** 71.50S 61.00E
Meppel Neth. **8** 52.42N 6.12E
Meppen W. Germany **8** 52.42N 7.17E
Mer France **9** 47.42N 1.30E
Merano Italy **12** 46.41N 11.10E
Merauke Indonesia **44** 8.30S140.22E
Merbein Australia **46** 34.11S142.04E
Mercato Saraceno Italy **9** 43.57N 12.12E
Merced U.S.A. **54** 37.18N120.29W
Mercedes Buenos Aires Argentina **63** 34.40S 59.25W
Mercedes Corrientes Argentina **62** 29.15S 58.05W
Mercedes San Luis Argentina **63** 33.40S 65.30W
Mercedes Uruguay **63** 33.16S 58.01W
Mercy, C. Canada **51** 65.00N 63.30W
Mere U.K. **5** 51.05N 2.16W
Meredith Australia **46** 37.50S144.05E
Merefa U.S.S.R. **19** 49.49N 36.05E
Mergenevo U.S.S.R. **19** 49.59N 51.19E
Mergui Burma **29** 12.26N 98.34E
Mergui Archipelago is. Burma **29** 11.30N 98.15E
Meribah Australia **46** 34.42S140.53E
Meriç r. Turkey **13** 40.52N 26.12E
Mérida Mexico **57** 20.59N 89.39W
Mérida Spain **10** 38.55N 6.20W
Mérida Venezuela **60** 8.24N 71.08W
Mérida, Cordillera de mts. Venezuela **60** 8.30N 71.00W
Meridian U.S.A. **53** 32.21N 88.42W
Mérignac France **11** 44.50N 0.42W
Merikarvia Finland **17** 61.51N 21.30E
Merino Australia **46** 37.45S141.35E
Merir i. Caroline Is. **27** 4.19N132.18E
Merirumã Brazil **61** 1.15N 54.50W
Merksem Belgium **8** 51.14N 4.25E
Merlo Argentina **63** 34.40S 58.45W
Merne Merna Australia **46** 31.45S138.21E
Merredin Australia **43** 31.29S118.16E
Merrick mtn. U.K. **6** 55.08N 4.29W
Merrill Oreg. U.S.A. **54** 42.01N121.36W
Merrill Wisc. U.S.A. **53** 45.12N 89.43W
Merriwa Australia **47** 32.08S150.20E
Merrygoen Australia **47** 31.51S149.16E
Mersch Lux. **8** 49.44N 6.05E
Mersea I. U.K. **5** 51.47N 0.58E
Merseburg E. Germany **14** 51.22N 12.00E
Mersey r. U.K. **4** 53.22N 2.37W
Merseyside d. U.K. **4** 53.28N 3.00W
Mersin Turkey **30** 36.47N 34.37E
Mersing Malaysia **26** 2.25N103.50E
Merthyr Tydfil U.K. **5** 51.45N 3.23W
Mértola Portugal **10** 37.38N 7.40W
Merton U.K. **5** 51.25N 0.12W
Méru France **9** 49.14N 2.08E
Meru mtn. Tanzania **37** 3.15S 36.44E
Méry France **9** 48.30N 3.53E
Merzifon Turkey **30** 40.52N 35.28E
Merzig W. Germany **8** 49.26N 6.39E
Mesa U.S.A. **54** 33.25N111.50W
Mesagne Italy **13** 40.33N 17.49E
Mesewa Ethiopia **35** 15.36N 39.29E
Meslay-du-Maine France **9** 47.57N 0.33W
Mesocco Switz. **9** 46.23N 9.14E
Mesolóngion Greece **13** 38.23N 21.23E
Mesopotamia f. Iraq **31** 33.30N 44.30E
Messalo r. Mozambique **37** 11.38S 40.27E
Messina Italy **12** 38.13N 15.34E
Messina R.S.A. **39** 22.20S 30.03E
Messina, Stretto di str. Italy **12** 38.10N 15.35E
Messíni Greece **13** 37.03N 22.00E
Messiniakós, Kólpos g. Greece **13** 36.50N 22.05E
Mesta r. Bulgaria see Néstos r. Greece **13**
Mestre Italy **9** 45.29N 12.15E
Meta r. Venezuela **60** 6.10N 67.30W
Metán Argentina **62** 25.30S 65.00W
Metangula Mozambique **37** 12.41S 34.51E
Metković Yugo. **13** 43.03N 17.38E
Métsovon Greece **13** 39.46N 21.11E
Metz France **11** 49.07N 6.11E
Meulaboh Indonesia **26** 4.10N 96.09E
Meulan France **9** 49.01N 1.54E
Meuse r. Belgium see Maas r. Neth. **8**
Mexicali Mexico **54** 32.40N115.29W
Mexico C. America **56** 20.00N100.00W
México d. Mexico **56** 19.45N 99.30W
Mexico, G. of N. America **56** 25.00N 90.00W
Mexico City see Ciudad de México Mexico **56**
Meymaneh Afghan. **28** 35.54N 64.43E
Mezen U.S.S.R. **18** 65.50N 44.20E
Mezen r. U.S.S.R. **18** 65.50N 44.18E
Mézenc, Mont mtn. France **11** 44.54N 4.11E
Mezenskaya Guba g. U.S.S.R. **18** 66.30N 44.00E
Mezőkövesd Hungary **15** 47.50N 20.34E
Mezzolombardo Italy **9** 46.13N 11.05E
Miahuatlán Mexico **56** 16.20N 96.36W
Miami Fla. U.S.A. **53** 25.45N 80.10W
Miāndow Āb Iran **31** 36.57N 46.06E
Miāneh Iran **31** 37.23N 47.45E
Miānwāli Pakistan **28** 32.32N 71.33E
Mianyang Sichuan China **24** 31.28N104.46E
Miass U.S.S.R. **20** 55.00N 60.00E
Mibu r. Japan **23** 35.49N137.57E
Mica R.S.A. **39** 24.09S 30.49E
Michalovce Czech. **15** 48.45N 21.55E
Michelson, Mt. U.S.A. **50** 69.19N144.17W
Michigan d. U.S.A. **55** 44.00N 85.00W
Michigan, L. U.S.A. **55** 44.00N 87.00W
Michigan City U.S.A. **55** 41.43N 86.54W
Michikamau L. Canada **51** 54.00N 64.00W
Michipicoten Canada **55** 47.57N 84.55W
Michipicoten I. Canada **55** 47.40N 85.48W
Michoacán d. Mexico **56** 19.20N101.00W
Michurin Bulgaria **13** 42.09N 27.51E
Michurinsk U.S.S.R. **18** 52.54N 40.30E
Micronesia is. Pacific Oc. **40** 8.00N160.00E
Middelburg Neth. **8** 51.30N 3.36E
Middelburg C.P. R.S.A. **39** 31.29S 25.00E
Middelburg Trans. R.S.A. **39** 25.45S 29.27E
Middelharnis Neth. **8** 51.46N 4.09E
Middenmeer Neth. **8** 52.51N 4.59E
Middlebury U.S.A. **55** 44.01N 73.10W
Middle I. Australia **43** 34.07S123.12E
Middlesboro U.S.A. **53** 36.37N 83.43W
Middlesbrough U.K. **4** 54.34N 1.13W
Middletown N.Y. U.S.A. **55** 39.31N 84.13W
Mid Glamorgan d. U.K. **5** 51.38N 3.25W
Midi-Pyrénées d. France **11** 44.10N 2.00E
Midland Canada **55** 44.45N 79.53W
Midland Mich. U.S.A. **55** 43.38N 84.14W
Midland Tex. U.S.A. **52** 32.00N102.09W
Midland Junction Australia **43** 31.54S115.57E
Midleton Rep. of Ire. **7** 51.55N 8.10W
Midwest U.S.A. **54** 43.25N106.16W
Midyan f. Saudi Arabia **32** 27.50N 35.30E
Midye Turkey **13** 41.37N 28.07E
Midžor mtn. Yugo. **13** 43.23N 22.42E
Mie d. Japan **23** 34.42N136.08E
Miechów Poland **15** 50.23N 20.01E
Miedzychód Poland **14** 52.36N 15.55E
Mielec Poland **15** 50.18N 21.25E
Mienga Angola **39** 17.16S 19.50E
Mieres Spain **10** 43.15N 5.46W
Mijares r. Spain **10** 39.58N 0.01W
Mikhaylov U.S.S.R. **18** 54.14N 39.00E
Mikhaylovgrad Bulgaria **13** 43.25N 23.11E
Mikhaylovka U.S.S.R. **19** 50.05N 43.15E
Miki Japan **23** 34.48N134.59E
Mikínai Greece **13** 37.44N 22.45E
Mikindani Tanzania **37** 10.16S 40.05E
Mikkeli Finland **18** 61.44N 27.15E
Míkonos i. Greece **13** 37.29N 25.25E
Mikumi Tanzania **37** 7.22S 37.00E
Mikun U.S.S.R. **18** 62.20N 50.01E
Milagro Ecuador **60** 2.11S 79.36W
Milan see Milano Italy **9**
Milange Mozambique **37** 16.09S 35.44E
Milano Italy **9** 45.28N 9.10E
Milâs Turkey **13** 37.18N 27.48E
Mildenhall U.K. **5** 52.20N 0.30E
Mildura Australia **46** 34.14S142.13E
Miles Australia **44** 26.40S150.11E
Miles City U.S.A. **54** 46.25N105.51W
Milford Utah U.S.A. **54** 38.24N113.01W
Milford Haven town U.K. **5** 51.43N 5.02W
Milford Sound town New Zealand **48** 44.41S167.56E
Milgarra Australia **44** 18.10S140.55E
Miliana Algeria **34** 36.15N 2.15E
Miling Australia **43** 30.27S116.20E
Milk r. U.S.A. **52** 48.05N106.15W
Millau France **11** 44.06N 3.05E
Mille Lacs, Lac des l. Canada **55** 48.48N 90.34W
Mille Lacs L. U.S.A. **53** 46.15N 93.40W
Miller r. Australia **46** 30.05S136.07E
Millerovo U.S.S.R. **19** 48.55N 40.25E
Millersburg Mich. U.S.A. **55** 45.21N 84.02W
Milleur Pt. U.K. **6** 55.01N 5.07W
Millicent Australia **46** 37.36S140.22E
Millie Australia **47** 29.49S149.34E
Millinocket U.S.A. **55** 45.39N 68.43W
Millom U.K. **4** 54.13N 3.16W
Milne Inlet town Canada **51** 72.30N 80.59W
Mílos Greece **13** 36.45N 24.27E
Mílos i. Greece **13** 36.40N 24.26E
Milparinka Australia **46** 29.45S141.55E
Milton Australia **47** 35.19S150.24E
Milton Keynes U.K. **5** 52.03N 0.42W
Milwaukee U.S.A. **53** 43.03N 87.56W
Milwaukie U.S.A. **54** 45.27N122.38W
Milyatino U.S.S.R. **18** 54.30N 34.20E
Mim Ghana **38** 6.55N 2.34W
Mina U.S.A. **54** 38.24N118.07W
Mīnā 'al Aḥmadī Kuwait **28** 29.04N 48.08E
Mīnāb Iran **31** 27.07N 57.05E
Minas Uruguay **63** 34.23S 55.14W
Minas de Corrales Uruguay **63** 31.35S 55.28W
Minas de Ríotinto Spain **10** 37.41N 6.37W
Minas Gerais d. Brazil **59** 18.00S 45.00W
Minatitlán Mexico **56** 17.59N 94.32W
Mindanao i. Phil. **27** 7.30N125.00E
Mindanao Sea Phil. **27** 9.10N124.25E
Mindarie Australia **46** 34.51S140.12E

inden W. Germany 14 52.18N 8.54E
inderoo Australia 42 21.59S115.04E
indif Cameroon 38 10.25N 14.23E
ndiptana Indonesia 27 5.45S140.22E
ndona L. Australia 46 33.09S142.09E
ndoro i. Phil. 27 13.00N121.00E
ndoro Str. Pacific Oc. 27 12.30N120.10E
ndra mtn. Romania 15 45.20N 23.32E
nehead U.K. 5 51.12N 3.29W
nerva Australia 44 24.00S148.05E
ngan Canada 51 50.18N 64.02W
ngary Australia 46 32.09S140.46E
ngela Australia 44 19.53S146.40E
ingenew Australia 43 29.11S115.26E
ingin Burma 29 22.52N 94.39E
inhe China 24 36.20N102.50E
inidoka U.S.A. 54 42.46N113.30W
inigwal, L. Australia 43 29.35S123.12E
inna Nigeria 38 9.39N 6.32E
inneapolis U.S.A. 53 45.00N 93.15W
innedosa Canada 51 50.14N 99.51W
innesota d. U.S.A. 53 46.00N 95.00W
innipa Australia 46 32.51S135.09E
iño r. Spain 10 41.50N 8.52W
inobu-sanchi mts. Japan 23 35.05N138.15E
ino-kamo Japan 23 35.26N137.01E
ino-mikawa-kōgen mts. Japan 23 35.16N137.10E
inorca i. see Menorca i. Spain 10
inot U.S.A. 52 48.14N101.18W
insen W. Germany 8 53.44N 7.59E
insk U.S.S.R. 15 53.51N 27.30E
inta Cameroon 38 4.37N 12.47E
into, L. Canada 51 51.00N 73.37W
inturno Italy 12 41.15N 13.45E
inûf Egypt 32 30.28N 30.56E
inyā al Qamḥ Egypt 32 30.31N 31.21E
inyar U.S.S.R. 18 55.06N 57.29E
iquelon Canada 55 49.24N 76.29W
ira Italy 9 45.26N 12.08E
irābād Afghan. 31 30.32N 61.52E
iracema Brazil 59 21.22S 42.09W
irah, Wādī al r. Iraq 30 32.27N 41.21E
iraj India 28 16.51N 74.42E
iranda de Ebro Spain 10 42.41N 2.57W
iranda do Douro Portugal 10 41.30N 6.16W
irande France 11 43.31N 0.25E
irandela Portugal 10 41.28N 7.10W
irandola Italy 9 44.53N 11.04E
irbāṭ Oman 28 17.00N 54.45E
irecourt France 11 48.18N 6.08E
iri Malaysia 26 4.28N114.00E
irim, L. Brazil 59 33.10S 53.30W
ironovka U.S.S.R. 15 49.40N 30.59E
iroşi Romania 15 44.25N 24.58E
irpur Khās Pakistan 28 25.33N 69.05E
iryeny U.S.S.R. 15 47.00N 29.06E
irzāpur India 29 25.09N 82.34E
ishawaka U.S.A. 55 41.38N 86.10W
ishima Japan 23 35.07N138.55E
ishkino U.S.S.R. 18 55.34N 56.00E
isima I. P.N.G. 44 10.40S152.45E
isiones d. Argentina 62 27.00S 54.40W
iskolc Hungary 15 48.07N 20.47E
isoöl i. Indonesia 27 1.50S130.10E
isr al Jadīdah Egypt 32 30.06N 31.20E
iṣrātah Libya 34 32.24N 15.04E
iṣr Baḥrī f. Egypt 32 30.30N 31.00E
issinaibi r. Canada 55 50.44N 81.29W
ississippi d. U.S.A. 53 33.00N 90.00W
ississippi r. U.S.A. 53 28.55N 89.05W
ississippi Delta U.S.A. 53 29.00N 89.10W
issoula U.S.A. 54 46.52N114.01W
issouri d. U.S.A. 53 39.00N 93.00W
issouri r. U.S.A. 53 38.40N 90.20W
istake Creek town Australia 42 17.06S129.04E
istassini Canada 55 48.54N 72.13W
istassini r. Canada 55 48.54N 72.13W
istassini, Lac l. Canada 55 51.15N 73.10W
istretta Italy 12 37.56N 14.22E
itchell Australia 44 26.29S147.58E
itchell r. N.S.W. Australia 47 29.40S152.18E
itchell r. Qld. Australia 44 15.12S141.35E
itchell r. Vic. Australia 47 37.53S147.41E
itchell Oreg. U.S.A. 54 44.34N120.09W
itchell S.Dak. U.S.A. 52 43.40N 98.01W
itchell, Mt. U.S.A. 53 35.57N 82.16W
itchell River town Australia 44 15.28S141.44E
itchelstown Rep. of Ire. 7 52.16N 8.17W
it Ghamr Egypt 32 30.43N 31.16E
itilíni Greece 13 39.06N 26.34E
itla, Mamarr pass Egypt 32 30.00N 32.53E
itla Pass see Mitla, Mamarr pass Egypt 32
ittagong Australia 47 34.27S150.25E
ittelandkanal W. Germany 8 52.24N 7.52E
itú Colombia 60 1.08N 70.03W
itumba, Monts mts. Zaïre 37 3.00S 28.30E
itzic Gabon 36 0.48N 11.30E
iura Japan 23 35.08N139.37E
iya r. Japan 23 34.32N136.44E
iyako jima i. Japan 25 24.45N125.25E
iyakonojō Japan 25 31.43N131.02E
iyazaki Japan 25 31.58N131.50E
izen Head Rep. of Ire. 7 51.27N 9.50W
izil Romania 15 45.00N 26.26E
izoch U.S.S.R. 15 50.30N 25.50E
izoram d. India 29 23.40N 92.40E
izpe Ramon Israel 32 30.36N 34.48E
izukaidō Japan 23 36.01N139.59E
izunami Japan 23 35.22N137.15E
jölby Sweden 17 58.19N 15.08E
jösa l. Norway 17 60.40N 11.00E
kata Tanga Tanzania 37 5.47S 38.18E
kushi Zambia 37 13.40S 29.26E
kuze R.S.A. 39 27.10S 32.00E
kwaja Tanzania 37 5.46S 38.51E
kwiti Tanzania 37 10.27S 39.18E
ladá Boleslav Czech. 14 50.26N 14.55E
ława Poland 15 53.06N 20.23E
Mljet i. Yugo. 13 42.45N 17.30E
Mneni Zimbabwe 39 20.38S 30.03E
Moab U.S.A. 54 38.35N109.33W
Moama Australia 47 36.05S144.50E
Moamba Mozambique 39 25.35S 32.13E
Moapa U.S.A. 54 36.40N114.39W
Moatize Mozambique 37 16.10S 33.40E
Moba Zaïre 37 7.03S 29.42E
Mobara Japan 23 35.25N140.18E
Mobert Canada 55 48.41N 85.40W
Mobile U.S.A. 53 30.40N 88.05W
Mobile B. U.S.A. 53 30.30N 87.50W
Mobridge U.S.A. 52 45.31N100.25W
Moçambique town Mozambique 37 15.00S 40.47E
Mochudi Botswana 39 24.26S 26.07E
Mocimboa da Praia Mozambique 37 11.19S 40.19E
Mocimboa do Ruvuma Mozambique 37 11.05S 39.15E
Moclips U.S.A. 54 47.14N124.13W
Mococa Brazil 59 21.28S 47.00W
Moctezuma Mexico 56 30.10N106.28W
Mocuba Mozambique 37 16.52S 37.02E
Modane France 11 45.12N 6.40E
Modder r. R.S.A. 39 29.03S 23.56E
Modena Italy 9 44.39N 10.55E
Modena U.S.A. 54 37.48N113.57W
Modesto U.S.A. 54 37.39N121.00W
Modica Italy 12 36.51N 14.51E
Moe Australia 47 38.10S146.15E
Moebase Mozambique 37 17.04S 38.41E
Moelv Norway 17 60.56N 10.42E
Moffat U.K. 6 55.20N 3.27W
Mogadisho Somali Rep. 37 2.02N 45.21E
Mogaung Burma 29 25.20N 97.00E
Mogi das Cruzes Brazil 59 23.33S 46.14W
Mogi-Guaçu Brazil 59 20.55S 48.06W
Mogilev U.S.S.R. 15 53.54N 30.20E
Mogilev Podolskiy U.S.S.R. 15 48.29N 27.49E
Mogil-Mogil Australia 47 29.21S148.44E
Mogilno Poland 15 52.40N 17.58E
Mogi-Mirim Brazil 59 22.29S 46.55W
Mogincual Mozambique 37 15.33S 40.29E
Mogliano Veneto Italy 9 45.33N 12.14E
Mogok Burma 29 23.00N 96.40E
Mogollon Rim f. U.S.A. 54 32.30N111.00W
Mogumber Australia 43 31.01S116.02E
Mohács Hungary 15 45.59N 18.42E
Mohawk Ariz. U.S.A. 54 32.41N113.47W
Mohéli i. Comoros 37 12.22S 43.45E
Mohon France 9 49.45N 4.44E
Mohoro Tanzania 37 8.09S 39.07E
Mohoru Kenya 37 1.01S 34.07E
Moi Norway 17 58.28N 6.32E
Mointy U.S.S.R. 20 47.10N 73.18E
Mo-i-Rana Norway 16 66.19N 14.10E
Mõisaküla U.S.S.R. 17 58.06N 25.11E
Moisdon France 9 47.37N 1.22W
Moisie r. Canada 51 50.13N 66.02W
Moissac France 11 44.07N 1.05E
Mojave U.S.A. 54 35.03N118.10W
Mojave Desert U.S.A. 54 35.00N117.00W
Mokau New Zealand 48 38.41S174.37E
Mokmer Indonesia 27 1.13S136.13E
Mokpo S. Korea 25 34.50N126.25E
Mol Belgium 8 51.11N 5.09E
Molchanovo U.S.S.R. 20 57.39N 83.45E
Mold U.K. 4 53.10N 3.08W
Moldavskaya S.S.R. d. U.S.S.R. 15 47.30N 28.30E
Molde Norway 16 62.44N 7.08E
Molepolole Botswana 39 24.26S 25.34E
Molfetta Italy 13 41.12N 16.36E
Molina de Aragón Spain 10 40.50N 1.54W
Moline U.S.A. 53 41.31N 90.26W
Molinella Italy 9 44.37N 11.40E
Moliro Zaïre 37 8.11S 30.29E
Molise d. Italy 12 41.40N 15.00E
Mollendo Peru 62 17.02S 72.01W
Mölndal Sweden 17 57.39N 12.01E
Molodechno U.S.S.R. 15 54.16N 26.50E
Molokai i. Hawaii U.S.A. 52 21.20N157.00W
Molong Australia 47 33.08S148.53E
Molopo r. R.S.A. 39 28.30S 20.22E
Moloundou Cameroon 38 2.03N 15.14E
Molteno R.S.A. 39 31.23S 26.21E
Moluccas is. Indonesia 27 4.00S128.00E
Molucca Sea see Maluku, Laut sea Pacific Oc. 27
Moma Mozambique 37 16.40S 39.10E
Mombasa Kenya 37 4.04S 39.40E
Mommark Denmark 14 54.55N 10.03E
Mompós Colombia 60 9.15N 74.29W
Mön i. Denmark 17 55.00N 12.20E
Mona i. Puerto Rico 57 18.06N 67.54W
Monaco Europe 11 43.40N 7.25E
Monadhliath Mts. U.K. 6 57.09N 4.08W
Monaghan Rep. of Ire. 7 54.15N 6.58W
Monaghan d. Rep. of Ire. 7 54.10N 7.00W
Moncalieri Italy 9 45.00N 7.40E
Monchegorsk U.S.S.R. 18 67.55N 33.01E
Mönchen-Gladbach W. Germany 8 51.12N 6.25E
Monchique Portugal 10 37.19N 8.33W
Monclova Mexico 56 26.55N101.20W
Moncton Canada 51 46.06N 64.50W
Mondo Tanzania 37 5.00S 35.54E
Mondoubleau France 9 47.59N 0.54E
Mondovì Italy 9 44.24N 7.50E
Mondrain I. Australia 43 34.08S122.15E
Monessen U.S.A. 55 40.08N 79.54W
Monet Canada 55 48.10N 75.40W
Monfalcone Italy 12 45.49N 13.32E
Monforte Spain 10 42.32N 7.30W
Monga Zaïre 35 4.05N 22.56E
Mong Cai Vietnam 26 21.36N107.55E
Monger, L. Australia 43 29.15S117.05E
Monghyr India 29 25.24N 86.29E
Mongo Chad 34 12.14N 18.45E
Mongolia Asia 24 46.30N104.00E
Mongoro Chad 35 12.22N 22.26E
Mongu Zambia 36 15.17S 23.06E
Monifieth U.K. 6 56.29N 2.50W
Monitor Range mts. U.S.A. 54 38.45N116.30W
Monmouth U.K. 5 51.48N 2.43W
Monmouth Oreg. U.S.A. 54 44.51N123.14W
Mono L. U.S.A. 54 38.00N119.00W
Monopoli Italy 13 40.56N 17.19E
Monor Hungary 15 47.21N 19.27E
Monreal del Campo Spain 10 40.47N 1.20W
Monroe La. U.S.A. 53 32.31N 92.06W
Monroe Mich. U.S.A. 55 41.56N 83.21W
Monrovia Liberia 34 6.20N 10.46W
Mons Belgium 8 50.27N 3.57E
Monselice Italy 9 45.14N 11.45E
Mönsterås Sweden 17 57.02N 16.26E
Montabaur W. Germany 8 50.27N 7.51E
Montagnana Italy 9 45.14N 11.28E
Montalbán Spain 10 40.50N 0.48W
Montalto di Castro Italy 12 42.21N 11.37E
Montana Switz. 9 46.18N 7.29E
Montana d. U.S.A. 52 47.14N109.26W
Montargis France 9 48.00N 2.44E
Montauban France 11 44.01N 1.20E
Montbard France 9 47.37N 4.20E
Montbéliard France 11 47.31N 6.48E
Montbrison France 11 45.37N 4.04E
Montceau-les-Mines France 11 46.40N 4.22E
Mont Cenis, Col du pass France 11 45.15N 6.55E
Montcornet France 9 49.41N 4.01E
Mont de Marsan town France 11 43.54N 0.30W
Montdidier France 9 49.39N 2.34E
Monte Alegre town Brazil 61 2.01S 54.04W
Monte Azul town Brazil 59 15.53S 42.53W
Monte Carlo Monaco 11 43.44N 7.25E
Monte Caseros Argentina 63 30.15S 57.38W
Montecatini Terme Italy 9 43.53N 10.46E
Montecollina Australia 46 29.22S139.56E
Montecristo i. Italy 12 42.20N 10.19E
Montego Bay town Jamaica 57 18.27N 77.56W
Montélimar France 11 44.33N 4.45E
Montemor-o-Velho Portugal 10 40.10N 8.41W
Montenegro see Crna Gora d. Yugo. 13
Montepuez Mozambique 37 13.09S 39.33E
Montereau France 9 48.22N 2.57E
Monterey Calif. U.S.A. 54 36.37N121.55W
Monterey B. U.S.A. 54 36.45N121.55W
Montería Colombia 60 8.45N 75.54W
Montero Bolivia 62 17.20S 63.15W
Monteros Argentina 62 27.10S 65.30W
Monterrey Mexico 56 25.40N100.20W
Monte Santu, Capo di c. Italy 12 40.05N 9.44E
Montes Claros Brazil 59 16.45S 43.52W
Montevideo Uruguay 63 34.53S 56.11W
Montfort-sur-Meu France 9 48.08N 1.57W
Montgomery U.K. 5 52.34N 3.09W
Montgomery Ala. U.S.A. 53 32.22N 86.20W
Montguyon France 11 45.13N 0.11W
Monthey Switz. 9 46.15N 6.57E
Monthois France 9 49.19N 4.43E
Monticello Utah U.S.A. 54 37.52N109.21W
Montichiari Italy 9 45.25N 10.23E
Montiel, Campo de f. Spain 10 38.46N 2.44W
Montigny-le-Roi France 11 48.00N 5.30E
Montijo Portugal 10 38.42N 8.59W
Montijo Dam Spain 10 38.52N 6.20W
Montilla Spain 10 37.36N 4.40W
Montivilliers France 9 49.33N 0.12E
Mont Joli town Canada 55 48.36N 68.14W
Mont Laurier town Canada 55 46.33N 75.31W
Mont Louis town Canada 55 49.15N 65.46W
Montluçon France 11 46.20N 2.36E
Montmagny Canada 55 46.56N 70.28W
Montmédy France 8 49.31N 5.21E
Montmirail France 9 48.52N 3.32E
Montmorillon France 11 46.26N 0.52E
Montmort France 9 48.55N 3.49E
Monto Australia 44 24.52S151.07E
Montoro Spain 10 38.02N 4.23W
Montpelier Idaho U.S.A. 54 42.20N111.20W
Montpelier Vt. U.S.A. 55 44.16N 72.35W
Montpellier France 11 43.36N 3.53E
Montreal Canada 55 45.30N 73.36W
Montreal r. Canada 55 47.14N 84.39W
Montrejeau France 11 43.05N 0.33E
Montreuil France 11 50.28N 1.46E
Montreux Switz. 14 46.27N 6.55E
Montrichard France 9 47.21N 1.11E
Montrose U.K. 6 56.43N 2.29W
Montrose Colo. U.S.A. 54 38.29N107.53W
Montsant, Sierra de mts. Spain 10 41.20N 1.00E
Montserrat i. Leeward Is. 57 16.45N 62.14W
Mont Tremblant Prov. Park Canada 55 46.30N 74.35W
Monument Valley f. U.S.A. 54 36.50N110.20W
Monveda Zaïre 36 2.57N 21.27E
Monywa Burma 29 22.07N 95.11E
Monza Italy 9 45.35N 9.16E
Monze Zambia 36 16.16S 27.28E
Monzón Spain 10 41.52N 0.10E
Moolawatana Australia 46 29.55S139.43E
Mooloogool Australia 42 26.06S119.05E
Moomin r. Australia 47 29.35S148.45E
Moonbi Range mts. Australia 47 31.00S151.10E
Moonie Australia 45 27.40S150.19E
Moonie r. Australia 45 29.30S148.40E
Moonta Australia 46 34.04S137.37E
Moora Australia 43 30.40S116.01E
Mooraberree Australia 44 25.12S140.57E
Moorarie Australia 42 25.56S117.35E
Moore r. Australia 43 31.22S115.29E
Moore, L. Australia 43 29.30S117.30E
Moorfoot Hills U.K. 6 55.43N 3.03W
Moorhead U.S.A. 53 46.51N 96.44W
Moorlands Australia 46 35.20S139.40E
Moornanyah L. Australia 46 33.02S143.58E
Mooroopna Australia 47 36.24S145.22E
Moosehead L. U.S.A. 55 45.40N 69.40W
Moose Jaw Canada 50 50.23N105.35W
Moosonee Canada 55 51.18N 80.40W
Mootwingee Australia 46 31.52S141.14E
Mopti Mali 38 14.29N 4.10W
Mopti d. Mali 38 15.20N 3.35W
Moquegua Peru 62 17.20S 70.55W
Mora Cameroon 38 11.02N 14.07E
Mora Spain 10 39.41N 3.46W
Mora Sweden 17 61.00N 14.33E
Morādābād India 29 28.50N 78.45E
Moralana Australia 46 31.42S138.12E
Moramanga Madagascar 36 18.56S 48.12E
Morar, Loch U.K. 6 56.56N 4.00W
Morava r. Czech. 15 48.10N 16.59E
Morava r. Yugo. 15 44.43N 21.02E
Moravské Budějovice Czech. 14 49.03N 15.49E
Morawhanna Guyana 60 8.17N 59.44W
Moray Firth est. U.K. 6 57.35N 5.15W
Morbach W. Germany 8 49.49N 7.05E
Morbegno Italy 9 46.08N 9.34E
Morcenx France 11 44.02N 0.55W
Morden Australia 46 30.30S142.23E
Morden Canada 51 49.15N 98.10W
Mordialloc Australia 47 38.00S145.05E
Mordovo U.S.S.R. 19 52.06N 40.45E
Moreau r. U.S.A. 52 45.18N100.43W
Morecambe U.K. 4 54.03N 2.52W
Morecambe B. U.K. 4 54.05N 3.00W
Moree Australia 47 29.29S149.53E
Morée France 9 47.55N 1.15E
Morehead U.S.A. 55 38.11N 83.27W
Morelia Mexico 56 19.40N101.11W
Morella Spain 10 40.37N 0.06W
Morelos d. Mexico 56 18.40N 99.00W
Morena, Sierra mts. Spain 10 38.10N 5.00W
Morenci U.S.A. 54 33.05N109.22W
Möre og Romsdal d. Norway 16 63.00N 9.00E
Moreton I. Australia 45 27.10S153.25E
Morez France 11 46.31N 6.02E
Mórfou Cyprus 32 35.12N 33.00E
Mórfou, Kólpos b. Cyprus 32 35.15N 32.50E
Morgan Australia 46 34.02S139.40E
Morgan City U.S.A. 53 29.41N 91.13W
Morgantown U.S.A. 55 39.38N 79.57W
Morghāb r. Afghan. 28 36.50N 63.00E
Moriki Nigeria 38 12.55N 6.30E
Morioka Japan 25 39.43N141.08E
Morisset Australia 47 33.06S151.29E
Moriyama Japan 23 35.04N135.59E
Morkalla Australia 46 34.22S141.10E
Morlaix France 11 48.35N 3.50W
Mormon Range mts. U.S.A. 54 37.08N114.20W
Mornington Australia 47 38.12S145.05E
Mornington I. Australia 44 16.33S139.24E
Mornington Mission Australia 44 16.40S139.10E
Morobe P.N.G. 27 7.45S147.35E
Morocco Africa 34 31.00N 5.00W
Moro G. Phil. 27 6.30N123.20E
Morogoro Tanzania 37 6.47S 37.40E
Morogoro d. Tanzania 37 8.30S 37.00E
Moroleón Mexico 56 20.08N101.12W
Morón Argentina 63 34.39S 58.37W
Morón Cuba 57 22.08N 78.39W
Mörön Mongolia 24 49.36N100.08E
Morón Spain 10 37.06N 5.28W
Moroni Comoros 37 11.40S 43.19E
Morotai i. Indonesia 27 2.10N128.30E
Moroto Uganda 37 2.32N 34.41E
Moroto, Mt. Uganda 37 2.30N 34.46E
Morpeth U.K. 4 55.10N 1.40W
Morrinsville New Zealand 48 37.39S175.32E
Morristown Ariz. U.S.A. 54 33.51N112.37W
Morrumbene Mozambique 39 23.41S 35.25E
Morsbach W. Germany 8 50.52N 7.44E
Mortagne France 9 48.32N 0.33E
Mortain France 9 48.39N 0.56W
Mortara Italy 9 45.15N 8.44E
Mortes r. Brazil 59 21.09S 45.06W
Mortes r. see Manso r. Brazil 62
Mortlake town Australia 46 38.05S142.48E
Morundah Australia 47 34.56S146.18E
Moruya Australia 47 35.56S150.06E
Morven Australia 44 26.25S147.05E
Morvern f. U.K. 6 56.37N 5.45W
Morwell Australia 47 38.14S146.25E
Morzhovets i. U.S.S.R. 18 66.45N 42.30E
Mosby Norway 17 58.14N 7.54E
Moscow U.S.A. 54 46.44N117.00W
Moscow see Moskva U.S.S.R. 18
Mosel r. W. Germany 8 50.23N 7.37E
Moselle r. see Mosel r. France/Lux. 8
Moses Lake town U.S.A. 54 47.08N119.17W
Mosgiel New Zealand 48 45.53S170.22E
Moshi Tanzania 37 3.20S 37.21E
Mosjöen Norway 16 65.50N 13.10E
Moskenes Norway 16 67.55N 13.00E
Moskenesöy i. Norway 16 67.55N 13.00E
Moskva U.S.S.R. 18 55.45N 37.42E
Moskva r. U.S.S.R. 18 55.08N 38.50E
Mosquera Colombia 60 2.30N 78.29W
Mosquitia Plain Honduras 57 15.00N 84.00W
Mosquitos, Costa de f. Nicaragua 57 13.00N 84.00W
Mosquitos, Golfo de los g. Panama 57 9.00N 81.00W
Moss Norway 17 59.26N 10.42E
Mossburn New Zealand 48 45.41S168.15E
Mosselbaai R.S.A. 39 34.11S 22.08E
Mossgiel Australia 47 33.18S144.05E
Mossman Australia 44 16.28S145.22E
Mossoró Brazil 61 5.10S 37.18W
Mossuril Mozambique 37 14.58S 40.42E
Most Czech. 14 50.31N 13.39E
Mostar Yugo. 13 43.20N 17.50E
Mösting, Kap c. Greenland 51 64.00N 41.00W
Mostiska U.S.S.R. 15 49.48N 23.05E
Mosul see Al Mawşil Iraq 30
Motagua r. Guatemala 57 15.56N 87.45W
Motala Sweden 17 58.33N 15.03E
Motherwell U.K. 6 55.48N 4.00W
Motīhāri India 29 26.39N 84.55E
Motloutse r. Botswana 39 22.15S 29.00E
Motol U.S.S.R. 15 52.25N 25.05E
Motril Spain 10 36.44N 3.37W
Motueka New Zealand 48 41.08S173.01E
Moúdhros Greece 13 39.52N 25.16E
Mouka C.A.R. 35 7.16N 21.52E
Moulamein Australia 46 35.03S144.05E
Moulins France 11 46.34N 3.20E
Moulins-la-Marche France 9 48.39N 0.29E
Moulmein Burma 29 16.30N 97.40E
Moundou Chad 34 8.36N 16.02E
Moundsville U.S.A. 55 39.54N 80.44W
Mountain Ash U.K. 5 51.42N 3.22W
Mountain City U.S.A. 54 41.50N115.58W
Mountain Home Idaho U.S.A. 54 43.08N115.41W
Mountain Village U.S.A. 50 62.05N163.44W
Mount Barker town S.A. Australia 46 35.06S138.52E
Mount Barker town W.A. Australia 43 34.36S117.37E
Mount Bellew town Rep. of Ire. 7 53.28N 8.30W
Mount Brown town Australia 46 29.45S141.52E
Mount Darwin town Zimbabwe 37 16.46S 31.36E
Mount Douglas town Australia 44 21.31S146.50E
Mount Drysdale town Australia 47 31.11S145.51E
Mount Eba town Australia 46 30.12S135.33E
Mount Fletcher town R.S.A. 39 30.41S 28.30E
Mount Gambier town Australia 46 37.51S140.50E
Mount Goldsworthy town Australia 42 20.20S119.31E
Mount Hagen town P.N.G. 27 5.54S144.13E
Mount Hope town N.S.W. Australia 47 32.49S145.48E
Mount Hope town S.A. Australia 46 34.07S135.23E
Mount Isa town Australia 44 20.50S139.29E
Mount Ive town Australia 46 32.24S136.10E
Mount Lofty Range mts. Australia 46 34.40S139.03E
Mount Magnet town Australia 43 28.06S117.50E
Mountmellick Rep. of Ire. 7 53.08N 7.21W
Mount Morgan town Australia 44 23.39S150.23E
Mount Murchison town Australia 46 31.23S143.42E
Mount Newman town Australia 42 23.20S119.40E
Mount Nicholas town Australia 42 22.54S120.27E
Mount Pleasant town Mich. U.S.A. 55 43.36N 84.46W
Mount's B. U.K. 5 50.05N 5.25W
Mount Sturgeon town Australia 44 20.08S144.00E
Mount Swan town Australia 44 22.31S135.00E
Mount Vernon town Australia 42 24.09S118.10E
Mount Vernon town Wash. U.S.A. 54 48.25N122.20W
Mount Willoughby Australia 46 27.58S134.08E
Moura Brazil 60 1.27S 61.38W
Mourdi, Dépression de f. Chad 35 18.10N 23.00E
Mourne Mts. U.K. 7 54.10N 6.02W
Mouscron Belgium 8 50.46N 3.10E
Moussoro Chad 34 13.41N 16.31E
Moy r. Rep. of Ire. 7 54.10N 9.09W
Moyale Kenya 37 3.31N 39.04E
Moyeni Lesotho 39 30.24S 27.41E
Moyobamba Peru 60 6.04S 76.56W
Moyowosi r. Tanzania 37 4.59S 30.58E
Mozambique Africa 36 17.30S 35.45E
Mozambique Channel Indian Oc. 36 16.00S 42.30E
Mozdok U.S.S.R. 19 43.45N 44.43E
Mozyr U.S.S.R. 15 52.02N 29.10E
Mpala Zaïre 37 6.45S 29.31E
Mpanda Tanzania 37 6.21S 31.01E
Mpésoba Mali 38 12.31N 5.39W
Mphoengs Zimbabwe 39 21.10S 27.51E
Mpika Zambia 37 11.52S 31.30E
Mponela Malaŵi 37 13.32S 33.43E
Mporokoso Zambia 37 9.22S 30.06E
Mpunde mtn. Tanzania 37 6.12S 33.48E
Mpwapwa Tanzania 37 6.23S 36.38E
Msaken Tunisia 34 35.44N 10.35E
Mseleni R.S.A. 39 27.21S 32.33E
Msingu Tanzania 37 4.52S 39.08E
Msta r. U.S.S.R. 18 58.28N 31.20E
Mtakuja Tanzania 37 7.21S 30.37E
Mtama Tanzania 37 10.20S 39.19E
Mtito Andei Kenya 37 2.32S 38.10E
Mtsensk U.S.S.R. 18 53.18N 36.35E
Mtwara Tanzania 37 10.17S 40.11E
Mtwara d. Tanzania 37 10.00S 38.30E
Muaná Brazil 61 1.32S 49.13W
Muang Chiang Rai Thailand 29 19.56N 99.51E
Muang Khammouan Laos 29 17.25N104.45E
Muang Khon Kaen Thailand 29 16.25N102.50E
Muang Lampang Thailand 29 18.16N 99.30E
Muang Nakhon Phanom Thailand 26 17.22N104.45E
Muang Nakhon Sawan Thailand 29 15.35N100.10E
Muang Nan Thailand 29 18.52N100.42E
Muang Ngoy Laos 29 20.43N102.41E
Muang Pak Lay Laos 29 18.12N101.25E
Muang Phichit Thailand 29 16.29N100.21E
Muang Phitsanulok Thailand 29 16.50N100.15E
Muang Phrae Thailand 29 18.07N100.09E
Muang Ubon Thailand 29 15.15N104.50E
Muar Malaysia 26 2.01N102.35E
Muara Brunei 26 5.01N115.01E
Muara Indonesia 26 0.32S101.20E
Muarakaman Indonesia 26 0.02S116.45E
Muaratewe Indonesia 26 0.57S114.53E
Mubende Uganda 37 0.30N 31.24E

Mubi Nigeria **38** 10.16N 13.17E
Muchea Australia **43** 31.36S115.57E
Muchinga Mts. Zambia **37** 12.15S 31.00E
Muck *i.* U.K. **6** 56.50N 6.14W
Mucojo Mozambique **37** 12.05S 40.26E
Mudanjiang China **25** 44.36N129.42E
Mudgee Australia **47** 32.37S149.36E
Mudyuga U.S.S.R. **18** 63.45N 39.29E
Muèda Mozambique **37** 11.40S 39.31E
Mufulira Zambia **37** 12.30S 28.12E
Muganskaya Step *f.* U.S.S.R. **31** 39.40N 48.30E
Mugía Spain **10** 43.06N 9.14W
Muğla Turkey **13** 37.12N 28.22E
Muḩammad, Ra's *c.* Egypt **32** 27.42N 34.13E
Mühldorf W. Germany **14** 48.15N 12.32E
Mühlhausen E. Germany **14** 51.12N 10.27E
Mühlig Hofmann fjella *mts.* Antarctica **64** 72.30S 5.00E
Muhola Finland **16** 63.20N 25.05E
Muhos Finland **16** 64.48N 25.59E
Muhu *i.* U.S.S.R. **17** 58.32N 23.20E
Muhu Väin *str.* U.S.S.R. **17** 58.45N 23.30E
Mui Ca Mau *c.* Vietnam **26** 8.30N104.35E
Muine Bheag *town* Rep. of Ire. **7** 52.42N 6.58W
Muir, L. Australia **43** 34.30S116.30E
Mukachevo U.S.S.R. **15** 48.26N 22.45E
Mukah Malaysia **26** 2.56N112.02E
Mukawa P.N.G. **44** 9.48S150.00E
Mukinbudin Australia **43** 30.52S118.08E
Muko *r.* Japan **23** 34.41N135.23E
Mukwela Zambia **39** 17.02S 26.39E
Mulanje Mts. Malaŵi **37** 15.57S 35.33E
Mulchén Chile **63** 37.43S 72.14W
Mulde *r.* E. Germany **14** 51.10N 12.48E
Mulgathing Australia **46** 30.15S134.00E
Mulgrave Canada **51** 45.37N 61.23W
Mulgrave I. Australia **44** 10.07S142.08E
Mulhacén *mtn.* Spain **10** 37.04N 3.22W
Mülheim N.-Westfalen W. Germany **8** 50.58N 7.00E
Mülheim N.-Westfalen W. Germany **8** 51.25N 6.50E
Mulhouse France **11** 47.45N 7.21E
Mull *i.* U.K. **6** 56.28N 5.56W
Mull, Sd. of *str.* U.K. **6** 56.32N 5.55W
Mullaghanattin *mtn.* Rep. of Ire. **7** 51.56N 9.51W
Mullaghareirk Mts. Rep. of Ire. **7** 52.19N 9.06W
Mullaghmore *mtn.* U.K. **7** 54.51N 6.51W
Mullaley Australia **47** 31.06S149.55E
Mullengudgery Australia **47** 31.40S147.23E
Mullet Pen. Rep. of Ire. **7** 54.12N 10.04W
Mullewa Australia **43** 28.33S115.31E
Mullingar Rep. of Ire. **7** 53.31N 7.21W
Mullion Creek *town* Australia **47** 33.09S149.09E
Mull of Galloway *c.* U.K. **6** 54.39N 4.52W
Mull of Kintyre *c.* U.K. **6** 55.17N 5.45W
Mullovka U.S.S.R. **18** 54.12N 49.26E
Mullumbimby Australia **47** 28.32S153.30E
Mulobezi Zambia **39** 16.49S 25.09E
Muloorina Australia **46** 29.10S137.51E
Muloowurtina Australia **46** 30.06S140.04E
Multān Pakistan **28** 30.10N 71.36E
Multyfarnham Rep. of Ire. **7** 53.37N 7.25W
Mulyungarie Australia **46** 31.30S140.45E
Muna *i.* Indonesia **27** 5.00S122.30E
Munābāo India **28** 25.45N 70.17E
Münchberg W. Germany **14** 50.11N 11.47E
München W. Germany **14** 48.08N 11.35E
Muncie U.S.A. **55** 40.11N 85.23W
Mundaring Weir Australia **43** 31.59S116.13E
Münden W. Germany **14** 51.25N 9.39E
Mundiwindi Australia **42** 23.50S120.07E
Mundo *r.* Spain **10** 38.20N 1.50W
Mungallala *r.* Australia **45** 28.53S147.05E
Mungari Mozambique **39** 17.12S 33.31E
Mungbere Zaïre **37** 2.40N 28.25E
Mungerannie Australia **46** 28.00S138.36E
Mungindi Australia **47** 28.58S148.56E
Munich *see* München W. Germany **14**
Muniz Freire Brazil **59** 20.25S 41.23W
Munkfors Sweden **17** 59.50N 13.32E
Munning *r.* Australia **47** 31.50S152.30E
Münster N.-Westfalen W. Germany **8** 51.58N 7.37E
Muntadgin Australia **43** 31.41S118.32E
Muonio Finland **16** 67.57N 23.42E
Muonio *r.* Finland / Sweden **16** 67.10N 23.40E
Mupa *r.* Mozambique **39** 19.07S 35.50E
Mur *r.* Austria *see* Mura *r.* Yugo. **14**
Mura *r.* Yugo. **14** 46.18N 16.53E
Muralón *mtn.* Argentina / Chile **63** 49.48S 73.25W
Muranga Kenya **37** 0.43S 37.10E
Murashi U.S.S.R. **18** 59.20N 48.59E
Murchison *r.* Australia **42** 27.30S114.10E
Murchison New Zealand **48** 41.48S172.20E
Murcia Spain **10** 37.59N 1.08W
Murcia *d.* Spain **10** 38.30N 1.45W
Mureş *r.* Romania **15** 46.16N 20.10E
Muret France **11** 43.28N 1.19E
Murewa Zimbabwe **39** 17.40S 31.47E
Murgon Australia **44** 26.15S151.57E
Murguía Spain **10** 42.57N 2.49W
Muriaé Brazil **59** 21.08S 42.33W
Müritzsee *l.* E. Germany **14** 52.25N 12.45E
Murjek Sweden **16** 66.29N 20.50E
Murmansk U.S.S.R. **18** 68.59N 33.08E
Murom U.S.S.R. **18** 55.04N 42.04E
Muroran Japan **25** 42.21N140.59E
Murrah al Kubrā, Al Buḩayrah al *l.* Egypt **32** 30.20N 32.20E
Murra Murra Australia **47** 28.18S146.48E
Murray *r.*S.A. Australia **46** 35.23S139.20E
Murray *r.*W.A. Australia **43** 32.35S115.46E
Murray Utah U.S.A. **54** 40.40N111.53W
Murray, L. P.N.G. **27** 7.00S141.30E
Murray Bridge *town* Australia **46** 35.10S139.17E
Murrayville Australia **46** 35.16S141.14E
Murringo Australia **47** 34.19S148.36E
Murrumbidgee *r.* Australia **46** 34.38S143.10E
Murrumburrah Australia **47** 34.33S148.21E
Murrurundi Australia **47** 31.47S150.51E
Murtee Australia **46** 31.05S143.35E
Murtoa Australia **46** 36.40S142.31E
Murud *mtn.* Malaysia **26** 3.45N115.30E
Murwāra India **29** 23.49N 80.28E
Murwillumbah Australia **47** 28.20S153.24E
Muş Turkey **30** 38.45N 41.30E
Mūsá, Jabal *mtn.* Egypt **32** 28.31N 33.59E
Musala *mtn.* Bulgaria **13** 42.11N 23.35E
Musay'īd Qatar **31** 24.47N 51.36E
Muscat *see* Masqaţ Oman **31**
Musgrave Australia **44** 14.47S143.30E
Musgrave Ranges *mts.* Australia **42** 26.10S131.50E
Mushin Nigeria **38** 6.33N 3.22E
Musi *r.* Indonesia **26** 2.20S104.57E
Muskegon U.S.A. **55** 43.13N 86.15W
Muskegon *r.* U.S.A. **55** 43.13N 86.16W
Muskegon Heights *town* U.S.A. **55** 43.03N 86.16W
Muskogee U.S.A. **53** 35.45N 95.21W
Muskoka, L. Canada **55** 45.00N 79.25W
Musoma Tanzania **37** 1.31S 33.48E
Musselburgh U.K. **6** 55.57N 3.04W
Musselkanaal Neth. **8** 52.57N 7.01E
Musselshell *r.* U.S.A. **54** 47.21N107.58W
Mustang Nepal **29** 29.10N 83.55E
Mustjala U.S.S.R. **17** 58.28N 22.14E
Muswellbrook Australia **47** 32.17S150.55E
Mut Turkey **30** 36.38N 33.27E
Mutala Mozambique **37** 15.54S 37.51E
Mutare Zimbabwe **39** 18.59S 32.40E
Mutoko Zimbabwe **39** 17.23S 32.13E
Mutooroo Australia **46** 32.30S140.58E
Mutoray U.S.S.R. **21** 61.20N100.32E
Muwale Tanzania **37** 6.22S 33.46E
Muya U.S.S.R. **21** 56.28N115.50E
Muyinga Burundi **37** 2.48S 30.21E
Muynak U.S.S.R. **20** 43.46N 59.00E
Muzaffarnagar India **28** 29.28N 77.42E
Muzaffarpur India **29** 26.07N 85.23E
Muzhi U.S.S.R. **18** 65.25N 64.40E
Muztag *mtn.* China **24** 36.25N 87.25E
Mvomero Tanzania **37** 6.18S 37.26E
Mvuma Zimbabwe **39** 19.16S 30.30E
Mwanza Tanzania **37** 2.30S 32.54E
Mwanza *d.* Tanzania **37** 3.00S 32.30E
Mwaya Mbeya Tanzania **37** 9.33S 33.56E
Mweka Zaïre **36** 4.51S 21.34E
Mwene Ditu Zaïre **36** 7.01S 23.27E
Mwenezi *r.* Mozambique **39** 22.42S 31.45E
Mwenezi Zimbabwe **39** 21.22S 30.45E
Mweru, L. Zaïre / Zambia **37** 9.00S 28.40E
Mwingi Kenya **37** 1.00S 38.04E
Mwinilunga Zambia **36** 11.44S 24.24E
Myanaung Burma **29** 18.25N 95.10E
Myingyan Burma **29** 21.25N 95.20E
Myitkyinā Burma **29** 25.24N 97.25E
Mymensingh Bangla. **29** 24.45N 90.23E
Myrdal Norway **17** 60.44N 7.08E
Myrdalsjökull *ice cap* Iceland **16** 63.40N 19.06W
Myrtle Creek *town* U.S.A. **54** 43.01N123.17W
Myrtleford Australia **47** 36.35S146.44E
Myrtle Point *town* U.S.A. **54** 43.04N124.08W
Myślenice Poland **15** 49.51N 19.56E
Mysore India **28** 12.18N 76.37E
My Tho Vietnam **26** 10.21N106.21E
Mytishchi U.S.S.R. **18** 55.54N 37.47E
Mziha Tanzania **37** 5.53S 37.48E
Mzimba Malaŵi **37** 12.00S 33.39E

N

Naab *r.* W. Germany **14** 49.01N 12.02E
Naantali Finland **17** 60.27N 22.02E
Naas Rep. of Ire. **7** 53.13N 6.41W
Näätämö *r.* Norway **16** 69.40N 29.30E
Nababeep R.S.A. **39** 29.36S 17.44E
Nabadwīp India **29** 23.25N 88.22E
Nabari *r.* Japan **23** 34.45N136.01E
Nabingora Uganda **37** 0.31N 31.11E
Naboomspruit R.S.A. **39** 24.31S 28.24E
Nabq Egypt **32** 28.04N 34.26E
Nābulus Jordan **32** 32.13N 35.16E
Nacala Mozambique **37** 14.34S 40.41E
Nachingwea Tanzania **37** 10.21S 38.46E
Nackara Australia **46** 32.51S139.13E
Nadiād India **28** 22.42N 72.55E
Nadūshan Iran **31** 32.03N 53.33E
Nadvoitsy U.S.S.R. **18** 63.56N 34.20E
Nadvornaya U.S.S.R. **15** 48.37N 24.30E
Nadym U.S.S.R. **20** 65.25N 72.40E
Naeröy Norway **16** 64.48N 11.17E
Naestved Denmark **17** 55.14N 11.46E
Nafada Nigeria **38** 11.08N 11.20E
Nafīshah Egypt **32** 30.34N 32.15E
Naft-e Safīd Iran **31** 31.38N 49.20E
Naga Phil. **27** 13.36N123.12E
Nāgāland *d.* India **29** 26.10N 94.30E
Nagambie Australia **47** 36.48S145.12E
Nagano Japan **25** 36.39N138.10E
Nagano *d.* Japan **23** 35.33N137.50E
Nagaoka Japan **25** 37.30N138.50E
Nāgappattinam India **29** 10.45N 79.50E
Nagara *r.* Japan **23** 35.01N136.43E
Nagasaki Japan **25** 32.45N129.52E
Nāgaur India **28** 27.12N 73.44E
Nagele Neth. **8** 52.39N 5.43E
Nāgercoil India **28** 8.11N 77.30E
Nagles Mts. Rep. of Ire. **7** 52.06N 8.26W
Nagorskoye U.S.S.R. **18** 58.18N 50.50E
Nagoya Japan **23** 35.10N136.55E
Nāgpur India **29** 21.10N 79.12E
Nagqên China **29** 32.15N 96.13E
Nagykanizsa Hungary **15** 46.27N 17.01E
Naha Japan **25** 26.10N127.40E
Nahanni Butte *town* Canada **50** 61.03N123.31W
Nahariyya Israel **32** 33.01N 35.05E
Nahāvand Iran **31** 34.13N 48.23E
Nahe *r.* W. Germany **8** 49.58N 7.54E
Nain Canada **51** 56.30N 61.45W
Nā'īn Iran **31** 32.52N 53.05E
Nairn U.K. **6** 57.35N 3.52W
Nairobi Kenya **37** 1.17S 36.50E
Naivasha Kenya **37** 0.44S 36.26E
Najd *f.* Saudi Arabia **30** 25.00N 45.00E
Naj 'Hammādī Egypt **30** 26.04N 32.13E
Nakatsugawa Japan **23** 35.29N137.30E
Nakhichevan U.S.S.R. **31** 39.12N 45.24E
Nakhodka U.S.S.R. **25** 42.53N132.54E
Nakhon Pathom Thailand **29** 13.50N100.01E
Nakhon Ratchasima Thailand **29** 14.59N102.12E
Nakhon Si Thammarat Thailand **29** 8.29N100.00E
Nakina Canada **55** 50.11N 86.43W
Nakło Poland **15** 53.08N 17.35E
Naknek U.S.A. **50** 58.45N157.00W
Nakop Namibia **39** 28.05S 19.57E
Nakskov Denmark **17** 54.50N 11.09E
Näkten *l.* Sweden **16** 65.50N 14.35E
Nakuru Kenya **37** 0.16S 36.04E
Nalchik U.S.S.R. **19** 43.31N 43.38E
Nalón *r.* Spain **10** 43.35N 6.06W
Nālūt Libya **34** 31.53N 10.59E
Namacurra Mozambique **37** 17.35S 37.00E
Namakī *r.* Iran **31** 31.02N 55.20E
Namanga Kenya **37** 2.33S 36.48E
Namangan U.S.S.R. **24** 40.59N 71.41E
Namanyere Tanzania **37** 7.34S 31.00E
Namapa Mozambique **37** 13.48S 39.44E
Namaponda Mozambique **37** 15.51S 39.52E
Namarroi Mozambique **37** 15.58S 36.55E
Namatele Tanzania **37** 10.01S 38.26E
Nambour Australia **45** 26.40S152.52E
Nambucca Heads *town* Australia **47** 30.38S152.59E
Nam Co *l.* China **24** 30.40N 90.30E
Nam Dinh Vietnam **26** 20.25N106.12E
Namecala Mozambique **37** 12.50S 39.38E
Nametil Mozambique **37** 15.41S 39.30E
Namib Desert Namibia **39** 23.00S 15.20E
Namibe Angola **36** 15.10S 12.10E
Namibia Africa **36** 21.30S 16.45E
Namin Iran **31** 38.25N 48.30E
Namlea Indonesia **27** 3.15S127.07E
Namoi *r.* Australia **47** 30.14S148.28E
Nampa U.S.A. **54** 43.44N116.34W
Nam Phong Thailand **29** 16.45N102.52E
Namp'o N. Korea **25** 38.40N125.30E
Nampula Mozambique **37** 15.09S 39.14E
Nampula *d.* Mozambique **37** 15.00S 39.00E
Namsen *r.* Norway **16** 64.27N 12.19E
Namsos Norway **16** 64.28N 11.30E
Namuchabawashan *mtn.* China **29** 29.30N 95.10E
Namungua Mozambique **37** 13.11S 40.30E
Namur Belgium **8** 50.28N 4.52E
Namur *d.* Belgium **8** 50.20N 4.45E
Namutoni Namibia **39** 18.48S 16.58E
Nanaimo Canada **50** 49.08N123.58W
Nanango Australia **45** 26.42S151.58E
Nanchang China **25** 28.38N115.56E
Nanchong China **24** 30.54N106.06E
Nancy France **11** 48.42N 6.12E
Nanda Devi *mtn.* India **29** 30.21N 79.50E
Nānded India **28** 19.11N 77.21E
Nandewar Range *mts.* Australia **47** 30.20S150.45E
Nandyāl India **29** 15.29N 78.29E
Nanga Eboko Cameroon **38** 4.41N 12.21E
Nānga Parbat *mtn.* Jammu & Kashmir **28** 35.10N 74.35E
Nangapinoh Indonesia **26** 0.20S111.44E
Nangqên China **24** 32.15N 96.13E
Nanjing China **25** 32.00N118.40E
Nan Ling *mts.* China **25** 25.20N110.30E
Nannine Australia **42** 26.53S118.20E
Nanning China **25** 22.50N108.19E
Nannup Australia **43** 33.57S115.42E
Nanortalik Greenland **51** 60.09N 45.15W
Nanping Fujian China **25** 26.40N118.07E
Nansei shotō *is.* Japan **25** 26.30N125.00E
Nanshan *is.* S. China Sea **26** 10.30N116.00E
Nantes France **9** 47.14N 1.35W
Nanteuil-le-Haudouin France **9** 49.08N 2.48E
Nanticoke U.S.A. **55** 41.12N 76.00W
Nantong China **25** 32.05N120.59E
Nantua France **14** 46.09N 5.37E
Nantucket I. U.S.A. **55** 41.16N 70.03W
Nantucket Sd. U.S.A. **55** 41.30N 70.15W
Nantwich U.K. **4** 53.05N 2.31W
Nanyang China **25** 33.06N112.31E
Nanyuki Kenya **37** 0.01N 37.03E
Naococane, Lac *l.* Canada **51** 52.52N 70.40W
Napa U.S.A. **54** 38.18N122.17W
Napadogan Canada **55** 46.25N 67.01W
Napier New Zealand **48** 39.29S176.58E
Naples *see* Napoli Italy **12**
Napo *r.* Peru **60** 3.30S 73.10W
Napoleon U.S.A. **55** 41.24N 84.09W
Napoli Italy **12** 40.50N 14.14E
Napoli, Golfo di *g.* Italy **12** 40.42N 14.15E
Naqb Ishtar Jordan **32** 30.00N 35.30E
Nara Japan **23** 34.41N135.50E
Nara *d.* Japan **23** 34.27N135.55E
Nara Mali **34** 15.13N 7.20W
Naracoorte Australia **46** 36.58S140.46E
Naradhan Australia **47** 33.39S146.20E
Naran Mongolia **25** 45.20N113.41E
Narathiwat Thailand **29** 6.25N101.48E
Nārāyanganj Bangla. **29** 23.36N 90.28E
Narbada *r. see* Narmada *r.* India **28**
Narbonne France **11** 43.11N 3.00E
Nardò Italy **13** 40.11N 18.02E
Narembeen Australia **43** 32.04S118.23E
Nares Str. Canada **51** 78.30N 75.00W
Naretha Australia **43** 31.01S124.50E
Narita Japan **23** 35.47N140.19E
Narmada *r.* India **28** 21.40N 73.00E
Narodichi U.S.S.R. **15** 51.11N 29.01E
Narodnaya *mtn.* U.S.S.R. **18** 65.00N 61.00E
Narok Kenya **37** 1.04S 35.54E
Narooma Australia **47** 36.15S150.06E
Narrabri Australia **47** 30.20S149.49E
Narrabri West Australia **47** 30.22S149.47E
Narran *r.* Australia **47** 29.45S147.20E
Narrandera Australia **47** 34.36S146.34E
Narran L. Australia **47** 29.40S147.25E
Narrogin Australia **43** 32.58S117.10E
Narromine Australia **47** 32.17S148.20E
Narsimhapur India **29** 22.58N 79.15E
Narubis Namibia **39** 26.56S 18.36E
Narva U.S.S.R. **18** 59.22N 28.17E
Narvik Norway **16** 68.26N 17.25E
Naryan Mar U.S.S.R. **18** 67.37N 53.02E
Naryilco Australia **46** 28.41S141.50E
Naryn U.S.S.R. **20** 41.24N 76.00E
Nasa *mtn.* Norway **16** 66.29N 15.23E
Nasarawa Nigeria **38** 8.35N 7.44E
Naseby New Zealand **48** 45.01S170.09E
Nashua Mont. U.S.A. **54** 48.08N106.22W
Nashua N.H. U.S.A. **55** 42.46N 71.27W
Nashville U.S.A. **53** 36.10N 86.50W
Našice Yugo. **15** 45.29N 18.06E
Näsijärvi *l.* Finland **17** 61.37N 23.42E
Nāsik India **28** 20.00N 73.52E
Nāşir, Buḩayrat *l.* Egypt **30** 22.40N 32.00E
Naşr Egypt **32** 30.36N 30.23E
Nassau Bahamas **57** 25.03N 77.20W
Nasser, L. *see* Nāşir, Buḩayrat *l.* Egypt **30**
Nassian Ivory Coast **38** 8.33N 3.18W
Nässjö Sweden **17** 57.39N 14.41E
Nata Botswana **39** 20.12S 26.12E
Natal Brazil **61** 5.46S 35.15W
Natal Indonesia **26** 0.35N 99.07E
Natal *d.* R.S.A. **39** 28.30S 30.30E
Natanes Plateau *f.* U.S.A. **54** 33.35N110.15W
Naţanz Iran **31** 33.30N 51.57E
Natashquan Canada **51** 50.12N 61.49W
Natchez U.S.A. **53** 31.22N 91.24W
National City U.S.A. **54** 32.40N117.06W
Natitingou Benin **38** 10.17N 1.19E
Natron, L. Tanzania **37** 2.18S 36.05E
Naţrūn, Wādī an *f.* Egypt **32** 30.25N 30.18E
Naturaliste, C. Australia **43** 33.32S115.01E
Naturaliste Channel Australia **42** 25.25S113.00E
Naubinway U.S.A. **55** 46.05N 85.27W
Naumburg E. Germany **14** 51.09N 11.48E
Nā'ūr Jordan **32** 31.53N 35.50E
Nauru Pacific Oc. **40** 0.32S166.55E
Naustdal Norway **17** 61.31N 5.43E
Nauta Peru **60** 4.30S 73.40W
Nautla Mexico **56** 20.13N 96.47W
Navalmoral de la Mata Spain **10** 39.54N 5.33W
Navan Rep. of Ire. **7** 53.39N 6.42W
Navarre Australia **46** 36.54S143.09E
Navarro Argentina **63** 35.00S 59.10W
Naver *r.* U.K. **6** 58.32N 4.14W
Navlya U.S.S.R. **18** 52.51N 34.30E
Navoi U.S.S.R. **20** 40.04N 65.20E
Navojoa Mexico **56** 27.06N109.26W
Návpaktos Greece **13** 38.24N 21.49E
Návplion Greece **13** 37.33N 22.47E
Navrongo Ghana **38** 10.51N 1.03W
Nawá Syria **32** 32.53N 36.03E
Nawābshāh Pakistan **28** 26.15N 68.26E
Náxos Greece **13** 37.06N 25.23E
Náxos *i.* Greece **13** 37.03N 25.30E
Nayarit *d.* Mexico **56** 21.30N104.00W
Nāy Band Iran **31** 32.20N 57.34E
Nāy Band Iran **31** 27.23N 52.38E
Nāy Band, Kūh-e *mtn.* Iran **31** 32.25N 57.30E
Nazaré Brazil **61** 13.00S 39.00W
Nazarovka U.S.S.R. **18** 54.19N 41.20E
Nazas *r.* Mexico **56** 25.34N103.25W
Nazca Peru **60** 14.53S 74.54W
Nazerat Israel **32** 32.41N 35.16E
Nazilli Turkey **30** 37.55N 28.20E
Nchanga Zambia **37** 12.30S 27.55E
Ncheu Malaŵi **37** 14.50S 34.45E
Ndali Benin **38** 9.53N 2.45E
Ndasegera *mtn.* Tanzania **37** 1.58S 35.41E
Ndélé C.A.R. **35** 8.24N 20.39E
Ndélélé Cameroon **38** 4.03N 14.55E
N'Dendé Gabon **36** 2.23S 11.23E
Ndikiniméki Cameroon **38** 4.46N 10.49E
N'Djamena Chad **38** 12.10N 14.59E
Ndola Zambia **37** 12.58S 28.39E
Ndungu Tanzania **37** 4.25S 38.04E
Nea *r.* Norway **16** 63.15N 11.00E
Neagh, Lough U.K. **7** 54.36N 6.25W
Néa Páfos Cyprus **32** 34.45N 32.25E
Neápolis Greece **13** 36.30N 23.04E
Neath U.K. **5** 51.39N 3.49W
Nebit-Dag U.S.S.R. **31** 39.31N 54.24E
Nebraska *d.* U.S.A. **52** 41.30N100.00W
Nebraska City U.S.A. **53** 40.41N 95.50W
Nebrodi, Monti *mts.* Italy **12** 37.53N 14.32E
Neches *r.* U.S.A. **53** 29.55N 93.50W
Neckar *r.* W. Germany **14** 49.32N 8.26E
Necochea Argentina **63** 38.31S 58.46W
Necuto Angola **36** 4.55S 12.38E
Needles U.S.A. **54** 34.51N114.37W
Neerpelt Belgium **8** 51.13N 5.28E
Neftegorsk U.S.S.R. **19** 44.21N 39.44E
Nefyn U.K. **4** 52.55N 4.31W
Negaunee U.S.A. **55** 46.31N 87.37W
Negele Ethiopia **35** 5.20N 39.36E
Negev *des. see* HaNegev *des.* Israel **32**
Negoiu *mtn.* Romania **15** 45.36N 24.32E
Negomano Mozambique **37** 11.26S 38.30E
Negombo Sri Lanka **29** 7.13N 79.50E
Negotin Yugo. **15** 44.14N 22.33E
Negrais, C. Burma **29** 16.00N 94.30E
Negritos Peru **60** 4.42S 81.18W
Negro *r.* Argentina **63** 40.50S 63.00W
Negro *r.* Brazil **60** 3.00S 59.55W
Negro *r.* Uruguay **63** 33.27S 58.20W
Negros *i.* Phil. **27** 10.00N123.00E
Negru-Vodă Romania **15** 43.50N 28.12E
Neijiang China **24** 29.32N105.03E
Nei Monggol *d.* China **25** 41.30N112.00E
Neisse *r.* Poland / E. Germany **14** 52.05N 14.42E
Neiva Colombia **60** 2.58N 75.15W
Nekső Denmark **17** 55.04N 15.09E
Nelidovo U.S.S.R. **18** 56.13N 32.46E
Nelkan U.S.S.R. **21** 57.40N136.04E
Nelligen Australia **47** 35.39S150.06E
Nellore India **29** 14.29N 80.00E
Nelson Australia **46** 38.04S141.05E
Nelson Canada **50** 49.29N117.17W
Nelson *r.* Canada **51** 57.00N 93.20W
Nelson New Zealand **48** 41.18S173.17E
Nelson *d.* New Zealand **48** 41.40S172.20E
Nelson U.K. **4** 53.50N 2.14W
Nelson U.S.A. **54** 35.30N113.16W
Nelson, C. Australia **46** 38.27S141.35E
Nelson, Estrecho *str.* Chile **63** 51.33S 74.40W
Nelspoort R.S.A. **39** 32.07S 23.00E
Nelspruit R.S.A. **39** 25.27S 30.58E
Néma Mauritania **34** 16.32N 7.12W
Neman *r.* U.S.S.R. **17** 55.18N 21.23E
Nembe Nigeria **38** 4.32N 6.25E
Nemours France **9** 48.16N 2.41E
Nenagh Rep. of Ire. **7** 52.52N 8.13W
Nenana U.S.A. **50** 64.35N149.20W
Nene *r.* U.K. **4** 52.49N 0.12E
Nenjiang China **25** 49.10N125.15E
Nepal Asia **29** 28.00N 84.30E
Nephi U.S.A. **54** 39.43N111.50W
Nephin Beg *mtn.* Rep. of Ire. **7** 54.02N 9.38W
Nephin Beg Range *mts.* Rep. of Ire. **7** 54.00N 9.37W
Nera *r.* Italy **12** 42.33N 12.43E
Nérac France **11** 44.08N 0.20E
Nerekhta U.S.S.R. **18** 57.30N 40.40E
Neretva *r.* Yugo. **13** 43.02N 17.28E
Neriquinha Angola **36** 15.50S 21.40E
Nero Deep Pacific Oc. **27** 12.40N145.50E
Néronde France **11** 45.50N 4.14E
Nerriga Australia **47** 35.10S150.03E
Nerva Spain **10** 37.42N 6.30W
Nes Neth. **8** 53.27N 5.46E
Nesbyen Norway **17** 60.34N 9.09E
Nesle France **9** 49.46N 2.51E
Nesna Norway **16** 66.13N 13.04E
Nesöy *i.* Norway **16** 66.35N 12.40E
Ness, Loch U.K. **6** 57.16N 4.30W
Nestaocano *r.* Canada **55** 48.40N 73.25W
Nesterov U.S.S.R. **15** 50.04N 24.00E
Néstos *r.* Greece **13** 40.51N 24.48E
Nesttun Norway **17** 60.19N 5.20E
Nesvizh U.S.S.R. **15** 53.16N 26.40E
Netanya Israel **32** 32.20N 34.51E
Netherlands Europe **8** 52.00N 5.30E
Netherlands Antilles S. America **57** 12.30N 69.00W
Neto *r.* Italy **13** 39.12N 17.08E
Nettilling L. Canada **51** 66.30N 70.40W
Neubrandenburg E. Germany **14** 53.33N 13.16E
Neubrandenburg *d.* E. Germany **14** 53.30N 13.15E
Neuchâtel Switz. **14** 47.00N 6.56E
Neuchâtel, Lac de *l.* Switz. **14** 46.55N 6.55E
Neuenhaus W. Germany **8** 52.30N 6.58E
Neufchâteau Belgium **8** 49.51N 5.26E
Neufchâtel France **9** 49.44N 1.26E
Neuillé-Pont-Pierre France **9** 47.33N 0.33E
Neumarkt W. Germany **14** 49.16N 11.28E
Neumünster W. Germany **14** 54.06N 9.59E
Neuquén Argentina **63** 39.00S 68.05W
Neuquén *d.* Argentina **63** 38.30S 70.00W
Neuquén *r.* Argentina **63** 39.02S 68.07W
Neuruppin E. Germany **14** 52.55N 12.48E
Neuse *r.* U.S.A. **53** 35.04N 77.04W
Neusiedler See *l.* Austria **14** 47.52N 16.45E
Neuss W. Germany **8** 51.12N 6.42E
Neustadt Bayern W. Germany **14** 49.44N 12.11E
Neustrelitz E. Germany **14** 53.22N 13.05E
Neuvic France **11** 45.23N 2.16E
Neuwied W. Germany **8** 50.26N 7.28E
Nevada *d.* U.S.A. **54** 39.50N116.10W
Nevada, Sierra *mts.* Spain **10** 37.04N 3.20W
Nevada, Sierra *mts.* U.S.A. **52** 37.30N119.00W
Nevanka U.S.S.R. **21** 56.31N 98.57E
Nevel U.S.S.R. **18** 56.00N 29.59E
Nevers France **11** 47.00N 3.09E
Nevertire Australia **47** 31.52S147.47E
Nevinnomyssk U.S.S.R. **19** 44.38N 41.59E
Nevşehir Turkey **30** 38.38N 34.43E
Newala Tanzania **37** 10.56S 39.15E
New Albany Ind. U.S.A. **55** 38.17N 85.50W
New Amsterdam Guyana **61** 6.18N 57.30W
Newark N.J. U.S.A. **55** 40.44N 74.11W
Newark N.Y. U.S.A. **55** 43.03N 77.06W
Newark Ohio U.S.A. **55** 40.03N 82.25W
Newark-on-Trent U.K. **4** 53.06N 0.48E
New Bedford U.S.A. **55** 41.38N 70.56W
Newberg U.S.A. **54** 45.18N122.58W
New Bern U.S.A. **53** 35.05N 77.04W
Newberry Mich. U.S.A. **55** 46.22N 85.30W
Newbiggin-by-the-Sea U.K. **4** 55.11N 1.30W
New Braunfels U.S.A. **52** 29.43N 98.09W
New Britain *i.* P.N.G. **41** 6.00S150.00E
New Brunswick *d.* Canada **55** 46.30N 66.15W
New Brunswick U.S.A. **55** 40.29N 74.27W
Newburgh U.S.A. **55** 41.30N 74.00W
Newbury U.K. **5** 51.24N 1.19W
New Bussa Nigeria **38** 9.53N 4.29E
Newcastle Australia **47** 32.55S151.46E
Newcastle N.B. Canada **55** 47.01N 65.36W
Newcastle Ont. Canada **55** 43.55N 78.35W
Newcastle R.S.A. **39** 27.44S 29.55E
Newcastle U.K. **7** 54.13N 5.53W
New Castle Penn. U.S.A. **55** 41.00N 80.22W

wcastle Wyo. U.S.A. **52** 43.50N104.11W
wcastle B. Australia **44** 10.50S142.37E
wcastle Emlyn U.K. **5** 52.02N 4.29W
wcastle-under-Lyme U.K. **4** 53.02N 2.15W
wcastle upon Tyne U.K. **4** 54.58N 1.36W
wcastle Waters *town* Australia **44** 7.24S133.24E
wcastle West Rep. of Ire. **7** 52.26N 9.04W
wdegate Australia **43** 33.06S119.01E
w Delhi India **28** 28.37N 77.13E
w England Range *mts.* Australia **47** 0.30S151.50E
wenham, C. U.S.A. **50** 58.37N162.12W
went U.K. **5** 51.56N 2.24W
w Forest *f.* U.K. **5** 50.50N 1.35W
wfoundland Australia **47** 30.53S144.38E
wfoundland *d.* Canada **51** 55.00N 60.00W
wfoundland *i.* Canada **51** 48.30N 56.00W
w Galloway U.K. **6** 55.05N 4.09W
w Guinea *i.* Austa. **27** 5.00S140.00E
w Hampshire *d.* U.S.A. **55** 43.35N 71.40W
w Hanover *i.* Pacific Oc. **41** 2.00S150.00E
whaven U.K. **5** 50.47N 0.04E
w Haven U.S.A. **55** 41.18N 72.55W
w Ireland *i.* P.N.G. **41** 2.30S151.30E
w Jersey *d.* U.S.A. **55** 40.15N 74.30W
w Liskeard Canada **55** 47.30N 79.40W
w London Conn. U.S.A. **55** 41.21N 72.06W
wmarket Australia **46** 34.43S144.31E
wmarket Rep. of Ire. **7** 52.13N 9.00W
wmarket U.K. **5** 52.15N 0.23E
wmarket on Fergus Rep. of Ire. **7** 52.46N .55W
w Martinsville U.S.A. **55** 39.39N 80.52W
w Meadows U.S.A. **54** 44.58N116.32W
w Mexico *d.* U.S.A. **52** 33.30N106.00W
w Norcia Australia **43** 30.58S116.15E
w Norfolk Australia **45** 42.46S147.02E
w Orleans U.S.A. **53** 30.00N 90.03W
w Philadelphia U.S.A. **55** 40.31N 81.28W
w Plymouth New Zealand **48** 39.03S174.04E
wport Mayo Rep. of Ire. **7** 53.53N 9.34W
wport Tipperary Rep. of Ire. **7** 52.42N 8.25W
wport Dyfed U.K. **5** 52.01N 4.51W
wport Essex U.K. **5** 51.58N 0.13E
wport Gwent U.K. **5** 51.34N 2.59W
wport Hants. U.K. **5** 50.43N 1.18W
wport Ark. U.S.A. **53** 35.35N 91.16W
wport Maine U.S.A. **55** 44.50N 69.17W
wport N.H. U.S.A. **55** 43.21N 72.09W
wport Oreg. U.S.A. **54** 44.38N124.03W
wport R.I. U.S.A. **55** 41.13N 71.18W
wport News U.S.A. **53** 36.59N 76.26W
w Providence *i.* Bahamas **57** 25.03N 77.25W
wquay U.K. **5** 50.24N 5.06W
w Quay U.K. **5** 52.13N 4.22W
w Radnor U.K. **5** 52.15N 3.10W
w Romney U.K. **5** 50.59N 0.58E
w Ross Rep. of Ire. **7** 52.24N 6.57W
wry U.K. **7** 54.11N 6.21W
w Scone U.K. **6** 56.25N 3.25W
w South Wales *d.* Australia **47** 32.40S147.40E
wton Kans. U.S.A. **53** 38.02N 97.22W
wton Abbot U.K. **5** 50.32N 3.37W
wton Aycliffe U.K. **4** 54.36N 1.34W
wtonmore U.K. **6** 57.04N 4.08W
wton Stewart U.K. **6** 54.57N 4.29W
wtown U.K. **5** 52.31N 3.19W
wtownabbey U.K. **7** 54.39N 5.57W
wtownards U.K. **7** 54.35N 5.41W
wtown Butler U.K. **7** 54.12N 7.22W
wtown St. Boswells U.K. **6** 55.35N 2.40W
wtownstewart U.K. **7** 54.43N 7.25W
w Westminster Canada **50** 49.12N122.55W
w York U.S.A. **55** 40.40N 73.50W
w York *d.* U.S.A. **55** 43.00N 75.00W
w Zealand Austa. **48** 41.00S175.00E
ya U.S.S.R. **18** 58.18N 43.40E
yagawa Japan **23** 34.46N135.38E
yrīz Iran **31** 29.12N 54.17E
yshābūr Iran **31** 36.13N 58.49E
zhin U.S.S.R. **15** 51.03N 31.54E
jala Nigeria **38** 12.21N 14.10E
jami, L. Botswana **39** 20.32S 22.38E
jamiland *f.* Botswana **39** 20.00S 22.30E
jangla Ringco *l.* China **29** 31.40N 83.00E
janglong Kangri *mtn.* China **24** 32.45N 81.12E
Gao Congo **36** 2.28S 15.40E
jaoundéré Cameroon **38** 7.20N 13.35E
aruawahia New Zealand **48** 37.40S175.09E
aruroro *r.* New Zealand **48** 39.34S176.54E
auruhoe *mtn.* New Zealand **48** 39.10S175.35E
'iro, Mt. Kenya **37** 2.06N 36.44E
jiva Angola **39** 17.03S 15.47E
jomba Tanzania **37** 8.16S 32.51E
jomeni Kenya **37** 3.00S 40.11E
jong Kenya **37** 1.22S 36.40E
jorongoro Crater *f.* Tanzania **37** 3.13S 35.32E
jozi Burundi **37** 2.52S 29.50E
juigmi Niger **38** 14.00N 13.11E
junza Angola **36** 11.11S 13.52E
juru Nigeria **38** 12.53N 10.30E
juruka Tanzania **37** 5.08S 30.58E
jwerere Zambia **37** 15.18S 28.20E
haccongo Mozambique **39** 24.18S 35.14E
hachengue Mozambique **39** 22.52S 35.10E
handugue *r.* Mozambique **39** 18.47S 34.30E
ha Trang Vietnam **26** 12.15N109.10E
hill Australia **46** 36.20S141.40E
afounké Mali **38** 15.56N 4.00W
agara Falls *town* U.S.A. **55** 43.06N 79.02W
ah Malaysia **26** 3.52N113.44E
amey Niger **38** 13.32N 2.05E
amey *d.* Niger **38** 14.00N 1.40E
a-Nia Zaïre **37** 1.30N 27.41E
apa, Gunung *mtn.* Indonesia **26** 1.45N117.30E
as *i.* Indonesia **26** 1.05N 97.30E
assa *d.* Mozambique **37** 13.00S 36.30E
caragua C. America **57** 13.00N 85.00W
Nicaragua, Lago de *l.* Nicaragua **57** 11.30N 85.30W
Nicastro Italy **12** 38.58N 16.16E
Nice France **11** 43.42N 7.16E
Nichelino Italy **9** 44.59N 7.38E
Nicholson Australia **42** 18.02S128.54E
Nicholson *r.* Australia **44** 17.31S139.36E
Nicobar Is. India **29** 8.00N 94.00E
Nicolls Town Bahamas **57** 25.08N 78.00W
Nicosia *see* Levkosía Cyprus **32**
Nicoya, Golfo de *g.* Costa Rica **57** 9.30N 85.00W
Nicoya, Península de *pen.* Costa Rica **57** 10.30N 85.30W
Nid *r.* Norway **17** 58.24N 8.48E
Nida *r.* Poland **15** 50.18N 20.52E
Nidzica Poland **15** 53.22N 20.26E
Niederösterreich *d.* Austria **14** 48.20N 15.50E
Niedersachsen *d.* W. Germany **8** 52.55N 7.40E
Niekerkshoop R.S.A. **39** 29.19S 22.48E
Niéllé Ivory Coast **38** 10.05N 5.28W
Nienburg W. Germany **14** 52.38N 9.13E
Niers *r.* Neth. **8** 51.43N 5.56E
Nieuw Nickerie Surinam **61** 5.57N 56.59W
Nieuwpoort Belgium **8** 51.08N 2.45E
Niğde Turkey **30** 37.58N 34.42E
Niger Africa **34** 17.00N 9.30E
Niger *d.* Nigeria **38** 9.50N 6.00E
Niger *r.* Nigeria **38** 4.15N 6.05E
Niger Delta Nigeria **38** 4.00N 6.10E
Nigeria Africa **38** 9.00N 9.00E
Nightcaps New Zealand **48** 45.58S168.02E
Niigata Japan **25** 37.58N139.02E
Niiza Japan **23** 35.48N139.34E
Nijmegen Neth. **8** 51.50N 5.52E
Nikel U.S.S.R. **16** 69.20N 30.00E
Nikiniki Indonesia **42** 9.49S124.29E
Nikki Benin **38** 9.55N 3.18E
Nikolayev U.S.S.R. **19** 46.57N 32.00E
Nikolayevskiy U.S.S.R. **19** 50.05N 45.32E
Nikolayevsk-na-Amure U.S.S.R. **21** 53.20N140.44E
Nikolsk U.S.S.R. **18** 59.33N 45.30E
Nikopol U.S.S.R. **19** 47.34N 34.25E
Niksar Turkey **30** 40.35N 36.59E
Nīkshahr Iran **31** 26.14N 60.15E
Nikšić Yugo. **13** 42.48N 18.56E
Nīl, An *r.* Egypt **32** 31.30N 30.25E
Nila *i.* Indonesia **27** 6.45S129.30E
Nile *r. see* Nīl, An *r.* Egypt **32**
Nile Delta Egypt **32** 31.00N 31.00E
Niles Mich. U.S.A. **55** 41.51N 86.15W
Nilgiri Hills India **28** 11.30N 77.30E
Nimbin Australia **47** 28.35S153.12E
Nîmes France **11** 43.50N 4.21E
Nindigully Australia **47** 28.20S148.47E
Ninety Mile Beach *f.* Australia **47** 38.07S147.30E
Ninety Mile Beach *f.* New Zealand **48** 34.45S173.00E
Nineveh *ruins* Iraq **30** 36.24N 43.08E
Ningbo China **25** 29.54N121.33E
Ningde China **25** 26.41N119.32E
Ningnan China **24** 27.03N102.46E
Ningwu China **25** 39.00N112.19E
Ningxia Huizu *d.* China **24** 37.00N106.00E
Ninh Binh Vietnam **26** 20.14N106.00E
Niningarra Australia **42** 20.35S119.58E
Ninove Belgium **8** 50.50N 4.02E
Niobrara *r.* U.S.A. **52** 42.45N 98.10W
Nioro Mali **34** 15.12N 9.35W
Niort France **11** 46.19N 0.27W
Nipāni India **28** 16.24N 74.23E
Nipigon Canada **55** 49.00N 88.17W
Nipigon, L. Canada **55** 49.50N 88.30W
Nipigon B. Canada **55** 48.53N 87.50W
Nipissing, L. Canada **55** 46.17N 80.00W
Niquelândia Brazil **59** 14.27S 48.27W
Nirasaki Japan **23** 35.42N138.27E
Niš Yugo. **13** 43.20N 21.54E
Nisa Portugal **10** 39.31N 7.39W
Nishinomiya Japan **23** 34.43N135.20E
Nisko Poland **15** 50.35N 22.07E
Nissedal Norway **17** 59.10N 8.30E
Nisser *l.* Norway **17** 59.10N 8.30E
Niţā' Saudi Arabia **31** 27.13N 48.25E
Niterói Brazil **59** 22.54S 43.06W
Nith *r.* U.K. **6** 55.00N 3.35W
Nitra Czech. **15** 48.20N 18.05E
Niue *i.* Cook Is. **40** 19.02S169.52W
Niut, Gunung *mtn.* Indonesia **26** 1.00N110.00E
Nivala Finland **16** 63.55N 24.58E
Nivelles Belgium **8** 50.36N 4.20E
Nizāmābād India **29** 18.40N 78.05E
Nizhneangarsk U.S.S.R. **21** 55.48N109.35E
Nizhne Kolymsk U.S.S.R. **21** 68.34N160.58E
Nizhneudinsk U.S.S.R. **21** 54.55N 99.00E
Nizhnevartovsk U.S.S.R. **20** 60.57N 76.40E
Nizhniy Tagil U.S.S.R. **18** 58.00N 60.00E
Nizhnyaya Tunguska *r.* U.S.S.R. **21** 65.50N 88.00E
Nizhnyaya Tura U.S.S.R. **18** 58.40N 59.48E
Nizke Tatry *mts.* Czech. **15** 48.54N 19.40E
Nizza Monferrato Italy **9** 44.46N 8.21E
Njombe Tanzania **37** 9.20S 34.47E
Njombe *r.* Tanzania **37** 7.02S 35.55E
Njoro Tanzania **37** 5.16S 36.30E
Nkalagu Nigeria **38** 6.28N 7.46E
Nkawkaw Ghana **38** 6.35N 0.47W
Nkayi Zimbabwe **39** 19.00S 28.54E
Nkhata Bay *town* Malaŵi **37** 11.37S 34.20E
Nkhotakota Malaŵi **37** 12.55S 34.19E
Nkongsamba Cameroon **38** 4.59N 9.53E
Nkungwe Mt. Tanzania **37** 6.15S 29.54E
Noatak U.S.A. **50** 67.34N162.59W
Noce *r.* Italy **9** 46.09N 11.04E
Nogales Mexico **56** 31.20N110.56W
Nogara Italy **9** 45.11N 11.04E
Nogayskiye Step *f.* U.S.S.R. **19** 44.25N 45.30E
Nogent-le-Rotrou France **9** 48.19N 0.50E
Nogent-sur-Seine France **9** 48.29N 3.30E
Nogoyá Argentina **63** 32.22S 59.49W
Noguera Ribagorçana *r.* Spain **10** 41.27N 0.25E
Noirmoutier, Île de *i.* France **11** 47.00N 2.15W
Nojima-zaki *c.* Japan **23** 34.56N139.53E
Nokia Finland **17** 61.28N 23.30E
Nok Kundi Pakistan **28** 28.48N 62.46E
Nokomis Canada **50** 51.30N105.00W
Nokou Chad **38** 14.35N 14.47E
Nolinsk U.S.S.R. **18** 57.38N 49.52E
Noma Omuramba *r.* Botswana **39** 19.14S 22.15E
Nome U.S.A. **50** 64.30N165.30W
Nomgon Mongolia **24** 42.50N105.13E
Nonancourt France **9** 48.47N 1.11E
Nonburg U.S.S.R. **18** 65.32N 50.37E
Nong Khai Thailand **29** 17.50N102.46E
Nongoma R.S.A. **39** 27.58S 31.35E
Nonning Australia **46** 32.30S136.30E
Nonthaburi Thailand **26** 13.48N100.31E
Noojee Australia **47** 37.57S146.00E
Noongaar Australia **43** 31.21S118.55E
Noonkanbah Australia **42** 18.30S124.50E
Noord Beveland *f.* Neth. **8** 51.35N 3.45E
Noord Brabant *d.* Neth. **8** 51.37N 5.00E
Noord Holland *d.* Neth. **8** 52.37N 4.50E
Noordoost-Polder *f.* Neth. **8** 52.45N 5.45E
Noordwijk Neth. **8** 52.16N 4.29E
Noorvik U.S.A. **50** 66.50N161.14W
Nora Sweden **17** 59.31N 15.02E
Noranda Canada **55** 48.18N 79.01W
Nord *d.* France **8** 50.17N 3.14E
Nordaustlandet *i.* Arctic Oc. **64** 79.55N 23.00E
Norddeich W. Germany **8** 53.35N 7.10E
Norden W. Germany **8** 53.34N 7.13E
Nordenham W. Germany **14** 53.30N 8.29E
Norderney W. Germany **8** 53.43N 7.09E
Norderney *i.* W. Germany **8** 53.45N 7.15E
Nordfjord *est.* Norway **17** 61.54N 5.12E
Nordfjordeid Norway **17** 61.54N 6.00E
Nordfold Norway **16** 67.48N 15.20E
Nordfriesische Inseln *is.* W. Germany **14** 54.30N 8.00E
Nordhausen E. Germany **14** 51.31N 10.48E
Nordhorn W. Germany **8** 52.27N 7.05E
Nordkapp *c.* Norway **16** 71.11N 25.48E
Nordkinnhalvöya *pen.* Norway **16** 70.55N 27.45E
Nordland *d.* Norway **16** 66.50N 14.50E
Nord-Ostsee-Kanal W. Germany **14** 53.54N 9.12E
Nordreisa Norway **16** 69.46N 21.00E
Nordrhein-Westfalen *d.* W. Germany **8** 51.18N 6.32E
Nord Tröndelag *d.* Norway **16** 64.20N 12.00E
Nordvik U.S.S.R. **21** 73.40N110.50E
Nore Norway **17** 60.10N 9.01E
Nore *r.* Rep. of Ire. **7** 52.25N 6.58W
Norfolk *d.* U.K. **5** 52.39N 1.00E
Norfolk Va. U.S.A. **53** 36.54N 76.18W
Norfolk Broads *f.* U.K. **4** 52.43N 1.35E
Norheimsund Norway **17** 60.22N 6.08E
Norilsk U.S.S.R. **21** 69.21N 88.02E
Norman *r.* Australia **44** 17.28S140.49E
Normanby *r.* Australia **44** 14.25S144.08E
Normanby New Zealand **48** 39.32S174.16E
Normanby I. P.N.G. **44** 10.05S151.05E
Normandie, Collines de *hills* France **9** 48.50N 0.40W
Normanton Australia **44** 17.40S141.05E
Norman Wells Canada **50** 65.19N126.46W
Nornalup Australia **43** 34.58S116.49E
Norquinco Argentina **63** 41.50S 70.55W
Norrahammar Sweden **17** 57.42N 14.06E
Norra Kvarken *str.* Sweden / Finland **16** 63.36N 20.43E
Norra Storfjället *mtn.* Sweden **16** 65.52N 15.18E
Norrbotten *d.* Sweden **16** 67.00N 19.50E
Nörresundby Denmark **17** 57.04N 9.56E
Norris L. U.S.A. **53** 36.20N 83.55W
Norristown U.S.A. **55** 40.07N 75.20W
Norrköping Sweden **17** 58.36N 16.11E
Norrsundet Sweden **17** 60.56N 17.08E
Norrtälje Sweden **17** 59.46N 18.42E
Norseman Australia **43** 32.15S121.47E
Norsk U.S.S.R. **21** 52.22N129.57E
Norte, C. Brazil **61** 1.40N 49.55W
Norte, Punta *c.* Argentina **63** 36.17S 56.46W
Northallerton U.K. **4** 54.20N 1.26W
Northam Australia **43** 31.41S116.40E
Northampton Australia **43** 28.21S114.37E
Northampton U.K. **5** 52.14N 0.54W
Northamptonshire *d.* U.K. **5** 52.18N 0.55W
North Battleford Canada **50** 52.47N108.19W
North Bay *town* Canada **55** 46.19N 79.28W
North Bend Oreg. U.S.A. **54** 43.24N124.14W
North Berwick U.K. **6** 56.04N 2.43W
North Bourke Australia **47** 30.01S145.59E
North C. Antarctica **64** 71.00S166.00E
North C. New Zealand **48** 34.28S173.00E
North Canadian *r.* U.S.A. **53** 35.30N 95.45W
North Carolina *d.* U.S.A. **53** 35.30N 79.00W
North Channel *str.* Canada **55** 46.02N 82.50W
North Channel U.K. **7** 55.15N 5.52W
North China Plain *f. see* Huabei Pingyuan *f.* China **25**
Northcliffe Australia **43** 34.36S116.04E
North Dakota *d.* U.S.A. **52** 47.00N100.00W
North Dorset Downs *hills* U.K. **5** 50.46N 2.25W
North Downs *hills* U.K. **5** 51.18N 0.40E
North Eastern *d.* Kenya **37** 1.00N 40.00E
Northern *d.* Ghana **38** 9.00N 1.30W
Northern Ireland *d.* U.K. **7** 54.40N 6.45W
Northern Territory *d.* Australia **44** 20.00S133.00E
North Esk *r.* U.K. **6** 56.45N 2.25W
North Foreland *c.* U.K. **5** 51.23N 1.26E
North French *r.* Canada **55** 51.03N 80.52W
North Frisian Is. *see* Nordfriesische Inseln *is.* W. Germany **14**
North Horr Kenya **37** 3.19N 37.00E
North I. New Zealand **48** 39.00S175.00E
Northiam U.K. **5** 50.59N 0.39E
North Korea Asia **25** 40.00N128.00E
Northland *d.* New Zealand **48** 35.25S174.00E
North Las Vegas U.S.A. **54** 36.12N115.07W
North Ogden U.S.A. **54** 41.18N112.00W
North Platte U.S.A. **52** 41.09N100.45W
North Platte *r.* U.S.A. **52** 41.09N100.55W
North Powder U.S.A. **54** 45.13N117.55W
North Ronaldsay *i.* U.K. **6** 59.23N 2.26W
North Sea Europe **3** 56.00N 5.00E
North Sporades *see* Vorïai Sporádhes *is.* Greece **13**
North Taranaki Bight *b.* New Zealand **48** 38.45S174.15E
North Tawton U.K. **5** 50.48N 3.55W
North Tonawanda U.S.A. **55** 43.02N 78.54W
North Uist *i.* U.K. **6** 57.35N 7.20W
Northumberland *d.* U.K. **4** 55.12N 2.00W
Northumberland, C. Australia **46** 38.04S140.40E
Northumberland Is. Australia **44** 21.40S150.00E
North Walsham U.K. **4** 52.49N 1.22E
Northway U.S.A. **50** 62.58N142.00W
North West C. Australia **42** 21.48S114.10E
North West Highlands U.K. **6** 57.30N 5.15W
North West River *town* Canada **51** 53.30N 60.10W
Northwest Territories *d.* Canada **51** 66.00N 95.00W
Northwich U.K. **4** 53.16N 2.30W
North York Moors *hills* U.K. **4** 54.21N 0.50W
North Yorkshire *d.* U.K. **4** 54.14N 1.14W
Norton Sound *b.* U.S.A. **50** 63.50N164.00W
Nort-sur-Erdre France **9** 47.26N 1.30W
Norwalk Conn. U.S.A. **55** 41.07N 73.25W
Norwalk Ohio U.S.A. **55** 41.14N 82.37W
Norway Europe **16** 65.00N 13.00E
Norway House *town* Canada **51** 53.59N 97.50W
Norwegian Dependency Antarctica **64** 77.00S 10.00E
Norwegian Sea Europe **64** 65.00N 5.00E
Norwich U.K. **5** 52.38N 1.17E
Norwood Ohio U.S.A. **55** 39.12N 84.21W
Noshul U.S.S.R. **18** 60.04N 49.30E
Nosovka U.S.S.R. **15** 50.55N 31.37E
Noşratābād Iran **31** 29.54N 59.58E
Noss Head U.K. **6** 58.28N 3.03W
Nossob *r.* R.S.A. / Botswana **36** 26.54S 20.39E
Noteć *r.* Poland **14** 52.44N 15.26E
Noto Italy **12** 36.53N 15.05E
Notodden Norway **17** 59.34N 9.17E
Notre Dame, Monts *mts.* Canada **55** 48.00N 69.00W
Nottawasaga B. Canada **55** 44.40N 80.30W
Nottaway *r.* Canada **55** 51.25N 78.50W
Nottingham U.K. **4** 52.57N 1.10W
Nottinghamshire *d.* U.K. **4** 53.10N 1.00W
Notwani *r.* Botswana **39** 23.46S 26.57E
Nouadhibou Mauritania **34** 20.54N 17.01W
Nouakchott Mauritania **34** 18.09N 15.58W
Nouméa New Caledonia **40** 22.16S166.27E
Nouna Burkina Faso **38** 12.44N 3.54W
Noupoort R.S.A. **39** 31.11S 24.56E
Nouveau-Comptoir Canada **51** 53.00N 78.42W
Nouvelle Calédonia *is.* Pacific Oc. **40** 21.30S165.30E
Nouzonville France **9** 49.49N 4.45E
Novafeltria Bagnodi Romagna Italy **9** 43.53N 12.17E
Nova Friburgo Brazil **59** 22.16S 42.32W
Nova Gaia Angola **36** 10.09S 17.35E
Nova Iguaçu Brazil **59** 22.45S 43.27W
Nova Lima Brazil **59** 19.59S 43.51W
Novara Italy **9** 45.27N 8.37E
Nova Scotia *d.* Canada **51** 45.00N 64.00W
Nova Sofala Mozambique **39** 20.09S 34.24E
Novato U.S.A. **54** 38.06N122.34W
Novaya Ladoga U.S.S.R. **18** 60.09N 32.15E
Novaya Lyalya U.S.S.R. **20** 59.02N 60.38E
Novaya Sibir, Ostrov *i.* U.S.S.R. **21** 75.20N148.00E
Novaya Ushitsa U.S.S.R. **15** 48.50N 27.12E
Novaya Zemlya *i.* U.S.S.R. **20** 74.00N 56.00E
Novelda Spain **10** 38.24N 0.45W
Nové Zámky Czech. **15** 47.59N 18.11E
Novgorod U.S.S.R. **18** 58.30N 31.20E
Novgorod Severskiy U.S.S.R. **18** 52.00N 33.15E
Novi di Modena Italy **9** 44.54N 10.54E
Novigrad Yugo. **14** 45.19N 13.34E
Novi Ligure Italy **9** 44.46N 8.47E
Novi Pazar Yugo. **13** 43.08N 20.28E
Novi Sad Yugo. **15** 45.16N 19.52E
Novoalekseyevka U.S.S.R. **19** 46.14N 34.36E
Novoanninskiy U.S.S.R. **19** 50.32N 42.42E
Novo Arkhangel'sk U.S.S.R. **15** 48.34N 30.50E
Novocherkassk U.S.S.R. **19** 47.25N 40.05E
Novofedorovka U.S.S.R. **19** 47.04N 35.18E
Novograd Volynskiy U.S.S.R. **15** 50.34N 27.32E
Novogrudok U.S.S.R. **15** 53.35N 25.50E
Novo Hamburgo Brazil **59** 29.37S 51.07W
Novokazalinsk U.S.S.R. **20** 45.48N 62.06E
Novokuznetsk U.S.S.R. **20** 53.45N 87.12E
Novomoskovsk R.S.F.S.R. U.S.S.R. **18** 54.06N 38.15E
Novomoskovsk Ukr.S.S.R. U.S.S.R. **19** 48.38N 35.15E
Novorossiysk U.S.S.R. **19** 44.44N 37.46E
Novoshakhtinsk U.S.S.R. **19** 47.46N 39.55E
Novosibirsk U.S.S.R. **20** 55.04N 82.55E
Novosibirskiye Ostrova *is.* U.S.S.R. **21** 76.00N144.00E
Novouzensk U.S.S.R. **19** 50.29N 48.08E
Novo-Vyatsk U.S.S.R. **18** 58.30N 49.40E
Novozybkov U.S.S.R. **15** 52.31N 31.58E
Novska Yugo. **14** 45.21N 16.59E
Nový Jičín Czech. **15** 49.36N 18.00E
Novyy Bykhov U.S.S.R. **15** 53.20N 30.21E
Novyy Port U.S.S.R. **20** 67.38N 72.33E
Nowa Ruda Poland **14** 50.34N 16.30E
Nowa Sól Poland **14** 51.49N 15.41E
Nowendoc Australia **47** 31.35S151.45E
Nowgong Assam India **29** 26.20N 92.41E
Nowingi Australia **46** 34.36S142.15E
Nowra Australia **47** 35.54S150.36E
Nowy Dwór Mazowiecki Poland **15** 52.26N 20.43E
Nowy Korczyn Poland **15** 50.19N 20.48E
Nowy Sącz Poland **15** 49.39N 20.40E
Nowy Targ Poland **15** 49.29N 20.02E
Nowy Tomśyl Poland **14** 52.20N 16.07E
Noxon U.S.A. **54** 48.01N115.47W
Noyant France **9** 47.31N 0.08E
Noyon France **9** 49.35N 3.00E
Nozay France **9** 47.34N 1.38W
Nsanje Malaŵi **37** 16.55S 35.12E
Nsawam Ghana **38** 5.49N 0.20W
Nsombo Zambia **37** 10.50S 29.56E
Nsukka Nigeria **38** 6.51N 7.29E
Nuatja Togo **38** 6.59N 1.11E
Nubian Desert Sudan **35** 21.00N 34.00E
Nueces *r.* U.S.A. **53** 27.55N 97.30W
Nueltin L. Canada **51** 60.20N 99.50W
Nueva Gerona Cuba **57** 21.53N 82.49W
Nueva Helvecia Uruguay **63** 34.19S 57.13W
Nueva Palmira Uruguay **63** 33.53S 58.25W
Nueva Rosita Mexico **56** 27.57N101.13W
Nueve de Julio Argentina **63** 35.30S 60.50W
Nuevitas Cuba **57** 21.34N 77.18W
Nuevo, Golfo *g.* Argentina **63** 42.42S 64.35W
Nuevo Berlín Uruguay **63** 32.59S 58.03W
Nuevo Laredo Mexico **56** 27.30N 99.30W
Nuevo León *d.* Mexico **56** 26.00N 99.00W
Nuevo Rocafuerte Ecuador **60** 0.56S 75.24W
Nu Jiang *r.* China *see* Salween *r.* Burma **29**
Nukha U.S.S.R. **31** 41.12N 47.10E
Nuku'alofa Tonga **40** 21.07S175.12W
Nulato U.S.A. **50** 64.43N158.06W
Nullagine Australia **42** 21.56S120.06E
Nullarbor Australia **43** 31.26S130.55E
Nullarbor Plain *f.* Australia **43** 31.30S128.00E
Numalla, L. Australia **46** 28.45S144.21E
Numan Nigeria **38** 9.30N 12.01E
Numazu Japan **23** 35.06N138.52E
Numedal *f.* Norway **17** 60.06N 9.06E
Numurkah Australia **47** 36.05S145.26E
Nundle Australia **47** 31.28S151.08E
Nuneaton U.K. **5** 52.32N 1.29W
Nungo Mozambique **37** 13.25S 37.45E
Nunivak I. U.S.A. **50** 60.00N166.30W
Nunthurungie Australia **46** 30.55S142.29E
Nuoro Italy **12** 40.19N 9.20E
Nuqūb S. Yemen **35** 14.59N 45.48E
Nürburg W. Germany **8** 50.20N 6.59E
Nure *r.* Italy **9** 45.03N 9.49E
Nürnberg W. Germany **14** 49.27N 11.05E
Nurri, Mt. Australia **47** 31.44S146.04E
Nusa Tenggara *is.* Indonesia **26** 8.30S118.00E
Nusa Tenggara Barat *d.* Indonesia **26** 8.50S117.30E
Nusa Tenggara Timur *d.* Indonesia **27** 9.30S122.00E
Nusaybin Turkey **30** 37.05N 41.11E
Nutak Canada **51** 57.30N 61.59W
Nuuk *see* Godthåb Greenland **51**
Nuwaybi'al Muzayyinah Egypt **32** 28.58N 34.38E
Nuweveldberge *mts.* R.S.A. **39** 32.15S 21.50E
Nuyts, Pt. Australia **43** 35.02S116.32E
Nuyts Archipelago *is.* Australia **45** 32.35S133.17E
Nxaunxau Botswana **39** 18.19S 21.04E
Nyabing Australia **43** 33.32S118.09E
Nyahua Tanzania **37** 5.25S 33.16E
Nyahururu Falls *town* Kenya **37** 0.04N 36.22E
Nyainqêntanglha Shan *mts.* China **24** 30.10N 91.00E
Nyakanazi Tanzania **37** 3.05S 31.16E
Nyaksimvol U.S.S.R. **18** 62.30N 60.52E
Nyala Sudan **35** 12.01N 24.50E
Nyamandhlovu Zimbabwe **39** 19.50S 28.15E
Nyamapanda Zimbabwe **39** 16.59S 32.50E
Nyamtukusa Tanzania **37** 3.03S 32.44E
Nyandoma U.S.S.R. **18** 61.33N 40.05E
Nyanza *d.* Kenya **37** 0.30S 34.30E
Nyanza Rwanda **37** 2.20S 29.42E
Nyashabozh U.S.S.R. **18** 65.28N 53.42E
Nyaunglebin Burma **29** 17.57N 96.44E
Nyborg Denmark **17** 55.19N 10.48E
Nybro Sweden **17** 56.45N 15.54E
Nyda U.S.S.R. **20** 66.35N 72.58E
Nyeri Kenya **37** 0.22S 36.56E
Nyhammar Sweden **17** 60.17N 14.58E
Nyika Plateau *f.* Malaŵi **37** 10.25S 33.50E
Nyimba Zambia **37** 14.33S 30.49E
Nyíregyháza Hungary **15** 47.59N 21.43E
Nyköbing Falster Denmark **17** 54.46N 11.53E
Nyköbing Jylland Denmark **17** 56.48N 8.52E
Nyköbing Sjaelland Denmark **17** 55.55N 11.41E
Nyköping Sweden **17** 58.45N 17.00E
Nylstroom R.S.A. **39** 24.42S 28.24E
Nymagee Australia **47** 32.05S146.20E
Nymboida Australia **47** 29.57S152.32E
Nymboida *r.* Australia **47** 29.39S152.30E
Nymburk Czech. **14** 50.11N 15.03E
Nynäshamn Sweden **17** 58.54N 17.57E
Nyngan Australia **47** 31.34S147.14E
Nyong *r.* Cameroon **38** 3.15N 9.55E
Nyons France **11** 44.22N 5.08E
Nysa Poland **15** 50.29N 17.20E
Nysa Kłodzka *r.* Poland **15** 50.49N 17.50E
Nyssa U.S.A. **54** 43.53N117.00W
Nyuksenitsa U.S.S.R. **18** 60.24N 44.08E
Nyunzu Zaïre **37** 5.55S 28.00E
Nyurba U.S.S.R. **21** 63.18N118.28E
Nzega Tanzania **37** 4.13S 33.09E
N'zérékoré Guinea **34** 7.49N 8.48W
Nzeto Angola **36** 7.13S 12.56E

O

Oahe Resr. U.S.A. 52 45.45N100.20W
Oahu *i.* Hawaii U.S.A. 52 21.30N158.00W
Oakbank Australia 46 33.07S140.33E
Oakesdale U.S.A. 54 47.08N117.15W
Oakey Australia 45 27.26S151.43E
Oak Harbour U.S.A. 54 48.18N122.39W
Oakland Calif. U.S.A. 54 37.47N122.13W
Oakland Oreg. U.S.A. 54 43.25N123.18W
Oaklands Australia 47 35.25S146.15E
Oakley U.S.A. 54 42.15N113.53W
Oakridge U.S.A. 54 43.45N122.28W
Oak Ridge *town* U.S.A. 53 36.02N 84.12W
Oakvale Australia 46 33.01S140.41E
Oakville Canada 55 43.27N 79.41W
Oamaru New Zealand 48 45.07S170.58E
Oates Land *f.* Antarctica 64 70.00S155.00E
Oaxaca Mexico 56 17.05N 96.41W
Oaxaca *d.* Mexico 56 17.30N 97.00W
Ob *r.* U.S.S.R. 18 66.50N 69.00E
Oba Canada 55 49.04N 84.07W
Oban U.K. 6 56.26N 5.28W
Obbia Somali Rep. 35 5.20N 48.30E
Oberá Argentina 62 27.30S 55.07W
Oberhausen W. Germany 8 51.28N 6.51E
Oberösterreich *d.* Austria 14 48.15N 14.00E
Obi *i.* Indonesia 27 1.45S127.30E
Obidos Brazil 61 1.55S 55.31W
Obitsu *r.* Japan 23 35.24N139.54E
Obo C.A.R. 35 5.18N 26.28E
Obodovka U.S.S.R. 15 48.28N 29.10E
Oboyan U.S.S.R. 19 51.13N 36.17E
Obozerskiy U.S.S.R. 18 63.28N 40.29E
Obruk Platosu *f.* Turkey 30 38.00N 33.30E
Obskaya Guba *g.* U.S.S.R. 20 68.30N 74.00E
Ōbu Japan 23 35.00N136.58E
Obuasi Ghana 38 6.15N 1.36W
Obudu Nigeria 38 6.42N 9.07E
Ocala U.S.A. 53 29.11N 82.09W
Ocaña Colombia 60 8.16N 73.21W
Ocaña Spain 10 39.57N 3.30W
Occidental, Cordillera *mts.* Colombia 60 5.00N 76.15W
Occidental, Cordillera *mts.* S. America 62 17.00S 69.00W
Oceanside Calif. U.S.A. 54 33.12N117.23W
Oceanside N.Y. U.S.A. 55 40.38N 73.38W
Ochamchire U.S.S.R. 19 42.44N 41.30E
Ochil Hills U.K. 6 56.16N 3.25W
Ochsenfurt W. Germany 14 49.40N 10.03E
Ockelbo Sweden 17 60.53N 16.43E
Ocotal Nicaragua 57 13.37N 86.31W
Ocotlán Mexico 56 20.21N102.42W
Octeville France 9 49.37N 1.39W
Ocua Mozambique 37 13.40S 39.46E
Oda Ghana 38 5.55N 0.56W
Odádhahraun *mts.* Iceland 16 65.00N 17.30W
Odawara Japan 23 35.15N139.10E
Odda Norway 17 60.04N 6.33E
Ödeborg Sweden 17 58.33N 12.00E
Odemira Portugal 10 37.36N 8.38W
Ödemiş Turkey 13 38.12N 28.00E
Odense Denmark 17 55.24N 10.23E
Odenwald *mts.* W. Germany 14 49.40N 9.20E
Oder *r.* E. Germany *see* Odra *r.* Poland 14
Oderzo Italy 9 45.47N 12.29E
Odessa Tex. U.S.A. 52 31.50N102.23W
Odessa U.S.S.R. 15 46.30N 30.46E
Odorhei Romania 15 46.18N 25.18E
Odra *r.* Poland 14 53.30N 14.36E
Odžak Yugo. 15 45.03N 18.18E
Odzi *r.* Zimbabwe 39 19.46S 32.22E
Oegstgeest Neth. 8 52.12N 4.31E
Oeiras Brazil 61 7.00S 42.07W
Oenpelli Australia 44 12.20S133.04E
Ofanto *r.* Italy 12 41.22N 16.12E
Ofaqim Israel 32 31.19N 34.37E
Offa Nigeria 38 8.09N 4.44E
Offaly *d.* Rep. of Ire. 7 53.15N 7.30W
Offenbach W. Germany 14 50.06N 8.46E
Offenburg W. Germany 14 48.29N 7.57E
Offerdal Sweden 16 63.28N 14.03E
Offranville France 9 49.52N 1.03E
Ofir Portugal 10 41.31N 8.47W
Ofotfjorden *est.* Norway 16 68.25N 17.00E
Ōgaki Japan 23 35.21N136.37E
Ogbomosho Nigeria 38 8.05N 4.11E
Ogden Utah U.S.A. 54 41.14N111.58W
Ogeechee *r.* U.S.A. 53 32.54N 81.05W
Ogilvie Mts. Canada 50 65.00N139.30W
Oginskiy, Kanal *canal* U.S.S.R. 15 52.25N 25.55E
Oglio *r.* Italy 9 45.02N 10.39E
Ognon *r.* France 11 47.20N 5.37E
Ogoja Nigeria 38 6.40N 8.45E
Ogoki *r.* Canada 55 51.38N 85.57W
Ogoki Resr. Canada 55 50.50N 88.26W
Ogooué *r.* Gabon 36 1.00S 9.05E
Ogosta *r.* Bulgaria 13 43.44N 23.51E
Ogulin Yugo. 14 45.17N 15.14E
Ogun *d.* Nigeria 38 6.50N 3.20E
Ohai New Zealand 48 45.56S167.57E
Ohanet Algeria 34 28.45N 8.55E
Ohey Belgium 8 50.26N 5.06E
O'Higgins, L. Chile 63 48.03S 73.10W
Ohio *d.* U.S.A. 55 40.15N 82.45W
Ohio *r.* U.S.A. 55 36.59N 89.08W
Ōhito Japan 23 34.59N138.56E
Ohře *r.* Czech. 14 50.32N 14.08E
Ohrid Yugo. 13 41.06N 20.48E
Ohrid, L. Albania / Yugo. 13 41.00N 20.43E
Ōi *r.* Japan 23 34.45N138.18E
Oil City U.S.A. 55 41.26N 79.42W
Oise *d.* France 9 49.30N 2.30E
Oise *r.* France 9 49.00N 2.10E
Oisterwijk Neth. 8 51.34N 5.10E
Ojai U.S.A. 54 34.27N119.15W
Ojocaliente Mexico 56 22.35N102.18W
Ojo de Agua Argentina 62 29.30S 63.44W
Ojos del Salado *mtn.* Argentina / Chile 62 27.05S 68.05W
Oka Nigeria 38 7.28N 5.48E
Oka *r.* U.S.S.R. 18 56.09N 43.00E
Okaba Indonesia 27 8.06S139.46E
Okahandja Namibia 39 21.58S 16.44E
Okanogan U.S.A. 54 48.39N120.41W
Okanogan *r.* U.S.A. 52 48.22N119.35W
Okaputa Namibia 39 20.08S 16.58E
Okarito New Zealand 48 43.14S.170.07
Okaukuejo Namibia 39 19.12S 15.56E
Okavango *r.* Botswana 39 18.30S 22.04E
Okavango Basin *f.* Botswana 39 19.30S 22.30E
Okayama Japan 25 34.40N133.54E
Okazaki Japan 23 34.57N137.10E
Okeechobee, L. U.S.A. 53 27.00N 80.45W
Okefenokee Swamp *f.* U.S.A. 53 30.40N 82.40W
Okehampton U.K. 5 50.44N 4.01W
Okere *r.* Uganda 37 1.37N 33.53E
Okha U.S.S.R. 21 53.35N142.50E
Okhansk U.S.S.R. 18 57.42N 55.20E
Okhotsk U.S.S.R. 21 59.20N143.15E
Okhotsk, Sea of U.S.S.R. 21 55.00N150.00E
Okhotskiy Perevoz U.S.S.R. 21 61.55N135.40E
Okiep R.S.A. 39 29.36S 17.49E
Oki guntō *is.* Japan 25 36.30N133.20E
Okinawa jima *i.* Japan 25 26.30N128.00E
Okino Torishima *i.* Pacific Oc. 27 20.24N136.02E
Okipoko *r.* Namibia 39 18.40S 16.03E
Okitipupa Nigeria 38 6.31N 4.50E
Oklahoma *d.* U.S.A. 53 35.00N 97.00W
Oklahoma City U.S.A. 53 35.28N 97.33W
Oknitsa U.S.S.R. 15 48.22N 27.30E
Okola Cameroon 38 4.03N 11.23E
Oksskolten *mtn.* Norway 16 65.59N 14.15E
Oktyabr'sk U.S.S.R. 19 49.30N 57.22E
Oktyabrskiy B.S.S.R. U.S.S.R. 15 52.35N 28.45E
Oktyabrskiy R.S.F.S.R. U.S.S.R. 18 54.30N 53.30E
Oktyabr'skoy Revolyutsii, Ostrov *i.* U.S.S.R. 21 79.30N 96.00E
Okuru New Zealand 48 43.56S168.55E
Okuta Nigeria 38 9.13N 3.12E
Ólafsvík Iceland 16 64.53N 23.44W
Olancha U.S.A. 54 36.17N118.01W
Öland *i.* Sweden 17 56.45N 16.38E
Olary Australia 46 32.18S140.19E
Olascoaga Argentina 63 35.14S 60.37W
Olavarría Argentina 63 36.57S 60.20W
Oława Poland 15 50.57N 17.17E
Olbia Italy 12 40.55N 9.29E
Old Crow Canada 50 67.34N139.43W
Oldenburg Nschn. W. Germany 8 53.08N 8.13E
Oldenburg Sch.-Hol. W. Germany 14 54.17N 10.52E
Oldenzaal Neth. 8 52.19N 6.55E
Old Forge Penn. U.S.A. 55 41.22N 75.44W
Old Gumbiro Tanzania 37 10.00S 35.24E
Oldham U.K. 4 53.33N 2.08W
Old Head of Kinsale *c.* Rep. of Ire. 7 51.37N 8.33W
Old Town U.S.A. 55 44.56N 68.39W
Olean U.S.A. 55 42.05N 78.26W
Olecko Poland 15 54.03N 22.30E
Olekma *r.* U.S.S.R. 21 60.20N120.30E
Olekminsk U.S.S.R. 21 60.25N120.00E
Olema U.S.S.R. 18 64.25N 40.15E
Olenëk U.S.S.R. 21 68.38N112.15E
Olenëk *r.* U.S.S.R. 21 73.00N120.00E
Olenëkskiy Zaliv *g.* U.S.S.R. 21 74.00N120.00E
Oléron, Île d' *i.* France 11 45.55N 1.16W
Oleśnica Poland 15 51.13N 17.23E
Olevsk U.S.S.R. 15 51.12N 27.35E
Olga U.S.S.R. 25 43.46N135.14E
Olga L. Canada 55 49.37N 77.26W
Ölgiy Mongolia 24 48.54N 90.00E
Olgopol U.S.S.R. 15 48.10N 29.30E
Olhão Portugal 10 37.01N 7.50W
Olifants *r.* Namibia 39 25.28S 19.23E
Olifants *r.* C.P. R.S.A. 39 31.42S 18.10E
Olifants *r.* Trans. R.S.A. 39 24.08S 32.39E
Ólimbos *mtn.* Cyprus 32 34.55N 32.52E
Ólimbos Greece 13 35.44N 27.11E
Ólimbos *mtn.* Greece 13 40.04N 22.20E
Olinda Brazil 61 8.00S 34.51W
Oliva Argentina 62 32.05S 63.35W
Oliva Spain 10 38.58N 0.15W
Olivares Spain 10 39.45N 2.21W
Oliveira Brazil 59 20.39S 44.47W
Olivenza Spain 10 38.41N 7.09W
Olney U.K. 5 52.09N 0.42W
Olofström Sweden 17 56.16N 14.30E
Olomouc Czech. 15 49.36N 17.16E
Olonets U.S.S.R. 18 61.00N 32.59E
Oloron France 11 43.12N 0.35W
Olot Spain 10 42.11N 2.30E
Olovyannaya U.S.S.R. 25 50.58N115.35E
Olpe W. Germany 8 51.02N 7.52E
Olsztyn Poland 15 53.48N 20.29E
Olsztynek Poland 15 53.36N 20.17E
Olt *r.* Romania 15 43.43N 24.51E
Oltenița Romania 15 44.05N 26.31E
Olteț *r.* Romania 15 44.13N 24.28E
Olympia U.S.A. 54 47.03N122.53W
Olympic Mts. U.S.A. 54 47.50N123.45W
Olympic Nat. Park U.S.A. 54 47.48N123.30W
Olympus *mtn. see* Ólimbos *mtn.* Greece 13
Olympus, Mt. U.S.A. 54 47.48N123.43W
Omae-zaki *c.* Japan 23 34.36N138.14E
Omagh U.K. 7 54.36N 7.20W
Omaha U.S.A. 53 41.15N 96.00W
Oman Asia 28 22.30N 57.30E
Oman, G. of Asia 31 25.00N 58.00E
Omarama New Zealand 48 44.29S169.58E
Omaruru Namibia 39 21.25S 15.57E
Omate Peru 62 16.40S 70.58W
Ombrone *r.* Italy 12 42.40N 11.00E
Omdurman *see* Umm Durmān Sudan 35
Omegna Italy 9 45.53N 8.24E
Ometepec Mexico 56 16.41N 98.25W
Ōmi-hachiman Japan 23 35.08N136.06E
Omitara Namibia 39 22.18S 18.01E
Ōmiya Japan 23 35.54N139.38E
Ommen Neth. 8 52.32N 6.25E
Omolon *r.* U.S.S.R. 21 68.50N158.30E
Omsk U.S.S.R. 20 55.00N 73.22E
Omulew *r.* Poland 15 53.05N 21.32E
Omuramba Omatako *r.* Namibia 39 18.19S 19.52E
Omuta Japan 25 33.02N130.26E
Oña Spain 10 42.44N 3.25W
Onda Spain 10 39.58N 0.16W
Ondangua Namibia 39 17.59S 16.02E
Ondo *d.* Nigeria 38 7.10N 5.20E
Onega U.S.S.R. 18 63.57N 38.11E
Onega *r.* U.S.S.R. 18 63.59N 38.11E
Oneida U.S.A. 55 43.06N 75.39W
Onezhskaya Guba *b.* U.S.S.R. 18 63.55N 37.30E
Onezhskoye Ozero *l.* U.S.S.R. 18 62.00N 35.30E
Ongerup Australia 43 33.58S118.29E
Ongole India 29 15.31N 80.04E
Onitsha Nigeria 38 6.10N 6.47E
Onjiva Angola 36 17.03S 15.41E
Onslow Australia 42 21.41S115.12E
Onstwedde Neth. 8 53.04N 7.02E
Ontario *d.* Canada 51 52.00N 86.00W
Ontario Calif. U.S.A. 54 34.04N117.39W
Ontario Oreg. U.S.A. 54 44.02N116.58W
Ontario, L. Canada / U.S.A. 55 43.45N 78.00W
Ontonagon U.S.A. 55 46.52N 89.18W
Oodnadatta Australia 45 27.30S135.27E
Ooldea Australia 45 30.27S131.50E
Oostelijk-Flevoland *f.* Neth. 8 52.30N 5.40E
Oostende Belgium 8 51.13N 2.55E
Oosterhout Neth. 8 51.38N 4.50E
Oosterschelde *est.* Neth. 8 51.35N 3.57E
Oosthuizen Neth. 8 52.33N 5.00E
Oostmalle Belgium 8 51.18N 4.45E
Oost Vlaanderen *d.* Belgium 8 51.00N 3.45E
Oost Vlieland Neth. 8 53.18N 5.04E
Opaka Bulgaria 13 43.28N 26.10E
Opala U.S.S.R. 21 51.58N156.30E
Oparino U.S.S.R. 18 59.53N 48.10E
Opasatika Canada 55 49.32N 82.53W
Opasatika *r.* Canada 55 50.23N 82.26W
Opava Czech. 15 49.56N 17.54E
Opochka U.S.S.R. 18 56.41N 28.42E
Opole Poland 15 50.40N 17.56E
Oporto *see* Porto Portugal 10
Opotiki New Zealand 48 38.00S177.18E
Oppdal Norway 16 62.36N 9.41E
Oppland *d.* Norway 17 61.30N 9.00E
Opportunity U.S.A. 54 47.39N117.15W
Opthalmia Range *mts.* Australia 42 23.25S120.00E
Opunake New Zealand 48 39.27S173.51E
Ora Italy 9 46.21N 11.18E
Ora Banda Australia 43 30.27S121.04E
Oradea Romania 15 47.03N 21.55E
Öraefajökull *mtn.* Iceland 16 64.02N 16.39W
Orai India 29 26.00N 79.26E
Oran Algeria 34 35.45N 0.38W
Orán Argentina 62 23.07S 64.16W
Orange Australia 47 33.19S149.10E
Orange France 11 44.08N 4.48E
Orange *r.* R.S.A. 39 28.38S 16.38E
Orange Tex. U.S.A. 53 30.05N 93.43W
Orange, C. Brazil 61 4.25N 51.32W
Orangeburg U.S.A. 53 33.28N 80.53W
Orange Free State *d.* R.S.A. 39 28.00S 28.00E
Orangevale U.S.A. 54 38.41N121.13W
Oranienburg E. Germany 14 52.45N 13.14E
Oranjefontein R.S.A. 39 23.27S 27.40E
Oranjemond Namibia 39 28.35S 16.26E
Oras Phil. 27 12.09N125.22E
Orbetello Italy 12 42.27N 11.13E
Orbost Australia 47 37.42S148.30E
Örbyhus Sweden 17 60.14N 17.42E
Orchies France 8 50.28N 3.15E
Orchila *i.* Venezuela 57 11.52N 66.10W
Orco *r.* Italy 9 45.10N 7.52E
Ord *r.* Australia 42 15.30S128.30E
Ordu Turkey 30 41.00N 37.52E
Orduña Spain 10 43.00N 3.00W
Ordzhonikidze U.S.S.R. 19 43.02N 44.43E
Örebro Sweden 17 59.17N 15.13E
Örebro *d.* Sweden 17 59.30N 15.00E
Oregon *d.* U.S.A. 54 43.49N120.36W
Oregon City U.S.A. 54 45.21N122.36W
Öregrund Sweden 17 60.20N 18.26E
Orekhovo-Zuyevo U.S.S.R. 18 55.47N 39.00E
Orel U.S.S.R. 18 52.58N 36.04E
Orem U.S.A. 54 40.19N111.42W
Orenburg U.S.S.R. 18 51.50N 55.00E
Orense Spain 10 42.20N 7.52W
Oressa *r.* U.S.S.R. 15 52.33N 28.45E
Orestiás Greece 13 41.30N 26.33E
Orfanoú, Kólpos *g.* Greece 13 40.40N 24.00E
Orford U.S.A. 55 43.54N 72.10W
Orfordness *c.* Australia 44 11.22S142.50E
Orford Ness *c.* U.K. 5 52.05N 1.36E
Orgeyev U.S.S.R. 15 47.24N 28.50E
Orick U.S.A. 54 41.17N124.04W
Orient Australia 46 28.10S142.50E
Oriental, Cordillera *mts.* Bolivia 62 17.00S 65.00W
Oriental, Cordillera *mts.* Colombia 60 5.00N 74.30W
Origny France 9 49.54N 3.30E
Orihuela Spain 10 38.05N 0.56W
Orillia Canada 55 44.37N 79.25W
Orimattila Finland 17 60.48N 25.45E
Orinduik Guyana 60 4.42N 60.01W
Orinoco *r.* Venezuela 60 9.00N 61.30W
Orinoco, Delta del *f.* Venezuela 60 9.00N 61.00W
Orissa *d.* India 29 20.15N 84.00E
Oristano Italy 12 39.53N 8.36E
Oristano, Golfo di *g.* Italy 12 39.50N 8.30E
Orizaba Mexico 56 18.51N 97.08W
Orkanger Norway 16 63.17N 9.52E
Orkney Is. *d.* U.K. 6 59.00N 3.00W
Orlândia Brazil 59 20.55S 47.54W
Orlando U.S.A. 53 28.33N 81.21W
Orléans France 9 47.54N 1.54E
Orléans, Canal d' France 9 47.54N 1.55E
Ormāra Pakistan 28 25.12N 64.38E
Ormoc Phil. 27 11.00N124.37E
Ormond New Zealand 48 38.35S177.58E
Ormskirk U.K. 4 53.35N 2.53W
Orne *d.* France 9 48.40N 0.05E
Orne *r.* France 9 49.17N 0.10W
Örnsköldsvik Sweden 16 63.17N 18.50E
Orobie, Alpi *mts.* Italy 9 46.03N 10.00E
Orocué Colombia 60 4.48N 71.20W
Orodara Burkina Faso 38 11.00N 4.54W
Oromocto Canada 55 45.50N 66.28W
Oron Israel 32 30.55N 35.01E
Oron Nigeria 38 4.49N 8.15E
Orono U.S.A. 55 44.53N 68.40W
Orosei Italy 12 40.23N 9.40E
Orosei, Golfo di *g.* Italy 12 40.15N 9.45E
Orosháza Hungary 15 46.34N 20.40E
Orotukan U.S.S.R. 21 62.16N151.43E
Oroville Calif. U.S.A. 54 39.31N121.33W
Oroville Wash. U.S.A. 54 48.56N119.26W
Orroroo Australia 46 32.46S138.39E
Orsa Sweden 17 61.07N 14.37E
Orsha U.S.S.R. 18 54.30N 30.23E
Orsières Switz. 9 46.02N 7.09E
Orsk U.S.S.R. 18 51.13N 58.35E
Orşova Romania 15 44.42N 22.22E
Orta Nova Italy 12 41.19N 15.42E
Orthez France 11 43.29N 0.46W
Ortigueira Spain 10 43.41N 7.51W
Ortona Italy 12 42.21N 14.24E
Oruro Bolivia 62 17.59S 67.09W
Oruro *d.* Bolivia 62 18.00S 72.30W
Oryakhovo Bulgaria 13 43.42N 23.58E
Orzinuovi Italy 9 45.24N 9.55E
Os Norway 16 62.31N 11.11E
Osa, Península de *pen.* Costa Rica 57 8.20N 83.30W
Osage *r.* U.S.A. 53 38.35N 91.57W
Ōsaka Japan 23 34.40N135.30E
Ōsaka *d.* Japan 23 34.24N135.25E
Ōsaka-wan *b.* Japan 23 34.30N135.18E
Osby Sweden 17 56.22N 13.59E
Osen Norway 16 64.18N 10.32E
Osh U.S.S.R. 20 40.37N 72.49E
Oshawa Canada 55 43.54N 78.51W
Ō shima *i.* Tosan Japan 23 34.43N139.24E
Oshmyany U.S.S.R. 15 54.22N 25.52E
Oshnovīyeh Iran 31 37.03N 45.05E
Oshogbo Nigeria 38 7.50N 4.35E
Oshtorān, Kūh *mtn.* Iran 31 33.18N 49.15E
Oshvor U.S.S.R. 18 66.59N 62.59E
Osijek Yugo. 13 45.35N 18.43E
Osipovichi U.S.S.R. 15 53.19N 28.36E
Oskarshamn Sweden 17 57.16N 16.26E
Oskol *r.* U.S.S.R. 19 49.08N 37.10E
Oslo Norway 17 59.56N 10.45E
Oslofjorden *est.* Norway 17 59.20N 10.35E
Osmancik Turkey 30 40.58N 34.50E
Osmaniye Turkey 30 37.04N 36.15E
Osnabrück W. Germany 8 52.17N 8.03E
Osorno Chile 63 40.35S 73.14W
Osorno Spain 10 42.24N 4.22W
Osöyra Norway 17 60.11N 5.30E
Osprey Reef Australia 44 13.55S146.38E
Oss Neth. 8 51.46N 5.31E
Ossa *mtn.* Greece 13 39.47N 22.41E
Ossa, Mt. Australia 45 41.52S146.04E
Osse *r.* Nigeria 38 5.55N 5.15E
Ostashkov U.S.S.R. 18 57.09N 33.10E
Ost-Berlin *d.* E. Germany 14 52.30N 13.25E
Ostend *see* Oostende Belgium 8
Oster U.S.S.R. 15 50.55N 30.53E
Oster *r.* U.S.S.R. 15 53.47N 31.46E
Österdal *r.* Sweden 17 61.03N 14.30E
Österdalen *f.* Norway 17 61.15N 11.10E
Östergötland *d.* Sweden 17 58.25N 15.35E
Österö *i.* Faroe Is. 16 62.10N 7.00W
Osteröy *i.* Norway 17 60.33N 5.35E
Östersund Sweden 16 63.10N 14.40E
Östfold *d.* Norway 17 59.20N 11.10E
Ostfriesische Inseln *is.* W. Germany 8 53.45N 7.00E
Östhammar Sweden 17 60.16N 18.22E
Ostrava Czech. 15 49.50N 18.15E
Ostróda Poland 15 53.43N 19.59E
Ostrog U.S.S.R. 15 50.20N 26.29E
Ostrołeka Poland 15 53.06N 21.34E
Ostrov U.S.S.R. 18 57.22N 28.22E
Ostrowiec-Świetokrzyski Poland 15 50.57N 21.23E
Ostrów Mazowiecka Poland 15 52.50N 21.51E
Ostrów Wielkopolski Poland 15 51.39N 17.49E
Ostuni Italy 13 40.44N 17.35E
Osŭm *r.* Bulgaria 13 43.41N 24.51E
Ōsumi shotō *is.* Japan 25 30.30N131.00E
Osuna Spain 10 37.14N 5.06W
Oswego U.S.A. 55 43.27N 76.31W
Oswestry U.K. 4 52.52N 3.03W
Otago *d.* New Zealand 48 45.10S169.20E
Otago Pen. New Zealand 48 45.48S170.45E
Otaki New Zealand 48 40.45S175.08E
Otaru Japan 25 43.14N140.59E
Otavalo Ecuador 60 0.14N 78.16W
Otavi Namibia 39 19.37S 17.21E
Otelec Romania 15 45.36N 20.50E
Otematata New Zealand 48 44.37S170.11E
Oti *r.* Ghana 38 8.43N 0.10E
Otira New Zealand 48 42.51S171.33E
Otiwarongo Namibia 39 20.30S 16.39E
Otjiwarongo Namibia 36 20.29S 16.36E
Otjiwero Namibia 39 17.59S 13.22E
Otju Namibia 39 18.15S 13.18E
Otočac Yugo. 14 44.52N 15.14E
Otra *r.* Norway 17 58.09N 8.00E
Otradnyy U.S.S.R. 18 53.26N 51.30E
Otranto Italy 13 40.09N 18.30E
Otranto, Str. of Med. Sea 13 40.10N 19.00E
Otrokovice Czech. 15 49.13N 17.31E
Otsego U.S.A. 55 42.26N 85.42W
Otsego Lake *town* U.S.A. 55 44.55N 84.41W
Ōtsu Japan 23 35.02N135.52E
Ōtsuki Japan 23 35.36N138.57E
Otta Norway 17 61.46N 9.32E
Ottawa Canada 55 45.25N 75.43W
Ottawa *r.* Canada 55 45.20N 73.58W
Ottawa Kans. U.S.A. 53 38.35N 95.16W
Ottawa Is. Canada 51 59.50N 80.00W
Otter *r.* U.K. 5 50.38N 3.19W
Otterbäcken Sweden 17 58.57N 14.02E
Otterburn U.K. 4 55.14N 2.10W
Otterndorf W. Germany 14 53.48N 8.53E
Otteröy *i.* Norway 16 62.45N 6.50E
Ottosdal R.S.A. 39 26.48S 26.00E
Ottumwa U.S.A. 53 41.02N 92.26W
Oturkpo Nigeria 38 7.13N 8.10E
Otway, C. Australia 46 38.51S143.34E
Ouachita *r.* U.S.A. 53 33.10N 92.10W
Ouachita Mts. U.S.A. 53 34.40N 94.30W
Ouadda C.A.R. 35 8.04N 22.24E
Ouagadougou Burkina Faso 38 12.20N 1.40W
Ouahigouya Burkina Faso 38 13.31N 2.21W
Ouallam Niger 38 14.23N 2.09E
Ouallene Algeria 34 24.37N 1.14E
Ouargla Algeria 34 32.00N 5.16E
Ouarzazate Morocco 34 30.57N 6.50W
Ouassouas *well* Mali 38 16.01N 1.26E
Ouddorp Neth. 8 51.49N 3.57E
Oudenaarde Belgium 8 50.50N 3.37E
Oudenbosch Neth. 8 51.35N 4.30E
Oude Rijn *r.* Neth. 8 52.14N 4.26E
Oudon *r.* France 9 47.47N 1.02W
Oudtshoorn R.S.A. 39 33.35S 22.11E
Ouellé Ivory Coast 38 7.26N 4.01W
Ouessant, Île d' *i.* France 11 48.28N 5.05W
Ouezzane Morocco 34 34.52N 5.35W
Oughter, Lough Rep. of Ire. 7 54.01N 7.28W
Ouimet Canada 55 48.43N 88.35W
Ouistreham France 9 49.17N 0.15W
Oujda Morocco 34 34.41N 1.45W
Oulu Finland 16 65.01N 25.28E
Oulu *d.* Finland 16 65.00N 27.00E
Oulu *r.* Finland 16 65.01N 25.25E
Oulujärvi *l.* Finland 16 64.20N 27.15E
Oum Chalouba Chad 35 15.48N 20.46E
Oumé Ivory Coast 38 6.25N 5.23W
Ounas *r.* Finland 16 66.30N 25.45E
Oundle U.K. 5 52.28N 0.28W
Our *r.* Lux. 8 49.53N 6.16E
Ouray U.S.A. 54 40.06N109.40W
Ourcq *r.* France 9 49.01N 3.01E
Ourinhos Brazil 59 23.00S 49.54W
Ouro Fino Brazil 59 22.16S 46.25W
Ouro Prêto Brazil 59 20.54S 43.30W
Ourthe *r.* Belgium 8 50.38N 5.36E
Ouse *r.* Humber. U.K. 4 53.41N 0.42W
Outardes, Rivière aux *r.* Canada 55 49.04N 68.25W
Outer Hebrides *is.* U.K. 6 57.40N 7.35W
Outjo Namibia 39 20.07S 16.10E
Ouyen Australia 46 35.06S142.22E
Ouzouer-le-Marché France 9 47.55N 1.32E
Ovalle Chile 62 30.36S 71.12W
Ovamboland *f.* Namibia 39 17.45S 16.00E
Ovar Portugal 10 40.52N 8.38W
Ovens *r.* Australia 47 36.20S146.18E
Overath W. Germany 8 50.56N 7.18E
Overflakkee *i.* Neth. 8 51.45N 4.08E
Overijssel *d.* Neth. 8 52.25N 6.30E
Överkalix Sweden 16 66.21N 22.56E
Overton U.S.A. 54 36.33N114.27W
Övertorneå Sweden 16 66.23N 23.40E
Ovidiopol U.S.S.R. 15 46.18N 30.28E
Oviedo Spain 10 43.21N 5.50W
Ovinishche U.S.S.R. 18 58.20N 37.00E
Ovruch U.S.S.R. 15 51.20N 28.50E
Owaka New Zealand 48 46.27S169.40E
Owando Congo 36 0.30S 15.48E
Owel, Lough Rep. of Ire. 7 53.34N 7.24W
Owen Falls Dam Uganda 37 0.30N 33.07E
Owensboro U.S.A. 53 37.45N 87.05W
Owens L. U.S.A. 54 36.25N117.56W
Owen Sound *town* Canada 55 44.34N 80.56W
Owen Stanley Range *mts.* P.N.G. 44 9.30S148.00E
Owerri Nigeria 38 5.29N 7.02E
Owo Nigeria 38 7.10N 5.39E
Owosso U.S.A. 55 43.00N 84.11W
Owyhee *r.* U.S.A. 54 43.46N117.02W
Oxelösund Sweden 17 58.40N 17.06E
Oxford U.K. 5 51.45N 1.15W
Oxfordshire *d.* U.K. 5 51.46N 1.10W
Oxley Australia 46 34.11S144.10E
Oxnard U.S.A. 54 34.12N119.11W
Oyapock *r.* Guiana 61 4.10N 51.40W
Oyem Gabon 36 1.34N 11.31E
Öyer Norway 17 61.12N 10.22E
Öyeren *l.* Norway 17 59.48N 11.14E
Oykel *r.* U.K. 6 57.53N 4.21W
Oymyakon U.S.S.R. 21 63.30N142.44E
Oyo Nigeria 38 7.50N 3.55E
Oyo *d.* Nigeria 38 8.10N 3.40E
Oyonnax France 11 46.15N 5.40E
Ozamiz Phil. 27 8.09N123.59E
Ozarichi U.S.S.R. 15 52.28N 29.12E
Ozark Plateau U.S.A. 53 36.00N 93.35W
Özd Hungary 15 48.14N 20.18E
Ozernoye U.S.S.R. 18 51.45N 51.29E
Ozersk U.S.S.R. 15 54.26N 22.00E
Ozinki U.S.S.R. 19 51.11N 49.43E

niut see Frederikshåb Greenland 51
l R.S.A. 39 33.44S 18.58E
ianice Poland 15 51.40N 19.22E
na Bangla. 29 24.00N 89.15E
araima, Sierra mts. Venezuela 60 4.00N 30W
asmayo Peru 60 7.27S 79.33W
nuca Mexico 56 20.10N 98.44W
kwood U.S.A. 54 46.36N 121.40W
y-sur-Eure France 9 49.01N 1.23E
ang Indonesia 26 0.55S 100.21E
angpanjang Indonesia 26 0.30S 100.26E
angsidempuan Indonesia 26 1.20N 99.11E
any U.S.S.R. 18 63.12N 33.20E
auari r. Brazil 60 0.15S 64.05W
erborn W. Germany 14 51.43N 8.44E
illa Bolivia 62 19.19S 64.20W
lei Canada 51 62.00N 96.50W
loping Island town Canada 51 67.00N .50W
ova Italy 9 45.27N 11.52E
re I. U.S.A. 53 27.00N 97.20W
stow U.K. 5 50.33N 4.57W
thaway Australia 46 36.37S 140.28E
ua see Padova Italy 9
ucah U.S.A. 53 37.03N 88.36W
roa New Zealand 48 37.23S 175.41E
iri Mozambique 39 22.27S 31.21E
i. Yugo. 14 44.28N 15.00E
adian Phil. 27 7.50N 123.30E
ai Selatan i. Indonesia 26 3.00S 100.18E
ai Utara i. Indonesia 26 2.42S 100.05E
an i. Mariana Is. 27 18.08N 145.46E
e U.S.A. 54 36.57N 111.27W
er r. Uganda 37 3.05N 32.28E
wa River town Canada 55 50.02N 85.14W
ala Hawaii U.S.A. 52 19.12N 155.28W
iatua New Zealand 48 40.26S 175.49E
lavi Dezh Iran 31 35.51N 46.02E
ole U.K. 6 57.35N 7.27W
de U.S.S.R. 17 58.54N 25.33E
nia New Zealand 48 35.16S 174.05E
änne l. Finland 17 61.35N 25.30E
nboeuf France 11 47.14N 2.01W
nan Indonesia 26 1.21S 100.34E
nesville U.S.A. 55 41.43N 81.15W
ns Brazil 59 20.23S 45.38W
sley U.K. 6 55.50N 4.26W
ala Sweden 16 67.11N 23.22E
ule Uganda 37 2.58N 32.53E
anbaru Indonesia 26 0.33N 101.20E
karaima Mts. Guyana 60 5.00N 60.00W
ki Nigeria 38 11.33N 8.08E
kistan Asia 28 30.00N 70.00E
ks Hungary 15 46.39N 18.53E
kwach Uganda 37 2.27N 31.18E
kxé Laos 26 15.05N 105.50E
a Chad 38 9.25N 15.05E
aiokhóra Greece 13 35.14N 23.41E
aiseau France 9 48.43N 2.15E
amós Spain 10 41.51N 3.08E
ana U.S.S.R. 21 59.05N 159.59E
angkaraya Indonesia 26 2.16S 113.56E
anguinos Spain 10 42.27N 5.31W
anpur India 28 24.10N 72.26E
apye Botswana 39 22.33S 27.07E
awan i. Phil. 26 9.30N 118.30E
diski U.S.S.R. 17 59.20N 24.06E
eleh Indonesia 27 1.04N 121.57E
embang Indonesia 26 2.59S 104.50E
encia Spain 10 42.01N 4.34W
enque Mexico 56 17.32N 91.59W
ermo Italy 12 38.09N 13.22E
imé Togo 38 6.55N 0.38E
isades Resr. U.S.A. 54 43.15N 111.05W
it, Kep-i- c. Albania 13 41.24N 19.23E
izada Mexico 56 18.15N 92.05W
k Str. India / Sri Lanka 29 10.00N 79.40E
linup r. Australia 43 34.29S 118.54E
liser, C. New Zealand 48 41.35S 175.15E
ma Mozambique 37 10.48S 40.25E
ma Spain 10 39.36N 2.39E
ma, Bahía de b. Spain 10 39.30N 2.40E
ma del Río Spain 10 37.43N 5.17W
manova Italy 9 45.54N 13.19E
mares Brazil 61 8.41S 35.36W
mas, C. Liberia 34 4.30N 7.55W
mas, Golfo di g. Italy 12 39.00N 8.30E
meira dos Indios Brazil 61 9.25S 36.38W
mer r. Australia 42 24.46S 133.25E
lmer U.S.A. 50 61.36N 149.07W
mer Land Antarctica 64 74.00S 61.00W
lmerston New Zealand 48 45.29S 170.43E
merston, C. Australia 44 21.32S 149.29E
merston North New Zealand 48 0.20S 175.39E
mi Italy 12 38.22N 15.50E
lmira Colombia 60 3.33N 76.17W
lm Is. Australia 44 18.48S 146.37E
lms U.S.A. 55 43.37N 82.46W
lm Springs town U.S.A. 54 33.50N 116.33W
lmyras Pt. India 29 20.40N 87.00E
loh Indonesia 26 1.46N 109.17E
lojoensuu Finland 16 68.17N 23.05E
lomani mtn. Bolivia 62 14.38S 69.14W
lopo Indonesia 27 3.01S 120.12E
lu Turkey 30 38.43N 39.56E
ma Burkina Faso 38 11.15N 0.44E
mekasan Indonesia 26 7.11S 113.50E
miers France 11 43.07N 1.36E
mir mts. U.S.S.R. 24 37.50N 73.30E
mpa U.S.A. 52 35.32N 100.58W
mpas f. Argentina 63 34.00S 64.00W
mplona Colombia 60 7.24N 72.38W
mplona Spain 10 42.49N 1.39W
naca U.S.A. 54 37.47N 114.23W
Panaji India 28 15.29N 73.50E
Panama C. America 57 9.00N 80.00W
Panamá town Panama 57 8.57N 79.30W
Panama Sri Lanka 29 6.46N 81.47E
Panamá, Golfo de g. Panama 57 8.30N 79.00W
Panama City U.S.A. 53 30.10N 85.41W
Panamint Range mts. U.S.A. 54 36.30N 117.20W
Panaro r. Italy 9 44.55N 11.25E
Panay i. Phil. 27 11.10N 122.30E
Pandan Phil. 27 11.45N 122.10E
Pando d. Bolivia 62 11.20S 67.40W
Pando Uruguay 63 34.43S 55.57W
Panevežys U.S.S.R. 17 55.44N 24.21E
Panfilov U.S.S.R. 24 44.10N 80.01E
Panga Zaïre 36 1.51N 26.25E
Pangani Tanga Tanzania 37 5.21S 39.00E
Pangkalpinang Indonesia 26 2.05S 106.09E
Pang Long Burma 29 23.11N 98.45E
Pangnirtung Canada 51 66.05N 65.45W
Pankshin Nigeria 38 9.22N 9.25E
Páno Lévkara Cyprus 32 34.55N 33.10E
Páno Plátres Cyprus 32 34.53N 32.52E
Pantano del Esla l. Spain 10 41.40N 5.50W
Pantelleria i. Italy 12 36.48N 12.00E
Pánuco Mexico 56 22.03N 98.10W
Paola Italy 12 39.21N 16.03E
Pápa Hungary 15 47.19N 17.28E
Papeete Tahiti 40 17.32S 149.34W
Papenburg W. Germany 8 53.05N 7.25E
Paphos see Néa Páfos Cyprus 32
Papua, G. of P.N.G. 44 8.30S 145.00E
Papua New Guinea Austa. 41 6.00S 144.00E
Papun Burma 29 18.05N 97.26E
Para d. Brazil 61 4.00S 53.00W
Paracatu Brazil 59 17.14S 46.52W
Paracatu r. Brazil 59 16.30S 45.10W
Paracel Is. S. China Sea 26 16.20N 112.00E
Parachilna Australia 46 31.09S 138.24E
Paraćin Yugo. 15 43.52N 21.24E
Pará de Minas Brazil 59 19.53S 44.35W
Paradise Calif. U.S.A. 54 39.46N 121.37W
Paradise Nev. U.S.A. 54 36.09N 115.10W
Paragonah U.S.A. 54 37.53N 112.46W
Paragua r. Venezuela 60 6.55N 62.55W
Paraguaçu r. Brazil 61 12.35S 38.59W
Paraguaná, Península de pen. Venezuela 60 11.50N 69.59W
Paraguarí Paraguay 59 25.36S 57.06W
Paraguay r. Argentina 59 27.30S 58.50W
Paraguay S. America 59 23.00S 57.00W
Paraiba d. Brazil 61 7.30S 36.30W
Paraíba r. Brazil 59 21.45S 41.10W
Paraibuna Brazil 59 23.29S 45.32W
Paraisópolis Brazil 59 22.33S 45.48W
Parakou Benin 38 9.23N 2.40E
Paramagudi India 29 9.33N 78.36E
Paramaribo Surinam 61 5.52N 55.14W
Paramonga Peru 60 10.42S 77.50W
Paraná Argentina 63 31.45S 60.30W
Paraná r. Argentina 63 34.00S 58.30W
Paranã Brazil 61 12.33S 47.48W
Paraná d. Brazil 59 24.30S 52.00W
Paranã r. Brazil 61 12.30S 48.10W
Paranaguá Brazil 59 25.32S 48.36W
Paranaíba Brazil 59 19.44S 51.12W
Paranaíba r. Brazil 59 20.00S 51.00W
Paranapanema r. Brazil 59 22.30S 53.03W
Paranapiacaba, Serra mts. Brazil 59 24.30S 49.15W
Paranavaí Brazil 59 23.02S 52.36W
Parangaba Brazil 61 3.45S 38.33W
Paraparaumu New Zealand 48 40.55S 175.00E
Paratoo Australia 46 32.46S 139.40E
Paray-le-Monial France 11 46.27N 4.07E
Parchim E. Germany 14 53.25N 11.51E
Parczew Poland 15 51.39N 22.54E
Pardo r. Bahia Brazil 59 15.40S 39.38W
Pardo r. Mato Grosso Brazil 59 21.56S 52.07W
Pardo r. São Paulo Brazil 59 20.10S 48.36W
Pardubice Czech. 14 50.03N 15.45E
Parecis, Serra dos mts. Brazil 60 13.30S 58.30W
Parent Canada 55 47.55N 74.36W
Parent, Lac l. Canada 55 48.40N 77.00W
Parepare Indonesia 26 4.03S 119.40E
Párga Greece 13 39.17N 20.23E
Pargas Finland 17 60.18N 22.18E
Paria, Golfo de g. Venezuela 60 10.30S 62.00W
Paria, Península de pen. Venezuela 60 10.45N 62.30W
Pariaguán Venezuela 60 8.51N 64.43W
Pariaman Indonesia 26 0.36S 100.09E
Parichi U.S.S.R. 15 52.48N 29.25E
Parigi Indonesia 27 0.49S 120.10E
Parika Guyana 60 6.51N 58.25W
Parima, Sierra mts. Venezuela 60 2.30N 64.00W
Parinari Peru 60 4.35S 74.25W
Paringa Australia 46 34.10S 140.49E
Parintins Brazil 61 2.36S 56.44W
Paris France 9 48.52N 2.20E
Paris Ky. U.S.A. 55 38.13N 84.15W
Paris Tex. U.S.A. 53 33.41N 95.33W
Parisienne d. France 9 48.50N 2.20E
Parkano Finland 17 62.01N 23.01E
Parker Ariz. U.S.A. 54 34.09N 114.17W
Parker, C. Canada 51 75.04N 79.40W
Parker Dam U.S.A. 54 34.18N 114.10W
Parkersburg U.S.A. 55 39.17N 81.33W
Parkes Australia 47 33.10S 148.13E
Parkland U.S.A. 54 47.09N 122.26W
Parlākimidi India 29 18.46N 84.05E
Parma Burkina 38 11.15N 0.44E
Parma Italy 9 44.48N 10.18E
Parma r. Italy 9 44.56N 10.26E
Parma U.S.A. 55 41.24N 81.44W
Parnaguá Brazil 61 10.17S 44.39W
Parnaíba Brazil 61 2.58S 41.46W
Parnaíba r. Brazil 61 2.58S 41.47W
Parnassós mtn. Greece 13 38.33N 22.35E
Parndana Australia 46 35.44S 137.14E
Pärnu U.S.S.R. 17 58.24N 24.32E
Pärnu r. U.S.S.R. 17 58.23N 24.29E
Paroo r. Australia 46 31.30S 143.34E
Páros i. Greece 13 37.04N 25.11E
Parral Chile 63 36.09S 71.50W
Parramatta Australia 47 33.50S 150.57E
Parras Mexico 56 25.25N 102.11W
Parrett r. U.K. 5 51.10N 3.00W
Parry, C. Greenland 51 76.50N 71.00W
Parry Is. Canada 51 76.00N 102.00W
Parry Sound town Canada 55 45.21N 80.02W
Parseta r. Poland 14 54.12N 15.33E
Parsons Kans. U.S.A. 53 37.20N 95.17W
Parthenay France 11 46.39N 0.14W
Partille Sweden 17 57.44N 12.07E
Partinico Italy 12 38.03N 13.07E
Partry Mts. Rep. of Ire. 7 53.40N 9.30W
Paru r. Brazil 61 1.33S 52.38W
Parys R.S.A. 39 26.54S 27.26E
Pasadena Calif. U.S.A. 54 34.09N 118.09W
Pasadena Tex. U.S.A. 53 29.42N 95.14W
Pasaje Ecuador 60 3.23S 79.50W
Paşcani Romania 15 47.15N 26.44E
Pasco U.S.A. 54 46.14N 119.06W
Pasewalk E. Germany 14 53.30N 14.00E
Pasinler Turkey 30 39.59N 41.41E
Pasir Puteh Malaysia 26 5.50N 102.24E
Påskallavik Sweden 17 57.10N 16.27E
Pasley, C. Australia 43 33.55S 123.30E
Pasmore r. Australia 46 31.07S 139.48E
Paso de los Libres town Argentina 63 29.45S 57.05W
Paso de los Toros town Uruguay 63 32.49S 56.31W
Paso Robles U.S.A. 54 35.38N 120.41W
Paspébiac Canada 55 48.03N 65.17W
Passau W. Germany 14 48.35N 13.28E
Passero, C. Italy 12 36.40N 15.08E
Passo Fundo Brazil 59 28.16S 52.20W
Passos Brazil 59 20.45S 46.38W
Pastaza r. Peru 60 4.50S 76.25W
Pasto Colombia 60 1.12N 77.17W
Pasuruan Indonesia 26 7.38S 112.44E
Patagonia f. Argentina 63 42.20S 67.00W
Patea New Zealand 48 39.46S 174.29E
Pategi Nigeria 38 8.44N 5.47E
Pate I. Kenya 37 2.08S 41.02E
Paternò Italy 12 37.34N 14.54E
Paterson U.S.A. 55 40.55N 74.10W
Pathānkot India 28 32.17N 75.39E
Pathfinder Resr. U.S.A. 54 42.30N 106.50W
Patía r. Colombia 60 1.54N 78.30W
Patiāla India 28 30.21N 76.27E
Patkai Hills Burma 29 26.30N 95.40E
Pátmos i. Greece 13 37.20N 26.33E
Patna India 29 25.37N 85.12E
Patos Brazil 61 6.55S 37.15W
Patos, Lagoa dos l. Brazil 59 31.00S 51.10W
Patos de Minas Brazil 59 18.35S 46.32W
Patquía Argentina 62 30.02S 66.55W
Pátrai Greece 13 38.15N 21.45E
Patraïkós Kólpos g. Greece 13 38.15N 21.35E
Patrasuy U.S.S.R. 18 63.35N 61.50E
Patrickswell Rep. of Ire. 7 52.36N 8.43W
Pattani Thailand 29 6.53N 101.16E
Patuca r. Honduras 57 15.50N 84.18W
Pau France 11 43.18N 0.22W
Pauillac France 11 45.12N 0.44W
Paulina U.S.A. 54 44.09N 119.58W
Paulistana Brazil 61 8.09S 41.09W
Paulo Afonso Brazil 61 9.25S 38.15W
Pavia Italy 9 45.10N 9.10E
Pavilly France 9 49.34N 0.58E
Pavlodar U.S.S.R. 20 52.21N 76.59E
Pavlograd U.S.S.R. 19 48.34N 35.50E
Pavlovo U.S.S.R. 18 55.58N 43.05E
Pavlovsk U.S.S.R. 19 50.28N 40.07E
Pavlovskaya U.S.S.R. 19 46.18N 39.48E
Pavullo nel Frignano Italy 9 44.20N 10.50E
Paxoí i. Greece 13 39.12N 20.12E
Payette U.S.A. 54 44.05N 116.56W
Payne, L. Canada 51 59.25N 74.00W
Paynes Find Australia 43 29.15S 117.41E
Paysandú Uruguay 63 32.19S 58.05W
Pays de Caux f. France 9 49.40N 0.40E
Pays de la Loire d. France 11 47.30N 1.00W
Pazardzhik Bulgaria 13 42.10N 24.22E
Peace r. Canada 50 59.00N 111.26W
Peace River town Canada 50 56.15N 117.18W
Peach Springs town U.S.A. 54 35.32N 113.25W
Peacock Hills Canada 50 66.05N 110.45W
Peake r. Australia 46 28.05S 136.07E
Peak Hill town N.S.W. Australia 47 32.47S 148.13E
Peak Hill town W.A. Australia 42 25.40S 118.41E
Peak Range mts. Australia 44 23.18S 148.30E
Peale, Mt. U.S.A. 54 38.26N 109.14W
Pearl r. U.S.A. 53 30.15N 89.25W
Peary Land f. Greenland 64 82.00N 35.00W
Pebane Mozambique 37 17.14S 38.10E
Pebas Peru 60 3.17S 71.55W
Peć Yugo. 13 42.40N 20.17E
Pechenga U.S.S.R. 16 69.28N 31.04E
Pechora U.S.S.R. 18 65.14N 57.18E
Pechora r. U.S.S.R. 18 68.10N 54.00E
Pechorskaya Guba g. U.S.S.R. 18 69.00N 56.00E
Pechorskoye More sea U.S.S.R. 18 69.00N 55.00E
Pecos U.S.A. 52 31.25N 103.30W
Pecos r. U.S.A. 52 29.45N 101.25W
Pécs Hungary 15 46.05N 18.14E
Peddie R.S.A. 39 33.12S 27.07E
Pedregulho Brazil 59 20.15S 47.29W
Pedreiras Brazil 61 4.32S 44.40W
Pedrinhas Brazil 61 11.12S 37.41W
Pedro Afonso Brazil 61 8.59S 48.11W
Pedro de Valdivia Chile 62 22.36S 69.40W
Pedro Juan Caballero Paraguay 59 22.30S 55.44W
Peebinga Australia 46 34.55S 140.57E
Peebles U.K. 6 55.39N 3.12W
Peebles U.S.A. 55 38.57N 83.14W
Peel r. Canada 50 68.13N 135.00W
Peel U.K. 4 54.14N 4.42W
Peel Inlet Australia 43 32.35S 115.44E
Peel Pt. Canada 50 73.22N 114.35W
Peene r. E. Germany 14 53.53N 13.49E
Peera Peera Poolanna L. Australia 44 26.43S 137.42E
Peery L. Australia 46 30.44S 143.34E
Pegasus B. New Zealand 48 43.15S 173.00E
Pegu Burma 29 17.18N 96.31E
Pegunungan Van Rees mts. Indonesia 27 2.35S 138.15E
Pegu Yoma mts. Burma 29 18.40N 96.00E
Pehuajó Argentina 63 35.50S 61.50W
Peixe Brazil 61 12.03S 48.32W
Pekalongan Indonesia 26 6.54S 109.37E
Peking see Beijing China 25
Pelat, Mont mtn. France 11 44.17N 6.41E
Peleaga mtn. Romania 15 45.22N 22.54E
Peleng i. Indonesia 27 1.30S 123.10E
Peleniya U.S.S.R. 15 47.58N 27.48E
Pelkum W. Germany 8 51.38N 7.44E
Pello Finland 16 66.47N 24.00E
Pelly r. Canada 50 62.50N 137.35W
Pelly Bay town Canada 51 68.38N 89.45W
Pelly L. Canada 51 65.59N 101.12W
Pelotas Brazil 59 31.45S 52.20W
Pematangsiantar Indonesia 26 2.59N 99.01E
Pemba Mozambique 37 13.02S 40.30E
Pemba I. Tanzania 37 5.10S 39.45E
Pemberton Australia 43 34.28S 116.01E
Pembroke Canada 55 45.49N 77.07W
Pembroke U.K. 5 51.41N 4.57W
Peñaranda de Bracamonte Spain 10 40.54N 5.13W
Penarth U.K. 5 51.26N 3.11W
Peñas, Cabo de c. Spain 10 43.42N 5.52W
Penas, Golfo de g. Chile 63 47.20S 75.00W
Pendine U.K. 5 51.44N 4.33W
Pendleton U.S.A. 54 45.40N 118.47W
Penedo Brazil 61 10.16S 36.33W
Penetanguishene Canada 55 44.47N 79.55W
Penganga r. India 29 18.52N 79.56E
Pengshui China 25 29.17N 108.13E
Penicuik U.K. 6 55.49N 3.13W
Peninsular Malaysia d. Malaysia 26 5.00N 102.00E
Penneshaw Australia 46 35.42S 137.55E
Pennines, Alpes mts. Switz. 9 46.08N 7.34E
Pennsylvania d. U.S.A. 55 40.45N 77.30W
Penn Yan U.S.A. 55 42.41N 77.03W
Penny Highland mtn. Canada 51 67.10N 66.50W
Penobscot r. U.S.A. 55 44.30N 68.50W
Penola Australia 46 37.23S 140.21E
Penong Australia 43 31.55S 133.01E
Penonomé Panama 57 8.30N 80.20W
Penrith Australia 47 33.47S 150.44E
Penrith U.K. 4 54.40N 2.45W
Penryn U.K. 5 50.10N 5.07W
Pensacola U.S.A. 53 30.30N 87.12W
Pensacola Mts. Antarctica 64 84.00S 45.00W
Penshurst Australia 46 37.52S 142.20E
Penticton Canada 50 49.29N 119.38W
Pentland Australia 44 20.32S 145.24E
Pentland Firth str. U.K. 6 58.40N 3.00W
Pentland Hills U.K. 6 55.50N 3.20W
Penza U.S.S.R. 18 53.11N 45.00E
Penzance U.K. 5 50.07N 5.32W
Penzhinskaya Guba g. U.S.S.R. 21 61.00N 163.00E
Peoria Ariz. U.S.A. 54 33.35N 112.14W
Peoria Ill. U.S.A. 53 40.43N 89.38W
Perabumulih Indonesia 26 3.29S 104.14E
Perche, Collines du hills France 9 48.30N 0.40E
Percival Lakes Australia 42 21.25S 125.00E
Pereira Colombia 60 4.47N 75.46W
Perekop U.S.S.R. 19 46.10N 33.42E
Perené r. Peru 62 11.02S 74.19W
Perevolotskiy U.S.S.R. 18 51.10N 54.15E
Pereyaslav-Khmelnitskiy U.S.S.R. 15 50.05N 31.28E
Pergamino Argentina 63 33.53S 60.35W
Pergine Valsugana Italy 9 46.04N 11.14E
Péribonca r. Canada 55 48.45N 72.05W
Périers France 9 49.11N 1.25W
Périgueux France 11 45.12N 0.44E
Perija, Sierra de mts. Venezuela 60 10.30N 72.30W
Perm U.S.S.R. 18 58.01N 56.10E
Pernambuco d. Brazil 61 8.00S 39.00W
Pernatty L. Australia 46 31.31S 137.14E
Pernik Bulgaria 13 42.35N 23.03E
Perniö Finland 17 60.12N 23.08E
Péronne France 8 49.56N 2.57E
Perosa Argentina Italy 9 44.58N 7.10E
Perpignan France 11 42.42N 2.54E
Perranporth U.K. 5 50.21N 5.09W
Perryton U.S.A. 52 36.23N 100.48W
Persepolis ruins Iran 31 29.55N 53.00E
Perth Australia 43 31.58S 115.49E
Perth Canada 55 44.54N 76.15W
Perth U.K. 6 56.24N 3.28W
Perth Amboy U.S.A. 55 40.32N 74.17W
Peru S. America 60 10.00S 75.00W
Perugia Italy 12 43.06N 12.24E
Péruwelz Belgium 8 50.32N 3.36E
Pervomaysk U.S.S.R. 15 48.03N 30.50E
Pervouralsk U.S.S.R. 18 56.59N 59.58E
Pesaro Italy 9 43.54N 12.54E
Pescara Italy 12 42.27N 14.13E
Pescara r. Italy 12 42.28N 14.13E
Pescia Italy 9 43.54N 10.41E
Peshāwar Pakistan 28 34.01N 71.40E
Pesqueira Brazil 61 8.24S 36.38W
Pessac France 11 44.48N 0.38W
Peşteana Jiu Romania 15 44.50N 23.15E
Pestovo U.S.S.R. 18 58.32N 35.42E
Petah Tiqwa Israel 32 32.05N 34.53E
Petaluma U.S.A. 54 38.14N 122.39W
Pétange Lux. 8 49.32N 5.56E
Petare Venezuela 60 10.31N 66.50W
Petatlán Mexico 56 17.31N 101.16W
Petauke Zambia 37 14.16S 31.21E
Petawawa Canada 55 45.54N 77.17W
Peterborough S.A. Australia 46 33.00S 138.51E
Peterborough Vic. Australia 46 38.36S 142.55E
Peterborough Canada 55 44.18N 78.19W
Peterborough U.K. 5 52.35N 0.14W
Peterhead U.K. 6 57.30N 1.46W
Peterlee U.K. 4 54.45N 1.18W
Petermann Ranges mts. Australia 42 25.00S 129.46E
Petersburg W.Va. U.S.A. 55 39.00N 79.07W
Petersfield U.K. 5 51.00N 0.56W
Petitot r. Canada 50 60.14N 123.29W
Petit St. Bernard, Col du pass France / Italy 9 45.40N 6.53E
Petitsikapau L. Canada 51 54.45N 66.25W
Petoskey U.S.A. 55 45.22N 84.59W
Petra ruins Jordan 32 30.19N 35.26E
Petrich Bulgaria 13 41.25N 23.13E
Petrikov U.S.S.R. 15 52.09N 28.30E
Petrodvorets U.S.S.R. 18 59.50N 29.57E
Petrolina Brazil 61 9.22S 40.30W
Petropavlovsk U.S.S.R. 20 54.53N 69.13E
Petropavlovsk Kamchatskiy U.S.S.R. 21 53.03N 158.43E
Petrópolis Brazil 59 22.30S 43.06W
Petroşani Romania 15 45.25N 23.22E
Petrovaradin Yugo. 15 45.16N 19.55E
Petrovsk U.S.S.R. 18 52.20N 45.24E
Petrovsk Zabaykal'skiy U.S.S.R. 21 51.20N 108.55E
Petrozavodsk U.S.S.R. 18 61.46N 34.19E
Petrus Steyn R.S.A. 39 27.38S 28.08E
Peureulak Indonesia 26 4.48N 97.45E
Pevek U.S.S.R. 21 69.41N 170.19E
Pézenas France 11 43.28N 3.25E
Pezinok Czech. 15 48.18N 17.17E
Pezmog U.S.S.R. 18 61.50N 51.45E
Pfaffenhofen W. Germany 14 48.31N 11.30E
Pfalzel W. Germany 8 49.47N 6.41E
Pforzheim W. Germany 14 48.53N 8.41E
Phangan, Ko i. Thailand 26 9.50N 100.00E
Phangnga Thailand 29 8.29N 98.31E
Phan Rang Vietnam 26 11.35N 109.00E
Pharenda India 29 27.06N 83.17E
Phenix City U.S.A. 53 32.28N 85.01W
Phet Buri Thailand 29 13.01N 99.55E
Philadelphia Penn. U.S.A. 55 39.57N 75.07W
Philippeville Belgium 8 50.12N 4.32E
Philippines Asia 27 13.00N 123.00E
Philippine Sea Pacific Oc. 40 18.00N 135.00E
Philippine Trench Pacific Oc. 27 8.45N 127.20E
Philipstown R.S.A. 39 30.25S 24.26E
Phillip I. Australia 47 38.29S 145.14E
Phillips r. Australia 43 33.55S 120.01E
Phillips Maine U.S.A. 55 44.49N 70.21W
Phillipson, L. Australia 46 29.28S 134.28E
Phnom Penh see Phnum Pénh Kampuchea 26
Phnum Pénh Kampuchea 26 11.35N 104.55E
Phoenix Ariz. U.S.A. 54 33.27N 112.05W
Phoenix I. Kiribati 40 4.00S 172.00W
Phôngsali Laos 29 21.40N 102.06E
Phukao Miang mtn. Thailand 29 16.50N 101.00E
Phuket Thailand 29 8.00N 98.28E
Phuket, Ko i. Thailand 29 8.10N 98.20E
Phumĭ Sâmraông Kampuchea 26 14.12N 103.31E
Phu Quoc i. Kampuchea 26 10.10N 104.00E
Phu Tho Vietnam 26 21.23N 105.13E
Piacá Brazil 61 7.42S 47.18W
Piacenza Italy 9 45.03N 9.42E
Pian r. Australia 47 30.03S 148.18E
Piana France 11 42.14N 8.38E
Piangil Australia 46 35.04S 143.20E
Pianoro Italy 9 44.22N 11.20E
Pianosa i. Italy 12 42.35N 10.05E
Piatra-Neamţ Romania 15 46.56N 26.22E
Piauí d. Brazil 61 7.45S 42.30W
Piauí r. Brazil 61 6.14S 42.51W
Piave r. Italy 9 45.33N 12.45E
Piawaning Australia 43 30.51S 116.22E
Pic r. Canada 55 48.36N 86.28W
Picardie d. France 8 49.47N 3.12E
Pickering U.K. 4 54.15N 0.46W
Pickle Crow Canada 51 51.30N 90.04W
Pickwick L. resr. U.S.A. 53 35.00N 88.10W
Picola Australia 47 35.59S 145.06E
Picos Brazil 61 7.05S 41.28W
Picquigny France 9 49.57N 2.09E
Picton Australia 47 34.12S 150.35E
Picton Canada 55 44.01N 77.09W
Picton New Zealand 48 41.17S 174.02E
Picún Leufú Argentina 63 39.30S 69.15W
Pidálion, Akrotírion c. Cyprus 32 34.56N 34.05E
Piedecuesta Colombia 60 6.59N 73.03W
Piedras r. Peru 60 12.30S 69.10W
Piedras, Punta c. Argentina 63 35.25S 57.07W
Piedras Negras Mexico 56 28.40N 100.32W
Piedra Sola Uruguay 63 32.04S 56.21W
Pielavesi Finland 16 63.14N 26.45E
Pielinen l. Finland 18 63.20N 29.50E
Piemonte d. Italy 9 44.45N 8.00E
Pierce U.S.A. 54 46.29N 115.48W
Pierre U.S.A. 52 44.23N 100.20W
Piesseville Australia 43 33.11S 117.12E
Piešt'any Czech. 15 48.36N 17.50E
Pietarsaari Finland 16 63.40N 22.42E
Pietermaritzburg R.S.A. 39 29.36S 30.23E
Pietersburg R.S.A. 39 23.54S 29.27E
Pietrasanta Italy 9 43.57N 10.14E
Piet Retief R.S.A. 39 27.00S 30.49E
Pietrosu mtn. Romania 15 47.36N 24.38E
Pietrosul mtn. Romania 15 47.08N 25.11E
Pieve di Cadore Italy 9 46.26N 12.22E

Pigailoe *i.* Caroline Is. **27** 8.08N146.40E
Pigna Italy **9** 43.56N 7.40E
Pihtipudas Finland **16** 63.23N 25.34E
Pikalevo U.S.S.R. **18** 59.35N 34.07E
Pikes Peak *mtn.* U.S.A. **52** 38.51N105.03W
Piketberg R.S.A. **39** 32.54S 18.43E
Piketon U.S.A. **55** 39.03N 83.01W
Pila Argentina **63** 36.00S 58.10W
Piła Poland **14** 53.09N 16.44E
Pilar Paraguay **59** 26.52S 58.23W
Pilar do Sul Brazil **59** 23.48S 47.45W
Pilcomayo *r.* Argentina / Paraguay **62** 25.15S 57.43W
Pilica *r.* Poland **15** 51.52N 21.17E
Pilliga Australia **47** 30.23S148.55E
Pílos Greece **13** 36.55N 21.40E
Pilsum W. Germany **8** 53.29N 7.06E
Pimba Australia **46** 31.18S136.47E
Pimenta Bueno Brazil **60** 11.40S 61.14W
Pinang, Pulau *i.* Malaysia **26** 5.30N100.10E
Pinarbaşi Turkey **30** 38.43N 36.23E
Pinar del Río Cuba **57** 22.24N 83.42W
Píndhos Óros *mts.* Albania / Greece **13** 39.40N 21.00E
Pindiga Nigeria **38** 9.58N 10.53E
Pine Bluff *town* U.S.A. **53** 34.13N 92.00W
Pine Creek *town* Australia **42** 13.51S131.50E
Pinega U.S.S.R. **18** 64.42N 43.28E
Pinega *r.* U.S.S.R. **18** 63.51N 41.48E
Pinerolo Italy **9** 44.53N 7.21E
Pinetown R.S.A. **39** 29.49S 30.52E
Piney France **9** 48.22N 4.20E
Ping *r.* Thailand **29** 15.45N100.10E
Pingaring Australia **43** 34.45S118.34E
Pingdingshan Liaoning China **25** 41.26N124.46E
Pingdong Taiwan **25** 22.40N120.30E
Pingelly Australia **43** 32.34S117.04E
Pingliang China **24** 35.25N107.14E
Pingrup Australia **43** 33.33S118.30E
Pingxiang Guang. Zhuang. China **24** 22.05N106.46E
Pinhal Brazil **59** 22.10S 46.46W
Pinhel Portugal **10** 40.46N 7.04W
Pini *i.* Indonesia **26** 0.10N 98.30E
Piniós *r.* Greece **13** 39.51N 22.37E
Pinjarra Australia **43** 32.37S115.53E
Pinnaroo Australia **46** 35.18S140.54E
Pinos, Isla de *i.* Cuba **57** 21.40N 82.40W
Pinrang Indonesia **26** 3.48S119.41E
Pinsk U.S.S.R. **15** 52.08N 26.01E
Pinto Argentina **62** 29.09S 62.38W
Pinyug U.S.S.R. **18** 60.10N 47.43E
Piombino Italy **12** 42.56N 10.30E
Piorini, L. Brazil **60** 3.34S 63.15W
Piotrków Trybunalski Poland **15** 51.25N 19.42E
Piove di Sacco Italy **9** 45.18N 12.02E
Pipinas Argentina **63** 35.30S 57.19W
Pipmouacane, Résr. Canada **55** 49.35N 70.30W
Piqua U.S.A. **55** 40.08N 84.14W
Piracicaba Brazil **59** 22.45S 47.40W
Piracicaba *r.* Brazil **59** 22.35S 48.14W
Piracuruca Brazil **61** 3.56S 41.42W
Piraeus *see* Piraiévs Greece **13**
Piraiévs Greece **13** 37.56N 23.38E
Pirassununga Brazil **59** 21.59S 47.25W
Pírgos Greece **13** 37.42N 21.27E
Pirna E. Germany **14** 50.58N 13.58E
Pirot Yugo. **13** 43.10N 22.32E
Piryatin U.S.S.R. **19** 50.14N 32.31E
Pisa Italy **12** 43.43N 10.24E
Pisciotta Italy **12** 40.08N 15.12E
Pisco Peru **60** 13.46S 76.12W
Písek Czech. **14** 49.19N 14.10E
Pishan China **24** 37.30N 78.20E
Pistoia Italy **9** 43.55N 10.54E
Pisuerga *r.* Spain **10** 41.35N 5.40W
Pisz Poland **15** 53.38N 21.49E
Pita Guinea **34** 11.05N 12.15W
Pitalito Colombia **60** 1.51N 76.01W
Pitarpunga, L. Australia **46** 34.23S143.32E
Pite *r.* Sweden **16** 65.14N 21.32E
Piteå Sweden **16** 65.20N 21.30E
Piteşti Romania **15** 44.52N 24.51E
Pithāpuram India **29** 17.07N 82.16E
Pithiviers France **9** 48.10N 2.15E
Pitlochry U.K. **6** 56.43N 3.45W
Pittsburg N.H. U.S.A. **55** 45.03N 71.26W
Pittsburgh U.S.A. **55** 40.26N 80.00W
Pittsfield U.S.A. **55** 42.27N 73.15W
Pittston U.S.A. **55** 41.19N 75.47W
Pittville U.S.A. **54** 41.03N121.20W
Piũí Brazil **59** 20.28S 45.58W
Piura Peru **60** 5.15S 80.38W
Placentia Canada **51** 47.14N 53.58W
Plains U.S.A. **54** 47.27N114.53W
Plainview U.S.A. **52** 34.12N101.43W
Plampang Indonesia **26** 8.48S117.48E
Planá Czech. **14** 49.52N 12.44E
Plana Cays *is.* Bahamas **57** 21.31N 72.14W
Plasencia Spain **10** 40.02N 6.05W
Plassen Norway **17** 61.08N 12.31E
Plaster Rock *town* Canada **55** 46.55N 67.24W
Platani *r.* Italy **12** 37.24N 13.15E
Plate, R. *est. see* La Plata, Río de Argentina / Uruguay **63**
Plateau *d.* Nigeria **38** 8.50N 9.00E
Platí, Ákra *c.* Greece **13** 40.26N 23.59E
Platinum U.S.A. **50** 59.00N161.50W
Plato Colombia **60** 9.54N 74.46W
Platte *r.* U.S.A. **53** 41.05N 96.50W
Plattling W. Germany **14** 48.47N 12.53E
Plattsburgh U.S.A. **55** 44.42N 73.28W
Plauen E. Germany **14** 50.29N 12.08E
Plavsk U.S.S.R. **18** 53.40N 37.20E
Pleasantville U.S.A. **55** 39.23N 74.32W
Pleiku Vietnam **26** 13.57N108.01E
Plenty, B. of New Zealand **48** 37.40S176.50E
Plesetsk U.S.S.R. **18** 62.42N 40.21E
Pleshchenitsy U.S.S.R. **15** 54.24N 27.52E
Pleszew Poland **15** 51.54N 17.48E
Pleven Bulgaria **13** 43.25N 24.39E
Pljevlja Yugo. **13** 43.22N 19.22E
Płock Poland **15** 52.33N 19.43E
Ploieşti Romania **15** 44.57N 26.02E
Plomb du Cantal *mtn.* France **11** 45.04N 2.45E
Plombières France **11** 47.58N 6.28E
Plön W. Germany **14** 54.09N 10.25E
Płońsk Poland **15** 52.38N 20.23E
Ploudalmézeau France **11** 48.33N 4.39W
Plovdiv Bulgaria **13** 42.09N 24.45E
Plumtree Zimbabwe **39** 20.30S 27.50E
Plymouth U.K. **5** 50.23N 4.09W
Plymouth Ind. U.S.A. **55** 41.20N 86.19W
Plzeň Czech. **14** 49.45N 13.22E
Pô Burkina Faso **38** 11.11N 1.10W
Po *r.* Italy **9** 44.51N 12.30E
Pobé Benin **38** 7.00N 2.56E
Pobeda, Gora *mtn.* U.S.S.R. **21** 65.20N145.50E
Pobla de Segur Spain **10** 42.15N 0.58E
Pocatello U.S.A. **54** 42.52N112.27W
Pocklington U.K. **4** 53.56N 0.48W
Poços de Caldas Brazil **59** 21.48S 46.33W
Poděbrady Czech. **14** 50.08N 15.07E
Podgaytsy U.S.S.R. **15** 49.19N 25.10E
Podkamennaya Tunguska U.S.S.R. **21** 61.45N 90.13E
Podkamennaya Tunguska *r.* U.S.S.R. **21** 61.40N 90.00E
Podolsk U.S.S.R. **18** 55.23N 37.32E
Podor Senegal **34** 16.35N 15.02W
Podporozhye U.S.S.R. **18** 60.55N 34.02E
Pofadder R.S.A. **39** 29.08S 19.22E
Pogrebishche U.S.S.R. **15** 49.30N 29.15E
Poh Indonesia **27** 1.00S122.50E
P'ohang S. Korea **25** 36.00N129.26E
Poinsett, C. Antarctica **64** 65.35S113.00E
Point Arena *f.* U.S.A. **54** 38.55N123.41W
Pointe-à-Pitre Guadeloupe **57** 16.14N 61.32W
Pointe aux Anglais *town* Canada **55** 49.38N 67.11W
Pointe-aux-Trembles *town* Canada **55** 45.40N 73.30W
Pointe Noire *town* Congo **36** 4.46S 11.53E
Point Hope *town* U.S.A. **50** 68.21N166.41W
Point Lookout *town* Australia **47** 30.33S152.20E
Point Pleasant *town* W.Va. U.S.A. **55** 38.53N 82.07W
Poissy France **9** 48.56N 2.03E
Poitiers France **11** 46.35N 0.20E
Poitou-Charentes *d.* France **11** 46.00N 0.00
Poix France **9** 49.47N 2.00E
Poix-Terron France **9** 49.39N 4.39E
Pokataroo Australia **47** 29.37S148.44E
Pokhara Nepal **29** 28.14N 83.58E
Polacca U.S.A. **54** 35.50N110.23W
Pola de Lena Spain **10** 43.10N 5.49W
Polān Iran **31** 25.29N 61.15E
Poland Europe **15** 52.30N 19.00E
Polatli Turkey **30** 39.34N 32.08E
Polch W. Germany **8** 50.18N 7.19E
Polda Australia **46** 33.30S135.10E
Polesye *f.* U.S.S.R. **15** 52.15N 28.00E
Poli Cameroon **38** 8.30N 13.15E
Policastro, Golfo di *g.* Italy **12** 40.00N 15.35E
Poligny France **11** 46.50N 5.42E
Pólis Cyprus **32** 35.02N 32.26E
Políyiros Greece **13** 40.23N 23.27E
Pollino *mtn.* Italy **12** 39.53N 16.11E
Pollock Reef Australia **43** 34.28S123.40E
Polnovat U.S.S.R. **20** 63.47N 65.54E
Polonnoye U.S.S.R. **15** 50.10N 27.30E
Polotsk U.S.S.R. **18** 55.30N 28.43E
Polperro U.K. **5** 50.19N 4.31W
Polson U.S.A. **54** 47.41N114.09W
Poltava U.S.S.R. **19** 49.35N 34.35E
Polunochnoye U.S.S.R. **18** 60.52N 60.28E
Polyarnyy U.S.S.R. **18** 69.14N 33.30E
Polynesia *is.* Pacific Oc. **40** 4.00S165.00W
Pomarkku Finland **17** 61.42N 22.00E
Pombal Brazil **61** 6.45S 37.45W
Pombal Portugal **10** 39.55N 8.38W
Pomene Mozambique **39** 22.53S 35.33E
Pomeroy Wash. U.S.A. **54** 46.28N117.36W
Pomona Namibia **39** 27.09S 15.18E
Pomona U.S.A. **54** 34.04N117.45W
Pompey's Pillar *town* U.S.A. **54** 45.59N107.56W
Ponca City U.S.A. **53** 36.41N 97.04W
Ponce Puerto Rico **57** 18.00N 66.40W
Pondicherry India **29** 11.59N 79.50E
Pond Inlet *str.* Canada **51** 72.30N 75.00W
Ponferrada Spain **10** 42.32N 6.31W
Pongani P.N.G. **44** 9.05S148.35E
Pongola *r.* Mozambique **39** 26.13S 32.38E
Ponnāni India **28** 10.46N 75.54E
Ponoy U.S.S.R. **18** 67.02N 41.03E
Ponoy *r.* U.S.S.R. **18** 67.00N 41.10E
Ponta Grossa Brazil **59** 25.00S 50.09W
Pont-à-Mousson France **11** 48.55N 6.03E
Ponta Porã Brazil **59** 22.27S 55.39W
Pont-Audemer France **9** 49.21N 0.31E
Pont Canavese Italy **9** 45.25N 7.36E
Pontchartrain, L. U.S.A. **53** 30.50N 90.00W
Pont-d'Ain France **11** 46.03N 5.20E
Pontedera Italy **12** 43.40N 10.38E
Pontefract U.K. **4** 53.42N 1.19W
Ponte Nova Brazil **59** 20.25S 42.54W
Pontevedra Spain **10** 42.25N 8.39W
Pontiac Mich. U.S.A. **55** 42.39N 83.18W
Pontianak Indonesia **26** 0.05S109.16E
Pontivy France **11** 48.05N 3.00W
Pont l'Évêque France **9** 49.18N 0.11E
Pontoise France **9** 49.03N 2.05E
Pontorson France **9** 48.33N 1.31W
Pontremoli Italy **9** 44.22N 9.53E
Pontresina Switz. **9** 46.28N 9.53E
Pontrilas U.K. **5** 51.56N 2.53W
Pont-sur-Yonne France **9** 48.17N 3.12E
Pontypool U.K. **5** 51.42N 3.01W
Pontypridd U.K. **5** 51.36N 3.21W
Ponziane, Isole *is.* Italy **12** 40.56N 12.58E
Poochera Australia **46** 32.42S134.52E
Poole U.K. **5** 50.42N 2.02W
Pooncarie Australia **46** 33.23S142.34E
Poopelloe, L. Australia **46** 31.39S144.00E
Poopó, Lago de *l.* Bolivia **62** 19.00S 67.00W
Popayán Colombia **60** 2.27N 76.32W
Poperinge Belgium **8** 50.51N 2.44E
Popilta Australia **46** 33.15S141.49E
Popilta L. Australia **46** 33.09S141.45E
Poplar Bluff *town* U.S.A. **53** 36.40N 90.25W
Popocatépetl *mtn.* Mexico **56** 19.02N 98.38W
Popondetta P.N.G. **44** 8.45S148.15E
Poprad Czech. **15** 49.03N 20.18E
Popricani Romania **15** 47.18N 27.31E
Porbandar India **28** 21.40N 69.40E
Porcupine *r.* U.S.A. **50** 66.25N145.20W
Pordenone Italy **9** 45.57N 12.39E
Pori Finland **17** 61.29N 21.47E
Porirua New Zealand **48** 41.08S174.50E
Porjus Sweden **16** 66.57N 19.50E
Porkhov U.S.S.R. **18** 57.43N 29.31E
Porkkala Finland **17** 59.59N 24.26E
Porlamar Venezuela **60** 11.01N 63.54W
Pornic France **11** 47.07N 2.05W
Porog U.S.S.R. **18** 63.50N 38.32E
Poronaysk U.S.S.R. **21** 49.13N142.55E
Porosozero U.S.S.R. **18** 62.45N 32.48E
Porretta Terme Italy **9** 44.09N 10.59E
Porsangen *est.* Norway **16** 70.58N 25.30E
Porsangerhalvöya *pen.* Norway **16** 70.50N 25.00E
Porsgrunn Norway **17** 59.09N 9.40E
Porsuk *r.* Turkey **30** 39.41N 31.56E
Portachuela Bolivia **62** 17.21S 63.24W
Port Adelaide Australia **46** 34.52S138.30E
Portadown U.K. **7** 54.25N 6.27W
Portaferry U.K. **7** 54.23N 5.33W
Portage la Prairie *town* Canada **51** 49.58N 98.20W
Port Albert Australia **47** 38.09S146.40E
Portalegre Portugal **10** 39.17N 7.25W
Port Alfred R.S.A. **39** 33.36S 26.52E
Port Alice Canada **50** 50.23N127.27W
Port Angeles U.S.A. **54** 48.07N123.27W
Port Antonio Jamaica **57** 18.10N 76.27W
Port Arthur Australia **45** 43.08S147.50E
Port Arthur U.S.A. **53** 29.55N 93.56W
Port Augusta Australia **46** 32.30S137.46E
Port-au-Prince Haiti **57** 18.33N 72.20W
Port Austin U.S.A. **55** 44.04N 82.59W
Port Blair India **29** 11.40N 92.30E
Portbou Spain **10** 42.25N 3.09E
Port Bouet Ivory Coast **38** 5.14N 3.58W
Port Bradshaw *b.* Australia **44** 12.30S136.42E
Port Broughton Australia **46** 33.36S137.56E
Port Campbell Australia **46** 38.37S143.04E
Port Cartier Canada **55** 50.01N 66.53W
Port Chalmers New Zealand **48** 45.49S170.37E
Port Curtis Australia **44** 23.50S151.13E
Port-de-Paix Haiti **57** 19.57N 72.50W
Port Edward R.S.A. **39** 31.03S 30.13E
Portela Brazil **59** 21.38S 41.59W
Port Elizabeth R.S.A. **39** 33.57S 25.34E
Port Ellen U.K. **6** 55.38N 6.12W
Port-en-Bessin France **9** 49.21N 0.45W
Port Erin U.K. **4** 54.05N 4.45W
Porterville R.S.A. **39** 33.01S 19.00E
Porterville U.S.A. **54** 36.04N119.01W
Port Fairy Australia **46** 38.23S142.17E
Port Germein Australia **46** 33.01S138.00E
Portglenone U.K. **7** 54.52N 6.30W
Port Harcourt Nigeria **38** 4.43N 7.05E
Port Harrison *see* Inoucdjouac Canada **51**
Port Hawkesbury Canada **51** 45.37N 61.21W
Porthcawl U.K. **5** 51.28N 3.42W
Port Hedland Australia **42** 20.24S118.36E
Port Henry U.S.A. **55** 44.03N 73.28W
Porthmadog U.K. **4** 52.55N 4.08W
Port Huron U.S.A. **55** 42.59N 82.28W
Portimão Portugal **10** 37.08N 8.32W
Port Isaac B. U.K. **5** 50.36N 4.50W
Portiţei, Gura *f.* Romania **13** 44.40N 29.00E
Port Jervis U.S.A. **55** 41.22N 74.40W
Port Keats Australia **42** 14.15S129.35E
Port Kenny Australia **46** 33.09S134.42E
Portland N.S.W. Australia **47** 33.20S150.00E
Portland Vic. Australia **46** 38.21S141.38E
Portland Maine U.S.A. **55** 43.39N 70.17W
Portland Oreg. U.S.A. **54** 45.33N122.36W
Port-la-Nouvelle France **11** 43.01N 3.03E
Port Laoise Rep. of Ire. **7** 53.03N 7.20W
Port Lavaca U.S.A. **53** 28.36N 96.39W
Port Lincoln Australia **46** 34.43S135.49E
Port MacDonnell Australia **46** 38.03S140.46E
Port Macquarie Australia **47** 31.28S152.25E
Port Maitland N.S. Canada **55** 43.59N 66.04W
Portmarnock Rep. of Ire. **7** 53.25N 6.09W
Port Moresby P.N.G. **44** 9.30S147.07E
Port Musgrave *b.* Australia **44** 11.59S142.00E
Portnaguiran U.K. **6** 58.15N 6.10W
Port Neill Australia **46** 34.07S136.20E
Port Nelson Canada **51** 57.10N 92.35W
Port Nolloth R.S.A. **39** 29.16S 16.54E
Port-Nouveau Québec Canada **51** 58.35N 65.59W
Porto Portugal **10** 41.09N 8.37W
Pôrto Alegre Brazil **59** 30.03S 51.10W
Porto Alexandre Angola **36** 15.55S 11.51E
Porto Amboim Angola **36** 10.45S 13.43E
Pôrto de Moz Brazil **61** 1.45S 52.13W
Pôrto Esperança Brazil **59** 19.36S 57.24W
Pôrto Feliz Brazil **59** 23.11S 47.32W
Portoferraio Italy **12** 42.49N 10.19E
Port of Ness U.K. **6** 58.30N 6.13W
Pôrto Franco Brazil **61** 6.21S 47.25W
Port of Spain Trinidad **57** 10.38N 61.31W
Porto Grande Brazil **61** 0.42N 51.24W
Portogruaro Italy **9** 45.47N 12.50E
Pörtom Finland **16** 62.42N 21.37E
Portomaggiore Italy **9** 44.42N 11.48E
Pôrto Mendes Brazil **59** 24.30S 54.20W
Pôrto Murtinho Brazil **59** 21.42S 57.52W
Porton U.K. **5** 51.08N 1.44W
Pôrto Nacional Brazil **61** 10.42S 48.25W
Porto-Novo Benin **38** 6.30N 2.47E
Porto San Giorgio Italy **12** 43.11N 13.48E
Porto Tolle Italy **9** 44.56N 12.22E
Porto Torres Italy **12** 40.49N 8.24E
Pôrto Valter Brazil **60** 8.15S 72.45W
Porto Vecchio France **11** 41.35N 9.16E
Pôrto Velho Brazil **60** 8.45S 63.54W
Portoviejo Ecuador **60** 1.07S 80.28W
Portpatrick U.K. **6** 54.51N 5.07W
Port Phillip B. Australia **47** 38.05S144.50E
Port Pirie Australia **46** 33.11S138.01E
Port Radium Canada **50** 66.05N118.02W
Portree U.K. **6** 57.24N 6.12W
Port Renfrew Canada **54** 48.30N124.20W
Portrush U.K. **7** 55.12N 6.40W
Port Said *see* Būr Sa'īd Egypt **32**
Port St. Louis France **11** 43.25N 4.40E
Port Shepstone R.S.A. **39** 30.44S 30.27E
Portsmouth U.K. **5** 50.48N 1.06W
Portsmouth N.H. U.S.A. **55** 43.04N 70.46W
Portsmouth Ohio U.S.A. **55** 38.45N 82.59W
Portsoy U.K. **6** 57.41N 2.41W
Port Stanley Canada **55** 42.40N 81.13W
Portstewart U.K. **7** 55.11N 6.43W
Port Sudan *see* Būr Sūdān Sudan **35**
Port Talbot U.K. **5** 51.35N 3.48W
Porttipahdan tekojärvi *resr.* Finland **16** 68.08N 26.40E
Port Townsend U.S.A. **54** 48.07N122.46W
Portugal Europe **10** 39.30N 8.05W
Port Vendres France **11** 42.31N 3.06E
Port Victoria Australia **46** 34.30S137.30E
Port Wakefield Australia **46** 34.12S138.11E
Porvenir Chile **63** 53.18S 70.22W
Porz W. Germany **8** 50.53N 7.05E
Posada Italy **12** 40.38N 9.43E
Posadas Argentina **62** 27.25S 55.48W
Poschiavo Switz. **9** 46.18N 10.04E
Posht *r.* Iran **31** 29.09N 58.09E
Poso Indonesia **27** 1.23S120.45E
Posse Brazil **59** 14.05S 46.22W
Postavy U.S.S.R. **18** 55.07N 26.50E
Poste-de-la-Baleine *town* Canada **51** 55.20N 77.50W
Poste Maurice Cortier Algeria **34** 22.18N 1.05E
Postmasburg R.S.A. **39** 28.19S 23.03E
Postojna Yugo. **14** 45.47N 14.13E
Postoli U.S.S.R. **15** 52.30N 28.00E
Potchefstroom R.S.A. **39** 26.42S 27.05E
Potenza Italy **12** 40.40N 15.47E
Potgietersrus R.S.A. **39** 24.11S 29.00E
Poti *r.* Brazil **61** 5.01S 42.48W
Poti U.S.S.R. **19** 42.11N 41.41E
Potiskum Nigeria **38** 11.40N 11.03E
Potosí Bolivia **62** 19.35S 65.45W
Potosí *d.* Bolivia **62** 21.00S 67.00W
Pototan Phil. **27** 10.54N122.38E
Potsdam E. Germany **14** 52.24N 13.04E
Potsdam *d.* E. Germany **14** 52.30N 12.45E
Potsdam U.S.A. **55** 44.40N 74.59W
Pottstown U.S.A. **55** 40.15N 75.38W
Pouancé France **9** 47.47N 1.11W
Poughkeepsie U.S.A. **55** 41.43N 73.56W
Pouso Alegre Brazil **59** 22.13S 45.49W
Poŭthĭsăt Kampuchea **26** 12.33N103.55E
Povenets U.S.S.R. **18** 62.52N 34.05E
Póvoa de Varzim Portugal **10** 41.22N 8.46W
Povorino U.S.S.R. **19** 51.12N 42.15E
Powder *r.* U.S.A. **54** 46.44N105.26W
Powder River *town* U.S.A. **54** 43.03N106.58W
Powell U.S.A. **54** 44.45N108.46W
Powell, L. U.S.A. **54** 37.25N110.45W
Powell Creek *town* Australia **42** 18.05S133.40E
Powers U.S.A. **55** 45.42N 87.31W
Powys *d.* U.K. **5** 52.26N 3.26W
Poyang Hu *l.* China **25** 29.05N116.20E
Požarevac Yugo. **15** 44.38N 21.12E
Poza Rica de Hidalgo Mexico **56** 20.34N 97.26W
Poznań Poland **14** 52.25N 16.53E
Pozoblanco Spain **10** 38.23N 4.51W
Prachuap Khiri Khan Thailand **29** 11.50N 99.49E
Pradera Colombia **60** 3.23N 76.11W
Prades France **11** 42.38N 2.25E
Praestö Denmark **17** 55.07N 12.03E
Prague *see* Praha Czech. **14**
Praha Czech. **14** 50.05N 14.25E
Prainha Amazonas Brazil **60** 7.16S 60.23W
Prainha Para Brazil **61** 1.48S 53.29W
Prairie City U.S.A. **54** 44.28N118.43W
Prang Ghana **38** 8.02N 0.58W
Prato Italy **9** 43.52N 11.06E
Pravia Spain **10** 43.30N 6.12W
Predazzo Italy **9** 46.19N 11.36E
Pré-en-Pail France **9** 48.27N 0.12W
Preesall U.K. **4** 53.55N 2.58W
Pregel *r.* U.S.S.R. **15** 54.41N 20.22E
Premer Australia **47** 31.26S149.54E
Prenzlau E. Germany **14** 53.19N 13.52E
Preparis *i.* Burma **29** 14.40N 93.40E
Přerov Czech. **15** 49.27N 17.27E
Prescott Ariz. U.S.A. **54** 34.33N112.28W
Presidencia Roque Sáenz Peña Argentina **62** 26.50S 60.30W
Presidente Epitácio Brazil **59** 21.56S 52.07W
Presidente Hermes Brazil **62** 11.17S 61.55W
Presidente Prudente Brazil **59** 22.09S 51.24W
Presidio U.S.A. **52** 29.34N104.23W
Prešov Czech. **15** 49.00N 21.15E
Prespa, L. Albania / Greece / Yugo. **13** 40.53N 21.02E
Presque Isle *town* Maine U.S.A. **55** 46.41N 68.01W
Prestea Ghana **38** 5.26N 2.07W
Presteigne U.K. **5** 52.17N 3.00W
Preston U.K. **4** 53.46N 2.42W
Preston Idaho U.S.A. **54** 42.06N111.53W
Prestonpans U.K. **6** 55.57N 3.00W
Prestwick U.K. **6** 55.30N 4.36W
Prêto *r.* Brazil **59** 22.00S 43.21W
Pretoria R.S.A. **39** 25.43S 28.11E
Préveza Greece **13** 38.58N 20.43E
Prey Vêng Kampuchea **26** 11.29N105.19E
Priboj Yugo. **13** 43.35N 19.31E
Příbram Czech. **14** 49.42N 14.00E
Price Utah U.S.A. **54** 39.36N110.48W
Prieska R.S.A. **39** 29.40S 22.43E
Prijedor Yugo. **13** 44.59N 16.43E
Prikaspiyskaya Nizmennost *f.* U.S.S.R. **19** 47.00N 48.00E
Prilep Yugo. **13** 41.20N 21.32E
Priluki R.S.F.S.R. U.S.S.R. **18** 63.05N 42.05E
Priluki Ukr.S.S.R. U.S.S.R. **19** 50.35N 32.24E
Primorsk R.S.F.S.R. U.S.S.R. **18** 60.18N 28.35E
Primstal W. Germany **8** 49.33N 6.59E
Prince Albert Canada **50** 53.13N105.45W
Prince Albert R.S.A. **39** 33.14S 22.02E
Prince Albert Sd. Canada **50** 70.25N115.00W
Prince Alfred C. Canada **50** 74.30N125.00W
Prince Charles I. Canada **51** 67.50N 76.00W
Prince Edward Island *d.* Canada **51** 46.15N 63.10W
Prince George Canada **50** 53.55N122.49W
Prince of Wales, C. U.S.A. **50** 66.00N168.30W
Prince of Wales I. Australia **44** 10.40S142.10E
Prince of Wales I. Canada **51** 73.00N 99.00W
Prince of Wales I. U.S.A. **50** 55.00N132.30W
Prince Patrick I. Canada **50** 77.00N120.00W
Prince Regent Inlet *str.* Canada **51** 73.00N 90.30W
Prince Rupert Canada **50** 54.09N130.20W
Princess Charlotte B. Australia **44** 14.25S144.00E
Princeton Ind. U.S.A. **55** 38.21N 87.33W
Príncipe *i.* São Tomé & Príncipe **38** 1.37N 7.27E
Príncipe da Beira Brazil **60** 12.23S 64.28W
Prinzapolca Nicaragua **57** 13.19N 83.35W
Priozersk U.S.S.R. **18** 61.01N 50.08E
Pripet Marshes *see* Polesye *f.* U.S.S.R. **15**
Pripyat *r.* U.S.S.R. **15** 51.08N 30.30E
Priština Yugo. **13** 42.39N 21.10E
Pritzwalk E. Germany **14** 53.09N 12.10E
Privas France **14** 44.44N 4.36E
Privolzhskaya Vozvyshennost *f.* U.S.S.R. **18** 53.15N 45.45E
Prizren Yugo. **13** 42.13N 20.42E
Proddatūr India **29** 14.44N 78.33E
Progreso Mexico **57** 21.20N 89.40W
Prokopyevsk U.S.S.R. **20** 53.55N 86.45E
Prome Burma **29** 18.50N 95.14E
Propriá Brazil **61** 10.15S 36.51W
Proserpine Australia **44** 20.24S148.34E
Prostějov Czech. **15** 49.29N 17.07E
Provence-Côte d'Azur *d.* France **11** 43.45N 6.00E
Providence U.S.A. **55** 41.50N 71.25W
Providence Mts. U.S.A. **54** 34.55N115.35W
Providencia, Isla de *i.* Colombia **57** 13.21N 81.22W
Provins France **9** 48.34N 3.18E
Provo U.S.A. **54** 40.14N111.39W
Prozor Yugo. **15** 43.49N 17.37E
Prudhoe Bay *town* U.S.A. **50** 70.20N148.25W
Prüm W. Germany **8** 50.12N 6.25E
Prüm *r.* W. Germany **8** 49.50N 6.29E
Pruszcz Gdański Poland **15** 54.17N 19.40E
Pruszków Poland **15** 52.11N 20.48E
Prut *r.* Romania / U.S.S.R. **15** 45.29N 28.14E
Pruzhany U.S.S.R. **15** 52.23N 24.28E
Prydz B. Antarctica **64** 68.30S 74.00E
Przemyśl Poland **15** 49.48N 22.48E
Przeworsk Poland **15** 50.05N 22.29E
Przhevalsk U.S.S.R. **24** 42.31N 78.22E
Psará *i.* Greece **13** 38.34N 25.35E
Psel *r.* U.S.S.R. **19** 49.00N 33.30E
Pskov U.S.S.R. **18** 57.48N 28.00E
Pskovskoye, Ozero *l.* U.S.S.R. **18** 58.00N 27.55E
Ptich U.S.S.R. **15** 52.15N 28.49E
Ptich *r.* U.S.S.R. **15** 52.09N 28.52E
Ptolemaís Greece **13** 40.31N 21.41E
Puán Argentina **63** 37.30S 62.45W
Pucallpa Peru **60** 8.21S 74.33W
Pucarani Bolivia **62** 16.23S 68.30W
Pucheng China **25** 27.55N118.31E
Pudasjärvi Finland **16** 65.25N 26.50E
Pudozh U.S.S.R. **18** 61.50N 36.32E
Pudozhgora U.S.S.R. **18** 62.18N 35.54E
Puebla Mexico **56** 19.03N 98.10W
Puebla *d.* Mexico **56** 18.30N 98.00W
Pueblo U.S.A. **52** 38.16N104.37W
Pueblo Hundido Chile **62** 26.23S 70.03W
Puelches Argentina **63** 38.09S 65.58W
Puelén Argentina **63** 37.32S 67.38W
Puente Alta Chile **63** 33.37S 70.35W
Puente-Genil Spain **10** 37.24N 4.46W
Puerto Aisén Chile **63** 45.27S 72.58W
Puerto Ángel Mexico **56** 15.40N 96.29W
Puerto Armuelles Panama **57** 8.19N 82.15W
Puerto Ayacucho Venezuela **60** 5.39N 67.32W
Puerto Barrios Guatemala **57** 15.41N 88.32W
Puerto Bermúdez Peru **60** 10.20S 75.00W
Puerto Berrío Colombia **60** 6.28N 74.28W
Puerto Cabello Venezuela **60** 10.29N 68.02W
Puerto Cabezas Nicaragua **57** 14.02N 83.24W
Puerto Carreño Colombia **60** 6.08N 67.27W
Puerto Casado Paraguay **62** 22.20S 57.55W
Puerto Coig Argentina **63** 50.54S 69.15W
Puerto Cortés Costa Rica **57** 8.58N 83.32W
Puerto Cortés Honduras **57** 15.50N 87.55W
Puerto de Nutrias Venezuela **60** 8.07N 69.18W
Puerto de Santa Maria Spain **10** 36.36N 6.14W

erto Heath Bolivia 60 12.30S 68.40W
erto Juárez Mexico 57 21.26N 86.51W
erto La Cruz Venezuela 60 10.14N 64.40W
erto Leguízamo Colombia 60 0.12S 74.46W
ertollano Spain 10 38.41N 4.07W
erto Lobos Argentina 63 42.01S 65.04W
erto Madryn Argentina 63 42.46S 65.02W
erto Maldonado Peru 60 12.37S 69.11W
erto Melendez Peru 60 4.30S 77.30W
erto Montt Chile 63 41.28S 73.00W
erto Natales Chile 63 51.44S 72.31W
erto Páez Venezuela 60 6.13N 67.28W
erto Peñasco Mexico 56 31.20N113.33W
erto Pinasco Paraguay 59 22.36S 57.53W
erto Plata Dom. Rep. 57 19.48N 70.41W
erto Princesa Phil. 26 9.46N118.45E
erto Quepos Costa Rica 57 9.28N 84.10W
erto Rey Colombia 60 8.48N 76.34W
erto Rico C. America 57 18.20N 66.30W
erto Rico Trench Atlantic Oc. 57 19.50N 6.00W
erto Saavedra Chile 63 38.47S 73.24W
erto Santa Cruz Argentina 63 50.03S 68.35W
erto Sastre Paraguay 59 22.02S 58.00W
erto Siles Bolivia 62 12.48S 65.05W
erto Tejado Colombia 60 3.16N 76.22W
erto Vallarta Mexico 56
erto Varas Chile 63 41.20S 73.00W
gachev U.S.S.R. 18 52.02N 48.49E
glia d. Italy 13 41.00N 16.40E
isaye, Collines de la hills France 9 47.34N .28E
kaki, L. New Zealand 48 44.00S170.10E
kekohe New Zealand 48 37.12S174.56E
keuri New Zealand 48 45.02S171.02E
khovichi U.S.S.R. 15 53.28N 28.18E
la Yugo. 14 44.52N 13.53E
lacayo Bolivia 62 20.25S 66.41W
lawy Poland 15 51.25N 21.57E
lkkila Finland 16 64.16N 25.52E
llman U.S.A. 54 46.44N117.10W
log mtn. Phil. 27 16.50N120.50E
lozero U.S.S.R. 18 68.22N 33.15E
ltusk Poland 15 52.42N 21.02E
ma Tanzania 37 5.02S 34.46E
ncak Jaya mtn. Indonesia 27 4.00S137.15E
ne India 28 18.34N 73.58E
njab d. India 28 30.30N 75.15E
no Peru 60 15.53S 70.03W
nta Alta town Argentina 63 38.50S 62.00W
nta Arenas town Chile 63 53.10S 70.56W
ntabie Australia 46 32.15S134.13E
nta Delgada town Argentina 63 42.43S 3.38W
nta Gorda town Belize 57 16.10N 88.45W
ntarenas Costa Rica 57 10.00N 84.50W
nto Fijo Venezuela 60 11.50N 70.16W
olanka Finland 16 64.52N 27.40E
quio Peru 60 14.44S 74.07W
r r. U.S.S.R. 20 67.30N 75.30E
rari r. P.N.G. 27 7.49S145.10E
ri India 29 19.49N 85.54E
rnea India 29 25.47N 87.28E
rros Namibia 39 18.38S 12.59E
rúlia India 29 23.20N 86.24E
rus r. Brazil 60 3.58S 61.25W
san S. Korea 25 35.05N129.02E
shkin U.S.S.R. 18 59.43N 30.22E
shkino U.S.S.R. 19 51.16N 47.09E
spökladány Hungary 15 47.19N 21.07E
stoshka U.S.S.R. 18 56.20N 29.20E
tao Burma 29 27.22N 97.27E
taruru New Zealand 48 38.03S175.47E
tian China 25 25.32N119.02E
ting, Tanjung c. Indonesia 26 3.35S111.52E
toran, Gory mts. U.S.S.R. 21 68.30N 96.00E
tsonderwater R.S.A. 39 29.14S 21.50E
ttalam Sri Lanka 29 8.02N 79.50E
ttgarden W. Germany 14 54.30N 11.13E
tumayo r. Brazil 60 3.05S 68.10W
ulavesi l. Finland 17 61.50N 26.42E
yallup U.S.A. 54 47.11N122.18W
y de Dôme mtn. France 11 45.46N 2.56E
ysegur Pt. New Zealand 48 46.10S166.35E
vani d. Tanzania 37 7.00S 39.00E
veto Zaïre 37 8.27S 28.52E
vllheli U.K. 4 52.53N 4.25W
yaozero, Ozero l. U.S.S.R. 18 66.00N 31.00E
yapon Burma 29 16.15N 95.40E
yasina r. U.S.S.R. 21 73.10N 84.55E
yatigorsk U.S.S.R. 19 44.04N 43.06E
yhä r. Finland 16 64.28N 24.13E
yhäjärvi l. Oulu Finland 16 63.35N 25.57E
yhäjärvi l. Turku-Pori Finland 17 61.00N 22.20E
yhäjoki Finland 16 64.28N 24.14E
yinmana Burma 29 19.45N 96.12E
yöngyang N. Korea 25 39.00N125.47E
yramid U.S.A. 54 40.05N119.43W
yramid Hill town Australia 46 36.03S144.24E
yramid L. U.S.A. 54 40.00N119.35W
yrénées mts. France/Spain 11 42.40N 0.30E
yrzyce Poland 14 53.10N 14.55E
yttegja mtn. Norway 17 62.13N 7.42E

Q

aanaaq see Thule Greenland 51
ā'emshahr Iran 31 36.28N 52.53E
agcaka China 29 32.32N 81.49E
ahā Egypt 32 30.17N 31.12E
alāt Afghan. 28 32.07N 66.54E
al'eh-ye Now Afghan 31 34.58N 63.04E
alyūb Egypt 32 30.11N 31.12E
amdo China 24 31.11N 97.18E
anâtir Muhammad 'Alī Egypt 32 30.12N 31.08E
andahār Afghan. 28 31.36N 65.47E
andala Somali Rep. 35 11.23N 49.53E
aquortoq see Julianehåb Greenland 51
ārah Egypt 30 27.37N 26.30E
Qareh Sū Iran 31 34.52N 51.25E
Qareh Sū r. Iran 31 35.58N 56.25E
Qarqan He r. China 24 40.56N 86.27E
Qārūn, Birkat l. Egypt 32 29.30N 30.40E
Qasigiannguit see Christianshåb Greenland 51
Qaşr al Farâfirah Egypt 30 27.15N 28.10E
Qaşr-e Qand Iran 31 26.13N 60.37E
Qatanā Syria 32 33.27N 36.04E
Qatar Asia 31 25.20N 51.10E
Qaṭrānī, Jabal mts. Egypt 32 29.40N 30.36E
Qattara Depression see Qaṭṭārah, Munkhaf. f. Egypt 30
Qaṭṭārah, Munkhafaḍ al f. Egypt 30 29.40N 27.30E
Qāyen Iran 31 33.44N 59.07E
Qazvīn Iran 31 36.16N 50.00E
Qeqertarsuaq see Godhavn Greenland 51
Qeqertarsuatsiaat see Fiskenaesset Greenland 51
Qeshm Iran 31 26.58N 57.17E
Qeshm i. Iran 31 26.48N 55.48E
Qezel Owzan r. Iran 31 36.44N 49.27E
Qezi'ot Israel 32 30.52N 34.28E
Qianjiang China 25 29.31N108.46E
Qiemo China 24 38.08N 85.33E
Qilian Shan mts. China 24 38.30N 99.20E
Qimantag mts. China 24 37.45N 89.40E
Qinā Egypt 30 26.10N 32.43E
Qinā, Wādī r. Egypt 30 26.07N 32.42E
Qingdao China 25 36.04N120.22E
Qinghai d. China 24 36.15N 96.00E
Qinghai Hu l. China 24 36.40N100.00E
Qingjiang China 25 28.02N115.23E
Qingxu China 25 37.36N112.21E
Qingyang China 24 36.06N107.49E
Qing Zang Gaoyuan f. China 24 34.00N 84.30E
Qinhuangdao China 25 39.55N119.37E
Qin Ling mts. China 25 33.40N109.00E
Qinzhou China 25 21.57N108.37E
Qiqihar China 25 47.23N124.00E
Qira China 24 37.02N 80.53E
Qiryat Gat Israel 32 31.37N 34.47E
Qiryat Shemona Israel 32 33.13N 35.35E
Qishn S. Yemen 28 15.25N 51.40E
Qom Iran 31 34.40N 50.57E
Qornet'es Sauda mtn. Lebanon 32 34.17N 36.04E
Qoṭūr Iran 31 38.28N 44.25E
Quairading Australia 43 32.00S117.22E
Quakenbrück W. Germany 8 52.41N 7.59E
Quambatook Australia 46 35.52S143.36E
Quambone Australia 47 30.54S147.55E
Quang Ngai Vietnam 26 15.09N108.50E
Quang Tri Vietnam 26 16.46N107.11E
Quan Long Vietnam 26 9.11N105.09E
Quanzhou Fujian China 25 24.57N118.36E
Qu'Appelle r. Canada 51 51.13N 98.05W
Quaraí Brazil 63 30.23S 56.27W
Quaraí r. Brazil 63 30.12S 57.36W
Quartu Sant'Elena Italy 12 39.14N 9.11E
Quartzsite U.S.A. 54 33.40N114.13W
Qūchān Iran 31 37.04N 58.29E
Queanbeyan Australia 47 35.24S149.17E
Québec Canada 55 46.50N 71.15W
Québec d. Canada 51 52.00N 72.00W
Quebracho Uruguay 63 31.57S 57.53W
Quedlinburg E. Germany 14 51.48N 11.09E
Queen Charlotte Is. Canada 50 53.00N132.30W
Queen Charlotte Str. Canada 50 51.00N129.00W
Queen Elizabeth Is. Canada 51 78.30N 99.00W
Queen Maud G. Canada 51 68.30N 99.00W
Queen Maud Range mts. Antarctica 64 86.20S165.00W
Queens Channel Australia 42 14.46S129.24E
Queenscliff Australia 47 38.17S144.42E
Queensland d. Australia 44 23.30S144.00E
Queenstown Australia 45 42.07S145.33E
Queenstown New Zealand 48 45.03S168.41E
Queenstown R.S.A. 39 31.52S 26.51E
Queguay Grande r. Uruguay 63 32.09S 58.09W
Queimadas Brazil 61 10.58S 39.38W
Quela Angola 36 9.18S 17.05E
Quelimane Mozambique 37 17.53S 36.57E
Quemado U.S.A. 54 34.20N108.30W
Quequén Argentina 63 38.34S 58.42W
Querétaro Mexico 56 20.38N100.23W
Querétaro d. Mexico 56 21.03N100.00W
Quesnel Canada 50 53.03N122.31W
Quetta Pakistan 28 30.15N 67.00E
Quettehou France 9 49.36N 1.18W
Quevedo Ecuador 60 0.59S 79.27W
Quezaltenango Guatemala 56 14.50N 91.30W
Quezon City Phil. 27 14.39N121.01E
Quibdo Colombia 60 5.40N 76.38W
Quiberon France 11 47.29N 3.07W
Quilán, C. Chile 63 43.16S 74.27W
Quilengues Angola 36 14.09S 14.04E
Quillabamba Peru 60 12.50S 72.50W
Quillacollo Bolivia 62 17.26S 66.17W
Quillota Chile 63 32.53S 71.16W
Quilon India 28 8.53N 76.38E
Quilpie Australia 44 26.37S144.15E
Quilpué Chile 63 33.03S 71.27W
Quimilí Argentina 62 27.35S 62.25W
Quimper France 11 48.00N 4.06W
Quimperlé France 11 47.52N 3.33W
Quincy Ill. U.S.A. 53 39.55N 91.22W
Quincy Wash. U.S.A. 54 47.14N119.51W
Qui Nhon Vietnam 26 13.47N109.11E
Quintanar de la Orden Spain 10 39.36N 3.05W
Quintana Roo d. Mexico 57 19.00N 88.00W
Quinto Spain 10 41.25N 0.30W
Quionga Mozambique 37 10.37S 40.31E
Quirigua ruins Guatemala 57 15.20N 89.25W
Quissanga Mozambique 37 12.24S 40.33E
Quissico Mozambique 39 24.42S 34.44E
Quiterajo Mozambique 37 11.46S 40.25E
Quito Ecuador 60 0.14S 78.30W
Quorn Australia 46 32.20S138.02E
Qurayyah, Wādī r. Egypt 32 30.26N 34.01E
Qurdūd Sudan 35 10.17N 29.56E
Qu Xian China 25 28.57N118.52E

R

Raahe Finland 16 64.41N 24.29E
Raalte Neth. 8 52.22N 6.17E
Raasay i. U.K. 6 57.25N 6.05W
Rába r. Hungary 15 47.42N 17.38E
Raba Indonesia 26 8.27S118.45E
Rabat Morocco 34 34.02N 6.51W
Rābor Iran 31 29.18N 56.56E
Racconigi Italy 9 44.46N 9.46E
Race, C. Canada 51 46.40N 53.10W
Rach Gia Vietnam 26 10.02N105.05E
Racibórz Poland 15 50.06N 18.13E
Racine U.S.A. 53 42.42N 87.50W
Rădăuţi Romania 15 47.51N 25.55E
Radebeul E. Germany 14 51.06N 13.41E
Radekhov U.S.S.R. 15 50.18N 24.35E
Radium Hill town Australia 46 32.30S140.32E
Radom Poland 15 51.26N 21.10E
Radomir Bulgaria 13 42.32N 22.56E
Radomsko Poland 15 51.05N 19.25E
Radomyshl U.S.S.R. 15 50.30N 29.14E
Radöy i. Norway 17 60.38N 5.05E
Radstock U.K. 5 51.17N 2.25W
Radstock, C. Australia 46 33.11S134.21E
Raḍwā, Jabal mtn. Saudi Arabia 30 24.36N 38.18E
Rae Canada 50 62.50N116.03W
Raeren W. Germany 8 50.41N 6.07E
Raeside, L. Australia 43 29.30S122.00E
Rafaela Argentina 62 31.16S 61.44W
Rafaḥ Egypt 32 31.18N 34.15E
Rafaï C.A.R. 35 4.56N 23.55E
Rafḥā Saudi Arabia 30 29.38N 43.30E
Rafsanjān Iran 31 30.24N 56.00E
Ragged, Mt. Australia 43 33.27S123.27E
Ragunda Sweden 16 63.06N 16.23E
Ragusa Italy 12 36.56N 14.44E
Raha Indonesia 27 4.50S122.43E
Raḥá, Ḥarrat ar f. Saudi Arabia 32 28.00N 36.35E
Rāichūr India 28 16.15N 77.20E
Raiganj India 29 25.38N 88.11E
Raigarh India 29 21.53N 83.28E
Rainbow Australia 46 35.56S142.01E
Rainier, Mt. U.S.A. 54 46.52N121.46W
Raipur India 29 21.16N 81.42E
Ra'is Saudi Arabia 30 23.35N 38.36E
Rājahmundry India 29 17.01N 81.52E
Rajang r. Malaysia 26 2.10N112.45E
Rājapālaiyam India 28 9.26N 77.36E
Rājasthān d. India 28 27.00N 74.00E
Rājgarh Madhya P. India 28 23.56N 76.58E
Rājkot India 28 22.18N 70.53E
Rakaia New Zealand 48 43.45S172.01E
Rakaia r. New Zealand 48 43.52S172.13E
Rakhov U.S.S.R. 15 48.02N 24.10E
Rakitnoye U.S.S.R. 15 51.18N 27.10E
Rakops Botswana 39 21.00S 24.32E
Rakov U.S.S.R. 15 53.58N 26.59E
Rakulka U.S.S.R. 18 62.19N 46.52E
Råkvåg Norway 16 63.47N 10.10E
Rakvere U.S.S.R. 18 59.22N 26.28E
Raleigh U.S.A. 53 35.46N 78.39W
Rama Nicaragua 57 12.09N 84.15W
Rāmah Saudi Arabia 31 25.33N 47.08E
Rām Allāh Jordan 32 31.55N 35.12E
Ramallo Argentina 63 33.28S 60.02W
Ramat Gan Israel 32 32.05N 34.48E
Rambouillet France 9 48.39N 1.50E
Rame Head U.K. 5 50.18N 4.13W
Ramelton Rep. of Ire. 7 55.02N 7.40W
Rāmhormoz Iran 31 31.14N 49.37E
Ramillies Belgium 8 50.39N 4.56E
Ramingstein Austria 14 47.04N 13.50E
Ramla Israel 32 31.56N 34.52E
Ramlo mtn. Ethiopia 35 13.20N 41.45E
Ramona Calif. U.S.A. 54 33.08N116.52W
Ramore Canada 55 48.27N 80.20W
Ramos Arizpe Mexico 56 25.35N100.59W
Rāmpur Uttar P. India 29 28.48N 79.03E
Ramree I. Burma 29 19.10N 93.40E
Rāmsar Iran 31 36.54N 50.41E
Ramsey England U.K. 5 52.27N 0.06W
Ramsey I.o.M. U.K. 4 54.19N 4.23W
Ramsey L. Canada 55 47.15N 82.16W
Ramsgate U.K. 5 51.20N 1.25E
Rāmshīr Iran 31 30.54N 49.24E
Ramsjö Sweden 17 62.11N 15.39E
Ramu r. P.N.G. 27 4.00S144.40E
Ranau Malaysia 26 5.58N116.41E
Rancagua Chile 63 34.10S 70.45W
Rānchī India 29 23.22N 85.20E
Rand Australia 47 35.34S146.35E
Randalstown U.K. 7 54.45N 6.20W
Randers Denmark 17 56.28N 10.03E
Randsburg U.S.A. 54 35.22N117.39W
Randsfjorden l. Norway 17 60.25N 10.24E
Råne r. Sweden 16 65.52N 22.19E
Råneå Sweden 16 65.52N 22.18E
Rangely U.S.A. 54 40.05N108.48W
Rangemore Australia 46 35.19S144.22E
Rangia India 29 26.28N 91.38E
Rangiora New Zealand 48 43.18S172.38E
Rangitaiki r. New Zealand 48 37.55S176.50E
Rangoon Burma 29 16.45N 96.20E
Rankin Inlet town Canada 51 62.52N 92.00W
Rankins Springs town Australia 47 33.52S146.18E
Rannoch, Loch U.K. 6 56.41N 4.20W
Rann of Kutch f. India 28 23.50N 69.50E
Ranong Thailand 29 9.59N 98.40E
Rantauparapat Indonesia 26 2.05N 99.46E
Rantekombola mtn. Indonesia 26 3.30S119.58E
Rapallo Italy 9 44.20N 9.14E
Rapid Bay town Australia 46 35.33S138.09E
Rapid City U.S.A. 52 44.05N103.14W
Raquette Lake town U.S.A. 55 43.49N 74.41W
Ra's al Ḥadd c. Oman 28 22.32N 59.49E
Ra's al Khaymah U.A.E. 31 25.48N 55.56E
Ra's an Nabq town Egypt 32 29.36N 34.51E
Ra's an Naqb town Jordan 32 30.30N 35.29E
Ra's Banās c. Egypt 35 23.54N 35.48E
Ras Dashen mtn. Ethiopia 35 13.20N 38.10E
Râs Ghârib Egypt 32 28.22N 33.04E
Rashīd Egypt 32 31.25N 30.25E
Rasht Iran 31 37.18N 49.38E
Raška Yugo. 13 43.17N 20.37E
Rason, L. Australia 43 28.46S124.20E
Ratangarh India 28 28.05N 74.36E
Rat Buri Thailand 26 13.30N 99.50E
Rathcormack Rep. of Ire. 7 52.05N 8.18W
Rathdrum Rep. of Ire. 7 52.56N 6.15W
Rathenow E. Germany 14 52.37N 12.21E
Rathlin I. U.K. 7 55.17N 6.15W
Rath Luirc Rep. of Ire. 7 52.21N 8.41W
Rathmullen Rep. of Ire. 7 55.06N 7.32W
Ratlām India 28 23.18N 75.06E
Ratnāgiri India 28 16.59N 73.18E
Ratno U.S.S.R. 15 51.40N 24.32E
Raton U.S.A. 52 36.54N104.24W
Rattlesnake Range mts. U.S.A. 54 42.45N107.10W
Rattray Head U.K. 6 57.37N 1.50W
Rättvik Sweden 17 60.53N 15.06E
Rauch Argentina 63 36.47S 59.05W
Raufoss Norway 17 60.43N 10.37E
Raul Soares Brazil 59 20.04S 42.27W
Rauma Finland 17 61.08N 21.30E
Rauma r. Norway 16 62.32N 7.43E
Raurkela India 29 22.16N 85.01E
Rautas Sweden 16 68.00N 19.55E
Rāvar Iran 31 31.14N 56.51E
Rava-Russkaya U.S.S.R. 15 50.15N 23.36E
Ravena U.S.A. 55 42.29N 73.49W
Ravenna Italy 9 44.25N 12.12E
Ravensburg W. Germany 14 47.47N 9.37E
Ravenshoe Australia 44 17.37S145.29E
Ravensthorpe Australia 43 33.35S120.02E
Ravenswood Australia 44 20.05S146.52E
Ravī r. Pakistan 28 30.30N 72.13E
Rāwalpindi Pakistan 28 33.40N 73.08E
Rawāndūz Iraq 31 36.38N 44.32E
Rawene New Zealand 48 35.24S173.30E
Rawicz Poland 14 51.37N 16.52E
Rawlinna Australia 43 31.00S125.21E
Rawlins U.S.A. 54 41.47N107.14W
Rawson Argentina 63 34.40S 60.02W
Raya mtn. Indonesia 26 0.45S112.45E
Rāyen Iran 31 29.34N 57.26E
Raymond U.S.A. 54 46.41N123.44W
Raymond Terrace Australia 47 32.47S151.45E
Razan Iran 31 35.22N 49.02E
Razdelnaya U.S.S.R. 15 46.50N 30.02E
Razgrad Bulgaria 15 43.32N 26.30E
Ré, Île de i. France 11 46.10N 1.26W
Reading U.K. 5 51.27N 0.57W
Reading U.S.A. 55 40.20N 75.56W
Realicó Argentina 63 35.02S 64.14W
Reay Forest f. U.K. 6 58.17N 4.48W
Rebi Indonesia 27 6.24S134.07E
Reboly U.S.S.R. 18 63.50N 30.49E
Recalde Argentina 63 36.39S 61.05W
Recherche, Archipelago of the is. Australia 43 34.05S122.45E
Rechitsa U.S.S.R. 15 52.21N 30.24E
Recife Brazil 61 8.06S 34.53W
Recklinghausen W. Germany 8 51.36N 7.11E
Reconquista Argentina 62 29.08S 59.38W
Recreo Argentina 62 29.20S 65.04W
Red r. Canada 51 50.30N 96.50W
Red r. U.S.A. 53 31.10N 92.00W
Red r. see Hong Hà r. Vietnam 26
Red Bluff U.S.A. 54 40.11N122.15W
Redcar U.K. 4 54.37N 1.04W
Red Cliffs town Australia 46 34.22S142.13E
Red Deer Canada 50 52.15N113.48W
Redding U.S.A. 54 40.35N122.24W
Redditch U.K. 5 52.18N 1.57W
Rede r. U.K. 4 55.08N 2.13W
Red Hill town Australia 46 33.34S138.12E
Red L. U.S.A. 53 48.00N 95.00W
Red Lake town Canada 51 50.59N 93.40W
Redlands U.S.A. 54 34.03N117.11W
Red Lodge U.S.A. 54 45.11N109.15W
Redmond U.S.A. 54 44.17N121.11W
Red Oak U.S.A. 53 41.01N 95.15W
Redondela Spain 10 42.15N 8.38W
Redondo Portugal 10 38.39N 7.33W
Redondo Beach town U.S.A. 54 33.51N118.23W
Redrock U.S.A. 54 32.35N111.19W
Redruth U.K. 5 50.14N 5.14W
Red Sea Africa/Asia 35 20.00N 39.00E
Red Volta r. Ghana 38 10.32N 0.31W
Redwood City U.S.A. 54 37.29N122.13W
Ree, Lough Rep. of Ire. 7 53.31N 7.58W
Reed City U.S.A. 55 43.54N 85.31W
Reedsport U.S.A. 54 43.42N124.06W
Reefton New Zealand 48 42.07S171.52E
Reese r. U.S.A. 54 40.39N116.54W
Reftele Sweden 17 57.11N 13.35E
Rega r. Poland 14 54.10N 15.18E
Regensburg W. Germany 14 49.01N 12.07E
Reggane Algeria 34 26.30N 0.30E
Reggio Calabria Italy 12 38.07N 15.38E
Reggio Emilia-Romagna Italy 9 44.40N 10.37E
Reghin Romania 15 46.47N 24.42E
Regina Canada 50 50.30N104.38W
Regnéville France 9 49.01N 1.33W
Rehoboth Namibia 39 23.19S 17.10E
Rehovot Israel 32 31.54N 34.46E
Reigate U.K. 5 51.14N 0.13W
Reims France 9 49.15N 4.02E
Reindeer L. Canada 50 57.00N102.20W
Reinosa Spain 10 43.01N 4.09W
Remanso Brazil 61 9.41S 42.04W
Remarkable, Mt. Australia 46 32.48S138.10E
Rembang Indonesia 26 6.45S111.22E
Remeshk Iran 31 26.52N 58.46E
Remich Lux. 8 49.34N 6.23E
Remiremont France 11 48.01N 6.35E
Remscheid W. Germany 8 51.10N 7.11E
Rena Norway 17 61.08N 11.22E
Rendsburg W. Germany 14 54.19N 9.39E
Renfrew Canada 55 45.28N 76.41W
Rengat Indonesia 26 0.26S102.35E
Rengo Chile 63 34.25S 70.52W
Renheji China 25 31.56N115.07E
Reni U.S.S.R. 15 45.28N 28.17E
Renkum Neth. 8 51.59N 5.46E
Renmark Australia 46 34.10S140.45E
Renner Springs town Australia 44 18.20S133.48E
Rennes France 9 48.06N 1.40W
Reno r. Italy 9 44.36N 12.17E
Reno U.S.A. 54 39.31N119.48W
Renton U.S.A. 54 47.30N122.11W
Réo Burkina Faso 38 12.20N 2.27W
Repki U.S.S.R. 15 51.47N 31.06E
Republic Wash. U.S.A. 54 48.39N118.44W
Republican r. U.S.A. 53 39.05N 94.50W
Republic of Ireland Europe 7 53.00N 8.00W
Republic of South Africa Africa 39 28.30S 24.50E
Repulse B. Australia 44 20.36S148.43E
Repulse Bay town Canada 51 66.35N 86.20W
Requa U.S.A. 54 41.34N124.05W
Requena Peru 60 5.05S 73.52W
Requena Spain 10 39.29N 1.08W
Resistencia Argentina 62 27.28S 59.00W
Reşiţa Romania 15 45.17N 21.53E
Resolute Canada 51 74.40N 95.00W
Resolution I. Canada 51 61.30N 65.00W
Resolution I. New Zealand 48 45.40S166.30E
Restigouche r. Canada 55 48.02N 66.22W
Rethel France 9 49.31N 4.22E
Réthimnon Greece 13 35.22N 24.29E
Reus Spain 10 41.10N 1.06E
Reusel Neth. 8 51.21N 5.09E
Reutlingen W. Germany 14 48.30N 9.13E
Reutte Austria 14 47.29N 10.43E
Revda U.S.S.R. 18 56.49N 59.58E
Revelstoke Canada 50 51.02N118.12W
Revilla Gigedo, Islas de is. Mexico 56 19.00N111.00W
Revin France 8 49.58N 4.40E
Revue r. Mozambique 39 19.58S 34.40E
Rexburg U.S.A. 54 43.49N111.47W
Rexford U.S.A. 54 48.53N115.13W
Rey Iran 31 35.35N 51.27E
Reykjavík Iceland 16 64.09N 21.58W
Reynosa Mexico 56 26.09N 97.10W
Rezā'īyeh Iran 31 37.32N 45.02E
Rezé France 11 47.12N 1.34W
Rēzekne U.S.S.R. 18 56.30N 27.22E
Rhayader U.K. 5 52.19N 3.30W
Rheden Neth. 8 52.01N 6.02E
Rhein r. Europe 8 51.53N 6.03E
Rheinbach W. Germany 8 50.39N 6.59E
Rheine W. Germany 8 52.17N 7.26E
Rheinland-Pfalz d. W. Germany 8 50.05N 7.09E
Rhenen Neth. 8 51.58N 5.34E
Rheydt W. Germany 8 51.10N 6.25E
Rhine see Rhein r. Europe 8
Rhinelander U.S.A. 53 45.39N 89.23W
Rhino Camp town Uganda 37 2.58N 31.20E
Rho Italy 9 45.32N 9.02E
Rhode Island d. U.S.A. 55 41.40N 71.30W
Rhodes i. see Ródhos i. Greece 13
Rhodopi Planina mts. Bulgaria 13 41.35N 24.35E
Rhondda U.K. 5 51.39N 3.30W
Rhône r. France 11 43.25N 4.45E
Rhône-Alpes d. France 11 45.20N 5.45E
Rhosneigr U.K. 4 53.14N 4.31W
Rhum i. U.K. 6 57.00N 6.20W
Rhyl U.K. 4 53.19N 3.29W
Riachão Brazil 61 7.22S 46.37W
Riau d. Indonesia 26 0.00 102.35E
Riau, Kepulauan is. Indonesia 26 0.50N104.00E
Ribadeo Spain 10 43.32N 7.04W
Ribarroja, Embalse de resr. Spain 10 41.12N 0.20E
Ribauè Mozambique 37 14.57S 38.27E
Ribble r. U.K. 4 53.45N 2.44W
Ribe Denmark 17 55.21N 8.46E
Ribeauvillé France 11 48.12N 7.19E
Ribécourt France 9 49.31N 2.55E
Ribécourt France 8 49.31N 2.52E
Ribeirão Prêto Brazil 59 21.09S 47.48W
Ribérac France 11 45.14N 0.22E
Riberalta Bolivia 62 10.59S 66.06W
Ribnitz-Damgarten E. Germany 14 54.15N 12.28E
Riccione Italy 9 43.59N 12.39E
Rice U.S.A. 54 34.06N114.50W
Richard's Bay town R.S.A. 39 28.47S 32.06E
Richfield Idaho U.S.A. 54 43.03N114.09W
Richfield Utah U.S.A. 54 38.46N112.05W
Richland U.S.A. 54 46.17N119.18W
Richmond N.S.W. Australia 47 33.36S150.46E
Richmond Qld. Australia 44 20.44S143.08E
Richmond New Zealand 48 41.20S173.10E
Richmond C.P. R.S.A. 39 31.24S 23.56E
Richmond U.K. 4 54.24N 1.43W
Richmond Ind. U.S.A. 55 39.50N 84.51W
Richmond Utah U.S.A. 54 41.55N111.48W
Richmond Va. U.S.A. 53 37.34N 77.27W
Richmond Hill town Canada 55 43.53N 79.26W
Richmond Range mts. Australia 47 29.00S152.48E
Ricobayo, Embalse de resr. Spain 10 41.40N 5.50W
Ridderkerk Neth. 8 51.53N 4.39E

Rideau Lakes Canada 55 44.45N 76.14W
Ridgway U.S.A. 55 41.26N 78.44W
Ried Austria 14 48.13N 13.30E
Riemst Belgium 8 50.49N 5.38E
Riesa E. Germany 14 51.18N 13.18E
Rieti Italy 12 42.24N 12.53E
Rifle U.S.A. 54 39.32N107.47W
Rift Valley d. Kenya 37 1.00N 36.00E
Riga U.S.S.R. 17 56.53N 24.08E
Riga, G. of see Rīgas Jūras Līcis g. U.S.S.R. 17
Rīgān Iran 31 28.40N 58.58E
Rīgas Jūras Līcis g. U.S.S.R. 17 57.30N 23.35E
Rīgestān f. Afghan. 28 31.00N 65.00E
Riggins U.S.A. 54 45.25N116.19W
Rīg Matī Iran 31 27.40N 58.11E
Rigo P.N.G. 44 9.50S147.35E
Rigolet Canada 51 54.10N 58.30W
Riihimäki Finland 17 60.45N 24.46E
Riiser-Larsenhalvöya pen. Antarctica 64 68.00S 35.00E
Rijeka Yugo. 12 45.20N 14.25E
Rijssen Neth. 8 52.19N 6.31E
Rijswijk Neth. 8 52.03N 4.22E
Riley U.S.A. 54 43.31N119.28W
Rimah, Wādī ar r. Saudi Arabia 30 26.10N 44.00E
Rimavská Sobota Czech. 15 48.23N 20.02E
Rimbo Sweden 17 59.45N 18.22E
Rimini Italy 9 44.01N 12.34E
Rîmnicu-Sărat Romania 15 45.24N 27.06E
Rîmnicu-Vîlcea Romania 15 45.06N 24.22E
Rimouski Canada 55 48.27N 68.32W
Rinconada Argentina 62 22.26S 66.10W
Rindal Norway 16 63.04N 9.13E
Ringebu Norway 17 61.31N 10.10E
Ringerike Norway 17 60.10N 10.12E
Ringim Nigeria 38 12.09N 9.08E
Ringköbing Denmark 17 56.05N 8.15E
Ringling U.S.A. 54 46.16N110.49W
Ringsted Denmark 17 55.27N 11.49E
Ringvassöy i. Norway 16 69.55N 19.10E
Ringwood Australia 47 37.51S145.13E
Ringwood U.K. 5 50.50N 1.48W
Riobamba Ecuador 60 1.44S 78.40W
Rio Branco Brazil 60 9.59S 67.49W
Rio Bueno Chile 63 40.20S 72.55W
Rio Casca Brazil 59 20.13S 42.38W
Rio Claro Brazil 59 22.19S 47.35W
Río Cuarto Argentina 63 33.08S 64.20W
Rio de Janeiro Brazil 59 22.53S 43.17W
Rio de Janeiro d. Brazil 59 22.00S 42.30W
Río Gallegos Argentina 63 51.37S 69.10W
Río Grande town Argentina 63 53.50S 67.40W
Rio Grande town Brazil 59 32.03S 52.08W
Rio Grande r. Mexico/U.S.A. 56 25.55N 97.08W
Río Grande r. Nicaragua 57 12.48N 83.30W
Rio Grande do Norte d. Brazil 61 6.00S 36.30W
Rio Grande do Sul d. Brazil 59 30.15S 53.30W
Ríohacha Colombia 60 11.34N 72.58W
Rio Largo Brazil 61 9.28S 35.50W
Río Negro d. Argentina 63 40.00S 67.00W
Rio Negro Brazil 59 26.06S 49.48W
Río Negro, Embalse del resr. Uruguay 63 32.45S 56.00W
Rio Novo Brazil 59 21.15S 43.09W
Rio Piracicaba Brazil 59 19.54S 43.10W
Rio Pomba Brazil 59 21.15S 43.12W
Rio Prêto Brazil 59 22.06S 43.52W
Ríosucio Colombia 60 7.27N 77.07W
Río Tercero Argentina 62 32.10S 64.05W
Rio Verde town Brazil 62 17.50S 50.55W
Ripley N.Y. U.S.A. 55 42.16N 79.43W
Ripon U.K. 4 54.08N 1.31W
Rirapora Brazil 59 17.20S 45.02W
Risbäck Sweden 16 64.42N 15.32E
Riscle France 11 43.40N 0.05W
Rishā, Wādī ar r. Saudi Arabia 31 25.40N 44.08E
Rishon LeZiyyon Israel 32 31.57N 34.48E
Risle r. France 9 49.26N 0.23E
Risör Norway 17 58.43N 9.14E
Riti Nigeria 38 7.57N 9.41E
Ritzville U.S.A. 54 47.08N118.23W
Riva Italy 9 45.53N 10.50E
Rivadavia Argentina 62 24.11S 62.53W
Rivarolo Canavese Italy 9 45.25N 7.36E
Rivas Nicaragua 57 11.26N 85.50W
Rivera Uruguay 63 30.54S 55.31W
River Cess town Liberia 34 5.28N 9.32W
Rivergaro Italy 9 44.55N 9.36E
Riverhead U.S.A. 55 40.55N 72.40W
Riverina f. Australia 47 34.30S145.20E
Rivers d. Nigeria 38 4.45N 6.35E
Riversdale R.S.A. 39 34.05S 21.15E
Riverside U.S.A. 54 33.59N117.22W
Riverton Australia 46 34.08S138.24E
Riverton Canada 51 50.59N 96.59W
Riverton New Zealand 48 46.21S168.01E
Riverton U.S.A. 54 43.02N108.23W
Riviera di Levante f. Italy 9 44.00N 9.40E
Riviera di Ponente f. Italy 9 43.40N 8.00E
Rivière-du-Loup town Canada 55 47.49N 69.32W
Rivière Pentecôte town Canada 55 49.46N 67.12W
Rivoli Italy 9 45.04N 7.31E
Riyadh see Ar Riyāḍ Saudi Arabia 31
Rize Turkey 30 41.03N 40.31E
Rizokárpason Cyprus 32 35.35N 34.24E
Rizzuto, Capo c. Italy 13 38.54N 17.06E
Rjukan Norway 17 59.52N 8.34E
Roa Norway 17 60.17N 10.37E
Roag, Loch U.K. 6 58.14N 6.50W
Roanne France 11 46.02N 4.05E
Roanoke r. U.S.A. 53 36.00N 76.35W
Roanoke Va. U.S.A. 53 37.15N 79.58W
Robāṭ Iran 31 30.04N 54.49E
Robe Australia 46 37.11S139.45E
Robe, Mt. Australia 46 31.39S141.16E
Roberts, Mt. Australia 47 28.12S152.21E
Robertson R.S.A. 39 33.48S 19.52E
Robertsport Liberia 34 6.45N 11.22W
Robertstown Australia 46 33.59S139.03E
Roberval Canada 55 48.31N 72.16W
Robin Hood's Bay town U.K. 4 54.26N 0.31W
Robinson r. Australia 44 16.03S137.16E
Robinson Ranges mts. Australia 42 25.45S119.00E
Robinvale Australia 46 34.37S142.50E
Robledo Spain 10 38.46N 2.26W
Roboré Bolivia 62 18.20S 59.45W
Robson, Mt. Canada 50 53.00N119.09W
Roccella Italy 13 38.19N 16.24E
Rocciamelone mtn. Italy 9 45.12N 7.05E
Rocha Uruguay 59 34.30S 54.22W
Rocha da Gale, Barragem dam Portugal 10 37.42N 7.35W
Rochdale U.K. 4 53.36N 2.10W
Rochechouart France 11 45.49N 0.50E
Rochefort Belgium 8 50.10N 5.13E
Rochefort France 11 45.57N 0.58W
Rochester Australia 47 36.22S144.42E
Rochester Kent U.K. 5 51.22N 0.30E
Rochester Minn. U.S.A. 53 44.01N 92.27W
Rochester N.Y. U.S.A. 55 43.12N 77.37W
Rochfort Bridge Rep. of Ire. 7 53.25N 7.19W
Rock U.S.A. 55 46.03N 87.10W
Rockefeller Plateau Antarctica 64 80.00S140.00W
Rockford U.S.A. 53 42.16N 89.06W
Rockhampton Australia 44 23.22S150.32E
Rockingham Australia 43 32.16S115.21E
Rock Island town U.S.A. 53 41.30N 90.34W
Rockland Idaho U.S.A. 54 42.34N112.53W
Rockland Maine U.S.A. 55 44.06N 69.06W
Rockland Mich. U.S.A. 55 46.44N 89.12W
Rocklands Resr. Australia 46 37.13S141.52E
Rockport U.S.A. 54 39.45N123.47W
Rock Sound town Bahamas 57 24.54N 76.11W
Rock Springs Wyo. U.S.A. 54 41.35N109.13W
Rockville U.S.A. 55 39.05N 77.09W
Rocky Ford U.S.A. 52 38.03N103.44W
Rocky Gully town Australia 43 34.31S117.01E
Rocky Island L. Canada 55 46.56N 82.55W
Rocky Mts. N. America 52 43.21N109.50W
Rocky Pt. Australia 43 33.30S124.01E
Rocroi France 8 49.56N 4.31E
Rod Pakistan 28 28.10N 63.05E
Rödby Denmark 17 54.42N 11.24E
Rodel U.K. 6 57.44N 6.58W
Rodez France 11 44.21N 2.34E
Ródhos i. Greece 13 36.12N 28.00E
Ródhos town Greece 13 36.24N 28.15E
Rodonit, Kep-i- c. Albania 13 41.34N 19.25E
Roe, L. Australia 43 30.40S122.10E
Roebourne Australia 42 20.48S117.10E
Roebuck B. Australia 42 19.04S122.17E
Roermond Neth. 8 51.12N 6.00E
Roeselare Belgium 8 50.57N 3.06E
Rogachev U.S.S.R. 15 53.05N 30.02E
Rogaland d. Norway 17 59.00N 6.15E
Rogerson U.S.A. 54 42.14N114.47W
Rogliano France 11 42.57N 9.25E
Rogue r. U.S.A. 54 42.26N124.25W
Rohtak India 28 28.54N 76.35E
Rojas Argentina 63 34.15S 60.44W
Rokan r. Indonesia 26 2.00N101.00E
Rola Co l. China 29 35.26N 88.24E
Röldal Norway 17 59.49N 6.48E
Rolla Mo. U.S.A. 53 37.56N 91.55W
Rolleston Australia 44 24.25S148.35E
Rolleville Bahamas 57 23.41N 76.00W
Rolvsöya i. Norway 16 70.58N 24.00E
Roma Australia 44 26.35S148.47E
Roma Italy 12 41.54N 12.29E
Roma Sweden 17 57.32N 18.28E
Romain, C. U.S.A. 53 33.01N 79.23W
Romaine r. Canada 51 50.20N 63.45W
Roman Romania 15 46.55N 26.56E
Romang i. Indonesia 27 7.45S127.20E
Romania Europe 15 46.30N 24.00E
Romano, C. U.S.A. 53 25.50N 81.42W
Romans France 11 45.03N 5.03E
Rome see Roma Italy 12
Rome Ga. U.S.A. 53 34.01N 85.02W
Rome N.Y. U.S.A. 55 43.13N 75.27W
Romeo U.S.A. 55 42.47N 83.01W
Romilly France 9 48.31N 3.44E
Romney Marsh f. U.K. 5 51.03N 0.55E
Romorantin France 9 47.22N 1.44E
Rona i. U.K. 6 57.33N 5.58W
Ronan U.S.A. 54 47.32N114.06W
Roncesvalles Spain 10 43.01N 1.19W
Ronda Spain 10 36.45N 5.10W
Rondane mtn. Norway 17 61.55N 9.45E
Rondônia d. Brazil 60 12.10S 62.30W
Rondonópolis Brazil 61 16.29S 54.37W
Rongcheng China 25 37.09N122.23E
Rönne Denmark 17 55.06N 14.42E
Ronneby Sweden 17 56.12N 15.18E
Ronse Belgium 8 50.45N 3.36E
Ronuro r. Brazil 61 11.56S 53.33W
Roof Butte mtn. U.S.A. 54 36.28N109.05W
Roosendaal Neth. 8 51.32N 4.28E
Roosevelt r. Brazil 60 7.35S 60.20W
Roosevelt U.S.A. 54 40.18N109.59W
Roosevelt I. Antarctica 64 79.00S161.00W
Ropcha U.S.S.R. 18 62.50N 51.55E
Roper r. Australia 44 14.40S135.30E
Roper Valley town Australia 44 14.56S134.00E
Roque Pérez Argentina 63 35.23S 59.22W
Roraima d. Brazil 60 2.00N 62.00W
Roraima, Mt. Guyana 60 5.14N 60.44W
Röros Norway 16 62.35N 11.23E
Rosa, Monte mtn. Italy/Switz. 9 45.56N 7.51E
Rosamond U.S.A. 54 34.52N118.10W
Rosario Argentina 63 32.57S 60.40W
Rosário Brazil 61 3.00S 44.15W
Rosario Uruguay 63 34.19S 57.21W
Rosario de la Frontera Argentina 62 25.50S 64.55W
Rosario del Tala Argentina 63 32.20S 59.10W
Rosário do Sul Brazil 59 30.15S 54.55W
Roscoff France 11 48.44N 4.00W
Roscommon Rep. of Ire. 7 53.38N 8.13W
Roscommon d. Rep. of Ire. 7 53.38N 8.11W
Roscrea Rep. of Ire. 7 52.57N 7.49W
Roseau Dominica 57 15.18N 61.23W
Rosebud Australia 47 38.21S144.54E
Roseburg U.S.A. 54 43.13N123.20W
Rosenheim W. Germany 14 47.51N 12.09E
Roses Spain 10 42.19N 3.10E
Rosetown Canada 50 51.34N107.59W
Rosetta R.S.A. 39 29.18S 29.58E
Roseville Calif. U.S.A. 54 38.45N121.17W
Rosières France 9 49.49N 2.43E
Rosignano Marittimo Italy 12 43.24N 10.28E
Roşiori-de-Vede Romania 15 44.07N 25.00E
Rositsa Bulgaria 15 43.57N 27.57E
Roska r. U.S.S.R. 15 49.27N 29.45E
Roskilde Denmark 17 55.39N 12.05E
Roslags-Näsby Sweden 17 59.26N 18.04E
Roslavl U.S.S.R. 18 53.55N 32.53E
Ross New Zealand 48 42.54S170.49E
Rossano Italy 13 39.35N 16.39E
Ross Dependency Antarctica 64 75.00S170.00W
Rossing Namibia 39 22.31S 14.52E
Rossiyskaya S.F.S.R. d. U.S.S.R. 20 62.00N 80.00E
Rosslare Rep. of Ire. 7 52.17N 6.23W
Ross-on-Wye U.K. 5 51.55N 2.36W
Rossosh U.S.S.R. 19 50.12N 39.35E
Rössvatnet l. Norway 16 65.45N 14.00E
Rosta Norway 16 68.59N 19.40E
Rosthern Canada 50 52.40N106.17W
Rostock E. Germany 14 54.06N 12.09E
Rostock d. E. Germany 14 54.15N 12.30E
Rostov R.S.F.S.R. U.S.S.R. 18 57.11N 39.23E
Rostov R.S.F.S.R. U.S.S.R. 19 47.15N 39.45E
Rota i. Mariana Is. 27 14.10N145.15E
Rotem Belgium 8 51.04N 5.44E
Rothbury U.K. 4 55.19N 1.54W
Rotherham U.K. 4 53.26N 1.21W
Rothes U.K. 6 57.31N 3.13W
Rothesay Canada 55 45.23N 66.00W
Rothesay U.K. 6 55.50N 5.03W
Roti i. Indonesia 42 10.30S123.10E
Roto Australia 47 33.04S145.27E
Rotondella Italy 13 40.10N 16.32E
Rotorua New Zealand 48 38.07S176.17E
Rotorua, L. New Zealand 48 38.00S176.00E
Rotterdam Neth. 8 51.55N 4.29E
Rottnest I. Australia 43 32.01S115.28E
Rottweil W. Germany 14 48.10N 8.37E
Roubaix France 8 50.42N 3.10E
Rouen France 9 49.26N 1.05E
Rougé France 9 47.47N 1.26W
Rouku P.N.G. 44 8.40S141.35E
Round Mt. Australia 47 30.26S152.15E
Roundup U.S.A. 54 46.27N108.33W
Rousay i. U.K. 6 59.10N 3.02W
Rouyn Canada 55 48.14N 79.01W
Rovaniemi Finland 16 66.30N 25.40E
Rovato Italy 9 45.34N 10.00E
Rovereto Italy 9 45.53N 11.02E
Rovigo Italy 9 45.04N 11.47E
Rovinj Yugo. 14 45.06N 13.39E
Rovno U.S.S.R. 15 50.39N 26.10E
Rowena Australia 47 29.49S148.54E
Rowley Shoals f. Australia 42 17.30S119.00E
Roxburgh New Zealand 48 45.33S169.19E
Roxen l. Sweden 17 58.30N 15.41E
Royale, Isle i. U.S.A. 55 48.00N 89.00W
Royal Leamington Spa U.K. 5 52.18N 1.32W
Royal Tunbridge Wells U.K. 5 51.07N 0.16E
Royan France 11 45.37N 1.02W
Roye France 9 49.42N 2.48E
Royston U.K. 5 52.03N 0.01W
Rozhishche U.S.S.R. 15 50.58N 25.15E
Rožňava Czech. 15 48.40N 20.32E
Rtishchevo U.S.S.R. 18 52.16N 43.45E
Ruahine Range mts. New Zealand 48 40.00S176.00E
Ruapehu mtn. New Zealand 48 39.20S175.30E
Ruapuke I. New Zealand 48 46.45S168.30E
Rub 'al Khali des. see Ar Rub 'al Khālī des. Saudi Arabia 28
Rubino Ivory Coast 38 6.04N 4.18W
Rubio Colombia 60 7.42N 72.23W
Rubryn U.S.S.R. 15 51.52N 27.30E
Rubtsovsk U.S.S.R. 20 51.29N 81.10E
Ruby Mts. U.S.A. 54 40.25N115.35W
Rūdān r. Iran 31 27.02N 56.53E
Rūdbār Afghan. 31 30.10N 62.38E
Rudewa Tanzania 37 6.40S 37.08E
Rudki U.S.S.R. 15 49.40N 23.28E
Rudnaya Pristan U.S.S.R. 25 44.18N135.51E
Rudnichnyy U.S.S.R. 18 59.10N 52.28E
Rudnik Poland 15 50.28N 22.15E
Rudnyy U.S.S.R. 20 53.00N 63.05E
Rudolstadt E. Germany 14 50.44N 11.20E
Rue France 11 50.15N 1.40E
Ruffec France 11 46.02N 0.12E
Rufiji r. Tanzania 37 8.02S 39.19E
Rufino Argentina 63 34.16S 62.45W
Rufunsa Zambia 37 15.02S 29.35E
Rugao China 25 32.27N120.35E
Rugby U.K. 5 52.23N 1.16W
Rugby U.S.A. 52 48.24N 99.59W
Rügen i. E. Germany 14 54.30N 13.30E
Ruhr f. W. Germany 8 51.22N 7.26E
Ruhr r. W. Germany 8 51.27N 6.41E
Ruinen Neth. 8 52.47N 6.21E
Rukwa d. Tanzania 37 7.05S 31.25E
Rukwa, L. Tanzania 37 8.00S 32.20E
Ruma Yugo. 15 44.59N 19.51E
Rum Cay i. Bahamas 57 23.41N 74.53W
Rumford U.S.A. 55 44.33N 70.33W
Rum Jungle Australia 42 13.01S131.00E
Rummānah Egypt 32 31.01N 32.40E
Runcorn U.K. 4 53.20N 2.44W
Rundvik Sweden 16 63.30N 19.24E
Rungwa r. Tanzania 37 7.38S 31.55E
Rungwa Singida Tanzania 37 6.57S 33.35E
Rungwe Mt. Tanzania 37 9.10S 33.40E
Runka Nigeria 38 12.28N 7.20E
Ruoqiang China 24 39.00N 88.00E
Ruo Shui r. China 24 42.15N101.03E
Rupert r. Canada 55 51.30N 78.45W
Rupununi r. Guyana 60 4.00N 58.30W
Rur r. Neth. 8 51.12N 5.58E
Rusape Zimbabwe 39 18.30S 32.08E
Ruse Bulgaria 13 43.50N 25.59E
Rushden U.K. 5 52.17N 0.37W
Rushworth Australia 47 36.38S145.02E
Russell Pt. Canada 50 73.30N115.00W
Russell Range mts. Australia 43 33.15S123.30E
Russkaya Polyana U.S.S.R. 20 53.48N 73.54E
Rustavi U.S.S.R. 19 41.34N 45.03E
Rustenburg R.S.A. 39 25.39S 27.13E
Rutana Burundi 37 3.58S 30.00E
Rütenbrock W. Germany 8 52.51N 7.06E
Ruteng Indonesia 27 8.35S120.28E
Rutenga Zimbabwe 39 21.15S 30.46E
Ruth U.S.A. 54 39.17N114.59W
Ruthin U.K. 4 53.07N 3.18W
Rutland U.S.A. 55 43.36N 72.59W
Rutog China 29 33.30N 79.40E
Rutshuru Zaïre 37 1.10S 29.26E
Ruvu Coast Tanzania 37 6.50S 38.42E
Ruvuma r. Mozambique/Tanzania 37 10.30S 40.30E
Ruvuma d. Tanzania 37 10.45S 36.15E
Ruwenzori Range mts. Uganda/Zaïre 37 0.30N 30.00E
Ruyigi Burundi 37 3.26S 30.14E
Ruzayevka U.S.S.R. 18 54.04N 44.55E
Ruzitgort U.S.S.R. 18 62.51N 64.52E
Ružomberok Czech. 15 49.06N 19.18E
Rwanda Africa 37 2.00S 30.00E
Ryan, Loch U.K. 6 54.56N 5.02W
Ryasna U.S.S.R. 15 54.00N 31.14E
Ryazan U.S.S.R. 18 54.37N 39.43E
Ryazhsk U.S.S.R. 18 53.40N 40.07E
Rybachiy, Poluostrov pen. U.S.S.R. 18 69.45N 32.30E
Rybachye U.S.S.R. 24 46.27N 81.30E
Rybinskoye Vodokhranilishche resr. U.S.S.R. 18 58.30N 38.25E
Rybnik Poland 15 50.06N 18.32E
Rybnitsa U.S.S.R. 15 47.42N 29.00E
Ryd Sweden 17 56.28N 14.41E
Rye U.K. 5 50.57N 0.46E
Rye r. U.K. 4 54.10N 0.44W
Ryki Poland 15 51.39N 21.56E
Rylstone Australia 47 32.48S149.58E
Ryūgasaki Japan 23 35.54N140.11E
Ryukyu Is. see Nansei shotō is. Japan 25
Rzeszów Poland 15 50.04N 22.00E
Rzhev U.S.S.R. 18 56.15N 34.18E

S

Saa Cameroon 38 4.24N 11.25E
Saale r. E. Germany 14 51.58N 11.53E
Saanich Canada 54 48.28N123.22W
Saar r. W. Germany 8 49.43N 6.34E
Saarbrücken W. Germany 14 49.15N 6.58E
Saarburg W. Germany 8 49.36N 6.33E
Saaremaa i. U.S.S.R. 17 58.25N 22.30E
Saarijärvi Finland 16 62.43N 25.16E
Saariselkä mts. Finland 16 68.15N 28.30E
Saarland d. W. Germany 8 49.30N 6.50E
Saba i. Leeward Is. 57 17.42N 63.26W
Šabac Yugo. 15 44.45N 19.41E
Sabadell Spain 10 41.33N 2.07E
Sabah d. Malaysia 26 5.30N117.00E
Sabalān, Kūhhā-ye mts. Iran 31 38.15N 47.50E
Sabana, Archipiélago de Cuba 57 23.30N 80.00W
Sabanalarga Colombia 60 10.38N 75.00W
Sabaudia Italy 12 41.18N 13.01E
Sabbioneta Italy 9 45.00N 10.39E
Sabhā Libya 34 27.04N 14.25E
Sabi r. Zimbabwe 39 21.16S 32.20E
Sabinas Mexico 56 26.33N101.10W
Sabinas Hidalgo Mexico 56 26.33N100.10W
Sabine r. U.S.A. 53 29.40N 93.50W
Sabkhat al Bardawīl l. Egypt 32 31.10N 33.15E
Sablayan Phil. 27 12.50N120.50E
Sable, C. Canada 51 43.30N 65.50W
Sable I. Canada 51 44.00N 60.00W
Sablé-sur-Sarthe France 9 47.50N 0.20W
Sabon Birni Nigeria 38 13.37N 6.15E
Sabongidda Nigeria 38 6.54N 5.56E
Sabrina Coast f. Antarctica 64 67.00S120.00E
Sabzevār Iran 31 36.13N 57.38E
Sacaca Bolivia 62 18.05S 66.25W
Sacajawea mtn. U.S.A. 54 45.15N117.17W
Sacedón Spain 10 40.29N 2.44W
Sachigo r. Canada 51 55.06N 88.58W
Saco U.S.A. 55 43.29N 70.28W
Sacramento Brazil 59 19.51S 26.47W
Sacramento U.S.A. 54 38.35N121.30W
Sacramento r. U.S.A. 54 38.03N121.56W
Sacramento Valley f. U.S.A. 54 39.15N122.00W
Sádaba Spain 10 42.19N 1.10W
Sadani Tanzania 37 6.00S 38.40E
Sadiya India 29 27.49N 95.38E
Şafājah des. Saudi Arabia 30 26.30N 39.30E
Şafāniyah Egypt 32 28.49N 30.48E
Şafarābād Iran 31 38.59N 47.25E
Säffle Sweden 17 59.08N 12.56E
Saffron Walden U.K. 5 52.02N 0.15E
Safi Morocco 34 32.20N 9.17W
Safid r. Iran 31 37.23N 50.11E
Safonovo R.S.F.S.R. U.S.S.R. 18 55.08N 33.1
Safonovo R.S.F.S.R. U.S.S.R. 18 65.40N 48.1
Sagaing Burma 29 22.00N 96.00E
Sagala Mali 38 14.09N 6.38W
Sagami r. Japan 23 35.14N139.23E
Sagamihara Japan 23 35.32N139.23E
Sagami-nada b. Japan 23 34.55N139.30E
Sāgar India 29 23.50N 78.44E
Sagara Japan 23 34.41N138.12E
Sage U.S.A. 54 41.49N110.59W
Saginaw U.S.A. 55 43.25N 83.54W
Saginaw B. U.S.A. 55 43.56N 83.40W
Sagiz U.S.S.R. 19 47.31N 54.55E
Saglouc Canada 51 62.10N 75.40W
Sagres Portugal 10 37.00N 8.56W
Sagua la Grande Cuba 57 22.55N 80.05W
Saguenay r. Canada 55 48.10N 69.45W
Sagunto Spain 10 39.40N 0.17W
Sahagún Spain 10 42.23N 5.02W
Sahand, Kūh-e mtn. Iran 31 37.37N 46.27E
Sahara des. Africa 34 18.00N 12.00E
Sahāranpur India 28 29.58N 77.33E
Sahbā, Wādī as r. Saudi Arabia 31 23.48N 49.50E
Sāhīwāl Punjab Pakistan 28 31.57N 72.22E
Saibai i. Australia 44 9.24S142.40E
Sa'īdābād Iran 31 29.28N 55.43E
Saidpur Bangla. 29 25.48N 89.00E
Saimaa l. Finland 18 61.20N 28.00E
Saimbeyli Turkey 30 38.07N 36.08E
St. Abb's Head U.K. 6 55.54N 2.07W
St. Agapit Canada 55 46.34N 71.26W
St. Albans U.K. 5 51.46N 0.21W
St. Albans Vt. U.S.A. 55 44.49N 73.05W
St. Amand France 8 50.27N 3.26E
St. Amand-Mont-Rond town France 11 46.43N 2.29E
St. Andrews U.K. 6 56.20N 2.48W
St. Andries Belgium 8 51.12N 3.10E
St. Ann's Bay town Jamaica 57 18.26N 77.12W
St. Anthony Canada 51 51.24N 55.37W
St. Anthony U.S.A. 52 43.59N111.40W
St. Arnaud Australia 46 36.40S143.20E
St. Augustine U.S.A. 53 29.54N 81.19W
St. Augustin Saguenay Canada 51 51.14N 58.39W
St. Austell U.K. 5 50.20N 4.48W
St. Barthélemy i. Leeward Is. 57 17.55N 62.50
St. Bees Head U.K. 4 54.31N 3.39W
St. Boniface Canada 51 49.54N 97.07W
St. Brides B. U.K. 5 51.48N 5.03W
St. Brieuc France 11 48.31N 2.45W
St. Calais France 9 47.55N 0.45E
St. Catharines Canada 55 43.10N 79.15W
St. Catherine's Pt. U.K. 5 50.34N 1.18W
St. Céré France 11 44.52N 1.53E
St. Cloud U.S.A. 53 45.34N 94.10W
St. Croix i. U.S.V.Is. 57 17.45N 64.35W
St. David's U.K. 5 51.54N 5.16W
St. David's Head U.K. 5 51.55N 5.19W
St. Denis France 9 48.56N 2.21E
St. Dié France 11 48.17N 6.57E
St. Dizier France 9 48.38N 4.58E
Sainte-Agathe-des-Monts Canada 55 46.03N 74.19W
Sainte Anne de Beaupré Canada 55 47.02N 70.58W
St. Elias, Mt. U.S.A. 50 60.20N139.00W
St. Éloi Canada 55 48.03N 69.14W
Sainte Marguerite r. Canada 55 50.10N 66.40W
Sainte Marie, Cap c. Madagascar 36 25.36S 45.08E
Sainte Menehould France 14 49.05N 4.54E
Sainte Menehould France 9 49.05N 4.54E
Sainte Mère-Église France 9 49.24N 1.19W
Saintes France 11 45.44N 0.38W
Sainte-Thérèse-de-Blainville Canada 55 45.38 73.50W
St. Étienne France 11 45.26N 4.26E
St. Fargeau France 9 47.38N 3.04E
St. Feliu de Gixols Spain 10 41.47N 3.02E
Saintfield U.K. 7 54.28N 5.50W
St. Florent France 11 42.41N 9.18E
St. Florentin France 9 48.00N 3.44E
St. Flour France 11 45.02N 3.05E
St. Gallen Switz. 14 47.25N 9.23E
St. Gaudens France 11 43.07N 0.44E
St. George Australia 45 28.03S148.30E
St. George N.B. Canada 55 45.08N 66.56W
St. George U.S.A. 54 37.06N113.35W
St. George Head Australia 47 35.11S150.40E
St. Georges Belgium 8 50.37N 5.20E
St. George's Grenada 57 12.04N 61.44W
St. Georges Guiana 61 3.54N 51.48W
St. George's Channel Rep. of Ire./U.K. 7 51.30 6.20W
St. Germain France 9 48.53N 2.04E
St. Gheorghe's Mouth est. Romania 13 44.51N 29.37E
St. Gilles-Croix-de-Vie France 11 46.42N 1.56
St. Girons France 11 42.59N 1.08E
St. Gotthard Pass Switz. 11 46.30N 8.55E
St. Govan's Head U.K. 5 51.36N 4.55W
St. Helena B. R.S.A. 39 32.35S 18.05E
St. Helens U.K. 4 53.28N 2.43W
St. Helens U.S.A. 54 45.52N122.48W
St. Helier U.K. 5 49.12N 2.07W
St. Hilaire-du-Harcouët France 9 48.35N 1.06W
St. Hubert Belgium 8 50.02N 5.22E
St. Hyacinthe Canada 55 45.38N 72.57W
St. Ignace U.S.A. 55 45.53N 84.44W
St. Ives U.K. 5 50.13N 5.29W
St. Jean Canada 55 45.18N 73.16W
St. Jean France 11 45.17N 6.21E
St. Jean, Lac l. Canada 55 48.35N 72.00W
St. Jean de Matha Canada 55 46.14N 73.33W
St. Jean Pied-de-Port France 11 43.10N 1.14W
St. Jérôme Canada 55 45.47N 74.01W
St. John Canada 55 45.16N 66.03W

. John *r.* Canada **55** 45.15N 66.04W
. John's Antigua **57** 17.07N 61.51W
. John's Canada **51** 47.34N 52.41W
. Johns U.S.A. **54** 34.30N109.22W
. Johnsbury U.S.A. **55** 44.25N 72.01W
. John's Pt. U.K. **7** 54.14N 5.39W
. Jordi, Golf de *g.* Spain **10** 40.50N 1.10E
. Joseph Mich. U.S.A. **55** 42.05N 86.30W
. Joseph Mo. U.S.A. **53** 39.45N 94.51W
. Joseph, L. Canada **51** 51.05N 90.35W
. Junien France **11** 45.53N 0.55E
. Just-en-Chaussée France **9** 49.30N 2.26E
. Kitts-Nevis Leeward Is. **57** 17.20N 62.45W
. Laurent Que. Canada **55** 45.31N 73.42W
. Laurent du Maroni Guiana **61** 5.30N 54.02W
. Lawrence *r.* Canada **55** 48.45N 68.30W
. Lawrence, G. of Canada **51** 48.00N 62.00W
. Lawrence I. U.S.A. **50** 63.00N170.00W
. Lô France **9** 49.07N 1.05W
. Louis Senegal **34** 16.01N 16.30W
. Louis U.S.A. **53** 38.40N 90.15W
. Lucia Windward Is. **57** 14.05N 61.00W
. Lucia, L. R.S.A. **39** 28.05S 32.26E
. Maixent France **11** 46.25N 0.12W
. Malo France **9** 48.39N 2.00W
. Malo, Golfe de *g.* France **11** 49.20N 2.00W
.-Marc Haiti **57** 19.08N 72.41W
. Margaret's Hope U.K. **6** 58.49N 2.57W
. Maries U.S.A. **54** 47.19N116.35W
. Martin *i.* Leeward Is. **57** 18.05N 63.05W
. Martin U.K. **5** 49.27N 2.34W
. Martin's *i.* U.K. **5** 49.57N 6.16W
. Mary U.K. **5** 49.14N 2.10W
. Marys Australia **45** 41.33S148.12E
. Mary's *i.* U.K. **5** 49.55N 6.16W
. Matthew I. U.S.A. **50** 60.30N172.45W
. Maur France **9** 48.48N 2.30E
. Maurice *r.* Canada **55** 46.21N 72.31W
. Moritz Switz. **14** 46.30N 9.51E
. Nazaire France **11** 47.17N 2.12W
. Neots U.K. **5** 52.14N 0.16W
. Niklaas Belgium **8** 51.10N 4.09E
. Omer France **11** 50.45N 2.15E
. Pacôme Canada **55** 47.24N 69.58W
. Pascal Canada **55** 47.32N 69.48W
. Paul Pyr. Or. France **11** 42.49N 2.29E
. Paul Minn. U.S.A. **53** 45.00N 93.10W
. Paul du Nord Canada **55** 48.27N 69.16W
. Peter Port U.K. **5** 49.27N 2.32W
. Petersburg U.S.A. **53** 27.45N 82.40W
. Pierre Char. Mar. France **11** 45.57N 1.19W
. Pierre S. Mar. France **9** 49.48N 0.29E
. Pierre and Miquelon *is.* N. America **51** 47.00N 56.15W
. Pierre-Église France **9** 49.40N 1.24W
. Pölten Austria **14** 48.13N 15.37E
. Quentin France **9** 49.51N 3.17E
. Seine-l'Abbaye France **9** 47.26N 4.47E
. Siméon Canada **55** 47.56N 69.58W
. Stephen Canada **55** 45.12N 67.18W
. Thomas Canada **55** 42.47N 81.12W
. Thomas *i.* U.S.V.Is. **57** 18.22N 64.57W
. Tropez France **11** 43.16N 6.39E
. Truiden Belgium **8** 50.49N 5.11E
. Valéry France **9** 49.52N 0.43E
. Vallier France **11** 45.11N 4.49E
. Vincent, G. Australia **46** 35.00S138.05E
. Vincent and the Grenadines Windward Is. **57** 13.00N 61.15W
. Vith Belgium **8** 50.15N 6.08E
. Wendel W. Germany **8** 49.27N 7.10E
. Yrieix France **11** 45.31N 1.12E
aipan *i.* Mariana Is. **27** 15.12N145.43E
aitama *d.* Japan **23** 35.55N139.00E
ajama *mtn.* Bolivia **62** 18.06S 69.00W
aka Kenya **37** 0.09S 39.18E
akai Japan **23** 34.35N135.28E
akākah Saudi Arabia **30** 29.59N 40.12E
akania Zaïre **37** 12.44S 28.34E
akarya *r.* Turkey **30** 41.08N 30.36E
akété Benin **38** 6.45N 2.45E
akhalin *i.* U.S.S.R. **25** 50.00N143.00E
akivier R.S.A. **36** 30.50S 20.26E
akrivier R.S.A. **39** 30.53S 20.24E
akuma Japan **23** 35.05N137.48E
al *r.* U.S.S.R. **19** 47.33N 40.40E
ala Sweden **17** 59.55N 16.36E
alaca *r.* U.S.S.R. **17** 57.45N 24.21E
alacgriva U.S.S.R. **17** 57.45N 24.21E
alado *r.* Buenos Aires Argentina **63** 35.44S 57.22W
alado *r.* Santa Fé Argentina **63** 31.40S 60.41W
alado *r.* La Pampa Argentina **63** 36.15S 66.55W
alado *r.* Mexico **56** 26.46N 98.55W
alaga Ghana **38** 8.36N 0.32W
alālah Oman **28** 17.00N 54.04E
alamanca Spain **10** 40.58N 5.40W
alamina Colombia **60** 5.24N 75.31W
alatiga Indonesia **26** 7.15S110.34E
albris France **9** 47.26N 2.03E
alcombe U.K. **5** 50.14N 3.47W
aldaña Spain **10** 42.32N 4.48W
aldanha R.S.A. **39** 33.00S 17.56E
aldanha B. R.S.A. **39** 33.05S 17.50E
aldus U.S.S.R. **17** 56.40N 22.30E
ale Australia **47** 38.06S147.06E
alekhard U.S.S.R. **18** 66.33N 66.35E
alem India **29** 11.38N 78.08E
alem Ind. U.S.A. **55** 38.38N 86.06W
alem Oreg. U.S.A. **54** 44.57N123.01W
älen Sweden **17** 61.10N 13.16E
alerno Italy **12** 40.41N 14.45E
alerno, Golfo di *g.* Italy **12** 40.30N 14.45E
alford U.K. **4** 53.30N 2.17W
algótarján Hungary **15** 48.07N 19.48E
algueiro Brazil **61** 8.04S 39.05W
alima Malaŵi **37** 13.45S 34.29E
alim's Tanzania **37** 10.37S 36.33E
alina Cruz Mexico **56** 16.11N 95.12W
Salinas Ecuador **60** 2.13S 80.58W
Salinas U.S.A. **54** 36.40N121.38W
Salinas *r.* U.S.A. **52** 36.45N121.48W
Salinópolis Brazil **61** 0.37S 47.20W
Salins France **11** 46.56N 5.53E
Salisbury U.K. **5** 51.04N 1.48W
Salisbury Md. U.S.A. **55** 38.22N 75.36W
Salisbury Plain *f.* U.K. **5** 51.15N 1.55W
Şalkhad Syria **32** 32.29N 36.42E
Salmās Iran **31** 38.13N 44.50E
Salmi U.S.S.R. **18** 61.19N 31.46E
Salmon U.S.A. **54** 45.11N113.55W
Salmon *r.* U.S.A. **54** 45.51N116.46W
Salmon Gums Australia **43** 32.59S121.39E
Salmon River Mts. U.S.A. **54** 44.45N115.30W
Salo Finland **17** 60.23N 23.08E
Salò Italy **9** 45.36N 10.31E
Salobreña Spain **10** 36.45N 3.35W
Salome U.S.A. **54** 33.47N113.37W
Salon France **11** 43.38N 5.06E
Salonta Romania **15** 46.48N 21.40E
Salsk U.S.S.R. **19** 46.30N 41.33E
Salso *r.* Italy **12** 37.07N 13.57E
Salsomaggiore Terme Italy **9** 44.49N 9.59E
Salt *r.* U.S.A. **54** 33.23N112.18W
Salta Argentina **62** 24.47S 65.24W
Salta *d.* Argentina **62** 25.00S 65.00W
Saltdal Norway **16** 67.06N 15.25E
Saltee Is. Rep. of Ire. **7** 52.08N 6.36W
Saltfjorden *est.* Norway **16** 67.15N 14.10E
Saltfleet U.K. **4** 53.25N 0.11E
Salt Fork *r.* U.S.A. **53** 36.41N 97.05W
Saltillo Mexico **56** 25.30N101.00W
Salt Lake City U.S.A. **54** 40.46N111.53W
Salto Argentina **63** 34.17S 60.15W
Salto Brazil **59** 23.10S 47.16W
Salto *r.* Italy **12** 42.23N 12.54E
Salto Uruguay **63** 31.23S 57.58W
Salto da Divisa Brazil **61** 16.04S 40.00W
Salton Sea *l.* U.S.A. **54** 33.19N115.50W
Saluzzo Italy **9** 44.39N 7.29E
Salvador Brazil **61** 12.58S 38.29W
Salween *r.* Burma **29** 16.30N 97.33E
Salyany U.S.S.R. **31** 39.36N 48.59E
Salzbrunn Namibia **39** 24.23S 18.00E
Salzburg Austria **14** 47.54N 13.03E
Salzburg *d.* Austria **14** 47.25N 13.15E
Salzgitter W. Germany **14** 52.02N 10.22E
Salzwedel E. Germany **14** 52.51N 11.09E
Samālūt Egypt **32** 28.18N 30.43E
Samaná Dom. Rep. **57** 19.14N 69.20W
Samana Cay *i.* Bahamas **57** 23.05N 73.45W
Samanga Tanzania **37** 8.24S 39.18E
Samannūd Egypt **32** 30.58N 31.14E
Samar *i.* Phil. **27** 11.45N125.15E
Samara *r.* U.S.S.R. **18** 53.17N 50.42E
Samarai P.N.G. **44** 10.37S150.40E
Samarinda Indonesia **26** 0.30S117.09E
Samarkand U.S.S.R. **20** 39.40N 66.57E
Sāmarrā Iraq **31** 34.13N 43.52E
Sambalpur India **29** 21.28N 84.04E
Sambor U.S.S.R. **15** 49.31N 23.10E
Samborombón, Bahía *b.* Argentina **63** 36.00S 57.00W
Sambre *r.* Belgium **8** 50.29N 4.52E
Samburu Kenya **37** 3.46S 39.17E
Samch'ŏk S. Korea **25** 37.30N129.10E
Same Tanzania **37** 4.10S 37.43E
Samobor Yugo. **14** 45.48N 15.43E
Samorogouan Burkina Faso **38** 11.21N 4.57W
Sámos *i.* Greece **13** 37.44N 26.45E
Samothráki *i.* Greece **13** 40.26N 25.35E
Sampit Indonesia **26** 2.34S112.59E
Samsang China **29** 30.22N 82.50E
Samsun Turkey **30** 41.17N 36.22E
Samtredia U.S.S.R. **19** 42.10N 42.22E
Samui, Ko *i.* Thailand **29** 9.30N100.00E
Samur *r.* U.S.S.R. **19** 42.00N 48.20E
Samut Sakhon Thailand **29** 13.32N100.17E
San Mali **38** 13.21N 4.57W
San *r.* Poland **15** 50.25N 22.20E
Şan'ā' Yemen **35** 15.23N 44.14E
Sana *r.* Yugo. **14** 45.03N 16.23E
Sanaba Burkina Faso **38** 12.25N 3.47W
Sanaga *r.* Cameroon **38** 3.35N 9.40E
Sanandaj Iran **31** 35.18N 47.01E
San Andreas U.S.A. **54** 38.12N120.41W
San Andrés, Isla de *i.* Colombia **57** 12.33N 81.42W
San Andrés Tuxtla Mexico **56** 18.27N 95.13W
San Angelo U.S.A. **52** 31.28N100.28W
San Antonio Chile **63** 33.35S 71.38W
San Antonio Tex. U.S.A. **52** 29.25N 98.30W
San Antonio, C. Cuba **57** 21.50N 84.57W
San Antonio, Cabo *c.* Argentina **63** 36.40S 56.42W
San Antonio, Punta *c.* Mexico **56** 29.45N115.41W
San Antonio Abad Spain **10** 38.58N 1.18E
San Antonio de Areco Argentina **63** 34.16S 59.30W
San Antonio Oeste Argentina **63** 40.44S 64.57W
San Benedetto Italy **12** 42.57N 13.53E
San Benedetto Po Italy **9** 45.02N 10.55E
San Benito Guatemala **57** 16.55N 89.54W
San Bernardino U.S.A. **54** 34.06N117.17W
San Bernardo Chile **63** 33.36S 70.43W
San Blas, C. U.S.A. **53** 29.40N 85.25W
San Bonifacio Italy **9** 45.24N 11.16E
San Carlos Chile **63** 36.25S 71.58W
San Carlos Mexico **56** 29.01N100.51W
San Carlos Nicaragua **57** 11.07N 84.47W
San Carlos Phil. **27** 15.59N120.22E
San Carlos Venezuela **60** 1.55N 67.04W
San Carlos Venezuela **60** 9.39N 68.35W
San Carlos de Bariloche Argentina **63** 41.08S 71.15W
San Carlos del Zulia Venezuela **60** 9.01N 71.55W
Sancerre France **9** 47.20N 2.51E
Sancerrois, Collines du *hills* France **9** 47.25N 2.45E
San Clemente U.S.A. **54** 33.26N117.37W
San Clemente *i.* U.S.A. **54** 32.54N118.29W
San Cristóbal Argentina **62** 30.20S 61.14W
San Cristóbal Dom. Rep. **57** 18.27N 70.07W
San Cristóbal Venezuela **60** 7.46N 72.15W
Sancti Spíritus Cuba **57** 21.55N 79.28W
Sand Norway **17** 59.29N 6.15E
Sanda *i.* U.K. **6** 55.17N 5.34W
Sandakan Malaysia **26** 5.52N118.04E
Sanday *i.* U.K. **6** 59.15N 2.33W
Sandbach U.K. **4** 53.09N 2.23W
Sandefjord Norway **17** 59.08N 10.14E
Sanders U.S.A. **54** 35.13N109.20W
Sandgate Australia **47** 27.18S153.00E
Sandhornöy *i.* Norway **16** 67.05N 14.10E
Sandia Peru **60** 14.14S 69.25W
San Diego U.S.A. **54** 32.43N117.09W
San Diego, C. Argentina **63** 54.38S 65.05W
Sand Lake *town* Canada **55** 47.46N 84.31W
Sandnes Norway **17** 58.51N 5.44E
Sandness U.K. **6** 60.18N 1.38W
Sandö *i.* Faroe Is. **16** 61.50N 6.45W
Sandoa Zaïre **36** 9.41S 22.56E
Sandomierz Poland **15** 50.41N 21.45E
San Donà di Piave Italy **9** 45.38N 12.34E
Sandover *r.* Australia **44** 21.43S136.32E
Sandoway Burma **29** 18.28N 94.20E
Sandown U.K. **5** 50.39N 1.09W
Sandpoint *town* U.S.A. **54** 48.17N116.34W
Sandringham U.K. **4** 52.50N 0.30E
Sandstone Australia **43** 27.59S119.17E
Sandusky Ohio U.S.A. **55** 41.27N 82.42W
Sandveld *f.* Namibia **39** 21.25S 20.00E
Sandviken Sweden **17** 60.37N 16.46E
Sandy U.S.A. **54** 40.35N111.53W
Sandy Bight *b.* Australia **43** 33.53S123.25E
Sandy C. Australia **44** 24.42S153.17E
Sandy Creek *town* U.S.A. **55** 43.39N 76.05W
Sandy L. Ont. Canada **51** 53.00N 93.07W
San Enrique Argentina **63** 35.47S 60.22W
San Felipe Chile **63** 32.45S 70.44W
San Felipe Colombia **60** 1.55N 67.06W
San Felipe Mexico **56** 31.00N114.52W
San Felipe Venezuela **60** 10.25N 68.40W
San Fernando Argentina **63** 34.26S 58.34W
San Fernando Chile **63** 34.35S 71.00W
San Fernando Phil. **27** 16.39N120.19E
San Fernando Spain **10** 36.28N 6.12W
San Fernando Trinidad **60** 10.16N 61.28W
San Fernando de Apure Venezuela **60** 7.35N 67.15W
San Fernando de Atabapo Venezuela **60** 4.03N 67.45W
Sanford *r.* Australia **42** 27.22S115.53E
Sanford Fla. U.S.A. **53** 28.49N 81.17W
San Francisco Argentina **62** 31.29S 62.06W
San Francisco U.S.A. **54** 37.48N122.24W
San Francisco *r.* U.S.A. **54** 32.59N109.22W
San Francisco, C. Ecuador **60** 0.50N 80.05W
San Francisco de Macorís Dom. Rep. **57** 19.19N 70.15W
Sanga-Tolon U.S.S.R. **21** 61.44N149.30E
Sanggan He *r.* China **25** 40.23N115.18E
Sangha *r.* Congo **36** 1.10S 16.47E
Sangihe *i.* Indonesia **27** 3.30N125.30E
Sangihe, Kepulauan *is.* Indonesia **27** 2.45N125.20E
San Gil Colombia **60** 6.35N 73.08W
San Giovanni in Persiceto Italy **9** 44.38N 11.11E
Sangkulirang Indonesia **26** 1.00N117.58E
Sāngli India **28** 16.55N 74.37E
Sangmélima Cameroon **38** 2.55N 12.01E
Sangonera *r.* Spain **10** 37.58N 1.04W
San Gottardo, Passo del *pass* Switz. **14** 46.30N 8.55E
San Gregorio Uruguay **63** 32.37S 55.40W
Sangri China **24** 29.18N 92.05E
San Ignacio Bolivia **62** 16.23S 60.59W
San Ignacio Paraguay **62** 26.52S 57.03W
San Isidro Argentina **63** 34.29S 58.31W
Sanīyah, Hawr as *l.* Iraq **31** 31.52N 46.50E
San Javier Argentina **63** 30.40S 59.55W
San Javier Bolivia **62** 16.22S 62.38W
San Javier Chile **63** 35.35S 71.45W
San Joaquin *r.* U.S.A. **54** 38.03N121.50W
San Jorge, Golfo *g.* Argentina **63** 46.00S 66.00W
San José Costa Rica **57** 9.59N 84.04W
San José Guatemala **56** 13.58N 90.50W
San Jose U.S.A. **54** 37.20N121.53W
San José de Chiquitos Bolivia **62** 17.53S 60.45W
San José de Feliciano Argentina **63** 30.25S 58.45W
San José de Guanipa Venezuela **60** 8.54N 64.09W
San José del Guaviare Colombia **60** 2.35N 72.38W
San José de Mayo Uruguay **63** 34.20S 56.42W
San José de Ocuné Colombia **60** 4.15N 70.20W
San Juan Argentina **62** 31.30S 68.30W
San Juan *d.* Argentina **62** 31.00S 68.30W
San Juan *r.* Costa Rica **57** 10.50N 83.40W
San Juan Dom. Rep. **57** 18.40N 71.05W
San Juan Peru **62** 15.20S 75.09W
San Juan Phil. **27** 8.25N126.22E
San Juan Puerto Rico **57** 18.29N 66.08W
San Juan *r.* U.S.A. **54** 37.18N110.28W
San Juan, C. Argentina **63** 54.45S 63.50W
San Juan Bautista Spain **10** 39.05N 1.30E
San Juan del Norte Nicaragua **57** 10.58N 83.40W
San Juan de los Morros Venezuela **60** 9.53N 67.23W
San Juan del Río Querétaro Mexico **56** 20.23N100.00W
San Juan Mts. U.S.A. **54** 37.35N107.10W
San Julián Argentina **63** 49.19S 67.40W
San Justo Argentina **63** 30.47S 60.35W
Sankt Niklaus Switz. **9** 46.11N 7.48E
San Lázaro, Cabo *c.* Mexico **56** 24.50N112.18W
San Leonardo Spain **10** 41.49N 3.04W
San Lorenzo Argentina **63** 32.45S 60.44W
San Lorenzo *mtn.* Chile **63** 47.37S 72.19W
San Lorenzo Ecuador **60** 1.17N 78.50W
San Lorenzo de El Escorial Spain **10** 40.34N 4.08W
Sanlúcar de Barrameda Spain **10** 36.46N 6.21W
Sanlúcar la Mayor Spain **10** 37.26N 6.18W
San Lucas Bolivia **62** 20.06S 65.07W
San Lucas, Cabo *c.* Mexico **56** 22.50N109.55W
San Luis Argentina **63** 33.20S 66.20W
San Luis *d.* Argentina **63** 34.00S 66.00W
San Luis Cuba **57** 20.13N 75.50W
San Luis Obispo U.S.A. **54** 35.17N120.40W
San Luis Potosí Mexico **56** 22.10N101.00W
San Luis Potosí *d.* Mexico **56** 23.00N100.00W
San Marcos U.S.A. **52** 29.54N 97.57W
San Marino Europe **9** 43.55N 12.27E
San Marino *town* San Marino **9** 43.55N 12.27E
San Martín *r.* Bolivia **62** 12.25S 64.25W
San Mateo U.S.A. **54** 37.35N122.19W
San Matías Bolivia **60** 16.22S 58.24W
San Matías, Golfo *g.* Argentina **63** 41.30S 64.00W
Sanmenxia China **25** 34.46N111.17E
San Miguel *r.* Bolivia **62** 12.25S 64.25W
San Miguel *r.* Bolivia **60** 13.52S 63.56W
San Miguel El Salvador **57** 13.28N 88.10W
San Miguel del Monte Argentina **63** 35.25S 58.49W
San Miguel de Tucumán Argentina **62** 26.49S 65.13W
San Miguelito Panama **57** 9.02N 79.30W
Sannār Sudan **35** 13.31N 33.38E
Sannicandro Italy **12** 41.50N 15.34E
San Nicolas Argentina **63** 33.20S 60.13W
Sanok Poland **15** 49.35N 22.10E
San Pablo Phil. **27** 13.58N121.10E
San Pedro Buenos Aires Argentina **63** 33.40S 59.41W
San Pedro Jujuy Argentina **62** 24.14S 64.50W
San Pedro Dom. Rep. **57** 18.30N 69.18W
San Pedro Paraguay **59** 24.08S 57.08W
San Pedro, Punta *c.* Costa Rica **57** 8.38N 83.45W
San Pedro, Sierra de *mts.* Spain **10** 39.20N 6.20W
San Pedro de las Colonias Mexico **56** 25.50N102.59W
San Pedro Sula Honduras **57** 15.26N 88.01W
San Pellegrino Terme Italy **9** 45.50N 9.40E
San Pietro *i.* Italy **12** 39.09N 8.16E
Sanquhar U.K. **6** 55.22N 3.56W
San Quintín Mexico **56** 30.28N115.58W
San Rafael U.S.A. **54** 37.59N122.31W
San Raphael Argentina **63** 34.40S 68.21W
San Remo Italy **9** 43.48N 7.46E
San Salvador Argentina **63** 31.37S 58.30W
San Salvador *i.* Bahamas **57** 24.00N 74.32W
San Salvador El Salvador **57** 13.40N 89.10W
San Salvador de Jujuy Argentina **62** 24.10S 65.20W
San Sebastián Argentina **63** 53.15S 68.30W
San Sebastián Spain **10** 43.19N 1.59W
San Severo Italy **12** 41.40N 15.24E
Santa *r.* Peru **60** 9.00S 78.35W
Santa Ana Argentina **62** 27.20S 65.35W
Santa Ana Bolivia **62** 13.45S 65.35W
Santa Ana El Salvador **57** 14.00N 89.31W
Santa Ana U.S.A. **54** 33.44N117.54W
Santa Bárbara Mexico **56** 26.48N105.49W
Santa Barbara U.S.A. **54** 34.25N119.42W
Santa Catarina *d.* Brazil **59** 27.00S 52.00W
Santa Clara Cuba **57** 22.25N 79.58W
Santa Clara Calif. U.S.A. **54** 37.21N121.57W
Santa Clara Utah U.S.A. **54** 37.08N113.39W
Santa Clotilde Peru **60** 2.25S 73.35W
Santa Comba Dão Portugal **10** 40.24N 8.08W
Santa Cruz *d.* Argentina **63** 48.00S 69.30W
Santa Cruz *r.* Argentina **63** 50.03S 68.35W
Santa Cruz Bolivia **62** 17.45S 63.14W
Santa Cruz *d.* Bolivia **62** 17.45S 62.00W
Santa Cruz Canary Is. **34** 28.27N 16.14W
Santa Cruz U.S.A. **54** 36.58N122.08W
Santa Cruz *i.* U.S.A. **54** 34.01N119.45W
Santa Cruz Is. Solomon Is. **40** 10.30S166.00E
Santa Domingo Mexico **54** 25.32N112.02W
Santa Elena Argentina **63** 31.00S 59.50W
Santa Elena, C. Costa Rica **57** 10.54N 85.56W
Santa Fé Argentina **63** 31.40S 60.40W
Santa Fé *d.* Argentina **62** 30.00S 61.00W
Santa Fe U.S.A. **52** 35.42N106.57W
Santa Filomena Brazil **61** 9.07S 45.56W
Santa Inés, Isla *i.* Chile **63** 53.40S 73.00W
Santa Isabel Argentina **63** 36.15S 66.55W
Santa Isabel do Morro Brazil **61** 11.36S 50.37W
Santa Lucía Uruguay **63** 34.27S 56.24W
Santa Lucía *r.* Uruguay **63** 34.48S 56.22W
Santa Lucia Range *mts.* U.S.A. **54** 36.00N121.20W
Santa Margherita Ligure Italy **9** 44.20N 9.12E
Santa Maria Brazil **59** 29.40S 53.47W
Santa Maria U.S.A. **54** 34.57N120.26W
Santa Maria di Leuca, Capo *c.* Italy **13** 39.47N 18.24E
Santa Maria Madalena Brazil **59** 21.58S 42.02W
Santa Marta Colombia **60** 11.18N 74.10W
Santa Marta, Sierra Nevada de *mts.* Colombia **60** 11.20N 73.00W
Santa Monica U.S.A. **54** 34.01N118.30W
Santana do Livramento Brazil **63** 30.53S 55.31W
Santander Colombia **60** 3.00N 76.25W
Santander Spain **10** 43.28N 3.48W
Santañy Spain **10** 39.20N 3.07E
Santarém Brazil **61** 2.26S 54.41W
Santarém Portugal **10** 39.14N 8.40W
Santa Rosa Argentina **63** 36.00S 64.40W
Santa Rosa Bolivia **60** 10.36S 67.25W
Santa Rosa Brazil **59** 27.52S 54.29W
Santa Rosa Honduras **57** 14.47N 88.46W
Santa Rosa *i.* U.S.A. **54** 33.58N120.06W
Santa Rosa Calif. U.S.A. **54** 38.26N122.34W
Santa Rosa de Cabal Colombia **60** 4.52N 75.37W
Santa Rosalía Mexico **56** 27.19N112.17W
Santa Rosa Range *mts.* U.S.A. **54** 41.00N117.40W
Santa Vitória do Palmar Brazil **59** 33.31S 53.21W
Santhià Italy **9** 45.22N 8.10E
Santiago Chile **63** 33.27S 70.40W
Santiago Dom. Rep. **57** 19.30N 70.42W
Santiago Panama **57** 8.08N 80.59W
Santiago *r.* Peru **60** 4.30S 77.48W
Santiago de Compostela Spain **10** 42.52N 8.33W
Santiago de Cuba Cuba **57** 20.00N 75.49W
Santiago del Estero Argentina **62** 27.50S 64.15W
Santiago del Estero *d.* Argentina **62** 27.40S 63.30W
Santiago Vázquez Uruguay **63** 34.48S 56.21W
Santo Amaro Brazil **61** 12.35S 38.41W
Santo André Brazil **59** 23.39S 46.29W
Santo Angelo Brazil **59** 28.18S 54.16W
Santo Antônio do Içá Brazil **60** 3.05S 67.57W
Santo Domingo Dom. Rep. **57** 18.30N 69.57W
Santoña Spain **10** 43.27N 3.26W
Santos Brazil **59** 23.56S 46.22W
Santos Dumont Brazil **59** 21.30S 43.34W
Santo Tomás Peru **60** 14.34S 72.30W
Santo Tomé Argentina **62** 28.31S 56.03W
Santpoort Neth. **8** 52.27N 4.38E
San Valentín, Cerro *mtn.* Chile **63** 46.40S 73.25W
San Vicente El Salvador **57** 13.38N 88.42W
San Vito al Tagliamento Italy **9** 45.54N 12.52E
São Borja Brazil **59** 28.35S 56.01W
São Caetano do Sul Brazil **59** 23.36S 46.34W
São Carlos Brazil **59** 22.01S 47.54W
São Francisco *r.* Brazil **61** 10.20S 36.20W
São Francisco do Sol Brazil **59** 26.17S 48.39W
São Gabriel Brazil **59** 30.20S 54.19W
São Gonçalo do Sapucaí Brazil **59** 21.54S 45.35W
Sao Hill *town* Tanzania **37** 8.21S 35.10E
São João da Boa Vista Brazil **59** 21.59S 46.45W
São João da Madeira Portugal **10** 40.54N 8.30W
São João del Rei Brazil **59** 21.08S 44.15W
São João do Piauí Brazil **61** 8.21S 42.15W
São Joaquim da Barra Brazil **59** 20.36S 47.51W
São José do Calçado Brazil **59** 21.01S 41.37W
São José do Rio Prêto Brazil **59** 20.50S 49.20W
São José dos Campos Brazil **59** 23.07S 45.52W
São Leopoldo Brazil **59** 29.46S 51.09W
São Lourenço Brazil **59** 22.08S 45.05W
São Luís Brazil **61** 2.34S 44.16W
São Manuel Brazil **59** 22.40S 48.35W
São Manuel *r. see* Teles Pires *r.* Brazil **61**
São Miguel d'Oeste Brazil **59** 26.45S 53.34W
Saona *i.* Dom. Rep. **57** 18.09N 68.42W
Saône *r.* France **14** 45.46N 4.52E
São Paulo Brazil **59** 23.33S 46.39W
São Paulo *d.* Brazil **59** 22.05S 48.00W
São Paulo de Olivença Brazil **60** 3.34S 68.55W
São Roque Brazil **59** 23.31S 47.09W
São Sebastião Brazil **59** 23.48S 45.26W
São Sebastião, Ilha de *i.* Brazil **59** 23.53S 45.17W
São Sebastião do Paraíso Brazil **59** 20.54S 46.59W
São Tiago Brazil **59** 20.54S 44.30W
São Tomé *i.* São Tomé & Príncipe **34** 0.19N 6.43E
São Tomé & Príncipe Africa **34** 1.00N 7.00E
São Vicente Brazil **59** 23.57S 46.23W
São Vicente, Cabo de *c.* Portugal **10** 37.01N 8.59W
São Vicente de Minas Brazil **59** 21.40S 44.26W
Sapé Brazil **61** 7.06S 35.13W
Sapele Nigeria **38** 5.53N 5.41E
Sapporo Japan **25** 43.05N141.21E
Sapri Italy **12** 40.04N 15.38E
Saqqārah Egypt **32** 29.51N 31.13E
Saqqez Iran **31** 36.14N 46.15E
Sarāb Iran **31** 37.56N 47.35E
Sarābiyūm Egypt **32** 30.23N 32.17E
Sara Buri Thailand **29** 14.32N100.53E
Sarajevo Yugo. **15** 43.52N 18.26E
Saranac Lake *town* U.S.A. **55** 44.20N 74.08W
Sarandí del Yi Uruguay **63** 33.21S 55.38W
Sarandí Grande Uruguay **63** 33.44S 56.20W
Sārangarh India **29** 21.38N 83.09E
Saranpaul U.S.S.R. **18** 64.15N 60.58E
Saransk U.S.S.R. **18** 54.12N 45.10E
Sarapul U.S.S.R. **18** 56.30N 53.49E
Sarasota U.S.A. **53** 27.20N 82.32W
Sarata U.S.S.R. **15** 46.00N 29.40E
Saratoga U.S.A. **54** 37.16N122.02W
Saratoga Springs U.S.A. **55** 43.05N 73.47W
Saratov U.S.S.R. **19** 51.30N 45.55E
Sarawak *d.* Malaysia **26** 2.00N113.00E
Saraychik U.S.S.R. **19** 47.29N 51.42E
Sarbāz Iran **31** 26.39N 61.20E
Sarcelles France **9** 49.00N 2.23E
Sardegna *d.* Italy **12** 40.05N 9.00E
Sardegna *i.* Italy **12** 40.00N 9.00E
Sardinia *i. see* Sardegna *i.* Italy **12**
Sarek *mtn.* Sweden **16** 67.25N 17.46E
Sareks Nat. Park Sweden **16** 67.15N 17.30E
Sargodha Pakistan **28** 32.01N 72.40E
Sarh Chad **34** 9.08N 18.22E
Sarī Iran **31** 36.33N 53.06E
Sarigan *i.* Mariana Is. **27** 16.43N145.47E

Sarikamiş Turkey **30** 40.19N 42.35E
Sarikei Malaysia **26** 2.07N111.31E
Sarina Australia **44** 21.26S149.13E
Sark *i.* U.K. **5** 49.26N 2.22W
Sarlat France **11** 44.53N 1.13E
Sărmasu Romania **15** 46.46N 24.11E
Sarmi Indonesia **27** 1.51S138.45E
Sarmiento Argentina **63** 45.35S 69.05W
Särna Sweden **17** 61.41N 13.08E
Sarnia Canada **55** 42.58N 82.23W
Sarny U.S.S.R. **15** 51.21N 26.31E
Saronno Italy **9** 45.38N 9.02E
Saros Körfezi *g.* Turkey **13** 40.32N 26.25E
Sárospatak Hungary **15** 48.19N 21.34E
Sarpsborg Norway **17** 59.17N 11.07E
Sarrebourg France **11** 48.43N 7.03E
Sarreguemines France **11** 49.06N 7.03E
Sarria Spain **10** 42.47N 7.25W
Sarro Mali **38** 13.40N 5.05W
Sartène France **11** 41.36N 8.59E
Sarthe *d.* France **9** 48.00N 0.05E
Sarthe *r.* France **9** 47.29N 0.30W
Sartilly France **9** 48.45N 1.27W
Sartynya U.S.S.R. **20** 63.22N 63.11E
Şarūr Oman **31** 23.25N 58.10E
Sárvár Hungary **14** 47.15N 16.57E
Saryshagan U.S.S.R. **24** 46.08N 73.32E
Sarzana Italy **9** 44.07N 9.58E
Sasebo Japan **25** 33.10N129.42E
Saser *mtn.* Jammu & Kashmir **28** 34.50N 77.50E
Saskatchewan *d.* Canada **50** 55.00N105.00W
Saskatchewan *r.* Canada **51** 53.25N100.15W
Saskatoon Canada **50** 52.10N106.40W
Sasovo U.S.S.R. **18** 54.21N 41.58E
Sassandra Ivory Coast **38** 4.58N 6.08W
Sassari Italy **12** 40.43N 8.33E
Sassnitz E. Germany **14** 54.32N 13.40E
Sasso Marconi Italy **9** 44.24N 11.15E
Sassuolo Italy **9** 44.33N 10.47E
Sasyk, Ozero *l.* U.S.S.R. **15** 45.38N 29.38E
Sātāra India **28** 17.43N 74.05E
Satna India **29** 24.33N 80.50E
Sátoraljaújhely Hungary **15** 48.24N 21.39E
Sātpura Range *mts.* India **28** 21.50N 76.00E
Satu Mare Romania **15** 47.48N 22.52E
Sauce Argentina **63** 30.05S 58.45W
Sauda Norway **17** 59.39N 6.20E
Saudi Arabia Asia **30** 26.00N 44.00E
Saulieu France **9** 47.17N 4.14E
Sault Sainte Marie Canada **55** 46.31N 84.20W
Sault Sainte Marie U.S.A. **55** 46.29N 84.22W
Saumarez Reef Australia **44** 21.50S153.40E
Saumlaki Indonesia **44** 7.59S131.22E
Saumur France **9** 47.16N 0.05W
Saurimo Angola **36** 9.38S 20.20E
Sava *r.* Yugo. **15** 44.50N 20.26E
Savalou Benin **38** 7.55N 1.59E
Savannah *r.* U.S.A. **53** 32.10N 81.00W
Savannah Ga. U.S.A. **53** 32.09N 81.01W
Savannakhét Laos **26** 16.34N104.55E
Savant L. Canada **55** 50.48N 90.20W
Savant Lake *town* Canada **55** 50.20N 90.40W
Savé Benin **38** 8.04N 2.37E
Save *r.* Mozambique **39** 20.59S 35.02E
Sāveh Iran **31** 35.00N 50.25E
Savelugu Ghana **38** 9.39N 0.48W
Saverdun France **11** 43 14N 1.35E
Savigliano Italy **9** 44.38N 7.40E
Savigny-sur-Braye France **9** 47.53N 0.49E
Savona Italy **9** 44.18N 8.28E
Savonlinna Finland **18** 61.52N 28.51E
Savoonga U.S.A. **50** 63.42N170.27W
Savu Sea *see* Sawu, Laut *sea* Pacific Oc. **27**
Sawākin Sudan **35** 19.04N 37.22E
Sawbridgeworth U.K. **5** 51.50N 0.09W
Sawdā', Qurnat as *mtn.* Lebanon **32** 34.17N 36.04E
Sawhāj Egypt **30** 26.33N 31.42E
Sawston U.K. **5** 52.07N 0.11E
Sawtooth Mts. U.S.A. **54** 44.03N114.35W
Sawu *i.* Indonesia **27** 10.30S121.50E
Sawu, Laut *sea* Pacific Oc. **27** 9.30S122.30E
Saxmundham U.K. **5** 52.13N 1.29E
Saxon Switz. **9** 46.09N 7.11E
Say Mali **38** 13.08N 2.22E
Say Niger **38** 13.08N 2.22E
Sayama Japan **23** 35.51N139.24E
Şaydā Lebanon **32** 33.32N 35.22E
Sayers Lake *town* Australia **46** 32.46S143.20E
Saynshand Mongolia **25** 44.58N110.10E
Sayula Mexico **56** 19.52N103.36W
Sázava *r.* Czech. **14** 49.53N 14.21E
Scafell Pike *mtn.* U.K. **4** 54.27N 3.12W
Scalea Italy **12** 39.49N 15.48E
Scalloway U.K. **6** 60.08N 1.17W
Scammon Bay *town* U.S.A. **50** 61.50N165.35W
Scapa Flow *str.* U.K. **6** 58.53N 3.05W
Scarborough Tobago **60** 11.11N 60.45W
Scarborough U.K. **4** 54.17N 0.24W
Sceale Bay *town* Australia **46** 33.00S134.15E
Schaerbeek Belgium **8** 50.54N 4.20E
Schaffhausen Switz. **14** 47.42N 8.38E
Schagen Neth. **8** 52.47N 4.47E
Schefferville Canada **51** 54.50N 67.00W
Schelde *r.* Belgium **8** 51.13N 4.25E
Schell Creek Range *mts.* U.S.A. **54** 39.10N114.40W
Schenectady U.S.A. **55** 42.47N 73.53W
Scheveningen Neth. **8** 52.07N 4.16E
Schiedam Neth. **8** 51.55N 4.25E
Schiermonnikoog *i.* Neth. **8** 53.28N 6.15E
Schio Italy **9** 45.43N 11.21E
Schleiden W. Germany **8** 50.32N 6.29E
Schleswig W. Germany **14** 54.32N 9.34E
Schleswig-Holstein *d.* W. Germany **14** 54.00N 10.30E
Schouten, Kepulauan *is.* Indonesia **27** 0.45S135.50E
Schouwen *i.* Neth. **8** 51.42N 3.45E
Schreiber Canada **55** 48.48N 87.17W
Schwandorf W. Germany **14** 49.20N 12.08E
Schwaner, Pegunungan *mts.* Indonesia **26** 0.45S113.20E
Schwarzrand *mts.* Namibia **39** 25.40S 16.53E
Schwarzwald *f.* W. Germany **14** 48.00N 7.45E
Schwedt E. Germany **14** 53.04N 14.17E
Schweich W. Germany **8** 49.50N 6.47E
Schweinfurt W. Germany **14** 50.03N 10.16E
Schwelm W. Germany **8** 51.17N 7.18E
Schwerin E. Germany **14** 53.38N 11.25E
Schwerin *d.* E. Germany **14** 53.30N 11.30E
Schwyz Switz. **14** 47.02N 8.40E
Sciacca Italy **12** 37.31N 13.05E
Scilla Italy **12** 38.15N 15.44E
Scilly, Isles of U.K. **5** 49.55N 6.20W
Scone Australia **47** 32.01S150.53E
Scotia Calif. U.S.A. **54** 40.26N123.31W
Scotland U.K. **6** 55.30N 4.00W
Scott *r.* Australia **46** 30.41S137.50E
Scottburgh R.S.A. **39** 30.17S 30.45E
Scott Reef Australia **42** 14.00S121.50E
Scottsbluff U.S.A. **52** 41.52N103.40W
Scottsdale Australia **45** 41.09S147.31E
Scottsdale U.S.A. **54** 33.30N111.56W
Scranton U.S.A. **55** 41.24N 75.40W
Scugog, L. Canada **55** 44.10N 78.51W
Scunthorpe U.K. **4** 53.35N 0.38W
Scutari, L. Yugo. / Albania **13** 42.10N 19.18E
Seabrook, L. Australia **43** 30.56S119.40E
Seaford U.S.A. **55** 38.39N 75.37W
Seahouses U.K. **4** 55.35N 1.38W
Sea Isle City U.S.A. **55** 39.09N 74.42W
Seal *r.* Canada **51** 59.00N 95.00W
Sea Lake *town* Australia **46** 35.31S142.54E
Searchlight U.S.A. **54** 35.28N114.55W
Seascale U.K. **4** 54.24N 3.29W
Seaside Calif. U.S.A. **54** 36.37N121.50W
Seaside Oreg. U.S.A. **54** 46.02N123.55W
Seaton U.K. **5** 50.43N 3.05W
Seattle U.S.A. **54** 47.36N122.20W
Seaview Range *mts.* Australia **44** 18.56S146.00E
Sebastián Vizcaíno, Bahía *b.* Mexico **56** 28.00N114.30W
Sebba Burkina Faso **38** 13.27N 0.33E
Sebeş Romania **15** 45.58N 23.34E
Sebidiro P.N.G. **27** 9.00S142.15E
Sebinkarahisar Turkey **30** 40.19N 38.25E
Sechura, Desierto de *des.* Peru **60** 6.00S 80.30W
Seclin France **8** 50.34N 3.01E
Sêda *r.* Portugal **10** 38.55N 7.30W
Sedalia U.S.A. **53** 38.42N 93.15W
Sedan Australia **46** 34.34S139.19E
Sedan France **9** 49.42N 4.57E
Seddon New Zealand **48** 41.40S174.04E
Sédhiou Senegal **34** 12.44N 15.30W
Sedom Israel **32** 31.04N 35.23E
Seeheim Namibia **39** 26.50S 17.45E
Sées France **9** 48.38N 0.10E
Ségou Mali **38** 13.28N 6.18W
Ségou *d.* Mali **38** 13.55N 6.20W
Segovia Spain **10** 40.57N 4.07W
Segozero, Ozero *l.* U.S.S.R. **18** 63.15N 33.40E
Segré France **9** 47.41N 0.53W
Segre *r.* Spain **10** 41.25N 0.21E
Séguédine Niger **34** 20.12N 12.59E
Segura Portugal **10** 39.50N 6.59W
Segura *r.* Spain **10** 38.07N 0.14W
Segura, Sierra de *mts.* Spain **10** 38.00N 2.50W
Seiches-sur-le-Loir France **9** 47.35N 0.22W
Seiland *i.* Norway **16** 70.25N 23.10E
Seinäjoki Finland **16** 62.47N 22.50E
Seine *r.* France **9** 49.28N 0.25E
Seine, Baie de la *b.* France **9** 49.25N 0.15E
Seine-et-Marne *d.* France **9** 48.30N 3.00E
Seine-Maritime *d.* France **9** 49.45N 1.00E
Sekaju Indonesia **26** 2.58S103.58E
Seki Japan **23** 35.29N136.55E
Sekoma Botswana **39** 24.41S 23.50E
Sekondi-Takoradi Ghana **38** 4.57N 1.44W
Sekūheh Iran **31** 30.45N 61.29E
Selaru *i.* Indonesia **44** 8.09S131.00E
Selatan, Tanjung *c.* Indonesia **26** 4.20S114.45E
Selbu Norway **16** 63.14N 11.03E
Selby U.K. **4** 53.47N 1.05W
Seldovia U.S.A. **50** 59.27N151.43W
Sele *r.* Italy **12** 40.30N 14.50E
Selebi-Pikwe Botswana **36** 22.01S 27.50E
Selenga *r.* U.S.S.R. **24** 52.20N106.20E
Selenge Mörön *r.* *see* Selenga Mongolia **24**
Sélestat France **11** 48.16N 7.28E
Seligman U.S.A. **54** 35.20N112.53W
Seljord Norway **17** 59.29N 8.37E
Selkirk U.K. **6** 55.33N 2.51W
Selkirk Mts. Canada / U.S.A. **50** 49.00N116.00W
Selles-sur-Cher France **9** 47.16N 1.33E
Selma Calif. U.S.A. **54** 36.34N119.37W
Selseleh ye Safīd Kūh *mts.* Afghan **31** 34.30N 63.30E
Selsey Bill *c.* U.K. **5** 50.44N 0.47W
Selty U.S.S.R. **18** 57.19N 52.12E
Sélune *r.* France **9** 48.35N 1.15W
Selva Argentina **59** 29.50S 62.02W
Selvas *f.* Brazil **60** 6.00S 65.00W
Selwyn Australia **44** 21.32S140.30E
Selwyn Mts. Canada **50** 63.00N130.00W
Selwyn Range *mts.* Australia **44** 21.35S140.35E
Seman *r.* Albania **13** 40.53N 19.25E
Semara W. Sahara **34** 26.44N 11.41W
Semarang Indonesia **26** 6.58S110.29E
Sembabule Uganda **37** 0.08S 31.27E
Seminoe Resr. U.S.A. **54** 42.00N106.50W
Semiozernoye U.S.S.R. **20** 52.22N 64.06E
Semipalatinsk U.S.S.R. **20** 50.26N 80.16E
Semirom Iran **31** 31.31N 52.10E
Semiyarka U.S.S.R. **20** 50.52N 78.23E
Semliki *r.* Zaïre **37** 1.12N 30.27E
Semmering Pass Austria **14** 47.40N 16.00E
Semnān Iran **31** 35.31N 53.24E
Semois *r.* France **8** 49.53N 4.45E
Semporna Malaysia **26** 4.27N118.36E
Semu *r.* Tanzania **37** 3.57S 34.20E
Semur-en-Auxois France **9** 47.29N 4.20E
Sena Mozambique **37** 17.36S 35.00E
Senador Pompeu Brazil **61** 5.30S 39.25W
Senaja Malaysia **26** 6.49N117.02E
Sena Madureira Brazil **60** 9.04S 68.40W
Sendai Tōfuku Japan **25** 38.16N140.52E
Sendenhorst W. Germany **8** 51.52N 7.50E
Seneca Oreg. U.S.A. **54** 44.08N118.58W
Senegal Africa **34** 14.30N 14.30W
Sénégal *r.* Senegal / Mauritania **34** 16.00N 16.28W
Senekal R.S.A. **39** 28.18S 27.37E
Senhor do Bonfim Brazil **61** 10.28S 40.11W
Senica Czech. **15** 48.41N 17.22E
Senigallia Italy **14** 43.42N 13.14E
Senise Italy **12** 40.09N 16.18E
Senj Yugo. **14** 45.00N 14.58E
Senja *i.* Norway **16** 69.15N 17.20E
Senlis France **9** 49.12N 2.35E
Sennan Japan **23** 34.22N135.17E
Sennen U.K. **5** 50.04N 5.42W
Senneterre Canada **55** 48.24N 77.14W
Sens France **9** 48.12N 3.18E
Senta Yugo. **15** 45.56N 20.04E
Sentinel U.S.A. **54** 32.53N113.12W
Seoni India **29** 22.05N 79.32E
Seoul *see* Sŏul S. Korea **25**
Sepik *r.* P.N.G. **27** 3.54S144.30E
Sepopa Botswana **39** 18.45S 22.11E
Sept Îles *town* Canada **55** 50.13N 66.22W
Sepúlveda Spain **10** 41.18N 3.45W
Seraing Belgium **8** 50.37N 5.33E
Seram *i.* Indonesia **27** 3.10S129.30E
Seram, Laut *sea* Pacific Oc. **27** 2.50S128.00E
Serang Indonesia **26** 6.07S106.09E
Serbia *d.* *see* Srbija *d.* Yugo. **15**
Seremban Malaysia **26** 2.42N101.54E
Serengeti Nat. Park Tanzania **37** 2.30S 35.00E
Serengeti Plain *f.* Tanzania **37** 3.00S 35.00E
Serenje Zambia **37** 13.12S 30.50E
Serenli Somali Rep. **37** 2.19N 42.15E
Sergach U.S.S.R. **18** 55.32N 45.27E
Sergipe *d.* Brazil **61** 11.00S 37.00W
Sergiyevsk U.S.S.R. **18** 53.56N 50.01E
Seria Brunei **26** 4.39N114.23E
Serian Malaysia **26** 1.10N110.35E
Sericho Kenya **37** 1.13N 39.06E
Sérifos *i.* Greece **13** 37.11N 24.31E
Serle, Mt Australia **46** 30.34S138.55E
Sermata *i.* Indonesia **27** 8.30S129.00E
Serodino Argentina **63** 32.37S 60.57W
Serov U.S.S.R. **18** 59.42N 60.32E
Serowe Botswana **39** 22.25S 26.42E
Serpa Portugal **10** 37.56N 7.36W
Serpentine *r.* Australia **43** 32.33S115.46E
Serpent's Mouth *str.* Venezuela **60** 9.50N 61.00W
Serpukhov U.S.S.R. **18** 54.53N 37.25E
Serra do Navio Brazil **61** 0.59N 52.03W
Sérrai Greece **13** 41.04N 23.32E
Serra Talhada Brazil **61** 8.01S 38.17W
Serravalle Scrivia Italy **9** 44.43N 8.51E
Serre *r.* France **8** 49.40N 3.22E
Serrinha Brazil **61** 11.38S 38.56W
Serui Indonesia **27** 1.53S136.15E
Serule Botswana **39** 21.54S 27.20E
Serviceton Australia **46** 36.22S141.02E
Şes, Munţii *mts.* Romania **15** 47.05N 22.30E
Seseganaga L. Canada **55** 50.02N 90.08W
Sese Is. Uganda **37** 0.20S 32.30E
Sesepe Indonesia **27** 1.30S127.59E
Sesheke Zambia **39** 17.27S 24.19E
Sesia *r.* Italy **9** 45.05N 8.37E
Sesimbra Portugal **10** 38.26N 9.06W
Sestao Spain **10** 43.18N 3.00W
Sestri Levante Italy **9** 44.16N 9.24E
Sète France **11** 43.25N 3.43E
Sete Lagoas Brazil **59** 19.29S 44.15W
Sete Quedas, Salto das *f.* Brazil **59** 24.00S 54.10W
Sétif Algeria **34** 36.09N 5.26E
Seto Japan **23** 35.14N137.06E
Settat Morocco **34** 33.04N 7.37W
Setté Cama Gabon **36** 2.32S 9.46E
Settimo Torinese Italy **9** 45.09N 7.46E
Settle U.K. **4** 54.05N 2.18W
Setúbal Portugal **10** 38.31N 8.54W
Setúbal, Baía de *b.* Portugal **10** 38.20N 9.00W
Sevan, Ozero *l.* U.S.S.R. **31** 40.22N 45.20E
Sevastopol' U.S.S.R. **19** 44.36N 33.31E
Sevenoaks U.K. **5** 51.16N 0.12E
Sévérac France **11** 44.20N 3.05E
Severn *r.* Australia **47** 29.08S150.50E
Severn *r.* Canada **51** 56.00N 87.40W
Severn *r.* U.K. **5** 51.50N 2.21W
Severnaya Zemlya *is.* U.S.S.R. **21** 80.00N 96.00E
Severnyy U.S.S.R. **18** 69.55N 49.01E
Severnyy Donets *r.* U.S.S.R. **19** 49.08N 37.28E
Severnyy Dvina *r.* U.S.S.R. **18** 57.03N 24.00E
Severodvinsk U.S.S.R. **18** 64.35N 39.50E
Severomorsk U.S.S.R. **18** 69.05N 33.30E
Sevier *r.* U.S.A. **54** 39.04N113.06W
Sevier L. U.S.A. **54** 38.55N113.09W
Sevilla Spain **10** 37.24N 5.59W
Sèvre-Nantaise *r.* France **11** 47.12N 1.35W
Sèvre Niortaise *r.* France **11** 46.35N 1.05W
Sevrey Mongolia **24** 43.33N102.13E
Seward U.S.A. **50** 60.05N149.34W
Seward Pen. U.S.A. **50** 65.00N164.10W
Seydhisfjördhur *town* Iceland **16** 65.16N 14.02W
Seym *r.* U.S.S.R. **19** 51.30N 32.30E
Seymour Australia **47** 37.01S145.10E
Sézanne France **9** 48.44N 3.44E
Sfax Tunisia **34** 34.45N 10.43E
Sfîntu-Gheorghe Romania **15** 45.52N 25.50E
'sGravenhage Neth. **8** 52.05N 4.16E
Shaanxi *d.* China **25** 35.00N109.00E
Shaba *d.* Zaïre **37** 8.00S 27.00E
Shache China **24** 38.27N 77.16E
Shafter U.S.A. **54** 35.30N119.16W
Shaftesbury U.K. **5** 51.00N 2.12W
Shahbā' Syria **32** 32.51N 36.37E
Shahdād Iran **31** 30.27N 57.44E
Shāh Jahān, Kūh-e *mts.* Iran **31** 37.00N 58.00E
Shāhjahānpur India **29** 27.53N 79.55E
Shāh Kūh *mtn.* Iran **31** 31.38N 59.16E
Shahr-e Bābak Iran **31** 30.08N 55.04E
Shahrezā Iran **31** 32.00N 51.52E
Shahr Kord Iran **31** 32.40N 50.52E
Shahsavār Iran **31** 36.49N 50.54E
Sha'īb Abā al Qūr *wadi* Saudi Arabia **30** 31.02N 42.00E
Shakawe Botswana **39** 18.22S 21.50E
Shaker Heights *town* U.S.A. **55** 41.29N 81.36W
Shakhty U.S.S.R. **19** 47.43N 40.16E
Shakhunya U.S.S.R. **18** 57.41N 46.46E
Shaki Nigeria **38** 8.41N 3.24E
Shakshūk Egypt **32** 29.28N 30.42E
Shala, L. Ethiopia **35** 7.25N 38.30E
Shām, Jabal ash *mtn.* Oman **31** 23.14N 57.17E
Shāmat al Akbād *des.* Saudi Arabia **30** 28.15N 43.05E
Shamokin U.S.A. **55** 40.47N 76.34W
Shamva Zimbabwe **37** 17.20S 31.38E
Shandong *d.* China **25** 35.45N117.30E
Shandong Bandao *pen.* China **25** 37.00N121.30E
Shanghai China **25** 31.13N121.25E
Shanghai *d.* China **25** 31.14N121.28E
Shangrao China **25** 28.28N117.54E
Shangshui China **25** 33.33N114.38E
Shannon *r.* Rep. of Ire. **7** 52.39N 8.43W
Shannon, Mouth of the *est.* Rep. of Ire. **7** 52.29N 9.57W
Shanshan China **24** 42.52N 90.10E
Shantarskiy Ostrova *is.* U.S.S.R. **21** 55.00N138.00E
Shantou China **25** 23.23N116.39E
Shanwa Tanzania **37** 3.09S 33.48E
Shanxi *d.* China **25** 36.45N112.00E
Shaoguan China **25** 24.54N113.33E
Shaoxing China **25** 30.02N120.35E
Shaoyang China **25** 27.43N111.24E
Shap U.K. **4** 54.32N 2.40W
Shapinsay *i.* U.K. **6** 59.03N 2.51W
Shapur *ruins* Iran **31** 29.42N 51.30E
Shaqrā' Saudi Arabia **31** 25.17N 45.14E
Shaqrā' S. Yemen **35** 13.21N 45.42E
Shark B. Australia **42** 25.30S113.30E
Sharlyk U.S.S.R. **18** 52.58N 54.46E
Sharm ash Shaykh Egypt **32** 27.51N 34.16E
Sharon U.S.A. **55** 41.16N 80.30W
Sharqī, Al Jabal ash *mts.* Lebanon **32** 34.00N 36.25E
Sharqīyah, Aş Şaḥrā' ash *des.* Egypt **32** 27.40N 32.00E
Sharya U.S.S.R. **18** 58.22N 45.50E
Shashi *r.* Botswana / Zimbabwe **39** 22.10S 29.15E
Shashi China **25** 30.16N112.20E
Shasta, Mt. U.S.A. **54** 41.20N122.20W
Shatt al Arab *r.* Iraq **31** 30.00N 48.30E
Shaunavon Canada **50** 49.40N108.25W
Shaw I. Australia **44** 20.29S149.05E
Shawinigan Canada **55** 46.33N 72.45W
Shaykh, Jabal ash *mtn.* Lebanon **32** 33.24N 35.52E
Shchara *r.* U.S.S.R. **15** 53.27N 24.45E
Shchelyayur U.S.S.R. **18** 65.16N 53.17E
Shchors U.S.S.R. **15** 51.50N 31.59E
Shebelle *r.* Somali Rep. **37** 0.30N 43.10E
Sheboygan U.S.A. **53** 43.46N 87.44W
Shebshi Mts. Nigeria **38** 8.30N 11.45E
Sheeffry Hills Rep. of Ire. **7** 53.41N 9.42W
Sheelin, Lough Rep. of Ire. **7** 53.48N 7.20W
Sheep Range *mts.* U.S.A. **54** 36.45N115.05W
Sheffield U.K. **4** 53.23N 1.28W
Shefford U.K. **5** 52.02N 0.20W
Sheki U.S.S.R. **19** 41.12N 47.10E
Sheksna *r.* U.S.S.R. **18** 60.00N 37.49E
Shelburne N.S. Canada **51** 43.46N 65.19W
Shelburne B. Australia **44** 11.49S143.00E
Shelby Mich. U.S.A. **55** 43.36N 86.22W
Shelby Mont. U.S.A. **54** 48.30N111.51W
Shelbyville Ind. U.S.A. **55** 39.31N 85.46W
Sheldrake Canada **55** 50.18N 64.54W
Shelikof Str. U.S.A. **50** 58.00N153.45W
Shelley U.S.A. **54** 43.23N112.07W
Shellharbour Australia **47** 34.35S150.52E
Shelton U.S.A. **54** 47.13N123.06W
Shenandoah *r.* U.S.A. **55** 39.19N 78.12W
Shenandoah Va. U.S.A. **55** 38.29N 78.37W
Shëngjin Albania **13** 41.49N 19.33E
Shengze China **25** 30.55N120.39E
Shenkursk U.S.S.R. **18** 62.05N 42.58E
Shenyang China **25** 41.50N123.26E
Shepetovka U.S.S.R. **15** 50.12N 27.01E
Shepparton Australia **47** 36.25S145.26E
Sheppey, Isle of U.K. **5** 51.24N 0.50E
Sherborne U.K. **5** 50.56N 2.31W
Sherbrooke Canada **55** 45.24N 71.54W
Sherburne U.S.A. **55** 42.41N 75.30W
Sheridan U.S.A. **54** 44.48N106.58W
Sheringa Australia **46** 33.51S135.15E
Sheringham U.K. **4** 52.56N 1.11E
Sherkin I. Rep. of Ire. **7** 51.28N 9.25W
Sherman Tex. U.S.A. **53** 33.39N 96.35W
Sherman Mills U.S.A. **55** 45.52N 68.23W
Sherridon Canada **51** 57.07N101.05W
'sHertogenbosch Neth. **8** 51.42N 5.19E
Shetland Is. *d.* U.K. **6** 60.20N 1.15W
Shetpe U.S.S.R. **19** 44.09N 52.06E
Shevchenko U.S.S.R. **19** 43.37N 51.11E
Shibīn al Kawm Egypt **32** 30.33N 31.00E
Shibīn al Qanāţir Egypt **32** 30.19N 31.19E
Shiel, Loch U.K. **6** 56.48N 5.33W
Shiga *d.* Japan **23** 34.55N136.00E
Shijiazhuang China **25** 38.04N114.28E
Shikārpur Pakistan **28** 27.58N 68.42E
Shikoku *i.* Japan **25** 33.30N133.30E
Shilka U.S.S.R. **25** 51.55N116.01E
Shilka *r.* U.S.S.R. **25** 53.20N121.10E
Shillong India **29** 25.34N 91.53E
Shima Japan **23** 34.13N136.51E
Shimada Japan **23** 34.49N138.11E
Shima-hantō *pen.* Japan **23** 34.25N136.45E
Shimizu Japan **23** 35.01N138.29E
Shimoda Japan **23** 34.40N138.57E
Shimoga India **28** 13.56N 75.31E
Shimonoseki Japan **25** 33.59N130.58E
Shimpek U.S.S.R. **24** 44.50N 74.10E
Shin, Loch U.K. **6** 58.06N 4.32W
Shīndand Afghan. **28** 33.18N 62.08E
Shingleton U.S.A. **55** 46.21N 86.28W
Shinshār Syria **32** 34.36N 36.45E
Shinshiro Japan **23** 34.54N137.30E
Shinyanga Tanzania **37** 3.40S 33.20E
Shinyanga *d.* Tanzania **37** 3.30S 33.00E
Shipka Pass Bulgaria **13** 42.45N 25.25E
Shippensburg U.S.A. **55** 40.03N 77.31W
Shiprock U.S.A. **54** 36.47N108.41W
Shipston on Stour U.K. **5** 52.04N 1.38W
Shiqian China **25** 27.30N108.20E
Shirakskaya Step *f.* U.S.S.R. **31** 41.40N 46.20E
Shirane san *mtn.* Japan **23** 35.40N138.15E
Shīrāz Iran **31** 29.36N 52.33E
Shirbīn Egypt **32** 31.13N 31.31E
Shire *r.* Mozambique **37** 17.46S 35.20E
Shīr Kūh *mtn.* Iran **31** 31.38N 54.07E
Shīrvān Iran **31** 37.24N 57.55E
Shivpuri India **28** 25.26N 77.39E
Shiyan Hubei China **25** 32.34N110.47E
Shizuishan China **24** 39.17N106.52E
Shizuoka Japan **23** 34.58N138.23E
Shizuoka *d.* Japan **23** 35.00N138.00E
Shklov U.S.S.R. **15** 54.16N 30.16E
Shkodër Albania **13** 42.03N 19.30E
Shkumbin *r.* Albania **13** 41.01N 19.26E
Shoal C. Australia **43** 33.51S121.10E
Sholāpur India **28** 17.43N 75.56E
Shōnai *r.* Japan **23** 35.04N136.50E
Shoshone Calif. U.S.A. **54** 35.58N116.17W
Shoshone Idaho U.S.A. **54** 42.57N114.25W
Shoshone Mts. U.S.A. **54** 39.25N117.15W
Shoshoni U.S.A. **54** 43.14N108.07W
Shostka U.S.S.R. **18** 51.53N 33.30E
Show Low U.S.A. **54** 34.15N110.02W
Shpola U.S.S.R. **15** 49.00N 31.25E
Shreveport U.S.A. **53** 32.30N 93.46W
Shrewsbury U.K. **5** 52.42N 2.45W
Shropshire *d.* U.K. **5** 52.35N 2.40W
Shuangliao China **25** 43.30N123.29E
Shuangyashan China **25** 46.37N131.22E
Shubrā al Khaymah Egypt **32** 30.06N 31.15E
Shuksan U.S.A. **54** 48.55N121.43W
Shule China **24** 39.25N 76.06E
Shumagin Is. U.S.A. **50** 55.00N160.00W
Shumerlya U.S.S.R. **18** 55.30N 46.25E
Shumikha U.S.S.R. **20** 55.15N 63.14E
Shumyachi U.S.S.R. **15** 53.52N 32.25E
Shunde China **25** 22.50N113.16E
Shur *r.* Khorāsān Iran **31** 34.05N 60.22E
Shūr *r.* Kermān Iran **31** 31.14N 55.29E
Shūr *r.* Khorāsān Iran **31** 34.11N 60.07E
Shūrāb Iran **31** 28.09N 60.18E
Shūrāb *r.* Iran **31** 31.30N 55.18E
Shurugwi Zimbabwe **39** 19.40S 30.00E
Shūshtar Iran **31** 32.04N 48.53E
Shuttleton Australia **47** 32.08S146.08E
Shuwak Sudan **35** 14.23N 35.52E
Shuya U.S.S.R. **18** 56.49N 41.23E
Shwebo Burma **29** 22.35N 95.42E
Shyok Jammu & Kashmir **29** 34.11N 78.08E
Siāhān Range *mts.* Pakistan **28** 27.25N 64.30E
Siālkot Pakistan **28** 32.29N 74.35E
Sian *see* Xi'an China **25**
Siargao *i.* Phil. **27** 9.55N126.05E
Siau *i.* Indonesia **27** 2.42N125.24E
Šiauliai U.S.S.R. **17** 55.56N 23.19E
Sibasa R.S.A. **39** 22.56S 30.28E
Šibenik Yugo. **12** 43.45N 15.55E
Siberut *i.* Indonesia **26** 1.30S 99.00E
Sibi Pakistan **28** 29.31N 67.54E
Sibiti *r.* Tanzania **37** 3.47S 34.45E
Sibiu Romania **13** 45.47N 24.09E
Sibolga Indonesia **26** 1.42N 98.48E
Sibu Malaysia **26** 2.18N111.49E
Sibut C.A.R. **36** 5.46N 19.06E
Sicasica Bolivia **62** 17.22S 67.45W
Siccus *r.* Australia **46** 31.26S139.30E
Sichuan *d.* China **24** 30.30N103.00E
Sicilia *d.* Italy **12** 37.30N 14.00E
Sicilia *i.* Italy **12** 37.30N 14.00E
Sicily *i.* *see* Sicilia *i.* Italy **12**
Sicuani Peru **60** 14.21S 71.13W
Sidaouet Niger **38** 18.34N 8.03E
Sīdī Barrānī Egypt **30** 31.38N 25.58E
Sidi bel Abbès Algeria **34** 35.15N 0.39W
Sidi Ifni Morocco **34** 29.24N 10.12W
Sīdī Sālim Egypt **32** 31.16N 30.47E
Sidlaw Hills U.K. **6** 56.31N 3.10W
Sidley, Mt. Antarctica **64** 77.30S125.00W
Sidmouth U.K. **5** 50.40N 3.13W
Sidney Canada **54** 48.39N123.24W
Sidney Nebr. U.S.A. **52** 41.09N102.59W
Sidney Ohio U.S.A. **55** 40.16N 84.10W
Sidon *see* Şaydā Lebanon **32**
Sidra, G. of *see* Surt, Khalīj *g.* Libya **34**
Siedlce Poland **15** 52.10N 22.18E
Sieg *r.* W. Germany **8** 50.49N 7.11E
Siegburg W. Germany **8** 50.48N 7.13E
Siegen W. Germany **8** 50.52N 8.02E
Siemiatycze Poland **15** 52.26N 22.53E
Siena Italy **12** 43.19N 11.20E

eradz Poland 15 51.36N 18.45E
erck-les-Bains France 8 49.28N 6.20E
erpc Poland 15 52.52N 19.41E
erra Colorada Argentina 63 40.35S 67.50W
erra Leone Africa 34 9.00N 12.00W
erra Mojada *town* Mexico 56 27.17N103.42W
erra Nevada *mts.* U.S.A. 54 37.45N119.30W
erre Switz. 9 46.18N 7.32E
nos *i.* Greece 13 36.59N 24.60E
g U.S.S.R. 18 65.31N 34.16E
ghetul Marmaţiei Romania 15 47.56N 23.54E
ghişoara Romania 15 46.13N 24.49E
gli Indonesia 26 5.23N 95.57E
glufjördhur Iceland 16 66.12N 18.55W
gny France 9 49.42N 4.25E
güenza Spain 10 41.04N 2.38W
guiri Guinea 34 11.28N 9.07W
ka *r.* Finland 16 64.50N 24.44E
rt Turkey 30 37.56N 41.56E
kar India 28 27.33N 75.12E
kasso Mali 38 11.18N 5.38W
kasso *d.* Mali 38 11.20N 6.05W
khote Alin *mts.* U.S.S.R. 25 44.00N135.00E
kinos *i.* Greece 13 36.39N 25.06E
kkim *d.* India 29 27.30N 88.30E
r. Spain 10 42.24N 7.15W
char India 29 24.49N 92.47E
garhi-Doti Nepal 29 29.14N 80.58E
ifke Turkey 30 36.22N 33.57E
iguri India 29 26.42N 88.30E
ing Co *l.* China 29 31.40N 88.30E
istra Bulgaria 13 44.07N 27.17E
jan *l.* Sweden 17 60.50N 14.45E
keborg Denmark 17 56.10N 9.34E
le-le-Guillaume France 9 48.12N 0.08E
loth U.K. 4 54.53N 3.25W
ogui Indonesia 26 1.10S 98.46E
ver Bow U.S.A. 54 46.00N112.40W
ver City U.S.A. 54 32.46N108.17W
ver Lake *town* U.S.A. 54 43.08N120.56W
verstone U.K. 5 52.05N 1.03W
verton Australia 46 31.53S141.13E
verton U.S.A. 54 45.01N122.47W
vi Italy 12 42.34N 14.05E
manggang Malaysia 26 1.10N111.32E
mard, Lac *l.* Canada 55 47.38N 78.40W
mav *r.* Turkey 13 40.24N 28.31E
mba Kenya 37 2.10S 37.37E
mcoe Canada 55 42.50N 80.18W
mcoe, L. Canada 55 44.20N 79.20W
menga U.S.S.R. 21 62.42N108.25E
meria Romania 13 45.51N 23.01E
meulue *i.* Indonesia 26 2.30N 96.00E
mferopol' U.S.S.R. 19 44.57N 34.05E
mitli Bulgaria 13 41.51N 23.09E
miyu *r.* Tanzania 37 2.32S 33.25E
mla India 28 31.07N 77.09E
mleul Silvaniei Romania 15 47.14N 22.48E
mmern W. Germany 8 49.59N 7.32E
mo *r.* Finland 16 65.37N 25.03E
mojärvo *l.* Finland 16 66.06N 27.03E
monstown R.S.A. 39 34.12S 18.26E
moom Sound *town* Canada 50 50.45N126.45W
mplon Pass Switz. 11 46.15N 8.03E
mplon Tunnel Italy / Switz. 12 46.20N 8.05E
mpson Desert Australia 44 25.00S136.50E
mrishamn Sweden 17 55.33N 14.20E
muco Mozambique 37 14.00S 40.35E
nā', Shibh Jazīrat *pen.* Egypt 32 29.00N 34.00E
nai *see* Sīnā', Shibh Jazīrat *pen.* Egypt 32
naloa *d.* Mexico 56 25.00N107.30W
nan China 25 27.56N108.22E
ncelejo Colombia 60 9.17N 75.23W
nclair U.S.A. 54 41.47N107.07W
nes Portugal 10 37.58N 8.52W
nfra Ivory Coast 38 6.35N 5.56W
ngapore Asia 26 1.20N103.45E
ngapore *town* Singapore 26 1.20N103.45E
ngaraja Indonesia 26 8.06S115.07E
ngida Tanzania 37 4.45S 34.42E
ngida *d.* Tanzania 37 6.00S 34.30E
nging India 29 28.53N 94.47E
ngitikós Kólpos *g.* Greece 13 40.12N 24.00E
ngkaling Hkamti Burma 29 26.00N 95.42E
ngkang Indonesia 27 4.09S120.02E
ngkawang Indonesia 26 0.57N108.57E
ngkep *i.* Indonesia 26 0.30S104.20E
ngleton Australia 47 32.33S151.11E
ngosan N. Korea 25 38.50N127.27E
nj Yugo. 13 43.42N 16.38E
nnicolau Mare Romania 13 46.05N 20.38E
nnūris Egypt 32 29.25N 30.52E
nop Turkey 30 42.02N 35.09E
nsheim W. Germany 14 49.15N 8.53E
ntang Indonesia 26 0.03N111.31E
nt Eustatius *i.* Leeward Is. 57 17.33N 63.00W
nt Maarten *i.* *see* St. Martin *i.* Leeward Is. 57
nūiju N. Korea 25 40.04N124.25E
nyavka U.S.S.R. 15 52.58N 26.30E
nyukha *r.* U.S.S.R. 15 48.03N 30.51E
ocon Phil. 27 7.42N122.08E
ófok Hungary 15 46.54N 18.04E
on Switz. 9 46.14N 7.21E
oux City U.S.A. 53 42.30N 96.28W
oux Falls *town* U.S.A. 53 43.34N 96.42W
oux Lookout *town* Canada 51 50.07N 91.54W
phaqeni R.S.A. 39 31.05S 29.29E
ping Jilin China 25 43.15N124.25E
pura *i.* Indonesia 26 2.10S 99.40E
ra *r.* Norway 17 58.17N 6.24E
racusa Italy 12 37.05N 15.17E
rasso Ivory Coast 38 9.16N 6.06W
r Edward Pellew Group *is.* Australia 44 15.40S136.48E
iret *r.* Romania 13 45.28N 27.56E
irhān, Wādī as *f.* Saudi Arabia 30 31.00N 37.30E
Sir James MacBrien, Mt. Canada 50 62.07N127.41W
Síros *i.* Greece 13 37.26N 24.56E
Sirrah, Wādī as *r.* Saudi Arabia 31 23.10N 44.22E
Sisak Yugo. 12 45.30N 16.21E
Sishen R.S.A. 39 27.46S 22.59E
Sisimiut *see* Holsteinsborg Greenland 51
Sisŏphŏn Kampuchea 26 13.37N102.58E
Sissonne France 9 49.34N 3.54E
Sisteron France 11 44.16N 5.56E
Sitka U.S.A. 50 57.05N135.20W
Sittang *r.* Burma 29 17.30N 96.53E
Sittard Neth. 8 51.00N 5.52E
Sittwe Burma 29 20.09N 92.55E
Siuruan *r.* Finland 16 65.20N 25.55E
Sīvan *r.* Iran 31 29.50N 52.47E
Sivas Turkey 30 39.44N 37.01E
Sivomaskinskiy U.S.S.R. 18 66.45N 62.44E
Sivrihisar Turkey 30 39.29N 31.32E
Sīwah Egypt 30 29.12N 25.31E
Sīwah, Wāḥat *oasis* Egypt 30 29.10N 25.40E
Siwa Oasis *see* Sīwah, Wāḥat *oasis* Egypt 30
Sixmilecross U.K. 7 54.34N 7.08W
Siya U.S.S.R. 18 63.38N 41.40E
Sjaelland *i.* Denmark 17 55.30N 11.45E
Sjötorp Sweden 17 58.50N 13.59E
Skagafjördhur *est.* Iceland 16 65.55N 19.35W
Skagen Denmark 17 57.44N 10.36E
Skagerrak *str.* Denmark / Norway 17 57.45N 8.55E
Skagway U.S.A. 50 59.23N135.20W
Skaill U.K. 6 58.56N 2.43W
Skála Oropoú Greece 13 38.20N 23.46E
Skala Podolskaya U.S.S.R. 15 48.51N 26.11E
Skalat U.S.S.R. 15 49.20N 25.59E
Skanderborg Denmark 17 56.02N 9.56E
Skånevik Norway 17 59.44N 5.59E
Skara Sweden 17 58.22N 13.25E
Skaraborg *d.* Sweden 17 58.20N 13.30E
Skarnes Norway 17 60.15N 11.41E
Skarżysko-Kamienna Poland 15 51.08N 20.53E
Skeena *r.* Canada 50 54.10N129.08W
Skegness U.K. 4 53.09N 0.20E
Skellefte *r.* Sweden 16 64.42N 21.06E
Skellefteå Sweden 16 64.46N 20.57E
Skelleftehamn Sweden 16 64.41N 21.14E
Skelmersdale U.K. 4 53.34N 2.49W
Skene Sweden 17 57.29N 12.38E
Skerries Rep. of Ire. 7 53.35N 6.07W
Skhíza *i.* Greece 13 36.42N 21.45E
Ski Norway 17 59.43N 10.50E
Skiddaw *mtn.* U.K. 4 54.40N 3.09W
Skidel U.S.S.R. 15 53.37N 24.19E
Skien Norway 17 59.12N 9.36E
Skierniewice Poland 15 51.58N 20.08E
Skikda Algeria 34 36.50N 6.58E
Skipness U.K. 6 55.45N 5.22W
Skipton U.K. 4 53.57N 2.01W
Skíros Greece 13 38.53N 24.33E
Skíros *i.* Greece 13 38.50N 24.33E
Skive Denmark 17 56.34N 9.02E
Skjálfanda Fljót *r.* Iceland 16 65.55N 17.30W
Skjálfandi *est.* Iceland 16 66.08N 17.38W
Skjönsta Norway 16 67.12N 15.45E
Skoghall Sweden 17 59.19N 13.26E
Skole U.S.S.R. 15 49.00N 23.30E
Skopje Yugo. 13 41.58N 21.27E
Skotterud Norway 17 59.59N 12.07E
Skövde Sweden 17 58.24N 13.50E
Skovorodino U.S.S.R. 21 54.00N123.53E
Skreia Norway 17 60.39N 10.56E
Skull Rep. of Ire. 7 51.32N 9.33W
Skuodas U.S.S.R. 17 56.16N 21.32E
Skutskär Sweden 17 60.38N 17.25E
Skvira U.S.S.R. 15 49.42N 29.40E
Skye *i.* U.K. 6 57.20N 6.15W
Slagelse Denmark 17 55.24N 11.22E
Slalowa Wola Poland 15 50.40N 22.05E
Slamet *mtn.* Indonesia 26 7.10S109.10E
Slaney *r.* Rep. of Ire. 7 52.21N 6.30W
Slantsy U.S.S.R. 18 59.09N 28.09E
Slatina Romania 13 44.26N 24.23E
Slave *r.* Canada 50 61.10N113.30W
Slavgorod B.S.S.R. U.S.S.R. 15 53.25N 31.00E
Slavgorod R.S.F.S.R. U.S.S.R. 20 53.01N 78.37E
Slavuta U.S.S.R. 15 50.20N 26.58E
Slavyansk U.S.S.R. 19 48.51N 37.36E
Slawno Poland 14 54.22N 16.40E
Sleaford U.K. 4 53.00N 0.22W
Sleaford B. Australia 46 35.00S136.50E
Sleat, Sd. of *str.* U.K. 6 57.05N 5.48W
Sledmere U.K. 4 54.04N 0.35W
Sleetmute U.S.A. 50 61.40N157.11W
Sliedrecht Neth. 8 51.48N 4.46E
Slieve Aughty Mts. Rep. of Ire. 7 53.05N 8.31W
Slieve Bloom Mts. Rep. of Ire. 7 53.03N 7.35W
Slieve Callan *mtn.* Rep. of Ire. 7 52.51N 9.18W
Slieve Donard *mtn.* U.K. 7 54.11N 5.56W
Slieve Gamph *mts.* Rep. of Ire. 7 54.06N 8.52W
Slievekimalta *mtn.* Rep. of Ire. 7 52.45N 8.17W
Slieve Mish *mts.* Rep. of Ire. 7 52.48N 9.48W
Slieve Miskish *mts.* Rep. of Ire. 7 51.41N 9.56W
Slievenamon *mtn.* Rep. of Ire. 7 52.25N 7.34W
Slieve Snaght *mtn.* Donegal Rep. of Ire. 7 55.12N 7.20W
Sligo Rep. of Ire. 7 54.17N 8.28W
Sligo *d.* Rep. of Ire. 7 54.10N 8.35W
Sligo B. Rep. of Ire. 7 54.18N 8.40W
Slite Sweden 17 57.43N 18.48E
Sliven Bulgaria 13 42.41N 26.19E
Slobodka U.S.S.R. 15 47.56N 29.18E
Slobodskoy U.S.S.R. 18 58.42N 50.10E
Slonim U.S.S.R. 15 53.05N 25.21E
Slough U.K. 5 51.30N 0.35W
Slovechna *r.* U.S.S.R. 15 51.41N 29.41E
Slovechno U.S.S.R. 15 51.23N 28.20E
Slovenija *d.* Yugo. 12 46.10N 14.45E
Slovenjgradec Yugo. 12 46.31N 15.05E
Słubice Poland 14 52.20N 14.32E
Sluch *r.* U.S.S.R. 15 52.08N 27.31E
Sluis Neth. 8 51.18N 3.23E
Slunj Yugo. 14 45.07N 15.35E
Słupsk Poland 15 54.28N 17.01E
Slurry R.S.A. 39 25.48S 25.49E
Slutsk U.S.S.R. 15 53.02N 27.31E
Slyne Head Rep. of Ire. 7 53.25N 10.12W
Slyudyanka U.S.S.R. 24 51.40N103.40E
Smederevo Yugo. 13 44.40N 20.56E
Smela U.S.S.R. 19 49.15N 31.54E
Smilde Neth. 8 52.58N 6.28E
Smilovichi U.S.S.R. 15 53.45N 28.00E
Smith Arm *b.* Canada 50 66.15N124.00W
Smithfield R.S.A. 39 30.11S 26.31E
Smiths Falls *town* Canada 55 44.54N 76.01W
Smithton Australia 45 40.52S145.07E
Smithtown Australia 47 31.03S152.53E
Smoky Bay *town* Australia 46 32.22S133.56E
Smoky C. Australia 47 30.55S153.05E
Smoky Hill *r.* U.S.A. 52 39.03N 96.48W
Smöla *i.* Norway 16 63.20N 8.00E
Smolensk U.S.S.R. 18 54.49N 32.04E
Smolevichi U.S.S.R. 15 54.00N 28.01E
Smólikas *mtn.* Greece 13 40.06N 20.55E
Smolyan Bulgaria 13 41.34N 24.45E
Smorgon U.S.S.R. 15 54.28N 26.20E
Snaefell *mtn.* Iceland 16 64.48N 15.34W
Snaefell *mtn.* U.K. 4 54.16N 4.28W
Snake *r.* Idaho U.S.A. 52 43.50N117.05W
Snake *r.* Wash. U.S.A. 54 46.12N119.02W
Snake Range *mts.* U.S.A. 54 39.00N114.15W
Snake River *town* U.S.A. 54 44.10N110.40W
Snake River Plain *f.* U.S.A. 54 43.00N113.00W
Snåsa Norway 16 64.15N 12.23E
Snåsavatn *l.* Norway 16 64.05N 12.00E
Sneek Neth. 8 53.03N 5.40E
Sneem Rep. of Ire. 7 51.50N 9.54W
Sneeuwberg *mtn.* R.S.A. 39 32.30S 19.09E
Śniardwy, Jezioro *l.* Poland 15 53.46N 21.44E
Snina Czech. 15 48.59N 22.07E
Snizort, Loch U.K. 6 57.35N 6.30W
Snöhetta *mtn.* Norway 17 62.20N 9.17E
Snov *r.* U.S.S.R. 15 51.45N 31.45E
Snowdon *mtn.* U.K. 4 53.05N 4.05W
Snowdrift Canada 50 62.23N110.47W
Snowflake U.S.A. 54 34.30N110.05W
Snowtown Australia 46 33.47S138.13E
Snowy *r.* Australia 47 37.49S148.30E
Snowy Mts. Australia 47 36.30S148.20E
Snyatyn U.S.S.R. 15 48.30N 25.50E
Soacha Colombia 60 4.35N 74.13W
Soalala Madagascar 37 16.06S 45.20E
Soasiu Indonesia 27 0.40N127.25E
Sob *r.* U.S.S.R. 15 48.42N 29.17E
Sobat *r.* Sudan / Ethiopia 35 9.30N 31.30E
Sobernheim W. Germany 8 49.47N 7.40E
Sobral Brazil 61 3.45S 40.20W
Sochi U.S.S.R. 19 43.35N 39.46E
Socorro Colombia 60 6.30N 73.16W
Socorro, Isla *i.* Mexico 56 18.45N110.58W
Socotra *i.* *see* Suquṭrá *i.* Indian Oc. 35
Socuéllamos Spain 10 39.16N 2.47W
Sodankylä Finland 16 67.29N 26.32E
Söderhamn Sweden 17 61.18N 17.03E
Söderköping Sweden 17 58.29N 16.18E
Södermanland *d.* Sweden 17 59.10N 16.35E
Södertälje Sweden 17 59.12N 17.37E
Sodium R.S.A. 39 30.10S 23.08E
Sodo Ethiopia 35 6.52N 37.47E
Södra Vi Sweden 17 57.45N 15.48E
Soest W. Germany 8 51.34N 8.06E
Sofala Australia 47 33.05S149.42E
Sofala *d.* Mozambique 39 19.00S 34.39E
Sofia *see* Sofiya Bulgaria 13
Sofiya Bulgaria 13 42.41N 23.19E
Sofiysk U.S.S.R. 21 52.19N133.55E
Sofporog U.S.S.R. 18 65.47N 31.30E
Sogamoso Colombia 60 5.43N 72.56W
Sögel W. Germany 8 52.51N 7.31E
Sognefjorden *est.* Norway 17 61.06N 5.10E
Sogn og Fjordane *d.* Norway 17 61.30N 6.50E
Söğüt Turkey 30 40.02N 30.10E
Soignies Belgium 8 50.35N 4.04E
Soissons France 9 49.23N 3.20E
Sokal U.S.S.R. 15 50.30N 24.10E
Söke Turkey 13 37.46N 27.26E
Sokodé Togo 38 8.59N 1.11E
Sokol U.S.S.R. 18 59.28N 40.04E
Sokółka Poland 15 53.25N 23.31E
Sokolo Mali 38 14.53N 6.11W
Sokolov Czech. 14 50.09N 12.40E
Sokoto Nigeria 38 13.02N 5.15E
Sokoto *d.* Nigeria 38 11.50N 5.05E
Sokoto *r.* Nigeria 38 13.05N 5.13E
Solbad Hall Austria 14 47.17N 11.31E
Solec Kujawski Poland 15 53.06N 18.14E
Soledad Venezuela 60 8.10N 63.34W
Solesmes France 8 50.12N 3.32E
Solginskiy U.S.S.R. 18 61.07N 41.30E
Solheim Norway 17 60.53N 5.27E
Soligalich U.S.S.R. 18 59.02N 42.15E
Solikamsk U.S.S.R. 18 59.40N 56.45E
Sol-Iletsk U.S.S.R. 18 51.09N 55.00E
Solingen W. Germany 8 51.10N 7.05E
Sollefteå Sweden 16 63.12N 17.20E
Sollentuna Sweden 17 59.28N 17.54E
Sóller Spain 10 39.47N 2.41E
Sollia Norway 17 61.47N 10.24E
Solola Somali Rep. 37 0.08N 41.30E
Solomon Is. Pacific Oc. 40 8.00S160.00E
Solomon Sea Pacific Oc. 41 7.00S150.00E
Solon U.S.A. 55 44.57N 69.52W
Solothurn Switz. 14 47.13N 7.32E
Solovetskiye, Ostrova *is.* U.S.S.R. 18 65.05N 35.30E
Šolta *i.* Yugo. 12 43.23N 16.17E
Solṭānābād Iran 31 36.25N 58.02E
Soltau W. Germany 14 52.59N 9.49E
Sölvesborg Sweden 17 56.03N 14.33E
Solway Firth *est.* U.K. 4 54.50N 3.30W
Solzach *r.* Austria 14 48.35N 13.30E
Soma Turkey 13 39.11N 27.36E
Somabhula Zimbabwe 39 19.40S 29.38E
Somali Republic Africa 35 5.30N 47.00E
Sombor Yugo. 13 45.48N 19.08E
Sombrerete Mexico 56 23.38N103.39W
Somerset *d.* U.K. 5 51.09N 3.00W
Somerset East R.S.A. 39 32.43S 25.33E
Somerset I. Canada 51 73.00N 93.30W
Someš *r.* Hungary 15 48.40N 22.30E
Somme *r.* France 11 50.01N 1.40E
Sommen *l.* Sweden 17 58.01N 15.15E
Sompuis France 9 48.41N 4.23E
Son *r.* India 29 25.55N 84.55E
Sönderborg Denmark 17 54.55N 9.47E
Sondershausen E. Germany 14 51.22N 10.52E
Söndreströmfjord Greenland 51 66.30N 50.52W
Sondrio Italy 9 46.10N 9.52E
Songa *r.* Norway 17 59.45N 7.59E
Songea Tanzania 37 10.42S 35.39E
Songhua Jiang *r.* China 25 47.46N132.30E
Songkhla Thailand 29 7.13N100.37E
Song Xian China 25 34.02N111.48E
Son La Vietnam 26 21.20N103.55E
Sonneberg E. Germany 14 50.22N 11.10E
Sonora *d.* Mexico 56 29.30N110.40W
Sonora *r.* Mexico 56 28.50N111.33W
Sonsorol *i.* Caroline Is. 27 5.20N132.13E
Son Tay Vietnam 26 21.06N105.32E
Sopi Indonesia 27 2.40N128.28E
Sopot Poland 15 54.28N 18.34E
Sopotskin U.S.S.R. 15 53.49N 23.42E
Soppero Sweden 16 68.07N 21.40E
Sopron Hungary 14 47.41N 16.36E
Sorel Canada 55 46.03N 73.06W
Sörfjorden Norway 16 66.29N 13.20E
Sörfold Norway 16 67.30N 15.30E
Sorgono Italy 12 40.01N 9.06E
Soria Spain 10 41.46N 2.28W
Soriano Uruguay 63 33.24S 58.19W
Sor Kvalöy *i.* Norway 16 69.40N 18.30E
Sörli Norway 16 64.15N 13.50E
Sor Mertvyy Kultuk *f.* U.S.S.R. 19 45.30N 54.00E
Sorocaba Brazil 59 23.29S 47.27W
Sorochinsk U.S.S.R. 18 52.29N 53.15E
Soroki U.S.S.R. 15 48.08N 28.12E
Sorol *i.* Caroline Is. 27 8.09N140.25E
Sorong Indonesia 27 0.50S131.17E
Soroti Uganda 37 1.40N 33.37E
Söröya *i.* Norway 16 70.35N 22.30E
Sorraia *r.* Portugal 10 39.00N 8.51W
Sorrento Italy 12 40.37N 14.22E
Sör-Rondane *mts.* Antarctica 64 72.30S 22.00E
Sorsele Sweden 16 65.30N 17.30E
Sortavala U.S.S.R. 18 61.40N 30.40E
Sortland Norway 16 68.44N 15.25E
Sör Tröndelag *d.* Norway 16 63.00N 10.20E
Sosnogorsk U.S.S.R. 18 63.32N 53.55E
Sosnovo U.S.S.R. 18 60.33N 30.11E
Sosnovyy U.S.S.R. 18 66.01N 32.40E
Sosnowiec Poland 15 50.18N 19.08E
Sosva U.S.S.R. 18 59.10N 61.50E
Sosyka U.S.S.R. 19 46.11N 38.49E
Sotik Kenya 37 0.40S 35.08E
Sotra *i.* Norway 17 60.15N 5.10E
Sotteville France 9 49.25N 1.06E
Souflíon Greece 13 41.12N 26.18E
Sŏul S. Korea 25 37.30N127.00E
Sources, Mont-aux- *mtn.* Lesotho 39 28.44S 28.52E
Soure Portugal 10 40.04N 8.38W
Souris *r.* Canada 52 49.38N 99.35W
Sousa Brazil 61 6.41S 38.14W
Sousse Tunisia 34 35.48N 10.38E
Soustons France 11 43.45N 1.19W
Southampton Canada 55 44.29N 81.23W
Southampton U.K. 5 50.54N 1.23W
Southampton I. Canada 51 64.30N 84.00W
South Auckland-Bay of Plenty *d.* New Zealand 48 38.00S176.00E
South Australia *d.* Australia 46 30.00S137.00E
South Bend Ind. U.S.A. 55 41.40N 86.15W
South Bend Wash. U.S.A. 54 46.40N123.48W
South Branch U.S.A. 55 44.29N 83.36W
Southbridge New Zealand 48 43.48S172.15E
South Carolina *d.* U.S.A. 53 34.00N 81.00W
South Cerney U.K. 5 51.40N 1.55W
South China Sea Asia 26 12.30N115.00E
South Dakota *d.* U.S.A. 52 44.30N100.00W
South Dorset Downs *hills* U.K. 5 50.40N 2.25W
South Downs *hills* U.K. 5 50.04N 0.34W
South East C. Australia 45 43.38S146.48E
South East Is. Australia 43 34.23S123.30E
Southend-on-Sea U.K. 5 51.32N 0.43E
Southern Alps *mts.* New Zealand 48 43.20S170.45E
Southern Cross Australia 43 31.14S119.16E
Southern Indian L. Canada 51 57.10N 98.40W
Southern Uplands *hills* U.K. 6 55.30N 3.30W
Southern Yemen Asia 35 16.00N 49.30E
South Esk *r.* U.K. 6 56.43N 2.32W
Southesk Tablelands *f.* Australia 42 20.50S126.40E
South Glamorgan *d.* U.K. 5 51.27N 3.22W
South-haa U.K. 6 60.34N 1.17W
South Haven U.S.A. 55 42.25N 86.16W
South Horr Kenya 37 2.10N 36.45E
South I. Kenya 37 2.36N 36.38E
South I. New Zealand 48 43.00S171.00E
South Korea Asia 25 36.00N128.00E
South Lake Tahoe *town* U.S.A. 54 38.57N119.57W
Southland *d.* New Zealand 48 45.40S168.00E
South Molton U.K. 5 51.01N 3.50W
South Nahanni *r.* Canada 50 61.00N123.20W
Southport Australia 47 27.58S153.20E
Southport U.K. 4 53.38N 3.01W
South Ronaldsay *i.* U.K. 6 58.47N 2.56W
South Shields U.K. 4 55.00N 1.24W
South Tyne *r.* U.K. 6 54.59N 2.08W
South Uist *i.* U.K. 6 57.15N 7.20W
Southwest C. New Zealand 48 47.15S167.30E
South Windham U.S.A. 55 43.44N 70.26W
Southwold U.K. 5 52.19N 1.41E
South Yorkshire *d.* U.K. 4 53.28N 1.25W
Soutpansberge *mts.* R.S.A. 39 22.58S 29.50E
Sovetsk Lit.S.S.R. U.S.S.R. 17 55.05N 21.53E
Sovetsk R.S.F.S.R. U.S.S.R. 18 57.39N 48.59E
Sovetskaya Gavan U.S.S.R. 21 48.57N140.16E
Soweto R.S.A. 39 26.16S 27.51E
Soyo Angola 36 6.12S 12.25E
Sozh *r.* U.S.S.R. 15 51.57N 30.48E
Spa Belgium 8 50.29N 5.52E
Spain Europe 10 40.00N 4.00W
Spalding Australia 46 33.29S138.40E
Spalding U.K. 4 52.47N 0.09W
Spandau W. Germany 14 52.32N 13.13E
Spanish Fork U.S.A. 54 40.07N111.39W
Sparks U.S.A. 54 39.32N119.45W
Spartanburg U.S.A. 53 34.56N 81.57W
Spárti Greece 13 37.04N 22.28E
Spartivento, Capo *c.* Calabria Italy 12 37.55N 16.04E
Spartivento, Capo *c.* Sardegna Italy 12 38.53N 8.50E
Spátha, Ákra *c.* Greece 13 35.42N 23.43E
Speculator U.S.A. 55 43.30N 74.17W
Speke G. Tanzania 37 2.20S 33.30E
Spence Bay *town* Canada 51 69.30N 93.20W
Spencer Idaho U.S.A. 54 44.21N112.11W
Spencer Iowa U.S.A. 53 43.08N 95.08W
Spencer, C. Australia 46 35.18S136.53E
Spencer G. Australia 46 34.00S137.00E
Sperrin Mts. U.K. 7 54.49N 7.06W
Spétsai *i.* Greece 13 37.15N 23.10E
Spey *r.* U.K. 6 57.40N 3.06W
Speyer W. Germany 14 49.18N 8.26E
Spiekeroog *i.* W. Germany 8 53.48N 7.45E
Spilimbergo Italy 9 46.07N 12.54E
Spilsby U.K. 4 53.10N 0.06E
Spina *ruins* Italy 9 44.42N 12.08E
Spinazzola Italy 12 40.58N 16.06E
Spišská Nova Ves Czech. 15 48.57N 20.34E
Spithead *str.* U.K. 5 50.45N 1.05W
Spitsbergen *is.* Arctic Oc. 64 78.00N 17.00E
Spittal an der Drau Austria 14 46.48N 13.30E
Split Yugo. 13 43.32N 16.27E
Spokane U.S.A. 54 47.40N117.23W
Spokane *r.* U.S.A. 54 47.44N118.20W
Spratly *i.* S. China Sea 26 8.45N111.54E
Spray U.S.A. 54 44.50N119.48W
Spree *r.* E. Germany 14 52.32N 13.15E
Springbok R.S.A. 39 29.40S 17.50E
Springerville U.S.A. 54 34.08N109.17W
Springfield Australia 44 25.52S143.06E
Springfield New Zealand 48 43.20S171.56E
Springfield Ill. U.S.A. 53 39.49N 89.39W
Springfield Mass. U.S.A. 55 42.07N 72.35W
Springfield Miss. U.S.A. 53 37.11N 93.19W
Springfield Ohio U.S.A. 55 39.55N 83.48W
Springfield Oreg. U.S.A. 54 44.03N123.01W
Springfield Vt. U.S.A. 55 43.18N 72.29W
Springfontein R.S.A. 39 30.15S 25.41E
Springs *town* R.S.A. 39 26.16S 28.27E
Springsure Australia 44 24.07S148.05E
Springville Utah U.S.A. 54 40.10N111.37W
Spry U.S.A. 54 37.55N112.28W
Spurn Head U.K. 4 53.35N 0.08E
Squamish Canada 50 49.42N123.09W
Squillace Italy 13 38.46N 16.31E
Srbija *d.* Yugo. 13 44.30N 20.30E
Srednekolymsk U.S.S.R. 21 67.27N153.35E
Sredne Russkaya Vozvyshennost *f.* U.S.S.R. 18 53.00N 37.00E
Sredne Sibirskoye Ploskogor'ye *f.* U.S.S.R. 21 66.00N108.00E
Sretensk U.S.S.R. 25 52.15N117.52E
Srīkākulam India 29 18.18N 83.54E
Sri Lanka Asia 29 7.30N 80.50E
Srinagar Jammu & Kashmir 28 34.08N 74.50E
Srnetica Yugo. 13 44.26N 16.40E
Staaten *r.* Australia 44 16.24S141.17E
Stadskanaal Neth. 8 53.02N 6.55E
Stadtkyll W. Germany 8 50.21N 6.32E
Stadtlohn W. Germany 8 52.00N 6.58E
Staffa *i.* U.K. 6 56.26N 6.21W
Stafford U.K. 4 52.49N 2.09W
Staffordshire *d.* U.K. 4 52.40N 1.57W
Staines U.K. 5 51.26N 0.31W
Stainforth U.K. 4 53.37N 1.01W
Stakhanov U.S.S.R. 19 48.34N 38.40E
Stalina Kanal *canal* U.S.S.R. 18 64.33N 34.48E
Stamford U.K. 5 52.39N 0.28W
Stamford Conn. U.S.A. 55 41.03N 73.32W
Stamford N.Y. U.S.A. 55 42.25N 74.37W
Standerton R.S.A. 39 26.57S 29.14E
Stanger R.S.A. 39 29.20S 31.17E
Stanley Canada 50 55.45N104.55W
Stanley Falkland Is. 63 51.42W 57.51W
Stanley U.K. 4 54.53N 1.42W
Stanley Idaho U.S.A. 54 44.13N114.35W
Stanovoy Khrebet *mts.* U.S.S.R. 21 56.00N125.40E
Stanthorpe Australia 47 28.37S151.52E
Starachowice Poland 15 51.03N 21.04E
Stara Dorogi U.S.S.R. 15 53.02N 28.18E
Stara Planina *mts.* Bulgaria 13 42.50N 24.30E
Staraya Russa U.S.S.R. 18 58.00N 31.22E
Staraya Sinyava U.S.S.R. 15 49.38N 27.39E
Stara Zagora Bulgaria 13 42.26N 25.37E
Stargard Szczecinski Poland 14 53.21N 15.01E
Staritsa U.S.S.R. 18 56.29N 34.59E
Starnberg W. Germany 14 48.00N 11.20E
Starobin U.S.S.R. 15 52.40N 27.29E
Starogard Gdański Poland 15 53.59N 18.33E

Starokonstantinov U.S.S.R. 15 49.48N 27.10E
Start Pt. U.K. 5 50.13N 3.38W
Staryy Oskol U.S.S.R. 19 51.20N 37.50E
State College U.S.A. 55 40.48N 77.52W
Staten I. *see* Estados, Isla de los *i.* Argentina 63
Staunton U.S.A. 53 38.10N 79.05W
Stavanger Norway 17 58.58N 5.45E
Stavelot Belgium 8 50.23N 5.54E
Staveren Neth. 8 52.53N 5.21E
Stavropol' U.S.S.R. 19 45.03N 41.59E
Stavropolskaya Vozvyshennost *mts.* U.S.S.R. 19 45.00N 42.30E
Stawell Australia 46 37.06S142.52E
Stawiski Poland 15 53.23N 22.09E
Steamboat Springs *town* U.S.A. 54 40.29N106.50W
Steelpoort R.S.A. 39 24.44S 30.13E
Steelton U.S.A. 55 40.14N 76.49W
Steenbergen Neth. 8 51.36N 4.19E
Steenvoorde France 8 50.49N 2.35E
Steenwijk Neth. 8 52.47N 6.07E
Steep Rock Lake *town* Canada 51 48.50N 91.38W
Steiermark *d.* Austria 14 47.10N 15.10E
Steilloopbrug R.S.A. 39 23.26S 28.37E
Steinkjer Norway 16 64.00N 11.30E
Steinkopf R.S.A. 39 29.16S 17.41E
Stella R.S.A. 39 26.32S 24.51E
Stellenbosch R.S.A. 39 33.56S 18.51E
Stenay France 9 49.29N 5.11E
Stendal E. Germany 14 52.36N 11.52E
Stenträsk Sweden 16 66.20N 19.50E
Stepan U.S.S.R. 15 51.09N 26.18E
Stepanakert U.S.S.R. 31 39.48N 46.45E
Stepnyak U.S.S.R. 20 52.52N 70.49E
Sterkstroom R.S.A. 39 31.32S 26.31E
Sterling Colo. U.S.A. 52 40.37N103.13W
Sterling Mich. U.S.A. 55 44.02N 84.02W
Sterlitamak U.S.S.R. 18 53.40N 55.59E
Šternberk Czech. 15 49.44N 17.18E
Stettler Canada 50 52.21N112.40W
Steuben U.S.A. 55 46.12N 86.27W
Steubenville U.S.A. 55 40.22N 80.39W
Stevenage U.K. 5 51.54N 0.11W
Stevenston U.K. 6 55.39N 4.45W
Stewart Canada 50 55.56N130.01W
Stewart I. New Zealand 48 47.00S168.00E
Stewart River *town* Canada 50 63.19N139.26W
Steynsburg R.S.A. 39 31.17S 25.48E
Steyr Austria 14 48.04N 14.25E
Stikine *r.* Canada 50 56.45N132.30W
Stikine Mts. Canada 50 59.00N129.00W
Stiklestad Norway 16 63.48N 11.22E
Stilbaai R.S.A. 39 34.22S 21.22E
Stillwater Range *mts.* U.S.A. 54 39.50N118.15W
Stilton U.K. 5 52.29N 0.17W
Stimson Canada 55 48.58N 80.37W
Stinchar *r.* U.K. 6 55.06N 5.00W
Stînisoara, Munţii *mts.* Romania 15 47.10N 26.00E
Štip Yugo. 13 41.44N 22.12E
Stirling U.K. 6 56.07N 3.57W
Stirling Range *mts.* Australia 43 34.23S117.50E
Stjernöya *i.* Norway 16 70.17N 22.40E
Stjördalshalsen Norway 16 63.29N 10.51E
Stockaryd Sweden 17 57.18N 14.35E
Stockbridge U.K. 5 51.07N 1.30W
Stockerau Austria 14 48.23N 16.13E
Stockett U.S.A. 54 47.21N111.10W
Stockholm Sweden 17 59.20N 18.03E
Stockholm *d.* Sweden 17 59.40N 18.10E
Stockinbingal Australia 47 34.03S147.53E
Stockport U.K. 4 53.25N 2.11W
Stocksbridge U.K. 4 53.30N 1.36W
Stockton Australia 47 32.55S151.47E
Stockton Calif. U.S.A. 54 37.57N121.17W
Stockton-on-Tees U.K. 4 54.34N 1.20W
Stoeng Tréng Kampuchea 26 13.31N105.58E
Stoffberg R.S.A. 39 25.25S 29.49E
Stoke-on-Trent U.K. 4 53.01N 2.11W
Stokes Bay *town* Canada 55 44.55N 81.21W
Stokhod *r.* U.S.S.R. 15 51.52N 25.38E
Stokksund Norway 16 64.03N 10.05E
Stolac Yugo. 13 43.05N 17.58E
Stolberg W. Germany 8 50.47N 6.12E
Stolbtsy U.S.S.R. 15 53.30N 26.44E
Stolin U.S.S.R. 15 51.52N 26.51E
Stone U.K. 4 52.55N 2.10W
Stonehaven U.K. 6 56.58N 2.13W
Stooping *r.* Canada 55 52.08N 82.00W
Stora Lulevatten *l.* Sweden 16 67.10N 19.16E
Stora Sjöfallets Nat. Park Sweden 16 67.44N 18.16E
Storavan *l.* Sweden 16 65.40N 18.15E
Storby Finland 17 60.13N 19.34E
Stord *i.* Norway 17 59.53N 5.25E
Store Baelt *str.* Denmark 17 55.30N 11.00E
Stor Elvdal Norway 17 61.32N 11.02E
Stören Norway 16 63.03N 10.18E
Storlien Sweden 16 63.20N 12.05E
Stornoway U.K. 6 58.12N 6.23W
Storozhevsk U.S.S.R. 18 62.00N 52.20E
Storozhinets U.S.S.R. 15 48.11N 25.40E
Storsjön *l.* Sweden 16 63.10N 14.20E
Storuman Sweden 16 65.06N 17.06E
Storuman *l.* Sweden 16 65.10N 16.40E
Stour *r.* Dorset U.K. 5 50.43N 1.47W
Stour *r.* Kent U.K. 5 51.19N 1.22E
Stour *r.* Suffolk U.K. 5 51.56N 1.03E
Stourport-on-Severn U.K. 5 52.21N 2.16W
Stowmarket U.K. 5 52.11N 1.00E
Stow on the Wold U.K. 5 51.55N 1.42W
Strabane U.K. 7 54.50N 7.30W
Stradbally Laois Rep. of Ire. 7 53.01N 7.09W
Stradbroke I. Australia 45 27.38S153.45E
Stradella Italy 9 45.05N 9.18E
Straelen W. Germany 8 51.27N 6.14E
Strahan Australia 45 42.08S145.21E
Strakonice Czech. 14 49.16N 13.55E
Stralsund E. Germany 14 54.18N 13.06E
Strand R.S.A. 39 34.07S 18.50E
Stranda Norway 16 62.19N 6.58E
Strangford Lough U.K. 7 54.28N 5.35W
Strangways Springs *town* Australia 46 29.08S136.35E
Stranraer U.K. 6 54.54N 5.02W
Strasbourg France 11 48.35N 7.45E
Stratford Australia 47 37.57S147.05E
Stratford Canada 55 43.22N 80.57W
Stratford New Zealand 48 39.20S174.18E
Stratford-upon-Avon U.K. 5 52.12N 1.42W
Strathalbyn Australia 46 35.16S138.54E
Strathclyde *d.* U.K. 6 55.45N 4.45W
Strathmore *f.* Tayside U.K. 6 56.44N 2.45W
Strathspey *f.* U.K. 6 57.25N 3.25W
Straubing W. Germany 14 48.53N 12.35E
Straumnes *c.* Iceland 16 66.30N 23.05W
Streaky B. Australia 46 32.36S134.08E
Streaky Bay *town* Australia 46 32.48S134.13E
Street U.K. 5 51.07N 2.43W
Stresa Italy 9 45.53N 8.32E
Stretton Australia 43 32.30S117.42E
Strimon *r.* Greece 13 40.47N 23.51E
Stromboli *i.* Italy 12 38.48N 15.14E
Stromeferry U.K. 6 57.21N 5.34W
Stromness U.K. 6 58.57N 3.18W
Strömö *i.* Faroe Is. 16 62.08N 7.00W
Strömsbruk Sweden 17 61.53N 17.19E
Strömstad Sweden 17 58.56N 11.10E
Strömsund Sweden 16 63.51N 15.35E
Strömsvattudal *f.* Sweden 16 64.15N 15.00E
Stronsay *i.* U.K. 6 59.07N 2.36W
Stroud U.K. 5 51.44N 2.12W
Stroud Road *town* Australia 47 32.18S151.58E
Struan Australia 46 37.08S140.49E
Struer Denmark 17 56.29N 8.37E
Struga Yugo. 13 41.10N 20.41E
Struma *r.* Bulgaria *see* Strimon *r.* Greece 13
Strumica Yugo. 13 41.26N 22.39E
Strydenburg R.S.A. 39 29.56S 23.39E
Stryker U.S.A. 54 48.40N114.44W
Stryy U.S.S.R. 15 49.16N 23.51E
Strzelecki Creek *r.* Australia 46 29.37S139.59E
Strzelno Poland 15 52.38N 18.11E
Stuart Creek *town* Australia 46 29.43S137.01E
Stuart L. Canada 50 54.32N124.35W
Stuart Range *mts.* Australia 46 29.10S134.56E
Stuart Town Australia 47 32.51S149.08E
Sturgeon Falls *town* Canada 55 46.22N 79.55W
Sturgeon L. Ont. Canada 55 49.47N 90.40W
Sturminster Newton U.K. 5 50.56N 2.18W
Sturt B. Australia 46 35.24S137.32E
Sturt Creek *r.* Australia 42 20.08S127.24E
Sturt Desert Australia 46 28.30S141.12E
Sturt Plain *f.* Australia 44 17.00S132.48E
Stutterheim R.S.A. 39 32.32S 27.25E
Stuttgart W. Germany 14 48.47N 9.12E
Stviga *r.* U.S.S.R. 15 52.04N 27.54E
Stykkishólmur Iceland 16 65.06N 22.48W
Styr *r.* U.S.S.R. 15 52.07N 26.35E
Subotica Yugo. 13 46.04N 19.41E
Suceava Romania 15 47.39N 26.19E
Suck *r.* Rep. of Ire. 7 53.16N 8.04W
Suckling, Mt. P.N.G. 44 9.45S148.55E
Sucre Bolivia 62 19.02S 65.17W
Sucuriu *r.* Brazil 59 20.44S 51.40W
Sudan Africa 35 14.00N 30.00E
Sudbury Canada 55 46.30N 81.00W
Sudbury U.K. 5 52.03N 0.45E
Sudety *mts.* Czech./Poland 14 50.30N 16.30E
Sudirman, Pegunungan *mts.* Indonesia 27 3.50S136.30E
Sueca Spain 10 39.12N 0.21W
Suez *see* As Suways Egypt 32
Suez, G. of *see* Suways, Khalīj as *g.* Egypt 32
Suez Canal *see* Suways, Qanāt as *canal* Egypt 32
Şufaynah Saudi Arabia 30 23.09N 40.32E
Suffolk *d.* U.K. 5 52.16N 1.00E
Sugarloaf Pt. Australia 47 32.25S152.30E
Şuḩār Oman 31 24.23N 56.43E
Suhl E. Germany 14 50.37N 10.43E
Suhl *d.* E. Germany 14 50.40N 10.30E
Suibin China 25 47.19N131.49E
Suide China 25 37.32N110.12E
Suihua China 25 46.39N126.59E
Suileng China 25 47.15N127.05E
Suipacha Argentina 63 34.47S 59.40W
Suiping China 25 33.09N113.59E
Suippes France 9 49.08N 4.32E
Suir *r.* Rep. of Ire. 7 52.17N 7.00W
Suita Japan 23 34.45N135.32E
Sui Xian Hubei China 25 31.43N113.22E
Sukabumi Indonesia 26 6.55S106.50E
Sukadana Indonesia 26 1.15S110.00E
Sukaraja Indonesia 26 2.23S110.35E
Sukhinichi U.S.S.R. 18 54.07N 35.21E
Sukhona *r.* U.S.S.R. 18 61.30N 46.28E
Sukhumi U.S.S.R. 19 43.01N 41.01E
Sukkertoppen Greenland 51 65.40N 53.00W
Sukkur Pakistan 28 27.42N 68.54E
Sula *i.* Norway 17 61.08N 4.55E
Sula, Kepulauan *is.* Indonesia 27 1.50S125.10E
Sulaimān Range *mts.* Pakistan 28 30.50N 70.20E
Sulak *r.* U.S.S.R. 19 43.18N 47.35E
Sulawesi *i.* Indonesia 27 2.00S120.30E
Sulawesi Selatan *d.* Indonesia 27 3.45S120.30E
Sulawesi Utara *d.* Indonesia 27 1.45S120.30E
Sulechów Poland 14 52.06N 15.37E
Sulejów Poland 15 51.22N 19.53E
Sulina Romania 13 45.08N 29.40E
Sulitjelma Norway 16 67.10N 16.05E
Sullana Peru 60 4.52S 80.39W
Sully France 9 47.46N 2.22E
Sulmona Italy 12 42.04N 13.57E
Sultan Canada 55 47.36N 82.47W
Sultan Hamud Kenya 37 2.02S 37.20E
Sulu Archipelago Phil. 27 5.30N121.00E
Sulu Sea Pacific Oc. 27 8.00N120.00E
Sumatera *i.* Indonesia 26 2.00S102.00E
Sumatera Barat *d.* Indonesia 26 1.00S100.00E
Sumatera Selatan *d.* Indonesia 26 3.00S104.00E
Sumatera Utara *d.* Indonesia 26 2.00N 99.00E
Sumatra *see* Sumatera *i.* Indonesia 26
Sumatra U.S.A. 54 46.38N107.31W
Sumba *i.* Indonesia 26 9.30S119.55E
Sumbar *r.* U.S.S.R. 31 38.00N 55.20E
Sumbawa *i.* Indonesia 26 8.45S117.50E
Sumbawanga Tanzania 37 7.58S 31.36E
Sumburgh Head U.K. 6 59.51N 1.16W
Šumen Bulgaria 13 43.15N 26.55E
Sumgait U.S.S.R. 31 40.35N 49.38E
Šumperk Czech. 14 49.58N 16.58E
Sumusţā al Waqf Egypt 32 28.55N 30.51E
Sumy U.S.S.R. 19 50.55N 34.49E
Sunart, Loch U.K. 6 56.43N 5.45W
Sunbury Australia 47 37.36S144.45E
Sunda, Selat *str.* Indonesia 26 6.00S105.50E
Sundarbans *f.* India/Bangla. 29 22.00N 89.00E
Sundays *r.* R.S.A. 39 33.43S 25.50E
Sunderland U.K. 4 54.55N 1.22W
Sundsvall Sweden 17 62.23N 17.18E
Sungaipakning Indonesia 26 1.19N102.00E
Sungaipenuh Indonesia 26 2.00S101.28E
Sungguminasa Indonesia 26 5.14S119.27E
Sungurlu Turkey 30 40.10N 34.23E
Sunne Sweden 17 59.50N 13.09E
Sunnyside U.S.A. 54 46.20N120.00W
Suntar U.S.S.R. 21 62.10N117.35E
Sun Valley *town* U.S.A. 52 43.42N114.21W
Sunwu China 25 49.40N127.10E
Sunyani Ghana 38 7.22N 2.18W
Suoyarvi U.S.S.R. 18 62.02N 32.20E
Superior Mont. U.S.A. 54 47.12N114.53W
Superior Wisc. U.S.A. 53 46.42N 92.05W
Superior Wyo. U.S.A. 54 41.46N108.58W
Superior, L. Canada/U.S.A. 55 48.00N 88.00W
Süphan Dagi *mtn.* Turkey 19 38.55N 42.55E
Süphan Daglari *mtn.* Turkey 30 38.55N 42.55E
Suquţrá *i.* Indian Oc. 35 12.30N 54.00E
Şūr Lebanon 32 33.16N 35.12E
Şūr Oman 31 22.23N 59.32E
Sur, Punta *c.* Argentina 63 36.53S 56.41W
Sura U.S.S.R. 18 53.52N 45.45E
Surabaya Indonesia 26 7.14S112.45E
Surakarta Indonesia 26 7.32S110.50E
Şūrān Syria 32 35.18N 36.44E
Surany Czech. 15 48.06N 18.14E
Surat India 28 21.10N 72.54E
Sūratgarh India 28 29.19N 73.54E
Surat Thani Thailand 29 9.03N 99.28E
Surazh U.S.S.R. 15 53.00N 32.22E
Sûre *r.* Lux. 8 49.43N 6.31E
Surfer's Paradise Australia 47 27.58S153.26E
Surgut U.S.S.R. 20 61.13N 73.20E
Surigao Phil. 27 9.47N125.29E
Surin Thailand 29 14.50N103.34E
Surinam S. America 61 4.00N 56.00W
Suriname *r.* Surinam 61 5.52N 55.14W
Surrey *d.* U.K. 5 51.16N 0.30W
Surt Libya 34 31.10N 16.39E
Surt, Khalīj *g.* Libya 34 31.45N 17.50E
Surtsey *i.* Iceland 16 63.18N 20.30W
Surud Ad *mtn.* Somali Rep. 35 10.41N 47.18E
Suruga-wan *b.* Japan 23 34.45N138.30E
Susa Italy 9 45.08N 7.03E
Susanino U.S.S.R. 21 52.46N140.09E
Susanville U.S.A. 54 40.25N120.39W
Susquehanna *r.* U.S.A. 55 39.33N 76.05W
Sussex Wyo. U.S.A. 54 43.42N106.19W
Sutherland R.S.A. 39 32.23S 20.38E
Sutherlin U.S.A. 54 43.25N123.19W
Sutlej *r.* Pakistan 28 29.26N 71.09E
Sutton England U.K. 5 51.22N 0.12W
Sutton W. Va. U.S.A. 55 38.41N 80.43W
Sutton in Ashfield U.K. 4 53.08N 1.16W
Suva Fiji 40 18.08S178.25E
Suwałki Poland 15 54.07N 22.56E
Suwanee *r.* U.S.A. 53 29.15N 82.50W
Suways, Khalīj as *g.* Egypt 32 28.48N 33.00E
Suways, Qanāt as *canal* Egypt 32 30.40N 32.20E
Suwon S. Korea 25 37.16N126.59E
Suzhou China 25 31.21N120.40E
Suzuka Japan 23 34.51N136.35E
Suzuka *r.* Japan 23 34.54N136.39E
Suzuka-sammyaku *mts.* Japan 23 35.00N136.20E
Suzzara Italy 9 45.00N 10.45E
Svalyava U.S.S.R. 15 48.33N 23.00E
Svanvik Norway 16 69.25N 30.00E
Svappavaara Sweden 16 67.39N 21.04E
Svarhofthalvöya Norway 16 70.35N 26.00E
Svartenhuk Halvo *c.* Greenland 51 71.55N 55.00W
Svartisen *mtn.* Norway 16 66.40N 13.56E
Svatovo U.S.S.R. 19 49.24N 38.11E
Svedala Sweden 17 55.30N 13.14E
Sveg Sweden 17 62.02N 14.21E
Svelgen Norway 17 61.47N 5.15E
Svendborg Denmark 17 55.03N 10.37E
Svenstrup Denmark 17 56.59N 9.52E
Sverdlovsk U.S.S.R. 18 56.52N 60.35E
Svetlograd U.S.S.R. 19 45.25N 42.58E
Svetogorsk U.S.S.R. 18 61.07N 28.50E
Svetozarevo Yugo. 13 43.58N 21.16E
Svinö *i.* Faroe Is. 16 62.17N 6.18W
Svir *r.* U.S.S.R. 18 60.09N 32.15E
Svishtov Bulgaria 13 43.36N 25.23E
Svisloch U.S.S.R. 15 53.28N 29.00E
Svitavy Czech. 14 49.45N 16.27E
Svobodnyy U.S.S.R. 25 51.24N128.05E
Svolvaer Norway 16 68.15N 14.40E
Swaffham U.K. 5 52.38N 0.42E
Swain Reefs Australia 44 21.40S152.15E
Swakop *r.* Namibia 39 22.38S 14.30E
Swakopmund Namibia 39 22.40S 14.34E
Swale *r.* U.K. 4 54.05N 1.20W
Swan *r.* Australia 43 32.03S115.45E
Swanage U.K. 5 50.36N 1.59W
Swan Hill *town* Australia 46 35.23S143.37E
Swansea Australia 45 42.08S148.00E
Swansea U.K. 5 51.37N 3.57W
Swan Vale *town* Australia 47 29.43S151.25E
Swastika Canada 55 48.07N 80.06W
Swaziland Africa 39 26.30S 32.00E
Sweden Europe 16 63.00N 16.00E
Swedru Ghana 38 5.31N 0.42W
Sweetwater U.S.A. 52 32.37N100.25W
Swidnica Poland 14 50.51N 16.29E
Swiebodzin Poland 14 52.15N 15.32E
Świętokrzyskie, Góry *mts.* Poland 15 51.00N 20.30E
Swift Current *town* Canada 50 50.17N107.49W
Swilly, Lough Rep. of Ire. 7 55.10N 7.32W
Swindon U.K. 5 51.33N 1.47W
Świnoujście Poland 14 53.55N 14.18E
Switzerland Europe 11 47.00N 8.00E
Syderö *i.* Faroe Is. 16 61.30N 6.50W
Sydney Australia 47 33.55S151.10E
Sydney Canada 51 46.10N 60.10W
Sydpröven Greenland 51 60.30N 45.35W
Syktyvkar U.S.S.R. 18 61.42N 50.45E
Sylhet Bangla. 29 24.53N 91.51E
Sylt *i.* W. Germany 14 54.50N 8.20E
Sylte Norway 16 62.31N 7.07E
Syracuse N.Y. U.S.A. 55 43.03N 76.09W
Syr Darya *r.* U.S.S.R. 20 46.00N 61.12E
Syria Asia 30 35.00N 38.00E
Syriam Burma 26 16.45N 96.17E
Syrian Desert *see* Bādiyat ash Shām *des.* Asia 30
Syzran U.S.S.R. 18 53.10N 48.29E
Szarvas Hungary 15 46.52N 20.34E
Szczecin Poland 14 53.25N 14.32E
Szczecinek Poland 14 53.42N 16.41E
Szczytno Poland 15 53.34N 21.00E
Szécsény Hungary 15 48.06N 19.31E
Szeged Hungary 13 46.16N 20.08E
Székesfehérvár Hungary 15 47.12N 18.25E
Szekszárd Hungary 13 46.22N 18.44E
Szentes Hungary 15 46.39N 20.16E
Szolnok Hungary 15 47.10N 20.12E
Szombathely Hungary 14 47.12N 16.38E
Sztutowo Poland 15 54.20N 19.15E

T

Tabagne Ivory Coast 38 7.59N 3.04W
Ţābah Saudi Arabia 30 27.02N 42.10E
Ţabas Khorāsān Iran 31 32.48N 60.14E
Ţabas Khorāsān Iran 31 33.36N 56.55E
Tabasco *d.* Mexico 56 18.30N 93.00W
Tābask, Kūh-e *mtn.* Iran 31 29.51N 51.52E
Tabili Zaïre 37 0.04N 28.01E
Table B. R.S.A. 39 33.52S 18.26E
Tábor Czech. 14 49.25N 14.41E
Tabora Tanzania 37 5.02S 32.50E
Tabora *d.* Tanzania 37 5.30S 32.50E
Tabou Ivory Coast 34 4.28N 7.20W
Tabrīz Iran 31 38.05N 46.18E
Tabūk Saudi Arabia 32 28.23N 36.36E
Tabulam Australia 47 28.50S152.35E
Tachikawa Japan 23 35.42N139.25E
Tacloban Phil. 27 11.15N124.59E
Tacna Peru 62 18.01S 70.15W
Tacoma U.S.A. 54 47.15N122.27W
Tacora *mtn.* Chile 62 17.40S 69.45W
Tacuarembó Uruguay 63 31.44S 55.59W
Tademaït, Plateau du *f.* Algeria 34 28.45N 2.10E
Tadmor New Zealand 48 41.26S172.47E
Tadoussac Canada 55 48.09N 69.43W
Tadzhikskaya S.S.R. *d.* U.S.S.R. 24 39.00N 70.30E
Taegu S. Korea 25 35.52N128.36E
Taejŏn S. Korea 25 36.20N127.26E
Tafalla Spain 10 42.31N 1.40W
Tafí Viejo Argentina 62 26.45S 65.15W
Taftān, Kūh-e *mtn.* Iran 31 28.38N 61.08E
Taganrog U.S.S.R. 19 47.14N 38.55E
Taganrogskiy Zaliv *g.* U.S.S.R. 19 47.00N 38.30E
Tagaytay City Phil. 27 14.07N120.58E
Tagbilaran Phil. 27 9.38N123.53E
Tagish Canada 50 60.18N134.16W
Tagliamento *r.* Italy 9 45.38N 13.06E
Taglio di Po Italy 9 45.00N 12.12E
Tagula I. P.N.G. 44 11.30S153.30E
Tagum Phil. 27 7.33N125.53E
Tagus *r.* Portugal/Spain *see* Tejo *r.* Portugal 10
Tahara Japan 23 34.40N137.16E
Tahat *mtn.* Algeria 34 23.20N 5.40E
Tahe China 25 52.35N124.48E
Tahiti Îs. de la Société 40 17.37S149.27W
Tahoe, L. U.S.A. 54 39.07N120.03W
Tahoua Niger 38 14.57N 5.16E
Tahoua *d.* Niger 38 15.38N 4.50E
Ţahţā Egypt 30 26.46N 31.30E
Tahuna Indonesia 27 3.37N125.29E
Taibai Shan *mtn.* China 29 34.00N107.40E
Taidong Taiwan 25 22.49N121.10E
Taihape New Zealand 48 39.40S175.48E
Tailai China 25 46.23N123.24E
Tain U.K. 6 57.48N 4.04W
Tainan Taiwan 25 23.01N120.14E
Taínaron, Ákra *c.* Greece 13 36.22N 22.28E
Taipei Taiwan 25 25.05N121.32E
Taiping Malaysia 26 4.54N100.42E
Taito, Península de *pen.* Chile 63 46.30S 74.25W
Taivalkoski Finland 16 65.34N 28.15E
Taiwan Asia 25 23.30N121.00E
Taiyuan China 25 37.50N112.30E
Taizhong Taiwan 25 24.09N120.40E
Taizhou China 25 32.30N119.50E
Ta'izz Yemen 35 13.35N 44.02E
Tajimi Japan 23 35.19N137.08E
Tajo *r.* Spain *see* Tejo *r.* Portugal 10
Tajrish Iran 31 35.48N 51.20E
Tajuna *r.* Spain 10 40.10N 3.35W
Tak Thailand 29 16.47N 99.10E
Takachu Botswana 39 22.37S 21.58E
Takaka New Zealand 48 40.51S172.48E
Takalar Indonesia 26 5.29S119.26E
Takamatsu Japan 25 34.20N134.01E
Takapuna New Zealand 48 36.48S174.47E
Takarazuka Japan 23 34.49N135.21E
Takatsuki Japan 23 34.51N135.37E
Tākestān Iran 31 36.02N 49.40E
Takhādīd *well* Iraq 31 29.59N 44.30E
Taklimakan Shamo *des.* China 24 38.10N 82.00E
Talā Egypt 32 30.41N 30.56E
Tala Uruguay 63 34.21S 55.46W
Talagante Chile 63 33.40S 70.56W
Talangbetutu Indonesia 26 2.48S104.42E
Talara Peru 60 4.38S 81.18W
Talasskiy Alatau *mts.* U.S.S.R. 24 42.20N 73.20E
Talata Mafara Nigeria 38 12.37N 6.05E
Talaud, Kepulauan *is.* Indonesia 27 4.20N126.50E
Talavera de la Reina Spain 10 39.58N 4.50W
Talbragar *r.* Australia 47 32.12S148.37E
Talca Chile 63 35.26S 71.40W
Talcahuano Chile 63 36.43S 73.07W
Taldom U.S.S.R. 18 56.49N 37.30E
Taldy Kurgan U.S.S.R. 24 45.02N 78.23E
Talia Australia 46 33.16S134.53E
Taliabu *i.* Indonesia 27 1.50S124.55E
Talkeetna U.S.A. 50 62.20N150.09W
Ţalkhā Egypt 32 31.04N 31.22E
Tallahassee U.S.A. 53 30.28N 84.19W
Tallangatta Australia 47 36.14S147.19E
Tallard France 11 44.28N 6.03E
Tallinn U.S.S.R. 17 59.22N 24.48E
Tall Kalakh Syria 32 34.40N 36.18E
Tall Kūshik Syria 30 36.48N 42.04E
Tall Salḩab Syria 32 35.15N 36.22E
Talmont France 11 46.28N 1.36W
Talnoye U.S.S.R. 15 48.55N 30.40E
Talsi U.S.S.R. 17 57.15N 22.36E
Taltal Chile 62 25.24S 70.29W
Talvik Norway 16 70.05N 22.52E
Talwood Australia 47 28.29S149.25E
Talyawalka *r.* Australia 46 31.49S143.25E
Tama *r.* Japan 23 35.32N139.47E
Tamala Australia 42 26.42S113.47E
Tamale Ghana 38 9.26N 0.49W
Tamanrasset Algeria 34 22.50N 5.31E
Tamar *r.* U.K. 5 50.28N 4.13W
Tamaské Niger 38 14.55N 5.55E
Tamaulipas *d.* Mexico 56 24.00N 98.20W
Tamazunchale Mexico 56 21.16N 98.47W
Tambacounda Senegal 34 13.45N 13.40W
Tambara Mozambique 37 16.42S 34.17E
Tambellup Australia 43 34.03S117.36E
Tambo Australia 44 24.53S146.15E
Tambo *r.* Australia 47 37.51S147.48E
Tambohorano Madagascar 37 17.30S 43.58E
Tambov U.S.S.R. 18 52.44N 41.28E
Tambre *r.* Spain 10 42.50N 8.55W
Tambura Sudan 35 5.36N 27.28E
Tamchaket Mauritania 34 17.25N 10.40W
Tâmega *r.* Portugal 10 41.04N 8.17W
Tamil Nadu *d.* India 29 11.15N 79.00E
Ţāmiyah Egypt 32 29.29N 30.58E
Tam Ky Vietnam 26 15.34N108.29E
Tammisaari Finland 17 59.58N 23.26E
Tampa U.S.A. 53 27.58N 82.38W
Tampa B. U.S.A. 53 27.48N 82.15W
Tampere Finland 17 61.30N 23.45E
Tampico Mexico 56 22.18N 97.52W
Tamsagbulag Mongolia 25 47.10N117.21E
Tamworth Australia 47 31.07S150.57E
Tamworth U.K. 5 52.38N 1.42W
Tana *r.* Kenya 37 2.32S 40.32E
Tana Norway 16 70.26N 28.14E
Tana *r.* Norway 16 69.45N 28.15E
Tana, L. Ethiopia 35 12.00N 37.20E
Tanacross U.S.A. 50 63.12N143.30W
Tanafjorden Norway 16 70.54N 28.40E
Tanahgrogot Indonesia 26 1.55S116.12E
Tanahmerah Indonesia 27 6.08S140.18E
Tanami Australia 42 19.59S129.43E
Tanana U.S.A. 50 65.11N152.10W
Tanana *r.* U.S.A. 50 65.09N151.55W
Tananarive *see* Antananarivo Madagascar 36
Tanaro *r.* Italy 9 45.01N 8.46E
Tanda Ivory Coast 38 7.48N 3.10W
Tăndărei Romania 15 44.38N 27.40E
Tandil Argentina 63 37.18S 59.10W
Tandou L. Australia 46 32.38S142.05E
Tanezrouft *f.* Algeria 34 22.50N 1.05E
Tanga Tanzania 37 5.07S 39.05E
Tanga *d.* Tanzania 37 5.20S 38.30E
Tangalla Sri Lanka 29 6.02N 80.47E
Tanganyika, L. Africa 37 6.00S 29.30E
Tanger Morocco 34 35.48N 5.45W
Tanggula Shan *mts.* China 29 32.40N 92.30E
Tangier *see* Tanger Morocco 34
Tangra Yumco *l.* China 24 31.00N 86.22E
Tangshan China 25 39.37N118.05E
Tanguiéta Benin 38 10.37N 1.18E
Tanimbar, Kepulauan *is.* Indonesia 27 7.50S131.30E
Tanjay Phil. 27 9.31N123.10E
Tanjona Vilanandro *c.* Madagascar 37 16.11S 44.27E
Tanjung Indonesia 26 2.10S115.25E
Tanjungbalai Indonesia 26 2.59N 99.46E
Tanjungkarang Indonesia 26 5.28S105.16E
Tanjungpandan Indonesia 26 2.44S107.36E
Tanjungredeb Indonesia 26 2.09N117.29E
Tankapirtti Finland 16 68.16N 27.20E
Tännäs Sweden 17 62.27N 12.40E
Tannin Canada 55 49.40N 91.00W
Tannu Ola *mts.* U.S.S.R. 21 51.00N 93.30E

annūrah, Ra's c. Saudi Arabia 31 26.40N 50.10E
ano r. Ghana 38 5.07N 2.54W
anout Niger 38 14.55N 8.49E
anṭā Egypt 32 30.48N 31.00E
anzania Africa 37 5.00S 35.00E
ao'an China 25 45.25N122.46E
aoudenni Mali 34 22.45N 4.00W
apachula Mexico 56 14.54N 92.15W
apajós r. Brazil 61 2.25S 54.40W
apaktuan Indonesia 26 3.30N 97.10E
apalquén Argentina 63 36.20S 60.02W
apanahoni r. Surinam 61 4.20N 54.25W
apanui New Zealand 48 45.57S169.16E
apauá r. Brazil 60 5.40S 64.20W
apirapecó, Serra mts. Venezuela/Brazil 60 1.00N 64.30W
apolca Hungary 15 46.53N 17.27E
apti r. India 28 21.05N 72.45E
apurucuara Brazil 60 0.24S 65.02W
aquari r. Brazil 59 19.00S 57.27W
aquaritinga Brazil 59 21.23S 48.33W
ara U.S.S.R. 20 56.55N 74.24E
ara r. U.S.S.R. 20 56.30N 74.40E
ara r. Yugo. 13 43.23N 18.47E
arabuco Bolivia 62 19.10S 64.57W
arābulus Lebanon 32 34.27N 35.50E
arābulus Libya 34 32.58N 13.12E
arābulus f. Libya 34 29.45N 14.30E
arago Australia 47 35.05S149.10E
arakan Indonesia 26 3.20N117.38E
aranaki d. New Zealand 48 39.00S174.30E
arancón Spain 10 40.01N 3.01W
aranto Italy 13 40.28N 17.14E
aranto, Golfo di g. Italy 13 40.00N 17.20E
arapacá Colombia 60 2.52S 69.44W
arapoto Peru 60 6.31S 76.23W
arashcha U.S.S.R. 15 49.35N 30.20E
arasovo U.S.S.R. 18 66.14N 46.43E
arauacá Brazil 60 8.10S 70.46W
arauacá r. Brazil 60 6.42S 69.48W
arawera New Zealand 48 39.02S176.36E
arbagatay, Khrebet mts. U.S.S.R. 24 47.00N 83.00E
arbat Ness c. U.K. 6 57.52N 3.46W
arbert Rep. of Ire. 7 52.34N 9.24W
arbert Strath. U.K. 6 55.51N 5.25W
arbert W. Isles U.K. 6 57.54N 6.49W
arbes France 11 43.14N 0.05E
arcento Italy 9 46.13N 13.13E
arcoola N.S.W. Australia 46 33.31S142.40E
arcoola S.A. Australia 46 30.41S134.33E
arcoon Australia 47 30.19S146.43E
arcutta Australia 47 35.17S147.45E
aree Australia 47 31.54S152.26E
arella Australia 46 30.55S143.06E
arendö Sweden 16 67.10N 22.38E
arfā, Wādī aṭ r. Egypt 32 28.36N 30.50E
arfaya Morocco 34 27.58N 12.55W
arifa Spain 10 36.01N 5.36W
arija Bolivia 62 21.31S 64.45W
arija d. Bolivia 62 21.40S 64.20W
arim He r. China 24 41.00N 83.30E
aritatu r. Indonesia 27 2.54S138.27E
arkwa Ghana 38 5.16N 1.59W
arlac Phil. 27 15.29N120.35E
arm Denmark 17 55.55N 8.32E
arma Peru 60 11.28S 75.41W
arn r. France 11 44.15N 1.15E
ärnaby Sweden 16 65.43N 15.16E
arnica mtn. Poland 15 49.05N 22.44E
arnobrzeg Poland 15 50.35N 21.41E
arnów Poland 15 50.01N 20.59E
aro r. Italy 9 45.00N 10.15E
aroom Australia 44 25.39S149.49E
arragona Spain 10 41.07N 1.15E
arran Hills Australia 47 32.27S146.27E
arsus Turkey 30 36.52N 34.52E
artagal Argentina 62 22.32S 63.50W
artu U.S.S.R. 18 58.20N 26.44E
arṭūs Syria 32 34.55N 35.52E
arutino U.S.S.R. 15 46.09N 29.04E
arutung Indonesia 26 2.01N 98.54E
ashauz U.S.S.R. 20 41.49N 59.58E
ashkent U.S.S.R. 24 41.16N 69.13E
asiilaq see Ammassalik Greenland 51
asikmalaya Indonesia 26 7.20S108.16E
asjön Sweden 16 64.15N 15.47E
asman B. New Zealand 48 41.00S173.15E
asmania d. Australia 45 42.00S147.00E
asman Mts. New Zealand 48 41.00S172.40E
asman Pen. Australia 45 43.08S147.51E
atabánya Hungary 15 47.34N 18.26E
atarsk U.S.S.R. 20 55.14N 76.00E
atarskiy Proliv g. U.S.S.R. 21 47.40N141.00E
ateyama Japan 23 34.59N139.52E
athra Australia 47 36.44S149.58E
atnam, C. Canada 51 57.00N 91.00W
atong Australia 47 36.46S146.03E
atvan Turkey 30 38.31N 42.15E
aubaté Brazil 59 23.00S 45.36W
aumarunui New Zealand 48 38.53S175.16E
aumaturgo Brazil 60 8.57S 72.48W
aung R.S.A. 39 27.32S 24.46E
aung-gyi Burma 29 20.49N 97.01E
aunton U.K. 5 51.01N 3.07W
aunus mts. W. Germany 14 50.07N 7.48E
aupo New Zealand 48 38.42S176.06E
aupo, L. New Zealand 48 38.45S175.30E
aurage U.S.S.R. 17 55.15N 22.17E
auranga New Zealand 48 37.42S176.11E
aurianova Italy 12 38.21N 16.01E
aurus Mts. see Toros Dağlari mts. Turkey 30
avani Canada 51 62.00N 93.20W
avda U.S.S.R. 20 58.04N 65.12E
avda r. U.S.S.R. 20 57.40N 67.00E
aveta Kenya 37 3.23S 37.42E
avira Portugal 10 37.07N 7.39W
avistock U.K. 5 50.33N 4.09W
Tavoy Burma 29 14.07N 98.18E
Taw r. U.K. 5 51.05N 4.05W
Tawas City U.S.A. 55 44.16N 83.33W
Tawau Malaysia 26 4.16N117.54E
Tawitawi i. Phil. 27 5.10N120.05E
Ṭawkar Sudan 35 18.26N 37.44E
Tay r. U.K. 6 56.21N 3.18W
Tay, L. Australia 43 33.00S120.52E
Tay, Loch U.K. 6 56.32N 4.08W
Tayabamba Peru 60 8.15S 77.15W
Tayan Indonesia 26 0.02S110.05E
Taylor, Mt. U.S.A. 54 35.14N107.37W
Taymā' Saudi Arabia 30 27.37N 38.30E
Taymyr, Ozero l. U.S.S.R. 21 74.20N101.00E
Taymyr, Poluostrov pen. U.S.S.R. 21 75.30N 99.00E
Tayport U.K. 6 56.27N 2.53W
Tayshet U.S.S.R. 21 55.56N 98.01E
Tayside d. U.K. 6 56.35N 3.28W
Taytay Phil. 26 10.47N119.32E
Taz r. U.S.S.R. 20 67.30N 78.50E
Taza Morocco 34 34.16N 4.01W
Tazovskiy U.S.S.R. 20 67.28N 78.43E
Tbilisi U.S.S.R. 31 41.43N 44.48E
Tchad, Lac see Chad, L. Africa 38
Tchamba Togo 38 9.05N 1.27E
Tcholliré Cameroon 38 8.25N 14.10E
Tczew Poland 15 54.06N 18.47E
Te Anau New Zealand 48 45.25S167.43E
Te Anau, L. New Zealand 48 45.10S167.15E
Teapa Mexico 56 17.33N 92.57W
Te Araroa New Zealand 48 37.38S178.25E
Tea Tree Australia 44 22.11S133.17E
Tebingtinggi Indonesia 26 3.20N 99.08E
Tebingtinggi Indonesia 26 3.37S103.09E
Tebulos Mta mtn. U.S.S.R. 19 42.34N 45.17E
Techiman Ghana 38 7.36N 1.55W
Tecuci Romania 15 45.49N 27.27E
Tees r. U.K. 4 54.35N 1.11W
Tefé Brazil 60 3.24S 64.45W
Tefé r. Brazil 60 3.35S 64.47W
Tegal Indonesia 26 6.52S109.07E
Tegelen Neth. 8 51.20N 6.08E
Tegina Nigeria 38 10.06N 6.11E
Tego Australia 47 28.48S146.47E
Tegouma well Niger 38 15.33N 9.19E
Tegucigalpa Honduras 57 14.05N 87.14W
Teguidda I-n-Tessoum Niger 38 17.21N 6.32E
Tehamiyam Sudan 35 18.20N 36.32E
Téhini Ivory Coast 38 9.39N 3.32W
Tehrān Iran 31 35.40N 51.26E
Tehuacán Mexico 56 18.30N 97.26W
Tehuantepec Mexico 56 16.21N 95.13W
Tehuantepec, Golfo de g. Mexico 56 16.00N 95.00W
Tehuantepec, Istmo de f. Mexico 56 17.00N 94.30W
Teifi r. U.K. 5 52.05N 4.41W
Teignmouth U.K. 5 50.33N 3.30W
Teixeiras Brazil 59 20.37S 42.52W
Tejo r. Portugal 10 39.00N 8.57W
Te Kaha New Zealand 48 37.44S177.52E
Tekapo, L. New Zealand 48 43.35S170.30E
Tekax Mexico 57 20.12N 89.17W
Tekirdag Turkey 13 40.59N 27.30E
Te Kuiti New Zealand 48 38.20S175.10E
Tela Honduras 57 15.56N 87.25W
Telavi U.S.S.R. 31 41.56N 45.30E
Tel Aviv-Yafo Israel 32 32.05N 34.46E
Telegraph Creek town Canada 50 57.56N131.10W
Telemark d. Norway 17 59.40N 8.30E
Teleneshty U.S.S.R. 15 47.35N 28.17E
Teles Pires r. Brazil 61 7.20S 57.30W
Telford U.K. 5 52.42N 2.30W
Telfs Austria 14 47.19N 11.04E
Telgte W. Germany 8 51.59N 7.46E
Telichie Australia 46 31.43S139.54E
Tell Atlas mts. Algeria 34 36.10N 4.00E
Tell City U.S.A. 55 37.56N 86.46W
Teller U.S.A. 50 65.16N166.22N
Telok Anson Malaysia 26 4.00N101.00E
Telpos-Iz mtn. U.S.S.R. 18 63.56N 59.02E
Telsen Argentina 63 42.25S 67.00W
Telšiai U.S.S.R. 17 55.59N 22.15E
Telukbetung Indonesia 26 5.28S105.16E
Tema Ghana 38 5.41N 0.01W
Temagami, L. Canada 55 47.00N 80.05W
Tembo Aluma Angola 36 7.42S 17.15E
Teme r. U.K. 5 52.10N 2.13W
Temir U.S.S.R. 19 49.09N 57.06E
Temirtau U.S.S.R. 20 50.05N 72.55E
Témiscaming Canada 55 46.44N 79.06W
Temora Australia 47 34.27S147.35E
Tempe U.S.A. 54 33.25N111.56W
Tempino Indonesia 26 1.55S103.23E
Tempio Italy 12 40.54N 9.06E
Temple U.S.A. 53 31.06N 97.22W
Temple B. Australia 44 12.10S143.04E
Templemore Rep. of Ire. 7 52.48N 7.51W
Templin E. Germany 14 53.07N 13.30E
Temuco Chile 63 38.44S 72.36W
Tenabo Mexico 56 20.03N 90.14W
Tenasserim Burma 29 12.05N 99.00E
Tenby U.K. 5 51.40N 4.42W
Tende France 11 44.05N 7.36E
Tende, Col de pass France/Italy 9 44.09N 7.34E
Ten Degree Channel Indian Oc. 29 10.00N 92.30E
Tenenkou Mali 38 14.25N 4.58W
Tenerife i. Canary Is. 34 28.10N 16.30W
Tengchong China 29 25.02N 98.28E
Tengiz, Ozero l. U.S.S.R. 20 50.30N 69.00E
Teng Xian China 25 35.10N117.14E
Tenke Zaïre 36 10.34S 26.12E
Tenkodogo Burkina Faso 38 11.47N 0.19W
Tennant Creek town Australia 44 19.31S134.15E
Tennessee d. U.S.A. 53 36.00N 86.00W
Tennessee r. U.S.A. 53 37.10N 88.25W
Tenosique Mexico 56 17.29N 91.26W
Tenryū Japan 23 34.52N137.49E
Tenryū r. Japan 23 34.39N137.47E
Tenterfield Australia 47 29.01S152.04E
Teófilo Otoni Brazil 59 17.52S 41.31W
Tepa Indonesia 27 7.52S129.31E
Tepelenë Albania 13 40.18N 20.01E
Tepic Mexico 56 21.30N104.51W
Teplice Czech. 14 50.40N 13.50E
Ter r. Spain 10 42.02N 3.10E
Téra Niger 38 14.01N 0.45E
Tera r. Portugal 10 38.55N 8.01W
Teramo Italy 12 42.40N 13.43E
Terassa Spain 10 41.34N 2.00E
Tercan Turkey 30 39.47N 40.23E
Terebovlya U.S.S.R. 15 49.18N 25.44E
Terekhova U.S.S.R. 15 52.13N 31.28E
Teresina Brazil 61 5.09S 42.46W
Teresópolis Brazil 59 22.26S 42.59W
Tergnier France 9 49.39N 3.18E
Termez U.S.S.R. 20 37.15N 67.15E
Termination I. Australia 43 34.25S121.53E
Termini Italy 12 37.59N 13.42E
Términos, Laguna de b. Mexico 56 18.30N 91.30W
Termoli Italy 12 41.58N 14.59E
Ternate Indonesia 27 0.48N127.23E
Terneuzen Neth. 8 51.20N 3.50E
Terni Italy 12 42.34N 12.44E
Ternopol U.S.S.R. 15 49.35N 25.39E
Terra Bella U.S.A. 54 35.58N119.03W
Terracina Italy 12 41.17N 13.15E
Terralba Italy 12 39.43N 8.38E
Terre Adélie f. Antarctica 64 80.00S140.00E
Terre Haute U.S.A. 55 39.27N 87.24W
Terschelling i. Neth. 8 53.25N 5.25E
Teruel Spain 10 40.21N 1.06W
Tervola Finland 16 66.05N 24.48E
Teryaweynya Australia 46 32.18S143.29E
Tešanj Yugo. 15 44.37N 18.00E
Teslin Canada 50 60.10N132.42W
Teslin r. Canada 50 62.00N135.00W
Tessaoua Niger 38 13.46N 7.55E
Tessy-sur-Vire France 9 48.58N 1.04W
Test r. U.K. 5 50.55N 1.29W
Têt r. France 11 42.43N 3.00E
Tete Mozambique 37 16.10S 33.30E
Tete d. Mozambique 37 15.30S 33.00E
Teterev r. U.S.S.R. 15 51.03N 30.30E
Teterow E. Germany 14 53.46N 12.34E
Teteven Bulgaria 13 42.55N 24.16E
Tetiyev U.S.S.R. 15 49.22N 29.40E
Tétouan Morocco 34 35.34N 5.22W
Tetovo Yugo. 13 42.01N 20.58E
Teulada Italy 12 38.58N 8.46E
Teun i. Indonesia 27 6.59S129.08E
Teuva Finland 16 62.29N 21.44E
Tevere r. Italy 12 41.45N 12.16E
Teverya Israel 32 32.48N 35.32E
Teviot r. U.K. 6 55.36N 2.27W
Teviotdale f. U.K. 4 55.26N 2.46W
Teviothead U.K. 6 55.20N 2.56W
Tewkesbury U.K. 5 51.59N 2.09W
Texarkana Ark. U.S.A. 53 33.28N 94.02W
Texas Australia 47 28.50S151.09E
Texas d. U.S.A. 52 32.00N100.00W
Texel i. Neth. 8 53.05N 4.47E
Texoma, L. U.S.A. 53 34.00N 96.40W
Tezpur India 29 26.38N 92.49E
Thabana Ntlenyana mtn. Lesotho 39 29.28S 29.17E
Thabazimbi R.S.A. 39 24.36S 27.23E
Thādiq Saudi Arabia 31 25.18N 45.52E
Thailand Asia 29 16.00N102.00E
Thailand, G. of Asia 29 10.30N101.00E
Thai Nguyen Vietnam 26 21.31N105.55E
Thal Pakistan 28 33.22N 70.33E
Thale Luang l. Thailand 29 7.30N100.20E
Thallon Australia 47 28.39S148.49E
Thamarīt Oman 28 17.39N 54.02E
Thames r. Canada 55 42.19N 82.28W
Thames New Zealand 48 37.08S175.35E
Thames r. U.K. 5 51.30N 0.05E
Thāna India 28 19.14N 73.02E
Thane Australia 47 28.08S151.39E
Thanh Hóa Vietnam 26 19.50N105.48E
Thành Pho Ho Chí Minh Vietnam 26 10.46N106.43E
Thanjāvūr India 29 10.46N 79.09E
Thar Desert India 28 28.00N 72.00E
Thargomindah Australia 45 27.59S143.45E
Tharrawaddy Burma 29 17.37N 95.48E
Tharthār, Wādī ath r. Iraq 30 34.18N 43.07E
Thásos Greece 13 40.47N 24.42E
Thásos i. Greece 13 40.40N 24.39E
Thatcher U.S.A. 54 32.51N109.56W
Thaton Burma 29 17.00N 97.39E
Thaungdut Burma 29 24.26N 94.45E
Thayetmyo Burma 29 19.20N 95.18E
Thazi Burma 29 20.51N 96.05E
Thebes ruins Egypt 30 25.41N 32.40E
The Bight town Bahamas 57 24.19N 75.24W
The Cherokees, L. O' U.S.A. 53 36.45N 94.50W
The Cheviot mtn. U.K. 4 55.29N 2.10W
The Cheviot Hills U.K. 4 55.22N 2.24W
The Coorong g. Australia 46 36.00S139.30E
The Dalles town U.S.A. 54 45.36N121.10W
The Everglades f. U.S.A. 53 26.00N 80.30W
The Fens f. U.K. 5 55.10N 4.13W
The Granites town Australia 42 20.35S130.21E
The Gulf Asia 31 27.00N 50.00E
The Hague see 'sGravenhage Neth. 8
The Little Minch str. U.K. 6 57.40N 6.45W
Thelon r. Canada 51 64.23N 96.15W
The Machers f. U.K. 6 54.45N 4.28W
The Minch str. U.K. 6 58.10N 5.50W
The Needles c. U.K. 5 50.39N 1.35W
Theodore Australia 44 24.57S150.05E
Theodore Roosevelt L. U.S.A. 54 33.30N110.57W
The Pas Canada 51 53.50N101.15W
The Pennines hills U.K. 4 55.40N 2.20W
Thérain r. France 9 49.15N 2.27E
Theresa U.S.A. 55 44.13N 75.48W
The Rhinns f. U.K. 6 54.50N 5.02W
Thermaïkós Kólpos g. Greece 13 40.10N 23.00E
Thermopolis U.S.A. 54 43.39N108.13W
Thermopylae, Pass of Greece 13 38.47N 22.34E
The Rock town Australia 47 35.16S147.07E
The Salt L. Australia 46 30.05S142.10E
The Solent str. U.K. 5 50.45N 1.20W
The Sound str. Denmark/Sweden 17 55.35N 12.40E
Thessalon Canada 55 46.20N 83.34W
Thessaloníki Greece 13 40.38N 22.56E
Thetford U.K. 5 52.25N 0.44E
Thetford Mines town Canada 55 46.06N 71.18W
The Twins town Australia 46 30.00S135.16E
The Wash b. U.K. 4 52.55N 0.15E
The Weald f. U.K. 5 51.05N 0.20E
Thiene Italy 9 45.42N 11.29E
Thiers France 11 45.51N 3.33E
Thika Kenya 37 1.04S 37.04E
Thimbu Bhutan 29 27.29N 89.40E
Thingvallavatn l. Iceland 16 64.10N 21.10W
Thionville France 11 49.22N 6.11E
Thíra i. Greece 13 36.24N 25.27E
Thirsk U.K. 4 54.15N 1.20W
Thisted Denmark 17 56.57N 8.42E
Thistilfjördhur b. Iceland 16 66.11N 15.20W
Thistle I. Australia 46 35.00S136.09E
Thívai Greece 13 38.21N 23.19E
Thjórsá r. Iceland 16 63.53N 20.38W
Tholen i. Neth. 8 51.34N 4.07E
Thomas U.S.A. 55 39.09N 79.30W
Thomasville Fla. U.S.A. 53 30.50N 83.59W
Thompson Canada 51 55.45N 97.45W
Thompson Utah U.S.A. 54 38.58N109.43W
Thompsonville U.S.A. 55 44.32N 85.57W
Thomson r. Australia 44 25.11S142.53E
Thonburi Thailand 29 13.43N100.27E
Thórisvatn l. Iceland 16 64.15N 18.50W
Thorshavn Faroe Is. 16 62.02N 6.47W
Thorshöfn Iceland 16 66.12N 15.17W
Thouars France 11 46.59N 0.13W
Thrapston U.K. 5 52.24N 0.32W
Three Forks U.S.A. 54 45.54N111.33W
Three Rivers town Australia 42 25.07S119.09E
Three Sisters Mt. U.S.A. 54 44.10N121.46W
Thuin Belgium 8 50.21N 4.20E
Thule Greenland 51 77.30N 69.29W
Thun Switz. 14 46.46N 7.38E
Thunder Bay town Canada 55 48.25N 89.14W
Thunkar Bhutan 29 27.55N 91.00E
Thüringer Wald mts. E. Germany 14 50.40N 10.50E
Thurles Rep. of Ire. 7 52.41N 7.50W
Thurloo Downs town Australia 46 29.18S143.30E
Thursday I. Australia 27 10.45S142.00E
Thurso U.K. 6 58.35N 3.32W
Thury-Harcourt France 9 48.59N 0.29W
Tia Australia 47 31.15S151.40E
Tianjin China 25 39.08N117.12E
Tianjin d. China 25 39.08N117.12E
Tianjun China 24 37.16N 98.52E
Tian Shan mts. Asia 24 42.00N 80.30E
Tianshui China 24 34.25N105.58E
Tibati Cameroon 38 6.25N 12.33E
Tiber r. see Tevere r. Italy 12
Tiberias see Teverya Israel 32
Tiberias, L. see Yam Kinneret l. Israel 32
Tibesti mts. Chad 34 21.00N 17.30E
Tibet d. see Xizang d. China 24
Tibetan Plateau see Qing Zang Gaoyuan f. China 24
Tibooburra Australia 46 29.28S142.04E
Tiburón, Isla Mexico 56 29.00N112.20W
Tichît Mauritania 34 18.28N 9.30W
Ticino r. Italy 9 45.09N 9.12E
Ticonderoga U.S.A. 55 43.51N 73.26W
Tidaholm Sweden 17 58.11N 13.57E
Tidjikdja Mauritania 34 18.29N 11.31W
Tiel Neth. 8 51.53N 5.26E
Tieling China 25 42.18N123.49E
Tielt Belgium 8 51.00N 3.20E
Tienen Belgium 8 50.49N 4.56E
Tiénigbé Ivory Coast 38 8.11N 5.43W
Tientsin see Tianjin China 25
Tierp Sweden 17 60.20N 17.30E
Tierra Blanca Mexico 56 18.28N 96.12W
Tierra del Fuego d. Argentina 63 54.30S 67.00W
Tierra del Fuego i. Argentina/Chile 63 54.00S 69.00W
Tietar r. Spain 10 39.50N 6.00W
Tietê Brazil 59 23.04S 47.41W
Tiger U.S.A. 54 48.42N117.24W
Tigil U.S.S.R. 21 57.49N158.40E
Tignère Cameroon 38 7.23N 12.37E
Tigre r. Venezuela 60 9.20N 62.30W
Tigris r. see Dijlah r. Asia 31
Tīh, Jabal at f. Egypt 32 28.50N 34.00E
Tihāmah f. Saudi Arabia 35 20.30N 40.30E
Tijuana Mexico 56 32.32N117.01W
Tikaré Burkina Faso 38 13.16N 1.44W
Tikhoretsk U.S.S.R. 19 45.52N 40.07E
Tikhvin U.S.S.R. 18 59.35N 33.29E
Tikitiki New Zealand 48 37.47S178.25E
Tiksha U.S.S.R. 18 64.04N 32.35E
Tiksi U.S.S.R. 21 71.40N128.45E
Tilburg Neth. 8 51.34N 5.05E
Tilbury U.K. 5 51.28N 0.23E
Tilemsi, Vallée du f. Mali 38 16.15N 0.02E
Till r. Northum. U.K. 4 55.41N 2.12W
Tillabéri Niger 38 14.28N 1.27E
Tillamook U.S.A. 54 45.27N123.51W
Tílos i. Greece 13 36.25N 27.25E
Tilpa Australia 46 30.57S144.24E
Timanskiy Kryazh mts. U.S.S.R. 18 66.00N 49.00E
Timaru New Zealand 48 44.23S171.41E
Timashevsk U.S.S.R. 19 45.38N 38.56E
Timbákion Greece 13 35.04N 24.46E
Timboon Australia 46 38.32S143.02E
Timbuktu see Tombouctou Mali 38
Timimoun Algeria 34 29.14N 0.16E
Timiș r. Yugo./Romania 15 44.49N 20.28E
Timișoara Romania 15 45.47N 21.15E
Timișul r. Yugo. 13 44.49N 20.28E
Timmins Canada 55 48.30N 81.20W
Timok r. Yugo. 13 44.13N 22.40E
Timor i. Indonesia 42 9.30S125.00E
Timor Sea Austa. 42 11.00S127.00E
Timor Timur d. Indonesia 27 9.00S125.00E
Timpahute Range mts. U.S.A. 54 37.38N115.34W
Tinahely Rep. of Ire. 7 52.48N 6.19W
Tindouf Algeria 34 27.50N 8.04W
Tingha Australia 47 29.58S151.16E
Tingo María Peru 60 9.09S 75.56W
Tingréla Ivory Coast 38 10.26N 6.20W
Tingsryd Sweden 17 56.32N 14.59E
Tinguipaya Bolivia 62 19.11S 65.51W
Tinian i. Mariana Is. 27 14.58N145.38E
Tinne r. Norway 3 59.05N 9.43E
Tinnenburra Australia 47 28.40S145.30E
Tinnoset Norway 17 59.43N 9.02E
Tínos i. Greece 13 37.36N 25.08E
Tinsukia India 29 27.30N 95.22E
Tintinara Australia 46 35.52S140.04E
Tioman, Pulau i. Malaysia 26 2.45N104.10E
Tionaga Canada 55 48.05N 82.06W
Tione di Trento Italy 9 46.02N 10.43E
Tipperary Rep. of Ire. 7 52.29N 8.10W
Tipperary d. Rep. of Ire. 7 52.37N 7.55W
Tirān, Jazīrat Saudi Arabia 32 27.56N 34.34E
Tiranë Albania 13 41.20N 19.48E
Tirano Italy 9 46.12N 10.10E
Tiraspol U.S.S.R. 15 46.50N 29.38E
Tirat Karmel Israel 32 32.46N 34.58E
Tirebolu Turkey 30 41.02N 38.49E
Tiree i. U.K. 6 56.30N 6.50W
Tîrgovişte Romania 15 44.56N 25.27E
Tîrgu-Jiu Romania 15 45.03N 23.17E
Tîrgu-Lăpuş Romania 15 47.27N 23.52E
Tîrgu Mureş Romania 15 46.33N 24.34E
Tîrgu-Neamţ Romania 15 47.12N 26.22E
Tîrgu-Ocna Romania 15 46.15N 26.37E
Tîrgu-Secuiesc Romania 15 46.00N 26.08E
Tírnavos Greece 13 39.45N 22.17E
Tirol d. Austria 14 47.15N 11.20E
Tir Pol Afghan. 31 34.38N 61.19E
Tirso r. Italy 12 39.52N 8.33E
Tiruchchirāppalli India 29 10.50N 78.43E
Tirunelveli India 28 8.45N 77.43E
Tirupati India 29 13.39N 79.25E
Tiruppur India 28 11.05N 77.20E
Tisa r. Yugo. 15 45.09N 20.16E
Tis'ah Egypt 32 30.02N 32.35E
Tisdale Canada 50 52.51N104.01W
Tisza r. Hungary see Tisa r. Yugo. 15
Titicaca, L. Bolivia/Peru 62 16.00S 69.00W
Titiwa Nigeria 38 12.14N 12.53E
Titograd Yugo. 13 42.30N 19.16E
Titovo Užice Yugo. 13 43.52N 19.51E
Titov Veles Yugo. 13 41.43N 21.49E
Titran Norway 16 63.42N 8.22E
Titusville Penn. U.S.A. 55 41.38N 79.41W
Tiverton U.K. 5 50.54N 3.30W
Tivoli Italy 12 41.58N 12.48E
Tizimín Mexico 57 21.10N 88.09W
Tizi Ouzou Algeria 34 36.44N 4.05E
Tiznit Morocco 34 29.43N 9.44W
Tjeuke Meer l. Neth. 8 52.55N 5.51E
Tjörn i. Sweden 17 58.00N 11.38E
Tlaxcala d. Mexico 56 19.45N 98.20W
Tlemcen Algeria 34 34.53N 1.21W
Tmassah Libya 34 26.22N 15.47E
Toab U.K. 6 59.53N 1.16W
Toamasina Madagascar 36 18.10S 49.23E
Toano Italy 9 44.23N 10.34E
Toba Japan 23 34.29N136.51E
Toba, Danau l. Indonesia 26 2.45S 98.50E
Toba Kākar Range mts. Pakistan 28 31.15N 68.00E
Tobar U.S.A. 54 40.53N114.54W
Tobelo Indonesia 27 1.45N127.59E
Tobermory Canada 55 45.15N 81.39W
Tobermory U.K. 6 56.37N 6.04W
Tobi i. Caroline Is. 27 3.01N131.10E
Toboali Indonesia 26 3.00S106.30E
Tobol r. U.S.S.R. 20 58.15N 68.12E
Tobolsk U.S.S.R. 20 58.15N 68.12E
Tobseda U.S.S.R. 18 68.34N 52.16E
Tocantinópolis Brazil 61 6.20S 47.25W
Tocantins r. Brazil 61 1.50S 49.15W
Töcksfors Sweden 17 59.30N 11.50E
Tocopilla Chile 62 22.05S 70.12W
Tocorpuri mtn. Bolivia/Chile 62 22.26S 67.53W
Tocumwal Australia 47 35.51S145.34E
Tocuyo r. Venezuela 60 11.03N 68.23W
Todenyang Kenya 37 4.34N 35.52E
Togian, Kepulauan is. Indonesia 27 0.20S122.00E
Togo Africa 38 8.00N 1.00E
Toijala Finland 17 61.10N 23.52E
Tokaj Hungary 15 48.08N 21.27E
Tokala mtn. Indonesia 27 1.36S121.41E
Tokat Turkey 30 40.20N 36.35E
Tokelau Is. Pacific Oc. 40 9.00S171.45W
Toki Japan 23 35.21N137.11E
Toki r. Japan 23 35.12N136.52E
Tokmak U.S.S.R. 24 42.49N 75.15E
Tokoname Japan 23 34.53N136.51E
Tokoroa New Zealand 48 38.13S175.53E
Tokuno shima i. Japan 25 27.40N129.00E
Tōkyō Japan 23 35.42N139.46E

Tōkyō-wan *b.* Japan **23** 35.25N139.45E
Tolaga Bay *town* New Zealand **48** 38.22S178.18E
Tolbukhin Bulgaria **13** 43.34N 27.52E
Toledo Spain **10** 39.52N 4.02W
Toledo U.S.A. **55** 41.40N 83.35W
Toledo, Montes de *mts.* Spain **10** 39.35N 4.30W
Toliara Madagascar **36** 23.21S 43.40E
Tolmezzo Italy **9** 46.24N 13.01E
Tolo, Teluk *g.* Indonesia **27** 2.00S122.30E
Tolosa Spain **10** 43.09N 2.04W
Tolstyy-Les U.S.S.R. **15** 51.24N 29.48E
Toluca Mexico **56** 19.20N 99.40W
Toluca *mtn.* Mexico **56** 19.10N 99.40W
Tol'yatti U.S.S.R. **18** 53.32N 49.24E
Tomar Portugal **10** 39.36N 8.25W
Tomás Gomensoro Uruguay **63** 30.26S 57.26W
Tomaszów Lubelski Poland **15** 50.28N 23.25E
Tomaszów Mazowiecki Poland **15** 51.32N 20.01E
Tombigbee *r.* U.S.A. **53** 31.05N 87.55W
Tombos Brazil **59** 20.53S 42.03W
Tombouctou Mali **38** 16.49N 2.59W
Tomé Chile **63** 36.37S 72.57W
Tomelilla Sweden **17** 55.33N 13.57E
Tomelloso Spain **10** 39.09N 3.01W
Tomingley Australia **47** 32.06S148.15E
Tomini Indonesia **27** 0.31N120.30E
Tomini, Teluk *g.* Indonesia **27** 0.30S120.45E
Tominian Mali **38** 13.17N 4.35W
Tomintoul U.K. **6** 57.15N 3.24W
Tomkinson Ranges *mts.* Australia **42** 26.11S129.05E
Tom Price Australia **42** 22.49S117.51E
Tomra Norway **16** 62.34N 6.55E
Tomsk U.S.S.R. **20** 56.30N 85.05E
Toms River *town* U.S.A. **55** 39.57N 74.12W
Tonalá Mexico **56** 16.08N 93.41W
Tonalea U.S.A. **54** 36.20N110.58W
Tonasket U.S.A. **54** 48.42N119.26W
Tonbridge U.K. **5** 51.12N 0.16E
Tondano Indonesia **27** 1.19N124.56E
Tönder Denmark **17** 54.56N 8.54E
Tondibi Mali **38** 16.39N 0.14W
Tondoro Namibia **39** 17.45S 18.50E
Tone *r.* Japan **23** 35.44N140.51E
Tonga Pacific Oc. **40** 20.00S175.00W
Tongaat R.S.A. **39** 29.34S 31.07E
Tongeren Belgium **8** 50.47N 5.28E
Tongguan Shaanxi China **25** 34.36N110.21E
Tonghai China **29** 24.07N102.45E
Tonghua China **25** 41.40N126.52E
Tongking, G. of Asia **26** 20.00N107.50E
Tongling China **25** 30.57N117.40E
Tongo Australia **46** 30.30S143.47E
Tongoy Chile **62** 30.15S 71.30W
Tongue U.K. **6** 58.28N 4.25W
Tongue *r.* U.S.A. **54** 46.24N105.25W
Tongyu China **25** 44.48N123.06E
Tonk India **28** 26.10N 75.50E
Tônlé Sap *l.* Kampuchea **26** 12.50N104.00E
Tonnerre France **9** 47.51N 3.59E
Tonopah U.S.A. **54** 38.04N117.14W
Tonota Botswana **39** 21.28S 27.24E
Tönsberg Norway **17** 59.17N 10.25E
Tonstad Norway **17** 58.40N 6.43E
Tonto Basin *town* U.S.A. **54** 33.55N111.18W
Toobeah Australia **47** 28.22S149.50E
Toodyay Australia **43** 31.35S116.26E
Tooele U.S.A. **54** 40.32N112.18W
Tooligie Australia **46** 33.51S135.41E
Toolondo Australia **46** 36.55S142.00E
Toowoomba Australia **45** 27.35S151.54E
Topeka U.S.A. **53** 39.03N 95.41W
Topko *mtn.* U.S.S.R. **21** 57.20N138.10E
Toplița Romania **15** 46.55N 25.21E
Topock U.S.A. **54** 34.44N114.27W
Topolovgrad Bulgaria **13** 42.05N 26.20E
Topozero, Ozero *l.* U.S.S.R. **18** 65.45N 32.00E
Toppenish U.S.A. **54** 46.23N120.19W
Tora-Khem U.S.S.R. **21** 52.31N 96.13E
Tor B. Australia **43** 35.00S117.40E
Torbat-e Heydariyeh Iran **31** 35.16N 59.13E
Torbat-e Jām Iran **31** 35.15N 60.37E
Torbay *town* U.K. **5** 50.27N 3.31W
Tördal Norway **17** 59.10N 8.45E
Tordesillas Spain **10** 41.30N 5.00W
Töre Sweden **16** 65.54N 22.39E
Töreboda Sweden **17** 58.43N 14.08E
Torgau E. Germany **14** 51.34N 13.00E
Torhout Belgium **8** 51.04N 3.06E
Toride Japan **23** 35.53N140.04E
Torington Australia **47** 29.20S151.40E
Torino Italy **9** 45.04N 7.40E
Tormes *r.* Spain **10** 41.18N 6.29W
Torne *r.* Sweden *see* Tornio *r.* Finland **16**
Torneträsk Sweden **16** 68.15N 19.30E
Torneträsk *l.* Sweden **16** 68.20N 19.10E
Tornio Finland **16** 65.52N 24.10E
Tornio *r.* Finland **16** 65.53N 24.07E
Tornquist Argentina **63** 38.06S 62.14W
Toro Spain **10** 41.31N 5.24W
Toronaios Kólpos *g.* Greece **13** 40.05N 23.38E
Toronto Canada **55** 43.39N 79.23W
Toropets U.S.S.R. **18** 56.30N 31.40E
Tororo Uganda **37** 0.42N 34.13E
Toros Dağlari *mts.* Turkey **30** 37.15N 34.15E
Torrance U.S.A. **54** 33.50N118.19W
Torreblanca Spain **10** 40.14N 0.12E
Torre de Moncorvo Portugal **10** 41.10N 7.03W
Torrelavega Spain **10** 43.21N 4.00W
Torremolinos Spain **10** 36.38N 4.30W
Torrens *r.* Australia **44** 22.22S145.09E
Torrens, L. Australia **46** 31.00S137.50E
Torrens Creek *town* Australia **44** 20.50S145.00E
Torreón Mexico **56** 25.34N103.25W
Torre Pellice Italy **9** 44.49N 9.13E
Torres Str. Australia **44** 10.30S142.20E
Torres Vedras Portugal **10** 39.05N 9.15W
Torrevieja Spain **10** 37.59N 0.40W
Torrey U.S.A. **54** 38.18N111.25W
Torridge *r.* U.K. **5** 51.01N 4.12W
Torridon U.K. **6** 57.23N 5.31W
Torridon, Loch U.K. **6** 57.35N 5.45W
Torriglia Italy **9** 44.31N 9.10E
Torsby Sweden **17** 60.08N 13.00E
Tortola *i.* B.V.Is. **57** 18.28N 64.40W
Tortona Italy **9** 44.54N 8.52E
Tortosa Spain **10** 40.49N 0.31E
Tortue, Île de la *i.* Cuba **57** 20.05N 72.57W
Toruń Poland **15** 53.01N 18.35E
Tory I. Rep. of Ire. **7** 55.16N 8.13W
Tory Sd. Rep. of Ire. **7** 55.14N 8.15W
Torzhok U.S.S.R. **18** 57.02N 34.51E
Toscana *d.* Italy **12** 43.35N 11.10E
Tosen Norway **16** 65.16N 12.50E
Tosno U.S.S.R. **18** 59.38N 30.46E
Tostado Argentina **62** 29.15S 61.45W
Totana Spain **10** 37.46N 1.30W
Tôtes France **9** 49.41N 1.03E
Totma U.S.S.R. **18** 59.59N 42.44E
Totora Bolivia **62** 17.42S 65.09W
Tottenham Australia **47** 32.14S147.24E
Tottori Japan **25** 35.32N134.12E
Toubkal *mtn.* Morocco **34** 31.03N 7.57W
Toucy France **9** 47.44N 3.18E
Tougan Burkina Faso **38** 13.05N 3.04W
Touggourt Algeria **34** 33.08N 6.04E
Toul France **11** 48.41N 5.54E
Toulnustouc *r.* Canada **55** 49.35N 68.25W
Toulon France **11** 43.07N 5.53E
Toulouse France **11** 43.33N 1.24E
Toummo Niger **34** 22.45N 14.08E
Toungoo Burma **29** 19.00N 96.30E
Touques *r.* France **9** 49.22N 0.06E
Tourcoing France **8** 50.44N 3.09E
Tournai Belgium **8** 50.36N 3.23E
Tournon France **11** 45.04N 4.50E
Tournus France **11** 46.33N 4.55E
Tours France **9** 47.23N 0.42E
Toury France **9** 48.11N 1.56E
Touwsrivier *town* R.S.A. **39** 33.20S 20.02E
Towamba Australia **47** 37.09S149.43E
Towcester U.K. **5** 52.07N 0.56W
Towerhill *r.* Australia **44** 22.29S144.39E
Townsend, Mt. Australia **47** 36.24S148.15E
Townshend, C. Australia **44** 22.10S150.30E
Townshend I. Australia **44** 22.15S150.30E
Townsville Australia **44** 19.13S146.48E
Towson U.S.A. **55** 39.24N 76.36W
Towyn U.K. **5** 52.37N 4.08W
Toyama Japan **25** 36.42N137.14E
Toyo *r.* Japan **23** 34.47N137.20E
Toyohashi Japan **23** 34.46N137.23E
Toyokawa Japan **23** 34.49N137.24E
Toyota Japan **23** 35.05N137.09E
Tozeur Tunisia **34** 33.55N 8.08E
Traben-Trarbach W. Germany **8** 49.57N 7.07E
Trabzon Turkey **30** 41.00N 39.43E
Trafalgar, Cabo *c.* Spain **10** 36.11N 6.02W
Traiguén Chile **63** 38.15S 72.41W
Trail Canada **50** 49.04N117.39W
Trajanova Vrata *pass* Bulgaria **13** 42.13N 23.58E
Trakt U.S.S.R. **18** 62.40N 51.26E
Tralee Rep. of Ire. **7** 52.16N 9.42W
Tralee B. Rep. of Ire. **7** 52.18N 9.55W
Tranås Sweden **17** 58.03N 14.59E
Trang Thailand **29** 7.35N 99.35E
Trangan *i.* Indonesia **27** 6.30S134.15E
Trangie Australia **47** 32.03S148.01E
Trani Italy **12** 41.17N 16.26E
Tranqueras Uruguay **63** 31.12S 55.45W
Transkei *f.* R.S.A. **39** 32.12S 28.20E
Transvaal *d.* R.S.A. **39** 24.30S 29.30E
Transylvanian Alps *see* Carpații Meridionalimts. *mts.* Romania **13**
Trapani Italy **12** 38.02N 12.30E
Traralgon Australia **47** 38.12S146.32E
Traryd Sweden **17** 56.35N 13.45E
Trasimeno, Lago *l.* Italy **12** 43.09N 12.07E
Traunstein W. Germany **14** 47.52N 12.38E
Travellers L. Australia **46** 33.18S142.00E
Travers, Mt. New Zealand **48** 42.05S172.45E
Traverse City U.S.A. **55** 44.46N 85.38W
Travnik Yugo. **13** 44.14N 17.40E
Trayning Australia **43** 31.09S117.46E
Trbovlje Yugo. **14** 46.10N 15.03E
Trebbia *r.* Italy **9** 45.04N 9.41E
Třebíč Czech. **14** 49.13N 15.55E
Trebinje Yugo. **13** 42.43N 18.20E
Trebišov Czech. **15** 48.40N 21.47E
Třeboň Czech. **14** 49.01N 14.50E
Trecate Italy **9** 45.26N 8.44E
Tredegar U.K. **5** 51.47N 3.16W
Tregaron U.K. **5** 52.14N 3.56W
Tregosse Islets and Reefs Australia **44** 17.41S150.43E
Tréguier France **11** 48.47N 3.16W
Treinta-y-Tres Uruguay **59** 33.16S 54.17W
Treis W. Germany **8** 50.10N 7.20E
Trélazé France **9** 47.27N 0.28W
Trelew Argentina **63** 43.15S 65.20W
Trelleborg Sweden **17** 55.22N 13.10E
Trélon France **8** 50.04N 4.05E
Tremadog B. U.K. **4** 52.52N 4.14W
Tremp Spain **10** 42.10N 0.52E
Trenčín Czech. **15** 48.54N 18.04E
Trenque Lauquen Argentina **63** 35.56S 62.43W
Trent *r.* U.K. **4** 53.41N 0.41W
Trentino-Alto Adige *d.* Italy **9** 46.30N 11.20E
Trento Italy **9** 46.04N 11.08E
Trenton Canada **55** 44.06N 77.35W
Trenton N.J. U.S.A. **55** 40.15N 74.43W
Trepassey Canada **51** 46.44N 53.22W
Tres Árboles Uruguay **63** 32.24S 56.43W
Tres Arroyos Argentina **63** 38.26S 60.17W
Três Corações Brazil **59** 21.44S 45.15W
Três Lagoas Brazil **59** 20.46S 51.43W
Três Marias, Represa *resr.* Brazil **59** 18.15S 45.15W
Três Pontas Brazil **59** 21.23S 45.29W
Três Rios Brazil **59** 22.07S 43.12W
Treuchtlingen W. Germany **14** 48.57N 10.55E
Treviglio Italy **9** 45.31N 9.35E
Treviso Italy **9** 45.40N 12.14E
Tribulation, C. Australia **44** 16.03S145.30E
Trida Australia **47** 33.00S145.01E
Trier W. Germany **8** 49.45N 6.39E
Trieste Italy **12** 45.40N 13.47E
Triglav *mtn.* Yugo. **12** 46.21N 13.50E
Trikala Greece **13** 39.34N 21.46E
Trikomon Cyprus **32** 35.17N 33.53E
Trincomalee Sri Lanka **29** 8.34N 81.13E
Trinidad Bolivia **62** 14.47S 64.47W
Trinidad Colombia **60** 5.25N 71.40W
Trinidad Cuba **57** 21.48N 80.00W
Trinidad Uruguay **63** 33.32S 56.54W
Trinidad U.S.A. **52** 37.10N104.31W
Trinidad & Tobago S. America **57** 10.30N 61.20W
Trinity *r.* U.S.A. **53** 29.55N 94.45W
Trinity B. Australia **44** 16.56S145.50E
Trinity Range *mts.* U.S.A. **54** 40.13N119.12W
Trino Italy **9** 45.12N 8.18E
Tripoli *see* Țarābulus Lebanon **32**
Tripoli *see* Țarābulus Libya **34**
Trípolis Greece **13** 37.31N 22.21E
Tripolitania *f. see* Țarābulus *f.* Libya **34**
Tripura *d.* India **29** 23.45N 91.45E
Trivandrum India **28** 8.41N 76.57E
Trnava Czech. **15** 48.23N 17.35E
Troarn France **9** 49.11N 0.11W
Trobriand Is. P.N.G. **44** 8.35S151.05E
Troglav *mtn.* Yugo. **13** 43.57N 16.36E
Troisdorf W. Germany **8** 50.50N 7.07E
Trois-Rivières *town* Canada **55** 46.21N 72.33W
Troitsk U.S.S.R. **20** 54.08N 61.33E
Troitsko-Pechorsk U.S.S.R. **18** 62.40N 56.08E
Troitskoye R.S.F.S.R. U.S.S.R. **18** 52.18N 56.26E
Troitskoye UKr.S.S.R. U.S.S.R. **15** 47.38N 30.19E
Trölladyngja *mtn.* Iceland **16** 64.54N 17.16W
Trollhättan Sweden **17** 58.16N 12.18E
Trollheimen *mts.* Norway **16** 62.50N 9.15E
Troms *d.* Norway **16** 69.20N 19.30E
Tromsö Norway **16** 69.42N 19.00E
Trondheim Norway **16** 63.36N 10.23E
Trondheimsfjorden *est.* Norway **16** 63.40N 10.30E
Troödos *mts.* Cyprus **32** 34.57N 32.50E
Troon U.K. **6** 55.33N 4.40W
Tropic U.S.A. **54** 37.37N112.05W
Trosh U.S.S.R. **18** 66.24N 56.08E
Trostan *mtn.* N. Ireland **7** 55.03N 6.10W
Trostyanets U.S.S.R. **15** 48.35N 29.10E
Trout Creek *town* Canada **55** 45.59N 79.22W
Trouville France **9** 49.22N 0.55E
Trowbridge U.K. **5** 51.18N 2.12W
Troy Mont. U.S.A. **54** 48.28N115.53W
Troy N.Y. U.S.A. **55** 42.43N 73.40W
Troy Ohio U.S.A. **55** 40.02N 84.12W
Troyes France **9** 48.18N 4.05E
Troy Peak *mtn.* U.S.A. **54** 38.19N115.30W
Trpanj Yugo. **13** 43.00N 17.17E
Truchas Peak *mtn.* U.S.A. **52** 35.58N105.39W
Truckee U.S.A. **54** 39.20N120.11W
Trujillo Honduras **57** 15.55N 86.00W
Trujillo Peru **60** 8.06S 79.00W
Trujillo Spain **10** 39.28N 5.53W
Trujillo Venezuela **60** 9.20N 70.37W
Trundle Australia **47** 32.54S147.35E
Truro Australia **46** 34.23S139.09E
Truro Canada **51** 45.24N 63.18W
Truro U.K. **5** 50.17N 5.02W
Truslove Australia **43** 33.19S121.40E
Trustrup Denmark **17** 56.21N 10.47E
Trust Territory of the Pacific Is. Pacific Oc. **40** 10.00N155.00E
Trysil Norway **17** 61.19N 12.16E
Trysil *r.* Norway **17** 61.03N 12.30E
Trzemeszno Poland **15** 52.35N 17.50E
Tsaratanana, Massif de *mts.* Madagascar **36** 14.00S 49.00E
Tsau Botswana **39** 20.10S 22.29E
Tsavo Nat. Park Kenya **37** 2.45S 38.45E
Tselinograd U.S.S.R. **20** 51.10N 71.28E
Tses Namibia **39** 25.58S 18.08E
Tsévié Togo **38** 6.28N 1.15E
Tshabong Botswana **39** 26.03S 22.25E
Tshane Botswana **39** 24.02S 21.54E
Tshesebe Botswana **39** 20.45S 27.31E
Tsimlyansk U.S.S.R. **19** 47.40N 42.06E
Tsimlyanskoye Vodokhranilishche *resr.* U.S.S.R. **19** 48.00N 43.00E
Tsingtao *see* Qingdao China **25**
Tsiribihina Madagascar **39** 19.42S 44.31E
Tsivilsk U.S.S.R. **18** 55.50N 47.28E
Tskhinvali U.S.S.R. **19** 42.14N 43.58E
Tsna *r.* B.S.S.R. U.S.S.R. **15** 52.10N 27.03E
Tsna *r.* R.S.F.S.R. U.S.S.R. **18** 54.45N 41.54E
Tsobis Namibia **39** 19.27S 17.30E
Tsu Japan **23** 34.43N136.31E
Tsuchiura Japan **23** 36.05N140.12E
Tsudakhar U.S.S.R. **19** 42.20N 47.11E
Tsumeb Namibia **39** 19.12S 17.43E
Tsuru Japan **23** 35.30N138.56E
Tsushima Japan **23** 35.10N136.43E
Tsushima *i.* Japan **25** 34.30N129.20E
Tuam Rep. of Ire. **7** 53.32N 8.52W
Tuamotu, Îles *is.* Pacific Oc. **40** 17.00S142.00W
Tuapse U.S.S.R. **19** 44.06N 39.05E
Tuatapere New Zealand **48** 46.08S167.41E
Tuba City U.S.A. **54** 36.08N111.14W
Tubarão Brazil **59** 28.30S 49.01W
Țubayq, Jabal aț *mts.* Saudi Arabia **32** 29.30N 37.15E
Tubbercurry Rep. of Ire. **7** 54.03N 8.45W
Tübingen W. Germany **14** 48.32N 9.04E
Țubjah, Wādī *r.* Saudi Arabia **30** 25.35N 38.22E
Țubruq Libya **35** 32.06N 23.58E
Tucacas Venezuela **60** 10.48N 68.19W
Tuchola Poland **15** 53.35N 17.50E
Tucson U.S.A. **52** 32.13N110.58W
Tucumán *d.* Argentina **62** 26.30S 65.20W
Tucumcari U.S.A. **52** 35.10N103.44W
Tucupita Venezuela **60** 9.02N 62.04W
Tucuruí Brazil **61** 3.42S 49.44W
Tudela Spain **10** 42.04N 1.37W
Tudmur Syria **30** 34.36N 38.15E
Tuen Australia **47** 28.33S145.38E
Tufi P.N.G. **44** 9.05S149.20E
Tugela R.S.A. **39** 29.10S 31.25E
Tuguegarao Phil. **27** 17.36N121.44E
Tugur U.S.S.R. **21** 53.44N136.45E
Tukangbesi, Kepulauan *is.* Indonesia **27** 5.30S124.00E
Tukayyid *well* Iraq **31** 29.47N 45.36E
Țūkh Egypt **32** 30.21N 31.12E
Tuktoyaktuk Canada **50** 69.27N133.00W
Tukums U.S.S.R. **17** 57.00N 23.10E
Tukuyu Tanzania **37** 9.20S 33.37E
Tula Mexico **56** 23.00N 99.43W
Tula U.S.S.R. **18** 54.11N 37.38E
Tulare U.S.A. **54** 36.13N119.21W
Tulare L. *resr.* U.S.A. **54** 36.03N119.49W
Tulcán Ecuador **60** 0.50N 77.48W
Tulcea Romania **13** 45.10N 28.50E
Tulchin U.S.S.R. **15** 48.40N 28.49E
Tuli Indonesia **27** 1.25S122.23E
Tuli Zimbabwe **39** 21.50S 29.15E
Tuli *r.* Zimbabwe **39** 21.49S 29.00E
Țūlkarm Jordan **32** 32.19N 35.02E
Tullamore Australia **47** 32.39S147.39E
Tullamore Rep. of Ire. **7** 53.17N 7.31W
Tulle France **11** 45.16N 1.46E
Tullins France **11** 45.18N 5.29E
Tullow Rep. of Ire. **7** 52.49N 6.45W
Tully Australia **44** 17.55S145.59E
Tully U.S.A. **55** 42.47N 76.06W
Tuloma *r.* U.S.S.R. **18** 68.56N 33.00E
Tulsa U.S.A. **53** 36.07N 95.58W
Tuluá Colombia **60** 4.05N 76.12W
Tulumbasy U.S.S.R. **18** 57.27N 57.40E
Tulun U.S.S.R. **21** 54.32N100.35E
Tulungagung Indonesia **26** 8.03S111.54E
Tum Indonesia **27** 3.28S130.21E
Tumaco Colombia **60** 1.51N 78.46W
Tumba Sweden **17** 59.12N 17.49E
Tumbarumba Australia **47** 35.49S148.01E
Tumbes Peru **60** 3.37S 80.27W
Tumby Bay *town* Australia **46** 34.20S136.05E
Tumeremo Venezuela **60** 7.18N 61.30W
Tummel, Loch U.K. **6** 56.43N 3.55W
Tump Pakistan **28** 26.06N 62.24E
Tumuc Humac Mts. S. America **61** 2.20N 54.50W
Tumut Australia **47** 35.20S148.14E
Tunari *mtn.* Bolivia **62** 17.18S 66.22W
Tūnat al Jabal Egypt **32** 27.46N 30.44E
Tunceli Turkey **30** 39.07N 39.34E
Tunduma Tanzania **37** 9.19S 32.47E
Tunduru Tanzania **37** 11.08S 37.21E
Tundzha *r.* Bulgaria **13** 41.40N 26.34E
Tungabhadra *r.* India **28** 16.00N 78.15E
Tungsten U.S.A. **54** 40.48N118.08W
Tunis Tunisia **34** 36.47N 10.10E
Tunisia Africa **34** 34.00N 9.00E
Tunja Colombia **60** 5.33N 73.23W
Tunnsjöen *l.* Norway **16** 64.45N 13.25E
Tunuyán *r.* Argentina **63** 33.33S 67.30W
Tuoy-Khaya U.S.S.R. **21** 62.33N111.25E
Tupã Brazil **59** 21.57S 50.28W
Tupelo U.S.A. **53** 34.15N 88.43W
Tupinambaranas, Ilha *f.* Brazil **61** 3.00S 58.00W
Tupiza Bolivia **62** 21.27S 65.43W
Tuquan China **25** 45.22N121.41E
Túquerres Colombia **60** 1.06N 77.37W
Tura Tanzania **37** 5.30S 33.50E
Tura U.S.S.R. **21** 64.05N100.00E
Turangi New Zealand **48** 38.59S175.48E
Turbaco Colombia **60** 10.20N 75.25W
Turbanovo U.S.S.R. **18** 60.05N 50.46E
Turbo Colombia **60** 8.06N 76.44W
Turda Romania **15** 46.34N 23.47E
Turek Poland **15** 52.02N 18.30E
Turgeon *r.* Canada **55** 50.00N 78.54W
Tŭrgovishte Bulgaria **13** 43.14N 26.37E
Turgutlu Turkey **13** 38.30N 27.43E
Turhal Turkey **30** 40.23N 36.05E
Türi U.S.S.R. **17** 58.48N 25.26E
Turia *r.* Spain **10** 39.27N 0.19W
Turiaçu Brazil **61** 1.41S 45.21W
Turiaçu *r.* Brazil **61** 1.36S 45.19W
Turin *see* Torino Italy **9**
Turka U.S.S.R. **15** 49.10N 23.02E
Turkana, L. Kenya **37** 4.00N 36.00E
Turkestan U.S.S.R. **24** 43.17N 68.16E
Turkey Asia **30** 39.00N 35.00E
Turkey Creek *town* Australia **42** 17.04S128.15E
Turkmenskaya S.S.R. *d.* U.S.S.R. **20** 40.00N 60.00E
Turks Is. Turks & Caicos Is. **57** 21.30N 71.10W
Turku Finland **17** 60.27N 22.17E
Turku-Pori *d.* Finland **17** 61.00N 22.35E
Turkwel *r.* Kenya **37** 3.08N 35.39E
Turneffe Is. Belize **57** 17.30N 87.45W
Turnhout Belgium **8** 51.19N 4.57E
Turnu Măgurele Romania **13** 43.43N 24.53E
Turnu Roşu, Pasul *pass* Romania **13** 45.37N 24.17E
Turnu-Severin Romania **13** 44.37N 22.39E
Turon *r.* Australia **47** 33.03S149.33E
Turov U.S.S.R. **15** 52.04N 27.40E
Turpan China **24** 42.55N 89.06E
Turpan Pendi *f.* China **24** 43.40N 89.00E
Turquino *mtn.* Cuba **57** 20.05N 76.50W
Turret Range *mts.* Australia **46** 29.43S136.42E
Turriff U.K. **6** 57.32N 2.28W
Turtkul U.S.S.R. **31** 41.30N 61.00E
Turukhansk U.S.S.R. **21** 65.21N 88.05E
Turya *r.* U.S.S.R. **15** 51.48N 24.52E
Tuscaloosa U.S.A. **53** 33.12N 87.33W
Tuscarora U.S.A. **54** 41.19N116.14W
Tuticorin India **29** 8.48N 78.10E
Tutóia Brazil **61** 2.45S 42.16W
Tutrakan Bulgaria **13** 44.02N 26.40E
Tuttlingen W. Germany **14** 47.59N 8.49E
Tutuala Indonesia **27** 8.24S127.15E
Tutubu Tanzania **37** 5.28S 32.43E
Tuțūn Egypt **32** 29.09N 30.46E
Tuul Gol *r.* Mongolia **24** 48.53N104.35E
Tuvalu Pacific Oc. **40** 8.00S178.00E
Tuxpan Mexico **56** 21.00N 97.23W
Tuxtla Gutiérrez Mexico **56** 16.45N 93.09W
Túy Spain **10** 42.03N 8.39W
Tuz Gölü *l.* Turkey **30** 38.45N 33.24E
Țūz Khurmātū Iraq **31** 34.53N 44.38E
Tuzla Yugo. **13** 44.33N 18.41E
Tvedestrand Norway **17** 58.37N 8.55E
Tveitsund Norway **17** 59.01N 8.32E
Tweed *r.* U.K. **6** 55.46N 2.00W
Twentynine Palms U.S.A. **54** 34.08N116.03W
Twin Bridges *town* U.S.A. **54** 45.33N112.20W
Twin Falls *town* U.S.A. **54** 42.34N114.28W
Twins Creek *r.* Australia **46** 29.10S139.27E
Twizel New Zealand **48** 44.15S170.06E
Twofold B. Australia **47** 37.06S149.55E
Twyford U.K. **5** 51.01N 1.19W
Tyler Tex. U.S.A. **53** 32.22N 95.18W
Tyndinskiy U.S.S.R. **21** 55.11N124.34E
Tyne *r.* U.K. **4** 55.00N 1.25W
Tyne and Wear *d.* U.K. **4** 54.57N 1.35W
Tynemouth U.K. **4** 55.01N 1.24W
Tynset Norway **17** 62.17N 10.47E
Tyre *see* Şūr Lebanon **32**
Tyrifjorden *l.* Norway **17** 60.02N 10.08E
Tyrone *d.* U.K. **7** 54.35N 7.15W
Tyrone U.S.A. **55** 40.40N 78.14W
Tyrrell *r.* Australia **46** 35.28S142.55E
Tyrrell, L. Australia **46** 35.22S142.50E
Tyrrhenian Sea Med. Sea **12** 40.00N 12.00E
Tysnesöy *i.* Norway **17** 60.00N 5.35E
Tyumen U.S.S.R. **20** 57.11N 65.29E
Tywi *r.* U.K. **5** 51.46N 4.22W
Tzaneen R.S.A. **39** 23.49S 30.10E

U

Uanda Australia **44** 21.34S144.54E
Uatumã *r.* Brazil **61** 2.30S 57.40W
Uaupés Brazil **60** 0.07S 67.05W
Uaupés *r.* Brazil **60** 0.00S 67.10W
Ubá Brazil **59** 21.08S 42.59W
Ubangi *r.* Congo/Zaïre **36** 0.25S 17.50E
Ubatuba Brazil **59** 23.26S 45.05W
Ubayyiḍ, Wādī al *r.* Iraq **30** 32.04N 42.17E
Ubeda Spain **10** 38.01N 3.22W
Uberaba Brazil **59** 19.47S 47.57W
Uberlândia Brazil **59** 18.57S 48.17W
Ubombo R.S.A. **39** 27.35S 32.05E
Ubort *r.* U.S.S.R. **15** 52.06N 28.28E
Ubundu Zaïre **35** 0.24S 25.28E
Ucayali *r.* Peru **60** 4.40S 73.20W
Udaipur India **28** 24.36N 73.47E
Udaquiola Argentina **63** 36.35S 58.30W
Uddevalla Sweden **17** 58.21N 11.55E
Uddjaur *l.* Sweden **16** 65.55N 17.49E
Udine Italy **9** 46.03N 13.15E
Udipi India **28** 13.21N 74.45E
Udon Thani Thailand **29** 17.29N102.46E
Uele *r.* Zaïre **36** 4.08N 22.25E
Uelzen W. Germany **14** 52.58N 10.34E
Ueno Japan **23** 34.45N136.08E
Ufa U.S.S.R. **18** 54.45N 55.58E
Ufa *r.* U.S.S.R. **18** 54.45N 56.00E
Uffculme U.K. **5** 50.45N 3.19W
Ugab *r.* Namibia **39** 21.12S 13.37E
Ugalla *r.* Tanzania **37** 5.43S 31.10E
Uganda Africa **37** 2.00N 33.00E
Ugep Nigeria **38** 5.48N 8.05E
Ughelli Nigeria **38** 5.33N 6.00E
Uglegorsk U.S.S.R. **21** 49.01N142.04E
Uglovka U.S.S.R. **18** 58.13N 33.30E
Ugoma *mtn.* Zaïre **37** 4.00S 28.45E
Ugra *r.* U.S.S.R. **18** 54.30N 36.10E
Uherske Hradiště Czech. **15** 49.05N 17.28E
Uig U.K. **6** 57.35N 6.22W
Uíge Angola **36** 7.40S 15.09E
Uil U.S.S.R. **19** 49.08N 54.43E
Uil *r.* U.S.S.R. **19** 48.33N 52.25E
Uinta Mts. U.S.A. **54** 40.45N110.05W
Uitenhage R.S.A. **39** 33.46S 25.23E
Uithuizen Neth. **8** 53.24N 6.41E
Uivlleq *see* Nanortalik Greenland **51**
Uji *r.* Japan **23** 34.53N135.48E
Ujiji Tanzania **37** 4.55S 29.39E
Ujjain India **28** 23.11N 75.50E
Ujpest Hungary **15** 47.33N 19.05E
Ujście Poland **14** 53.04N 16.43E
Ujung Pandang Indonesia **26** 5.09S119.28E
Uka U.S.S.R. **21** 57.50N162.02E
Ukerewe I. Tanzania **37** 2.00S 33.00E
Ukhta U.S.S.R. **18** 63.33N 53.44E
Ukiah U.S.A. **54** 39.09N123.13W
Ukmerge U.S.S.R. **15** 55.14N 24.49E
Ukrainskaya S.S.R. *d.* U.S.S.R. **15** 49.45N 27.00E
Ukwi Botswana **39** 23.22S 20.30E
Ulaanbaatar Mongolia **24** 47.54N106.52E
Ulaangom Mongolia **24** 49.59N 92.00E
Ulan Bator *see* Ulaanbaatar Mongolia **24**
Ulan-Ude U.S.S.R. **24** 51.55N107.40E
Ulan Ul Hu *l.* China **29** 34.45N 90.25E
Ulcinj Yugo. **13** 41.55N 19.11E
Ulenia, L. Australia **46** 29.57S142.24E

ásnagar India 28 19.13N 73.07E
astay Mongolia 24 47.42N 96.52E
r. Spain 10 42.38N 8.45W
adulla Australia 47 35.21S150.25E
inger Sweden 16 62.58N 18.16E
apool U.K. 6 57.54N 5.10W
swater l. U.K. 4 54.34N 2.52W
n W. Germany 14 48.24N 10.00E
ngwé Mozambique 37 14.34S 34.21E
cehamn Sweden 17 57.47N 13.25E
an S. Korea 25 35.32N129.21E
berg Norway 16 62.45N 9.59E
ma Australia 46 35.30S143.20E
a r. Honduras 57 15.50N 87.38W
guru Mts. Tanzania 37 7.05S 37.40E
erston U.K. 4 54.13N 3.07W
erstone Australia 45 41.09S146.10E
yanovsk U.S.S.R. 18 54.19N 48.22E
aisha Nigeria 38 8.01N 7.12E
ala Bolivia 62 17.21S 68.00W
an U.S.S.R. 15 48.45N 30.10E
bria d. Italy 12 42.55N 12.10E
e r. Sweden 16 63.47N 20.16E
e r. Zimbabwe 39 17.00S 28.22E
eå Sweden 16 63.45N 20.20E
fors Sweden 16 65.56N 15.00E
fuli r. Zimbabwe 39 17.32S 29.23E
iat U.S.A. 50 69.25N152.10W
m-al-Qaywayn U.A.E. 31 25.32N 55.34E
m Durmân Sudan 35 15.37N 32.59E
m el Fahm Israel 32 32.31N 35.09E
m Lajj Saudi Arabia 30 25.03N 37.17E
niati Zimbabwe 39 18.41S 29.45E
niati r. Zimbabwe 39 17.32S 29.23E
tata R.S.A. 39 31.35S 28.47E
uahia Nigeria 38 5.31N 7.26E
zimkulu R.S.A. 39 30.15S 29.56E
zimvubu R.S.A. 39 31.37S 29.32E
a r. Yugo. 13 45.16N 16.55E
alakleet U.S.A. 50 63.53N160.47W
ayzah Jordan 32 30.29N 35.48E
ayzah Saudi Arabia 31 26.05N 43.57E
ayzah, Jabal mtn. Iraq 30 32.15N 39.19E
cia Bolivia 62 18.27S 66.37W
compahgre Peak U.S.A. 54 38.04N107.28W
compahgre Plateau f. U.S.A. 54 8.30N108.25W
derberg R.S.A. 39 29.46S 29.26E
derbool Australia 46 35.10S141.50E
echa U.S.S.R. 15 52.52N 32.42E
garie Australia 47 33.38S147.00E
gava, Péninsule d' pen. Canada 51 60.00N 4.00W
gava B. Canada 51 59.00N 67.30W
ggi N. Korea 25 42.19N130.24E
ião Brazil 61 4.35S 42.52W
ião da Vitória Brazil 59 26.13S 51.05W
imak I. U.S.A. 50 54.50N164.00W
ini Peru 60 10.41S 73.59W
iondale R.S.A. 39 33.39S 23.07E
ion Gap U.S.A. 54 46.34N120.34W
ion of Soviet Socialist Republics Europe / Asia 5 50.00N 28.00E
iontown U.S.A. 55 39.54N 79.44W
ited Arab Emirates Asia 31 24.00N 54.00E
ited Kingdom Europe 3 54.00N 2.00W
ited States of America N. America 52 9.00N100.00W
na W. Germany 8 51.32N 7.41E
st i. U.K. 6 60.45N 0.55W
ye Turkey 30 41.09N 37.15E
ata Venezuela 60 8.02N 62.25W
ernavik Greenland 51 72.50N 56.00W
ington R.S.A. 39 28.26S 21.12E
per d. Ghana 38 10.30N 1.40W
per Egypt see Aş Şa'īd f. Egypt 30
per Hutt New Zealand 48 41.07S175.04E
per Klamath L. U.S.A. 54 42.23N122.55W
per Lough Erne N. Ireland 7 54.13N 7.32W
per Tean U.K. 4 52.57N 1.59W
per Yarra Dam Australia 47 37.43S145.56E
psala Sweden 17 59.52N 17.38E
psala d. Sweden 17 60.10N 17.50E
lat aş Şuqūr Saudi Arabia 30 25.50N 42.12E
ruins Iraq 31 30.55N 46.07E
acoa Venezuela 60 9.03N 62.27W
aga-suido str. Japan 23 35.10N139.42E
al r. U.S.S.R. 19 47.00N 52.00E
alla Australia 47 30.40S151.31E
al Mts. see Uralskiy Khrebet mts. U.S.S.R. 18
al'sk U.S.S.R. 19 51.19N 51.20E
alskiy Khrebet mts. U.S.S.R. 18 60.00N 59.00E
ana Australia 47 35.21S146.19E
ana, L. Australia 47 35.21S146.19E
andangi Australia 44 21.36S138.18E
anium City Canada 50 59.32N108.43W
aricoera r. Brazil 60 3.10N 60.30W
awa Japan 23 35.51N139.39E
ay U.S.S.R. 20 60.11N 65.00E
bino Italy 12 43.43N 12.38E
cos Peru 60 13.40S 71.38W
da U.S.S.R. 19 48.44N 47.30E
dzhar U.S.S.R. 20 47.06N 81.33E
e r. U.K. 4 54.05N 1.20W
echye U.S.S.R. 15 52.59N 27.50E
en U.S.S.R. 18 57.30N 45.50E
engoy U.S.S.R. 20 65.59N 78.30E
es Mexico 56 29.26N110.24W
fa Turkey 30 37.08N 38.45E
güp Turkey 30 38.39N 34.55E
ibia Colombia 60 11.43N 72.16W
imbin Australia 46 28.15S143.46E
isino Australia 46 29.44S143.49E
jala Finland 17 61.05N 23.32E
k Neth. 8 52.40N 5.36E
lingford Rep. of Ire. 7 52.44N 7.35W
mia, L. see Daryācheh-ye Rezā'īyeh l. Iran 31
nograč Yugo. 14 45.10N 15.57E
Ursus Poland 15 52.12N 20.53E
Uruaçu Brazil 61 14.30S 49.10W
Uruapan Mexico 56 19.26N102.04W
Urubamba Peru 60 13.20S 72.07W
Urubamba r. Peru 60 10.43S 73.55W
Urucará Brazil 61 2.32S 57.45W
Uruçui Brazil 61 7.14S 44.33W
Uruguaiana Brazil 63 29.45S 57.05W
Uruguay r. Argentina / Uruguay 63 34.00S 58.30W
Uruguay S. America 59 33.15S 56.00W
Ürümqi China 24 43.43N 87.38E
Urun P.N.G. 44 8.36S147.15E
Urunga Australia 47 30.30S152.28E
Urup r. U.S.S.R. 19 44.59N 41.12E
Urzhum U.S.S.R. 18 57.08N 50.00E
Urziceni Romania 13 44.43N 26.38E
Usa r. U.S.S.R. 18 65.58N 56.35E
Uşak Turkey 30 38.42N 29.25E
Usakos Namibia 39 22.02S 15.35E
Usambara Mts. Tanzania 37 4.45S 38.25E
Ushant i. see Ouessant, Île d' i. France 11
Ush-Tobe U.S.S.R. 24 45.15N 77.59E
Ushuaia Argentina 63 54.47S 68.20W
Ushumun U.S.S.R. 21 52.48N126.27E
Usisya Malaŵi 37 11.10S 34.12E
Usk r. U.K. 5 51.34N 2.59W
Uskedal Norway 17 59.56N 5.52E
Üsküdar Turkey 13 41.00N 29.03E
Usman U.S.S.R. 19 52.02N 39.43E
Usovo U.S.S.R. 15 51.20N 28.01E
Uspenskiy U.S.S.R. 20 48.41N 72.43E
Ussuriysk U.S.S.R. 25 43.48N131.59E
Ustaoset Norway 17 60.30N 8.04E
Ustica i. Italy 12 38.42N 13.11E
Ust'-Ilga U.S.S.R. 21 54.59N105.00E
Ústí nad Labem Czech. 14 50.41N 14.00E
Ustinov U.S.S.R. 18 56.49N 53.11E
Ust Ishim U.S.S.R. 20 57.45N 71.05E
Ustka Poland 14 54.35N 16.50E
Ust'kamchatsk U.S.S.R. 21 56.14N162.28E
Ust-Kamenogorsk U.S.S.R. 20 50.00N 82.40E
Ust Kulom U.S.S.R. 18 61.34N 53.40E
Ust Kut U.S.S.R. 21 56.40N105.50E
Ust Lyzha U.S.S.R. 18 65.45N 56.38E
Ust'Maya U.S.S.R. 21 60.25N134.28E
Ust Nem U.S.S.R. 18 61.38N 54.50E
Ust Olenëk U.S.S.R. 21 72.59N120.00E
Ust-Omchug U.S.S.R. 21 61.08N149.38E
Ust Port U.S.S.R. 20 69.44N 84.23E
Ust Tapsuy U.S.S.R. 18 62.25N 61.42E
Ust'Tsilma U.S.S.R. 18 65.28N 53.09E
Ust-Tungir U.S.S.R. 21 55.25N120.15E
Ust Ura U.S.S.R. 18 63.06N 44.41E
Ust Vaga U.S.S.R. 18 62.42N 42.45E
Ust Vym U.S.S.R. 18 62.15N 50.25E
Ustyurt, Plato f. U.S.S.R. 19 43.30N 55.00E
Usu China 24 44.27N 84.37E
Usumacinta r. Mexico 56 18.22N 92.40W
U.S. Virgin Is. C. America 57 18.30N 65.00W
Ut U.S.S.R. 15 52.18N 31.10E
Utah d. U.S.A. 54 39.37N112.28W
Utah L. U.S.A. 54 40.13N111.49W
'Utaybah, Buḩayrat al l. Syria 32 33.31N 36.37E
Utengule Tanzania 37 8.55S 35.43E
Utete Tanzania 37 8.00S 38.49E
Utiariti Brazil 60 13.02S 58.17W
Utica N.Y. U.S.A. 55 43.05N 75.14W
Utiel Spain 10 39.33N 1.13W
Utopia Australia 44 22.14S134.33E
Utrecht Neth. 8 52.04N 5.07E
Utrecht d. Neth. 8 52.04N 5.10E
Utrecht R.S.A. 39 27.38S 30.19E
Utrera Spain 10 37.10N 5.47W
Utsjoki Finland 16 69.53N 27.00E
Utsunomiya Japan 25 36.33N139.52E
Utta U.S.S.R. 19 46.24N 46.01E
Uttaradit Thailand 29 17.38N100.05E
Uttar Pradesh d. India 29 27.40N 80.00E
Uummannarsuaq see Farvel, Kap c. Greenland 51
Uusikaupunki Finland 17 60.48N 21.25E
Uusimaa d. Finland 17 60.30N 25.00E
Uvalde U.S.A. 52 29.14N 99.49W
Uvarovichi U.S.S.R. 15 52.35N 30.44E
Uvat U.S.S.R. 20 59.10N 68.49E
Uvinza Tanzania 37 5.08S 30.23E
Uvira Zaïre 37 3.22S 29.06E
Uvs Nuur l. Mongolia 24 50.30N 92.30E
Uwajima Japan 25 33.13N132.32E
Uwayl Sudan 35 8.46N 27.24E
Uyo Nigeria 38 5.01N 7.56E
Uyuni Bolivia 62 20.28S 66.50W
Uyuni, Salar de f. Bolivia 62 20.20S 67.42W
Uzbekskaya S.S.R. d. U.S.S.R. 20 42.00N 63.00E
Uzda U.S.S.R. 15 53.28N 27.11E
Uzh r. U.S.S.R. 15 51.15N 30.12E
Uzhgorod U.S.S.R. 15 48.38N 22.15E

V

Vaagö i. Faroe Is. 16 62.03N 7.14W
Vaal r. R.S.A. 39 29.04S 23.37E
Vaala Finland 16 64.26N 26.48E
Vaal Dam R.S.A. 39 26.51S 28.08E
Vaasa Finland 16 63.06N 21.36E
Vaasa d. Finland 16 62.50N 22.50E
Vác Hungary 15 47.49N 19.10E
Vadodara India 28 22.19N 73.14E
Vado Ligure Italy 9 44.17N 8.27E
Vadsö Norway 16 70.05N 29.46E
Vaduz Liech. 14 47.08N 9.32E
Vaeröy i. Norway 16 67.40N 12.40E
Vaga r. U.S.S.R. 18 62.45N 42.48E
Vågåmo Norway 17 61.53N 9.06E
Vaggeryd Sweden 17 57.30N 14.07E
Váh r. Czech. 15 47.40N 17.50E
Vahsel B. Antarctica 64 77.00S 38.00W
Vailly-sur-Aisne France 9 49.25N 3.31E
Vakarai Sri Lanka 29 8.08N 81.26E
Vålådalen Sweden 16 63.09N 13.00E
Valavsk U.S.S.R. 15 51.40N 28.38E
Valcheta Argentina 63 40.40S 66.10W
Valdagno Italy 9 45.39N 11.18E
Valday U.S.S.R. 18 57.59N 33.10E
Valdayskaya Vozvyshennost mts. U.S.S.R. 18 57.10N 33.00E
Valdemārpils U.S.S.R. 17 57.22N 22.35E
Valdemarsvik Sweden 17 58.12N 16.36E
Valdepeñas Spain 10 38.46N 3.24W
Valdés, Pen. Argentina 63 42.30S 64.00W
Valdez U.S.A. 50 61.07N146.17W
Val d'Isère France 9 45.27N 6.59E
Valdivia Chile 63 39.46S 73.15W
Val d'Oise d. France 9 49.10N 2.10E
Val d'Or town Canada 55 48.07N 77.47W
Valença Bahia Brazil 61 13.22S 39.06W
Valença R. de Janeiro Brazil 59 22.14S 43.45W
Valença Portugal 10 42.02N 8.38W
Valence France 11 44.56N 4.54E
Valencia Spain 10 39.29N 0.24W
Valencia d. Spain 10 39.30N 0.40W
Valencia Venezuela 60 10.14N 67.59W
Valencia, Golfo de g. Spain 10 39.38N 0.20W
Valencia de Alcántara Spain 10 39.25N 7.14
Valenciennes France 8 50.22N 3.32E
Vale of Evesham f. U.K. 5 52.05N 1.55W
Vale of Pewsey f. U.K. 5 51.21N 1.45W
Vale of York f. U.K. 4 54.12N 1.25W
Valera Venezuela 60 9.21N 70.38W
Valga U.S.S.R. 18 57.44N 26.06E
Valinco, Golfe de g. France 11 41.40N 8.50E
Valjevo Yugo. 15 44.16N 19.56E
Valkeakoski Finland 17 61.16N 24.02E
Valkenswaard Neth. 8 51.21N 5.27E
Valladolid Mexico 57 20.41N 88.12W
Valladolid Spain 10 41.39N 4.45W
Vall de Uxó town Spain 10 39.49N 0.15W
Valle Norway 17 59.12N 7.32E
Valle d'Aosta d. Italy 9 45.45N 7.25E
Valle de la Pascua Venezuela 60 9.15N 66.00W
Valledupar Colombia 60 10.31N 73.16W
Valle Edén Uruguay 63 31.50S 56.09W
Vallegrande Bolivia 62 18.29S 64.06W
Vallenar Chile 62 28.35S 70.46W
Valletta Malta 12 35.53N 14.31E
Valley City U.S.A. 52 46.57N 97.58W
Valley Falls town U.S.A. 54 42.29N120.16W
Valleyfield Canada 55 45.15N 74.08W
Vallgrund i. Finland 16 63.12N 21.14E
Valls Spain 10 41.18N 1.15E
Valmiera U.S.S.R. 18 57.32N 25.29E
Valnera mtn. Spain 10 43.10N 3.40W
Valognes France 9 49.31N 1.28W
Valparaíso Chile 63 33.02S 71.38W
Valparaíso Mexico 56 22.46N103.34W
Vals, Tanjung c. Indonesia 27 8.30S137.30E
Valverde Dom. Rep. 57 19.37N 71.04W
Valverde del Camino Spain 10 37.35N 6.45W
Vammala Finland 17 61.20N 22.54E
Van Turkey 30 38.28N 43.20E
Van Blommestein Meer, W.J. resr. Surinam 61 4.45N 55.05W
Vancouver Canada 50 49.13N123.06W
Vancouver U.S.A. 54 45.39N122.40W
Vancouver I. Canada 50 50.00N126.00W
Vanderbilt U.S.A. 55 45.09N 84.39W
Vanderlin I. Australia 44 15.44S137.02E
Van Diemen, C. Australia 44 16.31S139.41E
Van Diemen G. Australia 44 11.50S132.00E
Vandry Canada 55 47.50N 73.34W
Vänern l. Sweden 17 59.00N 13.15E
Vänersborg Sweden 17 58.22N 12.19E
Vang Norway 17 61.10N 8.40E
Vanga Kenya 37 4.37S 39.13E
Van Gölü l. Turkey 30 38.35N 42.52E
Vanimo P.N.G. 27 2.40S141.17E
Vankarem U.S.S.R. 21 67.50N175.51E
Vanna i. Norway 16 70.10N 19.40E
Vännäs Sweden 16 63.58N 19.48E
Vannes France 11 47.40N 2.44W
Vanrhynsdorp R.S.A. 39 31.37S 18.42E
Vansbro Sweden 17 60.31N 14.13E
Vantaa Finland 17 60.13N 25.01E
Vanua Levu i. Fiji 40 16.33S179.15E
Vanuatu Pacific Oc. 40 16.00S167.00E
Van Wert U.S.A. 55 40.53N 84.36W
Vanzylsrus R.S.A. 39 26.51S 22.03E
Vapnyarka U.S.S.R. 15 48.31N 28.44E
Var r. France 14 43.39N 7.11E
Varades France 9 47.23N 1.02W
Varallo Italy 9 45.49N 8.15E
Varāmīn Iran 31 35.20N 51.39E
Vārānasi India 29 25.20N 83.00E
Varangerfjorden est. Norway 16 70.00N 30.00E
Varangerhalvöya pen. Norway 16 70.25N 29.30E
Varaždin Yugo. 12 46.18N 16.20E
Varazze Italy 9 44.22N 8.34E
Varberg Sweden 17 57.06N 12.15E
Vardar r. Yugo. see Axiós r. Greece 13
Varde Denmark 17 55.38N 8.29E
Varel W. Germany 8 53.24N 8.08E
Varennes France 11 46.19N 3.24E
Varese Italy 9 45.48N 8.48E
Varese Ligure Italy 9 44.22N 9.37E
Varginha Brazil 59 21.33S 45.25W
Värmland d. Sweden 17 59.55N 13.00E
Varna Bulgaria 15 43.13N 27.57E
Värnamo Sweden 17 57.11N 14.02E
Várpalota Hungary 15 47.12N 18.09E
Vartofta Sweden 17 58.06N 13.40E
Varzo Italy 9 46.12N 8.15E
Varzy France 9 47.21N 3.23E
Vasa see Vaasa Finland 16
Vascongadas y Navarra d. Spain 10 43.00N 2.45W
Vashka r. U.S.S.R. 18 64.55N 45.50E
Vasilkov U.S.S.R. 15 50.12N 30.15E
Vaslui Romania 15 46.38N 27.44E
Västerås Sweden 17 59.37N 16.33E
Västerbotten d. Sweden 16 64.50N 18.10E
Västerdal r. Sweden 17 60.33N 15.08E
Västernorrland d. Sweden 16 63.20N 17.30E
Västervik Sweden 17 57.45N 16.38E
Västmanland d. Sweden 17 59.50N 16.15E
Vasto Italy 12 42.07N 14.42E
Vatan France 11 47.05N 1.48E
Vatiua Mozambique 37 14.15S 37.22E
Vatnajökull mts. Iceland 16 64.20N 17.00W
Vatneyri Iceland 16 65.36N 23.59W
Vatra Dornei Romania 15 47.21N 25.21E
Vättern l. Sweden 17 58.30N 14.30E
Vaughn Mont. U.S.A. 54 47.35N111.34W
Vaughn N.Mex. U.S.A. 52 34.36N105.13W
Vaupés r. Colombia 60 0.20N 69.00W
Vavuniya Sri Lanka 29 8.45N 80.30E
Växjö Sweden 17 56.52N 14.49E
Vaygach U.S.S.R. 20 70.28N 58.59E
Vaygach, Ostrov i. U.S.S.R. 18 70.00N 59.00E
Vecht r. Neth. 8 52.39N 6.01E
Vecsés Hungary 15 47.26N 19.19E
Veddige Sweden 17 57.16N 12.19E
Veendam Neth. 8 53.08N 6.52E
Veenendaal Neth. 8 52.03N 5.32E
Vega i. Norway 16 65.39N 11.50E
Veghel Neth. 8 51.37N 5.35E
Vegreville Canada 50 53.30N112.02W
Veinticinco de Mayo Argentina 63 35.25S 60.11W
Vejen Denmark 17 55.29N 9.09E
Vejer Spain 10 36.15N 5.59W
Vejle Denmark 17 55.42N 9.32E
Velddrif R.S.A. 39 32.47S 18.09E
Vélez Málaga Spain 10 36.48N 4.05W
Vélez Rubio Spain 10 37.41N 2.05W
Velhas r. Brazil 59 17.20S 44.55W
Velikiye-Luki U.S.S.R. 18 56.19N 30.31E
Velikiy Ustyug U.S.S.R. 18 60.48N 45.15E
Veliko Tŭrnovo Bulgaria 13 43.04N 25.39E
Velizh U.S.S.R. 18 55.36N 31.13E
Velletri Italy 12 41.41N 12.47E
Vellore India 29 12.56N 79.09E
Velsen Neth. 8 52.28N 4.39E
Velsk U.S.S.R. 18 61.05N 42.06E
Veluwe f. Neth. 8 52.17N 5.45E
Vemdalen Sweden 16 62.29N 13.55E
Venado Tuerto Argentina 63 33.45S 61.56W
Venaria Italy 9 45.08N 7.38E
Vence France 9 43.43N 7.07E
Vendas Novas Portugal 10 38.41N 8.27W
Vendeuvre-sur-Barse France 9 48.14N 4.28E
Vendôme France 9 47.48N 1.04E
Veneto d. Italy 9 45.25N 11.50E
Venev U.S.S.R. 18 54.22N 38.15E
Venezia Italy 9 45.26N 12.20E
Venezuela S. America 60 7.00N 65.20W
Venezuela, Golfo de g. Venezuela 60 11.30N 71.00W
Vengurla India 28 15.52N 73.38E
Veniaminof Mtn. U.S.A. 50 56.05N159.20W
Venice see Venezia Italy 9
Venice, G. of Med. Sea 14 45.20N 13.00E
Venlo Neth. 8 51.22N 6.10E
Venraij Neth. 8 51.32N 5.58E
Venta r. U.S.S.R. 17 57.24N 21.33E
Ventersdorp R.S.A. 39 26.19S 26.48E
Ventimiglia Italy 9 43.47N 7.36E
Ventnor U.K. 5 50.35N 1.12W
Ventspils U.S.S.R. 17 57.24N 21.36E
Ventuari r. Venezuela 60 4.00N 67.35W
Venus B. Australia 47 38.40S145.43E
Vera Argentina 59 29.31S 60.30W
Vera Spain 10 37.15N 1.51W
Veracruz Mexico 56 19.11N 96.10W
Veracruz d. Mexico 56 18.00N 95.00W
Verāval India 28 20.53N 70.28E
Verbania Italy 9 45.56N 8.33E
Vercelli Italy 9 45.19N 8.26E
Verde r. Argentina 63 42.10S 65.03W
Verde r. Brazil 62 19.11S 50.44W
Verden W. Germany 14 52.55N 9.13E
Verdon r. France 11 43.42N 5.39E
Verdun Canada 55 45.28N 73.35W
Verdun Meuse France 11 49.10N 5.24E
Vereeniging R.S.A. 39 26.40S 27.55E
Vergelee R.S.A. 39 25.46S 24.09E
Verín Spain 10 41.55N 7.26W
Verkhniy Baskunchak U.S.S.R. 19 48.14N 46.44E
Verkhniy Lyulyukary U.S.S.R. 18 65.45N 64.28E
Verkhniy Shar U.S.S.R. 18 68.21N 50.45E
Verkhniy Ufaley U.S.S.R. 18 56.05N 60.14E
Verkhnyaya Taymyra r. U.S.S.R. 21 74.10N 99.50E
Verkhnyaya Tura U.S.S.R. 18 58.22N 59.50E
Verkhovye U.S.S.R. 18 52.49N 37.14E
Verkhoyansk U.S.S.R. 21 67.25N133.25E
Verkhoyanskiy Khrebet mts. U.S.S.R. 21 66.00N130.00E
Vermenton France 9 47.40N 3.42E
Vermilion Canada 50 53.21N110.52W
Vermilion U.S.A. 55 41.24N 82.21W
Vermont d. U.S.A. 55 43.50N 72.45W
Vernal U.S.A. 54 40.27N109.32W
Verneuil France 9 48.44N 0.56E
Vernon Canada 50 50.16N119.16W
Vernon France 9 49.05N 1.29E
Véroia Greece 13 40.31N 22.12E
Verona Italy 9 45.27N 10.59E
Verónica Argentina 63 35.24S 57.22W
Verrès Italy 9 45.40N 7.42E
Versailles France 9 48.48N 2.08E
Vert, Cap c. Senegal 34 14.45N 17.25W
Vertou France 11 47.10N 1.28W
Vertus France 9 48.54N 4.00E
Verviers Belgium 8 50.36N 5.52E
Vervins France 9 49.50N 3.54E
Vesanto Finland 16 62.56N 26.25E
Veselí nad Lužnicí Czech. 14 49.11N 14.43E
Vesle r. France 9 49.23N 3.38E
Vesoul France 14 47.38N 6.09E
Vest-Agder d. Norway 17 58.30N 7.10E
Vestfjorden est. Norway 16 68.10N 15.00E
Vestfold d. Norway 17 59.20N 10.10E
Vestmanhavn Faroe Is. 16 62.09N 7.11W
Vestmannaeyjar is. Iceland 16 63.30N 20.20W
Vestvågöy i. Norway 16 68.10N 13.50E
Vesuvio mtn. Italy 12 40.48N 14.25E
Vesyegonsk U.S.S.R. 18 58.38N 37.19E
Veszprém Hungary 15 47.06N 17.55E
Vésztő Hungary 15 46.55N 21.16E
Vetka U.S.S.R. 15 52.35N 31.13E
Vetlanda Sweden 17 57.26N 15.04E
Vetluga U.S.S.R. 18 57.50N 45.42E
Vetluga r. U.S.S.R. 18 56.18N 46.19E
Vettore, Monte mtn. Italy 12 42.50N 13.18E
Veurne Belgium 8 51.04N 2.40E
Vevelstad Norway 16 65.43N 12.30E
Vézelise France 11 48.29N 6.05E
Vézère r. France 11 44.53N 0.55E
Vezhen mtn. Bulgaria 13 42.45N 24.22E
Viacha Bolivia 60 16.40S 68.17W
Viadana Italy 9 44.56N 10.31E
Viana Brazil 61 3.13S 45.00W
Viana Portugal 10 38.20N 8.00W
Viana do Castelo Portugal 10 41.41N 8.50W
Viangchan Laos 29 18.01N102.48E
Viar r. Spain 10 37.45N 5.54W
Viareggio Italy 9 43.52N 10.14E
Viborg Denmark 17 56.26N 9.24E
Vibo Valentia Italy 12 38.40N 16.06E
Vibraye France 9 48.03N 0.44E
Vic Spain 10 41.56N 2.16E
Vicente López Argentina 63 34.32S 58.29W
Vicenza Italy 9 45.33N 11.32E
Vichada r. Colombia 60 4.58N 67.35W
Vichuga U.S.S.R. 18 57.12N 41.50E
Vichy France 11 46.07N 3.25E
Vicksburg U.S.A. 53 32.21N 90.51W
Viçosa Alagoas Brazil 61 9.22S 36.10W
Viçosa Minas Gerais Brazil 59 20.45S 42.53W
Victor Harbour Australia 46 35.36S138.35E
Victoria Argentina 63 32.40S 60.10W
Victoria d. Australia 47 37.20S145.00E
Victoria r. Australia 42 15.12S129.43E
Victoria Canada 50 48.26N123.20W
Victoria Chile 63 38.13S 72.20W
Victoria U.S.A. 53 28.49N 97.01W
Victoria, L. Africa 37 1.00S 33.00E
Victoria, L. Australia 46 34.00S141.15E
Victoria, Mt. P.N.G. 44 8.55S147.35E
Victoria Beach town Canada 51 50.43N 96.33W
Victoria de las Tunas Cuba 57 20.58N 76.59W
Victoria Downs town Australia 44 20.44S146.21E
Victoria Falls f. Zimbabwe / Zambia 39 17.58S 25.45E
Victoria I. Canada 50 71.00N110.00W
Victoria L. Australia 46 32.29S143.22E
Victoria Nile r. Uganda 37 2.14N 31.20E
Victoria River Downs town Australia 44 16.24S131.00E
Victoriaville Canada 55 46.04N 71.57W
Victoria West R.S.A. 39 31.24S 23.07E
Victorica Argentina 63 36.15S 65.25W
Videle Romania 15 44.16N 25.31E
Viderö i. Faroe Is. 16 62.20N 6.30W
Vidin Bulgaria 15 43.58N 22.51E
Viedma Argentina 63 40.50S 63.00W
Viedma, L. Argentina 63 49.40S 72.30W
Vienna see Wien Austria 14
Vienne France 11 45.32N 4.54E
Vienne r. France 11 47.13N 0.05W
Vientiane see Viangchan Laos 29
Vieques i. Puerto Rico 57 18.08N 65.30W
Viersen W. Germany 8 51.16N 6.22E
Vierwaldstätter See l. Switz. 14 47.10N 8.50E
Vierzon France 9 47.14N 2.03E
Vietnam Asia 26 15.00N108.00E
Vieux-Condé France 8 50.29N 3.31E
Vigan Phil. 27 17.35N120.23E
Vigevano Italy 9 45.19N 8.51E
Vignemale, Pic de mtn. France 11 42.46N 0.08W
Vigo Spain 10 42.15N 8.44W
Vigrestad Norway 17 58.34N 5.42E
Vijayawāda India 29 16.34N 80.40E
Vijosë r. Albania 13 40.39N 19.20E
Vik Norway 16 65.19N 12.10E
Vikajärvi Finland 16 66.37N 26.12E
Vikersund Norway 17 59.59N 10.02E
Vikna i. Norway 16 64.52N 10.57E
Vikulovo U.S.S.R. 20 56.51N 70.30E
Vila Vanuatu 40 17.44S168.19E
Vila da Maganja Mozambique 37 17.25S 37.32E
Vila Franca Portugal 10 38.57N 8.59W
Vilaine r. France 11 47.30N 2.25W
Vilanculos Mozambique 39 21.59S 35.16E
Vilanova la Geltrú Spain 10 41.13N 1.43E
Vila Real Portugal 10 41.17N 7.45W
Vila Real de Santo António Portugal 10 37.12N 7.25W
Vila Velha Brazil 59 20.20S 40.17W
Vileyka U.S.S.R. 15 54.30N 26.50E
Vilhelmina Sweden 16 64.37N 16.39E
Vilhena Brazil 60 12.40S 60.08W
Viliga Kushka U.S.S.R. 21 61.35N156.55E
Viljandi U.S.S.R. 18 58.22N 25.30E
Vilkavišhkis U.S.S.R. 15 54.39N 23.02E
Vil'kitskogo, Proliv str. U.S.S.R. 21 77.57N102.30E
Vilkovo U.S.S.R. 15 45.28N 29.32E
Villa Angela Argentina 62 27.34S 60.45W
Villa Bella Bolivia 62 10.23S 65.24W
Villablino Spain 10 42.57N 6.19W
Villacañas Spain 10 39.38N 3.20W
Villach Austria 14 46.37N 13.51E
Villa Clara Argentina 63 31.46S 58.50W

Villa Constitución Argentina 63 33.14S 60.21W
Villa Dolores Argentina 62 31.58S 65.12W
Villafranca di Verona Italy 9 45.21N 10.50E
Villagarcía Spain 10 42.35N 8.45W
Villaguay Argentina 63 31.55S 59.00W
Villahermosa Mexico 56 18.00N 92.53W
Villa Hernandarias Argentina 63 31.15S 59.58W
Villa Huidobro Argentina 63 34.50S 64.34W
Villaines-la-Juhel France 9 48.21N 0.17W
Villajoyosa Spain 10 38.31N 0.14W
Villalba Spain 10 43.18N 7.41W
Villa María Argentina 62 32.25S 63.15W
Villa Montes Bolivia 62 21.15S 63.30W
Villanueva de la Serena Spain 10 38.58N 5.48W
Villaputzu Italy 12 39.28N 9.35E
Villarrica Chile 63 39.15S 72.15W
Villarrica Paraguay 59 25.45S 56.28W
Villarrobledo Spain 10 39.16N 2.36W
Villa San José Argentina 63 32.12S 58.15W
Villasayas Spain 10 41.24N 2.39W
Villavicencio Colombia 60 4.09N 73.38W
Villaviciosa Spain 10 43.29N 5.26W
Villazón Bolivia 62 22.06S 65.36W
Villedieu France 9 48.50N 1.13W
Villefranche France 11 46.00N 4.43E
Villena Spain 10 38.39N 0.52W
Villenauxe-la-Grande France 9 48.35N 3.33E
Villeneuve France 11 44.25N 0.43E
Villeneuve d'Ascq France 8 50.37N 3.10E
Villeneuve-St. Georges France 9 48.44N 2.27E
Villeneuve-sur-Yonne France 9 48.05N 3.18E
Villers-Bocage France 9 49.05N 0.39W
Villers-Cotterêts France 9 49.15N 3.04E
Villers-sur-Mer France 9 49.21N 0.02W
Villeurbanne France 14 45.46N 4.54E
Vilnius U.S.S.R. 15 54.40N 25.19E
Vilvoorde Belgium 8 50.56N 4.25E
Vilyuy r. U.S.S.R. 21 64.20N126.55E
Vilyuysk U.S.S.R. 21 63.46N121.35E
Vimianzo Spain 10 43.07N 9.02W
Vimmerby Sweden 17 57.40N 15.51E
Vimoutiers France 9 48.55N 0.12E
Vina r. Chad 38 7.43N 15.30E
Viña del Mar Chile 63 33.02S 71.34W
Vinaroz Spain 10 40.30N 0.27E
Vincennes France 9 48.51N 2.26E
Vincennes U.S.A. 55 38.42N 87.30W
Vindel r. Sweden 16 63.54N 19.52E
Vindeln Sweden 16 64.12N 19.44E
Vinderup Denmark 17 56.29N 8.47E
Vindhya Range mts. India 28 22.55N 76.00E
Vineland U.S.A. 55 39.29N 75.02W
Vingåker Sweden 17 59.02N 15.52E
Vinh Vietnam 26 18.42N105.41E
Vînju Mare Romania 15 44.26N 22.52E
Vinkovci Yugo. 13 45.17N 18.38E
Vinnitsa U.S.S.R. 15 49.11N 28.30E
Vinson Massif Antarctica 64 78.00S 85.00W
Vioolsdrif R.S.A. 39 28.45S 17.33E
Vipava Yugo. 14 45.51N 13.58E
Viqueque Indonesia 27 8.42S126.30E
Virac Phil. 27 13.35N124.15E
Viranşehir Turkey 30 37.13N 39.45E
Vire France 11 48.50N 0.53W
Vire r. France 9 49.20N 0.53W
Vírgenes, C. Argentina 63 52.00S 68.50W
Virgin Gorda i. B.V.Is. 57 18.30N 64.26W
Virginia U.S.A. 53 47.30N 92.28W
Virginia d. U.S.A. 53 37.30N 79.00W
Virginia City Mont. U.S.A. 54 45.18N111.56W
Virginia City Nev. U.S.A. 54 39.19N119.39W
Virovitica Yugo. 15 45.51N 17.23E
Virrat Finland 16 62.14N 23.47E
Virserum Sweden 17 57.19N 15.35E
Virton Belgium 8 49.35N 5.32E
Virtsu U.S.S.R. 17 58.34N 23.31E
Virunga Nat. Park Zaïre 37 0.30S 29.15E
Vis Yugo. 12 43.03N 16.21E
Vis i. Yugo. 12 43.03N 16.10E
Visalia U.S.A. 54 36.20N119.18W
Visayan Sea Phil. 27 11.35N123.51E
Visby Sweden 17 57.38N 18.18E
Visconde do Rio Branco Brazil 59 21.00S 42.51W
Viscount Melville Sd. Canada 50 74.30N104.00W
Visé Belgium 8 50.44N 5.42E
Višegrad Yugo. 13 43.47N 19.20E
Viseu Brazil 61 1.12S 46.07W
Viseu Portugal 10 40.40N 7.55W
Viseu de Sus Romania 15 47.44N 24.22E
Vishākhapatnam India 29 17.42N 83.24E
Viso, Monte mtn. Italy 9 44.38N 7.05E
Visp Switz. 9 46.18N 7.53E
Vista U.S.A. 54 33.12N117.15W
Vistula r. see Wisła r. Poland 15
Vitarte Peru 60 12.03S 76.51W
Vitebsk U.S.S.R. 18 55.10N 30.14E
Viterbo Italy 12 42.26N 12.07E
Vitim U.S.S.R. 21 59.28N112.35E
Vitim r. U.S.S.R. 21 59.30N112.36E
Vitória Espírito Santo Brazil 59 20.19S 40.21W
Vitoria Spain 10 42.51N 2.40W
Vitória da Conquista Brazil 61 14.53S 40.52W
Vitré France 9 48.07N 1.12W
Vitry-le-François France 9 48.44N 4.35E
Vitteaux France 9 47.24N 4.30E
Vittoria Italy 12 36.57N 14.21E
Vittorio Veneto Italy 9 45.59N 12.18E
Vivonne Australia 46 35.58S137.10E
Vivonne B. Australia 46 36.00S137.00E
Vizcaíno, Desierto de des. Mexico 56 27.40N114.40W
Vizianagaram India 29 18.07N 83.30E
Vizinga U.S.S.R. 18 61.06N 50.05E
Vlaardingen Neth. 8 51.55N 4.20E
Vladimir U.S.S.R. 18 56.08N 40.25E
Vladimirets U.S.S.R. 15 51.28N 26.03E
Vladimir Volynskiy U.S.S.R. 15 50.51N 24.19E
Vladivostok U.S.S.R. 25 43.09N131.53E
Vlasenica Yugo. 15 44.11N 18.56E
Vlieland i. Neth. 8 53.15N 5.00E
Vlissingen Neth. 8 51.27N 3.35E
Vlorë Albania 13 40.28N 19.27E
Vltava r. Czech. 14 50.22N 14.28E
Voerde W. Germany 8 51.37N 6.39E
Vogelkop f. see Jazirah Doberai f. Indonesia 27
Voghera Italy 9 44.59N 9.01E
Voi Kenya 37 3.23S 38.35E
Voiron France 11 45.22N 5.35E
Volborg U.S.A. 54 45.50N105.40W
Volda Norway 17 62.09N 6.06E
Volga r. U.S.S.R. 19 45.45N 47.50E
Volgograd U.S.S.R. 19 48.45N 44.30E
Volgogradskoye Vodokhranilishche resr. U.S.S.R. 19 51.00N 46.05E
Volkhov U.S.S.R. 18 59.54N 32.47E
Volkhov r. U.S.S.R. 18 60.15N 32.15E
Völklingen W. Germany 14 49.15N 6.50E
Volkovysk U.S.S.R. 15 53.10N 24.28E
Vollenhove Neth. 8 52.41N 5.59E
Volnovakha U.S.S.R. 19 47.36N 37.32E
Volochanka U.S.S.R. 21 70.59N 94.18E
Volochisk U.S.S.R. 15 49.34N 26.10E
Volodarsk U.S.S.R. 18 56.14N 43.10E
Vologda U.S.S.R. 18 59.10N 39.55E
Volokolamsk U.S.S.R. 18 56.02N 35.56E
Vólos Greece 13 39.22N 22.57E
Volovets U.S.S.R. 15 48.44N 23.14E
Volsk U.S.S.R. 18 52.04N 47.22E
Volta d. Ghana 38 7.30N 0.25E
Volta r. Ghana 38 5.50N 0.41E
Volta, L. Ghana 38 7.00N 0.00
Volta Blanche r. Burkina Faso see White Volta r. Ghana 38
Volta-Noire d. Burkina Faso 38 12.30N 3.25W
Volta Noire r. Burkina Faso see Black Voltar. r. Ghana 38
Volta Redonda Brazil 59 22.31S 44.05W
Volta Rouge r. Burkina Faso see Red Volta r. Ghana 38
Volterra Italy 12 43.24N 10.51E
Voltri Italy 9 44.26N 8.45E
Volturno r. Italy 12 41.02N 13.56E
Volzhskiy U.S.S.R. 19 48.48N 44.45E
Voorburg Neth. 8 52.05N 4.22E
Vopnafjördhur est. Iceland 16 65.50N 14.30W
Vopnafjördhur town Iceland 16 65.46N 14.50W
Vorarlberg d. Austria 14 47.15N 9.55E
Vordingborg Denmark 17 55.01N 11.55E
Voríai Sporádhes is. Greece 13 39.00N 24.00E
Vorkuta U.S.S.R. 18 67.27N 64.00E
Vormsi i. U.S.S.R. 17 59.00N 23.20E
Voronezh U.S.S.R. 19 51.40N 39.13E
Voronovo U.S.S.R. 15 54.09N 25.19E
Voroshilovgrad U.S.S.R. 19 48.35N 39.20E
Vosges mts. France 14 48.10N 7.00E
Voss Norway 17 60.39N 6.26E
Vostochno Sibirskoye More sea U.S.S.R. 21 73.00N160.00E
Vostochnyy Sayan mts. U.S.S.R. 24 51.30N102.00E
Votkinsk U.S.S.R. 18 57.02N 53.59E
Votkinskoye Vodokhranilishche resr. U.S.S.R. 18 57.00N 55.00E
Votuporanga Brazil 62 20.26S 49.53W
Vouga r. Portugal 10 40.41N 8.38W
Vouillé France 11 46.38N 0.10E
Vouziers France 9 49.24N 4.42E
Voves France 9 48.16N 1.37E
Voxna Sweden 17 61.20N 15.30E
Voxna r. Sweden 17 61.17N 16.26E
Voyvozh U.S.S.R. 18 64.19N 55.12E
Vozhega U.S.S.R. 18 60.25N 40.11E
Voznesensk U.S.S.R. 19 47.34N 31.21E
Vrangelya, Ostrov i. U.S.S.R. 21 71.00N180.00
Vranje Yugo. 13 42.34N 21.52E
Vratsa Bulgaria 13 43.12N 23.33E
Vrbas r. Yugo. 13 45.06N 17.29E
Vrede R.S.A. 39 27.24S 29.09E
Vredendal R.S.A. 39 31.40S 18.28E
Vresse Belgium 8 49.53N 4.57E
Vries Neth. 8 53.06N 6.35E
Vrnograč Yugo. 12 45.10N 15.56E
Vršac Yugo. 15 45.08N 21.18E
Vryburg R.S.A. 39 26.57S 24.42E
Vught Neth. 8 51.39N 5.18E
Vukovar Yugo. 15 45.21N 19.00E
Vung Tau Vietnam 26 10.21N107.04E
Vyatka r. U.S.S.R. 20 55.40N 51.40E
Vyatskiye Polyany U.S.S.R. 18 56.14N 51.08E
Vyazma U.S.S.R. 18 55.12N 34.17E
Vyazniki U.S.S.R. 18 56.14N 42.08E
Vyborg U.S.S.R. 18 60.45N 28.41E
Vychegda r. U.S.S.R. 18 61.15N 46.28E
Vychodné Beskydy mts. Europe 15 49.30N 22.00E
Vygozero, Ozero l. U.S.S.R. 18 63.30N 34.30E
Vyrnwy, L. U.K. 4 52.46N 3.30W
Vyshka U.S.S.R. 31 39.19N 54.10E
Vyshniy-Volochek U.S.S.R. 18 57.34N 34.23E
Vytegra U.S.S.R. 18 61.04N 36.27E

W

Wa Ghana 38 10.07N 2.28W
Waal r. Neth. 8 51.45N 4.40E
Waalwijk Neth. 8 51.42N 5.04E
Wabag P.N.G. 27 5.28S143.40E
Wabash U.S.A. 55 40.47N 85.48W
Wabash r. U.S.A. 53 38.25N 87.45W
Wabrzeźno Poland 15 53.17N 18.57E
Wabush City Canada 51 53.00N 66.50W
Waco U.S.A. 53 31.33N 97.10W
Wad Pakistan 28 27.21N 66.30E
Waddeneilanden is. Neth. 8 53.20N 5.00E
Waddenzee b. Neth. 8 53.15N 5.05E
Wadderin Australia 43 31.57S118.27E
Waddington, Mt. Canada 50 51.30N125.00W
Wadhurst U.K. 5 51.03N 0.21E
Wādī Ḥalfā' Sudan 30 21.56N 31.20E
Wadikee Australia 46 33.18S136.12E
Wādī Mūsá town Jordan 32 30.19N 35.29E
Wad Madanī Sudan 35 14.24N 33.30E
Wafrah Kuwait 31 28.39N 47.56E
Wageningen Neth. 8 51.58N 5.39E
Wager B. Canada 51 65.26N 88.40W
Wager Bay town Canada 51 65.55N 90.40W
Wagga Wagga Australia 47 35.07S147.24E
Wagin Australia 43 33.18S117.21E
Wāh Pakistan 28 33.50N 72.44E
Wahai Indonesia 27 2.48S129.30E
Wahiba Sands des. Oman 28 21.56N 58.55E
Wahpeton U.S.A. 53 46.16N 96.36W
Waiau New Zealand 48 42.39S173.03E
Waidhofen Austria 14 47.58N 14.47E
Waigeo i. Indonesia 27 0.05S130.30E
Waihi New Zealand 48 37.24S175.50E
Waikato r. New Zealand 48 37.19S174.50E
Waikerie Australia 46 34.11S139.59E
Waikokopu New Zealand 48 39.05S177.50E
Waikouaiti New Zealand 48 45.36S170.41E
Waimakariri r. New Zealand 48 43.23S172.40E
Waimate New Zealand 48 44.45S171.03E
Waingapu Indonesia 27 9.30S120.10E
Wainwright U.S.A. 50 70.39N160.00W
Waiouru New Zealand 48 39.39S175.40E
Waipara New Zealand 48 43.03S172.45E
Waipawa New Zealand 48 39.56S176.35E
Waipiro New Zealand 48 38.02S178.21E
Waipu New Zealand 48 35.59S174.26E
Waipukurau New Zealand 48 40.00S176.33E
Wairau r. New Zealand 48 41.32S174.08E
Wairoa New Zealand 48 39.03S177.25E
Waitaki r. New Zealand 48 44.56S171.10E
Waitara New Zealand 48 38.59S174.13E
Waiuku New Zealand 48 37.15S174.44E
Wajir Kenya 37 1.46N 40.05E
Wakatipu, L. New Zealand 48 45.10S168.30E
Wakayama Japan 23 34.13N135.11E
Wakefield U.K. 4 53.41N 1.31W
Wakkanai Japan 25 45.26N141.43E
Wakre Indonesia 27 0.30S131.05E
Walamba Zambia 37 13.27S 28.44E
Wałbrzych Poland 14 50.48N 16.19E
Walcha Australia 47 31.00S151.36E
Walcheren f. Neth. 8 51.32N 3.35E
Wałcz Poland 14 53.17N 16.28E
Waldbröl W. Germany 8 50.52N 7.34E
Waldeck W. Germany 14 51.12N 9.04E
Walden U.S.A. 54 40.34N106.11W
Waldorf U.S.A. 55 38.37N 76.54W
Waldport U.S.A. 54 44.26N124.04W
Wales d. U.K. 5 52.30N 3.45W
Walgett Australia 47 30.03S148.10E
Walikale Zaïre 37 1.29S 28.05E
Walker L. U.S.A. 54 38.44N118.43W
Wallace Idaho U.S.A. 54 47.28N115.55W
Wallaceburg Canada 55 42.36N 82.23W
Wallachia f. Romania 15 44.35N 25.00E
Wallambin, L. Australia 43 30.58S117.30E
Wallangarra Australia 47 28.51S151.52E
Wallaroo Australia 46 33.57S137.36E
Walla Walla Australia 47 35.48S146.52E
Walla Walla U.S.A. 54 46.08N118.20W
Wallis, Îles is. Pacific Oc. 40 13.16S176.15W
Wallowa U.S.A. 54 45.34N117.32W
Wallowa Mts. U.S.A. 54 45.10N117.30W
Wallsend Australia 47 32.55S151.40E
Walpole Australia 43 34.57S116.44E
Walsall U.K. 5 52.36N 1.59W
Walsenburg U.S.A. 52 37.37N104.47W
Walton on the Naze U.K. 5 51.52N 1.17E
Walton on the Wolds U.K. 4 52.49N 0.49W
Walvis B. R.S.A. 39 22.55S 14.30E
Walvisbaai R.S.A. 39 22.57S 14.30E
Walvis Bay d. R.S.A. 39 22.56S 14.35E
Walvis Bay town R.S.A. 36 22.50S 14.31E
Walvis Bay town see Walvisbaai R.S.A. 39
Wamanfo Ghana 38 7.16N 2.44W
Wamba Kenya 37 0.58N 37.19E
Wamba Nigeria 38 8.57N 8.42E
Wamba Zaïre 37 2.10N 27.59E
Wami r. Tanzania 37 6.10S 38.50E
Wamsasi Indonesia 27 3.27S126.07E
Wan Indonesia 44 8.23S137.55E
Wāna Pakistan 28 32.20N 69.32E
Wanaaring Australia 46 29.42S144.14E
Wanaka New Zealand 48 44.42S169.08E
Wanaka, L. New Zealand 48 44.30S169.10E
Wan'an China 25 26.27N114.46E
Wanapiri Indonesia 27 4.30S135.50E
Wanapitei r. Canada 55 46.02N 80.51W
Wanapitei L. Canada 55 46.45N 80.45W
Wanbi Australia 46 34.46S140.19E
Wandana Australia 46 32.04S133.45E
Wandoan Australia 44 26.09S149.51E
Wanganella Australia 47 35.13S144.53E
Wanganui New Zealand 48 39.56S175.00E
Wangaratta Australia 47 36.22S146.20E
Wangary Australia 46 34.30S135.26E
Wangerooge i. W. Germany 8 53.50N 7.50E
Wangianna Australia 46 29.42S137.32E
Wantage U.K. 5 51.35N 1.25W
Wanxian China 29 30.52N108.20E
Wanyuan China 29 32.04N108.02E
Warangal India 29 18.00N 79.35E
Waranga Resr. Australia 47 36.32S145.04E
Waratah B. Australia 47 38.55S146.04E
Warburton r. Australia 45 27.55S137.15E
Warburton Range mts. S.A. Australia 46 30.30S134.32E
Warburton Range mts. W.A. Australia 42 26.09S126.38E
Ward Rep. of Ire. 7 53.26N 6.20W
Warden R.S.A. 39 27.49S 28.57E
Wardenburg W. Germany 8 53.04N 8.11E
Wardha India 29 20.41N 78.40E
Waren E. Germany 14 53.31N 12.40E
Warendorf W. Germany 8 51.57N 8.00E
Warialda Australia 47 29.33S150.36E
Wark Forest hills U.K. 4 55.06N 2.24W
Warkopi Indonesia 27 1.12S134.09E
Warkworth New Zealand 48 36.24S174.40E
Warley U.K. 5 52.29N 2.02W
Warmbad Namibia 39 28.26S 18.41E
Warminster U.K. 5 51.12N 2.11W
Warm Springs town U.S.A. 54 39.39N114.49W
Waroona Australia 43 32.51S115.50E
Warracknabeal Australia 46 36.15S142.28E
Warragamba Resr. Australia 47 33.54S150.36E
Warragul Australia 47 38.11S145.55E
Warrakalanna, L. Australia 46 28.13S139.23E
Warrambool r. Australia 47 30.04S147.38E
Warramutty Australia 46 30.30S144.04E
Warrego r. Australia 47 30.25S145.18E
Warrego Range mts. Australia 44 24.55S146.20E
Warren Australia 47 31.44S147.53E
Warren Mich. U.S.A. 55 42.28N 83.01W
Warren Ohio U.S.A. 55 41.15N 80.49W
Warren Penn. U.S.A. 55 41.51N 79.08W
Warrenpoint U.K. 7 54.06N 6.15W
Warrenton R.S.A. 39 28.07S 24.49E
Warri Nigeria 38 5.36N 5.46E
Warrina Australia 46 28.10S135.49E
Warriners Creek r. Australia 46 29.15S137.03E
Warrington U.K. 4 53.25N 2.38W
Warri Warri Australia 46 29.00S141.56E
Warrnambool Australia 46 38.23S142.03E
Warrumbungle Range mts. Australia 47 31.20S149.00E
Warsaw see Warszawa Poland 15
Warsaw Ind. U.S.A. 55 41.13N 85.52W
Warszawa Poland 15 52.15N 21.00E
Warta r. Poland 14 52.45N 15.09E
Warwick Australia 47 28.12S152.00E
Warwick U.K. 5 52.17N 1.36W
Warwickshire d. U.K. 5 52.13N 1.30W
Wasatch Plateau f. U.S.A. 54 39.20N111.30W
Wasco Calif. U.S.A. 54 35.36N119.20W
Wasco Oreg. U.S.A. 54 45.35N120.42W
Washburn L. Canada 50 70.03N106.50W
Washington U.K. 4 54.55N 1.30W
Washington d. U.S.A. 54 47.43N120.00W
Washington D.C. U.S.A. 55 38.55N 77.00W
Washington Ind. U.S.A. 55 38.40N 87.10W
Washington N.C. U.S.A. 53 35.33N 77.04W
Washington Utah U.S.A. 54 37.08N113.30W
Washington Va. U.S.A. 55 38.43N 78.10W
Wasian Indonesia 27 1.51S133.21E
Wasior Indonesia 27 2.38S134.27E
Wassenaar Neth. 8 52.10N 4.26E
Wassy France 9 48.30N 4.59E
Waswanipi Lac l. Canada 55 49.36N 76.39W
Watampone Indonesia 27 4.33S120.20E
Watchet U.K. 5 51.10N 3.20W
Waterbury U.S.A. 55 41.33N 73.03W
Waterford Rep. of Ire. 7 52.16N 7.08W
Waterford d. Rep. of Ire. 7 52.10N 7.40W
Waterford Harbour est. Rep. of Ire. 7 52.12N 6.56W
Waterloo Belgium 8 50.44N 4.24E
Waterloo Canada 55 43.28N 80.31W
Waterloo Iowa U.S.A. 53 42.30N 92.20W
Watertown N.Y. U.S.A. 55 43.59N 75.55W
Watertown S.Dak. U.S.A. 53 44.54N 97.08W
Watervale Australia 46 33.58S138.39E
Waterville Rep. of Ire. 7 51.50N 10.11W
Waterville Maine U.S.A. 55 44.33N 69.38W
Waterville Wash. U.S.A. 54 47.39N120.04W
Watford U.K. 5 51.40N 0.25W
Watrous Canada 50 51.40N105.29W
Watsa Zaïre 37 3.03N 29.29E
Watson Lake town Canada 50 60.07N128.49W
Watsonville U.S.A. 54 36.55N121.45W
Wattiwarriganna r. Australia 46 28.57S136.10E
Wattle Vale town Australia 46 30.00S143.30E
Wau P.N.G. 27 7.22S146.40E
Wauchope Australia 47 31.27S152.43E
Waukaringa Australia 46 32.18S139.27E
Wausau U.S.A. 53 44.58N 89.40W
Wave Hill town Australia 42 17.29S130.57E
Waveney r. U.K. 5 52.29N 1.46E
Wavre Belgium 8 50.43N 4.37E
Wāw Sudan 35 7.40N 28.04E
Waxweiler W. Germany 8 50.08N 6.20E
Waycross U.S.A. 53 31.08N 82.22W
Waynesboro Penn. U.S.A. 55 39.45N 77.35W
Waziers France 8 50.24N 3.05E
Wear r. U.K. 4 54.55N 1.21W
Weda Indonesia 27 0.30N127.52E
Wedderburn Australia 46 36.26S143.39E
Wedgeport Canada 55 43.44N 66.00W
Wedmore U.K. 5 51.14N 2.50W
Wedza Zimbabwe 39 18.37S 31.33E
Weebo Australia 42 28.01S121.03E
Weelde Belgium 8 51.25N 5.00E
Weemelah Australia 47 29.02S149.15E
Weert Neth. 8 51.14N 5.40E
Wee Waa Australia 47 30.34S149.27E
Wegorzyno Poland 14 53.32N 15.33E
Wegrów Poland 15 52.25N 22.01E
Weichang China 25 41.56N117.34E
Weiden in der Oberpfalz W. Germany 14 49.40N 12.10E
Weifang China 25 36.44N119.10E
Weihai China 25 37.30N122.04E
Weilmoringle Australia 47 29.16S146.55E
Weimar E. Germany 14 50.59N 11.20E
Weipa Australia 44 12.41S141.52E
Weir r. Australia 47 29.10S149.06E
Weiser U.S.A. 54 44.37N116.58W
Weissenfels E. Germany 14 51.12N 11.58E
Weiya China 24 41.50N 94.24E
Wejherowo Poland 15 54.37N 18.15E
Welbourn Hill town Australia 45 27.21S134.06E
Weldon U.S.A. 54 35.40N118.20W
Welkom R.S.A. 39 27.59S 26.42E
Welland Canada 55 42.59N 79.14W
Welland r. U.K. 4 52.53N 0.00
Wellesley Is. Australia 44 16.42S139.30E
Wellin Belgium 8 50.05N 5.07E
Wellingborough U.K. 5 52.18N 0.41W
Wellington N.S.W. Australia 47 32.33S148.59E
Wellington S.A. Australia 46 35.21S139.23E
Wellington New Zealand 48 41.17S174.47E
Wellington d. New Zealand 48 40.00S175.30E
Wellington Shrops. U.K. 5 52.42N 2.31W
Wellington Somerset U.K. 5 50.58N 3.13W
Wellington Nev. U.S.A. 54 38.45N119.22W
Wellington, Isla i. Chile 63 49.30S 75.00W
Wells U.K. 5 51.12N 2.39W
Wells Nev. U.S.A. 54 41.07N114.58W
Wellsboro U.S.A. 55 41.45N 77.18W
Wells-next-the-Sea U.K. 4 52.57N 0.51E
Wellton U.S.A. 54 32.40N114.08W
Wels Austria 14 48.10N 14.02E
Welshpool U.K. 5 52.40N 3.09W
Welwyn Garden City U.K. 5 51.48N 0.13W
Wem U.K. 4 52.52N 2.45W
Wembere r. Tanzania 37 4.07S 34.15E
Wenatchee U.S.A. 54 47.25N120.19W
Wenchi Ghana 38 7.40N 2.06W
Wendel U.S.A. 54 40.20N120.14W
Wendover U.S.A. 54 40.44N114.02W
Wenebegon L. Canada 55 47.24N 83.08W
Wenlock r. Australia 44 12.02S141.55E
Wenquan China 29 33.13N 91.50E
Wenshan China 29 23.25N104.15E
Wensleydale Australia 46 38.24S144.01E
Wensleydale f. U.K. 4 54.19N 2.04W
Wentworth Australia 46 34.06S141.56E
Wenzhou China 25 28.02N120.40E
Weott U.S.A. 54 40.19N123.54W
Wepener R.S.A. 39 29.43S 27.01E
Werda Botswana 39 25.15S 23.16E
Werdohl W. Germany 8 51.16N 7.47E
Weri Indonesia 27 3.10S132.30E
Werne W. Germany 8 51.39N 7.36E
Werra r. W. Germany 14 51.26N 9.39E
Werribee Australia 47 37.54S144.40E
Werris Creek town Australia 47 31.20S150.41E
Wesel W. Germany 8 51.39N 6.37E
Weser r. W. Germany 14 53.15N 8.30E
Wesiri Indonesia 27 7.30S126.30E
Wessel, C. Australia 44 10.59S136.46E
Wessel Is. Australia 44 11.30S136.25E
West Bengal d. India 29 23.00N 87.40E
West-Berlin d. W. Germany 14 52.30N 13.20E
West Bromwich U.K. 5 52.32N 2.01W
Westbrook U.S.A. 55 43.41N 70.21W
Westby Australia 47 35.29S147.27E
Westende Belgium 8 51.10N 2.46E
Western d. Ghana 38 6.00N 2.40W
Western d. Kenya 37 0.30N 34.30E
Western Australia d. Australia 42 24.20S122.30E
Western Ghāts mts. India 28 15.30N 74.30E
Western Isles d. U.K. 6 57.40N 7.10W
Western Sahara Africa 34 25.00N 13.30W
Western Samoa Pacific Oc. 40 13.55S172.00W
Westerschelde est. Neth. 8 51.25N 3.40E
Westerstede W. Germany 8 53.15N 7.56E
Westerwald f. W. Germany 8 50.40N 8.00E
West Falkland i. Falkland Is. 63 51.40W 60.00W
West Felton U.K. 4 52.49N 2.58W
Westfield Mass. U.S.A. 55 42.07N 72.45W
Westfield Penn. U.S.A. 55 41.55N 77.32W
West Frisian Is. see Waddeneilanden Neth. 14
West Germany Europe 14 51.00N 8.00E
West Glamorgan d. U.K. 5 51.42N 3.47W
West Lafayette U.S.A. 55 40.26N 86.56W
Westland d. New Zealand 48 43.15S170.10E
West Linton U.K. 6 55.45N 3.21W
Westmeath d. Rep. of Ire. 7 53.30N 7.30W
West Midlands d. U.K. 5 52.28N 1.50W
Westmoreland Australia 44 17.18S138.12E
West Nicholson Zimbabwe 39 21.06S 29.25E
Weston Malaysia 26 5.14N115.35E
Weston-Super-Mare U.K. 5 51.20N 2.59W
West Palm Beach town U.S.A. 53 26.42N 80.05W
Westport New Zealand 48 41.46S171.38E
Westport Rep. of Ire. 7 53.48N 9.32W
Westport Wash. U.S.A. 54 46.53N124.06W
Westray i. U.K. 6 59.18N 2.58W
West Siberian Plain f. see Zapadno-Sibirskaya Ravnina f. U.S.S.R. 20
West Sussex d. U.K. 5 50.58N 0.30W
West Terschelling Neth. 8 53.22N 5.13E
West Virginia d. U.S.A. 53 38.45N 80.30W
West Vlaanderen d. Belgium 8 51.00N 3.00E
West Wyalong Australia 47 33.54S147.12E
West Yellowstone U.S.A. 54 44.30N111.05W
West Yorkshire d. U.K. 4 53.45N 1.40W
Wetar i. Indonesia 27 7.45S126.00E
Wetaskiwin Canada 50 52.57N113.20W
Wetteren Belgium 8 51.00N 3.51E
Wetzlar W. Germany 14 50.33N 8.30E
Wewak P.N.G. 27 3.35S143.35E
Wexford Rep. of Ire. 7 52.20N 6.28W
Wexford d. Rep. of Ire. 7 52.20N 6.25W
Wexford B. Rep. of Ire. 7 52.27N 6.18W
Weyburn Canada 50 49.41N103.52W
Weymouth U.K. 5 50.36N 2.28W
Weymouth, C. Australia 44 12.32S143.36E
Whakatane New Zealand 48 37.56S177.00E
Whale Cove town Canada 51 62.30N 93.00W
Whallon r. Australia 47 29.10S148.42E
Whalsay i. U.K. 6 60.22N 0.59W
Whangarei New Zealand 48 35.43S174.20E
Wharfe r. U.K. 4 53.50N 1.07W
Wharfedale f. U.K. 4 54.00N 1.55W
Whataroa New Zealand 48 43.16S170.22E

heeler Peak mtn. Nev. U.S.A. 54 8.59N114.19W
heeler Peak mtn. N.Mex. U.S.A. 52 6.34N105.25W
heeler Ridge town U.S.A. 54 35.06N119.01W
heeler Springs town U.S.A. 54 4.30N119.18W
heeling U.S.A. 55 40.05N 80.43W
hernside mtn. U.K. 4 54.14N 2.25W
hidbey Pt. Australia 46 34.35S135.07E
hitburn U.K. 6 55.52N 3.41W
hitby Canada 55 43.52N 78.56W
hitby U.K. 4 54.29N 0.37W
hitchurch Shrops. U.K. 4 52.58N 2.42W
hite r. Ark. U.S.A. 53 33.53N 91.10W
hite r. Ind. U.S.A. 55 38.29N 87.45W
hite r. S.Dak. U.S.A. 52 43.40N 99.30W
hite r. Utah U.S.A. 52 40.04N109.41W
hite, L. Australia 42 21.05S129.00E
hite Cliffs town Australia 46 30.51S143.05E
hitefish U.S.A. 54 48.25N114.20W
hitefish B. U.S.A. 55 46.32N 84.45W
hitehall Mont. U.S.A. 54 45.52N112.06W
hitehaven U.K. 4 54.33N 3.35W
hitehorse Canada 50 60.41N135.08W
hitemark Australia 45 40.07S148.00E
hite Mountain Peak U.S.A. 54 37.38N118.15W
hite Mts. Calif. U.S.A. 54 37.30N118.15W
hite Plains town U.S.A. 55 41.02N 73.46W
hite Sea see Beloye More sea U.S.S.R. 18
hite Volta r. Ghana 38 9.13N 1.15W
hitewater Baldy mtn. U.S.A. 54 3.20N108.39W
hitfield Australia 47 36.49S146.22E
hithorn U.K. 6 54.44N 4.25W
hitianga New Zealand 48 36.50S175.42E
hitley Bay town U.K. 4 55.03N 1.25W
hitney Canada 55 45.30N 78.14W
hitney, Mt. U.S.A. 54 36.35N118.18W
hitstable U.K. 5 51.21N 1.02E
hitsunday I. Australia 44 20.17S148.59E
hittier U.S.A. 50 60.46N148.41W
hittlesea Australia 47 37.31S145.08E
itton U.K. 4 53.42N 0.39W
oldaia L. Canada 50 60.43N104.10W
yalla Australia 46 33.02S137.35E
yjonta Australia 46 29.42S142.30E
chita U.S.A. 53 37.43N 97.20W
chita Falls town U.S.A. 52 33.55N 98.30W
ck U.K. 6 58.26N 3.06W
ckenburg U.S.A. 54 33.58N112.44W
ckepin Australia 43 32.45S117.31E
cklow Rep. of Ire. 7 52.59N 6.03W
cklow d. Rep. of Ire. 7 52.59N 6.25W
cklow Head Rep. of Ire. 7 52.58N 6.00W
cklow Mts. Rep. of Ire. 7 53.06N 6.20W
dgiemooltha Australia 43 31.30S121.34E
dnes U.K. 4 53.22N 2.44W
ehl W. Germany 8 50.57N 7.32E
eluń Poland 15 51.14N 18.34E
en Austria 14 48.13N 16.22E
ener Neustadt Austria 14 47.49N 16.15E
eprz r. Poland 15 51.34N 21.49E
esbaden W. Germany 14 50.05N 8.15E
gan U.K. 4 53.33N 2.38W
ght, Isle of U.K. 3 50.40N 1.17W
gton U.K. 4 54.50N 3.09W
gtown U.K. 6 54.47N 4.26W
gtown B. U.K. 6 54.47N 4.15W
lcannia Australia 46 31.33S143.24E
ldhorn mtn. Switz. 11 46.22N 7.22E
ldon Austria 14 46.53N 15.31E
ldspitze mtn. Austria 14 46.55N 10.55E
ldwood U.S.A. 55 38.59N 74.49W
lgena Australia 46 30.46S134.44E
lhelm, Mt. P.N.G. 27 6.00S144.55E
lhelm II Land Antarctica 64 68.00S 89.00E
lhelmshaven W. Germany 8 53.32N 8.07E
lkes-Barre U.S.A. 55 41.15N 75.50W
lkes Land f. Antarctica 64 69.00S120.00E
lkie Canada 50 52.27N108.42W
lkinsburg U.S.A. 55 40.27N 79.53W
lkinson Lakes Australia 45 29.40S132.39E
llandra Billabong r. Australia 46 3.08S144.06E
llara Australia 46 29.14S144.30E
llemstad Neth. Antilles 60 12.12N 68.56W
lleroo Australia 42 15.17S131.35E
lliam, Mt. Australia 46 37.20S142.41E
lliam Creek town Australia 46 28.52S136.18E
lliams Australia 43 33.01S116.45E
lliams r. Australia 43 32.59S116.24E
lliams Lake town Canada 50 52.08N122.09W
lliamsport Penn. U.S.A. 55 41.14N 77.00W
llie's Range hills Australia 46 28.30S144.00E
llis Group is. Australia 44 16.18S150.00E
lliston R.S.A. 39 31.21S 20.53E
lliston U.S.A. 52 48.09N103.37W
lliston L. Canada 50 55.00N126.00W
llits U.S.A. 54 39.25N123.21W
llmar U.S.A. 53 45.06N 95.00W
llochra Australia 46 32.12S138.10E
llochra r. Australia 46 31.57S137.52E
llow U.S.A. 50 61.42N150.08W
llowmore R.S.A. 39 33.18S 23.28E
llow Ranch U.S.A. 54 41.55N120.21W
llunga Australia 46 35.18S138.33E
lmington Del. U.S.A. 55 39.44N 75.33W
lmington N.C. U.S.A. 53 34.14N 77.55W
lmslow U.K. 4 53.19N 2.14W
lpena r. Australia 46 31.13S139.25E
lson's Promontory c. Australia 47 9.06S146.23E
lton r. Australia 44 14.45S134.33E
lton U.K. 5 51.05N 1.52W
ltshire d. U.K. 5 51.20N 0.34W
ltz Lux. 8 49.59N 5.53E
luna Australia 42 26.36S120.13E
mmera r. Australia 46 36.05S141.56E
Winam b. Kenya 37 0.15S 34.30E
Winbar Australia 47 30.49S144.50E
Winburg R.S.A. 39 28.30S 27.01E
Wincanton U.K. 5 51.03N 2.24W
Winchester U.K. 5 51.04N 1.19W
Winchester Va. U.S.A. 55 39.11N 78.10W
Winchester Wyo. U.S.A. 54 43.51N108.10W
Windermere l. U.K. 4 54.20N 2.56W
Windhoek Namibia 39 22.34S 17.06E
Windorah Australia 44 25.26S142.39E
Wind River Range mts. U.S.A. 54 43.05N109.25W
Windsor Ont. Canada 55 42.18N 83.01W
Windsor Que. Canada 55 45.35N 72.01W
Windsor U.K. 5 51.29N 0.38W
Windward Is. C. America 57 13.00N 60.00W
Windward Passage str. Carib. Sea 57 20.00N 74.00W
Wingen Australia 47 31.43S150.54E
Wingham Australia 47 31.50S152.20E
Wingham Canada 55 43.53N 81.19W
Winifred U.S.A. 54 47.34N109.23W
Winisk Canada 51 55.15N 85.12W
Winisk r. Canada 51 55.20N 85.20W
Winisk L. Canada 51 52.55N 87.22W
Winneba Ghana 38 5.22N 0.38W
Winnebago, L. U.S.A. 53 44.00N 88.25W
Winnemucca U.S.A. 52 40.58N117.45W
Winnemucca L. U.S.A. 54 40.09N119.20W
Winnininnie Australia 46 32.35S139.40E
Winnipeg Canada 51 49.53N 97.10W
Winnipeg, L. Canada 51 52.45N 98.00W
Winnipegosis, L. Canada 51 52.00N100.00W
Winona Minn. U.S.A. 53 44.02N 91.37W
Winooski U.S.A. 55 44.29N 73.11W
Winschoten Neth. 8 53.07N 7.02E
Winsford U.K. 4 53.12N 2.31W
Winslow Ariz. U.S.A. 54 35.01N110.42W
Winslow Maine U.S.A. 55 44.32N 69.38W
Winston U.S.A. 54 46.28N111.38W
Winston-Salem U.S.A. 53 36.05N 80.05W
Winsum Neth. 8 53.20N 6.31E
Winterswijk Neth. 8 51.58N 6.44E
Winterthur Switz. 14 47.30N 8.45E
Winthrop Wash. U.S.A. 54 48.29N120.11W
Winton Australia 44 22.22S143.00E
Winton New Zealand 48 46.10S168.20E
Winton U.S.A. 54 41.45N109.10W
Wirrabara Australia 46 33.03S138.18E
Wirraminna Australia 46 31.11S136.04E
Wirrappa Australia 46 31.28S137.00E
Wirrega Australia 46 36.11S140.37E
Wirrida, L. Australia 46 29.45S134.39E
Wirulla Australia 46 32.24S134.33E
Wisbech U.K. 5 52.39N 0.10E
Wisconsin d. U.S.A. 53 45.00N 90.00W
Wisconsin Rapids town U.S.A. 53 44.24N 89.55W
Wisdom U.S.A. 54 45.37N113.27W
Wisła r. Poland 15 54.23N 18.52E
Wismar E. Germany 14 53.54N 11.28E
Wisznice Poland 15 51.48N 23.12E
Witham r. U.K. 4 52.56N 0.04E
Withernsea U.K. 4 53.43N 0.02E
Witkowo Poland 15 52.27N 17.47E
Witney U.K. 5 51.47N 1.29W
Witsand R.S.A. 39 34.23S 20.49E
Witten W. Germany 8 51.26N 7.19E
Wittenberg E. Germany 14 51.53N 12.39E
Wittenberge E. Germany 14 52.59N 11.45E
Wittenoom Australia 42 22.19S118.21E
Wittlich W. Germany 8 49.59N 6.54E
Witu Kenya 37 2.22S 40.20E
Witvlei Namibia 39 22.25S 18.29E
Wiveliscombe U.K. 5 51.02N 3.20W
Wkra r. Poland 15 52.27N 20.44E
Władysławowo Poland 15 54.49N 18.25E
Włocławek Poland 15 52.39N 19.01E
Włodawa Poland 15 51.33N 23.31E
Wodgina Australia 42 21.12S118.48E
Wodonga Australia 47 36.08S146.09E
Woerden Neth. 8 52.07N 4.55E
Wokam i. Indonesia 27 5.45S134.30E
Woking U.K. 5 51.20N 0.34W
Wolf Creek town U.S.A. 54 46.50N112.20W
Wolfenbüttel W. Germany 14 52.10N 10.33E
Wolf Point town U.S.A. 54 48.05N105.39W
Wolfsberg Austria 14 46.51N 14.51E
Wolfsburg W. Germany 14 52.27N 10.49E
Wolin Poland 14 53.51N 14.38E
Wollaston L. Canada 50 58.15N103.30W
Wollaston Pen. Canada 50 70.00N115.00W
Wollongong Australia 47 34.25S150.52E
Wolmaransstad R.S.A. 39 27.11S 25.58E
Wolomin Poland 15 52.21N 21.14E
Wolseley Australia 46 36.21S140.55E
Wolvega Neth. 8 52.53N 6.00E
Wolverhampton U.K. 5 52.35N 2.06W
Wondai Australia 44 26.19S151.52E
Wongan Hills town Australia 43 30.55S116.41E
Wŏnsan N. Korea 25 39.07N127.26E
Wonthaggi Australia 47 38.38S145.37E
Woocalla Australia 46 31.44S137.10E
Woodbridge U.K. 5 52.06N 1.19E
Woodbridge U.S.A. 55 38.39N 77.15W
Woodburn Australia 47 29.04S153.21E
Wooded Bluff f. Australia 47 29.22S153.22E
Woodenbong Australia 47 28.28S152.35E
Woodland U.S.A. 54 38.41N121.46W
Woodlark I. P.N.G. 44 9.05S152.50E
Woodroffe, Mt. Australia 44 26.20S131.45E
Woods, L. Australia 44 17.50S133.30E
Woods, L. of the Canada/U.S.A. 51 49.15N 94.45W
Woodside Australia 47 38.31S146.52E
Woodstock Canada 55 43.08N 80.45W
Woodstock U.K. 5 51.51N 1.20W
Woodville New Zealand 48 40.20S175.52E
Wooler U.K. 4 55.33N 2.01W
Woolgangie Australia 43 31.13S120.30E
Woolgoolga Australia 47 30.07S153.12E
Woolibar Australia 43 31.03S121.45E
Wooltana Australia 46 30.28S139.26E
Woomera Australia 46 31.11S136.54E
Woonsocket U.S.A. 55 42.00N 71.31W
Wooramel Australia 42 25.42S114.20E
Wooramel r. Australia 42 25.47S114.10E
Woorong, L. Australia 46 29.24S134.06E
Wooroorooka Australia 47 28.59S145.40E
Worcester R.S.A. 39 33.39S 19.25E
Worcester U.K. 5 52.12N 2.12W
Worcester U.S.A. 55 42.16N 71.48W
Workington U.K. 4 54.39N 3.34W
Worksop U.K. 4 53.19N 1.09W
Workum Neth. 8 53.00N 5.26E
Worland U.S.A. 54 44.01N107.57W
Worms W. Germany 14 49.38N 8.23E
Worthing U.K. 5 50.49N 0.21W
Worthington Minn. U.S.A. 53 43.37N 95.36W
Worthington Ohio U.S.A. 55 40.03N 83.03W
Worthville U.S.A. 55 38.38N 85.05W
Wosi Indonesia 27 0.15S128.00E
Woutchaba Cameroon 38 5.13N 13.05E
Wowoni i. Indonesia 27 4.10S123.10E
Wragby U.K. 4 53.17N 0.18E
Wrangel I. see Vrangelya, Ostrov i. U.S.S.R. 21
Wrangell U.S.A. 50 56.28N132.23W
Wrangell Mts. U.S.A. 50 62.00N143.00W
Wrangle U.K. 4 53.03N 0.09E
Wrath, C. U.K. 6 58.37N 5.01W
Wrexham U.K. 4 53.05N 3.00W
Wrightville Australia 47 31.36S145.53E
Wrigley Canada 50 63.16N123.39W
Wrocław Poland 15 51.05N 17.00E
Wronki Poland 14 52.43N 16.23E
Września Poland 15 52.20N 17.34E
Wubin Australia 43 30.06S116.38E
Wuchang China 25 30.32N114.18E
Wudham 'Alwā' Oman 31 23.48N 57.33E
Wudinna Australia 46 33.03S135.28E
Wuhan China 25 30.35N114.19E
Wuhu China 25 31.23N118.25E
Wu Jiang r. China 24 30.10N107.26E
Wukari Nigeria 38 7.57N 9.42E
Wuliang Shan mts. China 24 24.27N100.43E
Wum Cameroon 38 6.25N 10.03E
Wumbulgal Australia 47 34.25S146.16E
Wuppertal R.S.A. 39 32.16S 19.12E
Wuppertal W. Germany 8 51.15N 7.10E
Wurno Nigeria 38 13.20N 5.28E
Wurung Australia 44 19.14S140.23E
Würzburg W. Germany 14 49.48N 9.57E
Wutongqiao China 24 29.21N103.48E
Wuwei China 24 38.00N102.54E
Wuxi Jiangsu China 25 31.35N120.19E
Wuzhan China 25 50.14N125.18E
Wuzhou China 25 23.30N111.21E
Wyalkatchem Australia 43 31.21S117.22E
Wyalong Australia 47 33.55S147.17E
Wyandotte U.S.A. 55 42.11N 83.10W
Wyandra Australia 45 27.15S146.00E
Wyangala Resr. Australia 47 33.58S148.55E
Wyara, L. Australia 46 28.42S144.16E
Wye U.K. 5 51.11N 0.56E
Wye r. U.K. 5 51.37N 2.40W
Wymondham U.K. 5 52.34N 1.07E
Wynbring Australia 45 30.33S133.32E
Wyndham Australia 42 15.29S128.05E
Wyoming d. U.S.A. 52 43.10N107.36W
Wyong Australia 47 33.17S151.25E
Wyszków Poland 15 52.36N 21.28E

X

Xainza China 24 30.56N 88.38E
Xai-Xai Mozambique 39 25.05S 33.38E
Xam Nua Laos 29 20.25N104.04E
Xangongo Angola 36 16.43S 15.01E
Xanten W. Germany 8 51.40N 6.29E
Xánthi Greece 13 41.07N 24.55E
Xau, L. Botswana 39 21.15S 24.50E
Xenia U.S.A. 55 39.41N 83.56W
Xhora R.S.A. 39 31.58S 28.40E
Xiaguan China 24 25.33N100.09E
Xiamen China 25 24.26N118.07E
Xi'an China 25 34.16N108.54E
Xiangfan China 25 32.20N112.05E
Xiangkhoang Laos 29 19.11N103.23E
Xiangtan China 25 27.55N112.47E
Xiangyin China 25 28.40N112.53E
Xianyang China 25 34.23N108.40E
Xiao Hinggan Ling mts. China 25 48.40N128.30E
Xichang China 24 27.53N102.18E
Xigazê China 24 29.18N 88.50E
Xi Jiang r. China 25 22.23N113.20E
Xilin China 29 24.30N105.03E
Ximeng China 29 22.45N 99.29E
Xinfeng Jiangxi China 25 25.27N114.58E
Xing'an China 25 25.37N110.40E
Xingkai Hu l. see Khanka, Ozero U.S.S.R./China 25
Xingtai China 25 37.08N114.29E
Xingu r. Brazil 61 1.40S 52.15W
Xinhe Xin. Uygur China 24 41.34N 82.38E
Xining China 24 36.35N101.55E
Xinjiang-Uygur d. China 24 41.15N 87.00E
Xinjin Liaoning China 25 39.25N121.58E
Xin Xian China 25 38.24N112.47E
Xinxiang China 25 35.16N113.51E
Xinyu China 25 27.48N114.56E
Xinzhu Taiwan 25 24.48N120.59E
Xique Xique Brazil 61 10.47S 42.44W
Xixabangma Feng mtn. China 29 28.21N 85.47E
Xizang d. China 29 32.20N 86.00E
Xorkol China 24 39.04N 91.05E
Xuanhua China 25 40.36N115.01E
Xuchang China 25 34.03N113.48E
Xueshuiwen China 25 49.15N129.39E
Xugou China 25 34.42N119.28E
Xuyong China 24 28.10N105.24E
Xuzhou China 25 34.17N117.18E

Y

Ya'an China 29 30.00N102.59E
Yaapeet Australia 46 35.48S142.07E
Yabassi Cameroon 38 4.30N 9.55E
Yablonovyy Khrebet mts. U.S.S.R. 21 53.20N115.00E
Yabrūd Syria 32 33.58N 36.40E
Yacheng China 25 18.30N109.12E
Yacuiba Bolivia 62 22.00S 63.25W
Yādgīr India 28 16.46N 77.08E
Yagaba Ghana 38 10.13N 1.14W
Yagoua Cameroon 38 10.23N 15.13E
Yahagi r. Japan 23 34.50N136.59E
Yaizu Japan 23 34.52N138.20E
Yajua Nigeria 38 11.27N 12.49E
Yakima U.S.A. 54 46.36N120.31W
Yaksha U.S.S.R. 18 61.51N 56.59E
Yakutat U.S.A. 50 59.33N139.44W
Yakutsk U.S.S.R. 21 62.10N129.20E
Yala Thailand 29 6.32N101.19E
Yalgoo Australia 43 28.20S116.41E
Yalinga C.A.R. 35 6.31N 23.15E
Yallourn Australia 47 38.09S146.22E
Yalong Jiang r. China 24 26.35N101.44E
Yalpunga Australia 46 29.04S142.05E
Yalta U.S.S.R. 19 44.30N 34.09E
Yalutorovsk U.S.S.R. 20 56.41N 66.12E
Yamal, Poluostrov pen. U.S.S.R. 20 70.20N 70.00E
Yamanashi Japan 23 35.40N138.40E
Yamanashi d. Japan 23 35.30N138.35E
Yaman Tau mtn. U.S.S.R. 18 54.20N 58.10E
Yamato Japan 23 35.29N139.29E
Yamato-takada Japan 23 34.31N135.45E
Yamba N.S.W. Australia 47 29.26S153.22E
Yamba S.A. Australia 46 34.15S140.54E
Yambio Sudan 35 4.34N 28.23E
Yambol Bulgaria 13 42.28N 26.30E
Yamdena i. Indonesia 27 7.30S131.00E
Yamethin Burma 29 20.24N 96.08E
Yam Kinneret l. Israel 32 32.49N 35.36E
Yamma Yamma, L. Australia 44 26.20S141.25E
Yamoussoukro Ivory Coast 38 6.51N 5.18W
Yampol U.S.S.R. 15 48.13N 28.12E
Yamuna r. India 29 25.20N 81.49E
Yan Nigeria 38 10.05N 12.11E
Yana r. U.S.S.R. 21 71.30N135.00E
Yanac Australia 46 36.09S141.29E
Yanbu'al Baḩr Saudi Arabia 30 24.07N 38.04E
Yancannia Australia 46 30.16S142.50E
Yancheng China 25 33.23N120.10E
Yanchep Australia 43 31.32S115.33E
Yanchuan China 25 36.55N110.04E
Yanco Australia 47 34.36S146.25E
Yanda Australia 47 30.18S145.44E
Yanda r. Australia 47 30.22S145.38E
Yangarey U.S.S.R. 18 68.46N 61.29E
Yangjiang China 25 21.51N111.58E
Yangquan China 25 37.52N113.29E
Yangtze r. see Chang Jiang r. China 25
Yanji China 25 42.45N129.25E
Yanko r. Australia 47 35.25S145.27E
Yanko Glen town Australia 46 31.43S141.39E
Yanqi China 24 42.00N 86.30E
Yanshan China 29 23.36N104.20E
Yanskiy Zaliv g. U.S.S.R. 21 72.00N136.10E
Yantabulla Australia 47 29.13S145.01E
Yantai China 25 37.30N121.22E
Yao Chad 34 12.52N 17.34E
Yao Japan 23 34.37N135.36E
Yaoundé Cameroon 38 3.51N 11.31E
Yap i. Caroline Is. 27 9.30N138.09E
Yapen i. Indonesia 27 1.45S136.10E
Yaqui r. Mexico 56 27.37N110.39W
Yar U.S.S.R. 18 58.13N 52.08E
Yaraka Australia 44 24.53S144.04E
Yaransk U.S.S.R. 18 57.22N 47.49E
Yardea Australia 46 32.23S135.32E
Yare r. U.K. 5 52.34N 1.45E
Yaremcha U.S.S.R. 15 48.26N 24.29E
Yarensk U.S.S.R. 18 62.10N 49.07E
Yargora U.S.S.R. 15 46.25N 28.20E
Yaritagua Venezuela 60 10.05N 69.07W
Yarkant He r. China 24 40.30N 80.55E
Yarlung Zangbo Jiang r. China see Brahmaputra r. Asia 29
Yarmouth Canada 55 43.50N 66.08W
Yaroslavl U.S.S.R. 18 57.34N 39.52E
Yarra r. Australia 47 37.51S144.54E
Yarram Australia 47 38.30S146.41E
Yarran Range mts. Australia 44 18.08S136.40E
Yarrawonga Australia 47 36.02S145.59E
Yarrow r. U.K. 6 55.32N 2.51W
Yar Sale U.S.S.R. 20 66.50N 70.48E
Yartsevo R.S.F.S.R. U.S.S.R. 18 55.06N 32.43E
Yartsevo R.S.F.S.R. U.S.S.R. 21 60.17N 90.02E
Yarumal Colombia 60 6.59N 75.25W
Yaselda r. U.S.S.R. 15 52.07N 26.28E
Yasen U.S.S.R. 15 53.10N 28.55E
Yashi Nigeria 38 12.23N 7.54E
Yashkul U.S.S.R. 19 46.10N 45.20E
Yasinya U.S.S.R. 15 48.12N 24.20E
Yasothon Thailand 29 15.46N104.12E
Yass Australia 47 34.51S148.55E
Yatakala Niger 38 14.52N 0.22E
Yaví, Cerro mtn. Venezuela 60 5.32N 65.59W
Yavorov U.S.S.R. 15 49.59N 23.20E
Ya Xian China 25 18.20N109.31E
Yazd Iran 31 31.54N 54.22E
Ybbs Austria 14 48.11N 15.05E
Ye Burma 29 15.15N 97.50E
Yea Australia 47 37.12S145.25E
Yecla Spain 10 38.35N 1.05W
Yedintsy U.S.S.R. 19 48.09N 27.18E
Yeeda River town Australia 42 17.36S123.39E
Yefremov U.S.S.R. 18 53.08N 38.08E
Yegorlyk r. U.S.S.R. 19 46.30N 41.52E
Yegoryevsk U.S.S.R. 18 55.21N 39.01E
Yegros Paraguay 59 26.24S 56.25W
Yei Sudan 35 4.05N 30.40E
Yei r. Sudan 35 7.40N 30.13E
Yelets U.S.S.R. 18 52.36N 38.30E
Yeletskiy U.S.S.R. 18 67.04N 64.00E
Yell i. U.K. 6 60.35N 1.05W
Yellowdine Australia 43 31.19S119.36E
Yellowhead Pass Canada 50 52.53N118.28W
Yellowknife Canada 50 62.30N114.29W
Yellow Mt. Australia 47 32.19S146.50E
Yellow Sea Asia 25 35.00N123.00E
Yellowstone r. U.S.A. 54 47.58N103.59W
Yellowstone r. U.S.A. 52 47.55N103.45W
Yellowstone L. U.S.A. 54 44.25N110.38W
Yellowstone Nat. Park U.S.A. 54 44.30N110.35W
Yell Sd. U.K. 6 60.30N 1.11W
Yelma Australia 42 26.30S121.40E
Yelsk U.S.S.R. 15 51.50N 29.10E
Yelwa Nigeria 38 10.48N 4.42E
Yemen Asia 35 15.15N 44.30E
Yemilchino U.S.S.R. 15 50.58N 27.40E
Yenagoa Nigeria 38 4.59N 6.15E
Yendi Ghana 38 9.29N 0.01W
Yenisey r. U.S.S.R. 21 69.00N 86.00E
Yeniseysk U.S.S.R. 21 58.27N 92.13E
Yeniseyskiy Zaliv g. U.S.S.R. 20 73.00N 79.00E
Yenyuka U.S.S.R. 21 57.57N121.15E
Yeo, L. Australia 43 28.04S124.23E
Yeovil U.K. 5 50.57N 2.38W
Yeppoon Australia 44 23.08S150.45E
Yerbent U.S.S.R. 31 39.23N 58.35E
Yercha U.S.S.R. 21 69.34N147.30E
Yerepol U.S.S.R. 21 65.15N168.43E
Yerevan U.S.S.R. 31 40.10N 44.31E
Yerington U.S.A. 54 38.59N119.10W
Yermak U.S.S.R. 20 52.03N 76.55E
Yermitsa U.S.S.R. 18 66.56N 52.20E
Yermo U.S.A. 54 34.54N116.50W
Yershov U.S.S.R. 19 51.22N 48.16E
Yertom U.S.S.R. 18 63.31N 47.51E
Yerushalayim Israel/Jordan 32 31.47N 35.13E
Yeşil r. Turkey 30 41.22N 36.37E
Yessey U.S.S.R. 21 68.29N102.15E
Yetman Australia 47 28.55S150.49E
Yeu Burma 29 22.49N 95.26E
Yeu, Île d' i. France 11 46.43N 2.20W
Yevpatoriya U.S.S.R. 19 45.12N 33.20E
Yevstratovskiy U.S.S.R. 19 50.07N 39.45E
Yeysk U.S.S.R. 19 46.43N 38.17E
Yí r. Uruguay 63 33.17S 58.08W
Yiannitsá Greece 13 40.48N 22.25E
Yibin China 24 28.50N104.35E
Yichang China 25 30.43N111.22E
Yilan China 25 46.22N129.31E
Yilehuli Shan mts. China 25 51.20N124.20E
Yilliminning Australia 43 32.54S117.22E
Yinchuan China 24 38.30N106.19E
Yindarlgooda, L. Australia 43 30.45S121.55E
Yingde China 25 24.20N113.20E
Yingkou China 25 40.40N122.17E
Yingtan China 25 28.14N117.00E
Yinkanie Australia 46 34.21S140.20E
Yinning China 24 43.57N 81.23E
Yíthion Greece 13 36.46N 22.34E
Yiyang Hunan China 25 28.36N112.20E
Ylitornio Finland 16 66.19N 23.40E
Ylivieska Finland 16 64.05N 24.33E
Yodo r. Japan 23 34.41N135.25E
Yogyakarta Indonesia 26 7.48S110.24E
Yokadouma Cameroon 38 3.26N 15.06E
Yokkaichi Japan 23 34.58N136.37E
Yoko Cameroon 38 5.29N 12.19E
Yokohama Japan 23 35.27N139.39E
Yokosuka Japan 23 35.18N139.40E
Yola Nigeria 38 9.14N 12.32E
Yongxiu China 25 29.03N115.49E
Yonkers U.S.A. 55 40.56N 73.54W
Yonne d. France 9 47.55N 3.45E
Yonne r. France 9 48.22N 2.57E
York Australia 43 31.55S116.45E
York U.K. 4 53.58N 1.07W
York Penn. U.S.A. 55 39.58N 76.44W
York, C. Australia 44 10.42S142.31E
Yorke Pen. Australia 46 35.00S137.30E
Yorketown Australia 46 35.02S137.35E
York Factory town Canada 51 57.08N 92.25W
Yorkshire Wolds hills U.K. 4 54.00N 0.39W
Yorkton Canada 50 51.12N102.29W
Yoro Honduras 57 15.09N 87.07W
Yōrō Japan 23 35.32N140.04E
Yosemite Nat. Park U.S.A. 54 37.45N119.35W
Yoshino r. Japan 23 34.22N135.40E
Yoshkar Ola U.S.S.R. 18 56.38N 47.52E
Yos Sudarsa, Pulau i. Indonesia 27 8.00S138.30E
Yŏsu S. Korea 25 34.46N127.45E
Youghal Rep. of Ire. 7 51.58N 7.51W
You Jiang r. Guang. Zhuang. China 25 23.25N110.00E
Young Australia 47 34.19S148.20E
Young r. Australia 43 33.45S121.12E
Young Uruguay 63 32.41S 57.38W
Young U.S.A. 54 34.06N110.57W
Younghusband, L. Australia 46 30.51S136.05E
Younghusband Pen. Australia 46 36.00S139.15E
Youngstown U.S.A. 55 41.05N 80.40W
Yoxford U.K. 5 52.16N 1.30E
Yozgat Turkey 30 39.50N 34.48E
Yreka U.S.A. 54 41.44N122.38W
Ystad Sweden 17 55.25N 13.49E
Ythan r. U.K. 6 57.21N 2.01W
Ytterhogdal Sweden 17 62.12N 14.51E
Yu'alliq, Jabal mtn. Egypt 32 30.21N 33.31E
Yuan Jiang r. Hunan China 25 29.00N112.12E

Yuan Jiang *r.* Yunnan China *see* Hong Hà *r.* Vietnam **24**
Yuba City U.S.A. **54** 39.08N121.27W
Yucatán *d.* Mexico **57** 19.30N 89.00W
Yucatan Channel Carib. Sea **57** 21.30N 86.00W
Yucatan Pen. Mexico **56** 19.00N 90.00W
Yucca U.S.A. **54** 34.52N114.09W
Yuci China **25** 37.40N112.44E
Yudino U.S.S.R. **20** 55.49N 48.54E
Yuexi China **24** 28.36N102.35E
Yugorskiy Poluostrov *pen.* U.S.S.R. **18** 69.00N 62.30E
Yugoslavia Europe **13** 44.00N 20.00E
Yukon *r.* U.S.A. **50** 62.35N164.20W
Yukon Territory *d.* Canada **50** 65.00N135.00W
Yuleba Australia **44** 26.37S149.20E
Yuma Ariz. U.S.A. **54** 32.43N114.37W
Yumen China **24** 40.19N 97.12E
Yungas *f.* Bolivia **62** 16.20S 65.00W
Yungera Australia **46** 34.48S143.10E
Yunnan *d.* China **24** 24.30N101.30E
Yunta Australia **46** 32.37S139.34E
Yuribey U.S.S.R. **20** 71.02N 77.02E
Yurimaguas Peru **60** 5.54S 76.07W
Yuryuzan U.S.S.R. **18** 54.51N 58.25E
Yushkozero U.S.S.R. **18** 64.45N 32.03E
Yushu China **24** 33.06N 96.48E
Yūtō Japan **23** 34.42N137.38E
Yuzhno Sakhalinsk U.S.S.R. **25** 46.58N142.45E
Yuzhnyy Bug *r.* U.S.S.R. **15** 46.55N 31.59E
Yvelines *d.* France **9** 48.50N 1.50E
Yvetot France **9** 49.37N 0.45E

Z

Zaandam Neth. **8** 52.27N 4.49E
Zābol Iran **31** 31.00N 61.32E
Zābolī Iran **31** 27.08N 61.36E
Zabrze Poland **15** 50.18N 18.47E
Zacapa Guatemala **57** 15.00N 89.30W
Zacatecas Mexico **56** 22.48N102.33W
Zacatecas *d.* Mexico **56** 24.00N103.00W
Zadar Yugo. **12** 44.08N 15.14E
Zafra Spain **10** 38.25N 6.25W
Zagorsk U.S.S.R. **18** 56.20N 38.10E
Zagreb Yugo. **12** 45.49N 15.58E
Zāgros, Kūhhā-ye *mts.* Iran **31** 32.00N 51.00E
Zagros Mts. *see* Zāgros, Kūhhā-ye *mts.* Iran **31**
Zāhedān Iran **31** 29.32N 60.54E
Zaḩlah Lebanon **32** 33.50N 35.55E
Zaindeh *r.* Iran **31** 32.40N 52.50E
Zaïre Africa **36** 2.00S 22.00E
Zaïre *r.* Zaïre **36** 6.00S 12.30E
Zaječar Yugo. **13** 43.55N 22.15E
Zakataly U.S.S.R. **31** 41.39N 46.40E
Zákinthos *i.* Greece **13** 37.46N 20.46E
Zakopane Poland **15** 49.19N 19.57E
Zalaegerszeg Hungary **14** 46.51N 16.51E
Zalău Romania **15** 47.11N 23.03E
Zaleshchiki U.S.S.R. **15** 48.39N 25.50E
Zambezi *r.* Mozambique / Zambia **36** 18.15S 35.55E
Zambezi Zambia **36** 13.33S 23.09E
Zambezia *d.* Mozambique **37** 16.30S 37.30E
Zambia Africa **36** 14.00S 28.00E
Zamboanga Phil. **27** 6.55N122.05E
Zambrów Poland **15** 53.00N 22.15E
Zambue Mozambique **37** 15.09S 30.47E
Zamfara *r.* Nigeria **38** 12.04N 4.00E
Zamora Mexico **56** 20.00N102.18W
Zamora Spain **10** 41.30N 5.45W
Zamość Poland **15** 50.43N 23.15E
Zamtang China **29** 32.26N101.06E
Zaña Peru **60** 7.00S 79.30W
Záncara *r.* Spain **10** 38.55N 4.07W
Zanda China **29** 31.32N 79.50E
Zanesville U.S.A. **55** 39.55N 82.02W
Zanjān Iran **31** 36.40N 48.30E
Zanthus Australia **43** 31.02S123.34E
Zanzibar Tanzania **37** 6.10S 39.16E
Zanzibar I. Tanzania **37** 6.00S 39.20E
Zaozhuang China **25** 34.40N117.30E
Zapadno-Sibirskaya Ravnina *f.* U.S.S.R. **20** 60.00N 75.00E
Zapadnyy Sayan *mts.* U.S.S.R. **21** 53.00N 92.00E
Zapala Argentina **63** 38.55S 70.05W
Zaporozhye U.S.S.R. **19** 47.50N 35.10E
Zara Turkey **30** 39.55N 37.44E
Zaragoza Spain **10** 41.39N 0.54W
Zarand Iran **31** 30.50N 56.35E
Zárate Argentina **63** 34.05S 59.02W
Zaraza Venezuela **60** 9.23N 65.20W
Zard Kūh *mtn.* Iran **31** 32.21N 50.04E
Zarghūn Shahr Afghan. **28** 32.51N 68.25E
Zari Nigeria **38** 13.03N 12.46E
Zaria Nigeria **38** 11.01N 7.44E
Zaruma Ecuador **60** 3.40S 79.30W
Zary Poland **14** 51.40N 15.10E
Zarzal Colombia **60** 4.24N 76.01W
Zaslavl U.S.S.R. **15** 54.00N 27.15E
Zatishye U.S.S.R. **15** 47.20N 29.58E
Zave Zimbabwe **37** 17.14S 30.02E
Zavitinsk U.S.S.R. **25** 50.08N129.24E
Zāwiyat al Amwāt Egypt **32** 28.04N 30.50E
Zāyandeh *r.* Iran **31** 32.40N 52.50E
Zaysan U.S.S.R. **24** 47.30N 84.57E
Zaysan, Ozero *l.* U.S.S.R. **24** 48.00N 83.30E
Zbarazh U.S.S.R. **15** 49.40N 25.49E
Zborov U.S.S.R. **15** 49.40N 25.09E
Zdolbunov U.S.S.R. **15** 50.30N 26.10E
Zduńska Wola Poland **15** 51.36N 18.57E
Zebediela R.S.A. **39** 24.19S 29.17E
Zeebrugge Belgium **8** 51.20N 3.13E
Zeehan Australia **45** 41.55S145.21E
Zeeland *d.* Neth. **8** 51.30N 3.45E
Zeerust R.S.A. **39** 25.32S 26.04E
Zefa' Israel **32** 31.07N 35.12E
Zefat Israel **32** 32.57N 35.27E
Zeila Somali Rep. **35** 11.21N 43.30E
Zeist Neth. **8** 52.03N 5.16E
Zeitz E. Germany **14** 51.03N 12.08E
Zelechów Poland **15** 51.49N 21.54E
Zelenodolsk U.S.S.R. **18** 55.50N 48.30E
Zelenogorsk U.S.S.R. **18** 60.15N 29.31E
Zelenokumsk U.S.S.R. **19** 44.25N 43.54E
Zelentsovo U.S.S.R. **18** 59.51N 44.59E
Zell W. Germany **8** 50.02N 7.11E
Zelts U.S.S.R. **15** 46.38N 30.00E
Zelzate Belgium **8** 51.12N 3.49E
Zemio C.A.R. **35** 5.00N 25.09E
Zemun Yugo. **13** 44.51N 20.23E
Zenica Yugo. **15** 44.12N 17.55E
Zenne *r.* Belgium **8** 51.04N 4.25E
Zetel W. Germany **8** 53.28N 7.57E
Zeven W. Germany **14** 53.18N 9.16E
Zevenaar Neth. **8** 51.57N 6.04E
Zevenbergen Neth. **8** 51.41N 4.42E
Zeya U.S.S.R. **21** 53.48N127.14E
Zeya *r.* U.S.S.R. **21** 50.20N127.30E
Zêzere *r.* Portugal **10** 39.28N 8.20W
Zgierz Poland **15** 51.52N 19.25E
Zgorzelec Poland **14** 51.12N 15.01E
Zhailma U.S.S.R. **20** 51.37N 61.33E
Zhanatas U.S.S.R. **24** 43.11N 69.35E
Zhanghua Taiwan **25** 24.06N120.31E
Zhangjiakou China **25** 41.00N114.50E
Zhangye China **24** 38.56N100.27E
Zhangzhou China **25** 24.57N118.36E
Zhanjiang China **25** 21.05N110.12E
Zhashkov U.S.S.R. **15** 49.12N 30.05E
Zhdanov U.S.S.R. **19** 47.05N 37.34E
Zhejiang *d.* China **25** 29.15N120.00E
Zheleznodorozhnyy R.S.F.S.R. U.S.S.R. **18** 62.39N 50.59E
Zheleznodorozhnyy R.S.F.S.R. U.S.S.R. **18** 67.59N 64.47E
Zhengzhou China **25** 34.35N113.38E
Zhenjiang China **25** 32.05N119.30E
Zherdnoye U.S.S.R. **15** 51.40N 30.11E
Zhidachov U.S.S.R. **15** 49.20N 24.22E
Zhigansk U.S.S.R. **21** 66.48N123.27E
Zhitkovichi U.S.S.R. **15** 52.12N 27.49E
Zhitomir U.S.S.R. **15** 50.18N 28.40E
Zhlobin U.S.S.R. **15** 52.50N 30.00E
Zhmerinka U.S.S.R. **15** 49.00N 28.02E
Zhob *r.* Pakistan **28** 31.40N 70.54E
Zhongba China **29** 29.56N 84.20E
Zhongdian China **29** 28.00N 99.30E
Zhupanovo U.S.S.R. **21** 53.40N159.52E
Zhuzhou China **25** 27.53N113.07E
Žiar nad Hronom Czech. **15** 48.36N 18.52E
Zibo China **25** 36.50N118.00E
Ziel, Mt. Australia **42** 23.24S132.23E
Zielona Góra Poland **14** 51.57N 15.30E
Ziftā Egypt **32** 30.43N 31.14E
Zigong China **29** 29.18N104.45E
Zile Turkey **30** 40.18N 35.52E
Žilina Czech. **15** 49.14N 18.46E
Zillah Libya **34** 28.33N 17.35E
Zima U.S.S.R. **21** 53.58N102.02E
Zimatlán Mexico **56** 16.52N 96.45W
Zimba Zambia **39** 17.19S 26.12E
Zimbabwe Africa **36** 18.55S 30.00E
Zimbor Romania **15** 47.00N 23.16E
Zimnicea Romania **15** 43.38N 25.22E
Zimniy Bereg *f.* U.S.S.R. **18** 65.50N 41.30E
Zinder Niger **38** 13.46N 8.58E
Zinder *d.* Niger **38** 14.20N 9.30E
Zinga Mtwara Tanzania **37** 9.01S 38.47E
Ziniaré Burkina Faso **38** 12.34N 1.12W
Ziro India **29** 27.38N 93.42E
Zitundo Mozambique **39** 26.45S 32.49E
Ziway, L. Ethiopia **35** 8.00N 38.50E
Zlatograd Bulgaria **13** 41.23N 25.06E
Zlatoust U.S.S.R. **18** 55.10N 59.38E
Zloczew Poland **15** 51.25N 18.36E
Złotów Poland **15** 53.22N 17.02E
Zlynka U.S.S.R. **15** 52.24N 31.45E
Zmeinogorsk U.S.S.R. **20** 51.11N 82.14E
Zmiyevka U.S.S.R. **18** 52.40N 36.22E
Znamenka U.S.S.R. **19** 48.42N 32.40E
Znin Poland **15** 52.52N 17.43E
Znojmo Czech. **14** 48.52N 16.05E
Zobia Zaïre **36** 2.58N 25.56E
Zobue Mozambique **37** 15.35S 34.26E
Zoétélé Cameroon **38** 3.17N 11.54E
Zogno Italy **9** 45.48N 9.40E
Zohreh *r.* Iran **31** 30.04N 49.32E
Zolochev U.S.S.R. **15** 49.48N 24.51E
Zolotonosha U.S.S.R. **19** 49.39N 32.05E
Zomba Malaŵi **37** 15.22S 35.22E
Zonguldak Turkey **30** 41.26N 31.47E
Zorritos Peru **60** 3.50S 80.40W
Zouar Chad **34** 20.27N 16.32E
Zoutkamp Neth. **8** 53.21N 6.18E
Zrenjanin Yugo. **13** 45.22N 20.23E
Zuénoula Ivory Coast **38** 7.34N 6.03W
Zug Switz. **14** 47.10N 8.31E
Zuid Beveland *f.* Neth. **8** 51.30N 3.50E
Zuidelijk-Flevoland *f.* Neth. **8** 52.22N 5.22E
Zuid Holland *d.* Neth. **8** 52.00N 4.30E
Zuidhorn Neth. **8** 53.16N 6.25E
Zújar *r.* Spain **10** 38.58N 5.40W
Zújar, Embalse del *resr.* Spain **10** 38.57N 5.30
Zülpich W. Germany **8** 50.42N 6.36E
Zululand *f.* R.S.A. **39** 27.30S 32.00E
Zumbo Mozambique **37** 15.36S 30.24E
Zungeru Nigeria **38** 9.48N 6.03E
Zunyi China **29** 27.41N106.50E
Zurich Neth. **8** 53.08N 5.25E
Zürich Switz. **14** 47.23N 8.33E
Zuru Nigeria **38** 11.26N 5.16E
Zushi Japan **23** 35.18N139.35E
Zutphen Neth. **8** 52.08N 6.12E
Zuwārah Libya **34** 32.56N 12.06E
Zvenigorodka U.S.S.R. **15** 49.05N 30.58E
Zverinogolovskoye U.S.S.R. **20** 48.01N 40.09
Zvishavane Zimbabwe **39** 20.20S 30.05E
Zvolen Czech. **15** 48.35N 19.08E
Zwettl Austria **14** 48.37N 15.10E
Zwickau E. Germany **14** 50.43N 12.30E
Zwischenahn W. Germany **8** 53.13N 7.59E
Zwoleń Poland **15** 51.22N 21.35E
Zwolle Neth. **8** 52.31N 6.06E
Zyryanovsk U.S.S.R. **20** 49.45N 84.16E
Zywiec Poland **15** 49.41N 19.12E

THE WORLD : Physical

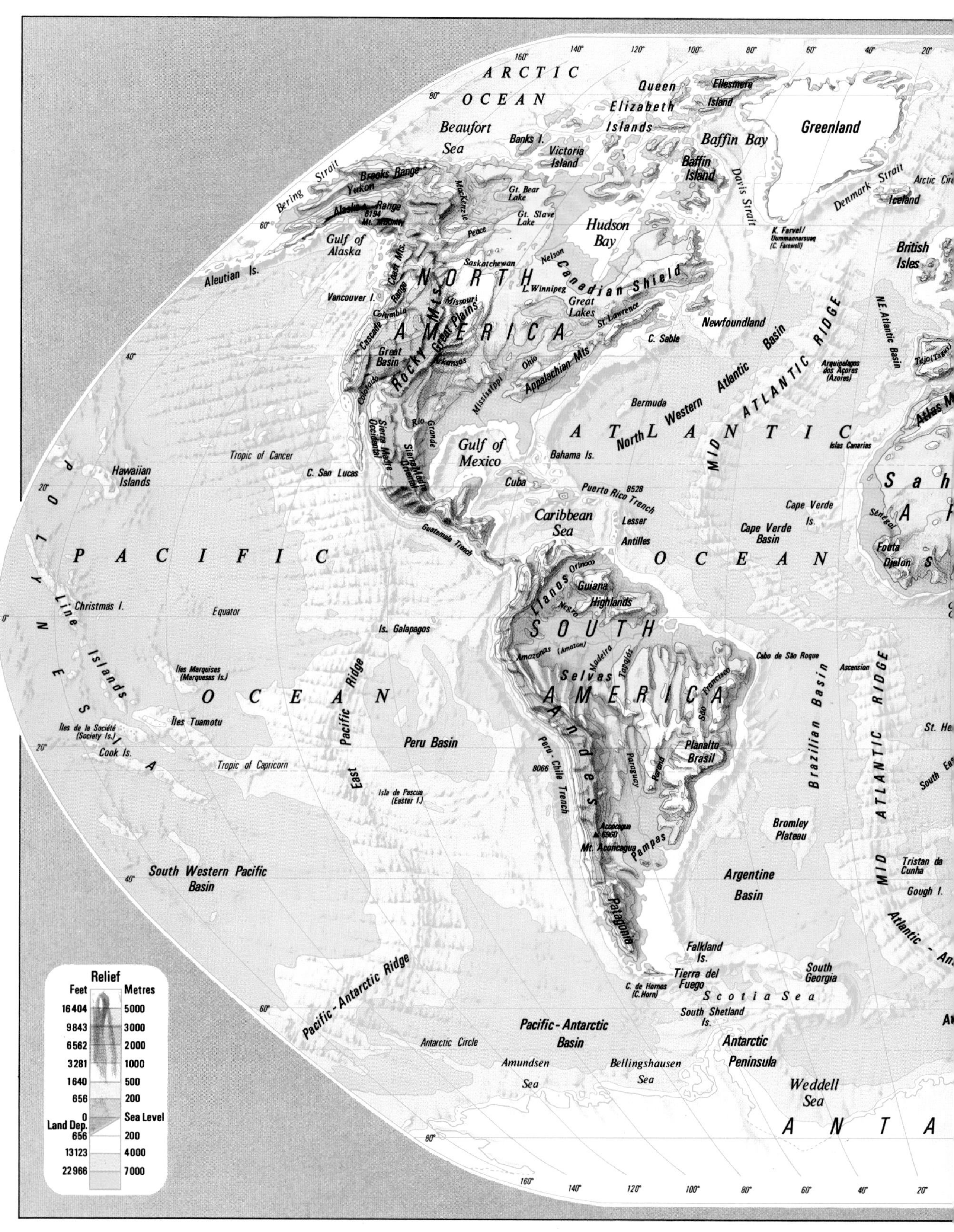

ARCTIC OCEAN
Beaufort Sea
Queen Elizabeth Islands
Ellesmere Island
Greenland
Baffin Bay
Baffin Island
Banks I.
Victoria Island
Bering Strait
Brooks Range
Yukon
Alaska Range
6194 Mt. McKinley
Gulf of Alaska
Aleutian Is.
Gt. Bear Lake
Gt. Slave Lake
Hudson Bay
Davis Strait
Denmark Strait
Iceland
Arctic Circle
K. Farvel/ Uummannarsuaq (C. Farewell)
British Isles
Peace
Saskatchewan
Nelson
Canadian Shield
NORTH AMERICA
Vancouver I.
L. Winnipeg
Great Lakes
St. Lawrence
Newfoundland
C. Sable
Columbia
Cascade
Great Basin
Rocky Mts
Great Plains
Missouri
Arkansas
Colorado
Ohio
Appalachian Mts
Mississippi
Rio Grande
Sierra Madre Occidental
Sierra Madre Oriental
Gulf of Mexico
Bahama Is.
Cuba
Bermuda
North Western Atlantic Basin
N.E. Atlantic Basin
MID ATLANTIC RIDGE
Arquipélagos dos Açores (Azores)
Tejo (Tagus)
Atlas Mts
Islas Canarias
ATLANTIC OCEAN
Tropic of Cancer
Hawaiian Islands
C. San Lucas
Puerto Rico Trench
8528
Caribbean Sea
Lesser Antilles
Cape Verde Is.
Cape Verde Basin
Sahara
Sénégal
Fouta Djalon
Guatemala Trench
PACIFIC OCEAN
POLYNESIA
Orinoco
Llanos
Guiana Highlands
Negro
SOUTH AMERICA
Christmas I.
Equator
Line Islands
Is. Galapagos
Amazonas (Amazon)
Madeira
Tapajós
Selvas
São Francisco
Cabo de São Roque
Ascension
Îles Marquises (Marquesas Is.)
Îles Tuamotu
Îles de la Société (Society Is.)
Cook Is.
Tropic of Capricorn
East Pacific Ridge
Peru Basin
Isla de Pascua (Easter I.)
Andes
Peru-Chile Trench
8066
Paraguay
Paraná
Planalto Brasil
Brazilian Basin
St. Helena
Aconcagua 6960
Mt. Aconcagua
Pampas
Bromley Plateau
Tristan da Cunha
Gough I.
South Western Pacific Basin
Argentine Basin
Patagonia
Falkland Is.
Tierra del Fuego
C. de Hornos (C. Horn)
South Georgia
Scotia Sea
South Shetland Is.
Pacific-Antarctic Ridge
Pacific-Antarctic Basin
Antarctic Circle
Antarctic Peninsula
Amundsen Sea
Bellingshausen Sea
Weddell Sea
ANTA
Relief
Feet
Metres
16404
5000
9843
3000
6562
2000
3281
1000
1640
500
656
200
0
Sea Level
Land Dep.
656
200
13123
4000
22966
7000

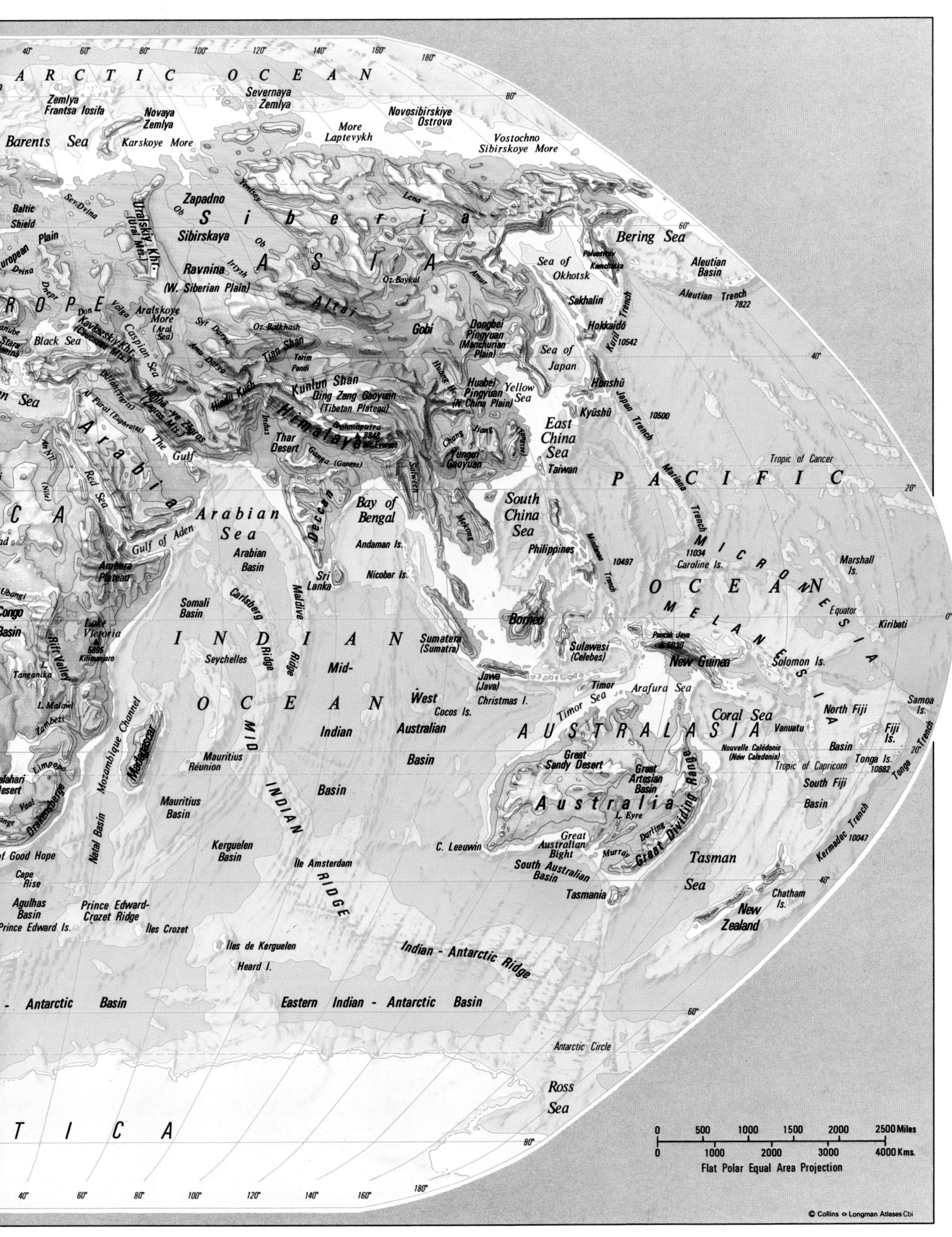

ARCTIC OCEAN
Zemlya Frantsa Iosifa
Severnaya Zemlya
Novaya Zemlya
Novosibirskiye Ostrova
More Laptevykh
Barents Sea
Karskoye More
Vostochno Sibirskoye More
Baltic Shield
Zapadno Sibirskaya Ravnina (W. Siberian Plain)
Siberia
ASIA
Uralskiy Khr. (Ural Mts.)
Bering Sea
Sea of Okhotsk
Aleutian Basin
Aleutian Trench
7822
European Plain
Oz. Baykal
Altai
Sakhalin
Hokkaidō
Kuril Trench
10542
Black Sea
Aralskoye More (Aral Sea)
Caspian Sea
Oz. Balkhash
Tian Shan
Gobi
Dongbei Pingyuan (Manchurian Plain)
Sea of Japan
Kunlun Shan
Qing Zang Gaoyuan (Tibetan Plateau)
Himalaya
Huabei Pingyuan (N. China Plain)
Yellow Sea
Honshū
Japan Trench
Kyūshū
10500
East China Sea
Thar Desert
The Gulf
Arabia
Yungui Gaoyuan
Taiwan
Tropic of Cancer
PACIFIC
Mariana Trench
11034
Arabian Sea
Deccan
Bay of Bengal
South China Sea
Philippines
Mindanao Trench
10497
Gulf of Aden
Andaman Is.
Nicobar Is.
Caroline Is.
Marshall Is.
MICRONESIA
OCEAN
Arabian Basin
Sri Lanka
Amhara Plateau
Somali Basin
Carlsberg Ridge
Maldive Ridge
Borneo
Equator
Kiribati
MELANESIA
Lake Victoria
5895 Kilimanjaro
Rift Valley
INDIAN
Seychelles
Mid-
Sumatera (Sumatra)
Sulawesi (Celebes)
Puncak Jaya 5030
New Guinea
Solomon Is.
OCEAN
Jawa (Java)
Christmas I.
Timor
Timor Sea
Arafura Sea
Coral Sea
West Australian Basin
Cocos Is.
Indian
AUSTRALASIA
Vanuatu
North Fiji Basin
Fiji Is.
Samoa Is.
Mozambique Channel
Madagascar
Mauritius
Réunion
Great Sandy Desert
Great Artesian Basin
Great Dividing Range
Nouvelle Calédonie (New Caledonia)
Tropic of Capricorn
Tonga Is.
10882
Tonga Trench
South Fiji Basin
Mauritius Basin
Australia
L. Eyre
MID INDIAN RIDGE
Kerguelen Basin
C. Leeuwin
Great Australian Bight
South Australian Basin
Darling
Murray
Tasman Sea
Kermadec Trench
10047
Natal Basin
Île Amsterdam
Tasmania
Chatham Is.
New Zealand
Cape Rise
Agulhas Basin
Prince Edward-Crozet Ridge
Prince Edward Is.
Îles Crozet
Îles de Kerguelen
Heard I.
Indian - Antarctic Ridge
Antarctic Basin
Eastern Indian - Antarctic Basin
Antarctic Circle
Ross Sea
TICA
0 500 1000 1500 2000 2500 Miles
0 1000 2000 3000 4000 Kms.
Flat Polar Equal Area Projection